HISTORY

OF

SOUTHEAST MISSOURI

A Narrative Account of its Historical Progress,
Its People and its Principal Interests.

By

Robert Sidney Douglass, A. B., LL. B.
Professor of History, State Normal School, Cape Girardeau, Mo.

VOLUME I

ILLUSTRATED

Publishers:
THE LEWIS PUBLISHING COMPANY
Chicago and New York
1912

R.S. Douglass

PREFACE

This territory of Southeast Missouri was first visited by De Soto about the year 1540. The next white men who saw it were the adventurous voyagers from Canada who reached the Mississippi from the north and passed down toward its mouth. Marquette and Joliet and La Salle all visited this section, or at least saw it as their canoes floated down the great stream. No attention however was paid to the district until Renault, the agent of the Company of the West came with his miners and four hundred slaves to Fort Chartres with instructions to explore the country for the precious metals. This was about 1720. In his search for gold and silver he penetrated to what is now the county of Ste. Genevieve, finding no traces of gold or silver, but finding abundant deposits of lead ore. These desposits he began to work. Mine a Breton was opened, Old Mine located, La Motte was discovered, and in other places attempts were made to work the rich deposits of lead ore, destined long afterward to be famous as among the greatest and richest deposits of lead in the world. These settlements for the purpose of mining naturally attracted other people, and about the year 1732 there was formed, in the great common field three miles south of the present site of Ste. Genevieve, the first permanent settlement within the limits of the state and one of the half dozen oldest towns in the Mississippi valley. This settlement known as "le vieux village de Ste. Genevieve," was also called "Misere" because of the troubles its inhabitants experienced with floods of the river.

Ste. Genevieve proved to be only the first of a number of settlements within this territory of Missouri. The magnificent plans of La Salle, long neglected by the French, at last began to be appreciated. France was arming herself for the great struggle impending with the English and preparing to shut them up in the territory occupied by them along the Atlantic coast. And so not alone along the Ohio and near the Alleghany mountains, but also along the course of the great river itself, settlements were planned, forts built, the favor of the Indians courted, in order to hold the country, if possible, against the inevitable attempt at expansion on the part of the English. Besides this organized attempt to settle and hold the country for political reasons, the country itself invited settlers. Missouri, at that time as always, was among the most attractive parts of the great continent. Here were all the things to attract settlers, and accordingly, at St. Charles, St. Louis, Cape Girardeau, and New Madrid settlements were planted, and the wilderness began to be brought under the dominion of the white man. Forests were cleared away, mines were opened, towns laid out, commerce began to stir, grain was grown, mills built, religion was not forgotten and the cross was lifted from many an humble church spire. The territory of New France was fondly believed to be destined to great things.

In 1762, however, by the secret treaty of Fontainebleau ceded all her territory west of the river to Spain, and the Spanish soon entered into possession. The transfer was very distasteful to the French settlers here, but in reality the rule of the Spanish was better than that of the French. The Spanish government undoubtedly dreamed of a great Spanish colonial empire west of the river, and gave much consideration to the task of building it up. Her governors here were instructed to do all in their power to secure settlers, especially those from east of the Mississippi who had had some experience in the life of the pioneer. The Ordinance of 1787 which prohibited slavery in the Northwest Territory of the United States, turned a part of the tide of imigration across the river to the Spanish territory where no such restriction was in force. Spain sent to this country some of the ablest of her colonial administrators who gave much thought and effort to the task set them of building up her western possessions.

In 1800, the territory passed again into the control of France, and there were again dreamed the dreams of a new and glorious France in the New World. However it was a time of great stress and storm in France. Napoleon was engaged in his herculean struggle with the English. He needed all the resources of his vast empire to support him in that struggle. The command of the sea was denied to France. Nelson and his fleets cut France off from her oversea dominions. Napoleon saw the inevitable consequence of trying to hold the great territory in America, known as Louisiana. It must fall into the hands of the English. To prevent this, to help build up a rival for England, and to gain money which he needed, he sold the immense territory of Louisiana to the United States for the sum of $15,000,000. And so on a day in 1804 the flag of France was once more hauled down from her American possessions and the banner of the republic took its place.

That transaction marks an epoch not alone in the history of the western territory, but also in the history of the United States. The territory thus acquired from France, contains some of the best and fairest parts of the vast domains of our country. Of course the transfer meant much to Louisiana. The restrictions on trade, on religious freedom, on local self government which France and Spain had imposed on settlers within the territory, were at once removed and there poured into the new possessions a constantly increasing stream of immigration from the older sections of the union. State after state was carved from the new territory. Missouri was admitted to the Union in 1820, taking her place at once among the great states.

The subsequent history of the state is a story of marvellous growth. Its vast resources have been developed, roads and railroads built, cities and towns have everywnere sprung up, the population has multiplied until now there are more than 3,000,000 people within the borders of Missouri alone. He who can close his eye to the present, sweep away all that civilization has brought, and with the imagination call again into existence the country as it appeared to De Soto or La Salle, awake from the grave the savage Indians who were once its sole population, then reclothe the land with its boundless forests and repeople them with the wild animals that once swarmed in countless numbers throughout all this region, fill the air again with the countless wild fowl that amazed the traveler, and then having restored the past as it was, can trace again the steps by which civilization came, sees before him one of the most stirring pages of history. It is the ever interesting story of man's conflict with the savage forces of nature, with savage man himself, of his conquest of mighty forests, his mastery of the streams, of the expansion of little settlements and frontier towns to great cities, the change of the rude and hard conditions of frontier life for the comforts and luxuries of civilization, the building of governments of systems of education, the spread of religion—in a word, he lives again the experience of the race in its struggle up from the savage conditions of the wilderness to the height of civilization.

To recount this wonderful story in part is the purpose of this work. No one can appreciate more than the author how imperfectly the task has been performed. The field is vast, the difficulty of sorting and selecting historical material great, and the time which might be devoted to the task, limited. He is conscious of many faults of omission, and doubts not that many of commission are present.

The sources of material are varied. For the early period the monumental work of Houck, The History of Missouri, must for many years be indispensable to the historian of Missouri. It is a rich mine of information. Goodspeed's History of Southeast Missouri is also valuable. The period of the Civil war is adequately covered as yet only by the official reports in War of the Rebellion Records published by the government. Conard's Encyclopaedia of the History of Missouri has been freely used. Where possible actual research work has been relied upon.

The author's thanks are due and are hereby tendered to Hon. Louis Houck of Cape Girardeau, for encouragement and assistance; to Rev. J. C. Maple, D. D., whose long acquaintance with Southeast Missouri and scholarly attainments render him peculiarly fitted for assistance in preparing its history; to Rev. Geo. W. Harlan of Farmington, for permission to use his unpublished History of the Presbytery of Potosi; to Dr. J. S. Dalton of New Madrid; to H. W. Watson of Memphis, for permission to print the account prepared by his grandfather, Judge Goah Watson.

It remains to be said that none of these, here named, are in anyway responsible for the errors in the work. For them the author is solely responsible and toward them he begs the kindly indulgence of the reader.

Windham Press is committed to bringing the lost cultural heritage of ages past into the 21st century through high-quality reproductions of original, classic printed works at affordable prices.

This book has been carefully crafted to utilize the original images of antique books rather than error-prone OCR text. This also preserves the work of the original typesetters of these classics, unknown craftsmen who laid out the text, often by hand, of each and every page you will read. Their subtle art involving judgment and interaction with the text is in many ways superior and more human than the mechanical methods utilized today, and gave each book a unique, hand-crafted feel in its text that connected the reader organically to the art of bindery and book-making.

We think these benefits are worth the occasional imperfection resulting from the age of these books at the time of scanning, and their vintage feel provides a connection to the past that goes beyond the mere words of the text.

As bibliophiles, we are always seeking perfection in our work, and so please notify us of any errors in this book by emailing us at corrections@windhampress.com. Our team is motivated to correct errors quickly so future customers are better served. Our mission is to raise the bar of quality for reprinted works by a focus on detail and quality over mass production.

To peruse our catalog of carefully curated classic works, please visit our online store at www.windhampress.com.

INTRODUCTION

The term, Southeast Missouri, like most terms made up from geographical expressions, is of indefinite application, being used in quite different ways by different people and at different times. In its widest significance it designates the east half of that part of the state south of the Missouri river, which contains somewhat more than a quarter of the entire area of the state. Sometimes its use is restricted to the counties lying in the alluvial plains of the Mississippi river, frequently called the swamps. Other meanings are given to the term also, but all of them have a vagueness of application which can be avoided only by arbitrary definition. As here used the term includes the counties of Jefferson, Washington, Iron, St. Francois, Madison, Ste. Genevieve, Perry, Reynolds, Wayne, Bollinger, Stoddard, Scott, Cape Girardeau, Carter, Ripley, Butler, Mississippi, New Madrid, Pemiscot, and Dunklin. These counties have an area of twelve thousand square miles and in 1910 their population was 362,453.

As the term is here used it is of course an arbitrary one, but definiteness in its use may not be secured without arbitrary limits being set. There are, however, certain considerations which led to the restriction of the term in the manner here proposed. In the first place the area chosen is practically that included within the three districts of Ste. Genevieve, Cape Girardeau, and New Madrid as laid out by the French and Spanish; with but few exceptions all the counties mentioned were settled before the transfer of the territory to the United States; and the larger number of the early settlements within the state are contained within Southeast Missouri as the term is here defined.

Another consideration which led to the selection of these limits is the fact that notwithstanding many striking differences in topography the section of the state here chosen for discussion has had a fairly uniform development. The causes which led to the settlements in one part of the section are substantially the same which led to settlements in other parts, and the general character of the settlements and the life of the people do not exhibit any great diversities.

Southeast Missouri, as here defined, consists of two sections differing widely in physical features. The line dividing the two sections runs from the Mississippi river at Cape Girardeau, southwest through Cape Girardeau, Stoddard, Butler, and Ripley counties dividing the latter two into almost equal parts; and reaches the state line about half way between the east and west lines of Ripley county. This line is marked throughout most of its course by bluffs averaging from seventy to one hundred feet in height and known as the Mississippi escarpment. East and south of this line of bluffs are the alluvial bottoms of the Mississippi, the St. Fran-

INTRODUCTION

cois, and Little rivers; west and north of the line is the Ozark plateau. In the alluvial bottoms are the counties of Scott, Mississippi, New Madrid, Pemiscot, and Dunklin together with parts of Cape Girardeau, Stoddard, Butler, and Ripley. In the Ozark uplift are Washington, Jefferson, Iron, Madison, Ste. Genevieve, Perry, Carter, Wayne. Bollinger, Reynolds and St. Francois counties and the remaining parts of Cape Girardeau, Stoddard, Butler, and Ripley. The former section includes about 3,800 square miles, the latter about 8,200 square miles.

The latter of these two sections, which has more than twice the area of the former, is a high land region being a part of an elevated plateau extending through Missouri and Arkansas and sending off ridges into other states. This plateau has been variously designated as the Ozark mountains, the Ozark upland, the Ozark uplift, and the Ozark plateau. Of late years there has been a tendency to restrict the term Ozark mountains to a part of the plateau in southern Missouri and Arkansas and to apply different names to other parts. In this discussion the term Ozark plateau is most frequently used as being the most appropriate name by which to designate such an elevated region as that we are here considering.

This plateau extends from the Mississippi river at St. Louis to the southwest and reaches into Arkansas, its eastern and southern boundary in Missouri is marked by a distinct escarpment or line of elevated, often precipitous bluffs. From St. Louis to Cape Girardeau, this escarpment is found on or near the bank of the Mississippi river, but south of Cape Girardeau the escarpment turns to the southwest and leaves the river. This elevated plateau or plain resembles in its general outline, an elevated dome; by some it has been compared to an upturned canoe, its central axis stretching from the northeast to the southwest. The plain is about five hundred miles in length and two hundred miles in

CAPAHA BLUFFS, ROCK LEVEE DRIVE, CAPE GIRARDEAU

INTRODUCTION

width, and has a total area of about seventy-five thousand square miles.

The central part of this plain does not resemble a mountainous country, most of it being free from any great differences of elevation. It is simply an elevated plateau. At its edges, however, the plain bears considerable resemblance to mountains, due to the action of the streams which have worn down their valleys at the edge of the plateau, leaving the land between the valleys to stand up as elevated and distinct hills or mountains. Through the central part of the plateau the fall of the streams is not very great, and consequently their action of wearing down their valleys has been slow. At the edge of the plateau, however, the slope is great, the average descent from the plateau to the Mississippi plain being about one hundred feet at the present time. Formerly it was more than this, and the streams of the plateau have carved their valleys rapidly thus making great differences of level between their beds and the untouched soil between them.

The average elevation of the Ozark plateau is about one thousand feet though there are places where the elevation is greater than this. From this central elevated part the slope extends to the northeast to the southeast and to the west.

Breaking away from this elevated dome-like region are a number of ridges extending in several directions. One of these ridges extends across the Mississippi river at Grand Tower and another at Thebes. Some other of the ridges extend to the south and cross into Arkansas, while others strike off to the southwest into Kansas and Oklahoma.

The ridge which is broken by the river at Grand Tower is called the Shawnee hills. It extends through Illinois and crosses the Ohio river into Kentucky where it gradually fades away into the other physical features of the state. It received the name Shawnee hills from the early explorers in Missouri and Illinois, who found the Shawnee Indians living along the hills. The Indians at that time were called Oshawando and this name was given at first to the hills. The point where the Mississippi river breaks through this ridge, now known as Grand Tower, is one of the most interesting places within the Mississippi valley. Even a casual examination of the spot discloses the fact that within comparatively recent times the Mississippi river flowed considerably east of its present channel. On the Illinois side above the town of Grand Tower is a great isolated rocky hill known as Fountain Bluff, which rises to a height of 635 feet above the ordinary level of the river. The channel of the river was evidently at one time to the north and east of this great bluff. One of the remarkable things connected with the formation at this place is the fact that the strata in Fountain Bluff dip are in an opposite direction from those found in the rock known as Grand Tower and the other rocks on the west side of the river. The strata are the same in general character indicating, that the formation was once continuous from Fountain Bluff to the hills on the west side, but the fact of the changed direction of the dip of the strata together with the narrowness of the channel and its precipitous sides, indicate that the break in the hills was formed by some violent upheaval.

Another of these ridges extends across the Mississippi river at Commerce, evidently having been broken here within comparatively recent times as the bed of the river is still formed of rocks and boulders, not having been worn away by the action of the

INTRODUCTION

stream nor covered with sediment as would have been the case if this part of the stream bed were as old as most of it. A part of this ridge extends into the alluvial section and is known as the Scott county hills. Other ridges make off from the central dome of the upland to the southwest extending into Arkansas and Oklahoma.

Within recent years the name St. Francois mountains has been applied to the hills in St. Francois, Iron, Wayne, and Washington counties. These hills are not only among the highest in the Ozark region of Missouri, but they are perhaps the only true mountains found within the state. They seem to have been formed not by the wearing down of the plain as is the case with most of the Ozark hills, but to have been thrust up from beneath by forces within the earth and thus are true mountains in their origin. In these mountains are exposed the only Azoic rocks in Missouri. The granites which form the primordial base on which this Ozark region was built, have been thrust up in the formation of these mountains until they are now at the surface: Iron Mountain, Shepherd Mountain, Pilot Knob, and others in their vicinity are some of the best known of these St. Francois mountains. The hill just west of Knob Lick in St. Francois county in the vicinity of the granite quarries known as Syenite, is a good example of these mountains formed by uplift. The name St. Francois mountains is peculiarly appropriate to them since most of them are found in St. Francois county and since also they form the source of the St. Francois river. The name because it is appropriate and describes a distinct formation will probably come into general acceptation and use. The upthrust which created these mountains brought the hard granite and basalt to the surface or near it in many places, and in places dikes of these rocks were formed crosswise of the ridges previously existing. The streams of the section occur for the most part in the folds in the ridges formed within the

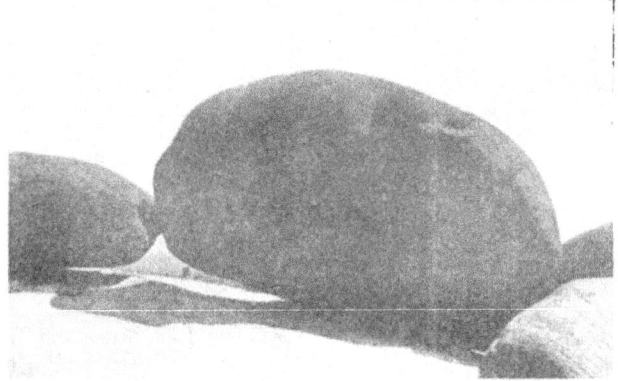

ELEPHANT ROCKS, GRANITEVILLE

material lying above the Azoic formation; the action of these streams has worn down their bed until in some cases they have come to the dikes of hard rock lying transversely across the stream bed. The hardness of the granite has prevented its wearing away as rapidly as the other portions of the valley and this fact has given rise to rather peculiar formations. The stream has ordinarily carved this wall of rock thrust across its course, but carved it much more slowly than

Southeast Missouri are Shepherd Mountain having an elevation of twelve hundred feet, Pilot Knob with an elevation of 1,118 feet covering an area of three hundred and sixty acres and Iron Mountain which rises 228 feet above the plain and covering an average of five hundred acres.

This Ozark region contains one of the greatest mineral regions in all the world. Judged by the variety of minerals as well as by the immense quantities of some of them,

SCENE AT THE SHUT-IN NEAR ARCADIA

the remaining parts of its stream bed so that it is hemmed into close quarters at these places. They are locally called "shut-ins." One of them is to be seen on Stout's creek in the vicinity of Arcadia and there are many others in the same region.

The Ozark region of Missouri has its highest elevation along the line extending from Jefferson county to the southwest through Iron and into Barry and White counties: east and west of this line the elevation gradually becomes less. The highest points in

the area deserves to take first place among mineral sections. The precious metals are not found in paying quantities, but a large number of other minerals are so found. The mineral which exists in this region in greatest abundance is lead which has attracted the attention of miners from the very earliest times; perhaps the greatest deposits of lead ore to be found in the entire world are in this section. Lead, however, is not the only mineral which is produced in paying quantities, iron is found in a number of these counties, notably Iron, St. Francois and Wayne. Copper and zinc are also taken in connection with lead and other minerals are mined on a smaller scale.

There exist great quantities of fine clays and some of the largest deposits of sand fit for glass making in the United States. Besides these there are immense quantities of valuable building stone both lime stone and granite and also considerable quantities of a good quality of sand stone.

The north part of this district is drained largely by the Maramec river which has its source in Maramec springs in Dent county and flows north and east emptying into the Mississippi on the line dividing Jefferson county from St. Louis county. It is a picturesque and beautiful stream and with it are connected some of the earliest events in the history of the state. It receives a number of small tributaries from both north and south. The principal tributary of the Maramec on the south is Big river which rises in Washington county, flows north through Washington and Jefferson counties and empties into the Maramec in Jefferson county. It is not navigable but is a very beautiful stream and has considerable water-power yet undeveloped. All the eastern part of the district is drained by streams which flow to the east and empty into the Mississippi. South of the Maramec are Saline creek, Aux Vases, Cinquehomme, Apple Creek and Cape LaCroix creek; these streams with other smaller ones have their source within the Ozark upland and flow down its eastern border into the Mississippi.

The rest of this district is drained principally by streams flowing to the south, the easternmost of these are Castor and Whitewater both of which have their origin in St. Francois county flowing toward the south and uniting to form Little river in New Madrid county. The St. Francois river also rises in St. Francois county and flows in a general southerly direction receiving the waters of Little river in Arkansas and finally flowing into the Mississippi. West of the St. Francois river are Black river and Little Black; these streams rise in Reynolds and Iron counties, flowing to the south into Arkansas and finally uniting with White river. The most westerly of the streams of the district is Current river, perhaps the most beautiful stream in the entire state, its general direction is south and east, it is a tributary of Black river.

South and east of the line which we have indicated, from Cape Girardeau to the Arkansas line, is found the alluvial bottoms of the Mississippi, Little River, the St. Francois, and Black River. With the exception of two areas, this section is practically level and all alluvial soil. These two areas are the Scott county hills and Crowley's ridge. The Scott county hills lie just south of what is called the Big swamp south of Cape Girardeau and extend a distance of about 15 miles from the neighborhood of Gray's Point to near Morley in Scott county. These hills are a part of the Paleozoic uplift and were doubtless connected with the ridge in Illinois at the time when the Mississippi river flowed to the southwest from Cape Girardeau. They are essentially the same in structure and geologic origin with the Ozark plateau.

The other elevated land in this part of Southeast Missouri is Crowley's ridge, extending from a point in Scott county not far from Bell City in a southwesterly direction, crossing the state line near Campbell, and ending at the Mississippi river near the mouth of the St. Francois. This ridge varies in width, being about ten miles wide in the central part of Stoddard county and becoming very narrow between Dexter and Malden. It is broken in two places, in the north by Castor and further south by the St. Francois river which crosses it just west of Campbell in Dunklin county. This ridge is geologically unlike the Ozark upland and most certainly had a different origin. It is composed principally of clay and seems the remains of alluvial soil which had been thrust up from below and sculptured down again by the action of the rivers, leaving this ridge. The ridge itself slopes from east to west having its greatest height on the eastern edge, where it is about one hundred feet in elevation.

The remainder of the land in Southeast Missouri is practically level but falls into a number of divisions. The first of these from east to west is the low country bordering along the Mississippi river. There is extending south from below the Scott county hills a sand ridge called the Sikeston ridge which reaches the river at New Madrid and extends almost to the south line of New Madrid county. This ridge is elevated some 10 or 15 feet above the level of the bottom lands and its soil is principally sandy loam. East of it in the neighborhood of Charleston, there are two other similar ridges of sandy loam.

West of the Sikeston ridge extending to Crowley's ridge in the north part and to the sandy ridge of Stoddard and Dunklin counties in the southern part, is the low bottom of Little River, which lies from 15 to twenty feet below the level of the sand ridges and is a heavily timbered section with a great deal of humus and exceedingly productive.

West of this bottom of Little River is another sand ridge which extends from just south of Dexter to the state line near Hornersville in Dunklin county. On this ridge are situated the towns of Bernie, Malden, Clarkton, and Kennett. The ridge is from 5 to 10 miles in width, is from 10 to 15 feet higher than the bottoms of Little river, and has a very rich and productive sandy loam soil.

West of this ridge lying between it and Crowley's ridge in the north part is what is known as West swamp, while in the south in Dunklin county the St. Francois river is between the sand ridge and Crowley's ridge. The bottom of St. Francois river is not unlike that of Little river.

West of Crowley's ridge in Stoddard county is the valley of the St. Francois river and Black river. These are heavily timbered regions with a soil considerably heavier than the sand ridges above mentioned.

The drainage in this alluvial section of Southeast Missouri is principally from north to south. Of course on its eastern edge it is drained by the Mississippi which forms its eastern boundary. The Scott county hills are the source of two creeks, Ramsey creek which flows north emptying into the Mississippi, and Caney creek which flows to the north and then west and is a tributary of Little river. Mississippi county and the eastern part of New Madrid county are drained in part by St. James and St. John's bayous. The other streams of the alluvial section are principally those which have their origin in the Ozark upland and enter the alluvial district at its northern limit. In the neighborhood of Allenville, Crooked creek and Whitewater river combine and the stream thus formed is called Whitewater until it receives the waters of Caney creek and the East Fork after which it takes the name of Little river. This stream flows to the southeast and then to the southwest and crosses the state line into Arkansas finally pouring its waters into the St. Francois.

West of Crooked creek a number of other smaller streams flow into the alluvial district. The first of these of importance is Castor river which enters the alluvial district near Zalma in Bollinger county. Castor flows south and southeast through parts of Stoddard and New Madrid counties and finally empties into Little river.

Two other streams of importance having their source in the Ozarks make their way through the alluvial district. The easternmost of these, the St. Francois river, leaves the hills in the edge of Wayne county and flows directly through Stoddard and forms the state line between Dunklin county and Arkansas. West of St. Francois river, Black river enters the alluvial district at Poplar Bluff. It, together with a number of smaller tributary streams, most of them rising in the hills, cross the state line into Arkansas from Bollinger county.

Besides these more important streams there are several other smaller ones such as Varner river, Buffalo creek, Taylor slough, and Chilletecaux in Dunklin county, Pemiscot bayou in Pemiscot county and Portage bay and Open bay in New Madrid and Pemiscot counties.

With the exception of part of the sand ridges in Scott, New Madrid, and Dunklin counties this entire alluvial section was formerly heavily timbered, the entire country being covered with a heavy growth of oak, gum, cottonwood, hickory, ash and other varieties of trees in the higher portions, and with cypress in those parts of the bottoms where water stood. There are still vast quantities of timber in this section, but it is fast being denuded of its timber.

This alluvial region presents an interesting geological problem. Those who have studied the region are not in agreement as to how the vast Mississippi embayment was formed. It has been suggested by some students that this great plain stretching from the mouth of the Mississippi to Cape Girardeau and varying in width from five to forty miles, is a coastal plain formed by the action of the waves against the land surface. No doubt a plain so formed would bear some resemblance to the alluvial plain of the Mississippi valley, but it is difficult to believe that such a plain as this could have been formed by wave action; the resulting debris from the destruction of the land surface must have retarded the action of the waves long before they sculptured a plain extending so far into the land.

Without attempting to go into minute details the probabilities are that the alluvial section as it now exists is a river valley. Early in geologic times the head of the Gulf of Mexico was near the site of Cape Girardeau and there was thus thrust into the heart of the North American continent a great triangular gulf. This gulf has been filled with alluvial soil from Cape Girardeau to the present southern limit of the delta. It is not possible to determine how deep the alluvial deposits are since there have been made no borings deep enough to find the bed of rock. Certain borings made for artesian wells and at New Madrid for the purpose of finding support for a bridge, indicate that the alluvial soil is more than two hundred feet in depth though there is very good reason to believe that it is very much deeper than this. A boring made at Cairo, Illinois, extended to a depth of 1,200 feet without striking bed rock.

It is plainly evident that the amount of alluvial material deposited in this gulf is enormous. It was brought down doubtless in large part by the great rivers which occupied the present position of the Mississippi and Ohio, perhaps at one time much larger than the present streams.

The soil now found in the alluvial section is not, however, the original deposits. There seems good reason for believing that the clay ridge known as Crowley's ridge is a remnant of the original deposit in the valley. This first deposit was raised up by the action of the forces beneath the surface and was then sculptured down by the action of the stream. This action has been going on for many thousands of years doubtless and the original deposits have been removed in large part except Crowley's ridge. Not only has the river sculptured the original deposits, it seems to have meandered back and forth across this great valley now washing the bluffs along the eastern side and now those along the western side, alternately sculpturing away deposits of alluvium and reforming them in other places.

The alluvial plains as they now exist then represent two separate cycles of stream action. The first consisted in filling in the arm of the Gulf of Mexico with alluvial deposits. This was separated from the second cycle of the stream action by the uplift of the deposited material above their former level; in the second cycle they are wearing down and redistributing this uplifted material into its present position. There seems no reason to doubt that within a comparatively short geologic time Crowley's ridge will entirely disappear under the action of the forces now at work upon it.

It is evident that there exists a complete contrast in physical characteristics between these two sections of Southeast Missouri. The most obvious of these differences is the fact that there are no hills in the alluvial section, while the whole Ozark uplift is dotted with them. There is also a marked difference in the streams; those of the plateau having their origin in springs of clear limpid water, flow between banks which are sometimes steep and even rugged in appearance. They have a swift current, are narrow and deep, but such of them like Castor, Whitewater, and the St. Francois which pass from the uplift to the alluvial plains undergo a complete change of character. They are no longer deep, narrow, and swift of current, with well marked banks, but they become wide and shallow and spread out over many miles.

The soils, too, are different. In the upland are the clays. They follow the outline of the hills on which they were deposited. The characteristic soil of the plains is a sandy loam, while gravels, clays and marl are to be found in places. The distinct characteristic soil is that which makes the great ridges on which are situated the flourishing towns of the district.

In minerals, also, the contrast between the sections is striking. No other section of equal size in the world contains a greater variety and wealth of minerals than the Ozark plateau. Here are to be found the great deposits of copper, zinc, lead, iron, and others. The alluvial plains on the other hand have no minerals except bog ore. The materials of which the plains are formed are the loose clastics. While the plains are lacking in mineral wealth, they possess great supplies of timber. The hills are covered in many places with timber, but the valuable trees in greatest numbers are to be found in the rich soil of the low lands. Here flourish the cotton wood, oak, gum, cypress, and hickory in great abundance. No other part of the United States possesses more valuable timbers than the low lands in Southeast Missouri.

This contrast between sections is also to be seen in their climate. Spring visits the lowlands at least two weeks earlier than it does the uplands. The winters, too, are not so cold on the plains, and the rain-fall is considerably greater. In fact the line marking forty inches of annual precipitation coincides quite closely with the escarpment which separates the plateau from the plain. These differences of climate and soil have resulted in certain differences in the crops cultivated in the two sections. The great staple crops, wheat and corn, are extensively grown in both sections, but in addition to these the alluvial soil produces large crops of cotton and melons which cannot be grown successfully in the hills.

CONTENTS

SECTION I

CHAPTER I
ARCHAEOLOGY

Mounds in Southeast Missouri—Great Numbers Known to Exist — Distribution of Mounds—Size of Mounds—Shape—Arrangement — Various Mounds Described — An Ancient Wharf—Contents of Mounds—Who Built the Mounds—The Mound Builder Theory—The Work of the Indians—Probable Origin—Collections of Relics—Beckwith's Great Collection—Plates Found Near Malden—Other Remarkable Pieces. 3

CHAPTER II
ADVENTURES OF DE SOTO

Is Made Governor of Florida—Lands in Florida—Discovers the Mississippi — Place of Crossing—Direction of March—The Casquins—Religious Service—Attack on Capahas—Search for Salt—Probable Situation of Capaha Camp—Return to the South—Quigate—Location of Caligoa—Further Travels and Death—Interest Concerning Exact Route. 13

CHAPTER III
FRENCH EXPLORERS

Why Spaniards Did not Take and Hold the Country—Vague Ideas of the West—News of the Mississippi—Radisson and Groseilliers—Joliet and Marquette—Discovery of the Mississippi—Extent of Their Voyage—The Return—Illness of Marquette — Why Joliet Was Not Given Credit for Expedition — Early Voyage of La Salle — French Ideas of the New World—Views of the English — La Salle's Purpose — Friendship With Frontenac—Visit to France—Start of the Expedition — Loss of the Griffon—Creve Coeur—He Reaches the Mississippi—Passes to its Mouth—The Colony at Starved Rock—Goes to France—Colony on the Gulf—Death of LaSalle—Estimate of His Character. 22

CONTENTS

CHAPTER IV
INDIAN HISTORY

IMPORTANCE OF INDIANS IN OUR HISTORY—INDIAN TRADE—INDIANS IN SOUTHEAST MISSOURI WHEN DESOTO CAME—THE CAPAHAS—THE SIOUAN FAMILY AND ITS BRANCHES — THE OSAGES—THEIR HOMES—THEIR FARMS—OSAGE HOUSES — FURNITURE AND CLOTHING — POLYGAMY—WEAPONS—PECULIAR CUSTOMS OF THE OSAGES — PAINTING OF THE BODY — THEIR GOVERNMENT—WARS WITH OTHER INDIANS—DEFEATED BY SACS AND FOXES—THEIR REMOVAL FROM THE STATE—DELAWARES AND SHAWNEES—THEIR HISTORY OUTSIDE MISSOURI—WHY THE SPANIARDS BROUGHT THEM TO MISSOURI—CHARACTER—THEIR VILLAGES—TECUMSEH'S SISTER — CHILLETECAUX — WITCHCRAFT DELUSION—THE MASHCOUX TRIBE—TREATIES WITH THE INDIANS—INDIAN EDUCATION. 33

SECTION II

CHAPTER V
STE. GENEVIEVE DISTRICT

THE NAME LOUISIANA—THE ILLINOIS— THE FRENCH AND SPANISH DISTRICTS WITH THEIR LIMITS—THE APPEARANCE AND CHARACTER OF THE COUNTRY—STE. GENEVIEVE—PROBABLE DATE OF FIRST SETTLEMENT—"THE OLD VILLAGE OF STE. GENEVIEVE" — ORIGINAL SETTLERS—OFFICIALS AND LEGAL PROCEEDINGS—OCCUPATIONS — THE "BIG FIELD" — INDIAN TROUBLES—LIFE OF THE FRENCH PIONEERS—POPULATION—PITTMAN'S ACCOUNT — VISIT OF PAUL ALLIOY—AS PECK SAW THE TOWN—IMPRESSIONS OF FLAG—FERDINAND ROZIER — JOHN JAMES AUDUBON—JOHN SMITH T.—HENRY DODGE—JOHN RICE JONES—NEW BOURBON—NEW TENNESSEE—TABLE OF SETTLEMENTS—FIRST SETTLERS IN IRON COUNTY—THE COOK AND MURPHY SETTLEMENTS—ST. MICHAEL'S—OLD MINES—FIRST SETTLERS IN JEFFERSON COUNTY—PERRY COUNTY SETTLEMENTS—LONG'S ACCOUNT. 49

CHAPTER VI
CAPE GIRARDEAU DISTRICT

ITS LIMITS—LIFE OF LORIMIER—FIRST SETTLEMENT AT CAPE GIRARDEAU—INFLUENCE WITH THE INDIANS—GRANTS OF AUTHORITY AND LAND—LORIMIER'S TOMB—NAME OF CAPE GIRARDEAU—COUSIN—EARLY SETTLERS—THE TOWN LAID OFF—SOME OF THE EARLY BUILDINGS—FIRST INCORPORATION, 1808—EARLY SETTLERS WITHIN THE DISTRICT—THE RAMSAYS—THE GIBONEYS—OTHER EARLY FAMILIES—SETTLEMENTS IN VARIOUS PARTS OF THE DISTRICT. 67

CHAPTER VII
DISTRICT OF NEW MADRID

ITS BOUNDARIES—"L'ANSE A LA GRAISE"—THE LESIEURS—SITUATION OF NEW MADRID—COLONEL GEORGE MORGAN—GRANT TO MORGAN—HIS EXPECTATION OF PROFIT — HIS DESCRIPTION OF THE SITE—THE SURVEY OF THE TOWN—OPPOSITION OF WILKINSON AND MIRO—NEW MADRID FALLS INTO HANDS OF MIRO—LETTER OF LA FORGE—THE COMMANDANTS

CONTENTS   xix

OF THE POST—EMIGRANTS WHO CAME WITH MORGAN—THE LESIEUR FAMILY—THE LA
FORGES—JOSEPH MICHEL—ROBERT MCCOY—RICHARD JONES WATERS—TARDIVEAU—OTHER
SETTLERS—ROBERT GOAH WATSON—MILITARY COMPANIES—OTHER SETTLEMENTS IN NEW
MADRID COUNTY—LITTLE PRAIRIE—SETTLEMENTS IN SCOTT COUNTY—TOWN NEAR SIKESTON
—BENTON—JOSEPH HUNTER—TYWAPPITY BOTTOMS—MISSISSIPPI COUNTY SETTLEMENTS—
SPANISH LAND GRANTS—THE KING'S HIGHWAY.   81

CHAPTER VIII

GOVERNMENT UNDER FRANCE AND SPAIN

LOUISIANA UNDER LA SALLE—THE PROVINCE OF LOUISIANA—CAPITALS AND GOVERNORS—CESSION TO SPAIN—PROVIDENCE OF UPPER LOUISIANA — LIEUTENANT GOVERNORS OF UPPER LOUISIANA—DISTRICTS AND COMMANDANTS—SYNDICS—AUTHORITY OF OFFICIALS—FRENCH LAW RETAINED—CHARACTER OF GOVERNMENT—THE CABILDO AT NEW ORLEANS—ORGANIZATION OF MILITIA—"L' ANNEE DU COUP" ATTACK ON ST. LOUIS—TREACHERY OF GOVERNOR LEYBA—ACTION OF THE STE. GENEVIEVE COMPANY—EXPEDITION TO NEW MADRID—PUNISHMENT OF INDIANS—ORDERS CONCERNING TAVERNS AND SALE OF LIQUOR TO INDIANS.   111

CHAPTER IX

SOCIAL LIFE

POPULATION IN 1804—SETTLEMENTS—OCCUPATIONS—DIFFERENCES BETWEEN FRENCH AND AMERICA SETTLEMENTS—HOUSES OF THE FRENCH—STOCKADES—FOOD AND COOKING—DIFFERENCES IN THE FRENCH PRODUCED BY RESIDENCE IN THIS COUNTRY—SOCIAL LIFE—DRESS—AMUSEMENTS—LA GUIGNOLEE—CONTENTED CHARACTER OF THE FRENCH—TRADE—AMERICAN SETTLERS—CHARACTERISTIC LIFE—HOUSES—CLOTHING—FOOD — LAW-ABIDING CHARACTERS—GERMAN SETTLERS—ABSENCE OF SPANISH SETTLERS—MERCHANTS—PRICES—PRODUCTS—TRAVEL—ROADS—RIVER TRAVEL—KEEL-BOATS—RELIGIOUS CONDITIONS—FIRST SERVICES—RESTRICTIVE LAWS OF SPAIN—RECORDS OF THE CATHOLIC CHURCH IN STE. GENEVIEVE—FATHER MEURIN—FATHER GIBAULT—JAMES MAXWELL—FIRST CHURCH BUILDINGS—SUPPORT OF PRIESTS—BISHOP DUBOURG—DE ANDREIS—FOUNDING OF ST. MARY'S SEMINARY — DANGER OF MISUNDERSTANDING THE CHARACTER OF THE PEOPLE.   117

CHAPTER X

TRANSFER TO THE UNITED STATES

FEELING OF THE FRENCH SETTLERS—SETTLEMENTS FOUNDED UNDER THE RULE OF FRANCE—EMIGRATION FROM THE WESTERN STATES—WHY SPAIN FOSTERED THE MOVEMENT OF AMERICANS ACROSS THE RIVER—QUESTION OVER THE NAVIGATION OF THE MISSISSIPPI—RESTRICTIONS ON COMMERCE—TREATY OF ILDEFONSO — NEGOTIATIONS FOR PURCHASE OF NEW ORLEANS—OFFER OF ALL LOUISIANA—MOTIVES OF NAPOLEON IN SELLING LOUISIANA—CEREMONIES ATTENDING THE ACTUAL TRANSFER—CAPTAIN AMOS STODDARD AND HIS AUTHORITY—SIGNIFICANCE OF THE TRANSFER.   139

CONTENTS

SECTION III

CHAPTER XI

AMERICAN TERRITORIAL GOVERNMENT

GOVERNMENT OF THE LOUISIANA TERRITORY—THE TERRITORY OF ORLEANS—THE DISTRICT OF LOUISIANA — FIRST GOVERNOR — COURTS OF COMMON PLEAS — OFFICERS AT THE VARIOUS POSTS—CAUSES OF DISSATISFACTION WITH THE GOVERNMENT OF THE UNITED STATES—MEMORIAL OF GRIEVANCES—THE TERRITORY OF LOUISIANA—CONFIRMATION OF LAND GRANTS—COURTS—WILKINSON AS GOVERNOR—LEWIS—CLARK—THE TERRITORY OF MISSOURI — POWERS OF THE GOVERNOR—MEETINGS OF THE TERRITORIAL LEGISLATURE—VARIOUS LAWS—RICHARD S. THOMAS—JOHN SCOTT—JOHNSON RANNEY—GENERAL WATKINS—GREER W. DAVIS—ALEXANDER BUCKNER—OTHER PROMINENT MEN—THE BYRD FAMILY—CIRCUIT COURTS—OFFICERS IN STE. GENEVIEVE—CAPE GIRARDEAU DISTRICT AND COUNTY—NEW MADRID DISTRICT AND COUNTY—CREATION OF NEW COUNTIES—LAWRENCE — WAYNE — MADISON — JEFFERSON — WASHINGTON — PERRY — MILITARY HISTORY. 147

CHAPTER XII

PERIOD FROM 1804 TO 1821

POPULATION—CHARACTER OF IMMIGRANTS—SETTLEMENTS IN VARIOUS PARTS OF THE SECTION — EARLY SETTLERS — INDUSTRIES — FARMING—MINING — MERCHANDISING — PREVAILING HIGH PRICES — MANUFACTURING — HUNTING — TRANSPORTATION — STEAMBOATS — SOCIAL LIFE — LAWLESSNESS — GAMBLING — DUELING — SOME FAMOUS DUELS — HOSPITALITY — POSTOFFICES AND RATES OF POSTAGE — NEWSPAPERS—SCHOOLS—LIBRARIES—DRESS. 175

CHAPTER XIII

PROTESTANT IMMIGRATION

VISITS OF PROTESTANT MINISTERS—JOHN CLARK — JOSIAH DODGE—THOMAS JOHNSON—ANDREW WILSON—RELIGIOUS CONDITION OF THE SETTLERS—MOTIVES WHICH BROUGHT THEM TO LOUISIANA — THE WORK OF THE BAPTISTS — DAVID GREENE — BETHEL CHURCH NEAR JACKSON — ITS EARLY MEMBERS — THE FIRST MEETING HOUSE — RELICS OF OLD BETHEL CHURCH—MEMORIAL SERVICES IN 1906—GROWTH OF THE CHURCH—OTHER CHURCHES ORGANIZED BY MEMBERS OF BETHEL—EARLY MINISTERS OF THE CHURCH—WILSON THOMPSON—THOMAS STEPHENS—THOMAS P. GREENE—THE FIRST MISSIONARY COLLECTION—THE FORMATION OF AN ASSOCIATION OF CHURCHES IN MISSOURI—JOHN M. PECK—THE WORK OF THE METHODIST CHURCH — FIRST PREACHERS — JOHN TRAVIS—ORGANIZATION OF MCKENDREE—EARLY MEMBERS—FIRST MEETING HOUSE—JESSE WALKER — THE FIRST CIRCUITS — FIRST SERMON IN CAPE GIRARDEAU—CAMPMEETING AT MCKENDREE IN 1810 — HARBISON — NEW CIRCUITS FORMED—ORGANIZATION OF THE MISSOURI CONFERENCE — RUCKER TANNER — THE FIRST CONFERENCE HELD IN MISSOURI—THE WORK OF THE PRESBYTERIANS—HEMPSTEAD'S LETTER — A CHURCH ORGANIZED IN WASHINGTON COUNTY, 1816 — ORGANIZATION OF THE PRESBYTERY OF MISSOURI — EARLY MINISTERS — TIMOTHY FLINT — THE COLUMBIAN BIBLE SOCIETY—FLINT'S WRITINGS—DISCIPLES OF CHRIST—WILLIAM MCMURTRY—FIRST ORGANIZATION IN MISSOURI, 1822 — DIFFICULTIES UNDER WHICH EARLY MINISTERS LABORED — PROGRESS MADE—PECK'S DESCRIPTION—DEBT OWED TO PIONEER MINISTERS. 196

CHAPTER XIV
NEW MADRID EARTHQUAKE

TIME AND AREA—UNIQUE AMONG EARTHQUAKES—CONTEMPORARY ACCOUNTS MENTIONED—THE SCENE DESCRIBED—DIRECTION OF THE SHOCKS—SIZE OF AFFECTED AREA—CHARACTER OF DISTURBANCES—SMALL LOSS OF LIFE EXPLAINED—A DEATH FROM FRIGHT—PERSONS DROWNED—APPEARANCE OF THE AIR—VAPORS—LIGHTS AND GLOWS—EARTH CHANGES—FISSURES—LIGNITE—AREAS OF SURFACE RAISED—SUNK-LANDS — OBSERVATIONS MADE BY LYELL—DISTRIBUTION OF SUNK-LANDS—EFFECT ON TIMBER — EXPULSION OF MATERIAL FROM THE EARTH — WATER-SAND—SAND BLOWS—SAND-SLOUGHS — SINKS — SUGGESTED CAUSES—CONTEMPORARY ACCOUNTS—MRS. ELIZA BRYAN — LONG—BRADBURY—FLINT—FAUX—LESIEUR—COL. JOHN SHAW—LETTER OF AN UNKNOWN WRITER—LONG—NUTTALL—FLAGG—FORMER DRAINAGE AS DESCRIBED BY LESIEUR—GOVERNMENT ASSISTANCE TO SUFFERERS—THE NEW MADRID CLAIMS—DELISLE VS. STATE OF MISSOURI—LOSS OF POPULATION. 212

CHAPTER XV
STATEHOOD ATTAINED

PETITION FOR ORGANIZATION AS A STATE—BILL TO ORGANIZE A STATE GOVERNMENT — THE SLAVERY CONTROVERSY—THE TALLMADGE AMENDMENT—DEBATE OVER THE AMENDMENT—DEADLOCK OF THE TWO HOUSES—THE MISSOURI COMPROMISE—FEELING IN THE STATE—THE CONSTITUTIONAL CONVENTION—MEMBERS FROM THE SOUTHEAST—THE CONSTITUTION IN CONGRESS—FURTHER OPPOSITION TO ADMISSION — THE DEBATE — CLAY'S COMPROMISE — THE SOLEMN PUBLIC ACT—THE PRESIDENT'S PROCLAMATION ADMITTING THE STATE—PECULIARITIES OF THE TRANSACTION—STATE BOUNDARIES — MISSOURI — ARKANSAS — WOLF ISLAND. 234

SECTION IV
CHAPTER XVI
GENERAL DEVELOPMENT

ANALYSIS OF POPULATION, 1820-1830—COMPARATIVE CENSUS TABLE, 1820-1860—FRENCH AND GERMAN ELEMENTS—PERIOD OF TOWN GROWTH. 247

CHAPTER XVII
STE. GENEVIEVE AND ST. MARYS.

SHIPPING CENTER OF MINERAL REGION—STE. GENEVIEVE-IRON MOUNTAIN PLANK ROAD—150TH ANNIVERSARY CELEBRATED—U. S. SENATORS FROM STE. GENEVIEVE—STE. GENEVIEVE OF TODAY—ST. MARYS. 251

CHAPTER XVIII
CAPE GIRARDEAU COUNTY TOWNS

CAPE GIRARDEAU A STEAMBOAT TOWN—INCORPORATED AS A CITY—PROSPERITY AFTER THE WAR—STATE NORMAL SCHOOL LOCATED—STAGE OF STAGNATION—REALLY REMARKABLE PROGRESS—FOUNDING OF JACKSON—FIRST INSTITUTIONS AND PERSONS—CIVIL GOVERNMENT—PRESENT COUNTY SEAT—BURFORDVILLE—APPLETON—POCAHONTAS AND OAK RIDGE. 256

CONTENTS

CHAPTER XIX
NEW MADRID AND MADISON COUNTIES

Blows to New Madrid—Incorporated as a City—Long the County Seat—Point Pleasant—Portageville—Fredericktown.   265

CHAPTER XX
WASHINGTON AND PERRY COUNTIES

Potosi Laid Out and Incorporated—Old Mines—Caledonia—Perryville—Longtown—Altenburg.   269

CHAPTER XXI
WAYNE AND JEFFERSON COUNTIES

Greenville, Early and Late—Piedmont—Patterson—DeSoto—Crystal City—Herculaneum—Hillsboro—Kimmswick—Hematite.   272

CHAPTER XXII
ST. FRANCOIS, BOLLINGER AND PEMISCOT COUNTIES

Present-Day Bismarck—Libertyville—Farmington—Marble Hill—Lutesville—Gayoso—Caruthersville.   277

CHAPTER XXIII
DUNKLIN AND MISSISSIPPI

Old-Time Kennett—Modern Town Dates from Railroad—Clarkton—Hornersville—Mississippi County Seat—Charleston of the Present—Belmont.   284

CHAPTER XXIV
TOWNS OF SIX COUNTIES

Commerce Incorporated—Benton, Scott County Seat—Sikeston—Doniphan, County Seat of Ripley—Poplar Bluff, Butler County's Seat of Justice—Bloomfield, Stoddard County—Ironton, County Seat of Ironton—Arcadia—Lesterville—Smaller Settlements.   290

CHAPTER XXV
POLITICAL, CIVIL AND MILITARY

The First State Election—Contest for the Senatorship—The Eight Counties—Courts in Each County—Organization of New Counties—Southeast Missouri in the Mexican War.   299

CONTENTS

CHAPTER XXVI
CREATION OF NEW COUNTIES

St. Francois County—Scott County—Organization and Settlement of Stoddard County—Ripley County—Pioneers of Dunklin County—Reynolds, Butler and Bollinger Counties—Pemiscot County—St. Francois Levee District — Courts of the County and Prominent Citizens—Iron and Carter Counties—Founders of the Eight Old Counties. 302

SECTION V

CHAPTER XXVII
GENERAL MOVEMENTS

Position of the State—Number of Soldiers Furnished—Appointment of a Major-General of the State Guards—General S. Watkins—General Thompson—Skirmishes in August, 1861—General Grant—Fortifications at Cape Girardeau—Martial Law—Thompson's Raid into Jefferson County—Situation in November, 1861—Battle of Belmont—Early Months of 1862—Capture of New Madrid and Island Ten—Skirmishes and Raids of 1863—Marmaduke's Invasion—Capture of General Jeff Thompson—Price's Raid Conditions After the War. 327

CHAPTER XXVIII
REGIMENTAL HISTORIES

Union Troops Organized—Home Guards and State Militia—Third, Fifth, Sixty-Fourth, Sixty-eighth, Seventy-eighth, Seventy-ninth, Second, Twenty-ninth, Thirtieth and Forty-seventh Infantry—Sixth and Tenth Missouri Cavalry—Engineer Regiment, West Missouri Volunteers—Twenty-third and Twenty-ninth Regiments of Enrolled Militia—Other Commands of State Guards—Ninth and Second Infantry—Noted Confederate Organizations. 341

SECTION VI

CHAPTER XXIX
MOVEMENTS SINCE THE CIVIL WAR

Railroad Building—Drainage—Wealth — Manufacturing — Mining — Transportation—Resources—Schools and Churches — Local Option — Population — Organizations — Spanish-American War. 357

CONTENTS

CHAPTER XXX

TOWNS FOUNDED SINCE CIVIL WAR

Marquand — Glenallen — Zalma — Bessville — Neeleyville — Fisk — Harviel — Van Buren — Ellsinore — Grandin — Hunter — Pocahontas — Allenville—Whitewater — Burfordville — Millerville —Oakridge — Gordonville — Malden—Campbell — Gibson — Holcomb — Senath—Whiteoak — Glennonville — Cardwell — Caruth — Cottonplant — Des Arc — Sabula — Belleview — Annapolis — Festus — House's Spring — Morse Mill — Peveley — Victoria — Mine LaMotte — Cornwall — Diehlstadt — East Prairie — Bertrand — Marston — Gideon — Parma — Lilbourn — Como — Morehouse — Hayti — Holland — Cottonwood Point — Steele —Calryville — Lithium — Wittenberg — Longtown — Schumer Springs — Bunker — Ellington — Naylor — Flat River — Desloge — Leadwood — Elvins — Bonne Terre — Bismarck — DeLassus — Knob Lick—Libertyville — Doe Run — Oran — Fornfelt — Illmo—Crowder — Kelso — Blodgett — Morley — Chaffee — Vanduser — Dexter — Advance — Bernie — Puxico — Irondale — Mineral Point —Richwoods — Chaonia — Leeper — Mills Ring—Williamsville. 371

SECTION VII

CHAPTER XXXI

EARLY SCHOOLS

Work of the Subscription Schools — Academies at Ste. Genevieve, Jackson, Potosi, New Madrid, Perryville, Point Pleasant, Cape Girardeau, Bloomfield, Poplar Bluff and Charleston. 397

CHAPTER XXXII

PUBLIC SCHOOLS

Foundation of Public System—The State Commission—Sale of Lands—Laws of 1853—Provisions of 1874—Growth of the System — Southeast Missouri Teachers' Association—First Schools in Various Counties. 404

CHAPTER XXXIII

INSTITUTIONS OF HIGHER LEARNING

St. Mary's Seminary—St. Vincent's College—Will Mayfield College—Elmwood Seminary—Farmington College—Marvin Collegiate Institute—Carleton College—Arcadia College—The State Normal School at Cape Girardeau. 412

SECTION VIII

CHAPTER XXXIV

SOCIAL LIFE AND INDUSTRIES

Isolation of Many Communities—Deprivations Suffered—Houses—Food—Dress—Household Implements—Schools and Churches—Amusements—Unity of Feeling—Treatment of Disease—Versatility of the Pioneer—Development of Character—Farming—Mining—Manufacturing. 439

CHAPTER XXXV

RELIGIOUS HISTORY—Continued

Catholics—Methodists: Quarterly Meetings, Circuits and Districts—Baptists: Associations—Evangelical Lutherans—Protestant Episcopal Churches—Congregationalists—German Evangelical and German Methodist Churches—New School Presbyterians—Cumberland Presbyterian Churches—Christians (Disciples of Christ)—Southeast Missouri Presbyterian Churches—Presbyterianism in 1854-64—1864-1874—Division in Presbytery—Decade from 1884 to 1894—History Since 1894. 448

CHAPTER XXXVI

RAILROADS

Beginning of Railroad Agitation—Companies Formed—The First Railroad—St. Louis, Iron Mountain & Southern—Cairo & Fulton—Present Condition of the Iron Mountain—The Cape Girardeau, Pilot Knob & Belmont—The Houck Lines—The 'Frisco System—the St. Louis Southwestern—The Illinois & Missouri Bridge Company—Mississippi River & Bonne Terre Railroad Company—The Williamsville, Greenville & St. Louis Railroad Company—St. Louis, Kennett & Southeastern—The St. Louis & Missouri Southern—The Paragould Southeastern—The Illinois Southern—The Missouri Southern—The Paragould & Memphis—The Butler County Railroad—The St. Francois County Interurban. 496

CHAPTER XXXVII

GENERAL STATUS

Location—Area—Topography—Timber—Industries—Transportation—Towns—Population—Schools—Wealth—Bollinger—Butler—Cape Girardeau—Carter—Dunklin—Iron—Jefferson—Madison—Mississippi—New Madrid—Pemiscot—Perry—Reynolds—Ripley—St. Francois—Ste. Genevieve—Scott—Stoddard—Washington—Wayne. 510

CONTENTS

CHAPTER XXXVIII

THE NEWSPAPERS

Cape Girardeau — The First Paper — Bollinger — Butler — Carter — Dunklin — Iron — Jefferson — Madison — Mississippi — New Madrid — Pemiscot — Perry — Reynolds — Ripley — St. Francois — Ste. Genevieve — Scott — Stoddard — Washington — Wayne — The Great Work of Newspapers. 529

CHAPTER XXXIX

SOME BIOGRAPHIES

Louis Houck—Lownes H. Davis—Robert H. Whitelaw — William B. Wilson — Judge John W. Emerson—Samuel S. Hildebrand—Samuel Byrns—B. B. Cahoon—James D. Fox—J. J. Russell—H. J. Deal—Absalom McElmurry — William Dawson — Joseph Hunter—John A. Mott—Robert A. Hatcher—Eliza A. Carleton—William Carter—Placide DeLassus—James R. McCormack—Milton P. Cayce—Gustavus St. Gem—Charles S. Hertich— M. L. Clardy— Marshall Arnold — James P. Walker — N. B. Henry—F. P. Graves—Firmin Desloge. 548

INDEX

Abbey, Daniel, 291, 342
Abel, Ezekiel, 74, 75, 257
Abel, Wilson, 290
Abernathy, Albert G., 402
Abernathy, Clayton D., 270
Able, Wilson, 171
Abshier, Claude E., 821
Academies, 400
Adams, Benjamin H., 530
Adams, J. W., 912
Adams, James T., 293
Adams, Jefferson D., 1279
Adams, Joel, 1094
Adelphi Literary Society, 430
Advance, 391
"Advance Guard," 544
"Advertiser," 532
Ake, Eli D., 534
Akers, Alfred H., 618
Albert, H. L., 431
Albert, J., 256
Albert, John, 262
Albert, Leon J., 433, 588
Albert, R., 267
Albert, S., 256
Albright, George W., 753
Alderson, James, 410
Alexander, Harry E., 695
Alexander, John H., 282
Alexander, William, 302
Alford, George G., 265
Algonquins, 34
Allen, Albert O., 537, 1052
Allen, B. B., 411
Allen, Benjamin F., 976
Allen, Edward, 913
Allen, Russell L., 1163
Allen, Samuel, 265
Allen, Thomas, 497
Allen, Thomas C., 1149
Allen, William R., Jr., 821
Allenville, 373, 374
Alleys Mines, 177
Allstun, Hiram B., 1117
Ally, John, 63
Altenburg, 271
Altenberg Evangelical Lutheran Church, 479
Alvey, William T., 923
Amoreaux, Michael, 164

Amusements, 122
Anderson, Benjamin F., 1224
Anderson, Ed, 901
Anderson, Henry, 949
Anderson, I. E., 478
Anderson, M. S., 1251
Andrew, Lyman B., 402
Andrews, John, 302
Andrews, L. H., 402
Annapolis, 378
Anthony, Benjamin, 171
Anthony, Edward D., 576
Anthony, John, 249
Anthony, Robert A., 650
Antioch Christian Church, 494
Appleberry, Daly, 780
Appleberry, Reuben, 780
Apple Creek, xii
Apple Creek, 66
Apple Creek First Presbyterian Church, 489
Apple Creek German M. E. Church, 483
Applegate, H. A., 308
Appleton, 264
Arcadia, 297
Arcadia College, 420
Arcadia College and Ursuline Seminary, 842
Arcadia Congregational Church, 482
"Arcadia Prospect," 534
"Arcadia Valley Enterprise," 534
Arent, Cornelius, 79
Arenz, Oscar, 1283
"Argus," 530
Arion Literary Society, 430
Arkansas River, 26
Armour, David, 194, 262
Armstrong, John, 262
Arnold, J. L., 1050
Arnold, Marshall, 556
Arthur, William C., 960
Asa, A. Frank, 1186
Ashabranner, 183
Asherbramer, Daniel, 80
Ashley, John, 1078
Ashley, John L., 1090
Ashley, W. H., 257
Ashley, William H., 162, 261, 402
Audubon, John James, 60, 213
Austin, 181
Austin, A. C., 308

xxvii

Austin, James, 160, 302, 402
Austin, Moses, 64, 159, 169, 183, 269, 402
Austin, Stephen F., 154, **155**
Aux Vases, xii
Averill, Harvey E., 538
Azar (Breton), Francois, 182
Azoic Rocks, x

Bagby, Robert J., 756
Bage, Samuel E., 985
Bailey, J. A., 1136
Bailey, Ralph E., 1240
Baird, Ely D., 985
Baird, Francis M., 1072
Baird, James M., 893
Baird, Martin V., 473, 1067
Baker, E., 678
Baker, Elisha, 62
Baker, Henry, 178
Baker, James, 307
Baker, Moses, 290
Baker, Peter, 178
Baker, Rebecca, 63
Baker, W. L., 957
Baldwin, Hartwell, 291
Baldwin, Joseph, 421
Baldwin, J. W., 403
Baldwin, Paul, 560
Baldwin, T. E., 285
Baldwin, Thomas E., 559
Ball, J. Morgan, 1192
Ballard, James M., 929
Ballew, James, 161
Ballou, (Mrs.) Agnes, 197
Bancroft, C. B., 307
Bancroft, Thomas S., 402
Baptists, 198, 207, 463
"Baptist Headlight," 530
"Baptist Journal," 534
Barber, Moses B., 703
Barham, William H., 1068
Barkley, Richard, 402
Barley, Absolom, 295
Barnard, James Underwood, 426
Barnard, W. P., 287
Barnes, C. M., 1035
Barnes, Goah S., 1046
Barnes, John N., 1033
Barnes, William A., 1270
Barnett, Silas J., 1108
Barnhart, Adam, 307
Barren Church, 201
"Barrens, The," 66, 177
Barrett, A. M., 742
Barrett, William L., 566
Barrow, Abner, 674
Barsaloux, Jean Baptiste, 107
Barsaloux, John B., 115
Barsaloux, John Baptiste, 66
Barth, Phillip H., 1017
Bartlett, G. T., 403, 531
Bartlett, Orson, 295, 296, 403
Bartlett, Thomas, 291
Barton, David, 63, 169, 238, 299
Bateaus (pirogues), 131
Bates, Elijah, 169
Bates, Moses, 402
Battery F, Second Illinois Light Artillery, **347**
Battle of Belmont, 332

Baumblatt, C. F., 894
Baxter, Francois, 282
Bayou Portage, 230
Bayou, St. John, 6
Beattie, George M., 262
Beauvais, Jean, 52
Beauvais, J. S. J., 150
Beauvais, St. Gem, 52
Beck, Arnold, 341
Beckwith, Newman, 303
Bedford, A. M., 288, 295, **498**
Bedford, H. H., 350
Bedford, Henry Hale, 305
Belchamber, James, 794
Bell City, 391
Bell, Huey F., 789
Bell Telephone Co., 261
Belleview, 378
Bellevue Collegiate Institute, 461
Bellevue Presbyterian Church, 488
Bellevue Settlement, 207
Bellevue Valley, 64, 178
Bellon, Tolbert E., 1058
Belmont, 289
Belmont Branch, The, 497
Belt, Harry B., 1029
Beverly, Nathaniel, 168
Benedict, Horace D., 613
Bennett, Carroll P., 676
Bennett, Joseph, 267
Bennett, L. D., 476
Benton, 290, 449
"Benton Express," 542
"Benton Express Record," 542
Benton-Lucas Duels, 190
Benton Presbyterian Church, 484
"Benton Record," 542
Benton, Thomas H., 190, 299
Bequette, Joseph, 52
Bergmann, William C., 660
Bergmann, William F., 637
Bernie, 391
"Bernie Star," 544
Berry, J. A., 371, 784
Berryman, Jerome C., 461, 725
Berthaume, Marie, 73
Bertling, Daniel, 480
Bertrand, 379
Bessville, 372
Bethel Association of the Baptist Church, 463
Bethel Baptist Association, 475
Bethel Baptist Church, 162
Bethel Church, 198
Bethel Church Monument, 200
Bethlehem Baptist Church, 476
Bettis, Elijah, 238
Bettis, Overton, 167
Bidewell, Charles F., 643
Bidewell, George, 662
Biffle, A. L., 1193
Big Creek Baptist Church, 477
"Big Field," 7, 119
Bigham, William, 282
Big River, xii
Big River, 331
Big River Mills, 63
Big Swamp, 76
Bird, Abraham, 109, 179
Bird's Point, 109, 179, 379

INDEX   xxix

Bird, Thompson, 288
Bishop, Pleasant, 267
Bismark, 277, 386
"Bismark Gazette," 541
Bismark Presbyterian Church, 491
Bisplinghoff, George H., 694
Black, John, 314
Black River, xii, xiv
Black River Baptist Association, 469
Black River Baptist Church, 469
"Black River Country," 531
"Black River News," 531
Blackwell, 331
Blake, Ross, 871
Blakemore, A. F., 1076
Blakemore, J. B., 285, 507
Blaine, Albert, 733
Blair, Governor, 243
Blair, Robert, 74
Blair, Thomas, 204
Blanton, J. Thompson, 605
Blanton Plank-Road, 265
Blanton, William H., 724
Blaylock, Richard D., 848
Blaylock, W. M., 865
Bledsoe, John H., 966
Bledsoe, J. S., 288
Bledsoe, Richard, 254
Bledsoe, William B., 953
Block, Hiram, 402
Block, Levi, 270
Blodgett, 388
Bloom, Peter, 62
Bloomfield, 295, 335, 337, 453, 454, 462, 526
"Bloomfield Argus," 543
Bloomfield Baptist Church, 473
Bloomfield Educational Society, 403
"Bloomfield Herald," 295, 543
Bloomfield Mission, 454
"Bloomfield Vindicator," 296, 545
Blount, Jacob C., 293, 311
Boaz, Herbert L., 1210
Bocarie, Phyllis, 65
Bogliolo, Etienne, 97
Bogliolo, Matteo, 265
Bogy, Joseph, 154
Bogy, Leon, 344
Bogy, Lewis V., 253
Boise Brule Bottom, 66
Bolduc, Louis, 56
Boli, E. M., 273
Boli, John, 65
Boli, William, 125
Boli, Williams, 65
Bollinger County, 79, 313, 510, 531
Bollinger, Charles F., 770
Bollinger, Frederick, 150
Bollinger, George Frederick, 79, 153, 154, 155, 177, 313
Bollinger, H. A., 1220
Bollinger, Henry E., 827
Bollinger, Henry F., 1005
Bollinger, Major, 128
Bollinger, Phillip, 80
Bollinger, Solomon, 167
Bollinger, Walter A., 1183
Bollinger, William, 80, 1183
Bond, George, 344
Bond, George H., 741

Bone, William M., 965
Bonne Terre, 385, 450
Bonne Terre Congregational Church, 482
"Bonne Terre Register," 541
"Bonne Terre Star," 541
Booker, Charles O., 1273
Boon, Pinkney E., 1288
Booth, James, 1133
Boutin, Samuel, 671
Bowen, John S., 351
Bowers, James M., 997
Bowman, Arthur C., 564
Bowman, B. L., 477
Boyce, William, 66
Boyden, Charles, 1179
Boyden, John R., 1179
Boyer, Barton H., 857
Boyer, Jaques, 52
Brackenridge, William T., 913
Bradbury, John, 213
Bradley, James, 307
Bradley, James A., 1092
Bradley, John H., 655
Bragg, W. G., 285
Bragg, William G., 813
Bramblet, Clarence R., 794
Brand, Eli T., 841
Brandon, James D., 915
Brandt, John, 413
Branham, Adolphus, 1041
Branum, Lizzie, 306
Branum, Tecumseh, 306
Branum, Victorine, 306
Brasher, J. M., 314
Brasher, Joseph M., 641
Bray, William, 715
Bray, William G., 907
Brayton, Rev., 468
Brazeau Presbyterian Church, 488
Breckenkamp, August H., 747
Bredensteiner, William, 917
Breid, David W., 661
Breton, Francois, 269
Brevard, A. H., 262
Brevard, A. J., 263
Brewer, Robert M., 343
Brickey, Franklin W., 730
Brickey, John S., 169
Bridgeman, John, 270
Bridges, A. D., 307
Bridges, Ambrose D., 918
Bridges, J. H., 288
Bridges, L. L., 761
Bridges, William, 977
Bringier, L., 213
Brissenden, Ralph, 1271
Brooks, Elmer O., 895
Brooks, Harry T., 1026
Brooks, James A., 410
Brooks, Thomas I., 964
Brown, Allen C., 969
Brown, B. Gratz, 329
Brown, James, 317
Brown, John, 290
Brown, John L., 1077
Brown, John W., 473
Brown, Robert T., 170, 270
Brown, R. T., 238
Brown, Thomas J., 1046

INDEX

Browne, David S., 782
Browne, Joseph, 151
Browne, Lionel, 154, 190, 402
Browne, Wilson, 78
Brownell, John W., 266
Brownwood, 391
Brunke, Abraham, 402
Bryan, (Mrs.) Eliza, 213
Bryant, Bert P., 841
Bryant, P. P., 877
Brydon, Doc, 1126
Buck, Charles, 1093
Buck, James B., 1141
Buck, John L., 295, 1141
Buckner, Alexander, 157, 238, 242
Buckner, Robert, 171
Buehrman, Otto, 249
Buenger, E. E., 271
Buerkle, John C., 727
Buffalo Creek, xiv
Buford, John, 317
Bull, Thomas, 162, 198, 199
Bullett, George, 153
Bullock, James R., 1048
Bunker, 383
Bunte, Theodore L., Jr., 674
Bunyard, E. J., 476
Burchitt, J. G., 863
Burdette, John, 267
Burford, D. W., 1032
Burfordville, 264, 374
Burger, Moritz, 479
Burgess, William J., 990
Burke, Edward, 291
Burlison, Ed., 839
Burnham, B. P., 587
Burns, Robert F., 1056
Burnside, DeWitt L., 1232
Burris, Levi, 1252
Burrough, Jacob H., 422
Burrow, John W., 1195
Burrow, William A., 1088
Burton, C. E., 561
Butler County, 179, 248, 311, 511, 531
Butler County Educational Society, 403
Butler County Railroad Company, 508
Butler, Elisha C., 682
Butler, Frederick C., 402
Butler, John, 816
Butler, Mann, 193
Butler, W. A., 312
"Buzz-Saw," 546
Byrd, Abraham, 78, 162
Byrd, Amos, 78
Byrd, A. R., 410
Byrd Family, 78, 158
Byrd, John, 78, 161, 498
Byrd Settlement, 77
Byrd, Spencer, 153
Byrd, Stephen, 78, 150, 154, 238
Byrd's Creek, 78, 178
Byrns, Sam, 759
Byrns, Samuel, 551

Cabildo (Council), 114
Cahoon, Benjamin Benson, 351 ✗
Cain, Jesse, 161
Cairo & Fulton Railroad, 287, 498
Caldwell, Isaac W., 991
Caldwell, James, 80, 154, 299
Caldwell, Thomas, 154
Caldwell, William C., 1109
Caledonia, 64, 270
Caledonia Presbyterian Church, 270
Callaway, John, 63
Calvin, Lula, 1191
Calvin, Robert L., 1190
Cameron, Donald H., 635
Campbell, 375
"Campbell Citizen," 533
Campbell, Alexander, 310
Campbell, C. C., 311
Campbell, J. P., 539
Campbell, John M., 1017
Camp Rowdy, 254
Camren, James T., 1215
Canaan Cumberland Presbyterian Church, 494
Canada, 27, 28
Canada, Mark, 56
Canalou, 381
Cane Creek, 179, 312
Cane Creek Baptist Association, 470, 477
Caneer, W. T., Jr., 667
Caney Creek, xiii
"Capaha Arrow," 431
Capaha Bluffs, Rock Levee Drive, Cape Girardeau (view), viii
Capahas, 16, 34, 35
Cape Girardeau, 21, 34, 51, 71, 73, 74, 139, 140, 152, 161, 162, 164, 176, 177, 178, 186, 192, 249, 261, 318, 329, 409, 420, 453, 455, 460, 504
Cape Girardeau—A steamboat town, 256; incorporated as a city, 257; prosperity after the war, 258; State Normal School located, 259; remarkable progress, 260
Cape Girardeau Association of Baptists, 464
"Cape Girardeau Censor," 530
Cape Girardeau Circuit, 455
Cape Girardeau County, 178, 511
"Cape Girardeau Courier," 530
"Cape Girardeau Democrat," 530
Cape Girardeau District, 49, 117, 125, 197, 207— First settlement within, 67; water mills on Cape La Croix and Hubble creeks, 72; origin of name, 73; limits of the town, 75
Cape Girardeau German M. E. Church, 483
"Cape Girardeau Herald," 531
"Cape Girardeau News," 531
"Cape Girardeau Patriot," 530
Cape Girardeau Presbyterian Church, 489, 484
"Cape Girardeau Progress," 531
Cape Girardeau, Pilot Knob & Belmont Railroad Company, 501
Cape Girardeau & Jackson Interurban Company, 509
Cape Girardeau & Thebes Bridge Terminal Railway Company, 503
Cape Girardeau & State Line Railroad Company, 501
Cape Le-Croix Creek, xii
Cape La Crux Creek, 77
"Capote," 122
Capuchin, 133
Cardwell, 376
Carleton College, 420
Carleton, Eliza A., 553
Carleton, (Miss) E. A., 420
Carleton, George W., 282, 315
Carleton, G. W., 314

INDEX   xxxi

Carleton, Major, 315
Carondelet, Baron, 62
Carr, William C., 159
Carrington, W. T., 410
Carroll, William L., 1287
Carter County, 248, 306, 317, 409, 512
Carter Family, 554
Carter, Francis M., 827
Carter, William, 554, 886
Carter, Zimri, 180
Carter, Zimri A., 317
Cartobona, Don Francisco, 114
Carty, Moses, 311
Caruth, 377
Caruthers, Edgar P., 625
Caruthers, E. P., 533, 535
Caruthers, Sam, 282
Caruthers, Samuel, 322
Caruthersville, 282
"Caruthersville Republican," 538
Case, Theodore, 313
Cashion, Arthur V., 583
Cashion, Charles E., 760
Casquins, 14
Cassilly, E. V., 257
Castor Creek, xii
Castor River, xiv
Cates, William M., 773
Cato, Sanford, 1199
Caulk, Richard, 150
Cavender, John S., 344
Cavinor, Joseph, 153
Cayce, Milton P., 555
Cedar Hill Baptist Church, 476
Cellini, Francois, 449
Centerville, 311, 329
Cerre, Gabriel, 65, 72
Central Missouri Baptist Association, 475
Chaffee, 389
"Chaffee Signal," 542
Chalk Bluff, 335
Chambers, J. O., 1169
Chandler, Lewis, 307
Chaonia, 392
Chapman, Alvin, 1012
Chapman, Reuben, 314
Chapman, Reuben S., 1011
Chapman, Samuel, 291, 295
Chaponga, 52
Chapoosa Creek, 82
Charless, Joseph, 192
Charleston, 287, 516
Charleston Baptist Association, 478
"Charleston Call," 537
Charleston Classical Academy, 403
"Charleston Courier," 536
"Charleston Gazette," 536
Charleston M. E. Church, 460
Charleston Presbyterian Church, 485
"Charleston Republican," 536
"Charleston Sentinel," 536
"Charleston Star," 537
Charpentier, John, 65, 115
Chasteen, John B., 1129
Chatham, Alfred T., 1009
Cheney, L. H., 422, 423
Cheney, (Mrs.), 423
Cherokees, 35, 40, 41
Chevalier, Peter, 64

Chickasaw Bluffs, 14
Chilletecaux, xiv
Chilletecaux, 42, 44, 284, 306, 307
Chilletecaux River, 42
Chilton, Joseph F., 590
Chookalee (corn meal), 43
Chouteau, August, 150
Chouteau, Pierre, 39
Christians, 208, 494
Christian Indians, 41
"Chronicle," 537
Cinquehomme, xii
Cinque Homme, 42, 66, 81
Circuit Court, 159, 304
Cissell, Bernard, 270
"Citizen-Democrat," 532
Civil War, 327
Claiborne, William, 142
Clamorgan, Jacques, 65
Clardy, Martin L., 556
"Clarion," 535
Clark, B., 470
Clark, Francis, 80
Clark, George B., 374
Clark, Henry E., 286
Clark, H. C., 370
Clark, John, 65, 197
Clark, W. C., 1193
Clarke, C. B., 423
Clarkson, Riley, 307, 308
Clarkton, 164, 286
Clarkton Presbyterian Church, 491
Clary, Claude L., 1250
Claryville, 382
Clay, Henry, 239
Clements, Charles B., 1118
Clevenger, E. L., 696
Clifton, James D., 1287
Clifton & Mothershead, 262
Climate, xvi
Cline, Benjamin J., 1137
Clippard, F. G., 633
Clowd, Robert E., 282
Cluley, John M., 341
Cluley, J. M., 409
Coats, O. B., 1030
Coburn, John, 151
Cohen, D., 273
Coker, A. S., 410
Cole, Charles A., 672
Cole, Oscar R., 935
Cole, Phillip, 169
Cole, Rolla A., 1003
Cole, William L., 626
Cole, W. N., 820
Coleman, Francois, 52
Coleman, F. M., 317
Collins, Cicero, 898
Columbian Bible Society, 208
"Columbian Reciprocity," 534
"Comet," 530
Commerce, 290, 303
"Commerce Dispatch," 542
Commercial Clubs, 370
Common Fields, 118
Common Pleas Court, 159, 164
Como, 381
Concord Baptist Association, 474
Concordia Seminary, Altenberg, 480

INDEX

Confederate Organizations (Civil War), 348
Confederate Veterans, 369
Congregational Churches, 482
Conrad, Arthur O., 818
Conrad, David R., 618
Conrad, Daniel E., 618
Conrad, D. J., 682
Conrad, George E., 743
Conrad, J. J., 313
Conrad, Peter R., 668
Conran, James V., 1231
Conran, Matt J., 1050
"Conservative," 535
"Constitution," 188
Cook Settlement, 177
Cook, Allen, 342
Cook, John D., 155, 158, 238, 299, 304, 310, 311
Cook, L. C., 1153
Cook, Mrs. M. K., 1291
Cook, Nathaniel, 63, 154, 238, 267, 299
Cook, Richard, 307
Cooke, Mrs. L. A., 1021
Cook's Settlement, 63
Cooksey, Guy E., 537
Cooley, W. G., 288
Cooper, Samuel, 164
Cooper, T. S., 968
Cooper, Thomas W., 717
Cooper, William A., 575
Coppage, Robert F., 932
Coppedge, George S., 1062
Corbin, Abel R., 405
Corbin, Daniel B., 1187
Cordrey, Henry L., 1225
Cordrie, Charles, 342
Corn Measured by Horses (view), 517
Cornwall, 379
Cornyn, F. M., 346
"Correspondent and Record," 541
"Cosmos," 543
Cottard, Francis, 150
Cottle, Warren, 150
Cottonplant, 7, 377
Cotton Plant Baptist Church, 473
Cottonwood Point, 382
Couch, Lewis J., 890
Cousin, Barthelimi, 74
Cox, Caleb, 267
Cox, John J., 267
Cox, Moses, 267
Cox, William, 171
Cowdon, Emma E., 425
Craig, Peter, 171
Craig, William L., 941
Craighead, E. B., 428
Crain, George A., 1090
Crain, Nancy, 934
Cramer, George H., 250, 341, 409
Cramer, William, 249
Cramer, Wilson, 250
Cravens, George L., 311
Cravens, L. B., 1078
Creek Indians, 43
Creeks, 41
Creighton, James A., 419
"Creole," 541
Criddle, Edward, 163, 262
Criddle, (Mrs.) Edward, 402
Crites, Charles M., 673

Crites, Peter, 80
Crittenden, John J., 243
Crittenden, Thomas T., 190
Crockett, Robert L., 1039
Croke, James J., 830
Crooked Creek, xiii
Crooked Creek, 334
Crow, William E., 768
Crowder, 388
Crowe, Bennette D., 941
Crowley's Ridge, xii, xv
Crowley's Ridge, 14
Crumb, George H., 543
Crutcher, William J., 1095
Crutchfield, William H., 1134
Crystal City, 274
Cude, James, 284
Culmer, Frederick A., 575
Cumberland Presbyterians, 493
Cummings, Henry G., 287, 311
Cummins, John, 65
Cunningham, J. A., 314
Cupples, Samuel, 262
Current River, 292, 318, 513
"Current Local," 532
Cushion Lake, 231

Daffron, Isaac N., 656
Daffron, William H., 722
Dale, John C., 696
Daley, John, 450
Dallas, 313
Dalton, George, 972
Dalton, Jesse S., 1040
Dalton, Robert P., 620
Danby, Edward L., 1089
Danforth, L. W., 1256
Daniels, James, 342
Daniels, Rev., 468
Darlington, Thomas P., 1017
Davault, W. A., 687
David, Nathan, 312
Davidson, Alexander, 1116
Davidson, Hugh C., 1115
Davidson, Isaac M., 1117
Davidson, John, 154, 155
Davidson, J. T., 532
Davis, Albert S., 1020
Davis, A. M., 284
Davis, Charles, 267
Davis, Edward L., 958
Davis, Garret, 243
Davis, Greer W., 157
Davis, John, 162
Davis, Lowdes H., 549
Davis, Orren L., 1086
Davis, Timothy, 157
Davis, W. J., 1192
Davis, Will E., 1297
Davis, William L., 1169
Daugherty, Abraham, 171
Daugherty, Colonel, 329
Daugherty, G. R., 1272
Daugherty, Ralph, 79
Daugherty Settlement, 77
Daugherty, William, 77, 161, 261
Dawson Family, 533, 1065
Dawson, George W., 96, 1066
Dawson, Robert A., 1066

INDEX

Dawson, Robert D., 96, 105, 154, 155, 238, 265, 315, 402
Dawson. William, 96, 1066
Day, Jacob, 858
Deal, Henry J., 344, 552
Dean, William D., 1285
De Andreis, Father, 137, 448
Dearmont, W. S., 427, 428
Dearmont, Washington S., 563
Deck, Jacob M., 692
Deck, John, 178
Deckwith, Thomas, 11
Decyperi, 89
Deem, David B., 1128
DeField, C. S., 1280
De Guire, Andrew, 64
De Guire, Baptiste, 64
De Guire, Paul, 64, 183
De Guire, Michael, 669
Delaroderie, Alphonse, 265, 266
De 'Lashmutt, Lindsay, 78
De Lashmutt, Van B., 194
De Lassus, Camille, 115
De Lassus, Charles DeHault, 89, 95, 110
Delassus, Governor, 64, 72, 386
DeLassus, Leon, 270
DeLassus, Placide, 554
Delawares, 40, 41, 170
DeLisle Family, 232
DeLisle, Alfonse, 1031
DeLisle, Alfred, 1286
DeLisle, Alphonso, 314
DeLisle, Charles A., 1161
DeLisle, Edward, 267
DeLisle, George, 1054
DeLisle, James E., 1175
DeLisle, Jesse J., 1202
DeLisle, Jonah, 1162
Delorederi, Alphonso, 402
De Luziere, Pierre De Hault De Lassus, 62
"Democrat," 532, 539
"Democrat-News," 536
"Democracy," 530
De Mun, Augustine, 154
Denman, Clint, 540
Denman, Harry, 540
Denman. Harry E., 1177
Denny, William, 79
De Reign, Albert, 1266
Des Arc, 298, 377
DesLoge, 384
DesLoge, Firmin, 557
"DesLoge Sun," 541
De Soto, 1, 82, 133, 273, 514
De Soto's Adventures—Route, 14; timber, 15; first religious service, 16; the Capahas, 16; Quigate, 20; death, 21; exact route, 21
De Soto Congregational Church, 482
De Soto Episcopal Church, 482
"DeSoto Facts," 535
De Soto German M. E. Church, 483
DeSoto Home Guards, 342
"DeSoto Press," 535
Detchemendy House, 401
Detchemendy, P., 150
"Deutscher Volks Freund," 530
Dexter, 389, 526
Dexter Christian Church, 495
"Dexter Enterprise," 543

"Dexter Messenger," 544
"Dexter Statesman," 544
Dick, F. A., 243
Dickinson, J. J., 370
Dickinson, Lewis, 478
Diehlstadt, 379
Digges, T. H., 266
Digges, William L., 1038
Dill, A. R., 343
Dinkins, John T., 853
Dinning, Louis F., 1244
District of St. Louis, 49
Dittlinger, Michael, 341, 347, 409
D'Lashnutt, E., 262
Dodge, Augustus C., 253, 399
Dodge, Henry, 61, 171, 238, 399
Dodge, Israel, 66, 124, 197
Dodge, John, 124
Dodge, Josiah, 197
Dodge, Thomas, 66
Dodson, N. C., 349
Doerner, H. E., 955
Doe Run, 387
Doe Run Presbyterian Church, 491
Doeselman, Charles, 480
Dohogne, Leo, 1253
Donaldson, Humphrey, 308
Donaldson, I. F., 882
Donaldson, Thomas F., 882
Doniphan, 292, 522
Doniphan, Alexander William, 292
"Doniphan News," 539
"Doniphan Prospect," 539
"Doniphan Prospect-News," 539
"Doniphan Republican," 539
Doniphan's Expedition, 300
Donnell, Thomas, 207
Donohoe, Thomas, 201
Dooley, A. J., 349
Doris, James H., 722
Dorris, Timothy, 1142
Dorsay, Samuel, 105
Dorsey, Richard, 270
Dougherty, John, 307
Douglas, A. E., 426
Douglas, R. E., 536
Douglass, A. B., 308
Douglass, Alexander T., 570
Douglass, A. T., 307
Douglass, A. W., 996
Douglass, James M., 571
Douglass, R. H., 473, 474
Douglass, R. S. (Frontispiece)
Douglass, Thomas J., 1015
Douthitt, Thomas, 495
Dowd, Thomas, 265
Dowdy, Robert A., 1139
Downing, Ben R., 826
Downing, James L., 927
Downing, John M., 1286
Downs, Thomas J., 735
Drainage, 360
Drainage Movements, 357
Drerup, John B., 1007
Dress, 195
Drum, T. B., 837
Drury, Amos L., 1267
Dubourg, 448
Dubourg, W. F., 137

Duckworth, Buren, 783
Dudley, William, 306
Dueling, 189
Dufour, Parfait, 52
Duncan, Burwell A., 1209
Duncan, J., 476
Duncan, John E., 1058
Dunham Hall, 269
Dunklin County, 284, 306, 310, 513
"Dunklin County Advocate," 532
"Dunklin County Herald," 532
"Dunklin County Mail," 533
"Dunklin County News," 533
Dunklin County Publishing Company, 533
Dunklin, Daniel, 169, 322, 405
"Dunklin Democrat," 533
Dunmire, George T., 615
Dunn, John, 154
Dunn, S. G., 162
Dunscomb, Daniel E., 925
Dunscombe, James K., 952
Durham Hall, 169
Dutcher, C. H., 426, 428, 434
Duval, John, 66
Duvall, Rev., 468
Dye, Dave, 1055

Eagle's Nest, 257
Ease's, Jim, Camp, 42
East Prairie, 379
"East Prairie Eagle," 537
Easton, Rufus, 151
Eastwood, James, 313
Eating Up the Flax (illustration), 129
Eaton, R. S., 476
Ebert, A. A., 1281
"Echo," 536
Echols, Joseph W., 290
Eckhardt, 262
Eckhardt, Otto, 426
Edgar, William R., 599
Edmonds, Moses, 316
Education—Work of the subscription schools, 398; parochial schools, 400; academies, 400. (See also Public Schools and Higher Learning.)
Edwards, Casper M., 533
Edwards, James, 262
Edwards, James P., 203
Edwards, John F. T., 297, 316
Edwards, Mike, 1285
Ehrichs, Theodore, 896
Eighty-third Battalion, 348
"El Camino Real" (King's Highway), 110
Eldridge, L. P., 349
Elephant Rocks, Graniteville (view), x
Ellington, 383
"Ellington Press," 540
Elliott, Benjamin, 402
Elliott, Henry, 299
Ellis, Alfred P., 256
Ellis, Erastus, 74, 155
Ellis, Solomon, 74
Ellis, William H., 1285
Ellis, W. W., 1258
Ellrodt, Christian, 342
Ellsinore, 373
Elmer, J. B., 342
Elmwood, 78
Elmwood Seminary, 419

Elvins, 384
Elvins, Jesse M., 644
Elvins, Polite, 645
Ely, T. R. R., 607
"Embarras," 132
Emerson, John W., 297, 550
Emory, Arthur R., 1124
Engineer Regiment, West Missouri Volunteers, 347
England, R. E., 846
English, 27
English, James H., 754
English, Robert, 154, 155
English, Thomas, 199
English, Thomas B., 158, 293
Enler, George W., 270
"Enterprise," 532, 536
"Enterprise-Messenger," 544
Episcopal Churches, 481
Epps, Daniel, 179
Ernst, Joseph A., 542, 741
"Espial," 535
Essary, Calvin L., 1156
"Essex Leader," 544
Establishment Creek, 66
Eubanks, J. Oliver, 706
Eudaly, James, 312
Eudaly, John, 312
Evangelical Lutheran Churches, 479
Evans, Enoch, 303
Evans, Evan, 307
Evans, E. P., 257
Evans, Horace D., 601
Evans, James, 74, 238
Evans, John James, 242
Evans, W. H., 277
"Evening Shade," 533
Ewing, H. C., 422
Ewing, Thomas, Jr., 337

"Fairplay," 541
Fallenwider, Caleb B., 262
Faris, Charles B., 1174
"Farmer & Miner," 535
"Farmers' Union Advocate," 534
Farming, 364
Farming Machinery and Implements, 445
Farmington, 277, 337, 450
Farmington Circuit, 453, 455, 463
Farmington College, 419
"Farmington District Messenger," 545
"Farmington Eagle," 540
"Farmington Herald," 540
"Farmington News," 540
Farmington Presbyterian Church, 489
"Farmington Progress," 540
"Farmington Times," 540
"Farmington Times-Herald," 540
Farnham, A. C., 317
Farnsworth, Albert A., 677
Farquhar, J. S. N., 918
Farr, S., 476
Farrar, B. J., 345
Farrar, John, 203
Farrar, George W., 422
Farrar, Moses, 308, 310
Farris, Absolom, 307
Fath, Leonard, 270
Faughn, James, 307
Felts, John W., 1180

INDEX

Felts, Robert G., 1180
Feltz, Lawrence L., 778
Fenwick-Crittenden Duel, 190
Fenwick, Ezekiel, 78
Fenwick Settlement, 66
Fenwick, Walter, 190
Ferguson, James S., 293
Ferguson, J. S., 403
Ferguson, N. G., 470
Ferguson, Patrick, 1223
Ferrell, J. F., 729
Ferries, 161
Festus, 378
"Festus News," 535
Fields, William R., 1296
Fifteenth Regiment, Missouri Enrolled Militia, 347
Fifth Missouri Regiment, 343
Fiftieth Missouri Infantry, 346
Fifty-sixth Missouri Regiment, 343
Figari, H., 413
Finch, James A., 1272
Finger, B. F., 371
Finley, David, 307, 308
Finney, James G., 531
Finney, John M., 623
Finney, Reynolds M., 776
Finney, T. M., 461
Finney, William B., 770
Finney, W. E., 1240
First Association of Baptist Churches, 203
First Bank in Cape Girardeau, 256
First Bank in Jackson, 262
First Baptism, 56
First Baptist Church in Louisiana, 198
First Brick House Built West of the Mississippi (view), 50
First Circuit Court in Butler County, 312
First Conference West of the Mississippi, 206
First Congregational Church in Southeast Missouri, 482
First County (state) Court, 160
First English School West of the Mississippi River, 77
First Grist Mill, 52
First Masonic Lodge, 157
First Methodist Society West of the Mississippi, 204
First Presbyterian Church, 207
First Protestant Baptism, 197
First Religious Service, 16
First School in Southeast Missouri, 193
First Schools in Bloomfield, 402
First Schools in Various Counties, 409
First Steamboat up the Mississippi, 188
Fisher, Alvin B., 1155
Fisher, T. D., 540
Fisk, 372
Flanary, Hugh M., 1093
Flat River, 384
Fleege, William B., 872
Flentge, Edward W., 606
Flentge, William, 343
Fletcher, Governor, 501
Fletcher, C. E., 273
Fletcher, James W., 345
Fletcher, John W., 273
Fletcher, Thomas C., 273, 345
Flint, Timothy, 207, 208, 261
Florence, Oscar S., 810
Floyd, J. H., 473

Fly, Christopher C., 1219
Flynn, Ebenezer, 163
Flynn, Joseph, 530, 542
Fonville, William T., 1217
Forcher, Pierre, 89
Fordyce, S. W., 505
Fornfelt, 387
Fort, James L., 567
Fort A, 329
Fort B, 329
Fort Celeste, 89
Fort Creve, 30
Fort Davidson, 338
Fort Joachim, 52
Fort Osage, 44
Forty-seventh Missouri Infantry, 345
Forty-seventh Regiment, Missouri Volunteers, 347
"Forum," 539
Foster, F. P., 1277
Fourche a Renault Church, 478
Four Mile Baptist Church, 473
Foust, A. L., 1177
Fowlkes, R. W., 1176
Fox, Burwell, 616
Fox, James D., 551
Foxes, 35, 40, 70, 150, 170
Frank, Jacob J., 1150
Franklin Baptist Association, 469
Franklin, J. R., 293
Franklin, Robert G., 267
Frazer, Theodore F., 1263
Fredericktown, 64, 177, 186, 267, 268, 349, 420, 453, 454, 455
Fredericktown Baptist Church, 477
"Fredericktown Conservative," 538
"Fredericktown Democrat," 535
"Fredericktown Journal," 535
Fredericktown Northern Presbyterian Church, 493
"Fredericktown Standard," 535
Fremont's Rangers, 342
French, 50
French, Bristol, 705
French Explorers—From the great lakes, 22; French in Canada, 23; Joliet and Marquette, 24; La Salle, 27; Indian trade, 28; Tonti and Hennepin, 29; La Salle's death, 31
French, George R., 342
French Settlers, 248
Frie, Philip A., 885
Friend, Charles, 108, 179
Frissell, Elizabeth Bollinger, 318
Frizzell, Joseph, 194, 262
Frohna Evangelical Lutheran Church, 479
Fromentin, Eligius, 150
Frontenac, 23, 27, 28
Fry, Henry, 63, 179
Fulkerson, James P., 256
Fur Trade, 124

Gabouri, Laurent, 51, 52
Gaither, Benjamin B., 290
Gaither, J. W., 987
Gale, C. F., 256
Gallivan, Thomas, 1062
Gambling, 189
Game, 50
Garaghty, Eugene, 256
Gardiner, J. J., 402
Gardner, Dempsey, 1180

Gardner, Samuel, 1155
Gardoqui, Diego, 83
Gargas, James W., 795
Garner, Levi, 1205
Garner, William J., 1184
Garrett, H. Clay, 1061
Garrett, Peter R., 262
Gary, Walter, 1269
Gaskin, John W., 1130
Gay, W. T., 799
Gayle, John W., 262
Gayoso, 108, 179, 282
"Gayoso Democrat," 538
Geaslin, Hiram P., 582
Gee, John T., 1260
Genesauz, 52
George, Solomon, 62
"General Pike," 188
Gerhard, Ernst, 479
German Evangelical Churches, 482
German Methodists, 483
German Settlers, 249
Germans in Upper Louisiana, 128
Gibault, Father, 135
Gibler, Frederick, 74
Giboney Family, 77
Giboney, Alexander, 77
Giboney, Andrew, 256, 319
Giboney, Rebecca (Ramsay), 77
Gibson, 376
Gibson, Dean, 536
Giddings, N. J., 463
Giddings, Solomon, 207
Gideon, 379
Gideon Anderson Lumber & Manufacturing Company, 1251
Gilbert, Charles E., 713
Gilbert, Miles A., 254
Gilbow, William N., 1285
Giles, John, 171
Gill, Ralph, 262
Gillen, Edward D., 951
Gilley, Jesse A., 293
Gillispie, Grant, 370
Girardot, 73
Girvin, J. T., 314
Gissel and Company, 270
Glascock, Charnel, 204
Glascock, John, 262
Glascock, Robert L., 307
Glascock, Sarah A., 308
Glassey, James A., 1198
Glen Allen, 178, 371
Glennonville, 377
Goad, Henry S., 1013
Godt, William J., 1142
Goff, David P., 721
Goff, James L., 830
Gorg, Albert J., 1293
Golden, John, 291
Golder, Solomon D., 288, 344
Gomache, August, 65
Gomache, Jean Baptiste, 65
Goodale, C. T., 410
Goodman, Laurin C., 1192
Gordon, Joseph F., 1042
Gordon, Nellie, 426
Gordonville, 77, 79, 178, 374
Gordonville German M. E. Church, 483

Gorman, Kuran, 287, 288
Gossage, William F., 1008
Governor, 152
Government Under France—Province of Upper Louisiana, 112; question of language, 113; procedure, 113; intoxicants to Indians, 116; excise tax, 116
Govreau, Joseph, 52
Grace Episcopal Church, Crystal City, 482
Graham, C. T., 476, 477
Graham, Clara E., 1261
Graham, Margaret A., 1173
Graham, Napoleon B., 1173
Graham, Pinkney, 477
Graham, William, 1278
Graham, William F., 262
Grand Army of the Republic, 369
Grand Tower, ix
Grand Tower, 24
Grandin, 373
Grandin Congregational Church, 482
Grant, John F., 1001
Grant, U. S., 329
Grasey, William, 290
Gratiot, Charles, 150
Graves, Fayette P., 819
Graves, F. P., 557
Gray, Alexander, 320
Gray, David, 105
Gray, Drakeford, 171
Gray, John, 171
Great Osages, 39
Green, B. W., 1113
Green, Ernest A., 1154
Green, Samuel M., 319
Green, Thomas P., 193, 465
Greene, David, 199, 201
Greene, Robert, 161
Greene, Samuel M., 203
Greene, Thomas Parish, 202
Greenville, 272, 333
Greenville Circuit, 454
"Greenville Democrat," 545
"Greenville Reporter," 545
"Greenville Sun," 545
Greenwell, Leo A., 1060
Greer, Alfred W., 1172
Gregory, James, 374
Gregory, William, 349
Gregory, William N., 297
Gresham, Milo, 1276
Griffin, Edward, 656
Grimsly, William C., 313
Grisham, Lin, 628
Grojean, Constantine, 342
Groseilliers, 23
Grove, F. M., 409
Gruelle, William, 530
Gudger, William M., 707
Guerthing, John, 164
Guess, Harry A., 709
Guffy, B. L., 982
Guibeault, Charles, 107
Guibord, Eugene, 411
Guibord, Jacques, 159
"Guignolee, La," 123
Guignon, S. A., 267
Guild, Ralph, 163, 318
Gulf Railroad System, 259
Gulf System, 260

INDEX xxxvii

Gunnells, John, 307
Guthrie, Orlando F., 370
Guy, R. L., 1188
Gwyn, Oliver B., 622

Haden, Anthony, 162
Hafner, Phil A., 542
Haines, Bert, 1077
Haines, Edward C., 1036
Haines, Frank, 1059
Haley, Oba, 630
Hall, Joseph, 206
Hall, Robert, 162
Ham, Thomas H., 732
Hamburg, 328
Hamilton, A. V., 410
Hamilton, George A., 66
Hammersley, George O., 786
Hammond, Daniel, 238
Hammond, Samuel, 148, 275
Hand, William, 262
Handy, Noah, 288
Hanesworth, Henry, 461
Hanover Evangelical Lutheran Church, 480
Happy Missouri Corn Grower (view), 181
Harbin, James A., 1191
Harbin, John W., 1148
Harbison & Christie, 282
Harbison, George C., 158
Harbison, John, 291
Harbison, John C., 74, 205, 206
Hardemann, Letcher, 370
Harden, Joseph, 155
Harkey, Daniel, 308
Harkey, Daniel D., 308
Harkey, J. H., 308
Harkey, W. M., 308
Harkey, Wells R., 823
Harkey, Wilbur D., 308
Harlan, George W., 485
Harlow, Alonzo T., 857
Harms, Ernst, 480
Harper & Christy, 295
Harper, Robert, 80
Harper, W. B., 265
Harrington, George W., 531
Harris & Chinn, 297
Harris, Charles, 1267
Harris, James, 307
Harris, John W., 1030
Harris, O. B., 740
Harris, Samuel Stanhope, 319, 349
Harris, Van Leslie, 1268
Harrison, Allan J., 1260
Harrison, Arthur S., 888
Harrison, N. C., 409
Harrison, Van H., 286, 877
Hart, George W., 154
Hart, John, 115
Hartshorn, Carr, 664
Harty, Alfred L., 1200
Harty, William C., 1199
Harviel, 372
Hase, Frederick, 270
Hatcher, Robert A., 553
Hatcher (R. A.) & Co., 265
Hatcher, William H., 749
Hatley, Thomas, 307
Haw, J. L., 288

Haw, Marvin T., 461
Haw, U. L., 461
Haw, Uriel, 452
Hawkins, H. P., 346
Hawkins, Jesse M., 854
Hawkins, John, 159, 402
Hawkins, Milton, 835
Hawn, Daniel, 776
Hawks, Edward L., 1185
Hawthorn, Edward, 80
Hayden, Anthony, 158
Hayden, Blevins, 77
Hayes & Bartlett, 288
Hayes, Hartford, 288, 410
Haynes, Daniel, 374, 905
Haynes, Henry, 747
Hays, Christopher, 79, 84, 150, 161, 162
Hays, George, 78
Hays, John, 161
Hayti, 381
"Hayti Signal," 538
Hazel Run Lead District, 183
Head, James, 65
"Headlight," 531, 539, 540
Heeb, John W., 1186
Heeb, Rosa L., 1186
Hematite, 65, 276
Hembree, J. C., 477
Hemme, Charles A. F., 804
Hempstead, Benjamin R., 855
Hempstead, Stephen, 207
Henderson & Lawson, 293
Henderson, A. S., 291
Henderson, George, 74, 257
Henderson, Harry, 1045
Henderson, J. M., 403
Hendricks, A. F., 573
Hendrickson, William, 342
Henn, Susan, 56
Hennepin, 29
Henry, Nelson B., 426, 557
Henry, S., 539
Hensley, Oliver E., 1147
Henson, Elbert H., 979
Henson, James A., 597
Henson, Samuel D., 305
Hepzibah Church, 201
"Herald," 531
Herculaneum, 168, 177, 193, 275
Herkstroeter, Henry A., 598
Herrman, James, 307
Hertich, Charles S., 556
Hertich, Joseph, 193, 405
Heuchan, Robert B., 1234
Hickman, E. A., 370
Hickman, J., 468
Hickman, John A., 1159
Hicks, Z. T., 748
Higdon, William H., 773
High School, Farmington (view), 279
Higher Learning—St. Mary's seminary, 412; St. Vincent's college, 413; Will Mayfield college, 418; Elmwood seminary, 419; Farmington college, 419; Marvin Collegiate institute, 419; Carleton college, 420; Arcadia college, 420
Highest Point on Pilot Knob (view), 298
Higginbotham, James L., 1102
Higginbotham, Thomas, 825
Highfill, B. F., 781

INDEX

Highfill, Charles W., 998
Highfill, Sadie E., 998
Hildebrand, John, 64, 124
Hildebrand, Samuel S., 550
Hilgert, John J. A., 899
Hill, Alonzo D., 1253
Hillsboro, 275
Himmelberger, John H., 646
Hindman, Emma P., 879
Hindman, James M., 879
Hinrichs, Belle C., 1163
Hinrichs, Charles F., 1162
Hitchcock, Ethan Allen, 274
Hitt, Benjamin, 199
Hitt, William, 199
Hodges, Thomas L., 859
Hodgmeiller, James, 344
Hoffmann, August W., 1145
Hogan, Edmund, 162
Hogan, Peter, 343
Hogue, John A., 982
Holbert, James, 302
Holbrook, F. M., 477
Holcomb, 376
Holcomb, Lewis, 307, 310
Holden, Edward M., 402
Holland, 382
Holland, James H., 1114
Holley, Ulysses G., 1257
Holliday-Klotz Land and Lumber Company, 507
Holliday Land & Lumber Company, 272
Holliday, Sallie H., 419
Holliman, A. W., 317
Hollister, Edward, 208
Holly, W. N., 960
Home of Our Fathers (view), 126
Honey, John, 65
Hoos, Thomas, 343
Hopewell Baptist Church, 476
Hopkins, Joseph A., 303
Hopper, Gillum M., 950
Horine, Thomas M., 300
Horner, John J., 948
Horner, Russell, 307
Horner, William B., 889
Horner, William H., 287, 307
Hornersville, 287
"Hornersville Courier," 287
Hornsby, J. C., 477
Horrell, B. M., 256, 319
Horrell, Thomas, 481
Hoskins, John, 290
Hoskins, Thomas L., 1204
Hostetler, Henry S., 986
Houck, Louis, 78, 259, 422, 428, 434, 501, 503, 548
Houck's Missouri & Arkansas Railroad, 502
Hough, Harrison, 312, 315, 498
House, Adam, 65
Houses of Louis Bolduc and Louis Guibourd, Ste. Genevieve (views), 57
House's Spring, 65, 378
Houston, Hiram J., 891
Houston, John S., 284
Houston, Joseph S., 310
Houston, W. H., 981
Houts, Christopher G., 238, 262, 291
Houts, James, 303
Houts, John, 290
Howard, William N., 685

Hubbard, Charles T., 911
Hubbard, Michael, 286
Hubbard, Robert G., 940
Hubbard, Walter M., 922
Hubbard, William W., 697
Hubbell Creek, 79
Hubbell, Ithamar, 79
Hubble's Mill, 161
Hudspeth, Ayers, 311
Huebner, John H., 1188
Huff, Henderson, 293
Huffman, Jesse D., 892
Huffman, Samuel, 462
Hug, Stephen, 909
Hughes, A., 476
Hughes, Benjamin H., 666
Hulser, H. M., 342
Humboldt Literary Society, 430
Hummel, John A., 1054
Humphreys, Joshua, 164
Hunot, Joseph, 115
Hunter, 373
Hunter, Abraham, 108, 303
Hunter, Albert B., 1079
Hunter & Mathewson, 266
Hunter & Watson, 265
Hunter, Eva P., 1249
Hunter, Ben. F., 292
Hunter, David, 291
Hunter, E. C., 895
Hunter, J. H., 349
Hunter, Joseph, 108, 153, 154, 179, 290, 553
Hunter, Lewis F., 1249
Hunter, Mary, 78
Hunter, Shapley R., Jr., 1055
Hunting, 187
Hurley, Moses, 108, 165
Huskey, Thomas, 732
"Hustler," 537, 539
Hutchings, John, 238
Hux, William J., 1121

Illinois, 24
Illinois, Missouri & Texas Railway Company, 501
Illinois Southern Railroad, 508
Illmo, 388
"Illmo Headlight," 543
Impeachment Proceeding, 155
"Independent," 534, 541
"Independent Patriot," 192, 529
Indian Grove School, 288, 410
Indian Agriculture, 36
Indian Moccasin, 38
Indian Mound (view), 4
Indian Plates, 11
Indian Relics, 11
Indian Roads, 82
Indian Trade, 27, 33
Indian Wars, 170
Indians, 9, 150, 170
Indians—Trade with, 33; tribes, 34; agriculture, 36; houses of the Osages, 36; women, 36; weapons, 37; knowledge of the stars, 37; pipe, clothing and Indian moccasin, 38; government of the Osages, 38; witchcraft, 43
Industries, 180
Industries—Farming, 444; trade, 445; mining interests, 446
In the Bonne Terre Lead Mining District (view), 385

INDEX

In the Thick Timber (view), 511
Iowas, 70, 170
Iron, 183
Iron County, 178, 316, 513
"Iron County Register," 534
Irondale, 392
Irondale Presbyterian Church, 491
Iron Mountain Evangelical Lutheran Church, 481
Ironton, 296
"Ironton Forge," 534
"Ironton Furnace," 534
Iroquois, 30, 31, 40
Island No. 10, 333
Ivers, John, 257

Jackson, 162, 178, 186, 193, 261, 401
Jackson—Founding of, 261; first institutions and persons, 262; civil government, 263; present county seat, 263
Jackson Academy, 194, 402
Jackson Baptist Church, 465
Jackson Branch Railroad Company, 500
"Jackson Courier," 530
"Jackson Eagle," 529
Jackson German Evangelical Church, 482
Jackson M. E. Church, 455, 460
"Jackson Review," 529
Jackson, Albert, 315, 343
Jackson, John W., 1173
Jackson, Lyman F., 533
Jackson, Sanford, 282, 315
Jackson, Thomas M., 686
Jackson, Wingate, 202, 463
Jacobs, John, 78
James, Henry, 308
James, M. T., 1239
Janis, B. N., 52
Janis, Henry J., 542
Janis, Nicholas, 53
Jarvis, Daniel O., 1127
Jasper, Henry, 266
"Jeans," 127
Jecko, F. J., 288
Jeffers, W. L., 334, 349, 350
Jefferson, 141
Jefferson County, 168, 176, 179, 514—First settler in, 64; first mill in Jefferson county, 65; first Protestant services within Jefferson county, 65
Jefferson County Baptist Association, 475
"Jefferson County Crystal Mirror," 535
"Jefferson County Democrat," 535
"Jefferson County Record," 535
"Jefferson County Republican," 535
"Jeffersonian," 529, 535
Jennings, Daniel L., 349
Jennings, James M., 349
Jennings, R. E., 688
Jesuits, 133
Joachim, 177
Joachim Creek, 273
Johns, William L., 595
Johnson, Albert L., 610
Johnson, Benjamin, 193
Johnson, John, 179, 751
Johnson, John M., 295
Johnson, Joseph, 109
Johnson, Thomas, 197, 198
Johnson, T., 256
Johnson, William H., 1157

Johnson, Winifred, 426, 1242
Johnson, W. H., 1211
Johnson, W., 256
Johnston, Frank A., 749
Jokerst, Leon, 51
Joliet, 14
Joliet, Louis, 24
Jones, Andrew, 349
Jones, Augustus, 253
Jones, Benjamin C., 1165
Jones, Charles, 65
Jones, Charles L., 906
Jones, E. E., 1032
Jones, E. M., 1041
Jones, F. M., 807
Jones, George H., 1103
Jones, George W., 252
Jones, Isaiah, 307, 308
Jones, John Rice, 61, 154, 169, 238, 252, 269, 299, 322, 402
Jones, Joseph L., 1203
Jones, Langdon, 787
Jones, N. G. H., 295
Jones, O. C., 543
Jones, Robert H., 787
Jones, R. H., 285, 507
Jones, Thomas D., 864
Jones, William T., 1297
Jones, W. P., 349
Jordan, G. W., 493
Jordan, J. S., 468
Joslyn, Clarence L., 1073
"Journal," 545
Joyce, J. R., 1279
Joyce, T. E., 410
Juden, John, Sr., 199
Juden, John, Jr., 155, 199
Juden, John, 262

Kahmann, Guy F., 700
Kalfus, C. C., 288
Kansas, 34
Karnes, John M., 1002
Kaskaskia, 51
Kaskaskias, 14, 26
Kaths, Frederick, 814
Kayser, George M., 344
Keaton, Cornelius L., 1212
Kelch, L. E., 1184
Keel-boat, 132
Keep, Frederick, 171
Keith, Abram W., 755
Keith, Frank L., 755
Keller, Daniel J., 533, 994
Kelley, John R., 1005
Kelley & Taylor, 293
Kelly, Jacob, 80
Kelly, N. F., 711
Kelly, William V., 711
Kelso, 388, 450
Kelso, I. R., 1232
Kendree Chapel, 453
Kennedy, John E., 1156
Kennedy, Matthew, 54, 124
Kennett, 284
Kennett Baptist Church, 473
"Kennett Clipper," 533
Kennett Presbyterian Church, 491
Kent & Sparrow, 254

INDEX

Kent, Thomas B., 923
Keyl, Wilhelm, 479
Keyte, William A., 270
Kibby, Timothy, 150
Kiefner, Charles E., 692
Kiefner, Samuel B., 619
Killian, George, 270
Killian, Joseph C., 343
Killion, William M., 1057
Killough, W. W., 488
Kimball, Charles A., 282
Kimbrow, James H., 1068
Kimm, Theodore, 275
Kimmell, G. G., 409
Kimmell, J. Q. A., 410
Kimmswick, 275
Kinder, Emanuel, 1164
King's Highway, 65, 108, 110, 291
Kinsolving, Herschel P., 946
Kinsolving, Thomas B., 763
Kinsolving, Timothy F., 871
Kirkman, Albert, 1120
Kirkman, Thomas P., 768
Kitchen, Solomon G., 78, 293, 296, 304, 312, 349, 350, 403, 499
Kittrell, Lemuel, 305
Kittrell, Solomon, 179, 311
Kittredge, W. Herbert, 1196
Klepman, Frank, 342
Kneibert, Jacob, 262
Knob Lick, 386
Knowd, James, 415
Knowles, John A., 764
Kochtitzky, John S., 736
Kochtitzky, Otto, 560
Kohl, John H., 1271
Koons, M. B., 295
Kopp, F., 266
Koppitz, Albert, 766
Kreps, W. P., 292
Krone, George, 585
Krueger, Louis, 631
Krueger, Martin C., 640
Kuennel, John, 271
Kurreville Evangelical Lutheran Church, 480

"Labor Herald," 541
Labriere, Julien, 51
Lacy, George A., 759
Lacey, Jordan, 307
Lacey, W. R., 538
Ladd, Pierre D., 370
La Fleur, Lambert, 55
Lafont, Lafayette F., 1208
La Forge, Alexander, 96
La Forge, Antoine, 148
La Forge, A. C., 96
La Forge, Pierre, 115
La Forge, Pierre Antoine, 89, 96
Laidlaw, John, 410
Lakeville Presbyterian Church, 485
Lalond, Jeanette, 53
Lambert, Felix G., 654
Lambert, Warren C., 1264
La Motte Mine, 59
Land, A., 476
Land Grants, 148
Landry, T. & L., 270
Lane, Albert, 811

Lane, Adam, 317
Lane, Hardage, 154
Lane, Isaac, 474, 475
Lane, M. M., 539
Lane, Thomas F., 726
Langdon, Edwin J., 307, 308
Langdon, Hiram, 307
Langley, DeWitt C., 1131
Langley, L., 476
Langlois, Francis, 107
L'Annee des Grandes Eaux, 59
"L'Annee du Coup," 114
Lanpher, George W., Sr., 688
Laque Terrible, 231
Laramie Station, 67
Larsen, Martin, 1098
Larsen, William H., 1099
Larson, Louis, 1275
LaRue, John P., 1111
La Salle, 27
Lasieur, Francois, 43
Lasley, C. N., 308
Lasswell, W. D., 507, 897
Latham, H. C., 266
Latimer, R. T., 1259
Latimer, William H., 1259
La Valle, E. P., 290
Lavalle, John, 95, 115
Lawlessness, 189
Lawrence County, 154, 166
Lawson, A. W., 410
Lawson, Moses, 275
Lawson, William, 317
Layton, Bernard, 270
Layton, John, 402
Layton, John E., 170
Lazear, Benjamin F., 343
Leach, John, 295
Lead Belt, 363
"Lead Belt Banner," 541
"Lead Belt News," 541
Lead Mines (1804-1821), 183
Leadwood, 384
Leavenworth, F., 344
Lebanon Baptist Church, 476
Lebermuth, Adolph, 919
LeCompte, Elroy S., 410
Lee, Frank, 307
Lee, George, 306
Lee, Isaac H., 1070
Lee, Robert E., 370
Leech, A. D., 256, 422
Leedy, D. H., 291
Lefler, Leonard L., 1035
Leeper, 392
Leeper, William T., 342
Legislative Council, 152
Legrand, Joseph A., 1224
Lehman, A., 480
Lemmon, G. T., 423
Leopold, 449
LeRoy, Lewis B., 1146
LeSieur, Francois, 81, 107, 266
LeSieur, F. V., 265
LeSieur, Godfrey, 213, 402
LeSieur, G. V., 266
LeSieur, Joseph, 81
Lesieur, Lewis F., 1284
LeSieur, Napoleon, 265

INDEX

Lesieur, Philo, 1284
Lesterville, 298, 311
Levees, 313
Leveque, J. A., 415
Levi Mercantile Company, 919
Lewis, Lilburn, 266
Lewis, William H., 742
Leyba, Ferdinand, 114
"Liberal," 534
Libertyville, 277, 387
Liberty Baptist Church, 473
Libraries, 195
Light, Peter, 84
Lilbourn, 380
Liles, William J., 1230
Limbaugh, Frederick, 80, 161
Lindsay, 335
Lindsay, James, 348, 530
Linn, Lewis F., 213, 321, 399
Literary Societies, 430
Lithium, 383
Little Black River, xii
Little, Kos, 694
Little Osages, 39
Little Prairie, 95, 107, 178, 233, 282, 315
Little River, xii
Little River, 230
Little, William, 306, 470
Lix, Louis W., 870
Local Option Movement, 367
Loeber, Gotthold H., 479
Logan, Charles, 80
Logan, David, 80
Logan, James, 167
Logan, James M., 839
Logan, John, 270
Logan, J. V., 316
Logan, Mary L., 1171
Logan, Oliver, 1171
Logan, Robert A., 80
Loggrear, Del, 538
Loignon, Charles, 107
Loisel, Joseph, 52
London, William, 477
London, William, 895
Long, Mayor, 213
Long, Frank L., 712
Long, Jesse, 307
Longtown, 271
Longtown, 383
Lorance, John, 178
Lorimer, Charlotte P. B., 73
Lorimer, Louis, 34, 41, 67, 74, 115
Lorimier, Louis, 161, 164
Louisiana, 49
Louisiana Purchase, 139
Lower Louisiana, 49
Lowery, John, 307
Lowery, John J., 405
Lowry, William, 66
Lucas, Charles, 169, 190
Lucas, James B. C., 151
Lucas, John B. C., 299
Luckey, Frank S., 891
Lutes, Eli, 280
Lutes, Jacob, 371
Lutesville, 280
"Lutesville Banner," 531
Lutherans, 479

Lyell, Charles, 213
Lynch, Orton C., 609
Lynn, James W., 1028
Lynn, W. A., 288

Mabrey, Thomas, 1292
McAlister, Alexander, 206
McAnally, Edward D., 738
McArthur, John, 154
McBride, Albert, 1053
McCarthy, E. S., 285, 507
McCarty, Sterling H., 574
MacChesney, F. L., 410
McCleary, H. S., 410
McClendon, H. B., 710
McColgan, John W., 1241
McCollum, Jesse W., 1105
McCombs, John, 295
McCombs, William, 402
McConachie, L. G., 426
McCormack, James R., 555
McCormack, Peter, 65
McCormick, Emmett C., 847
McCormick, James R., 846
McCourtney, Joseph, 105
McCown, Thomas D., 1290
McCoy, Ananias, 64
McCoy, Robert, 96, 115, 265
McCoy, Mollie, 1182
McCulloch, Colonel, 328
McCulloch, Robert, 350
McCullough, E. E., 410
McCullough, J. R., 284
McCutchen, Louis, 1216
McDaniel, C. P., 650
McDaniel, J., 307
McDaniel, W. I., 649
MacDonald, John, 329
McElmurry, Absalom, 311, 552
McElmurry, Henry, 469
McElvain, Jerry M., 914
McFarland, James A., 282
McFarland, Thomas, 980
McFerron, Joseph, 74, 157, 161, 190, 238, 401
McFerron-Ogle Duel, 157, 190
McGready, Israel, 153, 169
McGee, Charles, 1288
McGee, John S., 426, 435
McGee, Samuel T., 701
McGehan, George, 302
McGerry, J. F., 413
McGerry, John F., 415
McGhee, J. S., 427
McGinthy, Fleety, 988
McGlothlin, Jesse A., 648
McGrew, Elias V., 1113
McGuire, F. A., 530
McGuire, J. S., 262
McGuire, William, 262
McHaney, T. C., 659
McHaney, T. N., 834
Machen, Harry L., 580
McIlvaine, John, 402
McKay, Benjamin A., 888
McKay, John T., 663
McKay, Virgil, 507, 1298
McKendree, 204
McKendree Chapel, 463
McKendree, William, 204

INDEX

McKenzie, David H., 807
Mackley, Andrew P., 863
McLane, William, 270
McLane, W. H., 343
McLaughlin, Michael, 290
Maclird, Thomas H., 342
McMasters, John, 307
McMillan, Albert C., 1016
McMillan, William J., 1056
McMinn, Sam J., 658
McMullin, Frank M., 1104
McMullin, R. W., 535, 796
McMurtry, William, 208
McNails, Joseph, 311
McNelly, Eugene T., 425
McNeil, John, 335
McNiel, Oscar, 1082
Macom, William, 469
Madden, Thomas, 62
Madison County, 167, 177, 514
Magness, Perry G., 155
Malls, 192
Maisonville, 42
Malcolm, Pleasant M., 1264
Malden, 374
Malden Christian Church, 495
"Malden Clipper," 533
Malden Cumberland Presbyterian Church, 493
Malone, Elias J., 1194
Maltus, C. F., 482
Malugen, John H., 771
Manitous, 24
Mann Brothers, 266
Mann, David H., 1076
Mantler, S. C., 277
Mantz, Ernst, 480
Manufactures, 362
Manufacturing, 446
Maple, J. C., 199, 465
Maramec Baptist Association, 478
Maramec River, xii
Marble City Guards, 348
Marble City Mill, 256
"Marble City News," 530
Marble Hill, 280, 313
Marble Hill Northern Presbyterian Church, 492
Marbury, Benjamin H., 584
Marbury, H. L., 885
Marks, David F., 155
Marlow, Roy S., 596
Marmaduke, John S., 337
Marmaduke's Raid, 335
Marquand, 371
"Marquand Leader," 536
Marquette, 14, 24, 133
Marquette Among the Mississippi Valley Indians (view), 25
Marsh, John, 307
Marsh, John H., 284, 310
Marshall, Brannon, 308
Marshall, John I., 822
Marston, 372
Martin, George, 536
Martin, John, 315, 402
Martin, Tom, 1072
Marvin Collegiate Institute, 419, 461
Massey, Drury, 313
Mason, Charles H., 1002
Mason, Charles J., 1289

Mason, E., 257
Mason, Nellie J., 1003
Mason Gang of Robbers, 96
Mason's and Murrell's Men, 102
Master, Henry, 164
Mathews, Richard, 303
Mathews Prairie, 109, 179, 452
Matkin, William M., 874
Matthews, Ezekiel, 297
Matthews, John, 207
Matthews, William, 371
Mattox, W. H., 476
Maulsby, H. D., 402
Maulsby, H. T., 265
Maurice, Francois, 52
Maurice, Henri, 52
Maurice, Jean Baptiste, 52
Mauthe, John J., 617
May, Henry A., 691
Mayes, F. A., 1027
Mayfield College, Will, 572
Mayfield, John J., 1073
Mayfield, Pinkney M., 1073
Maxwell, James, 136, 153, 154
Maxwell, I. Newton, 1070
Mead, Robert L., 992
Meador, A. R. L., 476
Meador, J. Frank, 637
Meigs, Return J., 148
Menard, Mrs., 51
Menard, Pierre, 56
Menard & Valle, 56
"Mercury," 529
Merrill, William, 306
"Messenger," 543, 545
Metcalfe, Richard L., 532
"Methodist Advocate," 542
Methodists, 452
Meurin Father, 134
Meurin, J. L., 56
Mexican War, 300
Meyers, Benjamin, 107
Meyers, Jacob, 105
Meyers, William, 108, 290
Michel, Joseph, 96
Michie, Ive, 962
Michie, L. S., 1069
Middle Brook, 298
Milem, Jacob A., 1235
Miller, Daniel, 295
Miller, D. H., 293, 312, 413
Miller, Elijah, 295
Miller, Harry A., 655
Miller, Henry, 296, 403
Miller, Isadore W., 900
Miller, James S., 1249
Miller, John, 311
Miller, John A., 1099
Miller, John N., 1123
Miller, John W., 316
Miller, Otis W., 1280
Miller, Robert J., 1279
Miller, Trentis V., 1254
Miller, William H., 569
Millerville, 374
Mills, J. N., 1262
Mill Spring, 393
Milsepen, Henry, 450
Milster, A. W., 410

Mine a Breton, 64, 169, 182
Mine a Gerboree, 183
Mine a Platte (Doggett mine), 183
Mine LaMotte, 178, 182, 378
"Mine LaMotte Advertiser," 535
Mineral District of Louisiana, 181
Mineral Point, 292, 337
Minerals, xv
"Miners' Prospect," 544
Mineral Regions, xi
Mining, 181
Mining Industry, 362
Minter, Martin B., 758
Mintrup, Joseph A., 604
Miro, (Governor,) 88
Mississippi, 24
Mississippi Bottoms, 26
Mississippi County, 109, 179, 311, 516
Mississippi embayment, xiv
Mississippi River & Bonne Terre Railway, 506
"Mississippi Valley Globe," 530
"Missouri Cash Book," 530
Missouri Compromise, 237, 240
"Missouri Democrat," 541
"Missouri Democracy," 532
"Missouri Gazette," 153, 192, 541
"Missouri Herald," 192, 529
Missouri M. E. Conference, 206
Missouri Orchards in Bearing (views), 519
Missouri Presbytery, 207
Missouris, 34, 35
Missouri State Guards, 328
Missouri State Hospital from Superintendent's Residence (view), 279
Missouri State Militia, 342
Mitchell, John N., 295
Mitchell, Samuel, 262
Mitchell, Samuel E., 911
Mitchim, C. C., 777
Mobley, A. B., 285
Mohrstadt, E. C., 1126
Molder, H. M., 498
Monroe, 141
Monteith, John, 422
Montgomery, (Mrs.) Floyd, 307
Montgomery, Grover C., 1233
Montgomery, Maude, 419
Montgomery, Samuel, 346
Monticello, 275
Moonshine, Captain, 43
Moore, B. J., 288
Moore, Curtis, 999
Moore, David H., 306, 718
Moore, George, 482
Moore, Howard, 306
Moore, Isadore, 66
Moore, Isidore, 154, 155
Moore, James L., 288
Moore, J. L., 288
Moore, Joseph, 287
Moore, Joseph C., 288
Moore, Joseph H., 1213
Moore, Joseph L., 1214
Moore, Joseph R., 793
Moore, P. B., 536
Moore, Sam C., 288
Moothart, George W., 806
Morean & Burgess, 290

Morehouse, 381, 537
"Morehouse Sun," 537
Morgan, Fred, 984
Morgan, George, 82
Morley, 389
Morrill, Joseph W., 1114
Morris, Ira M., 967
Morris, John W., 983
Morrison, D. L., 410
Morrison, E., 1249
Morrison, James, 171
Morrison, Robert, 262
Morrison, T. J. O., 265, 315, 422
Morrow, James R., 994
Moseley, Clay A., 1087
Moseley, William S., 314
Moser, John R., 481
Mott, John A., 553
Mound Builders, 8
Mounds—De Soto's discovery of, 1; distribution of, 2; material of, 3; pottery, 7; burial, 8; mound builders, 8; age of, 9.
Mt. Tabor, 76
Mt. Zion Chapel, 452
Mozley, Charles N., 1265
Mueller, George, 271
Mueller, Jacob, 483
Murdock, Lindsay, 342, 521
Murphy, D., 302
Murphy, David, 277
Murphy, Jesse, 302
Murphy, Richard, 154
Murphy, (Mrs.) Sarah, 63, 410
Murphy Settlement, 177, 206, 410
Murphy, William, 63
Muse, William, 286
Musgrave, Elzie H., 953
Musick, David, 150
Myers, William, 1051
Myrick, Frank, 288

Naeter Brothers, 531
Nall, G. B., 297
Nancy Hunter Chapter, D. A. R., Cape Girardeau, 369
Nanson, H. Clem, 939
Napper, William H., 1043
Nations, Gilbert O., 571
Navarro, Angelo, 415
Naylor, 384
"Naylor Nail," 539
Neal, George F., 274
Neal, James P., 307
Neal, Thomas, 194, 262
Neale, Thomas, 262, 295, 401
Neel, Thomas, 307
Neel, Thomas, Jr., 306
Neeley, William, 153, 154
Neely, William, 261
Neeleyville, 372
Neiswanger, Joseph, 80
Netherton, George, 291
Newberry, Frank, 791
Newberry, William, 791
Newberry, William M., 791
New Bourbon, 66, 124, 177
New Bourbon (Novelle Bourbon), 62
"New Era," 530, 531, 535, 540
New France, 28
New Hamburg, 449

New Hartford, 65
New Madrid, 16, 21, 34, 51, 82, 106, 114, 125, 139, 152, 165, 176, 177, 178, 186, 192, 232, 333, 334—Early history, 265; blows to New Madrid, 265; incorporated as a city, 266; long the county seat, 266
New Madrid Academy, 402
New Madrid Baptist Association, 478
New Madrid Circuit, 455
New Madrid County, 164, 165, 178, 517
New Madrid District, 49, 117, 125, 176—Its boundaries, 81; "L'Anse a la Graise," 82; Indian transfer, 83; Pemiscot county, 107; Scott county, 108; Mississippi county, 109
New Madrid Earthquake—Area of, 214; fissures, 218; sand blows, 222; sinks, 222; cause, 223
"New Madrid Gazette," 537
New Madrid Presbyterian Church, 490
"New Madrid Record," 537
"New Madrid Times," 537
Newman, Arthur R., 287
Newspapers, 192, 529, 547
New River, 231
"New Southeast," 544
New Tennessee, 62, 454
New Tennessee Christian Church, 494
Neybour, Joseph, 65
Nichols, James A., 1226
Nickey, Emmett C., 1161
Ninth Missouri Infantry, 351
Nipper, Simon G., 876
Nixon, Burton S., 1175
Nixon, Frank B., 1175
Noblesse, Peter, 107
Noel, Thomas E., 323
Noell, John W., 322
Normal Dormitory Company, 428
Norman, Moses, 307
Northern Judicial Circuit, 300
Northern Judicial (territorial) Circuit, 154
Northern Presbyterians, 491
Northwest Ordinance, 139
Norton, Richard C., 426, 435
Null, William, 65

Oakes, Clyde, 760
Oak Grove Baptist Church, 473
Oakridge, 264, 374
"Oakridge Indicator," 531
Oak Ridge Presbyterian Church, 491
O'Bannon, Welton, 96
O'Connor, John N., 734
Odin, John, 413
Odin, J. M., 448
Oertel, Maximilian, 249
Oglesby, Joseph, 206
Ohio River, 24, 27
O'Kelley, H. T., 797
Oldest House in Cape Girardeau (view), 258
Old-Fashioned Ore Hoisters in Action (views), 120
Ogle, William, 74, 157, 190
Old Mines, 64, 270, 449
Old-Time Windlass (view), 119
Olive, John Baptiste, 96, 116, 164
Oliver, Arthur L., 887
Omahas, 35
Open Bay, xiv
Oran, 387
"Oran Leader," 542

O'Reilly, 53
O'Reilly, Count, 139
Orr, D., 463
Orth, John, 342
Osage Indians, 54, 63, 183—Agriculture, 36; furniture and implements, 36; polygamy, 37; stealing horses, 37; religion, 37; pipe, 38; clothing, 38; Great and Little Osages, 39; treaty, 44
Osages, 23, 34, 35, 40, 70
Osborn, Stephen, 276
Otter Bayou, 230
Otto, George H., 737
Our Lady of Perpetual Help Church, 451
Outagamies, 37, 40
Overall, Asa, 206
Overall, B. W., 533
Overton, James M., 311
Owen, David W., 662
Owen, Given, 307, 309
Owen, Reuben, 309
Owen, R. P., 295
Oxley, James, 308
Ozark Plateau, Elevation of, ix

Pacahas, 35
Page, Thomas J. E., 944
Painter, Louis, 262
Painter, (Mrs.) Louis, 78
"Palladium," 531
Palmer, Aaron, 636
Panker, D. B., 507
Pankey, David Young, 309
Pankey, D. B., 836
Pankey, D. Y., 285, 349
Paquin, Joseph, 413
Paragould & Memphis Railroad, 508
Paragould Southeastern Railroad, 508
Paramore & McDaniel, 295
Parish, Joseph, 80
Parker, A. F., 1283
Parker, Henry B., 851
Parkin, Felix J., 659
Parks & Akin, 266
Parks, F. C., 995
Parma, 380
"Parma Victor," 537
Parrott, James, 291
Parochial Schools, 400
Parsons, Charles B., 591
Parsons, Roscoe R. S., 595
Pascola, 381
Patterson, 178, 273
"Patterson Times," 545
Patterson, Andrew, 171
Patterson, John, 74
Pawnees, 41
Payne, Joseph, 107
Pease & Hill, 297
Peck, 58
Peck, Elmer H., 962
Peck, George W., 374, 961
Peck, John Mason, 203
Peckham, James, 344
Peers, John D., 302
Pelts, Charles L., 601
Pelts, John A., 600
Pelts, Joseph, 307, 600
"Pemiscot Argus," 538
Pemiscot Bayou, xiv

INDEX

Pemiscot Bayou, 231
Pemiscot County, 107, 178, 242, 282, 313, 518, 538
Penny, Gilbert T., 970
Peorias, 40, 41
Perkins, Amos B., 1181
Perkins, William F., 1069
Perry County, 66, 169, 177, 249, 518
"Perry County Republican," 536, 539
"Perry County Sun," 539
Perry, Samuel, 154, 155, 169, 238
Perry, William, 402
Perryman, David E., 169
Perryville, 138, 270, 451, 520
"Perryville Chronicle," 539
"Perryville Democrat," 539
"Perryville Union," 538
Peter, Sherwood T., 802
Peterson, B. H., 344
Pettis, William G., 238
Petty, Harry V., 890
Petty, William G., 883
Petty, William H., 1101
Petty, W. G., 314
Pevely, 378
Peyroux, Henri, 95, 96
Pfefferkorn, William, 1235
Pharr, N. H., 314
Phelan, William G., 305, 349
Phelps, C. P., 293
Phelps, John D., 904
Phillips, Henry N., 1168
Phillips, Levi B., 931
Phillips, Murray, 1063
Phillips, Samuel, 153, 164
Phillipson, Joseph, 256
Philomathean Literary Society, 430
Physicians, 442
Pickard, Taylor, 349
Pickawilly, 67
Picker, Frederick, 249
Piedmont, 272, 527
"Piedmont Banner," 545
"Piedmont Leader," 545
"Piedmont Rambler," 545
"Piedmont Weekly Banner," 545
Piernas, 53
Pierrepont, William, 265
Pigg, P. T., 531
Pigg, T. P., 540
Pikey, Ben, 1051
Pikey, Grace, 1052
Pilgrim's Rest Baptist Church, 476
Pillow, General, 328
Pilot Knob, xi
Pilot Knob, 178, 338
Pilot Knob Evangelical Lutheran Church, 481
"Pioneer," 541
Pioneer Spinning Wheel (illustration), 129
Pipe, 38
Pirtle, Isaac J., 860
Pitman, W. A., 1028
Pittman, 56
"Plaindealer," 535
"Pleasant Dealer," 541
Pleasant Hill Presbyterian Church, 490
Plumb, William, 342
Pocahontas, 264, 373
Poe, Elton W., 744
Poe, Isaiah, 204

Poe, Simon, 204
Point Pleasant, 178, 230, 266, 334
Polack, Theodore H., 425
Polk, Charles K., 843
Pollock, L. N., 942
Ponder, Abner, 306
Ponder, William S., 351
Ponder's Mill, 337
Pontiac, 38
Pope, Nathaniel, 158
Poplar Bluff, 292, 312, 511
"Poplar Bluff Citizen," 531
Poplar Bluff Christian Church, 495
Poplar Bluff High School (view), 294
Poplin, Green L., 403
Poplin, G. L., 531
"Poplin's Black River News," 531
Population, 53, 56
Population (1804-1821), 175
Population (1820-1830), 247
Poor, T. C., 28
Portage Bay, xiv
Portage Bay, 107
Portageville, 178, 267
"Portageville Critic," 537
"Portageville Push," 537
Portell, Thomas E., 89
Porter, Charles E., 786
Porterfield, John D., 675
Porterfield, J. M., 680
Postage, 192
Postoffices, 192
Poston, Charles P., 578
Poston, Harry P., 998
Poston, Henry, 302
Potosi, 169, 193, 269, 329, 337, 401, 527
Potosi Academy, 402
"Potosi Eagle," 544
"Potosi Free Press," 544
Potosi Home Guards, 342
"Potosi Independent," 544
Potosi Presbytery, 489
"Potosi Republican," 544
Powell, B., 265
Powell, John E., 266
Powell, John W., 347
Powell, Isaac W., 1040
Powell, William H., 930
Powers, William A., 1024
Pratt, Charles R., 782
Pratte, Bernard, 171
Pratte, J. B. T., 52
Pratte, James W., 160
Pratte, Joseph, 115, 413
Pratte, John B., 53, 183
Pratte, S. B., 267
Prentiss, 330
Presbyterians—Presbytery of Missouri formed, 483; Southeast Missouri Presbyterian churches, 484; Presbyterianism in 1854-94, 484; 1864-74, 485; division in Presbytery, 486; decades from 1884 to 1904, 487; general review, 488; Northern Presbyterians, 491; Cumberland Presbyterians, 493.
Preslar, J. P., 1014
Press (see newspapers).
"Press," 531, 538
Price, Charles B., 349
Priest, J. V., 318
Priest, Zenas, 262, 401

Pritchard, Charles M., 1044
Pritchard, Columbus E., 989
Pritchard, Thomas E., 989
Protestants, 196
Provenchere, P., 150
Providence Church, 201
Provines, William C., 410
Pruente, E., 450
Pryor, Herbert, 598
Public Schools—Foundation of public system, 404; the State Commission, 405; sale of lands, 406; curriculum, 406; laws of 1853, 406; provisions of 1874, 407; growth of the system, 407; Southeast Missouri Teachers' Association, 409; first schools in various counties, 409.
Pulliam, Thomas, 306
Punch, Jasper N., 1085
Purtels, James, 290
Puxico, 392
"Puxico Index," 544

Quapas, 35
Quigate, 20
Quinby, N. E., 288

Radisson, 23
Railroads—Railroad building since the war, 357; St. Louis & Iron Mountain Railway Company, 496; the Belmont branch, 497; Cairo & Fulton, 498; Jackson Branch Railroad Company, 500; Cape Girardeau, Pilot Knob & Belmont Railroad Company, 501; Cape Girardeau & State Line Railroad Company, 501; Illinois, Missouri & Texas Railway Company, 501; Houck's Missouri & Arkansas Railroad, 502; St. Louis & Gulf Railroad, 502; St. Louis & San Francisco Railroad Company, 502; Cape Girardeau & Thebes Bridge Terminal Railway Company, 503; St. Louis & San Francisco system, 503; St. Louis, Memphis & Southeastern Railroad, 504; St. Louis Southwestern Railroad Company, 505; Mississippi River & Bonne Terre Railway, 506; Holliday-Knotz Land and Lumber Company, 507; St. Louis, Kennett & Southeastern Railroad, 507; St. Louis & Missouri Southern Railroad, 507; Paragould Southeastern Railroad, 508; Illinois Southern Railroad, 508; Paragould & Memphis Railroad, 508; Butler County Railroad Company, 508; Cape Girardeau & Jackson Interurban Company, 509.
Rainbolt, W. K., 478
Ramsay, Andrew, 77, 150, 171
Ramsay, Andrew, Jr., 171
Ramsay, Andrew M., 303
Ramsay, James, 171
Ramsay, John, 78
Ramsay Settlement, 76
Ramsay, W. C., 78
Ramsay, William, 171
Ramsey Creek, xiii
Ramsey, Robert G., 802
Ramsey, Samuel L., 1248
Randoff, S. M., 476
Randol, Enos, 79
Randol, John, 79, 214
Randol, Medad, 79, 171
Randol, Samuel, 79
Randol Settlement, 77
Randol, Thankful, 287
Randolph, George E., 1288

Raniller, Baptiste, 65
Rankin, Lewis J., 273
Ranney, Johnson, 155
Ranney, Rhoda, 402
Ranney, Robert G., 611
Ranney, W. C., 257, 295, 501
Rau, Gustav C., 775
Rauls, John H., 1135
Ravenscroft, James, 155
Rawls, Hardy, 107
Ray, David M., 1122
Rayburn, M. B., 310, 995
Rayburn, W. C., 310
Read, T. W., 803
Reagan, George K., 115
Reagan, Mathias M., 803
Reaves, George A., 1268
Reavis, G. H., 410
Reck, Edward B., 586
Redden, George W., 627
Reddick, John R., 1107
Red House, 71, 74
Redman, S. E., 973
Reed, Charles W., 1047
Reed, D. C., 317
Reed, Harmon, 295
Reed, Jacob, 188
Reed, Mary E., 1154
Reed, Simpson, 1153
Reed, William, 62
Reeves, Everett, 881
"Reflector," 531
"Reformer," 540
Regimental Histories (Civil War)—Home Guards, 341 Missouri State Militia, 342; Third Missouri Regiment, 343; Fifth Missouri Regiment, 343; Fifty-sixth Missouri Regiment, 343; Sixty-fourth Missouri Regiment, 343; Sixty-eighth Missouri Regiment, 344; Seventy-ninth Missouri Regiment, 344; Second Missouri Infantry, 344; Twenty-ninth Missouri Infantry, 344; Thirteenth Missouri Infantry, 345; Forty-seventh Missouri Infantry, 345; Fiftieth Missouri Infantry, 346; Sixth Missouri Cavalry, 346; Tenth Missouri Cavalry, 346; Engineer Regiment, West Missouri Volunteers, 347; Second Regiment Missouri Volunteers, 347; Forty-seventh Regiment Missouri Volunteers, 347; Fifteenth Regiment, Enrolled Missouri Militia, 347; Twenty-third Regiment, Missouri Enrolled Militia, 348; Thirty-ninth Regiment, Missouri Enrolled Militia, 348; Eighty-third Battalion, 348; Confederate organizations, 348; Ninth Missouri Infantry, 351; Second Missouri Infantry, 351; Second Missouri Cavalry, 352.
Reid, James, 410
Reinecke, Frederick, 74, 97
Relfe, James H., 322
Religious History (see also churches)—Catholics, 448; Methodists, 452; Baptists, 463; Lutherans, 479; Episcopal, 481; Congregational, 482; German Evangelical Church, 482; German Methodists, 483; Presbyterians, 483; Presbyterianism in 1854-64, 484; Presbyterians, 1864-74, 485; division in Presbytery, 486; decades from 1884 to 1904, 487; general review, 488; Northern Presbyterians, 491; Cumberland Presbyterians, 493; Christians, 494.
Renault, 270
Renault, Philip Francois, 182
Rench, Daniel R., 716

Renick, Joseph A., 1010
"Renovator," 532
Reppy, John H., 535
Reppy, Samuel A., 785
"Representative," 541
"Republic," 532
"Republican," 261, 532, 534
Resources, 366
Revelle, John W., 370, 1004
Revelle, L. W., 477
"Review," 534
Reyburn, Joseph A., 832
Reynol, A., 150
Reynolds County, 179, 311, 520
"Reynolds County Outlook," 539
Reynolds, James, 256
Reynolds, Thomas, 311
Rhodes, Horatio S., 1198
Rice, David, 308, 310
Rice, James, 402
Rice, Jimer E., 606
Rice, John F., 1120
Rice, John T., 1021
Rice, Pascal, 306
Richards, Cap B., 1072
Richardson, J. N., 473
Richardson, Mack, 370
Richardson, W. B., 478
Richwoods, 392
Riddle, J. F., 1274
Rider, R. P., 423
Rigby, J., 257
Rigdon, D. M., 748
Rigdon, Thomas J., 800
Riney, Thomas, 270
Ring, Thomas, 80
Ringer, Louis, 295
Ringo, Mann, 619
Ripley County, 180, 248, 305, 521
Ripley, Eleazer W., 306
Ripley Mission, 453
Rishe, John, 74
Risher, John, 74
Ritton, J., 257
Rivard, Francois, 51
"River of the Conception," 133
River St. Louis, 49
River Transportation, 364
Rivers, D. L., 1018
Riverside, 65
Riviere, Baptiste, 65
Riviere Petite (Little River), 230
Riviere Zenon, 79
Roberson, C. A., 1160
Roberts, DeWitt, 426
Roberts, Frank D., 920
Roberts, Thomas, 290, 303
Robertson, Edward, 108
Robertson, J. R., 1132
Robidaux, Joseph, 153
Robins, M., 477
Robinson, C. S., 207
Robinson, William P., 1288
Rocheblave, Phillip, 53
Rodney family, 79
Rodney, Michael, 171, 295
Rodney settlement, 77
Rodney, Thomas J., 256, 257
Rogers, Edmond, 290

Rogers, James A., 702
Rogers, John J., 896
Roland, Dan W., 724
Romain, John, 65
Romine, Abraham, 293
Romines, James R., 697
Rood, Lee W., 899
Roper, G. L., 1167
Rosati, Father, 412, 448
Rosati, Joseph, 137
Rosecrans, General, 337
Rosenberg, L., 288
Rosenthal, Moses, 707
Ross, Alexander, 1170
Ross, A. M., 468
Ross, Steel, 165
Ross, Stephen, 155
Roth, Caspar, 480
Roth, Louis, 480
Rotrock, C. P., 545
Rowe, C. E., 280
Roy, Barbeau A., 652
Roy, Joachim, 65
Roy, Pierre, 53
Rozier, Charles, 415
Rozier, Charles C., 321, 422, 433
Rozier, Edward A., 817
Rozier, Ferdinand, 56, 60, 270, 402
Rozier, Firmin A., 115, 301, 320
Rozier, Francois C., 410
Rozier, Frederick, 413
Ruddell, George, 43, 107
Ruddell, John, 107
Rudy, J. F., 477
Ruebottom, Ezekiel, 167
Ruether, Fred J., 728
Ruggles, Martin, 169
Rui, 53
Runels, Will M., 1013
Rush's Ridge, 179
Russell, James, 78, 79
Russell, Joseph, 318
Russell, J. J., 288, 551
Russell, William, 78, 79
Ruth, Andrew F., 781
Rutledge, James A., 402
Rutter, John B., 290
Rutter, John P., 303
Ryan, Abram J., 417
Ryan, Dawsey, 1115

Sabula, 378
Sacs, 35, 40, 70, 150, 170
Sadd, Joseph M., 492
Sadler, Stephen H., 973
St. Aubin, Lewis, 107
St. Charles, 51, 140, 152
St. Charles District, 49
St. Francis Levee District, 314
St. Francisville, 333
St. Francois County, 177, 277, 302, 522
"St. Francois County Democrat," 540
"St. Francois County Republican," 541
St. Francois Mountains, x
St. Francois River, xii, xiv
St. Francois River, 42
St. Gem, Gustavus, 555
St. Gem, Jean Baptiste, 51, 52
St. Gem, J. B., 171

St. Gem, Vital, 53
Ste. Genevieve, 21, 50, 56, 114, 137, 139, 140, 152, 176, 177, 182, 186, 190, 192, 193, 197, 254; shipping center of mineral region, 251; Ste. Genevieve-Iron Mountain Plank Road, 251; 150th anniversary celebrated, 252; U. S. Senators from Ste. Genevieve, 252; Ste. Genevieve of today, 254.
Ste. Genevieve Academy, 193, 194, 257, 320, 401
Ste. Genevieve Asylum, 399
Ste. Genevieve Circuit, 454, 455
"Ste. Genevieve Correspondent and Record," 192
Ste. Genevieve County, 177, 523
Ste. Genevieve District, 49, 66, 125, 159; population, 53, 56; trade of, 54; military expedition, 55; social life and amusement, 55; common field, 56; dates of settlement, 62; houses of French settlers, 119; food and cooking, 121; French Canadians, 121; houses of American settlers, 125; food of the Americans, 127.
Ste. Genevieve Evangelical Lutheran Church, 481
"Ste. Genevieve Herald," 542
St. John's Bayou, xiii
St. John's Bayou, 82, 229
St. James Bayou, xiii
St. James Bayou, 229
St. Joseph Lead Company, Bonne Terre, 506
St. Louis, 57, 114, 140, 152
St. Louis & Gulf Railroad, 502
St. Louis & Iron Mountain Railway Company, 496
St. Louis & Iron Mountain Railroad, 259, 506
St. Louis & Missouri Southern Railroad, 507
St. Louis & San Francisco Railroad Company, 502
St. Louis & San Francisco System, 503
St. Louis, Kennett & Southeastern Railroad, 507
St. Louis, Memphis & Southeastern Railroad, 504
St. Louis Southwestern Railroad Company, 505
St. Mary, Augustus S., Jr., 878
St. Marys, 254
St. Mary's Academy, 193
"St. Mary's Progress," 542
"St. Mary's Review," 542
St. Mary's Seminary, 412, 448
"St. Mary's Times," 542
St. Michael's, 64, 126, 139, 201, 449
St. Paul's Episcopal Church, Ironton, 482
St. Philip River, 49
St. Vincent's Church, 448
St. Vincent's College, 413
St. Vincent's College (views), 414
Saline Creek, xii
Saline Creek, 18, 65, 177
Sand Blows, 222
Sandlin, Jonathan R., 311
Sandlin, Martin, 179
Sandy Creek, 193
Sanford, Daniel, 295
Sans Oreille, 39
Satterfield, W. M., 308
Saucier, F., 150
Saukees, 40
Sayres, William, 311
Scene at the Shut-in near Arcadia (view), xi
Scene on Black River near Poplar Bluff (view), 294
Schaaf, John F., 254
Schadt, Otto, 345
Schaper, Jesse H., 903
Schell, Casper, 178
Schiller Verein, 431
Schleich, L. C., 423

Schmitz, Ferdinand, 342
Schneider, Charles W., 829
Schonhoff, C. A., 1229
Schonhoff, J. H., 1247
Schools (see Education)
Schrader, Anthony, 480
Schramm, Emil C., 684
Schrum, Eugene G., 1189
Schult, Hina C., 314
Schult, H. C., 956
Schult, W. D., 314
Schulte, Frank, 678
Schultz, Thomas W., 634
Schultze, Andrew T., 578
Schulz, Gustav B., 665
Schwartz, John, 342
Scoggin, George W., 809
Scott, Andrew, 154, 402
Scott, Jonathan, 315
Scott, John, 153, 155, 237, 238, 242, 307, 313
Scott, J. B., 410
Scott, John G., 323
Scott, Thomas, 311
Scott, Thomas B., 148
Scott County, 108, 156, 179, 290, 303, 342, 524
Scott County Hills, xii
"Scott County Agricultural Wheel," 542
"Scott County Banner," 543
"Scott County Democrat," 543
"Scott County Kicker," 542
"Scott County Newsboy," 543
Scripps, George H., 262
Scripps, John, 205
Scripps, (Mrs.) John, 402
Seabaugh, A. Frank, 1254
Seabaugh, Oda L., 779
Seavers, David, 74
Seavers, Nicholas, 77
Seawell, Joseph, 261, 401
Second Missouri Cavalry, 352
Second Missouri Infantry, 344, 351
Second Regiment, Missouri Volunteers, 347
Seelitz Evangelical Lutheran Church, 479
Segal, Louis, 1064
Seindre, John, 65
Sellers, Benjamin, 282
Selma, 275
Senath, 376
"Senath Leader," 534
"Senath Star," 534
Seneca Slough, 42
Sergeant, Ichabod, 411
Settle, V. T., 477
Settle, W. W., 476, 477
Seventy-ninth Missouri Regiment, 344
Sewell, Joseph, 154, 155
Sexton, J. W., 643
Sexton, Lafayette, 307
Shady Grove Baptist Church, 473
Shafer, Sophia, 65
Shaner, Henry, 295
Shannon, William, 155
Sharp, E. F., 1278
Sharp, James J., 946
Sharp, Thomas B., 699
Shaw, John, 172, 228
Shaw, Thomas M., 290
Shawnee Hills, ix
Shawnees, 40, 41, 170

Shearer, J. G., 478
Sheehy, John T., 1060
Shelby, Jo, 335, 337
Shelby, Reuben, 270, 402
Shell, Benjamin, 162
Shelton, Enoch, 308
Shelton, Lee, 562
Shelton, William H., 308
Shelton, W. F., 823
Shelton, W. F., Jr., 824
Shepherd Mountain, xi
Sheppard, Isaac, 199
Sheppard, Jesse C., 1282
Sheppard, John, 162
Sheppard, William, 262
Sherrill, L., 277
Shields, Charles W., 926
Shields, S. A., 808
Shipley, Hugh, 307
Shivers, J. A., 965
Short, John, 178
Shot Tower, 65
Shrader, John, 153
Shreve, Israel, 84
Shultz, Thomas J., 853
Shurlds, Henry, 169
Siege of New Madrid (1862), 265
Sigler, Charles L., 1220
Sikes, John, 291
Sikeston, 108, 291, 525
"Sikeston Herald," 542
Sikeston M. E. Church, 460
Sikeston Presbyterian Church, 491
Sikeston Ridge, xiii
"Sikeston Standard," 542
"Sikeston Star," 542
Simply a Big Oil Tank (view), 518
Simpson, A. E., 288
Simpson, A. P., 1052
Simpson, Doda B., 1052
Simpson, Jeremiah, 77
Simpson, Samuel P., 343
Sink Hole, 172
Sinks, 222
Siouan, 34
Sioux, 170
Sixth Missouri Cavalry, 346
Sixty-fourth Missouri Regiment, 343
Sixty-eighth Missouri Regiment, 244
Sixth Regiment (Spanish-American War), 370
Skaggs, Dick, 307
Skaggs, Dr., 286
Skaats, Lillie E., 426
Slinkard, Frederick, 80
Slinkard, J. V., 873
Sloan, Albert D., 370
Sloan, H. L., 256, 262
Sloan, William, 169
Smart, John C., 349
Smelting of Lead, 363
Smith & Love, 297
Smith, Ashael, 265
Smith, Harry A., 539
Smith, Henry H., 154
Smith, H. M., 478
Smith, James, 288
Smith, James W., 160, 302
Smith, John, 350
Smith, John T., 169

Smith, Joseph, 290, 303
Smith, J. S., 290
Smith, Melbourne, 746
Smith, Owen A., 835
Smith, Reuben, 313
Smith, S. Henry, 535
Smith, Tilman, 80
Smith, T. John, 60, 190
Smith T.-Browne duel, 190
Smith, William, 199
Smyth, James A., 308
Smyth, R. Lee, 1096
Snider, Frank M., 954
Snider, G. B., 667
Snider, Jacob, 307
Snider, John A., 1143
Snider, Oliver E., 313
Snoddy, John, 293
Social Life—Population of Louisiana in 1804, 117; Ste. Genevieve district, 118, 119, 121; American settlers, 119; houses of French settlers, 119; Indians, 119; food and cooking, 121; French Canadians, 121; dress of the French, 122; amusements, 122; personal property, 124; wealth (personal property), 124; trade, 124; fur trade of Upper Louisiana, 124; American immigration, 125; houses of American settlers, 125; clothing, 127; food of the Americans, 127; general conditions, 439; houses, 440; food, 440; dress, 440; household implements, 441; amusements, 441; physicians, 442.
Son, Thomas A., 752
Sorosis Society, 430
Soulard, Antonio, 65
Southeast District Agricultural Society, 257
"Southeast Gazette," 530
"Southeast Missourian," 532, 537
"Southeast Missouri Enterprise," 534
Southeast Missouri Teachers' Association, 409
"Southeast Missouri Statesman," 538
"South Missouri," 530
South Missouri Guards, 301
"Southern Advocate and State Journal," 529
"Southern Democrat," 529
Southern Judicial (territorial) Circuit, 154
Southern Mississippi Steamer (view), 365
"Southern Missouri Argus," 540
"Southern Pemiscot News," 538
"Southern Scimetar," 538
Southern, William A., 720
Spanish-American War, 370
Spanish Government over Louisiana—Merchants, 130; prices, 130; products, 130; travel, 131; religion, 133.
Sparks, Daniel, 164
Spear, Edward, 171, 199
Speer, Asier J., 1189
Spence, James M., 293
Spence, J. M., 403
Spence, William A., 1152
Spence, W. W., 493
Spencer, Edward, 307, 310
Spencer, H., 307
Spencer, Urban C., 402
Spencer, Wade H., 282
Spiggott, Joseph, 206
Spiller, Elbert C., 284
Spiller, S. W., 374
Sprigg Street, 329

INDEX

Stacy, William L., 1047
Stady, William C., 568
Stallcup, James A., 1208
Stallcup, Lynn M., 1207
Stallcup, Mark H., 291, 1206
Stanberry, Henry, 243
Stancil, Martin L., 313
"Standard," 531
Stanfill, J. H., 371
Stanley, Rufus H., 937
Stanton, John, 169
Starett, William S., 957
Starved Rock, 30, 31
Statehood—Memorial for, 234; Missouri Compromise, 237, 240; solemn public act, 239; state boundaries, 242.
State Normal School, Cape Girardeau, 259, 367, 409; established, 420; courses of study, 428; literary societies, 430; the Young Men's Christian Association, 431; library, 431; enrollment, 432; faculty, 432; board of regents, 433; former presidents, 434; place of the normal school, 436.
State Normal School, Cape Girardeau (view), 421
Statler, Conrad, 79
Statler, Peter, 79
Stear, Jacob, 290
Steck, Emil, 1236
Steele, 382
Stein, Louis, 652
Steinback, B., 74, 97
Steinback, F., 74, 97
Stephens, John W., 932
Stephens, L. L., 473
Stephens, Thomas, 202
Stevens, John, 313
Stevenson, John, 311
Stevenson, J. Henry, 763
Stevenson, William J., 341
Stevenson, William T., 879
Steward, Ambrose S., 1292
Steward, James, 65
Stewart, Robert, 313
Stewart, Thomas, 262, 401
Stierberger, Edward A., 642
Stiver, Christian E., 629
Stoddard, Amos, 142, 143, 304
Stoddard County, 180, 295, 304, 525
Stoddard County Baptist Association, 478
"Stoddard County Republican," 543
Stokes, Amzi L., 1023
Stokes, Charles E., 543
Stokes, John E., 963
Stokes, Robert W., 992
Stokes, R. W., 286, 308
Stokes, T. C., 286
Stokes, William C., 881
Stone, John H., 317
Storey, O. H., 639
Story, Joseph, 105, 107, 165
Stout, Ephraim, 80, 178
Stout, Thankful, 79
Strange, Tubal E., 192
Strange, T. E., 262, 529
Street, William, 167, 203
Stricklin, John W., 1210
Strother, Benjamin, 159
Stumpe, Frederick W., 681
Sturdivant, Robert, 256, 318
Subscription Schools, 398

Sugg, H. A., 856
Summers, Andrew, 79
Summers, John, 105
Summers, John C., 948
Sumpter, Bert, 818
"Sunnyside," 541
Surrell, William, 195, 262
Sutherland, George W., 1049
Swan, Clarence M., 729
Swashing Baptist Church, 476
Swearingen, William A., 963
Sweazea, Thomas J., 685
Swinger, Jacob M., 1178
Syenite Granite Company, 820
Syenite Presbyterian Church, 491

Tarkington, William W., 974
Tallmadge Amendment, 237
Tanner, Rucker, 206
Tanot, Pierre, 65
Tarlton, George W., 699
Tate, C. J., 468
Tatum Brothers, 285
Tatum, James F., 657
Tatum, Luther F., 933
Tatum, Luther P., 562
Tatum, Ira B., 934
Tatum, Richard M., 658
Taverns, 191
Tawney, John, 1101
Taylor, (Captain), 349
Taylor, Edward O., 1032
Taylor, John P., 308
Taylor, Lee, 349
Taylor, Lee J., 1000
Taylor, Luther, 270
Taylor, M. W., 476
Taylor Slough, xiv
Taylor Slough, 231, 307
Taylor, T., 400
Taylor, William R., 1097
Taylor, William T., 980
Tecumseh, 42
Templeton, James D., 938
Templeton, William A., 943
Tennille, Benjamin, 162
Tenney, David, 208
Tenth Missouri Cavalry, 346
Territorial Government of Louisiana—Governor and general assembly, 152; courts, 158
Territorial House, 152
Terry, Philip S., 1025
Test Oath, 417
Tetweiler, S. G., 536
Thebes, 260
Theel, Levi, 65
Theilmann, Louis, 915
Thiele, Frederick, 858
Thilenius, Edward, 797
Thilenius, E. M., 902
Thilenius, G. C., 343, 501
Third Missouri Regiment, 343
Thirtieth Missouri Infantry, 345
Thirty-ninth Regiment, Missouri Enrolled Militia, 348
Thomas, Jesse B., 237
Thomas, John C., 288, 498
Thomas, John L., 867
Thomas, Judge, 170
Thomas, Richard S., 153, 154, 155, 238, 242, 300

INDEX

Thomasson, Bettie G., 1075
Thomasson, J. W., 1074
Thompson, A., 307
Thompson, Benjamin, 410
Thompson, Benjamin F., 792
Thompson, General, 330, 331
Thompson, James, 171
Thompson, John, 171
Thompson, Samuel H., 206
Thompson, Samuel T., 1152
Thompson's Fort, 335
Thompson, Sullivan S., 1039
Thompson, Wilson, 202
Thomure, Jean Baptiste, 52
Thornberry, Ephraim, 307
Thorne, Solomon, 74
Thrower, A. C., 1222
Tidwell, A., 477
Tidwell, A. G., 476
Tiedeman, D. F., 410
Timber, xv
Timber, 360
Timberman, J. W., 673
Timberman, John, 286
Timberman, John H., 1273
"Times," 540
Timon, John, 413, 448
Tindle, Albert, 1037
Tinnin, Edwin L., 828
Tinnin, Robert H., 790
Tipton, Samuel, 77
Tolds, James, 403
Tolle, B. A., 1065
Tolleson, Thomas R., 850
Toole, Thomas J., 1093
Toney, Henry, 402
Tong & Carson, 297
Tong, H. F., 477
Tong, Theodore F., 267, 316
Tonti, 29
Topping, Moses H., 614
Toriman, 35
Totty, Ulysses G., 1291
Tower, Rush, 275
Towl, Benjamin F., 838
Townships, 159, 163, 304
Trade, 27, 33, 124, 130, 140, 186, 445
Transfer to the United States-Louisiana Purchase, 139; trade, 140; land grants, 148
Transportation, 187, 364
Travis, John, 204
Traylor, George H., 1033
Treece, George W., 958
Tresenwriter, C. D., 531
Tribble, Pearl D., 1085
Tribble, Thomas E., 1083
"Tribune," 536
"Tri-City Independent," 535
Trogdon, J. R., 1204
Tromley, L. F., 532
Trotter, David, 44, 115
Trudeau, Zenon, 79
Tual, Charles J., 861
Tucker, Father, 451
Tucker, John, 164
Tucker, Joseph, 170, 270
Tucker, Marion F., 832
Tucker, Nathaniel B., 302
Tucker, Rufus C., 774

Tucker, William L., 566
Turley, John G., 1025
Turley, Lee, 762
Turnbaugh, J. J., 262
Turnbaugh, T. Ben, 1081
Turnbaugh, Thomas B., 1080
Turner, B. F., 403
Turner, Samuel E., 342
Tuttel, Joseph, 1151
Twenty-third Regiment, Missouri Enrolled Militia, 348
Twenty-ninth Missouri Infantry, 344
Tyler, Thomas, 65
Typical Stone Quarries (views), 515
Tywappity Bottoms, 81, 179

Uhl, Casper, 343
Union American Lead Company, 268
Union Literary Society, 430
United Daughters of the Confederacy, 369
Unity Masonic Lodge, 157
Upper Louisiana, 49
Ursuline Sisters, 420

Vail, John W., 1137
Valle Family, 269
Valle, Charles, 114
Valle, Felix, 410
Valle, Francisco, 52, 115, 159
Valle, Francisco, Jr., 115
Valle, Jean Baptiste, 52
Van Amburg, James H., 410
Van Buren, 180, 372
Vance, Robert L., 723
Vandenbenden, Joseph, 105
Vandenbenden, Louis, 97, 105
Van Denbenden, Lewis, 107
Vandiver, Willard D., 426, 427, 435
Vandover, William, 293
Vanduser, 389
VanFrank, P. R., 342
VanGilder, J. W., 1133
Van Guard Literary Society, 430
Vanhorn, Nathan, 163, 262
Van Lluytelaar, John, 449
Vardell, B. N., 822
Vardell, Drew, 875
Vasquez, Benito, 65
Vessells, Francis M., 805
Victoria, 378
Views—Capaha Bluffs, Rock Levee Drive, Cape Girardeau, viii; elephant rocks, Graniteville, x; scene at the Shut-in near Arcadia, xi; Indian mound, 4; Marquette among the Mississippi Valley Indians, 25; first brick house built west of the Mississippi, 50; old-time windlass, 119; home of our fathers, 126; happy Missouri corn grower, 181; oldest house in Cape Girardeau, 258; Missouri State Hospital from superintendent's residence, 279; high school, Farmington, 279; Will Mayfield College, Marble Hill, 281; Poplar Bluff High School and scene on Black River near Poplar Bluff, 294; highest point on Pilot Knob, Arcadia Heights, 298; southern Mississippi river steamer, 365; State Normal School, Cape Girardeau, 421; in the thick timber, 511; typical stone quarries, 515; corn measured by horses, 517; simply a big oil tank, 518; Missouri orchards in bearing, 519.

Vincennes, 51
"Vindicator," 543, 545
Vire, F. A., 539
Vitt, Alfred A., 632
Vossbrink, Henry C., 653
Voyageur, 24

Wabash River, 49
Wade, David, 74
Wade, Robert C., 971
Wade, Robert L., 908
Wagner, John F., 648
Wagner, L. M., 481
Wagster, Nofflit J., Sr., 815
Wahl, James S., 908
Waide, Robert, 288
Walker, Alexander S., 154
Walker, C. A., 705
Walker, Charles N., 537
Walker, Cyrus, 263
Walker, George W., 679
Walker, Irwin K., 342
Walker, James A., 349
Walker, James P., 556
Walker, Jesse, 204, 205, 461
Walker, J. H., 233, 282
Walker, John B., 307
Walker, John Hardeman, 107, 178, 242, 315
Walker, Thomas B., 343
Walker, Thomas M., 928
Walker, William S. C., 629
Wallace, John W., 968
Wallace, Newton, 312
Waller's Ferry, 163
Wallis, J. P., 476
Walls, Robert D., 714
Walser, David F., 1202
Walsh, M. C., 450
Walters, Jacob, 155
Walther, C. F., 271
Walther, Carl F. W., 480
Waltrip, I. A., 308
Waltrip, J. M., 308
Ward, E. D., 274
Ward, H. M., 498
Ward, M., 288
Ward, Robert L., 945
Ward, Samuel J., 348
Ward, W. J., 844
Ware, Hardy, 65
Warren, Humphrey, 287
Warren, Martin S., 892
Warrington & Pennell, 265, 282
Warner, Charles G., 505
Warner, John E., 1262
Warren, Robert L., 1015
Washington County, 153, 168, 176, 179, 269, 526
Washington County Baptist Association, 478
Washington County Battalion, 342
Washington County, first settlement in, 64
"Washington County Gazette," 545
"Washington County Journal," 544
"Washington County Miner," 544
Washington Female Seminary, 402
Waters, Richard Jones, 97, 115, 150, 164, 265, 402
Waters, Thomas W., 179
Waters, W. W., 537
Watervalley Presbyterian Church, 491
Watkins, Griffin, 717

Watkins, James H., 987
Watkins, Joseph, 80
Watkins, Martha E., 988
Watkins, Nathaniel W., 156
Watkins, N. M., 263
Watkins, N. W., 257, 316, 328
Watkins, W., 349
Wathen, I. R., 256
Wathen, Ignatius R., 290
Watrin, P. M., 56
Watson, Jason, 263
Watson, Robert Goah, 97, 265, 402
Watson, W. S., 257
Watts, H. S., 461
Watts, Napoleon B., 639
Wayne County, 80, 167, 176, 178, 203, 272, 527
Wayne County Baptist Association, 479
Weber, Carl, 1221
Weber, Charles A., 343
Weber, Emil M., 1220
Webb, George B., 986
Webb, W. J., 1222
Webster Literary Society, 430
"Weekly Journal," 545
Weiberg (Whybark), Samuel, 80
Weigel, E. F., 422
Weirick, Upton L., 709
Weiss, Henry F., 769
Welker, Leonard, 80
Welker, Wilbur M., 587
Wellborn, James, 290
Welling, Charles, 262, 263, 318
Wells, Francis M., 624
Wenom, Gustavus A., 866
Wernert, L. C., 842
West, Henry T., 581
West, John, 287
"Western Eagle, 530
"Westliche Post," 530
Whaley, Nathaniel C., 999
Wheeler, Doctor, 402
Wheeler, David, 402
Whitcomb, George, 287, 498
Whitcomb, G. W., 288
White, Cornelius C., 1074
White, Edmund, 295
White, Elbert C., 532
White, E. C., 308
White, G. M., 308
White, James B., 351
White, Josiah M., 745
White, J. W., 884
White, William, 74
Whiteaker, Robert A., 924
Whiteaker, William C., 1071
Whitehead, Samuel W., 1196
Whitehead, Thomas L., 1119
Whitelaw, James M., 319
Whitelaw, Robert H., 549, 704
Whitener, David A., 739
Whitener, Henry, 267, 371
Whitener, J. Q. A., 371
Whiteoak, 377
White Oak Grove Baptist Church, 478
Whiteside, Jacob, 206
Whitewater, 373, 492
Whitewater Creek, xii
Whitewater River, xiii
"Whitewater Times," 531

INDEX

Whittaker, M. J., 473, 474
Whitten, William H., 1083
Whitworth, Isaac G., 851
Whybark, Levi C., 343
Whybark, Levi E., 493
Whybark, John C., 313
Whybark, Samuel, 492
Wichterich, Robert F., 689
Wiggins, Levy, 66
Wiggs, Franklin A., 638
Wilcox, Edward, 204
Wilkinson, James, 142, 143
Wilkerson, Joel, 349
Wilkes, William C., 349, 872
Wilkins, Fabium M., 962
Wilkinson, James, 88
Wilkson, Charles P., 765
Willett, J. O., 468
Williams, A. B., 307
Williams, C. S., 799
Williams, Elisha G., 1125
Williams, George, 291
Williams, George B., 849
Williams, George K., 647
Williams, George W., 849
Williams, James, 469, 475
Williams, Justin, 403
Williams, J. J., 314
Williams, Lee, 1227
Williams, Lewis, 45
Williams, Luther H., 703
Williams, Matthew J., 1225
Williams, Philbert R., 731
Williams, Thomas, 291
Williams, William, 204
Williamson, James, 307
Williamsville, 893
"Williamsville Iron News," 546
Williford, Charles, 349
Willis, Riley, 1229
Will Mayfield College, 418
Will Mayfield College, Marble Hill, 479, 572
Will Mayfield College, Marble Hill (view), 281
Wills, Ernest S., 1138
Wilson, Andrew, 105
Wilson, A. W., 419
Wilson, Ben, 1111
Wilson, Charles D., 1092
Wilson, Eli, 1237
Wilson, Ellen, 425
Wilson, George, 164
Wilson, H. G., 409
Wilson, John O., 1289
Wilson, Michael A., 296, 403
Wilson, Mattie G., 1239
Wilson, Nicholas, 154
Wilson, Parrish G., 1110
Wilson, Thomas G., 753
Wilson, T. M., 410
Wilson, Ward, 370
Wilson, William B., 550
Winchester, 291

Winchester, Abraham, 291
Winchester, Henderson, 291
Windsor, Elisha, 164
Windsor, Thomas, 164
Winn, Lulu May, 419
Winningham, S., 469
Winston, P. S., 988
Winter, H. F., 480
Wisecarver, John, 312
Wisecarver, Nathan, 312
Witchcraft, 43
Witt, Christian, 65
Wittenberg, 383
Wittenberg Evangelical Lutheran Church, 479
Wofford, Moses, 921
Wolf Island, 243
Wolff, Joseph S., 621
Wolverton, Levy, 74
Wood, Fred C., 714
Wood, S. N., 346
Wood's Battalions, State Guards, 349
Woodward, John, 266, 267, 402
Workman, Elmer S., 1086
Workman, Henry A., 1270
Worsham, J. V., 487
Worth, Charles, 1296
Worthington, Robert, 74
Wright, Campbell, 284
Wright, C., 346
Wright, Edward A., 1043
Wright, E. A., 537
Wright, (Mrs.) Ellen, 257
Wright, John, 308
Wright, J. L., 975
Wright, Thomas, 204, 205, 206, 207
Wright, Will D., 545
Wulfert, Albert, 869

Yankeetown, 254
Yarber, John N., 293
Yesberg, John H., 1081
Yorke Chapel, 452
Young, Charles A., 882
Young, David, 205
Young, David B., 1258
Young, John A., 1227
Young, J. R., 1236
Young, L. Willis, 1048
Young, Robert C., 936

Zalma, 371
Zenonian Literary Society, 430
Zimmerman, Aaron R., 927
Zimmerman, Daniel C., 767
Zimmerman, John H., 1027
Zion Evangelical Lutheran Church, Gravelton, 481
Zoellner Brothers, The, 1022
Zoellner, Adolph H., 1022
Zoellner, August B., 1023
Zoellner, Frank H., 1023
Zoellner & Zoellner, 539

SECTION I

Archaeology—De Soto—French Explorers—Indians

HISTORY OF SOUTHEAST MISSOURI

CHAPTER I

ARCHAEOLOGY

MOUNDS IN SOUTHEAST MISSOURI—GREAT NUMBERS KNOWN TO EXIST — DISTRIBUTION OF MOUNDS—SIZE OF MOUNDS—SHAPE—ARRANGEMENT — VARIOUS MOUNDS DESCRIBED — AN ANCIENT WHARF—CONTENTS OF MOUNDS—WHO BUILT THE MOUNDS—THE MOUND BUILDER THEORY—THE WORK OF THE INDIANS—PROBABLE ORIGIN—COLLECTIONS OF RELICS—BECKWITH'S GREAT COLLECTION—PLATES FOUND NEAR MALDEN—OTHER REMARKABLE PIECES. .

In every part of the world are found evidences of the early existence of man. The dwellers in Europe find constant evidence that many centuries ago, long before the beginning of recorded history, there were men living who left behind them traces of their existence in the form of tools and implements of stone, of heaps of shells, of earthen mounds and stone burial places. This is true also of the other continents, even of Asia and Africa, whose recorded history goes so far back into the past. It is also true of America. Here are to be found numerous remains, some of them centuries old, unmistakable evidence of man's residence here in ages long since past. These remains, or at least the most conspicuous of them, are great mounds of earth. They are to be found in most parts of the United States, though not in all places. Many of them are in Southeast Missouri.

Here the remains are mostly earthen mounds and their contents. Some of these mounds are large, many of them are small. They exist in great numbers. In fact we now know that there are a great many more of them than was suspected a few years ago. They have been here many years. They were here when the earliest explorers visited the country. DeSoto found a large hill, perhaps in the immediate neighborhood of New Madrid. At any rate it was within the alluvial region of the southeast where no natural hills are to be found. It was doubtless one of the ancient mounds. All the early explorers noted them. They were old at that distant date. Some of them give evidence of great age. Large trees are growing upon them which could not, in the nature of things, have developed short of centuries. They are to a close observer one of the most striking features of the topography of this section for they exist by thousands. Few people have any idea as to the vast numbers of mounds. There are single counties which have within their borders more than three thousand mounds. This is true of Bollinger county and of Scott county. Our knowledge of the vast numbers of mounds has been rendered exact in recent years by the work of Hon. Louis Houck. In the preparation of his "History of Missouri" he had the mounds of the state counted. Even this enumeration, carefully formed the basis of more widely divergent views. An entire theory of the early history of this country has been built up around them. They have been regarded, at times, as the evidence of the existence of a mighty and civilized race of people who existed here before the coming of the Indians; and who, for some unknown reason, perished completely from the land before the discovery by Columbus. A great empire with organized government, with a mighty capital, with swarming millions of population, has been pictured as

INDIAN MOUND

made as it was, does not give all the mounds. He found, however, within the bounds of Southeast Missouri, as defined in this book, more than eighteen thousand mounds, and it is doubtless safe to say that were all of them known we should find the number to exceed twenty thousand. Such vast figures are overwhelming when we consider what an enormous amount of work is represented by them.

These mounds have formed a fruitful subject of controversy. Few subjects connected with history have evoked more discussions or the condition of the people who built them. On the other hand other views have been advanced concerning them. An examination of some of the principal facts and theories concerning these prehistoric remains cannot fail to be of interest to all those who have a regard for the past.

In the first place, it is to be said, that these mounds are to be found in every county in this district. There seems to have been no part of Southeast Missouri where the people who constructed mounds did not live and work. It is true that they are more abundant in some parts of the section than in others. It is pointed out by Houck, that they are most abundant on a line extending southwest along the border of the lowlands from Cape Girardeau to Arkansas. Along this line they exist in great numbers. They are found also in large numbers in all the lowland region bordering the Mississippi. Another fact that concerns their distribution is that they were often constructed on the bank of creek or river.

Many of them are found, it is true, away from bodies of water, and yet so many of them are found in relation to water that we are justified in concluding that proximity to some body of water helped often to determine the location of the mounds.

Another fact of interest in connection with them is that they vary greatly in size. Some of them are very large. One which stands about two miles south of the present site of New Madrid is nearly circular in form, having a diameter of about two hundred feet and is probably thirty feet high. It is surrounded by many smaller mounds. The largest mound in the section, if not in the state, is in Pemiscot county. It is four hundred feet long, two hundred and fifty feet wide and thirty-five feet high. It has an approach from the south leading up to the top. It is higher at the north end than at the south by fifteen feet. There are many other large mounds in the same vicinity, some of them being more than two hundred feet in length. One of them is six hundred feet long and two hundred feet wide but only eight feet high. From these large mounds they vary in size to the very small ones only a few feet in length and in some cases only a few inches high.

The mounds vary in shape as well as in size. Some of them are rudely conical. This is perhaps the most common form. Others are somewhat elliptical in form having one axis much longer than the other. This is the case of the great mound in Pemiscot county. Others, still, are almost square at the base with tapering sides in the form of a pyramid. These mounds however are very much less numerous than the conical ones. It is rather remarkable that few if any of the countless mounds here show any resemblance to bird or beast. In other parts of the country, where mounds exist in such numbers as here, some are usually found bearing unmistakable resemblance to the form of some animal. This is true of the great serpent mound of Ohio. One mound in Pemiscot bears some resemblance to the handle of a gourd. A few others in this part of the state bear some real or fancied resemblance to some natural object. Most of them, however, have no such resemblance.

Another fact that is true of a very large number of these mounds is that they are earth mounds. In many parts of the country there are mounds which have rude structures of stones at their base. There are some of this character in Southeast Missouri, but the great number are built entirely of earth. It is plainly evident, in many cases, just where the earth which entered into the construction of the mound was secured, for the depression or excavation made in taking up the earth is still to be seen in the immediate neighborhood of the earthwork itself. No matter who built them, nor for what purpose, it is still true that they were built of earth taken in most if not all cases from near the site of the mound itself.

These mounds are often grouped in rather significant ways. They are as we have said often situated on the bank of a stream or pond. They are nearly always grouped together in numbers. Not many are solitary. Often one large mound is surrounded by many smaller ones. Sometimes a number of larger ones are found near together. It is the all but universal rule that they are not found singly. In some cases the group of mounds is surrounded by a wall. Mention is made elsewhere of a group in New Madrid county around which a wall of some height was constructed. Beckwith, in his history of the Indians of Missouri, mentions another similar group in Mississippi county which is also inclosed within a wall.

On Bayou St. John, about eighteen miles from New Madrid, is a group of interesting mounds. They lie on the west side of the bayou and are situated on the sloping ground that rises from the bayou to the prairie land above. It seems that in early times an area of about fifty acres was here inclosed by a wall. This wall may be traced in part yet, though much of it has disappeared. It is from three to five feet in height and about fifteen thick at the base. It is built of earth. Inside the inclosure made by this wall and near its western side is an oblong mound about three hundred feet long by one hundred in width and twenty feet high. Near this mound is a depression in the earth about ten feet in depth. Within the memory of men now living this depression had very steep sides so that a ladder was necessary to reach its bottom. In the center of the inclosure is another mound, circular in shape, seventy-five feet in diameter and twenty feet in height. Directly in line with these two is another circular mound, one hundred feet in diameter and twelve feet high. Surrounding this one are a number of smaller mounds, while still within the inclosure are a large number of shallow depressions about three feet in average depth.

In connection with these mounds there was to be seen at one time a curious formation of the banks of the bayou. Conant, from whom this description is taken, says that small tongues of the land had been carried out into the water, from fifteen to thirty feet in length and ten to fifteen in width, with open spaces between. These are quite similar, says Conant, to the wharves of a seaport town. It is Conant's theory that this bayou was once the channel of the Mississippi river, which no doubt it was, that with the recession of the waters of the river, a lake was formed and that upon the shores of this lake the builders of the mounds and the inclosing wall built these miniature walls for the convenience of handling their fishing boats.

Conant further describes an excavation lying about one mile from the mounds here described. This excavation is in the form of an oval, one hundred and fifty feet by seventy-five feet and six feet deep. It has an embankment around it. On the northern side this embankment is eight feet high while at the south it is only five. On the southern side there is a narrow opening in the wall and from this opening a curved dump or fill, such as are erected by railroads, leads to the swamp. At the end of this fill and within the swamp the dirt taken from the excavation was deposited, until a circular mound or wharf was raised about twenty feet in diameter and five feet high. The same opening and elevated way extends from the northern end of the excavation to the water. (Switzler's "History of Missouri.")

In addition to the mounds which we have described there are a large number of other striking ones to be seen in several of the counties. One of these is a group of mounds south of the present site of Ste. Genevieve. They are found within the "Big Field" and are very evidently of artificial origin. Immediately around them the ground is perfectly level being alluvial soil. The mounds vary in size, the largest being about thirty feet in height and probably one hundred and fifty feet by one hundred feet. There are a number of other smaller mounds some of these too being of considerable size. Most of these mounds have been partly explored and have yielded some material to the work of the explorers.

In Dunklin county, just south of the town of Cottonplant on the main county road, there is a large mound probably thirty feet in height and one hundred feet in diameter at the base. This mound has been dug into at various times and considerable quantities of Indian relics taken from it. It was evidently a burial ground for there have been found vessels containing bones in the mound. This mound is the site of the substantial dwelling of C. V. Langdon.

Still another group of mounds is on the main road between Bernie and Dexter not far from the line of the Cotton Belt Railway. Just as is true of all the others we have described, this group of mounds is found on perfectly level ground. There are four of them varying in size from a small heap of earth to the largest which is perhaps twenty-five feet in height. Different persons have dug in this group of mounds at various times and in 1900 some persons living in Malden opened the largest of these mounds and took from it a quantity of Indian relics. Among these relics are some specimens of Indian pottery that are unusually good. There were found water bottles, pots and urns of a very high class of workmanship. Some of these pieces are in the possession of the Malden High school.

It is evident that these mounds present to the student of history and archæology a most fascinating problem. Here are thousands of mounds of earth, scattered throughout every county of this section, varying in size from the tiny one of a few feet in diameter and a few inches in height, to the giant earthwork hundreds of feet in dimensions large enough to be mistaken for natural hills, and yet bearing unmistakable evidence of artificial origin. These structures are grouped in some order, follow the water-courses, are inclosed sometimes by walls of earth, are of such age in many cases as to bear upon their summits or sides great trees hundreds of years old. Who built these mounds? For what purpose were they built? These questions presented themselves at once to those who first recognized their artificial character.

An answer to these questions was sought in the mounds themselves. Many of them were excavated. They returned to the researches of those who dug in them very different rewards. Some of them contained absolutely nothing at all. In many of them nothing was found except the evidences of fire. Burned pieces of wood and ashes constituted the entire contents of many of the mounds. But some of the mounds contained other and very interesting remains. Pottery of every character and size, bones of persons and of beasts, implements and tools, and weapons of war, all these have been found in mounds. Most numerous of all are the mounds which contain bones and pottery. In some cases the bones are found in the earth itself, in others they are in vessels of pottery. Many people have engaged in the exploration of these mounds and many mounds have been opened. There are still others in this section which have not been touched as yet. These are for the most part owned by persons who do not wish them disturbed. It is quite probable that there exist large numbers of mounds, some of them not yet known, which contain many interesting remains such as those mentioned.

So many bones are found in some of the mounds that they are classified as burial mounds. In some of them there are evidences of two or more distinct burials, leading us to believe that after the first bodies were placed in the mound and covered, other bodies were then placed above and the mound carried on to its completed form. The condition of the bones leads to the belief that most of the bodies were denuded of flesh before being placed in the mounds, and that frequently only a part of the bones were buried at all. Often only the skull and some of the large bones of the legs are found. In some cases a large number of bones are found together, comprising parts of a number of skeletons. The probability is that in such cases a large number of bones were gathered together and then put into the mound without separation. The tools and implements sometimes found in the mounds are often associated with bones, showing them to have been buried together, and suggesting some connection between their presence and the rites of burial. The pottery found in these mounds is of various shapes and sizes. A few large urns containing bones have been found, other and smaller vessels seem to have been made to hold food or water.

As has been said, these mounds and their contents have given rise to a great deal of discussion and many theories have been advanced to explain their origin. Archaeologists believed for a long time that they were the work of a vanished race whom they called the "Mound Builders." These people were regarded as having lived in this country prior to the coming of the Indians and to have been a much superior race. The grouping of the mounds has suggested to some the arrangement of cities and villages about a center which was a great capital. It was insisted that the Indians could not have built the mounds for a number of reasons. One reason was that their arrangement indicated an organization, a nation with a capital. This organized national life the Indians did not have; consequently they did not build the mounds. Another reason was that the Indians could not have built mounds of such great size as some of the works. Still another advanced was that the age of the mounds precludes the idea that they were the work of the Indians.

The balance of opinion inclines however, at this time, to the idea that the mounds are the work of Indians. It is difficult to accept the hypothesis of the Mound Builders, with their high state of civilization, their organized government and their great capital. There is not sufficient evidence of such a state of civilization. The excavation of the mounds did not disclose any evidence at all of a high state of civilization supposed by those who believe the Mound Builders to have existed. There has been little or nothing found in the mounds which was not entirely familiar to the Indian of this country. No such finds were made in these mounds as in the somewhat similar appearing mounds of the Tigris-Euphrates valley. There the spade of the archaeologist turned up all the external evidences of a great civilization. Mighty palaces and temples; the walls and streets of great cities, libraries, inscriptions; the record of long years of existence and civilization, were all uncovered. bearing silent but unmistakable evidence to the existence of mighty and wealthy nations. Contrast this with the meager contents, the implements of stone, the vessels of pottery, and the masses of bones found in the mounds of this country, and we see at once how strong is the negative argument against the existence of a great civilized race of people antedating the Indians. It is true that in Central America some ruins are found approaching the constructions unearthed in the East, but such is not the case in North America. We may wonder at the industry that reared the mounds of such great size, we find some things difficult to explain in any way about them, but we cannot believe them to have been the work of civilized people.

On the other hand there are reasons for believing that they are the work of the Indians. One of these is the fact of their arrangement. The Indian, for many reasons, selected most frequently as a site for his habitation or village, the bank of a stream or lake. This is the situation of many of the mounds. Another evidence of the Indian origin of the mounds is the fact that the utensils and implements found in some of them are similar to those used by the Indians. Yet another is the fact that the Indians of this country were accustomed to practice mound burial. They placed the dead body on a scaffold or in a tree until it was denuded of flesh, then gathered up the bones and placed them in a mound. That is evidently what the builders of the mounds did. The age of some of the mounds also indicates their Indian origin. Many of the mounds, it is true, are very old. On the other hand many of them bear unmistakable evidence of having been built in recent times. The mound described by Conant near Bayou St. John in New Madrid county, cannot be very old for within very recent times the pit, from which the earth was taken for the mound, had very steep sides; so steep, in fact, that a ladder was needed to descend into it. This would not have been the case if the mound had not been of recent origin. The natural action of the elements would have partly filled it up and reduced the steepness of its sides. In fact this has happened within the memory of those living when Conant wrote.

These facts, while not conclusive, point to the Indians as the builders of the mounds. There are other facts pointing in the same direction. Many of the mounds contain traces of what seems to be the mud plastering from a wall constructed of canes or sticks. Such walls were built by the Indians of the Mississippi valley having been copied, doubtless, from the Indians of the southwest.

It has been objected to this theory that some of the mounds are too old. It is pointed out that many of them must have been in existence for centuries before the coming of the white men, for at the time when DeSoto was here these mounds had trees growing on them. This objection assumes the Indians to have lived here but a short time. That is not known to be true. On the contrary we have strong reason for believing that they must have lived in North America for many hundreds of years. If they have not been here for a long time, it is difficult or even impossible to explain how they became scattered over the great continent. They were found to be living in practically every part of this country. No matter how they first reached the continent it required a long period of years for them to people such a vast expanse of territory.

It is objected too that the Indians had no reason for building the mounds. We may not understand just why they were built by Indians, but neither do we know why they were built by Mound Builders or anyone else. It is just as difficult to explain the motive of their construction, if we assume them to have been reared by the Mound Builders, as it is if we ascribe them to the Indians. To imagine another race of people does not lessen the difficulty of explaining the reason for their construction.

It is not, however, impossible to give a reasonable explanation of the existence of these mounds on the theory that they were the work of the Indians. When the ancient Assyrians began to rear buildings, they put them on mounds of earth and constructed them of sun-dried brick, and this, in spite of the fact that their country contained many hills suitable for building purposes and plenty of wood and stone which might have been utilized for building. The explanation of these remarkable facts is found when we remember that they were imitating the work of an older civilized people, the Babylonians. These Babylonians had neither hills as sites, nor wood or stone as building materials. They found substitutes for them. The Assyrians, who began later, simply copied what they had seen others do. It is highly probable that the Indians who build mounds were simply imitating a form of village arrangement with which they had become familiar elsewhere. Perhaps in the southwest, where the Pueblo Indians placed their dwellings on the top of cliffs and utilized the tall rocks for lookout stations, there was formed the notion that the suitable place for a dwelling was on an elevation. The Indians who went out from there carried this idea into places where no natural elevation was to be found. In lieu of this they reared artificial mounds. In time it came to be accepted that a mound of earth was the proper place for the location of the house or temple. This idea, in turn, was carried from the alluvial plains where it was formed into the hills where again mounds were reared.

In considering this, which is advanced simply as a theory which may explain the building of mounds, it should be remembered that mounds are not found in all parts of the country. A careful investigation may disclose the fact that they are found in those parts of the country where the inhabitants had some connections with the south and southwest.

What seems the best and most reasonable explanation of the existence of the mounds is this. The Indians selected as a site for their village the vicinity of some stream or lake. They then erected mounds. One was for the house of the chief; another, sometimes pyramidal in shape for the temple; another was for the burial of the dead; still another formed a station for the priests and orators of the tribe, and one was for the purpose of a lookout from which to observe the approach of enemies. The size of the mounds depended in part upon the number of Indians in the village and in part upon their inclination and industry. In the course of years the dwellings and temples, of frail construction as they were, disappeared, leaving only a heap of earth to puzzle those who found them.

The contents of these mounds, as we have said, are interesting as being the record of the degree of civilization of the people who built them. Many of the mounds have yielded interesting and curious returns to the spade of the investigator. Hundreds of mounds have been explored more or less completely. The relics taken from them have been carried to museums and the collections of private individuals in many parts of the country. There are a great many of these relics owned in Southeast Missouri. Most of them are scattered, but there are several good collections.

Perhaps the largest collection of Indian relics in Southeast Missouri, if not in the entire state, is that owned by Thomas Beckwith, of Charleston. This collection has been gathered by Mr. Beckwith through a period of more than thirty years, and now comprises about ten thousand different pieces; some of them of the every finest workmanship and of the greatest value. Practically all of these were found in Mississippi county and by far the larger number on Mr. Beckwith's own farm. This collection is described and pictured in his book, "Indians of North America." There are a number of other collections, most of them smaller, owned by residents of this section. Louis Houck in his book, "History of Missouri," described some unique pieces which he has seen, one of which, a pipe bearing a carved head, has disappeared. Another of these was a statuette, the figure of a woman carved in sandstone, about eight inches in height and bearing considerable resemblance to the Venus de Melos. Unfortunately this remarkable piece of sculpture has been lost. Another of these unique pieces is a figure in the collection of Mr. Beckwith. It represents some animal and is also carved from sandstone and evidences considerable skill on the part of the artist.

There are other collections not so large as this, but containing many things of interest. Some collections which formerly existed have been broken up and the pieces dispersed. It seems unfortunate that at some central point in this part of the state, there might not be gathered a great and complete collection of Indian relics of this section to be permanently retained as a memorial for all time of the presence of the aborigines.

Besides these collections having a general interest, there have been found occasionally certain pieces which have been deemed of great importance owing to the fact that they were different from the usual character of Indian relics. In —— there was found on a farm just south of Malden a very remarkable series of Indian plates. Ray Groomes while plowing on the farm of Mrs. Baldwin, turned up a piece of metal which attracted his attention by being caught on the point of his plow. On examination he found that there had been thrown out of the furrow some metal plates. He searched about and picked up eight of these plates which had been buried to a depth of about sixteen inches. There was nothing to mark the spot and he is confident that there was nothing else buried in connection with the plates. He dug about hoping to find some other relics, but the only thing that he discovered was a kind of white powder in the place where the plates had been lying. This powder he did not preserve as he could make nothing of it at all. The plates were taken by him to the town of Malden and offered for sale. They were finally bought by A. S. Davis and kept by him for a time, and then disposed of to J. M. Wulfing, of St. Louis, who now owns them. These plates are the most remarkable of the Indian relics found in Southeast Missouri. They are of thin copper and represent what seemed to be eagles having faces of men. One of them seems to be a double eagle. They at once suggest, from their appearance and workmanship, the work of the Indians of Mexico. There is nothing else like them to be found in the Mississippi valley. How or why they were put into the place where they were discovered are questions which cannot now be answered. No one who has examined them has been able to solve the mystery of their presence in this part of America.

There existed in Southeast Missouri two or three other unusually good collections of Indian relics. Dr. G. W. Travis, of Cape Girardeau, at one time owned one of these large collections. On his removal from Cape Girardeau the collection was broken up and sold, part of it coming into the possession of the State Normal School. Another large collection was owned by Dr. L. P. Ruff. This collection has been removed from this part of the state.

CHAPTER II

ADVENTURES OF DE SOTO

Is Made Governor of Florida—Lands in Florida—Discovers the Mississippi — Place of Crossing—Direction of March—The Casquins—Religious Service—Attack on Capahas—Search for Salt—Probable Situation of Capaha Camp—Return to the South—Quigate—Location of Caligoa—Further Travels and Death—Interest Concerning Exact Route.

It seems probable that De Soto was the first white man to set foot on the soil of Missouri. Certain difficulties are in the way of an exact determination of the question of his visit to this state. One of these is the somewhat romantic style of the Spanish chroniclers who wrote the earliest accounts of his journey; another is the difficulty of telling, from their accounts, just what places are referred to. It is no easy matter to identify with certainty, from the description given of places visited, where these places are. Yet, while we may not be sure, it seems highly probable that the travels of De Soto and his companions brought them into the Southeast Missouri.

Ferdinand De Soto was one of the most daring and able of the Spanish soldiers of fortune who explored the continent of America. He was with Avila on the isthmus of Darien, with Cordoba in Nicaragua; explored, independently, the coasts of Guatemala and Yucatan, seeking doubtless for a waterway to the west. In 1532, he accompanied Pizarro to Peru and was one of the boldest members of the remarkable band of men that overturned the empire of the Incas. From these expeditions De Soto returned to Spain with a large fortune, apparently willing to settle down to a life of ease. In 1537, however, he was appointed by Charles V, governor of Florida and Cuba and in May, 1539, he landed at Tampa bay, Florida, with an expedition for the exploration of that country. He had with him a well-equipped army of six hundred men, the largest and most complete expedition that Spain had sent to the New World. His purpose was to explore and conquer the country. Especially was he desirous of finding the great and populous cities which the imagination of the Spaniards, stimulated by their experiences in Mexico and Peru, pictured as existing in the great and unknown continent to the north. Strange stories were told by the Indians of these cities and returning wanderers of the Spanish had heard of Quivira, a great and rich city where there was gold enough to satisfy even the Spaniards.

De Soto plunged into the wilderness with his little army and for nearly three years pursued his journey through the unexplored wilderness of North America. For a time he was in the Carolinas; then he explored the

Alabama river; then he came to the great river, the Mississippi, and crossed it. From this time on his wanderings have an interest for the student of Missouri history, for, from a careful study of the narrative of his further wanderings, we are led to the conclusion that he penetrated the territory of the present state of Missouri. It is not possible to determine with absolute accuracy the precise point where he crossed the Mississippi. Some students of journey, among them Bancroft, Nuttall and Schoolcraft, think he must have crossed at the Chickasaw Bluffs, near the present site of Memphis. Others, however, including Elliot, Winsor and Martin, consider it more probable that he crossed lower down. Houck, reasoning from the fact stated by Garcillasso that heavy timber existed where they crossed the river, concludes that the crossing must have been at a place of alluvial soil and consequently not at Chickasaw Bluffs, which were not then timbered. He thinks the crossing was at some point between the mouth of the St. Francois and the mouth of the Arkansas, and in view of all the facts this seems the most reasonable supposition.

Having crossed the river the expedition wandered for four days through a flat country intersected with swamps. On the fifth day from their crossing they reached a high ridge from whose summit they saw a river. Upon its banks was an Indian town surrounded by fields of maize. To this place the march of the party had been to the north. Garcillasso says they kept "northward" or "marched directly to the north." This probably means that after crossing the Mississippi they did not strike into the forest away from it, but continued their journey in a general direction parallel to the course of the river itself. It was quite natural for them to do this, because we know that the trails or traces of the Indians were accustomed to follow the general course of the river. If, then, De Soto after the crossing, continued to the north near or along the bank of the Mississippi, we may inquire as to the location of the ridge which the expedition climbed and from which was seen another river with a village encircled with fields of maize.

It seems highly probable that this ridge was what is now called Crowley's ridge, one of the offshoots of the Ozark range which continues into Arkansas, forming a divide between the alluvial bottom of the St. Francois and that of the White and the Cache. This ridge terminates at the Mississippi river not far from Helena, Arkansas, and along its eastern border flows the St. Francois. Crowley's ridge is the only ridge on the west side of the river between the Ohio and the Arkansas. If the expedition then proceeded north from their point of crossing, and that point was south of the mouth of the Arkansas as we believe it to have been, then it was to this ridge they came. From its summit the course of the St. Francois could be seen, and in the alluvial soil at its base would likely be found the fields of maize mentioned by the chroniclers of the expedition.

De Soto and his men spent some time in the village which they had seen form the summit of the ridge resting and recovering from the effects of their long march through the wilderness. These Indians are called Casquins by the members of the expedition. They were probably a part of the tribe of the Kaskaskias. They later made their home on the Illinois where they were found by Joliet and Marquette. It was not an unusual thing for the Indian tribes to change their place of residence, however. In fact, this was a habit that marked them, so that we may believe that the Indians found by De Soto dwelling on the St. Francois, later moved to the country of the Illinois. These Indians received De Soto and his men with great hospitality showing the utmost friendliness and desire to please. They opened their houses, such as they were, for the use of De Soto's men, and provided provisions for men and beasts.

The Indians of this village told De Soto that their great chief, or cacique, resided some distance to the north. Indeed two messengers from this chief came to the village during the stay of the expedition and invited De Soto to visit the cacique. This he determined to do. He marched north along the banks of the Mississippi river, finding higher ground than formerly and the richest alluvial soil they had yet seen. This soil was a sandy loam, black in color and very rich. It was covered with forests of timber in places, diversified with prairies and broken in places by swamps. The pecan tree, the wild plum and the mulberry were everywhere abundant, while the fields abounded in maize. After two days of marching they came to the chief town of the country where the cacique of the Casquins resided. It seems evident that this ridge up which they marched was the sandy ridge that runs parallel to the river from near the mouth of the St. Francois to the hills of the Ozark region near Cape Girardeau. It has the same soil as that described by De Soto's men, the trees are the same, and it runs in the direction of the course taken by them. On this ridge are situated many flourishing towns in southeast Missouri, to-day. Among them are Caruthersville, New Madrid and Charleston. Then, of course, it was a wilderness broken by the small clearings of the Indians and traversed by the celebrated trace that led to the great crossing of the river near Commerce.

The expedition was received by the Indians with great kindness. The chief invited De Soto to lodge in his house. This dwelling stood on a high artificial mound and consisted of a number of houses for the accommodation of his numerous wives and their children. This invitation was declined by De Soto and he and most of his men were lodged by the natives in arbors or booths of brush. Presents were exchanged and the utmost good feeling prevailed.

On the fourth day of their stay occurred an incident which attested the impression made by the expedition upon the savages. On the morning of that day there appeared before De Soto the cacique, accompanied by his principal followers, who addressed the leader of the Spaniards in these words: "Senor, as you are superior to us in prowess and surpass us in arms, we likewise believe that your God is better than our god. We supplicate you to pray to your God that our fields, which are now parched may receive rain and our crops be saved."

In response to this request, De Soto caused a large pine tree to be procured, and from it the carpenter of the expedition constructed a large cross. This cross was erected, and, there in the midst of the forest, a solemn procession was formed which marched to the cross, and while the wondering Indians looked on in astonishment the services of the church were performed and a supplication sent up to God for the needed rain. The Indians seemed profoundly impressed by the solemnity of the occasion. Many of them knelt upon the ground, some were moved to tears by the service, and others still inquired for an explanation of the mysteries which they beheld for the first time. The solemn service was closed with the singing of a Te Deum and the forest aisles echoed for the first time with the sound of men's voices lifted up in the service of song to God. In the middle of the night the long drought was broken and a copious rain fell upon the earth.

Such was the first religious service of the Christian church held in Missouri. Speaking of it Irving says:* "More than three centuries ago the cross, the type of our beautiful religion, was planted on the banks of the Mississippi, and its silent forests wakened by the Christian's hymn of gratitude and praise. The effect was vivid but transitory. The voice cried in the wilderness and reached and was answered by every heart, but it died away and was forgotten; and was not to be heard in that savage region again for many generations. It was as if a lightning's gleam had broken for a moment upon a benighted world, startling it with sudden effulgence, only to leave it in ten-fold more gloom. The real dawning was yet afar off from the benighted valley of the Mississippi."

That the place of this first service was within the limits of Missouri we may not doubt. It is impossible to fix the precise spot. The high hill, doubtless an artificial mound, has probably disappeared. The pine tree, which was made into a cross, was probably a cypress which resembles the pine in some respects, and might have been found anywhere in a vast extent of territory. From these things, then, it is impossible to determine the place of this Indian village, but, judging from the direction of their travel, from the distance probably covered in the two days of their march, they were within the limits of Missouri, perhaps according to the opinion of

* "Conquest of Florida," p. 114.

Nuttall near the present site of New Madrid. At an early day a mound stood near the town. This mound has been swept away by the river, but it may well have been the scene of this service.

On the next morning after the service and the rain, De Soto made ready to continue his journey to the north. He was still led onward by the hopes which had brought him into the wilderness. Great cities were yet to be found, gold was to be discovered. These things lay in the distance before him, as he fondly thought. From time to time, during their journey, they had found in the possession of the Indians various trinkets and other things made of gold; and these served to confirm them in their belief that somewhere in the mighty and unconquered wilderness there was much of the yellow metal waiting for the fortunate men who might be led to find it. And so to seek gold and adventure, after the days of rest and pleasure with their new friends of the Casquin Indians, they made ready to depart.

The cacique, however, a wily savage of about fifty years of age, had no idea of allowing his good and great friends to depart without conferring on him other tokens of their friendship and power. He had been greatly impressed with the evident power of the Spaniards and meditated on turning it to his own account.

For many years enmity had existed between the Casquins or Kaskaskias and the Capahas, a tribe living further to the north. Lately the fortunes of war had inclined to the side of the Capahas, and the cacique of the Casquins and his people had been compelled to accept the yoke of their enemies and to pay tribute and render service to them. In the undoubted prowess and power of his new-found friends, the Spaniards, the cacique saw a means by which he and his people might be liberated from the power of the Capahas. Accordingly when De Soto was ready to depart toward the north the cacique begged leave to accompany him with two bodies of his people. "For," he said, "the way is long and arduous. Roads are to be cut, the swamps are to be crossed, and the baggage of the army to be carried through the rough woods of the way." Accordingly, De Soto was accompanied by three thousand Indians, who carried the luggage of the expedition, and by a body of five thousand warriors, gay with plumes and war-paint and armed with all the weapons of savage warfare. Of course we are to understand that these numbers have been greatly exaggerated in the telling by the chroniclers of the expedition. No such numbers of savages could have been gathered together in that region. Still we are to suppose that many accompanied the expedition, perhaps the whole force which the cacique could muster, for he meant, now to avenge himself on his hated enemies, the Capahas.

On taking up the march, the cacique took the lead with his men, dividing them into squadrons and marching in what the Spanish called good military array. The reason given for the arrangement of men was that the Indians were to clear the roads and prepare the camps in advance of the expedition. On the third day of the march they came to a miry swamp which contained within its center a lake or gulf which was probably a part of the old channel of the Mississippi. This swamp discharged itself into the river and was about half a bowshot across and was deep and sluggish. Over this the Indians constructed a bridge of logs, over which the men passed while the horses of the expedition swam. This lake with a miry swamp about its edge was quite probably one of the sluggish streams which break the sandy ridge up which De Soto was pursuing his march. This ridge extends through the counties of New Madrid, Mississippi, and Scott. It is broken at a number of places by streams which carry part of the drainage from the basin of Little river to the Mississippi. It is impossible to know which one of these is meant from the early accounts, but it is evident that one of them is referred to, if we accept the general course of his march as here outlined. That march must have carried him from near the site of New Madrid across lakes, bayous, swamps, along the sandy ridge through the edge of Mississippi county, east of the hills in Scott county, to the swamp lying southwest of Cape Girardeau.

Having crossed on the improvised bridge of of logs, De Soto and his men found themselves on what is described as meadows. Here they encamped, charmed by the beauty of the landscape, the luxuriance of the foliage and the abundance of the flowers. From this place he continued his journey north for two days. On the third day he came to some elevated ridges from which he saw the fortified camp of the chief of the Capahas. This town was itself on a high hill or mound. "It was nearly encircled by a deep moat fifty paces in breadth; and where the moat did not extend, was defended by a strong wall of plaster and timber such as has already been described. The moat was filled with water by a canal cut from the Mississippi river, which was three leagues distant. The canal was deep and sufficiently wide for two canoes to pass abreast without touching one another's paddles. The canal and moat were filled with fish, so as to supply all the wants of the army and village, without any apparent diminution of the number."[*]

It is evident that, in thus describing the situation and character of the Indian camp, the Spaniards were transferring to America, as they often did, the scenes and customs of Europe. The moat and canal to supply it were doubtless nothing more than natural channels, perhaps a bayou or former channel of the river. The Indians of America seem never to have constructed castles defended by moats, and while the situation of the Capaha village may have resembled the artificial moats with which the Spaniards were familiar, they were not constructed by the hand of man. It would be interesting to know the exact site of this camp of Capaha Indians for these were among the most interesting of all the Indians encountered by De Soto and his party; but it is not possible to determine from the description given what the site of the camp was. If we have been correct in our conjectures as to the general route followed thus far in the wanderings, then the camp thus reached must have been not far from the neighborhood of Cape Girardeau. Of course many places in the foothills of the Ozarks might fit in a general way the description here given, but two circumstances in addition to the course pursued in reaching this place lead us to believe that it was in the vicinity mentioned. One of these is a journey, hereafter described, of a part of the expedition to a stream, which from the presence of salt we suspect to have been Saline creek in Ste. Genevieve county. The other is the fact that one of the varieties of fish described as having been present in the moat and canal was the spadefish or Platyrostra edentula, sometimes known as the shovel-bill cat. The latter fish is characteristic of the

[*] Irving, "Conquest of Florida," p. 117.

regions we have mentioned and its presence lends weight to the theory that the place of the Capahas was at least within the limits of Southeast Missouri. This town of the Capahas contained, according to the account of the Spaniards, about five hundred houses, and was situated nearly three leagues from the Mississippi river.

The chief of the Capahas had received notice through his scouts of the coming of the Casquins with their new allies, and on their near approach to the town, being unable, because of the absence of his warriors, to defend it, he escaped in a canoe, making his way down the canal to the river and taking refuge on an island in the vicinity. All who could, followed him to this retreat, others fled into the woods, while many remained in the village and waited with alarm the approach of the Casquins. The cacique of the Casquins, marching with his men in advance of the expedition, entered the Capaha village and proceeded to take vengeance for former defeats. All the men who were found were immediately killed and scalped, the women and children were taken as prisoners, among them being two wives of the cacique who had failed to flee with him, owing to the confusion and alarm into which the village was thrown by the approach of their enemies. These women are described by the Spaniards as being young and beautiful—a description which we may be pardoned for doubting, for it was their invariable custom to find beautiful women among the Indians, just as they found among them almost all the manners and customs with which they were acquainted at home. The houses of the Capahas were plundered, and even the dead were not safe from insult and disturbance. Within the public square there was situated a mausoleum or burial place in which had been deposited the remains of the ancestors of the chief, the great men of the tribe and the trophies won by them in war. The Casquins broke open this sacred place, stripped arms and trophies from the walls, heaped insult and abuse on the dead bodies contained within it, trampled upon the bones and scattered them upon the ground. They replaced the heads of slain enemies, some of them Casquins, with these of freshly slain Capahas. There was no insult or indignity which the minds of savages could devise which was not put upon all that the Capahas held sacred.

Now these outrages were committed, we are told, before the arrival of De Soto and his men. They were in the rear and came to the village only in time to save it from utter destruction as the maddened Casquins were proceeding to fire the houses. De Soto resented these actions, for he was impressed with the evidences of the power of the Capahas and learning of the presence of the chief on the island to which he had fled, he sent envoys there to disavow the actions of his savage allies, and to beg for a friendly alliance with him. These envoys were not received by the Capaha chief, and De Soto learned that he was making every effort to gather warriors that he might take vengeance for the outrages inflicted upon his village. Accordingly De Soto prepared to attack the Capahas on their island. He caused to be gathered all the available canoes and, filling these with his own men and the warriors of the Casquins, he made an attack on the island. He found that the Capahas had fortified themselves strongly, and it was only with great difficulty that he was able to effect a landing at all. The Casquins were unwilling to fight and, after a brief engagement, retreated to their canoes leaving the brunt of the battle to fall upon the Spaniards. It was only after a desperate struggle that De Soto and his men were able to retreat from the island and make their way back to the village. In fact, it seems they would not have been able to embark in their canoes at all had not the Capaha chief ordered his men not to press their attack upon the Spaniards and allowed them to depart.

De Soto was very much displeased because of the cowardly desertion of the Casquins and when on the following day envoys arrived from the Capahas, asking for peace and signifying the desire of their cacique to visit him, he determined to accept the offered friendship and agree to an amnesty despite the objections of the Casquins.

The cacique of the Casquins feeling the displeasure of De Soto and fearing to lose the help of such powerful allies as the Spaniards had proved themselves to be, attempted to appease the Adelantado (as De Soto is called by the chroniclers) by gifts of skins and even of his daughter as handmaid. In spite of these evidences of friendship, De Soto was distrustful of the cacique and contrasted his conduct most unfavorably with that of the Capaha, and he caused the cacique to send most of his warriors home.

On the day appointed the Capaha chief, accompanied by a hundred of his warriors, dressed in handsome skins and beautiful plumes came to pay his court to De Soto. He proved to be a young man of noble and splendid bearing with handsome face and physique. He was vastly moved by the indignities which had been offered to his dead, and his first care was to gather the scattered bones, and return them reverently to their resting place. He then sought De Soto who came forth to meet him accompanied by the Casquin.

He brought presents for the Adelantado,

and offered himself as a vassal, but refused to have anything to do with Casquin, except to threaten him with a day of retribution, until upon the interposition of De Soto he finally agreed to settle his quarrel with him.

In this village the expedition remained for several days as the situation was pleasant, the Indians friendly, and the supplies of food and of skins for clothing were very grateful to the members of the expedition who were worn and ragged from their long wanderings. It was De Soto's wish to find out about the country he had not visited. To this end he made many inquiries of the Indians concerning the country to the north and its inhabitants. He was told that much of the country was barren, but hearing that salt was to be obtained in that direction, he sent de Silvera and Morena in search of it. The Spaniards had suffered much on the expedition from lack of salt. Many of those who had died on the way declared that they thought they would recover if only they could have meat with plenty of salt on it. At the end of eleven days, the men who had been detached returned, almost starved, having passed through a thinly settled and sterile country where they found little to eat except roots and wild plums. They brought with them, however, supplies of salt and some copper. It is quite probable that these men had reached Saline creek for the Indians of later, and doubtless of that time also, were accustomed to secure salt from the banks of that stream.

From this place the expedition returned to the village of the Casquins where they remained for four or five days, and then De Soto determined to travel to the westward. He was led to this decision by the reports of a country called Quigate. On leaving the village of the Casquins he travelled one day's march and then rested at another village of the Casquins near a river, which in all probability was Little river. Crossing this river, he found himself upon another ridge, that which extends through Dunklin county, and after travelling for about four days he reached Quigate. His march carried him through a fruitful country where large fields of maize were to be seen and all the evidences of a large Indian population. Quigate, the largest town visited by the Spaniards since leaving Florida, was perhaps at the lower end of the ridge over which they had been traveling, near the line which separates Dunklin county from Arkansas. From here De Soto turned to the northwest to reach a town called Caligoa, where he expected, from what he had been told, he would find stores of gold and other precious metals. One difference is noted by the chroniclers in the march that was made to Caligoa and that is that no paths were found, but that the expedition made its way through the unbroken wilderness. We may infer from this, what we should conclude otherwise, that the former marchings had followed the trails or traces made by the Indians. The country from Quiquate to Caligoa is described as marshy and swampy with morasses and lagoons, and then as hilly and mountainous. Garcillasso says they marched forty leagues before reaching Caligoa. They found this town to be on a small river. Here they remained for some days. They were told that to north a distance of six days' journey the country was level, devoid of trees, and covered with buffalo. We may only speculate as to the location of Caligoa. If we are correct in conjecturing Quiguate to have been on lower end of the ridge running through Dunklin county, and the march of De Soto was toward the north and west, he probably followed the ridge to the low hills in the neighborhood of Campbell, crossed these into the lowlands of Stoddard and Butler county, then reached the foothills of the Ozarks and followed them to near the headwaters of the St. Francois or the Black, in the granite hills of St. Francois county. This is the conclusion of most of the men who have made a study of the probable course of De Soto's wanderings, among them Nuttall, Schoolcraft, and Houck. Some others, however, conclude that he was farther west, perhaps in Southwest Missouri.

From Caligoa the expedition turned to the south and west seeking now for the Cayas or Kansas Indians, and with this part of his journey he is carried from out the territory of Southeast Missouri. With his subsequent wanderings, the sufferings and hardships he encountered, and his tragic fate we are not directly concerned. Suffice it to say that after long wanderings he reached the Mississippi near the mouth of the Red river, sick, broken in mind and body. Here, to his consternation, he was told that the lower reaches of the river instead of being populated with towns and settlements where he could find for his men food and shelter, were practically uninhabited and impassable, that he might hope for little help or guidance there and less of food and other supplies. And, so, at last, after three years of wanderings, after untold hardships, after having surmounted countless obstacles, and traversed enormous reaches of the great continent where the foot of white men had never before trod, after having inflicted untold suffering and cruelty on the helpless Indians, his dreams of wealth and conquest all dissipated, having conquered no great cities and found no El Dorado, the spirit of the great Conquistador, the companion of Avila and Cortez was at last broken. In the midst of the savage forest, surrounded by hostile Indians, far from his home, disappointed, and despairing, he lay down to die. At night, by the dim light of torches, clad in full armor, his broken and wasted body was lowered into the great river which he discovered, and the long wanderings, the brilliant hopes, the troubled, cruel life of De Soto were at an end.

It will always be a matter of regret to those who are interested in the history of their country, that the exact route of De Soto cannot be traced with certainty. Surely we should be glad if we might but know what his exact course through Southeast Missouri was. It would be interesting to retrace the route over which he wandered, to compare the places now, with the description given of them by the Spaniards who followed him. But such certainty is no longer possible. Time has swept away the last traces of his expedition. The very surface of the earth has changed in the nearly four hundred years that have elapsed. The great river has changed its course from side to side of the wide alluvial bottom since then, sweeping away the very ground, a mighty earthquake has changed some of the topography of the country through which he passed, mighty forests have sprung up, all the forces of nature have combined through the years to change the character of the surface of the earth. And so it is that we may never be sure of the way over which he passed. Time was when it might have been ascertained. Doubtless when the first Missouri settlements were formed at Ste. Genevieve, New Madrid, St. Louis, Cape Girardeau, traces of that first historic march through Missouri might have been found. But our fathers were too much occupied with the struggle for existence to give their time to hunting for traces of long vanished men.

CHAPTER III

FRENCH EXPLORERS

WHY SPAINARDS DID NOT TAKE AND HOLD THE COUNTRY—VAGUE IDEAS OF THE WEST—NEWS OF THE MISSISSIPPI—RADISSON AND GROSEILLIERS—JOLIET AND MARQUETTE—DISCOVERY OF THE MISSISSIPPI—EXTENT OF THEIR VOYAGE—THE RETURN—ILLNESS OF MARQUETTE — WHY JOLIET WAS NOT GIVEN CREDIT FOR EXPEDITION — EARLY VOYAGE OF LA SALLE — FRENCH IDEAS OF THE NEW WORLD—VIEWS OF THE ENGLISH — LA SALLE'S PURPOSE — FRIENDSHIP WITH FRONTENAC—VISIT TO FRANCE—START OF THE EXPEDITION — LOSS OF THE GRIFFON—CREVE COEUR—HE REACHES THE MISSISSIPPI—PASSES TO ITS MOUTH—THE COLONY AT STARVED ROCK—GOES TO FRANCE—COLONY ON THE GULF—DEATH OF LASALLE —ESTIMATE OF HIS CHARACTER.

It was in 1540 that De Soto and his band were in Southeast Missouri. They came as we have seen from the south, having landed in Florida and penetrated the country in a vain search for gold. The next white men who came to Missouri were French explorers from the great lakes. These came from the north and entered the country to find the great river whose existence was made known to them by the Indians, to search out places for trade, and to secure the country for France. Some of them were priests who were moved by the desire to carry the Gospel to the savages—by whatever motives moved they came, pushing their adventurous way into the wilderness and blazing the trail over which civilization and settlement were destined to enter the bounds of the state. It is somewhat surprising that the Spanish did not take possession of the valley of the Mississippi since De Soto had discovered the river and explored a part of its valley, and since the Spanish claimed the Gulf of Mexico as a sea belonging to them. They did little or nothing to make good their claims, however, as it was the great misfortune of the Spanish to be occupied in this country, at the first, with a search for gold and for cities to conquer, rather than with attempts to settle the country and to develop those resources which were destined to produce wealth far greater than the mines and cities of which they dreamed.

It was thus left to France to begin the settlement and development of the valley of the great river. One characteristic of all grants made in this country was their indefinite extension toward the west. Little idea was had as to the extent of the continent in that direction, and, accordingly, kings and trading companies calmly made grants whose western limits were undefined and undetermined, and whose extent, if carried to the western sea, was vast beyond the very conception of those making them. Thus the French in Canada, having little idea of the extent of the country to the west of them, came to regard it as only an extension of Canada. When reports came to them of the great river that very probably emptied into the western sea or the Sea of Japan, they were moved to accept it as part of New France and laid claim to it accordingly.

No more adventurous or hardy men were concerned with the early settlement and exploration of the new world than these same French in Canada. Better than any one else they understood and sympathized with the Indian; for better than any one else they entered into and shared his life. The mighty forests, the unexplored regions, the wild life had no terrors but rather attractions for them. Thus it was that the hardy woodsmen, traders, trappers, and canoe men of Canada explored and hunted throughout a wide expanse of territory. They set their traps and hunted in all the woods, they pushed the prows of the adventurous canoes into all the waters about them, they found the secret trails of the Indians and followed them into the west. They took part in the long hunts of the Indian, lived his life, traded to him the beads, the calico, the hatchets, and sometimes the arms of the white men, and received in turn the choicest furs caught in the wide domain that stretched from the lakes far to west and south and north.

To these men, fitted by nature and experience for daring adventure and exploration in distant territories, the news of the mighty river of the west, so great that it dwarfed all the other rivers of the continent and poured a mighty flood of waters to an unknown sea, came like a challenge, and, in response to that challenge, we find them making their way farther and farther into the west.

It is probable that some of these men made their way into Missouri and perhaps penetrated to the southeast corner of the state. It seems certain from the narrative of Radisson, one of the most famous of these hardy and daring explorers, that he and Groseilliers made their way once, if not oftener, to Missouri, coming at least as far as the mouth of the Missouri. He speaks of the 'forked river' —perhaps, if not certainly, the Mississippi; of the tribe of Indians living upon one branch of it, "of extraordinary height and biggnesse," referring no doubt to the Osages who were celebrated for their height and size. Others probably came, also, lured by the hope of riches, and the desire of adventure, but little is known of them and their wanderings. They established no trading posts or settlements within the state and left, with the exception of Radisson, no accounts of their wanderings to enable us to judge with any certainty concerning the course of their travels.

But these obscure and almost unknown voyages and explorations, barren of any tangible result in one way, produced a great effect in another way, and were, therefore, of importance. The reports which they brought back of the country through which they travelled, of its soil, its rivers, the Indians and the rich trade which might be secured with them, of the mighty river that poured its flood southward and perhaps westward, of an empire that might be won for France and for New France, induced the French authorities of Canada to arrange for the exploration of the wilderness and of the great river.

In 1672, Frontenac, the newly appointed and energetic governor of Canada, determined to send an expedition to explore the course of the great river and to take possession of the country it traversed, for France. No man seemed better suited for such an expedition than Louis Joliet. He was a Canadian by birth, was educated at the Jesuit school at Quebec and intended for the life of a priest; but was so attracted by the wild country about him that he abandoned the idea of the church and began the adventurous life of a voyageur. Previous to 1672 he had made several expeditions to the west, having explored a part of the western shores of Quebec and been present when that country was taken possession of in the name of France. He had also explored a part of the Hudson Bay territory, and was looked upon by those who knew him well, as a hardy, daring, and reliable man. To him Frontenac intrusted the command of the expedition to the great river. He had instruction to take Father Marquette with him. Marquette was a Jesuit priest who had long contemplated a visit to the Indians of the Mississippi, and was assigned to accompany Joliet in accordance with the usual policy of the French in sending priests to accompany expeditions into the wilds. Joliet was commissioned to proceed to the river, to make a voyage down its course, at least far enough to determine into what body of water it emptied, and to its mouth if possible.

Joliet began his voyage from Point St. Ignace on May 17, 1673. The expedition consisted of Joliet himself, Father Marquette, and five other Frenchmen. They had two canoes and a somewhat scanty stock of provisions. They made their way along the shores of Lake Michigan to Green Bay, passed up the Fox river to Lake Winnebago then the limit of French explorations, secured here Indian guides, made their way through lakes and streams to the height of land separating streams flowing into the lakes from those which empty into the Mississippi. Here they carried their canoes across the divide, which is narrow at this point, and launched them again on the Wisconsin, and on the 17th day of June they entered the Mississippi. After proceeding down its current for some distance they came to a settlement of Indians where they landed and were kindly received. Then they came to the mouth of the Illinois and saw on the face of the great rocks which line the stream on the eastern side, painted monsters, described by Marquette as dreadful in appearance and suggestive of the devil. These were two specimens of the art of the Indians and represented manitous or gods. While they meditated on these they came to the mouth of the Missouri. They seem to have reached it during flood time and were amazed and frightened at the tremendous flood of water, bearing on its tide trees and logs and all the debris common to high water in the great and turbulent Missouri. With difficulty they passed safely through. They next observed a place where the river was narrowed by rocks, part of it pouring into a narrow gorge and then returning with fury on itself. Doubtless this is the first description of the narrows at Grand Tower. The description is not quite accurate for the present condition there, but the place has doubtless changed in appearance in the years that have passed.

Day after day the voyagers pursued their way, floating tranquilly down the tide of the great river. They passed the mouth of the Ohio, which they called Ouabouskiaou, or the Beautiful river. Sometimes they came to the camps of Indians, and, on displaying the calumet which one of their Indian friends had given them, they were kindly received. What a scene was presented to their eyes—the wide expanse of the majestic river, the boundless forests that lined its course unbroken by the dwellings of men, and peopled only by the wild and savage life of the woods. The nights

Marquette Among the Mississippi Valley Indians

they passed in their boats or lying on the shore by the river, beneath the stars, listening to the sounds of the mighty current sweeping its way to an unknown sea.

The scenes changed as they made their way farther and farther south. The high and rocky bluffs which had lined one or both sides of the river, from the top of which the country stretched in rolling verdure for miles on either side, gave way to the low and marshy land of the Mississippi bottoms. Cane brakes were seen and mosquitos appeared in great clouds and made life miserable for them. They came at last to the mouth of the Arkansas. Here they met with Indians who displayed the greatest hostility for a long time, but were finally induced to receive them with something like civility. One member of the tribe spoke the language of the Illinois and through him Marquette preached the Christian faith to the assembled savages. They told him, in return for presents given them, what they knew concerning the lower reaches of the river. According to their account, the lower Mississippi was infested by tribes of fierce Indians, so formidable that they themselves dared not hunt the buffalo but contented themselves with fish and corn.

Joliet and Marquette determined to turn back from this place. They had performed a part of their tasks. They had seen the great river, had voyaged for hundreds of miles upon its bosom, and had approached near its mouth as they believed, though in reality they were seven hundred miles from the Gulf. They had gone at least far enough to make sure that it did not empty into the sea of Virginia, the Vermillion or California sea, but into the Gulf of Mexico. Further progress was doubtful. Their supplies were limited, the hot weather was coming on, the Indians farther down were reported as hostile,—all these considerations induced them to relinquish their hope of continuing to the mouth of the river. They began the return trip on the seventeenth of July. The return voyage was far from pleasant. It was midsummer and the heat was great. They might no longer drift, but must urge their canoes against all the force of the river. Father Marquette fell ill and was like to die before the voyage could be completed. At last they reached the Illinois, entered its mouth, and made their way up its beautiful course. They were entertained by a tribe of the Illinois Indians, called Kaskaskias, perhaps the Casquins of De Soto's time. One of the members of the tribe guided them to Lake Michigan which they reached in September, having voyaged more than two thousand miles in the four months since their departure.

Joliet and Marquette separated at Green Bay, Marquette remaining to recruit his health while Joliet hastened homeward. The good fortune which had been his for so many months deserted him at the last and he was almost drowned near Montreal by the upsetting of his canoe. All his papers were lost by this accident, and he made only an oral report to Governor Frontenac concerning his trip. It is partly due to this circumstance that he has received so little of the credit justly due him for his exploit, since Marquette afterward published an account of the voyage and it is his name that is most closely associated with the enterprise. In reality he had no official connection with it, but was present as a volunteer under the direction of Joliet.

Frontenac was much gratified at the success of the voyage and reported to the government of France the results with a recommendation that it be followed up and the country held.

We have now to consider the work of the greatest of the French explorers whose travels and voyages brought them to Southeast Missouri. Robert Cavelier de La Salle was a man who would have made his mark in any place or situation of life, for he was rarely gifted in many ways. He was born in France in 1643, received a good education and emigrated to Canada at the age of twenty-three. Here he heard the reports current among the French and Indians of a great river that flowed to the south and west and perhaps entered into the western sea, called the Vermillion sea, or Sea of California. La Salle was fired by the desire to discover and explore this river and thus open the long sought and eagerly desired way to China and the East. He accordingly interested Courcelles, the governor, and Talon, the intendant of Canada, in his schemes. He spent several years in exploring the lakes and rivers, discovering in the course of his travels the Ohio river and descending it as far as the present site of Louisville and perhaps to its juncture with the Mississippi. At any rate he became convinced that the Mississippi did not flow to the west nor to the east but toward the south and emptied into the Gulf of Mexico.

La Salle had become a friend of the new governor of Canada, Frontenac, and was able to interest him in his schemes of exploration and settlement. Frontenac was a man of energy and resource and gave great assistance to La Salle. Through his help and encouragement La Salle secured from the government of France certain grants of land in Canada, the income of which enabled him to carry on the work which he had undertaken. In the course of his negotiations he made a trip to France and was able to interest many of his friends in the work he was attempting to perform. That work was a great and noble one.

La Salle seems to have been one of the few men at that time connected with the colonies in this country, either French or English, who had a clear grasp of the situation and saw the possibilities of the country. At the time the colonies of France were confined to Canada. The French were devoting their energy to the exploration and settlement of the country around the Great Lakes, to the fur trade with the Indians, and to the enjoyment of the wild and adventurous life of the woods. The country to which the French were devoting their time and energies was a great and wonderful country in many respects. It contained the Great Lakes, and a wonderful system of rivers and water-ways, the soil was fertile in places, and the Indian trade was most profitable and destined to grow for many years. But there was one great obstacle to the development of the French country and that was the severe climate. The winters were long and very cold. Snow was plentiful and deep, for weeks the lakes and rivers we coated with ice, and the shortness of the summer precluded the possibility of growing many of the desirable food plants. It was not a country to develop rapidly, nor to support a large population. When La Salle came to Canada, the French had been in possession for nearly two generations, but had done little or nothing looking to securing land to the south of them.

While the French were thus confining themselves to the region of the Lakes and ignoring the other parts of the continent, the English were planted along the Atlantic coast. They, too, for many generations, were content with the narrow strip which they held and made no efforts to secure the territory to the west. It was a case of short-sightedness in both the colonizing nations, and yet not a surprising case by any means. The continent was so vast, the distances so great, the forest so unconquerable, the dangers from Indians so real that it was natural for both French and English to hesitate before attempting the conquest of the interior of the continent. To them the attempt seemed almost useless as well. The colonies grew slowly. New France seemed large enough for all the French who would ever live there. The problem as the men of that time saw it, was, not to secure and hold new lands, but to people and subdue those they already held. The English were similarly situated. The Atlantic seaboard seemed ample for all the English there, or that were likely to come. Such were the generally accepted opinions of the times. It was, of course, the policy of short-sighedness, but then most men are short-sighted.

Now, however, there had come to America and interested himself its future, a man who was not short-sighted, but on the contrary gifted with remarkable powers to see into the future. La Salle rejected the idea that Canada was large enough for the French. He saw clearly the expansion that must come, and he believed that the Ohio valley which he had discovered and explored, offered, by far, the best field for that inevitable expansion. The soil in that valley was rich, the climate very favorable for agriculture, the opportunities for trade with the Indians were tempting. It must be remembered that at that time trade with the Indians was almost indispensable in the opening up of a new section of the country. It was largely to this trade that settlers looked for support while they cleared away the forests and made the country ready for the practice of agriculture. No part of the country offered any better opportunities for trade than the Ohio valley, and no part of the country was more fertile or better adapted to agriculture. Here, then La Salle believed he saw the seat of a New France more glorious than would ever be possible in Canada. He believed, too, that soon the English would be forced to expand; that the Atlantic seaboard must soon be too contracted for them. Their natural expansion would be to the westward. This movement, when it came, would bring the English across the Alleghanies and into the valley of the Ohio.

To forestall this movement, to explore the country, to claim it for the king of France, to open it for settlers, plant chains of forts and fortified posts, secure the friendship of the Indians and develop trade with them, to make the power of France supreme in the new lands which he had discovered and render them forever outside the power of the English to possess—this was the dream of La Salle. It was not the dream of a visionary. La Salle could dream the most splendid visions. but he was no mere dreamer. On the contrary he was one of the most active, tireless. and practical of men. His plan once formed he proceeded to put it into execution. He determined to organize an expedition, explore the great river to its mouth, found on its banks trading posts, and with the proceeds of this trade to open the country for settlement. He had a wonderful power of persuasion, and was able to make Frontenac see the greatness of his plans and secure his help in his undertakings. This help of the governor was almost indispensable to him, for Frontenac was a powerful and energetic man, fond of bold and daring schemes and desirous himself of achieving riches and distinction in the work of trading and colonizing. But useful as was the aid of Frontenac to La Salle, friendship with the governor brought one drawback with it. It made Frontenac's enemies, La Salle's enemies. These enemies of the governor were by no means few nor powerless. In the first place he had offended the traders of Canada, by embarking in trade on his own account and establishing posts for this purpose on the western lakes. He had been unfortunate enough, also, to incur the displeasure of the Jesuits by some opposition to their plans. The Jesuits were both numerous and powerful and their opposition to the scheme of La Salle, induced in part by their dislike of the governor, was destined to cost La Salle very dear. The Jesuits had long had attention directed to the valley of the great river. Here they had planned to evangelize the Indians and to found a province like that of Paraguay in South America where they should be supreme. La Salle's dream of colonization and settlement ran counter to this plan of the Jesuits and they were accordingly opposed to him and all that he attempted to do.

In spite of all opposition, however, La Salle persisted in his work. In 1673 he received from Frontenac the grant of a new seignory in the west. This was called Fort Frontenac and was situated near the present site of Kingston. This grant carried with it a practical monopoly of the fur trade in that part of Canada. In 1674 and again in 1677 he visited France. Here his enthusiasm, his knowledge of the country of America, and above all persistence and determination won approval for his schemes. He received from the King of France a patent of authority, giving him the right to explore the country at his own expense, to build and equip forts, and to exercise a monopoly of the trade in buffalo skins for a period of five years. Armed with this concession, La Salle made the greatest exertion to raise enough funds to equip his expeditions. In this he was successful, and returned to Canada after having organized his expedition. He arrived in Quebec in August, 1678, and secured men and supplies for his projected expedition to the Mississippi. One man who accompanied him, and who was destined to be closely associated with all his enterprises, was Tonti. He also secured the friendship and help of Father Hennepin.

On landing at Quebec, La Salle immediately set to making arrangements for the expedition and sent Father Hennepin and Tonti with men and supplies, as an advance guard. Starting on November 18th, from Fort Frontenac, they landed at Lewiston and continued up the Niagara river to the Falls. Here they concluded to wait, and arrange for the further course of the expedition. They were joined by La Salle in January, 1679. La Salle had come to Lewiston, in the vessel which he designed to use for the purpose of the expediton, but this vessel was wrecked in the attempt. The early part of 1679 was spent by the party in building a boat for use on the upper lakes. This boat was launched in the spring, above the Falls of Niagara. The party suffered very greatly from the hostility of the Iroquois Indians. In fact it was almost impossible to prevent the destruction of the vessel which they were building.

La Salle left the party in the spring, and returned to Fort Frontenac to secure further supplies and funds. He found that all of his property had been attached by his creditors, at the instigation of his enemies, for the payment of his debts. Nevertheless, La Salle returned to Lake Erie to continue the expedition, and on August the seventh, embarked on the new vessel which he had named the "Griffon." They sailed through Lake Huron and down Lake Michigan to Green Bay. Here La Salle collected a cargo of valuable furs, with which he loaded the "Griffon," and then sent the vessel back to Niagara, instructing the pilot to dispose of the furs, procure additional supplies, and then return.

La Salle, with the remainder of the expedition, left Green Bay in canoes, and made their way to the mouth of the St. Joseph. Here they proceeded to build a boat and awaited the return of the "Griffon." Not having heard any news of this vessel by the beginning of December, La Salle was filled with apprehension concerning her fate. The cargo of furs was necessary for a part of the expense of his journey. Notwithstanding this, he determined to continue, and on the 3rd of December the canoes made their way up the St. Joseph, and were carried over the five mile portage which separates the headwaters of the St. Joseph from those of the Illinois. They found the country of the Illinois practically deserted; and, while there was abundant sign of deer and buffalo, they nearly starved owing to their failure to find food. Finally they found an Indian village at the great rock on the Illinois river, known as Starved Rock. Here La Salle held a council with representatives of many of the tribes of the Illinois country. He outlined to them his plans, one of which was an alliance with the Indians for the purpose of trade.

The Indians discouraged his attempt, telling him that it would be impossible to reach the mouth of the Mississippi, owing to the hostility of the tribes on its lower course, and warning him of the dangers of such an undertaking. This opposition of the Indians, as La Salle afterward found, was caused by a rumor which his enemies had started, that he was the secret agent of the Iroquois. However, La Salle finally overcame their opposition with the threat that if they did not consent to accompany and help him in his schemes, he would "go to the Osages who were men and not women." This offer interested the Illinois and gained their consent, for they were bitterly hostile to the Osages.

Having secured supplies from these Indians, La Salle started down the river, reaching the place which he named Fort Creve Coeur in January, 1680. Here he was deserted by a number of his men and received the message which told of the loss of the "Griffon" with all its cargo. He then began the construction of a vessel in which to navigate the Mississippi. He found it necessary to return to Canada for certain supplies for the building of this vessel, and on March 1st set out alone for Canada. His return journey was one of the most terrible ever made; but he reached Fort Frontenac in safety, and, having made provision for the necessary supplies, started on the return trip in August. He had left the expedition at Fort Creve Coeur under the command of Tonti, but when he reached that point he found the camp entirely deserted. There were abundant signs that the Indians had made an attack upon the camp, and destroyed it. Only a part of the vessel which had been built was left, and since it was impossible to proceed, La Salle returned to the St. Joseph. Here he held a great council with the Miamis and the Shawnees, and with them he formed a league for the furtherance of his purpose in regard to the Illinois Indians. He returned to Canada, meeting on the way with Tonti, who, after most remarkable dangers and struggles, had succeeded in escaping from the Indians and returning by way of the upper lakes.

This experience, which would have shaken the resolution of a less resolute man, but confirmed La Salle in his intention to explore the great river. In October, 1681, he returned to Lake Michigan, entered the Chicago river and reached the Mississippi, February 6, 1682. This time he did not attempt the construction of a large vessel, but made his way down the river in canoes. He reached the mouth of the river, October 6th and took possession of the entire country in the name of the king of France.

Having returned from this voyage of discovery, La Salle set out upon the execution of the remainder of his great scheme. This included the project of fur trade among the Illinois Indians. He had become convinced that this was possible only after organizing the Indians, and offering them protection against the raids of the Iroquois. He had selected as the site for his trading post, the great rock known as Starved Rock. Here he planted a colony, and the Indians having fallen in with his scheme, he won their friendship and established a flourishing trade in that territory. Leaving his little colony, he made his way back to Canada to secure still further supplies, but here he found things changed. His friend, Frontenac had been superseded as governor of Canada, and the new governor was under the influence of La Salle's enemies. He did all he could to hinder and discourage La Salle who found it necessary once more to go to France. Here, in spite of the misrepresentations of the governor, he once more won the confidence of the king and his ministers and received still more valuable patents and grants in the new territory.

He organized a new expedition. It was planned to sail to the Gulf of Mexico, locate the mouth of the river, and then proceed up its course to some suitable place where a colony would be founded. In this way he intended to take and hold all the valley of the Mississippi.

The officer in command of the ships was both incompetent, and hostile to La Salle. He failed to find the mouth of the river, and after cruising back and forth for a time, he insisted on landing the expedition on the coast of the gulf some four hundred miles west of the mouth of the river. The ships then sailed away to France leaving La Salle and the members of the expedition helpless in an unknown and entirely unpromising region. La Salle made the best of the situation. A colony was formed, houses and shelters erected and the beginnings of a settlement formed. It was La Salle's intention to search for and find the river from this place. After numerous attempts he became convinced that he was so far from the river and so ignorant of its position and direction that he could not any longer hope to be successful in his search. The colony in the meantime was in a deplorable condition. Food supplies were limited; the region in which they were was barren and inhospitable. Many members of the expeditions were dissatisfied and hostile to their leader.

At last La Salle formed a desperate resolution. He despaired of finding the river. He saw that the colony could not long survive. No help could be expected from France direct. He determined to go overland to Canada and there secure ships and provisions for saving his men. On foot, then, accompanied by a few members of the expedition to set out a walk a thousand miles through an unknown country, to cross rivers and lakes, to meet the Indians and to confront all the dangers of the wilderness. Nothing shows better the unconquerable determination of the man than this last projected journey. He had gone but a little way until he was shot and killed by one of those accompanying him. This man had cherished a secret grudge against La Salle and had found an opportunity for satisfying his hatred.

So there died, in the prime of his life and in the midst of the execution of great plans, the greatest of the French explorers. Had he lived to carry out his plans and had the French government caught something of his idea and his enthusiasm, it is quite probable that the history of the Mississippi valley would have been quite different. It was long, however, before the government of France came to have much appreciation of the great territory of Louisiana. She regarded it with little care or concern; left it without attention, or granted it with careless indifference to various applicants.

CHAPTER IV

INDIAN HISTORY

IMPORTANCE OF INDIANS IN OUR HISTORY—INDIAN TRADE—INDIANS IN SOUTHEAST MISSOURI WHEN DESOTO CAME—THE CAPAHAS—THE SIOUAN FAMILY AND ITS BRANCHES — THE OSAGES—THEIR HOMES—THEIR FARMS—OSAGE HOUSES — FURNITURE AND CLOTHING — POLYGAMY—WEAPONS—PECULIAR CUSTOMS OF THE OSAGES — PAINTING OF THE BODY — THEIR GOVERNMENT—WARS WITH OTHER INDIANS—DEFEATED BY SACS AND FOXES—THEIR REMOVAL FROM THE STATE—DELAWARES AND SHAWNEES—THEIR HISTORY OUTSIDE MISSOURI—WHY THE SPANIARDS BROUGHT THEM TO MISSOURI—CHARACTER—THEIR VILLAGES—TECUMSEH'S SISTER — CHILLETECAUX — WITCHCRAFT DELUSION—THE MASHCOUX TRIBE—TREATIES WITH THE INDIANS—INDIAN EDUCATION.

Constant reference has been made in earlier chapters to the Indians, as the aboriginal inhabitants of America were incorrectly named by Columbus, and other early explorers, because they believed America to be the Indies. These Indians are interesting as being the earliest inhabitants of the country and also because they played a considerable part in its history after the white man came here. They were always to be taken into consideration. Whether friendly or hostile, whether disposed to help or hinder those who came, they were always to be reckoned with. It is difficult, perhaps impossible, for us who live in the security of the present, even to imagine the time when the savage warwhoop of the Indians was a sound of terror, often heard and always to be dreaded. We cannot reconstruct, except imperfectly, the conditions of life, here, when trade with the Indians was one of the prime motives for the coming of white people to this part of the world.

And yet, difficult as it is to realize these things, both of these conditions once existed There was a time in Southeast Missouri when every home was in some ways a fortress, when the inhabitants listened for the warwhoop, and when life and property were not safe from the savage attacks of the red men. It is true that the depredations committed here were not so extensive as those suffered by the people of the eastern part of this country, but they were sufficient in number to form a bloody chapter in our history.

There was time, also, when trade with the Indians was very profitable. The western country was once the home of many fur-bearing animals. Perhaps nowhere else in the world did there ever exist such a great number of animals valuable for their fur or for their flesh as in the western part of North America. Until the coming of the white people the Indians had done little to destroy these animals. It is true they lived largely by hunting, but they hunted only to supply the immediate needs for food, and so vast was the animal life of the country that its natural increase more than compensated for all the Indians killed for food and skins. But when the Indians found it possible to trade furs to the whites for those things which they desired, they became the agents for the destruction of the game of the country. It was relentlessly pursued and vast quantities of furs were every year bartered away to the traders. The fur trade was exceedingly profitable to the white men engaged in it, for it was possible to buy with a hatchet, a string of beads, some calico, or other inexpensive articles, valuable furs. To secure this trade and hold it became a prize, contended for, not alone by individuals and companies, but by nations themselves. A part of the colonial policy of France, of England, and of Spain was directed by a desire to secure or hold the trade in furs.

In order to accomplish these objects settlements were made, expeditions and wars carried on. Some of the early settlements in the state were made as trading points. This is true of Cape Girardeau. Here Louis Lorimier early established himself to carry on trade with the Indians. New Madrid was originally a trading post of the La Sieurs.

It is clear that much of the early history of this part of the state was determined and given course by the presence of the Indians. It is the purpose of this chapter to give an account of the various tribes that lived here, their character, habits, manner of life, relation to the settlers, and the final disposition made of them.

When DeSoto came to Southeast Missouri he found living within its borders at least three tribes of Indians. Those whose principal place of dwelling was in the neighborhood of New Madrid he called Casquins. These we believe to have been identical with the Kaskaskias later found on the other side of the river in what is now the state of Illinois. If this is correct the Casquins were a part of the great Algonquin group of Indians who were formerly to be found scattered over a considerable part of the eastern portion of the United States. Their removal from New Madrid county to Illinois is not a matter of surprise, for such removals were not at all uncommon among the Indians. In fact it was a custom with most of them to change their place from time to time. This was due, in part, to their roving disposition and constant love of change; in part, to the necessity of finding new hunting grounds where proper supplies of food might be had; and, in part, to the constant and bitter warfare waged between Indians of different tribes.

It was probably some such war which caused the Casquins to abandon their seat in Southeast Missouri and migrate to the other side of the great river. In fact we know that between them as Algonquins and the Siouan family (represented by the Osages, the Kansas, the Missouris and others) there was bitter hatred and constant warfare. It was the interference of DeSoto in the quarrel of the Casquins that bought him into contact with the Capahas.

These Capahas were doubtless living in the neighborhood of Cape Girardeau. They belonged, it seems, to the great Siouan family. It was a tradition among the Siouan Indians west of the river that their original seat was in the valley of the Ohio; that owing to trouble with other Indians they migrated down the Ohio to its mouth. Here they divided part of them turning to the south and others to the north. Those who went to the South were called Quapas, Capahas, Pacahas, and other similar names; all meaning "downstream Indians" and having reference to their going down the river from the time of their separation. Those who turned to the north were called Omahas, meaning "upstream Indians." These Omahas made their way to the Missouri river, where some of them settled and long remained. These were called Missouris. Others of them passed up this river toward the west. Some of them settled on that branch of the Missouri afterward called for them the Osage. These were the famous Osage Indians whose doings fill such a large part of the aboriginal history of Missouri. Still others of these Indians pressed their way further west to become known as the Kansas and Omahas.

If this legendary account as preserved by the Indians themselves is correct, there existed a close relation between all the Indians named. That this relation did exist is shown by the similarity of their language. They spoke, it is true, different dialects, but these were not so dissimilar as to preclude all communication. Indeed it was possible for one speaking either of these various dialects to learn the others in a very short space of time.

The third tribe of Indians found by DeSoto were these Osages, who at this time lived in the great bend of the Missouri, but whose hunting ground extended east to the Mississippi and south to the Arkansas.

When the French came, the Casquins had migrated to a new seat on the Illinois river, if indeed the Kaskaskias of Illinois were identical with the Casquins described by DeSoto. The Capahas had moved down the Mississippi to the Arkansas where they continued to reside. Others think, however, that their principal seat was on the St. Francois and that one of their villages, called Toriman, was in Dunklin county. This is the conclusion of Houck who has given the matter very careful study. (Houck's "History of Missouri," Vol. I, p. 173).

Of all these early aboriginal inhabitants of Southeast Missouri none are more interesting than the Osages. A part as we have seen of that great Siouan family which at an early date migrated from their original home in the valley of the Ohio to its mouth where they divided; the Osages, at the time of the French, were living on the Missouri and the Osage. From here their hunting parties went out to cover that great stretch of territory extending east to the Mississippi and south to the Arkansas. They continued to reside on the Osage until, with the Missouris, the tribe which for a time lived near the mouth of the Missouri but which afterward moved up the stream and united with the Osages, they came into conflict with Sacs and Foxes. A deadly strife ensued between these Indians, and later, between the Osages and the Cherokees when the latter were moved to this side of the river by the government. The Osages resented the coming of the Cherokees to their hunting grounds and tried to drive them out. They gradually degenerated, however, and finally disappeared from the Missouri country.

During the time of their prosperity they had been induced by the Indian traders to found some settlements on the Arkansas, and, when the pressure of other tribes and the whites became too strong for them, the remnant made their way to the south. Some of their descendants reside yet in Oklahoma.

These Indians lived principally by hunting, but they also cultivated little patches of soil. Usually each band of them had two or more places of residence. Near one of them they had some cleared land. Here, usually in April, they planted maize and squashes, or pumpkins and beans. When this planting was made, they then set out on a hunting expedition which lasted for two or three months. Returning usually in August they harvested their crops which, during their absence, had been uncultivated. The corn was usually shelled and stored in pots or hollow trunks of trees, the squashes and pumpkins were dried, the latter being cut into long strips and hung in the upper part of their houses. Beans were also kept by being shelled and stored. The crop harvested and stored for winter, the Indians were accustomed to depart again for another hunting expedition. The meat procured on these expeditions, such as was not immediately used, was dried or jerked, or else was partly cooked and covered with grease from the fat of some animal, usually the bear or deer. The skins which they secured were prepared for trading at the nearest post, for beads, hatchets, calico, powder, guns, or whiskey. This hunt lasted until about January when the Indians returned to their villages to remain during the colder wealther of winter, living principally upon the stores of food laid up during the summer. With the return of spring they engaged in still another hunt, coming back to the practice of their rude agriculture.

The houses of the Osages were rude cabins, not unlike a tent in shape and appearance but constructed of poles and matting. Two forks each about twenty feet high were stuck into the ground, a ridge pole laid across these, smaller forks put up on each side, and a framework of poles arranged to these, furnishing a support for the mats. These mats were often woven of rushes or reeds, sometimes skins or bark took the place of the matting, or even sod was sometimes used. Of course not all the houses were alike. Some of them were conical in shape. All were, without exception, rude in appearance, and greatly lacking in comfort. None possessed a chimney, the fire being kindled on the earth floor in the center of the house, or upon a hearth of stones, and the smoke was allowed to escape through a hole in the center of the roof.

The furniture was exceedingly limited, consisting principally of beds. These were made of skins or mats placed upon a shelf built along the walls. The beds served as seats in the day time, though the Indians, frequently, or most often, sat on the ground or on mats placed as a sort of carpet. Their household implements were those common to most American Indians and consisted of pottery vessels, stone knives, stones for grinding or pounding corn, and similar utensils, most if not all of them the product of the skill and industry of the Indian women. The men felt it to be beneath their dignity as warriors and hunters to engage in manual labor of any kind and deputed practically all of it, including the building and care of the house, the construction of the necessary implements and the cultivation of the fields, to the women.

These women were not uncomely in youth, but their life of toil and hardship brought upon them a premature old age. One custom concerning the women of the Osages is noted by many travellers among them and that is the way in which the married woman was distinguished from the unmarried. The Indian maiden was accustomed to bestow great attention upon the arrangement and adornment of her hair. It was arranged in two braids and ornamented with strings of wampum and such other beautiful objects as might be possessed. Upon marriage, however, the ornaments were laid aside to be kept for a daughter, and the hair was confined in one braid.

A curious form of polygamy was practiced among them. When a man took a wife he acquired rights over the persons of her sisters, and might bestow them in marriage as he wished or else add them to his own household. In spite of this privilege, monogamy was not uncommon among them and there frequently existed between husband and wife a strong and lasting tie of affection.

The Osages possessed the ordinary weapons of the Indians, the bow and arrow, the war-club, the tomahawk, and the scalping knife. They soon learned the superior power of the gun, and after coming into contact with the traders they equipped themselves, where possible, with guns. In common with most of the Indians of the continent they looked upon bravery in war as the chief virtue. Scalping was the one act that conferred the greatest distinction on a brave, and next to this stealing the enemy's horses. The young braves often spent their leisure time in boasting of their skill and prowess in handling the scalping knife and in carrying away horses. This latter accomplishment was held in high repute among them, for the Osages were distinguished among Indians for their knowledge of and regard for the horse. They possessed large numbers of them and held them as their chief riches. Nuttall ("Journal," p. 247) records the fact that once they purchased the temporary friendship of their bitter enemies, the Outagamies, by the present of a hundred head of horses. "A present," Nuttall remarks, "which though valuable was not costly to the givers, for in a raid undertaken immediately afterward they brought back three hundred horses either stolen from the Pawnees or else caught wild upon the prairies."

According to Nuttall ("Journal," p. 238), who spent sometime with them, they possessed some knowledge of the stars. They recognized the pole star and had observed that it was stationary in the heavens, they called Venus the harbinger of day, they knew the Pleiades and the three stars in Orion's belt, and they spoke of the Galaxy as the heavenly road or way.

The religion of the Osages was not unlike that of many other of the American Indians. They believed in a Great Spirit, and looked forward to a Happy Hunting Ground after death. In accordance with this belief they frequently buried with the deceased warrior his hunting implements and his weapons of war, that he might enjoy his favorite pastime in the land of the dead. Coupled with this religion was a gross form of superstition which manifested itself in an observance of omens, a belief in the efficacy of charms and amulets, and a constant effort to propitiate evil spirits. Before going on the war-path they were accustomed to spend a night in lamentation and in penitential exercises, in the course of which they inflicted upon themselves sundry forms of punishments in an endeavor to ward off misfortune in the time of war.

One of their peculiar customs, seemingly unique, was a morning lamentation indulged in by some or all of the members of the tribe, each morning about sun rise. This custom prevailed to the very great annoyance of their white visitors. Long speaks also of "a vesper hymn of doleful sound," chanted at sun-down during one his visits. (Long's "Expedition," Vol. 4, p. 266).

In common with other Indians they were exceedingly fond of tobacco and attached great importance to the pipe. It formed a part of all their great meetings, and no treaty was concluded and no formal act relating to the tribe ever performed without recourse to the pipe which was passed from hand to hand and smoked by each in turn.

Their clothing was made from skins, principally deer-skins, which were tanned by the women and made into garments for both men and women. They also possessed the art of weaving, and utilized for this purpose lint from the bark of the mulberry, the elm, or the paw-paw. Sometimes they wove a sort of cloth from feathers, and after they began to secure cloth from the white people they would frequently unravel an old piece of cloth and use the thread again. The men usually wore the breech clout made of skins, leggings, and moccasins. The women wore a short skirt, leggings, and moccasins, and sometimes a covering for the upper part of the body, either a shirt made of their cloth or a blanket. They adorned themselves with feathers, worked various patterns into their cloth, wore shells and beads, and, as far as their conditions allowed, exhibited all the signs of vanity of dress found among civilized people. The men of the tribe were fond of paint. They sometimes painted the entire body, staining it with colors derived from clay. The face was especially treated and was sometimes streaked and painted in a dreadful and hideous manner. This was true of all who went upon the warpath. Indeed the hideous painting of the face was usually a sign of war, though sometimes indulged in during their celebrations of various kinds.

The Indian moccasin deserves a more extended notice than any other part of their wearing apparel. Perhaps no other footgear ever devised, by either savage or civilized man, was quite so well adapted to the peculiar purposes for which it was intended, as this moccasin. Made of tanned deer-skin, it was soft and pliable, enabling its wearer to pass with wonderful celerity and absence of noise through the woods and over the rude trails, and yet it was durable and lasting. Its superiority is shown in the fact that all white men who have passed much time among the Indians have adopted it in preference to the shoe or boot of civilization.

The government of the Osages was a patriarchal despotism. The leader was frequently, though not always, succeeded by his son. This right of heredity was often disregarded and never was vested exclusively in the eldest son. In fact they refused to regard the right of primogeniture. The chief was, first of all, the leader in war. He was usually the most daring and ruthless of the warriors of the tribe. His retention of the leadership depended upon his hold upon the respect and confidence of his fellows. This could not long be retained, in such a state of society as existed among the Indians, by any one not recognized as brave and skilful in war. The chief was supposed to exercise authority over his warriors in time of peace, also, but this authority was mainly shadowy and vague. The real fact of the matter was that the character of the Indians of almost every tribe prevented anything like a firm government. They could not submit themselves to the rule of anyone else, even though he was chosen by themselves for that purpose. It was this fatal defect, coupled with their unreasonable delight in war that rendered all the resistance of the Indians to the encroachment of the white men so futile. Even the great chiefs, such as Pontiac and Tecumseh, found their influence often set at naught and their plans wrecked by the perverse and unstable character of their fellows. Many of their chiefs retained their hold upon their men by cunning and a practice of all the arts of the political demagogue. Brackenridge, says of Sans Oreille, chief of the Little Osages, that he was, "as usual with the ambitious among these people, the poorest man in the nation; for to set the heart upon goods and chattels was thought to indicate a mean and narrow soul. He, therefore, gave away everything he could get, even though he should beg and rob to procure it; and this to purchase popularity. Such is ambition. Little they knew of this state of society, who believe that it is free from jealousies, from envy, detraction, or guilty ambition. No demagogue, no Cataline, ever used more art and finesse, ever displayed more policy than this cunning savage. The arts of flattery and bribery by which the unthinking multitude is seduced, are nearly the same everywhere, and passion for power and distinction seems inherent in human nature." (Brackenridge "Journal," p. 58).

In person the Osages were perhaps the most finely developed of any of the Indians of North America. They were tall, above the average height of both whites and Indians. Few of the men were under six feet and they were large and strong in proportion to their great height. They were comely in appearance for Indians, and evoked the admiration of most travellers among them. They possessed great powers of endurance. Nuttall ("Journal," p. 246) speaks of their hunting and foraging expeditions extending for three hundred miles or more, and says that it was not uncommon for them to walk from their camp on the Verdigris river in Arkansas to the trading post on the Arkansas in a single day. This is a distance of sixty miles.

As we have said, these Indians established themselves on the Osage river in Missouri. They early separated into three bands the Great Osages living on the Osage and numbering at time about one thousand warriors; the Little Osages who dwelt further west, numbering from two hundred and fifty to four hundred; and the Arkansas band, which settled on the Verdigris, a tributary of the Arkansas river. These last were induced to make settlement there by Pierre Chouteau of St. Louis. One DeLisa had secured from the government of Spain a monopoly of the Indian trade in Missouri, and Chouteau induced a part of the Osages to emigrate to Arkansas that he might trade with them. While thus the main camps of these Indians were outside the territory of Southeast Missouri as here defined, they had much to do with the history of this section of the state, for they roamed over all this territory and were for many years the dread of all the inhabitants. The French were accustomed to deal with the utmost leniency with the Indians, and this policy was inherited by the Spanish when they came into possession here. As a consequence the Indians were not forced to submit to the authority of either government and for years committed many depredations upon the inhabitants. They were especially troublesome in the matter of horse-stealing. Their fondness for horses, as noted elsewhere, caused them to take possession of good horses without regard to the ownership of them. They had a custom, too, of resenting any intrusion on their chosen hunting grounds, and many a white hunter and trapper was beaten, his property seized, or destroyed, because he was found by the Osages within territory which they claimed as their own. Often, too, these outrages did not stop short of the murder of the luckless hunter or trapper. This was almost certainly the fate of the man caught on their warpaths. These they held with tenacity and resented any intrusion upon them.

Constant struggle was carried on by the Osages with other Indians seeking to come into this territory. There was a general movement of the Indians from east to west. We have seen that the Osages themselves were the descendants of Siouan Indians who formerly lived in the valley of the Ohio. Many causes impelled this migration toward the west. Chief of these was terrible ferocity and power of Iroquois or Five Nations of New York. These fierce Indians, the strongest and most powerful of all the natives on the continent, carried on ruthless war against most of the tribes of the north and east. Many of these sought to escape this warfare by moving to the west. Those who came after the settlement of white men in Missouri found their way barred by the Osages, but little inferior in prowess and ferocity to the dreaded Iroquois themselves. Against these new comers the Osages waged bitter war. The Peorias, a little remnant flying across the river to find homes, were compelled to live in constant fear. A little band of thirty of these took up their abode under the protection of the white men at Ste. Genevieve, but they hunted but little we are told, owing to their fear of the Osages. The Saukees and Outgamies, or Sacs and Foxes, who settled in Iowa and north Missouri, attempted to extend their territory south of the Missouri and became involved in a bitter and relentless struggle with the Osages. Coming from another direction were the Cherokees, a part of that great nation of the southern Alleghenies. With all of these, as well as with the Delawares and Shawnees, the Osages contended with varying fortunes. None of the invaders surpassed them in bravery, ferocity, or skill in warfare, but the Sacs and Foxes brought with them the arms of the white men, and in the end this superiority of arms prevailed, and the lessened remnant of the great and haughty tribe of Osages made their way to the west. A remnant of them still live in Oklahoma.

A melancholy interest attaches to these few and feeble descendants of a once powerful and numerous race. The defects of Indian character were many and grave. Their society and government was most primitive, they inflicted upon the settlers untold suffering and most barbaric cruelties. Their going made way for the civilization and progress of the white race. No one would call back the Indians even if that were possible, but the chapter of history which records the dealings of our government with the Indians is a most painful one. We cannot forget that the Indian was fighting for his home, for his hunting grounds, for that state of life and society which seemed to him best and most desirable, and we cannot close our eyes to the fact that the treatment he received from those who took his land was often marked by the extreme of cruelty and treachery. Perhaps it was inevitable that he should disappear before the superior gifts of the white man, but surely it was not necessary that bad faith and cruelty and even treachery should mark our treatment of him.

The Osages were perhaps the most formidable and troublesome of all the savage neighbors of the people of this section of the state, but they were by no means the only Indians who were here. The constant drift of the aborigines westward across the river brought many of them through Missouri or near its borders, and of these passing through, some remained. Thus we find constant reference in the annals of the time to Creeks and Cherokees, Pawnees, Peorias and others of the many tribes of the western Indians. Some of these made their residence within the borders of the section, others were only occasional visitors, whose hunting or trading parties came and went as the whim seized them. These, as they traded or hunted or pursued other and less legitimate occupation, entered little into the real life of the people and had but little influence on the development of the country, further than the inducement of settlers for their trade.

Two other tribes than those mentioned, however, settled within the limits of Southeast Missouri in considerable numbers, and they came into closer relations with the people of this part of the state and probably were more important in its early history than any others of the savages. These two tribes were the Delawares and the Shawnees. Both nees. Both of these are Algonquin Indians and closely related to each other.

The Delawares were originally found on both sides of the Delaware river in Pennsylvania and Delaware. They were the Indians who were dealt with by William Penn and others of the early settlers in Pennsylvania. They early came into conflict with the Iroquois, and were subjugated by them. During the period of their subjugation they lost much of their former spirit and courage, and lived in a state of abject fear of their red masters. They finally moved further west into the present state of Ohio. Here they recovered their spirit and their love for war and became among the most formidable of the tribes. Part of them were converted to Christianity through the efforts of Moravian missionaries and became known as the Christian Indians. Those who refused Christianity joined with the French in the French and Indian wars, and with the British during the Revolution. They committed great depredations during the war all along the western borders, until an expedition under "Mad Anthony" Wayne laid waste their country and destroyed their power. They gradually drifted further west into Indiana and Iowa. During the Spanish regime in Missouri they were invited to settle in Missouri, or in Upper Louisiana as the country west of the river was then called.

This invitation to settle under the power of Spain was prompted by two motives. The Spanish wished them to be a bulwark against the constant encroachments of the Osages whose thieving and plundering expeditions harried all of Upper Louisiana and kept its inhabitants in a state of constant alarm. Spain greatly feared for her colonies, too, because of the American desire for the possession of the Mississippi. There was a feeling along our western border at that time that the United States should seize the river, and perhaps some of the territory of the western side, and hold it. To have the help of the savage allies whom she had brought to her colonies was one of the motives which prompted Spain to bring the Delawares to this side. Louis Lorimier, the founder of Cape Girardeau, was one of the principal agents in the Spanish dealing with the Indians.

The Shawnees who came to Missouri at the same time with the Delawares were quite probably an offshoot of the Delawares, who had been for some time separated from them but who again united with them just before their emigration to the west. They resembled the Delawares in language and tribal habits and acted with them in many of their dealings with the white men.

When these Indians came across the Mississippi they settled principally in the territory between the Cinque Homme and Flora creek. Their settlement extends west to Whitewater river. Two large villages were located on Apple creek, on the north line of what is now Cape Girardeau county. There were also villages of these Indians along Castor river, near the present site of Bloomfield in Stoddard county, and at Chilletecaux in Dunklin county. They settled at other places in various counties of the district, and most of the Indians known to the later settlers in this territory belonged to these two tribes, or else to the Cherokees concerning whose history some facts are given later. These Delawares and Shawnees were nearly always peaceful and inoffensive in their relations with the white people. Many of them cultivated little patches of corn or pumpkins, the work as was usual with Indians being virtually done by the women. They hunted and trapped, selling their furs to the various traders, using the flesh of animals for their food.

Many places through the lower counties of the district have names which perpetuate the memory of these Indians. Chilletecaux river in Dunklin county, Jim Ease's camp in New Madrid, and Seneca slough are a few of them. Along Apple creek, where were located the principal villages of the Indians, are many traces of their residence.

The largest of the villages on this creek contained about four hundred inhabitants. The houses were built of logs and the openings were filled with mud. They were superior in some ways to many of the tribes of the west. Most of them were fine looking well-made men, fond of war and the chase. They possessed considerable skill in war, and made even the fierce Osages respect the prowess of their arms. For a long time the Shawnees cherished a bitter hatred for Americans.

This village called Chillecathee, was situated on Apple creek in Cape Girardeau county. It was the largest village in the entire section. More than five hundred Indians made their homes here for many years. They were principally Shawnees and Delawares. Among these Indians was the sister of the celebrated Chief Tecumseh. This Indian woman, who is said to have been very beautiful and possessed of a great fluency of speech and considerable eloquence, during a visit to an Indian camp at New Madrid, formed the acquaintance of a creole named Francois Maisonville. They became attached to one another and were married after the Indian marriage customs. When Tecumseh heard of this he came to New Madrid and forced his sister to leave Maisonville and return to the village of Apple creek. However, within a few months, while Tecumseh was absent in the south attempting to form his great alliance of the southern Indians, his sister returned to New Madrid and to her husband. There are living today, in New Madrid county, some of the descendants of Maisonville and his Indian wife. She outlived her husband and seemed never to recover from her grief for the death of her brother, who was killed by Colonel Johnson in Indiana.

Another one of these Indian villages was called Chilletecaux. It was situated on a branch of the St. Francois river not far from the present site of Kennett, and a third village was located near the present site of Point Pleasant in New Madrid county.

The usual relation of the Indians and the white people was one of friendship and good feeling, but some times circumstances arose which led to trouble. Just before the earthquake of 1811 a war party of Creek Indians, under the leadership of a chief named Captain George, crossed the Mississippi river four miles below Little Prairie. They were on the warpath and showed great hostility toward the whites. They planned the capture of Little Prairie and subsequently New Madrid. They were foiled in their efforts by the actions of a Delaware Indian. He was a friend of the whites, and having discovered the intention of the Creeks reported their purpose to Francois Lasieur and Captain George Ruddell, each of whom commanded a company of militia. The militia were ordered out and all preparations made to repel the attack of the Indians. It was just at this time, when the whites and Indians were confronting one another, that the first shock of the earthquake was felt. The Indians were so alarmed by this that they fled across the river, and were doubtless among those who were chastised by General Jackson.

Lasieur in his writing on the early history of New Madrid (*New Madrid Record*, 1893) calls attention to the fact that the Indians were armed with good rifles which they had secured at Kaskaskia, and that they never bought any lead. In fact all Indians of this district were accustomed to secure their supplies of lead from some place in the immediate vicinity. The Indians remaining in the town of Chilletecaux would depart in the morning and return in the evening with baskets full of lead ore. They went in the direction of the St. Francois river. The source of their supplies of lead in this part of the district has never been discovered. One of these Indians named Chookalee, or Corn Meal, returned from the reservation to which the Indians had been removed, and in 1837 came to Point Pleasant. He had been induced to return by the La Sieurs and had promised to show them the site of the lead mine. Unfortunately he died on the very day of his arrival at Point Pleasant and the secret of his mine died with him. One of the famous chiefs of these Indians was Captain Moonshine whose son, Billy Moonshine, appeared in the battle of Big River during the Civil war.

The Indians of this district were seized during the close of the eighteenth century by a belief in witchcraft. This belief, which was widely distributed among them, led to the same results as the belief in witchcraft among the white people in Salem, Massachusetts. Many persons among the Indians suffered arrest, persecution and even death, because they were accused of being witches. The most trivial circumstance was liable to draw suspicion upon a person, and, once being suspected, he was almost certain to be convicted and put to death. It is difficult to say how far this delusion would have carried the Indians and how many victims it would have required had it not been for the fortunate visit of Tecumseh who was at this time organizing the Indians for an assault upon the whites, and in the course of his journeys for this purpose came to Southeast Missouri. Tecumseh had no belief in witches, and he was unwilling to see the lives of his people sacrificed to this delusion. He needed the energies of the Indians to assist him in his purpose. Such was his influence and power that he brought about the cessation of the punishment of those accused of witchcraft.

Outside of the Osages, the most troublesome Indians to the people of Southeast

Missouri were, very probably, the members of a band of Creeks. De Lassus, in a letter to Major Stoddard at the time of the transfer of Upper Louisiana to the United States, says that these Creek Indians had been expelled from their tribes on account of crimes and that they had spent about ten years wandering up and down on both sides of the Mississippi river, covering the territory from New Madrid to the Maramec and constantly slaying, killing, and burning houses. De Lassus calls them the Mashcoux Indians. It was some of this band that killed David Trotter and burned his house.

After the punishment of the Indians for the killing of Trotter, and some representations made by De Lassus to their chief, the band seems to have given up the larger part of their depredations and no longer to have troubled the inhabitants.

In 1808 the government made a treaty with the Osages, by which it was agreed that the boundary between them and the United States should begin at Fort Osage on the Mississippi river, run due south to the Arkansas river and down the Arkansas to the Mississippi. All the land east of this line was to pass from the Indians to the government of the United States. They also ceded to the government their lands north of the Mississippi river and two square leagues west of this line, to contain Fort Osage. This treaty left to the Osages only the western part of the territory now embraced in Missouri. In 1825 the Osages made another treaty by which they gave up their rights to all the lands in Missouri.

In 1793 Spain, by action of Baron Carondelet, granted to the Shawnees and Delawares a tract of land situated between the Cinque Homme and Cape Girardeau. This tract extended as far west as White river. This territory was claimed by the Osage Indians and was relinquished by them in their treaty of 1808. The government of the United States, however, did not press this claim to this particular tract, for one of the clauses in the treaty by which Louisiana was ceded to the United States bound this country to the fulfilment of all treaties and agreements between Spain or France and the Indian tribes. In 1815 there began a movement of the Shawnees and Delawares to the west. They seemed to have been promised other lands in consideration of their removal. Some of them went to Castor and St. Francois rivers; some of them settled on White river not far from Springfield. In 1825 a treaty was made with the Shawnees by which they exchanged their Spanish grants in the Cape Girardeau district for a tract of fifty square miles west of Missouri. They removed to these lands in what is now the Indian territory. In 1829 the Delawares gave up their title to the Cape Girardeau lands and moved further west. In 1832 the allied Delawares and Shawnees made a treaty by which they relinquished the very last of their lands and improvements in Southeast Missouri. This act extinguished the last title held by the Indians to the territory of Missouri.

While the Indians' lands were all transferred by this date (1832), not all the Indians themselves disappeared from this section of the state at that time. There are many persons now living who well remember when there were scattered bands of the Indians in Southeast Missouri. One of the last of these bands was that at the village of Chilletecaux, near Kennett. They remained here until game practically disappeared and it became impossible for them longer to live by hunting. Some of them died, and the survivors moved away, a few at a time, to the west. Most of them went to the Indian territory.

Some effort was made to educate the Indians, even in the early time. Rev. John Ficklin, a Baptist preacher of Kentucky, was sent by the Kentucky Mission Society to Missouri to secure some of the children in order to establish an Indian school in Scott county, Kentucky. He had an interview with the chief of a band of Shawnees and Delawares on the Maramec river. This chief was named Rogers. He was a white man, but had been taken prisoner by the Indians in boyhood and had been so trained by them that he was practically an Indian himself. He had married a young woman, a daughter of the chief, and because of his influence and talents had succeeded to the office. The Indians, under instructions of Captain Rogers, cultivated farms and opened a school in the village, which was attended by the children of the American settlers and of the Indians. These children studied their books in school hours and then engaged in shooting with a bow and arrow and other Indian pastimes, at intermission. One of the white children who began his early education in this mixed school was Rev. Louis Williams, who afterwards became a distinguished minister.

About the time of the cession Captain Rogers and his band had removed to Big Spring, at the head of the Maramec river. They intended to reside in this place, but the country was not suited to them and many of them died. They attributed these deaths to the influence of the evil spirit and moved away, settling in Franklin county, not far south of Union. The sons of Captain Rogers and Captain Fish, who succeeded him as chief, discussed with Reverend Ficklin the question of sending some of their children to Kentucky. Louis Rogers, a son of Captain Rogers, who could already read and write, offered to go to Kentucky, provided he were permitted to take his family with him. This was assented to, and some of the Indians went to Kentucky to this school. Peck ("Life of Peck," p. 111) says that this band of Indians were very thrifty farmers and brought the best cattle to the St. Louis market that the butchers received.

The Indian has now disappeared from Southeast Missouri. He no longer pursues the hunt through the forests, or causes the settler to tremble at the sound of the warhoop. His wigwam, his lodge of poles and mats, his implements of warfare, his tools and utensils no longer exist, or are found only in museums and collections of relics. The very mounds he reared as places for the burial of his dead, as sites for home or temple, are no longer sacred to the purposes for which he dedicated them, but are desecrated by the spade of the explorer and relic hunter, and his very erection of them is denied.

Most of those now living within the borders of the state never saw an Indian in his native haunts, and cannot reconstruct the life of the time when he formed an important part in the making of the history of the country. And yet we cannot give more than mere casual attention to the story of the development of Southeast Missouri, without discovering that the Indian once played a great part here. He has left ineffaceable traces of his life, and no one can ever hope to come to a complete understanding of our history without a study of Indian life and character.

SECTION II

Under France and Spain

CHAPTER V

STE. GENEVIEVE DISTRICT

THE NAME LOUISIANA—THE ILLINOIS— THE FRENCH AND SPANISH DISTRICTS WITH THEIR LIMITS—THE APPEARANCE AND CHARACTER OF THE COUNTRY—STE. GENEVIEVE—PROBABLE DATE OF FIRST SETTLEMENT—"THE OLD VILLAGE OF STE. GENEVIEVE" — ORIGINAL SETTLERS—OFFICIALS AND LEGAL PROCEEDINGS—OCCUPATIONS — THE "BIG FIELD" — INDIAN TROUBLES—LIFE OF THE FRENCH PIONEERS—POPULATION—PITTMAN'S ACCOUNT — VISIT OF PAUL ALLIOY—AS PECK SAW THE TOWN—IMPRESSIONS OF FLAG—FERDINAND ROZIER — JOHN JAMES AUDUBON—JOHN SMITH T.—HENRY DODGE—JOHN RICE JONES—NEW BOURBON—NEW TENNESSEE—TABLE OF SETTLEMENTS—FIRST SETTLERS IN IRON COUNTY—THE COOK AND MURPHY SETTLEMENTS—ST. MICHAEL'S—OLD MINES—FIRST SETTLERS IN JEFFERSON COUNTY—PERRY COUNTY SETTLEMENTS—LONG'S ACCOUNT.

La Salle applied to the territory along the Mississippi the name Louisiana. It was early divided by the French into two parts, Upper Louisiana which was north of the Arkansas river and Lower Louisiana which was south of the Arkansas. It should be said here that the whole territory on both sides of the river north of the Ohio was frequently called the country of the Illinois, and so various settlements and rivers were spoken of as being in the Illinois. They applied different names, also, to the rivers of the district. They called the Mississippi the river St. Louis, the Missouri they named the St. Philip, and the Wabash was called the St. James.

Upper Louisiana was divided into five districts: first, the district of St. Louis between the Missouri and the Maramec; second the district of Ste. Genevieve between the Maramec and Apple Creek; third the district of Cape Girardeau extending from Apple Creek to Tywappity bottom; fourth the district of New Madrid which reached south to the Arkansas river; and fifth the district of St. Charles which lay north of the Missouri river. All of these districts fronted on the Mississippi and extended an unknown distance to the west.

This country of Upper Louisiana, at the time the French began their settlements, was one of wonderful beauty and attractiveness. All explorers and travelers who visited it were enraptured with the country and the prospects of its development. Its hills and forests, its streams and springs were all of unusual beauty. The openness of the woods, the comparative absence of undergrowth made the woods both attractive and easy to travel through. The alluvial plains not yet changed by the earthquakes with their wide stretches of level woodland, with their great trees, were esteemed by many of the early travelers as the choicest part of all Upper

Louisiana. The country possessed many attractions for the French and especially for the French Canadians. The climate was milder than that of Canada, the rivers were open during the most of the year, and the forests abounded with game. Buffalo, deer, and turkeys were the most important of these. The streams were full of fish and the whole country swarmed in season with almost incredible flocks of geese, ducks, swans, and wild pigeons. It was a hunter's paradise, and to it were attracted many men because of the abundance of wild game. But there were other more solid attractions for the settlers. The district of Ste. Genevieve was exceedingly rich in minerals; that of New Madrid in fine soil and timber.

Within Upper Louisiana the French, attracted by all of these opportunities for acquiring wealth, planted settlements. The earliest of these were grouped about the mines. They were transient in nature. The first permanent settlement was made at Ste. Genevieve.

It is not possible to fix the exact date of the first settlement of Ste. Genevieve. Our records are not sufficient for us to determine the precise year in which it was founded. But while this is impossible we are able to carry the history of the town back to a date previous to that of any other settlement in the state, so that it is evident that here was made the first settlement of white men within the limits of Missouri. Not only is this true, but it was, in fact, the first French settlement west of the river and one of the first in

FIRST BRICK HOUSE BUILT WEST OF THE MISSISSIPPI
(Used as a Court House in 1785)

the valley of the Mississippi. Kaskaskia, Vincennes, and a few others are older, but only a few of them. Before there was a settlement at St. Louis, or St. Charles, or Cape Girardeau, or New Madrid, Ste. Genevieve was a thriving and prosperous village.

The original town was not located on the present site of Ste. Genevieve, but in the great common field about three miles south of the present town. This old town was called "le vieux village de Ste. Genevieve"— the old village of Ste. Genevieve. The site on which it stood has been swept away by the river. This old site was abandoned in 1785 owing to an unprecedented rise in the river which overflowed the entire town. So great was the flood and so vivid the impression it made on the people that this year was ever afterward known as the year of the great flood. By 1791 the removal to the new site was completed and the place where the old village had stood was gradually washed away by the river.

It is a matter of regret that we cannot fix the precise time when the first settlement here was begun. This, as has been stated, is not possible. Several considerations, however, enable us to fix the approximate date.

In the year 1881 there was discovered an old well on the bank of the river in the Big Field of Ste. Genevieve. The river had eaten away the earth from about the well until it stood up like a stone chimney. On a stone in the top of this well was the date 1732. A part of the stone containing the date was chipped off by Leon Jokerst, who discovered the old well, and preserved by him. The remainder of the old well was swept away by the currents of the river. This old well evidently belonged to some house in the outskirts of the old town, and the date is very probably the year in which the well was constructed. If this is the case then the first settlement was made sometime prior to 1732.*
There is still to be seen in the office of the recorder of deeds an affidavit made in 1825, by Julien Labriere, in which he deposes that he is fifty-six years of age, that he was born in the old village of Ste. Genevieve, that he remembered to have seen as a small child the first settler in the village, one Baptiste La Rose, then very old. The affidavit sets out also the recollections of Labriere concerning the removal to the new site.

Pittman who visited Ste. Genevieve in 1765 says that the first settlers came to Ste. Genevieve about twenty-eight years ago from Cascasquias attracted by the goodness of the soil and the plentiful harvests.†

Mrs. Menard of Ste. Genevieve as late as 1881 had in her possession what was perhaps the oldest legal document relating to the town. It was an account of the sale of a house and lot belonging to the estate of Laurent Gabouri. Jean Baptiste St. Gem was the purchaser. The property is described as located in the village of Ste. Genevieve which must have been an established village at the time of the transfer. The bill of sale is dated in December, 1754. The terms used in describing the property leave no doubt that the settlement was an old and well established one at that remote date and had been in existence for many years.‡

In the collection known as the Guibour Papers now in the Missouri Historical Society files are to be seen copies of petitions to the commandants of the district for land. In one of these Francois Rivard asks for a grant of land, which from the terms of the petition, must have been located near the vil-

* "History of Southeast Missouri," p. 241.
† "Mississippi Settlements," p. 95.
‡ Houck, "History of Missouri," Vol. I, p. 239.

lage for the petitioner promises to set aside a certain part of it for a church. The grant was made as requested and is dated 1752. It appears that at this time one Chaponga cultivated a part of what is now the Big Field of Ste. Genevieve. In the same year one Geneaux prays for a grant of land along the Saline Creek adjoining the land of one Dorlac who must have been in the Big Field also.

A fort named Fort Joachim was located in the old village during the year 1759. A reference to this old fort is to be found in the register of the Catholic church of Ste. Genevieve. Numerous other references to old events are found scattered through church records, in court proceedings and the letters and books of private persons. None of them give an exact date for the founding of the town, but all of them indicate that it was settled early in the eighteenth century.

The original settlers of the old village of Ste. Genevieve were Francisco Valle, Jean Baptiste Valle, Joseph Loisel, Jean Baptiste Maurice, Francois Maurice, Francois Coleman, Jaques Boyer, Henri Maurice, Parfait Dufour, Joseph Bequette, Jean Baptiste Thomure, Joseph Govreau, Louis Boldue, Jean Baptiste St. Gem, Laurent Gabouri, Jean Beauvais, B. N. Janis and J. B. T. Pratte.

Of these settlers the Valle family were very prominent, Francois Valle, Sr., and his sons Francois, Jr., and Jean Baptiste were all commandants of the post at various times. Francois, Jr., lived for many years in a large one story frame building on South Gabouri Creek. This house is still standing and is a typical French residence of that time. It is low but has large porches making it comfortable. The wife of Francois Valle was Louise Carpentier whom he married in 1777. They reared a number of children. One of the daughters of the family married Robert T. Brown of Perry county, another married Dr. Walter Fenwick who was afterward killed in a duel, a third daughter became the wife of Joseph Pratte, and the fourth married Captain Wilkinson. Francois Valle, Jr., died March 6, 1804, and was buried under his pew in the old Catholic church.

Jean Baptiste Valle, the brother of Francois, Jr., married Jane Barbau. He was a prosperous merchant and lived in Ste. Genevieve for a number of years. Another of the sons of Francois Valle, Sr., was named Charles. He married Pelagie Carpentier in 1769, and Marie Louise Valle the only daughter of Francois Valle, Sr., was married to Francois LeClerc in 1776.

Another of the influential families of the old village was the St. Gems, or as they are frequently known St. Gem Beauvais a shortening of St. Gem de Beauvais. Some members of the family finally discontinued the use of St. Gem in their name and became known as Beauvais. The founder of the family in this country was Jean Baptiste, who came to Kaskaskia about 1720 and was married in 1725 to Louise LaCrois at Fort Chartres. Their family consisted of five sons and two daughters. Two of the sons, Jean Baptiste, Jr., and Vital St. Gem, or as he was often called, Vital Beauvais, removed from Kaskaskia when that place was captured by Clark, to Ste. Genevieve. The former of the two brothers built what was perhaps the first grist mill west of the Mississippi. The house in which he lived for many years is still standing in Ste. Genevieve. He was an office holder for a number of years being one of the first judges of the Court of Common Pleas and Quarter Sessions remaining in office until his death. He was the father of six sons, Raphael, Joseph M. D., Bartholomew, Vital, John B. and August.

Vital St. Gem, the brother of Jean Baptiste, lived for a time at the Saline but came to Ste. Genevieve in 1791, the house in which he lived until his death was afterward occupied by Mrs. Menard and is still standing. He died in 1816.

John B. Pratte, who came to Ste. Genevieve about 1754, was one of the most successful merchants in the early history of the town. He held a number of local offices among them the chairmanship of the Board of Trustees of the town. His sons were Bernard, Joseph, Antoine, Bileron and Henry. The Pratte family now prominent in Ste. Genevieve county are descendents of John B. Pratte.

The Janis family, many of whose descendants are still to be found in Ste. Genevieve, came to the district very early in its history. The founder of the family was Nicholas Janis, who lived for a time in Kaskaskia. His sons were Francois, Antoine and Baptiste, his daughters were Felicite, who married Vital St. Gem; Catherine, who married Stephen Bolduc, and Francoise who became Madam Durocher.

The population of Ste. Genevieve increased very rapidly after the delivery of the territory east of the river from France to England. The French of Kaskaskia, Fort Chartres, Prairie du Rocher and Cahokia, unwilling to live under the government of England removed in large numbers across the river to St. Louis and Ste. Genevieve. This was from the years 1765 to 1769. Of course at this time the territory of Upper Louisiana had been transferred to Spain, but this change was not known to the French in this country, and accordingly they believed they were moving back under the flag of France. The first legal proceedings at Ste. Genevieve were had on the 19th day of May, 1766. In that year Rocheblave was Commandant, and M. Robinet was the notary and greffier. They were both officers of France and held office until November 22, 1769, when they gave way to the officers of Spain. This first legal proceeding was the drawing up of a marriage contract between Pierre Roy and Jeanette Lalond.

The court records and the official correspondence of the French and Spanish officials both at St. Louis and at New Orleans contain abundant evidence that Ste. Genevieve was a prosperous and flourishing village during the latter half of the eighteenth century. In 1769 Rui in a report to Governor O'Rielly says that the town contains fifty-five or sixty citizens, and Piernas in the same year says the population is about 600. Other statements made from time to time to the various Spanish Governors indicate that the town grew steadily, especially after its removal to its present site.

Among early officials was Phillip Rocheblave, who had been commandant at Kaskaskia at the time that post was taken by the Americans under George Rogers Clark, and after a somewhat adventurous life had made his way to St. Louis; he was there appointed commandant both civil and military of the post of Ste. Genevieve. He was succeeded by Francois Valle a member of one of the oldest and most influential families of Ste. Genevieve. Valle was succeeded by Francisco Cartabona de Oro, and he by Henri Peyroux De La Coudeniere. In 1796 Francois Valle, Jr., became commandant with both civil and military authority. He was succeeded by his brother Jean Baptiste who held the post until the transfer to the United

States and was continued in office by Governor William Henry Harrison. This Jean Baptiste was one of the most interesting characters in the early history of the town. He lived to a very great age and his descendants still occupy the old homestead in Ste. Genevieve.

The early settlers in Ste. Genevieve, while the town occupied the old site in the big field and which has long since been swept away by the river, were engaged principally in the cultivation of the soil of that big field. They had been attracted there largely by the richness of that soil, and in part by the opportunities for trade with the Indians, and in part also because of the nearness to the new mines then being opened up by Renault and his agents. These mines were situated on the Maramec river in what is now Washington county and at Mine La Motte. The lead produced by these mines was carried on horseback to Ste. Genevieve for transportation either down the river to New Orleans or else up the river to the Spanish post at St. Louis, which was then called Paincourt. Owing to the peculiar manner by which the pigs of lead were carried to Ste. Genevieve they were not cast in the usual shape but were moulded into a form resembling the collar of a horse and were then hung on the neck of the horse for transport. One of these peculiar pigs of lead was found some years ago by the side of the old road leading from the mines on the Maramec to Ste. Genevieve. It seems that some of the inhabitants of the town were engaged in mining and in the transportation of the lead. Others of them were early engaged in milling. They shipped flour and meal by way of the river to all the posts about them and as far south as New Orleans. In 1771 Matthew Kennedy, a merchant at Ste. Genevieve, shipped 1200 pounds of flour to a post on the Arkansas River. This shows that the trade of Ste. Genevieve, even at that early date, was extensive. It is a remarkable fact that the merchants and traders at St. Louis were accustomed to purchase a considerable part of their supplies in Ste. Genevieve.

In common with other settlers in Southeast Missouri, the people of Ste. Genevieve were much troubled by the Osage Indians. These Indians, whose principal camp was on the Osage river, extended their hunting and plundering operations over all the section, and were exceedingly troublesome. They were great thieves, being especially fond of horse stealing. They were accustomed to make raids upon the exposed farms and even upon houses in the outskirts of the village, to seize the horses and other property which attracted their attention and to carry it away. If resisted they frequently murdered the owner and burned his house. To assist in protecting themselves against these unpleasant raids the people of Ste. Genevieve procured the settlement of the old band of Peorias. These Indians from Illinois lived for many years in the vicinity of the town and took part in the resistance to the raids of the Osage Indians. They of course incurred the deadly hatred of the fierce and savage Osages and lived themselves in constant fear of them. They were afraid to venture on hunting expeditions which took them away from the immediate vicinity of the town and bewailed the fact that they were compelled to live like women on fish and the produce of the soil instead of living the life of men and warriors. The French, so long as they remained in control of the territory treated the outbreaks and outrages of the Osages with a great deal of leniency, but the Spanish on taking over the territory dealt with a firm hand with these matters and so we find that Baron Carondelet while in command in St. Louis organized the inhabitants of the various posts throughout his territory into companies of militia for the purpose of resisting and chastising the Indians. One of these companies was organized at Ste. Genevieve and we find records of its actual participation in the Indian troubles. On one occasion induced by a particularly flagrant outrage committed near New Madrid, all the companies of Southeast Missouri assembled for the purpose of inflicting punishment on the authors of the outrage and we find the little army composed of companies from St. Louis, Ste. Genevieve, Cape Girardeau and New Madrid assembling at Cape Girardeau and making its way to the south where the murderers were apprehended and summarily dealt with.

Life in Ste. Genevieve in these early years was not very different from pioneer life in other parts of the country. It was at first a typical French village. Some of the inhabitants were members of the old French families, but the greater part of them were of the peasant class. They were so shut off from the world, in the midst of a vast continent their nearest neighbors being sixty-five miles away at the little village of St. Louis, that they were dependent, almost entirely, upon themselves. News reached them from Europe only after the long voyage across the Atlantic and the almost equally as long and tedious voyage up the Mississippi, and so cut off from the world in an isolation difficult for us to comprehend, there developed the characteristic life of the frontier. The people were happy and industrious. They were religious by nature and provided liberally for the church. Their priests were held in high esteem and religion entered into all the affairs of their daily lives. They lived the free open life of a new country. They tilled the soil or voyaged on the river, they hunted or trapped in the great woods, or traded with the Indians, and somehow from it all they managed not only to live in considerable comfort, but to accumulate property. We find that Lambert La Fleur, who died in 1771, left an estate of about $14,000.00, all of which had been accumulated while a resident in Ste. Genevieve. But their industries and even their religion did not form all, or perhaps even the greatest part, of the life of the people of Ste. Genevieve. Being French they were fond of pleasure and amusement and they found both, even in the midst of the life in a frontier town. Their games, their social meetings, their dancing, their jests amused some of the courtly travelers who visited them direct from the King's court at Paris. They, no doubt, found all these things crude and even disagreeable to cultivated and refined tastes. Some of these travelers who were received by Ste. Genevieve with openhearted hospitality were rude enough to forget the duties of a guest and to write of their entertainment in a most sarcastic and cutting way. In spite of this, however, the people of the town found in their simple amusement and pleasure that relaxation from toil and care which is necessary to a healthy and sane life.

The first legal proceedings under Commandant Rocheblave were had on the 19th of May, 1766, it was the drawing up of a marriage contract between Pierre Roy and Jeanette Lalond. After that there was a record of the sale of land, the first sale of land was made by Pierre Aritfone to Henri Carpentier, another land sale was by Joseph LeDon to Le Febre du Couquette. In the same year there is a record of the sale of salt works on the Saline river with ten negroes and a lot of cattle by John LaGrange to one Blowin. In the year 1767 an appeal was prosecuted from the decision of the Commandant to the Cabildo at New Orleans.

One of the peculiar customs of old Ste. Genevieve was that of bringing all persons charged with crime to church on Sunday and exhibiting them before the congregation after the service in order that they might be known and recognized by the whole community.

The first baptism in the old village of Ste. Genevieve was performed by a Jesuit Missionary named P. M. Watrin, February 24, 1760; the first religious marriage was celebrated on October 30, 1764, by Father J. L. Meurin the parties were Mark Canada and Susan Henn, both of these persons had lived among the Indians, the woman for five years as a prisoner. This marriage was witnessed by Jean Ganion and T. Tebriege.

The great common field south of Ste. Genevieve was the most valuable possession of the inhabitants, this land was fenced at the expense of the entire town and at the beginning of each year a portion of the field was assigned to each resident who was expected to cultivate this and keep the fence in repair near his part of the field. If any one abandoned his land it was sold at a public sale at the church door. Plowing was done with a wooden plow and horses were seldom used but generally oxen were attached to the plow. Horses were used for pulling the charrette or cart; this cart had no iron fastenings or iron tires, the wheels were usually made of seasoned white oak with the hub of gum. From one to three horses were driven to the cart; when more than one horse was used they were driven tandem, the traces being of twisted rawhide. This cart was used for all kinds of work as well as for family use; when women traveled in them they were seated in chairs that were tied to the rail of the cart.*

Ste. Genevieve had a population of 945 in the year 1799 and 1,300 in 1804, one-third of the population were slaves. The trade was fairly large in early times, principal things bought and sold were lead and furs. The commercial men of Ste. Genevieve during the period from 1804 to 1820 were remarkably active and successful in their business pursuits. Ferdinand Rozier was one of the early merchants and was very successful in business; Louis Bolduc was another merchant who became very wealthy. It is said that at one time an American named Madden, who was also rich, offered to wager that he had more money than Bolduc; the latter, however, retorted by asking Madden to bring a half bushel measure in order to measure the silver money in Bolduc's cellar. Another wealthy trading firm was Menard & Valle. This firm was established in 1817, the year that the first steamboat made its way up the Mississippi river. Pierre Menard, one of the partners of this firm, was the Indian agent and controlled a great amount of trade throughout the west.

Pittman, who visited Ste. Genevieve in 1769 says that the town was settled 28 years previously by persons from Kaskaskia attracted by the goodness of the soil and the plentiful harvest and describes the situation of the village as very convenient, being within one league of the salt spring, which was for the general use of the French subjects. There were a number of works at the spring and large quantities of salt were made for the Indian hunters and other settlers. He says also that a lead mine which supplied the

* Rozier, "History of Mississippi Valley," p. 123.

Louis Boulduc's House, Ste. Genevieve

Louis Guibourd's House, Ste. Genevieve

whole country with shot was about 15 leagues distant. He further says: "The village of St. Louis is supplied with salt and other provisions from here. An officer appointed by the French Commandant as the entire regulation of the police here, is a company of militia commanded by a Mons. Vallet, who resides at this place and is the richest inhabitant of the country of the Illinois; he raises great quantities of corn and provisions of every kind, he has a hundred negroes besides hired white people constantly employed. The village is about one mile in length and contains about seventy families. Here is a very fine water mill for corn and plants belonging to Mons. Vallet."*

It is possible that the Vallet mentioned was a member of the family afterwards known as Valle.

In 1803 Paul Alliot visited Ste. Genevieve and says of it: "It is inhabited by twelve hundred people who are especially engaged in the cultivation of wheat and in the chase; they own lead mines from which they derive great profits. In their forests they find bears prodigiously fat and large, the oil from which is much sought after by the inhabitants, even by those of New Orleans. They raise good vegetables and make excellent butter and cheese. That city is large enough and rich enough to support a priest, yet it does not have any and the people are dying. They are governed by a Commandant who always terminates in a friendly manner the quarrels which arise among them.†

Peck, who visited the place in 1819, gives the following account of the place.

Ste. Genevieve is the oldest French Village in Missouri. When Laclede and the Chouteaus

* Pittman, "Mississippi Settlements," p. 96.
† Robertson, "Louisiana," Vol. I, p. 103.

came from New Orleans to establish a trading-post at St. Louis, in 1763, they stopped at Ste. Genevieve, which contained about twelve or fifteen families, in as many small cabins, but finding no warehouse or other building in which they could store their goods, they went on to Fort Chartres and wintered. We date the commencement of Ste. Genevieve as a village from the period of the erection of Fort Chartres, the second, about 1756. Very probably there were previous to this, as there were in the lead-mining districts, what are called in patois French, cabanes, a term expressing the idea of "shanties," a cluster of shelters for temporary purposes. Such cabanes were in the lead-mining district when Philip Francis Renault had his exploring parties out at various points in the upper valley of the Mississippi. And, by the way, I find no evidence that lead-mining was followed in the mining country after Renault, disappointed, and a "broken merchant," quit the business about 1740, until the possession of Illinois by the British about twenty-five years thereafter. Many of the French inhabitants who held slaves left the Illinois country; some went to the newly established town of St. Louis; others to Lower Louisiana. Many families also went to the lead mines in Missouri, while others stopped at Ste. Genevieve and New Bourbon with their servants. This gave an impulse to the former town, which before 1770 became the depot and shipping-port for the lead business. The French at St. Louis, as a nom-de-nique, called Ste. Genevieve Misere, as they did Cardondelet, Vide Poche; and in their turn received the nick-name of Pain Court, to indicate they were short of bread.

The old town of which I am writing was near the Mississippi, and about one mile below the ferry and landing. From this point, where the rock forms a landing, for seven miles down the river, was an extensive tract of alluvial bottom about three miles in width. On this rich alluvial the French of Ste. Genevieve and New Bourbon made one of the largest "common fields" to be found along the Upper Mississippi. It contained within the common enclosure from three thousand to four thousand acres. The repeated inundations of high water, and especially the great flood of 1784, drove the inhabitants to the high ground in the rear, where they built the old residences of the new town, or the existing Ste. Genevieve. Each successive flood tore away the rich bottom along the river, until that of 1844 about "used up" the great common field of the village. No passenger in passing up or down the great expansive bend of the river would hardly realize that the largest steamers now float in a channel that is more than two miles from the Mississippi river as it ran in 1780.*

When Flagg visited the Ste. Genevieve district in 1836, he says that the town then contained about eight hundred inhabitants though its population was once said to have exceeded two thousand. Among the persons whom he met at that time was Jean Baptiste Valle who was one of the chief proprietors of Mine La Motte, and though at that time more than ninety years of age, was almost as active as when he was fifty. Flagg gave this description of Ste. Genevieve at that time: "Ste. Genevieve is situated about one mile from the Mississippi, upon a broad alluvial plain lying between branches of a small stream called the Gabourie; beyond the first botton rises a second stepped and behind this is a third attaining an elevation of more than one hundred feet from the water edge. Upon this elevation was erected some twenty years since a handsome structure of stone commanding a noble prospect of the river, the broad American bottom on the opposite side and the bluffs beyond Kaskaskia. It was intended for a literary structure but owing to unfavorable reports with regard to the health of its situation, the design was abandoned and the structure was never completed. is now in a state of ruins and enjoys the reputation, however, of being haunted, in very sooth its aspect viewed from the river at twilight, with its broken windows outlined against the western sky is wild enough to warrant such an idea or any other. The court house and Catholic chapel constitute the public buildings. To the south of the village and looking upon the river is situated the common field originally comprising two thousand arpents, but it is now much less in extent and is yearly diminishing from the action of the current upon the alluvial banks. These common fields were granted by the Spanish government as well as the French to every village started under their domination. A single enclosure at the expense of the villagers, was erected and kept in repair; the lot of every individual was separated from his neighbors by double furrow. Near this field the village was formerly located but in the inundation of 1785, called by the habitants, L'annee des grandes eaux, when so much of the bank was washed away that the settlers were forced to secure a more elevated site. The Mississippi was at this time swelled thirty feet above the highest water mark before known and the town of Kaskaskia and the whole American bottom was inundated."†

Flagg says that at the time he visited, in 1836, the immense caves of pure white sand,

* "Life of Peck," p. 78.

† Flagg's "Far West," p. 95.

at not a great distance from Ste. Genevieve, were being opened and quantities of sand sent to Pittsburg for the manufacture of flint glass. He speaks also of a number of beautiful fountains in the neighborhood, one of them of surpassing loveliness.

Flagg also comments on the shot factories at Herculaneum and speaks with very great delight of the great rocks above Herculaneum called "Cornice" rocks.

One of the prominent citizens of Ste. Genevieve was Ferdinand Rozier. He was born in the city of Nantes, France. He had been in the French navy and came to America, settling first in Philadelphia, afterward in Kentucky, and finally removing to Ste. Genevieve in 1812. Rozier engaged in trade immediately upon his arrival, and continued in business to the end of his life. He was a man of enterprise and ability and had branch stores at Perryville and Potosi. Many of the goods bought and sold in those days came from the East and in the course of his trade Rozier made six trips between Ste. Genevieve and Philadelphia on horseback. A single trip of this kind at the present date would be considered a very great undertaking, to say nothing of six of them. Rozier left a large family, many of whose members have been, and are still, prominent in Missouri.

Associated with Rozier, for a number of years, was the famous naturalist, John James Audubon. Like the family of Rozier, his family lived in Nantes; the naturalist was born, however, in Louisiana, where the family resided for a short time. When John James Audubon was but a child, the family returned to France, and he was educated in the French schools. One of his teachers was the famous painter, David. Audubon and Rozier entered the navy together during the French Revolution. They served in the navy for only a short time and finally decided to emigrate to' America. They first lived in Pennsylvania, then in Kentucky, visiting in Springfield and Louisville, and spending in this state the time from 1807 to 1810. In 1810 they purchased a keel-boat, loaded it with provisions and whiskey and voyaged in it to Ste. Genevieve. Audubon's account of this voyage up the Mississippi river is a very interesting one. He pictures the scenes on the river and the slow progress of the keel-boat in a very remarkable manner. The two men embarked in business in Ste. Genevieve, together, and were very successful. The success of the business, however, depended entirely upon Rozier, for Audubon had no taste for business at all, but spent his time in the woods hunting and painting birds. In 1811 he sold his interest in the business and returned to Kentucky. Here he devoted himself for a time to business, but finally gave up entirely to the study of nature, becoming one of the greatest ornithologists of the world.

One of the famous men of this period in Missouri was the celebrated John Smith T. He was a native of Georgia, but had lived in Tennessee before coming to Missouri. He removed to Ste. Genevieve about the year 1800 and afterwards lived at a little town called Shibboleth, in Washington county. Smith was a tall, slender man, of the mildest appearance and the most courteous manners, the very last man, judging by his appearance only, to be considered at all dangerous. He was, however, a man of terrible passions and when aroused he was one of the most dangerous men in the history of the state. He was famous for his skill with the pistol and the rifle, and he had many encounters of a most serious and bloody character. His house resembled an arsenal, for it was filled with arms and weapons of every kind. He, himself, was a skilled mechanic, and kept slaves who were expert in the making of weapons. Smith's principal business was that of mining. He had at first entered into Burr's schemes for invading Mexico, but withdrew from that when they were warned by the proclamation of President Jefferson. Col. Smith was selected at one time to visit Washington, and represent the people of the territory before Congress. In 1806 he was appointed one of the Territorial Judges of the court of General Quarter Sessions. In spite of his numerous difficulties and duels, and in spite of the enemies which he had, Smith finally died a natural death, and was buried in St. Louis.

Henry Dodge was born at Vincennes, October 12, 1782. He was the son of Israel Dodge and his wife, Nancy Hunter. Israel Dodge, it will be remembered, was one of the first American settlers in Upper Louisiana, having come to the Ste. Genevieve district prior to 1800. The family engaged in the manufacture of salt on Saline creek. Henry Dodge was a very prominent and influential man. He served for a time as sheriff of Ste. Genevieve county; his greatest service, however, was rendered in a military way. On the breaking out of the Indian troubles, about the time of the war of 1812, Dodge was appointed as a general in the territory of militia. During that time he was exceedingly active in protecting the frontiers from the Indians. He lived in Ste. Genevieve until the year 1827, when he removed to Wisconsin. During the Black Hawk war, he was in command of some of the American troops, and defeated Black Hawk and the Indians. He also served in the army during the campaign against the Indians in the south and in 1835 was in charge of the expedition of the west. He was appointed Governor of Wisconsin territory for two terms and afterward was elected to the senate from Wisconsin. During his residence in Missouri he served as a member of the constitutional convention, and was prominent among those who helped to frame the constitution.

The first resident of Washington county, during this period, was a native of Wales. This was John Rice Jones, who was born in Wales in 1759. He was a soldier in the Revolutionary army, and assisted George Rogers Clark in the capture of Vincennes. Before coming to Missouri, he lived for a time in Vincennes and also in Kaskaskia. In 1804 he removed to Ste. Genevieve where he continued in the practice of law. He afterward fixed his residence at Potosi. He acquired a large practice, for he was a good lawyer, and full of energy and devotion to his clients. He was one of the prominent members of the constitutional convention, representing Washington county. He lived to the age of sixty-five, and two of his sons, John Augustus Jones and Hon. George W. Jones, were very prominent in public life, the latter being, at one time, United States senator from Iowa.

As we have seen Ste. Genevieve was the administrative center of a district and the residence of a commandant. This district included a large territory. Within it were the present counties of Ste. Genevieve, Perry, Jefferson, Washington, Madison, and Iron. During the period with which we are now engaged, extending from the visit of DeSoto to 1804, settlements were made in all these counties. All these settlements were under the authority of the commandant of Ste. Genevieve. Within the present county of Ste. Genevieve only two settlements besides Ste. Genevieve itself were made at this time.

They were "Novelle Bourbon" or New Bourbon and New Tennessee.

New Bourbon was situated about two and one-half miles from the old village of Ste. Genevieve. Its site was on a hill which overlooked a strip of plain about one league in width, lying between it and the river. The settlement here was made in 1793 by order of Baron Cardondelet. Cardondelet was at this time lieutenant governor of Upper Louisiana with headquarters at St. Louis. He founded this colony and made it a separate administrative division in order to give a place to Pierre De Hault De Lassus De Luziere who was made the commandant of New Bourbon. It was the intention to bring to this new settlement the colony of French nobles who had emigrated from France during the Revolution and had formed a settlement in Ohio called Gallipolis. The scheme for bringing these French nobles was never carried into effect fully, but some of them came and made their home here near Ste. Genevieve. The authority of the commandant at this place extended west to Mine La Motte. At New Bourbon there was a small mill erected in 1793 on the creek now called Dodge's creek. The mill was built by Francois Valle and afterward sold to Israel Dodge. It was the first mill west of the Mississippi river.

The settlement called New Tennessee was made in what is now Saline township. The first settlers here were Peter Bloom and Thomas Madden. Both of them had formerly lived at Ste. Genevieve. Others who lived in the vicinity were Nicholas Counts, Joseph Hughes, Jesse Bryant, William Painter, John and Edward Walsh, Elder Wingate Jackson. who was a Bapitst preacher, and John McFarland, who was a minister of the Methodist church. This settlement was made about the year 1800.

The following table gives the larger number of the settlements in the Ste. Genevieve district made before the transfer to the United States in 1804. The dates are as accurate as can now be given:

Ste. Genevieve 1735
Old Mines in Washington county......1748
Mine a Breton near Potosi............1775
In Bois Brule Bottom.................1787
On the Cinque Homme in Perry county.1788
New Bourbon near Ste. Genevieve.....1793
Ally's Mines on Big River in St. Francois county 1797
On the Aux Vases in Perry county.....1797
On the Brazeau in Perry county......1797
On Establishment creek in Perry county.1797
The Fenwick Settlement on Apple creek.1797
In Bellevue Valley....................1798
Murphy Settlement now Farmington...1798
Herculaneum 1798
Cook's Settlement southwest of Farmington 1799
On Joachim creek in Jefferson county..1799
St. Michael now Fredericktown........1800
On the Saline in Perry county........1800
Between Joachim and the Plattin......1801

William Reed was the first settler in the Bellevue Valley in Iron county. He came in 1798, having received permission of De Luziere the Spanish official in charge at New Bourbon. Solomon George came about the same time and made his home on the Little St. Francois. Elisha Baker came to the same settlement from the Bois Brule Bottom in 1798, being accompanied by his son Elijah. Joseph Reed, a nephew of William, was another of the early settlers. Near the vicinity of Big River Mills in St. Francois county, a settlement, was begun in the year 1796. The men who located there at that time were John Ally, Andrew Baker, Francis Starnater and John Andrews. They had marked out their claims two years earlier than this. At first they did not erect houses, but lived for a time in camps. This settlement grew rapidly and soon became one of great importance. On the first day of March, 1797, Henry Fry and Rebecca Baker, two inhabitants of this settlement, accompanied by a number of their friends, set out for Ste. Genevieve; they intended to be married at that place. There was no one nearer than Ste. Genevieve who was authorized to perform a marriage ceremony. While on their way in the vicinity of Terre Blue, they were met by a party of Osage Indians who stopped them and robbed them of everything they possessed. These circumstances compelled them to return to the settlement and postpone the intended marriage for one year.

In 1798, Reverend William Murphy, said to have been a Baptist minister, living in Tennessee, together with his son William and a friend named Cyrus George, came to Upper Louisiana and received permission from the authorities to form a settlement in St. Francois county. The site chosen by them is that of the present town of Farmington. William Murphy returned to Tennessee and died while there. In 1801 other sons of William Murphy came to the settlement and began to open farms on the land granted to them. Sarah Murphy, the widow of the minister, determined to make the trip from Tennessee to Louisiana and to take possession of the land which had been granted to her husband; this she did in 1803. The party with whom she came consisted of three sons, Isaac, Jesse and Dubart, a daughter, a grand-son, and a negro woman. The journey was made in a keel-boat down the Tennessee river and then up the Mississippi to Ste. Genevieve. It was a most arduous undertaking and it was only after very great difficulty and dangers that the party arrived at the settlement which came to be called Murphy's. Mrs. Murphy was a sister of David Barton, afterward United States senator from Missouri, and was a woman of great intelligence and force of character. She organized and taught the first Sunday school west of the Mississippi river. This was probably in the year 1807.

Some others who early settled in the vicinity were Michael Hart and his son Charles, his son-in-law Davis F. Marks, Isaac Mitchell, Isaac Burnham, James Cunningham and John Robinson.

The settlement which came to be called Cook's in the southeast part of St. Francois county, still bears the same name. The first settler here was Nathaniel Cook who came in the year 1800. Cook was a prominent and influential man, having been one of the first judges of the court of Quarter Sessions held at Ste. Genevieve and was also elected Lieutenant Governor of the state at the first election for state officers. He afterward resided in Madison county near Fredericktown. Others of the early settlers here were James Caldwell, William Holmes, Jesse Blackwell, Elliott Jackson, and James Davis.

The first people who came to Madison county were miners and their stay was ordinarily transitory; the first men who came to settle on a farm within the county was John Callaway, who came from Kentucky in 1799, and obtained a grant on Saline creek near the head of the Little St. Francois about the same time the sons of Nicholas Lachance settled on Castor creek. Their father lived at

New Bourbon in Ste. Genevieve county. Other early settlers were William Easum and James and Samuel Campbell, who at some time before 1803, built cabins near the St. Francois and cultivated the land. John Walther came to the county in 1882 as did Christopher Anthony, John L. Pettit, Daniel Phillips and William and Thomas Crawford.

In 1800 the Spanish authorities granted four hundred arpents of land to thirteen individuals, the land lying between Saline creek and the Little St. Francois. On the land so granted a settlement was soon made which was called St. Michael; it is now the town of Fredericktown. The early residents were Peter Chevalier, Paul, Andrew and Baptiste De Guire, four brothers, whose name was Caillot, called also Lachance, Gabriel Nicollo, Pierre Variat and three others whose names are not known. These settlers all came from other settlements in this district. They engaged in farming and also in lead mining at Mine LaMotte which is only a few miles distant.

The first settlement in Washington county was made at Mine a Breton about 1763. Those who made this settlement were miners interested in working the mine discovered by Breton. Near the same time work was begun in the mines known as Old Mines and a little settlement of miners sprung up there. Most of the settlers at both these places came from Ste. Genevieve, New Bourbon and Kaskaskia.

In 1799 the Spanish government made a grant of a large tract of land to Moses Austin covering a part of Mine a Breton. On his part he was to erect a smelter for the reduction of lead ores. By 1804 there were about twenty families living in the village on his grant. They mined and farmed but had no grants from the government. They seemed to have been either squatters on government land or else tenants of Austin. Austin brought his family to Mine a Breton in June, 1799, and says of the country at that time that the whole number of inhabitants on Renault's fork of Grand river did not exceed sixty-three or sixty-four persons. In 1802 fifteen French families settled at Old Mines and reopened the work there which had been suspended. One year later thirty-one residents of this place received from Gov. Delassus a grant of 400 arpents of land each. Other mines were opened in the county about the same time and a shifting and unstable population grew up around each of them.

Perhaps the first permanent settlement of persons intending to make the country their home and to engage in agriculture was made near the present town of Caledonia in 1798. In that year Ananias McCoy, Benjamin Crow, and Robert Reed, all from Tennessee, settled in the Bellevue valley about twelve miles south of Potosi. Others followed them and the settlement prospered. These men were farmers and the products of their soil were carried to Ste. Genevieve on horses or in carts. They soon built mills for themselves and became unusually prosperous. Their situation was very good and they enjoyed the advantages of fertile soil, plenty of water power and proximity to the mining region. By 1822 the county had a population of 2,769.

The first settler in Jefferson county was John Hildebrand, who was of French descent and who made a settlement on the Maramec near the farm of Isaac Sullens, in 1774. Hildebrand received a grant of a considerable tract of land from the Spanish government which was afterward confirmed by the United States.

In 1778 this grant passed into the possession of Thomas Tyler, another of the early settlers of the county. In 1776 the King of Spain began the opening of a road to extend from St. Louis to Ste. Genevieve and afterward to New Madrid; this road, which came to be called the King's highway, crossed the Maramec river not far from its mouth, passed near Kimswick, Sulphur Springs, Pevely, Horine, Rockfort Hill and on to Ste. Genevieve. In order to provide a ferry across the Maremec river a grant was made by the government to Jean Baptiste Gomache. In 1776 Gomache located 1,050 arpents of land at the mouth of the Maramec river and established a ferry about one mile above the mouth, which he operated for a number of years. In 1779 a settlement was made near Kimswick and in the same year one near Montesano Springs, the latter one was made for the purpose of obtaining salt. In 1786 Benito Vasquez located at the mouth of Saline creek.

By the close of the 18th century there were a number of settlers living along the Maramec river; west of the river near the settlement made by Hildebrand were John Boli, Benito Vasquez, John Cummins, Jacques Clamorgan, Antonio Soulard, John Charpenter, Levi Theel, John Seindre, John Romain, James Steward, Baptiste Raniller, August Gomache, Jean Baptiste Gomache and Hardy Ware; east of the river were William Boli, Gabriel Cerre, Joachim Roy, Pierre Tanot, Charles Jones, Joseph Neybour, Baptiste Riviere, Sophia Shafer and Phyllis Bocarie.

The first mill in Jefferson county was built in 1802 on Big river about three-quarters of a mile above Morse's mill, by Francis Widener. Some of the logs in the old dam are still to be seen.

The first town laid out in the county was New Hartford, which was situated not far from Riverside on the Mississippi river, the settlers were Christian Witt and John Honey, who in 1806 opened a store and built a shot tower on the site of their proposed town.

Other early settlers in the county besides those mentioned, were Peter McCormack who settled on the Plattin in 1802, James Head, who built a cabin near House's spring in 1805. A year later Head sold his cabin and claim to Adam House for whom the spring was afterward named; House was later brutally killed by some Indians during their raid. William Null settled Hematite in 1800 and John Boli on Romin's creek in 1788.

The first Protestant services within Jefferson county were held at Bates Rock on the Mississippi river in 1798 by John Clark, Clark was at that time an Independent Methodist preacher who lived in Illinois, he afterward became a Baptist and preached for many years in Missouri and Illinois. The first church house was a log cabin erected by the Baptists on the land of John Boli at the headwaters of Saline creek; in what is now known as Maramec settlement, this was not far from the place located by John Hildebrand. The date of the building of the first meeting house cannot now be determined but it was probably about 1825. In 1836 the Baptists built another log meeting house in Upper Sandy settlement and used it until 1840.

The oldest Catholic church in the county is the church of the Immaculate Conception at Maxville, and it was established in 1845.

A Lutheran church known as St. Johns was organized in Rock township in 1843; both these churches are still in existence.

The settlements in Perry county were made in the Bois Brule Bottom opposite Kaskaskia, along the Cinque Homme, the Saline, the Brazeau, the Aux Vases, on Establishment creek, and on Apple creek. The Bois Brule Bottom is one of the most fertile pieces of territory in the district of Ste. Genevieve. It was the fertility of this soil which attracted the early settlers. Some of these were John Baptist Barsaloux, who came in the year 1787, William Lowry, and on the Cinque Homme, Levy Wiggins, John Duval, William Boyce, Isadore Moore. Over on the Saline were a number of settlers from Kentucky. In memory of their Kentucky home they called the open territory on which they settled "The Barrens." Some of these settlers were Tuckers, Laytons, Moores, Haydens. Israel Dodge and his son who have been mentioned in connection with New Bourbon were operating a salt works at the mouth of the Saline in 1804. These salt works had been in operation more or less continuously for a long time, even at that early date; they probably were begun before the first permanent settlement in Upper Louisiana. Others on this stream were Thomas Madden, Job Westover and John Hawkins.

Thomas Dodge was, perhaps, the first man who lived on the Aux Vases. Other claims have been located on this stream before his time, but he seems to have been the first actual settler. He bought his claim from De Guire.

The Fenwick settlement was made on Brazeau creek; this is not far from the present town of Wittenberg; the grant was made to Joseph Manning, but the first settler was George A. Hamilton. General Harrison, who moved here from New Madrid, also had a grant on which is now located the town of Altenberg.

A little below the mouth of the Kaskaskia is a creek called the Saline entering on the west side a grant of a tract of land one league square made by the Spanish government in favor of a Frenchman named Pegreau, the founder of the deserted town called New Bourbon. The tract included a valuable brine spring near the mouth of the creek. The proprietor built a house near the bank of the Mississippi where he resided a long time and where he carried on the manufacture of salt, but having occasion to go to France he rented his works to a man who for want of funds or for some other reason, failed to keep them in operation.[*]

Long says[†] that when he visited Missouri, which was in 1819, that the important populous part of the section was the country immediately below the mouth of the Missouri including the town of St. Louis and the villages of Florissant, Carondelet, Herculaneum, Ste. Genevieve, Bainbridge, Cape Girardeau, Jackson, St. Michaels and the country in their immediate vicinity. The lead mine tract, including Mima, Berton, Potosi and Bellevue were also populous; besides these he says there were a number of other settlements and small villages in this part of the territory. This visit to New Madrid was made in 1811 just before the earthquake.

[*] "Long's Expedition," p. 99.
[†] "Long's Expedition," p. 126.

CHAPTER VI

CAPE GIRARDEAU DISTRICT

Its Limits—Life of Lorimier—First Settlement at Cape Girardeau—Influence With the Indians—Grants of Authority and Land—Lorimier's Tomb—Name of Cape Girardeau—Cousin—Early Settlers—The Town Laid off—Some of the Early Buildings—First Incorporation, 1808—Early Settlers Within the District—The Ramsays—The Giboneys—Other Early Families—Settlements in Various Parts of the District.

The district of Cape Girardeau was established about the year 1793, but its boundaries were not clearly defined. It was supposed to extend from Apple creek to Tywappity Bottoms. Its western boundary was not fixed. Considerable difficulty arose between commandants at Cape Girardeau and those at New Madrid concerning the boundary between their respective districts. The commandant at New Madrid insisted that the Cape Girardeau district extended west only to the St. Francois river, and that his authority extended west of that stream. The southern boundary of the Cape Girardeau district was also in dispute for a number of years. The Governor General of Louisiana finally fixed this boundary at a point five miles below the present town of Commerce. This line was afterward surveyed by Anthony Soulard the Surveyor-General of Louisiana.

The first settlement within the district as thus marked out was made early in the year 1793, by Louis Lorimier.

Little is known of the early life of Lorimier. For a long time it was not known where he was born. We now know that he was born near the city of Montreal, Canada. Just before the breaking out of the Revolutionary war, a man whose name was spelt "Loromie" and also "Laramie" came from Canada to Shelby county, Ohio, and established a trading station between the Miami and the Maumee. This station was called Pickawilly. It was also called from its founder, Laramie Station. Here was carried on an extensive trade with the Indians. Furs were bought from them, and fire-arms, food, ammunition, and whiskey sold to them. The man, Loromie, was a Tory and his place in Ohio became the headquarters for plots against the Americans. The Indians were incited here to make raids against the Americans. Loromie had great influence with them, having married an Indian woman and being possessed of great insight into Indian character. So well known was the place as the headquarters for plots and raids that, in 1782, General Clark of the American army came up from Kentucky with a force and destroyed the place. The following account is taken from the history of Ohio:

"At the time of the first settlement of Kentucky, a Canadian Frenchman, named Loramie, established a store or trading station among the Indians. This man was a bitter enemy of the Americans, and it was for a long time the headquarters of mischief toward the settlers.

"The French had the faculty of endearing themselves to the Indians, and no doubt Loramie was in this respect fully equal to any of his countrymen, and gained great influence over them. So much influence had Loramie with the Indians that, when Gen. Clark, from Kentucky, invaded the Miami valley in the autumn of 1782, his attention was attracted to the spot. He came on, burnt the Indian settlement there, and plundered and burnt the store of the Frenchman. Soon after this Loramie with a colony of the Shawnees immigrated to the Spanish territory west of the Mississippi and settled in the spot assigned them, at the junction of the Kansas and Missouri rivers, where the remaining part of the natives from Ohio have at different times joined them."

This account agrees with the following from "Knapp's History of the Miami Valley:"

"In 1769 a Canadian French trader, named Peter Loramie, established a store at Pickawillany, situated on the west side of the Great Miami river, at the mouth of Loramie's creek. He was a man of energy and a good hater of the Americans. For many years he exercised great influence among the Indians. After his arrival the place was called 'Loramie's Station.' During the Revolution Loramie was in full fellowship with the British. Many a savage incursion to the border was fitted out from his supply of war material. So noted had his place become as the headquarters of spies, emissaries, and savages, that Gen. Clark, of Kentucky, resolved to pay it a visit, which he did with a large party of Kentuckians in the fall of 1782. The post was taken by surprise, and Loramie barely escaped being made a prisoner. His store was rifled of its contents, and burned to the ground, as were all the other habitations in the vicinity. Poor Loramie shortly afterward removed with a party of Shawnese to a spot near the junction of the Kansas and Missouri rivers where he closed his days."

It will be seen that these two accounts agree in saying that this man, whose name is given as Peter Loramie, after the loss of his property in Ohio removed to Louisiana and settled on the Kansas and the Missouri. We find, however, that no Peter Loramie was known in Louisiana, and no man of that name lived at the junction of these two rivers. Doubtless these statements are erroneous, but they seem to refer to Louis Lorimier. The identity of Louis Lorimier with the man who had a trading post at Loramie's Station seems to be conclusively established by the following letter on file in Ste. Genevieve, in connection with the suit brought by Lorimier against a certain trading company:

"MIAMIS, 4th May, 1787.—Dear Sir: We learn from common report that you had left Port St. Vincents, with an intention to seize Mr. Louis Lorimier's goods. We have received from him about eight packs, and on our arrival here Mr. Sharp went to see him, on purpose to know his reasons for leaving this country. His reasons appeared to him pretty good, and as he had no property along with him, on purpose to get his peltry and gain his good will, we were induced to advance a few things, as he says, to assist him. A few days after Mr. Sharp left him, he got intelligence of your going to seize his goods, and he wrote a letter expressing his surprise at our duplicity.

"What we have to say on the subject is neither more nor less than this, that the Spaniards have invited the Delawares and Shawnese to their side of the Mississippi. With a tribe of the latter Mr. Lorimier goes, and expects the Spaniards will allow him to follow them. If this is the case and he well inclined, we think he may do better than was expected, and as the company means to have somebody there to do this business, it might in some measure atone for the loss of the Port Vincent's (Vincennes) trade, which will never be renewed.

"We wrote you yesterday at some length. You will be the best judge how to act in regard to Lorimier, but we think his intentions are honest.

"Sir, your very humble servants,
GEORGE SHARP.
THOMAS SHEPHERD.
"To Hugh Heward, Mouth Illinois."

We are unable to give many of the details of Lorimier's life previous to his coming to Missouri, but after that time we have reasonable grounds for believing that we know most of events in his life. In 1787 he settled on the Saline in Ste. Genevieve county where he made his home for six years.

The Spanish authorities soon recognized him as a man having great influence with the Indians, resulting in part from his long life of trading with them, in part from the real power and energy which he possessed. They saw in him a fit agent for carrying out their plans, which were to induce the Indians to settle west of the river. They wanted these Indians here because Spain and France were engaged in war, and Spain feared very greatly that the United States would take part in this war on the side of France. The Spanish officials hoped by securing the help of the Indians that they could use them to harass the Americans in such a way as to prevent their giving any assistance to the French and they further expected that their Indian allies would be very useful to them in securing information of hostile movements.

In 1792, the Spanish were in great fear of an invasion from across the river and Lorimier was employed to concert with the Spanish officials plans for defense. He was ordered to New Madrid in that year to confer with Portelle the commandant of the post of New Madrid. Lorimier had had some unpleasant experiences with Portelle arising over some of Lorimier's trading operations. He was reluctant to trust himself within Portelle's power at New Madrid and it was difficult to persuade him to do so. Finally he consented, however, and went to New Madrid where steps were taken to protect Spanish territory. He spent the fall and winter of that year engaged in these matters. He crossed the Mississippi, visited Indian chiefs, and induced many of them to come to this side. In all of this work he displayed great adaptability, energy, and loyalty. He was successful in his efforts with the Indians and large numbers of his friends, the Shawnees and Delawares came to Upper Louisiana.

In recognition of this service the following grant of authority was made to him, the text being a translation: "Baron of Carondelet, follower of the religion of St. John, Colonel of the royal armies, Governor, Intendant General, Vice-Regent of the Province of Louisiana and Western Florida, Inspector of the Army, etc.

"Know all men by these presents, that in consideration of the true and faithful services which Louis Lorimier has rendered to the state since he became a subject of her Catholic Majesty, we permit him to establish himself with the Delawares and Shawnese who are under his care, in such places as he may think proper in the province of Louisiana on the west bank of the Mississippi, from the Missouri to the River Arkansas, which may be unoccupied, with the right to hunt, and cultivate for the maintenance of their families, nor shall any commandant, officer or other subject of the king hinder them, nor occupy of the land for him and the said Indians, sown, planted or laid out, so much as is judged necessary for their maintenance; and be it further understood that in case they should remove elsewhere, the said lands shall become vacant and as for the house, which the said Sir Louis Lorimier has built at Girardeau, it will remain in his possession, nor can he be removed for any causes, except those of illicit trade or correspondence with the enemies of the State.

"In testimony of which we have given these presents, signed with our hand and the countersign of the secretary of the Government, and caused to be affixed our official seal at New Orleans, the 4th of January, 1793.

"THE BARON OF CARONDELET.

"By order of the Governor, Andres Lopez Armesto."

This grant of authority was accompanied by the following letter from Zenon Trudeau the Lieutenant-Governor:

"ST. LOUIS, Mo., May 1, 1793.—The within is a permit which the Governor-General gives you to make your trade with the Delawares and the Shawnese, so extended that there may be nothing more to desire, without fear that you will be troubled by any officer of the king as long as you do as you have heretofore done. He recommends you to maintain order among the savages, and to concentrate them, so that he may be sure that they will take position more on the frontier of our settlements in order to lend us help in case of a war with the whites, and they will thus also be opposite the Osages, against whom I shall declare war forthwith, a thing I have not yet done, because I have to take some precautions before that shall reach them. Inform the Delawares, Shawnese, Peorias, Potawattomies and the other nations which presented a memorial, last September, that it is on account of the bad treatment that they have suffered, that the Governor-General has determined upon the war, in order to procure quiet for our land; the Osages are at present deprived of aid and harassed by us and by them, they will surely be open to reason; that consequently all the red nations must agree to lend a hand; it is their good which the Government seeks; and it is of that that you must convince them, so that the offended nations will take some steps toward the others to secure their aid, and particularly that the Iowas, Sacs and Foxes shall not consent to let the Osages come so far as to trade on the river Des Moines, and that still less shall they allow the English to introduce themselves by that river, which is a possibility.

"Protected by the Government, you owe it your services in closely watching over all that tends to its prosperity, and averting everything which is to its detriment. At this moment we fear nothing from Congress, but from the ill-disposed which depend upon it, posted in advantageous places, to give advice of the least assemblage. I am confident that as soon as you are cognizant of it you will make it known to the commandants with whom you are connected, as much for our safety as for our defense.

"The Governor has approved of the distribution of the twenty thousand beads which I have given the Delawares, and to which you have contributed. It has been my intention to reimburse you, and to-day I can do it with greater facility, because they have offered me the means without looking for them elsewhere, so you may draw on me at the rate of six per thousand, which the king has agreed for me to pay.

"I am told that you are coming to St. Louis with your savages. Because I am deprived of all merchandise, their visit will be a little embarrassing. Therefore I ask you to come by yourself (when your presence here is necessary) and attend to it, that when the boats arrive you are here to make a suitable present to the savages.

"May God take you in His holy keeping.
"ZENON TRUDEAU.

"P. S.—I keep your permit for an occasion to which I can intrust it. It states that you shall not be troubled from the Missouri to the Arkansas in your trade, also in the settlements or encampments which you have formed with the savages, the Shawnese and Delawares, etc. and that you shall be protected at Cape Girardeau."

It will be seen that this grant conferred great privileges upon Lorimier. In the spring of 1793, in anticipation of this grant, he had removed from the Saline to Cape Girardeau. Here he built a house and established himself with his Indian friends and allies. They settled on unoccupied lands and engaged in hunting over a large part of Missouri and Arkansas.

In 1796, Lorimier made another trip east of the river gathering more Indians who were brought to this side of the river. He was an active and energetic man, and was moved not only by devotion to Spain, but also by hatred to the Americans. He had never forgotten nor forgiven the destruction of his property in Ohio, and he seemed to take great pleasure in doing everything he could to injure the people of the United States. In recognition of this and other services he received from time to time grants of land which, by the year 1797, aggregated 8,000 arpents. This land included the site of the city of Cape Girardeau. It will be seen that the Spanish had been liberal in their dealings with him. He was the owner of large bodies of productive land, and he had exclusive right to control of the Indians. This meant, of course, a monopoly of Indian trade. The only conditions annexed to the grants of land were that the land should be settled within a reasonable time and that roads and other public improvements should be made. In 1799 he was engaged in building a new house called The Red House on the present site of St. Vincent's church. Near his house, at the corner of the present William and Lorimier streets, was a large spring. The hills were covered with trees, and on these wooded hills in the vicinity of this spring, the Indians were accustomed to camp when they came for conferences with Lorimier. He was appointed commandant of the post of Cape Girardeau, holding this place until the transfer to the United States in 1804. He was held in high esteem by the Spanish officials, as is shown in the following letter written by De Lassus: "M. Louis Lorimier, the commandant at Cape Girardeau can neither read nor write, but he has a natural genius, since he has always had the judgment to have some one near him able to assist him in regard to his correspondence. He signs nothing without having it read to him two or three times, until he comprehends it, or it must be read again. He has maintained order in his post with incredible firmness against some inhabitants who designed to mutiny against him without cause. He is extremely zealous when employed. Although supposed to be interested, I have known him to neglect all his business to execute a commission which would cause him rather expense than profit. He is much experienced in Indian matters, particularly with the Shawnese and Delawares. It was through his influence with the latter tribe that the Delaware Indian, who had killed a citizen of the United States on the road to the Post Vincennes, was taken by his nation to Kaskaskia. I had an incontestible proof of his talent with the Indians at New Madrid, where, without his mediation, I would have been obliged to employ force to execute the Mascoux Indian. He is brave, and extremely well posted in the Indian method of warfare, feared and respected by the savages.'' In 1799 he presented a petition to De Lassus, setting out the service he had rendered to Spain, the expense and worry he had suffered, and the hardships and dangers he had been forced to undergo. He declared that for fifteen years he had faithfully served the Spanish government in every possible way, and that his services had been practically unrewarded. He called to mind the fact that it was owing to his efforts and his influence with the Indians that Upper Louisiana had received a large influx of Indian population. He asked that the governor should grant him 30,000 arpents of land, to be surveyed when he chose, and to be selected in any place whatsoever, so long as the selection did not interfere with persons having grants already established. This petition was granted by De Lassus and the land prayed for was given to him.

In 1798, Lorimier had a law suit concerning this land with Gabriel Cerre. Cerre was the trader who had sent the La Sieurs to New Madrid. He had extensive dealings with the Indians and considerable influence with them. The Spanish government recognized his service and was willing to reward him; however, his claim to the land of Lorimier was denied. In the decision, which was in Lorimier's favor, the Governor-General said that he was unwilling to deprive Lorimier of his land for the reason that his services had been so valuable. He ordered, however, that Cerre should be given an equal amount of land in another place.

Lorimier continued to trade with the Indians up to the time of his death. He bought the goods, which he sold them, in Kaskaskia. Besides trading, he engaged in farming and also in the operation of mills. He built a water mill on Cape La Croix creek, not far from where the Scott county road crosses this stream; later he built another mill on Hubble creek. Lorimier claimed as his right all the ponies and horses found in the woods on his extensive grants. After the cession of Louisiana to the United States an attempt was made to deprive him of his land. This grant, was afterward confirmed to Lorimier's heirs by the United States by an act dated July 4, 1826.

Lorimier was not an educated man; he could not read though he could write his name. His signature, which has been preserved on a large number of documents, is bold and firm, evidently the writing of a man of determination and character. All of his dealings were characterized by energy and perseverance, and he evinced a high degree of executive ability. He so conducted affairs in his district that it became rich and populous; he governed the Indians well and displayed at various times a great deal of military ability. Lorimier was buried in the old cemetery, called after him, in the city of Cape Girardeau. The graves of him and his wife are side by side. They are covered with flat slabs of stone and are most interesting relics of the old times. The slab above Lorimier's tomb has this inscription:

> To the Memory of
> Major Louis Lorimier,
> A native of Canada and first settler and commandant of the post of Cape Girardeau under the government of Spain. He departed this life the 26th day of June, 1812, aged 64 years three months.
> Ossa Habeant pacem tumulo cineresque sepulti: Immortali animae luceat alma dies.

These words may be translated: "Peace to his bones and his ashes interred in this grave; may the eternal day illumine his immortal soul."

The tomb of his wife bears this inscription:

> "To the Memory of
> Charlotte P. B. Lorimier,
> Consort of Major Louis Lorimier, who departed this life on the 23rd day of March, 1808, aged 50 years and 2 months, leaving 4 sons and 2 daughters.
> Vixit, Chaoniae praeses dignissima gentis;
> Et decus indigenum quam lapis iste tegit;
> Illa bonum dedicit natura—magistra. Et, duce natura, sponte secuta bonum est, Talis honos memorium, nullo cultore, quotannis Maturat frustus mitis oliva suos."

These words may be translated: "She lived the noblest matron of the Shawnese race, a native dignity covered her as does this slab. She chose nature as her guide and virtue, and with nature as her leader spontaneously followed good, as the olive, the pride of the grove without the planter's care, naturally brings its fruit to perfection."

This was Lorimier's first wife, if, indeed, he was married to her at all. He spoke of her in his will as the Indian woman with whom he had lived and whom he regarded with affection. They were probably married after the Indian custom. After her death he married Marie Berthaume. She was an Indian, or at any rate a half breed. After Lorimier's death his widow was married the second time to John Logan, the father of General John A. Logan. General Logan, however, was the son of another woman, his father's second wife.

Cape Girardeau was possibly named for one Girardot who was an ensign in the company of French soldiers stationed at Kaskaskia in 1704. He was a trader with the Indians and it seems probable that he came to the site of Cape Girardeau and traded at that place, from which circumstance it was called after him. Houck says that the church records at Ste. Genevieve show that one Girardeau was at Fort Chartres in 1765. It should be noted that the name of the place in early years was various ways spelled, sometimes it was written Girardot, sometimes Girardo, and again Girardeau. We may not be certain, but it seems quite probable, that it received its name from one of these two men. It had been named, it seems, before Lorimier settled here in 1793.

The site for the settlement was well chosen. The city is located on the foot-hills of the Ozarks and lies also on the border of the alluvial plain. The country about it possessed wonderful resources; there was an abundance of the finest timber; there were a great many fur bearing animals and many varieties of game; and more than all there was a great deal of the finest and most fertile soil; the district was well watered, having an abundance of creeks and springs and bordered on the Mississippi river. No other site along the river surpassed this as the place for a town. Nature seems to have destined it as the site of a considerable city.

It is a remarkable thing that the settlers of Cape Girardeau district were nearly all of them Americans. It is said that in 1804 there were only five French families in the district. One of the most remarkable of the French settlers was Barthelimi Cousin. He was the secretary for Lorimier and the official interpreter and surveyor. He was, perhaps, one of the most remarkable men ever in the district. He was a native of France and probably came directly to Cape Girardeau when he emigrated to this country. He was a highly educated man, spoke a number of languages fluently, was polished, cultivated, and knew the world. He had ability to meet people and to make friends with them. All the new settlers applied to Cousin for assistance. He drew up their petitions and their permits and was the means of inducing many of the early settlers to come to the district. He lived near the corner of the present Main and Themis streets. He was granted a large tract of land on White Water and Byrd's creek. It was said of him that he was a careful student of mathematics and physics; that he continued his mathematical studies during his entire life. One evidence of his knowledge of physical laws was the fact that he built a water mill on two flat boats which were anchored in the Mississippi, the action of the current generated the power to drive the mill. He died in 1824.

Some of the other settlers were Steinback and Reinecke who formed a partnership in trade. Their house was north of Cousin's, standing near the site of the Union Mills.

Solomon Thorne was a gun-smith, he also lived in the town; the town's blacksmith was John Rishe; David Wade was the carpenter and John Patterson and David Seavers were some of the other settlers in town.

Cape Girardeau was laid off as a town in February or March, 1806, by Barthelimi Cousin. At this time the entire town was owned by Louis Lorimier. As surveyed then, and its limits fixed, it extended from North street on the North to William street on the South, and from the river west to Middle street. The streets within its area were the same number and width as they are at the present time. The first lots were sold at $100 each. Among the early purchasers were John Risher, John Randol, Solomon Ellis, William Ogle, Ezekiel Abel, John C. Harbison, William White. Some of the other early residents were: B. & F. Steinback, Robert Blair, Dr. Erastus Ellis, James Evans, Frederick Gibler, Levy Wolverton, Robert Worthington, Frederick Reinecke, Joseph McFerron and George Henderson.

Louis Lorimier lived in a long, low frame house which had been constructed before the laying out of the town, on the lot now occupied by St. Vincent's academy. This house was called "The Red House" and was reported to be haunted. There were four or five brothers of the Ellis family who came to the district from Georgia. Charles G. Ellis built a large, two-story, log house on the corner where the Opera House now stands. This was for a good many years the leading hotel in the town. Ellis was also a merchant and carried a general stock of goods. He was also instrumental in organizing the Cape Girardeau Milling Company. This company built a small mill in the north part of the town. It followed the plan first used by Cousin in being built out over the water, and was propelled by a screw turned by the action of the current. Dr. Erasmus Ellis, another one of the brothers occupied a log house which stood at the side of the Baptist Church on Lorimier street. Solomon Ellis built a brick residence at the corner of Lorimier and Bellevue. D. P. Steinback, who was a son-in-law of Louis Lorimier, lived on the corner where the Sturdivant Bank now stands. He and Frederick Reinecke opened one of the first stores in the town. Robert Blair was another one of the prominent citizens. He was Judge of the Court of Quarter Sessions. He was a native of Ohio, and came to Cape Girardeau about the time of the establishment of the town. After his death, in December, 1810, his widow married George Henderson. Henderson, afterward, became Judge of the Probate Court, Recorder, Auditor, Treasurer, and was for a time the Judge of the County Court.

Ezekiel Abel was another one of the prominent citizens of the old town. By trade he was a blacksmith, but his principal business during the years he lived in Cape Girardeau was trading in land and land grants. He erected the first public buildings in this district. He had some financial difficulties, but finally became wealthy. In 1811 he constructed the first brick house in the town. It was finished just in time to be badly damaged by the earthquakes of that year. He left a large family, consisting of four sons and two daughters. His eldest daughter, Mary, became the wife of Gen. W. H. Ashley. The younger daughter, Elizabeth, married W. J. Stevenson.

The town was incorporated in 1808. The petition which was presented to the Court of Common Pleas, is as follows:

"Limits of the town of Cape Girardeau: The town of Cape Girardeau extends in front, 3,058 feet and 9 inches from Botany Street (North Street), the northern boundary, to the Street of Fortune (William Street), the southern limit, inclusively; and its depth is 1,773 feet 2 inches exclusive of Water Street, i. e. from the front of Water Street to the Street of Honor (Middle Street), inclusively, containing 126 acres and ¾, nearly, the divers parts and divisions of the town to be more particularly designated in the plan of the same.

"July 23rd, 1808.
(Signed) "LOUIS LORIMIER."

"To the Honorable Court of Common Pleas, For the District of Cape Girardeau: Your Petitioners pray that the court will appoint commissioners agreeable to a law, passed by the Legislature of the Territory of Louisiana, for the incorporating of towns and villages within the state. Territory agreeable to the above metes and bounds.

(Signed)

John Randol,	John C. Harbison,
James Evans,	William White,
A. Haden,	Isaac M. Bledsoe,
Rob't Worthington,	Joseph White,
Charles G. Ellis,	J. Morrison, Jr.,
D. F. Steinback,	Ezekiel Abel,
Levy Wolverton,	Frederick Gibler,
John Van Gilder."	

The court granted the petition, and ordered that an election be held for the selection of five trustees for the town. This election was held August 13th, 1808, at which time Joseph McFerron, Anthony Haden, Robert Blair, Daniel F. Steinback and Isaac M. Bledsoe were elected. These trustees immediately entered upon their duties, and under their direction the town continued to grow and prosper for a number of years. It received its first blow in the establishment of the county seat at Jackson. This took away from the town a great deal of its importance and built up a rival near it. It did not recover from this disaster until the development of the steamboat trade at a later time. In 1818 it had only two stores and about fifty houses.

Flagg visited Cape Girardeau in 1836 and describes the mills put in motion by a spiral water-wheel acted on by a current of the river; these are doubtless the wheels of which it is said that Barthelimi Cousin was the inventor. These wheels floated upon the surface of the water parallel to the shore rising and falling with the water and were connected with the gearing in the mill house by a long shaft. At the time of Flagg's visit there was a pottery in operation in Cape Girardeau using the clay from Tywappaty bottom,

Long, who visited Cape Girardeau in 1819, gives this description of the town and its site:[*] "The town comprises at this time about twenty log cabins, several of them in ruins, a log jail no longer occupied, a large unfinished brick dwelling falling rapidly into decay and a small one finished and occupied, it stands on the slope and part of the summit of a broad hill elevated about 150 feet above the Mississippi and having a deep primary soil resting on a strata of compact and sparry limestone. Near the place where boats usually land is a point of white rock jutting into the river and at very low stage of water producing a perceptible rapid, these are of white limestone abounding in the remains of marine animals; if you travel some distance they will be found to alternate with the common blue limestone so frequently seen in secondary districts. Through the substrata of this sparry lime-stone the rock is literally divided by seams and furrows and would undoubtedly effect a valuable marble not unlike the Daring marble qarry on the Hudson.

"The streets of Cape Girardeau are marked out with form of regularity intersecting each other at right angles but they are in some parts so gullied and torn by the rains as to be impassable; others overgrown with such thickets of gigantic vernonias and urticlas as to resemble small forests. The country back of the town is hilly covered with heavy forests of oak, tulip tree and nyssa intermixed in the valleys with the sugar tree and the sylvatica and on the hills with an undergrowth of American hazel and the shot bush. Settlements are considerably advanced and many well cultivated farms occur in various directions."

The principal population of the district however was outside the town itself. The district was large, embracing the present counties of Cape Girardeau, Bollinger, Wayne, and parts of others. The land, too, on which the town of Cape Girardeau was situated belonged to Lorimier who refused to dispose of it for a long time and thus kept away some settlers who might otherwise have come.

Besides Cape Girardeau the principal settlements within the limits of the present county of Cape Girardeau before the transfer to the United States in 1804 were the Ramsay settlement near Mt. Tabor, a chain of settlements extending from the Big Swamp south of Cape Girardeau around to the Jack-

* "Long's Expedition," p. 87.

son road, the Byrd settlement on Byrd's creek, the Rodney settlement near Gordonville, the Randol settlement on Randol creek, Gordonville on Hubble creek, a settlement near the headwaters of Cape La Crux creek, one on the river north of Cape Girardeau, the Daugherty settlement south of Jackson, and the settlement on Whitewater, now called Burfordville, but long known as Bollinger's Mill. An account of these various settlements is here given.

One of the earliest settlers outside the town was Andrew Ramsay who in 1795 settled land near Mt. Tabor and immediately adjoining Lorimier's grant. Ramsay was a Virginian, coming to Cape Girardeau from the neighborhood of Harper's Ferry. He was related by marriage to Daniel Morgan of Virginia. He had been a soldier, was among the Virginia troops at the time of Braddock's defeat, and it is quite probable that he was a soldier in the Revolution. He was induced to settle in the Cape Girardeau district by his acquaintance with Cousin whose scholarly ability and friendliness attracted him. Ramsay was followed by members of his family and friends.

William Daugherty and Samuel Tipton were sons-in-law of Ramsay. They came to the district soon after him. Daugherty settled near his father-in-law and Tipton near Jackson.

Among the friends of Ramsay who settled near him were Nicholas Seavers, Jeremiah Simpson, Alexander Giboney and Dr. Blevins Hayden. These settlers were very naturally followed by their friends and by the year 1804 their settlements reached from the Big Swamp south of the town around to the Jackson road. Stoddard, who visited the district in that year said that it was the richest settlement in Upper Louisiana.

Ramsay was a leader among these settlers and his place became the headquarters for all persons who came to the district. They made their way first of all to Ramsay's farm. He assisted many of them to secure good locations in the near-by country. In fact, it seems to have been a custom for the American settlers to gather at Ramsay's place, especially on Sunday, where the day was spent in the amusements that the country afforded. Ramsay became rich, owning the largest tract of land in the settlement and having also many slaves. He was interested in education and was influential in establishing the first English school west of the Mississippi river. This school was founded in 1799 at Mt. Tabor.

Ramsay's family was a large one. Besides the two married daughters who came with their families soon after his location, he had three other daughters and five sons. Margaret Ramsay married Stephen Jones and moved to Arkansas; Mary became the wife of Peter Craig who was afterward killed at the battle of the Sink Hole; Rachael married John Rodney.

Ramsay's sons were John, who married Hannah Lorimier; Andrew and James, who married two sisters, Pattie and Rebecca Worthington; William, who married Elizabeth Dunn and Ellen. The first three sons here mentioned subsequently removed to Mississippi county.

Among the settlers the Giboney family was prominent and numerous. They came to the district prior to 1797. The head of the family was Alexander Giboney. He was a Virginian and a man of great ability and influence. He died, however, shortly after his removal to the district, and the care of the family fell upon his widow Rebecca (Ramsay) Giboney. Mrs. Giboney was a remarkable woman, possessing a high degree of intelligence, great energy and enthusiasm, and no small amount of executive ability. She continued to reside upon her plantation which was granted by the Spanish in 1797 until her death in 1840.

This plantation is now called Elmwood, and is the home of Honorable Louis Houck. Mrs. Houck is a grand-daughter of Rebecca Giboney.

Alexander Giboney left seven children, four sons and three daughters. One of the sons, Robert, lived on an adjoining grant, which is still occupied by his descendants. Of his daughters, one married Judge W. C. Ramsay, and another Dr. Wilson Browne, who was prominent in Missouri politics, having been at one time state auditor, and at the time of his death was Lieutenant Governor of the state.

Another son, Alexander, was killed at the battle of the Sink Hole; a third son, whose name was John, lived a mile west of the grant to his father. His descendants are very numerous and still live in Cape Girardeau and adjoining counties. One of the daughters of John Giboney married Doctor Henderson of Scott county and another married Colonel Solomon G. Kitchen of Stoddard county. The youngest son of Alexander Giboney was named Andrew, he lived to the age of 82, dying in 1874. He was married in 1832 to Mary Hunter; Mrs. Louis Houck is a daughter of these two.

Of the daughters of Alexander Giboney, Arabella married John Jacobs; their descendants lived in Pemiscot county. Isabella became the wife of Doctor Ezekiel Fenwick and lived in the north part of Cape Girardeau county. Margaret Giboney married Lindsay De'Lashmutt.

Mrs. Louis Painter, who lived for many years in Jackson, was a niece of Andrew Ramsay. Her father, John Ramsay, came to Cape Girardeau accompanied by a large number of relatives and friends, but later removed to Scott county. She was an intelligent and interesting woman.

Another family that came in early times to the district was the Byrd family. Amos Byrd, the head of the family, was a native of North Carolina. He was born in 1737 and lived for a time in Virginia and in Tennessee. In the latter state he located Byrd's Station on a fort on the frontier of Knox county. One of the neighboring families in Tennessee was that of the Gillespies. The acquaintance between these two families grew until no fewer than three sons of Amos Byrd had married into the Gillespie family. In 1799 Amos Byrd accompanied by his family came to Upper Louisiana and settled on Bryd's creek. He was, doubtless, attracted by the easy terms on which land could be secured from Spain. The spot chosen by him for the settlement was an exceedingly attractive one. The sons of the family were Abraham, Stephen, John, and Amos, Jr. With them came the daughters, Pollie, who had married William Russell, Clarissa who afterward married James Russell, and Sallie, who afterward became the wife of George Hays. All of these settled on, or near, Byrd's creek. John Byrd conducted a mill, cotton gin, a still, and a blacksmith shop. Abraham and Stephen became prominent in political life after the transfer to the United States, both of them holding at various times important offices under the government. They both left large families and inter-married with the Birds of the New Madrid district and with the Horrels, Allens, Martins and Mintons.

William Russell, who became the husband of Pollie Byrd was a native of Scotland. Before coming to Cape Girardeau he had lived for a time in Virginia and in Tennessee. It was in Tennessee that he became acquainted with the Byrd family. He was the father of Honorable James Russell at one time sheriff of Cape Girardeau county, and member of the state legislature. William Russell was a man of education, a teacher, and conducted the first school in the Byrd settlement.

The Rodney family was another prominent and influential one. They settled about two miles southwest of Gordonville. They were Germans, the original form of the name seems to have been Rodner. The head of the family in this country was Martin Rodney, who came about 1801 or 1802. One of his sons married a daughter of Louis Lorimier.

The first settlement of Randol creek was made in 1797 by Enos Randol. His family consisted of himself and ten children, seven sons and three daughters. Mrs. C. B. Houts who lived for a long time in Cape Girardeau was a daughter of Anthony Randol the eldest son of Enos. Samuel Randol married Pollie Pierrpont. He was an influential man, one of the syndics under Louis Lorimier. He built one of the first mills in the county. Medad was the second son, and for his second wife he married Thankful Stout, in Scott county. After his death she purchased a farm on Matthews Prairie, and became a part owner of the city of Charleston; other members of the family continued to reside in the county.

In 1797 the first settlement was made on Hubbell Creek. The creek was then known as Riviere Zenon, having been so named in honor of Zenon Trudeau, lieutenant governor of Upper Louisiana. This settlement was made by Ithamar Hubbell, where the town of Gordonville is now located. Hubbell had been a soldier in the Revolutionary army from New York. Andrew Sumners located near the head waters of Hubbell creek and in 1800 Christopher Hays settled on a grant about eight miles north of Gordonville.

Cornelius Arent made an early settlement at the mouth of Indian creek. Joseph Chevalier from Kaskaskia settled on the river north of Cape Girardeau in 1799, and south of Chevalier George Henderson settled in 1808.

William Denny, a native of Wales, came to Cape Girardeau from Tennessee in 1808. He settled near Gordonville. He was a gunsmith and a very fine workman. There were seven children in the family; these settled in Cape Girardeau, in Stoddard, Scott and New Madrid counties.

South of Jackson in 1798, there came the family of Daughertys. There were four brothers of them and they located on adjoining farms. William Daugherty was the husband of Elizabeth Ramsay. He was an original abolutionist and would own no slaves of his own and controlled only those inherited by his wife. His son, Ralph Daugherty, was a son-in-law of George F. Bollinger.

The first settlement in Bollinger county was made by George Frederick Bollinger, a native of North Carolina, of Swiss descent. He came from North Carolina about 1796 or 97 and selected a location on Whitewater. Lorimier promised him a large tract of land on condition that he would bring a certain number of settlers to the district. In fulfilment of this agreement he made a trip back to North Carolina and on his return he was accompanied by twenty families. They crossed the Mississippi river at Ste. Genevieve on the first day of January, 1800, and later settled along Whitewater. Some of the men who came with him were Matthias, John, Henry, William. Daniel, and Phillip Bollinger, Peter and Conrad Statler, Joseph

Neiswanger, Peter Crites, Frederick Limbaugh, Leonard Welker and Frederick Slinkard. They were all Protestants, being members of the German Reformed church. In 1804 Colonel Bollinger induced Reverend Samuel Weiberg or Whybark, to come to the settlement and to become the minister of the colonists. Reverend Whybark remained until his death in 1833. He preached over very extensive districts in Illinois and Missouri.

Among these settlers Colonel Bollinger was a leader, and was appointed by Don Louis Lorimier as captain of the militia. He organized a very effective company, which was said by Lorimier to be a model company. Bollinger erected a mill after his arrival, which was the only one in the section, and it served farmers for a long distance around.

Bollinger was a large and powerful man, of generous disposition and very popular. He was a member of the Territorial assembly, and after the admission of Missouri to the Union he became a member of the state senate in 1828, and was president of the state senate, and a presidential elector in 1836. As was elsewhere stated, his only daughter, Sarah, became the wife of Ralph Daugherty. It is said that she was educated in North Carolina and that she was a musician and the owner of the first piano brought to Cape Girardeau county.

The next settlement in Bollinger county seems to have been made in 1800 on Castor river near where Zalma now stands. Irvin Asherbramer was probably the first settler and he erected a water-mill at this place which is still in operation. Other early settlers in the same neighborhood were: Daniel Asherbramer, Phillip and William Bollinger, Joseph Watkins, Robert Harper and Edward Hawthorn.

The first settlement in Wayne county was made in 1802; this was where the village of Patterson now stands and the settlers were: Joseph Parish, Thomas Ring, David, Charles and Robert A. Logan. Ephraim Stout receiving a grant on the St. Francois, below the settlement made by the Logans, but removed in a few years to Iron county and was the first settler in Arcadia valley. Jacob Kelly was one of the wealthy and influential settlers and was the first justice of the peace. Others who are mentioned as having lived here in early times were: Tilman Smith, James Caldwell and Francis Clark.

CHAPTER VII

DISTRICT OF NEW MADRID

ITS BOUNDARIES—"L'ANSE A LA GRAISE"—THE LESIEURS—SITUATION OF NEW MADRID—COLONEL GEORGE MORGAN—GRANT TO MORGAN—HIS EXPECTATION OF PROFIT — HIS DESCRIPTION OF THE SITE—THE SURVEY OF THE TOWN—OPPOSITION OF WILKINSON AND MIRO—NEW MADRID FALLS INTO HANDS OF MIRO—LETTER OF LA FORGE—THE COMMANDANTS OF THE POST—EMIGRANTS WHO CAME WITH MORGAN—THE LESIEUR FAMILY—THE LA FORGES—JOSEPH MICHEL—ROBERT MCCOY—RICHARD JONES WATERS—TARDIVEAU—OTHER SETTLERS—ROBERT GOAH WATSON—MILITARY COMPANIES—OTHER SETTLEMENTS IN NEW MADRID COUNTY—LITTLE PRAIRIE—SETTLEMENTS IN SCOTT COUNTY—TOWN NEAR SIKESTON—BENTON—JOSEPH HUNTER—TYWAPPITY BOTTOMS—MISSISSIPPI COUNTY SETTLEMENTS—SPANISH LAND GRANTS—THE KING'S HIGHWAY.

As originally defined by the Spanish in the grant to Morgan, the District of New Madrid extended from the Cinque Homme, south to the mouth of the St. Francois, and west a distance of ten or fifteen miles, though the western boundary was not exactly located. Out of the north part of this district was carved the District of Cape Girardeau and after this was done New Madrid District was bounded on the north by Tywappity Bottoms. The exact line between Cape Girardeau district and New Madrid district was, however, for a long time a matter of dispute. It was finally settled by the governor-general and located at a point about five miles south of the present town of Commerce. The western boundary was left unsettled; however, the district was generally understood to extend as far west as there were settlements. As we have seen in discussing the boundary of the District of Cape Girardeau, there was an attempt made by the commandants of New Madrid to extend their authority over all the territory west of the St. Francois river and to confine Cape Girardeau district between the St. Francois and the Mississippi. The southern boundary of the District of New Madrid was generally understood as about the present southern boundary of the state. It was fixed not by any order or enactment but by the fact that settlements extended only about that far to the south.

The first settlement in this district was made in 1783 by Francois and Joseph LeSieur, two Canadian trappers and traders who had been accustomed to come to the territory about the present site of New Madrid for the purposes of hunting and trading with the Indians. Other hunters and traders also visited this place which is situated in a great bend of the river. Before any settlement existed there, while it was only a temporary trading post, it was called "L'Anse a la Graise." This name, which means the "cove of grease," was given it by those who came there to trade. Just what reason there was for the name is a question. Some have said that it came from the fact that stores of bear meat were kept there for sale to the passing boats; others said that it was named because of the fact that the hunters there killed an abundance of game, among which were many bears. A third suggestion is that the name was applied because of the richness of the soil.

Whatever the reason for the early name, the settlement was made by the LeSieurs. It was situated on the east bank of the Chapoosa creek; this was the early name of St. John's Bayou. The situation was a splendid one for the town; the great ridge which extends from the foot of the Scott county hills to the mouth of the St. Francois river is one of the most fertile and desirable parts of all of Southeast Missouri. This ridge touches the river at several places, among them New Madrid and Caruthersville. In early times it formed a most attractive place for settlers. It had immense quantities of timber of the finest sorts; within a short distance of New Madrid there was a lake of clear, limpid water; the woods swarmed with game; the climate was mild; the soil was exceedingly rich and productive. Those who visited the place believed it to be the most attractive site along the whole course of the river. These advantages had not been overlooked in the early times. The whole country about New Madrid is dotted over with Indian mounds. There are so many of these that it has been conceived by those who believed the mounds to have been built by a race preceding the Indians, that New Madrid was perhaps the seat of government for the extensive empire which they believed to have been organized at that time. Whatever the truth may be about this, there can be no doubt that great numbers of people lived here at the time the mounds were being built. It was near this place, perhaps, that De Soto camped on his expedition. An Indian village was situated here at that time and even when the French began to come here to trade there seems to have been an Indian village still in existence. Along this ridge was one of the great Indian roads which led from the crossing at Commerce to the south as far, perhaps, as the mouth of the St. Francois.

The LeSieurs lived and traded here for several years and other hunters and traders came, attracted by the advantages of the place, until there was quite a settlement. The most remarkable thing connected with its early history was the attempt of Colonel George Morgan to found a great city which should be the capital of a principality.

Morgan was an American; he was fond of the life of the woods; had an adventurous spirit; was bold and daring and far-sighted. He visited the West about the time of the transfer from France to Spain, paddled up and down its rivers, selected promising sites for settlements, and doubtless dreamed of an empire which might be established in Upper Louisiana. He took part in the Revolutionary war and was a man of considerable influence and high position in the United States. However, he became indignant at the treatment accorded him by the government of the United States. He had acquired from the Indians a large tract of land, enough to make him independently wealthy, but the policy of the United States government was never to recognize the validity of an Indian transfer. In the view of the government, the Indians had no power or authority to alienate any lands. This invalidated Morgan's claims and he became practically penniless. He applied to the congress of the United States for redress, but this was denied him. He then conceived the plan of founding a settlement within Spanish territory. He seems to have been moved by a desire for wealth, and partly by a desire to revenge himself on the United States by helping to build up the power of Spain. He came into correspondence with Don Diego Gardoqui the Spanish minister at Washington. He pointed out to the minister the immense importance to Spain of colonizing her territory west of the Mississippi river and of inducing settlers from America to emigrate there. His familiarity with the West and his real ability caught the fancy of Gardoqui who entered into his scheme. Under the arrangement entered into between these persons, Morgan was to receive a grant of land reaching from the Cinque Homme to the mouth of the St. Francois river, a distance of about three hundred miles. The grant was to extend some twelve or fifteen miles westward from the river and thus to include between twelve and fifteen million acres of land. Morgan pointed out to the minister that if Americans were to be induced to settle on these lands certain things must be granted to them. It was accordingly agreed that Americans should be exempt from taxation and that they should have the right to self-government. In addition to these inducements Mr. Morgan held out to prospective colonists cheap land for he expected to sell parts of his enormous holdings for very small sums.

It was a part of Morgan's scheme to induce Indians from east of the river to settle in Spanish territory. This was to be done, in part, on account of trading with the Indians, and, in part, so that they might serve as a protection for the Spanish territory, especially against the Osage Indians who lived on the Missouri river. He promised Gardoqui that if the grant should be made on the terms agreed upon between them that within a very few years the population of the district should be at least one thousand persons. Morgan seems to have been deceived as to the authority of the minister to make the grant; he undoubtedly believed that he had secured from the Spanish government the grant of the lands mentioned. In the winter of 1789, he descended the Ohio river with a numerous party consisting of Americans and of Indians and selected for the site of his town the place now known as New Madrid. He was led to do this by the beauty of the situation and the probabilities that it would be a most desirable place for a prosperous trading village. Here he left a large part of the expedition while he, himself, in company with some other members of the party, made his way up the river to St. Louis to meet the lieutenant-governor of the district who resided there. The lieutenant-governor received him with great favor and entered into all of his schemes. He then returned and proceeded to carry out his plans for the settlement of the country.

Morgan's hope of wealth was founded on the expectation that a considerable trade would soon be developed at his post, which he named New Madrid, and that he would be able to dispose of large bodies of land. He evidently expected, also, to engage in the cultivation of the soil and in addition to this he had received a promise that if his scheme turned out successfully the Spanish government would grant him a pension in reward for his services. He proceeded to lay out the site of his village and to have the surrounding lands surveyed. The surveyors who did this work were Col. Israel Shreve, Peter Light, and Col. Christopher Hays. It seems that his instructions to these surveyors was really the beginning of the present system of land survey, and that the United States government adopted the method devised by Mr. Morgan, in a subsequent survey of the public lands.

*Morgan thus describes the site which he had chosen for his town of New Madrid: "We have unanimously resolved to establish our new city above-mentioned with the date (of this letter) some twelve leagues below the above-mentioned Ohio, at the place formerly called L'Ance la Graisse, below the mouth of the river called Chepousea or Sound river in Captain Hutchins's map. Here the banks of the Mississippi, for a considerable distance, are high, dry, and delicious, and the territory west of the San Francisco river is of the most desirable quality for corn, tobacco, hemp, cotton, flax, and indigo, although according to the opinion of some, too rich for wheat, in such manner, that we truly believe that there is not a single arpent of uncultivable land, nor does it show any difference throughout the space of one thousand square miles. The country rises gradually from the Mississippi and is a fine, dry, agreeable, and healthful land, superior, we believe, in beauty and quality to those of any part of America.

"The limits of our new city of Madrid will extend about four miles south on the bank of the river, and two to the west of it, so that it is divided by a deep lake of the purest fresh water, 80 varas wide and many

* Houck, "History of Missouri," Vol. II, p. 64.

leagues long, running north and south and empting by a constant and small current into the Mississippi after flowing through the center of the city. The banks of this lake, which is called Santa Anna, are high, beautiful and pleasant; its waters are deep, clear, and fresh; its bottom is of clean sand, without logs, grass, or other vegetables; and it abounds in fish.

"On each side of this fine lake, streets, one hundred feet broad, have been marked out, and a road of equal width about the same. Trees have been marked, which must be preserved for the health and recreation of the citizens.

"Another street, one hundred and twenty feet wide, has been marked out on the bank of the Mississippi, and also the trees noted which must be kept for the above-mentioned objects.

"Twelve acres have been kept in the center of the city for the purpose of a public park, whose plan and adornment the magistrates of the city will look after; and forty lots of one and one-half acres apiece, have been considered for those public works or uses which the citizens may request or the magistrate or chief order, and another twelve acres reserved for the disposition of the King. A ground-plot of one and one-half acres, and a lot of five acres, outside the city will be given to each one of the first six hundred settlers.

"Our surveyors are now working on the extensive plan and proving up the ground plots of the city and the outside lots, and measuring the lands into sections of 320 acres apiece, in addition to those which they choose for the settlement of the people who may come (here). These portions and the conditions of the settlements are also in accordance with a plan universally satisfactory, which will avoid the interminable lawsuits which a different method has caused in other countries to the posterity of the first settlers.

"We have constructed cabins and a storehouse for provisions, etc., and we are making gardens and clearing one hundred acres of land in the most beautiful meadow in the world, in order to sow corn, hemp, flax, cotton, tobacco, and potatoes.

"The timber here is different in some kinds of trees from those in the central states of America. However, we have found white oak, high and straight, of extraordinary size, as well as black oak, mulberry, ash, white poplar, persimmon, and apples in abundance, and larger than those which we have hitherto seen. Also hickory, walnut, etc. The sassafras, very straight and of extraordinary size, is commonly 24 inches in diameter. The shrubs are principally cane and spice-wood.

"The timbers unknown to you gentlemen, are the cypress, pecan, coffee (sic), cucumber, and some others. The cypress grows on the lowlands at the edge of the river; its quality is equal to that of white cedar. We have a fine grove of these trees in our neighborhood which Colonel Morgan has had divided into shares of a suitable size, in order to assign them to each farm.

"We are satisfied with the climate, and we have reason to congratulate ourselves that we have at last found a country which conforms to our most ardent desires."

*Morgan gives this account of the way the town is laid out and the manner in which lots are to be disposed of: "The first six hundred persons applying for city and out lots, who shall build and reside thereon one whole year, or place a family who shall so reside, shall have one city lot of half an acre, and one out lot of five acres, gratis; paying only one dollar for each patent. All other city and out lots shall be reserved for sale, to future applicants according to their value. In the choice of the city and out lots the first applicant shall have the first choice of each; the second applicant shall have the second, and so on. Forty lots of half an acre each shall be reserved for public uses, and shall be applied to such purposes as the citizens shall from time to time recommend, or the chief magistrate appoint; taking care that the same be so distributed in the different parts of the city that their uses may be general, and as equal as possible. There shall be two lots of twelve acres each laid out and reserved forever; viz.: one for the King, and one for public walks, to be ornamented, improved and regulated by or under the direction of the chief magistrate of the city, for the time being, for the use and amusement of the citizens and strangers. So soon as these lots shall be laid off, the timber, trees and shrubs, now growing thereon, shall be religiously preserved as sacred; and no part thereof shall be violated or cut down, but by the personal direction and inspection of the chief magistrate for the time being, whose reputation must be answerable for an honorable and generous discharge of this trust, meant to promote the health and pleasure of the citizens. There shall be a reserve of one acre at each angle of every intersection of public roads or highways, throughout the whole territory, according to the plan laid down for settlement of the country; by which means, no farm house can be more than two miles and a half from one of these reserves, which are made forever for the following uses, viz.: one acre on the northeast angle or the use of a school; one acre in the northwest angle for a church; one acre on the southwest angle

* Houck, "Spanish Regime," Vol. I, p. 137.

for the use of the poor of the district, and the remaining angle in the southeast angle for the use of the King.

"In laying out the city, all streets shall be at right angles and four rods wide, including the foot-paths on each side, which shall be fifteen feet wide, and shall be raised twelve or fifteen inches above the wagon road. No person shall be allowed to encroach on the foot-paths, with either porch, cellar door, or other obstruction to passengers.

"All the oblongs, or squares of the city, shall be of the same dimensions, if possible; viz.: extending from east to west eighty rods or perches, and from north to south twelve perches, so that each oblong or square will contain six acres, which shall be subdivided by meridian lines, into twelve lots of half an acre each; by this means every lot will have at least two fronts, and the end lots will have three fronts. The lots shall be numbered from No. 1 upward, on each side of every street; extending from east to west; commencing at the east end.

"The streets shall be distinguished by names in the following manner: the middle street shall be a continuation of the middle range or road, extending from the first meridional line to the Mississippi river, and shall be called King street; and the streets north of this, extending from east to west, shall be called first North street, second North street, and so on, reckoning from King's street or Middle street. In like manner all the streets south of Kings street or Middle street, extending from east to west, shall be called first South street, second South street, and so on, reckoning from King street; so also, all the streets extending North and South shall be distinguished by the names of first River street, second River street, and so on; reckoning the space between the eastmost squares and the river, as first or front River street.

"The space between the eastmost squares and the river, shall not be less than one hundred feet at any place, from the present margin or bank of the river, to be kept open forever for the security, pleasure and health of the city, and its inhabitants; wherefore religious care shall be taken to preserve all the timber growing thereon.

"The lots of each square shall be numbered from the above space fronting the river. The eastmost lot of each square being No. 1, and so on, to the westmost lot of the whole city; by which means every lot in the city may be easily known and pointed out by any person.

"The two lots No. 1 on each side of King street are hereby given forever to the citizens for market places. The two lots No. 13 on each side of King street are hereby given forever to the citizens; viz.: that on the south side for a Roman Catholic school, and that on the north side for a Roman Catholic church.

"The two lots No. 13 in the fifth North street are hereby given forever to the citizens, viz: that on the south side for an Episcopal school, and that on the north side for an Episcopal church.

"The two lots No. 13 in the fifth South street are hereby given forever to the citizens, viz.: that on the south side for a Presbyterian school, and that on the north side for a Presbyterian church.

"The two lots No. 13 in the tenth North street are hereby given forever to the citizens, viz.: that on the south side for a German Lutheran school, and that on the north side for a German Lutheran church.

"The two lots No. 13 on the fifteenth North street are hereby given forever to the citizens

—that on the south side for a German Calvanistic school, and that on the north side for a German Calvanistic church.

"In like manner the two lots No. 13 in every fifth North street, and in every fifth South street throughout the city, shall be reserved and given for churches and schools, to be governed by such religious denominations as shall settle in New Madrid, on their respective plans.

"All these lots, thus given, or reserved to be given are to be esteemed so many of these forty promised as before mentioned.

"Every landing on the river opposite the city shall be equally free for all persons; under regulation, however, of the magistrates of the police.

"No trees in any street of the city, nor in any road throughout the country, shall be injured or be cut down, but under the direction of the magistrates of the police, or an officer of their appointment, who shall be accountable in the premises; and no timber injured or cut down in any street or road, shall be applied to private uses under any plea whatsoever.

"The banks of the Mississippi, throughout the territory, including a space of four rods in breadth, shall be a highway and kept open forever as such; and the trees growing therein shall not be injured, nor be cut down, but by the magistrates of the police or their order, for the reasons given above in relation to other roads.

"No white person shall be admitted to reside in this territory who shall declare himself to be a hunter by profession, or who shall make a practice of killing buffaloes or deer without bringing all the flesh of every carcass to his own family, or to New Madrid, or carrying it to some other market. This regulation is intended for the preservation of those animals, and for the benefit of neighboring Indians, whose dependence is on hunting principally—this settlement being wholly agricultural and commercial, no encouragement shall be given to white men hunters.

"No person shall be concerned in contraband trade on any account. Care will be taken to instruct the inhabitants what is contraband, that they may not offend innocently.

"Every person having permission to settle in this territory shall be allowed to bring with him his family, servants, slaves and effects of every kind, but not to export any part thereof, deemed contraband to any other part of his Majesty's dominions.

"Every navigable river throughout the territory shall be esteemed a highway; and no obstruction to the navigation shall be made therein for the emolument of any person whatsoever.

"No transfer of lands within this territory shall be valid unless acknowledged, and a record thereof be made in an office to be erected for that purpose in the district. This is meant to prevent fraudulent sales, and not to obstruct those made bonafide to any person whatsoever, being a Spanish subject.

"All mortgages must in like manner be recorded at the same office for the same purpose; the fees of the office shall be reasonable, and the books, with alphabetical tables kept of the buyer and seller, and of the mortgagor and mortgagee, shall be open for examination.

"The foregoing regulations and directions are meant as fundamental stipulations for the government and happiness of all who shall become subjects of Spain, and shall reside in this Territory.

Given under my hand at New Madrid this sixth day of April, 1789.

GEORGE MORGAN."

A number of settlers were attracted by the generous conditions on which land was granted and by the real desirability of the site of New Madrid, and Morgan steered well on the way to the accomplishment of his desire. He came in conflict however with plans that had been formed by Governor Miro the Spanish governor of Louisiana whose headquarters were at New Orleans and who was engaged in intrigue with General James Wilkinson. Wilkinson was an officer in the army of the United States in command of the district along the Mississippi river. He had planned with Miro to incite a rebellion among the people of the United States west of the Alleghanies, with the intention of separating this territory from the United States and of joining it to the Spanish territory. Wilkinson was drawing a pension from the Spanish government and had hopes that his efforts in securing a part of the territory of the United States for Spain would result in his receiving some very great reward. Of course Morgan's plan of drawing settlers to New Madrid and making that a prosperous and flourishing center of trade for Upper Louisiana was in direct opposition to the hopes of Wilkinson. He saw in Colonel Morgan a rival and set to work to thwart his plans. He wrote Governor Miro that he had applied for a grant in the Yazoo country in order to destroy the place of a certain Colonel Morgan. He told Miro that Morgan was a man of education and intelligence, but a thorough speculator. He also said of Morgan that he had been twice in bankruptcy, and that he was very poor, but also very ambitious. He also said that he had had a spy searching out information concerning Morgan and his agreement with Don Diego Gardoqui and that he was convinced that Morgan's scheme would be successful unless steps were taken to counteract it. He assured Miro that their plans would be greatly hindered if Morgan would be allowed to carry on his settlement.

Acting on this information Governor Miro proceeded at once to try and put an end to the operations conducted by Morgan. On the 20th of May, 1789, he wrote to the Spanish government protesting against the grant that had been made to Morgan. He said that it formed a state within a state and asked the government to cancel this grant; at the same time he wrote to Morgan himself and charged him with having exceeded his powers and with having acted toward the government of Spain in bad faith. He said that Morgan had no authority to lay out a town and provide for a government. He informed Morgan that it was his intention to construct a fort at New Madrid and to place a detachment of soldiers there to control the situation. Morgan saw that this interference would very likely work the ruin of all of his hopes. He replied to the letter in a most apologetic manner, saying that if he had, indeed, exceeded his authority he had done so because of his zeal in the service of the King of Spain. He was unable to conceal the fact, however, from those colonists who had come and were coming to New Madrid, that he had fallen into disfavor with the government and they immediately began to fear that he would be unable to carry out his promise. It seems too that an emissary of Miro visited New Madrid and succeeded in stirring up some ill feeling against Morgan and his rule. The colonists complained about some of the regulations and finally sent an agent, one John Ward, to present a petition to Governor Miro. Acting on this petition Miro carried out his threat and sent a company of soldiers with orders to construct a fort at New Madrid and to take entire charge of the government of the post. This practically destroyed Morgan's influence, and with its loss went all his hope of making a settlement at New Madrid. The post was continued under the government of Spanish officials.

The officer whom Miro sent with the company of thirty soldiers to take charge of the post was Lieutenant Pierre Forcher who laid off a town between Bayou St. John and the Decyperi. The fort which he built on the bank of the river he named Fort Celeste, in honor of the wife of Governor Miro. Commandant Forcher was a man of energy and administrative ability and under his rule order and prosperity reigned in the community. He was succeeded after about eighteen months by Thomas Portell. Portell was a man well suited to the place, governed with justice, and was able to satisfy most of the people.

A letter is here inserted which was written in 1796 by Pierre Antoine La Forge to Charles DeHault De Lassus. De Lassus had been appointed military and civil commandant of the post and district of New Madrid. La Forge was a resident of the post and thoroughly acquainted with the entire situation. His letter cannot fail to be of interest as it covers the conditions at New Madrid at that time.

NEW MADRID, Dec. 31, 1796.—To Mr. Chas. Dehault DeLassus, Lieutenant-Colonel admitted into the Stationary Regiment of Louisiana and Military and Civil Commandant of the Posts and Districts of New Madrid— Sir, the Commandant:—Before handing you the first census of New Madrid under your commandment, I have ventured upon a sketch of the origin of the settlement of this post, and the courses which have retarded its growth and chiefly its cultivation. If former defects have kept it until this time in a species of stupefaction, your sagacious views and the zeal you exhibit to second the good will of Mr., the Governor General of this Province, towards this settlement, can in a little while efface the trouble it experienced in its birth.

I was present, Mr. Commandant, when you pronounced with effusion these words, which I wish that all of the inhabitants might have heard; words which depicted so frankly your kind intention, and the interest which Mr., the Governor, takes in us.

"The Governor," said you, "is surprised at the langour exhibited by this settlement and its little advance; he desires its prosperity. I will reflect upon its failure," added you, "and will endeavor to remedy it; I ask your assistance. If the inhabitants need encouragement, if they stand in need of help, let them inform me of their wants, and I will convey them to the Governor General." This offer was appreciated by those near you; little accustomed to hear the like, they wondered at you, and appeared to rest content. Nevertheless different statements were spread among those who heard you. Why, so long a silence since your generous offer? Is it distrust on their part? Is it mistrust of their own misunderstanding? Is it profound reflection to better further your views? or may it be self interest that induces some to remain silent? I am ignorant of their motives, and limit myself to the hope that they will eventually break their silence and make known to you their solitary reflections.

If my knowledge equalled my desires, I would hasten with all my power, sir, the commandant, to tender you the homage of my services, but they fall too far short to allow me to hope that they could be of any utility to you. I will confine myself solely to communicate to you such knowledge as I have acquired, and my reflections thereon since I have been at this post, and may a series of these reflections assist in your benevolent heart some happy idea that may tend to the advantage and prosperity of this colony.

Some traders in pursuit of gain, came to l'anse a la graissse (cove of fat or grease), a rendezvous or gathering place of several Indian nations, and where, as we are told by tradition, they found abundance of game, and especially bears and buffaloes, hence the name of l'anse a la graissse. A first year of success induced them to try a second, and to this others. Some of them, determined to establish their homes where they found a sure trade and unlimited advantages, divided there among themselves the land. The bayou, named since St. John, was the rallying point, and the land the nearest to this then became settled, therefore we find that Messrs. Francis and Joseph Lasieuer, Ambrose Dumay, Chattoillier, and others, divided among themselves this neighborhood; property which Mr. Foucher, the first commandant, considered as sacred, and which he did not disturb. The profits of the trade of l'anse a la graissse having been heard of as far as the Post Vincennes, the St. Maries, the Hunots, the Racines, the Barsaloux, etc., of that place accomplished for some years very advantageous trips. They congratulated themselves, moreover, that the Indians of l'anse a la graissse traded with them amicably, whilst those of the United States were treacherous towards them, and made them averse to inhabit a post where their lives were in constant danger.

Nevertheless an unfortunate anarchy, a singular disorder, prevailed, at l'anse a la graissse: all were masters, and would obey none of those who set themselves up a heads or commandants of this new colony. A murder was committed by an inhabitant on another—then their eyes were opened, they began to feel the necessity of laws, and some one at their head to compel their observance. They bound the culprit and sent him to New Orleans. Everything tends to the belief that the commandants of the posts of Ste. Genevieve and of St. Louis had, during these transactions, apprised the Governor-General of what was occuring at l'anse a la graissse; but a new scene was in preparation.

One Morgan, having descended the Ohio the first year that traders settled at l'anse a la graissse, examined, in passing, the land, and found it suitable to fix here a settlement Returning to America (U. S.), he removed and succeeded in bringing down to this post several families. He selected for the village the elevated ground, where at present are the habitations of Jackson and of Waters, near the Mississippi. They built some houses on the land, and, full of his enterprise and the success he expected from it, Morgan descended to New Orleans to obtain, not encouragement simply in his plans, but proprietary and honorary concessions beyond measure. He was baffled in his pretensions, and did not again set his foot in the colony.

These various occurrances determined the Governor General to send a commandant to this post, and M. Forcher was selected. Men are not gods, they all possess in some respects the weaknesses of human nature; the predominant one of the first commandant was self-interest; and who in his place would not have been so sent to a desert in the midst of savages, to bring the laws of a regulated government to new settlers as barbarous as the Indians themselves? What recompense would he have received for neglecting his personal interests? What obligation would the new colony have been under to him? None.

Mr. Forcher was the man that was wanted

for the creation of this new colony. Busying himself at the same time with his own interests as of those of the inhabitants; with his own amusements as well as theirs, but always after having attended first to his business; and by a singular address, if he sometimes plucked the fowl, he not only did it without making it squall, but set it dancing and laughing. M. Forcher remained but a very short time at this post, and did a great deal. In eighteen months he divided out the country, regulated the land necessary for the village and that of the inhabitants. He built an imposing fort, promulgated the laws of the King and made them respected. He was the father and friend of all, lamented, regretted and demanded again, from the Governor General down, by the unanimous voice of all the inhabitants.

In all his labors was Mr. Forcher assisted by anyone? Had he overseers at the head of the works he presented? Not at all; he alone directed everything; he laid out the work, penetrated the cypress swamps to select the useful trees; he walked with the compass in hand to align the streets and limit of lots; he demonstrated by his example to the perplexed workmen how much men with but little main strength, but with intelligence and dexterity, can multiply the extent of the same, and surmount obstacles. His administration was too brief to ascertain the good he might have done, had it continued the ordinary period. What is certain is that, during the eighteen months that he was in command, there came to New Madrid the largest portion of families that are still there, and it was he that attracted them there.

M. Portell, successor to M. Forcher, commanded this post during five years; the population did not increase under his administration, and the growth of agricultural labors was but slightly perceptible.

M. Portell did not value the inhabitants sufficiently to do them a substantial favor, nor did he use the proper means to improve the condition of the colony. He was not a man of the people, and when by chance his interest required him to assume the character, he was extremely awkward in it; they perceived that he could not play his part, and that a residence in court would have infinitely better suited him than one in a new settlement mostly ill composed. M. Portell had a good heart, he was by nature noble and generous, but his mind was somewhat mistrustful and suspicious, and his age placed him in a position to be influenced by his surroundings. I am convinced that if M. Portell had come alone to this colony, he would have exhibited much less weakness and that his time would have been much more to him for the public good than it had been.

The little progress made by the colony must not, however, be attributed to the apparent indifference which seemed to form the base of M. Portell's character; physical and moral courses retarded its advancement.

At the period when M. Portell assumed command he found the inhabitants of this post made up of traders, hunters and boatmen. Trade was still pretty fair for the first two years of his residence here, so that nearly everyone, high or low, would meddle with the trade and not a soul cultivated the soil. It was so convenient, with a little powder and lead, some cloth and a few blankets, which they obtained on credit at the stores, to procure themselves the meat, grease and suet necessary for their sustenance, and pay off a part of their indebtedness with some peltries. Some of them, but a very few, seeded, equally as well as badly, about an acre of corn, and they all found time to smoke their pipes and give balls and entertainments. How often have I heard them regretting those happy days, when they swam in grease, and when abundance of every description was the cause of waste and extravagance, and the stores of fish from their dragnets gave them whiskey at four or five reaux (bit of 12½) a gallon, and flour at four or five dollars a barrel, maintained and kept up these festivals and pleasures, which only came to an end when their purses were exhausted.

Mr. Forcher, a young man who, during his command of the post, never neglected his work or business for amusements, yet found time to be at them all, and often was the first to start them, but M. Portell was not so sociable in this respect. He found fault with this giddiness and folly, and judged that a colony, peopled by such individuals, could not attain a very brilliant success.

At last, game in these parts becoming scarcer, the Indians removed themselves further off, and were seldom here; the traders knew very well where to find them, but the inhabitants waited for them in vain; then grease, suet, meat and peltries being no longer brought by the Indians, it was only a few resident hunters and the traders themselves who provisioned the village; the unfortunate habit of not working had gained the day, it was too difficult to overcome it, so great distress was often seen in the country before they could snatch a few green ears of corn from a badly cultivated field. Three or four Americans, at most, as far back as 1793, had risqued the settlement of farms on large tracts of land. The Creoles undervalued them, did not eat their fill of dry corn bread, and smoked their pipes quietly. They were, however, surprised to see that, with several cows, they often had not a drop of milk, while these three or four Americans gorged themselves with it, and sold them butter, cheese, eggs, chickens, etc.

By dint of looking into the matter, and waiting in vain for the Indians to supply them with provisions, it struck them that the most prudent thing they could do would be to become farmers. It became, then, a species of epidemic, and the malady spreading from one to another, there was not a single one of them but who, without energy, spirit, animals or ploughs, and furnished only with his pipe and steel, must needs possess a farm.

It was towards the close of the year 1793 that this disease spread itself, and towards the spring of 1794 all the lands in the vicinity of New Madrid were to be broken up and torn into rags, to be seeded and watered by the sweat of these new farmers. Who can tell how far this newly awakened enthusiasm might have been carried? It might have produced a salutary crisis, and self-love and necessity combined, we should be supplied with farmers at all hazards, and whose apprenticeship might, perhaps, have resulted in some success.

An unlooked for occurrence calmed this effervescence; all were enrolled into a militia to be paid from January 1, 1794, and they found it much pleasanter to eat the King's bread, receive his pay, and smoke his pipes, than to laboriously grub some patches of land to make it produce some corn and potatoes. These militiamen were disbanded about the middle of 1794; their pay was already wasted. They found it a great hardship to be no longer furnished with bread by the King, the largest portion of them had neglected their planting, they found themselves at the year's end in want, and clamored as thieves against the King, saying it was all his fault. M. Portell knew his people and disregarded these outcries.

In the meantime five gallies had come up in the course of this year, and had passed all the summer at New Madrid, and they had caused a great consumption of food. M. Portell found nothing in the village for their subsistence, and drew his supplies for them in part from Illinois and from Kentucky. He did not let pass the opportunity of making it felt by those of the inhabitants of long residence, that should have been in a condition to have furnished a part of these supplies, but the blows he struck came too late, and made but little impression—the hot fever which had occasioned the delirium, where every one saw himself a farmer, had now subsided; no one thought any more of it, some of them who had made a trial of their experience at Lake St. Isidor, had so poorly succeeded, that the laugh was not on their side, and it needed but little for hunting, rowing, and smoking the pipe, to resume their ancient authority over nearly all the colony.

In 1795 a new fit of the fever struck the inhabitants. The settlement of Ft. St. Fernando occasioned a hasty cleaning out of the little corn there was in the colony. Kentucky furnished a little, and Ste. Genevieve supplied a great deal, even to New Madrid, that fell short after having consumed her own supply. This example struck the inhabitants; they saw that if they had harvested extensively, they could now well have disposed of their surplus—new desires to go on farms to raise stock and to make crops.

During these occurrances several American families came to New Madrid; some of them placed themselves at once on farms, and like children our Creoles, from a state of jealousy, clamored against the Americans, whom they thought too wonderful. Jealousy stimulated them, and they would also place themselves on farms.

It is in reality, then, only since the year 1796 that we may regard the inhabitants of this post as having engaged in cultivation, and that it is but yet absolutely in its infancy; a new scarcity they have just experienced before the last crops has convinced them of the importance of raising them, not only to provide against such affliction, to enable them also, with the surplus above their own consumption, they may procure their other indispensable necessaries.

The population of the years 1794, 1795 and 1796 is nearly about the same, but the crops have increased from year to year, and all tends to the belief that this increase will be infinitely more perceptible in future years.

In the year 1794 the corn crop was 6,000 bushels; in 1795, 10,000, and in 1796, 17,000.

It was in this condition of things that M. Portell left his command.

It was, perhaps, impossible, from the foregoing facts, that the settlement at New Madrid could have made greater progress than it has up to this time. It was not husbandmen who came and laid the foundation, it was tradesmen, cooks, and others, who would live there with but little expense and labor, who, being once fixed there, having their lands and their cattle, the Indians having removed themselves to a distance, and trade no longer within the reach of all the world, necessity taught them that to procure the means necessary to live, they must resort to tilling the soil. The first attempts were difficult, but the inducement of disposing with ease of their crops determined them to labor.

The first steps have been taken; nothing remains for a wise commandant, but to manage everything with prudence, according to the views of the government, to firmly repel idleness and laziness, to welcome and encourage activity, and exhibit to the industrious men that he is distinguished above others and has earned the protection of the government, in giving him tangible proof, either by preference in purchasing from him or some other manner of recompense. The honest man, the active and industrious man, is sensible of the slightest proceeding on the part of his superior, and it is to him a great expansion to reflect that his labors and fatigues have not been ignored, and that they have given him a claim on the good will and benevolence of the heads of a Providence.

What a vast field is open to a commandant who would reap advantage by these means, and gain the benediction of all the worthy inhabitants of a colony.

I stop here, Mr. Commandant; what I might say further would add but little to the good purposes you design for the progress and success of the place. I have made a concise narrative of the origin of the post of New Madrid, and the reasons of its slow growth in agriculture. The census which follows, will give you a correct view of its present situation. It will prove to you that courage and emulation need but a slight support to emerge from the giddiness where they have so long remained. But for certain the Creoles will never make this a flourishing settlement, it will be the Americans, Germans and other active people who will reap the glory of it.

Observe, if it please you, sir, that amongst the habitations granted long since, those given by Francis Racine, by Hunot, Sr., the Hunot sons, Paquin, Laderoute, deceased, Gamelin, Lalotte, etc., have not yet had a single tree cut on them; that those of the three brothers, Saint Marie, Meloche and other Creoles are barely commenced.

You will see, on the contrary, that the Americans who obtain grants of land have nothing more at heart but to settle on them at once and improve them to the extent of their ability, and from this it is easy to draw conclusions.

Another observation which will surely not escape you, sir, is that the total head of families amount, according to the census I exhibit to you, to 159, and that in this number there are fifty-three who have no property. This, I think, is an evil to which it would be for you to apply a remedy. In a county ned to agricultural pursuits, and to the breeding of domestic animals, it is too much that one-third of the inhabitants should stand isolated from the general interest, and that the other two-thirds should be exposed to be the victim of a set of idle and lazy people, always at hand at their slightest necessities to satiate their hunger by preying on the industrious.

I think, Mr. Commandant, that several habitations left by persons who have absented themselves from this post for a long time should be reunited to the domain.

The following are of this class:

One Enic Bolduc, absent for over two years, had a place at Lake St. Francis No. 2.

One John Easton, absent for over three years, had a place at Lake St. Eulalie; it is now abandoned. One Mr. Waters says he has claims on it. What are they?

One Tourney had a place at Lake St. Isidor; he associated with to cultivate it one Gamard. Tourney returned to France, and Gamard had worked for two years at Fort St. Fernando.

One M. Desrocher, why has he not worked his place in the Mill Prairie, which he holds for over four years? Has he not enough with the one he holds at St. Isidor?

One M. Chisholm holds three places; he lives on one he has just commenced to clear; a second is in litigation, and for over four years he has done nothing on a third near the village—has he not enough with two? Why hold land uselessly, and above all near the village?

The examination you will give the census, and the information concerning the property of each head of a family will lead you probably to other reflections. I append to the whole a new map of the village and its environs, as taken after the last abrasion of land by the Mississippi; this work claims your indulgence; it is not that of an artist, but one of the most zealous subjects of his majesty; and the only merit it may possess is to demonstrate to you with correctness the number of places that have been conceded in the village, the houses that are built thereon, and the names of the proprietors on the general list which correspond with the same numbers as those placed on each conceded place.

I pray you to believe me, with profound respect, sir, the commandant,

Your very affectionate and devoted servant,*

New Madrid, December 31, 1796.

PIERRE ANTOINE LAFORGE.

De Lassus remained as commandant at New Madrid until the spring of 1799 when he was transferred to St. Louis and became the lieutenant governor of Upper Louisiana. De Lassus was, perhaps, the most popular official ever in command at New Madrid, as he was, indeed, one of the most popular in all Louisiana. He was succeeded by Don Henri Peyroux who was transferred to the post from Ste. Genevieve. Peyroux landed

* "History of Southeast Missouri," p. 140.

in New Madrid in August, 1799, and was in command four years. He then resigned and returned to France.

John Lavalle succeeded Peyroux as commandant of the post and held the place until the transfer to the United States in March, 1804.

The emigrants who came to New Madrid with Colonel Morgan were mainly from Maryland and Pennsylvania. Among them were David Gray, Alex Samson, Joseph Story, Richard Jones Waters, John Hemphill, Elisha Windsor, Andrew Wilson, Samuel Dorsay, Benjamin Harrison, Jacob and Benjamin Meyers, William Chambers, Elisha Jackson, Ephraim Conner, John Hart, James Dunn, Lawrence Harrison, John Gregg, Nicholas and James Gerry, John Wallace, John Becket, John Summers, Louis and Joseph Vandenbenden, Joseph McCourtney, John Pritchett and David Shelby.

As we have seen the earliest French settlers were the two LeSieurs, Francois and Joseph. They were not only the first, but perhaps the most influential of all. Many of their descendants are still to be found in New Madrid county. These two were the sons of Charles LeSieur a native of the south of France who had emigrated to Three Rivers in Canada. Francois and Joseph came to St. Louis in 1785 and entered the employ of Gabriel Cerre who was a fur trader. It was in his interest that they visited the place where the town of New Madrid was afterward located. Joseph died in 1796 and left no children. Francois married on May 13, 1791, Cecile Guilbequet, a native of Vincennes. In 1794 they removed to Little Prairie, remaining there until the earthquakes of 1811 and '12 when they returned to New Madrid county and made their home at Point

Pleasant. Francois LeSieur died in 1826; he had been married three times. The children of the first marriage were Francois, Jr., whose wife was a LeGrand; Colestique, who became the wife of Noah Gambol; Marguerite, who married Hypolite Thiriat; Godfrey, who married Mary E. Loignon and reared a family of eleven children; Matilda who became Mrs. W. B. Nicholas; and Christine, who was married to George G. Alford. His second wife was a Miss Bowman, and their son was named Napoleon. In 1820 he was married for a third time to the widow of Charles Loignon. Another member of this family was Raphael LeSieur who was a nephew of the two brothers and came to Madrid in 1798.

Another of the other French settlers was Pierre Antoine La Forge who came from France. La Forge was an aristocrat by birth, had been educated to be a priest, but fell in love with his cousin Margaret Champagne. He resided in Paris, but was compelled to leave at the time of the Revolution. He came to America then. At first he lived in Gallipolis, Ohio; he then removed to New Madrid where he was appointed a public writer and interpreter. He was also an adjutant of militia and justice of the peace and a notary public. De Lassus thought very highly of La Forge and accounted him one of the best officers in the service of the Spanish. His descendants still live in New Madrid county and have always been influential citizens. Among them we mention Alexander La Forge, A. C. La Forge, Hon. William Dawson, Robert D. Dawson, Dr. Geo. W. Dawson, and Dr. Welton O'Bannon. Others also have attained prominence and wealth.

As we have seen, Francis and Joseph LeSieur are the first settlers in New Madrid. The third was Joseph Michel. Michel's son, also named Joseph, who was born in 1800, lived to be a very old man, dying in 1895. He lived in New Madrid until 1829, when he moved to Hales Point, Tennessee. He was a nephew by marriage of Captain Robert McCoy who was also his guardian. He married a daughter of John Baptiste Olive one of the early settlers in New Madrid.

Captain McCoy was one of the most prominent men in New Madrid, he came to the settlement with Morgan, and became an officer under the Spanish authorities, being in command of a Spanish galley, or revenue boat. There were several of these galleys stationed at New Madrid and they were charged with the execution of the Spanish commercial laws. All boats passing New Madrid were required to stop and to give an account of themselves, and to pay the required tax to the government. It was while in command of one of these boats that McCoy captured the celebrated Mason gang of robbers and river pirates who for a number of years committed depredations on the river commerce. Joseph Michel who visited New Madrid in 1887 had a vivid recollection of the encounter between McCoy and the Mason gang. The Spanish governor at that time was Peyroux. He ordered McCoy to Little Prairie where he found and captured Mason and his men. They were then brought to New Madrid, sent from there to New Orleans and were then ordered up the river again, and on the return while their boat was tied at the river bank with most of the crew on the bank, Mason and his men seized the boat, shot and wounded Captain McCoy and made their escape. McCoy was commandant at post of New Madrid in 1799, then he was commandant at Tywappaty Bottom. He died in New Madrid in 1840.

Another of the early French settlers was Etienne Bogliolo who had been a resident of St. Louis, but early moved to New Madrid and engaged in trading. He secured some large grants of land from the Spanish authorities, but lost his property and died poor.

Another of the French settlers was John B. Olive. He left numerous descendants who still live in New Madrid county. Still another was John LaValle. He came to New Madrid direct from France and was a man of education and of superior intellect. Of his descendants, many still live in the county.

Of the men who came with Morgan, one of the most prominent was Doctor Richard Jones Waters. Waters was a native of Maryland, he came to New Madrid about 1790 and began the practice of his profession. Besides being a physician he was also a trader, mill owner, and land speculator. He married the widow of Louis Vandenbenden. The Waters family of New Madrid are descendants of Richard Jones Waters. He left a large estate and was an energetic, enterprising man. De Lassus rated him as a good officer, but referred to his somewhat extravagant disposition.

Barthelemi Tardiveau was a Frenchman who came to New Madrid with Morgan. He was a native of France and lived in Holland and had been a merchant in Louisville. He was a very able, energetic man, and was probably the most cultured man in the early settlement. He was a master of several different languages including French, English, and Spanish, as well as a number of Indian tongues. The company with which he was associated was, perhaps, the most extensive trading company in New Madrid district. He came to New Madrid after some experience east of the river which satisfied him that if the French in America were to prosper they must remove to the west side of the Mississippi. While living in the east he had interested himself in securing large grants of land from Congress for the benefit of French settlers and in satisfaction of their claims which had originated from Indian grants. He was fairly successful in this matter, but he soon saw that the very land he had been granted slipped out of the hands of the French and into the possession of the Americans. This convinced him that the French people would not prosper unless they got further away from the Americans. This conviction led him to give his assistance and influence to the support of Morgan's scheme. He not only followed Morgan to New Madrid, but he induced others of his friends and acquaintances to do the same.

Steinbeck and Reinecke, the traders whom we have noted as being established in Cape Girardeau, had a trading post at New Madrid also, they were further interested at Little Prairie. Bogliolo was also a trader as was the firm of Derbigny, La Forge & Company.

About 1804 Robert Goah Watson, a Scotchman by birth, but who had resided in Vincennes, Indiana, and also in Nova Scotia moved to New Madrid. He engaged in trade and acquired a large fortune. He was a man of great energy and ability and had the respect and confidence of all the people of the community. He was noted for his kind and charitable disposition and rendered such service to the community that he was affectionately referred to as the Father of the Country. Watson was killed on his farm near Point Pleasant. He left a large family of children, consisting of four sons and five daughters. One of his daughters married John Nathaniel Watson, another Doctor Edmund La Valle, a third married Thomas L. Fontaine, a fourth married W. W. Hunter and the fifth daughter married Doctor Thomas A. Dow. Many of the Watsons, Fontaines, La Valles and Hunters of New Madrid county are descendants of Robert G. Watson.

Shortly before his death Judge Watson wrote a sketch of his life. It is inserted here because of the information it contains as to conditions existing in this part of the state, and especially for its presentation of the great difficulty attendant upon travel in that early day.

I am a Scotchman by birth. I left Auldearn, Scotland, a small town east of Iverness, in March, 1802. I came to this country when a lad with an elder brother of mine, Wm. G. Watson, under the guardianship of an uncle of ours, who had been in this country a number of years previous to our arrival, and was doing business as a merchant in Detroit, Michigan, then a small town. We took shipping at Greenoch, Scotland, and landed at Montreal, lower Canada, the latter part of May. From there we took passage on a batteau at a place called Sacchine, six or eight miles from Montreal. We crossed the small lake some six or eight miles wide, which brought us to the mouth of the river Magon. We proceeded on this batteau, which was loaded with merchandise, for Upper Canada, there being no other mode of conveyance at that period. After being fifteen days on the river, contending against a strong current and numerous falls, shoals, and other obstructions, we arrived at Queenstown on Lake Ontario, a small town settled by British subjects, with a garrison containing two or three companies. After remaining there four days we took a small vessel for passage to Niagara, a small town at the head of Lake Ontario, after being out six days. From there we walked to Queenstown Heights, a distance of ten miles. From Queenstown we took a wagon to Fort Erie. When we arrived we found a vessel waiting for freight for Detroit and Upper Canada. We remained some ten days before the vessel got in freight and was ready to sail. While waiting we had nothing to do only amuse ourselves by hunting and fishing. We crossed from Fort Erie to the mouth of Buffalo Creek on the American side and found there a tribe of Indians encamped on a hunting expedition. The city of Buffalo was not then spoken of, or had any connection with the state of New York, either by railroad, canal, turnpike or any other kind of road. The whole Lake country was claimed and owned by Indians, the only white settlement at that period on Lake Erie, was at a place then called Presque Isle, near the line dividing the state of New York from Pennsylvania. It was then the only good harbor on the Lake. After leaving Fort Erie we arrived at Detroit, eight days out in the latter part of August. I remained with my uncle, Robert Gouie Watson, in Detroit, one year. He sent my brother and myself to school during that time, which was pretty much all the school-going we ever received. My uncle had a small trading establishment on the British side opposite Detroit, and he sent me over there to take charge of it. I remained there about a year, he being connected with the Indian trade on the American side at Sandusky and Huron river along Lake Erie, then a considerable trading country owned and claimed by the Indians. I visited that country on business for my uncle in the year 1803. Where Cleveland and Sandusky are now located there were no white settlements or settlers, with the exception of a few Indian traders. My uncle also had an Indian trading establishment at New Madrid, Mo., under the management and control of a Frenchman by the name of Gabriel Hunot, who had numerous connections of that name in that place (New Madrid) and Fort Vincennes, Ind. From some cause my uncle was obliged to take charge of the trading establishment, and sent me out with an outfit of goods imported from London, expressly for the Indian trade, to take charge at New Madrid of the establishment. We left Detroit, I think, in July, 1805, with two pirogues loaded with Indian goods, myself, and four French Canadians for New Madrid. We found the river Maumee very low, making a long trip to Fort Wayne. No white inhabitants were on the banks from the time we left the foot of the rapids, with the exception of one Frenchman—a baker—at the mouth of the river Glase, called Fort Defiance, who furnished the Indians and traders who traveled up and down the river with bread. The length of time out in getting to Fort Wayne, I do not recollect. We found some Indian traders and a company of U. S. troops stationed there. We were then obliged to haul our goods and pirogues a distance of ten miles to the head waters of Little river, which empties into the Wabash. Those Indian traders at Fort Wayne were prepared with oxen and wagons to haul our goods and boats across, for which we had to pay them considerable and sometimes when the waters of Little river were very low, we had to haul our goods and boats a distance of forty miles, to where Little river empties into the Wabash. On one occasion I had to haul my goods and boats a distance of sixty miles to near the Missionary town, an Indian village on the Wabash where a Frenchman by the name of Godfrey from Detroit had located as a trader. The chief of this village was Thecomery, brother to the Prophet who held a power and sway over the different tribes, unparalleled in the history of Indian nations. I got to Vincennes after encountering extreme low water, having to carry our goods which were made up in small packages expressly to be carried from shoal to shoal by the hands, distance of one-quarter to one-half a mile, sometimes longer, and rolling our pirogues on rollers over every rapid until we got them in deep water. This was our daily occupation. We arrived at Vincennes after being out about two months. During our trip we were very much exposed, the weather being excessively warm and not having anything to protect us from the hot sun and bad weather; not even a tent, which latter was not used or hardly known at that early period, and being short of provisions, a little salt pork and a few hard biscuit and some lye hominy composed our diet, no tea, no coffee, no sugar; the latter article in those times was in but little use and scarcely known. From extreme exposure and hard living I was taken down violently with chills and fever. My hands knew that Gabriel Hunot, who was trading for my uncle at New Madrid, had a sister in Vincennes by the name of Pagey. I sent for one of her sons to come and see me. He did so, and seeing my critical situation invited me to his mother's house, and by his request I went there, and fortunate it was for me I did so. If I had remained where I was I must have died. Every care and attention and good nursing was given me night and day, by Mrs. Pagey and her kind sons. I owe my existence now to that kind lady's attention to me, which I shall forever remember with gratitude and esteem. I remained at Vincennes for some time to regain my strength. While there I became acquainted with a good many of the French settlers and Indian traders, Rupert Debois, Francois Langois, the Lazells, Bamon—Indian interpreter for Gen. Harrison—and a number of names not recollected. Not a white inhabitant except Indian traders, from the time we left Fort Wayne till we arrived at Vincennes, and from there to the mouth of the Wabash—with the exception of Coffee island, some French families lived there of the name of Leviletts. We arrived at New Madrid in October and found the place settled principally by the French, and the town or village beautifully laid off in lots of two and four arpens, each, well improved and the streets wide and running parallel with the river. The banks of the river then as now were encroaching upon the town. The first town laid off by the Spanish had all fallen in, and at the present writing we are living in the third town carefully laid off back of the second, which has also gone. When the encroachments of the river will stop is hard to conjecture. After a residence of 50 years in the place I find little or no change in the caving of the river banks. I have moved my possessions back three times and my first residence is now in Kentucky. When I arrived in New Madrid I took possession of my uncle's trading establishment and commenced trading with the Indians, French, and Americans, the place being a considerable trading point principally with the Indians. I continued buying peltries and furs during the winter until March. I then baled all my peltries and furs and shipped them in two pirogues containing 24 packs each. I started them in charge of some Frenchmen up the Ohio river, then up the Wabash, some 350 miles from its mouth to Little river, then up that river to its source, where we hauled again our pirogues and furs across to Ft. Wayne on the Maumee or the lake, and from there we proceeded to Detroit where everything was delivered up to my uncle. I followed my shipment by land by myself some three weeks after they started. I went by the way of Kaskaskia, Ill. After leaving that village, settled by French not a sign of a white inhabitant did I see until I got to Fort Vincennes out three nights. I expected at Vincennes to have found several traders ready to leave by land for Detroit. They, like myself, generally followed their shipments of skins by land. They had left some five days before I got there and I was obliged to continue the journey by myself.

When I left Vincennes I took the Terre Haute route. At that place I found an Indian village and two French traders. I spent the night with them and the next morning proceeded on my journey. I crossed a stream not far from Terre Haute, called Vermillion and the next place I came to was an Indian village where I found a Frenchman, a trader by the name of Langlois. The next place of note was the Missionary town where I found my old friend Godfrey, spoken of on my trip out from there. My next point was Fort Wayne. I had then been out six nights from Vincennes and four of these nights I lay out by myself and from Fort Wayne to the foot of the rapids, two nights. This was a hazardous undertaking for a youth of only about 16 years. From the foot of the rapids to Detroit, the country was more or less settled by the French. I remained at Detroit some two weeks and started back by land the same route I went out. I made three trips by water and three by land and worked and steered my own pirogues and continued in the trade until the war broke out between this country and Great Britain in 1812. The war stopped all communication between this country and Detroit, and I was then compelled to seek another channel of trade for my peltries and furs. In 18— I made a large shipment of peltries and furs in a keel boat, the largest shipment I ever made from this country, by the way of Chicago. The keel boat left New Madrid in March with a freight valued at $14,000. They went up the Mississippi, then up the Illinois, then up a stream I think they call Fox river, up that to within six miles of Chicago; my object in sending my skins that route was to meet a government vessel which the government generally sent out at the opening of navigation in the spring, with provisions and stores for the troops stationed there, but, unfortunately, when my furs and peltries got there the government boat had been there and left some five or six days before for Detroit. The hope of getting them to Detroit that season was hopeless. No vessels running the lake with the exception of one government vessel, spring and fall. My skins remained there all summer expecting to ship them in the fall. When we examined and commenced preparing them for shipment we found them all destroyed by moths or bugs. I did not realize one cent from the amount stored there. While at New Madrid trading with the Indians and shipping my skins to Detroit until 1812, I purchased stock and produce from 1808 up to 1825 and shipped it to New Orleans in flat boats. My first visit to New Orleans was in the year 1809 having consigned my first shipment in 1808. I loaded two flat boats with assorted articles of produce and steered one of them myself, but under the control and management of a pilot of Pierre Depron. I got to the city on my flat boats, but how to get back was the next question. No steam boats running at that time and but few barges and keel boats on the river. I bought a horse and started back by land; crossed Lake Ponchartrain in an open boat with my horse and took the road from Maisonville to Nashville, Tenn., passing through the Cherokee and Choctaw Indian country (owned and claimed by them) to the Tennessee river. In getting to New Madrid I was out six weeks, suffering much for the want of provisions for myself and feed for my horse, having to pay $1 per meal for myself and $1 per gallon for corn. My men had to wait some time at New Orleans before an opportunity offered to get back, and then they had to work their way home on a barge. From that period up to the present time I have continued visiting New Orleans every year and am of course well posted in being an eye witness to all improvements made in the city and coast since my first visit there. In 1810-11 I came up the Mississippi river in a pirogue with my hands that I had taken down on a flat boat. We left New Orleans the latter part of July with scant provisions or allowances of any kind for our trip having to rely on our guns and fishing tackle for a supply, not being particular as to what we killed or ate—Hobson's choice, that or none. Cranes, pelicans and cat fish, we considered a delicacy. We had not a tent or umbrella to protect us from the inclemency of the weather; when it rained so hard that we could not travel we put ashore and peeled the bark off the trees to make shelter from the rain. We were out 45 days. From 1808 to 1812 but few inhabitants were on the river. At Point Chicot we found two Frenchmen at White river and one at the mouth of St. Francois, Phillips and Mr. Joy; and a Spaniard on the side opposite Memphis. (Then Memphis was not known or spoken of.) One or two Indian traders were there at that time. At that early period the banks of the Mississippi were settled by robbers and counterfeiters. Flat boats descending the river then had to go in convoys well armed and under the lead of some experienced commander; if they did not they were sure to be attacked, killed, or robbed of their effects by these robbers who were settled at different points on the river. In returning in a dug out with my hands, in 1810, we were followed by one of Mason's and Murrell's men from a little below Lake Providence until a few miles below Point Chicot. He came up within half a mile of us and no nearer; he continued his pursuit by following us two days. He was going as we thought to apprize some of his colleagues of our approach near Point Chicot, and that we were no doubt in possession of considerable money, proceeds of produce shipped to New Orleans. This robber was one of Mason's surviving confederates in crime, etc. He was a French Canadian by the name of Revard, and his location was on the island below Lake Providence; there he watched and saw everything that passed up and down. We tried to pass in the night hoping not to be discovered but we could not. He was too watchful of us to evade his notice. We had some confidential advisers who instructed us how to act in the neighborhood of Lake Providence, where Mason had his general rendezvous, on or near Bayou Mason, back of Lake Providence, a remote and secluded place where he kept his headquarters. Nothing saved us that trip from being killed by the French robber only my crew being French and he, Rivard, being a Canadian, disliked attacking, robbing and killing us, being French, he having heard my French crew singing French songs which was a custom among the French boatmen. After following us two days he abandoned the chase. My long residence at New Madrid gave me an opportunity of becoming acquainted with a great many people and their acts whether good or bad. Not a day from 1809 to 1815 but some innocent man, the owner of some flat boat loaded with produce, had been imposed on by some of this class by purchasing of them for money, which they called good, and on good solvent banks, when in fact it was nothing but the basest kind of counterfeit money. There was scarcely a day but what there was large amounts presented to me for examination and inspection. Our whole country from Evansville, Indiana, to Natchez was full of such people. In fact they ruled and controlled the country at that period. They had the sway. We were from the necessity in the minority they being the strongest party and to express our opinion against them and their actions placed our lives and property in a dangerous situation. After an elapse of a certain time a better population commenced coming in. We saw after counting these we considered honest and would take an interest in securing and driving out of the country the despised class, we had from necessity to consult with the citizens of the country and ascertain from them what course we ought to adopt in order to get rid of this description of population. They put at defiance all laws proving themselves innocent of every crime and charge brought against them. A general meeting of the citizens of the country was called and the matter laid before them. They came to a conclusion and that conclusion by a unanimous vote of the people then in public council. "That these people must leave the country" and a committee was appointed by the meeting to carry the resolutions into effect, which was done and the country cleared of thieves and counterfeiters. The last difficulty we had with them they had their rendezvous at different places in the country, in the interior and on the river; they kept up a constant correspondence night and day with their leaders and strikers. They were numerous and their acquaintances on the Ohio and Mississippi rivers intimately connected with them in extending their dishonest operations was unprecedented in the history of this or any other country. We owe in a measure our complete success of clearing the country of this description of population to the energy and perseverance and determined action of a few honest and resolute men, one of them I will refer to with feelings of respect and pride as being one of the principal actors in accomplishing our object, that person was the deceased Capt. Dunklin, whose virtues and standing as a man and citizen is yet recollected and appreciated by a number of persons, yet in existence who were witnesses to his valuable service.

In the years 1812-13-14 being at New Orleans each of those years, I returned home as a passenger on board of a barge or keel boat, 50 and 60 days out. I preferred this mode of getting back to the land route. In the year 1815 I visited Cincinnati, Ohio, on my way to Detroit, Michigan. I bought a horse and outfit at Cincinnati for my trip. Cincinnati was then a small place; the Court House was upwards of a quarter of a mile out of the city. I visited the Court House to see what was to be done having seen in the morning posted up at the different corners of the street hand bills that a certain gentleman, a lawyer of some distinction, a resident of the city, by the name of Binhem, would address the citizens at the Court House at a certain hour of that day on the subject of charges brought against him and published while he was absent from the city on professional business. It appears that during the progress of the war with Great Britain he was drafted as a soldier to join the U. S. Army but from some cause he failed to comply with the request of the draft and the charges I think made against him were cowardice and not willing to expose his life in defense of his country. In addressing the citizens he proved to them conclusively that he had used every exertion to raise means to equip himself and proved that he was a minor and under the guardianship of a near relative of his and who had control of his person and his means, although he had made frequent applications to him for means, but in all cases refused to furnish him with any and was opposed to his joining the army. His appeal to the people was a very feeling one and being an able speaker his appeal was listened to with every attention. His excuse was approved of. The same trip I became acquainted with the agent of the United States Bank at Cincinnati. The bank owned and claimed considerable town property, vacant lots on which they built family residences and offered them for sale through their agent. I was offered one or two lots with their improvements on them on Second and Third streets for from $1,000 to $1,200, each lot. The improvements must have cost the money. The same property cannot now be bought for $60,000. I had means at the time and if I had bought this property at the time and let it remain it would have proved a source of considerable revenue to me now. My object was to take General Harrison's road through the black swamp to Detroit. Urbana was then a frontier town, there was a new county laid off and a county seat located at a place called Bellefontaine. Some few log cabins were put up in place, but there was no public house in the place at that time. Next morning I took the road cut by General Harrison through the black swamp and traveled by the Northwestern army, and where he encountered so many difficulties in getting along as commander of the Northwestern army. His object was to attack and beat back the British army that had crossed over and attacked the American army at the river Raisin, under General Winchester. I had to travel one hundred miles through this swamp until I got to Fort Meigs, on the Maumee river, foot of the rapids. I found three houses in crossing the swamp, where a traveller could stay all night about 35 miles apart. My object is to show you the great changes in the country now to what it was then—comparatively not known. In 1806 I visited St. Louis, a small French village. Little or no business was done, the principal men in the place were two Chouteaus. Their descendants are still there, all respectable and influential men. Fred Bates filled an office about that time under the territorial government, a recorder of land titles or secretary of state, under the acting governor. I knew him at Detroit, Michigan, in 1803 or 1804, one of those years Detroit was destroyed by fire, and I assisted Mr. Bates in saving from the devouring elements a few of his small effects. He was then a citizen of that place. I was intimately acquainted with him at St. Louis from his arrival up to his death. He was an intelligent business man and a gentleman in every sense of the word. The earthquakes visited New Madrid county in December, 1811. Their effect was felt all over the U. S. and more particularly in this and adjoining counties, and the injury produced from the effects was more combined to this county than any other, producing alarm and distress, depopulating generally the whole country. Plantations, stock of all kinds, cribs of corn, smoke houses full of meat, were offered for horses to live on. At that time I was carrying on the Indian trade pretty extensively. The whole white population, or all that could leave as well as the Indians, left largely in my debt, leaving me considerably indebted to persons here and in other places and little or no means to pay with. What little was left me I had to subsist on and divide with those that remained and could not get away. We had a trying time, our population having all left, no business doing and no capital to do business with. Heavy losses at different times at Chicago and on the Mississippi river in produce sent to New Orleans in flat boats and by the earthquakes upwards to $30,000, leaving me destitute and without any capital to operate on; and on having a small family to support, I came to the conclusion, after consulting with my wife, to remain in the country and await the result of circumstances. To leave without means and move to a new country, among strangers and be dependent on them for support, I could not reconcile it to myself. I proposed remaining and awaiting with patience the result of what was to take place, which I have done. I never left but stood up and persevered, in prosperity and adversity, contending against the misfortunes and privations of a new country, the Mason and Murrell counterfeiters and horse thieves, earthquakes, and with all these reverses and misfortunes staring me in the face, it never produced the least change in my general course of conduct, but stimulated me to additional exertions. The misfortunes and privations I endured at an early period would have driven hundreds to acts of desperation. With me they never produced the least change. I am what I was forty years ago. Nothing ever induced me to resort to dissipation, to take a glass of grog or smoke a cigar more than I did then. My general habits, if good or bad, are the same now, to which a long residence in the country and a general acquaintance with those now settled in the country, can testify. My friends who knew me, and I never deceived them, came forward to my assistance and relief; to them I owe the means I am in possession of. The staple of this country from 1805 to 1812 was cotton. The average yield of an acre was from 1000 to 1200 pounds of seed cotton. Since 1812 there has been a great change in our climate; the winters have grown colder and the other seasons more changeable. The raising of cotton has been entirely abandoned for the last thirty-five years; our staple, now, has been principally corn. Prejudices to some extent exist now in some of the states against this country. At an early period they had some grounds to speak rather lightly of this country, it being sickly and visited by earthquakes; inhabited by counterfeiters and horse thieves and but few inhabitants in the country. To a certain extent our country has been overlooked and misrepresented. Things have changed since then. The country has become healthy, our soil the best in the United States. It cannot be surpassed.

Doctor Samuel Dorsay, a native of Maryland, was appointed surgeon of the military post at New Madrid, a position which he held until the transfer to the United States. The position had attached to it a salary of $30.00 a month. On January 17, 1795, Dr. Dorsay was married to Marie J. Bonneau, a native of Indiana. He was afterward married to a daughter of Jeremiah Thompson of Cape Girardeau district.

Joseph Story, of Massachusetts, was one of the surveyors brought by Morgan to New Madrid, he assisted Morgan in laying off the city. He married a daughter of Jacob Beck in 1794.

Andrew Wilson, a native of Scotland, and a minister in the Presbyterian church, was also one of the early settlers. He seems to have given up his ministerial work before coming to New Madrid. His son, George W., was the first sheriff of the district.

Some of the other early settlers were John Summers, Joseph and Louis Vandenbenden. These brothers were merchants, and the widow of Louis afterward married Richard Jones Waters.

Jacob Meyers, Joseph McCourtney, David Gray and John La Valle were other of the early settlers. La Valle was the last commandant under the Spanish government; his descendants still live in New Madrid county.

Doctor Robert D. Dawson, who was a native of Maryland, came to New Madrid at an early date and engaged in the practice of medicine. He was, for a number of years, the leading physician of the town, and was a very popular man. His activities were not confined to the practice of his profession, but he had a great interest in politics. For a number of years he represented New Madrid county in the general assembly of the territory, and was elected a member of the Constitutional convention.

During the Spanish regime there were three military organizations in New Madrid. Two of these were companies of militia and the other was a dragoon company. One of the militia companies had for its officers La Valle as captain, La Forge as lieutenant, and Charpentier as ensign. The other militia company was officered by Captain McCoy, Lieutenant Joseph Hunot, and Ensign John Hart. Richard Jones Waters was captain of the company of dragoons, George N. Reagan was lieutenant, and John Baptiste Barsaloux was ensign.

Cuming, who visited New Madrid in 1808 gives the following description of the town at that time: "New Madrid contains about a hundred houses scattered on a fine plain two miles square on which, however, the river has so encroached during the twenty-two years since it was first settled, that the bank is now half a mile behind its old bounds and the inhabitants have had to move rapidly back. They are a mixture of French Creoles from Illinois, United States Americans and Germans. They have plenty of cattle but seem in other respects to be very poor. There is some trade with the Indian hunters of furs and peltry but of little consequence. Dry goods and groceries are enormously high and the inhabitants charge travelers immense prices for any common necessaries such as milk, butter, fowls, eggs, etc. There is a militia the officers of which wear cockades as a mark of distinction although the rest of their dress should be only a dirty ragged shirt and trousers. There is a church going to decay and no preacher and there are courts of Common Pleas and Quarter Sessions from which an appeal lies to the Supreme Court at St. Louis, the capital of the territory of Upper Louisiana, which is two hundred and forty miles to the northward by wagon road which passes through Ste. Genevieve which is 180 miles distant. On account of this distance from the capital New Madrid has obtained a right to have all trials for felony held and adjudged here without appeal. The inhabitants regret much the change of government from Spanish to American but this I am not surprised at as it is the nature of mankind to never be satisfied."*

Alliot who visited Louisiana in 1803 says: "A hundred leagues farther up the river the traveler comes to that charming river known by the name of Belle Riviere (the Ohio) which, like so many others, pays its tribute of respect to the mortal Mississippi by giving its limpid waters to it; at that place is built the fort l' Ance à la Graice where a commandant and 150 soldiers are stationed, there is a hamlet there inhabited by three score persons. That place is so much more remarkable in as much as its inhabitants were the first along the river to engage in the cultivation of wheat. Excellent meadows are seen there on which cows and steers feed, its inhabitants rear many hogs and fowls, the forests are full of all sorts of game and fallow-deer."†

Nuttall who visited New Madrid in 1820 has this account of the town: "We arrived before noon at New Madrid, we found both sides of the river lined with logs, some stationary and others in motion and we narrowly avoided several of considerable magnitude. New Madrid is an insignificant French hamlet containing little more than about twenty log houses and stores miserably supplied, the goods of which are retailed at exorbitant prices, for example, 18 cents per pound for lead which costs 7 cents at Herculaneum, salt $5.00 per bushel, sugar $31\frac{1}{4}$ cents per pound, whiskey $1.25 per gallon, apples 25 cents per dozen, corn 50 cents per bushel, fresh butter $37\frac{1}{2}$ cents per pound and eggs the same price per dozen, pork $6.00 per hundred, beef $5.00. Still the labor of the land seems to be of a good quality but

* Cuming's "Tour to the West," p. 281.
† Robertson, "Louisiana," Vol. I, p. 133.

the people have been discouraged by the earthquakes which, besides the memorable one of 1811, are very frequent experiences, two or three oscillations being sometimes felt in a day. The United States in order to compensate those who suffered in their property by the catastrophe granted to the settlers an equivalent of land in other parts of the territory."*

Besides those whom we have seen lived in the town of New Madrid itself and immediately about it, there were other settlements within the present territory of New Madrid county; some of these were made on Lake St. Ann, along the St. Johns Bayou, at Lake St. Mary and on Bayou St. Thomas. Some of the early settlers at these places were: Benjamin Meyers, Hardy Rawls, Lewis Van Denbenden and Joseph Story. These men opened up farms at the places mentioned and some of them erected mills and others were engaged principally in hunting and trapping.

The district of New Madrid, as we have seen, included not only New Madrid county, as it now exists, but also Pemiscot county, Mississippi county, Scott county and even the counties lying further west. During this period which we are studying settlements were made within the district in all the counties mentioned except those lying west of St. Francois river.

The first settlement in Pemiscot county was made at Little Prairie, a short distance below the present town of Caruthersville. The settlement was made in 1794 by Francois Le Sieur, who came to Little Prairie from New Madrid where he had formerly lived and on receiving the grant of land laid out about

* "Nuttall Journal," p. 77.

two hundred arpents into a town divided into lots each containing an arpent. Here a fort was also constructed called Fort St. Fernando. Among the early residents of the town and country in the immediate vicinity were: Francois Le Sieur, Jean Baptiste Barsaloux, George and John Ruddell, Joseph Payne, Lewis St. Aubin, Charles Guibeault, Charles Loignon, Francis Langlois and Peter Noblesse. The site of Little Prairie was well chosen it being situated at a place where the great ridge, of which we have previously spoken, touches the river, and the surrounding country was rich in soil, timber and game. There was considerable trade with the Indians; and the town, because of these advantages, prospered. The population was seventy-eight in 1799 and in 1803 it numbered one hundred and three. It continued to grow until the earthquakes of 1811 and 1812 by which it was almost destroyed. This earthquake seems to have had its center about Little Prairie and the shocks were probably more violent here than anywhere else. The greater part of the population moved away at the time of the earthquake so that the village was practically deserted, the only conspicuous settler who remained in the vicinity was Colonel John Hardeman Walker.

In 1808 Cuming visited Little Prairie of which he gives the following account: "We landed at the town of Little Prairie on the right containing twenty-four little log cabins scattered on a fine pleasant plain. Inhabitants chiefly being French creoles from Canada and Illinois, we were informed that there were several Anglo-American farmers all around in a circle of ten miles. We stopped at a tavern and store kept by European-Frenchmen, where we got some necessaries, everything is excessively dear here as in New Madrid, butter a quarter of a dollar per pound, milk half dollar per gallon, eggs a quarter of a dollar a dozen and fowls half to three-quarters of a dollar each.''*

Cuming says that at this time there was a camp of Delaware Indians about one mile below Little Prairie.

Besides this settlement at Little Prairie there were some three or four other settlements within Pemiscot county. One of them was in the vicinity of the town of Gayoso, afterward the county seat; another in the western part of the county on Little river; the third was just north of the lake called Big Lake and the fourth was located on Portage Bay. All of these settlements suffered greatly from the earthquake and most of them were practically depopulated by its effects.

With the opening of the King's Highway from Ste. Genevieve to New Madrid in 1789 there sprung up a number of settlements along the line of this road, some of them being in Scott county. One of the first of these was made in the vicinity of Sikeston by Edward Robertson and a son-in-law, Moses Hurley. Robertson was a shrewd and capable man. He traded with the Indians and also kept a stock of goods which he sold to other settlers, but he accumulated the greater part of his wealth by land speculation. At his death he left a considerable amount of property.

Another one of these early settlements was made in Scott county in 1796 near the present town of Benton by Captain Charles Friend, who was a native of Virginia. He received a grant from the Spanish government near Benton and located there with his family. There were nine sons and two daugh-

*Cuming's ''Tour to the West,'' p. 283.

ters in his family and most of them remained in the vicinity of the Spanish grant. Another settler in this neighborhood who came in 1811 was John Ramsay of Cape Girardeau.

Perhaps the most distinguished and influential family in Scott county in this period was the family of Joseph Hunter. He came to New Madrid in 1805 and located on a grant near New Madrid, but soon afterwards removed to Big Prairie not far from Sikeston and continued to reside in Scott county until the time of his death. The family of Joseph Hunter was a large one and was always wealthy and prominent in this part of the state; he, himself, was a member of the territorial council after the transfer to the United States and his son, Abraham, was one of the best known politicians in Southeast Missouri, holding office in the state legislature for about twenty years. He was the second son and married Sally Ogden. Their family consisted of three sons and three daughters; the sons were Isaac of Scott county, Joseph of New Madrid county, who has recently died, and Benjamin F., who lives near Sikeston. One of the daughters, Catherine, married Marmaduke Beckwith, Mary married Archibald Price. Another son of Joseph Hunter was named James; he married Lucy Beckwith. The youngest son of Joseph Hunter was Thomas; he married Eliza Meyers and to them were born two children, a daughter who became the wife of Colonel Thomas Brown, and Senator William Hunter of Benton. Of the daughters of Joseph Hunter, Mary married Andrew Giboney of Cape Girardeau, their daughter is the wife of Hon. Louis Houck, and Hannah married Mark H. Stallcup of New Madrid.

Another of the early settlers of Scott county was Captain William Meyers, who came to Missouri from Tennessee and made his home at what is now Benton.

Settlers began to locate in Tywappity Bottoms as early as 1798; among them were James Brady, James Curran, Charles Findley, Edmund Hogan, Thomas, John and James Wellborn and the Quimbys. Thomas W. Waters was the first settler on the site of Commerce, arriving there in 1802, here he began the sale of goods in partnership with Robert Hall and also operated a ferry across the Mississippi.

The first settlement in Mississippi county seems to have been made in 1800 by Joseph Johnson near Bird's Point. Other early settlements were made on Mathews Prairie called in the early times St. Charles Prairie. Those who lived there were: Edward Mathews and his sons Edward, Charles, Joseph, James and Allen, Charles Gray, Joseph Smith, John Weaver, George Hector and Absalom McElmurry. Johnson sold his land in 1805 to Abraham Bird whose name was given afterwards to the settlement known as Bird's Point.

All of these settlers whom we have named and many others whose names we cannot give were farmers and traders. Most of them were engaged in the actual cultivation of the soil. Even those who lived in towns and carried on trade with Indians and with other settlements in Louisiana owned and cultivated farms. With the well known liberality of the Spanish government, grants of land were very easy to secure. Anyone who had performed a service for the government or who promised to perform such a service in the future could obtain a grant of land. These grants were also given for the purpose of encouraging the development of industries. It is recorded in some cases, in connection with these grants, that they were made because the grantee expected to cut down timber on the land or because he expected to use the wood for smelting lead or other ores. These Spanish land grants varied in size. It was a custom in the mineral district to give every discoverer of a mine at least four arpents of land. Outside the mineral district large grants were frequently made. Twenty thousand and even thirty thousand arpents was not an unusual grant. These grants were made without any reference to the French surveys or to any particular system of lands surveyed. Generally they followed a line of a creek, or the meanderings of a swamp, or they included the tillable land in a certain valley, or they stretched from hill-top to hill-top in a most irregular way. It is a rather curious thing that practically the only trace of Spanish occupancy in Missouri consists in these old land grants. The name of New Madrid, of course, perpetuates the attempt of Morgan to found a great Spanish town and a few other settlements bear Spanish names. Outside of these, however, few memorials of Spain exist. No great public works were undertaken or carried through, no codes of laws were made, no great industries developed, only the grants testify to the presence of the Spaniard. These Spanish grants, owing to the irregularity of their boundaries and the apparently careless way in which they were recorded have been one of the most fruitful sources of legal controversy within the state. It has required a great deal of litigation to determine the ownership of much of the land covered by these grants.

About 1789 the Spanish government laid out a road running from New Madrid to St. Louis. This road crossed Big Prairie, passed through the "Rich Woods" across Scott county to Cape Girardeau and thence to St. Louis by way of Ste. Genevieve. Through the greater part of its course it followed the old Indian trace along which De Soto very probably travelled. The route was determined by the Spanish as it had been for the Indians by the great sandy ridge which stretches from south the "Big Swamp" south of Cape Girardeau to Caruthersville in Pemiscot county touching the river at New Madrid. This road was called by the Spanish "el camino real" the King's Highway. In 1803 the expedition which De Lassus led to New Madrid passed along this road, cutting it out wider as they went. In 1808 the Territorial assembly of the District of Louisiana which was the name by which Missouri was then known, ordered that a road be opened between St. Louis and New Madrid. This road, doubtless, followed the old Spanish road, the King's Highway.

Between Cape Girardeau and New Madrid the road is still in use for a great part of the way. Between Cape Girardeau and Perryville there is a part of the road still in use; that part between the Maramec river and the City of St. Louis is also used now. Its name is perpetuated in a boulevard in St. Louis, called King's Highway. This is, perhaps, the oldest road in the state.

CHAPTER VIII

GOVERNMENT UNDER FRANCE AND SPAIN

LOUISIANA UNDER LA SALLE—THE PROVINCE OF LOUISIANA—CAPITALS AND GOVERNORS—CESSION TO SPAIN—PROVIDENCE OF UPPER LOUISIANA — LIEUTENANT GOVERNORS OF UPPER LOUISIANA—DISTRICTS AND COMMANDANTS—SYNDICS—AUTHORITY OF OFFICIALS—FRENCH LAW RETAINED—CHARACTER OF GOVERNMENT—THE CABILDO AT NEW ORLEANS—ORGANIZATION OF MILITIA—"L'ANNEE DU COUP" ATTACK ON ST. LOUIS—TREACHERY OF GOVERNOR LEYBA—ACTION OF THE STE. GENEVIEVE COMPANY—EXPEDITION TO NEW MADRID—PUNISHMENT OF INDIANS—ORDERS CONCERNING TAVERNS AND SALE OF LIQUOR TO INDIANS.

We have seen something of the formation of the various settlements of Upper Louisiana, of the character and life of its people, and it is desired in this chapter to give a brief account of the government exercised by both France and Spain over the territory before its transfer to the United States.

In 1682, when La Salle reached the mouth of the Mississippi river, he took possession of all the territory drained by it and its tributaries in the name of the king of France. He bestowed upon this vast region, which was as extensive as the valley of the Mississippi, the name of Louisiana, and claimed to exercise over it authority as commandant of Louisiana.

In 1698 the French organized the province of Louisiana with the seat of government at Port Biloxi, near New Orleans. The capital of the province was kept here until 1701 when it was moved to Mobile, Alabama. There it remained until 1723, when it was returned to New Orleans. The governors of this province of Louisiana were as follows: Sauvolle, 1698 to 1701; Bienville, July 22, 1701, to May 17, 1713; LaMothe Cadillac, May 17, 1713, to 1717; De l'Epinay, March 9, 1717, to 1718; Bienville, March 9, 1718, to January 16, 1724; Boisbriant, January 16, 1724, to 1726; Perier, 1726 to 1733; Bienville, 1733 to May 10, 1743; De Vaudreuil, May 10, 1743, to February 9, 1753; Kerlerec, February 9, 1753, to June 29, 1763; D'Abbadie, June 29, 1763, to February 4, 1765; Aubry, February, 1765, acting governor.

In 1763, France ceded to England all of that part of Louisiana east of the Mississippi river. She had promised by the secret treaty of Ildefonso to give to Spain the western part of Louisiana, but the fact of this treaty was not generally known for many years and France continued to exercise authority over Louisiana west of the Mississippi river. Just before the transfer of the territory to Spain the province of Upper Louisiana was organized, including all that part of Louisiana north of the Arkansas river. It was sometimes called the country of the Illinois. The capital of Upper Louisiana was St. Louis. The government was administered by a commandant. Only one served; he was Louis St. Ange de Bellerive, from July 17, 1765, to May 20, 1770 (de facto).

On May 20, 1770, the Spanish officials acting under the treaty of November 3, 1762, took possession of Upper Louisiana. They styled the commandant of Upper Louisiana, the lieutenant governor of the province of Upper Louisiana, with capital at St. Louis. The following were the lieutenant governors of this province: Pedro Piernas, May 20, 1770, to May 19, 1775; Francisco Cruzat, May 19, 1775, to June 17, 1778; Fernando De Leyba, June 17, 1778, to June 8, 1780; Francisco de Cartabona, June 8, 1780, to September 24, 1789 (acting); Francisco Cruzat, September 24, 1780, to November 27, 1787; Manuel Perez, November 27, 1787, to July 21, 1792; Zenon Trudeau, July 21, 1792, to August 29, 1799; Carlos Dehault de Delassus, August 29, 1799, to March 9, 1804.

These lieutenant governors of Upper Louisiana were sometimes called in the Spanish official documents, lieutenant governors at St. Louis for "San Luis, San Genoveva and the District of the Ylinneses." The lieutenant governor of Upper Louisiana was regarded as subordinate to the governor and captain general of Louisiana who had his seat at New Orleans.

This province of Upper Louisiana under the authority of the lieutenant governor was, as we have seen, divided into districts. Over each one of these districts was stationed a commandant who had both civil and military authority. He was regarded as the subordinate of the lieutenant governor at St. Louis. An exception, however, was made in case of the commandant at New Madrid. He was a sub-delegate, was the direct subordinate of the governor general at New Orleans and was thus independent of the authority of the lieutenant governor at St. Louis. Each of these commandants had under him one or more subordinate officers known as syndics. In each one of the various settlements within the district there was appointed a syndic, usually the most prominent and influential citizen in the settlement, who became a personal representative of the commandant exercising a part of his authority.

Each commandant was charged with the administration of the law in his district. He had authority to try minor cases, both civil and criminal. His jurisdiction, however, was limited by the amount of property involved. All cases which involved a considerable amount fell under the direct jurisdiction of the lieutenant governor. The commandant was also charged with the care of all government papers relating to his district and was required to take possession of the estates of deceased persons and to make an inventory thereof. The commandant was, also, commander of the military force consisting, usually, of one or two companies of militia.

The law administered by all of these various officials, governors, lieutenant governors, commandants and syndics was very largely French law. When the province of Louisiana was granted to Cruzat it was with the express understanding that the law of Paris, called by the French "coutume de Paris," was to extend over Louisiana. It was clearly within the province of the Spanish authority to have entirely changed its law and to have substituted for it the Spanish system of law; this, however, they did not do. They made certain changes in the law, especially with regard to the granting of land and to the collection of revenue, but so far as those great provinces of the law which define the rights and duties of individuals and the holding and transfer of property were concerned, the Spanish retained almost unchanged, the French law. They did this because the settlers were, many of them, French; they were acquainted with the law of France; they had acquired and held property under it, and it was really less difficult for Spanish officials to continue the administration of this law than it would have been to make a change. They were the more inclined to this course because of the fact that the Spanish law and French law are quite similar. They were both derived from the old Roman civil law and in their fundamental principles were the same.

This law derived from the civil law is still in force in Louisiana, which is the only one of the states in the union where the English common law is not in force. The civil law differs from the common law in many vital respects, and it was this law, whether French or Spanish in its form, that was administered by the Spanish officials in the province of Louisiana. The question of language gave considerable trouble. There were three principal languages spoken in Upper Louisiana—Spanish, which was the language of the officials, and French, and English, the language of the settlers. Spanish was the official language, and trials and other official proceedings were supposed to be conducted in Spanish, but very frequently, owing to the prevalence of the French language, it was used even in the official proceedings. In each one of the districts there was an official interpreter who assisted the commandant in the hearing of cases by translating from one language to the other as necessity required. Cousin, it will be recalled, acted in this capacity in Cape Girardeau; he drew up petitions and other official papers for settlers, both French and American; these petitions were presented to the commandant, and were in French or Spanish, either being acceptable.

The government exercised by all of these various officials was in theory a practically absolute despotism; the power being in the hands of the officers. In fact, however, the rigor of the law was tempered to suit the times and occasions and the government was often paternal in character. The thing which bore most heavily on the American settlers and which made them most impatient of Spanish control was the dilatory character of some proceedings. This statement does not, however, apply to the proceedings before the various commandants. They were usually transacted with commendable despatch. In fact, most of the trials and other proceedings before the commandants are rather remarkable for the speed with which they were conducted. It was not unusual for the issues to be joined and a decision to be rendered within a very short time. Execution of the sentence was usually summary, but the authority of the commandant was sometimes exercised in order to postpone proceedings and to prevent unnecessary hardship. An instance of this is recorded in the life of Lorimier: One, Josiah Lee, had abandoned his wife and was ordered by Lorimier to leave the country. All persons were forbidden, under penalty, to harbor or help him in any way. Lee, however, presented a very humble petition in which he confessed his fault and prayed that he might be permitted to remain, on condition that he should not again offend. This petition seems to have been granted, for the name of Lee is found on the tax records for several years after this incident. It required but little time and no further formalities than an expression of the commandant's pleasure to dispose of this infraction of the law of the province.

It was quite otherwise, however, with regard to those matters which were within the jurisdiction of the officials at New Orleans. There the governor and captain general of Louisiana was assisted in his labors by a cabildo. This cabildo, or council, was composed of eleven persons, including an attorney general, a syndic and other officers. There was also an officer charged with the royal revenue, who was called the intendant. There were many other officers besides the cabildo and they enforced the cumbersome restrictions of trade with rigor. The Spanish were not a commercial people, and their regulations with regard to trade were the regulations of the middle ages. To carry a load of merchandise to New Orleans and turn it over for shipment to other parts of the world was a long and tedious process, so far as complying with the regulations of the port was concerned. These restricting and hampering regulations much retarded commerce—in fact, more than any other cause, perhaps, made the Americans impatient and intolerant of Spanish control of the Mississippi river.

The Spanish government required the commandant at each post in Upper Louisiana to organize all of the able-bodied citizens into military companies. All persons between the ages of fourteen and fifty were liable to this service and the companies were required to be ready for service at any time they were called upon. There were small bodies of regular Spanish troops maintained at St. Louis and New Madrid; the other posts were defended entirely by the military companies. These companies found employment in defending the posts from attack by Indians, and one purpose of their organization and maintenance was to be prepared in case of an attack by the Americans.

The year 1780 was known by the French inhabitants as "L'Annee du Coup," (the year of the attack). This was during the war of the Revolution and the English were stirring up the Indians throughout all the west to attack Americans, and it was rumored in the early part of this year that these British and Indians were contemplating an attack on St. Louis. The commandant at St. Louis was Lieutenant Governor Ferdinand Leyba. He was instructed by the Spanish authorities to prepare the post against the threatened attack. He accordingly ordered the military company at Ste. Genevieve, which at that time was the only company outside of St. Louis, to be sent to St. Louis. For the purpose of executing this order, Don Francisco Cartobona was sent to Ste. Genevieve. He gathered a company together consisting of sixty men under the command of Charles Valle, and embarked them on a keel-boat for St. Louis. The attack upon the town was made May 26, 1780. The attacking force numbered about fifteen hundred Indians, under command of a British officer. Governor Leyba acted in a very peculiar manner. Either he was cowardly and afraid to take part in the defense of the town, or else he was a traitor. It appears that on the very day the attack was made he was intoxicated, and instead of making any effort at defense, he merely did all in his power to prevent such defense. The citizens of the town, however, did all in their power to protect themselves. There has been a question raised regarding the conduct of the Ste. Genevieve company on this occasion. They have been charged with cowardice, but this was untrue. The facts in the case as presented by General Firmin A. Rozier, are these: Just before the attack was made, Governor Leyba refused to allow the Ste. Genevieve company to be supplied with ammunition. Captain Valle attempted to supply this lack by seizing three kegs of powder in the possession of a lady who resided in the town. She very reluctantly allowed the powder to be taken and conveyed to the company headquarters. While Captain Valle was temporarily absent, Governor Leyba ordered the company to spike their guns and to march up into a garret and remain. Captain Valle, however, returned and refused to allow the order to be obeyed. He and his company, then, did all they could to aid the citizens of St. Louis in the defense of the town; their efforts were successful, and the attack of the Indians failed.

In 1802 there occurred an incident which cast a light on the military arrangements of the Spanish. That year David Trotter, who lived in the New Madrid district, was killed by some Indians; they were members of a band of Creeks who had come from the eastern states and were engaged in thieving and plundering on both sides of the Mississippi. Through the efforts of Louis Lorimier, five of the Indians were captured and one of them was condemned to be executed. Lieutenant Governor De Lassus, who resided in St. Louis, determined to be present at the execution and to take personal charge of the affair. About two weeks before the date, he set out from St. Louis for New Madrid. On reaching Ste. Genevieve, he ordered the three companies of militia at that point to be assembled and to accompany him under arms to New Madrid. He did the same at Cape Girardeau and further increased his army by the addition of the three companies at New Madrid. He thus had almost a full regiment of soldiers for the occasion.

The order book used by Colonel De Lassus on this expedition is still in existence and it contains a great number and variety of orders. De Lassus was an officer, trained in the Spanish army, and he conducted his expedition after the most approved manner of Spanish warfare. The most rigid etiquette prevailed, and everything was performed with the utmost care. The second in command of the expedition was Don Francisco Valle. Don Joseph Pratte and Don Francisco Valle, Jr., and Don Camille De Lassus were commanders of companies and the last named was also an adjutant. There was a bodyguard for the lieutenant governor consisting of a mounted orderly from each company.

On arriving at New Madrid De Lassus appointed officers for the three companies at that place. One of these was a company of cavalry of which Richard Jones Waters was captain; George K. Reagan, lieutenant; and John B. Barsaloux, ensign. John La Valle was captain; Pierre La Forge, lieutenant, and John Charpentier, ensign of the first company of infantry. The officers of the second company were Robert McCoy, captain; Joseph Hunot, lieutenant; and John Hart, ensign.

The prisoner then under sentence of execution was brought forth and the detail of soldiers was ordered out, who proceeded to execute the sentence by shooting the prisoner. The corpse was then buried by the soldiers and the other four prisoners were turned over to the chief of the band under his promise that they should not again trouble the inhabitants of New Madrid district. The expedition then returned with the same care for etiquette with which it had been assembled.

While on this expedition Governor De Lassus issued some very strict orders regarding the sale of intoxicants to Indians. He pointed out that the Indians were usually peaceful and law-abiding, except when they had been inflamed by liquor. Trotter, himself, had been killed by the Indians to whom he had unlawfully sold liquor. In view of these circumstances the governor ordered that there should be only a limited number of tavern and dram-shop keepers; that they must have an appointment from the governor, himself, and must be persons of good conduct; that under no pretext whatever, were they to give or sell liquor to the Indians or slaves.

They were ordered to give immediate notice of any disorder in their houses to the commandant or nearest syndic. Any person found keeping an unauthorized tavern or dram-shop, or who should have sold liquor unlawfully, was to be both imprisoned and fined, and any person who, whether a keeper of a tavern or dram-shop or any other, should sell or give liquor to Indians was bound to be arrested and sent in irons, at his own expense, to New Orleans; all his property was to be seized until the matter was decided by the governor-general. The commanders of posts were held responsible for the enforcement of these orders.

At New Madrid the governor licensed John Baptiste Olive to keep a tavern, in the same district, on the road to Illinois, Mr. Edward Robertson, and at Little Prairie, Mr. Charles Guilbault. The license tax for these persons was to be such a sum as the governor general might fix and this tax was very appropriately to be used in the construction of a prison at New Madrid.

CHAPTER IX

SOCIAL LIFE

POPULATION IN 1804—SETTLEMENTS—OCCUPATIONS—DIFFERENCES BETWEEN FRENCH AND AMERICA SETTLEMENTS—HOUSES OF THE FRENCH—STOCKADES—FOOD AND COOKING—DIFFERENCES IN THE FRENCH PRODUCED BY RESIDENCE IN THIS COUNTRY—SOCIAL LIFE—DRESS—AMUSEMENTS—LA GUIGNOLEE—CONTENTED CHARACTER OF THE FRENCH—TRADE—AMERICAN SETTLERS—CHARACTERISTIC LIFE—HOUSES—CLOTHING—FOOD—LAW-ABIDING CHARACTERS—GERMAN SETTLERS—ABSENCE OF SPANISH SETTLERS—MERCHANTS—PRICES—PRODUCTS—TRAVEL—ROADS—RIVER TRAVEL—KEEL-BOATS—RELIGIOUS CONDITIONS—FIRST SERVICES—RESTRICTIVE LAWS OF SPAIN—RECORDS OF THE CATHOLIC CHURCH IN STE. GENEVIEVE—FATHER MEURIN—FATHER GIBAULT—JAMES MAXWELL—FIRST CHURCH BUILDINGS—SUPPORT OF PRIESTS—BISHOP DUBOURG—DE ANDREIS—FOUNDING OF ST. MARY'S SEMINARY—DANGER OF MISUNDERSTANDING THE CHARACTER OF THE PEOPLE.

By the time of the transfer to the United States, in 1804, there were living in the territory of Louisiana about 10,120 people. Of these, the greater number were in Southeast Missouri. Each of the five districts into which the Spanish had divided the country for purposes of administration was in a flourishing condition. There had been a considerable immigration into the district from the territory of the United States across the river, and, as we have seen, in a few places there were large numbers of French settlers. The following table gives as correctly as can be determined the population of the principal settlements at the time of the Louisiana Purchase: Cape Girardeau district, 1,470; Ste. Genevieve district, 2,350 whites and 520 slaves; New Madrid district, 1,350 whites and 120 slaves.

By this date settlements had been made in most of the present counties of this section. There were probably no settlements in Dunklin, Butler, Ripley, Carter, Stoddard, and Reynolds counties, but in all the other counties there were at least some attempts at settlement made. There were flourishing towns at New Madrid, Cape Girardeau and Ste. Genevieve. Ste. Genevieve was a distinctly French settlement; Cape Girardeau was just as distinctly an American settlement, while New Madrid was in part French and in part American.

As we have seen, these people were attracted here by a number of things. It is, perhaps, true that the greater number of them came on account of the richness of the soil and the possibility of obtaining land on easy terms from the Spanish government. The settlers were largely farmers. This is true of the districts of Cape Girardeau and New Madrid; in fact, outside of trading and the running of an occasional mill, there were no other settled industries besides agriculture. Some of the inhabitants depended in part upon hunting and trapping, but the greater number of them were almost entirely dependent upon agriculture. It was this fact that led the American settlers to open up farms and to scatter out over the country upon these farms, rather than to gather together in larger towns and villages. We find that in the Cape Girardeau district there were settlements in a large number of places extending over quite a part of the territory of the district. Nearly all the population of the district was to be found on scattered farms. This was, in part, due to that intense spirit of independence which rendered the American impatient of restraint and unwilling to be hampered or hindered in his activities within the towns.

The inhabitants of the district of Ste. Genevieve were, by no means, so entirely dependent upon agriculture. This was the district that contained the mineral region. Many of the settlers were engaged in mining; in fact, it seems true that more than half the people of the district were supported in part, at least, by the mines. It should be remembered that mining was carried on in a most primitive way. They were all surface mines, there having been no deep shafts sunk in the district. There was little use of machinery, so that the production of even relatively small quantities of lead required the work of a large number of persons. We find around each one of the larger mines a group of houses, a little settlement, where there were trading posts for the exchange of goods. We find, too, that considerable numbers of the inhabitants were engaged in transporting the lead from the mines to the river and on the river to the various places to which it was shipped. There were a number, too, who were engaged in trading. Commercial enterprises were developed more extensively in the district of Ste. Genevieve than any other part of the territory.

Another striking difference between the Ste. Genevieve district and the others, lay in the greater concentration of the population in the towns and villages. Travelers were struck by the contrast in this respect. This grouping of the inhabitants was a result of the French character. The French emigrants to America were in a great majority of cases industrious, hard working people. They were perfectly willing to undergo hardships and dangers in their attempts to gain wealth, but the French are a distinctly social people, and, while these settlers here were willing to endure privation and to face the dangers of the wilderness and to toil unceasingly for the accomplishment of their purposes, they were not willing to give up that social life which they loved. It was this social part of their nature which prevented them from scattering over the country and developing farms as did the Americans. The American family was satisfied to live upon a farm a long distance removed from others. Not so with the French family. There must be society and intermingling of the people. While the French developed agriculture and carried on farms in a considerable way, we find them living not on their farms but grouped together in towns. It was this fact that accounts for the common fields attached to the French towns. The people who lived in the town of Ste. Genevieve, many of them, were farmers. They were perfectly willing to cultivate the soil, provided it could be done without causing them to endure the isolation of farming life. A great tract of fertile land which lies just south of the town of Ste. Genevieve, which is now known as the Big

Field, was owned in common by the inhabitants of the town. It was divided up for the purposes of cultivation at the beginning of the year. It provided an opportunity for the pursuit of farming without demanding the sacrifice of social life.

These differences in the spirit and attitude of the French and the Americans was the cause of a great difference in development of the two sections of the country. It is evident, of course, that no new country can be thoroughly settled and reduced to the purposes of agriculture, except by people who are willing to settle upon the land itself. Here the American settlers possessed a very great advantage over the French.

We have referred to the fact that the French settlers lived in towns. Most of them of the well-to-do class built for themselves comfortable houses. These houses usually stood near the street or road, the front yard being small, but back of the house there was ordinarily a considerable enclosure, in which were to be found the family orchard, the garden in which was grown a variety of vegetables, the cabins for servants or slaves, and other buildings for the use and convenience of the inhabitants. The amount of ground depended, of course, upon the wealth of the owner. The well-to-do among the French usually enclosed a considerable space for these purposes. The house and grounds were

Old-Time Windlass

usually surrounded by a stout fence. This fence was in reality something of a stockade and was strongly built of pickets driven into the ground and sometimes reinforced with earth and stone. It really served as a means of protection against the Indians, for all of the people were exposed more or less to the danger of Indian assault. The various tribes of Indians living in the vicinity of Ste. Genevieve were accustomed, at times, when they came into possession of whiskey, to take the town. On these occasions the inhabitants usually retired within their houses, closed

Old-Fashioned Ore Hoisters in Action

the gates of their yards, barricaded the doors and windows and waited until the Indians tired of their pranks.

The houses themselves were usually one story in height. They were long and low, with a porch in front and rear and sometimes entirely around the house. They were built of wood, sometimes of logs and more often, perhaps, framed together and covered with boards running up and down on the framing. Plastering was used on the outside of some of these houses, and sometimes they were weather-boarded, though this was unusual. The houses were substantial and warmly built. Each room was lighted by one window with small panes of glass. There was generally no attic, or else if there was an attic provided for, it was rarely lighted by a window or reached by any permanent steps. The houses were ordinarily heated by open fires built in the fire places of great chimneys. These chimneys were usually made of sticks and earth. Four great poles were driven into the earth and drawn nearly together at the top and then the structure of sticks and earth built up between these poles. Sometimes, though, there was a stone chimney and fire place connected with the house. That the houses were substantial is shown by the fact that a number of them are still in use in Ste. Genevieve though more than a century old.

One of the differences between the French settlers and the American was in the character of the food and in cooking. The French people are noted for their skill as cooks, and the early French settlers in Missouri were no exception to the rule. American travelers among these French settlers were struck by the variety of food that there was prepared. Instead of the usual dishes of meat variously cooked and corn bread, such as was found on the tables of the Americans, the French had many salads, vegetables and soups. They cooked meat, it is true, but it by no means occupied so large a place on the bill of fare as it did among the Americans.

It should be said that most of the French settlers were French Canadians. Some of the families came direct from France. Some of these were of the nobility and left France during the turbulent times of the French Revolution. These settled at New Bourbon, near Ste. Genevieve, but the greater majority of the people were descendants of the French settlers in Canada. They retained many of the characteristics of the French; but long residence in America, in an entirely different environment, had produced some changes in them. This was noted by early travelers, especially in their language and in their bearing and habits of speech. The natural vivacity and liveliness of the French, especially those of the higher class, was modified among the settlers in Missouri. They were more vivacious than the Americans, it is true, but there was a suppression and restraint that was not observable among the original French settlers. The language, too, had lost something of its sharpness and had acquired a softness and musicalness in this country.

Contradictory accounts are given by early travelers concerning the habits and character of these French settlers. They impressed some of the early writers by their courtesy, their careful training of their children, their restraint and dignity, their openhanded hospitality and real culture and grace of manner. Some of these writers declared that nowhere else was to be found greater perfection of manners or of character than among these French. They were said to be very moderate in their use of wine; most genial and kind toward all who came in contact with them; crime was practically unknown among them, and the courts had little, even, of civil business to transact. Those who saw them in this favorable light were impressed by the dignity of the people which arose, in part, from the feeling of security in which they lived. They were in the midst of plenty, land was cheap, and the soil productive. The woods were full of game, and trade with the Indians was profitable. There was no reason for any to worry concerning a livelihood. From these conditions there seems to have developed among them an ease of manner and a dignity born of assured position that left its impress upon all that they did. The women were said to possess unusual refinement, to be devoted to their families and to have unusual ability as housekeepers.

On the other hand, some of the early travelers saw the French settlers with different eyes. They said that they were inclined to be slothful; that they were content with a bare living taken from the soil; that they were given to indulgence in strong drink; and that the children were not properly instructed, but allowed a great deal of freedom and liberty in their lives.

The dress of all the French, whether rich or poor, was distinguished by its simplicity. The men wore a long coat and cape, so designed that it could be thrown up over the head. From these circumstances it was called the "capote." They wore shirts of various kinds of cloth, usually linen trousers and Indian moccasins. The women, too, dressed with great simplicity, but tried to impress visitors that they were not altogether out of the fashion. The centers of fashion were many hundreds of miles away; yet, in spite of these conditions, the women of the French communities generally managed to know something of the styles. They, too, wore the Indian moccasins, and it was the custom of both men and women to cover the head with a handkerchief, usually blue in color. It should be said, too, that most of them were able to possess, even when they were comparatively poor, clothes which were set apart for Sunday wear and for holiday occasions. The inventory which has been preserved of the estate of some of the French settlers discloses that the love of dress was present among them.

All accounts agree that the great majority of the French settlers were noted for their devotion to truth and for strict honesty in their dealings with one another, and even with outsiders.

It is not to be supposed that, even in these remote places, amusement was not sought after with the same eagerness that it is pursued elsewhere. The French settlements almost universally observed a sort of carnival season, when a large part of the time was given up to celebrations, and to the pursuit of various amusements.

Of these amusements, the one most passionately followed was dancing. Sunday afternoon in these settlements was, usually, devoted to dancing. The children and young people came together under the supervision of their elders, and all of them engaged in that pastime which they most thoroughly loved. Some of the travelers say that these Sunday afternoon assemblies were really schools for the instruction of the children in good manners. Be that as it may, they were held, and it was a well known custom in Ste. Genevieve and other of the French towns.

The season of the year when amusement

was most sought was the beginning of the year. On New Year's Eve there was a custom, among the young men, to gather in a numerous group, arrayed in fantastic dress, some appearing as clowns, some as negroes, and others as Indians, but each carrying a bucket, box, basket or other receptacle. Thus dressed, the young men made their way from house to house, and at each place they sang what was called "La Guignolee." This was a jocular song in which there was demanded from the master and mistress of the house their eldest daughter, and also a contribution of some sort of food which was called "La Guignolee." After the donation had been given the young men danced before the house and then went on to the next house. At some central point, before day, the whole population of the settlement assembled and heard mass. After mass all the children and grandchildren made their way to their parents where they placed themselves upon their knees and implored a parental blessing. This pleasing custom of submitting themselves to the authority of their parents and of imploring a blessing upon them was one of the peculiar customs of the French settlements.

On January 6th, of each year, there was given at some selected house a supper and a dance. A cake was baked for this occasion which contained four beans. At some time during the festivity the cake was cut into small pieces and a piece given to each girl present. The girls who were fortunate enough to obtain a slice containing one of the beans were hailed as queens. Each queen then selected some young man as king. The selection was made known by the presentation to him of a bouquet. The four young men thus selected were charged with the preparation of the next ball. They made arrangements for it and bore the expenses of giving it. These balls were called Bals du Roi. At each one of them, arrangements were made for the holding of the next.[*]

One thing concerning the condition of these French people, which struck all observers, was the absence of anything like a caste, or even a class system among them. The people were almost all related by blood or by marriage, and this fact tended to produce a feeling of unity among them which very largely prevented the development of the class spirit. It was true, of course, that men of intelligence and wealth were more highly regarded than others, but this regard was largely a personal matter and was paid to the individual showing great attainments, and not to the class itself.

Innovations were not regarded with favor. There was something of a clannish spirit among them. They were satisfied with their conditions of life and they did not wish for changes. Their wants were easily supplied from the produce of the soil, and from the wealth obtained by traffic and from the mines. It is true everywhere, that among a population no larger than that of the French settlement, bound together by ties of blood and language in a country where plenty abounds for everyone, there is an absence of a stimulus to great progress. This feeling that they had no need to display very great activity, a feeling of security and well being, led some who visited the settlements to regard the people as lazy. They were not lazy —they were industrious and frugal—but they found that they had time for leisure, and need not devote all of their energies to the acquisition of wealth. They were simple

[*] Missouri Historical Society Collections, Vol. II, No. 1, p. 12.

people and had little desire for greater things than they found about them. That progress among them was slow is evidenced by the statement of Breckenridge. He was a native of Pennsylvania; and was sent at an early age by his father to live for three years in Ste. Genevieve, in order to study French. His record, in the form of a diary, of those years, is very valuable on account of the light it casts on the conditions there. He says that for many years there was no public bakery in all the French settlements; there was no loom or even a spinning wheel; there was not even a churn for butter making. Butter, when it was made at all, was made by shaking cream within a bottle, or a bag. There was very little money. These conditions resulted in all material for clothing being imported. The French of Louisiana bought the material for their clothing and blankets, their flax, their calimanco, in Philadelphia or in Baltimore. Among them was to be seen no home-spun cloth, such as distinguished the American settlement. Their principal trade, in the absence of money, was carried on by means of barter and exchange. As a substitute for money lead was sometimes used and more often peltry, or deer skins, supplied the place.

Among these people wealth was almost entirely in the form of personal property. Land was not regarded very highly as a form of wealth. This arose from the fact that land was abundant, that it might be had on very easy terms and was, consequently, very cheap. The principal form of this wealth was household furniture, clothing, and slaves. Some effort has been made to estimate the trade of these settlements. It is difficult to determine how extensive that trade was. It has been said that from 1789 to 1804 the fur trade of Upper Louisiana amounted to $200,-000. This amount, however, does not represent all of the trade, but only that part of it which passed through the hands of the Spanish officials. That large part of the Indian trade which went to the English is not included in this sum. Besides the fur trade, the settlers exported lead and provisions down the river, principally to New Orleans; they sent lead to Canada, and lead and salt to Philadelphia and Baltimore. It was in return for these exports that the settlers received their supplies of clothing and materials from the cities.

Communities situated as these French settlements were, developed a life of their own. They were cut off, as we have seen, from the centers of French influence by hundreds and even thousands of miles. They were divided by the river from the American settlements, and divided even more distinctly by differences in race and language. It is impossible to tell how far a civilization distinct in itself with social and political institutions might have developed in Upper Louisiana, had time been given for its development. We cannot now say that the French might not have cultivated institutions similar to those of the American colonies. Doubt, however, is cast on the probability of this, by the fact that they were careless with regard to matters of education. There were some private schools but they were limited in term and seemed to have produced no great results. Instruction in these schools was confined to reading. writing and a little arithmetic.

Matthew Kennedy, an American, was in Ste. Genevieve in 1771; John and Israel Dodge were in New Bourbon shortly after the founding of this settlement about 1794. and in 1774 John Hildebrand was on the Maramec river. In that same neighborhood.

a little later, was William Boli. These seem to have been the first American settlers in Upper Louisiana. The great tide of American immigration did not begin until about 1790. When Morgan had outlined his scheme for the forming of a great state, with its capital at New Madrid, he advertised very extensively the attractions of his new settlement, and induced a number of Americans to become interested in Louisiana. The surveyors whom he brought with him, among whom was Christopher Hays, induced many of their friends and acquaintances to settle in Louisiana. It happened that this scheme of Morgan's coincided in time with the great western movement into Kentucky. Some of the Spanish officials, even before the time of Morgan, saw that the probabilities were that the Americans would come in large numbers to Upper Louisiana, and that they would probably be unwilling to live long under the rule of Spain. When Americans became acquainted with the territory and all the advantages of life here, they came in large numbers. By 1804 half the population of the Ste. Genevieve district was American, two-thirds of the population of the New Madrid district was American, and of the population of the Cape Girardeau district, all were American with the exception of a few families.

The life of these Americans was quite different from that of their French neighbors. Most of the Americans were men who had had experience in a new country. They had been pioneers in Virginia, Kentucky, and Tennessee; they were accustomed to the life of the wilderness; and they had that bold, independent attitude which made them impatient of restraint. They did not possess the social nature of the French. They were entirely willing to do without neighbors and to forego the delights of social intercourse. We find them scattered about on farms, rather than crowded together into the towns. They took possession of the country and began at once to open up the soil for cultivation. They were men of energy and vitality. They seemed to have seen something of the future of the country and to have appreciated the importance of subduing the wilderness. They were not so much in sympathy with the Indians, nor with the life of the Indians as were the French. They did not have such a romantic attachment for the forest and for the life of nature. They liked the wilds of the new country, but they liked them on account of the possibilities they possessed. Accordingly, they set themselves to the task of clearing the land and putting it into cultivation. Their settlements lacked the charm that was present among the French, but they gave evidence of prosperity and an energy superior to that of the others. Many of the French officials who visited the American settlements about Cape Girardeau were struck by the evidence of thrift and energy. They wished the French settlers might exhibit something of this enterprising spirit.

The houses of these American settlers were the houses which have been characteristic of new settlements all over America. They consisted, usually, of two square pens built of logs. Between them was an open space usually about as large as one of the pens. Over all was a single roof usually extending far enough in both front and rear to form porches. Sometimes the porch at the rear of the house was boarded up forming another room. The cracks between the logs forming the house were filled with mud. There was usually one, and sometimes two, doors in each of these rooms, besides one or two openings for light. These openings were sometimes closed with board shutters, and occasionally were filled with glass. The rooms had puncheon floors. The space between the two rooms was left open for the circulation of light and air. It was not infrequently left without a floor. In each of the rooms there was a large fire place. The chimney was usually built of mud and sticks, sometimes of stone. One of these large rooms were not much concerned about religion, else they would not have said themselves to be good Catholics. They were most of them willing to set aside whatever convictions they had on religious subjects, in order to be admitted to the Spanish territory. The testimony of missionaries who traveled among them is that they were in a deplorable condition, religiously. They had no services of their own to attend, many of them were unwilling to at-

HOME OF OUR FATHERS

was used for the kitchen, the other was the family living room. The slaves owned by the family lived in small cabins in the rear of the house. The American family's wealth and importance was estimated by the size of the barns and the number of slave cabins on the place.

These American settlers were part of them Catholics, such as the settlers at St. Michaels and many of those who settled in Perry county; many of the others were Protestants, and some of them professed no religion at all. It is evident that many of the Protestants tend the services of the Catholic church, so they were without religious instruction. Sunday among them was too often a holiday given up to the pursuit of pleasure of one kind and another.

Unlike the French settlers, the Americans were people who depended largely upon their own resources. Instead of importing goods for their clothing from New Orleans, Philadelphia or Baltimore, each house of the American settler became a factory where thread was spun and cloth woven to supply the wants of the household. Nearly all of the settlers were accustomed to dress in the home-spun cloth called "jeans." This was woven from thread, spun at the house itself, and the garments were made from the cloth by the women of the household. This famous "jeans" was dyed various colors, perhaps the one most favored was known as "butter-nut." This cloth was almost indestructible. It was all wool; there was no mixture of cotton and wool such as is found in almost all the cloth of the present time. There was among these people no such careful attention to dress as distinguished the French. They were content if they had a sufficient amount of comfortable and presentable clothing. There was but little effort to follow the fashions, and no great pride was taken in a large collection of garments of one sort or other. The women wore the sun-bonnet and the men frequently covered the head with a cap made from coon skin or bear skin. Moccasins were frequently worn by both sexes. The Indian moccasin was so well suited to the life of the woods that it was adopted by practically all the people who lived among the Indians.

The food of the Americans was by no means so varied nor so daintily prepared and cooked as the food of the French. There was an abundance of it and most of it was wholesome, but there was not that attention to the minor and lighter items of diet that the French gave. Instead of soups, salads, vegetables and desserts, the staple items on the table of the American settlers were meat and corn bread. This meat was the meat of wild game, deer, turkey and other varieties, or it was the meat of the hog. Bacon was one of the favored dishes to be found on almost all tables.

American settlers were usually strong and robust. The men were distinguished for their strength of body, their vigor and their hardiness. These qualities were to be expected in a race of men who went out to subdue the wilderness. Many stories are

HOME-MADE LOOM AND OPERATOR

told of the feats of strength performed by them. They gloried in their strength. They were usually content in their brawls and quarrels with the weapons with which nature had provided them, and whatever disturbances took place among them, were usually settled by an appeal to personal prowess.

The American settlers were usually law-abiding people. They had something of a dread of the Spanish criminal law. There were stories told concerning the horrible sufferings endured by prisoners in Spanish dungeons and in Spanish mines where criminals were frequently sent. This account of Spanish authority had, perhaps, its wholesome effect in keeping the population quiet; but the thing that more than anything else operated to produce quiet and orderly settlements among the Americans was the law-abiding and independent character of the people themselves. Experience had shown them that people could not expect to be free unless they exercised the virtues of self control. Accordingly, we find the communities of American settlers were very largely self governing. They settled their disputes among themselves, where that was possible, without any appeal to the Spanish authorities or to Spanish law.

Strange as it may seem, nearly all of the American settlers were well affected toward the authority of the Spanish government, and it does not appear that they greeted the change from the authority of Spain to that of the United States with any great rejoicing. Spain had dealt liberally with them in respect to grants of land, and, so far as those of the settlers who were engaged in agriculture were concerned, the Spanish regulations did not hamper them very greatly. Opposition to Spain's control of the Mississippi did not come in any very large measure from west of the river. The opposition which made Spain's continued control of the river impossible arose in the states bordering along the river to the east. We find even expressions of dissatisfaction when the flag of Spain was replaced by that of the United States.

Beside the French and American settlers, of whom we have spoken, there were a few settlements of Germans in Upper Louisiana. We have mentioned some of them, especially those who came to the district of Cape Girardeau. Major Bollinger and the company of men who with him settled on Whitewater were among the earliest of these German settlers. They, too, were hardy and industrious people. They were distinguished for their thrift, for their ability to wring a living from the soil, and to accumulate property.

It is rather curious that in all the years from 1762 to 1802, while Spain was in control of the Louisiana territory, there were very few Spanish people who came to the territory. It seems that the Spanish would have seized the opportunity to settle Louisiana while it was owned and controlled by Spain; such, however, was not the case. There are to be found the names of only two or three families in all of Upper Louisiana who seem to have been of Spanish origin. There were a number of reasons why the Spanish did not settle here. The chief of these was the idea that the Spanish held that the new world was not a place so much for settlement and colonization as it was a place for searching for the precious metals. Long before the acquisition of the territory by Spain, it had become apparent that Upper Louisiana, while rich in lead, contained very little of the precious metals. It was for this reason principally

Pioneer Spinning Wheel

Eating up the Flax

that Spain neglected to colonize the territory. Of course there were other causes which joined with this to produce the same result. One of these was the greater interest which the southern part of the United States and even South America, had for the Spanish. They came from a different climate, and they found the warmer parts of the country more congenial to them.

The merchants who traded in these settlements were very different from the merchants of to-day. Some of them had very small warehouses, but most frequently, the goods of every kind were placed in a large box. They were brought out for inspection only on the demand of the customer. Within this box all kinds of things were kept—sugar, salt, dry goods, paints, tobacco, gunpowder, guns, hatchets; in fact, the whole store of the merchant was usually contained within a single receptacle. The merchant was usually not very enterprising, and was content to wait for the coming of customers and made no great effort to extend his trade. One result of this system of trading was the prevailing high prices of everything that was bought and sold. This was especially true of groceries which were imported from New Orleans, Canada, or the eastern part of the United States. Sugar sold at two dollars a pound, and tea at the same price; coffee was equally as dear. These high prices extended even to the products of the country; butter sold for from thirty to fifty cents a pound; eggs, twenty-five cents a dozen; chickens, forty to fifty cents a piece. All of the travelers of the time speak of these high prices. Cumings, who visited New Madrid in 1809, says that milk, butter, eggs and chickens were outrageously high and Bradbury, who a few years later made a voyage from St. Louis to New Orleans, found similar prices prevailing. It is probably true that these high prices were in part the result of the system of barter that prevailed in most parts of the country. During the Spanish regime the Spanish officials were accustomed to pay for goods, which they bought, in currency; and this attracted to the west side of the river a considerable amount of the produce from Illinois. These circumstances all combined to render the price of articles higher than would otherwise have been maintained.

Nearly all the settlers of the country were engaged in farming, as we have seen, and their principal products were cattle, wheat, corn, and horses. Other things were grown to a limited extent, but these were the staple products. We may well suppose that agriculture was in the primitive state. It is said that in 1804 the entire crop of corn grown by the settlers of New Madrid amounted to only 6,000 bushels. Crops in other settlements were proportionately small. The amount produced barely provided for the necessities of the settlers themselves and left only a small amount for export. Whatever surplus there was was sent east to New Orleans or to Canada. Cattle, of course, could be grown with little expense, owing to the vast range where they lived practically without being fed. This was true to some degree of horses also. It was noted, however, that both cattle and horses deteriorated in Louisiana. No attention was given to the breeding of stock and they decreased in size and quality. Horses were especially valuable on account of the fact that almost all travel on land was done either on foot or on horseback.

One of the great hardships endured by settlers in the new country is the isolation which is unavoidable. It is difficult for us to imagine the situation of the settlers in New Madrid, Cape Girardeau and Ste. Genevieve. They were separated from one another by many miles and they were cut off from the centers of wealth and power by hundreds and thousands of miles. To reach New Orleans or Canada required a journey whose difficulties cannot be measured by us. There were no roads. One who traveled by land must follow the trails or traces as laid out by the Indians and adopted for use by the settlers. These trails were simply paths which led through the woods. Often it was difficult to follow them, owing to their indistinctness; sometimes the trees along them were blazed to prevent them being entirely lost. There were no bridges over the streams; the traveler must make his way across these as best he might. There were no inns, or other provision for one who made his way along these trails. He must carry with him the supplies necessary for his subsistence. Travel along these trails was necessarily limited either to horseback or else on foot. It must have been a great undertaking to go from the settlements in Missouri to Quebec or Montreal in Canada. No matter at what time of year one traveled, he met with great hardships and dangers. The streams were frequently swollen and dangerous to cross; there were long stretches of country consisting of swamps; wild animals were abundant, and savages were still more to be dreaded. There was great suffering from cold in winter, and from heat and mosquitoes in summer; and yet, as difficult as such a journey over land must have been, it was frequently made. Traders found it necessary to go from Missouri to Canada. Some of them made annual trips covering 1,600 to 2,000 miles on land.

The traveler set out with his horse. On either side of his saddle he placed such things as were necessary for his comfort. He procured his provisions, in part, by hunting; he camped at night under the sky, in the forests or on the prairie. In winter time it was frequently necessary to shovel away the snow to find a little dry wood with which to kindle a fire. It was always necessary to be on constant guard against the dangers of the way.

Strange as it may seem, however, this life of travel came to have the very greatest attractions for some men. There was a fascination about the life of the woods, its hardships and even its dangers, which drew men irresistibly to it. This was true not only of men who were reared amid such surroundings; it was true of Europeans who came from the midst of a high state of civilization. They found something in the life of the woods which made their every-day existence at home seem tame and uninspiring by comparison. Scarcely a traveler of all of those who left a record of their wanderings in the west but reveals the influence of this peculiar charm of savage life. Some seemed to revel in it; to feel that for the first time they had come in contact with nature, and were living the life for which men were destined.

If we turn from travel on land, with its lack of roads and its inconveniences, to travel on the river, we find conditions improved indeed and yet arduous, still. In the early times travel on the river was in the large dug-outs called bateaus or pirogues. Nearly all of the early voyages up and down the river were made in these boats. They were copied from the Indian boats and were the hollowed out trunks of large trees. In such a boat it required from twenty-five to thirty days to make the trip from Ste. Genevieve to New Orleans, and it required from three to four months to make the trip from New Orleans to Ste. Genevieve. One of the Spanish commandants boasted that he had just come from New Orleans to St. Louis in one of the king's bateaus in the very short time of ninety-three days. It was in boats like these that the produce, the lead and food was exported from Ste. Genevieve to New Orleans. It was not a great while, however, until the pirogue gave way, as a carrier of freight, to the keel-boat.

The keel-boat was a large, flat bottomed boat, somewhat resembling a canal-boat. It was strongly built, equipped with a mast and sail, had space for carrying considerable cargo, and sometimes accommodation for a passenger or two. The bulwarks of the keel-boat were flat and usually from fourteen to eighteen inches in width, forming a walk entirely around the boat. It was fitted with a large oar, mounted in the rear, by which it was steered. It was propelled in a number of different ways. Sometimes it was rowed by means of oars; occasionally, when the wind was favorable, the sail was set and the boat propelled by the wind; sometimes it was towed as the canal boat was towed. A rope was fastened at the top of the mast, then brought down through a ring in the bow of the boat, and extended to the bank of the river where it was grasped by a number of men. They walked along the tow path and pulled the boat. Perhaps the most characteristic method of propelling the keel-boat, however, was the use of setting poles. These were long poles which were used in the following manner: If the water was of the right depth, the men engaged in propelling the boat, took their places along the bulwarks forming a line on either side as near as possible to the bow, with their faces toward the stern. Each man grasped in his hand one of the setting poles, planted one end against the bottom of the river, put the other to his shoulder and then the line of men pressing against these poles walked toward the rear of the boat. The leading man in each line, upon reaching the rear, dropped out of line, made his way quickly through the boat to the bow, took his place at the rear of the line of men and again walked toward the stern of the boat, pushing as he went. This method of procedure gave a continuous impulse to the boat and was the method most favored by the keel-boat men.

Whatever method was used for the propulsion of these boats, their progress was slow. Twelve to fourteen miles a day was considered a fair rate of travel and eighteen miles a day, remarkable. If the boats were towed by a cordelle or little rope, there was constant trouble, owing to the entangling of this rope in the tree limbs that lined the bank of the river. Constant stops must be made for the purpose of untangling these lines, and there were many other obstructions to be overcome, too. Very frequently at short intervals there were great rafts extending from the bank out into the river, sometimes for a distance of fifty or sixty feet formed of drift wood which had been caught by some obstruction. Such a raft was called by the French an *embarras*. Sometimes, too, great trees that had been washed down by the streams extended out for a distance of a hundred feet into the river. The keel-boat must make its way around all of these obstructions, and there was always found a swift and violent current around each of these. In spite of all of these difficulties, however, the keel boat continued for years to be the principal means of travel on the river. Large quantities of lead, corn, and wheat, and occasionally passengers were carried from St. Louis to Ste. Genevieve and New Orleans.

The social life and condition of these people must always be a matter of the very greatest interest. It is unfortunate that we do not have more complete records of their real condition. Enough, however, remains for us to form some idea of their surroundings, and the things in which they took the deepest and most vital interest. It is quite evident that one of these things was religion. We have seen before this time that the first service ever held within the limits of the state was that celebrated by De Soto and his companions at the request of the Indians. That religious service was held in 1541. It was destined to be many years before another was celebrated. We cannot be certain as to the date when the next religious celebration was held within the limits of the state. We have no accurate account as to the coming of any missionaries until, at least, the time of Marquette. We cannot, indeed, be certain that Marquette landed and held services on the soil of the state. We know, however, that he passed along its border upon the bosom of the great river, and we know that he was a most devout Christian and sincerely interested in spreading the Gospel among the Indians. In fact, he had vowed that should he discover the river, he intended to name it The Immaculate Conception, and to name the first post planted within the territory in the same way. He fulfilled this vow, and the Mississippi was known for a number of years as the "River of the Conception." We may rightfully infer, from these circumstances, that he did land in Missouri and hold religious services; but even if such was the case, it was like the service held so long before by De Soto, only an incident, long separated in time, from any regular series of religious services.

We are unable to fix the date when regular religious services were first held here. We may suppose that, as soon as settlers began to live about the mines and at Ste. Genevieve, the priests at Kaskaskia and Fort Chartres came to Missouri to hold services. There is one reference in the Jesuit Relations which seems to confirm this supposition. We do not, however, reach a certain period until the beginning of the church records of Ste. Genevieve. This was in the year 1759.

It should be said, of course, that all the early religious services held in the section were Catholic. The French dominated the territory until its transfer to Spain, and so long as the French were here, religious control was vested in the priests of the Jesuit order. After the transfer to Spain an order was issued banishing the Jesuits from Louisiana and the religious control of the territory was claimed by the Capuchin fathers whose establishment in this country was in New Orleans. The laws of Spain were very strict with regard to the settlement of Protestants in the territory and, of course, forbade under penalty the immigration of Protestant clergymen and the holding of Protestant services. It must be said, however, that the Spanish officials, who were charged with the execution of these laws, were very rarely bigoted, and they seem to have had little desire to enforce the laws in a harsh manner. What these laws were, may be ascertained from the following instructions issued by Manuel Gayoso, the governor of Louisiana, to the commandants of the various posts:

"6. The privilege of enjoying liberty of conscience is not to extend beyond the first generation. The children of those who enjoy it must positively be Catholic. Those who will not conform to this rule are not to be admitted, but are to be sent back out of the Province immediately, even though they possess much property."

"7. In the Illinois, none shall be admitted but Catholics of the class of farmers and artisans. They must, also, possess some property, and must not have served in any public character in the country from whence they came. The provisions of the preceding article shall be explained to the emigrants already established in the Province who are not Catholics, and shall be observed by them."

"8. The commandants will take particular care that no Protestant Preacher, or one of any sect other than Catholics, shall introduce himself into the Province. The least neglect in this respect will be a great reprehension."*

It must be kept in mind, however, that these rigid instructions were not rigidly enforced. The commandants of the various posts understood the very great desire of Spain for settlers in the new territory. That desire for settlers extended to the Americans, and it was the understanding that Americans should be admitted without any too rigid inquiry into their religion. Some questions were asked, but those questions could be answered in the affirmative by almost any believer in the Christian religion. Any person who answered these questions satisfactorily was pronounced a good Catholic and permitted to enter the settlement. This took the place, it seems, of a declaration in form that the settler was a Catholic. It was explained to all of these settlers that their children must be brought up in the Catholic faith. Of

* History of Southeast Missouri, p. 521.

course the open practice of the Protestant religion—the holding of public services—was forbidden. It seems, however, that no great diligence was exercised to prevent the holding of prayer meetings, and other assemblies within private houses. Occasionally a minister from the settlements of Illinois crossed the river and conducted these private services. It is said that more than one of these men was more than once warned, but the warning usually came at the close of the visit, and no great effort was made to arrest or punish for the violation of the law. Of course, under these circumstances, no Protestant church house could be erected and no formal organization made. For this reason the early religious history of the state is a history of the Catholic church.

That history began, as we have seen, in 1759, when there began to be kept in the village of Ste. Genevieve a record of church affairs. The records mentioned show the following persons to have had charge of the church in Ste. Genevieve at the dates given: Fathers P. F. Watrin, J. B. Salveneuve and John La Morinie, from 1760 to 1764; Father J. L. Meurin, from 1764 to 1768; Father Gibault, from 1768 to 1773; Father Hiliarie. from 1773 to 1777; Father Gibault, from 1778 to 1784; Father Louis Guiques, from 1786 to 1789; Father St. Pierre, from 1789 to 1797; and Father James Maxwell, from 1797 to 1814.

Father Meurin was a Jesuit, and was the only priest exempt in the order of 1763 which expelled the Jesuits from Louisiana. He remained in charge, and continued missionary work among the settlers and Indians for a number of years. He labored under exceedingly great difficulties. The property of the order to which he belonged had been confiscated and there were many persons within the district who were hostile to him, on account of the fact that he was a Jesuit. He was not in very good standing with the Spanish officials, though, the fact that an exception had been made in his favor shows him to have been appreciated at least to a degree by them. Meurin did not confine his labors to Ste. Genevieve, but ministered to the settlers on the east side of the river, also. He visited Kaskaskia, Fort Chartres, Fort St. Phillip and the settlements in the mining regions in Missouri. He was not only a missionary priest, he had been commissioned as vicar general of Louisiana, and this commission, which he attempted to exercise, resulted in a discussion concerning the authority under which he was commissioned. At the time of the transfer of Louisiana to Spain, the territory was under the spiritual jurisdiction of the bishop of Quebec, and it was from him that Meurin had received his commission. While the question of spiritual jurisdiction seems to have been a religious one, it was not so regarded at that time. The Spanish authorities considered it to be a political question, and they refused to concede that an appointee of the bishop of Quebec could exercise any spiritual authority in the territory of Spain. They no longer regarded the bishop of Quebec as the spiritual ruler of the territory, but conceived that place to be held by the bishop of San Domingo. In 1776 they asked for and obtained a formal transfer of the territory from the authority of the bishop of Quebec to the bishop of Santiago de Cuba. Later this was transferred to the bishop of New Orleans, Cardenas. This dispute over jurisdiction and the existing hostility to the order to which he belonged, made the work of Father Meurin a difficult and laborious one indeed.

Of the men mentioned as having been in charge at Ste. Genevieve, two, at least, deserve a more extended account. Father Gibault was a missionary who came to the Illinois country from Canada, about the year 1768. He bore with him a passport issued by Guy Carleton, lieutenant governor and commander-in-chief of the province of Quebec. Father Gibault lived in Kaskaskia, but he served as the priest of the church in Ste. Genevieve from 1768 until 1776, and again from 1778 until 1784. He did not confine his work to Ste. Genevieve, but seems to have visited Old Mines, La Salinas and, in fact, all the settlements on both sides of the river. Gibault deserves a place in history because of the service which he rendered to George Rogers Clark, on the occasion of Clark's capture of Vincennes. The priest went with Clark from Kaskaskia to Vincennes, and used his influence among the French people at that place to secure their submission to the authority of the United States and their adherence to its government. That this influence was very great, we may well suppose, Clark specially acknowledged the obligation he was under for the service rendered. In 1792 Father Gibault removed from Kaskaskia to New Madrid where he seems to have served as priest until his death in 1802. He was a man of considerable ability and energy. He was industrious and devoted to the work of preaching among all of the people of the territory. He was most probably a man of very tender heart and great sympathy, for we find that he was reproved at times by his superior, Father Maxwell, the vicar general of Upper Louisiana, for his failure to collect funds for marriages and other services. This reprimand came from Maxwell because he was entitled to a part of these fees.

Soon after Father Gibault's appointment to New Madrid and his removal there, he began and completed the erection of a building for church purposes, and a house for the residence of the priest. He has left a description of this early church building. It was constructed of wood and was ample and commodious in size and perfect in its appointments for all of the services of the church. Of course this building has long since disappeared, together with the very site on which it was erected.

The second man noted as among the priests of Ste. Genevieve deserving of a further mention was Father James Maxwell. He was a native of Ireland, an educated man and one of superior ability. He resided in New Bourbon a short distance from Ste. Genevieve, and rode to his services at that place. He was appointed vicar general of Upper Louisiana in 1792, and held this post for about seventeen years. He was held in the highest esteem and regard by the people among whom he labored, and he accomplished a great work for the church. He was killed by being thrown from the horse while riding home from the service at the church in Ste. Genevieve. Maxwell was very diligent in looking after the matter of land grants from the Spanish government. It is said that at one time he had received grants amounting to more than 120,000 arpents of land. The land thus claimed by him was scattered over a considerable part of the district of Ste. Genevieve, but his claim to the greater number of these tracts was finally denied and he was left in possession of only about three hundred and twenty arpents.

The first church building in Southeast Missouri was erected in the old village of Ste. Genevieve at a date which we are unable to fix. It was previous to the great flood, because after the year of that flood the village was moved to its present site. The church which had been erected was moved to the new site in 1794. It was a wooden structure, but large and well suited to the purposes for which it was dedicated. It was used by the inhabitants of Ste. Genevieve until the year 1835. It was then so old and dilapidated that it was torn down to make way for the erection of a larger and more suitable structure.

Until the transfer of Louisiana to the United States, the priests were supported by the government of Spain. The salaries were paid in this way and the government also looked after the erection and care of the different buildings. It is said that the ordinary pay of the priests was about six hundred dollars a year. Besides this there was usually furnished a priests' house, and there were some other minor compensations. This was a very small salary, of course, but considering the time and circumstances under which they were placed, it was sufficient for the support of priests. Of course this government support was discontinued with the transfer to the United States. From that time the money for buildings and for the pay of church officials had to be secured from the congregation itself. As was right, the property of the church was transferred or confirmed to the church. The buildings in Ste. Genevieve and New Madrid were in this way transferred to the proper officers of the church. There was also a tract of land in Little Prairie belonging to the church and the title to this was confirmed by the government. The work of these missionaries and priests was, of course, rendered more difficult by reason of the cutting off of the support of the government. They could no longer be assured that their salaries would be paid regularly and without any question, they must look to the congregation which they served, and the only revenues were voluntary gifts to the church. Just as the matter worked out everywhere, however, the change was made and the work of the church carried on in spite of this change.

We cannot fail to perceive that the work of the missionaries in Missouri at this early time was both arduous and dangerous. There were few roads. Those in existence were simply paths through the wilderness. The devoted priests often rode for hundreds of miles in the course of the year, traveling from one settlement to another along these paths through the woods and across the streams; they were exposed to all the dangers of the wilderness. They were sometimes attacked by the Indians, and sometimes in peril from the wild beasts. They must have suffered great hardships from exposure to the weather, and from their distance from civilization. There has never been a lack, however, of men willing to endure hardships and to face dangers in the work of spreading the gospel. The services that these men rendered cannot be fully estimated. They helped to redeem the wilderness and to plant standards of religion and morality in communities that must otherwise have been entirely unreclaimed.

Religious enterprise by no means ceased with the transfer of Louisiana in 1804. In the year 1815 the Reverend W. F. Dubourg, who had been an officer of the church at New Orleans, undertook a journey to Rome and while there was consecrated bishop of the diocese of New Orleans. The territory over which he was to exercise spiritual authority and jurisdiction included all of Louisiana, both Upper and Lower, and stretched from the Mississippi river to the Pacific ocean. It was an enormous task to be undertaken by any man, but the new bishop was fitted for the work. He possessed industry, learning and devotion to the work. He had also, what was indispensable to him in the work of his position, an insight into human character and the ability to select those assistants who would be useful to him in his work. While he was in Rome he chose a number of men and persuaded them to return with him to Louisiana. He had been greatly impressed at Rome by the preaching of Father De Andreis. This priest was a most remarkable man. He was highly educated, distinguished for his ability as an orator and as a teacher, and he occupied a high position at Rome. Nevertheless, he yielded to the persuasion of Bishop Dubourg and, accompanied by some others, among them Father Joseph Rosati, departed for the new scene of his labours.

The bishop, himself, was detained, but Father De Andreis, with the rest of the party, arrived in St. Louis in 1817. They had come by way of Bardstown, Kentucky, the residence of Bishop Flaget, who accompanied them on their trip to St. Louis. After remaining some days in St. Louis and making preparation for the coming of Bishop Dubourg, the party started back down the river. They met the bishop at Ste. Genevieve. Here in 1818, the Bishop celebrated the first pontifical high mass ever celebrated in Upper Louisiana. Dubourg fixed his seat at St. Louis and entered on the work of his great diocese with tremenduous energy and zeal. He had from at first seen the necessity of the establishment of a school for the training of priests. One of the purposes he had in mind in persuading Father De Andreis to come with him to this country was to make use of his great learning and ability as a teacher in the foundation of the seminary which he had in mind. Accordingly, six hundred and forty acres of land in Perry county near the site of Perryville was bought for the sum of eight hundred dollars. This was to be the site of the new seminary. The first structures located upon it were simply log cabins. In 1819 the first students were received for instruction. Father De Andreis was the first president of the seminary and conducted the work of organizing and equipping it. He served in this position until his death, when he was succeeded by Father Joseph Rosati.

It is somewhat difficult to avoid getting an incorrect notion of these people. It must not be supposed that all of them were rude or rough and turbulent. There were among them many excellent people. Sparks, on his biography of Daniel Boone, says that to avoid falling into this error people should remember that the west received emigrants of various sorts. "Small numbers of them had fled from the scene of crime," he continues, "but a large majority were peaceable, industrious, moral and well disposed, who, for various motives, had crossed the great river, some from love of adventure, some from that spirit of restlessness which belongs to a class of people, but a much larger number with the expectation of obtaining large tracts of land which the government gave to each settler for the trifling expense of surveying and recording.

"Under the Spanish government the Roman Catholic faith was the established religion of the province and no other christian sect was tolerated by the laws of Spain. Each emigrant was required to be *un bon Catholique*, as the French express it, yet by the connivance of the commandants of Upper Louisiana and by the use of a legal fiction in the examination of Americans who applied for land, toleration in fact existed.

Many Protestant families, communicants in Baptist, Methodist, Presbyterian and other churches, settled in the province and remained undisturbed in their religious principles. Protestant itinerant clergymen passed over from Illinois and preached in the log cabins of the settlers unmolested, though they were occasionally threatened with imprisonment; these threats were never executed. (*Spark's Biography*, Vol. 23, p. 166.)

CHAPTER X

TRANSFER TO THE UNITED STATES

FEELING OF THE FRENCH SETTLERS—SETTLEMENTS FOUNDED UNDER THE RULE OF FRANCE—EMIGRATION FROM THE WESTERN STATES—WHY SPAIN FOSTERED THE MOVEMENT OF AMERICANS ACROSS THE RIVER—QUESTION OVER THE NAVIGATION OF THE MISSISSIPPI—RESTRICTIONS ON COMMERCE—TREATY OF ILDEFONSO — NEGOTIATIONS FOR PURCHASE OF NEW ORLEANS—OFFER OF ALL LOUISIANA—MOTIVES OF NAPOLEON IN SELLING LOUISIANA—CEREMONIES ATTENDING THE ACTUAL TRANSFER—CAPTAIN AMOS STODDARD AND HIS AUTHORITY—SIGNIFICANCE OF THE TRANSFER.

We have thus seen that Spain neglected Louisiana territory, giving to it practically no consideration after the time of De Soto. France seized the opportunity which was hers and took possession of the country, but in 1759 France lost Canada to England, and having lost Canada she lost the key to Louisiana. In 1762, by the secret treaty of Fontainbleau, she ceded to Spain all her possessions in America; Spain, however, did not take full possession of the territory until in 1768. This delay was caused by the opposition of the French settlers of Louisiana. These settlers were unwilling to believe for a long time that France had sold them. The Spanish officers who came to take over the government at St. Louis met with resistance and returned to New Orleans without having received the country from France. Finally, however, Spain sent a governor in the person of Count O'Reilly, who came equipped with sufficient power to compel the acknowledgment of the authority of Spain.

It will be seen that French settlements in Upper Louisiana were confined to Ste. Genevieve and a few small settlements around the lead mines. St. Louis was founded by the French, it is true, but this was not until the year 1764, two years after the signing of the treaty that transferred the country to Spain. Cape Girardeau, New Madrid, St. Michaels, Cook's Settlement, Murphy's Settlement at Farmington, and Herculaneum, were all settled during the rule of Spain, some of them by the French, however, and some by Americans. The town of New Madrid was laid out by Colonel Morgan, an American in the service of the Spanish government. He brought to his new town a number of French settlers. These French who came to Louisiana after the transfer to Spain came for the most part from east of the Mississippi river. They did not wish to live under the power of Great Britain or of the United States; they preferred to emigrate to Louisiana which had once been a possession of France, though now belonging to Spain.

One of the motives, as we have seen, was to escape the Northwest ordinance of 1787. Many people who lived in the Northwest territory were slave owners and when slavery was prohibited by the ordinance they decided, instead of losing their slaves to emigrate across the river and live under the rule of Spain. Many of them doubtless came without thinking that in making the change they were in reality giving up their allegiance to the government of the United States and falling under the government of Spain. There seems to have been a feeling existing in the American people that the territory west of the river was not destined long to remain under Spanish control but that it would eventually become a part of the territory of the United States, and so these people, unwilling to lose their property and feeling that they would probably aid in a movement to secure for their country more territory, crossed the river and took up their life in Upper Louisiana.

The Spanish government fostered the movement of both French and Americans to their new territory. They developed the lead industry and were diligent in planning new settlements and in improving the resources and conditions of the country. It was fortunate for the United States, however, that the Spanish did not possess a talent for colonizing. They held to the "bullion theory" that is, that wealth consists in gold and silver only; and they believed that a colony existed for the benefit of the mother country. They looked to the colonists in Louisiana to produce supplies of gold and silver and other metals for the enrichment of Spaniards at home. In spite, however, of this false attitude, the government of Spain was, perhaps, as well adapted to the development of the country as was the government of France. Neither of these great nations possessed the real colonizing ability that distinguished the English.

The Spanish governed Louisiana from New Orleans. Here resided the governor; a lieutenant governor resided at St. Louis; and Ste. Genevieve, St. Charles, Cape Girardeau and New Madrid were the centers of districts and the places of residence for commandants. Very strict enforcement of law was insisted upon. We find the settlers at Ste. Genevieve afraid to chastise the Indians even when they had committed outrages, without at first receiving permission from the Spanish officials.

The period of Spanish rule in Louisiana was coincident with the growth of western United States. American settlers were pouring by the thousands into Kentucky and the Northwest territory. These settlers soon developed the resources of the country and came to have many things for export. The surplus products of the American settlers in the states just east of the Mississippi river were considerable in quantity and in value, but the way to the east was long; the roads led across the mountains; they were rough; travel was exceedingly difficult; the only possible method of shipment in large quantities was upon the river. The surplus products of the states on the river were loaded on flat boats and keel-boats and dispatched down the river to New Orleans; but the Spanish officials at New Orleans greatly hampered and restricted this trade. They were jealous of the growing power of the United States. They were afraid that the Americans on the east side would attempt to take possession of the territory on the west; and, too, the Spanish people were not a trading people. They had little or no sympathy with the quick and efficient American spirit; they were mediæval in their manners and customs; everything that was done must be done according to form and ceremony; taxes were imposed; the method of procedure was slow; all these things greatly irritated the Americans who traded through New Orleans. They were pushing and energetic, impatient of delay, placing a small value on forms and not inclined to submit to the exactions of the Spanish. It was not possible to carry on this trade without depositing goods which came down the river at New Orleans and awaiting the arrival of trading ships, but the jealousy of the Spanish led them to forbid the deposit of goods. Thus for a long time trade down the river was virtually denied to the Americans.

Such a situation could have but one result. Through the later part of the eighteenth century there arose a strong demand on the part of the people of the west that the United States should acquire from Spain the free navigation of the Mississippi river and the control of the port of New Orleans. These things were to be secured either by purchase or by war.

In 1800 Napoleon, then at the head of the government of France, began negotiations with the Spanish government for the transfer of the Spanish possessions in America to France, and on October 25th, of that year, there was signed a secret agreement between France and Spain by which Spain agreed to transfer Louisiana to France in exchange for certain territory in Italy. This agreement was kept secret, because Napoleon did not wish it to become known until he was ready to land a large army in New Orleans and thus take possession of the country. Some hint of this agreement, however, escaped and came to England. England, at that time engaged in a contest with Napoleon, objected seriously to the transfer and made such representations to the Spanish government as to prevent the consummation of the transfer for nearly two years. It was not until in 1802 that the formal treaty which transferred Louisiana to France was signed. Even at this date Napoleon was not ready to take possession of his new territory. He had decided that the island of San Domingo offered the best base for the operation of his fleet and army, and had, therefore, attempted to take possession of this island. His effort to do so was resisted by Toussaint L'Ouverture. He had found great difficulty in subduing this uprising in San Domingo, and was not prepared to enter New Orleans in force at the time of the signing of the treaty.

By this time the demand on the part of the West that the United States government should get possession of New Orleans had grown so greatly that it could not any longer be resisted. On January 11, 1803, Jefferson, then President, appointed James Monroe as minister extraordinary to France. Monroe was instructed by Jefferson to purchase New Orleans and the Floridas. He was expected to pay for this territory the sum of two million dollars. In fact, negotiations had been carried on for some time by Livingston, the minister to France. After Monroe's arrival negotiations proceeded, but on April 11, 1803, Talleyrand, the French minister of foreign affairs, said that he was ordered by Napoleon to offer to the American officials, not New Orleans alone, but the whole of Louisiana. This offer came as a very great surprise. It had not been the intention of the Americans to purchase all of Louisiana. The importance, however, of securing this territory for the United States was so felt by Livingston and Monroe that they agreed to the purchase of the entire territory for the sum of fifteen million dollars.

The motives which induced Napoleon to make this offer to the United States were various. He was terribly disgusted with his failure in San Domingo; he needed the funds for the prosecution of the Continental system which he was carrying on, and he did not like to see an alliance formed between England and the United States. Such an alliance had been threatened, for both countries were opposed to the holding of Louisiana by France. Perhaps, however, the principal reason why Napoleon consented to the sale of the territory was the fear that it might fall into the hands of Great Britain. He was then engaged in a war with Great Britain and he did not possess sufficient naval power to enable him to contest the control of territory on the other side of the sea. He is said to have remarked, after he signed the treaty which transferred Louisiana to the United States, that he had given Great Britain a rival.

On receipt in Washington of news that arrangements had been made for the purchase of Louisiana from France, President Jefferson called an extra session of congress to consider this question and to ratify the treaty. Congress assembled on the 17th of October, 1803, and proceeded to the ratification of the treaty. President Jefferson appointed Governor William Claiborne, of Mississippi, and Major General James Wilkinson, as commissioners of the United States to receive the transfer of the territory from France. The representative of the French government who was to receive the territory from Spain was M. Laussat. M. Laussat arrived in New Orleans in November and received from Governor de Casa Calvo the transfer of the territory from Spain. A considerable delay occurred, however, in taking over the territory in St. Louis. France did not wish to send a representative from New Orleans to St. Louis to receive the transfer from Governor De Lassus because of the time that would be required and the expense of the journey. Accordingly it was agreed among all the parties that the commissioners of the United States should designate a person with authority to receive the transfer from France. Governor Claiborne selected Captain Amos Stoddard, of the United States army. Upon his notification of the selection M. Laussat then designated Captain Stoddard as commissioner and agent of France to receive the transfer of Upper Louisiana. He then sent to Stoddard, a letter to Lieutenant Governor De Lassus containing the demand of France for the transfer of that territory. This letter also was a credential for Captain Stoddard. Stoddard also received instructions from Governor Claiborne to proceed to St. Louis and to carry out the orders issued to him, first as commissioner and agent of France to demand and receive possession of the country from Spain, and secondly as agent of the United States to occupy and hold the posts, territories and dependencies which had been transferred by France to the United States. Stoddard was further instructed by Governor Claiborne that until some permanent regulations could be made by congress for the government of the new province, all the functions, both civil and military, which had been previously exercised by the Spanish commandants of posts and districts would devolve upon him and his subordinates. It was carefully explained, however, that there was to be no further blending of civil and military functions, but that on the other hand they were to be kept entirely separate and distinct. That this fact might be made clear, Stoddard received two commissions, one from Governor Claiborne constituting him civil commandant of St. Louis and conveying instructions for his actions in such place, and also a commission from the commanding general of the

American army conveying instructions as to his actions in military affairs. He was further instructed that in the absence of precise definition of powers, he was to consider himself in possession of all authority accustomed to be exercised by his predecessors, the Spanish commandants, and was to govern himself by the circumstances under which he was placed and was given a wide discretion in his actions. In accordance with these grants of authority, Stoddard, who was at Kaskaskia, wrote to De Lassus informing him of his selection as an agent of France, and notifying him of his early arrival in St. Louis.

On receipt of the reply from Governor De Lassus, Stoddard proceeded to St. Louis, and on the 9th day of March, 1804, received from De Lassus the transfer from Spain to France. The occasion was made as dignified and formal as it was possible to be made under the circumstances. The Spanish soldiers were drawn up in line, the inhabitants of the town assembled in the street in front of the building, and Governor De Lassus then issued a brief proclamation. In it he set out the fact that the flag under which they had lived for a period of thirty-six years was to be withdrawn. He released them from their oath of allegiance to Spain and wished them prosperity. There was then executed a document in the nature of a memorial of the transactions which had taken place. After this had been signed, Governor De Lassus addressed Captain Stoddard as agent of the French republic, saluted him as such commissioner and formally transferred to him authority over the province. After Captain Stoddard's very brief response to this address, the flag of Spain which was floating from the staff was lowered and replaced by the flag of France. The Spanish soldiers then fired a salute and retired after having received the American troops who were in charge of an adjutant of Stoddard. When this was done, the flag of France was lowered and that of the United States was put in its place.

De Lassus then addressed a communication to the commandants at Ste. Genevieve, New Madrid, Cape Girardeau, and the other posts in Upper Louisiana informing them of the actions which had taken place on that day. It seems that the transfer of the other posts were made without any formality, except in the case of New Madrid. Here the flag was lowered and a salute was fired, but these were the only ceremonies observed, even there.

Captain Stoddard, having come into possession of the territory, informed his superiors, Governor Claiborne and General Wilkinson, of the fact and issued a rather lengthy address to the people of Upper Louisiana. This address is found in the archives of Madrid and is an interesting document. In it Stoddard congratulated the people of Louisiana on account of the change of government which they had undergone. He informed the people as to the probable provisions that would be made for their government, and he pointed out to them some of the differences which they would observe in the government under the United States. He described the change as a change from subjects to citizens and he assured them of his very great interest in their welfare and his very great desire to conduct affairs, so long as he was in charge, to the best interests of the people of the province.

By these acts the territory of Louisiana passed forever from the control of Spain. The hopes which had been built, first, upon the marvellous explorations of De Soto, and later upon the treaty of Fontainbleau, were finally dissipated. The dream of a great Spanish empire with its capital at New Orleans was dispelled. War between the United States and Spain for the possession of the Mississippi river was avoided.

It is quite clear that this transaction was one of the most momentous incidents in all history. The territory is a vast one embracing a million square miles and stretching from the Mississippi to the Rockies. The territory of Louisiana contained within its borders some of the richest mineral districts, some of the richest soil, and some of the greatest forests in the world and was, even at that date, exceedingly valuable. Fifteen million dollars was a large amount of money for the United States, in 1803, but fifteen million is the merest fraction of the value of Louisiana territory. Its value to the United States was not solely to be measured by the soil, or its forests, or the mineral wealth of the territory. It is difficult to say how our country would have become a great nation without the possession of Louisiana. Its possession carried with it the free and unobstructed use of the Mississippi river; it rounded out our territory; it gave us possession of the greatest tract of food producing soil in all the world. The Mississippi valley is the heart of our country and had the Louisiana purchase not been made the Mississippi valley would have been owned by the United States only in part. The purchase meant much for the people who lived in Louisiana at that time, but it meant a great deal more to the United States and to the people of our country at the present day. We can hardly imagine what our country would be now if the Louisiana territory had remained in the possession of Spain, or in the possession of France; instead of being one of the great powers of the world, the United States would have been one of the smaller nations and its wealth would be but a fraction of what it now is.

This purchase deserves and holds a great space in history. The restrictive laws of Spain, her unjust restrictions upon commerce, her censorship of religion, her oppression of free speech and the press, her antiquated machinery of government, her ideals, which were those of the middle ages, were all swept away with the coming of the United States government and a new era set in then for Louisiana. We may not say, of course, that all the results that immediately followed were good. As has been the case everywhere, new-found liberty was made an occasion for license, and the freedom with which the people of the territory of Louisiana found themselves clothed upon their transfer to the United States, was in some cases an excuse for lawlessness and violence. These disorders, however, were temporary in their character and when the ideas of Anglo-Saxon liberty, liberty restrained by law, of self-government, were realized, then followed good order throughout Louisiana. Not only did the change of ownership bring a greater degree of liberty, not only did it enable the people who lived in Louisiana to govern themselves and to carry on the concerns of their lives without interference and fear from the hampering regulations of Spain, the change of ownership brought a great flood of immigration. The river had acted as a barrier to the westward movement of our population, it had dammed that movement up and held it in the states on the east side of the river, and when the barrier was removed and Louisiana passed out from the control of Spain and into that of the United States immigration flowed into the district in streams, new towns sprung up, industries were revived and within a few years the population of Louisiana was doubled many times over.

SECTION III

As a United States Territory

CHAPTER XI

AMERICAN TERRITORIAL GOVERNMENT

GOVERNMENT OF THE LOUISIANA TERRITORY—THE TERRITORY OF ORLEANS—THE DISTRICT OF LOUISIANA — FIRST GOVERNOR — COURTS OF COMMON PLEAS — OFFICERS AT THE VARIOUS POSTS—CAUSES OF DISSATISFACTION WITH THE GOVERNMENT OF THE UNITED STATES—MEMORIAL OF GRIEVANCES—THE TERRITORY OF LOUISIANA—CONFIRMATION OF LAND GRANTS—COURTS—WILKINSON AS GOVERNOR—LEWIS—CLARK—THE TERRITORY OF MISSOURI — POWERS OF THE GOVERNOR—MEETINGS OF THE TERRITORIAL LEGISLATURE—VARIOUS LAWS—RICHARD S. THOMAS—JOHN SCOTT—JOHNSON RANNEY—GENERAL WATKINS—GREER W. DAVIS—ALEXANDER BUCKNER—OTHER PROMINENT MEN—THE BYRD FAMILY—CIRCUIT COURTS—OFFICERS IN STE. GENEVIEVE—CAPE GIRARDEAU DISTRICT AND COUNTY—NEW MADRID DISTRICT AND COUNTY—CREATION OF NEW COUNTIES—LAWRENCE — WAYNE — MADISON — JEFFERSON — WASHINGTON — PERRY — MILITARY HISTORY.

As soon as it was known that the transfer of Louisiana to the United States had been completed and all formalities complied with, Congress at once passed an act providing for the government of the newly acquired territory.

It was arranged that the law of Spain and France which had previously been in force in the territory should be superseded by the law of the United States. It divided the entire territory acquired into two parts. All that part of Louisiana south of the 33rd parallel of north latitude was made into a territory under the style of the Territory of Orleans. The remainder of the territory was denominated the District of Louisiana, and was attached for the purposes of government to the territory of Indiana. The authority of the governor of the territory of Indiana was caused to extend over the new district.

A legislative body was provided for the district of Louisiana which was to consist of the three judges of the territory of Indiana. They were clothed with authority to make all needful laws for the government of the people within the district. They were also empowered to hold two terms of court each year within Louisiana.

The governor of Indiana, who was thus made governor of the new district, was William Henry Harrison. The three judges in whose hands was placed the legislative power were Thomas Davis, Henry Vandenburg and John Griffin, who proceeded to make laws for the district. They accepted substantially the division of territory which had been in use by the Spanish. There was a lieutenant governor at the posts of St. Louis, New Madrid, St. Charles, Ste. Genevieve, and Cape Girardeau. There was also established in each one of these posts a court of common pleas and quarter sessions, and a provision was made for a recorder and a sheriff at each place.

The following officers were appointed at the various posts: Colonel Samuel Hammond was appointed lieutenant governor or commandant of St. Louis; Major Seth Hunt, lieutenant governor or commandant of Ste. Genevieve; Colonel Return J. Meigs, lieutenant governor or commandant of St. Charles, and Colonel Thomas B. Scott, lieutenant governor or commandant of Cape Girardeau. For New Madrid, Pierre Antoine La Forge acted as civil commandant.

Such was the form of government arranged for the new territory. It was reasonable, the selections for the various offices were good, and it was to be expected that the people of the territory would be happy and content under the government. It has been pointed out that there was little objection made by any of the people of the territory to the transfer; some few complaints were made and there were some who wished that Spain might have retained the territory; on the whole, however, the people were quiet and satisfied.

This condition did not last very long. There were several principal sources of complaint. One of them was the provision in the act of congress concerning Spanish land grants. We have seen that the Spanish officials were lavish with their grants of land. A great many inhabitants of Upper Louisiana had asked for concessions which were granted, but a number of these were granted after the secret treaty which had transferred Louisiana to France. The act provided that all Spanish grants should be given full force and effect by the officers of the United States, except those which had been made subsequent to the treaty between France and Spain. It was the opinion of the government of the United States that after the signing of that agreement by which Louisiana passed from Spain to France, the Spanish officials had no authority whatever to alienate for any purpose the lands of the territory. It was held that all grants attempted to be made between the transfer to France and the transfer to the United States were absolutely without any force whatever and that the settlers who held these grants had no title to their lands.

It may be supposed that the men who had received these grants were very much dissatisfied with this action of the government of the United States. This dissatisfaction, however, was not confined to the holders of these grants by any means. There were many questions which arose concerning these land titles, questions which could be settled only after the lapse of considerable time. The transfer thus acted as a disturber of the land titles, and a great many of the titles in the territory had a cloud over them for a period of many years. When these facts were appreciated by the people of the territory and especially by the French settlers, there was very great dissatisfaction. A meeting was held in St. Louis to protest to the government and a petition or memorial was drawn up setting forth the alleged grievance suffered by the inhabitants.

Another matter which created dissatisfaction among the settlers was the change in the method of jurisprudence. We have seen that the ordinary procedure in the courts of the Spanish commandants was entirely summary in its character. There was little delay and there was little opportunity for hampering suits by technicalities. The decision was vested in the power of one man and he ordinarily decided questions without much delay. The trial of cases before commandants proceeded informally, but while there was opportunity offered for appeal, such appeal was rarely prosecuted, and if prosecuted at all it usually did not go further than the Lieutenant Governor at St. Louis. This system of Spanish Law operated to produce great celerity of judicial action. For this system there was substituted the system of the English Common Law. That system provides for trial by jury, and it provides for the hampering of trials by the use of technicalities, and to the people of the territory accustomed to the celerity of Spanish justice the long delays and the great expense of the American system of courts came with an unpleasant shock.

Another thing which caused dissatisfaction among the settlers in Upper Louisiana was the fact that the territory was not erected into a separate government but was joined to Indiana. The settlers felt that they were sufficiently numerous and sufficiently intelligent to be a distinct territory of the United States, and they held it a grievance that they were not so treated.

A fourth grievance was the proposed settlement of the eastern Indians in Louisiana. One of the provisions of the Act of Congress for the government of the territory was that the land of the Indians then resident east of the Mississippi should be purchased from them and they should be settled in Louisiana. This provision gave great offence to the people of the territory. They had had sufficient experience with Indian population to cause them to dread the coming of any other Indian tribes.

This Indian question really settled itself in a very short time. The Government of the United States did not make any formal declaration as to its intentions, but the fact that it did purchase from the Sacs and Foxes the territory which they inhabited just north of the Missouri river and remove them further west seemed an evidence that it was not the intention of the United States to thrust the eastern Indians into that part of Louisiana inhabited by white people.

Although this particular complaint was thus disposed of, the others still remained, and on September 29th, 1804, there was held a meeting in the city of St. Louis as we have seen, which drew up a petition or memorial to the Government of the United States on these questions. The memorial set out at length the conditions that existed in the territory and called attention to all of the grievances which we have mentioned. The signers, fifteen in number, who declared themselves to be the representatives of the entire population of Upper Louisiana, requested that the act which had been passed providing for the government of the territory should be repealed. They further asked that Upper Louisiana be erected into a separate and distinct territory with a government of its own.

The territories of the United States, at this time, were divided into three distinct grades, first, second and third, the lowest grade of the territory. Those having the least rights were those of the first grade. This petition to the Congress asked that Upper Louisiana should be made into a territory of the second grade. The removal of the Indians was also objected to as well as the action with regard as to the Spanish land grants made subsequent to 1802. The petitioners further asked that their right to own slaves should be expressly recognized. This act had forbidden the inhabitants of the territory of Orleans, as Lower Louisiana was called, from importing slaves. Nothing had been said in the act, however, with regard to

Upper Louisiana, and it was assumed by the inhabitants that since the right was not expressly taken away, they still possessed it. This memorial prayed that this right should be expressly recognized. Another thing asked for was that funds and lands should be set aside by the Government of the United States for the support of a French and English school in every county of the district, and that further provision should be made at once for the establishment of a seminary where instruction should be given in the higher branches of learning. This memorial was signed by the following persons: Richard Jones Waters and Eligius Fromentin of New Madrid, Christopher Hays, Stephen Byrd, Andrew Ramsay and Frederick Bollinger of Cape Girardeau, J. S. J. Beauvais and P. Detchmendy of Ste. Genevieve, Charles Gratiot, P. Provenchere, August Chouteau, Richard Caulk, David Musick and Francis Cottard of St. Louis, Warren Cottle, A. Reynol, F. Saucier and Timothy Kibby of St. Charles; Choteau and Fromentin were appointed as deputies and agents to present the petition to the Congress of the United States.

It will be easily seen here that the men here represented as petitioners were among the most prominent and influential to be found in all of Upper Louisiana. Fromentin, who was one of the agents for the presentation of the petition was one of the most distinguished scholars in the whole territory. He occupied a number of positions and in 1812 was made a senator of the United States from Louisiana.

The petition was presented to Congress on January 4th, 1805. After some discussion and delay, a bill was passed on the third day of March, 1805, which regulated affairs in the territory. By the terms of this bill all of Upper Louisiana was made into a separate territory of the first or lowest grade and called the Territory of Louisiana. It provided in the act that the governor three judges should be appointed with po to make such rules and regulations conc ing affairs within the territory as should s to them to be necessary for its governm The act was silent on some of the matters were set out in the petition. We have alre seen that the Indian question was practic settled by the action of the United State regard to the Sacs and Foxes, which ac evinced the determination of the governn to remove the Indians to the far west. the other questions raised by the petitio and the other complaints put in by them not adjusted by the Act of Congress. No vision was made for confirming the dispu land grants and it is quite probable that question of land grants was of all the q tions concerning the territory the one r pressing and most troublesome. It is ra peculiar that this matter was not fully set until April, 1814. At that time Cong passed an act which confirmed the title of grants made by Spain previous to the 9th of March, 1804, that is, previous to the f relinquishment of the territory to the Un States. This action, though it was long layed, finally settled the question of the va ity of the grants made from 1802 to 1 but the question of these particular gr was by no means the only question regard the Spanish lands, in fact there existed fo great length of time considerable uncertai as to the validity of most of these gra There seemed to be no way of finally dete ining their validity, except by the action the courts and it required a long period time to dispose of the question of these l grants in a final and satisfactory way.

The act of 1805 which created the territ

of Louisiana, defined the powers of the governor and three judges, established courts, and made provision for the confirmation of the action of these various bodies. Under the terms of this act, General James Wilkinson was appointed governor of the territory, Joseph Browne of New York was made secretary, and James B. C. Lucas, John Coburn, and Rufus Easton were made judges of the court.

Wilkinson, the new governor, was a man about whom there has raged a great deal of controversy. We have seen that he was the commander of the American forces along the Mississippi river and that he had been one of the two commissioners appointed to receive the transfer of the territory. By some people he was regarded as a very able man. It was Wilkinson who denounced Burr, and he was one of the men responsible for Burr's arrest and trial. He did not testify in that case but attended the trial and was ready and even anxious to appear against Burr. It is now known that Wilkinson was for a long time in the pay of the Spanish government. It was his interference that caused Governor Miro to oppose Morgan's plan at New Madrid, and there seems to be no doubt that Wilkinson was for some years, even while in command of the forces of the United States, in correspondence with Spanish officials and considering with them a scheme by which the people of the western part of the United States along the Mississippi river, could be induced to throw off their allegiance to the government of the United States and attach themselves to Spain. For his services in these matters Wilkinson seems to have received a pension from the Spanish government, and there is no reason to doubt that he was very well disposed toward Spain.

His actions as governor of the new territory caused a great deal of antagonism and bitter feeling. He was accused of having tried to speculate in land even while he was governor, he seemed to have been opposed to the American settlers in the territory and to have been a friend to the French. He failed also to be able to deal successfully with his subordinates and was in constant trouble on account of differences with the men who served under him. It is said that he became so enraged against Easton, who had been one of the judges of the superior court and was later postmaster at St. Louis, that he refused to allow his mail to be sent through a postoffice over which Easton presided. He engaged in a feud with a number of the officers of the territory; he seemed to have no tact or ability to manage affairs at all. A very strenuous effort was made to have him removed from office; he was charged with oppression and neglect and with cruel conduct, and the charges against him were pressed with so much violence that finally Jefferson removed him from office on March 3, 1807.

Wilkinson was succeeded by Meriwether Lewis. Lewis' name will always be famous on account of his association with Clark on the celebrated expedition sent out by Jefferson to explore the northwestern part of the newly purchased territory of Louisiana. He found affairs in Louisiana in a deplorable state. The people were hostile to the government; they were divided into factions, and strife and bitter feeling raged everywhere. Lewis was an able man and a diplomat and he very soon established a feeling of respect for himself and the office which he held that went far toward restoring tranquility in the territory.

We have seen that the administration of Governor Lewis was successful, he possessed qualities which made him a valuable leader in any community and which enabled him to bring order out of the confusion existing in Missouri. In September, 1809, while traveling through Tennessee on his way to Washington, he committed suicide. After his death President Madison appointed General Benjamin Howard, of Kentucky, as governor of the territory. General Howard held office until 1810, when he resigned to accept a brigadier generalship in the army of the United States. Howard county was named in his honor.

William Clark who was a captain in the army of the United States and the other principal in the expedition of Lewis and Clark was appointed governor and held office until the admission of Missouri into the Union.

On the 4th day of June, 1812, Missouri was organized into a territory with a governor and general assembly. The territory had previously been organized as a territory of the first or lowest class. In the territory of this class, as we have seen, the sole power was vested in the governor and judges with other officers, all of whom were appointed by the president of the United States. In other words, the people of a territory of the first class had no right of self government so far as the administration of the general affairs of the territory was concerned. This, we remember, was one of the grievances of the people of Louisiana as set out in the petition presented to Congress in 1805, but by the act of 1812, the territory was raised to the second class. Under the provisions of that act, the legislative power of the territory was vested in the governor, legislative council, and a house of representatives.

The governor was to be appointed by the president of the United States. He had power of absolute veto over all the actions of the general assembly. The legislative council was to consist of nine members who were to hold their office for a period of five ye[ars]. The members of this council were selected [in] the following manner: The territorial ho[use] of representatives nominated eighteen [per]sons, and the president of the United St[ates] from this number selected nine members of [the] legislative council. The house of represen[ta]tives consisted of members who held office [for] a term of two years and were elected by [the] people of the territory. The unit of repres[en]tation was fixed at five hundred male citize[ns] with a further provision that the number [of] representatives could not exceed twenty-fi[ve]. The first house of representatives under t[his] act consisted of thirteen members. The ju[di]cial power of the territory was vested in [a] superior court, inferior courts and justices [of] the peace. There were three judges of [the] superior court whose term of office was fo[ur] years and who had original and appellate [ju]risdiction in civil and criminal cases. The [act] further provided that the territory should [be] represented in Congress by one territor[ial] delegate who, according to the Constituti[on] had the right to speak on matters pertaini[ng] to the territory, but was not allowed to vo[te].

Governor Clark, who was in office at [the] time of the passage of this act, issued a pr[oc]lamation, and, on October 1, 1812, reorga[n]ized the five districts in the state into f[ive] counties, known as the counties of St. Charl[es], St. Louis, Ste. Genevieve, Cape Girardeau a[nd] New Madrid. An election was ordered to [be] held on the 2nd Monday in November for [the] selection of the delegate to Congress and [the] members of the house of representatives. T[he] President of the United States appoint[ed] William Clark, who was already in office [as] the first governor of the re-organized ter[ri]tory. At the election in November, 1812, E[d]ward Hempstead was elected as the first t[er]ritorial delegate to Congress. Hempstead w[as] an able man. He was a native of Connecticut, received a good education, became a lawyer, and in 1804 removed to St. Louis, where he continued in the practice of law. He held a number of positions and was held in highest regard by all who knew him. His term of service in Congress was marked by no particular achievement, but he was regarded as an able and conscientious man, and his retirement, for he declined to serve a second term, was regretted by those with whom he had served. He was the author of the Act of 1812 which confirmed the titles and the holders in the Spanish grants, and provided for the support of schools by the Government of the United States.

The first General Assembly of the territory of Missouri was held in the house of Joseph Robidaux between Walnut and Elm streets in St. Louis on the 17th day of December, 1812. Southeast Missouri was represented by the following persons: George Bullett, Richard S. Thomas and Israel McGready from Ste. Genevieve; George F. Bollinger and Spencer Byrd represented Cape Girardeau; and John Shrader and Samuel Phillips represented New Madrid. Besides these members there were two from St. Charles and four from St. Louis. The house of representatives then nominated fourteen persons from which the President of the United States selected nine members of the council. The members of this council from Southeast Missouri were these: John Scott and James Maxwell from Ste. Genevieve; William Neeley and Joseph Cavinor from Cape Girardeau; and Joseph Hunter from New Madrid.

The first meeting of the legislature was held in St. Louis in July, 1813, on the first Monday. It is not possible to give a full account of the acts of this legislature. No account of the proceedings was officially kept, but a part of the laws were noticed and published in the *Missouri Gazette*, the first paper established west of the Mississippi river. From its files it is discovered that one of the first subjects which received the attention of the legislature was that of establishing and regulating weights and measures. Of course this was an exceedingly important matter, one which had never been adjusted in the territory of Louisiana. Some of the other matters which received the attention of the legislature were laws concerning the office of sheriff, taking of the census, the fixing of the seats of justice in the various counties, the compensation of members of the legislature, the incorporation of the bank of St. Louis. Besides these a criminal code was adopted and a law defining forcible entry and detainer was enacted, as well as one establishing courts of common pleas. The legislature also made provision for the organization of the county of Washington. This county was erected from a part of Ste. Genevieve, and Potosi was selected as the county seat.

The second session of the first general assembly was begun in St. Louis, December 10, 1813. George Bullett of Ste. Genevieve county, was elected speaker of the house and Washington county was for the first time represented by Israel McGready. Among the subjects considered by the legislature and upon which laws were passed, were the suppression of vice and immorality on the Sabbath day, public roads and highways, and the regulation of the financial affairs of the territory. The offices of territorial auditor and treasurer, and county surveyor were created. The legislature also defined the boundaries of the counties and created a new county known as Arkansas county.

The first session of the second general assembly met in St. Louis, December 5th, 1814. There were twenty members of the house, and James Caldwell of Ste. Genevieve was chosen speaker, and Andrew Scott, clerk. William Neeley of Cape Girardeau was the president of the council. The members from Southeast Missouri were: Nicholas Wilson and Phillip McGuire, from Washington county; Richard S. Thomas, Thomas Caldwell, and Augustine De Mun from Ste. Genevieve; Stephen Byrd, George F. Bollinger, Robert English, Joseph Sewell, and one other from Cape Girardeau; John Davidson, George W. Hart, and Henry H. Smith from New Madrid county. The only change in the representatives from Southeast Missouri in the council was the appointment of John Rice Jones, in place of James Maxwell.

The second session of the second general assembly met in St. Louis, January, 1815. At this session Washington county was represented by Hardage Lane and Stephen F. Austin, Ste. Genevieve county by Isidore Moore, New Madrid county by Doctor Robert D. Dawson. This session of the general assembly transacted considerable business. It ordered the establishment of county courts in the various counties, to be made up of the justices of the peace. The clerks of these courts were also to act as recorders for the counties; two judicial circuits were created, the northern and the southern. The counties of Ste. Genevieve, Cape Girardeau and New Madrid constituted the southern circuit, counties of St. Louis, St. Charles and Washington constituted the northern circuit. Besides these acts the assembly created a new county known as Lawrence county. This county was erected out of the western part of New Madrid county.

The third general assembly, which met in 1816, had the following representatives from Southeast Missouri: Hardage Lane Stephen F. Austin of Washington cou Nathaniel Cook, Isidore Moore, and John Arthur of Ste. Genevieve county; Georg Bollinger, Robert English, and John Dun Cape Girardeau county; Doctor Robert Dawson of New Madrid county; and ander S. Walker of Lawrence county. By time provision had been made by Congres the election of the members of the cou rather than their appointment. The mem of the council from Southeast Missouri w Samuel Perry from Washington county, eph Bogy from Ste. Genevieve county, Wil Neeley from Cape Girardeau county, Jo Hunter from New Madrid county, and R ard Murphy from Lawrence county. meeting of the assembly chartered the B of St. Louis and the Bank of Missouri. of these institutions were afterward or ized in St. Louis, and both of them authorized to issue notes to be used as rency. A charter was also granted for academy to be established in Potosi. bounty was also placed on the killing wolves, panthers and wild cats. It was provided that several lotteries might be h and it was this meeting of the assembly enacted the first law for the creation school board for the city of St. Louis. It in 1816 that an act was passed which in duced the common law into the territor Missouri. The act specified that the com law of England and the statutes of a gen nature enacted prior to the reign of Ja the First, should be enforced in the territ It was not provided that the former law France and Spain should be abrogated, were they repealed until a much later time.

The fourth, and last, general assembly in 1818. The representation from South Missouri was as follows: Lionel Browne

Stephen F. Austin from Washington county; Isidore Moore, David F. Marks, William Shannon, and Jacob Walters from Ste. Genevieve county; Johnson Ranney, Robert English, Joseph Sewell, Erastus Ellis, and James Ravenscroft from Cape Girardeau county; Stephen Ross from New Madrid county; Perry G. Magness, Joseph Harden, and John Davidson from Lawrence county. The following were members of the council: John D. Cook, Ste. Genevieve; Samuel Perry, Washington; George F. Bollinger, Cape Girardeau; Robert D. Dawson, New Madrid. This general assembly created a number of counties. Those in the southeast were Jefferson, Wayne, and Madison. It also abolished Lawrence county. It was at this meeting of the assembly that a memorial was prepared praying for the establishment of a state government. This memorial was afterward presented to Congress. The assembly also redistricted the state into three judicial circuits: Ste. Genevieve, Madison, Wayne, New Madrid, and Cape Girardeau composed the southern circuit, the other southeast counties became a part of the northern circuit; the third circuit, known as the northwestern, included no Southeast Missouri territory.

The first judge of the southern circuit was Honorable Richard S. Thomas. At the time of his appointment he was a resident of Ste. Genevieve, but afterward moved to Jackson, where he resided until his death. Judge Thomas was a native of Virginia, had lived some years in Ohio, where he married. He came to Ste. Genevieve in 1810, and engaged in the practice of law. In 1811 he appeared as counsel for the defendant in a murder case. Judge Thomas was not a lawyer of high rank, and he became very unpopular with the bar. As a consequence of this unpopularity, he was impeached and a number of charges were preferred against him in the impeachment proceeding. Most of them seem to have been rather trivial in nature, and to reflect the hostility which he aroused, rather than to exhibit any very grave errors in his conduct as a judge. One of the charges against him was that he had behaved in an arbitrary, oppressive, unjust and partial manner in refusing to recognize John Juden, Jr., as clerk of the circuit court. He took the position that the office was made vacant by the amendment to the constitution of 1822 and appointed his son, Claiborne S. Thomas, as clerk, and ordered that the records and papers of this office be delivered up to him. He was further charged with having illegally adjourned the April term of the court in 1823, on the pretense that his son, whom he had appointed clerk, had not received the records of the court. It was further charged that he had shown partiality toward his son in a suit between the son and Charles G. Ellis, and that he had entered into an agreement with the counsel for Doctor Ezekiel Fenwick, who had been charged with murder, to admit him to bail, on condition of his surrender to the sheriff. The articles of impeachment were presented to the house of representatives in February, 1825. Judge Thomas denied the charges, but was found guilty and removed from office on March 25th. He then resumed the practice of law at Jackson, but was killed within a short time by being thrown from his horse while on his way to attend court at Greenville.

The most conspicuous lawyer in the early days in Southeast Missouri was John Scott. He, too, was a Virginian, and had graduated at Princeton college. He lived for a short time in Vincennes, Indiana, and came to Ste. Genevieve in 1806. Scott was well versed in the law, was possessed of a great deal of energy and aggressiveness, and soon became one of the leading lawyers in the section. He was appointed a member of the territorial council and afterward made a canvass for the office of territorial delegate to Congress. His opponent in this canvass was Rufus Easton, of St. Louis. Easton had served one term as delegate, but was defeated by Scott on the face of the returns. Easton contested the election, however, on the ground that certain votes were improperly counted and the second election was held. At this election Scott increased his plurality from 15 to 392, and Easton gave up the contest. He served as territorial delegate until the admission to the Union, after which he was elected as a member of Congress. He served three terms and was a very popular and influential member. It was, perhaps, his speech indignantly rejecting the idea that the people of Missouri could be dictated to in the matter of their constitution that gave impulse to the movement of the state which resulted in the overwhelming victory of the slavery forces in the election of the constitutional convention. Scott lost his popularity, however, in 1825 when, in spite of the wishes of his constituents, he voted for John Quincy Adams for President. The people of Missouri were very strong in their support of Jackson, and this vote for Adams prevented Scott's retaining the place. After his retirement to private life he continued the practice of law. He was known all over the section, and attended court in practically every county. He was a thorough lawyer, and an impressive speaker. He was rather eccentric in his personal appearance and demeanor; he always went armed, but was never known to use these weapons. He was famous for his honesty and also for the great influence which he had over juries. He died in 1862,

at the age of eighty years. Scott county named for him.

One of the early lawyers in Cape G deau county was General Johnson Ran He was a native of Connecticut, had be teacher in early life, but studied law and moved to Jackson upon establishment of courts there in 1815. There existed at time quite a strong prejudice against ' kees, but General Ranney was a man of disposition and he very quietly went a his work and soon overcame this preju He was opposed to slavery, and during campaign in 1820 was threatened with lence, but he entrenched himself in his and defied his points. He was not a pa ularly brilliant speaker, but was a student and was very industrious and dev to the interests of his clients. He wa member of the legislature and a major gen of militia. He died in Jackson, Noven 11, 1849.

In 1819, General Nathaniel W. Wat came to Jackson and began the practice law. General Watkins was a half brothe Henry Clay and a native of Kentucky. was a man of fine appearance and reseml Clay in his general bearing. He was orator and had very great influence juries. No man in the southeast had a lai or more extended practice than he had. traveled, every spring and fall, on horse-b from one county seat to another. There scarcely an important case in any of tl counties in which he did not appear on side or the other. He served a number terms in the general assembly and in 1 was elected speaker of the house of repre tatives. He took part in the organization the Southeast District Agricultural Soci which was organized for the purpose of h ing a district fair. He was the first presid of this society. When war broke out General Watkins stood with the South and was appointed by Governor Jackson as brigadier general in the first military district which embraced Southeast Missouri. This was in 1861 and he proceeded to organize The Missouri State Guard in his district. He did not long retain command, however, as he found the place uncongenial to him. He resigned and was succeeded by General Jefferson Thompson. General Watkins afterward removed to Scott county where he lived until the time of his death in 1876. Just before his death, as a fitting recognition of his long and active service, he was chosen a member of the constitutional convention of 1875 and was made its president. His home in Scott county was called "Beechland," and was not far from Morley.

Another member of the famous bar at Jackson was Timothy Davis, who was a native of New Jersey but had lived two years in Kentucky and came to Jackson in 1818. He remained there for a year and a half. He then moved to Ste. Genevieve and later to Iowa, from which state he was sent to Congress. When he came to Jackson he was accompanied by a nephew who was destined to become one of the famous lawyers of the Southeast; this was Greer W. Davis. He was not admitted to the bar until 1820, but from that time on was a prominent lawyer. For seventeen years he was circuit attorney for the southeast circuit. He was very careful in attending to business and soon became wealthy. It was said of him that he was both fluent and logical, and that his addresses were models of concise, careful statements. He was a member of the Methodist church at Jackson for more than half a century. He was the last of the territorial lawyers in the state, dying in 1878. He was held in the highest esteem by his neighbors and by the bar of the entire Southeast.

In 1818 Alexander Buckner, who was a resident of Kentucky, removed to Cape Girardeau county and settled with his mother and sisters on Randol creek. He was a good lawyer, with a turn for political life. He was a pro-slavery advocate and soon took a prominent place in the political affairs of the territory. He was appointed circuit attorney shortly after his coming and was a member of the constitutional convention in 1820. He was afterward a member of the state senate and in 1831 was elected United States senator from Missouri. He was the organizer of Unity Lodge at Jackson, the first Masonic lodge in the territory of Missouri. This lodge was organized under a charter from the Grand Lodge of Indiana. Senator Buckner died in 1833 at Jackson, during the scourge of cholera.

One of the most prominent men in the Cape Girardeau district, during the early period, was Joseph McFerron. McFerron was an Irishman who came to America in early life, was a man of fine sense and possessed a superior education. He was reserved in manner and peculiar in appearance. He was the first clerk of the courts of the Cape Girardeau district and held the position for a number of years. After his duel with William Ogle, an account of which is given in another place, McFerron resigned from office. This resignation, however, was a test of public sentiment, which was soon shown to be in his favor. He was reelected and held the office until his death in 1821. He lived for a considerable time in Cape Girardeau, but removed to Jackson upon the establishment of the county seat at that place.

Among the first attorneys before the court held in Cape Girardeau were Anthony Hayden and George C. Harbison. Their names are found in the record of the year 1805. Hayden was one of the first trustees for the town of Cape Girardeau, chosen in 1808. Among the other early lawyers in Cape Girardeau were Nathaniel Pope, and James Evans. Evans was a very popular and able man, had a very large practice at one time, and was a member of the first constitutional convention. For a short time he served as circuit judge, but he ruined his career by becoming an habitual drunkard. He removed from Cape Girardeau to Perryville, from Perryville to Kentucky, where he afterward died.

The Byrd family of the Cape Girardeau district was one of the influential families during the early history of Missouri. The leading members of the family were Stephen and Abraham. They were brothers, being the sons of Amos Byrd. They came to Upper Louisiana from Tennessee about 1800. The home of the family was fixed at Byrd's creek, not far from Jackson. Stephen Byrd was frequently in office. He was a judge of the court of common pleas for the Cape Girardeau district, was one of the men who drew up the remonstrance concerning the organization of the Louisiana district and its connection with the Indian Territory, and was a number of times a member of the territorial assembly. He also took part in the convention that framed the constitution of the state and was afterward a representative of Cape Girardeau county in the general assembly of the state. Abraham Byrd was also a member of the state legislature at different times, and was a presidential elector in 1836. His family was a large one, and their descendants, many of them, still live in Cape Girardeau county.

In 1817 there came to Cape Girardeau a young man named Thomas B. English. He was a native of Louisiana and was educa[ted] at St. Mary's college. He studied law [with] General Johnson Ranney, and was afterw[ard] admitted to the bar. He was a man of g[reat] energy, and was modest and unassumin[g in] manner, but soon was able to take a [very] high rank in his profession. Mr. English [was] a Democrat, and had considerable poli[tical] experience. He was for a time circuit a[ttor]ney, and in 1860 was a member of the s[tate] senate. In 1865 he was appointed judg[e of] the tenth circuit, but died in 1866.

John D. Cook came to Cape Girardeau [dur]ing the time when Missouri was a terri[tory] and in 1820 was chosen a delegate to the convention which formed the constitutio[n of] the state. In 1822 he was appointed jud[ge of] the supreme court but held the position only about a year, resigning to accept the [po]sition of circuit judge of the southern [judi]cial circuit. At the meeting of the first [state] legislature Cook was placed in nomina[tion] for one of the senatorships but was not cho[sen.] He was a man of great ability and recogn[ized] to be of the highest integrity and his fri[ends] said of him that if he had been as enter[pris]ing as he was able he would have risen to [the] very highest places. He possessed, howe[ver,] but little ambition and was inclined t[o be] indolent. His homeliness was prove[rbial] among his friends. Younger members of [the] bar found in him a friend and he was al[ways] ready to give them advice and assista[nce.]

Under the territorial government as it [was] first organized the chief judicial autho[rity] was vested in a court of quarter session[s of] the peace. This court was to be compose[d of] all the justices of the peace in the cou[nty] who were to be appointed by the gover[nor;] not less than three were to constitute a q[uor]um. This court had general jurisdiction.

cept in capital cases, and it had also civil jurisdiction; besides its criminal and civil authority the court was charged with general administrative functions in the county; it was the authority for the letting of contracts, for levying taxes and supervising the expenditures of the county, thus having the powers and duties which are now vested in a county court.

Besides the court in general quarter sessions, there was also organized a court of common pleas composed of two or more justices of the peace and having civil jurisdiction in cases involving less than $100. There was also a probate court and justice courts presided over by single justices of the peace.

In 1813 all the courts, except the single justice courts, were combined to form a court of common pleas which thus had authority over both criminal and civil matters, over probate matters and was also vested with administrative authority in the county.

In 1816 circuit courts were organized in the territory which was divided into two circuits, the northern and southern; all judicial matters were put under the supervision of the circuit courts as well as a large part of the administrative business in each county. This organization marks the greatest concentration of judicial and administrative authority to be found in the history of the state. The circuit court with its powers to try both civil and criminal cases was also vested with all powers now held by probate and county courts; this great concentration of power lasted until the adoption of the state constitution in 1820.

Besides the courts which we have mentioned the principal county officers were the sheriff, who was also collector and treasurer, coroner, assessor, recorder and the constables of the townships. The duties of these officers were not very different from the duties which they discharge today, the sheriff is no longer collector and treasurer, though up until within very recent years he was in many counties the collector as well as sheriff.

The court of quarter sessions of the peace for Ste. Genevieve district was organized December 11, 1804. The judges of this court were: Moses Austin, Jacques Guibord, Benjamin Strother, John Hawkins and Francois Valle. William C. Carr was appointed as the acting prosecutor; Israel Dodge was the sheriff of the district and he brought in a jury which acted as a grand jury. The grand jury made no indictments at this first term of the court. The principal business transacted was the appointment of constables for the different sections of the district. They were: Andrew Morris for New Bourbon, Peter Laurel for Ste. Genevieve, Joseph Tucker for the territory on the Saline, Thomas Donohue between the Saline and Apple Creek, John Paul for Bellevue and Bernard Foster for Mine a Breton. The sheriff, Israel Dodge, was directed to receive bids for the building of a jail. It was to stand on the public square in Ste. Genevieve, was to be 25x15 feet and to have double walls of timber one foot in thickness with rock filling. This jail was reported finished in September, 1805. In the same year, the court made a levy for taxes for the district. Assessors were appointed for the different settlements, who were instructed to make lists of the property held by each citizen. The amount of the tax levy for all of Ste. Genevieve district was $1,171.94.

In 1807 the district was divided into six townships: Breton, Bellevue, St. Michaels, Big River, Ste. Genevieve and Cinque Homme. In 1814, Saline township was formed from parts of Ste. Genevieve and Cinque Homme and included the south part of the present county of Ste. Genevieve and the west part of

Perry county; in the same year Plattin township was laid out, it was east of Big River. There was no court house building in the district. During the period until 1820, the courts were usually held in the various dwellings. In 1808 we find the court to have met in the house of James Maxwell; John Price's tavern was frequently used, as was also the house of Henry Dodge.

This court of quarter sessions, as may be seen from the record of its work, had somewhat the same jurisdiction as the present county courts. It had also criminal jurisdiction. Felony cases were tried by courts of oyer and terminer. The first murder trial in the district was held in 1810. Peter Johnson was tried at this time for the murder of John Spear; Edward Hempstead was the attorney general and prosecuted the case, while Henry M. Breckenridge and James A. Graham appeared for the defendant. The trial resulted in the conviction of Johnson, and in execution of the sentence he was hanged on the third day of August. According to the barbarous custom of the time the hanging was public. It took place on the hill near the academy building and was witnessed by almost the entire population of the town. Only one other execution took place in Ste. Genevieve county during this period. There were other cases of homicide but only two persons were executed. One of the famous killings was that of Captain De Mun, who was the commander of the body of militia known as the Dragoons, who lived in New Bourbon, and was a very prominent citizen. He and William McArthur, who was a brother-in-law of Louis F. Linn, were candidates for the territorial house of representatives in 1816. A difficulty arose between them concerning some statements charging McArthur with connection with a band of counterfeiters. De Mun repeated these charges and was challenge McArthur to a duel. This was refused De Mun on the ground that the challe was not a gentleman. Threats were made on both sides and at the occasion of first meeting, which occurred on the stai in the house used by the court, they fired. McArthur was not hurt, but De was killed. No charge was preferred ag: McArthur, as he was very generally hel be justified in the killing. We have give account in another place of the celebr duel between Thomas T. Crittenden Doctor Walter Fenwick. Doctor Fen was buried in the Catholic cemetery an(grave is still to be seen.

The first county court under the state ernment met in Ste. Genevieve, May 21, It was composed of James Pratte, James tin and James W. Smith. The court pointed Thomas Oliver as clerk, and he tinued to hold the office until his deat 1826. At this first meeting of the cour county was divided into two townships. Genevieve and Saline; the former wa: vided in 1827 and the north part was er into the township called Jackson. In Beauvais township was formed from par Saline and Ste. Genevieve and named in l of St. Gem Beauvais; Union township created in 1834 from the western pa Jackson.

A jail was erected in 1875 at a cos $8,000 and at the same time a buildin the use of the county clerk was erected 1883 the present court house was built: a two-story brick building and cost $1(Ste. Genevieve county has a poor farm it bought in 1880 from Jules F. Janis.

The court of quarter sessions for Cape Girardeau district was organized on March 19, [18]05. The following judges were present and took part in the organization of the court: [Ch]ristopher Hays, Louis Lorimier, James [A]llew, Robert Greene, John Byrd and Frederic Limbaugh; Joseph McFerron was clerk [of] the court and John Hays was sheriff. A [gr]and jury was summoned which returned [ind]ictments for assault against William Har[ke]r, and for burglary against Baptiste Manie. [Bo]th of these men were tried and convicted [at] the next term of the court. The court appointed John Randall, Jeremiah Still, Will[ia]n Hand, William Ross, William Lorimier, [an]d Michael Limbaugh as constables.

At other meetings of the court licenses were [iss]ued to Louis Lorimier and Thomas W. [W]aters to run ferries across the Mississippi [riv]er. Rogers was also given a license to con[du]ct a tavern at Hubble's Mill. The settlers [of] Tywappaty Bottom presented a petition, [wh]ich was granted, for the opening of a road [fro]m that settlement to Cape Girardeau. An[oth]er petition asked for a road from Hubble's [Mi]ll by way of Andrew Ramsay's to Cape Girardeau; this petition was signed by a number [of] settlers and was granted. Another petition [pr]ayed for the extension of the road from Ste. [Ge]nevieve to pass the upper Delaware towns [to] John Byrd's thence to William Daugh[ert]y's, thence to Jeremiah Simpson's, thence [to] the edge of the Big Swamp, to meet the [Ne]w Madrid road. The court appointed [vie]wers who were ordered to make a report [at] the next term of the court.

The court also fixed rates of taxation. [Ea]ch house was taxed 25 cents, each head of [cat]tle 6½ cents, each slave 50 cents, and each [on]e hundred dollars' worth of property 25 [cen]ts. Besides these a poll tax of 50 cents [wa]s levied on each able bodied single man who shall not have taxable property to the amount of four hundred dollars. This is probably one of the first instances in the state of a tax on bachelors.

The courts convened in Cape Girardeau. This was in obedience to a proclamation made by Governor Harrison on January 1, 1805. In that proclamation Governor Harrison says that he was not in possession of sufficient information to determine the proper site for a permanent seat of justice but found it necessary to determine a temporary site. Accordingly, he directed that the courts of common pleas and general quarter sessions of the peace and the orphans' court be held at Cape Girardeau upon the lands of Louis Lorimier. The proclamation further appointed the justices of the court of quarter sessions as commissioners to receive proposals and to make recommendation concerning the selection of a permanent site.

The commissioners thus appointed for this selection of the seat of justice received proposals from Louis Lorimier, William Daugherty and Jesse Cain. Daugherty wanted the site to be placed on the Russell farm, which he then owned, near the site of Jackson; Cain wanted it established on the farm afterward owned by August Henecke; Lorimier proposed to give to the district four acres of land to be selected on any part of his grant north of his dwelling house, to furnish all necessary timber for the public buildings, and finally to give two hundred dollars and thirty days' labor of a man toward the erection of the buildings. As a further inducement he declared his purpose to reserve for the use of the inhabitants of the town, which he meant to lay off at Cape Girardeau, all the timber on a certain part of his land. The rather peculiar method of land description is seen in the manner in which Lorimier describes his land. In the proposition to furnish the timber for the public buildings, he says that it is to be taken off his land anywhere "between Thorne's creek and the Shawnee Path." The land on which timber was to be reserved for the people of Cape Girardeau is described as bounded on one side by a line from the mouth of Thorne's creek and the intersection of his boundary line to the Shawnee Path, and on the other side by the town and the river. This proposition of Lorimier was accepted by the commissioners and the governor issued a proclamation fixing the permanent seat of justice at Cape Girardeau. In January, 1806, the court of quarter sessions appointed the following commissioners to lay off the town and locate the site of the public buildings: Anthony Haden, Edmund Hogan, Christopher Hays, Robert Hall and Benjamin Tennille. Other commissioners were appointed to let the contract for the erection of a jail and court house. At the next session of court Commissioner Haden presented a plan of the town as laid off; three acres of the public square was divided into lots and sold. Ezekiel Abel bought lot No. 1 for $62.00, John Scott bought lots 2 and 4 for $77.00 and $89.00, Joseph Meterron lot No. 5 for $62.00, and John Risher lot No. 6 for $69.00. The public square thus left consisted of one acre which was cleared by order of the court. The jail was completed in December, 1806. It was built of oak timber and was 12x25 feet. It was never satisfactory as a jail, having been very poorly built. The grand jury reported in 1812 that prisoners did not stay in jail, but simply passed through it.

The courts of common pleas and general quarter sessions of the peace were superseded in 1813 by a court of common pleas with a jurisdiction equal to both the for[mer] courts. At the same time Cape Girard[eau] county was formed in the place of the [dis]trict of Cape Girardeau, and it was de[ter]mined to establish a new seat of justice. [In] a short period of time, in 1814, the co[urts] were held in Bethel Baptist church on Hu[bble] creek, about one and one-half miles sout[h of] Jackson. It was on the plantation of Tho[mas] Bull. In 1815 the circuit courts were or[gan]ized and the court of common pleas abolis[hed]. The circuit court, as then constituted, [had] jurisdiction over both civil and criminal m[at]ters, over all probate business, and was [also] vested with the oversight of county affa[irs]. Its jurisdiction was thus about as extensiv[e as] that of the present circuit courts, the pro[bate] courts and the county courts combined. T[he] court held its first session in the house w[hich] is now the residence of Mrs. Schmuke. T[his] was in May, 1815, and Hon. Richard [S.] Thomas, judge of the southern circuit, was [on] the bench.

The general assembly had appointed [as] commissioners, to establish the new seat [of] justice, John Davis, John Sheppard, S. [G.] Dunn, Abraham Byrd and Benjamin Sh[ell]. These commissioners selected as a site, a p[iece] of ground then belonging to William H. A[sh]ley on Hubble creek. They purchased f[our] acres of this land, and the house then sta[nd]ing on it was used as a court house. In 1[817] another building was erected for the purpo[se] of the court. It was a frame building, la[rge] and rough, and cost $2,250, and was built [by] John Davis. The jail cost $1,400, and [was] destroyed by fire in 1819; it was immediat[ely] replaced by another which was erected [by] William L. Byrd. The town of Jack[son] itself was located in 1815. This was just af[ter] the battle at New Orleans, and the town named in honor of Andrew Jackson. There was a sale of lots in the town, the sum of $900 being derived from this source.

The divisions of Cape Girardeau county were first made in 1806. At that time two districts, the northern and the southern, were formed and two assessors appointed for each. Charles G. Ellis and Abraham Byrd were assessors in the northern district and John Abernathy and Frederick Bollinger on the southern. In 1807 the entire district was divided into five townships: Tywappity, German, Byrd, Cape Girardeau and St. Francois. Tywappity was bounded on the north and west by the middle of the Big Swamp, on the south by the district line separating Cape Girardeau from New Madrid and on the east by the river. Cape Girardeau township was bounded on the east by the Mississippi river and on the south by the middle of the Big Swamp, and on the north and west by a line beginning at Joseph Waller's ferry on the Mississippi and running west and south to Hubble creek and down Hubble creek to the middle of the Big Swamp. Byrd township was bounded on the east by Cape Girardeau township on the north of the district line, on the south by the Big Swamp, on the west by Whitewater. German township extended from the district line on the north to the Big Swamp on the south and from Whitewater to Turkey creek. St. Francois township was west of Turkey creek, and included all the territory between the district line to the north and the middle of the Big Swamp on the south, extending as far west as there were any settlements. Tywappity township was thus practically the same as Scott county. German township included Bollinger and a part of Madison counties. St. Francois township included Wayne county, while Cape Girardeau and Byrd townships included the present county of Cape Girardeau.

Two of these townships, Tywappity and St. Francois, were later cut off to form Scott and Wayne counties. In 1872 a new township called Randol was formed from portions of Byrd and Cape Girardeau; Apple Creek was erected from a part of Byrd township two years later and at the same time Lorance was formed from the southern part of German township. No other changes were made in the township line until 1840, when Union was created from portions of Apple Creek and German; four years later a part of Lorance was taken to form a new township called Liberty. The whole system of townships was revised in 1848. At this time eleven townships were marked out; they were Lorance, Clubb, Union, German, Liberty, Hubbell, Cape Girardeau, Randol, Shawnee, Byrd and Apple Creek. Bollinger county was organized three years later and Lorance, Clubb, Union, German and part of Liberty townships becoming a part of Bollinger county. In 1852 Whitewater township was organized, in 1856 Welsh, and in 1872 Kinder.

The court house had become unfit for its purposes by 1837 and the court in that year appointed Edward Criddle, Nathan Vanhorn, Ralph Guild and Ebenezer Flynn as the commissioners to superintend the erection of a new building; it was built of brick and stone and was two stories in height. In 1870 this building was destroyed by fire, and in November of that year the court set aside $25,000 for the erection of a new building. It was a brick structure, standing on the public square in Jackson and was erected by Joseph Lansmann of Cape Girardeau. In 1905 it was determined to erect a larger building more suited to the use of the court; this building was completed in 1908 and is still in use.

The first jail, built in 1819, was used for thirty years, when a stone building two stories in height was erected on the public square west of the court house; it was in use only ten years and was superseded by the present brick jail.

At one time in Missouri the legislature created several courts called courts of common pleas; these were given limited jurisdiction coordinate in part with the circuit courts in civil matters. One of these courts was organized at Clarkton in Dunklin county and another in Cape Girardeau, and others at different places in this section of the state. Of all of them, however, created throughout the entire state, only two of them continue to exist, one of them being the court of common pleas at Cape Girardeau. Its sittings are held in the common pleas court house situated on a bluff overlooking the Mississippi river, one of the most beautiful situations in the entire state. This building has recently been the cause of a rather unusual controversy. It is built on land once owned by Louis Lorimier and given by him to Cape Girardeau for court purposes. Whether it is the property of the municipality of Cape Girardeau or the county is the question which has not yet been determined; neither county nor city desire to be vested with the ownership, for that carries with it the financial burden of repairs and maintenance. For a number of years the expense was divided but recently there is an agitation to determine who is the owner of the property.

Not only was Lorimier farsighted enough and patriotic enough to devote land in his new town for the purpose of building a court house, the terms of his will set aside certain tracts of land, also, to be used for school and also for recreation purposes, and the city of Cape Girardeau is fortunate in holding some very desirable park and school sites within bounds, owing to the generosity of its foun

The courts of common pleas and ger quarter sessions of the peace in New Ma district were organized in March, 1805; judges were Richard Jones Waters, E Windsor, Henry Master, John Baptiste C and Michael Amoreaux; Joshua Humpk was the clerk and George Wilson was sh The records of this court have been destr and there is practically no information a able concerning the work of this court. 1813 New Madrid district was changed New Madrid county. It then had the fo ing boundaries: On the north it was bou by the south line of Cape Girardeau cou this line was described as "commencin the Mississippi river at the head of Tywap bottom at the upper end of the tract of where James Brady now lives (near (merce), thence west to the south side o Big Swamp, thence on a direct line to Shawnee village on Castor river, thence west to the western boundary line of Osage purchase." On the east it was bou by the main channel of the Mississippi r on the south by a line commencing in the at Island No. 19, running thence in a d line to White river at the mouth of Little river; thence up Red river to the wes boundary of the Osage purchase.

In the organization of the county, Sar Cooper, Thomas Windsor, Daniel Sp John Guerthing and John Tucker named as a commission to locate a perma seat of justice.

Prior to this time the courts had me New Madrid and also at the house of Sar Phillips in Big Prairie. The court of (mon pleas as reorganized by the act chan the district into a county, was composec

Thomas Neal, John LaValle, William Winchester, and William Gray. This court divided New Madrid county into townships. The territory about New Madrid and Little Prairie was named New Madrid township; Big Prairie township was established to include the settlements about Sikeston; Tywappity township included the territory lying east of St. John's Bayou and extending as far north as the Lucas place; Moreland township embraced the territory between the north part of the Big Prairie and Cape Girardeau county. All the western part of the county of New Madrid was organized into a township called White River. The court also appointed judges of election in each of the townships. For New Madrid township John E. Hart, George Tennille and Robert McCoy were made judges and the house of Samuel Cooper was appointed as the polling place. For Big Prairie township the judges selected were Enoch Liggett, Samuel Phillips and Thomas Bartlett. The election was to be held at the house of Samuel Phillips. John Tucker, Drakeford Gray and John Brooks were the judges of the election of Tywappaty township; the polling place was the house of Edward N. Matthews. For Moreland township the polling place was at the house of Charles Friend and the judges of election were John Ramsay, Hugh Johnson and Timothy Harris. The house of Captain Harris on Spring river was the polling place in White River township and the judges were George Ruddell, Amos Musick and Captain Hines.

In March, 1814, the court, as reorganized, met at the house of Samuel Phillips in Big Prairie, and the June term was held at the house of Jesse Bartlett. In November, 1814, the commissioners for the seat of government selected fifty acres of land in Big Prairie which was donated by Steel Ross and Moses Hurley. This land lay about one-fourth mile south of the present town of Sikeston. Joseph Story was the county surveyor, and he was ordered by the court to lay the fifty acres off into lots. These lots were sold at public auction in November and December of that year. The money thus derived was used for the erection of a jail which was built in 1817. This place continued to be the county seat of New Madrid county until the organization of Scott county, when the county seat was removed to New Madrid. On the removal to New Madrid a new court house and jail became necessary; the old jail was sold on the orders of the court and the new commission, consisting of Mark H. Stallcup, John Shanks, Thomas Bartlett, Francois Le Sieur, and John Ruddell, were appointed. They proceeded to erect a court house and jail. This was the first court house in the county; they were both frame structures. The court house was used until 1854 and the jail until 1845.

This organization of New Madrid county into townships was maintained until 1822. In that year the area of the county having been very greatly reduced by the erection of new counties, townships were formed as follows: Big Prairie was all that part of the county north of a line running in a westerly direction north of Rawl's old mill to the western boundary of the county. New Madrid township was to consist of all of part of the county lying south of Big Prairie township and north of a line beginning on the Mississippi river and running west so as to divide the surveys of Robert McCoy and Joseph Vandenbenden; thence to the west just south of the plantations of Robert G. Watson and Aaron T. Spear on Lake St. Ann to the western boundary of the county. Le Sieur township was to include all the remainder of the county.

New Madrid county was made a part of the southern circuit at the time the territory was divided into judicial circuits, the presiding judge being Hon. Richard S. Thomas, of Jackson. The first session of court in New Madrid county was held in December, 1815, in the house of William Montgomery in Big Prairie. Colonel John D. Walker was sheriff and Greer W. Davis was circuit attorney. The most important case was that of the United States vs. William Gordon, for murder. Gordon was convicted and, afterwards, hanged.

In 1831 St. Johns township was formed in the eastern part of the county to include the territory along St. Johns Bayou. In 1834 Little Prairie township was organized and in 1839 Pemiscot township; in 1842 Woodland was erected from the south part of Big Prairie township and at the same time Big Lake township was formed from parts of Le Sieur and Little Prairie; Woodland township was divided in 1845, a part of it being attached to Big Prairie and the other part to New Madrid. When Pemiscot county was organized in 1851 the size of New Madrid county was considerably reduced and no more townships were organized until 1874, when Portage township was formed.

The court house was destroyed by fire in 1895 and since that time no special building for the use of the courts has been provided by the county. An effort has been made on several occasions to vote bonds for the erection of a court house and the measure has always been defeated. The last attempt was made in 1911; it failed, however, through the opposition of Lilbourn, Marston and some of the other towns of the county which desire a change of the county seat from New Mad At the present time the court offices are tributed in various buildings in the city New Madrid.

We have seen that in 1815 the territo legislature divided the county of New Ma and established, out of the western par that county, a new county to be knowr Lawrence. Its boundaries were describe follows: "Beginning at the mouth of L Red river on the line dividing said cor from the county of Arkansas; thence with line to the river St. Francois; thence up river St. Francois to the division line betv the counties of Cape Girardeau and New dried; thence with said last mentioned to the western boundary of the Osage chase; thence with the last mentioned lir the northern boundary of the county of kansas; thence with the last mentioned lir the place of beginning." A commission appointed to fix the seat of justice, bu December, 1818, an act was passed which ished this county and created another or

The new county was to include the eas part of Lawrence county and the south part of the county of Cape Girardeau. boundaries were described as follows: ' ginning at the southeast corner of the cor of Madison running southwesterly on road which divides the waters of Cro creek and Castor until it strikes the edg the Big Swamp between Jenkin's creek Castor; thence west to the river Cas thence down the main channel of the river Castor until it strikes New Ma county line; thence south so far that a west line will leave the plantation of Edw N. Mathews on the north; thence west to Osage boundary line; thence north with said line so far that a due east line would tersect the place of beginning." This county so bounded was called Wayne county and on account of its great size was often spoken of as the "State of Wayne." The commissioners to fix the seat of government were Overton Bettis, James Logan, Solomon Bollinger, William Street and Ezekiel Ruebottom. The courts were held at first in the house of Ransom Bettis.

When Wayne county was organized, in 1818, the commissioners selected as a site for the county seat the place where Greenville now is. The town was laid out in that year and has been the county seat ever since. For a number of years the courts were held in rooms rented for the purpose.

The first court house was a two-story log building which was replaced in 1849 by a brick structure; this was burned in 1853 and the county appropriated $2,500 to rebuild it. Jeremiah Spencer and L. H. Flinn were appointed to supervise its construction; they completed its erection in 1856. The first jail in the county was built of logs and stood on the south corner of the public square. It was moved away and a brick building erected in 1849; this was used until 1873, when a new jail costing $9,000 was built. The present court house was erected in 1894 at a cost of $7,000.

The first clerk of the courts in Wayne county was Solomon R. Bowlin. Another clerk in the early period of the county was Thomas Catron, who resigned the office in 1849; among his successors were Nixon Palmer and George W. Creath. One of the first sheriffs was Wiley Wallis.

Madison county was created by the territorial legislature by an act passed December 14, 1818. At that time, as in other counties, the principal court was the circuit court, which transacted much of the business of the county. The first meeting of the court was held in the house of Theodore F. Tong on July 12, 1819. Judge Thomas was on the bench; Charles Hutchings was clerk, but was afterwards succeeded by Nathaniel Cook; Joseph Montgomery was the sheriff. A grand jury was summoned and it returned indictments against a number of persons for larceny. The courts for a number of years were held in private houses. The county court of Madison county was organized in 1821; it met at the house of J. G. W. McCabe; William Dillon and Henry Whitener were the judges of the court, and Nathaniel Cook was clerk. The county boundary on the west was Black River, and up to the meeting of the county court in this year it had been divided into three townships: St. Michaels, on the west, Liberty, on the north, and Castor, on the east. In this year two new townships, Twelve Mile and German, were erected. In 1822 a court house was ordered to be erected and was built in the same year. It was built of brick and is still standing. The jail was built in 1820, and it was built of logs on the present jail lot.

From the organization of the county until the year 1822 the courts were held at private residences. In that year, however, the present brick court house was completed; it is the oldest structure of its kind now in use west of the Mississippi river. It was well built and is still in a good state of preservation. A jail had been built before the erection of the court house. It stood on what is still known as the jail lot. It was burned by an escaping prisoner and a new building of brick was erected; it was also destroyed by fire and since that time the county has never erected a jail.

In 1845 the township of St. Francois was erected; Arcadia township in 1848 and Union township in 1850. On the organization of

Iron county in 1857, Arcadia township, Union and Liberty were cut off to form a part of Iron county. Another township, known as Liberty, was later erected in Madison county and a new one created called Hope township.

The county early incurred a debt of more than $12,000 for the erection of the Fredericktown and Pilot Knob gravel road; the total indebtedness of the county in 1859 was $14,946. In the same year its receipts were $4,542, and expenditures $5,931. This shows a gain over the year of 1822, at which time the total receipts were $249.42 and the expenditures were $343.72.

Jefferson county was created December 8, 1818. Parts of Ste. Genevieve and St. Louis counties were cut off to form the new county. It was named in honor of Thomas Jefferson. William Bates, Peter McCormack, Thomas Evans, Henry Metz, Jacob Wise and William Noll were commissioners to select the permanent seat of justice for the county. They decided upon Herculaneum. This decision was made because Herculaneum was the principal town in the county, though at this time, as we have seen, it consisted of only a very few houses. The first court room was in the log cabin owned by a negro named Abe. After a time court was held in the back room of a store occupied by Mr. Glasgow. The officers of the court rented offices in various parts of the town, sometimes holding their deliberation, as we are told, in the shade of the trees.

The first county court met March 22, 1819. The members of the court were H. B. Boyd, Elias Bates and Samuel Hammond. A lot in Herculaneum was donated by James Bryant as a building site for the county buildings, and upon this lot a log jail was erected; no effort was made, however, to build a court house. After considerable agitation a vote was taken in August, 1832, on the proposit to establish the county seat at Montice When the returns of this election were fina canvassed in 1833 it was declared that proposition had been defeated, but in Septe ber, 1834, the returns were again gone o and the court declared that the proposit had carried. Commissioners were appoin to look after the erection of a log court hou Delays, however, occurred and it was not u April 7, 1838, that a building site was tained in Monticello. Hugh O'Neil and S uel Merry donated fifty acres of land for purpose. On February 8, 1839, the gene assembly passed an act establishing the s of justice at Hillsboro, the name Montic being changed because it was the name of county seat of Lewis county. The court pointed John J. Buren as commissioner erect a court house. The building was brick and stood near the present public sch building and cost $4,600. The first meet of the court was held in this building April, 1840. A jail was built in 1841, and 1865 the present court house and jail w erected at a cost of $16,000.

The first circuit court in Jefferson cou was held in 1819 by Judge Nathaniel Beve Tucker, who was judge of northern circ

The territory now composing Washing county was a part of the Ste. Genevieve trict and so remained until August 21, 18 when Washington county was organized an act of the territorial legislature. As was organized it included a great amount territory, being several times as large as present county; its limits were gradually duced as new counties were formed and 1868 its boundaries were finally fixed as th are now. The act creating the county pointed Lemuel Brown, Samuel Perry, Jo

Hawkins, Martin Ruggles and John Andrews to select the permanent seat of justice. They held a meeting in the fall of 1813 and selected Mine a Breton as a temporary meeting place for the court. The first judges of the court of common pleas were Martin Ruggles, William Sloan and John Stanton, who met on the first Monday in January, 1814, in the house of Benjamin Elliott, with John Brickey as clerk. The first sheriff was Lemuel Brown. Brown was a nephew of Colonel Burr and was afterward killed in a duel by John Smith T. The first business transacted by this court was the appointment of an administrator for the estate of William Blanford; John Perry was appointed. At a meeting on the 13th of January, 1814, Charles Lucas was granted permission to practice law before the courts of the county; he was the first lawyer admitted to the bar. For two years there was no court except the court of common pleas, but in 1815 the county court was organized and also the circuit court. At the time of the organization of these new courts a log jail was erected on the public square in the original town of Potosi. This town was laid out on a tract of land northeast of the old town of Mine a Breton and donated by Moses Austin and John Rice Jones. Lots were sold in this new town and the money from their sale was used for the building of a court house, the total cost of which was $5,595. The citizens of Potosi at this time wished to make the town the capital of the state and the court house was designed to be used as a capitol building. The contractor for the court house was unable to finish the work and the upper story was never completed. In 1849 a contract was let for the building of the present structure at a cost of $10,000.

The first term of the court was held at Mine a Breton in April, 1815, by David Barton, judge of the northern circuit, and Richard S. Thomas of the southern circuit. The lawyers who practiced before the courts of Washington county were, many of them, very able men; among them were Israel McGready, Daniel Dunklin, David E. Perryman, John S. Brickey, Phillip Cole and Henry Shurlds.

The county was divided into eleven townships: Belgrade, Bellevue, Breton, Concord, Harmony, Johnson, Kingston, Liberty, Richwoods, Union and Walton.

Potosi was made the county seat. It was originally a mining camp near Mine a Breton. Potosi was separated from the old village of Mine a Breton by a fork of Breton creek. It was a typical mining village in the early days and contained several rather pretentious dwellings and was rather better built and a more pleasant town than other towns of the district. There were three stores, two distilleries, a flour mill, some lead furnaces, one saw mill and post office. The mail was brought from St. Louis and also from Ste. Genevieve once each week. There was also a monthly mail from Arkansas. The most pretentious and commodious residence in town was Durham Hall, which we have previously described as the home of Moses Austin. Austin and his son, Samuel Perry, John Rice Jones, Elijah Bates, and Brickey, were among the principal residents of the town in the early times. The town grew slowly and was supported almost entirely by the lead mines. These mines in the immediate vicinity of Potosi produced in the period from 1798 to 1818 nearly ten million pounds of lead.

Perry county was created by the legislature by a law passed November 16, 1820, but the county court was not organized until May 21, 1821. The meeting was held at the house of Bede Moore, who lived about two and one-half miles north of the present site of Perryville. The judges of the court were: Louis Cissell, D. L. Caldwell and Samuel Anderson.

The first clerk of the court was Cornelius N. Slattery. The county was divided into three townships: Brazeau, including the territory between the Cinque Homme and Apple Creek; Bois Brule, in the northeast part of the county, and Cinque Homme, which included the remainder of the county. Robert T. Brown was the first sheriff, and Joseph Tucker was the first assessor. Commissioners were appointed to locate the seat of justice, and they selected the present site of Perryville. Provision for the building of a court house was not made until 1825. Up to this time the courts met in rooms which were rented for the purpose, though a log jail had previously been erected.

The second court house was erected in 1859. The court appropriated $8,000 for the building and John E. Layton was appointed as superintendent of construction. This court house still stands and is in a fair state of preservation. A jail was erected about 1825; it was built of logs. This jail was used until 1839, when it was superseded by a brick building 32 feet long and 22 feet wide, which was put upon the public square near the court house.

Judge Thomas organized the circuit court of Perry county June 4, 1821. There seems to have been but little business transacted by this court for a number of years. The first case of importance was the trial of Ezekiel Fenwick for the killing of William R. Bellamy; this was March 29, 1824. The circumstances under which Bellamy was killed are said to have been about these: Bellamy, who was a constable, had attempted to attach goods belonging to Fenwick, but found the goods on a boat about to be removed across the Mississippi river. Fenwick resist[ed] constable's efforts to tie the boat up. A [strug]gle ensued between the two men and [in] an exchange of shots Bellamy was w[ounded] in the arm; the wound finally resulted [in] death. Fenwick escaped to Cape Gir[ardeau] county, but afterwards surrendered [himself] on a promise made by Judge Thomas t[hat he] would be admitted to bail. It was this [prom]ise of Judge Thomas that formed one [of the] charges in the impeachment case again[st him]. Fenwick was afterward tried and acq[uitted].

This was the last of the counties org[anized] before the admission of the state in[to the] Union. The county was formed aft[er the] organization of the state governmen[t but] before the proclamation of the Preside[nt ad]mitting the state into the Union.

After the transfer to the United St[ates in] 1804 there was very little trouble wi[th the] Indians until just before the breaking [out of] the war of 1812 with Great Britain. [In] 1811 the British agents in the north an[d west] began to stir up the Indians and induc[e them] to commit depredations on the wester[n and] northern frontier. This brought the I[ndians] upon the inhabitants of Missouri in t[he dis]trict of St. Charles. Every effort was [made] to induce the Indians to give up thei[r arms] and in May, 1812, an assembly of the [chiefs] of a large number of tribes was held [at St.] Louis. Later these chiefs visited Wash[ington] and endeavors were made to pacify [them.] Tecumseh's influence was too stron[g over] them and many of the Indians, includi[ng the] Sacs, Foxes, Iowas, Sioux and some [of the] Shawnees, decided to go on the wa[rpath.] Most of the Shawnees and the Delaware[s were] either neutral or assisted the settlers i[n Mis]souri. This determination of the I[ndians] caused a very great increase in outrag[es] disturbances in the north part of the state. The militia of the St. Charles district did all that it could to protect that part of the territory and a large number of forts were built there and troops stationed to garrison them. These troops were, however, entirely inadequate to protect all the settlers, and accordingly a call was made on the districts south of the river for assistance.

In response to this call for help, companies were organized to take part in the Indian wars. One of the first of these companies was recruited in Cape Girardeau district by Andrew Ramsay, Jr.; this was in the spring of 1813. The officers were Andrew Ramsay, captain; James Morrison, first lieutenant; Peter Craig, second lieutenant; Drakeford Gray, third lieutenant; William Ramsay, ensign; Wilson Able, Edward Spear, John Giles, John Gray and James Ramsay, sergeants; Daniel Harklerood, George Simpson, Willis Flannagan, Michael Ault, Alexander Scott and Edward Tanner, corporals, and Solomon Fossett, trumpeter. This company took part in some of the Indian troubles, but soon was disbanded.

In the summer of 1814 General Henry Dodge of Ste. Genevieve, collected a force of about three hundred, including some forty or fifty Shawnee Indians. The force consisted of a company from St. Louis under Captain John Thompson; one from Cape Girardeau under Captain Abraham Daugherty; one from the Boone's Lick settlement under Captain Cooper; one from Ste. Genevieve under Captain Bernard Pratte, and the Indians who were under command of Captain J. B. St. Gem. This body of troops marched into the St. Charles district, were joined by another company under Captain Edward Hempstead, and attacked the camp of Miamis on the south side of the Missouri river. The camp was captured and the Indians, who had scattered in the woods, were taken prisoners; there were 152 of them. These were first sent to St. Louis and then to the site of every nation on the Wabash river. The company from Cape Girardeau and those from St. Louis then marched to Cape au Gris; they were then returned home. The officers of this Cape Girardeau company were: Abraham Daugherty, captain; Medad Randol, first lieutenant; Andrew Patterson, second lieutenant; Robert Buckner, third lieutenant; Frederick Keep, ensign; Michael Rodney, William Cox, James Thompson, Benjamin Anthony, sergeants; Jacob Yount, Henry Shaner, Hall Hudson, John Davis, Nero Thompson and John Ezell, corporals.

The most famous of these expeditions was that made in 1814 by a company of mounted rangers raised by Peter Craig of Cape Girardeau county. Many of the members of the company had served under Captain Ramsay in 1813; they were now enlisted for a period of one year to serve on the frontiers of Missouri and Illinois, and they became a part of a regiment commanded by Colonel William Russell. This company did very much service during these Indian troubles, and fought the famous battle of the Sink Hole. The officers of this company were: Peter Craig, captain; Drakeford Gray, first lieutenant; Wilson Able, second lieutenant; Edward Spear, third lieutenant; John Giles, ensign; John Rodney, Enos Randol, Daniel Harklerood, William Fugate, William Blakeney, sergeants; Abraham Letts, Perry W. Wheat, Jeremiah Able, William McCarty, Charles Sexton and Thomas S. Rodney, corporals.

The privates of the company were: James Atkinson, John Able, Stephen Byrd, Jonathan Brickey, John Brown, Tessant Barkume, James Brown, William B. Bush, George P.

Bush, Peter Barrado, Francois Barraboe, Thomas Boyce, Burrel Castly, John Cameron, Charles Cardinal, William Crump, John Cooper, Jesse Cochran, Baptiste Cotie, Alexander Cotie, James Cowan, Hugh Dowlin, Elias Davis, Ludwell Davis, John Dotson, Samuel Foster, Able Galland, Alexander Giboney, Louis Guliah, Charles Hamilton, Louis Heneaux, Abijah Highsmith, John Houk, Benjamin Hall, John Holcomb, James Hamilton, Frederick Hector, Thomas Hail, John Hodge, Stephen Jarboe, Jehoida Jeffrey, Andrew Johnson, Baptiste Janneaux, Jr., Baptiste Janneaux, Sr., William King, Charles Lloyd, Francis Lemmey, Joseph Lemmey, John Langston, Baptiste La Croy, Baptiste Labeaux, Stephen McKenzie, James Massey, Nathan McCarty, James Masterson, Mark Murphy, William Martin, Benjamin Ogle, Samuel Parker, James Putney, Samuel Philip, John Patterson, Antoine Pelkey, John Roach, Tessant Reeves, Robert Robertson, Joshua Simpson, John Sorrells, John Shepherd, Alexander St. Scott, Joseph Sivwaris, Edward Stephenson, Solomon Thorn, Hubbard Tayon, John D. Upham, John Vance, Louis Vanure, Pascal Valle, George Wilt, John Watkins, Isaac Williams, John Wiggs, David Wilt, William Wathen, Jenkin Williams, William Wells, Levi Wolverton, Michael Wigo, Frederick Webber, Isaac Gregory, George Vanleer.

After the company was organized and mustered into service it was sent to North Missouri and while there fought the battle of the Sink Hole. This was in Lincoln county, not far from Cape au Gris. The account here given of this battle was written by Colonel John Shaw of the Wisconsin Historical Society: "Captain Peter Craig commanded at Fort Howard. About noon five of the men went out of the fort to Byrne's deserted house on the bluff, about one-fourth of a mile below the fort, to bring in a grindstone. In co[nse]quence of back water from the Mississ[ippi] they went in a canoe, and on their return v[ere] fired on by a party supposed to be fifty [In]dians, who were under shelter of some b[rush] that grew along at the foot of the bluff [near] Byrne's house, and about fifteen rods dis[tant] from the canoe at that time. Three of [the] whites were killed and one mortally woun[ded] and as the water was shallow the Indians [ran] out and tomahawked their victims. The [peo]ple of the fort ran out and fired on the [In]dians across the back water, a few inches d[eep] while another party of about twenty-five [went] to the right of the water with a view of in[ter]cepting the Indians, who seemed to be mak[ing] toward the bluff or high plain west and no[rth] west of the fort. The party of twenty [five] and Captain Craig's soon united. On [the] bluff was the cultivated field and dese[rted] residence of Benjamin Allen. The field [was] about forty rods across, beyond which [was] pretty thick timber. Here the Indians ma[de a] stand and here the fight began. Both pa[rties] fired, and as the fight waxed warm the [In]dians slowly retired as the whites advan[ced.] After the fight had been going on perl[haps] some ten minutes the whites were reinfo[rced] by Captain David Musick, of Cape au G[ris] with about twenty men. He had been o[n a] scout toward the head of Cuiver river and [had] returned to within about one-half a mil[e of] the fort and about one and a half miles of [the] scene of the conflict, and had stopped with [his] men to graze their horses when, hearing [the] firing, they instantly remounted and da[shed] toward the place of battle. Dismountin[g at] the edge of the timber on the bluff, and hi[tch]ing their horses, they rushed through a [part] of the Indian line, and shortly after the en[emy] fled, a part bearing to the right of the s[ink] hole toward Bob's creek, but the most of th[em] taking refuge in the sink hole, which was close by where the main fighting had taken place. About the time the Indians were retreating, Captain Craig exposed himself about four feet beyond his tree and was shot through the body and fell dead. James Putney was killed before Captain Craig, and perhaps one or two others. Before the Indians retired to the sink hole the fighting had become animated; the loading was done quickly and shots rapidly exchanged, and when one of our party was killed or wounded it was announced aloud. The sink hole was about sixty feet in length, and from twelve to fifteen feet in width, and ten or twelve feet deep. Near the bottom, on the southeast side, was a shelving rock under which perhaps some fifty or sixty persons might have sheltered themselves. At the northeast end of the sink hole the descent was quite gradual, the other end much more abrupt, and the southeast side almost perpendicular, and the other side about like the steep roof of a house.

"On the southeast side the Indians, as a farther protection in case the whites should rush up, dug under the shelving rock with their knives. On the sides and in the bottom of the sink hole were some bushes, which also served as something of a screen for the Indians. Captain Musick and his men took part on the northeast side of the sink hole, and others occupied other positions surrounding the enemy. As the trees approached close to the sink hole, these served in part to protect our party. Finding we could not get a good opportunity to dislodge the enemy, as they were best protected, those of our men who had families at the fort gradually went there, not knowing but a large body of Indians might seize the favorable occasion to attack the fort while the men were mostly away engaged in the exciting contest. The Indians in the sink hole had a drum made of a skin stretched over the section of a hollow tree, on which they beat quite constantly, and some Indian would shake a rattle called She-shuqui, probably a dried bladder with pebbles within, and even for a moment would venture to thrust his head in view, with his hand elevated, shaking his rattle and calling out "peash! peash!" which was understood to be a sort of defiance, or as Blackhawk, who was one of the party says in his account of that affair, a kind of bravado to come and fight them in the sink hole. When the Indians would creep up and shoot over the rim of the sink hole they would instantly disappear, and while they sometimes fired effectual shots they in turn became occasionally the victims. From about 1 to 4 o'clock p. m. the firing was incessant, our men generally reserving their fire till an Indian would show his head, and all of us were studying how we could more effectually attack and dislodge the enemy. At length Lieutenant Spears suggested that a pair of cart wheels, axle and tongue, which were seen at Allen's place, be obtained, and a moving battery constructed. The idea was entertained favorably and an hour or more was consumed in its construction. Some oak floor puncheons from seven to eight feet in length were made fast to an axle in an upright position and port holes made through them. Finally the battery was ready for trial and was sufficiently large to protect some half a dozen or more men. It was moved forward slowly and seemed to attract the particular attention of the Indians, who had evidently heard the knocking and pounding connected with its manufacture, and who now frequently popped up their heads to make momentary discoveries, and it was at length moved up to within less than ten paces of the brink of the sink hole on the southeast side. The upright plank did not reach to the ground within some eighteen inches, the men calculating to shoot beneath the lower end at the Indians, but the latter from their position had decided advantage of this neglected aperture, for the Indians, shooting beneath the battery at an upward angle, would get shots at the whites before the latter could see them. The Indians also watched the port holes and directed some of their shots at them. Lieutenant Spear was shot dead through the head, and his death was much lamented, as he had proved himself an intrepid officer. John Patterson was wounded in the thigh, and some others were also wounded behind the battery. Having failed in its design, the battery was abandoned after sun-down. Our hope all along had been that the Indians would emerge from their covert and attempt to retreat to where we supposed their canoes were left, some three or four miles distant, in which case we were firmly determined to rush upon them and endeavor to cut them off totally. The men generally evinced the greatest bravery during the whole engagement.

"Night was now coming on and the reports of a half a dozen guns in the direction of the fort by a few Indians, who rushed out of the woods skirting Bob's creek not more than forty rods from the north end of the fort, was heard. This movement on the part of the few Indians who had escaped when the others took refuge in the sink hole was evidently designed to divert the attention of the whites and alarm them for the safety of the fort, and thus effectually relieve the Indians in the sink hole. This was the result, for Captain Musick and men retired to the fort, carrying the dead and wounded, and made every preparation to pel a night attack.

"The men at the fort were mostly up night, ready for resistance if necessary. Th was no physician at the fort and much ef was made to set some broken bones. Th was a well in the fort, and provisions ammunition to sustain a pretty formid attack. The women were greatly alarn pressing their infants to their breasts, fear they might not be permitted to behold ano morning's light, but the night passed a without seeing or hearing an Indian. next morning a party went to the sink l and found the Indians gone. They had ried off all their dead and wounded exc five dead bodies left on the northwest s From all signs it appeared some thirty them were killed or wounded. Lieuten Gray reported eight of our party killed, missing and five wounded. The dead w buried near the fort, and a man sent to Charles for medical assistance. Lieuten Gray assumed command."

Those who were killed in this battle we Captain Craig, Lieutenant Spear, Alexan Giboney, James Putney, Antoine Pell Hubbard Tayon and Francois Lemmey. J Patterson, Benjamin Hale and Abraham L were wounded. The company was soon n tered out and the men returned to their hon

In 1816 a regiment was formed in C Girardeau, Ste. Genevieve, St. Charles St. Louis. John Shaw was the colonel Levi Roberts was the major. They took part in the hostilities as the war ended fore they reached their destination in Illin

CHAPTER XII

PERIOD FROM 1804 TO 1821

POPULATION—CHARACTER OF IMMIGRANTS—SETTLEMENTS IN VARIOUS PARTS OF THE SECTION — EARLY SETTLERS — INDUSTRIES — FARMING—MINING — MERCHANDISING — PREVAILING HIGH PRICES — MANUFACTURING — HUNTING — TRANSPORTATION — STEAMBOATS — SOCIAL LIFE — LAWLESSNESS — GAMBLING — DUELING — SOME FAMOUS DUELS — HOSPITALITY — POSTOFFICES AND RATES OF POSTAGE — NEWSPAPERS—SCHOOLS—LIBRARIES—DRESS.

We have followed the changes in the government of Missouri under the United States, from the purchase in 1803 to the time when the territorial assembly petitioned Congress for the organization of a state government. We have seen that Louisiana was first made a district and attached to the territory of Indiana; that later it was organized as a territory of the first class, and known as the Territory of Louisiana; that in 1812 it was organized as a territory of the second class under the title of the Territory of Missouri; that in 1816 it became a territory of the third or highest class. We have further seen the organization of a government, the various governors who held executive authority in the territory; we have seen the formation of the general assembly and the gradual growth of self government among the people of the territory. We have now to recount the growth in population of the territory after its transfer to the United States.

At that time the total population of Upper Louisiana, including the settlements in Arkansas, was not more than 10,000; at the time we have now reached, 1818, it is probable that there were, in Missouri alone, nearly 40,000 people. This was a remarkable growth. It is not strange, however, that the population increased very rapidly. There was a great movement of population from east to west and Missouri was situated on the line of the principal part of this early movement. We may not forget the great part played in western immigration by the Ohio river. It offered a safe and easy road from east to west, and those who used this highway almost invariably came to Missouri. Not all of them remained within the borders of the state, but many of them did so, for not only was Missouri in the main highway of east-to-west travel, but it offered unusual attractions to settlers. Its soil, its climate, its timber, its minerals all combined to draw inhabitants. The fact that it had become a part of the United States, that restrictions on religion and on trade had been removed, were powerful inducements to immigrants.

These Americans who came to Missouri in this period were, for the most part, farmers. They came to cultivate the soil. Accordingly, we find them scattered over the state and opening up lands. The first settler in any community set himself down in the midst of the woods, cleared away a little space for his farm, and erected a rude log house. He was most probably miles and miles away from the nearest neighbor. This isolation, however, did not affect him very much. The very fact that he had made his way into a new country and faced the conditions of pioneer life was sufficient evidence that he was not to be daunted by the fact that neighbors were few. He was not long allowed, however, to dwell alone. Other people came, more of the forest was cleared away, and other log houses were erected. In a little while there was a settlement. The settlers, however, were not crowded into towns, they were scattered on their farms. There was something, however, of a community life. There were some attempts made to hold schools in the settlements, in some of them church houses were erected. Many of the settlements were made by persons previously acquainted; in some cases families came and opened up new lands. Where this was not true, it was not long until acquaintance was formed. The families thus living in the same communities intermarried and there came to be something of a solidarity and unity about the life of the community. The transformation was little less than marvelous; where all had been forest, and wild life had reigned supreme, there came to be cultivated fields and houses and even villages. This process went on all over Southeast Missouri.

These immigrants were almost all of them Americans. They came from Ohio, Kentucky, Tennessee, Virginia, and other states. They were moved by various motives. Some of them were attracted by the cheapness of the lands, others felt that the states in which they lived were becoming overcrowded, many of them had that spirit that moves people out on the frontier. They did not like to live in communities where neighbors were near to them. Whatever it was that brought them, they came, and in large and increasing numbers.

At the time of the transfer to the United States there were only a few settlements outside of the towns of Ste. Genevieve, Cape Girardeau and New Madrid. There were a few settlers in Jefferson, Perry, Wayne, Bollinger, Scott, Mississippi and Pemiscot counties, but the great numbers of population were in the towns or immediately adjoining them. The growth of population under the United States was not confined to the country; the towns grew rapidly in population. Those that were already established had, of course, the advantage; but other towns sprung up also.

In 1803 New Madrid district, including Little Prairie and Arkansas, contained 1,350 people, two-thirds of whom were Americans and one-third were French. Cape Girardeau had 1,470 white population, besides a few slaves. All of the white population, except a few French families, were Americans. In Ste. Genevieve there were 2,350 whites, 520 slaves, and more than one-half the population was American. In 1814 a census was taken of the white male population and the figures here given are those of this census: New Madrid had 1,548, Cape Girardeau 2,062, Ste. Genevieve 1,701, and Washington county had 1,010. It is probable that the entire adult population in each case was about twice the figures here given.

By the year 1820 one or more settlements had been made within the limits of most of the counties in southeast Missouri. Several of these counties, however, had not yet been created. There were in existence only Ste. Genevieve, Washington, Wayne, Jefferson,

Cape Girardeau, New Madrid, and Madison. The territory now in the limits of the other counties in the southeast, at that time, formed a part of one or the other of these counties. When the counties were created, during the organization of the government of the territory of Louisiana, they extended an unknown distance to the west. The western boundary was not determined and so the counties that bordered on the river—Ste. Genevieve, Cape Girardeau and New Madrid—included vast stretches of territory to the west. It was out of this western territory that most of the new counties were created. After the treaty with the Osage Indians, however, which established them at first in western Missouri, counties extended to the western boundary of the Osage purchase.

The principal settlements at this time in the various counties were these:

In Ste. Genevieve county there were settlements at Ste. Genevieve and New Bourbon, and there was also a settlement on the Saline creek, which was called for a long time New Tennessee.

In St. Francois county the principal settlements were Alleys Mines, the Murphy settlement, and the Cook settlement.

In Jefferson county there were a number of settlements. Among these were settlements on the Joachim, on Big river, and Herculaneum on the Mississippi river. This settlement at Herculaneum was noted on account of its manufacture of shot. Very early in the period of Missouri's territorial history the manufacture of shot was begun at this place. The high bluffs just north of the town were used for this purpose. The melted lead was dropped from the tops of the bluffs thus doing away with the necessity of a shot tower. The manufacture was so profitable that there were three different establishments for making shot.

In 1818 Peck visited Herculaneum, which he described as "a river town, a landing and a place of some importance." It was situated on the alluvial flat of the Joachim. This flat was very narrow, and was bounded on each end by perpendicular cliffs, rising two hundred feet high. It was these cliffs which were used in the manufacture of shot, in place of a shot tower. At that date there were four stores and about thirty dwelling houses in the town. On the Plattin, a short distance below the Joachim, there were water mills and distilleries. Herculaneum was, even then, the depot for the lead trade of the interior.

In Perry county there were a number of settlements, the chief of these were in the Bois Brule bottom, on the Barrens near Perryville, and on Apple creek near the line between Cape Girardeau and Perry counties.

The most flourishing of these settlements were those found in the bottoms. The soil was very rich there and attracted many settlers. The Barrens, as the land about the present site of Perryville was then called, was the place where Bishop DuBourg had founded the first Catholic seminary in Louisiana. This seminary began its operations just before the close of this territorial period.

The settlements in Madison county were those on Saline creek, and in the south part of the county; the first being St. Michaels. Owing to great damage caused by flood the settlers on the original site of St. Michaels removed the town about one and a half miles west and re-established it there. After the removal the town was renamed Fredericktown, being so called in honor of Colonel George Frederick Bollinger, one of the pioneers in Bollinger county. This town of Fredericktown grew very rapidly during this period, owing to activity in the operations of

Mine LaMotte, which is situated not far from Fredericktown.

In Iron county there were settlements made in Bellevue valley, and in 1805 Ephraim Stout settled near the present site of Arcadia. A little later John Short took up his residence close to where the town of Pilot Knob now stands.

There were other settlements within the limits of the county, but these were the principal ones.

In Cape Girardeau county the principal settlements were at Cape Girardeau and in the immediate vicinity; near Jackson on Byrd's creek; at Gordonville; on Randol's creek, and on Indian creek. The town of Jackson was founded during this period and so named in honor of President Andrew Jackson. In 1815 Jackson was made the county seat of Cape Girardeau county.

The settlements in Bollinger county were principally along the Whitewater river, on Crooked creek, and near the present towns of Lutesville and Glen Allen. The settlements along Whitewater river were those made by Colonel Bollinger and his friends. John Lorance began a settlement on Crooked creek in 1805; about that same date Daniel Hahn settled on the creek afterward called Hahn's creek, named for him, about one-half mile west of Lutesville. Casper Schell and Peter Baker lived in the same neighborhood. Henry Baker and John Deck were others who lived in this part of the county. The settlement at Glen Allen was made by families from North Carolina; some of these were George and Jacob Nifong, Jacob Hinkle and Jacob Clodfelter.

In Wayne county the first settlement seems to have been made about 1802, by settlers from Virginia. Among them were Joseph Parrish, Thomas Ring, David, Charles and Robert A. Logan. The latter had lived Kentucky. Some of these settled in neighborhood of the village of Patterson others on the St. Francois river. Some of other early settlers were Isaac E. Kelly, man Smith, James Caldwell and Fran Clark. Besides these there were Elijah thews, a man named Alston from North C lina; they lived on Otter creek. They bec involved in a difficulty and Alston was ki Elijah Ranson and Overton Beltis were ot who settled in the same neighborhood. was near Greenville.

The principal settlements in New Ma county were those at New Madrid and P Pleasant. Besides these two settlements t was a small settlement at Portageville. as we have previously said, a number of sons lived along St. John's bayou and in o parts of the county.

In Pemiscot county the principal settler was at Little Prairie, though there were ot scattered over the county. The settlemen Little Prairie was made in 1794 by Fran Le Sieur.

Some of the early settlers were Jean tiste Barsaloux, George and John Rud Joseph Payne, Louis Auvin, Charles Guib and Peter Noblesse. In 1799 there wer people in the settlement and 103 in 1803. was a prosperous village up to the time of earthquake in 1812, when it was almost tirely destroyed. About 1810 Colonel J Hardeman Walker came to Little Prairie was one of the few settlers who rema after the time of the earthquake. He sheriff of the county and later one of judges of the county court. He was the r prominent and influential citizen of county for many years. The other settlem of which we have spoken as being in exist in the county were merely collections of or three families. One of these was at Gayoso and another on Little river, and one not a great way from Big lake.

In Scott county the first settlement seems to have been made near Sikeston by Edward Robertson and his son-in-law, Moses Hurley. Robertson was a merchant and land speculator and became wealthy through his various operations. He probably came to the county about 1790. In 1796 Captain Charles Friend from Virginia settled near Benton. He brought with him a large family of sons. In 1811 John Ramsay came from Cape Girardeau and settled on what is now the county poor farm.

Joseph Hunter, who in 1805 located in New Madrid, removed about a year later to Big Prairie and located near Sikeston. Hunter was a Scotchman and was a very influential man in the territory. He acquired considerable wealth by trading and land speculation, and was appointed by President Madison as a member of the council of the territory.

Thomas W. Waters from South Carolina was the first settler on the site of Commerce. About 1803 he established a trading post and store there in partnership with Robert Hall; the firm also operated a ferry across the Mississippi. Tiwappity bottom, between Commerce and Bird's Point, was early settled. Some of the men who came were James Brady, James Curran, Charles Findlay, Edmund Hogan, Thomas, John and James Welbourn.

The first settlement in Mississippi county was made in 1800 by one John Johnson, who secured a grant of land and located on it near Bird's Point. In 1801 a settlement on what is now called Matthews' Prairie was made. This prairie was first called St. Charles but was changed in name in honor of Edward Matthews, who made the first settlement there. Others who came here within a few years were Charles Gray, Joseph Smith, John Weaver, George Becker and Absalom McElmurry. Abraham Bird bought the land which was first granted to Johnson, about 1805; Bird's Point was named for him. He remained there until 1815, when he sold the homestead to his son, John, and moved to Louisiana.

A settlement was made between Norfolk and Wolf Island in 1812 by Newman Beckwith of Virginia. In 1813 William Rush settled on Rush's Ridge. In 1802 James Lucas settled at the place afterwards called Lucas' Bend. The settlement at Norfolk was made in 1800 by John, Andrew and James Ramsay from Cape Girardeau. The first settlers on Wolf Island were John Gray, Drakeford Gray and Thomas Phillips, while William D. Bush was a pioneer in Long Prairie.

In 1819 the first settlement was made in Butler county. This was on Cane creek. The settlement was located by Solomon Kittrel, who was a Kentuckian, and took up a large tract of land and also operated a store, a distillery and a tan yard. Kittrel lived to be very old, dying in 1872. Other settlers on Cane creek were Thomas Scott and Malachi Hudspeth. Some of the other pioneers in the county were Daniel Epps, Martin Sandlin, Samuel Hillis, the Whittingtons, Samuel Poke, James Bramum and the Applebys and Vandovers.

The first settlement in Washington county was made at Potosi. This was near Mine a Breton. The settlers were attracted on account of the mines and the mine itself was opened in 1787. There were other settlements in the county but nearly all of them were grouped around the mines. When Washington county was separated from Ste. Genevieve in 1816, Potosi was made the seat of government for the county.

The first settlement in Reynolds county was made in 1812 by Henry Fry, who came from

Kentucky and settled on the middle fork of Black river. Some of the other early settlers were the families of Henry, Logan and Hyatt. The territory embraced in the county was first a part of Ripley county, but was later attached to Washington.

Zimri Carter made a settlement on Current river in 1820; this was not far from the present town of Van Buren. Other families, the Chiltons, Colemans and others, settled in the same vicinity at a somewhat later date. These were the beginnings of settlements in Carter county, which was named for Zimri Carter.

The first settlement in Ripley county was made about 1819 on Current river. The settlers of that date were George Lee, William Merrill, Joseph Hall, Willis Dudley and Abner Ponder. William Little and James Pulliam settled about the same date on La Fourche de Main.

According to this account we find that settlements had been made before the admission of the state, in all the counties in Southeast Missouri, except Stoddard and Dunklin. Stoddard county was settled in 1823, but no settlement was made in Dunklin county until about 1835. Owing to its location this latter county was very difficult of access. It was, therefore, not settled as soon as the other counties in the section. Of course it will be remembered that not all of these counties were in existence when the state was admitted. Most of them were organized after that time. The territory formed a part of some one or other of the existing counties.

The principal industry in this period, as in the one preceding it, was agriculture. A large part of the population was engaged in farming. It is quite evident that the methods used were very primitive and the crops corre-

spondingly small. The timber that grew the land selected was cut down, burne otherwise disposed of in the easiest way sible, and the land thus cleared was fa in a rude, inefficient way. In spite of handicaps, however, the crops obtained better than we might expect, owing to th the the land was exceedingly rich. wheat, oats, formed perhaps the prir grain crops that were grown. Nearly all ers were also stock raisers on a limited They were induced to grow cattle and l partly on account of the necessity of the and partly because it was possible to stock at comparatively little expense. I easy to raise both cattle and hogs and pr them in a way for market, with but very food other than they obtained in the v The vast forests offered the very best for stock, and it was not unusual for to stay out through the entire year. So them became almost wild. Such a ci stance, of course, made it easy for pers disposed to kill stock which did not belc them. So great was this abuse that the torial assembly passed a law providing any person who should kill any domesti mal in the woods should report the mat the justice of the peace within three day should bring to the justice the head c animal slain. This was done in ord identify the animal by any marks which be upon the head.

The produce of the soil was very l used by those who grew it. Some part was available for export and the towns territory derived their food supplies fro surrounding country, but the greater p all that was grown was used on the where it was produced. A number of mills were erected and operated at conv

...ces, and to these the farmers carried their ...in and received from the mill the flour or ...al ground from their own grain.

If farming was the most important of the ...lustries in Southeast Missouri during this ...riod of its history, mining was second in ...portance. Large numbers of families de-...nded in whole or in part upon mining for ...pport. Austin, who was given a great tract ...land by the Spanish for the erection of the ...st reverbatory furnace, says that it was the ...stom for the poor to resort to the mines ...ter harvest, and to spend several months ...gaged in labor in these mines. The rich ...milies sent their slaves about the same time, ...that the greater part of the mining was ...ne from August to December. This offered ...those who farmed an opportunity, which ...ey were not slow to use, to spend the months ...t needed upon the farms in labor at the ...ines.

The mines of the southeast had long been famous. They were worked by the French and were one of the prime motives for French exploration and settlement.

The region to which the early French seekers after mineral wealth gave most attention lies between the head waters of the St. Francois and the Mississippi and between the Maramec on the north and Apple creek. So full of mineral wealth was this district that it was early called the mineral district of Louis-iana. Within its 3,000 square miles are found many minerals. Lead, iron and zinc are those of most importance, but besides these are copper, manganese, salt, antimony, cobalt, plumbago and some others. All the early French explorers mention the richness of the lead mines. These deposits of lead were known and worked even by the Indians. The French began to take out lead in this district probably before the year 1700.

It is impossible to fix, with certainty, either the date when lead was first mined or the men who opened this first mine. Schoolcraft,

Happy Missouri Corn Grower

copied by Rozier, is of the opinion that Mine LaMotte was the earliest mine and was discovered by one LaMotte, a gentleman in the company of Renault. This was probably in the year 1720 or 21. Houck, however, believes that this mine was probably opened much earlier than this and that it was named for Cadillac De La Mothe, governor of Louisiana, who seems to have visited the mine in 1714. We may be sure of this, that early in the eighteenth century—perhaps before its beginning — the French overran this country in search for gold and silver. They failed to find the precious metals in any large quantities, but did find great quantities of lead in all the region about the Maramec and the St. Francois. The first mining in the district was probably done on the Maramec under the direction of Governor Lochan; and Mine La Motte near the present site of Fredericktown, if not the first was one of the first and most important of these mines.

In 1719, Philip Francois Renault left France with a well organized expedition for the mineral district of Louisiana. He brought with him supplies and material and 200 skilled miners. The expedition stopped on the way at San Domingo, where 500 slaves were purchased for work in the mines. These slaves were the first brought to Missouri. Renault came with his expedition to Kaskaskia and in 1720 built a village called St. Phillip, near Fort Chartres in Illinois. He proceeded with his search for mines, and discovered and opened a lead mine near Potosi in Washington county. This mine was called, after him, Mine a Renault.

Renault had been commissioned by the Royal Company of the Indies, which at this time held control of Louisiana. In 1723 the authorities at Kaskaskia granted him a territory six leagues by one and one-half leagues on the Maramec river, and two leagues Mine LaMotte. From this time until his turn to France in 1742 Renault was activ engaged in working these mines. The l from them was carried first to Fort Char and later to Ste. Genevieve and then ship by boat to New Orleans and to France. La quantities of ore were taken out of all tl mines during this period. They were v profitable. A road was constructed from river to the mines and it was in connec with the carrying of this lead and trade v miners that the town of Ste. Genevieve founded. It was located at the river end this road. This was the first road opened, only in Southeast Missouri, but in the en state, and is still in use.

When Renault returned to France in 1 he seems to have abandoned his interest in mines to others, and if his family or heirs received any part of his interests in the great tracts of valuable mining prop which were granted him, the fact is no record. A great many lawyers have inv gated the question of the ownership of Renault claims, but the claims have n been successfully prosecuted by any mer of Renault's family.

In 1773 Francois Azar or Breton, w engaged in hunting, found lead ore lyin; the ground near Potosi. He opened a r at this place, which was called after him N a Breton. It became a celebrated mining and attracted miners from all parts of state. Breton, who was a native of Fra had been a soldier in his youth and had ser under Marshal Saxe. He was present, with the Indians who defeated Braddocl Virginia. He came to Louisiana as a m and hunter and discovered this mine quit accident. He lived to be 111 years old for many years before his death resided miles above Ste. Genevieve. He died in 1821. At the time of his discovery he received a grant of four arpens. This was a very small recompense for the service he had rendered in the discovery of the mine.

In 1779 Moses Austin, an American miner, agreed to erect a smelter near this mine of Breton, and on consideration of doing so he was granted a tract to contain 7,000 arpens, including one-third of the original mine. In performance of his agreement he erected here the first reverberatory furnace west of the river. This furnace, on account of its superior qualities, soon superseded all others. In 1797, when it was erected, there were twenty French furnaces in the district. In 1802 the Austin furnace was the only one in operation. In 1804 Austin made to the United States government the first report of the lead mining industry in Missouri.

It seems certain, then, that Mine LaMotte, Mine a Renault and Mine a Breton were the great centers of the lead industry in early days, but there were other mines also in operation; many small ones were opened; settlements sprung up around them. Some of these mines are still in successful operation. Some of the settlements have become flourishing towns, others have entirely disappeared. The whole lead region of southeast Missouri has many traces of the activity of the early French miners.

Some of the famous lead mines which were operated during this period in addition to those already described are here mentioned:

Mine a Platte or Doggett mine was discovered in 1799, and was granted to DeLassus at one time. It was on Plattin creek in what is now St. Francois county. Mine a Gerboree, situated on the St. Francois river near De Lassus, is said to have been operated by Renault in 1745. The Hazel Run lead district was discovered about 1810; this district is in the northern part of St. Francois county. The mines now owned and operated by the St. Joe Lead company of Bonne Terre were also worked during this period. They seem to have been granted in 1800, together with 800 arpens of land, to John B. Pratte. This land was surveyed in the same year by Antoine Soulard, the surveyor general of Upper Louisiana.

These lead mines, together with some others, were all in operation in the period which we are now considering. Their output was considerable, when we remember the conditions under which they were worked. It was all surface mining and the greater part of the labor was performed by hand. While the output was small, measured by the standards of the present, it still meant a great deal to the people of Missouri. While the greatest mining activity was, of course, in the lead regions, there began to be iron smeltered before the year 1820. Some time prior to this date Paul De Guire and his partner, Ashabranner, built a furnace on the Fredericktown road near the Shut-In, in Iron county. On the creek near this smelter they set up a forge, and being thus equipped they proceeded to work the iron ore. This ore was taken from mines in the vicinity, there being considerable deposit of iron in this county, and it was treated at this smelter. Their method of reducing the ore was first to roast it; it was then beaten by hammers into a powder, which was then heated in the forge. This forge, situated as it was on the bank of the creek, had a blower attached, which was worked by water power. When the powdered ore had been fused in the forge, the mass was then placed under a heavy hammer, also operated by water power, and worked. This treatment secured iron of a fair grade in small quantities.

The great handicap to mining, both lead and iron, was the absence of sufficient capital to provide proper equipment. It is quite certain that even vast sums of capital could not have provided equipment such as in use today in mines, but it could have made a very great improvement in the methods of those days. It was, however, impossible to secure capital sufficient for the purpose. It was a new country and like all new countries, suffered from a scarcity of money. It was only by the slow process of growth and development that capital could be produced in sufficient quantities to operate the mines in any adequate or efficient way. We are inclined to smile at the modest efforts and poor facilities of the early miners, but we should not forget that their limited product was contributing to the formation of that store of wealth which makes possible the improved methods and splendid machinery of today.

The early French mining was even more wasteful and less carefully organized than that of which we have spoken. There were a great many shallow diggings in many parts of the mineral district in which ore was taken out, but the only furnace used in the early times was an "Ash" furnace, that could not have saved more than sixty per cent of the lead, the rest being lost in the slack.

When Louisiana was ceded to the United States, in 1803, the government reserved to itself all mines and salt springs in the entire territory. This was in accordance with the usual policy in such cases. It was the purpose to lease these mines and springs and to collect a rental charge upon them. It was discovered, however, that the cost of clearing the land was greater than the revenue obtain and the fact that the rental was not carefu collected explains the non-existence of ac rate statistics concerning the reduction. I said that in the year 1811 five million pou of ore were delivered at Shiboleth, but in 1 it was reported that only one million pou were yielded. Mine a Breton at one t yielded three million pounds a year, but 1819 the yield was not more than five h dred thousand pounds, and there were more than thirty miners at work through the year.

It was in 1819 that the government of United States sent Schoolcraft to the min region to study and make a report on condition of these mines. He found M. I ton, the discoverer of the mine which bears name, still living near Ste. Genevieve. was at that time one hundred and nine y old. This report which Schoolcraft prepa and submitted to the government is the n accurate and authentic source of informa concerning the mining industry which th is in existence.

Its author, Henry R. Schoolcraft, who born in Albany, New York, in 1793, and ceived rudimentary education, moved in 1 to Pittsburg. From his earliest years he very much interested in mining and geolo At his own expense he traveled over porti of the country west of the Mississippi and South, then came to St. Louis. He was pointed an agent of the government and m his headquarters for a time at Potosi. H he studied the conditions of the mines in the districts, especially in Washington cou and drew up a formal and elaborate rep concerning the entire mining region.

Most of the shafts were from ten to thi feet deep and were sunk in stiff, red clay i the lead here found imbedded. This ore

...) mixed with fragments—quartz, flint and (oth)er minerals. The shaft which had been (sun)k by Moses Austin was eighty feet deep (and) one other, that of John Rice Jones, with (tha)t of Austin, were the only ones in the (nei)ghborhood of Potosi extending into the (roc)k itself. In both cases it was found that (the)re were large quantities of ore in the cavi(ties) of the rock, and from appearances School(cra)ft concluded that the lower strata perhaps (also) contained lead.

The average yield of all the mines in that (dist)rict about Potosi, from 1803 to 1819, was (abo)ut three million pounds a year. It was (esti)mated that its value was equal to one-(fou)rth of the cost of all of the Louisiana ter(rito)ry. His list of mines, together with the (num)ber of persons employed and the pounds (of o)re raised during the year 1819, is as follows: "Mine a Breton, 1,500,000 pounds, 160 (min)ers; Shiboleth, 2,700,000 pounds, 240 (min)ers; LaMotte, 2,400,000 pounds, 210 (min)ers; Richwoods, 1,300,000 pounds, 140 (min)ers; Bryan and Daggat's, 910,000 pounds, (100)miners; Rock diggings, Citadel, Lamberts, (Aus)tin's and Jones' mines, 1,160,000 pounds, (120) miners; all others, 550,000 pounds, 90 (min)ers."

(A)t that time there was only one regular (hea)rth furnace and that not of the best char(acte)r. There were but four or five regular (pi)ts in the more than forty diggings then (wor)ked and there was not an engine of any (kin)d in use for pumping from the mines.

(It) was suggested by Schoolcraft that in all (prob)ability, judging from the European ex(peri)ence, that beneath the lead ores, copper (ore) would be found. This prediction has (been), in part, verified. He advised the govern(men)t to sell the mineral lands, or at least to (exte)nd the leases upon them for a number of (year)s.

At the time that Schoolcraft observed these mines the principal minerals taken out, besides lead, were zinc, tiff, spar, pyrites, quartz, cobalt, sulphur, and clay. Schoolcraft gives a very interesting account of how the ore was mined and smelted in this early day. The only tools and implements used at that time were the pick ax, shovel, drill, rammer and priming rod; after having determined on the site for the mine the miners were accustomed to lay off a square of eight feet and then throw out the dirt by the use of a hand shovel to a depth of from 8 to 15 feet; after that depth the windlass and bucket became necessary for further digging. When ore was struck it was broken up by the use of pick and sometimes by blasting, black powder being used for the purpose; this ore as taken to the top by means of the windlass and bucket. It was then cleaned and broken up into small particles and heated in a wood fire for from 24 to 36 hours; about 50 per cent of the lead was extracted by this first method of smelting.

A considerable part of the lead was lost in the ashes of the fire. It was the custom after considerable quantities of ashes had accumulated to wash them very carefully after they had been run through a sieve and then the ashes were mixed with sand, flinted gravel and lime, and the whole mass put into a furnace; first a layer of ashes and then of the sand, gravel and lime and fired for about eight hours. This resulted in the saving of about 15 per cent more of the lead.

In 1819 lead sold at $4.00 per cwt. at the mines; it was worth $4.50 per cwt. at St. Louis or Herculaneum on the river. At the same time the market price of lead at New Orleans was $5.50 per cwt. and at Philadelphia, $6.00.

He estimated there were received at Herculaneum during the year 1817 somewhat more than three million pounds of ore, which was probably about one-half of the entire product of the region during the year. At this time there were about 1,100 men engaged in mining, this being a considerably smaller number than had formerly worked in the mines. Schoolcraft's explanation of this decrease in the number of miners is that more men than formerly were engaged in manufacturing and in farming.

Besides farming and mining, perhaps the industries most important were trading and transportation. The stores of this period, while still small, with limited stock, were a great improvement over those of the earlier day, which we have described. There were to be found at Ste. Genevieve, Fredericktown, Cape Girardeau, Jackson, and New Madrid stores having considerable quantities of varied merchandise. A number of men were engaged in the business of buying and selling, and they were necessary to the growth of the country. They still continued to buy their goods in the east. We have noted the experience of the Jackson merchant who sent a team and wagon from Jackson to Baltimore, requiring three months to make the trip. These merchants acted as distributers of goods for other communities. Their profits were not large in the aggregate, because their total volume of sales was small. They usually realized a sufficient profit on each particular sale as it was made.

The conditions of trade in the territory are shown, in part, by the following advertisement, which appeared in the *Missouri Gazette* in 1811: "Cheap Goods. The subscriber has just opened a quantity of bleached country linen, cotton cloth, cotton and wool cards, German steel, smoothing irons, ladies' silk bonnets, artificial flowers, linen check muslins, white thread, wool and cotton, a l some new gig with plated harness, cable cordelle ropes, with a number of ar which suit the country, and which he sell on very low terms.

"He will take in pay, furs, hides, whi country made sugar and bees wax.

(Signed) John Arthu

"P. S. A negro girl, eighteen years o is also for sale. She is a good house serv

In 1806, the following prices were obta for articles in Cape Girardeau: C $1.00 a yard, linen 75 cents a yard, pins cents a paper, sugar 25 cents a pound, paper 50 cents a quire, and other ar proportionately high.

In 1818, when John M. Peck moved t Louis he found high prices still preva there. The houses, shops and stores wer small, most of them only one story and sisting of two or three rooms. For a s room, occupied by the family, he paid $ a month. The school room, which was teen by sixteen feet, cost them $14.0 month. It was at that time very difficu procure food at all. Butter sold from 50 cents a pound, sugar from 30 to 40 c coffee from 62 to 75 cents, flour, of a ferior grade, cost about $12.00 a barrel, in the ear was from $1.00 to $1.25 a bu pork raised on the range was regarde cheap at $6.00 or $8.00 a hundred pou There was a ready market for chickens cents each, and eggs from 37 to 50 cen dozen. These high prices were, in part, to the system of currency. The currenc use was what was afterward denomin "shin plaster." These bills were issued banks which had been instituted without adequate capital. The fact that the bills not secure made people reluctant to take t helped to produce the prevailing high 〈prices〉.*

Nuttall in speaking of the country about 〈Mount〉 Pleasant says the land "is of a superior quality but flat and no high grades have made their appearance since we passed the 〈Iron〉 banks; no rock is anywhere to be seen. 〈The〉 Banks are deep and friable, islands and 〈sand〉 bars, at this stage of the river, connected with the land are almost innumerable. 〈In〉 the midst of so much plenty provided by 〈nat〉ure the Canadian squatters are here, as 〈else〉where, in miserable circumstances; they 〈rai〉se no wheat and scarcely enough maize for 〈the〉ir support; superfine flour sold here at 〈$〉.00 per barrel. The dresses of the men 〈con〉sist of blanket capeaus, buckskin pan〈tal〉oons and moccasins."†

Besides these occupations, some men still 〈ma〉de their living by hunting and trapping. 〈As〉 more and more the forests disappeared 〈and〉 lands were cleared and settled, hunting 〈bec〉ame less and less profitable. There were 〈alw〉ays some men left to engage hunting as a 〈bus〉iness. They did not contribute greatly to 〈the〉 wealth of the state, but they, undoubtedly, 〈add〉ed something to it.

The day of the Indian was practically closed 〈by〉 the time of the admission of the state into 〈the〉 Union. During part of the period, how〈eve〉r, there was still money to be made by 〈tra〉ding and trapping with the Indians. Furs 〈we〉re still brought and offered to the trader 〈at〉 very low prices, and so there were few men 〈wh〉o were engaged very largely in this busi〈nes〉s of trading with the Indians.

A number of men were engaged in the very 〈im〉portant and necessary business of transpor〈tat〉ion. It required great labor and expense to 〈mo〉ve the products of the country to market. This was especially true of the lead and iron produced at the mines. It was true also of the goods sold by the merchant. These usually had to be transported for long distances before reaching him. The river continued to be the favorite route over which goods were carried when it was possible to use the river at all. This period of history saw the beginning of steamboat navigation. Its principal dependence was upon the keel-boat, but the keel-boat was destined to disappear before a better method of transportation.

In a former chapter we have examined the use of the river for transporting goods. Traffic on the river increased very rapidly after the cession to the United States. The American settlers very soon added largely to the exports. These exports, consisting of the various products of the country were sent usually by river to New Orleans and sometimes to Pittsburgh on the Ohio river. The river was covered with fleets of keel-boats and travel was brisk; however, the long time required for a trip from Ste. Genevieve to New Orleans and return was a very great handicap to trade. It is one of the remarkable things in history that at this time, when there arose a very great necessity for improved methods of transportation, there should have come into use the steamboat, which changed so greatly the traffic on the river. In 1807 Fulton had put in operation the first steamboat the world had ever seen, the Clermont.

Immediately upon the beginning of steam navigation, a suggestion was made to Fulton and his associates that the Clermont should be put in the Mississippi river trade. It was already known in the East that this trade was very extensive, and it seems that Fulton considered the question of bringing the Clermont to the Mississippi. It is not known how he

* Life of Peck, p. 84.
† Nuttall Journal, p. 78.

expected to do this, and if he ever really intended it. He soon gave up the idea because the Clermont was put into use on the Hudson river, where it found waiting for it the greatest river traffic in the world. But, if the Mississippi river was not to have the Clermont for its trade, it was not long to be deprived of steamboats. In 1811 a company of men built in Pittsburgh a boat which they called the New Orleans. This boat made the trip from Pittsburgh to New Orleans and was for some time concerned in the traffic on the Mississippi river.

In a very short time other boats were built and in 1816 the first steamboat passed up the Mississippi above the mouth of the Ohio. This was the General Pike and was commanded by Captain Jacob Reed. This steamboat was looked upon by all of the inhabitants as a very remarkable and wonderful thing indeed, but it was only a little while until there were a great number of steamboats in operation. They possessed such remarkable advantages over the keel-boat that they were adopted for traffic as fast as possible. The second boat to come up the river above the mouth of the Ohio was the Constitution; it reached St. Louis in 1817.

The change produced by these steamboats was remarkable. They lowered not only the time necessary for the journey, but they lowered in a remarkable way the expense of transportation. The rates on the steamboats, even, were enormous, but they were lower than the rates on the keel-boats. In 1819 a contract was entered into between the owners of two steamboats and the United States government to carry freight from St. Louis to Council Bluffs and the rate charged was $8.00 a hundred pounds. This is enormous compared to our present rates, but seemed reasonable in those days when compared to the rates necessarily charged by other means of tr portation.

Flint, who was a minister and traveled and down the river very many times, recorded the feeling of pleasure with w he took his first voyage on a steamboat. speaking of his experience, he says: "I now refreshing and imparts a feeling energy and power to the beholder, to see large and beautiful steamboats scudding the eddies, as though on the wing; and w they have run out the eddy, strike the rent. The foam bursts in a sheet quite the deck. She quivers for a moment the concussion, and then, as though she collected all her energy and vanquished enemy, she resumes her stately march mounts against the current five or six mile hour." And lost in admiration at the derful advance from the slow upward m ment of the keel-boat, at the rate of six n a day, he says, "A stranger to this mod traveling would find it difficult to desc his impressions upon first descending Mississippi in one of the better steamb He contemplates the prodigious estab ment, with all its fitting of deck, common, ladies' cabin apartments. Overhead, a him and below him all is life and moveme Then, speaking of the time when he first t eled on these western waters, and before era of the steamboat, he says, "This str instead of being plowed by a hundred st boats, had seen but one. The astonishing cilities for traveling, by which it is al changed to flying, had not been inven The thousand travelers for mere amusen that we now see on the roads, canals rivers, were then traveling only in books. stillness of the forest had not been broker the shouting of the turnpike makers. Mississippi forest had seldom resounded cept with the cry of wild beasts, the echo of thunder, or the crash of undermined trees, falling into the flood. Our admiration, our unsated curiosity at that time, would be a matter of surprise at the present to the thousands of hackneyed travelers on this stream, to whom this route and all its circumstances are as familiar as the path from the bed to the fire.'"*

It has been said that among all the settlers of Upper Louisiana there existed comparative quiet and freedom from disturbance, under Spanish rule. The French were by nature and by the circumstances of their relationship and close connection in the towns, peaceable and law abiding people, and little effort was required to keep peace among them. The Americans were scattered over the country, and while they were bolder in some respects and a more difficult population to govern, the troubles that arose among them were usually settled by an appeal to physical strength, with the use of nature's weapons, so that there was little crime which needed the attention of the officers of the law. They stood, too, as we have said, in wholesome respect of the Spanish authorities and had a dread of Spanish dungeons and mines. When the territory passed under the dominion of the United States, however, and when large numbers of immigrants from the states further to the east had filled up the country, there ensued a period of considerable lawlessness. It was, perhaps, the natural feeling of reaction after the repression of the Spanish government. Quarreling, fighting, and occasional crimes were present in all the settlements in the territory. The officers of the law had much to do in some of the settlements and the population was far from being as quiet and free from disturbance as it had been under the government of Spain.

We have seen that one of the subjects which early occupied the attention of the territorial assembly was that of the suppression of vice and immorality on the Sabbath, owing to the lack of religious teaching, and to that freedom of restraint of public opinion found in new communities. There was not a great deal of attention paid to the observance of the day of rest, so that the legislature endeavored to correct this evil.

One of the prevalent vices of the population was gambling. There seems to be some connection between the life of a new country and the existence of the gambling spirit. Something of the exhilaration of the free life and of the spirit of taking chances which is cultivated by the daily circumstances under which the people live seem to incline large numbers of them to the gaming table. Gambling was exceedingly popular; it was, perhaps, the most prevalent form of amusement. The territory itself authorized a lottery, so that gambling was regulated and authorized by the law.

But, perhaps, the thing that most impressed itself upon travelers from other countries with regard to the lawless condition of the territory was the habit of dueling. Men were accustomed to settle differences between them by an appeal to arms. Some one has pointed out that this method was not in use among all classes of people in the territory, the laboring class not being accustomed to resort to the duel, but professional men, especially lawyers and all those who regarded themselves as higher up in the scale of society were accustomed to look with contempt upon the man who appealed to the law for the settlement of

* Houck, Vol. III, p. 199.

difficulties. Gentlemen were supposed to settle their own troubles. The slightest ground for quarrel was sufficient to bring the parties face to face in a duel. These duels were not such as are said to exist in France today; they were not arranged for show, and there was nothing of the spectacular in them; the meeting was almost certain to result in the death of one or the other of the participants. The weapons most commonly used were pistols. The meeting between two persons was arranged by seconds and at the appointed time they met and proceeded to shoot at one another. Ordinarily the exchange of one or more shots or the wounding or killing of one or the other of the antagonists was looked upon as satisfying the code of honor which governed the duel. Not infrequently after an exchange of shots the parties shook hands and the quarrel between them was at an end; very many duels, however, resulted fatally. It was a time when men were accustomed to firearms. Most of those who engaged in duels were expert shots with the pistol and there were very many chances of being at least wounded in one of these duels. Some of them are famous. There came to be recognized dueling places that were resorted to frequently. One of these places, not, however, in Southeast Missouri, but one to which persons from this part of the state sometimes resorted for the purpose of dueling was Bloody Island, in the Mississippi river near St. Louis.

In 1811 a duel was fought in Ste. Genevieve between Dr. Walter Fenwick and Thomas T. Crittenden. Crittenden was a lawyer and had, in the course of a trial, denounced Ezekiel Fenwick, who was a brother of Dr. Walter Fenwick. Ezekiel Fenwick thereupon challenged Crittenden, who, however, refused a meeting on the ground that Ezekiel was not a gentleman. The challenge had been car[ried] to Crittenden by Dr. Walter Fenwick [and] this reply affronted Dr. Fenwick, who, the[re]upon, issued a challenge on his own beh[alf]. The duel was fought on Moreau Island [just] below Ste. Genevieve. Dr. Fenwick [was] killed at the first fire. This duel was fou[ght] with pistols.

In 1807 Joseph McFerron and Will[iam] Ogle fought a duel on Cypress Island op[po]site Cape Girardeau. McFerron was an Ir[ish]man, possessed good education and was c[lerk] of the court in the Cape Girardeau dist[rict]. He had been a teacher, but before accept[ing] the position with the court he was a merch[ant] in Cape Girardeau. For some reason t[here] arose difficulty between these men and O[gle] challenged McFerron to duel. It seems [that] McFerron had never even fired a pistol, [but] accepted the challenge. Ogle was killed, w[hile] McFerron was unhurt. The most fam[ous] duel, perhaps, fought in this period was [that] between citizens of Southeast Missouri, [it] took place between Thomas H. Benton [and] Charles Lucas. The first duel between t[hem] was fought in August, 1817. At this mee[ting] Benton was wounded in the knee and L[ucas] in the neck. According to the usual custo[m in] duels this exchange of shots would have en[ded] the matter, but when Benton was asked i[f he] were satisfied he declared that he was [not] and demanded a second meeting. Eff[orts] were made to bring about a reconciliation [be]tween the two men but all of them were fu[tile]. Benton seems to have been determined to [have] another duel with Lucas. The second m[eet]ing was held on Bloody Island on the [   ] day of September, 1817, and resulted in [the] death of Charles Lucas.

In 1819 John Smith T. and Lionel Bro[wn,] the latter a nephew of Aaron Burr an[d a] lawyer of Potosi, fought a duel on an isl[and] osite Herculaneum. Browne was instantly ...ed, while Smith escaped. There are but a ... instances of the use of these barbarous ...hods of settling disputes. They came from ...e ideas of honor; there had grown up in ... minds of men a notion that a man was in ...e way sullied if he did not resent an in... of any kind, even to the point of killing ... antagonist. It required long years of con-...it agitation to displace this false notion ... caused so many deaths.

...ne of the virtues which distinguished the ...y settlers was hospitality. Any traveler ... sure to be received with kindness in any ...t of the country. The reason for this is ...e found, in part, in the character of the ...ple themselves and, in part, in the fact ... there were no other provisions for trav-...s. It was not until after the transfer to ... United States that public taverns, as the ...es of entertainment were called, were to ... found except in a very few of the towns. ... traveler, even up to the admission of the ...e to the Union, must depend either upon ... own resources and sleep in the open and ... pare his own food, or else be received into ... homes of the people; it was usually the ...er that happened. It was regarded as a ...y and also a pleasure to care for the ...eler, a duty because they were unwilling ... turn those away in need of shelter and ...d, and a pleasure largely because of the ... that the inhabitants depended for news ...n the traveler. Newspapers were very ...ce and, as we have seen, postage was so ...h and mail so irregular as practically to ...id any but the most necessary correspond-...e and for these reasons such news as was ...ived was brought by persons traveling. It ... been said that a traveler was rarely ever ...ed away from any door. His reception

was not the most cordial in manner, the usual response to a request for accommodation being the laconic reply: "Well, I guess we could keep you;" but though the welcome was not as cordial as might have been expected it was, nevertheless, a welcome and ample provision was made for the unexpected guest. The best the house afforded was his. The mistress of the house, dressed in the garb which was made in the house itself, quiet and repressed in manner, without many of the graces of refined society, was yet kindly attentive to all the wants of the traveler. Any attempt at pay for these accommodations was repulsed and often looked upon as something in the nature of an insult. The head of the house disclaimed any idea of keeping tavern. Flint and Peck, both of them famous ministers in the early days, recount their experiences as travelers and the almost uniform kindness and hospitality with which they were treated. Flint records as the most remarkable and unusual circumstance that at one place he was refused accommodation.

The people, while not religious for the most part and in many settlements rude and boisterous in their behavior, had a respect for religion that prompted them to treat with consideration the ministers who came to hold services; this was true even of the roughest classes. The tavern-keepers, themselves, were frequently kindly disposed toward preachers. Both Flint and Peck were received in taverns and cared for.

These taverns, or places of public entertainment, combined a house for the care of travelers with a place for the sale of liquor. A place where liquor was sold apart from the inn was called a grocery. Taverns were not numerous in the early days. They were licensed by the Spanish officials and careful instructions were given as to the number of taverns permitted in any community. Effort seems to have been made to reduce the number as low as possible. In a number of instances licenses for keeping tavern were refused on the ground that the community was already sufficiently supplied. After the organization of the territorial government, accompanying the growth of population, there was an increase in the number of taverns.

By 1805 the United States government had established postoffices at Ste. Genevieve, Cape Girardeau and New Madrid. Provision was made for the carrying of mails between these points and for connecting these mail routes with those east of the river. The weekly mail which reached these and other points in the territory was, necessarily, irregular; the roads were very poor, and many of those engaged in carrying the mails had very long journeys to make. It is rather curious to observe the constant complaint of the inhabitants of the territory concerning the mails, they were too irregular and at too infrequent intervals. Even settlers at the oldest of the towns, who had seemed to be content under Spanish government without any mails at all, were unable to be satisfied with one mail a week after the transfer to the United States. Doubtless the establishment of these postoffices and the regular delivery of the mail into even remote communities was one of the powerful agencies by which the government fostered the growth of population in the new territory. Men who have enjoyed the advantages of the regular postal system are often unwilling to settle in a community where no postal facilities are provided. The government could have done nothing that would have offered greater inducement to many prospective settlers than to arrange to keep them in contact with civilization by providing for the delivery of

The rate for carrying letters and p was, of course, very high compared t present rates. The roads over which the were carried were very bad, and in cases hardly existed at all. As a consequ all mails were transported for a time on h back and this was for many years the cipal method of carrying them. There w fixed rate of postage for a letter at that The price was not fixed then as no weight. The distance it must be carrie termined the cost and not its weight. case was the amount charged by the go ment small. The ordinary rate on letter from twenty-five to seventy-five cents.

The first newspaper published in Sout Missouri was the *Missouri Herald*. It established at Jackson in 1818 by Tub Strange. It was a weekly newspaper, b publication was discontinued in 1819; i revived in 1820 under the name of the *pendent Patriot*, published by Stephen ington & Company. In 1825 a paper the title the *Ste. Genevieve Correspo and Record* was established at Ste. Gene

While these were the first papers act published in Southeast Missouri, the Missouri paper was established in St. Lo 1808 by Joseph Charless; this was the *souri Gazette*. It is still published unde title, *The St. Louis Republic*. This pape some circulation in Southeast Missouri, at this early date. The publication of papers in a new territory such as this w tended with very great difficulty; it wa most impossible to secure sufficient subs ers to pay the expense of publication. this reason we find a constant chang proprietors taking place in almost all the papers.

It is not now possible to fix the exact date of the first school taught in Southeast Missouri. There is some evidence that members of the Russell family conducted private schools in Cape Girardeau county about the year 1800; however, this date is not definitely determined. In 1806 Benjamin Johnson opened a private school on Sandy Creek in Jefferson county. In 1808 a number of citizens of Ste. Genevieve established the Ste. Genevieve Academy, and employed as teacher Mann Butler, afterward a distinguished teacher and writer of history. In 1815 Joseph Hertich opened a school in Ste. Genevieve. Hertich was the first to introduce the new principles of education and methods of teaching which had been worked out by Pestalozzi. According to Houck, Hertich was a very able man and his school in Ste. Genevieve exercised a remarkable influence for several years. A number of his students achieved considerable reputation, three of them having become, afterwards, members of the United States senate.*

There was a school conducted in Herculaneum in 1815 and one at Potosi in 1817. A number of persons conducted private schools in Jackson in the years 1817 to 1820. Flint, the minister who has been referred to often, was one of these. In 1820 Thomas P. Green, a Baptist minister, opened a school in Jackson which he conducted for a number of years. It was in 1818, as we have seen, that St. Mary's Academy was established near Perryville. We may be sure that all these early efforts at conducting schools were limited in scope. Equipment was exceedingly meagre or altogether absent. The number of students was small, and the compensation of the teachers correspondingly small. Some of those who undertook to teach were very poorly qualified for the work. The subjects of instruction in most cases were simply the merest rudiments of education. The terms of school were short, and perhaps the greatest handicap of all was the lack of continuous instruction. Perhaps a settlement had school for a few months in one year and then would have no school for two or three years. Under these conditions it was impossible for any systematic education to be secured. There were exceptions, of course, to this. Some of the men, notably Hertich and some of the ministers, were highly educated men and quite capable of conducting schools.

This lack of proper means for education was one of the great drawbacks to the country. Part of these conditions which were so unfavorable were inseparably connected with life in a new country; they could not be removed. One of the great difficulties, however, was in the failure of many people to appreciate the necessity for education. The life of the frontier has little in it to inspire children with desire for learning; it also fails to disclose the necessity for an education. A living was very easily made by manual labor, and there seemed to be little demand for educated men. Physical strength and skill and native shrewdness were sufficient to enable a man not alone to live, but to accumulate property. Some of the wealthy men in the time which we are considering were unable to read or write and others had the most meagre and limited education. It was possible for a boy, if taught in the ordinary things of life, to care for himself and family and yet have no knowledge of books at all. Flint, who was from the East, and perhaps not altogether free from prejudice in the matter, says that many of the people living in the more remote districts made no effort to teach their children; that boys at fourteen or fifteen had learned to use the axe and the rifle, to perform the simple

---

* Houck, Vol. III, p. 68.

operations of farming as it was then practiced, and that thus equipped they were independent and scorned any notion that they needed to know more than these things.

Peck says that "after having gained correct knowledge, by personal inspection in most of the settlements, or by the testimony of reliable persons * * * the conclusion was that at least one-third of the schools were really a public nuisance, and did the people more harm than good. Another third about balanced the account by doing about as much harm as good, and, perhaps, one-third were advantageous to the community in various degrees. Not a few drunken, profane, worthless Irishmen were perambulating the country and getting up schools, and yet they could neither speak, read, pronounce, spell or write the English language."*

Peck further says that there existed a custom of turning the schoolmaster out of the house at Christmas and Easter. He records one instance of a schoolmaster who provided a treat for the children, in order to be permitted to re-enter the house. The treat consisted of a drink known as "Cherry Bounce." Both teacher and pupils were partly intoxicated by their treat and the teacher was dismissed. Peck gives this picture of the life of some of the people in the frontier settlements. He is careful to discriminate and point out that not all the people, by any means, were like those described. After lamenting their deplorable condition, religiously, and their ignorance of the Bible, and their indifference to the calls made upon them, and saying of them that few could read and fewer had Bibles or other books to read, he says that they were almost equally as poorly off concerning other matters. A small corn field, he says, and a truck patch was the height of their ambition. Venison, bear meat, and hog meat

*Life of Peck, p. 128.

dressed, cooked in a most slovenly and filthy manner, with corn bread baked in the form of a pone, and when cold as hard as a brick bat, constituted their provisions. Coffee and tea, he says, were prohibited articles amongst this class, for had they possessed the articles, not one woman in ten knew how to cook them. He adds, however, "doubtless in a few years, when the land came into market, this class of squatters cleared out."

In June, 1808, the territorial assembly chartered the Ste. Genevieve Academy with the following as trustees: James Maxwell, John Baptiste Valle, Jacques Guibord, St. James Beauvais, Francois Janis, John Baptiste Pratte, Joseph Pratte, Walter Fenwick, Andrew Henry, Timothy Phelps, Aaron Elliott, Nathaniel Pope, Joseph Spencer, Jr., William James, Frank Oliver, Joshua Penniman, William Shannon, George Bullett, Henry Dodge and Harry Diel.

The trustees were authorized to receive and expend money for the use of the academy, and they were bound to have instruction given in both French and English. One clause of the act of incorporation forbade their making any distinction in the employment of teachers, or in filling vacancies in the board of trustees, regarding religious beliefs. The academy was a necessity for all people and no religious distinction was to be made. The trustees were further commanded to admit poor children and children of Indians to the academy free of any charge for instruction. Power was conferred on them, also, to arrange, whenever it seemed best to them, to open an institution for the instruction of girls.

On October 14th, 1820, the territorial assembly chartered the academy in Jackson with the following trustees: David Armour, Joseph Frizzell, Thomas Neal, Van B. De

Lashmutt and William Surrell. The same restriction was placed on them with regard to religious privileges and discrimination as in the case of the Ste. Genevieve academy.

In spite of these things, there was a feeling among the leading men in the territory that provision must be made for a system of public education. Congress was early asked to set aside lands for the support of schools.

We have seen that one of the early assemblies chartered an academy at Potosi and also organized a public school board for St. Louis. Ste. Genevieve and Little Prairie, along with one or two other towns, received grants of the land which was held in common, the income from the property to be used for school purposes. Out of these feeble beginnings and most unpromising circumstances there grew up a great system of public schools.

We may suppose that under the conditions we have described there were few libraries in the southeast part of the state. In fact, there was not a public library of any kind in all this section until 1820. There were only a few private libraries deserving of the name. In many homes there were no books of any kind whatever, in others there were copies of the Bible and very few other books. A few men who lived in the district, however, had good libraries; these were usually the ministers.

The dress of the people did not differ much from the dress as described in a former chapter; everybody wore home-spun. Every house was a factory, the women spun the thread and wove the cloth and made the garments for the entire family. By the close of the territorial period there had grown up in the larger towns something of the society that gave attention to dress. Some people began to bring clothing from the eastern states and to devote time and money to these matters. The great majority of people, however, were dressed as we have seen. To them dress was not an adornment nor a luxury, but a necessity. John Clark, the famous pioneer minister, who spent many years in traveling throughout Southeast Missouri, preaching, was always dressed in home-spun. He was a bachelor and his clothing was made for him by members of his congregations.

CHAPTER XIII

PROTESTANT IMMIGRATION

VISITS OF PROTESTANT MINISTERS—JOHN CLARK — JOSIAH DODGE—THOMAS JOHNSON—ANDREW WILSON—RELIGIOUS CONDITION OF THE SETTLERS—MOTIVES WHICH BROUGHT THEM TO LOUISIANA — THE WORK OF THE BAPTISTS — DAVID GREENE — BETHEL CHURCH NEAR JACKSON — ITS EARLY MEMBERS — THE FIRST MEETING HOUSE — RELICS OF OLD BETHEL CHURCH—MEMORIAL SERVICES IN 1906—GROWTH OF THE CHURCH—OTHER CHURCHES ORGANIZED BY MEMBERS OF BETHEL—EARLY MINISTERS OF THE CHURCH—WILSON THOMPSON —THOMAS STEPHENS—THOMAS P. GREENE—THE FIRST MISSIONARY COLLECTION—THE FORMATION OF AN ASSOCIATION OF CHURCHES IN MISSOURI—JOHN M. PECK—THE WORK OF THE METHODIST CHURCH — FIRST PREACHERS — JOHN TRAVIS—ORGANIZATION OF MCKENDREE— EARLY MEMBERS—FIRST MEETING HOUSE—JESSE WALKER — THE FIRST CIRCUITS — FIRST SERMON IN CAPE GIRARDEAU—CAMPMEETING AT MCKENDREE IN 1810 — HARBISON — NEW CIRCUITS FORMED—ORGANIZATION OF THE MISSOURI CONFERENCE — RUCKER TANNER — THE FIRST CONFERENCE HELD IN MISSOURI—THE WORK OF THE PRESBYTERIANS—HEMPSTEAD'S LETTER — A CHURCH ORGANIZED IN WASHINGTON COUNTY, 1816 — ORGANIZATION OF THE PRESBYTERY OF MISSOURI — EARLY MINISTERS — TIMOTHY FLINT — THE COLUMBIAN BIBLE SOCIETY—FLINT'S WRITINGS—DISCIPLES OF CHRIST—WILLIAM MCMURTRY—FIRST ORGANIZATION IN MISSOURI, 1822 — DIFFICULTIES UNDER WHICH EARLY MINISTERS LABORED — PROGRESS MADE—PECK'S DESCRIPTION—DEBT OWED TO PIONEER MINISTERS.

We have seen something of the work of the missionaries who came to the state in the early years, and have traced and outlined the growth of the Catholic church up to the time of the transfer in 1804. Of course, up to this time there was no religious history of the state, except of the activity of the Catholic church. While, as we have seen, there were other persons living in the state, they were required to conform to the Catholic religion, to rear their children in the Catholic faith, and they were forbidden to hold public services of any kind. These restrictions, while they did not prevent Protestant immigration, hindered it greatly. There are a number of cases of families moving to Upper Louisiana then, on finding what they were required to subscribe to, declining to stay and returning to the east side of the river. Of course, these restrictions were swept away with the transfer to the United States. The principle recognized by the American people of absolute toleration in religious matters was extended to Louisiana. It was not long before the activity of the Protestant ministers brought them to the new territory.

We have seen, in fact, that even before the transfer some ministers had, in violation of the provisions of the Spanish law, come to

Louisiana and held services. John Clark, a minister of the Methodist church, was one of these who as early as 1796 came to Louisiana and visited a number of the settlements. Clark is described as a man simple, unaffected, and wholly disinterested. He violated the Spanish law in holding these services, but the lieutenant governor, then at St. Louis, Zenon Trudeau, was very much in favor of the coming of American settlers and, in order not to discourage them, he was disposed to allow these visits. He seemed to have warned Clark on a number of occasions, but he never really molested him, though he threatened him with imprisonment. Clark at the time resided in Illinois; he died in 1813; he became a Baptist at some time subsequent to his visits to Louisiana.

Doubtless the earliest of these ministers was Josiah Dodge. Dodge lived in Kentucky and was a Baptist. He was a brother of Israel Dodge, who lived near Ste. Genevieve. During his visits to his brother, Rev. Josiah Dodge was accustomed to preach to the American settlers in the vicinity. It is possible that these sermons were the first non-Catholic sermons delivered west of the Mississippi river. This was in 1794. In the same year, it is recorded that he crossed the river to Illinois and baptized four persons in Fountain creek. Perhaps these were residents of Upper Louisiana who were thus baptized in the Illinois to avoid violating the law regarding baptisms in Upper Louisiana. In 1799 Rev. Thomas Johnson, another Baptist minister, came to Cape Girardeau district; he was a native of Georgia. In that year he baptized Mrs. Agnes Ballou in Randol creek. This was, doubtless, the first baptism, not performed by a Catholic priest, west of the river.

One of the men who came with Morgan to New Madrid was Andrew Wilson. He was a Scotchman and had been a Presbyterian minister. He never preached in New Madrid and it is probable that he had previously given up the ministry.

The testimony of almost all observers as to some of the American settlers prior to the transfer to the United States is that their condition, religiously considered, was deplorable. We cannot believe it to have been otherwise. In the first place, the fact that though they were Protestants they were willing to conform to the nominal requirements of the Spanish law with regard to the rearing of their children as Catholics, and the further fact that they were compelled to forego any public religious services, are sufficient to show that they were not distinctly or deeply religious. Cut off, as they were, from all religious teaching by their situation and the requirements of the laws under which they lived, they must have fallen into a deplorable condition. It was reported by some observers that in some cases they had even forgotten the days of the week and that they made no attempt whatever to observe the Sabbath in any way, and where it was observed, too often it was a day given up to amusements such as the country offered. Andrew Ramsay's place in Cape Girardeau was used as an assembly place for all the people of the neighborhood. They came together, not for worship, but for the purpose of whatever amusement could be found. The condition of the early settlers, as here set out, unfavorable as it was with regard to religion, must not be taken to represent the feelings and convictions of all the people of Upper Louisiana. While those who were Protestants in belief had to give up, as we have seen, the open practice of their religion, it should not be forgotten that the motives that impelled men to settle in the Louisiana territory were very strong. American settlers who lived in the Northwest territory and who owned slaves found that in order to continue holding them they must give up their homesteads and seek another territory after the passage of the Northwest Ordinance of 1787. Many of these men crossed the Mississippi river to Upper Louisiana; others came because they were attracted by the ease with which land might be secured from the Spanish government, and still others were moved by the love of adventure and of a free life in the open which characterized so many Americans in the early period of history. These motives were very strong and they induced many respectable, honest and upright people to give up their homes and to take up their residence in what is now Missouri.

These people no doubt felt the deprivation of religious service and experience. That they still meditated on religion and wished for an opportunity to exercise it openly is made evident by the cordial reception which was given to the few Protestant ministers who, in spite of the proclamation of Spain, made their way into the territory. In the life of John Clark, which was no doubt written by John Mason Peck, it is clearly set out that the American families were very glad indeed to receive Clark into their homes and to listen to him as he read and preached, and were rejoiced at an opportunity to hear the Gospel in their new territory and according to their own beliefs again.

It seems that the first Baptists in Missouri were Thomas Bull, his wife and mother-in-law, Mrs. Lee. They moved to the Cape Girardeau district from Kentucky in 1796. They were followed, in 1797, by Enos Randol and wife, and the wife of John Abernathy. For a number of years they lived without any religious services, except such as they held at private houses. At one time they were in fear of being required to leave the province on account of their religious belief, but Lorimier was favorable to them and they continued to reside here. Elder Thomas Johnson, of Georgia, was perhaps the first Baptist minister who preached in Upper Louisiana. He was a resident of Georgia. He came to the Cape Girardeau district on a visit in 1799, and while there he preached. He performed the first non-Catholic baptism west of the river. He baptized Mrs. Ballou in Randol's creek. In 1805, Elder David Greene, a native of Virginia, but at that time a resident of Kentucky, came to the district. Greene preached, first, about the settlements near Commerce. He organized a church in Tywappity bottom in 1805. This was the first Baptist church in Louisiana. It had only some six or seven members and soon disbanded. Elder Greene, after a visit of some months, returned to Kentucky. He was impressed, however, by the importance of the field in Upper Louisiana and came back to the Cape Girardeau district in 1806. He resided in the district with his family until the time of his death in 1809.

On July 19, 1806, Elder Greene gathered together the Baptists near Jackson and organized a church which was called Bethel. It is not definitely known just where the organization took place, but it is believed to have been made in the house of Thomas Bull. This church so organized was the center from which sprang the large number of early Baptist churches in Missouri. The members who took part in the organization of the church were David Greene, Thomas English, Leanna Greene, Jane English, Agnes Ballou, Thomas Bull, Edward Spear, Anderson Rogers, John Hitt, Clara Abernathy, Katherine Anderson,

Rebecca Randol, Frances Hitt and William Matthews.

The board which took part in the organization of the church was composed of Elder David Greene and Deacons George Laurence and Henry Cockerham. The officers of the church as organized were: David Greene, pastor; Thomas English, deacon. In August, after the organization, Thomas Bull was elected writing clerk, and in the following April, William Matthews was elected singing clerk.

Thomas English, who was thus one of the charter members of the church, was a native of Georgia. He came to Missouri about 1804, and lived in the Ramsay settlement. He remained a member of the church and a deacon until his death, May 16, 1829. He left a large family of sons and daughters, and his descendants still live in Cape Girardeau county. His wife, Jane, was also a member. He died in 1842.

William Hitt, who became a member of Bethel church in 1812, and who afterward served as its clerk for a number of years, was one of the prominent members. He was the grandfather of the late Deacon Smith Hitt of the Cape Girardeau Baptist church. Benjamin Hitt, who also united with Bethel church in 1812, was the father of the late Judge Samuel Hitt, of Cape Girardeau.

The Randol family was one of the early Baptist families in the district. Enos Randol united with Bethel church in 1808. His son, Enos, was a sergeant in Peter Craig's company of mounted rangers that fought the battle of the Sink Hole. The Randol family still live in Cape Girardeau county.

Edward Spear, who was one of the charter members of the church, was afterward a lieutenant in Craig's company, and was killed at the Sink Hole.

Some of the other members of the church in the early time were William Smith, John Sheppard and his wife, Nancy; Isaac Sheppard, who united with Bethel church in 1809. Isaac Sheppard was elected deacon and treasurer, and was also one of the judges both of the common pleas court at Cape Girardeau and the county court.

Ezekiel Hill, Rachel Hill, William Hill, the Thompson family, John Daugherty and Hiram C. Davis were also among the early members, having united with the church prior to the year 1820.

John Juden, Sr., was a native of England, and came from Baltimore in 1805 to Missouri. In 1820 he and John Juden, Jr., joined Bethel church. This family and its descendants were very prominent in Cape Girardeau county for many years.

On October 11, 1806, the congregation voted to erect a meeting house. In pursuance of this resolution, a small log house was built on the farm of Thomas Bull. It proved, however, to be too small and in 1812 was replaced by a hewn log building. This second house was well and strongly constructed of poplar logs. It was thirty feet by twenty-four feet in size. This house was used by the church until about 1861. The church then transferred its sessions to a house northwest of Jackson on Byrd's creek. Sometime, about the same date, the old house was sold to a resident in the neighborhood who moved it away, about the distance of a mile, and rebuilt it into a barn. Some of the logs of the old house were saved at the time of the sale, and from them were constructed a number of walking canes and two gavels. One of these gavels was presented to the Baptist General Association of the state at its meeting in St. Joseph in the year 1875 by the Rev. Dr. J. C. Maple. It was handsomely inscribed and is still in use by the moderator of the general association. The other of the two gavels made at the time remained in the possession of Dr. Maple until the year 1910, when it was presented by him to the moderator of the Cape Girardeau Baptist Association at its meeting in Crosstown, Perry county, in September of that year. The old house as rebuilt still stands. The site on which it was erected has been purchased and is now owned by the Baptist General Association of Missouri. In 1906 this association held its annual meeting in Cape Girardeau. This was the one hundredth anniversary of the founding of Bethel church. One reason for the selection of Cape Girardeau as the place of meeting was to hold appropriate exercises in commemoration of the founding at the site of the old church, and to unveil a monument which had been erected on the spot.

One day during the meeting of the body was set aside for a visit to the site. After a session held in the Baptist church in Jackson on the morning of October 24th, the Association adjourned to meet in the grove of trees on the spot where the old church stood. This is about two miles from the town of Jackson and was reached after some difficulties. The meeting was called to order by E. W. Stephens of Columbia, the moderator of the General Association. After prayer and singing, E. W. Stephens delivered an address on the subject, "The Reason for Baptist Existence and Baptist Work One Hundred Years Ago and Now." The monument was then unveiled by Mrs. E. W. Stephens and Miss Mae Brown of Jackson.

The monument which was erected by the association is four feet high of granite and bears this inscription: "Here stood Bethel Baptist church, the first permanent non-Catholic church west of the Mississippi river. Constituted July 19, 1806, with these members: David Green, Thomas English, William Matthews, Leanna Green, William Smith, Jane English, Agnes Ballou, Thomas Bull, Clara Abernathy, Catherine Anderson, Anderson Rogers, Edward Spear, Rebecca Randol, John Hitt, and Frances Hitt. What Hath God Wrought?"

The membership of the church had grown to eighty by the year 1812 and in 1813 it was one hundred eighty-six. In June, 1814, forty-five of its members were dismissed to organize a church in what is now St. Francois county, but even after this dismissal there remained one hundred seventy-three members. In 1809 Bethel church became a member of the Red River Association, which held its meeting that year at Red River church, near Clarksville, Tennessee. It remained a member of this association until 1816, when it was decided to form a new association of the churches in Missouri.

One thing which distinguished the members of Bethel church from the very day of the organization was their fervent missionary spirit. They were untiring in their efforts to have the gospel preached in every possible place within the bounds of Upper Louisiana. To this end they contributed money and encouraged their ministers to visit the different parts of the district. We find them organizing congregations wherever that was possible. These congregations remained for a time as members of Bethel church, and were looked after, as much as possible, by the pastor of that church. As soon as these congregations became large enough they were organized into regular churches and their direct connection with Bethel church ceased.

The first of these in point of time was organized in the Bois Brule Bottom in what was then Ste. Genevieve county, but what is now

Perry county. Members were received there in 1807. Among them was Thomas Donohoe, who afterward became a preacher. This congregation of members seems to have disappeared after the year 1815. Donohoe and, perhaps some of the other members, then joined a church called Barren church in the same vicinity. This church was constituted in 1816 at the house of Jesse Evans. It soon disappeared, also, and was succeeded by another church known as Hepzibah.

The second organization constituted by Bethel was that at St. Michaels. This was in October, 1812. On the same day John Farrar was obtained as a minister. He was a member of this congregation. In 1814 this congregation was organized into a church known as Providence church, and Farrar became its pastor.

In January, 1813, a committee was sent from Bethel to organize a congregation on Saline creek. This soon became a church and seems to have been united, later, with Barren church and still later with Hepzibah.

In 1813 there were twenty-three members of Bethel church who lived about twenty-five miles south of Fredericktown. In 1814 they were organized into a church called St. Francois.

A church was organized on Turkey creek in 1815. There had previously been a number of members of Bethel church living in that vicinity.

In June, 1820, an organization was established on Apple creek, near Oak Ridge, and it was formed into a church in September of that year. The committee which had charge of the organization of the church was composed of Elders T. P. Greene, James Williams, and J. K. Gile, and Isaac Sheppard, Benjamin Thompson, Abraham Randol, Thomas English and Benjamin Hitt.

In June, 1821, it was resolved to constitute a church in the Big Bend. The church so organized was called Ebenezer and was situated near the site of Egypt Mills.

On May 11, 1822, fourteen members of Bethel church were dismissed for the purpose of organizing Hebron church, five miles southeast of Jackson. These members so dismissed, were, most of them, of the Randol, Poe and Hitt families. Seven members of Bethel were dismissed in April, 1824, and they constituted a church at Jackson.

In the period from the organization of the church in 1806 to 1824, nine church were constituted through the efforts of Bethel church. Of these nine churches, only two seem to have survived to the present date. They are Providence church at Fredericktown and the Jackson church.

The ministers of Bethel church from its foundation were David Greene, 1806 to 1809; Wilson Thompson, 1812 to 1814; Thomas Stephens, 1817; Thomas P. Greene, 1818 to 1826; Benjamin Thompson, 1826 to 1853; John Canterbury, 1853 to 1861, and Joel Foster, 1866.

David Greene, who organized the church, had spent some years as a minister in the Carolinas. He loved the life of the frontier, and moved from Carolina to Kentucky, where he preached among the frontier settlers of that date. In 1805, as we have said, he visited Missouri and stopped for a time in the Tywappity Bottom. There were some Baptists living in the neighborhood, and he preached to them and organized a church. The members of this church were Henry Cockerham, John Baldwin, William Ross and a few others. After residing in this settlement for a few months, Elder Greene paid a visit to the vicinity of Jackson, but after preaching for a time he returned to Kentucky. The condition of the Baptists in Missouri, however, rested heavily on his mind, and, though he was old and had spent a long life in the ministry, he resolved to visit the Cape Girardeau district again. This time he moved and located with his family near Bethel church. He was the pastor of the church until his death in 1809.

The second pastor of Bethel church was Wilson Thompson. It was the work of Thompson that made the church a power in Missouri. Like so many other famous preachers, he was of Welsh descent. He was born in Woodford county, Kentucky, August 17, 1788. In 1810 he was married to Miss Mary Gregg, and in January, 1811, they moved to the Cape Girardeau district, settling near Jackson. They were accompanied by his father and mother, and the entire family united with Bethel church. He had begun preaching at the age of twenty, before his removal from Kentucky, and his preaching was attended with marvelous results. Shortly after he united with Bethel church there occurred the great earthquake at New Madrid, and the shocks were felt over a large part of Upper Louisiana. In the following February Thompson began a revival service in Bethel church. It was one of the most remarkable religious manifestations in Missouri. It covered a period of two years, and spread to almost all the congregations which had been organized by the church. There was evidence of the power of the revival at Bois Brule, Saline, Providence and St. Francois, and during its progress Thompson baptized about five hundred persons. Up to this time he had not been an ordained minister, but on April 11, 1825, a council composed of John Farrar and Stephen Stilly ordained him. The following July he was chosen pastor of the church and served until September, 1814. At that time he resigned, and with his family moved to Ohio. He died in Indiana in 1865. He was, doubtless, the most powerful of the preachers ever connected with the church.

For some years the church seems to have been without a regular pastor, but in February, 1817, it called Thomas Stephens, who was a resident of Louisville, Kentucky. He served the church until December of that year. In the following year Thomas Parish Greene, a native of North Carolina, who had lived for some time in Tennessee, was chosen as the fourth of the church's pastors. This was in March, 1818. Elder Greene had moved to Missouri in 1817. He served as pastor of the church for eight years, and it was under his leadership that an interest was aroused in missions and Sunday schools. Elder Greene was an ardent advocate of the church's duty to assist in preaching the gospel to the entire world. While he was pastor of the church it was voted that the association should correspond with the board of foreign missions. Under his leadership the church welcomed the visit of John Mason Peck, who had come from the east under the direction of the board of missions to evangelize Missouri. During Peck's visit to Bethel church he organized a missionary society, and on November 8, 1818, after a missionary sermon, he took up a collection for missions, amounting to $31.37. The entire work of the church prospered, so long as Greene was its pastor. He closed his pastorate of the church in 1826, when he was called to the care of Hebron church. In 1828 he removed to Rock Springs, Illinois, where he was associated with Peck in publishing the *Western Pioneer*. He was also at the time agent of the American Sunday School Union, and assisted in establishing Sunday schools and libraries in New Madrid, Scott, Cape Girrdeau, Perry, Madison, St. Francois, Wayne and Stoddard counties. He later became a missionary for the American Baptist Home Mission Society. In 1834 he organized a Baptist church at Cape Girardeau. There were nine members at that time and Elder Greene became the first pastor. After two years he moved to St. Louis, where he was pastor of the Second Baptist church. Elder Greene had been educated as a printer, and had at one time conducted a little weekly paper himself. This was a combination paper, being part a religious weekly and in part a newspaper. It was this training and experience which led to Greene's selection as an associate of John Mason Peck in the attempt to publish a paper at Rock Spring, Illinois. He was to look after the actual details of printing and publication.

Thomas P. Greene was a man of great ability. He is said to have resembled Senator Benton, and to have possessed something of Benton's oratorical capability. He had only limited opportunities for education, but continued his studies all through his life and became quite a scholar. Hon. Samuel M. Greene, of Cape Girardeau, is his son.

Some of the other ministers who were connected with Bethel church, or with the association during this period, were John Farrar, William Street, James P. Edwards and Wingate Jackson. William Street was one of the early settlers in Wayne county, and was held in high esteem both as a citizen and a minister. He died in 1843. John Farrar was a resident of Madison county until 1825, when he was removed to Washington county. He died there in 1829. In 1811 James P. Edwards moved to Cape Girardeau from Kentucky. He was a lawyer, but was ordained as a minister in 1812, and afterward removed to Illinois. Wingate Jackson was a Virginian.

He was born in 1776 and resided for a number of years in Kentucky. About 1804 he located at New Tennessee, Ste. Genevieve county, where he died in 1835. It was under his ministry that Hepzibah church was established in 1820. The constituent members were Wingate Jackson, Obadiah Scott, Noah Hunt, and Joel and Enos Hamers.

In 1814 a committee of Bethel church was appointed to draw up a plan for the organization of an association of the Missouri churches. Invitations were sent to the various churches to meet the committee from Bethel church and for the consideration of this matter the representatives of the various churches met in Bethel in June, 1816. Bethel church was represented by Thomas Bull, John Sheppard, Benjamin Thompson and Robert English. Tywappity church was represented by Henry Cockerham, John Baldwin, and William Ross. Providence church was represented by William Savage; Saline church, by Elder Thomas Donohoe and John Duvall; St. Francois church, by Elder William Street and Jonathan Hubble; Turkey Creek church, by William Johnson, Daniel Johnson, E. Revelle and S. Baker.

The organization thus effected was in the nature of a preliminary organization and it was decided to hold another meeting in September, 1816, at Bethel church. At this meeting, which was participated in by Bethel, Tywappity, Providence, Barren, Bellevue, St. Francois and Dry Creek churches, an association was constituted which was named Bethel association. These seven churches had an aggregate membership of 230, and there were five ministers included in the association.

One of the famous and most active Baptist ministers of this time was John Mason Peck.

He did not live in Southeast Missouri, but spent most of the years of his residence within the state, in St. Louis. On various occasions he visited the churches in Southeast Missouri and exercised a great influence on the development of religious work in this section. He resided for a time in New York and began his ministerial work there. He was appointed by the Home Missionary Society to prosecute the work of the church in Missouri. Accompanied by his family and by another minister named James E. Welch, he came to the state in 1817. The next twenty years of lis life were spent in teaching, preaching and organizing all over the section. He was a student and collected most copious notes on social, religious and political conditions of Missouri. He was an indefatigable writer. His influence was very great over the course of Baptist development, and he, more than any other man, was responsible for the missionary spirit that prevailed among the churches of the early day.

The itinerant preachers of the Methodist church have always been found among the first in every new country. As soon as the restrictions on religious worship were removed from the people of Louisiana by the transfer to the United States, arrangements began to be made for sending a Methodist preacher to the territory. The Western Conference, which included all the territory west of the Alleghany mountains, at its meeting in Greenville, Tennessee, in 1806, appointed John Travis to the Missouri circuit. He entered upon his work here and established two districts, the Missouri district and the Maramec district, the latter being south of the Missouri river. In 1807 Edward Wilcox was appointed to the Maramec circuit, and in 1808 Joseph Oglesby was appointed; he, however, did not take up the work and his place was supplied by Thomas Wright, and Z. Maddox was appointed as local preacher to look after the Cape Girardeau district.

The first Methodist society west of the Mississippi river was organized about 1806 at McKendree, three miles west of Jackson in Cape Girardeau county. Among the members of this church were William Williams and wife, John Randol and wife, Thomas Blair, Simon and Isaiah Poe, Charnel Glascock and the Seeleys. Within a short time after the organization of this church a meeting house was erected of large, hewn poplar logs. The house was in a beautiful situation near a spring and shaded by large oak trees. It soon became famous as a camp ground and was the site of many camp meetings. The house, with some alterations and repairs, is still in existence. It is, perhaps, the oldest Protestant meeting house west of the Mississippi river.

It is a question as to what minister organized this early Methodist society. When John Travis came to Missouri he found this church already in existence, and it seems probable that it had been organized by Rev. Jesse Walker, who, in 1804, was stationed near the mouth of the Cumberland river, and who afterward came to Missouri. In 1806, while the Western Conference sent Travis to Missouri, it also sent Walker to Illinois. It seems, however, to be fairly certain that he did not confine his labors to Illinois, but crossed over, preached, and organized churches in what is now Missouri. When the conference met in 1807, at Chillicothe, Ohio, Travis reported that the two circuits, Cape Girardeau and the Maramec, had one hundred and six members. At this time Walker was assigned to the Cape Girardeau circuit. He came to Missouri in the summer of that year and was accompanied on his trip by William McKendree, who was then presiding elder of

Illinois district. He held the first quar[terl]y meeting with Travis in that year on the [Ma]ramec river, it seems, at the place where [Tra]vis chapel is now located.

[I]n 1808 the Western Conference appointed Rev. Jesse Walker for the Cape Girar[dea]u circuit and Rev. David Young and Rev. [Tho]mas Wright for the Maramec circuit. [Thi]s territory was then part of the Indiana [dist]rict, over which Samuel Parker was pre[sidi]ng elder. Rev. Parker visited the Cape [Girar]deau circuit in that year, and came to the [tow]n of Cape Girardeau, where he preached [the] first sermon ever heard in the town. This [wa]s at the house of William Scripps, who was [an] Englishman, having come to America in [180]1 and to Cape Girardeau in 1808. Scripps [wa]s a tanner by trade and he and Rev. Parker [had] been acquainted in Virginia. One of the [son]s of William Scripps, whose name was [Joh]n, was admitted, at the conference in [181]4. as a preacher on trial. Later, he was [tak]en into full connection with the church [and] was active as a minister until his removal [to] Illinois in 1820.

[I]n 1810 Jesse Walker and John Scripps [cro]ssed the big swamp to the New Madrid dis[tric]t and organized the New Madrid circuit. [Th]ey traveled this circuit in connection with [the] Cape Girardeau circuit. There were thirty [me]mbers in this circuit the first year. In this [ye]ar, 1810, the first camp meeting in Cape [Gi]rardeau county was held on the camp [gro]und in connection with McKendree [cha]pel. Walker, Wright, and Presiding [El]der Parker were present and conducted the [ca]mp meeting.

The conference of 1810 assigned John Mc[Fa]rland to the Maramec circuit and reap[po]inted Walker to the Cape Girardeau circuit. [W]alker did not remain and McFarland ministered to both the circuits. In 1811 McFarland was placed in charge of both Cape Girardeau and New Madrid circuits and Thomas Wright was sent to the Maramec. In 1812 Cape Girardeau and the New Madrid circuits were divided. Benjamin Edge was appointed to the work at Cape Girardeau and William Hart to that at New Madrid. In 1813 Thomas Wright was assigned to Cape Girardeau and Thomas Nixon to New Madrid.

In 1812 a camp meeting was held in what is now Madison county, though it was then a part of Ste. Genevieve county. The meeting was conducted by Thomas Wright and it was the first camp meeting held in Ste. Genevieve county. Like the great revival meeting by Wilson Thompson, in Bethel Baptist church, it followed very closely after the earthquake at New Madrid.

In 1814 the conference received John C. Harbison on trial. Harbison had been a resident of the district since 1798, but up to this time had been employed as a teacher at Mt. Tabor, and had also practiced law for a short period. He was of Scotch-Irish descent and had lived in other states before coming to Missouri. His descendants still live in Scott county. It is said that Harbison had been, for a long time, addicted to gambling and drunkenness before he became a member of the church, and that after he was converted and living an exemplary life as a minister, he met some of his former companions who challenged him to play a game of poker. He agreed to do this, provided that after the game was over they would listen to the sermon which he was to preach at the church. They agreed to this, and he preached such a powerful and convincing sermon that those who heard abandoned their wicked courses of life.*

In the same year Thomas Wright was ap-

* Houck, Vol. III, p. 238.

pointed to the Cape Girardeau circuit, and Asa Overall began work in the New Madrid circuit. There was also formed this year a new circuit to include the territory between the Maramec and Apple creek. This was given the name of Saline circuit. Preaching was held at several points within this circuit, principally at the Murphy settlement, Cook settlement, Callaway settlement and new Tennessee.

The Murphy settlement was the oldest Methodist community west of the Mississippi river, and probably contained more Methodists than any other. The first Methodist sermon west of the river was preached in the Murphy settlement in 1804, by Joseph Oglesby. This was at the house of Mrs. Sarah Murphy. One of the early Methodist preachers in the Saline circuit was Jacob Whiteside. This circuit had, at the close of the year 1815, one hundred and fifteen members.

The conference in 1815 appointed Philip Davis to the New Madrid circuit, Jesse Haile for the Cape Girardeau circuit and Thomas Wright for the Saline circuit.

In 1816 a new conference was organized at Shiloh meeting house near Belleville, Illinois. It comprised Saline, Cape Girardeau, New Madrid and the St. Francois circuits and was called the Missouri Conference. Samuel H. Thompson was made presiding elder of the conference, and Bishop Roberts presided at the meeting. The conference appointed Thomas Wright and Alexander McAlister to the Cape Girardeau and New Madrid circuits, and John C. Harbison to Saline circuit. In 1817 Thomas Wright was sent to Saline circuit, Joseph Spiggott to New Madrid circuit and Rucker Tanner to St. Francois circuit, while the Cape Girardeau circuit was left to be supplied.

Tanner was a rather remarkable man. He had been a very reckless youth and had spent his early life in the New Madrid district. It is related of him that on one occasion he and an elder brother made a trip to New Orleans, and while there ran short of funds. After all their money was exhausted, it was arranged between them that R. Tanner, whose complexion was very dark, should be sold by his brother as a slave. This arrangement was carried out and the elder brother departed with the money. After a considerable difficulty, R. Tanner succeeded in regaining his freedom and escaped from the country. He started to walk home but on the way hired himself out to a local Methodist preacher. He lived with this preacher for some time, becoming converted and professing a desire to preach. It may be imagined that his return home was a great surprise to his friends, who had thought him long since dead. Almost immediately upon his return he announced an appointment to preach. It was such a surprising thing that this reckless youth should be preparing for the ministry, that a very large congregation assembled to hear his first attempt. He was very soon admitted to the conference and appointed, as we have said, to the St. Francois circuit. For the years 1818 and '19 Saline circuit was served by Thomas Wright, Cape Girardeau circuit by John Scripps and the St. Francois circuit by John McFarland.

There is a question as to when the first conference west of the river was held. September 14, 1819, is sometimes given as the date of the beginning of the first conference. This conference was held at McKendree chapel. There is some authority, however, for believing that there had been a conference held in 1818 at Mt. Zion church in the Murphy settlement, at which conference Bishop McKen-

presided. The appointments made in [1819] were John McFarland to the Saline circuit; Joseph Spiggott to the Bellevue circuit which had, in the meantime, been organized); Philip Davis to the St. Francois circuit; Samuel Glaize to the Cape Girardeau circuit, and William Townsend to the New Madrid circuit.

When the conference met in 1820 it was decided to create a new district. This was called the Cape Girardeau district and Thomas Wright was appointed as presiding elder. The preachers for the year were: Bellevue circuit, John Harris; Saline and St. Francois circuits, Samuel Bassett; Spring River, which was a new circuit, Isaac Brookfield; White River, another new circuit, W. H. Redman; Cape Girardeau circuit, Philip Davis; and New Madrid circuit, Jesse Haile.

When Missouri was admitted to the Union in 1821, Thomas Wright was continued as presiding elder, Thomas Davis was sent to Cape Girardeau circuit, Philip Davis to Saline circuit, John Cord to the St. Francois circuit, Abram Epler to Spring River, and Washington Orr to the New Madrid circuit.

The Presbyterians did not begin their work in Southeast Missouri quite so early as the Baptists and Methodists. The beginning of their interest in Missouri probably dates from the year 1812. In that year the Missionary Society of New England appointed two men, Rev. John T. Schermerhorn and the Rev. Samuel J. Mills, as agents to ascertain the religious conditions of the western country and the places most in need of religious instruction, and to formulate some plan for the preaching of the gospel in the destitute places. These two men seem to have intended to visit St. Louis, and perhaps other parts of the territory, but, for some reason, they abandoned their visit and contented themselves with writing a letter of inquiry to Stephen Hempstead, of St. Louis. In the letter they asked concerning the condition of religion in Upper Louisiana, the number of clergymen and the places where they were settled, whether there was much infidelity existing, whether the Sabbath was observed, and whether it was thought best to attempt to found a Bible society. They offered to send two or three hundred Bibles and some tracts for distribution among the poor, provided it was thought best to do so. Mr. Hempstead replied to these inquiries, and gave a picture of the religious conditions existing in the territory. He says that "the Catholic church has services; that there are some Methodists in the territory; that some of the Presbyterians, in the absence of their own preachers, have joined the Methodists, and that the Baptists have ten churches and two hundred and seventy-six members." And finally says that he "knows of no place in the United States that needs a Presbyterian missionary more than Missouri." He further requests that the Bibles and tracts be sent, which was done.

The first church in Southeast Missouri of the Presbyterian faith was organized in the Bellevue settlement in Washington county August 2, 1816. The Presbytery of Missouri was formed by the Synod of Tennessee and held its first meeting in St. Louis, December 18, 1817. Its territory was all of the United States west of the Cumberland river. The Presbytery of Missouri had, as its ministers, Solomon Giddings, Timothy Flint, Thomas Donnell and John Matthews. The only churches represented were those at Bellevue. Bonhomme, in St. Louis county, and St. Louis. In 1819 he number of ministers was increased by the addition of Rev. C. S. Robinson and the Rev. David Tenney. Mr. Tenney died in the same year. The Rev. Edward Hollister was connected with the Presbytery for a short time in 1821. The Rev. Timothy Flint was one of the most active of the Presbyterian ministers in Southeast Missouri in the early times. He seems to have organized a Bible society in Jackson about 1820 and also a Sunday school at the same place. This society was called the Columbian Bible Society. Its officers were Jason Chamberlain, president; Christopher G. Houts, treasurer; and A. Hayne, secretary. Rev. Timothy Flint seems to have traveled all through Upper Louisiana. He preached at Jackson, New Madrid, St. Charles and in Arkansas. He was a very vigorous, energetic and earnest man, had been thoroughly educated at Harvard college, and wrote a number of books bearing on Missouri history. He spent the winter of 1819 at New Madrid. He was a man who had considerable influence but, also, considerable trouble, as he was not always able to adapt himself to the conditions under which he found himself placed.

Among the publications written by Flint were the "Life of Daniel Boone," a "History and Geography of the Mississippi Valley," and "Recollections of the Last Ten Years in the Mississippi Valley."

In 1818 a presbytery was held at Potosi and a young man, who had been a ministerial student was ordained by Rev. Timothy Flint and Rev. Matthews. They rode from St. Louis to Potosi on horseback to perform this service.

That one of the Christian denominations known as Disciples, or simply Christians, seems to have begun its labors in Southeast Missouri in 1819. The teachings of this denomination had spread from Kentucky and Pennsylvania to the west, and in the year mentioned the Rev. William McMurtry came from Virginia and located in Madison county. He was a carpenter by trade, but preached also. He began to teach the doctrines of the church as soon as he was located within the state, and in 1822 organized a church in what is now the town of Libertyville. There were only three members of the church at that time, and they held their meetings in the log school house. The increase was slow at first, for in 1826 there were only nine members of the church.

We have thus recounted something of the beginning of effort by the Christian denominations in the early years in Missouri. We find that the only formal organization before 1804 was the organization of the Catholic church; that its teachings had spread in practically every community in Upper Louisiana; that its work had been organized and at least two houses of worship constructed. There were members of other denominations in Upper Louisiana before the transfer; that they held their regular services in private families, but were not allowed to build meeting houses or to perfect any kind of organizations. Upon the transfer to the United States, the Baptists and Methodists, and a little later the Presbyterians and Christians, or Disciples, began to prosecute the work of evangelism in a systematic way. There seem to have been two distinct methods of carrying on the work. The first Baptist church within the state was organized through the efforts of a visiting minister, and this church became the center for the sending out of the gospel to other parts and for the organization of other churches. In the same way the organization of the Disciples was begun. The first work performed by the Presbyterians within the state, as we have seen, was the result of the sending of missionaries from the East. A similar movement assisted and encouraged the work of the Baptists, when Peck and his companion, Welch, were sent into the territory. The work of the Methodists began in an organized form by the erection of part of the territory into a circuit, and the appointment of a minister to supply the needs in the vast territory included within his circuit.

By the time of the transfer to the United States these denominations were flourishing, their work was progressing and they were building houses of worship, establishing Sunday schools and schools in many parts of the territory. It is plain to be seen that they labored under very great difficulties. The territory over which the ministers were called to travel was very extensive, the means of transportation very poor, the roads were simply paths and there were but few accommodations provided, in most places, for visitors. Many of the ministers were accustomed to travel on foot for distances that seem almost impossible. It is said of Clark, who was an early minister of the Baptist church, that he would never ride to his appointments. Some of his friends presented him with a horse, but he was dissatisfied with it and returned it, preferring to walk from one place to another. Some of the Methodist circuit riders traveled over immense distances to reach their various appointments. Those who lived east of the river, not infrequently walked for miles to reach a place where the river might be crossed and, having crossed, walked a long distance on this side to the place where they were to preach.

Another thing which very greatly retarded and made more difficult the work of the early ministers, was a feeling among the people that these ministers should labor without pay. Not all of them were of this belief, but it was sufficiently prevalent to render the support of the ministers very meagre and very uncertain. Perhaps all of the preachers in the early time were compelled to recoup their salary by work of one kind or another, that they might support their families. We have seen that Elder McMurtry, an early minister of the Christian church, was a carpenter, and we find that Peck supported himself, in part, by teaching, as did Flint and many others.

Another thing which made their work difficult and their lives hard was the condition of many people among whom they must labor. Many of them were illiterate and could not appreciate the efforts which were being made for them. Some of these people lived under the most severe conditions of life, and some of them had no hope or ambition for better things. It was a work of the very greatest difficulty to arouse the people to action and to get them to accept the things which the ministers brought to them. Peck and Flint both relate amusing but unpleasant experiences concerning their visits in different parts of this section. They frequently were received into homes, if a single roomed log cabin may be so described, in which only the barest necessities were to be found.

These hardships are set out fully in the account which Peck gives in describing one of his trips from St. Louis, on horse back, to Bethel association in Cape Girardeau county. He made this trip in September, 1818, and the experience through which he passed induced him to moralize a little on the hardships which attended the life of the traveler. He says: "The route was the same one I last traveled until I got below Herculaneum, and then gradually bearing to the left and down the direction of the Mississippi, through an extensive tract of barrens very thinly settled. It was in passing through these barrens that Joseph Piggott, a Methodist circuit preacher, in the year 1820, came near freezing to death, on an extremely cold night, and without food for himself or his horse. He gave the writer a narrative of his sufferings that night, four years after, at his residence on the Macoupin, Illinois, and yet we were so hard hearted as not to express a word of sympathy. A few stunted and gnarled trees, and a sprinkling of brushwood, with now and then a decayed log, appeared above the snow. He was nearly chilled, after wandering about a long time in search of a path, and with great difficulty with his tinder-box, flint and steel, could he get a fire. He then scraped away what snow he could, and with his blanket lay down, broadside to the fire; but before he secured much warmth the other side was nearly frozen. Then he would turn over, but finding no relief would get up and stamp his feet, while the wind seemed to pass through him. When daylight appeared he was too cold to mount his horse, but led him while he attempted to find his way on to some lonely cabin, which proved to be not many miles distant. There he spent the day and enjoyed the hospitality of the squatter family. We listened to the distressing tale with amazement! This man was born and raised in Illinois and accustomed all his life to the frontiers, and yet had never learned one of the indispensable lessons of a backwoodsman—how to camp out, make a fire and keep warm. Eating was not so very important, for any man in the vigor of life in those days in this frontier country who could not go without food for twenty-four hours, and more especially a preacher of the Gospel, ought to be sent back where he came from, to the kind care of his friends.

"The writer had not been in the country one year before he had learned half a dozen lessons in frontier knowledge of great value in practical life. One branch was how Indians, hunters, surveyors, and all others who had to travel over uninhabited deserts, made their camping-place and kept themselves comfortable. The first thing is to select the right place—in some hollow or ravine, protected from the wind, and if possible behind some old forest giant which the storms of winter have prostrated. And then, reader, don't build your fire against the tree, for that is the place for your head and shoulders to lie, and around which the smoke and heated air may curl. Then don't be so childish as to lie on the wet, or cold frozen earth, without a bed. Gather a quantity of grass, leaves and small brush, and after you have cleared away the snow and provided for protection from the wet or cold earth, you may sleep comfortably. If you have a piece of jerked venison, and a bit of pone with a cup of water, you may make out a splendid supper—provided you think so—'for as a man thinketh so is he.' And if you have a traveling companion you may have a social time of it. So now offer your prayers like a Christian, ask the Lord to protect you, wrap around you your blankets with your saddles for pillows, and lie down to sleep under the care of a watchful Providence. If it rains, a very little labor with barks or even brush, with the tops sloping downward, will be no mean shelter. Keep your feet straight to the fire, but not near enough to burn your moccasins or boots, and your legs and whole body will be warm. The aphorism of the Italian physician, which he left in a sealed letter as a guide to all his former paents, contains excellent advice to all frontier people: 'Keep your feet warm, your back straight, and your head cool, and bid defiance to the doctors.' "—("Life of Peck," pp. 103 to 105.)

In spite of these and many other difficulties, of which we can have no proper appreciation at this time, the work progressed. There were men in the early days whose hearts were filled with enthusiasm for the work. They were not daunted by difficulties nor stopped by hardships. They labored unceasingly in season and out of season. The journals and diaries of these early men reveal to us a remarkable story of energy and of self-sacrificing devotion to the work which they had in hand; that their labors were abundantly blessed and that they exercised a great influence over the course of early history is amply evidenced. Under their ministrations hundreds, and even thousands, of men and women were changed in their lives; received something of inspiration and uplift; schools were founded by them and the beginning of culture, as well as of religion, were made under their direction. Many of these early ministers were educated men. They brought with them a knowledge of the world and they brought, also, the first libraries within the state. The example of their devotion and earnestness of purpose was contagious. The great religious denominations now within the state owe to the memory of these early pioneer preachers a debt which it is impossible for them to pay.

It should not be forgotten, either, that not only do the churches owe to them a debt; the state as a state is equally under obligations to them. If intelligence and morality are the twin pillars on which popular government rests, then these men who so largely contributed, not only to morality but also to the spread of education and the increase of intelligence, certainly deserve well at the hands of all the people in the state.

CHAPTER XIV

NEW MADRID EARTHQUAKE

Time and Area—Unique Among Earthquakes—Contemporary Accounts Mentioned—The Scene Described—Direction of the Shocks—Size of Affected Area—Character of Disturbances—Small Loss of Life Explained—A Death from Fright—Persons Drowned—Appearance of the Air—Vapors—Lights and Glows—Earth Changes—Fissures—Lignite—Areas of Surface Raised—Sunk-Lands — Observations Made by Lyell—Distribution of Sunk-Lands—Effect on Timber — Expulsion of Material from the Earth — Water-Sand—Sand Blows—Sand-Sloughs — Sinks — Suggested Causes—Contemporary Accounts—Mrs. Eliza Bryan — Long—Bradbury—Flint—Faux—LeSieur—Col. John Shaw—Letter of an Unknown Writer—Long—Nuttall—Flagg—Former Drainage as Described by LeSieur—Government Assistance to Sufferers—The New Madrid Claims—DeLisle vs. State of Missouri—Loss of Population.

On the night of December 15, 1811, there occurred the first of a series of severe earthquake shocks in the region about New Madrid, which caused great suffering and distress among the inhabitants, changed the surface of the earth in places, and resulted in the depopulation of parts of the region affected. This earthquake has been the subject of much contention among historians and scientists, and has recently been made the subject of much careful study.

Myron L. Fuller, a member of the United States Geological Survey, has given as much time and study to the phenomena of the New Madrid earthquake as any other person. In 1912 the Geological Survey issued a bulletin by Mr. Fuller, entitled "The New Madrid Earthquake." His introductory statement is as follows: "The succession of shocks designated collectively the New Madrid earthquake occurred in an area of the central Mississippi valley, including southeastern Missouri, northeastern Arkansas, and western Kentucky and Tennessee. Beginning December 16, 1811, and lasting more than a year, these shocks have not been surpassed or even equaled for number, continuance of disturbance, area affected, and severity by the more recent and better-known shocks at Charleston and San Francisco. As the region was almost unsettled at that time relatively little attention was paid to the phenomenon, the published accounts being few in number and incomplete in details. For these reasons, although scientific literature in this country and in Europe has given it a place among the great earthquakes of the world, the memory of it has lapsed from the public mind."

Shaler, writing of the earthquake in 1869, said: "The occurrence of such a shock in a egion like the Mississippi valley, on the borers of a great river, is probably unprecedented in the history of earthquakes. * * * Many of the events of that convulsion were without a parallel. Scientifically this earthquake may be regarded as a type, exhibiting in unusual detail the geologic effects of great disturbances upon unconsolidated deposits. For this reason its phenomena have an importance which, in the absence of any previous systematic discussion, warrants detailed consideration."

It is the intention here to give as full an account of the earthquake itself as collected from contemporary accounts as is possible, and a description of the condition of the lands affected by the shocks. It is fortunate that there are in existence a number of accounts written by eye witnesses, some of them being scientific men and some others, men of education and training. Perhaps the best known scientist who felt the shocks and described them, was the great naturalist, John James Audubon, who at the time was in Kentucky. John Bradbury, an English botanist, was on a keel boat in the Mississippi river a few miles below New Madrid; the expedition of Major Long was passing through the region on its way from Pittsburgh to the Rocky mountains; L. Bringier, an engineer and surveyor, was on the scene of the shocks; and Captain Roosevelt was on board a steamer going down the river. Besides these men of scientific training who were on the scene, there were others at a somewhat greater distance who made a record of the shocks, among them being Daniel Drake at Cincinnati and Jared Brooks at Louisville; while S. L. Mitchill, a well known geologist and member of congress, collected all the available information about the earthquakes. It was fortunate, too, that the scene was visited by Timothy Flint, a Presbyterian minister and a writer on geography, and by Sir Charles Lyell the great English geologist. In addition to these there were accounts written by a number of other persons; one of these accounts, that of Mrs. Eliza Bryan, is given in this chapter. Godfrey LeSieur, the former well-known citizen of New Madrid and a member of the famous French family that founded the town, was at the time at Little Prairie and has given a vivid and interesting account of his experiences; this account is abbreviated in this chapter, also. Senator Lewis F. Linn was interested in the catastrophe and collected information concerning it which he made public in a letter containing a full account of the shocks. Besides all these there exist fragmentary statements from a number of other persons, so that contemporary accounts of events are reasonably full.

A comparison of all these accounts discloses the fact that they are in reasonable accord in their description and the main facts concerning the earthquake shocks seem to rest on the concurring testimony of these witnesses. The night of December 15, 1811, was as quiet and undisturbed during its early hours as any other of the hundreds of nights that had passed. There seems to have been nothing to give warning of any change impending. Some who wrote afterwards speak as if there was a peculiar condition of the air, but these accounts indicate only that it was probably damp and foggy weather. About 2 o'clock in the morning of December 16, the earth suddenly shook and vibrated with terrific force; the houses, most of them built of logs, were greatly shaken, some of them being thrown into instant ruin. The inhabitants made their way as best they could out of their houses into the open. The shocks continued; they were accompanied by low rumbling sound; the earth was thrown into waves like the waves of the sea; this waving motion was so violent that it was impossible to stand or to walk. One man gives it that he attempted to return to the house for a member of the family who was sick; he was thrown down five or six times in attempting to walk a short distance owing to these waves. The crest of the waves was elevated some three or four feet above the usual level of the earth, forming long lines running from the southwest to the northeast, and having depressions between them; some of these waves or swells burst, forming fissures in the earth some three to seven feet in width and extending to an unknown depth. These fissures were in some cases short, but others of them extended for miles. Out of the fissures thus formed there spouted great quantities of water, sand, and a kind of charcoal or lignite. In many cases there seems to have been a sort of gas having a sulphurous smell. The banks of the rivers fell into the stream owing to their being split off by these fissures. The quantities of earth carried into the river were very great, hundreds of trees being swept down into the stream. The shaking of the earth and the rising and falling of these swells or waves threw down whole forests and inclined many of the trees left standing at an angle. Some of the timber was split and much of it snapped off, as told by Mrs. Bryan. In places on the side of the high bluffs faults were formed in the earth, resulting in occasional land slides; the surface of some areas seem to have been raised, while other areas were sunk several feet below their former level. In other places small craters were opened in the earth from which spouted quantities of sand and water, the sand being deposited on top of the alluvium forming sand blows. The river itself was greatly agitated. In many places there were falls formed in it, due to the faulting of the surface; these falls were in places six to eight feet in height and the pouring of the water of the streams over them produced tremendous and unusual sounds. In other places the bottom of the river seems to have been raised, ponding water before these places so that the level of the river was raised several feet in a very short time. The waters receded from either shore to the center of the river and were piled up there for a time, leaving boats stranded on the bare sands. In a moment the waves returned and washed up on the shore and out into the timber, carrying the boats with them. Through the depressions formed in the banks of the river great volumes of water made their way, covering parts of the country to a depth of several feet. The falling of trees into the river and the shaking loose from the bottom of thousands of logs previously accumulated, covered its whole surface with floating timbers; the waters were agitated and churned into a foam so that it was almost impossible for a boat to live upon its surface. The inhabitants of the country were of course exceedingly terrified by these things and even the wild animals and fowls were thrown into confusion and uttered cries of alarm. This shaking of the earth continued at intervals for more than a year, though the last severe shock of the series was felt on the 7th of February, 1812. The shaking was felt over great regions, extending to the lakes on the north and to the Atlantic seaboard on the east, being observed in such widely separated places as Charleston, N. C.; Cincinnati, Ohio; Savannah, Ga.; St. Louis, Mo.; Washington, D. C., and Pittsburgh, Pa. In all these places the shocks were violent and all of them were noted as occurring about the same time as the shocks at New Madrid.

The shocks seemed to travel from the southwest to the northeast, and a study of all the recorded evidence indicates that the center of the disturbance was within the alluvial region. It is the opinion of Mr. Fuller, who has made a careful study of the situation, that the line marking the center of disturbance extended from a point in New Madrid county just east of Parma, in a southwesterly direction, crossing the sand ridge just east of Kennett, and ending south of St. Francis lake in Arkansas.*

The area affected, as we have said, was very large, including perhaps the east half of the United States. The smaller area in which there was an unusual earth disturbance characterized by sunken lands, fissures, sinks, sand-blows, etc., includes the New Madrid region as it is called, which extends from a point west of Cairo on the north to the latitude of Memphis on the south, a distance of more than 100 miles, and from Crowley's ridge on the west to the Chickasaw bluffs on the east, a distance of over 50 miles, the total area affected in this striking way being from 30,000 to 50,000 square miles.

It is not possible to give the number of shocks that were felt, but there were probably at least a hundred that could be detected without the use of instruments, a number of them being severe.

Attempts have been made to determine the exact character of the disturbances that took place in the surface of the earth. Here dependence must be put upon the observations within the area of the great disturbances. It is difficult to reconcile the opinions of the different observers on this particular point differences arising, doubtless, from the difficulty experienced during the earthquake in observing and recording the facts as they actually existed; the feeling of terror was so great that it was almost a matter of impossibility to make accurate and exact observations. The disturbances of the crust is said by Bringier to have been like the blowing up of the earth accompanied by loud explosions.**

Casseday says: "It seems as if the surface of the earth was afloat and set in motion by a slight application of immense power and when this regular motion is moved by a sudden cross shove all order is destroyed and a boiling action is produced, during the continuance of which the degree of violence is greatest and the scene most dreadful."***

Flint was told by other witnesses that the movement was an undulation of the earth resembling waves, increasing in elevation as they advanced, and when they had attained a certain fearful height the earth would burst.†

This agrees with LeSieur's account also, and Haywood writes that the motions were undulating, the agitating surface quivering like the flesh of beef just killed, and the motion progressed from west to east and was sometimes perpendicular, resembling a house rising and suddenly let fall to the ground.‡

Audubon, describing his experiences in Kentucky, says that the ground rose and fell in successive furrows like the ruffled waters of a lake; the earth moved like a field of corn before the breeze.¶

This wave motion of the crust seems to have

* U. S. Geological Survey, Bulletin 494, Plate 1.
** Bringier, American Jour. of Science, 1st series, Vol. III (1821), p. 1546.
*** Casseday, History of Louisville, p. 122.
† Timothy Flint, Recollections of the Last Ten Years, p. 223.
‡ Haywood, Natural and Aboriginal History of Tennessee, p. 124.
¶ Audubon, J. J., Journal, Vol. II, p. 234.

been the most common form of disturbance though there were also certain vertical motions which seem, however, not to have been so destructive as the wave motion.

It is plainly evident that if these accounts of the waving of the earth are accurate the shocks must have been very severe and destructive. That such was the case is amply evidenced by the testimony of men who visited the scene shortly afterward, Flint, who saw the country within a short time after the shocks, says: "The country exhibited a melancholy aspect of chasms, of sand covering the earth, of trees thrown down, or lying at an angle of 45 degrees, or split in the middle. The earthquakes still recurred at short intervals, so that the people had no confidence to rebuild good houses, or chimneys of brick."*

One of the remarkable things connected with the earthquakees is that notwithstanding their very great violence, few people were killed. The inhabitants were very naturally greatly alarmed and for a time refused to live within their houses, but they finally came to pay little or no attention to them. It seems that the earthquakes killed only one person by means of falling walls. This remarkable fact, when we compare the record of this earthquake with the record of other shocks which were possibly no more severe, is due to a number of circumstances. In the first place the country was very thinly settled. Within the whole New Madrid region as we have defined it, there were only a few hundred persons living. The character of the buildings also contributed to this escape from death. There were no brick or stone buildings; most of the houses were built of logs and were only one story in height. These log houses were strongly built and at the same time were elastic and fitted to give before the shock of

* Flint, Recollections of the Last Ten Years.

the earthquake. Then, too, the most severe shocks came after the people had gotten out of their houses. Besides the person killed by the falling of a house, one woman died from the effects of fright. She was so terrified that she ran until she was entirely exhausted and died.†

A number of men seem to have been drowned, some of whom were in boats that were overthrown and sunk by the violence of the waves. And there were others who were drowned, it seems, by falling into the river from caving banks. Some men were drowned by the disappearance of Island No. 94 near Vicksburg. Broadhead says: "They tied up at this island on the evening of the 15th of December, 1811. In looking around they found that a party of river pirates occupied part of the island and were expecting Sarpy with the intention of robbing him. As soon as Sarpy found that out he quietly dropped lower down the river. In the night the earthquake came and next morning when the accompanying haziness disappeared, the island could no longer be seen. It had been quietly destroyed, as well as its pirate inhabitants."

Having given some of the general features of the earthquake, of the effect upon the people living within the district, it is now intended to give a more particular account of some of the phenomena that accompanied the shocks. Many of the observers speak of the darkness that accompanied the most severe disturbances. In the account of Eliza Bryan, given herewith, she speaks of the awful darkness of the atmosphere; Godfrey LeSieur says a dense black cloud of vapor overshadowed the land. At Herculaneum it is said that the "air was filled with smoke or fog so that a boat could not be seen twenty paces, nor a house fifty feet away; the air did not clear

† Flint, Recollections of the Last Ten Years, p. 223.

until the middle of the day after the shocks."*

At New Madrid it is said that at the time of the shock the air was clear but in five minutes it become very black and this darkness returned at each successive shock.†

Geologists have sought an explanation of this darkness and some have ascribed it to dust projected into the air by the agitation of the surface, the opening and closing of fissures in dry earth, land slides, and falling chimneys and buildings. Besides the dust it is probable that the water vapors coming from the warm water sent up from the cracks and small craters was condensed and helped to make the air foggy. The darkness observed in places outside of the earthquake area may very probably be ascribed to other causes than the earthquakes themselves; perhaps to storms and clouds.

Besides the darkness the shocks seem to have been accompanied by sulphurous or other obnoxious odors and vapors. Mrs. Bryan speaks of the saturation of the atmosphere with sulphurous vapors; other observers tell of sulphur gas escaping through the cracks and tainting the air and even the water so that it was not fit for use. These vapors or odors were probably due to buried organic matter which had been covered by the alluvium. Gas from this matter was released through the fissures and small craters formed by the earthquake.

Some accounts speak of the light flashes and glows in connection with the shocks. D— says that there issued no burning flames but flashes such as would result from an explosion of gas or of the passing of electricity from cloud to cloud, and Senator Linn says the shock was accompanied by flashes of electricity. Another observer says sparks of fire were emitted from the earth. Over all the affected area, indeed, there were reports of lights and flashes like lightning about the time of the earthquake shocks.

It is not possible to account for these lights and glows in any satisfactory way. Some have doubted their presence at all, but they are mentioned by so many observers as to make it difficult to deny their existence altogether. They might possibly have been lightning accompanying storms. There seems to be no good reason for ascribing them to burning gas. The suggestion has been made by some that the light was due to magnetic disturbances and was perhaps of electrical character.

One of the phenomena accompanying the earthquakes and one of the most noticeable of all, was the noise. This noise was remarked by many persons. Among the quotations given from contemporary accounts, a number speak of the tremendous sounds terrifying in their nature, Haywood says: "A murmuring noise, like that of fire disturbed by the blowing of a bellows, issued from the pores of the earth; a distant rumbling was heard almost without intermission and sometimes seemed to be in the air." (Haywood, Natural and Aboriginal History of Tennessee.) Senator Linn compares the sounds to those produced by a discharge of one thousand pieces of artillery and says also that hissing sounds accompanied the throwing out of the water from the crevices. Flint says the sounds of the ordinary shocks were like distant thunder, but that the vertical shocks were accompanied by explosions and terrible mixture of noises. Mrs. Bryan speaks of the "awful noises resembling loud and distant thunder but more hoarse and vibrating." The noise of the escap-

* Mitchill, Trans. Lit. and Philos. Soc., New York, Vol. I, p. 291.

† Mitchill, p. 297.

ing water is compared to the escape of steam from a boiler by some of the observers. Audubon speaks of the sound as if it were "the distant rumbling of a violent tornado," while Bradbury mentions the fact that he "was awakened by a tremendous noise" and noticed the fact that the sound which was heard at the time of every shock always preceding it at least a second and uniformly came from the same point and went off in the opposite direction.

Other observers describe the sound in different ways. One said "'when the shocks came on the stones on the surface of the earth were agitated by a tremulous motion, like eggs in a frying pan, and made a noise similar to that of the wheels of a wagon in a pebbly road." Others speak of the sound as resembling a blaze of fire acted upon by the wind, or the wind rushing through the trees, or a carriage passing along the street, or distant thunder.

The effects of the earthquake on the surface of the earth itself may be summed up as consisting of fissures, sand-blows, a rising of parts of the earth and sinking of other portions, faulting of the crust and in some cases land slides. One of the most common of these phenomena was fissuring; the earth waves which we have described as accompanying the shocks burst in many cases, leaving a fissure, some of these as long as five miles. This was an estimate made by LeSieur; others mention fissures 600 or 700 feet long and 20 to 30 feet wide.*

Flint says that some of the fissures were wide enough to swallow horses or cattle.† He also says that people fell into these fissures and were gotten out with great difficulty. In some instances the inhabitants felled trees crosswise of the fissures and took refuge on their trunks to prevent being swallowed up. Out of these fissures there were ejected quantities of water and sand; mixed with the sand in many cases were particles of coal or lignite. This lignite seems to have been a feature of the sand which was thrown out from the fissures, and much of it is still to be found in many places throughout the district. Most of the contemporary accounts speak of it as "carbonized wood" or lignite. The material seen by Lyell near New Madrid is described in one place as bituminous coaly shale (clay), such as outcrops in the river bank and is found in shallow wells 35 feet or so below the surface and in another as lignite. The best description of its behavior on combustion is given by Mitchill, who examined samples submitted by a correspondent. I found it very inflammable; it consumed with a bright and vivid blaze. A copious smoke was emitted from it, whose smell was not at all sulphurous, but bituminous in a high degree. Taken out of the fire in its ignited and burning state, it did not immediately become extinct, but continued to burn until it was consumed. While blowed upon, instead of being deadened it became brighter by the blast. The ashes formed during the combustion were of a whitish color and when put into water imparted to it the quality of turning to a green the blue corolla of a phlox whose juice was subjected to its action.

Some specimens of the lignite matter were coated with a whitish or yellowish substance, suggesting sulphur, but it was probably the sulphate of iron common in lignite and certain coals. Wood not lignitized was also reported by some observers.‡

Another form of fissure seems to have been formed only near banks of streams; the por-

---

* Foster, The Mississippi Valley, p. 19.
† Flint, Recollections of the Last Ten Years, p. 226.
‡ U. S. Geological Survey, Bulletin 46.

tion of the alluvial soil between the fissure and the stream bank moved in the direction of the stream and left a considerably larger fissure than would otherwise have been formed. All these fissures of both characters extend in the general direction of the earthquake shocks. To understand their formation and also to account for the depth to which they extended, it must be remembered that practically all of the country affected by the earthquake is underlain at a depth of 10 to 20 feet by quicksand and that over this quicksand is a coating of alluvial soil consisting at the top of loam and then of layers of sand and clay alternating. The fissures opened out usually to the layers of quicksand, a depth of 10 to 20 feet. There are numbers of these fissures still to be seen. They have been partly filled by the action of the weather and by blowing in of leaves.

When Lyell visited the New Madrid region in 1849 he saw a number of fissures still open, some of which he followed continuously for over a mile. They ranged in depth from five to six feet and from two to four feet in width. Lyell also saw a fault produced by the earthquake near Bayou St. John east of New Madrid, where the descent was eight to ten feet. Fuller says that at Beechwell, northeast of Campbell in Dunklin county, is a fine fissure filled with sand. Pieces of lignite and shaly clay were seen in the trench, which appears to have been pushed diagonally upward into the clay alluvium, but not with sufficient force at least on one side, to break through.* He also gives an account of various fissures seen by him near Caruthersville, near Blythesville, and many of them across the Arkansas line. They are also to be seen east of the Mississippi river.

These fissures in many cases were partly, if

* U. S. Geological Survey, Bulletin 494, p. 54.

not entirely, filled. This was caused by the caving in of banks or walls and also by the pushing up of material from below. As the walls of the fissure opened, sand and water below the alluvium were pushed up, in some cases overflowed the walls of the fissure. It seems evident, too, that many of these cracks or fissures did not extend entirely to the surface of the earth but were stopped before reaching it. Into these cracks sand was forced up from below, filling the cracks and forming what geologists term a dike. These dikes are sometimes seen in the digging of wells or cellars and take the form of a narrow streak of sand pressed in between the other materials. Thomas Beckwith of Charleston photographed a remarkable dike of this character in Mississippi county.†

Besides these fissures there were also formed what geologists term "faults" in the surface, though these were nothing like so common as the fissures. It was probably due to these that falls were formed in the Mississippi river, the faults running crosswise of the channel. Several accounts speak of these falls, some of them being as much as six feet in height and extending entirely across the river.

No other effect of the earthquake has caused so much discussion or so wide a difference of opinion as that effect which geologists call "warping," a term used to include the rising of part of the crust and the depression of other parts. The accounts given by several of those who witnessed the shocks speak of the uplifting of parts of the surface of the earth. In the account of Mrs. Bryan it is said that the beds of some ponds were lifted up so that the ponds were drained and their former beds raised several feet. A. N. Dillard says: "Previous to the earthquake keel boats would come up the St. Francois river and

† U. S. Geological Survey, Bulletin 494, plate 3.

pass into the Mississippi river three miles below New Madrid; the bayou is now dry land."*

Others mention the terrible depression in the river, which was probably due to the uplift of part of its bed.

More general and much more important, probably so far as Southeast Missouri is concerned, were the effects of the earthquake in producing a depression of the surface. Fuller divides the lands which were depressed and which are characterized as sunk lands, into three divisions—the first, those marked by sand-sloughs; second, those characterized by river swamps, and third, those covered by lakes of standing water.

The sand-sloughs are broad, shallow sloughs generally of considerable length, several feet in depth and marked by well defined ridges covered by extruded sand and interspersed with depressions, in which the timber has been killed by standing water.

The river swamps include the depressed areas along certain of the streams, the level of which is such that water stands over them for considerable periods but does not cover them so deep as to prevent the growth of timber. They are, therefore, characterized by wet-land timber, most of which is young growth. Often the stumps of characteristic upland varieties of trees killed by the subsidence may be seen.

The sunk-land lakes are broad, shallow and essentially permanent bodies of water occurring in depressions of the bottom lands near the Mississippi and other streams or along the depressed channels of streams like the St. Francois.†

The amount of depression caused by the earthquakes varied in different localities from

* Foster, The Mississippi Valley, p. 9.
† U. S. Geological Survey, Bulletin 494, p. 65.

two to probably twenty feet. According to Fuller the sunk lands are limited to the flat bottom lands in Mississippi, Little and St. Francois rivers. The testimony of those who were present is that the land where New Madrid now stands subsided fifteen feet. Lyell, who visited the region in 1846, when the evidences were much clearer than at present, says: "The largest area affected by the convulsions lies eight or ten miles westward of the Mississippi and inland from the town of New Madrid, in Missouri. It is called the 'sunk country' and is said to extend along the course of the White Water (Little river?) and its tributaries for a distance of between 70 and 80 miles north and south and 30 miles or more east and west. Throughout this area innumerable submerged trees—some standing leafless, others prostrate—are seen, and so great is the extent of the lake and marsh that an active trade in the skins of muskrats, minks, otters and other wild animals is now carried on there. In March, 1846, I skirted the borders of the sunk country nearest to New Madrid, passing along the Bayou St. John and Little Prairie, where dead trees of various kinds—some erect in the water, others fallen and strewed in dense masses over the bottom, in the shallows and near the shore—were conspicuous." (Lyell.)

Farther south similar conditions existed. Dillard says: "I have trapped there (in the region of the St. François) for thirty years. There is a great deal of sunken land caused by the earthquake of 1811. There are large trees of walnut, white oak and mulberry, such as grow on high land, which are now seen submerged ten and twenty feet beneath the water. In some of the lakes I have seen cypresses so far beneath the surface that with a canoe I have paddled among the branches."

According to the map published by the United States geological survey in 1912, the principal areas of depression due to the earthquake which are to be found in Southeast Missouri are as follows: The low land lying south of Morley and on both sides of the Sikeston ridge, two narrow strips between Sikeston and Charleston, a part of the valley of Little river lying west of Lilbourn, a small area northwest of Hayti and another similar area lying south of Hayti, the bed of Little river south of the crossing on the Frisco between Hayti and Kennett, the section called Lake Nicormy and extending south of Big lake, a large section lying east and south of Malden, the section west of Malden known as West Slough and extending as far as Chilletecaux Slough, a large part of the valley of Buffalo creek, the sloughs lying between Buffalo creek and the St. Francois river including Seneca and Kinnamore, the bed of Varner river, and a part of the valley of the St. Francois west and south of Kennett. These are the principal areas of land submerged at the time of the earthquake in Southeast Missouri. Other large areas are to be found in Craighead and Green counties in Arkansas and include the territory about Lake City and the St. Francis lake.

In some places the sinking was enough to cause the land to be covered with water during the entire year. This resulted in the death of the timber. Some of this was timber found only on high land. The stumps are still to be seen. In many places the remains of these old trees are still to be seen, sometimes standing up above the water and in other cases entirely submerged. The writer remembers to have seen the bed of Little river, east of Hornersville, at a time of low water, when the stumps of hundreds of trees were visible, showing conclusively that this channel of the river was at one time much higher land. Its level was in all probability changed by the earthquake and the timbers killed by the incoming of the water.

At other places throughout the submerged region old cypress trees are to be found growing in the water, having still a feeble, lingering life in them, although the large bole at the root of the tree which is characteristic of the cypress, is entirely submerged. Some of these old trees were at Coker Landing on Little river and at many other places along that stream.

The sinking of the land is evidenced not alone by the existence of the stumps and trunks of trees killed by the water, but also by the existence of parts of the old banks of Little river. It was said by the inhabitants of the section before the earthquake, that the territory now known as Little river swamps, extending from within New Madrid county to within Dunklin county, was formerly a level plain covered with timber, but not a swamp; and that through this level plain Little river made its way, a stream with high banks and a well defined channel. That this was the case seems to be shown by the fact that at a number of places along the course of Little river there are still to be seen parts of these high banks. Throughout the greater part and course of the river it spreads out over immense territory, with scarcely anything to define its banks; but at places there are seen what are believed to be the remains of its former banks.

One other effect of the earthquake on the land is still to be described, and that is the forcing out upon the surface of water, sand, mud and gas. Bringier says the water forced its way by blowing up the earth with loud explosions. "It rushed out in all quarters bringing with it enormous quantities of carbonized wood reduced mostly into dust, which was ejected to the height of 10 and 15 feet and fell in a black shower mixed with the sand which its rapid motion had forced along. At the same time the roar and whistling produced by the impetuosity of the air escaping from its confinement seemed to increase the horrible disorder. * * * In the meantime the surface was sinking and a black liquid was rising to the saddle-girths of my horse."*

Great quantities of this water were thrown out. Flint says that the amount ejected in the neighborhood of Little Prairie was sufficient to cover a tract many miles in extent from three to four feet deep. Some districts were still covered when he saw them seven years after the earthquake.†

Out of the fissures and small craters there was blown, along with other material of various kinds, great quantities of sand, which came from below the strata of clay which underlies the alluvial top soil of the district. It was in this sand that the lignite was principally contained.

The sand thus ejected formed the sand blows characteristic of part of the New Madrid area. The name seems to have been given them from the fact that the sand was blown out of the craters or fissures. The ordinary sand blow is a patch of sand nearly circular in shape, from 8 to 15 feet across, and a few inches higher than the surrounding soil. Some of them are much larger and many of them are not circular. The material contained in the sand blows is a white quartz sand, mixed in some cases with clay, and in nearly all cases with lignite.

These sand blows at the present time are

* Bringier, Amer. Jour. of Science, 1st Series, Vol. III, p. 15.
† Flint, Recollections of the Last Ten Years, p. 222.

found scattered over a considerable part of the area covered by the earthquake. They do not occur, however, in all parts of it. They are not found immediately along the river nor seldom upon the domes or uplifts previously described. Many of them are to be found in the neighborhood of New Madrid, along the railroad leading to Campbell, about Campbell, in the neighborhood of Lilbourn and Portageville. There are also many between Hayti and Caruthersville, and about Pascola, and some are found on the ridge extending south from Dexter, especially in the southern part of Dunklin county.

The origin of these sand blows, as we have said, seems fairly evident. Out of the cracks opened in the alluvial top soil was forced sand and water in the form of a fountain and the sand was distributed over a small area about this crack.

Besides the sand blows there are certain depressions three to five feet in depth bordered on either side by ridges of sand parallel with one another, which are called sand sloughs. Some of these sloughs are wide and they are found only in the lower lands of the district. It has been considered by some students that they were formed at the time of the earthquake. The fissures which were opened were in many cases large, and out of them were forced enormous quantities of sand, which was piled in ridges coinciding in part with the sides of the fissures and spread over the area between them, helping to form the channel now known as a sand slough.

Of the phenomena of the earthquake among the most interesting are the sinks still to be seen in some places of the earthquake area. They are perhaps the most conspicuous of all the evidences of the shocks and perhaps the rarest. They are circular depressions in the alluvium originally from a few feet up to fifteen yards or more in diameter, and from

5 to 30 feet in depth. Lyell gives this account of the cavities which he saw at New Madrid: "Hearing that some of these cavities still existed near the town, I went to see one of them, three-quarters of a mile to the westward. There I found a nearly circular hollow, 10 yards wide and 5 feet deep, with a smaller one near it, and I observed, scattered about over the surrounding level ground, fragments of black bituminous shale, with much white sand. Within a distance of a few hundred yards were five more of these sand-bursts, or sand blows, as they are sometimes termed here, and rather more than a mile farther west, near the house of Mr. Savors, my guide pointed out to me what he called 'the sink hole where the negro was drowned.' It is a striking object, interrupting the regularity of a flat plain, the sides very steep and 28 feet deep from the top to the water's edge. The water now standing in the bottom is said to have been originally very deep, but has grown shallow by the washing in of sand and the crumbling of the bank caused by the feet of cattle coming to drink. I was assured that many wagon loads of matter were cast up out of this hollow, and the quantity must have been considerable to account for the void; yet the pieces of lignite and the quantity of sand now heaped on the level plain near its borders would not suffice to fill one-tenth part of the cavity. Perhaps a part of the ejected substance may have been swallowed up again and the rest may have been so mixed with water as to have spread like a fluid over the soil."

Bringier says: "The whole surface of the country remained covered with holes which, to compare small things with great, resembled so many craters of volcanoes surrounded with a ring of carbonized wood and sand, which rose to the height of about seven feet. I had occasion a few months after to sound the depth of several of these holes and found them not to exceed 20 feet; but I must remark the quicksand had washed into them."

Perhaps the most noticeable of these sinks still to be found in the earthquake region are along the west side of the Little river bottoms. Just east of the town of Caruth in Dunklin county there are a number of these sinks well defined in portions and still known to the inhabitants as having been caused by the earthquake shocks. They exist, of course, in other parts of the section, but are not numerous. It is difficult to determine exactly how they were caused, but in all probability were the result of the forcing out of large quantities of sand through the cracks in the alluvium, or through the sinking away of the sand at the bottom into the nearby bed of some stream. It must be remembered that the sand was in a semi-fluid condition and would easily flow away through a crack opened in the bank of a stream.

Various conjectures as to the cause of these shocks have been suggested. A few persons at the time advanced the idea that they were caused by volcanic action. This idea was rejected, however, by those acquainted with the country, owing to the absence of any indication of volcanic action. Another opinion was that they were due to disturbances in the mountains to the west.

Some have thought the earthquakes were caused by some change taking place in the alluvial soil itself; they have suggested the caving of the banks of the river, the filling in of underground caverns, the explosion of masses of gas and oil. The quotation of Nuttall in another place refers to the earthquake as caused by the decomposition of beds of lignite near the level of the river and filled with pyrites.

It is sufficient to point out in an analysis of these suggested causes that they are entirely inadequate to account for the violence of the shocks and especially for the wide area over which they were felt. The caving of the banks of the river, no matter how extensive, could have affected the soil for only a few feet, and no explosion of gas could have shaken the western half of the United States. In fact, no disturbance of any character whatever, taking place within the alluvial soil, could have been communicated through the Appalachian mountains to the east coast. There seems to be but one alternative and that is to suppose the earthquakes to have been caused by a movement not in the alluvial soil but in the underlying rocks, which extend not only under the alluvium but also throughout the eastern half of the country. Faulting or other disturbances in these underlying rocks, no matter where originating, might have been communicated to any part of the country, Such movement seems on the whole to be the most probable origin of these tremendous disturbances.

There follow the accounts of a number of persons who witnessed the scenes of the earthquakes or studied them shortly afterward. They are given in order to preserve as many as possible of the facts of that time. The first of these is a letter written in 1816 by Mrs. Eliza Bryan, who at the time of the shock was at New Madrid.

NEW MADRID, Territory of Missouri, March 22, 1816.

On the 16th of December, 1811, about 2 o'clock a. m., we were visited by a violent shock of an earthquake, accompanied by a very awful noise resembling loud, distant thunder, but more hoarse and vibrating, which was followed in a few minutes by a complete saturation of the atmosphere with sulphurous vapor, causing total darkness.

The screams of the affrighted inhabitants running to and fro, not knowing where to go or what to do; the cries of the fowls and beasts of every species; the cracking of trees falling, and the roaring of the Mississippi, the current of which retrograded for a few minutes, owing as is supposed to an eruption in its bed, all formed a scene truly horrible. From that time until nearly sunrise a number of lighter shocks occurred, at which time one still more violent than the first took place, with the same accompaniments as the first, and the terror which had been excited in everyone, and indeed in all animal nature, was now, if possible, doubled. The inhabitants fled in every direction to the country, supposing that there was less danger at a distance from than near the river.

There were several shocks of a day, but lighter than those mentioned, until the 23d of January, 1812, when one occurred as violent as the severest one of the former ones, accompanied by the same phenomena as the former. From this time until the 4th of February the earth was in continual agitation, visibly waving as a gentle sea. On that day there was another shock nearly as hard as the preceding ones. Next day four shocks, and on the 7th about 4 o'clock a. m., a concussion took place so much more violent than those which had preceded it that it was denominated the hard shock. The awful darkness of the atmosphere, which was as formerly saturated with sulphurous vapor, and the violence of the tempestuous thundering noise that accompanied it, together with all the other phenomena mentioned, formed a scene the description of which required the most sublimely fanciful imagination. At first the Mississippi seemed to recede from its banks and its waters gathered up like a mountain, leaving for a moment many boats on the bare sand, in which time the poor sailors made their escape from them. It was then seen rising fifteen or twenty feet perpendicularly and expanding, as it were, at the same moment, the banks were overflowed with a retrograde current rapid as a torrent. The boats which before had been left on the sand were now torn from their moorings and suddenly driven up a creek at the mouth of which they laid, to the distance in some instances of nearly a quarter of a mile. The river falling as rapidly as it had risen, receded within its banks again with such violence that it took with it whole groves of young cottonwood trees which hedged its borders. They were broken off with such regularity in some instances that persons who had not witnessed the fact would be with difficulty persuaded that it had not been the work of art. A great many fish were left on the banks, being unable to keep pace with the water; the river was covered with the wrecks of boats.

In all the hard shocks mentioned the earth was horribly torn to pieces; the surface of hundreds of acres was from time to time covered over, of various depths, by sand which issued from the fissures which were made in great numbers all over this country, some of which closed up immediately after they had vomited forth their sands and water; in some places, however, there was a substance somewhat resembling coal or impure stone coal thrown up with the sands. It is impossible to say what the depth of the fissures or irregular breaks were; we have reason to believe that some of them are very deep. The site of this town was evidently settled down fifteen feet, and not more than half a mile below the town there does not appear to be any alteration on the bank of the river, but back from the river a short distance the numerous large ponds, or lakes, as they were called, were nearly all dried up. The beds of some of them are elevated above their former banks several feet, and lately it has been discovered that a lake was formed on the opposite side of the Mississippi river in the Indian country upwards of one hundred miles in length and from one to six miles in width, of the depth of from ten to fifty feet. It has connection with the river at both ends and it is conjectured the principal part of the Mississippi river will pass that way. We were constrained by the fear of our houses falling to live twelve or eighteen months after the first shocks in little light camps made of boards; but we gradually became callous and returned to our houses again. Most of them who fled from the country in time of the hard shocks have returned home. We have slight shocks occasionally. It is seldom we are more than a week without feeling one and sometimes three or four in a day. There were two this winter past much harder than we have felt them for two years before. Since, they appear to be lighter, and we begin to hope that ere long they will entirely cease.

There is one circumstance worthy of remark; this country was subject to very hard thunder, but for twelve months before the earthquake there was none at all, and but very little since.

Your humble servant,
ELIZA BRYAN.*

Long says that the Missouri Indians believed earthquakes to be the effort of a superior agency connected with the immediate operations of the Master of Life. The earth-

*Le Sieur, in *New Madrid Record*, October 4, 1892.

quakes which in the year 1811 almost destroyed the town of New Madrid on the Mississippi, were very sensibly felt on the upper portion of the Missouri country and occasioned much superstitious dread among the Indians.*

Bradbury, who at the time of the earthquake was on a keel boat not far south of the Chickasaw bluffs, says that on the night of the first shock they had tied their boat to a small island about 500 yards above the entrance to the channel known as the Devil's channel. He was awakened about 10 o'clock in the night by a most tremendous noise accompanied by so violent an agitation of the boat that it appeared in danger of upsetting. He found the other four men on the boat in very great alarm and almost unconscious from terror. When he reached the deck of the boat and could see the river he found it agitated as if by storm and although the noise was inconceivably loud and terrific, he could distinctly hear the fall of trees and the screaming of the wild fowl of the river. After some moments, during which all on the boat thought they would be destroyed, they made their way to the stern of the boat in order to put out a fire which had been kindled on the flat surface of a large rock. By this time the shock had ceased, but they were further frightened by the fact that the perpendicular banks, both above and below the boat, began to fall into the river in such vast masses as to nearly sink the boat by the large swells which it occasioned.

After some difficulty he managed to send two men up the bank of the island to which they were moored to see if the island itself had not been cut in two by the shock; they had suspected this was the fact, owing to the noise which they had heard. Bradbury himself went on shore at about half past two in the morning; just as he was making his way to the shore another shock came, terrible indeed, but not equal to the first. On reaching the shore he found that the bank to which his boat was tied was divided from the rest of the island by a chasm four feet in width and that the bank itself had sunk at least two feet; the chasm which had opened seemed to be about 80 yards in length. A number of other shocks were felt during the night but they were not so violent as the first two. It was noticed that the sound which was heard at the time of every shock always preceded it at least a second and that the sound came every time from the same point and went off in an opposite direction; the shocks seemed to travel from a little north of east to the westward. By daylight they had counted twenty-seven shocks but on landing they were unable to cross the channel, the river at that time was covered with foam and drift timber and had risen considerably, but the boat was still safe.

They observed two canoes floating down the river, in one of which there was some Indian corn and some clothes. They found later that the men who had been in these canoes, as well as some others, had been drowned at the time of the shock. Just as they loosened the boat, preparing to depart, there came another shock almost equal to the first. At intervals during the day there were other shocks, among them a very strong one occurred, and the river was very greatly agitated. Mr. Bridge, one of Bradbury's companions, was standing on the bank during one of these and the shock was so violent that he was almost thrown into the river.

At 11 o'clock that morning there came another violent shock that seemed to affect the men in the boat as seriously as if they had been on the land; the trees on both sides of the river were violently agitated and the

* Long Journal, p. 57.

banks in several places fell into the river, carrying with them innumerable trees. The sounds were very terrifying; the crash of falling timber, the sound of the shock itself, and the screaming of the wild fowl produced an idea that all nature was in a state of dissolution. The river was greatly agitated, so much so, in fact, that Bradbury's companions refused to remain in the boat though he himself was of the opinion that it was much safer there than on the land. The shocks continued from day to day until the 17th. They found the people on the river to be very much alarmed, many of them having fled away, and those that remained were very anxious to do so. Bradbury was told by some of them that a chasm had opened on the sand bar and on closing had thrown water to the height of a tall tree and that chasms had opened in the earth in several places back from the river.*

Flint, on visiting America in 1818, wrote an account of the New Madrid earthquake as reported to him at that time: "During the year 1812 two considerable shocks and many lesser vibrations were observed. It appeared that the center from which the convulsions proceeded were in the vicinity of New Madrid. At that place a dreadful commotion prevailed in December, 1812; the trees beat upon one another and were either twisted or broken, the site of the town subsided about eight feet, many acres of land sunk and were overflowed by the river and the water rushed in torrents from crevices opened in the land, boats were sunk and sunk logs of timber were raised from the bottom in such quantities that almost covered the surface of the river, and that at slight intervals of a few days slight vibrations were felt to the present time. Many of the people deserted their possessions and retreated to the Missouri where lands were granted them by congress.**

Faux quotes a man who lived in Ohio and whom he visited in 1818, as follows: "It shook people out of their beds, knocked down brick chimneys and made old log houses crack and rattle. On the Mississippi, too, the convulsive motion of the water was truly awful, running and rising mountains high and the solid land on the high banks was seen in an undulated agitation like the waters of the sea. New Madrid sunk down several feet, the land, however, in many parts around this town, is covered with water.†

From the proceeds of the land granted to him on account of the New Madrid earthquake, August Chouteau established the first distillery in St. Louis.‡

LeSieur says that at the time of the earthquake there was living on a bayou called Terre Rouge, one of the tributaries of Pemiscot bayou, a man by the name of Culberson. The bayou at that point formed a short curve or elbow and on the point was Culberson's house; between the house and the extreme point was his well and smoke house. On the morning of the 16th of December, 1811, just after a hard shock had subsided, Mrs. Culberson started to the well for water and to the smoke house for meat, and discovered that they were on the opposite side of the river; the shock had opened a new channel across the point between the house and the well.¶

In 1871 Professor Hager asked Mr. LeSieur certain questions concerning this earthquake and these answers, which shed some light on the situation, are reproduced here: "First—

* Bradbury's Travels, p. 204.

** Flint, Letters from America, p. 246.
† Faux, Journal, p. 180.
‡ Early Western Travel, Vol. IV, p. 138.
¶ LeSieur in Weekly Record, Oct. 4, 1893.

That earthquakes in this region of country mentioned in my former communications were never known, nor are there any signs left on the surface of the earth as in that of 1811 and 1812, to indicate that there had ever been any. And in many conversations had with the old men of several tribes—Shawnees, Delawares and Cherokees—all said they had no traditionary account that earthquakes had ever visited the country before.

"Second—With regard to the charcoal mentioned, it may be the kind you mention (albertine, or solidified asphaltum). The peculiar odor of the coal induced the belief that it was impregnated with sulphur, yet it may have been the odor of petroleum. Its smell was unknown to us at that period.

"Third—The water thrown up during the eruption of the 'land waves' was luke warm; so warm, indeed, as to produce no chilly sensation while wading and swimming through it. Since the year 1812 the shakes have been of frequent occurrence, appearing at intervals and not periodical, and seemingly growing less every year.

"Fourth—It would be difficult to say with any degree of certainty how high the water, coal and sand were thrown up. The numerous fissures opened were of different sizes, some twelve to fifteen feet wide, while others were not over four or five feet; by guess I would say the waters, etc., thrown up were from six to ten feet high. Besides these long and narrow fissures the water, sand and coal were thrown out to a considerable height in a circular form, leaving large and deep basins, some of them one hundred yards across and sufficiently deep to retain water during the driest seasons." (LeSieur, *Weekly Record*.)

In order to arrive at some conclusion as to the general and permanent effects of the shocks on the level and the drainage of the country, a description is here inserted of the drainage of the section before the earthquakes. The account as given is condensed from the articles written in 1893 by Mr. Godfrey LeSieur and published in the *Weekly Record* of New Madrid. Mr. LeSieur was familiar with the country and understood the system of drainage. It should be borne in mind that he is describing the streams and lakes as they were before the shocks.

St. James Bayou had its source in Scott county near the southern limit of the Scott County hills and flowed south through Scott, Mississippi and a part of New Madrid counties. It received its waters from cypress ponds and lakes, principally those in Mississippi county. It emptied into the Mississippi river about ten miles northeast of New Madrid.

St. John's bayou, which was from ten to fifteen miles west of St. James, flowed parallel to it. It received its waters from lakes and also from connection with Little river just south of the present town of Benton. This bayou was about forty miles long and emptied into the river at the east side of the town of New Madrid. Eight miles above its mouth it received East bayou. At the point where these two join, the Spaniards, during their occupation of the country, built a water mill, and on a branch of St. John's called Little bayou, which connected with the river, the French built a mill in about 1790. This mill site and, indeed, the entire bayou has dis-

---

The "Personal Narrative of Col. John Shaw of Marquette County, Wisconsin," contained in the second annual report and collections of the State Historical Society of Wisconsin, for the year 1855, gives an account of the New Madrid earthquake of 1811 and 1812: "While lodging about thirty miles north of New Madrid, on the 14th of December, 1811, about

appeared, having been carried away by the river. Both of these bayous, St. James and St. John's, were named by Francois and Joseph LeSieur.

The next stream east of St. John's bayou was Little river, called by the French *Riviere Petite*. It was about seven miles west of New Madrid. About eight miles above New Madrid it flowed for a distance of a mile from a ledge strewn with boulders of bog ore. It received the following tributaries from the east: Otter bayou, which drained the lakes in the north part of the district; the Decypri, a cypress swamp which leaves the Mississippi river at New Madrid and flows into cypress lakes and then into Little river. Two miles South of New Madrid, Bayou Fourche left the Mississippi river, entered Lakes St. Marie and St. Ann, then flowed past La Grande Cote or the Big Mound, and entered Little river. In the early days a ferry across this stream was maintained near this mound. Four miles further south, Bayou Portage flowed out from the Mississippi river, running to the southwest and entering Little river one mile south of Weaverville. This bayou was frequently used for the purposes of transportation.

Barges and keel-boats were accustomed to come up the St. Francois and Little rivers to Weaverville and then pass up through Bayou Portage to the Mississippi. In time of low water it was necessary to make a carry across the ridge which separated a part of the bayou from the Mississippi. This carry was usually made to a point on the river where there was an Indian village; this place was afterward called Point Pleasant. This strip of high ground over which the carry was made came to be called the Portage also. Four miles south of Point Pleasant a low place in the banks of the river allowed the water to flow into a lake which, from its grassy banks, was called Cushion lake. The outlet from Cushion lake to Bayou Portage was called Portage bay. It is upon the bank of this bay that the present town of Portageville is situated. Between Cushion lake and the next large bayou there were a number of small tributaries which flowed from cypress lakes into Little river. Pemiscot bayou drained the lakes and swamps of Pemiscot county and also received water in three different places from the Mississippi river, and finally flowed into Little river.

---

2 o'clock in the morning, occurred a heavy shock of an earthquake. The house where I was stopping was partly of wood and partly of brick structure; the brick portion all fell, but I and the family all fortunately escaped unhurt. At the still greater shock, about 2 o'clock in the morning of the 7th of February, 1812, I was in New Madrid, when nearly two thousand people of all ages, fled in terror from their falling dwellings in that place and the surrounding country, and directed their course north about thirty miles to Tywappity Hill, on the western bank of the Mississippi, and about seven miles back from the river.

This was the first high ground above New Madrid and here the fugitives formed an encampment. It was proposed that all should kneel and engage in supplicating God's mercy and all simultaneously—Catholic and Protestant—knelt and offered solemn prayer to their Creator.

"About twelve miles back towards New Madrid a young woman about seventeen years of age, named Betsy Masters, had been left by her parents and family, her leg having been broken below the knee by the falling of one of the weight poles of the roof of the cabin, and although a total stranger I was the

The tributaries of Little river on the west were principally those that it received from the St. Francois river and will be mentioned in connection with the St. Francois. The St. Francois, for the most of its course within the low lands, made its way east of Crowley's ridge; it entered the low lands from the hills of Upper Louisiana, coming into this section further west and south than Little river. It received many tributaries from the west, but sent out many outlets from its western side to Little river. The first of these western outlets was in the early times called Laque Terrible; it is now called Taylor's slough. It left the St. Francois river four miles south of Chalk bluff, then continued southeast and connected with Little river near the mouth of New river. From Taylor's slough, or Laque Terrible, as it was formerly called, two branches made out on the west side; the first of these was called New river, and the second Old river. Varner's river, which was formerly called Chillitecaux, makes out from the St. Francois, runs to the east, then south and then west, and joins with the St. Francois again. The island thus formed was the last

only person who would consent to return and see whether she still survived. Receiving a description of the locality of the place I started, and found the poor girl upon a bed, as she had been left, with some water and corn bread within her reach. I cooked up some food for her and made her condition as comfortable as circumstances would allow, and returned the same day to the grand encampment. Miss Masters eventually recovered.

"In abandoning their homes on this emergency the people only stopped long enough to get their teams and hurry in their families and some provisions. It was a matter of doubt among them whether water or fire would be most likely to burst forth and cover all the country. The timber land around New Madrid sunk five or six feet, so that the lakes and lagoons, which seemed to have their beds pushed up, discharged their waters over the sunken lands. Through the fissures caused by the earthquake were forced up vast quantities of a hard, jet black substance which appeared very smooth, as though worn by friction. It seemed a very different substance from either anthracite or bituminous coal.

"This hegira, with all its attendant appalling circumstances, was a most heartrending scene and had the effect to constrain the most wicked and profane earnestly to plead to God in prayer for mercy. In less than three months most of these people returned to their homes and though the earthquakes continued occasionally with less destructive effects, they became so accustomed to the recurring vibrations that they paid little or no regard to them, not even interrupting or checking their dances, frolics and vices."

A correspondent of the *Louisiana Gazette*, whose name is not known, wrote from Cape Girardeau on February 15, 1812, the following letter: "The concussions of the earthquake still continue, the shock on the 23rd ult. was more severe and longer than that of December 16th, and the shock of the 7th inst. was still more violent than any preceding and lasted longer perhaps than any on record (from 10 to 15 minutes)—the earth was not at rest for an hour; the ravages of this terrible convulsion having nearly depopulated the district of new Madrid, but few remain to tell the sad tale. The inhabitants have fled in every direction. It has done considerable damage in this place by demolishing chimneys and cracking cellar walls; some have been driven from their houses and a

refuge of the buffalo in this section of the country. This island was divided by a small stream which connected the St. Francois with Varner's river. It was on this stream that there was located the Indian village of Chillitecaux. Five miles south of this village there was another permanent bayou known as Buffalo creek, which finally emptied into Little river.

On the 17th of February, 1815, Congress passed an act for the relief of persons who had sustained losses of real property. This act provided that any person owning lands in New Madrid county on 10th day of November, 1812, and whose lands were materially injured by the earthquake, might locate a like quantity on any public lands of the territory, no location, however, to embrace more than 640 acres.

The provisions of this act led to the celebrated New Madrid claims. Locations were made on some of the most fertile lands in the state in Boone, Howard, Saline and other counties. Many of the claims were filed by persons who had no right to them and who

number are yet in tents. No doubt volcanoes in the mountains of the west which have been extinguished for ages are now reopened." (Goodspeed, History of Southeast Missouri.)

While Long was at Cape Girardeau in 1819 he says: "On the 9th at 4 P. M. a shock of earthquake was felt; the agitation was such as to cause considerable motion of furniture and other loose articles in the room where we were sitting. Several others occurred during our stay at the Cape, but they all happened at night and were all of short duration. Shakes, as these concussions are called by the inhabitants, are in this part of the country extremely frequent and are spoken of as matters of every day occurrence. It is said of some passengers on a steamboat who went on shore at New Madrid and were in one of the houses of the town looking at a collection of books, they felt the house so violently shaken that they were scarce able to stand upon their feet. Some consternation was of course felt, and as several of the persons were ladies, much terror was expressed. 'Don't be alarmed,' said the lady of the house, 'it is nothing but an earthquake.' Several houses in and about Cape Girardeau have frequently been shaken down, forests have been overthrown and other considerable changes produced by their agency. These concussions are felt through a great extent of country, from the settlements on Red river to the fall of the Ohio and from the mouth of the Missouri to New Orleans. Their extent and very considerable degree of violence with which they affect not only large portions of the valley of the Mississippi, but the adjacent hilly country, appear to us to be caused by causes far more efficient and deep seated than the decomposition of beds of lignite or wood coal situated near the bed of the river and filled with pyrites, according to the suggestion of Mr. Nuttall." (Long, Expedition, p. 88.)

In speaking of Point Pleasant, Nuttall says: "This place and several islands below were greatly convulsed by the earthquake and have in consequence been abandoned. I was shown a considerable chasm still far from being filled up, from whence the water of the river, as they say, rushed in an elevated column." He says, also: "In the evening we arrived at the remains of the settlement called Little Prairie, where there is now only a single house, all the rest, together with their foundations, having been swept away by the river soon after the convulsions of the earthquake, sustained their claims by perjury. This is evidenced by the fact that the claims located under this act, presumably by people owning land in New Madrid county, covered more than the entire area of the county.

Out of these grants there arose a very famous lawsuit. It is known in legal history as De Lisle vs. State of Missouri.

The De Lisle family was one of the earliest in New Madrid. Eustache De Lisle and John Baptiste De Lisle came to New Madrid in 1795 from Detroit. They were brothers of the third wife of Francois LeSieur. It should be said that the family continued to reside in New Madrid and that many of its descendants are among the prominent and influential citizens of the county now. In 1808 John Baptiste De Lisle left New Madrid for a visit to his sister, Mrs. Gremar, who then lived in Vincennes, Indiana. This was about the beginning of the war with Great Britain, and De Lisle enlisted in the United States army and served through the war. He then settled in New York, where he married, but was deprived of all of his family during the great epidemic of cholera in 1839. He returned to Vincennes in 1841 and found his sister yet living.

Up to this time he had supposed that his brother, Eustache, and his sister, the wife of Francois LeSieur, had been killed in the earthquakes; he was informed by his sister, however, that his relatives in New Madrid were still living. He at once communicated with them, to their very great astonishment, for they had considered him to be dead; in fact, after his leaving New Madrid in 1808, a report had come back to the post of his death, and they had sold the land that had been granted to him, consisting of 160 arpens of land, for a very small sum. This land had then passed into the hands of the persons who speculated in the land grants after the time of the earthquake. The state of Missouri had given to the purchasers of the Delisle land the right to locate an equal amount of land at some other place in the state and they had located this claim on the Missouri river where the city of Jefferson City now is. This grant from the state included within it the capitol grounds. Now, when John Baptiste De Lisle received this information that the land which he had possessed had passed away from him in this manner and that the state had given to the purchasers of his land a valuable grant, he brought suit against the state of Missouri to have the title to the lands thus granted declared to be in him. After various trials, the case was finally appealed to the Supreme court of the United States. It continued in that court from 1844 to 1862. In that year the court rendered a decision denying the claim of De Lisle to the land.

The earthquakes resulted in an immediate loss of population throughout all the region affected. Most people who could do so moved away at once. Those who remained were either the more determined and daring of the population or they were the poorest who could not afford to leave. The flourishing village

in consequence, as the inhabitants say and as was also affirmed in New Madrid, of the land having sunk 10 feet or more below its former level." (Nuttall Journal, pp. 78-79.)

The force of the shocks was felt over a very wide area and extended as far north as the Missouri river. Flagg, who visited Cape Girardeau in 1836, says that the great earthquake of 1811 agitated the site of Cape Girardeau very severely, many brick houses were shattered, chimneys thrown down and other damage effected, traces of the repairs of which are yet to be viewed. (Flagg, Far West, p. 87.)

of Little Prairie which, in 1803, had a population of 103, almost entirely disappeared. Only a few families remained. Among them was Col. J. H. Walker, who was not frightened enough to leave. New Madrid suffered greatly in the same way, the population showing a great falling off shortly after the shocks. The same thing was true of the settlements and small villages all over the district.

CHAPTER XV

STATEHOOD ATTAINED

Petition for Organization as a State—Bill to Organize a State Government — The Slavery Controversy—The Tallmadge Amendment—Debate Over the Amendment—Deadlock of the Two Houses—The Missouri Compromise—Feeling in the State—The Constitutional Convention—Members from the Southeast—The Constitution in Congress—Further Opposition to Admission — The Debate — Clay's Compromise — The Solemn Public Act—The President's Proclamation Admitting the State—Peculiarities of the Transaction—State Boundaries — Missouri — Arkansas — Wolf Island.

The territory of Missouri grew, as we have seen, very rapidly in wealth and population. The people, though living since 1816 under the third or highest form of territorial government, desired to be organized as a state and to be admitted to the Union. Accordingly, we find that in 1817 a number of petitions were drawn up and circulated among the people of the territory asking Congress to authorize the organization of a state government. Most of these petitions were lost, but recently Mr. Bartholdt, a member of Congress from St. Louis, found one of the copies and had it framed and preserved. It is set out below:

"Memorial of the Citizens of Missouri Territory—To the Honorable, the Senate and the House of Representatives of the United States of America in Congress Assembled:—The petition of the undersigned inhabitants of the Territory of Missouri respectfully showeth: That your petitioners live within that part of the Territory of Missouri which lies between the latitudes of 36 degrees and 30 minutes and 40 degrees north, and between the Mississippi river to the east and the Osage boundary to the west. They pray that they may be admitted into the Union of the states with these limits.

"They conceive that their numbers entitle them to the benefits and to the rank of a state government. Taking the progressive increase during former years as the basis of the calculation they estimate their present numbers at 40,000 souls. Tennessee, Ohio and the Mississippi state were admitted with smaller numbers, and the treaty of cession guarantees this great privilege to your petitioners as soon as it can be granted under the principles of the Federal Constitution. They have passed eight years in the first grade of territorial government, five in the second; they have evinced their attachment to the honor and integrity of the Union during the late war and they with deference urge their right to become a member of the great republic. They forbear to dilate upon the evils of the territorial government but will barely name among the grievances of this condition:

"1. That they have no vote in your honorable body and yet are subject to the indirect taxation imposed by you.

"2. That the veto of the territorial executive is absolute upon the acts of the territorial legislature.

"3. That the Superior Court is constructed on principles unheard of in any other system of jurisprudence, having primary cognizance of almost every controversy, civil and criminal, and subject to correction by no other tribunal.

"4. That the powers of the territorial legislature are limited to the passage of laws of a local nature owing to the paramount authority of Congress to legislate upon the same subject."

And after describing the boundaries of the proposed new state the memorialists say that the boundaries, as solicited, will include the country to the north and west to which the Indian title has been extinguished, also the body of the population; that the Missouri river will run through the center of the state; that the boundaries are adapted to the country; that "the woodland districts are found towards the great rivers; the interior is composed of vast ridges and naked and sterile plains stretching to the Shining mountains;" and that the country north and south of the Missouri is necessary to each other, the former possessing a rich soil destitute of minerals, the latter abounding in mines of lead and iron and thinly sprinkled with spots of ground fit for cultivation. In conclusion the memorialists say that they "hope that their voice may have some weight in the division of their country and in the formation of their state boundaries; and that statesmen ignorant of its localities may not undertake to cut out their territory with fanciful divisions which may look handsome on paper, but must be ruinous in effect."

This petition was signed by Jacob Petit, Isaac W. Jameson, Sam S. Williams and others, nearly all of whom were at the time citizens of Washington county. The memorial was presented to Congress in January, 1818, but no action seems to have been taken upon it, nor upon other similar or perhaps identical petitions presented at the same time. In December of the same year, however, the territorial assembly of Missouri drew up a memorial on the same subject, which was presented to Congress by John Scott of Ste. Genevieve, the territorial delegate. This memorial was thereupon presented to a committee for consideration and report. This committee reported in favor of the organization of a state government in Missouri, and a bill was drawn and presented to the house for that purpose. The consideration of this bill precipitated a great discussion and brought to the front for the first time, in an acute way, the slavery question.

To understand the history of this bill and the great controversy that raged over the admission of the state, we must recall the situation that existed in the Union. The slavery question was already exciting people. It had not yet come to be regarded with such passionate earnestness as a moral question as it was later destined to be considered, but as a political question it was already before the people. A fierce contest raged between the north and south for the control of Congress. Power in political affairs had for some years vacillated between slave and free states. A few years prior to the introduction of this bill the north had a preponderance in both houses of Congress. That preponderance still maintained so far as the house was concerned. The organization of Alabama and its pending admission, however, threatened to increase the already superior power of the south in the senate. It was this political situation, the desire to control Congress, rather than opposition to slavery as an institution, that caused the opposition to the organization of Missouri. If Missouri and Alabama should both come into the Union as slave states, as was very probable, then the balance of power would be destroyed and the south would have a very great preponderance in the senate. It was determined to prevent this if possible.

It was considered almost certain that if the people of Missouri were left free to determine the question of slavery in the state for themselves that the constitution of the state would permit the existence of the institution. Some way must be accordingly found by which the matter of determining the question could be taken out of the hands of the people and transferred to Congress. It had been suggested, in the case of Alabama, that a provision in the act permitting the organization of the state, require the prohibition of slavery as a condition precedent to its admission. It was objected to this course, however, that when Georgia ceded the territory out of which Alabama was subsequently organized it was stipulated that no restriction should be placed upon slavery. This was regarded as standing in the way of any attempt to dictate to the people of the state their attitude toward it. Accordingly nothing was said concerning slavery in the act authorizing the admission of Alabama. It was felt, however, that some provision must be made concerning slavery in Missouri.

Accordingly, Mr. Tallmadge of New York, moved to amend the bill by inserting the following provision: "And provided that the further introduction of slavery or involuntary servitude be prohibited, except for punishment of crimes, whereof the party shall have been duly convicted, and that all children born within the said state after the admission thereof into the Union shall be free at the age of twenty-five years."

The debate over this amendment was long and bitter. The opponents of the amendment contended that such action was contrary to the action of Congress in the admission of Kentucky, Tennessee, Louisiana, Mississippi and Alabama, all of which had been admitted as slave states without such provision; that it violated the treaty entered into with France at the time of the cession of Louisiana, one clause of which guaranteed to the people of that territory, including Missouri, the possession of their property. It was urged that if Congress had respected the provision made by Georgia in ceding Alabama, then it should respect the treaty obligations of the government of the United States. It was further urged that such a clause, hampering the free action of the people of a state, was beyond the power of Congress to make, and therefore unconstitutional; that it put a stigma upon the people of Missouri, in that it did not admit them upon equal terms with the other states; and finally, that if the clause were inserted in the state constitution it could be repealed or amended at any time by action of the people of Missouri.

The friends of the amendment contended that the very fact that Congress could admit or reject a state was sufficient evidence that it possessed the power to prescribe the terms of admission; that the fact that slavery was morally wrong; that it was a political and economic evil existing only by virtue of local laws, conferred on Congress the right and power to supersede, if necessary, treaty obligations, and take those measures needed for the best interests of the country.

After long debate the amendment passed the house, but the amended bill was rejected by the senate, and the fifteenth Congress adjourned with a deadlock between the houses. The question was presented to the sixteenth Congress in December, 1819. Neither house seemed ready to recede from its position, but a new element entered into the discussion. Maine had applied for admission to the Union. It would come in, if admitted, as a free state. Its admission was desired by those who wished to place a restriction on the admission of Missouri. The senate, therefore, at the suggestion of Senator Jesse B. Thomas, of Illinois, united the measures for the two states into one bill. It was declared by those opposed to the restriction on Missouri that, unless that restriction was abandoned and Missouri admitted on terms of equality with other states, Maine should not be admitted at all. The debate over this matter continued for several weeks. A deadlock again occurred between the two houses. Out of that disagreement came the measures which are collectively known as the Missouri Compromise.

Maine was admitted as a free state; the people of Missouri were authorized to form a government without any clause in the act referring to slavery, and it was stipulated that slavery should be excluded from "all the territory ceded by France to the United States, under the name of Louisiana, north of thirty-six degrees and thirty minutes north latitude," except, of course, Missouri.

This series of measures known as the Missouri Compromise was approved on March 6, 1820. As we have said, this authorized the formation of a state government in Missouri; but, contrary to the usual practice, did not provide for the admission of the state into the Union. The people had no sort of guarantee that they would be admitted, even after the formation of their government. In pursuance of the terms of the act, an election was held in the territory in May, 1820, to select members of a constitutional convention. This convention was empowered, by the terms under which its members were elected, to determine by majority whether it was expedient for them to frame a constitution, and, if considered expedient, to proceed to the work of making the constitution. If, on the other hand, they felt that it was not the time for this work, they were authorized to provide for the election of another convention.

It is quite probable that a constitution favoring slavery would have been adopted in the state, no matter at what time the members of the convention had been elected. What was a mere probability, however, became a certainty, owing to the feeling of irritation over the attempted restriction on what was felt to be the right of the people of the state to decide the slavery question for themselves free from the dictation of Congress. John Scott had declared during the discussion of the Tallmadge amendment that the proposed limitation of the power of the people was an insult to them, and this was the prevailing sentiment in the state. Under such conditions the members of the constitutional convention were chosen and they were for a slavery constitution by a large majority.

This convention met in St. Louis, June 12, 1820. Its sessions were held in the hotel at the corner of Third and Vine streets, known as the "Mansion House." There were forty-one members of the convention. The Southeast Missouri members were as follows: From

Cape Girardeau county, Stephen Byrd, James Evans, Richard S. Thomas, Alexander Buckner and Joseph McFerron; Jefferson county, Daniel Hammond; Madison county, Nathaniel Cook; New Madrid county, Robert D. Dawson and Christopher G. Houts; Ste. Genevieve county, John D. Cook, Henry Dodge, John Scott and R. T. Brown; Washington county, John Rice Jones, Samuel Perry and John Hutchings; Wayne county, Elijah Bettis. David Barton, of St. Louis, was made president of the convention and William G. Pettis, secretary.

The convention was in session for a little more than a month, adjourning July 19, 1820. It was at once agreed that a constitution should be framed and the month the convention was in session was devoted to this work. The constitution thus made was in force in this state until superseded by the Drake constitution in 1865. It was comparatively short, concise in statement, and was evidently the work of a statesman and thinker. It sanctioned slavery, as was almost certain in any case, but doubly so after the attempted restriction by Congress. This constitution, under the terms of the election of the members of the convention, did not require to be submitted to the people of the state for their approval; it became effective at once, upon the close of the convention.

The second session of the sixteenth Congress met November 13, 1820, and on the 16th of November Mr. Scott, the delegate from Missouri, presented to the house a copy of the constitution of the state. This constitution was referred to the committee which reported on the 23rd, reciting the fact that Congress had previously authorized the formation of the state government; that the people of the state had held the convention and formed the constitution; and that said constitution "is Republican and in conformity with the provisions of said act." Accompanying this preamble was a resolution to admit the state into the Union on equal terms with the other states.

Doubtless it was supposed by the people of the state that there would be no further difficulty over its admission. They had complied with the terms of the act authorizing the formation of a government. That act contained no prohibition on slavery and it would seem that there was no possible ground on which the state might be refused admission. In spite of these facts, the resolution to admit the state was very bitterly fought. The ostensible ground of objection was the following clause in the constitution itself: "It shall be their duty, as soon as may be, to pass such laws as may be necessary to prevent free negroes and mulattos from coming to and settling in this state under any pretext whatsoever."

The opponents of the admission of Missouri argued that this clause in the constitution of the state was in direct violation of that clause in the constitution of the United States which guarantees equal privileges in all the states to the citizens of each state, of which privileges the right of emigration is one. On the other hand, it was pointed out that similar clauses controlling emigration existed in the constitutions of a number of states and that no objection had ever been raised to them; and it was further pointed out that if this clause was in reality in opposition to the constitution of the United States, it would be declared null and void by the supreme court of the United States.

It is clear, of course, that the real ground of objection to the admission of Missouri was not this paragraph. The motive of the men who opposed Missouri was not to protect the rights of a few negroes who might possibly wish to move to Missouri. In spite of the fact that the Missouri Compromise had been agreed to, there were a large number of the members of the house who had determined that the state should never be admitted as a slave state, and their real motive was the desire to keep the state from being admitted until a constitution prohibiting slavery should be adopted.

The debate on this resolution was one of the fiercest that ever took place in Congress. The whole country was stirred to fever heat by the charges and counter charges, by the threats of cession and the breaking up of the Union that were made on both sides. The whole institution of slavery was attacked with utmost vehemence and the right of the people of the states to decide this question for themselves was defended with equal fervor. After several weeks of debate, and at a time when it seemed the very foundations of the government itself would crumble; when fear was present everywhere that the Union could not long survive, Henry Clay, of Kentucky, introduced a resolution, which was adopted, providing that a committee of twenty-three members should be appointed by the senate and the house, who should take the whole matter under consideration and make a report to Congress. After long discussion, this committee reported to each house of Congress, February 26, 1821, a resolution which provided that Missouri should be admitted to the Union on an equal footing with the original states upon the fundamental condition that the 4th clause of the 26th section of the 3rd article of the constitution—the clause which forbade immigration of negroes—should never be construed to authorize the passage of any law by which any citizen of either of the states should be excluded from the enjoyment of any of the privileges to which he is entitled under the constitution of the United States. The resolution further provided that the legislature of Missouri by a solemn public act should declare the assent of the state to this fundamental condition, and should transmit to the president of the United States a copy of their actions. The president was thereupon authorized to issue a proclamation reciting the fact that the legislature had passed such an act and that upon the making of this proclamation the admission to Missouri should be considered as complete.

The resolution so reported was adopted on February 28th. The reason for referring the matter to the president and making his proclamation the basis for the final admission of the state, rather than an act of Congress, was to avoid any further discussion or agitation of a question which was felt to be dangerous to the safety of the country. All that remained to be done, under the terms of this resolution was for the legislature of the state to publish the solemn public act required of it. In order to do this, Governor Clark convened the legislature in special session June 24, 1821, and on June 26th the legislature adopted the following act: "Forasmuch as the good people of this state have, by the most solemn and public act in their power, virtually assented to the said fundamental condition, when, by their representatives in full and free convention assembled, they adopted the constitution of this state, and consented to be incorporated into the federal Union, and governed by the constitution of the United States, which, among other things, provides that the said constitution and laws of the United States, made in pursuance thereof, and all treaties made or which shall be made under the authority of the United States, shall be the supreme law of the land; and the judges in every state shall be bound thereby, anything in the constitution or law of any state to the contrary notwithstanding. And although this general assembly do most solemnly declare that the Congress of the United States have no constittuional power to annex any condition to the admission of this state into the federal Union, and that this general assembly have no power to change the operation of the constitution of this state, except in the mode prescribed in the constitution itself, nevertheless, as the Congress of the United States has desired this general assembly to declare the assent of this state to said fundamental condition, and forasmuch as such declaration will neither restrain nor enlarge, limit nor extend, the operation of the constitution of the United States or of this state; but the said constitution will remain in all respects as if the said resolution had never passed, and the desired declaration was never made; and because such declaration will not divest any power or change the duties of any of the constitutional authorities of this state or of the United States, nor impair the rights of the people of this state, or impose any additional obligation upon them, but may promote an earlier enjoyment of their vested federal rights, and this state being, moreover, determined to give to her sister states and to the world the most unequivocal proof of her desire to promote the peace and harmony of the Union, therefore

"Be it enacted and declared by the general assembly of the state of Missouri, and it is hereby solemnly and publicly enacted and declared, That this state has assented and does assent that the fourth clause of the twenty-sixth section of the third article of the constitution of this state shall never be construed to authorize the passage of any law, and that no law shall be passed in conformity thereto, by which any citizen, of either of the United States, shall be excluded from the enjoyment of any of the privileges and immunities to which such citizens are entitled under the constitution of the United States."

This act was transmitted to the president who, on August 10, 1821, made a proclamation announcing the admission of Missouri into the Union.

It is evident that this is one of the most remarkable transactions ever made by a legislative body. The whole matter of the controversy over the admission of Missouri is a striking evidence of the terrible passion that stirred the minds of men over the question of slavery. Prejudices were so strong they seemed to have blinded men's eyes to some very obvious things.

The first of these compromises which is distinctly known as the Missouri Compromise, whose author was Honorable Jesse B. Thomas, provided that the people of the state should be left free to organize a state government, without any restriction as to their action concerning slavery. It was well known at the time that, in all human probability, the constitution so formed would permit the holding of slaves and in return for this permission, if it may be so considered, the friends of slavery agreed to the exclusion of it from all the vast domain of the Louisiana Purchase north of the parallel of 36 degrees and 30 minutes. It can hardly be called a compromise, for the friends of slavery conceded practically everything and gained nothing.

Under the terms of this act the people of the state framed a constitution which allowed slavery, and presented it to Congress, in the full expectation that the state would be admitted. They found themselves opposed by a large number of their original opponents; this time on the ground that one article in their proposed constitution was in opposition to the constitution of the United States. This opposition to the admission of Missouri was strong enough to prevent all action upon the bill for a number of weeks. Quite probably, it was strong enough to keep the state out of the Union for an indefinite period. The matter was settled by another compromise. It, too, can hardly be termed a compromise, for it was also one-sided. At this time, however, the opposition conceded practically everything. They agreed that the offending clause in the fundamental law of Missouri should remain as it was. This concession they made, provided the legislature of the state should pass a solemn public act setting aside a clause in the constitution of the state. The legislature evidently had no authority or power to amend or in any way change the constitution and any solemn public act of theirs which attempted to do so was a mere farce. The word solemn, indeed, would hardly be applied to an act having the preamble that this act carries with it, for the legislature of the state quite evidently regarded the thing they were attempting to do as entirely beyond their power and authority.

Out of all the contention and bitterness, out of the conflicting claims and so-called compromises, one fact emerges with clearness and distinctness, and that is that Missouri was admitted to the Union and became the twenty-fourth state.

The constitutional convention which closed its labors July 19, 1820, in accordance with the terms of the act of Congress providing for the organization of the state government in Missouri, framed and adopted an ordinance which was expressly declared by its terms to be forever irrevocable and binding on the people of the state. This ordinance had in it five sections, which were designed to carry into effect five different demands made on the people by Congress. The first of these sections set aside the 16th section of every township in the state for school purposes. The second section of the ordinance dedicated the salt springs of the state, not to exceed twelve in number with six sections of land adjoining each of these springs, to the state. The third section set aside five per cent of the net proceeds of the state land for the purpose of building roads and canals. The fourth section provided that four sections of land should be set aside at the point afterward to be selected for the state capitol. The fifth section provided that one entire township should be reserved and forever dedicated to the purpose of a seminary of learning.

The convention inserted in the ordinance, however, a request that Congress should so modify its demand that five per cent of the net proceeds of the land should be set aside for roads and canals, so as to permit the fund bonus arising to be used not only for roads and canals, but also for school purposes.

The southern boundary of the state, as suggested in the memorial presented to Congress asking for the organization of a state government, was fixed at the parallel of 36 degrees and 30 minutes north latitude. It was so fixed on the theory that this left 3½ degrees south of the state for the territory of Arkansas.

This boundary was not at all satisfactory to people who lived in Little Prairie, now called Caruthersville. The settlements along Black river and White river were also dissatisfied with the suggested boundary. They did not wish to be attached to the territory of Arkansas. Another petition was presented to Congress in March, 1818, asking that the territory south of Missouri river be formed into a separate state. It was to be extended further to the west than the proposed western boundary of Missouri which, at that time, was fixed at the western limit of the Osage Purchase.

In 1818, on November 22nd, the territorial legislature adopted a memorial to Congress for the admission of Missouri as a state, and proposed new boundaries for the state. It is probable that the agitation over the southern boundary was carried on in the legislature by Stephen Ross of New Madrid county, in the house of Dr. Robert D. Dawson, also of New Madrid county, in the legislative council, and by the members from Laurence county, as it was then constituted, which were: Perry Magness, Joseph Harden and John Davidson. It was their desire that the boundary should be moved far enough south to include the principal settlements on the Mississippi and also on White river. Owing, doubtless, to their influence, this memorial fixed the southern boundary as follows: "Beginning at a point in the middle of the main channel of the Mississippi river at the 36th degree of north latitude and running in a direct line to the mouth of Black river, a branch of White river; thence in the middle of the main channel of White river to where the parallel of 36 degrees and 30 minutes north latitude crosses the same; thence with that parallel of latitude due west."

This memorial, with its proposed boundaries, was the subject of considerable debate in Congress, and after this discussion, the southern boundary was fixed as it now stands, that is to say, running west from the Mississippi on the parallel of 36 degrees to the St. Francois river; thence up and in the middle of the main channel thereof to a parallel of 36 degrees and 30 minutes, and thence west. There can be no doubt that the man most influential in securing the joining of the territory now included in Dunklin and Pemiscot counties to Missouri, was J. Hardeman Walker. He was at that time a most influential, energetic resident of Little Prairie and he carried on a vigorous agitation to secure the extension of the southern boundary to include this territory. It is quite probable that he had the assistance of other representatives from Southeast Missouri, including John Scott, the territorial delegate, Alexander Buckner, John James Evans, Judge Richard S. Thomas and Dr. Dawson.

Those who were interested in this extension of the boundary and the inclusion of the territory in Missouri were actuated by a number of motives: one was the feeling that Little Prairie and the other settlements in what is now Pemiscot county were really a part of Missouri. They had been made about the same time of the Missouri settlements, they had practically the same population, and were engaged in the same general industries. Their trade and association had been very largely with Missouri, and for this reason they regarded themselves as a part of the territory of Missouri. It was natural, too, for them to wish to be a part of a territory which was about to be admitted into the Union as a state. The advantages of state government over territorial government are obvious, and it was felt that it might be some years before the territory of Arkansas would be admitted as a state. These reasons, along with others of a similar nature, moved the men mentioned to vigorous effort to fix the boundary of the state as it now stands.

The only other boundary dispute directly concerning Southeast Missouri occurred at a later date, but is here given as it rounds out the story of the state's boundaries in this section.

One of the longest boundary disputes in the history of the United States was carried on between Kentucky and Missouri over the possession of Wolf Island, which lies just below Belmont and is the largest in the Mississippi river, having an area of 15,000 acres. The main channel of the river lies east of the island and it is separated from the west bank by a narrow channel so that it seems to belong to Missouri. When the state boundaries were defined in 1820 Wolf Island was left as a part of Kentucky because at that time the channel of the river was west of the island. After a time, however, the channel shifted to the east and the island came to be claimed as a part of Missouri. Most people regard it as belonging to New Madrid county and at one time a man living on the island was elected sheriff of New Madrid county. Kentucky, however, claimed jurisdiction over the island and finally the state of Missouri, by its attorney general, brought suit in the supreme court of the United States for possession of the island. The case was tried by a number of distinguished lawyers on each side and was before the court for eleven years. Kentucky was represented by John J. Crittenden, Garret Davis and Henry Stanberry. Missouri was represented by Governor Blair and F. A. Dick. During the course of the trial a great many persons were examined and a great many old books and maps produced in evidence in order to determine the location of the channel of the river in the early days. It was shown by most of the maps that the main channel was east of the island and witnesses said that from 1850 back to 1830 the main channel was east of the island and that from 1830 to 1794 both channels were navigable. It was shown also that the land was surveyed by United States surveyor in 1821 as part of Missouri; other witnesses, however, introduced by Kentucky, testified that the channel of the river was west of the island during most of this period and that about the year 1830 there was enough water for boats between the island and Kentucky; it was also shown that Kentucky had exercised continuous authority over the island since 1792 when it came into the possession of the title formerly held by Virginia. The court also heard evidence to show that the soil and the plant life of the island were similar in character to those of the Kentucky side and dissimilar to those on the Missouri side. It was also shown that the level of the island was the same as that of the second bottom of the Kentucky side and four or five feet higher than the western bank. These considerations, together with the fact that Kentucky had had jurisdiction over the island for a great number of years, decided the question in favor of Kentucky.

SECTION IV

Period 1820-1860—Town Histories

CHAPTER XVI

GENERAL DEVELOPMENT

ANALYSIS OF POPULATION, 1820-1830—COMPARATIVE CENSUS TABLE, 1820-1860—FRENCH AND GERMAN ELEMENTS—PERIOD OF TOWN GROWTH.

In 1820, when the state was organized, just before its admission to the Union, the population of Southeast Missouri was as follows:

Cape Girardeau county.......5,968
Jefferson county............1,835
Madison county..............2,047
New Madrid county..........2,296
Ste. Genevieve county........4,962
Washington county...........2,769
Wayne county...............1,443

Of this population, the greater part were white people, but there were a few free negroes and several hundred slaves. The population grew very rapidly for a number of years after the admission of the state into the Union. Southeast Missouri still had all the advantages which had attracted men to it in the earlier days and, added to this now, was the fact that it was part of a regularly organized state which had been admitted into the Union. The people were, as far as possible, under our republican form of government, self-governing, and from every part of the Union there was a movement toward the new state.

In 1830 the population of the counties in the southeast was as follows:

Cape Girardeau county.......7,445
Jefferson county............2,592
Madison county..............2,371
New Madrid county..........2,350
Perry county................3,349
St. Francois county.........2,366
Scott county................2,136
Washington county...........6,784
Wayne county...............3,264
Ste. Genevieve county.......2,186

ANALYSIS OF POPULATION, 1820-1830

It will be observed that in this decade the principal growth of population was in Washington county. This was due, largely, to the development of the mining industry in this county. Some of the counties, notably Ste. Genevieve, decreased in population, but this was owing to a cutting off of some of the territory in order to form new counties and not to an actual loss of population in the county itself.

The population of Southeast Missouri increased steadily during this period of its history. This is especially true of the counties along the Mississippi river and the settlements in adjoining counties. Those which lay further back and were, consequently, more difficult of access, as was the case in Carter, Ripley, Butler and Dunklin counties, grew in population much more slowly. They were separated too far from river transportation, and they were unprovided with either railroads or ordinary roads over which traveling could be easily made and were, therefore, almost cut off from any easy or regular communication with the different parts of the country. It is true that even in these counties settlements were made during this period and that by the close of it there were considerable numbers of people to be found in their limits, but their growth was nothing like the rapid growth of the counties along the river. The same causes which operated to increase rapidly the population of the section after the purchase of Louisiana operated with even more force to increase the population after the admission of the state into the Union. More and more people were attracted by the richness of the soil, the advantages of the climate and the possibility of earning a living and a competence which was offered to rich and poor alike. Most of the settlers who came were farmers who scattered themselves over the territory, opening up new farms and clearing away the wilderness. The section was distinctly agricultural in its life, with the exception of the mining region, and even there, as we have noted, most of the people depended in part at least upon farming for a living. A table is here inserted showing the population of each of the counties in the southeast at each of the census periods from 1820 to 1860, and also the total population at each date:

COMPARATIVE CENSUS TABLE, 1820-1860

Counties.	1820	1830	1840	1850	1860
Bollinger	....	....	....	....	7,371
Butler	....	....	....	1.616	2,891
Cape Girardeau	5,968	7,445	9,359	13,912	15,547
Carter	....	....	....	....	1,235
Dunklin	....	....	....	1,229	5,026
Iron	....	....	....	....	5,842
Jefferson	1,835	2,592	4,296	6,928	10,344
Madison	2,047	2,371	3,395	6,003	5,664
Mississippi	....	....	....	3,123	4,859
New Madrid	2,296	2,350	4,554	5,541	5,654
Pemiscot	....	....	....	....	2,962
Perry	....	3,349	5,760	7,215	9,128
Reynolds	....	....	....	1,849	3,173
Ripley	....	....	2,856	2,830	3,747
St. Francois	....	2,366	3,211	4,964	7,249
Ste. Genevieve	4,962	2,186	3,148	5,313	8,029
Scott	....	2,136	5,974	3,182	5,247
Stoddard	....	....	3,153	4,277	7,877
Washington	2,769	6,784	7,213	8,811	9,023
Wayne	1,443	3,264	3,403	4,518	5,629
Total	21,320	34,843	56,322	81,311	130,497

FRENCH AND GERMAN ELEMENTS.

These figures show that increase in population had been both steady and rapid. The greater numbers of those who came to the territory came from other states, so that the population of Southeast Missouri, outside of the older settlements, was largely American. In a few counties there was a considerable sprinkling of other settlers. The greater number of French were to be found in Ste. Genevieve county, though there were considerable numbers of them in New Madrid county.

German settlers were found in Cape Girardeau county in large numbers, and in somewhat smaller numbers in Scott, Bollinger and Perry counties. Of course, there was a sprinkling of foreigners in other counties, but the population, with the exception of the counties noted, was very largely American in character. It is to be noted that the presence of large numbers of Germans and other foreign settlers in Cape Girardeau and surrounding counties was one of the things which determined the action of Missouri at the outbreak of the Civil War. If it had not been for the presence of these people who were loyal to the Union, it is highly probable that the movement for secession in the state would have been successful, and Missouri would have aligned herself with the Confederate States government.

The German element in the population of Southeast Missouri is found largely in Perry and Cape Girardeau counties. There were a few German families in Ste. Genevieve in its early years; the most prominent German family in Ste. Genevieve county was a family named Ziegler; there were three brothers of this name, Martin, Francis and Sebastian, who settled in the vicinity of Ste. Genevieve quite early in its history. About 1840 the German settlers came to New Offenburg and Zell; these German families were mostly Catholics.

In 1839 a colony of Germans made their home in Perry county. These were Lutherans and came to America largely on account of dissatisfaction with religious teachings at home. Their leader was Martin Stephan. They came from a number of places in Germany and numbered more than seven hundred at the time of their sailing from Bremen. One of the five ships on which the party sailed was lost at sea. The others arrived at New Orleans in January, 1839, and continued their travels until they reached St. Louis on February 19th of the same year and remained there until the following June. Before sailing from Germany the colonists had collected a common fund of more than $100,000, and after reaching St. Louis they purchased lands in the southeastern part of Perry county out of this fund; they secured 4,400 acres for the sum of $10,000, and most of the colonists removed to this place from St. Louis. They suffered very great hardships for a number of years, as the land had to be cleared and some of it was of very little value. Before they succeeded in building houses they lived in tents and log cabins and the exposure resulted in sickness and death. Stephan, who as their leader, had control of affairs, proved to be incapable and had to be deposed. Somewhat later the land which had been held in common was distributed among the colonists and this lead to very great improvements in their condition.

About 1840 another lot of colonists to the number of 75, under the leadership of Rev. Maximilian Oertel, established themselves at Wittenberg. They were Lutherans, also, but their leader, Oertel, soon afterward returned to New York and there became a Catholic priest.

The German settlers of Cape Girardeau county began to come to the county in 1834; the first of these were Otto Buehrman, William Cramer and Rev. Frederick Picker. They located on farms in the Big Bend. The Cramers and Picker came from Hanover and Buehrman from Brunswick. Shortly after his arrival, Rev. Mr. Picker removed to the settlement on Whitewater and Cramer and John Anthony removed to Cape Girardeau and engaged in the manufacture of cigars.

George H. Cramer, who was the son of William Cramer, lived in Cape Girardeau for a number of years and was a very highly respected citizen, holding the office of mayor on several occasions. Hon. Wilson Cramer of Jackson, is a son of George H. Cramer. Of the family of Otto Buehrman there are still descendants living within the county and until within a few years one of his grandsons was a merchant in Cape Girardeau. In 1835 William Bierwirth, with his family, Daniel Bertling, Henry Friese and Chris Schatte came to Cape Girardeau county from Germany and since that time there has been a stream of German immigration. The settlement in the neighborhood of Dutchtown was made about 1835-36 by families from Switzerland. It was among these families that the German Evangelical church was organized in 1838.

Growth of Towns

We have said that the period was principally one in which the population of the country increased and farms were opened, but there was also a growth of the towns. With the coming of larger numbers of people, trade increased and therefore the trading centers grew rapidly in population. More and more men became interested in buying and selling goods, in the establishment of banks, and in a few cases, the establishment of factories of various kinds. These things were concentrated in the towns of the section and, accordingly, we find all of these towns having a prosperous history, and the new towns constantly springing up in every part of the district. We have previously referred to the history of more important towns in the section, and it will be the purpose in this to continue the story of these towns, and to trace the founding, and history of those whose story begins within the period we are now discussing.

CHAPTER XVII

STE. GENEVIEVE AND ST. MARYS.

SHIPPING CENTER OF MINERAL REGION—STE. GENEVIEVE-IRON MOUNTAIN PLANK ROAD—150TH ANNIVERSARY CELEBRATED—U. S. SENATORS FROM STE. GENEVIEVE—STE. GENEVIEVE OF TODAY—ST. MARYS.

Ste. Genevieve, the oldest town in the state, continued its period of prosperity during the greater part of these years—1820 to 1860. The successful application of steam to the propulsion of boats on the Mississippi river added very greatly to the river commerce and all the towns situated on the river reaped the benefit of this increase. Ste. Genevieve in particular was fortunate in this matter.

SHIPPING CENTER OF MINERAL REGION.

Until the construction of the Iron Mountain railroad, Ste. Genevieve was the shipping point for almost all the mineral region. The lead from Washington and Jefferson counties, and the iron from Iron county was all brought to Ste. Genevieve to be reshipped upon boats. From 1846, when the iron industry became very important, until the year 1858, when the Iron Mountain Railroad reached that region the quantities of iron which went by Ste. Genevieve were very large, indeed. The town became one of the greatest commercial centers of the state. The lead and iron traffic was like a living stream of prosperity that poured by the town. The building of the railroad, however, and the consequent change in the shipping point from St. Genevieve to St. Louis marked the beginning of the town's decline. It is hardly too much to say that had the railroad been built from Ste. Genevieve to the mining region, rather than from St. Louis, the probabilities are that Ste. Genevieve, rather than the latter town, might have become the great commercial city of the state.

As is set out in the chapter on schools and education, one of the principal things which marks the history of the town during these years was the establishment and conduct of schools. The Ste. Genevieve academy, which was established by a corporation in 1808, was for many years a flourishing institution. The public schools were not neglected either, the first board of directors being chosen in 1846 and a public school conducted from that time until the present.

The first telegraph line in Missouri was the line which connected Nashville with St. Louis. It passed through Ste. Genevieve and was constructed in the year 1820. Its use, however, was abandoned after a short time.

STE. GENEVIEVE-IRON MOUNTAIN PLANK ROAD.

One of the most important improvements of the early period was the plank road built in 1851 between Ste. Genevieve and Iron

Mountain. This road was 42 miles in length; it was considered a very great enterprise and a number of good engineers were employed in its building, among them being James P. Kirkwood, chief engineer of the Missouri Pacific Railroad, William R. Singleton, one Sullivan and Joseph A. Miller. The road was for many years the scene of a great traffic, as most of the ore from the lead country was carried over it to Ste. Genevieve.

150TH ANNIVERSARY CELEBRATED.

In 1885, on the 21st of July, there was held in the city of Ste. Genevieve the 150th anniversary of the founding of the old town and the 100th anniversary of the settlement of the new town of Ste. Genevieve. It was made a very great occasion. Maxwell Hill was selected as the site for the exercises of the day, which consisted of drills by soldiers that were present and a sermon, a long procession consisting of bands, city officers and most of the inhabitants of the town, and addresses. There were more than 5,000 persons present at the celebration, which was a most delightful event, except for the coming up of a great storm near the close of the day which scattered the people to their homes. The addresses were delivered by Firmin A. Rozier, Hon. Alexander J. P. Garesche, Col. F. T. Laderberger, Major William Cozzens and Lyndon A. Smith.

This town more than any other in Southeast Missouri retains something of its original aspect; this is due to several facts, one of which is that it is the oldest town in the state and the buildings which were erected here in the early days were of a somewhat better class of architecture than the usual ones. They have been preserved, many of them, up to this time; the oldest of these is the house of Louis Bolduc which was erected in 1785 and is still standing in a good state of preservation; there are other houses which were built about the beginning of the nineteenth century. The town is strictly French in appearance, the streets are clean and well kept, and there are beautiful lawns about the houses. The old houses give an air of distinction to the town, as many of them are in a good state of preservation. Many descendants of the old families still reside here. There is much to remind a visitor of the past.

U. S. SENATORS FROM STE. GENEVIEVE

It is the peculiar good fortune of Ste. Genevieve to have reared four men who afterwards became members of the United States senate. Besides these men one other citizen of the southeast became a senator. This was George W. Jones, the son of John Rice Jones, for many years famous as a lawyer in this part of the state. John Rice Jones came to Missouri in 1810, and immediately became prominent in political circles. He was a member of the territorial legislature and also the constitutional convention, and later a member of the supreme court of the state. His son, George W. Jones, was born in Indiana, but came to Ste. Genevieve in 1809. He married a daughter of one of the early French families, received a good education, graduating in law at Transylvania University in Kentucky. On returning to Missouri he began the practice of his profession at Ste. Genevieve, and while living there was appointed clerk of the United States district court.

From Ste. Genevieve he removed to Iowa, and here he once more entered political life, becoming first postmaster, then delegate to Congress, and was then appointed surveyor-general of Wisconsin and Iowa. In 1841 he became clerk of the supreme court of the United States and was later reappointed surveyor-general in 1845.

On the admission of Iowa to the Union in 1848, he was selected to represent the state in the senate, and was later re-elected, serving out two terms. After the close of his second term he was appointed minister to Bogota, serving until the outbreak of the Civil war. Senator Jones was one of the most respected and influential citizens of the city of Dubuque, where he made his home during the latter part of his life.

His brother, Augustus Jones, himself became a famous man. He took part in the Indian wars and later removed to Texas, where he soon became famous and influential. He was made a general in the army of the United States and served with distinction.

The third one of the men who became senators from Ste. Genevieve was Augustus C. Dodge, the son of Henry Dodge. He was born in Ste. Genevieve January 12, 1812, and when twenty-seven years old, after considerable experience in both peace and war, removed to the territory of Wisconsin. Before his removal he married Miss Clara Hertich, the daughter of the famous teacher, Joseph Hertich. After removing to Wisconsin Mr. Dodge then made his home in Iowa. He enlisted in the army and served in the Black Hawk war under his father, Governor Henry Dodge, of Iowa.

In 1838 he was appointed registrar of the land office at Burlington, Iowa. In 1841 he became delegate to Congress, and in 1847 was elected United Senator, serving to 1855. Both he and his father were influential men and voted and worked for every measure having to do with the upbuilding of the west. General Dodge was a particularly strong advocate of the homestead bill, of the bills for the establishment of military forts in the west, and worked for the admission of California as a state, and the establishment of territorial governments in New Mexico and Utah.

It was rather an unusual scene in the senate at this time when a father and son represented two states, Wisconsin and Iowa. It is one of the few instances in the history of our country.

After the close of his term in the senate, Senator Dodge was appointed as minister to Spain, and he discharged the duties of this position with great credit to himself. He died at Burlington, Iowa, November 20, 1883, but until the time of his death was an influential man, well known throughout this part of the country.

The fifth native of Ste. Genevieve who became a senator of the United States was Lewis V. Bogy. His father, Joseph Bogy, was a native of Kaskaskia. He became a citizen of Ste. Genevieve in the early history of the state, and himself filled several places of trust under the Spanish and American governments. He was private secretary of Governor Morales, then a member of the territorial legislature, and afterwards a state senator of Missouri. His wife was a member of the family of Beauvais, one of the pioneer families of the state.

Lewis V. Bogy was born in Ste. Genevieve in 1813. He received a good education, studied law in Kentucky, and taught for a short time in Wayne county, Kentucky. He was a volunteer in the Black Hawk war of 1832, and established himself as a lawyer in Ste. Genevieve in 1835. He became a member of the legislature from St. Louis, to which place he removed in 1840. He was a Whig and a very strong supporter of Mr. Clay. In 1849 he returned to Ste. Genevieve, taking part in all the political disputes of that time, and was very strongly opposed to Senator Benton. He opposed Benton as a candidate for Congress in 1852, but was defeated. Later he was a candidate for the legislature from Ste. Genevieve county, but was defeated. A little later he announced himself as a candidate for the legislature on an anti-Benton ticket. His opponent was another of the famous citizens of Ste. Genevieve, Hon. Firman A. Rozier. The contest between these two men, both representatives of old French families, was a very bitter one. Bogy was successful and served a term in the legislature.

At the conclusion of his term he again removed to St. Louis, and ran for Congress in 1863 against Frank P. Blair. Blair defeated him. He was appointed commissioner of Indian affairs in 1867 by President Johnson, but retired from the position after six months of service, because the senate refused to confirm his appointment.

Soon after his retirement he became a candidate for the United States senate, and was elected in 1873, serving one term with great credit to himself and his constituents. He had become a Democrat by this time and was chosen as the representative of his party. He died in the city of St. Louis.

STE. GENEVIEVE OF TODAY

The present town is a prosperous and flourishing community of 2,000 inhabitants. It is supported chiefly by the farming country about it, though there are some manufacturing plants, among them two large flouring mills, an ice plant, electric light plant, cigar factories, and a lime kiln. There are about fifty other business establishments. The transportation facilities are good. Much freight is handled by the river, which is only half a mile from the town, and two railroads afford ample facilities for travel by rail. The main line of the Frisco passes through Ste. Genevieve, and it is on the Illinois Southern which crosses the Mississippi at this place and extends to Bismarck in St. Francois county to the west.

The banking interests are cared for by the Bank of Ste. Genevieve, organized in 1902, with a capital of $10,000, and Henry L. Rozier, organized in 1891, with a capital of $10,000. The Catholic church building is one of the largest structures of its kind in this part of the state.

Elsewhere an account of the schools has been given. There is a well-conducted public school employing six teachers, and the Catholic church maintains a large parochial school with an enrollment of more than 300.

There are two weekly papers published in the town: The *Fair Play* is owned and edited by Jules J. Janis, himself a descendant of one of the pioneer families, and is Democratic in politics; and the *Herald*, published by Joseph A. Ernst, is Republican.

ST. MARYS

St. Marys, on the Mississippi river not far from the mouth of Saline creek, has been a town for a number of years. It was first known as Camp Rowdy. Its most prominent citizen in the early days was General Henry Dodge. For some years it was important as the shipping place for Perryville and Mine La Motte. The first store in the town was opened by two men from the east under the firm name of Kent & Sparrow. Owing to the fact of their eastern origin, the settlement came to be known as Yankeetown. They were succeeded by Miles A. Gilbert. Another one of the merchants in the early history of the town was Richard Bledsoe. John F. Schaaf built a flouring mill about 1857 or '58. This mill was rebuilt after its destruction by fire and is still in operation.

The town has grown recently since the building of the St. Louis & San Francisco Railroad. It is the shipping point for a considerable area of farming country and the town is supported principally by the farming interests. There is a large flouring mill and other business interests of the usual character; the town supports several church organizations, the largest and most flourishing being the Catholic church, and a public school. The population at present is 702.

CHAPTER XVIII

CAPE GIRARDEAU COUNTY TOWNS

CAPE GIRARDEAU A STEAMBOAT TOWN—INCORPORATED AS A CITY—PROSPERITY AFTER THE WAR—STATE NORMAL SCHOOL LOCATED—STAGE OF STAGNATION—REALLY REMARKABLE PROGRESS—FOUNDING OF JACKSON—FIRST INSTITUTIONS AND PERSONS—CIVIL GOVERNMENT—PRESENT COUNTY SEAT—BURFORDVILLE—APPLETON—POCAHONTAS AND OAK RIDGE.

Cape Girardeau is described in 1817 as a village containing two stores and about fifty houses. Within a short time a tan yard was established by Moses McLain, near the corner of Spanish and Independence streets. Another tan yard on the Painter place was established by William Scripps and his son, John. This tan yard was afterwards purchased by the Painter brothers, who conducted it and also a saddler shop. A still was operated just north of the town by Levy L. Lightner.

In 1818 the estate of Louis Lorimier was divided and the commissioners made an addition to the town. These lots were sold at public auction, November 22, 1818. The prices paid for the lots were very high. Ninety-three lots brought $34,733.00 and twenty-one out lots brought $26,523.00. These prices indicate the fact that Cape Girardeau was coming to occupy a more important position and that its advantages were coming to be known.

A STEAMBOAT TOWN

Just as in the case of Ste. Genevieve, however, it was the steamboat which made Cape Girardeau prosperous. The steamboat traffic assumed large proportion in the decade lying between 1830 and 1840, and during these years Cape Girardeau experienced a remarkable expansion in its business. Some of the men who were in business here during these years were: Andrew Giboney, James P. Fulkerson, Alfred P. Ellis, I. R. Wathen, H. L. Sloan, Robert Sturdivant, Thomas J. Rodney, A. D. Leech, T. and W. Johnson, Joseph Phillipson, J. and S. Albert, Eugene Garaghty and C. F. Gale. The first bank in the town was established in 1853. This was a branch of the state bank, and had formerly been in operation at Jackson. The first president here was I. R. Wathen, with A. F. Lacy as cashier, Lacy being succeeded in 1857 by Robert Sturdivant. A steam flouring mill, the first of the town's manufacturing establishments of much importance, was built by James Reynolds and B. M. Horrell. The Marble City mill was erected a few years later by I. R. Wathen. Attention was paid during these years in the town to education, the first schools being taught in the log house not far from the site of the St. Charles hotel. The schools were of a purely elementary character, and there seems reason to believe that the instruction was not always the best at the time, for children were sometimes sent to Mt. Tabor school. Cape Girardeau Academy was established in 1843, and in 1849 the Washington Female Seminary was incorporated. Both of these institutions were conducted until the time of the war. In 1843, too, St. Vincent's College was established and is still in operation.

The Southeast District Agricultural Society was organized and incorporated in 1855; it was to include all the counties in the congressional district. General N. W. Watkins was the president and the first meeting was held at Cape Girardeau and a fair was held during the first year, which was on a small scale but fairly successful. The next president of the society was Judge W. C. Ranney, who was elected in 1856 and served until 1860. The society secured grounds and erected buildings and held fairs each year until the beginning of the war. During the war the society was disbanded and the grounds taken possession of by troops. It was later reorganized and is still in existence.

INCORPORATED AS A CITY

We have seen that the first incorporation of the village of Cape Girardeau was in the year 1808. In 1843 the legislature of the state incorporated Cape Girardeau as a city with a special charter. It was provided in the charter that a mayor and seven councilmen should have charge of the affairs of the city. E. Mason was the first mayor and the members of the first council were: W. S. Watson, Thomas J. Rodney, J. Rigby, John Ivers, J. Ritton, E. P. Evans and E. V. Cassilly. The mayors of the city since the administration of Mason have been as follows: G. W. Juden, 1844 to 1845; E. Mason 1845 to 1846; Thomas Johnson, 1846 to 1849; P. H. Davis, 1849 to 1851; Alfred T. Lacy, 1851 to 1852; Thomas Baldwin, 1852 to 1853; John C. Watson, 1853 to 1854; Amasa Alton, 1854 to 1855; C. T. Gale, 1855 to 1857; John Ivers, Jr., 1857 to 1860.

The first brick house in Cape Girardeau was built by Ezekiel Abel, who was the contractor for the building of the court house and jail; he completed the jail, but became insolvent and could not finish the work on the court house. After his financial troubles, however, he became successful in business and left a considerable fortune. He left four sons, William, John, Jeremiah and Ezekiel, and two daughters, Mary, who became the wife of General W. H. Ashley, and Elizabeth, who married W. J. Stepheson. This brick house built by Abel was at the corner of Lorimier and Bellevue and was known for many years as Eagle's Nest, owing to the fact that it was the residence of the editor of the *Western Eagle*. This house was damaged by the earthquake in 1811, and cracks in the walls caused by the shocks were still visible when the house was torn down about 1896.

The oldest house now standing in Cape Girardeau is at the corner of Themis and Middle streets and is owned by Mrs. Ellen Wright. The lot on which it stands was bought in 1807 by Judge George Henderson, the father of Mrs. Wright's first husband, and the present house, a frame structure, was erected in 1811. The large brick chimney which still stands was damaged by the earthquake on the night of December 25, 1811, the top of the chimney beink shaken off. At the same time the large stones in the cellar of the house were cracked entirely through by the shocks. This house was used for a time as the meeting place for the courts. They assembled on the large open porch, a part of which has since been boarded up. Mrs. Wright, who is now about 85 years old, has resided in this house since 1855. She has a fund of recollections concerning the early history of the town.

Abel's failure to build the court house for which he had contracted resulted in the removal of the seat of justice, and as we have seen, checked the growth of Cape Girardeau very greatly. In 1867 there were in the town 27 dry goods stores, 3 hardware stores, and around the town, an account of which appears in the chapter on the Civil war.

Prosperity After the War

For a time after the war closed the town enjoyed a great degree of prosperity. It had a number of enterprising men who pushed its advantages in every possible way. Those advantages were numerous and very powerful in the upbuilding of the town. In the first place, it enjoyed the immense advantage of

Oldest House in Cape Girardeau

12 grocery stores, 5 drug stores, 5 furniture stores, 12 shoe shops, 7 wagon shops, 11 blacksmith shops, 3 flouring mills, 5 breweries, a distillery, 2 tanneries, 2 cigar shops and one bank, the Sturdivant, organized by Mr. Robert Sturdivant in 1857.

During the war Cape Girardeau was headquarters for a considerable Union force. A military prison was established here to which numbers of southern prisoners were brought. Several important skirmishes were fought in river transportation, which at that time was of the highest importance. Steamboats carried the greater part of the commerce of the country. Much of it for this section centered here. It was before the day of railroads. Towns and communities away from the river received their supplies from abroad by boat, hauling them in wagons from the nearest and most accessible point. The second great advantage possessed by Cape Girardeau was its relation to much of the other country in

Southeast Missouri. To the west there is a great section of the country that did its trading here because this was the nearest river point. The merchants in Wayne, Bollinger, and counties further west were naturally supplied from the markets of this city. To the southeast the counties of Stoddard and Dunklin, while at a great distance from town, found it almost impossible to reach the river points in counties to the east of them. The great swamp of Little river shut them off from the Mississippi. Their only chance to get river transportation was by coming to the Cape. Now these counties were rapidly settling up and their growing inhabitants demanded large supplies of goods. All this trade contributed to the wealth and prosperity of Cape Girardeau. It was no unusual sight to the people of Cape Girardeau of that day to see upon their streets long trains of wagons loaded with cotton or other products of the lower counties. The only flouring mills were in this section of the state. This led to the purchase of flour made in Cape Girardeau or Jackson mills. So important was the trade of some of these counties considered that some of the larger stores and mills sent men into these counties to become acquainted with conditions and bring trade here.

State Normal School Located

In 1873, through the liberality and energy of some of its citizens, the Cape secured the establishment of the State Normal school. The state expended considerable sums of money in the erection of buildings and the support of the school and the students of this institution and St. Vincent's College brought other large sums to the town.

By this time, however, a falling off in the town's business was already to be seen. The day of the railroad had come. The construction of the St. Louis & Iron Mountain, with its branches, cut off the trade of the west and southeast. Towns sprung up at various points and cut off some of the trade that formerly came this way. Dexter, in Stoddard county, secured the trade of Stoddard and Dunklin counties and became a flourishing town. Attempts were made to reconstruct the Blanton plank road between New Madrid and Clarkton in Dunklin county. It had been destroyed during the war. The attempt did not succeed, but resulted in construction of a railroad between New Madrid and Malden. This was the beginning of the Southwestern system and still further tended to make the lower counties independent of Cape Girardeau.

The people of the town did not tamely sit by and see the great empire of trade which had been theirs slip from their grasp. Efforts were made to hold it. Railroads were projected. Finally, through the tireless endeavors of Louis Houck, a line was built running to the southwest. It did much for the town, but it could not stay the tide which was turning more and more away from it. The Iron Mountain had made the territory tributary to St. Louis and the possibility once seen of making Cape Girardeau the trade center of all Southeast Missouri was gone, if not for all time, at least for many years.

Stage of Stagnation

Deprived of this great and lucrative foreign trade, the town entered upon a stage of stagnation. It was always a good town, but it ceased for many years to grow. It was at a standstill. The schools, the splendid farming country about it, and its manufacturing interests were a guarantee that it would always be a good town. Satisfied with this assurance, the most of the population contented themselves with conditions as they were. The town dropped behind some of its rivals, so far as public improvements were concerned.

A few of the more enterprising men were never satisfied with this condition. They still worked and planned for the control of the rich trade regions once tributary to the town. Foremost of these men was Mr. Houck. In 1902 he projected and built the Gulf System of railroads through Scott, New Madrid, Dunklin and Pemiscot counties. This was a long step in the right direction. A little later these roads were sold to the St. Louis & San Francisco, which immediately began the construction of a through line from St. Louis to Memphis. These enterprises awoke again the energies of the people of the town. Public improvements were planned, sidewalks, sewers, paved streets became possibilities and then realities; new factories were erected, the state spent great sums in the construction of a new Normal School plant, the same man who had already done so much for the town projected and built the Cape Girardeau and Chester and the Thebes Terminal roads. A federal court was established and a federal building erected. The destruction of the monopoly of roads by toll companies did much for the town which had formerly been hemmed in by toll-gates.

All these things contributed much to the growth and prosperity of the town, the population increased rapidly and real estate values doubled.

Not all things were fortunate for the town, however, even during this period. A failure to secure the entrance of the St. Louis Southwestern Railway was destined to cost the town very dear, for it was one of the factors which determined the building of the great railroad bridge at Thebes rather than at Cape Girardeau. The Frisco, in spite of a contract to the contrary, removed its shops and division point to Chaffee in Scott county and thus took many families from the town.

REMARKABLE PROGRESS

Notwithstanding these things, the town made really remarkable progress. Its population was nearly doubled from 1900 to 1910, now being 8,545. Its business interests were more than doubled. At the present time the town has more than 150 business institutions of one sort or another. There are a number of large general and department stores, and every form of mercantile establishment is represented. It has a number of woodworking establishments, manufacturing lumber, staves, boxes, sash and doors. There are factories for making shoes, lime, brick, cement, flour, cigars, ice cream and candy. There is a large rock-crushing plant, stone quarries, cigar and tobacco plants, foundries, machine shops, and other smaller manufacturing establishments.

It is famous for its educational institutions, which include a good system of public schools, parochial schools of two or three churches, St. Vincent's Academy for Young Ladies, St. Vincent's College, Moothhardt's Business College, and the State Normal school. About three thousand students are enrolled in its schools every year.

There are church organizations of the following denominations: Baptist, Catholic, Christian, Christian Science, Evangelical, Lutheran, Methodist, Presbyterian, Episcopal, besides negro churches. Nearly all of these possess a house of worship and the Catholics have two and the Methodists three.

There are four banks in the town. The Sturdivant, which is the oldest bank in Southeast Missouri, was organized in 1866 and now has a capital stock of $100,000. The First National was organized in 1892 and has a capital of $100,000. The Farmers and Merchants

Bank was organized in 1904 and has a capital stock of $15,000. The Southeast Missouri Trust Company was organized in 1906, and its capital is $500,000. All these banks are housed in commodious and beautiful structures erected for them.

Another institution which contributes much to the town is the St. Francis Hospital conducted by the Catholic Sisters of St. Francis.

In 1905 was begun the construction of the Cape Girardeau and Jackson Interurban Railway. At present it operates electric street cars in Cape Girardeau alone, though it will ultimately be extended to connect other towns in this section.

At present there are three miles of paved streets and others are projected.

Some notable buildings beside those mentioned are the Elks Club, the Himmelberger-Harrison office building, the Federal building, the courthouse of the court of common pleas. This latter, which occupies a commanding site on the bluff above the river, has been a landmark of Cape Girardeau for many years.

The town is on the main line of the Frisco from St. Louis to Memphis, and is the terminal point for the Hoxie branch of the Frisco, the St. Louis & Gulf, also owned by the Frisco, the Chicago and Eastern Illinois, the Cape Girardeau-Chester, and the Thebes Terminal. Good roads radiate in every direction from the town and add much to its trade.

There are two papers published in the town, *The Cape County Herald*, a weekly, and *The Republican*, both daily and weekly. *The Herald* is published in a well-equipped and *The Republican* owns one of the most complete printing plants in the state. Another business institution is the Cape Girardeau Bell Telephone Co., operating exchanges at Cape Girardeau and Jackson, and toll lines through a considerable part of this section. The town has a good system of waterworks, electric lights and gas, all operated by the same company.

FOUNDING OF JACKSON

Jackson was founded, as we have said, in 1815. It was put upon an improved farm which was purchased from William H. Ashley. Surrounding the town there were a number of settlements. On the west was the farm of Col. William Neely, on the north that of Joseph Seawell and on the south that of William Daugherty. The town grew rapidly after the sale of lots and in 1818 its population was three hundred or more. Some one described it as a "considerable village on the hill with the Kentucky outline of dead trees and huge logs lying on all sides of the fields." The population of the town consisted largely of young people who had been gathered from every quarter. There were only a few stores, three or four in number, some blacksmith shops, several taverns and boarding houses, a tan yard, a printing office, a court house and jail, and there was also erected in the early times a little building constructed of logs which was used as a school house. Rev. Timothy Flint, who came to the town in 1819, was very unfavorably impressed and spoke in a very derogatory manner of the town and its inhabitants. He said of them that they were entirely without interest; that they were extremely rough, most of them ignorant and bigoted, and inclined to think that sectarianism should atone for the want of morals and decency. Flint, however, seems to have had some prejudice in the matter.

Long, who visited the town in 1819, says (Long's Expedition, p. 85): "On our April expedition we came to Jackson, the seat of justice for the county of Cape Girardeau, and after St. Louis and St. Charles one of the best towns of Missouri. It lies about eleven or twelve miles northwest of the old town of Cape Girardeau on the Mississippi, and is surrounded by hilly and fertile tracts of country, at this time rapidly increasing in wealth and population. Jackson is what is called a thriving village and contains at present more than fifty houses which, though built of logs, seem to aspire to a degree of importance unknown to the humble dwellings of the scattered and solitary settlers assumed an appearance of superiority similar to that we immediately distinguished in the appearance and manners of the people.''

FIRST INSTITUTIONS AND PERSONS

The first store was that of Eckhardt, who came to Jackson from Virginia. He sold his store later to Clifton and Mothershead. Another of the early merchants was Samuel Cupples, a son-in-law of Judge Thomas. Joseph Frizzell was another of these merchants. He was a son-in-law of Col. George F. Bollinger and opened his store about 1817. David Armour and John Juden were partners in a business conducted on the opposite corner from Frizzell. It is related of them that they sent Robert Morrison with a wagon and team to Baltimore and that he returned with a load of goods in about three months. Other merchants were George H. Scripps, Nathan Vanhorn, and Doctor Thomas Neal. Neal's store was at the corner of Main street and the public square. Col. William McGuire, who was one of the prominent citizens in the town, and afterward a member of the state legislature, came to Jackson in 1818. He operated a tan yard. A still house was conducted by Caleb B. Fullenwider; he was also a prominent citizen, being elected judge of the county court and afterward clerk of the court. A mechanic shop was conducted by John Delap. Taverns and houses of entertainment were kept by James Edwards, Thomas Stewart, William Sheppard, and John Armstrong. Some other residents of the town at this early date were Louis Painter, who was a saddler, two blacksmiths named John Glascock and Samuel Mitchell; Edward Criddle, William Surrell, William Hand, C. G. Houts and E. D'Lashnutt; the last named were merchants. Peter R. Garrett was clerk of the court and afterward clerk of the county court. We have already mentioned some of the prominent lawyers, and T. E. Strange who published the first paper, the *Missouri Herald.*

The first physicians in the town were Dr. Zenas Priest and Dr. Thomas Neale. The former came from New York and was for years one of the leading physicians of the county. Dr. Neale was from Virginia, but had formerly lived in New Madrid. Dr. Cannon was another early physician. He was a native of North Carolina and married a daughter of Governor Dunklin. He took great interest in politics and was elected lieutenant governor of the state in 1836.

During this period (1820-1860), Jackson, which had been made the county seat of Cape Girardeau county, continued to grow quite rapidly. Among the merchants prominent in the town during this period were: William F. Graham, who began business about 1822 and sold his stock to Ralph Gill about 1826; Charles Welling, H. L. Sloan, John W. Gayle, A. H. Brevard, Jacob Kneibert, George M. Beattie, John Albert and brother, J. J. Turnbaugh and J. S. McGuire.

Charles Welling began business in Jackson in 1831, and for a period of fifty-seven years carried it on at practically the same site on Main street.

The first bank in Jackson was opened in 1841. It was a branch of the state bank. Its president was A. H. Brevard, and Thomas P. English was cashier. The bank was very prosperous and did a very large business until its removal to Cape Girardeau in 1853. In 1852 it was examined by a committee from the legislature which reported that its assets then amounted to $340,850 and its circulation was $199,050. During the fifteen years of its existence its net profits were $79,628. This branch was disposed of in 1857 when its assets were purchased by Robert Sturdivant, who removed it to Cape Girardeau.

As we have said in another place, the first newspaper in Southeast Missouri was published at Jackson, and during this period there was published, almost constantly, a newspaper under some name or other. A list of these is given in the chapter on newspapers.

The town suffered very greatly from cholera. The first epidemic was in 1833. Among those who died were Col. Alexander Buckner and wife. The total deaths at this time were 128, and the cholera reappeared in 1849, but there was only one death at that time. It was again in town in 1852, and this time it swept away a large number of the inhabitants.

During this period before the war, the schools were private schools. They were taught either by some person who acted entirely on his own account, or else were conducted by chartered associations, as was true in the case of the Jackson Academy. This association was incorporated in 1820 and erected its first building, a two-story brick, in 1838.

CIVIL GOVERNMENT

Jackson was incorporated in 1819, but there seems to have been no organization of the government of the town until 1828. In that year Nathaniel Vanhorn, Franklin Cannon, G. W. Davis and Edward Criddle seem to have been the trustees or members of the council. They were chosen at an election held by William G. Kennett and Joel Blunt, commissioners appointed by the county court. They passed ordinances and rules for the government of the board. In 1831 George W. Juden was clerk, and Welton O'Bannon was town constable. The organization seems then to have lapsed and there is no record of any business transacted by it until 1847. At that time incorporation was revived, and an election held which resulted in the choice of N. M. Watkins, Charles Welling, A. J. Brevard, Jason Watson and Cyrus Walker as trustees. In 1859, the town secured a special charter from the legislature and the first trustees under the new organization were: Thomas B. English, John W. McGuire, Jacob Neidert and Chas. Litterer.

PRESENT COUNTY SEAT

Just as was the fate of all other towns of this section, Jackson suffered greatly during the war, though not to the extent of some others. It began to improve, however. The coming of the railroad, a branch of the Iron Mountain which was built from Allenville in 1884, added greatly to the town's prosperity. Its population is now 2,105, and is rapidly increasing. There are about fifty business establishments of various kinds, most of which are doing a flourishing business. There are a number of good general stores carrying large and varied stocks of goods. There are two large flouring mills, a creamery, packing house, heading factory, brick kiln, and other smaller factories. There are two banks in the town. The Cape County Savings Bank was organized in the 80's. It has a capital of $50,000. The Jackson Exchange Bank was organized in 1894. Its capital is $20,000.

The possession of the county seat adds much

to the importance of the town. The court house occupies a commanding site in the center of the public square. It was erected in 1908, and is a well-constructed and commodious building. The usual church organizations are found, most of which have good buildings. The largest and most costly church edifice is that of the Methodist Episcopal church, South, recently erected at a cost of $40,000.

Jackson has a good system of public schools with a well-organized high school. There are two weekly newspapers, *The Missouri Cashbook* and *The Volkesfreund*, which is a German paper. Besides the branch of the Iron Mountain the town is situated on the Cape Girardeau and Chester Railroad, which was constructed in 1904, from Cape Girardeau to Chester. There is a fine rock road from Jackson to Cape Girardeau.

Burfordville

Burfordville, in Cape Girardeau county, was known for a good many years as Bollinger's Mill. It is situated on Whitewater river at the place where Major George Frederick Bollinger made a settlement about the year 1800 and where he for many years operated a mill. Other families besides the Bollinger family, who lived in the vicinity in the early times, were the Daughertys and Frisselles. It was incorporated as a town in the year 1900 and the first mayor was F. B. Meyer. The town now has four general stores and a furniture making establishment and a large flour mill. Its population is 114.

Appleton

Appleton, a village on Apple Creek, in Cape Girardeau county was founded in 1824. The first residents seem to have been John McClain and John Schlotz. Among the early merchants were Kimmel and Taylor, George Clodfelter and W. H. McClain. The first mill was built by Alfred McClain.

Pocahontas and Oak Ridge

Pocahontas was first settled in 1856 and organized as a village in 1861.

Oak Ridge, in Apple Creek township, ten miles northwest of Jackson, was settled about 1852. It is now a flourishing town with a population of 256. It is surrounded by a good farming community, and has a large flouring mill. It supports a good public school and there are several stores and other business establishments. The Bank of Oak Ridge was organized in 1904, and has a capital stock of $10,000.

CHAPTER XIX

NEW MADRID AND MADISON COUNTIES

BLOWS TO NEW MADRID—INCORPORATED AS A CITY—LONG THE COUNTY SEAT—POINT PLEASANT—PORTAGEVILLE—FREDERICKTOWN.

We have set out that New Madrid was incorporated in 1808. It grew slowly, however, and in 1811 contained only two stores and a few houses. Many of the inhabitants of the town moved away after the earthquake, and for several years affairs were at a standstill. The town was greatly benefited, however, by being selected as the seat of justice for the county. This was in 1822. In 1834 the town was reincorporated by the county court, and again in 1868. The trustees in 1834 were: William Pierrepont, Geo. G. Alford, Dr. Robert D. Dawson, Ashael Smith and Alphonse Delaroderie.

The early merchants were: Robert G. Watson, Robert McCoy, Matteo Bogliolo and Geo. G. Alford. In the decade from 1840 to 1850 business was transacted by H. T. Maulsby, Napoleon LeSieur, B. Powell, Richard J. Waters, Samuel Allen, W. B. Harper and Thomas Dowd. In 1856 the merchants were: Allen, Waters, R. A. Hatcher & Co., Hunter & Watson, F. V. LeSieur, T. J. O. Morrison, and Warrington & Pennell.

BLOWS TO NEW MADRID

The town suffered greatly during the war, as did most southeast towns. It was the scene of several skirmishes and battles. During 1862 General Pope laid regular siege to it. The Confederate forces defending the town were numerous and well-armed and several Confederate gunboats were in the river. Pope landed near the town with a large force, but doubted his ability to carry it by assault or to hold it in face of the fire from the gunboats. He accordingly contented himself at first with surrounding it as far as possible and ordered heavy guns from Cairo for a siege. The attack on New Madrid was a part of the movement for opening the river, and had for its immediate object the capture of the strongly fortified post of Island Ten. Finally, not being able to dislodge the Confederates from New Madrid, he took possession of Point Pleasant and New Madrid was evacuated. It had been repeatedly fired upon and suffered from this and other attacks. Many houses were burned and much property destroyed.

One thing which dealt a blow to the prosperity of New Madrid during and after the war was the destruction of the Blanton plank road. This road led across the Little River swamp to West Prairie, near Clarkton. It offered the people of Dunklin and Stoddard counties access to river transportation at New Madrid and drew a considerable trade to that town. Its destruction cut off this trade and caused it to seek other outlets.

In spite of these various misfortunes, the

citizens did not lose faith in the final prosperity of their town and they did not abandon it. It grew slowly during the years, its prosperity keeping pace with the opening and improving of the land about it.

Incorporated as a City

In 1878 the town was incorporated as a city of the second class. John W. Brownell was mayor and the aldermen were H. C. Latham, T. H. Digges, John E. Powell, and F. Kopp. Since that time the city government has been maintained and the town has had a prosperous history.

Some of the merchants, following the incorporation, have been Mann Bros., G. V. LeSieur, H. C. Latham, Hunter & Mathewson, Lilburn Lewis, Henry Jasper, T. H. Digges, and Parks & Akin. At the present time there are some forty business establishments, including general stores, special mercantile establishments of various kinds, and some manufacturing plants. The latter include some woodworking plants, cotton gins, electric light and water works plant, and grist mills.

The town is situated on a branch of the St. Louis Southwestern, which runs from Lilbourn to New Madrid. There has just been constructed a new railroad from Marston on the Frisco to New Madrid. This was built by home capital, having been promoted by E. S. McCarty, who has built a number of lines in this part of the state and northeast Arkansas. This is an unusually well-constructed and equipped line and will probably be extended to connect with other systems.

Long the County Seat

New Madrid has been the county seat for many years, but has been unfortunate in having the court house destroyed by fire. Other towns have desired the removal of the county seat, and while they have not so far been able to secure its removal, they have been able to prevent the rebuilding of the court house at New Madrid.

There has recently been erected a new and commodious Catholic church, which is an ornament to the town. There are two other churches, the Methodists having recently built a well-arranged brick building for their use. The town maintains a good public school, having a large brick school building. There are two weekly papers, the *Weekly Record* and the *Southeast Missourian*. They are both well-edited and influential papers.

The present population is 1,882. New Madrid is well situated. It is at the lower end of the great sand ridge known as the Sikeston ridge. Its soil is fertile, there are some fine shade trees, and the town presents a pleasing appearance. Just south of the town is a great Indian mound, which local tradition says is the site of De Soto's camp. The site is not that of the original town, as that has long since been swept away by the river.

Point Pleasant

Point Pleasant, in New Madrid county, was settled in 1815 by Francois LeSieur. He conducted a store until his death in 1826. John Woodward operated a combined hotel and store at the same place. Steamboats, however, were prevented from landing at the town because of the formation of a sand bar in the river, and for this reason the business of the town was transferred to a new site about one mile further south. On this new site there had been a wood-yard in operation since 1817. It was conducted by Alphonse Delaroderie. It was in 1846 that the new town was laid off and building begun. The first houses erected for business were warehouses. They were built by John Woodward and Pleasant Bishop. The first merchant of the town was John J. Cox.

For years the town was an important and flourishing one. Large stores were erected. The population grew. An academy was chartered in the early days and all indications pointed to the place as designed for the site of a thriving city. Unfortunately for its inhabitants, the river began to encroach upon the town. At first the caving was just south of the main part of the town. Gradually it extended up the river, until many of the houses had to be moved back. So rapidly did the bank cave in at times that it was almost impossible to remove the houses fast enough to save them. After several successive removals, the site was abandoned by many of the residents, who were attracted by the growth of Portageville, which began to acquire importance through the construction of the Frisco Railroad through it. These causes greatly reduce the population of Point Pleasant and the historic name is preserved by only a handful of houses.

PORTAGEVILLE

Portageville, in the south part of New Madrid county, now a flourishing town, had its beginning in 1848, when Edward Meatte and Charles Davis established a store there. In 1851 Robert G. Franklin succeeded them.

Later Edward DeLisle became interested in the place and carried on a mercantile establishment for many years. Others came and the town grew slowly. Two causes at last made it an important and flourishing town: the ruin of Point Pleasant and subsequent removal of many of its inhabitants further from the river, and the building of the Frisco Railroad. The land about Portageville is fertile and when it was cleared up and drained, the farming interests thus made possible gave an impetus to the town. Its present population is 987 and is rapidly increasing. It has wood-working plants and cotton gins, besides general and other stores.

The Farmers Bank was organized in 1905 and has a capital of $20,000. The Portageville Bank was chartered in 1903. Its capital is $20,000. There is a good system of public schools and the usual church organizations.

FREDERICKTOWN

This town, which was the successor of St. Michaels, was laid off in 1819. The land was owned by Nathaniel Cook and the commissioners appointed to set out the limits of the town were Theodore F. Tong, John Burdette, Joseph Bennett and Henry Whitener. The first stores in the town were owned by S. A. Guignon, S. B. Pratte and Moses and Caleb Cox.

Not much growth was made by Fredericktown until after the building of the Belmont branch of the Iron Mountain Railroad. There was always some business transacted, and the list of merchants includes six or eight names at any particular time, but the growth was, on the whole, slow for many years. The first paper published in Fredericktown was a Free Soil paper, called *The Espial*. It was established in 1847 by James Lindsay. An account of the other newspaper enterprises of the town is given in the chapter on newspapers. The first lodge was organized November 25, 1848. This was Marcus Lodge, A. F. & A. M. The meetings were held in the court house for a time, and F. L. Sullivan was the first temporary master.

The town was incorporated for the first time in May, 1868, and on November 28, 1903, it was incorporated as a city of the third class. The first mayor was R. Albert. There are now four general stores in the town and about fifty other business institutions, but no factories of any considerable importance. There are three banks and the town is supplied with electric lights. The Union American Lead Company owns and has operated mines in the vicinity of the town, but the company has suspended operations for some time. Among the important interests of Fredericktown are Marvin college, and its good system of public schools. In another place we gave an account of the founding and some of the history of the college, which attracts to the town a number of students and families who come for the purpose of educating their children.

During the last four or five years Fredericktown has suffered in an unusual way from calamities, a number of destructive fires have swept away some of the best and most important buildings and, too, the town has been damaged by serious floods; it is situated on the Little St. Francois river and some of the town is on ground subject to inundation. Its situation is a delightful one and few places offer a more pleasant site for residence than Fredericktown. Its population is 2,632. It is situated on the Belmont branch of the Iron Mountain Railroad and is now and has been for many years the county seat of Madison county.

There are two weekly newspapers published in the town. *The Democrat-News* is Democratic in politics and *The Tribune* is Republican.

CHAPTER XX

WASHINGTON AND PERRY COUNTIES

Potosi Laid Out and Incorporated—Old Mines—Caledonia — Perryville — Longtown — Altenburg.

Potosi, the county seat of Washington county situated in Breton township at the end of the branch line of the Iron Mountain Railroad, is one of the oldest towns in this part of the state, the first settlement having been made in that town in 1763. At first it was called Mine a Breton, but the name was changed to Potosi when the town was incorporated in 1826. It is impossible to tell who erected the first house in Potosi, though it is supposed that it was a member of the Valle family of Ste. Genevieve. The first settlers at the place came because of the lead mine which was discovered by Francois Breton; the permanent settlement of the place dates from about 1790 and its principal growth began with the coming of Moses Austin, who secured a large grant of land from the Spanish government. Austin made his home at Potosi or Mine a Breton, as it was then called, and built for himself a stone house known as Durham Hall. It was the finest residence west of the Mississippi river for a great many years and was burned in 1872. Austin also erected a large smelting plant, being the first reverberatory furnace in Missouri. He was also interested in other enterprises and did much for the building up of the town. When Louisiana was transferred to the United States in 1808 there were twenty families at Mine a Breton and the town contained two grist mills, a saw mill, Austin's smelter and shot tower and a sheet lead factory operated by Elias Bates.

Potosi Laid Out and Incorporated

When Washington county was organized in 1813, Austin donated forty acres and John Rice Jones ten acres for a county seat; the town was laid out and called Potosi. For a time there were two villages adjoining, one known as Potosi, the other Mine a Breton; they were consolidated and incorporated in 1826 under the name of Potosi. At the time of the incorporation the town had a population of about 400. Among the buildings were a court house, a jail, a school, two churches, Catholic and Methodist Episcopal, besides a number of business buildings of various kinds. At the present time there are six churches, good public school building, the Bank of Potosi, with a capital of $15,000, Washington County Bank, with a capital of $10,000, a flouring mill and a number of business establishments of various kinds. The streets are graded and lighted. The present population is 772. There are two weekly papers, *The Independent*, a Democratic paper, and *The Journal*, which is Republican.

Old Mines

Old Mines was founded in 1802 by French settlers from Ste. Genevieve, though there had been people living in the vicinity at various times from the discovery of the mines by Renault about 1726. There were thirty-one families of the old French settlers and the greater part of the population was engaged in mining. The first Catholic church in Washington county was erected by the people at this village. At the present time there are two churches, Catholic and Baptist, a public school, a Catholic school, a hotel, several stores, a lead smelter, and a mill. It has a population of about 250 and is situated in Washington county six miles north of Potosi.

Caledonia

Caledonia, a village in Washington county about 12 miles south of Potosi, was founded in 1819 and is in the center of the famous Bellevue valley, the country around it being remarkable for its fertility. In 1899 it had three general stores, a wagon factory, a saw mill, a grist mill, a Methodist church and a Presbyterian church and a public school. At that time its population was 250, its present population is 128. The Presbyterian church is one of the oldest in Missouri, having been organized in 1825. The town was formerly the seat of Bellevue Collegiate Institute before its removal to Fredericktown. There is one bank, the Bank of Caledonia, with a capital of $10,000. It is the terminus of the Caledonia branch of the Iron Mountain Railway which runs from Mineral Point.

Perryville

Perryville is the county seat of Perry county; it is in Center township fourteen miles west of the Mississippi river on the Cape Girardeau & Chester Railway. The town was laid out in 1822 by Robert T. Brown, Joseph Tucker and Thomas Riney, commissioners appointed to select the seat of justice of Perry county. The land was owned by Bernard Layton, who donated fifty-one acres to the county as a site for the county seat. This land was surveyed and the town platted by William McLane. The lots were sold at public auction, fifty-three lots bringing a total of $1,468.25. The first merchant in the town was Ferdinand Rozier, of Ste. Genevieve, who opened a store on the north side of the public square in a wooden building; after a time he built a large brick building, which is still standing. The second merchant was Levi Block, and about 1840 Gissel and Company and T. & L. Landry began business. Among the early settlers were John Logan, who conducted a tan yard, Leonard Fath, a blacksmith, Dr. Richard Dorsey, Dr. Reuben Shelby, Luther Taylor and Frederick Hase, who was clerk of the court. The first incorporation of the town was made in 1831, the trustees being Clayton D. Abernathy, George Killian, Luther Taylor, Dr. Richard Dorsey and William A. Keyte. This organization was allowed to lapse after a short time and the town was not reincorporated until 1856; at that time the trustees were Leon DeLassus, John Bridgeman, George W. Enler, Bernard Cissell and Leonard Fath. At the breaking out of the Civil war the population was about 300; the town suffered some during the war, but not so greatly as many other towns in this part of the state. At this time there were about 60 business houses, including bank, flouring mill, brick and ice plants, hotels, general stores, etc. There are four churches and a good system of public schools. St. Marys Seminary, which was established in

1818, is a large and flourishing Catholic school, situated just outside of the city limits; the school owns valuable land and has several large buildings. The population of the town is 1,708. There are two banks in the town with a combined capital of $35,000. *The Perry County Sun* is a Democratic weekly, and *The Republican* is Republican in politics.

LONGTOWN

Longtown, a village in Perry county, was settled in 1860. The first residents were John Long, Emil Urban, Herman Funke, Valentine Bergmann, Frederick Schade and Oliver Abernathy. The place was incorporated in April, 1874, the first time and Valentine Bergmann was the first mayor. Emil Urban and Oliver Abernathy were the first merchants in the town. At the present time there are three general stores and one flouring mill. The town is situated on the Cape Girardeau & Chester Railroad and has a population of 158.

ALTENBURG

The town of Altenburg in Perry county, was founded in 1847, one of the first settlers being C. F. Walther. Shortly after the founding of the town stores were opened by Zachariah Mueller, George Mueller and John Kuennell. The town was settled by Germans who were Lutherans, and shortly after the settlement was made they founded the college, whose history we have given in another place. A building was erected and this building is still in existence and steps have been taken to preserve it on account of its historic interest. The town was incorporated July 5, 1870, and Dr. E. E. Buenger was its first mayor. At the present time there are three general stores, a swing factory and a creamery. The financial interests are cared for by the Bank of Altenburg with a capital of $10,000. The more important buildings of the town are the high school and Lutheran church building. The present population is 279.

CHAPTER XXI

WAYNE AND JEFFERSON COUNTIES

GREENVILLE, EARLY AND LATE—PIEDMONT—PATTERSON — DESOTO — CRYSTAL CITY — HERCULANEUM — HILLSBORO — KIMMSWICK—HEMATITE.

In 1819 Greenville was platted on the St. Francois river by the commissioners for establishing the seat of justice in Wayne county. The early merchants were Van Horn & Wheeler, William Creath, Lysander Flinn and Zenas Smith. The hotels of the early times were kept by Moses Timmons and Joseph Bennett. The first physicians were: E. W. Bennett, Drs. Payne, Capp and Dickey. The town grew very slowly. It was at a distance from any great number of people, and all the goods that were bought and sold there must be hauled from the Mississippi river, usually from Cape Girardeau. In 1826 it was damaged by an overflow of the St. Francois river, which covered the town to a depth of several feet. The town was built on level ground, and it is difficult to protect it from a rise in the river.

For a great many years Greenville was without any railroad facilities, being situated at a distance of twenty miles from the nearest point on the Iron Mountain Railroad. About 1894 the Holliday Land & Lumber Company, a corporation interested in timber lands, saw mills and mining, began the construction of a railroad from Williamsville to Greenville, and at Greenville erected the shops for the railroad and also a very large mill for the manufacture of lumber. This railroad was afterwards extended to the northwest a distance of twenty miles from Greenville. The building of the railroad, together with the establishment of the mill, brought about a considerable growth in the town. It became a prosperous mercantile community. The mills, however, are now no longer in operation and the town depends for its support almost entirely upon the farming community about it and upon its importance as the county seat. There are now two general stores in the town, but no factories. Greenville has two banks: the Citizens, with a capital of $10,000, and the Wayne County, with a capital of $25,000. Among the more important buildings are the court house, a two-story brick structure and a good public school building, which gives accommodation to about 600 pupils.

In 1899 it contained about 125 business houses, including two banks, opera house, two flouring mills, five carriage and wagon shops, machine shop, electric light and ice plants, three hotels, a number of general stores, and miscellaneous establishments.

The town is situated on the St. Francois river and a part of it is subject to overflow at the time of unusually high water. It has had one or two disastrous experiences with floods. It is laid out in a very irregular manner, it being a common tradition in the town that the streets were originally determined by corn rows. Its present population is 914. The papers in the town are the *Wayne County Journal,* which is Democratic in politics, and the *Greenville Sun*, Republican.

PIEDMONT

Piedmont is a city of the fourth class situated in Benton township, Wayne county, on the St. Louis, Iron Mountain & Southern Railway. It was laid out at the completion of the Iron Mountain road to that point about 1860. It was made the division point of the railroad, the repair shops were erected and the town prospered very greatly. In 1888 about one-half of the business part of the town was destroyed by fire, and it has had other destructive fires since that time. It has revived from these damages, however, and is now a prosperous and growing community. It has good streets and sidewalks, electric lights, four churches, a good public school, which is housed in a modern school building, two banks, a flouring mill and about twenty other business enterprises of various kinds. The *Piedmont Banner* is a weekly paper published by Bristol French.

There are three banks in the town with a combined capital of $55,000. The present population is 1,154.

PATTERSON

Patterson, a town in Logan township, Wayne county, dates its beginning back to the year 1854. It was then known as Isbell's store, owing to the fact that Isbell was the first, and for a number of years the only merchant in the town.

DESOTO

DeSoto, the largest town in Jefferson county, is situated on the St. Louis, Iron

HIGH SCHOOL, DESOTO

Mountain & Southern Railway forty-seven miles south of St. Louis. It is built partly in the valley of Joachim creek and partly on the hills overlooking the valley. The first resident on the site of the town was Van Horne, who opened a farm here in 1808. In 1855 Colonel John W. Fletcher built a residence and saw mill on the site; the town was not laid out until 1857, when Thomas C. Fletcher, afterward governor of Missouri, and Lewis J. Rankin had the site surveyed and began the sale of lots. A postoffice was established with C. E. Fletcher as the first postmaster; E. M. Boli in the same year opened the first store, and the first brick house in the town was built by D. Cohen. The population grew slowly at first and did not exceed 200 by 1861, but at the close of the war it began to increase rapidly and the town was incorporated in 1869. The car works and machine shops of the Iron Mountain Railway Company were located in DeSoto in 1872 on condition that necessary grounds should be donated by the citizens and that the property of the company should be forever exempt from taxation. Owing to certain irregularities the city was incorporated two or three times before 1883. Soon after the establishment of the town an educational institution known as DeSoto Academy was organized by Professor Trumble for which a large building was erected. He gave up the work in 1868 and the school was closed for a time and the building used for private school purposes until 1886 when it was burned. In 1882 a stone and brick public school building was erected on the hill above the town at a cost of $15,000, and in 1905 a high school building adjoining the older building was erected; the public school at present employs about twenty-five teachers and is well and thoroughly organized; there are also two other ward school buildings and a school for negroes. There are many churches in the town—the Baptist, Methodist, Southern Methodist, Presbyterian, Congregationalist, Episcopal, Roman Catholic, German Methodist and Evangelical — each having church buildings and organizations. There is also a fine building for the Young Men's Christian Association, the funds for which were provided in large part by Miss Helen Gould. The leading industry of the town is the car works of the railroad; other industries are flouring mills, ice plant, planing mill, machine factory, wagon factory and marble and bottling works. The Jefferson County bank and the Peoples' Bank of Desoto were organized in 1885 and the German-American bank was organized in 1898; they are all prosperous and enterprising institutions with ample capital. The newspapers of the town are *The Press* and *The Republican*. The town has a good system of electric lights and water works, being supplied from artesian wells. There are many beautiful residences and the population of the town is 4,721.

Crystal City

Crystal City is situated in Jefferson county on Plattin creek, thirty miles south of St. Louis. The land on which the town now stands was entered in 1834 by an eastern company with the expectation of finding mineral on it; the site, however, was not occupied nor were minerals found at that time. In 1868 the place was visited by three English expert glass makers, who shipped two barrels of sand to England, which when tested proved to be of a very superior quality. The first successful attempt to make use of this sand was made in 1871. At that time the American Plate Glass Company of Detroit, Michigan, with a capital of $150,000 was organized by Captain E. D. Ward. Theodore Luce was appointed as superintendent and a plant for the manufacture of glass was constructed and put in operation in 1872. Because of the fact that the owners were Michigan people the village which grew up around the plant was called New Detroit, but the workmen persisted in giving it the name of Crystal City, which was afterwards adopted. The financial panic of 1873 and the death of Captain Ward caused the plant to be sold; it was purchased by a St. Louis corporation—the Crystal Plate Glass Company, of which Ethan Allen Hitchcock was president—for $25,000. This company increased the capital stock to $1,500,000 and appointed George F. Neal superintendent, and purchased additional land. It is said that the company owns about 250 acres of almost pure sand besides other property. This company built the

Crystal City Railroad, extending from the works to Silica on the Iron Mountain, a distance of three and a half miles. The railroad was operated until the building of the Frisco south from St. Louis to Memphis. The plant later came under the control of the Pittsburg Plate Glass Company, who now own and operate it. About 2,000 people are employed by the company and the product of the plant amounts to a large sum each year. The present town is supported almost exclusively by the Company. There is a good public school and several business establishments, and one church building. This church building was erected by the Company and stands in the midst of about three acres of very beautiful, well kept grounds. It was first turned over to the Episcopalians but is now free for the services of all denominations. The population of Crystal City is about 1,200.

HERCULANEUM

A town in Jefferson county thirty miles south of St. Louis. It was at one time one of the most important settlements in the west. The land on which the town stands was purchased in 1808 by Samuel Hammond and Moses Lawson, who laid it out in town lots and began the sale of the lots. The advantage of the situation of the town was twofold. In the first place it was near the lead region and in the second place it was situated on bluffs overlooking the Mississippi river, on which it was possible to erect shot towers for the manufacture of shot at a very little cost; in fact, no tower was really necessary, as the melted lead could be dropped from the top of the bluff into the water below. The first establishment for making shot was erected at the mouth of Joachim creek by John M. Macklot of St. Louis. Other shot towers were erected within a short time and considerable quantities of lead and shot were manufactured.

Long says (p. 104) that there were three shot factories at Herculaneum in 1819, all of them built on the summits of perpendicular precipices, by which means the erecting of high towers has been avoided.

Flagg ("Far West," p. 93) gives this bit of description: "In a few moments the forest opened unexpectedly before me and at my feet rolled on the turbid floods of the Mississippi, beyond which went up the towering cliffs of limestone to the height of more than a hundred feet from the water's edge, were the cliffs of Herculaneum with their shot towers."

When Jefferson county was organized in 1818 Herculaneum was made the county seat and continued to grow and prosper until the lead which had been transported to Herculaneum for shipments on the river began to be sent from two other shipping points known as Selma and Rush Tower. They afforded somewhat better facilities for shipping than Herculaneum and the town began to decline. The county seat was taken away in 1836 and removed to Monticello, afterward called Hillsboro. The town lost a great deal of its importance until the establishment of plants for the smelting of lead. When the Mississippi River & Bonne Terre Railway was constructed a large smelting plant was built on the river at Herculaneum and great quantities of lead ore were brought from the mines to be smelted in this plant. It is still one of the important lead manufacturing towns in the state. The town is supported almost entirely by the lead company. It has a bank called the Bank of Herculaneum, with a capital of $10,000; a small public school, two churches, and half a dozen business establishments, and its population is about 800. The *Herculaneum Hustler* is a weekly newspaper and is Republican in politics.

There is still standing the chimney of the old house where Governor Thomas C. Fletcher was born, and also the remains of one of the first shot towers (about 1808).

Hillsboro

The first settler on the site of Hillsboro was a man named Hanson, who moved there in 1832 and laid out the town. The place was first called Monticello, but on the removal of the seat of justice from Herculaneum to this place the name was changed to Hillsboro. It is a typical country town, being without railroad facilities, the nearest shipping points being Desoto and Victoria on the Iron Mountain Railway. It has a church, a public school, a hotel, two weekly newspapers—the *Jefferson Democrat* and the *Jefferson County Record*—a bank with a capital stock of $10,000, and its population is 261.

Kimmswick

Kimmswick is situated on the Mississippi river, twenty-one miles south of St. Louis. It was laid out as a town by Theodore Kimm in 1859. At one time the town bid fair to become one of considerable importance; this was during the operation of iron mines at Pilot Knob and Iron Mountain. A large smelting plant was erected in Kimmswick and much of the ore from Pilot Knob was brought here for smelting; this was in 1873, and the plant was operated until 1882. At the present time the town is supported by the agricultural country about it. There are Presbyterian and Catholic churches and a public school. The town is on the St. Louis, Iron Mountain & Southern Railway and also on the St. Louis & San Francisco. Just north of the town is Montesano Springs, a summer resort. The Bank of Kimmswick has a capital stock of $10,000. The population of Kimmswick is 235.

Hematite

A town in Jefferson county on the St. Louis, Iron Mountain & Southern Railway, thirty-five miles southwest of St. Louis, was laid out in 1861 by Stephen Osborn of St. Louis. It contains Christian, Congregational and Methodist churches, a public school, a flour mill and some other business establishments. It is the shipping point for a large amount of building stone quarried in the vicinity of the town. Its population is about 200.

Main Street, Hillsboro

CHAPTER XXII

ST. FRANCOIS, BOLLINGER AND PEMISCOT COUNTIES

Present-Day Bismarck — Libertyville — Farmington—Marble Hill—Lutesville—Gayoso—Caruthersville.

Birmarck, in St. Francois county, was settled in 1860 and incorporated twenty years later. Among its early settlers were S. C. Mantler, W. H. Evans, L. Sherrill, the Dent family, the Cooleys and the Matkins. The first merchants in the town were Columbus Grider, Sims and Boss. The early importance of the town was due almost entirely to the construction of the Iron Mountain Railroad and its growth has depended principally upon the farming community in which it is situated and its railroad interests.

Present-Day Bismarck

Bismarck has now five general stores, but the only manufacturing establishment is a flouring mill. The more important buildings in the town are the hotel and the I. O. O. F. hall; it is the division point of the Iron Mountain Railroad and the western terminus of the Illinois Southern, and is also the connection point of the Belmont branch with the main line of the Iron Mountain. The town has a good public school and the usual church organizations. Its financial interests are cared for by the Bank of Bismarck, which has a capital stock of $25,000. The population of Bismarck is 848. The *Bismarck Gazette* is a weekly newspaper and is independent in politics. It is published by George Bisplinghoff.

Libertyville

This village in St. Francois county is situated in the Cook settlement, one of the oldest communities in Southeast Missouri. It is six miles from Knoblick on the railroad and has a large flouring mill, a brick school building and a church.

Farmington

The county seat of St. Francois county was located and surveyed as a town in February, 1822. It was located on land belonging to David Murphy, the site of the old Murphy settlement which was made about the year 1800. Murphy donated to St. Francois county fifty-two acres of land and the county appointed Henry Postom, John Andrews, William Shaw, Mark Dent and William Alexander as commissioners to locate the seat of justice. The survey of the town was made by Henry Poston. The first store was opened in 1823 in a small log building on the west side of the public square, by John D. Peers; later he removed to the east side of the square and in 1833 formed a partnership with M. P. Cayce. Among the other merchants at that time were Henry W. Crowell and J. J. Brady; a saddlery shop was owned and managed by a Mr. Day, and the hotel was conducted by

John Boaz. The town was incorporated as a village by order of the county court in 1856, with John Cobb and George W. Williams as trustees; William R. Taylor was city clerk. It was incorporated as a city of the fourth class in 1878, the first mayor being Alvin Rucker. The town grew slowly and depended upon the farming community about it and also upon its possession of the county seat. At the breaking out of the war it had a population of about 500. At this time the principal merchants were M. P. Cayce, S. A. Douthitt & Son, Peers & Company, and Arnold & Rucker. The first grist mill was built in 1856 by M. P. Cayce and S. A. Douthitt; this mill, afterward enlarged and remodeled, was known as the Farmington roller mills. The town suffered considerable injury by the fact that the St. Louis & Iron Mountain Railroad was built at a distance of two and a half miles to the west, owing to the fact that the town refused to subscribe to the stock of the railroad. However, the injury to the town was neither serious nor permanent, and contrary to general expectation the business was not moved to the new town of DeLassus. The principal merchants in the period from 1880 to 1890 were Dalton & Marks, J. Krieger, S. S. Smith, Cole & Hackaday, M. Rosenthal, Simon J. Copson, Thomas Williams; general merchants, Orten & Davis, F. E. Klein & Company, S. C. Gosson and J. H. Waide; grocers, J. R. McCormick, Brad Robinson, A. Rucker and A. Parkhurst; druggist, Robert Tetlay; jeweler, C. E. Barroll; stationer, Lang & Brother; lumber dealers, Giessing Brothers, proprietors of the Farmington Roller mills.

In 1887 the Bank of Farmington was organized, with A. Parkhurst as president and L. P. Cayce as cashier, with a capital stock of $15,000; it now has a capital of $50,000. The Farmers' Bank of Farmington was organized in April, 1904, and has a capital stock of $35,000. The St. Francois County bank was organized in April, 1907, and has a capital of $30,000. At the present time there are twelve general stores, two drug stores, two confectionery stores, three restaurants, one five- and ten-cent store, two express offices, one jewelry store, four barber shops, one book store and three newspapers.

The present manufacturing establishments are three wagon and buggy shops, three blacksmith shops, four lumber yards and one construction company. The town has a good system of electric lights and water works. The principal buildings are the court house, St. Francois hotel, the Realty building, the opera house and a high school building. The town now covers two and a half square miles and has a population of 2,800. Its assessed valuation is more than a million dollars. It is divided into four wards; there are eight aldermen. Hon. George M. Wilson is mayor of the town.

There are eight churches in Farmington— Methodist Episcopal, Methodist Episcopal South, negro Methodist, Christian, Baptist, Presbyterian, Lutheran and Catholic. The first newspaper published was the *Southern Missouri Argus*, which was established by Nichol, Crowell & Shuck in 1880. In 1889 its name was changed to *The Herald*, and in 1892 it was removed to Desoto. The *New Era*, a paper which began a publication at Libertyville, was removed to Farmington in 1871 and to Marble Hill in 1876. In 1872 *The Times* was started by C. E. Ware and J. H. Rodehaver; it is now published by Theodore D. Fisher. *The News* was established in 1884 by P. T. Pigg and *The Herald* in 1886 by Isaac Rodehaver.

Farmington has been famous for many years as a center of educational interest. Its system of public schools is not surpassed in Southeast Missouri. It has three good school

Missouri State Hospital from Superintendent's Residence

High School, Farmington

buildings, one of them—the high school building—having been recently completed at a cost of $50,000. Besides its system of public schools the town is the seat of Carleton College and of Elmwood Seminary, accounts of both of which appear in the chapter on education. The town is also the seat of the state hospital No. 4 for the insane. This institution is one of the best equipped in the state. It is situated on beautiful and commodious grounds and the buildings are costly and convenient.

The town is not on any line of railroad but is connected with the St. Louis & Iron Mountain, and also with the Mississippi River & Bonne Terre Railroad by the St. Francois County Interurban line, which was constructed in 1905. The present population is 2,613.

Marble Hill

Marble Hill, which was selected as the county seat of Bollinger county, was first named New California. It was laid off as a town in 1851 by Thomas Hamilton. The commissioners to choose the site of the county seat, who were David Ramsay, Isaac Shepherd and J. J. Daugherty, selected this place and laid off a town, including New California, which they named "Dallas." They proceeded to mark out a place for the public square, and title to the town site was obtained from the owners of the land, who were Joseph Baker, Jacob Lutes, Daniel Crader and Thomas Hamilton. The first store in the town was conducted by John C. Whybark. Some of the other early merchants were William Grimsey, Edward Wilson and George Clippard. The first hotel was opened by Calvin Cook. The town was not incorporated until during the Civil war. Its name was then changed to Marble Hill and Levy E. Whybark, F. J. Williams, J. J. Conrad, Lindsay Murdoch and J. J. Duffy were appointed as trustees for the town.

The town has not grown very rapidly in recent years, but still has experienced a steady increase. Its present population is 313; it is supported by the farming community about it. The principal importance of the town lies in the fact that it is the county seat of the county and that it is the seat of the Will Mayfield College. The Bank of Marble Hill was chartered in 1905 and has a capital stock of $5,000. The town is situated on the top of a hill and is separated from Lutesville by Crooked creek. It is a pleasant place of residence and has a public schools system and churches of the Baptist, Methodist and Catholic denominations. The Marble Hill *Press* is a weekly newspaper published by Hill & Chandler.

Lutesville

The town of Lutesville is situated on the west side of Crooked creek, about a half mile from Marble Hill. It was laid out as a town in 1860 by Eli Lutes, in whose honor the town was named. In order to secure a station on the Belmont branch of the St. Louis, Iron Mountain & Southern Railroad, Mr. Lutes gave to the railroad company ten acres of ground for station purposes, the right-of-way through the town, and one-third of the lots. The first merchant in town was C. E. Rowe, who began business in a small box house and continued until the time of his death. Eli Lutes was also one of the early merchants. The first mayor of the town was F. S. Trautwein. There are now five general stores and the usual number of smaller business establishments. There is one stave factory, which has been in operation for a number of years, and also a mill. The Bollinger County bank, with a capital of $25,000, was incorporated in 1891, and the Peoples' Bank of Lutesville, with a capital of $12,000 was incorporated in 1903. Among the principal buildings are

Will Mayfield College, Marble Hill

the Odd Fellows' hall and the business blocks of W. W. Sample and Robert Drum. The population of Lutesville is 551. The Lutesville *Banner* is a weekly paper and is Republican in politics.

GAYOSO

This town received its name in honor of the Spanish governor of Louisiana, Don Manuel Gayoso. When the site was selected for the county seat of Pemiscot county in April, 1851, there was not a house standing on the fifty acres of land purchased by the commissioners. This land was bought from James A. McFarland and the town was surveyed by William Bigham. No house was erected until 1854, when Sanford Jackson built a small residence. The next house was built by Charles A. Kimball. Warrington & Pennell of New Madrid were the first merchants. They began business in 1854 and were succeeded by Benjamin Sellers. John H. Kelly was another early merchant. The first hotel was built in 1856 by Wade H. Spencer. Francois Baxter, who was an Englishman, taught the first school in the school house, which was erected in 1859. Other schools had been taught prior to this time, but they were conducted in the court house. This court house was erected in 1854 and was a small frame building on the public square. This building was used until 1873, when it was moved away and used as a stable by George W. Carleton.

James A. McFarland, who owned the land on which the town was laid out, was one of the first physicians in Gayoso, as was Robert E. Clowd. In 1858 Dr. John H. Alexander came from Point Pleasant to Gayoso. He seems to have been the first graduate of a regular medical college in the county. The principal resident of the town during many years of its history was Major George W. Carleton, whose life is recorded in another chapter. To his enterprise and business ability was due in large measure the prosperity which the place enjoyed. Gayoso met the fate of many other river towns. The Mississippi gradually encroached upon it until little was left. The county seat was removed to Caruthersville and the place ceased to exist.

CARUTHERSVILLE

Caruthersville, the present county seat of Pemiscot county, is situated not far from the old village of Little Prairie. It was named in honor of Hon. Sam Caruthers of Madison county, and was laid out in 1857. G. W. Bushley and Col. J. H. Walker were the men instrumental in locating the new town. It grew very slowly and attained no real importance until after the war. Among the first merchants were Harbison & Christie, and Davidson & Edwards.

At present Caruthersville has a population of 3,655. The three banks in the town have a capital stock of $175,000, with large deposits. Among the business interests are an ice plant, four cotton gins, a cottonseed oil mill, a large egg case factory, heading factory, a handle mill, bottling works and about thirty general stores. Besides these there are a number of other business interests of minor importance. The town is lighted with electric lights and has a modern system of water works. The public schools of Caruthersville are in a good condition, there being one large brick building for the grades, and a new high school building. Seventeen teachers are employed. Besides the public schools there is a Catholic parochial school, which has a large attendance. There are church organizations of most of the denominations and several of them have church buildings.

There are published in the town the following papers: *The Democrat*, edited by W. R. Lacey; *The Argus*, edited by H. E. Averill, and *The Republican*, edited by Frank Abernathy.

Large lumber interests center here and the rich farming country about makes the future of the place secure. It enjoys the advantage of river traffic and is the southern terminus of the St. Louis & Gulf, a branch of the Frisco.

CHAPTER XXIII

DUNKLIN AND MISSISSIPPI

OLD-TIME KENNETT—MODERN TOWN DATES FROM RAILROAD — CLARKTON — HORNERSVILLE—
MISSISSIPPI COUNTY SEAT—CHARLESTON OF THE PRESENT—BELMONT.

Kennett, the county seat of Dunklin county, was laid out as a town in 1846. It was first called Chilletecaux, after the Indian village which was near. In 1849 the legislature of the state changed its name to Butler. A few years after that time it received its present name, in honor of Luther M. Kennett.

OLD-TIME KENNETT

The first merchant in the town of Kennett was Elbert C. Spiller. Some of the other early merchants were James Cude, A. M. Davis, J. R. McCullough, John S. Houston, John H. Marsh and Campbell Wright. The town grew slowly for a good many years and was supported in part by the business of the county seat. It is surrounded by very fertile land, but this land for many years was undeveloped and the population of the county was small. In 1847 a small log building was erected as a court house. It was placed in the center of the public square, about where the present court house stands. It was used until during the war, when it was destroyed. The first jail was built at the same time of the court house building. It, too, was of logs, and was used until after the war.

The town suffered greatly during the war, as it was in territory traversed by both armies and was sometimes in the hands of lawless men. After the war there was not much left except a small village. Progress was very slow for many years. The town was so far from river and rail transportation that it seemed practically impossible for it to develop. The population of the county grew but the great bulk of its trade went to Cape Girardeau. That was the nearest accessible point on the river. The cotton and other products of Dunklin county soil were hauled to that place, and the dry goods and supplies used by the people brought back in return. With the building of the Cairo & Texas Railroad from Cairo to Poplar Bluff, Dexter became the great trading point for Dunklin county. A little later Malden, the western terminus of the St. Louis, Arkansas & Texas Railway (later the St. Louis Southwestern) was the most important trading center.

There were always a few stores at Kennett during this period, but they carried small stocks of goods and made little effort to provide a market for the county's products. This failure to provide for handling the crops was due to a number of things. The distance from adequate means of transportation, the lack of sufficient capital, and the method then in vogue of handling cotton, which was the most important staple crop. At that time cotton was ginned before being sold by the farmer.

and was then usually consigned by him to some commission merchant in St. Louis to be sold on account. Furs were for many years an important item in the county's wealth and these were often bought by traveling agents for fur houses in the cities. All these conditions prevented the town from acquiring any considerable importance.

A few men, however, saw the possibilities of the development of trade and the building up of a town, and kept working and planning for their own and the town's prosperity. The foremost of these men was W. F. Shelton, whose early struggles and final success form a most interesting chapter in the town's history. Other men who held on and kept faith in the town's eventual success were Tatum Bros., T. E. Baldwin, W. G. Bragg, R. H. Jones, D. Y. Pankey, Dr. A. B. Mobley and J. B. Blakemore.

Modern Town Dates from Railroad

Many plans were made for ending the town's isolation by the building of a railroad, but nothing was actually done until 1891. In that year E. S. McCarthy and associates built a line from Campbell on the St. Louis Southwestern, to Kennett. The first train reached the town January 1, 1892. The road soon came into possession of Louis Houck. It was eventually extended to Caruthersville, giving an outlet to the river; later it was built to the south. Coupled with the coming of the railroads were other changes which added to the prosperity of the town. Population of the county grew rapidly, the products of the farms became more varied, new business methods were introduced, capital for opening up new enterprises became abundant. The timber, which was very abundant, became valuable, and its development brought large sums of money. The county became one of the most prosperous in this part of the state, and Kennett shared in this prosperity. Frame buildings were supplanted by brick, sidewalks were built, and other public improvements made, so that in the short time since the railroad reached the town it has been transformed from a country village with a population of 500 or 600 to a thriving and prosperous town with modern improvements, good schools, churches, handsome residences, good business establishments, and a population of more than 3,000.

It is now one of the fastest growing towns in Southeast Missouri, is situated in the midst of a most fertile farming country, and it has also the advantage of nearness to large bodies of timber. Its railroad facilities are good. It is on the St. Louis and Gulf line of the Frisco, which gives it connection with the Cotton Belt at Campbell, with the main line of the Frisco at Cape Girardeau and Hayti, and also connects it with the Paragould & Southeastern Railroad to the south. Besides the Frisco, the town is the terminus of the St. Louis, Kennett & Southeastern, which extends from Piggott, Arkansas, to Kennett. This line is owned by home capital and is important to the town because it opens up great bodies of timber and much valuable farming land. There are about fifty business establishments of various kinds, including some large general stores, office buildings, drug stores and furniture and hardware establishments. Besides these there are some large wood working plants engaged in the manufacture of staves, heading and lumber, and the town has one of the few cotton oil mills in Missouri. It possesses the usual church organizations, all of which have good buildings, and there are two banks in the town—the Bank of Kennett, which was organized in 1891 and has a capital stock of $25,000, and the

Cotton Exchange Bank, organized in 1900, which has a capital stock of $30,000. The town is the county seat of Dunklin county and one of the principal buildings is the court house, which occupies a commanding site in the center of the square. The business connected with the courts is one of the features of life in the town. The Dunklin *Democrat,* a Democratic newspaper edited by E. P. Caruthers, is one of the best county papers in the section. It has a large circulation and considerable influence. The town has a good system of public schools, there being at present two buildings—the Central school and the Shelton school. There is a fully accredited high school and this institution is one of the most popular in the town.

in New Madrid county to Dunklin county, its terminus being Clarkton. The first settler in the town was Dr. Skaggs. Other early settlers were John Timberman and his partner, William Muse; they operated the first store in the town. Dr. Van H. Harrison was one of the first physicians and R. W. and T. C. Stokes were merchants. The town grew rapidly for a time as it was surrounded by a fine farming country and its population soon grew to three hundred. It built the first good school

COURT HOUSE, KENNETT

building in the county. Its prosperity was very greatly checked, however, by the building of the St. Louis, Arkansas & Texas railroad from New Madrid to Malden. Most of the business of Clarkton was moved either to Malden or Kennett, and for many years the town was at a standstill. Only one or two stores were conducted during this period, the principal one being that owned by Michael Hubbard. About 1895 a railroad was built from Gibson to Cape Girardeau; this was a branch of the Frisco system and it passed

CLARKTON

Clarkton, in Dunklin county, was founded in 1860 and was named in honor of Henry E. Clark, who was one of the contractors of the building of the Plank road from Weaverville through the old village of Clarkton. It immediately revived and took on new life, and is now a prosperous and flourishing town, having several good general stores, two banks, and boasts a population of 682.

The people of Clarkton have recently constructed a new school building, which is justly the pride of the citizens of the town. At one time Clarkton was the largest town in Dunklin county and constructed the first building for school purposes of any pretentions whatever. This frame building was used for many years, but has recently been superseded by a new and better building. A well was bored near the town in 1910 in an effort to find oil or gas. This effort was unsuccessful, but at a depth of about 1,000 feet a strong flow of artesian water was found.

HORNERSVILLE

Hornersville, in the south part of Dunklin county, was established in 1840 by William H. Horner. Mr. Horner was the first merchant of the town and its most prominent citizen. The town received its name from him. It had a very limited growth prior to the war, there being only a few stores up to this time.

It is now on the line of the Paragould Southeastern Railroad and is a flourishing business community. It has a number of good stores, several cotton gins and its financial interests are cared for by the Bank of Hornersville, chartered in 1909; it has a capital stock of $10,000. Its present population is 390.

There are cotton gins and sawmills which contribute to the town's prosperity. Its system of schools is well organized. It is in the finest farming country in Southeast Missouri and will always be a prosperous community. There are two churches—Methodist and Baptist.

MISSISSIPPI COUNTY SEAT

Charleston, the county seat of Mississippi county, was laid off as a town in 1837, sixteen acres being surveyed in twelve blocks. The land on which it was laid off belonged to Thankful Randol, Joseph Moore and W. P. Barnard. The first person to reside on the town site seems to have been Humphrey Warren, who built a small log house there about 1830. His house and land was bought by Thankful Randol, who resided at the place until her death. After the town of Charleston was established she kept a hotel. The first store in the town was opened by John West and his partner, whose name was Neil. Other merchants were Arthur R. Newman, Henry G. Cummings, and Kuran Gorman. Gorman was one of the largest and most successful merchants in Charleston prior to the war, and is said to have become wealthy through his trading operations. One of the men who did much to build the town up and make it prosperous was George Whitcomb. He moved to Charleston shortly after the town was founded and built a large, double log house on the lot where Hon. J. J. Russell now lives. He was a public spirited man and accomplished a great deal for the town. It was largely due to his work and influence that the Cairo & Fulton Railroad was secured for Charleston. He was clerk of the courts for about twenty years and during most of that time was also a dealer in real estate.

The first newspaper in Charleston was established in 1857. It was known as *The Courier*, and its editor was George Whitcomb. *The Courier* was one of the few papers in Southeast Missouri that was published during the war. From 1858 to 1872 the manager, and for a part of the time the editor, was W. F.

Martin; though the paper continued to be the property of Mr. Whitcomb.

It is said that there was a school conducted in a log cabin near the site of Charleston prior to the laying off of the town. It was known as the Indian Grove school. Some of the first teachers were Hartford Hayes, James L. Moore and John C. Thomas.

There were fifteen business establishments in the town in 1859, including general and special stores. Among the merchants were K. Gorman, L. Rosenberg, Hayes & Bartlett, Frank Myrick, J. H. Bridges, W. G. Cooley, W. A. Lynn and F. J. Jecko. At this time the town's physicians were B. J. Moore, S. D. Golder, T. C. Poor, J. L. Haw and A. E. Simpson. There was a strong bar, and a number of attorneys made their homes here. Among them were Robert Waide, A. M. Bedford, N. E. Quinby, Sam C. Moore, Joseph C. Moore and M. Ward.

The first bank in the town was a branch of the old Union Bank organized in 1860. John Bird was made president and J. C. Moore cashier. The directors were among the most influential citizens of the town at that time. They were G. W. Whitcomb, C. C. Kalfus, Thompson Bird, J. S. Bledsoe, Noah Handy, James Smith, J. L. Moore and K. Gorman. The bank was taken possession of by Confederate soldiers under General Jeff. Thompson in 1862 and $58,000 in gold and silver was carried away and afterward turned over to the depositors. This action was taken to prevent the funds falling into the hands of the Federal forces. The next bank was the Bank of Charleston, chartered in October, 1887, with a capital stock of $15,000. A. H. Danforth was its first president and Scott Alexander cashier. This bank now has a capital of $100,000 and J. J. Russell is president; Scott Alexander is still cashier. The Mississippi County Bank was chartered in 1891 and has a capital of $40,000. In 1902 the Peoples' Bank was organized and its capital is $35,000.

Charleston of the Present

The town is one of the most pleasantly situated in Southeast Missouri; it is on a sandy ridge and in the midst of the most fertile and easily worked soil in the entire section. It is distinctly a city of homes and has developed the characteristic life of the older settled communities of this part of the state. It is at the crossing of the Belmont branch of the Iron Mountain and of the Cairo & Texas between Poplar Bluff and Cairo; it has ample railroad facilities and is not a great distance from the river. The general business interests are well represented and there is a large flouring mill and other smaller manufacturing plants. The town is distinguished on account of its interest in churches and school system; all the usual church organizations exist and the Methodists and Baptists have recently completed the erection of two unusually well constructed church buildings. The public school system is of the highest grade, there being two buildings, both of them new and well adapted to the work of the schools; a four years' high school course is fully accredited and takes high rank among the schools of the section. The population is 3,144. The town is the county seat of Mississippi county. The newspapers are *The Enterprise*, a Democratic weekly, and *The Republican*, which is Republican in politics.

Charleston is the headquarters of the Southeast Missouri Telephone Company, which operates exchanges in many of the principal towns of the southeast.

BELMONT

Belmont, which is the terminus of the Belmont branch of the Iron Mountain Railroad, is a little town in Mississippi county; it was laid out in 1853. The oldest town in Mississippi county, however, is Norfolk, which was surveyed a year before Charleston was, in 1836. It was established by James Ramsay and William Lester, and is situated on the Mississippi river about six miles below Bird's Point. It is famous as the scene of a fiercely fought battle during the Civil war.

CHAPTER XXIV

TOWNS OF SIX COUNTIES

COMMERCE INCORPORATED—BENTON, SCOTT COUNTY SEAT — SIKESTON—DONIPHAN, COUNTY SEAT OF RIPLEY—POPLAR BLUFF, BUTLER COUNTY'S SEAT OF JUSTICE—BLOOMFIELD, STODDARD COUNTY—IRONTON, COUNTY SEAT OF IRONTON — ARCADIA — LESTERVILLE — SMALLER SETTLEMENTS.

The town of Commerce, in Scott county, was laid out in 1823. The commissioners were Wilson Abel, James Purtels, Thomas Roberts, Joseph Smith and James Wellborn. It had been a trading post for about twenty years before it was regularly laid off as a town. The land on which it was built was the property of the heirs of Thomas W. Waters. The early merchants were Archibald Price, Weaver & Echols, Shaw & Pettit, and Ignatius Wathen. John Brown was hotel keeper, Lyon & Applegate were carpenters, and William and Samuel Graysey operated a pottery making establishment. In 1844 Benjamin B. Gaither began the operation of a tan yard. In 1856 a large mill was built by Ignatius R. Wathen, who was at that time a resident of Cape Girardeau. Other men who bought and sold goods during this period were Thomas M. Shaw, John Hoskins, Moses Baker, and Morean & Burgess.

COMMERCE INCORPORATED

The town was incorporated in July, 1834, with William Grasey, Jacob Stear, J. S. Smith, John Brown and Joseph W. Echols as trustees. The legislature of the state granted a charter to the town in 1857 and the government was organized in accordance with the provisions of this charter. It, however, fell into disuse during the war period.

This town is at that point on the ridge known as the Scott county hills and is also on the Mississippi river. It has river transportation and is also on the Gulf division of the Frisco railroad. It has several business establishments, the principal one being a flouring mill and a plant for the manufacture of tile. There are the usual church organizations in the town and a public school. The Farmers' Bank was chartered in 1892 and has a capital stock of $50,000. The population of Commerce is 544.

BENTON, SCOTT COUNTY SEAT

Benton, the county seat of Scott county, was laid out in 1822 on land owned by Colonel William Meyers. Among the early residents were Colonel Meyers, Edmond Rogers, John Houts, Michael McLaughlin and John B. Rutter. Rogers was a tavern owner, Houts ran a tan yard, McLaughlin was a merchant, and Rutter was a clerk of the court. The early houses were, most of them, log houses. The first frame house in the town was a store building erected about 1830 by Joseph Hunter. Some of the other merchants in the early history of the town were Dr. E. P. LaValle, John

Harbison, George Netherton, Abraham Winchester, Crow, McCrary, George and Thomas Williams. The first physicians were John Golden, Samuel Chapman and Dr. A. S. Henderson, who came to the town in 1842. The town was incorporated in 1860 by the county court, with James Parrott, A. S. Henderson, D. H. Leedy, Daniel Abbey and Edward Burke as trustees.

The principal thing about Benton is that it is the county seat of the county, and the court house is situated in the midst of the public square. It is a two-story brick building and was erected in 1883. There are about a half dozen business establishments, including a large flouring mill. On the court house square there is a large well, from which the town is supplied with water, and there is a good system of electric lights. There are three churches in the town and a public school building. The Benton Bank was organized in 1903 and has a capital stock of $15,000. The population is about 320.

Sikeston

The first town in the neighborhood of Sikeston was called Winchester, and was named in honor of Colonel Henderson Winchester, who lived in the vicinity. This town was laid out in 1814 about a half mile south of the present site of Sikeston. The first store in Winchester was opened by Thomas Bartlett, and Hartwell Baldwin kept the tavern at that time. Other stores were opened by David Hunter, Mark H. Stallcup, and Christopher Houts. The town grew rather rapidly for a time and was the seat of justice for New Madrid county. When the county seat was removed to New Madrid, however, the town practically ceased to exist. This was in 1822. Its successor as a town was laid out in Sikeston in 1860 by John Sikes. The site selected was the place where the Cairo & Fulton Railroad crosses the road called the King's Highway from Cape Girardeau to New Madrid. In the year that Sikeston was founded the Cairo & Fulton Railroad was completed to that place.

Sikeston has experienced the most rapid growth of any town in Southeast Missouri in the last ten years. In 1899 its population was about 500; its present population is 3,327. This rapid growth is due in part to its situation with regard to railroad transportation, it being on the main line of the Frisco and also on the Cairo & Texas branch of the Iron Mountain. It has prospered also because of the fact that the farming country about it has developed wonderfully in the last few years. There is no better soil than that on the Sikeston ridge; it produces large quantities of wheat, corn and melons. Sikeston has also been fortunate in having an unusual and exceptional group of business men, who have pushed the interests of the town very rapidly. At the present time there are about fifty business establishments, including several large general stores; there are two flouring mills, one of them being the largest in Southeast Missouri. The usual church organizations are to be found here and the Methodist church South has recently completed a very large, handsome building, perhaps the most costly in this part of the state. The Bank of Sikeston was organized in 1800 and has a capital stock of $250,000. The Citizens' Bank was organized in 1895 and has a capital stock of $150,000, and the People's Bank was organized in 1909 and has a capital of $50,000. The public school system of Sikeston is a good one and there are two new and commodious buildings and a four years' high school course fully accredited is maintained. *The Herald* is a Democratic paper and *The Standard* is an independent paper. Just south of the town is a very beautiful plot of ground laid out as a cemetery, and here are buried some of the pioneers of Southeast Missouri. The most prominent of these is Ben F. Hunter, a man well known in the early history of the state, and whose descendants are prominent in this section still.

DONIPHAN, COUNTY SEAT OF RIPLEY

The county seat of Ripley county was settled about the year 1847 and was named for General Alexander William Doniphan, the hero of the Mexican war. Among the families who lived in Doniphan in its early days were Ponders, Dudleys, Daltons, Pulliams, O'Neals, Stringers, Kents, Lawsons, Wheelers and Mulhollands; most of these early families were from Tennessee. The census of 1850 shows that there were more native Tennesseeans in Ripley county than natives of all other states combined. In 1856-57 a number of Irish families were located in a colony in this county by Father Hogan, a pastor from St. Louis. The earliest merchants in the town were Kitrell & Thannish and W. P. Kreps. The town grew slowly at first and was not incorporated until after the close of the war. It was made the county seat of Ripley county when Carter county was organized in 1859. Previous to this time Van Buren had been the county seat and was then made the county seat of Carter county. For many years the town was without railroad connections and it was so until 1883, when the Doniphan branch of the Iron Mountain was built from Naylor to Doniphan. This gave the town an impetus and it has had a steady growth since that time. There are now ten general stores, with other business interests of minor importance, an ice factory and a canning factory. The financial interests of the town are cared for by the Ripley County Bank with a capital of $15,000, and the Doniphan State Bank whose capital is $15,000. The more important buildings in the town are the two bank buildings and ten brick business blocks. There are the usual church organizations, most of them having houses of worship, and a good system of public schools. The town has a modern system of water works and boasts that it has more concrete sidewalks than any other town of its size in the state.

Doniphan is beautifully situated on the hills overlooking Current river, perhaps the most beautiful stream in the state. It is connected with the territory on the other side of Current river by a modern steel bridge, which was recently erected. Its population is now about 1,800 and it is one of the most pleasant residence towns in this part of the state. It has two good weekly papers—*The Prospect-News*, published by J. P. Campbell, and *The Democrat*, published by D. G. Cunningham. Both are Democratic in politics.

POPLAR BLUFF, BUTLER COUNTY'S SEAT OF JUSTICE

The following order appears on the record of the county court of Butler county, of the date August 13, 1850: "It is ordered that hereafter the courts of Butler county be held at a place known and designated as Poplar Bluff, and the sheriff give notice by putting up three hand bills." This record gives the selection of Poplar Bluff as the county seat of Butler county. Prior to this time the courts had met at different places; sometimes in Cane Creek township, at the house of Solomon Kittrell, and sometimes in Epps township, at the house of Daniel Epps. The county judges at this time were Jonathan Sandlin and Solomon Kittrell. Jacob C. Blount was the clerk and Newton Wallace was the sheriff.

On the 11th day of November, 1850, the

court assembled for its first meeting in Poplar Bluff. This meeting was held in a rail pen, or shed, on the bank of Black river, near the foot of what is now Vine street. The judges at this time were Abraham Romine, John N. Yarber and William Vandover. The place selected was in the woods, and is named because of the presence of large poplar trees.

A postoffice was established February 27, 1850, and the first postmaster was Jesse A. Gilley, who was succeeded in September of the same year by Jacob C. Blount. The postoffice was kept at the east end of the old county bridge, in a small one-room cabin. The mail was brought to this place on horseback but was so uncertain that the postoffice was discontinued in December, 1851. The only mercantile establishment in Poplar Bluff was a small cabin built of hickory logs at the corner of Second and Vine streets. Charles S. Henderson was the proprietor, and he sold whisky and tobacco and dealt in furs. Other merchants who conducted stores in Poplar Bluff during the early years were C. P. Phelps, who operated a general store, Kelley & Taylor, and Henderson & Lawson. The town grew slowly of course during the period before the war, and was almost depopulated during the war.

The first circuit courts in Poplar Bluff were presided over by the Hon. Henderson Huff. The sittings of the court were held in the house opposite the present court house square. General Watkins, Thomas B. English and a Mr. Hill were the lawyers who conducted most of the cases before the court. They were all from Cape Girardeau county. In 1859 a contract was let to S. G. Kitchen and D. B. Miller to build a brick court house. The work was supervised by William Ringer of Stoddard county. The building, which cost $6,000, was paid partly in cash and partly in lands.

The first frame house was built in 1859 by James S. Ferguson. By the year 1860 there were twelve houses and ten families in the town.

Among the early settlers one of the most prominent was John N. Yarber. He was a native of North Carolina and came to the vicinity of Poplar Bluff in 1844. He took part in all the activities of his time and held numerous offices in the county. He lived for many years after the war and was held in great esteem by those who knew him. Another man prominent in the early times was James S. Ferguson, who built the first frame house in the town. He also held a number of offices, being clerk of the courts and county judge. Other citizens were James M. Spence, Dr. J. R. Franklin, Dr. James T. Adams, John Snoddy and Jesse A. Gilley. They were all prominent in the life of the town in its early years.

We may well suppose that life in a community like this was hampered in many ways and that the growth of the county, and necessarily the towns, was slow. Possibly one of the most remarkable records ever entered by a court was made by one of the courts in Poplar Bluff, as follows: "It is ordered by the court that the sheriff borrow $20 from anybody who would loan it to him for the purpose of buying two seals, one for the circuit clerk and one for the county clerk." We are left in doubt as to whether anyone was good enough to lend this money, but as seals were used by the courts within a short time after this we may reasonably conclude that the loan was made.

At the present time there are in Poplar Bluff about seventy-five mercantile establishments of every kind; this large number indicates the amount of mercantile business transacted in the town. In addition to these there

Poplar Bluff High School

Scene on Black River near Poplar Bluff

are about thirty factories of one sort or another. Many of these are wood working establishments, consisting of stave mills, spoke factories, handle factories, furniture making establishments, wagon factories, machine shops, planing mills, bottle and ice plant, brick and tile factory and a factory for the manufacture of adding machines. There are four banks in the town, indicating the financial situation and needs. The town is lighted with electric lights and has a good system of waterworks. Up to the present time the streets have never been paved, but there is now a movement on foot which will probably lead to the beginning of this work in the summer of 1912. Among the important buildings are the city hall, court house, high school building and the Dalton Adding Machine Company's fireproof factory building.

One fact of interest which connects Poplar Bluff of today with the old town is the existence of a farm in the suburbs which was transferred from the government of the United States directly to Judge Yarber in the early days of the town and which has never been retransferred. The original patent from the government was signed by President Buchanan and is still in existence.

The town was incorporated in 1861 and its first mayor was Daniel Kitchen. Its population is now 6,916, and it is growing rapidly. Its two papers, *The Republican* and *The Citizen*—Democrat—are published both daily and weekly and are both enterprising papers.

BLOOMFIELD, STODDARD COUNTY

John McCombs, Michael Rodney and Henry Shaner, three citizens of Stoddard county were appointed as commissioners to locate the site for the county seat. A number of offers of land were made to them, and many persons were interested in securing the selection of their property for this purpose. After a considerable consultation, the commissioners decided to select fifty acres of land donated to the county by Absolom Barley. This they did, and proceeded to lay out a town, which they named Bloomfield, it is said, because of the fact that the field was then covered with flowers. After the selection of the site, the county court appointed William C. Ranney as special commissioner for the sale of lots. It is probable that Absolom Barley, who had previously owned the land, was the first resident of the town. He lived in a small log house on the southwest corner of the place, but afterward built a brick house on another site. Orson Bartlett was, perhaps, the first merchant, and Rev. John N. Mitchell, a Methodist preacher, and Thomas Neale, who operated a tan yard, were very early residents. The hotel was kept by Harmon Reed, and the early physicians were M. B. Koons, Daniel Sanford, and Samuel Chapman. Edmund White opened a store on the south side of the public square in 1844 and Daniel Miller about the same time, together with his brother Henry, also began the sale of goods. In 1854, John M. Johnson, R. P. Owen and N. G. H. Jones, began to operate stores. The other merchants prior to the war were: Elijah Miller, John L. Buck, Paramore & McDaniel, Louis Ringer, John Leach and Harper & Christy.

The *Herald*, the first newspaper in Bloomfield, was established in 1858 by A. M. Bedford, of Charleston. The purpose of the publication of this paper was to advocate the building of the Cairo & Fulton Railroad. The Methodist church was used for several years for the conduct of the schools. These were elementary in character, and the terms were short. In 1853 a number of gentlemen organized the Bloomfield Educational Society for the purpose of conducting a seminary for learning. Its trustees were S. G. Kitchen, Orson Bartlett, Henry Miller, D. B. Miller and Michael A. Wilson. The society built a two-story frame structure and carried on the school in it until the breaking out of the war.

The town was one of the most prosperous in the district. Perhaps no other town away from the river grew quite as rapidly and substantially during these years as did Bloomfield. It was surpassed in size, perhaps, only by Cape Girardeau. The war, however, put an end to the prosperity of the town, and in fact, resulted in its almost complete destruction. Practically every building was either torn down or burned.

The site was taken possession of by Federal forces who erected a fort soon after the fire. On the close of the war the town had practically ceased to exist but was reincorporated in 1869 and in 1870 a new court house was built at a cost of $25,000. The first newspaper published in the town was the *Herald*, established in 1858 by A. M. Bedford and J. O. Hall, it was discontinued in 1861; in 1866 the *Argus* was started by James Hamilton and published until 1873; in 1878 the *Cosmos* began to be published but was later discontinued; the *Bloomfield Vindicator*, the present paper, has been published since 1878. In 1899 the town had a population of 2,200, and there were about 40 business establishments at that time, there were also churches, Methodist Episcopal, Methodist Episcopal South and the Catholic.

Up to 1896 the town was without railroad facilities of any kind. In that year a line was built from Bloomfield to Zeta on the St. Louis Southwestern. In 1898 Mr. Houck built a line from Broomwood to Bloomfield and rebuilt the line to Zeta. The improved methods of transportation and the erection of large woodworking plants, chiefly stave mills, increased the town's prosperity very greatly and it grew rapidly for a number of years. It was well-built with substantial brick buildings, many public improvements were made, and it became one of the most rapidly advancing towns of the section. The practical exhaustion of the timber, however, led to the loss of the mills and this dealt the prosperity of the place a heavy blow. For a time its population began to decline. In 1910 there were only 1,147 people there. This condition is changing now and population is once more increasing.

There are about forty business establishments of various kinds. One of these is a pottery factory and kiln. There is a good system of public schools, and several church organizations. The farming country about the town will always support it and it has too the interests which gather about the county seat and add to its prosperity

One of the old papers of the southeast is the *Bloomfield Vindicator* an ably edited weekly, Democratic in politics. Bloomfield Bank was chartered in 1895 and has a capital stock of $50,000. The City Bank was organized in 1900. Its capital is $15,000.

Ironton, County Seat of Iron

The present county seat of Iron county, Ironton, was laid off as a town immediately after the organization of Iron county. At that time there were in the county only three villages: Arcadia, Middle Brook and Pilot Knob. Pilot Knob was a settlement of miners at the base of the mountain of the same name. Two men who were interested in the site of Ironton determined to lay off the town there, and if possible to secure the county seat. The election was held September 7th, 1857, and there were three places asking for the county seat: Arcadia, Middle Brook and the proposed town of Ironton. Ironton was selected, and Tong and Carson, who owned the site, and whose influence had caused its selection, laid off the town and donated alternate lots to the county. These lots were sold at auction and brought the sum of $10,600.00. The new town, though handicapped by its nearness to Arcadia and Pilot Knob, experienced a fair growth owing in part to the mining industry, and in part to the presence of the county seat. In 1859 the population was about three hundred. The first paper in the town was the *Furnace,* a Free Soil paper, established in 1858 by James Lindsay.

Ironton has not experienced anything in the nature of a boom, it has grown slowly and steadily being supported by the fact of its being the county seat and by the further fact that it is a delightful summer resort. The valley in which the town is situated is one of the most pleasant places in the state and it is perhaps the only town in Southeast Missouri that is used as a place of summer residence by a large number of people. It is on the main line of the St. Louis Iron Mountain and Southern railway and is sufficiently near St. Louis to render it easy of access. It has a system of public schools and three churches. The Bank of Ironton was chartered in 1905 and has a capital stock of $15,000, the Iron County Bank was chartered in 1896 and has a capital stock of $10,000. The *Iron County Register,* one of the oldest newspapers in Southeast Missouri, is published here by Eli D. Ake. It is Democratic in politics and Mr. Ake is the dean of newspaper profession in this part of the state. The population of the town is 721.

Arcadia

Arcadia was surveyed as a town in 1849 The first merchants were: Ezekiel Matthews, Smith & Love, John F. T. Edwards, William N. Gregory, G. B. Nall, Pease & Hill and Harris and Chinn. The first mill was erected in 1847 by Josiah and J. C. Berryman. It was a steam mill for grinding grain and sawing timber. The first newspaper in the town was the *Arcadia Prospect* established in 1859 by A. Coulter and W. L. Faber. The town was not incorporated until after this period. It is quite probable that Arcadia owes its existence as a town to the Arcadia high school. It was an institution founded by Rev. J. C. Berryman, and conducted under the auspices of the Methodist Episcopal Church South. The town grew up in part around this school. This school was transferred to the Ursuline Sisters and since operated by them. Ironton was laid off just a short distance north of Arcadia, became the county seat, and outstripped the older town. It soon took on its distinguishing character as a residence town. No more beautiful situation exists in Missouri than Arcadia valley. Many people came attracted by the many desirable residence features.

The town suffered some during the war, but not greatly. On the lawn of Judge John W. Emerson, then the Union headquarters, Ulysses S. Grant received the commission promoting him from the rank of colonel to that of brigadier-general and putting him into command of Southeast Missouri. It was occupied at times by forces from both sides.

After the war it resumed its normal course of development. Families of wealth from other parts of the state established summer homes for themselves amid the quiet and pleasant surroundings here. Finally the town attracted the attention of church people and there was established quarters for summer meetings and encampments of church people especially of the young peoples organizations in the church. The Epworth League of the Methodist church owns fine grounds and has a yearly encampment as does also the Baptist Young Peoples' Union. Doubtless this special feature of life will continue to develop until the town is a famous resort for conventions and societies holding their meetings in the summer time. The course so far taken has been to avoid the development of the usual forms of resort life with large and expensive hotels, but to encourage simpler living. Tents and small cottages are in most demand for these gatherings.

The present population is 289. The *Arcadia Valley Enterprise* is an influential weekly paper edited by Fuller Swaift and is Republican in politics. The town is situated on the main line of the St. Louis, Iron Mountain and Southern Railway.

LESTERVILLE

The town of Lesterville in Reynolds county was settled about 1860, but has never been incorporated as a town and it is now impossible to give the names of the first settlers. The first merchant in the town was William Bowen, there are now four general stores and a hub factory. The financial interests of the town are cared for by the Bank of Lesterville. The more important buildings are the school house and Masonic hall. The town is not situated on a railroad and is rather difficult of access. Its population is about 300.

SMALLER SETTLEMENTS

Des Arc, an incorporated village in Union township in Iron county, is twenty-nine miles south of Ironton on the Iron Mountain Railroad; it has a hotel, flouring mill and two general stores. Its population is about 200.

The little town of Middle Brook, a short distance north of Ironton and on the line between Iron county and St. Francois county, was laid out as a town in 1856.

CHAPTER XXV

POLITICAL, CIVIL AND MILITARY

THE FIRST STATE ELECTION—CONTEST FOR THE SENATORSHIP—THE EIGHT COUNTIES—COURTS IN EACH COUNTY—ORGANIZATION OF NEW COUNTIES—SOUTHEAST MISSOURI IN THE MEXICAN WAR.

The people of Missouri, after the adoption of the first of the two compromises, supposing that they would be admitted to the Union, proceeded to the formation of a government. The constitution was framed in July, 1820, and it called for a meeting of the general assembly in September of that year. The election was ordered to be held August 28th. The people were then to elect a governor, lieutenant governor, a representative in Congress for the sixteenth Congress, one for the seventeenth, members of the general assembly, and sheriffs and coroners in the various counties. The constitution fixed the number of senators in the state at fourteen and representatives at forty-three.

FIRST STATE ELECTION

The election was held on the date announced and the entire state government selected. This was nearly a year before the admission of the state into the Union, so that Missouri presented the unusual spectacle of a sovereign state with a duly authorized government under a constitution, but outside of the Union and still not independent.

The election resulted in the choice of Alexander McNair for governor, William H. Ashley for lieutenant governor, and John Scott as representative in Congress for both its sessions. Scott lived in Ste. Genevieve.

CONTEST FOR THE SENATORSHIP

The general assembly met in St. Louis in September, 1820. James Caldwell of Ste. Genevieve was the speaker of the house. Among the duties of the legislature were the election of two United States senators and the appointment of three supreme and four circuit judges. One of the judges of the supreme court was John D. Cook of Cape Girardeau. The contest for United States senator was a very interesting one. There were two senators to be selected. David Barton of St. Louis was elected on the first ballot by an unanimous vote, but a fierce contest was waged for the remaining place. The candidates were Thomas H. Benton, John B. C. Lucas, Henry Elliott, John Rice Jones and Nathaniel Cook. Of these candidates, Judges Lucas and Benton were the most prominent. After a long attempt to select a senator Benton was finally chosen.

THE EIGHT COUNTIES

When Missouri was admitted to the Union in 1821 there were only eight counties organized in Southeast Missouri. These were:

Washington, Perry, Ste. Genevieve, Cape Girardeau, Wayne, New Madrid, Jefferson and Madison counties. All the other territory of this section of the state was embraced in one or more of these counties. It is plainly evident that some of them were vastly larger in area than they are at present. This was true especially of Wayne county; out of it there were afterward created several large counties.

Courts in Each County

In each one of these counties, as in other counties of the state, there was a county court composed of justices of the peace, and having very limited jurisdiction. These county courts were not thoroughly organized, and the principal business of the court was conducted not by the county courts but by the circuit courts.

The counties of Ste. Genevieve, Madison, Wayne, New Madrid, Cape Girardeau and Perry were organized into the southern judicial circuit. One judge presided over the sittings of the court in each of these counties. Terms of the court were held at specified times, and these terms were so arranged as not to conflict with one another, and thus make it possible for one judge to hold court in all the counties of the circuit. Washington and Jefferson counties belonged to the northern circuit, which included besides these southeastern counties St. Louis, St. Charles and Franklin counties. The circuit courts, as organized in each one of these counties, was a body having wide jurisdiction and great power. In addition to the jurisdiction now exercised by circuit courts the early courts had a large part of the jurisdiction which now belongs to either the county court or the probate court. We have seen that the first judge of the southern circuit was Hon. Richard S. Thomas, who during his term of office was a resident of Jackson.

At the time of the organization of the state government each county was represented by one or more members in the legislative council. Upon the organization of the state government each county was then represented by one member of the house of representatives, and there were organized senatorial districts for the election of members of the upper house. There was at the time of admission only one member of the national house of representatives. The population of Missouri was not sufficient to entitle the state to more than one representative, and this condition lasted until about 1840.

Southeast Missouri in the Mexican War

From the close of the Indian troubles, which were connected with the war of 1812, until the breaking out of the Civil war, the people of Southeast Missouri had little opportunity to make military history. The only time in which they were called upon to become soldiers was during the Mexican war and not many from this section of the state took part in that struggle. Only a few companies were organized and not a very large number of the individuals joined commands in other parts of Missouri and in other states. In the summer of 1846 Captain Thomas M. Horine organized a company at Ste. Genevieve and marched with it to Fort Leavenworth. At Fort Leavenworth the company became part of the Second Missouri Regiment which was commanded by Colonel, afterward General Sterling Price. It took part in the remarkable expedition known as Doniphan's expedition. In company with the other regiment forming Doniphan's command these troops marched west from Fort Leavenworth and finally reached Santa Fe. It took part in the engagement in New Mexico and when General Price was left by Doniphan in command of the territory of Mexico the Missouri soldiers remained with him. They fought a number of skirmishes with the Mexicans and Indians. One of them was the Battle of Taos, lasting all day and resulting in the surrender of the entire force of the enemy.

On August 23, 1846, Captain Firmin A. Rozier organized a company of one hundred and fifteen men in Ste. Genevieve and Perry counties. The organization was known as the South Missouri Guards. They were recruited for service in California under General Kearney and made their way to Fort Leavenworth on the Kansas border. They there became part of a regiment which, by the time the organization was completed, was too late in the season, and no effort was made to cross the plains and the company remained at Fort Leavenworth. In 1847 Captain Robert H. Lane recruited a company at Fredericktown, and the company was mustered into service at Jefferson barracks as Company I of the Third Missouri Mounted Volunteers. John Ralls was colonel of this company and Captain Lane was elected lieutenant colonel. This left his position as captain of Company I vacant, and John Head was chosen to succeed him as captain. From Jefferson barracks the regiment was sent to Fort Leavenworth and from Fort Leavenworth was ordered to Mexico to reinforce the command of Colonel Doniphan. They went by way of Santa Fe and El Paso and joined Colonel Doniphan at the city of Chihuahua, which was then his headquarters. On March 16, 1848, this Third Missouri Regiment, with three other companies, fought a battle with the Mexicans at Santa Cruz. It was a hard fight and lasted all day, for the Mexicans were entrenched within the town and their possession was defended by artillery. In spite of this they were defeated with the loss of three hundred and thirty killed, and the rest of the Mexican force surrendered. The greater part of this regiment, including Company I, was then stationed at Santa Cruz until July, 1848, when they were ordered to return to Independence, Missouri, and were then mustered out in the following October.

CHAPTER XXVI

CREATION OF NEW COUNTIES

ST. FRANCOIS COUNTY—SCOTT COUNTY—ORGANIZATION AND SETTLEMENT OF STODDARD COUNTY—RIPLEY COUNTY—PIONEERS OF DUNKLIN COUNTY—REYNOLDS, BUTLER AND BOLLINGER COUNTIES—PEMISCOT COUNTY—ST. FRANCOIS LEVEE DISTRICT — COURTS OF THE COUNTY AND PROMINENT CITIZENS—IRON AND CARTER COUNTIES—FOUNDERS OF THE EIGHT OLD COUNTIES.

The state had hardly been admitted into the Union until new counties were formed. On December 19, 1821, a bill became law for the creation of part of the counties of Ste. Genevieve, Washington and Jefferson into a new county, to be known as St. Francois county.

ST. FRANCOIS COUNTY

The new county was named from the St. Francois river, which runs almost entirely through it. The governor of the state appointed James Austin, George McGehan and James W. Smith as the county court. They held the first meeting of the court February 25, 1822, at the house of Jesse Murphy, in the neighborhood of Farmington, and appointed John D. Peers as county clerk.

St. Francois county was attached to the northern circuit and the circuit court was organized April 1, 1822, by Judge Nathaniel B. Tucker of St. Charles county. There was no particular business before the court at this first meeting, nor at any early subsequent meetings. The commissioners for the selection of the seat of justice were Henry Poston. John Andrews, William Alexander and James Holbert. On September 22, 1822, fifty-three acres of land were donated by D. Murphy for the purpose of laying out a county seat. They thereupon laid out the present town of Farmington, which has continued to be the seat of justice since that time.

The county was divided into four townships: Perry, Pendleton, Liberty and St. Francois. The officers in these townships were: Perry—William Hale, constable; John Andrews Jr., assessor; Thomas Hale, Archibald McHenry and John Baker, judges of election. Pendleton—Wesley Garret, constable and assessor; James Milburn, Absalom Dent and John Sherrill, judges of election. Liberty—Robert Hays, constable; James Dunlap, assessor; Reuben McFarland, James Dunlap and Samuel Kincaid, judges of election. St. Francois—Benjamin Burnham, constable; Laken Walker, assessor; Richard Murphy. John Murphy and D. F. Marks, judges of election.

Until 1824 the courts were held in the Methodist church, which at that time stood on the hill south of town where the cemetery now is. In that year a brick court house was built on the public square and at the same time a log jail was erected on the site of the present jail.

This jail building was two stories in height and had a dungeon below, which was entered through a trap door. The jail was burned about 1850 by a prisoner. In 1856 it was replaced by a new structure at a cost of $4,400; the present jail was erected in 1870 under the supervision of William Carter and L. D. Walker. The first court house was used until 1850, when it was replaced by another building at a cost of $8,000, and was erected by H. H. Wright. In July, 1885, the contract was let for the construction of the present court house. James P. Killick was the contractor and he turned over the completed building on October 7, 1886, the total cost being $15,560.

The court created a new township in St. Francois county in August, 1836. This was called Marion township and was cut off from the north part of Perry township. In 1840 a township called Black River was created in that part of the county out of which Iron county was later formed. Of the other townships in the county Iron was formed in 1850, Randolph in 1858, and Big River in 1863.

Scott County

Scott county was created by an act of the legislature, December 28, 1821. It was organized from a part of New Madrid county and was named in honor of Hon. John Scott, the first congressman from Missouri. At that time it included the present county of Mississippi. The governor of the state appointed Richard Mathews, Andrew M. Ramsay, and James Houts as the county court, and John P. Rutter as clerk of the circuit court; Joseph A. Hopkins as sheriff; and the county court appointed John P. Rutter as its clerk, also.

Enoch Evans, Abraham Hunter, Thomas Roberts, Joseph Smith and Newman Beckwith were the commissioners to locate the county seat. They selected the site of the town of Benton, and here in a little log house were held the first meetings of the courts. At the time of the organization of the county there were but two townships: Tywappity, which included Mississippi county, and Moreland. The county court, however, soon created four new townships: Richland, Kelso, Mississippi and Wolf Island. In 1836 Tywappity township was divided and the southern part was called St. James township, and in 1839 a township known as St. James Bayou was created.

Scott county was made part of the southern judicial circuit and the circuit court was ganized February 11, 1822, by Judge Thomas; Joseph A. Hopkins was the first sheriff. He gave bond in the sum of five thousand dollars, and his sureties were John Hall and William Meyers. At the next term of the court, which was held in June, 1822, a grand jury was impaneled, and it returned indictments against Samuel Glove and James Ramsay for assault and battery, against Newman Beckwith for selling liquor to the Indians and against Anthony Wills for vagrancy.

The first court house in Scott county was a small log building erected on the public square at Benton. Shortly after the town was laid out a jail costing $500 was erected in 1837. Before that time prisoners had been kept in the jail at Jackson. The first court house was torn down in 1844 and a brick building erected. It was so poorly constructed, however, that it soon became unsafe and was replaced by a frame building. The legislature moved the county seat away from Benton in 1864, to Commerce. The old court house was then sold and a brick court building erected at Commerce. In 1866 a jail was constructed, costing nearly $4,000. However, the people of Scott county were not satisfied with Commerce as the county seat, since it was on one side of the county, in fact, almost in the northeast corner, and in 1878 the seat of justice was returned to Benton, where the present court house, costing $11,000, was erected in 1883. The present townships are Sandyland, Kelso, Sylvania, Tywappity, Commerce, Morley, Moreland and Richland.

ORGANIZATION AND SETTLEMENT OF STODDARD COUNTY

The general assembly passed an act in the year 1829 which defined the boundaries of a new county to be erected out of a part of Wayne county. It was to be named Stoddard, in honor of Captain Amos Stoddard, the agent of the United States government who received the transfer of the Louisiana territory. At this time, however, the county was attached to Cape Girardeau county and the court of that county divided the territory into two townships. That part of Stoddard county east of Castor river was called Pipe township and the part to the north and west Castor township. The first justices of the peace were Joseph Chapman and Thomas Wylie in Pike township, and Thomas Neale and John Eaker in Castor. Joel Ramsay and William Hardin were appointed constables in Pike and Castor townships, respectively.

Stoddard county remained under the jurisdiction of Cape Girardeau officials until January 2nd, 1835. At that time the legislature passed an act to organize a county government. The territory of the new county lay between St. Francois and Little rivers and to the south of Mingo, the Big Swamp.

The commissioners for fixing the seat of government selected the site of the present town of Bloomfield and the first meeting of the county court was held at the house of A. B. Bailey in the southwest part of the town. This was February 9, 1835. The court was composed of Jacob Taylor, Field Bradshaw and John Eaker, and Jonas Eaker was the clerk of the court. Within a short time the court arranged for the erection of a small brick building to be used as a court house. This was placed on the public square and a log jail was built southeast of the square; both of these buildings were used until 1856. At that time $10,000.00 was set aside for the erection of a new court house. It was constructed under the supervision of Solomon G. Kitchen.

The county court, at one of its earliest meetings, divided the county into four townships: Castor, Pike, St. Francois and Liberty. In 1850 Duck Creek township was created, and shortly afterward four more townships were laid out. They were named Prairie, Clay, Benton and Filmore. In 1853 the county was re-divided, owing to the fact that it had been considerably reduced in size. Only five townships were made, under these names: Liberty, Richland, Duck Creek, Castor and Pike. A little later New Lisbon was created.

The circuit court in Stoddard county was organized at the house of A. B. Bailey by John D. Cook, on March 21st, 1836. At this sitting of the court a grand jury was impaneled and consisted of the following men: Samuel Lesley, Andrew Neale, Benjamin Taylor, Frederick Varner, Ephraim Snider, Jacob Crites, William V. Carlock, George Slinkard, Frederick Slinkard, Peter Proffer, Levy Baker, Henry Miller, Henry Asherbranner, W. W. Hicks, Daniel Bollinger, Samuel Moore, Thomas Neale and Horatio Laurence.

This court house was burned during Price's raid in 1864. It was one of a number of court houses destroyed about the time of the Civil war, but unlike most of the other cases, the records of the county were not destroyed. They had been removed by Major H. H. Bedford, who took them to Arkansas and concealed them; they were returned after the war was over without the loss of a single book. The rebuilding of the court house was undertaken in 1867, when the court appointed William G. Phelan as superintendent. The contractors, George F. Miller and Samuel D. Henson, completed the building in 1870. In that same year the contract was let for the building of the jail at a cost of $8,000.

There has long been a strong rivalry between Dexter and Bloomfield and for a number of years an effort was made to move the county seat from Bloomfield to Dexter. Failing in this, the people of Dexter secured in 1895 the enactment of a law declaring that four terms of the circuit court should be held in Stoddard county, two of them at Bloomfield and two in Dexter, making Dexter practically one of two different county seats. The citizens of Dexter erected a handsome two-story brick building to be used as a court house. The arrangement, however, was found to be unsatisfactory and within a few years the law was repealed and Bloomfield became once more the sole county seat. This left the people of Dexter with a court house on their hands for which they had no particular use. It was finally transferred to the Christian church to be used for college purposes. For a short time an academy was conducted in the building, but in 1911 the building became the property of the school district of Dexter and is now in use as a high school building. The present townships are Pike, Elk, Liberty, New Lisbon, Richland, Castor and Duck Creek.

Henry Hale Bedford, who was for a number of years the leading lawyer in Stoddard county, was a native of Tennessee, where he was born November 27, 1821. He received a common school education in Tennessee and was employed for three years as a teacher. With the money which he saved from teaching he purchased a farm in Scott county, Missouri, at the foot of Wolf Island. While engaged in farming, he began the study of law under Judge Hough. The great flood of 1844 compelled him to leave his farm and he removed to Bloomfield in Stoddard county. Bloomfield then had a population of about 150 and Mr. Bedford combined the practice of his profession with school teaching for several years. Later he devoted himself exclusively to the law and soon built up a very extensive practice, as he was an able lawyer and one of the very first in that part of the state. At the beginning of the Civil war he enlisted in the Confederate army in the brigade commanded by General Jeff Thompson. He was promoted to be a major at the battle of Belmont and served until the close of the war. Major Bedford had considerable political experience, also. He was a member of the legislature for two terms before the war and served for twelve years as prosecuting attorney. He was a Democrat in politics and was for many years one of the most influential citizens of his county, taking a great interest in all matters looking to the upbuilding of the community and to public improvements.

Ripley County

As we have seen, the first permanent settler in Ripley county was probably Lemuel Kittrell, who settled near Current river about 1819. Shortly after he made this settlement, a road was laid out from Potosi in Washington county to Little Rock, Arkansas, and the first settlements in Ripley county were made along this road. Other early settlers besides

Kittrell were William Little and Thomas Pulliam, who located on a small creek which flows into Current river. Near the present town of Doniphan the early settlers were George Lee, Joseph Hall, William Dudley, William Merrill and Abner Ponder; the descendants of these families are still living in the county. The general assembly of the state organized Ripley county by an act passed January 5, 1833. It was named in honor of General Eleazer W. Ripley; previous to its organization the territory had been part of Wayne county. As first organized, the county was vastly larger than it is at the present time. It was reduced to its present size, finally, by the organization of Carter county in 1859. For many years the county seat of Ripley county was Van Buren in what is now Carter county and the principal population of that section was in Carter county. The whole country was slowly settled. In 1840 there were in all Ripley county, then much larger than it is now, only 2,856 people; and Van Buren, the county seat, had one store in 1837 and a log building for the courts.

When Carter county was created in 1859 Doniphan was selected as the seat of justice for Ripley county and has remained the county seat until this time. A court house was erected shortly after the selection of the county seat, but it was burned during the war, as was practically all of the town of Doniphan. The new court house was erected shortly after the close of the war and is still in use. There are now thirteen townships in the county, as follows: Current River, Doniphan, Gatewood, Harris, Johnson, Jordan, Kelley, Pine, Sherley, Thomas, Union, Varner and Washington.

PIONEERS OF DUNKLIN COUNTY

The first settlers in Dunklin county were Howard Moore and family, who were natives of Virginia. They came to the county in 1829, settling about four miles south of Malden. They lived here for a short time and later bought the cabin which had been erected by the Indian chief, Chilletecaux, near Kennett. Here Mr. Moore made his home until the time of his death. He left a large family and many of his descendants still live in the county. His son, David H. Moore, who was born July 10, 1832, was the second child born in the county.

Another of the pioneer citizens of the county was Pascal Rice, who moved to the county in 1830. He was at the time about 12 years of age and spent the rest of his life in the community to which he first moved, near Hornersville. At the time he came to the county it was the home of many Indians and he became well acquainted with these Indian chiefs and attended many of their war dances.

The first child born of white parents within the limits of Dunklin county was Thomas Neel, Jr., who was born in May, 1832, his father, Thomas Neel, having moved to the county in February preceding and settled in the south part of the county near the little town of Lulu. He grew up under the pioneer conditions of life and became acquainted with the Indians and knew all the customs which distinguished them.

One of the earliest settlers was Michael Branum, who moved to Dunklin county from New Madrid, having been in New Madrid during the time of the great earthquake. His family, including Tecumseh, named for the great Indian chief, and daughters, Lizzie and Victorine, who became Mrs. Horner, lived in

Dunklin county for many years. Mrs. Horner was for a number of years preceding her death the oldest citizen in the county.

Besides these whom we have mentioned, there came to the county in the early times Jacob Taylor and his family. He located close to the stream which is known is Taylor slough, named for Jacob Taylor. Branum, Taylor and Rice came in the same year and were assisted over the country and in the selection of places of settlement by the Indian chief, Chilletecaux. In 1831 Moses Norman settled on West Prairie and in 1832 Thomas Neel, Sr., and his father-in-law, Ray, came to the county and located near Hornersville. While moving to their destination, Mr. Ray was killed by being thrown from his cart and was buried at the old Hornersville burying ground near Hornersville and is said to have been the first white person buried in the county.

In 1833 James Baker and Riley Clarkson settled on Buffalo island and in the same year Russell and William H. Horner made a settlement at the place afterwards called Hornersville.

The home of Evan Evans was just in front of a row of cottonwood trees on the public road four miles south of Kennett. McCullough and Lafayette Sexton came to the county in early times, also. Adam Barnhart settled on the old Baker place. Among his neighbors were Hugh Shipley, the families of Suter, Shultz and Jackson. Frank Lee lived three miles north of Hornersville.

In the north end of the county Dr. Given Owen located a claim on Rush creek in 1841; in 1844 A. D. Bridges settled on a creek near Four Mile; Jordan Lacey, John Holtzhouser, James Faughn and William Greer were other early settlers in the north part of the county. Somewhat later, Dr. Allen and Thomas Hatley located near Malden. In the vicinity of Clarkton, about the same time, were John Gunnells, Jesse Long, Mrs. Floyd Montgomery, John McMasters and Dick Skaggs.

Among the settlers on West Prairie were Ephraim Thornberry and James Harris. Some settlers also came to Holcomb Island about the same time, among them families named Barnes, Holloways, Lewis Holcomb, Millers, Dr. Bozark, John Lowery, H. D. Flowers, Hiram Langdon, John Scott and Price. Johnson's Island, south of Kennett, was named for William Johnson, who was one of the early settlers there. In the neighborhood of Caruth the families were those of A. Thompson, Mrs. Welch, C. B. Bancroft, H. Spencer, Whitney, Joseph Pelts and Robert L. Glascock. Besides these, Riley Clarkson, James McGrew, Joseph Langdon and David Harkey had begun to open farms in the neighborhood of Cotton Plant.

Just west of Hornersville the settlers were James P. Neal, J. McDaniel, John B. Walker and James Williamson. All these that we have mentioned came to the county before 1850.

Within the next decade a large number of families, later prominent in the history of the county, moved within its bounds. It is not possible to give a complete list of these families, but the names of some of them as its pioneer settlers will be of interest. On the hills west of Malden, Dr. Jacob Snider settled in 1850; with him were Charles Vincent, William Cross and Mrs. Skaggs.

About the same time in Clay township there were the families of A. T. Douglass, E. J. Langdon, Edward Spencer, Lewis Chandler, Isaiah Jones, John Marsh, James Bradley, John Dougherty, Richard Cook, James Herrman, Absolom Farris, A. B. Williams and David Finley. In the north end of the county there were such well known families as that of John P. Taylor, Judge Hodges, Henry James, J. M. Waltrip, A. B. Douglass, James Oxley, H. A. Applegate, William H. Shelton, R. W. Stokes, John Wright, I. A. Waltrip, G. M. White and E. C. White.

Among the early settlers were also Daniel Harkey, Brannon Marshall, Enoch Shelton, Humphrey Donaldson, A. C. Austin, W. M. Satterfield, Moses Farrar, C. N. Lasley, David Rice and James A. Smyth.

All these men who came to the county in its early years have passed through the usual experiences of the pioneer days. The country was very different then from what it now is. Many of the pioneers made their living largely from hunting. Two of these men were Nathaniel Baker and Joseph Pelts. Baker was the son of James Baker, who settled on Buffalo Island in 1833 and later removed to Cotton Plant. Pelts came to the county about 1,840 and there made his home the rest of his life. Both of these men were typical pioneers; they farmed but were also fond of hunting.

Riley Clarkson, who came with his father to the county in 1834, lived on Horse Island. He was a famous hunter and helped to kill some of the last buffalo in the county. Buffalo Island was named from the fact that it was the home of a great many buffalo. Mr. Clarkson was also a great bear hunter, having killed as many as fifty bear in a single season. He and his family passed through all the experiences of pioneer life, at the time of their coming there being not a single physician, church or school or postoffice in the entire county.

One of the prominent and influential men in the early history of the county was Judge Donaldson, who came to the county in 1855. He was a man of education and became a well known and highly respected citizen of the county. He was a Tennesseean by birth, but thoroughly identified himself with all the interests of his adopted home and was elected to public office, being for a time a member of the county court of Dunklin county. His family are still prominent in county offices, his son was a well known citizen and one of his grandsons is now a practicing lawyer at Kennett.

In 1854 David Finley came with his family to Dunklin county, opening a farm not far from the present site of Cotton Plant. He was a typical pioneer, having interests in farming and in hunting and in all the affairs of the county.

One of the large and influential families in the south part of Dunklin county was the Harkey family, who were descendants of Daniel D. Harkey a native of North Carolina, who came to Dunklin county in 1853, settling on the land near Nesbit, where the family continues to reside. Among the members of this family were Judge J. H. Harkey, Wilbur D. Harkey and W. M. Harkey. They were sons of the founder of the family and their descendants are both numerous and influential at this time.

Perhaps the man who made the greatest impression on the life of his day in the county was Edwin J. Langdon, who was born August 7, 1819, at Middlebury, Vermont. The family was of Scotch descent and this son seems to have inherited the great qualities which distinguish the Scotch. Before coming to Dunklin county, E. J. Langdon received a good common school education and for a time taught school. In 1839 he made his home in Dunklin county near Cotton Plant; he soon formed a partnership with Isaiah Jones and together they conducted a carriage and blacksmith shop. In 1847 he was married to Sarah A. Glasscock, the daughter of Robert L. Glasscock, also one of the pioneers of the county.

From his business as a carriage builder young Langdon turned his attention to contracting and together with his father they built the first court house in the county, in 1846. One year later he secured the contract for building the levee across Buffalo creek on the main road south of Kennett. With the proceeds of this contract he opened a store at Cotton Plant and from this time until his death he conducted this business. While he was always interested in mercantile pursuits, Judge Langdon did not confine his attention to this form of business. He tried to develop water transportation and built one of the first flat boats on Little river at Hornersville. It was his intention also to encourage the raising of cotton and to do this he erected one of the first cotton gins in the county. He also became convinced of the value of land about Cotton Plant and invested largely in these lands. The town in which he lived was built entirely on his property. He refused to dispose of any of it largely because he wished to be able to prevent the sale of whiskey in the town. For many years he was the postmaster at Cotton Plant and at one time was presiding judge of the county court for a period of six years. Judge Langdon was interested in all matters looking to the improvement of the community and the county, building roads, establishing the cause of churches and other public matters received encouragement from him. At the time of his death he was the owner of large tracts of valuable land. The children of this family were William H. Langdon, who lives in Texas, C. V. Langdon of Cotton Plant, and A. J. Langdon of Hornersville, and one daughter, Hettie D.

In 1838 Judge Given Owen, then twenty years of age, came to Bloomfield from Hickman, Kentucky, and began the practice of medicine. A few years later he made his home on a farm in what was then the south part of Stoddard county. He was elected a member of the county court in Stoddard county, but in a short time that part of Stoddard county in which he lived was transferred to Dunklin county. After becoming a citizen of Dunklin county he was elected to various offices, being judge of the common pleas court at Clarkton and of the county probate court and also of the county court. During all his life in the county he continued the practice of medicine and was regarded as an able physician and a most highly respected and intelligent citizen of the county. He was the son of Ruben Owen, a native of Georgia. His second wife was Louisiana Bozark, who survived her husband a number of years and was perhaps as well acquainted with the early history of the county as any person living in it.

In 1859 David Young Pankey, a native of Virginia, came to Dunklin county and made his home near Clarkton. He had formerly lived for a short time in Tennessee, just across from New Madrid. He engaged in farming in Dunklin county and was successful and was popular with his friends and neighbors. On the breaking out of the war he became first lieutenant in a company organized by Captain Pickard; this company was made part of a regiment of which Mr. Pankey was made lieutenant colonel, seeing service with a regiment which was a part of the Missouri state guards. On the expiration of the term of the state guards, Colonel Pankey enlisted in the confederate service and took part in the engagement at Fort Pillow and was with General Price in several skirmishes and battles, winning credit and distinction for himself in all of them. At one time Colonel Pankey was collector of Dunklin county and during all his life was a respected and influential citizen. His son David Ballard Pankey is cashier of the Bank of Kennett and one of the most prominent citizens of the county.

No account of the pioneers of Dunklin county would be complete without a mention of Hon. David Rice, who was a native of Tennessee, and came to the county in 1853. At first he lived northwest of Campbell, where he married, but within a short time he removed to a farm east of Senath, where he lived until his death. He devoted himself principally to farming but was also interested and active in all affairs of public concern. Just before the war he was assessor of the county and from 1872 to 1876 was public administrator and later served a term in the general assembly.

Major W. C. Rayburn, a native of Alabama, came to Dunklin county in 1865, locating near Clarkton. He was immediately recognized as a man of ability and character and soon came to occupy a prominent place in the affairs of the county. He was always interested in schools and churches and served as a county surveyor for a number of years. His son, Moore M. Rayburn, served throughout the war in a regiment of Arkansas infantry and at its close came home to devote himself to farming and stock raising. He was for four years sheriff and constable of the county and carried on the activities which had for many years interested his father. One of his sons, M. B. Rayburn, is cashier of the Bank of Malden and a highly respected citizen of that town.

Dunklin county was created February 14, 1845. Stoddard county was divided by a line running on the parallel of 36 degrees and 30 minutes. All that part of Stoddard county south of this line of division was called Dunklin county. In 1853 the north line of the new county was moved to the north nine miles. The territory included within the limits of the county, with the exception of this nine mile strip, was a part of the territory which was originally left in Arkansas, but was added to Missouri through the efforts of John Hardeman Walker and others.

The town of Kennett was selected as the county seat of the new county. The town was named for Hon. Luther M. Kennett, though when it was laid out in 1846 it was called Chillitecaux. It was later known for a year or two as Butler and then received its present name, Kennett. The county was named for Hon. Daniel Dunklin, who was at one time governor of the state.

The circuit court was probably organized in 1845 by John D. Cook, who was the judge of the circuit which included this county.

The first county court in Dunklin county is said to have been composed of Moses Farrar, Edward Spencer and Alexander Campbell; Joseph S. Houston was the first clerk and Lewis Holcomb the first sheriff; Houston was soon succeeded by John H. Marsh, who held office until 1861. The first court house in the county was a log building erected in 1847 in the middle of the public square where the present court house stands. This building was destroyed during the war; it was not until 1870 that another was erected, which was a large frame building, and was burned in 1872. For a number of years this county had no court house and the courts were held in an old frame store building on the corner of the square now occupied by the Tatum building. In 1895 the present two-story brick court house building was erected. About the time of the building of the first court house a log jail was erected; it was destroyed by fire and another of the same character was built. In 1882 a frame building was erected on the corner now occupied by the Shelton office building. It was used as a jail until 1910, when the present structure was erected.

The present townships are Independence, Cotton Hill, Union, Freeborn, Holcomb, Salem, Buffalo, and Clay.

The legislature created Mississippi county on February 14, 1845; the territory being cut off from the south part of Scott county. The commissioner selected Charleston as the county seat, and the county court was organized there April 21, 1845. The judges of the court were: William Sayres, Absolom McElmurry and James M. Overton; George L. Cravens was the clerk of the court. The meetings of this court were, for a number of years, held in the store house of Henry G. Cummings. A court house was not erected until 1852. At the time the present building was erected by James T. Russell.

At the time of the organization, the county was divided into five townships. These were: Tywappity, Mississippi, St. James, St. James Bayou, and Wolf Island. In 1847 Mississippi township was divided and a new township created which was named Ohio. In 1858 Long Prairie township was formed from parts of Tywappity and St. James.

The circuit court was organized September 29, 1845, by John D. Cook. The meetings of the court were usually held in the Methodist church, until the erection of the court house.

Reynolds County

Until 1830 the territory now embraced in Reynolds county was a part of Ripley county. At that time it was attached to Washington county and later to Shannon. The legislative act organizing Reynolds county was approved February 25, 1845, and the county was named in honor of Governor Thomas Reynolds of Missouri. It then included a part of what is now Iron county which was afterwards cut off when that county was formed. The commissioners appointed to select the county seat were Ayers Hudspeth of Washington county, John Miller of Madison county, and Moses Carty of St. Francois county. It was provided also that until a county seat was located the court should be held in the house of Joseph McNails at Lesterville. The first term of the county court was held in this house in November, 1845, with H. Allen as the presiding judge; Marion Munger was sheriff and C. C. Campbell clerk. The commissioners selected Lesterville as the county seat and a small court house was erected. This building was burned during the war and the county seat was changed to Centerville, where another small building for court purposes was erected. This, too, was burned in 1872, and another building, now standing, was erected at a cost of $8,000. There are six townships in the county, Black River, Carroll, Jackson, Lesterville, Logan and Webb.

Butler County

Butler county was created by an act passed February 27, 1849. It had previously been a part of Wayne county, and at the time of the organization the larger part of the land in the county belonged to the government. The first session of the county court was held at the house of Thomas Scott, June 18, 1849. The judges were: John Stevenson, Solomon Kittrell, and Jonathan R. Sandlin; the clerk of the court was Jacob C. Blount. The commissioners selected the site of Poplar Bluff for the county seat and the court met there in November, 1850. Until 1852 the sessions of the court were held in various private houses and in that year a small frame court house was erected on the southeast corner of the public square. This building served the purposes of the courts until 1859, when D. B. Miller and Solomon G. Kitchen entered into a contract with the county for the erection of a new building.

As at first organized, there were only two townships, Black River and Otter Creek. In 1850 the county court created four townships, Beaverdam, Epps, Butler and Mud Creek. Later, the name of Mud Creek was changed to Black River, and a new township, called Polk, was formed in the southeast corner of the county. In 1856 the township of Ash Hills was established, and in 1860, Thomas township.

In 1866 the townships were relocated and established as follows: St. Francois, Black River, Cane Creek, Epps, Beaverdam, Thomas, Gillis Bluff, Ash Hills and Poplar Bluff. Thomas township was divided in 1871 and Neeley township formed from part of it; in 1886 Beaverdam township was divided, a part of it being erected into Harviell township.

In 1850 the records show that the collector had reported the entire amount of county revenue as $156.02. In the same year he had collected a total state tax of $122.28.

The first circuit court in Butler county was held September 15, 1849, at the house of Thomas Scott. Judge Harrison Hough presided over the court. The sheriff was Newton Wallace. A grand jury was impaneled at the next meeting of the court, which returned indictments against a number of persons for selling liquor without license.

Butler county was named in honor of W. A. Butler of Kentucky, and the county seat, Poplar Bluff, received its name from the fact that it was situated on the bluffs above Black River, which at that time were covered with a dense growth of the famous tulip tree, commonly called the poplar.

One of the earliest settlements in Butler county was made at the head waters of Cane creek, where there is fine farming land, by John Eudaly, who came to the neighborhood about 1841 from Tennessee. The land, at the time he came, was government land and he took up a homestead. He was accompanied by a number of his neighbors and friends and others came later. Among them were John and Nathan Wisecarver, Nathan Davis, Mr. Walton, Mr. Franklin and James Eudaly.

At the time these settlements were made the territory was a part of Wayne county, the present Stoddard county not having been created. The immediate vicinity near which the settlements were made was one of the few sections of Southeast Missouri which were not timbered, making the cultivation of the soil easy. The people lived the life of pioneers. There were no railroads in the vicinity. All their goods were hauled from Cape Girardeau. The houses that were constructed were of logs, as there was no saw mill within fifty miles. The produce of the county was used almost entirely by the settlers themselves, as there was no opportunity for shipping them away.

After the organization of Stoddard county John Eudaly was made assessor and made the first assessment in 1850. At that time the fees for making the assessment amounted to $34. There was not a village or community in the entire county. When Poplar Bluff was located and the land selected for a site of the county court, a commissioner was appointed to make a public sale of the lots and John Eudaly was the man that was appointed. A number of lots were sold within the present town of Poplar Bluff. The highest price obtained for a lot was for one at the corner of Vine and Second streets, which sold for $30. The two lots on the corner of Vine and Main streets were sold at $5 each and were afterwards resold for $2.50 each, while some lots located in what is the best business part of the town could not be sold at all.

Mr. Eudaly lived until his death in the neighborhood in which he settled, and was for many years postmaster, having been appointed on the establishment of the office in 1872.

BOLLINGER COUNTY

Bollinger county was organized in March, 1851, and was formed from parts of Wayne, Cape Girardeau and Stoddard counties. The commissioners appointed to select the seat of justice decided on Marble Hill, and a county court for the county was organized in the store of John C. Whybark, March 24, 1851. The members of the court were Reuben Smith, John Stevens, Drury Massey; Oliver E. Snider was clerk and William C. Grimsly the sheriff.

Shortly after the organization of the county a brick court house two stories in height was erected. It was used only a very short time and was burned. Another building similar to it in size and appearance was erected in the same year, the money having been raised by private subscription in part and in part an appropriation from the county. It, too, was destroyed by fire in March, 1884, though at the time it was practically abandoned, having been condemned as unsafe. For several months the county was without any court house building; an effort was made to remove the county seat from Marble Hill to the neighboring town, Lutesville. To prevent this, the citizens of Marble Hill raised a subscription amounting to $1,620, and the town itself contributed $1,000 for the rebuilding of the court house in that town. The proposition for removal was defeated and the county court appropriated $7,000 in addition to that raised, for the construction of the present building. It was erected under the supervision of J. J. Conrad. At present there are eight townships in the county, as follows: Crooked Creek, Fillmore, German, Liberty, Lorance, Union, Wayne and Whitewater.

The county was named in honor of Col. Geo. Frederick Bollinger, one of the early settlers in Cape Girardeau district and a most prominent and influential citizen. The county seat, which was long called Dallas, was named Marble Hill from the belief that the hill on which the town was built was composed of marble.

PEMSICOT COUNTY

On February 19th, 1851, the governor approved an act of the legislature for the establishment of Pemsicot county. It was erected from territory cut off from the south part of New Madrid county. The line between it and New Madrid county was to begin in the Mississippi river opposite Majors mill race, then through Cushion Lake bayou to Cushion lake to the head of Portage bay and through the bay to Little river and due west to the eastern boundary of Dunklin county. A county court was organized at the house of James Eastwood, who was its presiding justice, with Martin L. Stancil and John Scott as associate justices. Robert Stewart was the first sheriff and Theodore Case was the clerk of the court. When the question of the county levees came up, Judges Scott and Stancil resigned in 1855 and were succeeded by Ebenezer Oldham and Thomas Bartlett.

This question of levees was agitated by the people of Pemsicot county for a good many years. A large part of the county was subject to overflow from the Mississippi river. In fact, the name of the county is said to be an Indian word which signifies "liquid mud." An act of Congress was passed in 1850 which donated lands to the state for the purpose of reclaiming swamp lands within their limits. Large tracts of these lands were then given by the state to the counties for this purpose. The question of the reclamation of these swamp lands was early agitated in Pemsicot county. It was the desire of many of the people of the county to build a levee along the bank of the Mississippi river to protect it from the overflows. It was proposed by some that the levee should be built and paid for in lands at the price of $1.25 per acre. Stancil, who had been a judge of the county court, and who had resigned, opposed this plan of levee construction. He advocated the sale of the lands at a public auction, at a minimum price of $1.25, and that the money realized from this sale should be appropriated to the work of leveeing and draining the lands. He circulated a petition, which was afterward presented to the court, asking that this plan of disposing of the lands should be adopted. He was opposed by William S. Moseley, then a member of the legislature from New Madrid and Pemsicot counties, and the plan proposed was defeated. The court decided to build the levee, and to issue in payment for the work county scrip, which could be used in locating the land, at $1.25 per acre. After the plan was determined, there arose a contest over the location of the levee. Stancil believed that it should be placed on the west side of Cypress bayou and Big lake, but it was finally built along the bank of the river and extended, with two small breaks, along the entire length of the county. It was not long after its construction until it became evident that it was located too near the river, and it soon was washed away. This contest left some bitter feeling among the people of the county.

St. Francois Levee District

This state levee was completely destroyed by the caving of the banks of the river in 1893. The legislature created the St. Francis levee district of Missouri, embracing all that part of the state in the St. Francis valley lying in the counties of New Madrid, Pemiscot and Dunklin. A board of directors was appointed to manage the affairs of the district and to build a levee, consisting W. G. Petty, Reuben Chapman and John Black, of Dunklin county; Dr. J. J. Williams, J. T. Girvin and Alphonso DeLisle, of New Madrid county; and J. A. Cunningham, J. M. Brasher and G. W. Carleton, of Pemsicot county. The first meeting of the board was held in New Madrid March 29, 1893. Dr. J. J. Williams was made president, W. D. Schult, secretary; J. A. Cunningham, treasurer, and Captain N. H. Pharr, chief engineer. G. W. Carleton, of Pemsicot county, died March 30, 1893, and Hina C. Schult was appointed as his successor. In August of that year the building of the levee was commenced. It was raised to an average height of 7 feet in 1896 and 1897. Since that time there has been constant work done on the levee until it has been raised to an average of 11 feet. It extends from just south of the town of New Madrid to the state line and cost about $650,000. The United States government paid $120,000 of this, the state of Missouri $20,000, and the district, by taxation, $510,000.

Courts of the County

The circuit court in Pemsicot county was organized October 25, 1852, by Judge Harrison Hough. The court met at the house of Jonathan Scott. There was no court house erected for some years, the first being a small frame building which was put up in 1854. Sanford Jackson was the second clerk of the court, and he built, in the yard near his house, a clerk's office. It was a rail pen, sealed inside and out with cypress bark, and was covered with elm boards. It was used as an office until the court house was erected.

The first court house, erected in 1854, was a small frame building and was used until 1873. By that time it became inadequate for the purpose and was moved away and plans made for the erection of a new court building. This was destroyed by fire in 1882 and the legislature of the state appropriated the sum of $4,000 for the construction of another court house in Gayoso. This was used until the county seat was removed from Gayoso to Caruthersvile. The present building was then erected under the supervision of Charles B. Faris. Two jails were built in Gayoso and the present jail was constructed about the same time of the court house at Caruthersville.

From 1862 to 1865 there were no meetings of the county court, and in April of the former year the records of the county were removed to Memphis by Major Carleton, who was clerk of the court, and held there for safe keeping; they were returned to the county in August, 1865.

Owing to the fact that it was not possible to hold meetings of the county court in Pemsicot county during the war, a bill was passed by the legislature, through the efforts of T. J. O. Morrison, extending the jurisdiction of the courts of New Madrid county over Pemsicot county. This arrangement was continued until the close of the war.

The circuit courts were discontinued for an even longer period, no meetings of the court being held from 1860 to 1868. An attempt was made to hold circuit court in 1866 by Judge Albert Jackson, but Judge Jackson was not at all in sympathy with the people in Pemsicot county and very evidently hunted for some excuse to adjourn the court. He found that the seal used by the county had been broken and a new one put in its place. He declared that all instruments executed and attested by the use of the new seal were void and then adjourned court.

The present townships are Little Prairie, Pemsicot, Cooter, Virginia, Hayti, Braggadocio, Little River, Gayoso, Godair, Holland, Pascola and Butler.

PROMINENT CITIZENS

One of the earlier settlers and most prominent men in Pemiscot county was John Hardeman Walker. He came to the county about 1810 and made his home on Little Prairie. He was one of the few men who did not leave the section after the New Madrid earthquake. Colonel Walker remained and carried on his farming enterprises during all this period until the time of his death. He was sheriff of New Madrid county in 1821 and 1822 and was afterward a judge of the county court. One of his sisters married Dr. Robert D. Dawson of New Madrid, and another, John Martin of Point Pleasant.

One of the conspicuous settlers of Pemiscot county was Major George W. Carleton. He was born in Saratoga county, New York, April 19, 1830. He was educated in the public schools and high school and fitted himself for the position of civil engineer. He came to New Madrid October 10, 1852, and was at the time almost penniless. In the following spring he taught school for a time in New Madrid and was shortly afterward married to

Miss Summerville Tomlin and moved to Gayoso, Pemiscot county, in January, 1855. Here he rented a farm and began to cultivate it. However, in the same year he was appointed clerk of the county court of Pemiscot county and later in the same year was elected county surveyor. Again in 1860 he was made clerk of the county court and served for six years. He was a Union man at the breaking out of the war but was not in favor of abolition and when Captain Lyon seized Camp Jackson, Mr. Carleton decided to cast in his lot with the south. When the Federal forces took possession of New Madrid and Pemiscot counties Mr. Carleton put the records of the county in a dug-out and carried them across the Mississippi river and turned them over to the commander of the Confederate gunboats. The records were afterwards carried to Memphis, Tennessee, where they remained until the close of the war in 1865. He was appointed to a position in the Confederate States navy and entered upon active service. During the war he was at Yazoo, Mississippi and Charleston, South Carolina; in 1864 he was transferred to the engineering department with the rank and pay of major. When Macon, Georgia, was surrendered to the Federal forces he was made a prisoner and paroled April 26th. He returned home July 1, 1865, and at once took part in the reorganization of the government in Pemiscot county. During this time he acquired a knowledge of law but could not be admitted to the bar owing to his inability to take the test oath. In spite of this fact he was allowed to practice law before the courts of Pemiscot county and when the test oath was striken from the constitution of the state he was admitted to the bar and regularly enrolled as a practitioner.

In 1875 he was a member of the constitutional convention from the 23rd senatorial district in connection with General N. W. Watkins. He was a representative from Pemiscot county in four of the general assemblies of the state and was the author of several important bills, especially one creating drainage districts in the state. He was also in charge of the Hunter bill to indemnify the counties of Southeast Missouri for damages caused by the overflow of the Mississippi river.

In 1870 Major Carleton began the making of abstract of land titles in Pemiscot county. This abstract, which was brought up to date, proved to be of very great value owing to the destruction of the court house. The general assembly passed an act in 1885 making the Carleton abstracts legal evidence in all courts of record. In addition to his other activities Major Carleton at times controlled the publication of the Gayoso *Democrat,* and during all his life was interested in farming.

Iron County

The organization of Iron county dates from an act of the legislature approved February 17, 1857. It was created from parts of the counties of St. Francois, Madison, Washington, Dent, Reynolds and Wayne. It owes its peculiar shape to the fact that it was made up of parts of so many counties. This was necessary in order to avoid reducing any county below its constitutional limits. The first county court was composed of J. V. Logan, John W. Miller and Moses Edmonds. John F. T. Edwards was the clerk, and John Cole was sheriff. The first meeting of the court was on August 4, 1857. At that time the county was divided into seven townships: Dent, Kaolin, Iron, Pilot Knob, Arcadia, Liberty and Union. At this meeting of the court Theodore F. Tong was made school commissioner, A. C. Farnham county treasurer, and A. W. Holliman was county surveyor.

Arcadia was made the first county seat, but in August, 1857, the people voted to change the county seat to Ironton.

The first meeting of the circuit court was held May 17, 1858, and was presided over by Judge John H. Stone. A grand jury was summoned which returned indictments against two persons for grand larceny.

Iron county received its name from the fact that iron was being mined within its limits and was believed to exist in very large quantities.

The first county seat, Arcadia, was named by a lady who came from New England, and being struck by the beauty and simplicity of the surrounding country, and the delightful people, suggested that it be called Arcadia. The derivation of Ironton, the name of the present county seat, is apparent. It is situated quite near to what were then believed to be immense deposits of iron ore.

The county was made liable at its organization for a part of the stock subscribed for the building of the Fredericktown & Pilot Knob Gravel Road Company. This obligation was met by the issuance of bonds to the amount of $6,666. In January, 1858, an order of the county court was made for the erection of a court house. The contract was let to George S. Evans and William F. Mitchell in the sum of $14,000; John V. Logan was appointed as superintendent. The building was completed in 1860; six years later the present jail was built at a cost of $10,000.

The present townships are Iron, Kaolin, Liberty, Union, Dent, and Arcadia.

CARTER COUNTY

The first settlement made in Carter county was made in 1812 by Zimri A. Carter, who settled a few miles south of the present town of Van Buren. The county at this time was still a part of Wayne county and the country was wild and much of it rough. Zimri Carter was a man of ability and power and when he began to open up the country other settlers were attracted, among them the Chilton, Kennard, Snider and Kelley families. These all settled in the neighborhood of Carter and opened up considerable land. The population of the county grew slowly for a number of years, and it was not organized until March 10, 1859. The territory used in creating the county was cut off from the west part of Ripley and the eastern part of Shannon county and the legislature named the county in honor of its first settler.

On the erection of the county Adam Lane of Ripley, John Buford of Reynolds, and D. C. Reed of Shannon county, were appointed as commissioners to locate the seat of justice. They met in April, 1859, at the house of James Brown near Van Buren, and located the county seat at Van Buren. This had formerly been the county seat of Ripley county and the old log court house, which had been erected in 1853, was the meeting place for the courts until 1867. At that time a frame court house was built which is still in use.

At first the county was attached to Ripley county for the purpose of representation in the general assembly and the first member sent to the legislature from Carter county was William Lawson, who was elected in 1864 and served until 1870. He was succeeded at the latter date by F. M. Coleman.

Carter county has an area of about 321,000 acres, much of which is hilly and broken land and much of it is a low grade of fertility. It is drained by Current river, which flows through the central part of the county in a generally southern direction. On the west of Current river two creeks, Davis and Rogers, drain that part of the county. The northeast part of the county is drained by Brushy creek, which is a tributary of Current, and the southeastern part is drained by Little Black river and Cane creek. These streams or most of them are very beautiful. This is true, especially of Current river, which is famous for its clear sparkling waters. The streams afford great water power which is yet largely undeveloped, though some of it is used for running mills.

The chief resource of the county is timber, of which there are a number of varieties, the most abundant being pine and oak.

The county is divided into five townships: Carter, Jackson, Johnson, Kelly, and Pike.

Biographies

In a former chapter we have given the history of the settlement and organization of the eight counties organized before the admission of Missouri to the Union. It is desired to recall the names of some of the citizens of these counties who were especially active in building up this part of the state and whose names are connected with much of the progress which has been made. It is not possible to recite the lives of all of them; some are mentioned in connection with other matters, but some whose lives are of especial interest are referred to here.

Charles Welling was for many years one of the leading citizens of Cape Girardeau county. He was born in 1812 in New Jersey, was educated in the common schools and came to St. Louis county in 1830. One year later he removed to Jackson and became a clerk in the general store of Ralph Guild, and afterwards became a partner in this concern. He dissolved this partnership in 1848 and became associated with Joseph Russell and still later with J. V. Priest. Mr. Welling continued in the mercantile business until 1888, when he was appointed postmaster by President Cleveland. For a number of years he was cashier of the Cape Girardeau Savings Bank and was for twelve years treasurer of Cape Girardeau county. He was one of the best known citizens in the county and a man universally held in highest respect and esteem. He was of a most upright character and was known for his strict devotion to whatever duty he undertook. He was one of the first members and organizers of the First Presbyterian church at Jackson in 1856. He served the church as a leader and as superintendent of the Sunday school. Mr. Welling married Elizabeth Bollinger Frissell, a granddaughter of Colonel George Frederick Bollinger. Their descendants are prominent in Cape Girardeau county. He died at Jackson, June 20, 1900.

Few men have exercised a greater or better influence over affairs in Southeast Missouri than Robert Sturdivant. He was born March 31, 1817, in Lunnenberg county, Virginia, and died at Tallapoosa, Georgia, October 12, 1905. He came to Cape Girardeau in 1835. He received in his native state a good education for the time, having attended an academy, as the organized schools of the south were known.

On coming to Cape Girardeau he entered into a business partnership with Edmund White, who was his brother-in-law. Within a few years, however, he was forced into bankruptcy during a great panic which caused the financial wreck of hundreds of men. He was left penniless and made his way to Mississippi, where for a time he taught school and then worked with a construction gang on a railroad.

Through the kindness of Andrew Giboney,

who was his close friend, his affairs were arranged in Cape Girardeau and he returned. He taught school and for a time was associated in the publication of a newspaper. It is said that among his students were James M. Whitelaw and Samuel M. Green. From 1843 to 1846 he was engaged in the mercantile business with Andrew Giboney, under the firm name of Robert Sturdivant & Company. In the latter year he dissolved this partnership and began in connection with Ben M. Horrell, the operation of a mill. This was the White mill, as it was called, located on the river in the north part of town and was the first steam mill in Southeast Missouri. Later, Mr. Sturdivant established a commission and wholesale grocery house at the corner of Water and Themis streets. This business was exceedingly prosperous. In connection with it Mr. Sturdivant visited all the counties of Southeast Missouri, becoming acquainted with the leading men of every community and gaining a thorough knowledge of business conditions in this part of the state. It is an evidence of the sturdy honesty, which always characterized him, that during this period of his life he settled in full all the obligations of the firm of White & Sturdivant, though he was not legally bound to do so.

In 1857 he was elected cashier of the branch bank of the state of Missouri, which was at that time removed from Jackson to Cape Girardeau. He continued with the bank until it was closed up in 1867. Then he bought the assets of the branch bank and continued its operation as a private bank until 1882. In that year he organized a corporation known as the Sturdivant Bank. He was made its president and continued in office until some five years before his death.

During the sixty-five years of active business life, Mr. Sturdivant acquired a comfortable fortune, but while devoted to his business he never allowed it to interfere with the cultivation of friendship and that kindly spirit of helpfulness which distinguished him. He was always interested in the public welfare and no man did more to promote the enterprises of his town and community than he. For many years he served as the treasurer of the Southeast State Normal School and on many occasions advanced out of his own private fortune, as a loan, the funds with which to pay the teachers and expenses of that institution. He was very closely associated with Hon. Louis Houck in his railroad enterprises and it is quite probable that but for his assistance the railroads of Southeast Missouri could not have been built at that time.

Mr. Sturdivant, in spite of the esteem in which he was universally held and the influence which came in part from his real character and in part from his wealth, was a man who avoided all ostentation and display and was of a retiring and modest disposition. He lived simply and plainly and took a great interest in the simple pleasures of the time. His name is perpetuated in the great banking institution which he founded.

Samuel Stanhope Harris was born in Jackson December 26, 1836, and died in St. Louis December 6, 1891. His parents, Dr. E. W. and Mary Harris, were natives of North Carolina. He came to Missouri in 1821, first locating at Farmington and afterwards at Jackson. Samuel S. Harris was educated in the private academy at Pleasant Hill and later in Lexington college and then studied medicine at Bellevue Medical college in New York, being graduated at the age of twenty-one. He began the practice of medicine at Jackson in 1860 and was successful from the first. When the war broke out, Dr. Harris took the side of the south, organizing a company of cavalry famous as the Swamp Rangers, and afterward recruited a company of artillery with whom he took part in the battle of Fredericktown; later the company was sent to the south and participated in the engagements at Fort Pillow. Dr. Harris then became one of the crew of the iron clad ram Arkansas and served on board this vessel throughout the war. He distinguished himself for gallantry and ability as an officer. On the conclusion of the war he made his home for a short time at Watervalley, Mississippi, where he practiced medicine but later came to Cape Girardeau. Dr. Harris was not only a physician of great skill and energy, but was interested in all public matters. He contributed to medical journals and other publications and was an active member of the Democratic party. He was for a time postmaster at Cape Girardeau, but was never a candidate for any elective office. His first wife was Amanda Brown, daughter of Lieutenant Governor Brown; his second wife was Julia E. Russell of Jackson, a member of the old pioneer family of Cape Girardeau county; she was a great granddaughter of George Frederick Bollinger.

Alexander Gray, a native of Kentucky, served as a captain during the war of 1812 and came to Missouri at its close, making his home for a time at Cape Girardeau. From Cape Girardeau he went to St. Louis and was appointed by Governor Bates as judge of the St. Louis circuit court, holding two terms of the court under the territorial government and after the organization of the state government was appointed judge of the circuit court in Northern Missouri. Judge Gray was a highly educated man and a fine lawyer, especially able in criminal law.

General Firmin A. Rozier was born in Ste. Genevieve July 31, 1820. He was the son of Ferdinand Rozier, whose life we have given in another place. General Rozier was educated at St. Mary's College at Perryville and Bardstown, Kentucky. In 1846 he began to study law at the Transylvania Law School at Lexington, Kentucky. He gave up his studies, however, when the Mexican war broke out and raised a company of soldiers. He was elected captain of the company and stationed at Leavenworth, Kansas. After a time he was appointed major general of militia in Southeast Missouri. At the close of the war he returned to the law school and was graduated. In 1847 he began the practice of the law at Ste. Genevieve. General Rozier had some experiences in politics. In 1850 he was a candidate for Congress, but was defeated by a small majority. In 1856 he was a member of the state legislature and served two sessions. He was a delegate to the national Democratic convention at Chicago in 1860 and became a member of the state senate of Missouri in 1872, where he served four years, and was chairman of the committee on mines and mining. Besides this he held other minor offices, having been mayor of Ste. Genevieve and having held other positions of trust and honor. General Rozier was devoted to the public welfare of his town and community. He had a great interest in all matters pertaining to the public good. While very young he was a delegate to a convention which met at Memphis, Tennessee, in 1845, for the formation of plans regarding improvement of the Mississippi river. At this convention he read a report on the submerged lands of the Mississippi valley. Perhaps one of the things of which he was most justly proud was his interest in the establishment of the Ste. Genevieve Academy. He gave much of his time and money to this institution which prospered until the breaking out of the Civil war. General Rozier married Miss Mary M. Valle of

Ste. Genevieve in 1850, and to them six children were born. Another of the activities of General Rozier was the writing and publishing of the History of the Mississippi Valley. This book is devoted largely to the early times of Missouri and Illinois and especially in Ste. Genevieve. It is a valuable reference book on this early history.

Charles C. Rozier was the son of Ferdinand Rozier and was born September 1, 1830. He studied law, after his graduation from St. Vincents College in 1849, in the office of his brother, General Firmin A. Rozier. He purchased *The Democrat*, a weekly newspaper published at Ste. Genevieve in 1850, and continued its publication for a year. Then he went to St. Louis and edited a Fench paper, but discontinued its publication within a short time. In 1851 Mr. Rozier established *The Independent* at Ste. Genevieve and published it for three or four years. He then entered political life, holding the offices of circuit clerk, recorder and county clerk. He was appointed a member of the first board of regents of the State Normal school at Cape Girardeau and assisted in the location and establishment of that school. He was also administrator of Ste. Genevieve county and mayor of the town of Ste. Genevieve.

One of the most famous men ever connected with Southeast Missouri was Lewis F. Linn, who was born in 1796 near Louisville, Kentucky. He received a common school education and afterward studied medicine. At the breaking out of the war of 1812, he enlisted and served until its close. At that time he removed to Ste. Genevieve and began the practice of medicine. He was very successful in his practice, being gifted by nature with the power to make friends and acquaintances and to draw men to him. After devoting himself to his practice for a number of years and accumulating property, he became interested in politics and in 1827 was elected to the state senate, where he made a distinct impression for his ability and his devotion to the work given to him to do. In 1833 he was appointed by the governor of the state to fill a vacancy in the United States senate and was three times elected to the same position, holding it until his death in 1843. Mr. Linn was an unusual man in many respects. He gave the impression of honesty of purpose, of ability and of devotion to duty unequaled by many men. While in the senate he had to do with many matters of the utmost importance. Legislation affecting the west was constantly before Congress during this period and to all matters of this kind Senator Linn gave the closest study and the most careful attention. It was his conviction that the government of the United States owed it to itself as well as to the west to foster western territory and to encourage the building up of its population and to form and admit states into the Union. He was especially interested for a number of years in the Oregon territory and he was recognized as the champion of Oregon in the United States senate and was bitterly opposed to any suggestion that this territory should be abandoned to the English. On account of this fact the people of Oregon felt that they owed to Senator Linn a great debt of gratitude. Linn City in Oregon was named for him and in many other ways they have testified the debt which the people of the west felt was due to him. It was due to his efforts more than to the work of any one else that the Platte purchase was made for Missouri. In all his work he looked to the building up of the great west and especially to the interests of his own state. He died in 1843 and was buried at Ste. Genevieve, his home. Over his remains was erected the only monument provided for by the general assembly of Missouri out of the public funds. It is inscribed, "Here lies Lewis F. Linn, the model senator of Missouri."

John Rice Jones was born in Virginia in 1776. From 1781 to 1808 he practiced law in Vincennes. He became a resident of Potosi in 1808 and entered into the practice of law in partnership with Moses Austin. Mr. Jones was appointed a member and president of the legislative council of the territory and was also a member of the first constitutional convention. He was appointed by Governor McNair as one of the three judges of the supreme court, the other two being Matthias McGirk and John D. Cook. He held this position until his death in 1824. Mr. Jones was regarded as one of the ablest men in the territory. He was a man of upright character and had given a great deal of time to the study of the law.

Daniel Dunklin was born in South Carolina near Greenville in 1790, died August 25, 1844, in Jefferson county, and was buried on the bluff near Pevely. He removed to Kentucky when he was seventeen years old and at the age of twenty came to Missouri and established himself at Potosi. He was elected a member of the first constitutional convention in 1820 and in 1828 was elected lieutenant governor. At the close of his term he was elected governor and served until September, 1836, when he resigned three months before the close of the term in order to accept the position of surveyor general of Missouri, Illinois and Arkansas, which was offered to him by President Jackson. In this position he traced the boundary line between Missouri and Arkansas. Governor Dunklin is remembered chiefly on account of his very great interest in important work for the public school system of the state. It was largely due to him that the system exists in its present form. Dunklin county was named in his honor.

James H. Relfe who represented Missouri as one of its members of Congress in 1843 and 1845, was a native of Virginia. He came to Missouri at an early age and made his home at Caledonia in Washington county. His education was limited, owing to the character of the schools, but after becoming a man he studied medicine and engaged in the practice in Caledonia. He was a man of ability and won a place among his neighbors and acquaintances and received from them two elections to Congress. Mr. Relfe was a Democrat and supported the principles of that party.

Samuel Caruthers was born in Madison county, Missouri, October 13, 1820. He was educated in the common schools of the county and was graduated from Clinton College, Tennessee. After his graduation he entered upon the study of law and began his practice at Fredericktown. After practicing at Fredericktown for several years he moved to Cape Girardeau. It was at this place that he began his political career, holding several town and county offices. He was elected a member of Congress from the 7th district in 1853 and served in the 33rd and 34th Congresses as a Whig. When the campaign was made for election to the 35th Congress, Mr. Caruthers adopted the platform of the Democratic party and was again elected. He closed his political career with that session of Congress. He died at Cape Girardeau on July 20, 1860. Mr. Caruthers was a man of ability and stood well with the members of Congress with whom he served.

In 1859 John W. Noell was elected as the representative of the 7th congressional district to the 36th Congress. He was a native of Bradford county, Virginia, having been born in 1816. Mr. Noell received a good education in Virginia and moved to Missouri in 1832, making his home at Perryville. Here he entered a law office and after some years of study was admitted to the bar and became a successful practitioner. He entered politics, held several county offices and served as a member of the state senate for four years. He was elected to Congress as a Democrat and re-elected to the 37th and 38th Congresses. He died in Washington March 12th, 1863.

John G. Scott was born at Philadelphia, Pennsylvania, December 26th, 1819, and was educated in the schools of Philadelphia. He came to Missouri while a young man and settled in Jefferson county. He became interested in mine business. Mr. Scott accumulated considerable property and made his first venture in political life by becoming a candidate for the 38th Congress against John W. Noell. He was defeated by Noell, but was elected to fill the vacancy caused by Mr. Noell's death in office. Mr. Scott did not seek re-election at the close of his term.

Thomas E. Noel, who was born at Perryville, Mississippi, April 3rd, 1839, received a common school education and studied law in Perryville. He was successful in the practice of law and was made captain of the 19th Infantry of the United States army in 1862. He resigned from the army in 1863 and came to Missouri. He was elected as a member of Congress from the 3rd Missouri district in 1865 and served in the 39th and 40th Congresses. He was a radical in politics and supported the radical majority. Mr. Noel died at St. Louis October 4th, 1867.

SECTION V

The Civil War in Southeast Missouri

CHAPTER XXVII

GENERAL MOVEMENTS

Position of the State—Number of Soldiers Furnished—Appointment of a Major-General of the State Guards—General S. Watkins—General Thompson—Skirmishes in August, 1861—General Grant—Fortifications at Cape Girardeau—Martial Law—Thompson's Raid into Jefferson County—Situation in November, 1861—Battle of Belmont—Early Months of 1862—Capture of New Madrid and Island Ten—Skirmishes and Raids of 1863—Marmaduke's Invasion—Capture of General Jeff Thompson—Price's Raid Conditions After the War.

The position of Missouri during the Civil war was unique. The state is situated on the border line between the North and South. In fact nearly all the territory of this state is north of the Ohio river, which was in general the dividing line between slave and free territory. Under ordinary circumstances, Missouri would have been a northern state; on the other hand the great bulk of American immigrants were from the southern states, Virginia, Kentucky, and Tennessee perhaps furnishing more settlers for Missouri in the early period than all other states. These were southern in their sentiment. From this fact it was reasonable to expect Missouri to join with the South in secession. As we have pointed out in another chapter the thing which made Missouri take the position it did was doubtless the presence within the state of large numbers of foreign population. The American settlers who lived on farms were slave owners up to the time of the war. There were large numbers of slaves owned in this state, but the foreign population of the state, most of whom were gathered into towns, did not own slaves and their sympathies were very strongly in favor of the Union. The German population in Cape Girardeau, Cape Girardeau county, in Perry county, in Bollinger county and in St. Louis were almost to a man, favorable to the North. It was this fact that probably decided the course of Missouri. When the convention was held to determine what Missouri's action should be, there was a strong element in the state favorable to secession who desired that Missouri should join the seceded states, but their proposed action was bitterly opposed by the German element of her population, and as a compromise measure it was determined that the state should remain in the Union but should occupy the rather remarkable position of armed neutrality. It was determined that neither North nor South should invade the territory of the state and that Missouri should raise an army of its own for the purpose of protecting itself against the government of which it was a part and against its neighbor states that had seceded from the Union.

It is quite evident that this position was

one that it was impossible for the state long to hold. The tide of feeling on both sides rose too high to allow the state to remain neutral. Armies, both North and South, entered its borders and thousands of its citizens enlisted in the armies, some fighting for the Union, some for the South. Missouri contributed as many soldiers to both armies, according to its population, as almost any other state in the Union.

Not only did the state furnish many soldiers to the armies, it suffered as great damage and devastation as did any of the other states, except those like Virginia which were the scene of the greater military operations. In no other part of Missouri was the excitement greater or the consequent loss of property and life larger than in Southeast Missouri. The American population of this part of the state was very largely Southern and they desired to give all assistance possible to the South, but there were in two or three counties of this section large numbers of German people and they were just as loyal to the Union. The feeling between them grew very high and many depredations were committed on both sides.

To understand the military operations in Southeast Missouri, it is necessary to remember that St. Louis was made the headquarters of the Federal troops in the state. After the capture of Camp Jackson by Captain Lyon, the Confederates never had possession of St. Louis; it remained in the hands of Federal troops during all the war, and it was from St. Louis that there were sent out expeditions towards the South and Southwest to reduce those parts of the state which were held by the Confederates. Arkansas, the state immediately south of Missouri, seceded and from Arkansas a number of expeditions crossed the line into Missouri.

Southeast Missouri bordered on the river, which was made the highway for the transportation of troops and supplies and for the carrying on of certain operations against the South. This brought Southeast Missouri into the very center of the war.

In May, 1861, the state legislature passed an act providing for the organization of the Missouri State Guards. The state was divided into military districts; Southeast Missouri was made the first of these. The Governor appointed N. W. Watkins, of Cape Girardeau county as Brigadier-General to command this military district. It was his duty to organize the Missouri State Guards in this part of the state. General Watkins found the work uncongenial and soon resigned the position. He was succeeded by Jeff Thompson, whose headquarters for a time were established at Bloomfield.

The first plans of the Confederates for an invasion of Missouri provided that this invasion should be made by three separate bodies of troops. Colonel McCulloch was to enter the state in the southwest, General Hardee in the center and General Pillow in the east. Hardee brought 5,000 men and advanced as far as Greenville, while General Pillow reached and took possession of New Madrid. Neither of the forces penetrated any further into the state at this time, but General Thompson with the State Guards, was active and fought a number of skirmishes with the Federal troops. The Northern sympathizers who were not in the regular organized army, had been formed into Home Guards. Between these Home Guards and the Confederate State Guards there was constant hostility and warfare. On August 11, 1861, some of Thompson's men entered the village of Hamburg in Scott county. They there made an attack on a body of Home Guards of whom they killed one, wounded five and captured thirteen. On August 20th, there was a skirmish fought at Charleston between the forces under Jason H. Hunter and the 22nd Illinois Infantry under Colonel Daugherty. Hunter was defeated and retreated to the main body of Thompson's force where he was placed under arrest for having violated orders. He had been instructed that he was not to fight a superior force, but only to discover the position of the enemy.

Other skirmishes were fought during these months when each side was straining every nerve to make preparation for the great conflict which men were beginning to see was inevitable. On August 2, 1861, B. Gratz Brown, then in command at Ironton, made an advance toward Centerville in Reynolds county. When near Centerville a body of Confederates was found with whom a severe skirmish was fought. The Union forces then fell back toward Ironton.

On August 11th, a skirmish was fought at Potosi between Captain White of Fredericktown and the Potosi Home Guards.

On August 15th, John MacDonald of the Eighth Missouri made an expedition to Ste. Genevieve, captured the town, seized the money of the bank and carried it to St. Louis. August 19th, Col. Daugherty with Illinois troops fought a skirmish near Charleston with Confederates and defeated them. On the same date a skirmish was fought at Fish Lake near Charleston in which the Union forces were victorious.

It was the plan of the forces of the Federal army to make invasion into the southern part of the state from their headquarters at St. Louis. The first of these was made in July, 1861. A regiment under command of B. Gratz Brown was sent from St. Louis with orders to take possession of the town of Pilot Knob, which was then the terminus of the St. Louis & Iron Mountain Railroad. This was accomplished and Brown remained there with his forces until August 8th, when he was relieved by the 21st Illinois Regiment under command of Colonel U. S. Grant. Grant was at this time holding a colonel's commission; he had been appointed Brigadier-General, but had not received his commission. While he was staying at Pilot Knob he made his headquarters at the house of Colonel James Lindsay, now the property of Judge J. W. Emerson. It was here that he received his commission as a general. It was brought to him while he was standing under one of the great trees in the yard, and this spot is now marked by a monument erected by the members of this regiment. It was Grant's intention to begin a forward movement against General Hardee, but about the time he was ready to move he was relieved by General B. M. Prentiss. General Grant was then put in command of the district of Southeast Missouri which also included southern Illinois.

On being appointed to the command of this district, General Grant established temporary headquarters at Cape Girardeau where he remained for only a few days, then removing to Cairo, Illinois. Cape Girardeau had been taken possession of by Colonel Marsh with the 20th Illinois Regiment in July. Here he built four forts and named them A, B, C and D, commanding the approaches to the town on all sides. Fort A was on the high bluff near the Union Mill, now occupied as a residence site by I. B. Miller and James Reynolds. Fort B was situated on the hill where the Normal School now stands. This site is marked by a cannon presented to the school by the U. S. government. Fort C was at the south end of Sprigg street where there were small earth works, and Fort D was on the bank of the river south of St. Vincent's College. There was a line of rifle pits near the place now owned by Dr. Fullerton.

It was determined by those in command to make an effort to drive General Thompson out of the Southeast and if possible to capture him and disperse his forces. It was planned to send General Prentiss from Ironton to Cape Girardeau and then south, while General Grant was to cross the river at Cairo to Belmont and march to the west from that point. However, when General Prentiss reached Jackson he received orders from General Grant that he was to halt his troops at Jackson. He disregarded the orders and marched on to Cape Girardeau. Here he was met by Grant in person and ordered to return to Jackson. General Prentiss believed himself to be the senior officer and was quite indignant at these orders. He returned with his men to Jackson and left the command and went to St. Louis. This was the end of the projected expedition for the capture of General Thompson.

It should be said of this attempt to drive the Confederates out of Southeast Missouri that while the battles and skirmishes were not in themselves of very great importance, the attempt did have one result that is not usually considered. About the time that General Fremont took charge of the western department the invasion of Confederates from Arkansas into Missouri was threatened. The invasion was supposed to come by way of Springfield as it afterwards did come under the command of General Price. There was also the invasion that was spoken of in the direction of Birds Point and when General Fremont assumed command he was confronted with the question whether to defend Southeast Missouri or to defend Southwest Missouri. He elected to make his principal attempt against the forces invading Southeast Missouri and accordingly he sent a fleet of eight steamers carrying infantry and artillery to Birds Point and then returned them to St. Louis, finding nothing in particular for them to do. It was this expedition that resulted in part in the defeat of Lyon at Wilson's Creek.

When the Federal forces were defeated at Wilson's Creek it produced throughout the state a feeling that the Confederates were winning and a comparative depression among the friends of the Union. There arose a great deal of excitement and confusion within the borders of the state and on the 30th of August, General Fremont issued a proclamation declaring martial law and appointed J. McKinstry, a major in the United States army, as Provost Marshal of the state. He declared in the proclamation that the Union forces held a line extending from Leavenworth, Kansas, by way of Jefferson City, Rolla and Ironton, to Cape Girardeau and that all persons taken within the limits of this line with arms in their hands should be tried in court martial and shot, and that the property, real and personal, of all persons in Missouri who should be proved to have taken sides with the enemies of the Federal government should be confiscated to the public use and their slaves, if they had any, should be declared free men, and that persons who by speech of substance should be found guilty of giving aid to the Confederates in any way were warned of ill consequences to themselves.

The provost marshal then issued an order to carry into effect the proclamation of General Fremont and after issuing this order it became necessary for all persons traveling to carry with them a permit from the provost marshal. It would seem that martial law was thus extended over more than half of the state and that within the limits covered was a considerable part of the territory of Southeast Missouri. The enforcement of martial law greatly embarrassed the transaction of business and the travel of all persons within the limits mentioned. It is one of the things that caused such demoralization and loss of property throughout this part of the state.

In October, 1861, Thompson with his forces made an expedition from Stoddard county where he made his headquarters at that time, by way of Fredericktown into Jefferson county. He had two purposes in view. One was to destroy the Iron Mountain Railroad bridge over Big river and thus hamper the movement of Federal forces south from St. Louis, the other was to seize lead from the lead mines and carry it south for Confederate use. He separated his forces on the march, sending his infantry into Fredericktown while his cavalry made the raid into Jefferson county. They found the bridge which was near Blackwell guarded by Union soldiers and a fierce skirmish was fought. The bridge was destroyed and Thompson retreated to rejoin his forces at Fredericktown. Here he found that strong Union forces were closing in on him.

When news of his raid reached the Federal authorities they made plans for the capture of his force. Col. Plummer was sent from Cape Girardeau with about 1,500 men, while Col. Carlin advanced from Pilot Knob with about 3,000. On receiving news of these forces Thompson fell back from Fredericktown toward Greenville and fought an engagement with the Union forces about one mile outside of the town on the Greenville road, October 21, 1861. After the battle, which was fiercely contested on both sides, Thompson continued his retreat in good order and the Union forces occupied Fredericktown. During the disorder attendant upon their taking possession the town was fired and several houses were destroyed. Thompson made good his retreat and carried away about 18,000 pounds of lead.

October 14, 1861, a skirmish was fought at Underwood's farm near Bird's Point. It resulted in a Confederate victory.

On November 1, 1861, the situation in Southeast Missouri was as follows: General Grant was in command at Cairo with an army of about 20,000 soldiers, Colonel J. B. Plummer was at Cape Girardeau with about 1,500 soldiers including the 11th Missouri Volunteers and some Illinois troops, Colonel Carlin was at Ironton and Pilot Knob with 3,000 soldiers mostly from Illinois, Colonel R. J. Oglesby was in command at Bird's Point under direct supervision of General Grant. Besides the Union forces there were the following Confederate forces in this part of the state: General W. J. Hardee was at Greenville with about 3,000 men, General Pillow was at New Madrid with a force of about 5,000 and General Jeff Thompson was at Bloomfield with a force of about 1,500.

Keeping in mind this disposition of forces it is easy to understand the operations which resulted finally in the battle of Belmont. Grant was ordered by General Fremont at St. Louis to make a general advance and if possible take possession of all fortified posts in Southeast Missouri. Carrying out this instruction General Grant ordered Colonel Carlin with 3,000 men to march south from Ironton to Indian Ford where he was to meet and capture a detachment of Thompson's troops and then make his way toward Bloomfield to assist in the capture of Thompson's main forces. At the same time Colonel Plummer was ordered to march from Cape Girardeau to Bloomfield with his forces, and Colonel R. J. Oglesby with some 4,000 or 5,000 Illinois troops to take boat at Bird's Point, disembark at Commerce, and proceed to Bloomfield to operate against Thompson. These orders were carried out, Carlin starting from Ironton on November 3rd and reaching Indian Ford, twenty-five miles south of Greenville on the St. Francois river but finding no troops, from Indian Ford he was ordered to return to Ironton as it was found to be impracticable to cross from Indian Ford to Bloomfield with troops and a wagon train. Colonel Plummer marched from Cape Girardeau to Bloomfield expecting to capture Thompson and his command, but found they had retreated. Oglesby started from Bird's Point, landed at Commerce, marched across "Nigger Wool" swamp where he fought a skirmish with a few Confederate soldiers, and then to Bloomfield taking possession of that town. On the arrival of the Union troops, Thompson fell back from Bloomfield about ten miles to Camp Jackson and later to West Prairie in the vicinity of Clarkton. It was his intention, if pressed, to retreat across the Blanton plank road from Clarkton to New Madrid. When Plummer and Oglesby found that Thompson had retreated from Bloomfield they at first determined to follow him to New Madrid. They were, however, ordered by General Grant to return. Plummer then fell back to Cape Girardeau, and Oglesby returned to Bird's Point.

The battle of Belmont immediately followed these movements. General Grant had been ordered to stop the crossing of Confederate troops at Columbus and the battle was the result of this order.

The battle of Belmont was a fiercely fought and sanguinary contest. It was the purpose of General Grant to seize the Confederate post at Belmont and to hold it in order to prevent the crossing of troops from Kentucky.

On the evening of November 5th he embarked about 4,000 men on transports and accompanied by a convoy of gunboats dropped down from Cairo toward Belmont, a distance of twenty miles. Eleven miles from Belmont he made a feint at landing and remained anchored until daylight. Early in the morning the boats were dropped down to Hunter's farm three miles from Belmont, landed and marched against the latter place. The Confederate forces, while inferior in numbers to the attacking army, fought with great valor and were favored by the dense woods and marshy character of part of the ground. The fighting continued for four hours when the Confederates were driven out from their camp and took shelter under the river bank. They did not surrender, however, and kept up a desultory fire from their new position. The Union forces were disorganized by their capture of the camp and gave themselves up to pillage. Meantime the Confederates were hurrying reinforcements from Columbus on the other side of the river and soon began to press on the Federals. The camp was fired and the Confederate batteries at Columbus fired on the Union army. Finding the position untenable the Union forces fell back toward their transports and were attacked furiously by the Confederates. The Union forces suffered severely on this retreat and General Grant himself came near falling into the hands of the Confederates. He managed to reach the transport just as it pushed off.

The victory remained with the Confederates though they lost in all 642 men while the Union loss was 480.

While the Confederates were passing along the river bank a number of acts of heroism were performed; one of them was the act of a little boy who was attached to Tappan's Arkansas Regiment, one of the Confederate organizations, and took part in the retreat of the regiment along the river's bank. As he went he carried two flags, one in each hand. The Arkansas regiment was subjected to a terrific fire from the Union troops, many were killed and many men who were wounded fell into the river; among those struck was the little boy who bore the flags. He was not frightened by the terrific volley fired into the regiment nor was he dismayed by the wound he received. He waved the flags over his head, gave one last shout in honor of the flag which he carried and staggered into the river and was drowned. His death, which was witnessed by a great number on both sides, was very greatly deplored by all who saw it.

The remaining events of the year 1861 in Southeast Missouri consisted of skirmishes and desultory fighting. December 11th there was a skirmish at Bertrand, and on the next day one at Charleston. December 29th Thompson with forty men passed rapidly through Sikeston from Hunter's Farm to Commerce capturing stores and then retreated to New Madrid.

The year 1862 saw the war carried on in Southeast Missouri about as before. There were no great movements but skirmishes were fought and much property destroyed and suffering caused.

On January 7th, Col. Purcel with a Union force started from Bird's Point to Charleston. Just about daybreak he fell into an ambush and lost twenty-two men.

The Union forces more and more adopted the plan of sending out expeditions from the places in their possession into the lower counties of the district to seize suspected men and property. Many men who were accused of being bushwhackers and guerillas were shot on these expeditions, some were brought to Cape Girardeau and imprisoned. On January 15th of this year three of these expeditions were sent out. F. M. Smith led a force to Benton. Capt. Lindsay Murdoch to Bloomfield, and Maj. Rawalt to Dallas as Marble Hill was then called.

On January 23d, two hundred men were sent from Greenville then in possession of the Union forces to St. Francisville on the St. Francois river. They were beaten in a skirmish that ensued. On March 23d, Maj. Rawalt with a detachment of the 7th Illinois made an expedition from Point Pleasant to Little River. Here he fought a skirmish and then fell back to his headquarters. On April 3d, Col. Carlin defeated a Confederate force at Doniphan. He had led an expedition from Pilot Knob.

On April 13th Lindsay Murdoch conducted an expedition from Cape Girardeau to Jackson, Whitewater, and Dallas. No severe fighting occurred and no organized resistance encountered.

On March 3d of this year General Pope began the movements which resulted in the capture of the Confederate stronghold at Island No. 10.

With a strong force he reached New Madrid after a terrible march, March 3d. He found the town strongly defended, and protected by the guns of Confederate gunboats in the river. The situation was such that he was unwilling to risk an assault on the town for he feared that even if it could be carried the fire of the boats would render it impossible to hold it. He determined to lay siege to the place in form and accordingly sent for heavy siege guns from Cairo. Pending the arrival of these he directed Col. Plummer with the 11th Missouri to Point Pleasant, ten miles south of New Madrid. Plummer found Point Pleasant defended and entrenched himself.

Pope received his heavy guns from Cairo and put them into position and opened fire on the town March 13th. An artillery duel followed with the Confederate gunboats taking an active and vigorous part. That night the Confederate forces evacuated New Madrid and Point Pleasant. The possession of these places was of great importance to Pope in providing him a base for his attack of Island No. 10.

The purpose of taking this island was to open the Mississippi river to the passage of Federal transports and gunboats. So long as the Confederate forces held Island No. 10 it was not considered safe for Federal boats to pass that place. The task which General Pope had was one of considerable difficulty. It was thought that the only successful way of attacking the island was from below it, but such an attack was to be made only by the use of the gunboats and the transports and these were above the island. The difficulties of passing the island with the boats were very great. It was determined not to risk this passage but to cut a canal in such a way that the island could be passed without danger. The river makes a sharp bend near the island and as it was a high stage of water so that the bayous were overflowed, the engineers undertook to cut a channel across the narrow neck of the bend sufficient for the passage of the boats. There was not much digging because the water was so high, the trees were cut off and obstructions taken from the way, although in some places it was necessary to dig through the solid earth. Colonel J. W. Bissell, of the 1st Missouri Engineers, was in charge of the work and it was successfully completed on the 4th of April, having been begun March 17th. The canal was twelve miles long and for six miles it was cut through heavy timber. The small gunboats and the transports went through this canal while the two large gunboats, the Carondolet and the Pittsburg, ran the batteries of the island at night. As soon as the gunboats passed below the island the Confederates found their position untenable as it was fortified only on the upper side. They evacuated the position on the 7th of April and retreated to Tiptonville, Tennessee, where they were forced to surrender on April 9th. The forces consisted of 273 officers and 6,700 privates.

This was the only military operation of importance in Southeast Missouri during the year 1862, but there was a constant warfare going on between the Home Guards and the Confederate troops. Colonel W. L. Jeffers, who had been an officer in the Mexican war, organized a company of soldiers and gave the Federal troops a great deal of trouble. On April 6th he defeated a company of militia under Captain Wm. Flentge near Jackson. On August 24th with a hundred men he defeated four companies of the 12th Cavalry under Major B. F. Lazear on Crooked Creek in Bollinger county. On May 16th he defeated a Wisconsin regiment under Colonel Daniels at Chalk Bluff, Arkansas. This Colonel Daniels led his troops into Dunklin county and captured a small steamer on Little river at Hornersville. This steamer was called the Daniel E. Miller. Daniels had also previously defeated a detachment of Confederates under Colonel Phelan about twelve miles from Bloomfield. On October 29, 1862, near Clarkton in Dunklin county, there was a fight between some Illinois soldiers, who entered the county from Columbus and a company under Colonel John M. Clark. The Illinois soldiers retreated after the skirmish.

On December 22, 1862, the Thirty-second Iowa Regiment, then at New Madrid, made an expedition to Clarkton and Kennett seizing property and prisoners on the way.

December 27th New Madrid was evacuated by the Union forces owing to a curious misunderstanding. This blunder resulted in a court-martial because of the destruction of property ordered by some of the officers but they were held to have acted in good faith.

These were the principal incidents of the war in Southeast Missouri up to the beginning of the year 1863. The general tendency was to push the Confederate troops further and further back toward the Arkansas line and for the control of the country to pass into the hands of the Union forces. Some of the skirmishes and battles were victories for the Confederates but on the whole the fortunes of war in Southeast Missouri turned against them and from the beginning of 1863 to the close of the war the forces that fought battles in this part of the state were mostly those that came into the state from Arkansas. It is not to be understood, however, that these were Arkansas troops; they were, a good many of them, Missourians because the armies that operated in Arkansas as well as many of the armies of the east side of the river contained many Missourians.

On January 27, 1863, Col. Lindsay with the Sixty-eighth Regiment of Missouri Militia entered Bloomfield and destroyed much property in the town. On February 13th, part of the Twelfth Missouri cavalry went from Cape Girardeau to Dallas and Bloomfield. They reported no prisoners captured but a number killed.

On March 9th, John McNeil with the Second Missouri Cavalry made an expedition from Bloomfield to Chalk Bluff where a severe skirmish was fought. Seven men were killed in this fight. He then proceeded to Thompson's fort on Gum slough where he defeated some Confederate soldiers. From this place he proceeded to Kennett seizing a number of the inhabitants a number of whom were killed. March 23d part of McNeil's command went west from Bloomfield to Poplar Bluff and then to Pitman's Ferry. They fought several skirmishes on the way and were successful in them.

On April 17, 1863, began one of the memorable movements of the war—Marmaduke's invasion of Missouri. He entered the state with 5,000 men and ten pieces of artillery from Arkansas. His forces were organized into four brigades. Shelby's brigade of Missouri cavalry, Green's Missouri cavalry, Carter's Texas cavalry, and Burbridge's brigade of Missouri and Arkansas cavalry. These forces were organized into two columns. One of them commanded by Gen. Jo Shelby was composed of his own and Burbridge's brigade. The other made up of the brigades of Carter and Greene was commanded by Gen. Carter. Marmaduke's plans were for Shelby to enter the state to the west, pass by Van Buren in Carter county and then to Patterson reaching the latter place April 20, and if possible to capture the Federal force at that point. At the same time Carter with his column was to pass through Doniphan and reach Patterson on the 20th also.

These movements were performed on time and at midnight of April 20th, Carter, who was then near Patterson, detached a regiment under Col. Giddings to surprise Patterson. Giddings seized the picket guard of twenty-five men, but artillery fire was opened on the town at a distance of two miles and the Union force escaped in the direction of Pilot Knob.

From Patterson Shelby was sent to Fredericktown which he was to hold pending the arrival of Carter's column. Marmaduke himself accompanied Shelby. In the meantime Carter attacked Bloomfield, then held by Col. John McNeil with a considerable force. The plan was for Carter to defeat McNeil and if he retreated as it was supposed he would toward Pilot Knob for Shelby to intercept his retreat and capture his command.

Shelby was at Fredericktown April 22d, and while waiting for word from Carter sent a detachment to burn the railroad bridge over Big river. This was accomplished after a severe skirmish. Carter reached Bloomfield April 21st, and McNeil retreated as was supposed he would do in the direction of Pilot Knob by way of Dallas (Marble Hill). He was followed closely by Carter. On the retreat he learned of Shelby's presence at Fredericktown and turned to Cape Girardeau. Carter followed him to within four miles of the town and sent word to Shelby at Fredericktown for reinforcements. These messengers were captured and Marmaduke and Shelby were without news from Carter until the 25th. Shelby then led his column to Cape Girardeau. He approached by the Jackson road to make a demonstration while Marmaduke drew off Carter's men by the Bloomfield road. The demonstration became an artillery duel and Marmaduke brought Carter's men around to the Jackson road to support Shelby.

The brunt of the fighting fell on Fort B, the present site of the Normal school. Here there were four twenty-four pounder guns. There were four twelve pounder guns on a hill to the southwest of Fort B. These were brought during the engagement to the hill where the Fullerton house stands. Two of them were ultimately carried to Fort B. There was also a line of rifle pits near the Fullerton house. These were charged by the Confederates. Two of them were killed at this place. This house at the time was occupied by a family named Lacey. During the fighting they sought safety in the cellar. A shell fired the house, but the flames were extinguished.

Finding the town well defended and the fortifications strong, Marmaduke drew off his entire force to Jackson. While here he was threatened by a Union force under General Vandever in command of Iowa troops. These troops attacked Col. Newton's regiment as it encamped on the Jackson and Fredericktown road. Finding himself between the forces of McNeil at Cape Girardeau and Vandever on Whitewater, both being constantly reinforced, Marmaduke determined to retreat. He was followed until he crossed the St. Francois at Chalk Bluffs, fighting being continued during the retreat.

In August, 1863, a force of Federal troops comprising the Third cavalry of the Missouri state militia under command of Colonel R. G. Woodson started from Pilot Knob. They made their way to the south and at Pocahontas, Arkansas, they were able to surround and capture General Jeff Thompson and his entire staff. These prisoners were sent to the Gratiot prison in St. Louis. This capture came as a complete surprise and put an end to organized warfare in Southeast Missouri until the time of the great raid which General Price made through the state.

The last great movement of the Confederate troops through Missouri took place in 1864 and was known as Price's raid. At the beginning of this movement Price was in Arkansas with a considerable force of Confederate troops including a large number of Missourians. It was his intention to invade the state, to seize cities, among them St. Louis, if possible, and to arouse the enthusiasm and seek assistance for the Confederate cause from the people of Missouri. He entered the state, after having divided his troops into three divisions; the first of these divisions was under the command of Major General Fagan, who had under him Brigadier Generals Cabell, McRea, Stemmons and Dobbins; the second division was commanded by Major General John S. Marmaduke and consisted principally of Missourians; under Marmaduke were Brigadier Generals Clarke, Graham and Tyler and Colonels Freeman, Lowe, Bristow, Green, Jeffers, Burbridge and Kitchen. The third division of the army was commanded by General Jo Shelby and among the brigadiers who served under him was Jeff Thompson.

Opposed to Price's army were the Federal forces under General Thomas Ewing, Jr., who was stationed at St. Louis and had command over the district of Southeast Missouri, there being posts at Pilot Knob, Ste. Genevieve, Cape Girardeau and New Madrid.

The three divisions of Price's army comprising in all about 12,000 men and 14 pieces of artillery, entered the state at three different points. Shelby was on the left and marched by way of Doniphan. The Federal forces at Doniphan on his approach set fire to the town and retreated. They were followed by Shelby who defeated them in a skirmish at Ponder's Mill on the Little Black river. General Fagin entered the state to the east of Doniphan commanding as he did the central one of the three divisions; accompanied by General Price he reached Fredericktown September 24th. Marmaduke was in command of the most easterly of the divisions and his route was by Poplar Bluff, Castorville and Dallas. Orders were for all the divisions to drive the Federal forces before them, unite at Fredericktown and prepare for an attack on Pilot Knob where the most strenuous resistance was expected.

Shelby exceeded the fifteen miles a day which each division was supposed to march, reached Fredericktown in advance of the others, sent a detachment to Farmington, which place was taken after a skirmish with Federal forces in the courthouse at that place. Shelby waited for a time at Fredericktown and then took up the march toward the north. His command fought a severe skirmish at Mineral Point, destroyed the bridges at Big river, and tore up long stretches of railroad track, and reached Potosi. Here a force of Union troops holding the fortifications and the courthouse were captured. The railroad track from Mineral Point to Potosi was then torn up and Shelby awaited orders from Price. Not receiving them and hearing rumors of the fighting at Ironton he marched with his command in that direction in time to take part in the pursuit of Ewing.

As Marmaduke's division made its way to the north Jeffers was detached for an attack on Bloomfield. The Union forces withdrew on his approach and he followed them. On the 25th of September he fought a skirmish at Jackson and captured the town. He reached the rendezvous at Fredericktown September 26th. Price then with the divisions of Marmaduke and Fagan proceeded to the attack on Pilot Knob.

At this time General Rosecrans was department commander in Missouri with headquarters at St. Louis. When he was informed that Price contemplated entering the state, he called upon the authorities at Washington for reinforcements and received six thousand troops under command of General A. J.

Smith, a force that had been destined to General Sherman in Georgia. This gave General Rosecrans a force of about 12,000 soldiers, seemingly enough to defeat Price's intention and to preserve the state from the Confederate raid.

The forces came in conflict at Pilot Knob. General Rosecrans had directed General Ewing to gather his force, consisting of a brigade of the second division of the Sixteenth Army Corps then at Jefferson barracks and with this force to patrol the Iron Mountain railroad in preparation for the movement of the troops under General Smith. Carrying out these instructions Ewing left a part of his force at DeSoto and carried the Fourteenth Iowa through the country to Pilot Knob where he found Major James Wilson in command of a force of a thousand men; these were companies A, F, E, G, H and I of the Forty-seventh Missouri Infantry, Captain Lindsay's company of the Fiftieth Missouri, six companies of the Third Cavalry Missouri State Militia, Company L of the Second Cavalry, Company G of the First Cavalry and a battalion under command of Captain Montgomery; having assembled these forces General Ewing at once began the fortification of Pilot Knob.

There was already a fort just south of the village—Fort Davidson. It was about seven hundred yards in circumference and was defended by four thirty-two pound guns and three twenty-four pounders. This plain on which the fort stood is almost entirely surrounded by mountains, the only exceptions a gap between Shepherd Mountain and Pilot Knob, through which runs Stouts creek and a gap to the southeast known as the Shut-in through which passes the Fredericktown road. General Ewing obstructed the roads and cleared away the timber on the sides of the hills and dug two rifle pits in order to command the best approaches.

General Price and his army entered this valley by the Fredericktown road through the Shut-in. The first engagement took place on the 26th of September when a part of the Federal forces started from Pilot Knob in the direction of Fredericktown. They were driven back by Price's army into Ironton. General Price followed them and probably would have captured them at Ironton had it not been for the approach of night and a heavy rain storm. In spite of these handicaps the army of Price was in motion during most of the night and was concentrated about the town of Ironton. In the meantime the Federal forces had been busy moving their stores further up the railroad and in constructing fortifications. At daylight on the 27th of September, Major Wilson, who was in command at Ironton, was attacked by Price's troops and driven back into the gap between Pilot Knob and Shepherd's Mountain. Here he made a stand and during the assault on his position a detachment of the 14th Iowa was ordered by Ewing to take a position on the east end of Shepherd Mountain and then Wilson was ordered to fall back along the side of Pilot Knob so that the Confederate forces might be fired upon from the fort. A long and bloody engagement followed in which the losses were heavy on both sides. General Marmaduke was ordered by Price to take a position on the east side of Shepherd Mountain, which he did and planted two pieces of artillery. The fire from the artillery was very effective and he was able to drive the Federal forces out of the gap and to take possession of it. At the same time General Fagan marched from Pilot Knob and assaulted the fort from that side but was unable to take it. When night came on the operations of the forces were suspended, both sides feeling sure that the fort would not be able to hold out much longer. During the night General Ewing determined to evacuate the fort and if possible to draw his forces off in order to escape what seemed to be the inevitable, defeat and capture. The retreat was made without discovery and after the forces had withdrawn the magazine in the fort was fired and the fort destroyed, this feat was performed by Daniel Flood of the Third Cavalry Missouri State Militia. This battle at Pilot Knob was one of the most obstinately contended of any fought within the limits of Southeast Missouri during the war. It was a victory for the Confederate forces though both sides lost heavily.

After retreating from Pilot Knob General Ewing sent a detachment to Mineral Point where a small troop of Federal troops were, in order to warn them of his retreat, these troops, however, were attacked by Confederate soldiers under command of General Joe Shelby who had not participated in the battle at Pilot Knob but had marched from Fredericktown by the way of Farmington. This unexpected check caused General Ewing to change the plans of his retreat. He was no longer certain of being able to retreat in the direction of St. Louis and he turned toward Rolla. At Webster, however, he decided to march for Harrison, here he fought a skirmish with General Shelby and later retreated to Rolla.

Price's main force marched through Potosi and Richwoods which place was reached September 30. While on the march a number of men had been sent to DeSoto where they fought a skirmish and destroyed a depot of supplies. From Richwoods the command turned toward Washington, Hermann and Jefferson City and finally to Lexington and out of the state into Kansas.

The war left Southeast Missouri in a very deplorable condition. Its effects were the usual effects of war where it is brought home to the people. As we have said, Southeast Missouri was really on the border between the North and the South and while it was not the scene of great battles nor formed the pathway of great armies, it was ravaged by guerrilla bands from both sides. The fact that neighbors and friends and even members of the same family served on opposite sides tended to increase the bitterness that war naturally brings. There were hundreds of non-combatants who attempted to remain peaceably in their homes and who were killed during the war. The section was overrun by organized bands of lawless men who used the opportunity which war brings to live lawless and uncontrolled lives. The harried the whole country, they seized property when and where they pleased, and to resist them was almost certain to bring vengeance and perhaps death.

A country so disturbed was certain to suffer very greatly. Many flourishing towns were practically depopulated during the war. This was true of Bloomfield, Poplar Bluff, Fredericktown and other places in this district. The inhabitants were either killed in war or in the raids of the bands from either side, or else they were driven away from their homes and found shelter in other places. The population of the entire district was greatly diminished by the same causes. It is a fact that Southeast Missouri sent as large a proportion of its inhabitants into the armies of the North and South as any other part of the country; very many of whom never returned from the war.

But not only was the loss of life appalling and terrible, the country suffered a very great loss of property as well. Houses were destroyed and burned and even whole villages were practically wiped out of existence by the torch, fields were destroyed, in many cases all the fencing disappeared. Either it rotted away from neglect or else was burned for wood and fields left uncultivated grew up in briars and brush. The stock that existed at the time of the war was either killed or driven away by the soldiers and robber bands or else it became half wild in the woods and some died of starvation and of neglect.

These material losses were very great and it took many years for the country to recover from them. In many parts of Southeast Missouri a new conquest of nature had to be made. Fields were once more to be reclaimed, houses, fences and towns had to be rebuilt. But great as were these losses they were no greater than the damage brought to other interests not material in themselves. It is impossible to measure the ruin wrought by war viewed from the moral standpoint. It offered an opportunity for vicious men to reveal what was in them and live unrestrained lives. It took away in many cases the chance for making an honest living and substituted for it theft and robbery. Many men were demoralized by these conditions and it required years for the country to recover from the damage done to the country in this way. Civil authority had been to a very great extent done away with during the war. It was subordinated to the military power. Martial law prevailed and it was not for a long time that the courts could transact their business in the regular and usual way, and until the authority of the law came to be once more felt and recognized as it had been before.

It was certainly a most trying situation which the returned soldier from North or South was compelled to face as he came home from the war. He, in all probability, found his house in ashes, his horses and cattle dead or driven away, his fences in ruins, and his fields overgrown. He himself came home in most cases, practically penniless and must make a new start in life. Added to this was the fact that there was for sometime no secure protection for himself or property against these bands that were unwilling to give up their marauding and plundering even when the war closed.

But terrible and disheartening as these circumstances were the people of Southeast Missouri set themselves to rebuild their country, to develop its resources, and to make it once more a habitation fit for civilized men. In comparatively a short while the towns were rebuilt and houses once more arose from the ashes. The fields were reduced again to the purpose of agriculture, churches and schools were opened, and life resumed its ordinary condition. Out of the ruin which the war brought and out of its very demoralization there came vigor and splendor of enthusiasm that enabled men to make of this section of the state one of the richest and best parts of Missouri.

CHAPTER XXVIII

REGIMENTAL HISTORIES

UNION TROOPS ORGANIZED—HOME GUARDS AND STATE MILITIA—THIRD, FIFTH, SIXTY-FOURTH, SIXTY-EIGHTH, SEVENTY-EIGHTH, SEVENTY-NINTH, SECOND, TWENTY-NINTH, THIRTIETH AND FORTY-SEVENTH INFANTRY—SIXTH AND TENTH MISSOURI CAVALRY—ENGINEER REGIMENT, WEST MISSOURI VOLUNTEERS—TWENTY-THIRD AND TWENTY-NINTH REGIMENTS OF ENROLLED MILITIA—OTHER COMMANDS OF STATE GUARDS—NINTH AND SECOND INFANTRY—NOTED CONFEDERATE ORGANIZATIONS.

The Union troops organized in Missouri for service in the Civil war on the Union side were of five different kinds. The first of these were Home Guards, as they were called, enlisted for a period of three months. At a somewhat later period there began the enrollment of what was called the Six Months Militia. The third group of organizations was called the Missouri State Militia, the fourth group were the Missouri Volunteers. This group contained the principal number of regiments and of course, saw active, hard service in the campaigns of the war. Just about the close of the war, 1865, there were enlisted in Missouri a number of regiments known as the Enrolled Missouri Militia. These regiments served for a very short time, the organization of some of them was never even completed owing to the fact that peace was made almost immediately after they were enrolled.

An effort is made to furnish a statement of all the troops enlisted on both sides during the war. The information here given concerning Union troops is taken from reports of the Adjutant General of Missouri published in 1863 and 1865, and is as full and complete as it has been possible to make it. An account is given first of the troops enlisted for service in the Union armies. It has already been said that the Missouri State Militia was the term under which the state troops serving for the Union were known, while the Confederate troops under authority of the state were called the Missouri State Guard.

The first Union troops of Southeast Missouri were called at first Home Guards and their term of enlistment was three months. A battalion of four companies was organized in Cape Girardeau in June, 1861, under the command of Major George H. Cramer. The officers of the companies were as follows: Company A, John M. Cluley, captain; Company B, William J. Stevenson, captain; Company C, Michael Dittlinger, captain, and Company D, Arnold Beck, captain.

As the name implies these troops were intended for the defense of Cape Girardeau and the surrounding communities; they were to be in fact, as the name implies, home guards.

The battalion thus organized saw no particular service except in the town and county and they disbanded in the following September. Previous to this organization a battalion had been organized in Scott county in May, 1861, under Major Daniel Abbey, who was commissioned for the purpose by General Lyon. The captains of the four companies in this battalion were: John Orth, Constantine Grojean, James Daniels and Frank Klepman. When General Fremont came into command of the department of Missouri, he gave a commission of lieutenant colonel to Lindsay Murdock, of Bollinger county, and ordered him to recruit a battalion to be used in the defense of the post of Cape Girardeau. Four companies were raised under this order known as Fremont's rangers; they came from Bollinger, Scott and Cape Girardeau counties and their captains were: J. F. Burk, William P. Harris and Michael S. Eddlemon. These Fremont rangers served up to December 25th, 1861, and upon them fell the brunt of most of the work done in Southeast Missouri, especially the work of scouting. During their term of service they were not paid nor were they provided with clothing.

A company known as the Potosi Home Guards was organized in June, 1861, with George R. French as captain; Irwin K. Walker, first lieutenant; and Thomas H. Maclird as second lieutenant. The company consisted of 75 men and did guard duty in Washington county until August, 1861, when the term of enlistment expired. In the course of its guard duty it fought a skirmish at Potosi.

A company known as the DeSoto Home Guards was organized in June, 1861, and served until September of the same year. Allen Cook was captain; Christian Ellrodt, first lieutenant; and William Hendrickson, second lieutenant. This company was composed of 85 men and did guard service.

A company was organized at Pilot Knob in June, 1861, with Ferdinand Schmitz as captain; John Schwartz, first lieutenant; and Charles Cordrie, second lieutenant. This company was composed of 99 men and the only service that it saw was guard duty about Pilot Knob.

The Washington County Battalion was organized in July, 1861, and its lieutenant colonel was J. B. Elmer. Company A had the following officers: P. R. VanFrank, captain; Samuel E. Turner, first lieutenant; William Plumb, second lieutenant. The officers of Company B were Captain J. L. Page, and Lieutenants H. N. Cook and Isaac Benning. The officers of Company C were Captain H. M. Hulser, Lieutenants Charles MaClay and Gardner Henning. The officers of Company D were Captain Oscar Dover and Lieutenants Dugan and Williams. The officers of Company E were Captain T. C. Casselman, Lieutenants Samuel Weast and Eli Vincent. This battalion was organized at Potosi, September 19, 1861, and after doing scout duty and taking part in a number of skirmishes, was mustered out at Hillsboro in January, 1862.

The Missouri State Militia was not largely recruited in Southeast Missouri, but one regiment being organized here, the 12th cavalry. It was during the winter and spring of 1862 that the eight companies comprising this regiment were organized. Company A was recruited at Cape Girardeau and organized February 10, 1862. The captain was Lindsay Murdock; first lieutenant, George W. Hamil; second lieutenant, Erick Pape; Company B organized January 23, 1862, was from Wayne county; William T. Leeper, captain; Evan Francis, first lieutenant; C. W. Purcell, second lieutenant; Company C was recruited in Stoddard county and was organized February 4. Its captain was Thomas B. Walker; first lieutenant, Anthony Arnold; second lieutenant, John McMillan; Company D was organized February 27th, with William Flentge as captain; Henry Wolters, first lieutenant, and Louis Storts, second lieutenant; Company E from Perry county was organized March 26th, and had for its officers: captain, Peter Hogan; first lieutenant, Ferdinant Charveau and second lieutenant, Thomas Goin; Company F was recruited in Perry and Bollinger counties and organized on March 26th. Its officers were captain, Levi C. Whybark; first lieutenant, M. S. Eddlemon; second lieutenant, Samuel G. Bidwell. Bollinger and Wayne counties recruited Company G, which was organized March 29th. The officers were A. R. Dill, captain; Phillip Sutherlin, first lieutenant, and Henry W. Worth, second lieutenant; Company H was from Washington county and William T. Hunter was its captain.

The Third Regiment was organized May 14, 1862. Albert Jackson was made colonel; Samuel P. Simpson, lieutenant colonel; Benjamin F. Lazear, major; and H. M. Mathews, surgeon. Neither the colonel nor lieutenant colonel ever took active command of the regiment and during its existence Major Lazear was in actual charge of it. Owing to a combination of circumstances it was deemed best to break the regiment up and this was done February 2, 1863. Companies A, B, and H were made a part of the Third Cavalry; Companies D, E, and F, a part of the Fifth Cavalry; and Companies C and G were disbanded and distributed among the companies of the Fifth Cavalry. This Third Regiment was at this time at Pilot Knob. From there it went to Patterson in Wayne county, where it was attacked April 20, 1863, by General Marmaduke and driven back to Pilot Knob. This regiment took part in no other active fighting though it did duty as guard and escort in various ways and did some fighting against the guerrilla bands. This regiment was ordered to St. Louis after Price's raid and then to St. Joseph where it was employed until mustered out about May 1, 1865.

The Fifth Regiment, to which some of the companies of the 12th had been attached, was at Rolla. The regiment was engaged in scouting service up to the time of Price's raid and took part in the pursuit of Price, participating in the battles at Jefferson City, California, Booneville, Lexington, Big Blue, Independence, Hickmans Mills, and Fort Scott. They were later returned to Rolla and remained until they were mustered out of service.

Besides these there were a number of regiments of Enrolled Missouri Militia organized in Southeast Missouri. The Fifty-sixth Regiment was raised in Cape Girardeau county. It was organized October 4, 1862; and its general officers were: W. H. McLane, colonel; G. C. Thilenius, lieutenant colonel; and Casper Uhl, major. The company officers were: Company A, Captain A. P. Shriner; Company B, Captain William Regenhardt; Company C, Captain Lemon Haile; Company D, Captain William N. Wilson; Company E, Captain R. H. Ruhl; Company F, Captain S. W. Whybark; Company G, Captain J. S. Needham; Company H, Captain Elisha Sheppard; and Company I, Captain Adolph Tacke.

The Sixty-fourth Regiment was from Perry county and was organized October 27, 1862. Its general officers were Robert M. Brewer, colonel; Joseph C. Killian, lieutenant colonel; Charles A. Weber, major; and Thomas Hoos, adjutant. The captains were: Company A,

William T. Wilkinson, later John J. Seibel; Company B, Felix Layton, later W. H. Bennett; Company C, John C. Ochs, later Anthon Hunt; Company D, Thomas G. Chadwick; Company E, Henry Little; Company F, Joseph Meyer, later Henry B. Knox; Company H, Chris Feig; Company I, Emanuel Estel; Company K, Joseph Lukefahr.

The Sixty-eighth Regiment was organized November 20, 1862; it was made up of men from Iron and Wayne counties. Its general officers were: James Lindsay, colonel; George W. King, lieutenant colonel; Robert L. Lindsay, major; and C. R. Peck, adjutant. In March, 1864, John W. Emerson was appointed colonel in place of Lindsay. The captains were: Company A, William P. Adair; Company B, Ross Jekyll, later W. B. Connelly; Company C, E. A. Killian, later Franz Dinger; Company D, Morgan Mace; Company E, W. J. Ezell; Company F, W. W. Bunyard, later Pleasant W. Hodges; Company G, James E. Davis; Company H, H. H. Finley; Company I, Jasper Belkin and Company K, P. L. Powers.

The Seventy-eighth Regiment was organized principally from Ste. Genevieve and surrounding counties, was constituted April 21, 1863, with F. Leavenworth as colonel, George Bond lieutenant colonel, James Hodgmeiller major, and Leon Bogy adjutant. The captains were: Company A, C. H. Eddlemon; Company B, Thomas Stone; Company C, Phillip Wagner; Company D, John B. Eberett; Company E, Lawson Hughes; Company F, Andrew Miller; Company G, Herman Kustner; Company H, J. M. Benham; Company I, S. E. Montgomery, and Company K, William Roth.

The Seventy-ninth Regiment was organized in June, 1863, in Scott and Mississippi counties; Henry J. Deal was colonel; George M. Kayser, adjutant, and Solomon D. Golder, surgeon. The captains were: Company A, Edwin P. Deal; Company B, L. W. Prichett; Company C, Samuel Coleman; Company D, George C. Vail; Company E, W. W. Campbell, later C. Grojean; Company F, Samuel Tanner; Company G, James H. Howard; Company K, John L. Painsberry.

The Second Infantry was organized and mustered into service at St. Louis, September 10, 1861, and was composed in part of men from Southeast Missouri. It saw a great deal of hard service and took part in the battles in Southwest Missouri and then in the principal battles in Arkansas including Pea Ridge. Then it was transferred to Cape Girardeau and from there to Corinth, Riengi, Mississippi. In September, 1862, it was ordered to Cincinnati, and then to Lawrenceville. On October 1, 1862, it started for Nashville and took part in the great battle at Perryville; it reached Nashville in December, and participated in the battle of Murfreesboro. It was also engaged at Chickamauga and Chattanooga, at Charleston, Tennessee, and Dalton, Georgia. It was mustered out September 29, 1864.

In October, 1862, the Twenty-ninth Infantry was organized in Cape Girardeau. John S. Cavender was colonel, James Peckham, lieutenant colonel, and B. H. Peterson, major. Companies F, G, and H were recruited in Southeast Missouri; Christian Burkhardt was the first captain of Company F. He was made major of the regiment in November, 1864, and was succeeded as captain by Herman Bader. James McGarvey was captain of Company G, and Thomas Rhodes of Commerce, Missouri, was first lieutenant. The captains of Company H were: N. A. Cole, Thomas Jork, W. H. Gray and David Allen, Jr. This regiment also took part in many of the larger battles of the war, after its organization it was sent first to Patterson in Wayne county and then returned to Cape Girardeau. On December 8th, it was transferred to Helena; the regiment there became part of General Blair's brigade and took part in the campaign in Louisiana and Mississippi under Sherman. In the next summer it was engaged in the operations around Vicksburg and was present at the capture of that place. In September of that year it was ordered to Charleston and took part in the storming of Lookout Mountain and Missionary Ridge. Later the regiment was sent to Georgia and then to Alabama and on April 30, 1864, it became a part of the First Division of the Fifteenth Army Corps and was with that command in all the battles of the Atlanta campaign and the campaign against Hood; it was then mounted and took part in the campaign through the Carolinas. The regiment was mustered out in Washington and was returned to St. Louis in June, 1865.

The Thirtieth Regiment of Missouri Infantry was composed of eight companies recruited for this regiment and two of which had been raised for the 34th, which, however, was not organized. The general officers were: B. J. Farrar, colonel; Otto Schadt, lieutenant colonel, and James W. Fletcher, major. Company B was organized in Perry county in 1862, with William T. Wilkinson, captain; George S. Ziegler, first lieutenant, and C. M. French, second lieutenant; this regiment was also attached to Blair's brigade participating in the campaign along the Mississippi, and in the bordering states. It was in Louisiana in 1864, and in November of that year was made into a battalion of four companies and placed under the command of William T. Wilkinson who was made lieutenant colonel. After this change in organization it saw active service in Louisiana and about Mobile until it was transferred to Texas in June, 1865, and was there mustered out August 24 of that year.

The Forty-seventh Regiment was recruited by Colonel Thomas C. Fletcher, who had been authorized in August, 1864, to raise this regiment and was assigned to Southeast Missouri. The response to the call for soldiers was very prompt and more companies were offered than could be assigned one regiment, and out of the remaining companies the Fiftieth Regiment was formed. The officers of the 47th were: Thomas C. Fletcher, colonel; A. W. Maupin, lieutenant colonel, and John W. Emerson, major. Colonel Fletcher was elected governor of the state in November, 1864, and was succeeded as colonel by Lieutenant Colonel Maupin. The companies were recruited and officered as follows: Company A, Iron and Wayne counties, Captain J. S. McMurtry; first lieutenant, J. T. Sutton and second lieutenant, P. A. Hodges; Company B, Jefferson county; captain, W. J. Buxton; first lieutenant, J. C. Hamel; second lieutenant, B. F. Butler; Company C, Perry county; captain, C. A. Weber; first lieutenant, Felix Layton; second lieutenant, Thomas Stone; Company D, Washington county; captain, J. W. Maupin; first lieutenant, L. J. Crowe; second lieutenant, A. J. Gilchrist; Company E, Iron county; captain, F. Dinger; first lieutenant, George J. Fetley; second lieutenant, John Schwab; Company F, St. Francois county; captain, W. P. Adair; first lieutenant, C. Helber, second lieutenant, W. B. Connelly; Company G, Wayne and Bollinger counties; captain, Morgan Mace; first lieutenant, Samuel W. Whybark; second lieutenant, W. B. Wilson; Company H, Wayne county; captain, P. L. Powers; first lieutenant, W. P. Tate; second lieutenant, E. P. Settle; Company I, Madison county; Captain, H. W. Bradley; first lieutenant, C. H. Cummings; second lieuenant, W. A. Dunlap; Company K, Ste. Genevieve county; captain, Gustavus St. Gem; first lieutenant, Leon Bogy; second lieutenant, Robert D. Brown. The organization of this regiment was completed in September, 1864, and as soon as companies were ready they were sent to their respective counties and assisted in the defense against General Price; Companies A, G, and H were sent to Patterson and later returned to Pilot Knob where they were joined by Companies F and I and took part in the engagement at that place; later the regiment was sent to Rolla and was there joined to the command of General Thomas Nash; the regiment remained a part of the force under General Nash until mustered out in March, 1865.

The surplus companies which had been raised for the Forty-seventh Regiment were ordered to be organized into the 50th. The organization, however, had not been effected at the time of General Price's raid through the country and the companies were sent back to their counties before the organization was completed. After Price had passed on to north Missouri and work of organization was taken up and David Murphy was made lieutenant colonel at first and then in the spring of 1865, was made colonel of the regiment. B. Newey was the lieutenant colonel; the company officers were as follows: Company A, Mississippi county; captain, E. P. Deal; Company B, captain, Charles Perry; Company C, Cape Girardeau county; captain, Charles F. Bruihl; Company D, Scott county; captain, W. W. Campbell; Company E, captain, Arthur M. Kuson; Company F, Iron county; captain, Robert L. Lindsay; Company G, Perry county; captain, Christian Popp; Company H, captain, Lindsay Murdock; Company I, captain, William R. Vaughn; Company K, captain, Clinton Spencer. The only service the regiment saw was that of the respective companies in their own counties; in the summer of 1865, they were ordered to St. Louis and were a little later mustered out of service.

The Sixth Regiment Missouri Cavalry was organized February, 1862, by consolidating two battalions and a company; these battalions were known as Wright's and Wood's, and the company was the one raised by H. P. Hawkins. The regimental officers were: C. Wright, colonel; S. N. Wood, lieutenant colonel; H. P. Hawkins and Samuel Montgomery, majors; during the remainder of the year, 1862, the regiment saw service in southwest Missouri and Arkansas. It was then sent to Memphis, Tennessee, and took part in the battles around Vicksburg, some of these battles being Chickasaw Bayou, Arkansas Post, Greenville, Champions Hill, Black River and Bridgeport. From Vicksburg the regiment went to Jackson and then to Louisiana; it served in Louisiana until the close of the war when it was mustered out.

The Tenth Missouri Cavalry was organized at Camp Magazine near Jefferson Barracks, in December, 1862; its colonel was F. M. Cornyn; the regiment was made up in large part of men from Southeast Missouri. After its organization it was sent to the South and was divided for a time, parts of it being stationed at Helena, Memphis, Columbus, Kentucky. In the early part of 1863 the regiment was brought together at Memphis and then sent to Tuscumbia and took part in the operations against General Vandorn; its further service was confined to northern Mississippi and Alabama and won for itself an enviable record for bravery and activity.

The Engineer Regiment of West Missouri

Volunteers was recruited throughout most of the southern part of the state. One company of this regiment, the 3rd, was organized at Cape Girardeau in September, 1861, and took part in fortifying Cape Girardeau and Bird's Point. In March, 1862, this company was consolidated with three other companies to form a battalion which was then attached to General Pope's army as a pioneer corps; it took part in the engagements about New Madrid and Island No. 10. After Island No. 10 had been captured, the battalion was sent to northeast Mississippi with Pope's army and participated in the operations against Corinth, the rest of the year was spent in Tennessee, Mississippi and Alabama in repairing railroads, bridges, cars, locomotives, etc. During the year 1863, the regiment operated in two battalions the first against Vicksburg, the second was employed in keeping the railroad between Grand Junction and Corinth in repair. In December, 1863, the regiment was consolidated with the Fifth Missouri Volunteers and took part in the construction of the Nashville and Northwestern Railroad. It was then sent to Atlanta and took part in the fortification of that city after it was surrendered. The term of enlistment of many of the men expired while the regiment was in Atlanta and many of them were sent home; the remainder were organized into five companies and accompanied the Army of Tennessee in its march to the sea, having charge of the building of bridges on this march.

Battery F was recruited in Cape Girardeau and Scott counties and made a part of the Second Illinois Light Artillery, the organization being completed December 1st, 1861. The officers of the battery were: John W. Powell, captain; Michael Dittlinger and Joseph W. Mitchell, David Bliss, G. A. Tirmenstein, lieutenants; Fred Roeboeck, H. R. Henning, J. B. Walker, Lucius Moore, William Buchanan, Albert Gratenheim, W. H. Powell and Alfred S. Looker, sergeants. This battery was on duty in Cape Girardeau until March, 1862, when it was sent to Savannah, Tennessee; it took part in a number of engagements in Tennessee and Mississippi, and was later ordered to Louisiana, where it saw active service until the close of the war.

The Second Regiment of Missouri Volunteers was organized at St. Louis, September 10, 1861. Shortly after its organization it was sent to Southwest Missouri, where it took part in the battles at Pea Ridge, then in Arkansas where it fought at Batesville. Later the regiment returned to Missouri and was for a time stationed at Cape Girardeau; from Cape Girardeau it was sent east of the river and took part in the engagements at Corinth and Rienzi, Tennessee. In 1862 the regiment was sent to Cincinnati, Ohio, then to Louisville, Kentucky, and from there to Nashville, Tennessee; it took part in the great battles of Perryville, Murfreesboro, Chickamauga and Chattanooga.

The Forty-seventh Regiment of Missouri Volunteers was mustered in September 16, 1864, and disbanded March 30, 1865; the organization of the regiment was never entirely completed for as soon as the companies were enrolled they were dispersed in their counties where they saw active service for a time. Most of the companies of this regiment took part in the resistance of Price's raid. They fought in the battle of Pilot Knob and after Price had been driven from the state, they were sent to Tennessee and there formed part of Sherman's command on the march through Georgia.

Of the Enrolled Missouri Militia, most of which was recruited in 1865, the Fifteenth Regiments was raised in Jefferson county The regimental officers were colonel, Anthon Yerger; lieutenant colonel, C. C. Fletcher, and major, D. W. Bryant. The officers of the various companies of this regiment were as follows: Company A, captain, John Williams; lieutenants, John C. Powers, and R. W. McMillin; Company B, captain, B. F. Butler; lieutenant, S. F. McGee; Company C, lieutenants, Elbert Ogle, and R. M. Whitehead; Company D, captain, Eugene Armor, and lieutenants, George Martin and Xaver Kohler; Company E, captain, F. W. Fritter and lieutenant, J. J. McMillen; Company F, captain, J. W. Sullens and lieutenants, Philip Edniglo and C. M. VanGordon; Company G, lieutenant, William C. Alford; Company H, C. T. Edwards and lieutenant, Alfred Stewart; Company I, captain, F. D. Heaton and lieutenant, William Knapp; Company K, captain, E. F. Donnell.

Some of the companies of the Twenty-third Regiment of the Missouri Enrolled Militia were from Southeast Missouri also. The officers of these companies were as follows: Company B, captain, Joseph H. Vaughn and lieutenant, Ignaz Lutz; Company C, captain, J. H. Bridges, lieutenants, David Baker and William H. Bartlett; Company D, captain, Joseph M. Ayer; Company E, captain, S. R. Hoglan; Company F, captain, George W. Hutson; Company H, captain, Robert L. Bush.

The Twenty-third Regiment was raised principally in Iron county, its regimental officers were, colonel, James Lindsay, and afterward W. T. Leeper; lieutenant colonel, J. S. McMurtry; major, Warren E. Peck. The company officers were, Company A, captain, Martin G. Foster and lieutenant, Robert N. Spaugh; Company B, captain, W. Ake; Company C, captain, James G. Rauft; Company D, captain, William Russell; Company E, captain, John G. Imboden; company F, captain, D. E. Eddington; Company G, captain, Jacob Granthorn; Company H, captain, W. F. Mitchell, and lieutenants, Eli D. Ake and George Spitzmiller; Company I, lieutenant, Henry Schwan.

The Thirty-ninth Regiment of Missouri Enrolled Militia was raised principally in Cape Girardeau county; G. C. Thilenius was colonel, and another of the regimental officers was Patrick Gilroy. Company A of this regiment was commanded by Adolph Tacke. the organization of this regiment was never completed.

A regiment was also begun to be formed in Bollinger county and was known as the Eighty-third Battalion. It was never completed; the company officers were: of Company A, captain, James Rogers and lieutenants, Levi M. Lincoln and H. F. Rhodes; Company B, captain, Enoch Virgin, and lieutenants, S. J. Leesley and John A. Barks; Company C, captain, James G. Woodfin; lieutenants, Jonathan Couch and John Bess; Company D, captain, Erich Pape; lieutenants, Henry Samuels and James W. Stepp; Company E, captain, F. E. Witener, and lieutenant, John C. Krimminger; Company F, captain, W. A. Dunlap; lieutenants, Henry Yount and Jacob J. Conrad; Company G, captain, Andrew J. Horth.

CONFEDERATE ORGANIZATIONS

Before the war began a company of militia was organized at Cape Girardeau under command of Samuel J. Ward. This company was known as Marble City Guards. In the spring of 1861 after President Lincoln had made a call for troops, the Marble City Guards were divided. The organization contained in its ranks sympathizers with the South and men whose sympathies were with the North. The former of these became parts of Wood's battalions of State Guards which was organized at Jackson and enlisted for a term of six months. About the same time that this battalion was organized a company of cavalry was also formed at Jackson enlisted for the same length of time the captain of this company was W. L. Jeffers; first lieutenant, Dr. S. S. Harris; second lieutenant, W. Watkins, and third lieutenant, Joel Wilkerson. Within a short time the companies that were being organized in Southeast Missouri were formed into a battalion, the lieutenant colonel being W. L. Jeffers and Solomon G. Kitchen was major. The four companies which made up this battalion were from Stoddard, Bollinger, Washington and Cape Girardeau counties; the captains were: Solomon G. Kitchen, Edward Wilson, John J. Smith and W. L. Jeffers. The organization saw active service during its period of enlistment, but was disbanded at the end of the six months' term. The officers at once began to recruit independent companies. Lieutenant Harris organized an artillery company which was ordered to Fort Pillow in March, 1862, and took part in the fight, having been sent on board the flagship General Bragg. From here this company was sent to Yazoo City on the ram Arkansas and participated in the engagement with Porter's fleet, July 15, 1862. It was then made part of the regiment under command of Colonel Martin Green and served until the close of the war. In February, 1863, Jeffers, who had in the meantime been made a captain, organized a battery composed of Southeast Missourians at Camden, Arkansas, and this battery became part of Marmaduke's brigade. Also in 1861, a regiment of the State Guards was organized in Dunklin county. The regimental officers were: James A. Walker, colonel; D. Y. Pankey, lieutenant colonel; among the captains were: L. P. Eldridge, Lee Taylor, A. J. Dooley, W. P. Jones and Taylor Pickard.

The regimental organization was formed at Clarkton and after preliminary drill it became a part of the force under General Jeff Thompson and took part in the battle at Fredericktown; from there it was ordered to New Madrid and was mustered out at the end of the six months' period.

In the summer of 1862 a battalion was formed at Hornersville in Dunklin county, by Andrew Jones, who was soon afterward killed by deserters and was succeeded by Charles Williford. This battalion was composed of two companies; Williford commanded one and Lewis Chandler the other.

Another regiment of State Guards was organized at Bloomfield in Stoddard county by William G. Phelan; it was sent from Bloomfield to Camp Hunter, then to Belmont and Columbus and took part in the battle at Fredericktown and was disbanded January 1, 1862.

A battalion of the State Guards was organized in Butler county under command of Daniel L. Jennings. There were four companies commanded by James M. Jennings, John C. Smart, William Gregory and N. C. Dodson.

A company of State Guards was also raised in Bollinger county under command of J. H. Hunter. Two companies were organized in Mississippi county, one by Charles B. Price and another by Captain Taylor.

As we have seen the term of service for the State Guards was usually fixed at six months and most of the companies that were organized had disbanded at the end of that period. The organization of these troops was an attempt on the part of the state to be practically independent of both North and South and they were not a part of the Confederate troops though the men who formed the various organizations were southern sympathizers, the fact that they were disbanded at the end of their term of enlistment was a confession that the attitude assumed by Missouri was really an impossible one. A state with sympathies as widely divided as Missouri and as closely in touch with the South as well as with the North, could not hope to maintain long any armed neutrality. Men who composed the State Guards, almost without exception, entered one or another organization of Confederates and took the oath of allegiance, not to the state as before, but to the Confederate government itself. We have now to give an account of the principal ones of these organizations.

One of the first was a regiment organized at Belmont with John Smith as colonel, Solomon G. Kitchen, lieutenant colonel, and H. H. Bedford, major. Just before the battle was fought at Belmont, the regiment was ordered to New Madrid and took part in the skirmishes and battles around that place. In 1863 it was sent across the river to Memphis and made a part of Price's army. It operated under Price until the close of the war and took part in most of the battles fought by that command.

In the spring of 1862, W. L. Jeffers organized a company of cavalry with W. E. McGuire as first lieutenant and John A. Bennett as second lieutenant. This company took part in the operations in Southeast Missouri and northern Arkansas and became the basis of a regiment organized by Jeffers and known as the Eighth Missouri Cavalry; its regimental officers were: W. L. Jeffers, colonel; Samuel J. Ward, lieutenant colonel; James H. Parrott, major, and James Craig, sergeant major.

In 1862, Colonel Solomon G. Kitchen organized a battalion of four companies of volunteers and reported to Vandorn at Memphis. This battalion was then consolidated with troops from northern Missouri. A regiment of cavalry was organized with Robert McCulloch as colonel; S. G. Kitchen, lieutenant colonel, and H. A. Smith as major; this regiment was a part of General Price's command during the remainder of the war and participated in all his campaigns.

At a later date Colonel Kitchen returned to Stoddard county and recruited another regiment of which he was made colonel; Jesse Ellison, lieutenant colonel, and Captain Walker of Dunklin county, major. This regiment was united with a battalion which Colonel Kitchen organized in Arkansas and was known as the Missouri and Arkansas Legion: this legion was also joined to the forces of Price and took part with him in his engagements until the end of the war.

In 1861 a battalion of cavalry was organized at Bloomfield, composed in part of men from Ste. Genevieve and Madison counties. There were two companies in the battalion. one of them commanded by Captain John J. Casey and the other by Captain William Cousins. In the fall of 1861, they were sent to New Madrid and from there were transferred to Pocahontas, Arkansas, and made part of Colonel Lowe's regiment of infantry. In the spring of 1862, this regiment, with the exception of Captain Casey's company, was sent to the east side of the river with General Price's army. Captain Casey's company remained at Helena, Arkansas, during the summer of 1862. General Thompson crossed the Mississippi and took a part of the companies of Casey's and Cousins' with him and the remainder of these companies was placed under the command of James Surge and ordered to Brownsville, Arkansas. There the men were dismounted and were dissatisfied with this proceeding and they were then sent to Thomasville, Arkansas, where they were attached to the Third Missouri Cavalry under Colonel Green. They were later, after participating in the battles of Prairie Grove and Cane Hill, ordered to join General Porter and were then made a part of the command of General Marmaduke until the close of the war.

The Ninth Missouri Infantry was organized in September, 1862, at Little Black river bridge in Butler county, of which James B. White was colonel and William S. Ponder lieutenant colonel. It was made up of men from Southeast Missouri in large part; it marched to Pocahontas, Arkansas, then to Fort Smith and took part in the battle of Prairie Grove. It was then sent to Helena and to Camp Bragg where it was consolidated with the Tenth Infantry under Colonel Moore. The two regiments were then ordered to Shreveport, Louisiana, and in the following year took part in the battles of Mansfield and Pleasant Hill. They were then sent back to assist in the campaign against Steele and were in the fight at Jenkins Ferry; were then ordered to Camden and later to Shreveport, where they remained until the close of the war.

The Second Missouri Infantry was organized at Memphis, Tennessee, in 1861; it was made up of men principally from New Madrid and Pemiscot counties; its regimental officers were: Colonel, John S. Bowen; lieutenant colonel, L. L. Rich, and major, —— Campbell. Company A, Captain Sprague, from New Orleans; Company B, Captain Duffie, from St. Louis; Company C, Captain Hearst, from St. Louis, New Madrid and Pemiscot counties; Company D, Captain Burke, from St. Louis; Company E, Captain Rice, from Hickman, Kentucky, and Southeast Missouri; Company F, Captain Garland, from St. Louis; Company G, Captain John A. Gordon, from Pemiscot and New Madrid counties; Company H, Captain Hogan, from Pemiscot county; Company I, Captain Thomas J. Phillips, from New Madrid county; Company K, Captain John E. Averill, from Pemiscot.

This Second Missouri Regiment had a long and illustrious service from the place of its organization, New Madrid; it was sent to Fort Pillow then to New Madrid, Columbus, Kentucky, and to Camp Beauregard, taking part in all the battles and skirmishes on the way. On December 25, 1861, it was ordered from Camp Beauregard to Bowling Green, thence to Nashville, Murfreesboro, Iuka and Barnsby. The mention of these places is sufficient evidence that the regiment was seeing its share of fighting. This regiment was at Shiloh and after that battle it went into camp at Milldale not far from Corinth. The term for which the men had enlisted expired while the regiment was in this camp, most or all of them, however, reenlisted for three years or for the entire period of the war.

Colonel Bowen had been placed in command of a brigade before the battle of Shiloh and Lieutenant Colonel Rich was made colonel and A. C. Riley, first lieutenant of Company I, was made lieutenant colonel. This promotion of Riley offended some of the other officers who resigned their commissions. Lieutenant Colonel Riley was afterwards made Colonel of the regiment on the death of Colonel Rich, who was wounded at Shiloh. After the battle of Corinth the regiment was in camp at Lumpkins Mill near Holly Springs, and was there consolidated with the Fourth Missouri and assigned to Cockerill's brigade; it spent the winter of 1862-63 in

Mississippi and was then sent on an expedition to Louisiana and to Grand Gulf; it took part in the battle of Champions Hill and was surrendered with the army at Vicksburg on July 4th, 1863. From here it was sent into Parole Camp at Demopolis, Alabama, where it remained until it was exchanged in the following September. It was then sent to Mobile it went into winter quarters; from Mobile it went to Lauderdale Springs and then to Gainesville, Alabama. It was attached to Hood's army and took part in the great battles of Franklin and Nashville and the lesser engagements of that campaign. The regiment suffered very greatly at the battle of Franklin. Out of 140 men who went into the battle not more than thirty came out uninjured. It took part in all the campaigns about Atlanta; it was then sent to Mobile and was again captured at Fort Blakesly, which put an end to its active service. Colonel Riley was killed at New Hope Church and was succeeded by Captain Garland. When the latter was wounded the regiment was placed in command of Ambrose Keith, who had entered the service as lieutenant in Company H. The record of these two regiments was not surpassed by many in either army. They covered long distances in their marches, took part in many of the great battles and won for themselves a name for steadiness and bravery that is enviable.

One of the most famous of the Confederate organizations of Southeast Missouri was the Second Missouri Cavalry recruited in a number of counties in this part of the state. Its most famous colonel was Robert McCulloch, who was elected at Springfield in October, 1861. They took part in the battles in Missouri and Arkansas especially the one at Elk Horn Tavern, where the regiment displayed such courage and fortitude and such unusual steadiness as to attract the attention of officers even at this point in its career. In 1862, with the First and Third Regiments, it was assigned to the brigade commanded by General M. E. Green and sent to Arkansas. It made its headquarters at Van Buren and then crossed the river to the east with Generals Vandorn and Price. East of the river the First and Third Regiments were dismounted and became part of the Missouri Brigade, commanded by General Cockrell; the Second was retained as a cavalry regiment throughout the war. It took part in the great battle at Bolivar, Tennessee, in August, 1862, where it was commanded by General Armstrong. A little later it was at Iuka and with Bledsoe's Missouri battery checked the pursuit after the battle. The regiment distinguished itself at Corinth and later during the terrific fighting on Hatchie river. On this river when General Price's army seemed almost certain to fall into the hands of the enemy, the Second Missouri with Bledsoe's Battery, formed the rear guard and fought desperately for several days. At one time they formed an ambush and inflicted great damage and loss on the enemy.

In 1863 the regiment operated in Mississippi until in October when it took part on the raid of Tennessee, fighting at Savery and Collinsville. On the retreat from this raid the companies of Captains Savery, Thompson, and Lichlighter fought as the rear guard. It formed a part of the command of General Bedford Forrest and distinguished itself for bravery at Okalona in 1864. It led the charge made against Fort Pillow, and in every action which it took part, won new laurels for itself. Colonel McCulloch was wounded at Old Town creek, and Lieutenant Colonel R. A. McCulloch was chosen in his place as colonel. The regiment took part in the fighting around Memphis and went on Wilson's raid in Alabama and Georgia, surrendering at Gainesville, Alabama, in 1865.

The Missouri troops, including the First and Second Missouri Brigades and Marmaduke's Cavalry and the First and Second Missouri regiments, were everywhere recognized as among the finest soldiers of the South. General Maury in speaking on the repulse of Rosecrans' attack, says: "The glorious First Missouri Brigade." At one time there was a report that General Lovell, to whose negligence was probably due the defeat at Corinth, had spoken of Missouri troops as undisciplined. After the Corinth campaign, the troops were reviewed by Generals Vandorn and Price in the presence of President Davis. Davis said: "I have attended reviews of Generals Beauregard, Bragg, A. S. and J. E. Johnson, and the old United States service, but I have never seen a finer looking body of men nor of more soldierly appearance and efficiency, nor have I ever witnessed better drill or discipline among the soldiers belonging to any military service than these Missouri soldiers."

On another occasion he said: "I have never seen better fighters than Missouri troops or more gallant soldiers than General Price and his officers."

The attack on Corinth was made in three divisions, the First and Second Divisions carried out the plan and got into town. The Third in command of General Lovell, was inactive. Among those that entered the town were the Missouri troops. General Maury, in speaking of this attack on Corinth says of the Missouri troops: "General Price looked on the disorder of his darling troops with unmitigated anguish. The big tears coursed down his bronzed face and I have never witnessed such a picture of mute despair and grief as his countenance wore when he looked upon the defeat of those magnificent troops; he had never before known them to fail and they had never failed to carry the lines of any enemy in their front, nor did they ever to the very close of their noble career on April 9, 1865, fail to beat the troops before them. I mean no disparagement to any troops of the Confederacy when I say that the Missourians were not surpassed by any soldiers in the world."

SECTION VI

Since the Civil War—Movements and Towns Founded

CHAPTER XXIX

MOVEMENTS SINCE THE CIVIL WAR

Railroad Building—Drainage—Wealth — Manufacturing — Mining — Transportation—Resources—Schools and Churches — Local Option — Population — Organizations — Spanish-American War.

The period of the history of Southeast Missouri which extended from the close of the war in 1865 up to the present time is in many respects the most interesting period of our history. It differs widely from the other periods whose history we have already recounted. From 1820 to 1860, as we have seen, the population of Southeast Missouri increased from 20,000 to 130,000. This was a great increase in population and was accompanied by a like marvelous increase in resources and general social and industrial development; but the period from 1865 to 1912 not only saw a greater increase in population but also a vastly greater development of resources and of every side of the people's life. Doubtless few sections of the country anywhere have witnessed a more marvelous expansion of resources than Southeast Missouri in this period.

The period is distinguished for a number of great movements. The first of these, and perhaps the most powerful influence upon the building up of the country, was the building of railroads. In another place we have recounted in detail the story of railroad building. No one can study the figures of population or look over the map of the section or consider the figures which tell of industrial development without being at once struck with the very great part which the railroads played in the development of Southeast Missouri. Of course this was to be expected. So long as there were parts of the territory situated at great distances from river transportation, distances multiplied in a great many cases by the lack of roads, the developement of these parts of the district was greatly retarded, but with railroads penetrating to the farthest corner bringing every part of the section into connection with the centers and great markets by means of railroads, then development proceeded with leaps and bounds.

Another movement which distinguished this period of our study is the drainage movement. As we saw in the chapter on the geography of Southeast Missouri, nearly half of the area of this section lies within the Mississippi low lands or bottoms. Not all of this by any means, nor even half of it, is land that needed to be reclaimed, but in spite of this fact there were large bodies of the richest soil which could not be cultivated until steps were taken to protect it from overflow from the river and to drain from it the waters which it received from the streams entering it from the hills. Both of these things have received careful attention. To shut out the waters of the Mississippi river at flood time, levees have been built along the banks of the river, some of them miles in length and at such a height as to preclude the probability of their ever giving way. These levees were built under government supervision and in part at government expense, the greater part of their cost, however, was borne by the people whose lands were affected, who organized levee districts and placed a tax against lands for this purpose. This levee building was the first work done toward the reclamation of the swamp lands and while its results were very evident and very gratifying, it became evident that levee building alone was not sufficient. The levees saved from overflow thousands of acres and made it possible for land to be cultivated without fear of damage from the Mississippi river, but there were hundreds of thousands of acres in the swamps of Little river and other streams in the section, which could not be utilized without the cutting of drainage ditches. A realization of this fact coupled with a rise in the value of Southeast Missouri lands led to the organization of drainage districts and the cutting of drainage ditches and canals throughout the overflowed regions.

The effect of these drainage ditches was soon apparent, the ditches made it possible to cultivate large tracts of land which were before practically worthless and the productions of Southeast Missouri increased at a marvelous rate.

In order to understand the drainage system of Southeast Missouri it is necessary to keep in mind the physical condition of the alluvial plains. A line drawn from the Mississippi river at Cape Girardeau southwest to the Arkansas line at the southeast corner of Ripley county, follows practically the dividing line between the Ozark uplift and the Mississippi basin. The great stretch of territory lying south and east of this line is all alluvial flat land with the exception of two ridges. Beginning about two and a half miles south of Cape Girardeau and stretching along the bank of the river to a short distance below Commerce, is a ridge of hills known as the Scott county hills, and these and the ridge which extends through Stoddard county and part of Dunklin county into Arkansas and which is known as Crowley's ridge, form the only exception to the alluvial character of this part of Southeast Missouri.

The Scott county hills, which do not cover a very large area, have a rather rough surface, still much of the area is capable of cultivation. Crowley's ridge is principally composed of hills of clay sloping from the southeast to the northwest and being very rapidly worn by stream action.

The other physical features of the section are first of all, beginning at the river and going toward the west, an elevated level plain of high bottom land from 3 to 8 miles in width and extending south from the Scott county hills through Scott and New Madrid counties, reaching the river at New Madrid and then extending along the river to the south line of New Madrid county. This elevated ridge is generally known as the Sikeston ridge; it is the great corn, wheat and cotton producing area of the counties mentioned. Just east of Crowley's ridge stretching south from Dexter to the Arkansas line and lying between the St. Francois river and Little river, is another ridge somewhat similar in character to the Sikeston ridge; on this elevated land are situated the towns of Bernie, Malden, Kennett and others.

East of the Sikeston ridge and stretching to the Mississippi river is a territory which is sometimes called the Charleston district; much of this district at one time was subject to overflow by the river but was not disturbed very greatly by overflow from the local streams. This, too, is a very fertile and productive district containing some of the best farm land in this section of the state.

West of the Sikeston ridge, lying between it and the ridge in Stoddard and Dunklin counties, stretching north to the foothills in Cape Girardeau county and with an arm extending to the river at the town of Cape Girardeau, is Little river valley. This valley varies in width from 10 to 20 miles and is about 9 miles in length from its head at the foothills to the Arkansas line. This great area containing several hundred square miles was subject to overflow from Little river and the greater part of it not capable of being cultivated.

On the west side of Crowley's ridge extending to the Ozark hills is a flat bottom of the St. Francois and Black rivers, a strip of territory not much unlike the Little river bottom though not subject to such constant overflow.

As we have seen the first settlements in these alluvial districts were made on the hills in Scott county, on Crowley's ridge in the Charleston district and on the ridge extending south from Dexter; these were the parts of the district that were not subject to overflow and that could be cultivated without the drainage system; some of this territory, especially in the Charleston district and on Sikeston and Dexter ridges, was prairie land; not only was it high above overflow, but free from timber, being covered when the settlement was made upon it, by high, coarse grass and in some cases overgrown with bushes. Some of this prairie land retains the name as Mathews Prairie, Little Prairie, West Prairie and Grand Prairie. We see why settlements were being made both east and west of the Little river bottoms, which for a great many years formed a practically impassable barrier between the settlements on its east and west respectively, and it further explains the reason why Dunklin county and Stoddard county were settled much later than some other counties in the district. They were cut off from immigration from the east by the Little river bottoms and it was impossible to reach Dunklin county especially, except after traveling long distances out of the way. Another thing which is made evident by this study of the physical situation of Southeast Missouri is why Cape Girardeau became early an important trading point. The settlers in Dunklin county and in Stoddard county could not come in touch with river transportation except by coming to Cape Girardeau, and thus for many years that town was the principal shipping and distributing point for large areas of Southeast Missouri.

It has been estimated by competent authority, that Crowley's ridge and the Scott county hills near Commerce, together comprise about one-eighth of the total area of the alluvial section and that the dry bottom lands not subject to overflow which were found in Mississippi county, in Scott, in New Madrid, Stoddard and Dunklin taken together comprise also about one-eighth of the total area. If this estimate is correct only one-fourth of the vast area of the alluvial section, as it was seen by the first settlers, was capable of cultivation. This statement needs to be taken in this light that while some of the lands not included within this one-fourth made impossible to be cultivated, they were subject to overflow at times. Three-fourths of the district which we have under consideration was subject to overflow from the Mississippi river and from other streams in the territory. Most of this land was covered with heavy timber. Among the finest forests to be found in the state or in the whole country were growing on the overflowed lands of Southeast Missouri.

This timber became exceedingly valuable and much of it was cleared away, but the cutting of the timber was for many years the only thing that was done in connection with the overflowed lands. So long as the population in the alluvial district was sparse and so long as land was consequently cheap, but little attention was paid to the reclamation of the overflowed lands. In 1850 the United States donated to the several states the swamp lands contained within their limits. By an act of the General Assembly passed in 1852, Missouri conveyed to the different counties the title to the swamp lands within them to be disposed of in such a way as to promote their drainage. There thus came into control of these counties large bodies of overflowed lands at the time having no great value for any purpose whatever. The first disposition attempted to be made of them by the various counties was to grant them for the purpose of aiding the construction of roads and railroads. We have seen that when the Cairo & Fulton railroad was promoted that the counties affected by it subscribed to its capital stock in swamp lands. After the first excitement consequent upon the attempts to build railroads had somewhat subsided, the counties began to transfer their swamp lands to private owners usually in a way, ostensibly at least, to promote drainage. It was found very difficult, however, properly to drain these lands. The slope was usually about one foot a mile from north to south and the quantity of water to be handled at certain seasons of the year was so vast that local ditches were found to be entirely insufficient to handle it. On account of this fact the lands were for many years practically flood lands; they could not be sold for even the minimum price of $1.25 per acre, so that the greater part of the lands remained in the possession of the counties, and some of them were granted to aid in the construction of levees.

The inability to construct sufficient ditches was principally due to inadequate methods of construction and it was not until the invention of the dipper dredge, which since its improvement is capable of handling 2,000 cubic yards of earth a day and of cutting a canal through the swamp, that it became at all possible to drain these lands.

After this dipper dredge was invented and came to be known as an efficient instrument, a movement was begun in the counties having swamp lands, for the organization of districts for the purpose of digging ditches. The land in much of this district was taxed so much an acre for the purpose of digging and the ditches were dug to the southern limit of the district carrying the water to the next district. Some efficient work was done in this way and some land reclaimed. It was found, however, that there were other difficulties. there was no scheme for building a system of ditches and for this reason some of the work that was done in the early days was not productive of very good results. There was a failure to appreciate the magnitude of the enterprise and most of the early ditches were entirely too small for the purpose for which they were constructed. The construction. however, has gone on and up to this time there have been constructed more than 1,600 miles of canals at an approximate cost of $2,500 a mile. Most of these canals are from 12 to 20 feet in width and from 8 to 14 feet in depth. It has usually been estimated that each mile of ditch reclaims one section of land.

While much has been accomplished in the matter of drainage, there still remain a number of problems to be solved. The Charleston district has been levied and this protects from the overflow waters of the Mississippi river and it has been partly drained. It is possible that the levee will be extended to St. John's Bayou by which New Madrid and the lower part of this district will be drained.

Two great problems remain to be solved— the drainage of the Little river bottoms and the drainage of the basin of the St. Francois. The magnitude of the problem of the Little river is apparent when we consider the vast extent of these bottoms having an average width of from 12 to 15 miles and a length of nearly 90 miles. About 500,000 acres of land in these bottoms have been drained already by local ditches, but this drainage is to a certain extent inadequate and the great problem now is how to increase the efficiency of the drainage and add to the system. Two problems confront the engineers who would reclaim the remaining lands in the Little river bottoms. The bottoms receive an enormous quantity of water from Castor and Whitewater and the other streams which have their source in the Ozark hills and pour their water into the upper part of these bottoms. Some efficient means is to be found for the distribution of these waters. Besides this, however, the local drainage must be cared for. The rainfall from such a great area as the St. Francois bottoms is very large and provision must be made for taking care of this rainfall.

The problem of draining the St. Francois and Black river bottoms is a simpler one; it seems that the overflow waters of these rivers can be cared for by leveeing the banks of the rivers and confining the streams within the banks and by digging drainage ditches to the south. It is estimated that 200,000 acres of land in these bottoms may be reclaimed.

This period, along with many other changes which it has witnessed, has brought with it a very great increase in wealth. Land values have mounted up within the last few years to a height undreamed of by the people who lived here before the war. This increase in land values has been accompanied by a very great increase of other property. Perhaps in the first place the wealth of the district was enhanced by the cutting of the timber. Some of the most valuable timber in all the United States was found in Southeast Missouri; great forests of cotton wood, of white oak, of gum, of cypress and poplar existed. For a long time this timber of the finest quality was practically valueless. This was true because of the lack of facilities for manufacturing lumber and in a large degree because of the lack of facilities for transportation. The price, too, was low because of the existence in other parts of the country of vast bodies of timber. First other parts of the country worked up their timber, the price of lumber rose gradually, and there came to be more and more a demand for timber in Southeast Missouri. Those of the younger generation can hardly realize the vast extent of the forests that were once found here, nor can they appreciate the attitude which the early settlers and even of the settlers in the time immediately following the Civil war held toward this timber. It was looked upon not as an asset, but rather in the nature of an encumbrance. A body of land covered with timber was not as valuable by any means as a body of land without timber. The finest forests of gum or cottonwood were cut down and the timber destroyed in any way in order to get rid of it. Trees which would now be worth many dollars were regarded as so much encumbrance upon the soil, they were deadened and allowed to be blown down by the winds or to rot upon the surface of the ground or else burned. Sometimes they were cut down while yet green and cut up into logs which could be handled and thus burned in order to prepare the ground for cultivation.

For the year 1907 the surplus products of the Southeast Missouri counties reached a value of more than $60,000,000. The total is an impressive one and speaks more strongly than any other words could of the wealth contained within the borders of this territory. The mere amount of that wealth, however, is not in itself so significant as is the variety of its sources and the probability of a long continuance of its production. The wealth of Southeast Missouri not only does not depend upon one or two sources but is of such a character that it will continue. We have no reason to believe that the sources of wealth in this part of the state will fail. This is not true of course of some things that have added to our wealth in the last decade or two. The timber will be depleted and there will not be the immense shipments of lumber from some of the counties such as has been made within the years since 1890; but, as the timber fails, and this source of wealth disappears, its place will be taken by the products of the soil, for practically all the land which is being deforested is valuable for agricultural purposes. The probabilities are that the total of surplus products instead of being decreased by reason of the exhaustion of the timber, will be increased owing to the use of the land for farming purposes.

One striking development of the period we are now considering is the growth of manufactures. In other chapters we have discussed the very limited manufacturing interests of the section in former years. During the year 1910 the total of manufactured products for the twenty counties reached the sum of $39, 370, 538. The great items of manufacture were lead and other products of the mines, timber in its various forms, cotton and cotton-seed oil, flour and feed, and shoes. Many other things were manufactured, many of them in large quantities, but these were the great items which make up the total. No doubt this form of industry is destined to become more and more important. River transportation, nearness to the Illinois coal fields, and the existence of undeveloped water-power render certain the future of this part of the state as regards manufacturing.

The present period has witnessed the great developement of the mining industry. The principal minerals mined are iron and lead.

Southeast Missouri contains considerable deposits of iron ore, which is found in a belt crossing the state from the Mississippi on the east of the Osage river. The ore contained in the mineral region is of two principal characters, the specular ore which is of a concentrated character and the limonite or red. The specular ores are found in the southern part of St. Francois county and the northern part of Iron county. It was thought at one time that Iron Mountain in St. Francois county was a mass of specular ore and that Pilot Knob and Shepard Mountain in Iron county contained vast quantities of the same mineral; in fact a company was formed for the purpose of taking out the ore in Iron Mountain and large quantities of ore were mined at one period. It was found, however, that in none of these mountains was the quantity of ore so great as had been thought. Iron Mountain, which was considered at one time to be composed almost entirley of iron ore, has been found to contain no great quantities of high grade ore; mining is still carried on at these points but the ore is of an inferior grade, the best ore having been practically exhausted. There are also quantities of ore in Lewis Mountain near Arcadia, in Buford Mountain, also in Iron county, and in Boden Mountain in the same county. Besides these, such places as the Shut-In, Russell, Ackhurst and Big Bogy banks of iron also contain considerable quantities of iron ore. Limonite ores in large quantities are found in Wayne, Bollinger and Stoddard counties; the ore, however, is not so concentrated and the expense of working it is greater there than in the case of the specular ore. In spite of this disadvantage there is still going on a considerable amount of mining.

The last twenty years has witnessed a remarkable development of that section of the state known as the Lead Belt. About 1880 it was discovered that lead in large and paying quantities existed in what is known as the Flat River district. This discovery resulted in the opening of extensive mines first at Flat River then at DesLoge, Leadwood and Elvins. After the building of the Mississippi River & Bonne Terre railway to Bonne Terre, the necessity for providing transportation facilities for the products of the new mines resulted in the extension of this new railway through DesLoge and Flat River to Doe Run. The population of this Lead Belt increased very rapidly and in fact there is almost a continuous town from near Bonne Terre to Flat River. This large population rendered it almost imperative to construct an interurban line which was built in the year 1906, principally by capitalists of Farmington, from the Iron Mountain railway at DeLassus through Farmington to Flat River. This road has given an impetus to the building up of the section which has been very marked.

At the present time to a very much greater extent than formerly the lead belt is developing a characteristic life. Once those who worked in the mines were also interested in farming and the country depended about equally on its mines and its farms. The great extension of mining interests in recent years, however, has changed this; agricultural interests have become relatively unimportant throughout most of the section and a greater number of the population are directly dependent upon the mines and smelters. This has resulted in the development of the characteristic life of mining communities; the people are concentrated in the towns and these are all typical mining towns.

Of course the mining of lead on a large scale such as it is now conducted, differs very widely from the old system of mining which required little or no capital. In the former method any man with sufficient energy and strength could engage with some success in the digging of ore for himself independent of all other persons. The organization of great companies, however, and the almost universal use of improved machinery has made it practically impossible for any one to engage in mining independent of those companies or associations which control large amounts of capital. Accordingly we find practically all the mining in the entire district carried on by a few large companies.

It has been the policy of the mine owners in the district to concentrate the smelting of lead in one or two places. At the present time the great amount of smelting is carried on at Herculaneum. This point is a number of miles distant from any of the mines but the existence of the Mississippi & Bonne Terre railway renders the shipment of ore to one plant and its reduction there entirely practicable.

The quantity of ore produced in the lead belt is very great. In the year 1911 there was shipped from the single county of St. Francois, which contains most of the large mines, more than seven million dollars worth of mine products, principally lead. The deposits seem to be practically inexhaustible and the industry bids fair to continue to develop for a good many years even with the ore that is now in sight. There seems no reason to believe that all the ore has as yet been located, there are probably other fields in the district which await development.

Farming

The time has been, and that not far in the past, when farming in Southeast Missouri depended very largely upon a few staple products; corn, cotton and wheat were the great products and in some places the only crops grown. This dependence upon a few staples was due in part to distance from the market and to insufficient means of transportation. Today this dependence upon staple products, however, is disappearing. The improved facilities for transportation have made it possible for farmers to raise other crops than the so-called staples and ship them to market in such a way and at such a cost as to render them valuable. The soil and climate of Southeast Missouri are adapted to a variety of farm products and more and more this diversity of farm interests is appearing. It is clear to be seen that as farming becomes more diversified the value of farm products will increase and the degree of certainty of a good crop every year will also increase.

Outside of those two or three counties which produce enormous quantities of lead and other mineral products, it is clear that for many years the principal interest here will be agriculture. The time will come of course, when manufacturing will be developed. The water power which now goes to waste in many counties of the Southeast will be utilized and there is a sufficient quantity of power capable of development to make certain that manufacturing establishments of many kinds will be supported.

River Transportation

The history of river transportation in Missouri is a story of wonderful interest. The time was when it formed practically the only transportation possible. The products of Ste. Genevieve and of the mining region were transported by canoe or keel boats to New Orleans and then were shipped to various parts of the world. All the supplies used by the people of Missouri at one time came up the river by the same precarious means of transportation. The application of steam to the propelling of boats brought about a very great increase in the use of the river. From 1817, when the first steamboat made its appearance on the upper Mississippi until the period of railroad activity which really began in the state just before the Civil war. river transportation grew to almost unparalleled proportions. Hundreds of steamers were engaged in the business of transporting passengers and goods upon the river. River transportation was cheap, it was reasonably fast, and for these reasons reached a very remarkable development.

The building of railroads, however, practically put an end to the use of the river as a means of transportation. Today, instead of the hundreds of boats that once plied its waters, there are only a few, travel has been diverted from the river, steamboats are no longer crowded with passengers and overloaded with freight; the passengers travel by train and the freight is carried in the same way. The causes of this change in transportation are many. One of them is the greater speed of railroad traffic and another greater certainty. Railroad owners soon came to see that a great advantage could be obtained by operating their trains on a schedule. Railroads also had a great advantage in that they reached every part of the country so that steamboat owners. In a competition of this kind the advantage was all on the side of the railroads. They had a traffic which could not be taken from them by the steamboats under any circumstances, the inland traffic was all carried by rail and the money thus derived was used to enable railroad operators to fight steamboat transportation in those communities and towns situated along the river. There seems to be no doubt that the present failure to use the river transpor-

SOUTHERN MISSISSIPPI STEAMER

persons living away from the river might travel to their destination or ship their goods to market without transfer or reshipment. These advantages which the railroad possessed were natural and legitimate advantages. It is not quite clear, however, that the very great ascendancy which the railroads came to have was attained altogether by legitimate methods. The fierce competition between the river and the railroads no doubt impelled railroad owners and managers to resort to methods not legitimate in fighting tation is due in part at least, to unfair methods of competition on the part of the railroads.

No doubt, however, the decline of river traffic was due also in part to a failure on the part of the owners of boats to provide proper facilities for handling the traffic and to bring their methods to a high state of efficiency. The owners of steamboats today operate them in about the same way in which steamboats were operated before the war. Just as formerly the freight is still handled by hand

and there has been a failure to install freight handling machinery and to provide ample terminal facilities in the towns. There has been a failure to keep the equipment of the boats up to the standard demanded by the traveling public and to increase the speed or the comfort of travel on the river.

These are some of the causes which have brought about the virtual destruction of river traffic. We must not conclude, however, that these causes will continue to operate and to bring about the same result. There are reasons for believing that river transportation will once more become important and perhaps reach a degree of importance which it did not possess even in its most prosperous days. It is a serious situation which confronts the people of a country when there comes a congestion of traffic, when the means of transportation are inadequate to supply the needs of the country. Railroad owners in this country have themselves confessed that we have reached a point in our development when it is almost if not entirely, impossible, to build railroads sufficient to handle the traffic offered them. We are virtually compelled then to turn to the river for relief. Besides this there is a movement already on foot to provide terminal facilities and to equip boats with modern machinery and to bring them up to the high standard of efficiency displayed by the railroads. This movement will undoubtedly result in securing for the owners of boats a part at least of the traffic now carried by the railroads. More than all else, however, which leads us to believe in the coming importance of the river is a movement known as the deep waterway movement, by which it is planned to increase the depth of the channel of the Mississippi sufficiently to allow the operation of larger boats and even of sea-going vessels as far up as St. Louis.

If this proposed plan is ever carried out it will undoubtedly mean a great deal for Southeast Missouri. It will then be possible for residents of these counties to ship their products to almost any part of the world at very much less than the railroads now charge. Taken in connection with the opening of the Panama Canal and the consequent shortening and cheapening of transportation to the sea, such a use of the Mississippi would mean a great deal.

Resources

The great resources of Southeast Missouri are soil and climate, minerals, timber, and water-power. These do not exhaust the list, but they are the great items in the inventory of potential wealth. First place among these must be given to soil and climate. No part of the earth's surface has richer or more productive soil than is to be found in some counties of the section. This is not merely in small tracts, hundreds of square miles of fertile soil exist. Taken in connection with a climate, that by reasons of its rainfall and its long summers renders possible the production of both the great staple grains, corn and wheat, and of cotton, this soil is the greatest asset of the entire section.

Mineral wealth as we have seen is very great, and timber in the past has been one of the great resources. There is enough left of the great timbered areas to represent millions of dollars yet.

The water-power of these southeast counties is doubtless destined to be of great value and importance. It has as yet been developed except the smallest way, but it forms one of the sources of future wealth of the highest importance.

Not all the movements which have distinguished this period, however, have had to do with material wealth; railroad building and swamp reclamation were important in themselves and led to great consequences. They must have failed, however, of doing that for which they were intended had they not been associated with other movements in the life of the people. One of these was a movement looking toward the improvement of education. This movement while it had its beginning shortly after the war, and led, even then, to the organization and establishment of schools in every district through Southeast Missouri and brought a public school within reach of nearly every family, did not provide for a complete system of schools. It was possible for a state superintendent of education in 1894, to speak of Southeast Missouri as the educational low land of the state and to justify his characterization by pointing out that in all this great section of the state there existed only one, or at the most two schools, deserving of the name high school, and that in this section also there was only one school, the State Normal School at Cape Girardeau, that was doing any large amount of work above the common school branches. This situation has changed; and today, there is scarcely a town of any importance in Southeast Missouri that does not have a well organized and equipped high school. In rural communities, too, there is a movement for the organization of rural high schools and a consolidation of scattered and isolated districts into larger units for the maintainance of these country high schools.

Along with this increased interest in public education as evidenced in the establishment of public schools, the building of good schoolhouses, and the consolidation of rural schools, has come an increased interest in religious affairs. The time has come in Southeast Missouri when the various communities are no longer satisfied with a modified barn in which to hold religious services, but want comfortable, commodious, and even splendid structures erected for church purposes. This movement, too, has gone hand in hand with the spread of religious teaching and religious knowledge to every community. There is scarcely to be found within the bounds of Southeast Missouri a single settlement or community, no matter how remote, that does not have its regular gospel services carried on by one or another of the religious denominations.

One of the movements which has had a place in the history of Southeast Missouri in late years is known as the local option movement. In 1887 the General Assembly passed a law giving counties the right to determine for themselves whether intoxicating liquors should be sold within their limits. At that time campaigns were made by the temperance people in a number of southeast counties and part of them complied with the terms of the law and voted against dram shops. On appealing to the Supreme Court, however, the law was declared defective and the action of the counties null and void. At a later time, however, the General Assembly passed another law which is at present on the statute books, providing for local option elections. By its terms the county may vote on the question of local option, and each town within the county having a population of more than 2,500 may hold an election separate from the rest of the county. Under the provisions of this law local option elections have been held in a number of Southeast Missouri counties and many of them have become dry territory.

At the present time there are no saloons in Dunklin, Stoddard, Bollinger, Wayne, Iron and New Madrid.

There is presented a table showing the population of the various counties as shown at each census from 1860 to 1910. It is unfortunate that the figures are not obtainable for 1865 when the war closed. While this is not possible the figures that are given are highly instructive. Viewing them as a whole it is evident that all the counties have experienced a great growth and development of population since the close of the war. That growth has been marvelous and in some counties little short of incredible.

It is evident that beginning in 1900 the section entered on a different era. Up to that time with scarcely a single exception the counties showed a considerable increase during each decade. In the last decade a change takes place in some of the counties. The great growth in population was in the great agricultural counties of the alluvial bottoms, notably in Dunklin, New Madrid, Stoddard, Pemiscot, Scott, Mississippi and Butler; in the great mining county of St. Francois and in Jefferson county which is developing in both agriculture and manufacturing. The expansion of the agricultural counties is explained by the great increase in cultivated lands due to drainage and the removal of the timber. The population of St. Francois has kept pace with the great increase in its mining interests. Cape Girardeau with its growing city and its manufacturing interests, and Madison with the development of new mines showed considerable growth in the same period. Some of the counties lost population. This was doubtless due to the decided drift of population toward the cities, and in few cases to the closing of mills which had formerly supported numbers of people. It cannot be doubted that the population of Southeast Missouri will continue to increase. The opportunities are good, and the possibility of supporting much greater numbers is present in every section of the district.

Counties	1860	1870	1880	1890	1900	1910
Bollinger	7,126	8,162	11,130	13,121	14,650	14,576
Butler	2,839	4,298	6,011	10,152	16,769	20,624
Cape Girardeau	14,014	17,558	20,998	22,060	24,315	27,621
Carter	1,215	1,455	2,168	4,659	6,706	5,504
Dunklin	4,855	5,982	9,604	15,085	21,706	30,328
Iron	5,529	6,278	8,183	9,119	8,716	5,563
Jefferson	9,780	15,380	18,736	22,484	25,712	27,878
Madison	5,197	5,844	8,876	9,268	9,975	11,273
Mississippi	3,849	4,982	9,270	10,134	11,837	14,557
New Madrid	3,877	6,357	7,694	9,317	11,280	19,488
Pemiscot	2,694	2,059	4,299	5,975	12,115	19,559
Perry	8,389	9,877	11,895	13,237	15,134	14,898
Reynolds	3,135	3,756	5,722	6,803	8,161	9,592
Ripley	3,669	3,175	5,377	8,512	13,186	13,099
St. Francois	6,372	9,742	13,822	17,347	24,051	35,738
Ste. Genevieve	7,412	8,384	10,390	9,883	10,359	10,607
Scott	4,744	7,317	8,587	11,228	13,092	22,372
Stoddard	7,662	8,535	13,431	17,327	24,669	27,807
Washington	8,695	11,719	12,896	13,153	14,263	13,378
Wayne	5,868	6,068	9,096	11,927	15,309	15,181

ORGANIZATIONS

There are certain organizations within Southeast Missouri having somewhat dissimilar aims and purposes and yet all of them fitted for public services in some way or other. Some of them seek to keep alive the memory of great events while others, less historical in theory, have for their purpose the improvement of present conditions. One of these organizations is the Daughters of the American Revolution, a society of women who can trace their descent from some one or other of the Revolutionary soldiers. The purpose of this organization is to keep alive the memory of the Revolutionary struggle, of the men and women of our country who are descendants of Revolutionary patriots and to forward certain public movements within the state.

The only chapter in Southeast Missouri is

the Nancy Hunter Chapter at Cape Girardeau. The first member at Cape Girardeau, who was received October 7, 1897, and appointed a regent to organize a chapter. She began the organization but removed from the city before she completed the work. After her going Mrs. Louis Houck was appointed regent and completed the organization. The chapter was completed February 12, 1901, with the following charter members: Miss May H. Fee; Mrs. Jennie Allen Wilson, registrar; Mrs. Julia Allen Block; Mrs. Mary Hunter Giboney Houck, regent; Mrs. Marie Mount Green Houck, historian; Mrs. Mary Amanda Harris Blomeyer, secretary; Mrs. Mabel Ellen Hunter Howe, vice regent; Mrs. Clara Hunter Whitesell; Mrs. Mary Hunter Pierce; Mrs. Lucy Hunter Bird; Mrs. Mary B. Hunter Moore; Mrs. Virginia Hunter Houck, treasurer.

The chapter was named in honor of Nancy Hunter, daughter of Joseph Hunter, a distinguished soldier of the Revolution. Nancy Hunter herself rendered service to her country at Fort Jefferson. She married Isaac Dodge, the first American settler in Ste. Genevieve district; her sons were among the distinguished men of Missouri and other states. One of them was General Henry Dodge, another was Senator A. C. Dodge and another son by a second marriage was Senator Lewis F. Linn. The chapter is in a prosperous condition. It has accomplished a number of things of importance, among them the gathering of documents, the investigation of genealogical records and the beginning of a movement for the preservation of McKendree Chapel, a meeting house of the Methodist church, not far from Cape Girardeau which is the oldest Protestant house of worship now standing, west of the Mississippi river.

Another of these organizations is the United Daughters of the Confederacy. It is also an organization of women in this case of those who can establish their relationship to Confederate soldiers. Its purpose is principally historical, also to keep alive the memory of the Civil war, to secure correct treatment of the South and its struggles, and to perpetuate in every possible way the fame of those who fought for the South. It is also to a certain extent a social organization and concerns itself with progressive movements of every kind.

Among the societies and organizations founded in Southeast Missouri of a general public interest is the organization of Confederate Veterans. It has existed in Missouri since 1895 and the work of organization in this state was begun by General Joe Shelby. Its purpose is social, benevolent and historical, it holds annual reunions in order to preserve the memory of the struggles of its members, strives to render assistance to such as need it, and to collect and preserve all facts and incidents of the Civil war. At the present time there are camps at Doniphan, Greenville, Poplar Bluff, Farmington, Marble Hill, Jackson, Morley, Dexter, New Madrid, Kennett, Bloomfield and Fredericktown.

In many of the towns are camps of the Grand Army of the Republic composed of the veterans of the Union army in the great Civil war. The purpose of these camps is to keep alive the memory of the heroic deeds and sacrifices of the war, to provide opportunity for fellowship among those who stood together on the field of battle and to assist worthy historical and patriotic movements of every kind. The observance of Memoral Day is one of the means for accomplishing these purposes. Allied with the camps of the G. A. R. are organizations of women called the Women's Relief Corps. It was due to the initiative of a chapter of this organization that a statue fountain was recently placed in the courthouse square in Cape Girardeau and dedicated with appropriate ceremonies, the chief address being delivered by Governor Hadley.

There are also to be found in almost every community organizations of the great secret, social and philanthropic orders. As we have seen at a very early date lodges of the Masonic order were formed in Southeast Missouri and the activity of this order was soon followed by others. A detailed account of their organization cannot be presented here, but they have been and still are powerful and vital forces in the life of the people.

Every profession and business has its organizations. Commercial clubs exist in many of the larger towns, the club at Cape Girardeau being regarded as one of the most active and efficient organizations of the kind in the state. There are organizations of farmers, lawyers, physicians, dentists. All of them are active in advancing the interests of this part of the state.

Spanish-American War

The only regiment raised in Southeast Missouri was the Sixth Regiment which was mustered in at Jefferson Barracks, July 20 to 23, 1898. The regiment officers were Letcher Hardemann, Colonel; H. C. Clark, Lieutenant Colonel; Orlando F. Guthrie, Major; J. J. Dickinson, Major, and E. A. Hickman, Adjutant. Not all the companies of the regiment were from Southeast Missouri; Company D was recruited principally at Bloomfield and Stoddard county. Its officers were Mack Richardson, Captain; Grant Gillispie, First Lieutenant; Ward Wilson, Second Lieutenant. Company E was recruited at Doniphan and in Ripley county, its officers were Pierre D. Ladd, Captain; Giboney Houck, First Lieutenant; Walter F. Martin, Second Lieutenant. Company H was from Bollinger county being recruited principally at Lutesville; its officers were: Captain, John W. Revelle; First Lieutenant, Robert V. Cordell; Second Lieutenant, Stanley Gordon. Company I was from Dunklin county; its officers were: Albert D. Sloan, Captain; Robert A. Cox, First Lieutenant; W. H. Clopton. Second Lieutenant. Company K was recruited in Jefferson and St. Louis counties; its officers were: Captain, Robert E. Lee; First Lieutenant, Charles A. Conklin; Second Lieutenant, Arthur W. Brent.

This regiment was the last to take the field during the Spanish-American war, but it saw a more extensive service than any other of the Missouri regiments. It was mustered in at Jefferson Barracks July 20 to 23, 1898, and soon afterward was sent to Florida, where it stayed for sometime; the men being thoroughly drilled. It became a part of the army under General Lee and went with him to Cuba and took possession of Havana. The fact that its commanding officer, Colonel Hardeman, was an officer of the regular army and a skilled tactician, enabled the regiment to be brought to a high degree of discipline. It was regarded as the best regiment in General Lee's army. It remained on duty in Havana until May 10, 1899, when it was returned to Georgia and mustered out at Savannah. At the ceremony of mustering out the regiment presented a beautiful saber to Colonel Hardeman as a token of the esteem in which he was held.

CHAPTER XXX

TOWNS FOUNDED SINCE CIVIL WAR

MARQUAND — GLENALLEN — ZALMA — BESSVILLE — NEELEYVILLE — FISK — HARVIEL — VAN BUREN — ELLSINORE — GRANDIN — HUNTER — POCAHONTAS — ALLENVILLE—WHITEWATER — BURFORDVILLE — MILLERVILLE —OAKRIDGE — GORDONVILLE — MALDEN—CAMPBELL — GIBSON — HOLCOMB — SENATH—WHITEOAK — GLENNONVILLE — CARDWELL — CARUTH — COTTONPLANT — DES ARC — SABULA — BELLEVIEW — ANNAPOLIS — FESTUS — HOUSE'S SPRING — MORSE MILL — PEVELEY — VICTORIA — MINE LAMOTTE — CORNWALL — DIEHLSTADT — EAST PRAIRIE — BERTRAND — MARSTON — GIDEON — PARMA — LILBOURN — COMO — MOREHOUSE — HAYTI — HOLLAND — COTTONWOOD POINT — STEELE —CALRYVILLE — LITHIUM — WITTENBERG — LONGTOWN — SCHUMER SPRINGS — BUNKER — ELLINGTON — NAYLOR — FLAT RIVER — DESLOGE — LEADWOOD — ELVINS — BONNE TERRE — BISMARCK — DELASSUS — KNOB LICK—LIBERTYVILLE — DOE RUN — ORAN — FORNFELT — ILLMO—CROWDER — KELSO —BLODGETT — MORLEY — CHAFFEE — VANDUSER — DEXTER — ADVANCE — BERNIE — PUXICO — IRONDALE — MINERAL POINT —RICHWOODS — CHAONIA — LEEPER — MILLS RING—WILLIAMSVILLE.

That the founding of towns since the close of the Civil war has been quite a busy industry in Southeast Missouri, is evident from the record which follows.

Marquand in Bollinger county was settled in 1868. It is situated on the Belmont branch of the Iron Mountain Railroad. Among the early settlers were J. H. Stanfill, Henry Whitener and B. F. Finger. The first merchants were J. Q. A. Whitener, William Matthews, and Jacob Lutes. The town was not incorporated until 1908, the first mayor being F. J. Limbaugh. At the present time there are three general stores. Besides these there are wood working establishments, a flour mill, and a soda water factory. There is one bank in the town and among its important buildings are four churches. The population of Marquand now is 339.

GLENALLEN

The town of Glenallen in Bollinger county, was settled about 1870 and incorporated as a town in 1906. The first settler and also the first merchant was J. A. Berry. The first mayor of the town was R. Smith. There are now three general stores supported entirely by the farming community about it. It is situated on the Belmont branch of the Iron Mountain, and has a population of 106.

ZALMA

Zalma in the southern part of Bollinger county, is the terminus of the Frisco branch from Zalma by way of Brownwood to Bloomfield. Its population is 373. It has several stores, a flouring mill, and other interests. The Bank of Zalma with a capital stock of $12,000 was organized in 1905.

BESSVILLE

Bessville on the Belmont branch of the Iron Mountain, was laid out soon after the building of the railroad. Other villages in Bollinger county are Buchanan, Castor, Mayfield, Patton, Scopus, Sedwickville, Sturdivant, and Tallent.

NEELEYVILLE

Neeleyville in the southern part of Butler county, was laid out as a town in 1870. It is now the terminus of the Doniphan branch of the Iron Mountain Railroad. Its population is 241. It has stores, blacksmith shops, gins, and other business establishments. The Bank of Neeleyville was organized in 1910, and has a capital of $10,000. There are two churches in the town and a good public school.

FISK

Fisk, a village in Butler county, is situated not far from the Stoddard county line on the Cairo branch of the Iron Mountain. It is a flourishing community supported by timber and farming interest. Its population is 270 and it has stores and other small business establishments.

HARVIEL

Harviel, with a population of 201, is a town on the main line of the Iron Mountain, south of Poplar Bluff and on the Hoxie branch of the Frisco.

Other villages in Butler county are Hendrickson and Keener on the Iron Mountain, and Rombauer and Sawyer, new saw-mill towns on the Frisco.

MARSTON

The town of Marston in New Madrid county, was settled in October, 1898, the first settlers being George W. Coleman, H. L. Shidler, C. M. Barnes, R. W. Maxey, W. A. Barnes, R. D. Welshans, E. F. Sharp, S. S. Barnes and M. Foy. The first mayor of the town was E. F. Sharp. The early merchants were Barnes Store Company, M. H. Maxey, and Finsberry & Mennen. At the present time there are two general stores, six grocery stores and one drug store. In addition to these establishments there is a stave factory, one hoop factory, and a cotton gin. The Bank of Marston was organized in 1905 and has a capital stock of $10,000. The principal buildings in the town are the Fraternal Hall, opera house, a Methodist church building and a Baptist church building. Marston is on the main line of the Frisco and is the southern terminus of the St. Louis & Missouri Southern, a new railroad which has just been put into operation between Marston and New Madrid, but which it is proposed to extend to the Thebes bridge. The present population is 258.

VAN BUREN

Van Buren, the county seat of Carter county, is an unincorporated village. It is one mile from the Frisco and is on Current river. It has churches, school, five stores, mills, the *Current Local*, a weekly newspaper, and its population is about 500. The Carter County Bank was chartered in 1901, with a capital of $20,000. The most important buildings are those of the county.

ELLSINORE

The largest town in Carter county is Ellsinore which has a population of 813. It is in the eastern part of the county on the Frisco Railroad. It is the site of some large mills, has about twenty business establishments, and is growing rapidly. The Bank of Ellsinore was chartered in 1907, and has a capital of $10,000. The public school is in good condition.

GRANDIN

Grandin in Carter county, was at one time the most important saw-mill town in the state. Here were very large mills employing about 2,000 men, and cutting enormous quantities of lumber. The town was owned by the mill company which made extensive public improvements. With the decline in the timber interests, the town lost something of its importance. Its population is about 600. It has a school, six stores, three churches, sidewalks, electric lights, and is situated on the Frisco Railroad and Little Black river.

HUNTER

Hunter, a mill town in Carter county, is supported largely by timber interests. It has a population of 710 and is a rapidly growing and thriving town. It is on the Frisco Railroad, has fifteen business establishments and a public school.

POCAHONTAS

The first settlement at Pocahontas, Cape Girardeau county, was made before the war, but the town was not incorporated until 1893, at which time John Bonney was elected mayor. Among its early settlers were Robert Baldridge, Robert McNeely, and John Bonney. The first merchants were Robert McNeely and Samuel M. Green; Mr. Green afterwards removed to Cape Girardeau where he is now a practicing lawyer. There are three general stores and one flour mill. The town was unfortunate in its relation to the railroad. When the Cape Girardeau & Chester Railroad was built north from Jackson, it passed about one and three-quarter miles from Pocahontas. This has handicapped the town to a certain extent. Still it has continued to grow. Its population now is 239.

ALLENVILLE

The town of Allenville in Cape Girardeau county is situated at the junction of the Jackson branch of the Belmont branch of the Iron Mountain Railroad and was laid out as a town in 1869, the first mayor being H. C. Hinton. There are now three general stores in the town and some other minor business establishments. The population is 257.

WHITEWATER

The town of Whitewater is situated on the Belmont branch of the Iron Mountain Railroad in Cape Girardeau county. It was first settled as a town in 1866. Among its early settlers were William Devore, John Albert, William Steel, William and Thomas Wheeler, Dr. Dodson, Martin Lawrent, F. H. Stecker, Dr. S. M. McAnally, Miles Ax and P. N. O'Brien. The town was not incorporated until 1898, and its first mayor was P. N. O'Brien. Among the early merchants were Shell & Albert, Miles Ax, S. M. McAnally and P. N. O'Brien. There are now four general stores in the town. Besides these there is a flour mill, a saw mill and a mill devoted to the manufacture of butcher blocks. The Bank of Whitewater, with a capital of $10,000 supplies the financial wants of the citizens. The town is situated in a good farming community and is prosperous. It has a population of 250.

Allenville

Allenville, an incorporated village in Cape Girardeau county is situated at the junction of the Jackson branch of the Iron Mountain with the Belmont branch of the same line. It was laid out as a town in 1869 on the building of the railroad. It has a population of 257 with the usual business interests. There are Baptist and Methodist churches and a public school.

Burfordville is on Whitewater river near the old site of Bollinger's mill. It has been a village for many years and has two or three stores, a church and its population is about 150.

Millerville is in Whitewater township, Cape Girardeau county. It has stores, two churches and a school. Its population is 99.

Oakridge

Oakridge is in Apple Creek township. It was settled in 1852 and its present population is 256. Bank of Oakridge was organized in 1904 and its capital is $10,000. There are three churches, and business interests of various kinds. Oakridge has always supported a good school.

Gordonville

Gordonville is one of the oldest settlements in Cape Girardeau county, the first settlers having come to the vicinity during the Spanish regime. Its present population is 170. The Bank of Gordonville was chartered in 1910 and has a capital of $10,000. There are several church organizations and the town is on the Jackson branch of the Iron Mountain Railroad.

Other villages in Cape Girardeau county are Dutchtown, Pocahontas, Fruitland, New Wells, Shawneetown and Deray.

Malden

Malden, Dunklin county, was laid out in 1877 under the direction of Major George B. Clark. It was the western terminus for a time of the Little River Valley & Arkansas Railroad which then extended from New Madrid to Malden. The first house was built by S. W. Spiller and Daniel Haynes and was occupied by them as a store. They furnished supplies to the men engaged in building the railroad. Another early merchant was James Gregory and some who came with him were Jackson Erlick, William Harkey and Sisel and Plant. The J. S. Levi Mercantile Company was organized in Malden during its early years and has been one of its largest stores ever since that time. The town had the usual growth of a country town. Its situation on the railroad gave it an advantage and it attracted various interests from Clarkton and became for awhile the largest town in the county. It was built largely of wood and the greater part of the business interests in town were destroyed by fire in January, 1899. The burnt buildings were replaced by brick and the town has had a steady and substantial growth since that time. Malden was incorporated at the April term of the county court in 1878 and the first trustees were Daniel Haynes, James Gregory, S. W. Spiller, Samuel B. Dennis and J. P. Laswell.

One of the men most closely associated with the growth and prosperity of the town was George W. Peck, who was a native of New York, was educated in the State Normal School, taught for a time, equipped himself as a surveyor and came to Missouri as one of the engineers on the Little River Valley & Arkansas Railroad. He made his home in Malden and engaged in buying and selling grain. He added to his interests an insurance business and an ice plant and was for many years one of the foremost men of the town. In addition to his business interests he held various positions of trust having been mayor and for more than twenty years was president of the school board. Mr. Peck was a man of high public spiriit and did much to advance the interests of his community. No man deserved more at the hands of the town and none stood higher in the affection of the people. He died very suddenly in 1910.

At present the town has about fifty business establishments of one kind and another and is constantly adding to the number. There are several large general stores and many other business institutions of different kinds. Several large cotton gins take care of the cotton crop in the vicinity and there is a cotton oil mill. The town has also some large wood working establishments that manufacture lumber, staves and heading. A new electric light plant and water works system has recently been installed giving first class service. There are two banks. The Dunklin County Bank, the oldest in the county, was established in 1890. It now has a capital stock of $20,000. The Bank of Malden was chartered in 1903. Its capital stock is also $20,000. The town is situated on the main line of the St. Louis Southwestern Railway and a branch of this line runs from here to Cairo, Illinois. There is also a branch of the St. Louis & Gulf which reaches Malden from Clarkton. One of the large wood-working establishments has a tram road running for a number of miles into the East Swamp which is being converted into a standard gauge railroad. Malden has the usual church organizations all of them having buildings, and the Presbyterian church has recently completed the erection of a handsome brick structure. The public school system is well organized, the town has just completed a new building at a cost of $25,000. The farming country about the town is unusually rich and large quantities of cotton, melons and corn are shipped from this place every year. The population of Malden at the present time is 2,116.

CAMPBELL

The town of Campbell, Dunklin county, was established in 1881, the first residents in the town were L. McCutcheon, J. H. Bridges, H. A. Gardner, L. Walker, Dr. Hale, Dr. William R. Hughes, and the first merchants in the town were Lasswell Brothers, A. D. Bridges & Son, L. McCutcheon & Company, Levi Walker and William Bridges. The town grew slowly for a number of years but on the erection of a large wood working establishment the population increased very rapidly for a number of years. At the present time there are nineteen general stores besides restaurants, drug stores and other smaller business interests and there are ten factories, most of these are wood-working establishments of one kind or another, all of them taken together give employment to a large number of men and add considerable to the prosperity of the town. The town was incorporated May 18, 1894, and the first mayor was Charles Cheny. The Bank of Campbell was organized in 1897. It now has a capital stock of $30,000; the First National Bank of Campbell was organized in 1903 and also has a capital of $30,000. The town has a good system of electric lights and is completing a system of water works; the city water is to be taken from an artesian well, one of the few flowing wells in Southeast Missouri. Among the important buildings are the city hall and public school buildings. One of the things of which the city is especially proud is its system of public schools, employing ten teachers and giving opportunity for a good high-school education. Under the patronage of the school there have been held each year, for a number of years, an Old Settlers' day which has attracted many people and been the cause of great interest. In 1911 there was organized a Fair Association which that year gave the first of a series of fairs, which was very successful in every way. It is the purpose of the association to continue the custom of an annual fair. The association is pursuing a somewhat different course from other fairs in laying particular stress upon farm improvement and farm development.

Campbell is located on the main line of the St. Louis Southwestern Railway and on a branch of the St. Louis & San Francisco. It is situated in a prosperous farming community and doubtless has before it a considerable growth. Its present population is 1,781.

Four miles south of Campbell on the Frisco Railroad is the little town of Gibson. It is the junction point of two branches of the Frisco Railroad and is a flourishing village. It has three general stores, blacksmith shop, two churches and a school.

HOLCOMB

Two miles south of Gibson is the town of Holcomb, both in Dunklin county. This was laid out as a town about the year 1870. Owing to its situation with regard to the farming country about it has experienced a steady growth and now has a population of 279. It has good general stores, banks, and school such as are usually found in towns of this size. It is constantly growing and the resources of the country around it warrant the belief of its people that it will continue to grow.

SENATH

Ten miles south of Kennett, the county seat of Dunklin county, is the town of Senath. The first settler in the town was A. W. Douglas who moved there about 1878. The town had very slow growth, and was a mere village for a long time. It depended for its support entirely upon the farming community about it. The farms in this vicinity, however, are among the richest in Southeast Missouri and so the town continued to grow. A postoffice was established and some general stores opened, among the first being J. M. Baird & Company. Cotton gins were built and a market was formed for the purchase and selling of cotton. In 1897, Louis Houck, who built so many railroads in Southeast Missouri, extended his St. Louis, Kennett & Southern Railroad from Kennett to Senath, and this immediately brought about a growth of the town. Today it is a flourishing community of more than a thousand population and is substantially built of brick in its business section, and has all the evidences of a prosperous community.

CARDWELL

The town of Cardwell, Dunklin county, is situated on the line of the Paragould-Southeastern and Paragould & Memphis Railroad not far from the Arkansas line. It was first settled as a town in 1896 and was not incorporated until 1904. Among the early settlers were J. T. Meredith, J. A. Southers, W. D. Jackson, J. M. Barber and J. D. Washington. The first merchants were J. M. Seaborn, J. D. Hale, and the Bertig Mercantile Company; the latter two stores are still in existence and transact the greater part of the mercantile business of the town. The town has depended very largely on the farming country and also on the timber interests for support. When the settlement was first made at this point there were immense forests of timber about it and the town was made the location of some wood-working establishments employing large numbers of men. At the present time the Cardwell & Buffalo Stave Company operates the most important factory. The Peoples Bank with a capital of $15,000 supplies the financial wants of the citizens. The first mayor was J. R. Pool, who was also postmaster for a number of years. Cardwell is situated in the midst of fine farming country and will no doubt continue to have a steady growth. It now has a population of 874.

Whiteoak, a village in Dunklin county, situated nine miles north of Kennett on the St. Louis & Gulf Railroad, was settled in 1902 on the opening of this road. It has never been incorporated but exists only as a village without organized form. It contains at the present time three general stores and a saw mill. The country around Whiteoak is very fertile and much new farming land is being opened up so that the town will probably continue to be a good trading point.

Glennonville

The village of Glennonville in Dunklin county north of Campbell, was established in 1904. It was laid out on lands which had been purchased by the Catholic church in the name of Archbishop Glennon of St. Louis. The colony was composed of immigrants principally from Germany. It has had a considerable growth and is a flourishing town. The first merchant was L. M. Michlong. There are now three stores in the town and also three wood-working establishments manufacturing staves and handles.

Caruth

Caruth is an unincorporated village in Dunklin county. It has two stores, a mill, two churches and a population of about 100. The schoolhouse is the most important building in the place, being built of brick and having all modern improvements. It contains four rooms.

Cottonplant in Clay township was laid off as a town by E. J. Langdon who for a long time was the only merchant and the town's postmaster. At the present time there is a school, a church, one store and about 150 inhabitants.

Other villages in Dunklin county are Branum in the south part of the county, Octa on Varner river south of Kennett and a station on the Frisco Railroad, Hollywood south of Senath, McGuire near Malden on the Frisco, Paulding, Rushcreek on Crowley's ridge, Townley, a saw-mill town north of Malden on the Cotton Belt, Valleyridge north of Campbell, Vincit on Buffalo creek south of Kennett, and Wrightville.

Des Arc

The town of Des Arc, in Iron county, was settled first in the year 1800, the early settlers being David Shaver, Andrew Wallace and Major McFadden. The town was not incorporated as a town until 1889. The first mayor was Charles H. Collins. Some of the early merchants were David Shaver, Charles Collins and John and James Heifner. There are now seven general stores, two planing mills, two handle factories, two grist mills, one broom factory and two saw mills. The Bank of Des Arc was organized in 1907 and has a capital stock of $10,000. The town is lighted with electric lights and among the important buildings are the Woodman hall and three church buildings. It is on the main line of the St. Louis Iron Mountain & Southern and has a population of 287.

Sabula is a little village on the main line of the Iron Mountain Railroad in Iron county. It has a population of 70.

The old village of Belleview is situated west of Middlebrook and is an inland community having no railroad communications. It was for a long time famous as a place of residence, the surrounding country being esteemed unusually healthful and is also very beautiful.

Other villages in Iron county are Graniteville, Bixby, Hogan, Mann, Munger, Pippin and Tolu.

ANNAPOLIS

Annapolis in Iron county was settled about 1872. It was incorporated in 1902, but the incorporation was allowed to lapse. The first mayor was C. Hart. Among the early settlers were John Thomas Jackson, James Christopher and R. A. Clarkson. There are four general stores, a saw mill and a planing mill in the town. It has the usual number of hotels, restaurants and other minor interests and its present population is 160.

FESTUS

Festus is situated on the St. Louis & San Francisco and the Mississippi & Bonne Terre railways in Jefferson county, about thirty-five miles from St. Louis. It was laid out in 1878 by W. J. Adams and for several years known as Derby City. It contains a number of general stores and other business establishments and a good system of public schools, Catholic, Christian, Methodist and Presbyterian churches and a flouring mill. It is only two miles from Crystal City and many persons who are employed at that place make their homes in Festus. It has a system of electric lights and its present population is 2,556. The Citizens Bank was organized in 1889, and has a capital stock of $35,000. The Farmers and Merchants Bank, with a capital of $15,000, was organized in 1903.

House's Springs and Morse Mill are two small village communities in Jefferson county whose names perpetuate the memories of famous pioneers of that county. Both were settled very early in the history of that section and both were the scene of Indian attacks during the early days.

PEVELY

Pevely in Jefferson county is a station on the Mississippi river and Bonne Terre Railroad just south of Riverside. It has a population of 247. It is supported by farming country and its railroad interests. It has a school, several stores and a church. The Bank of Pevely was organized in 1906 and has a capital stock of $10,000.

Victoria, with a population of 150, Plattin. Riverside, Rushtower, High Ridge, Grubville, Frumet, Silica, Selma, and Wickes are other small villages. Valles Mines on the Mississippi river and Bonne Terre Railroad in the south part of the county is one of the old mining locations of this county. It bears the name of the pioneer French family long famous in the history of Ste. Genevieve district.

MINE LAMOTTE

Mine LaMotte, a village in Madison county four miles north of Frederickton and two miles from the Belmont branch of the Iron Mountain, is one of the oldest settlements in Southeast Missouri. We have elsewhere given the history of the mine situated here which is really the history of the town as it exists solely by virtue of the former. Its present population is estimated at 500 and it has churches, schools, a few stores and a hotel. Among the men closely associated with the place were the Valles of Ste. Genevieve who operated the mine for a time, one of whom was killed here by Indians, St. Gem Beauvais and J. B. Pratte.

Cornwall is a station on the Belmont branch south of Frederickton. Its population is 45.

Other villages in Madison county are White Springs, famous for its medicinal springs and used as a summer resort, and situated west of Cornwall off the railroad; French Mills, Roselle, Saco, Silvermine and Twelvemile.

DIEHLSTADT

The village of Diehlstadt in Mississippi county was settled in 1868 by John Kirkpatrick who also conducted the first store in the town. The town was incorporated in 1894 and its first mayor was John Rushing. There are at present five general stores besides minor business establishments of various kinds. The town has no factories of any kind and is supported wholly by the farming community in which it is situated. The land about the town is fertile and the community is a prosperous and growing one. Preparations are being made to organize a bank to care for the financial interests. The important buildings are the lodge hall and the church buildings belonging to the Methodists and Baptists. The town is situated on the Belmont branch of the Iron Mountain Railroad, and has a population of 160.

EAST PRAIRIE

East Prairie, an unincorporated village formerly known as Hibbard, in St. James township in Mississippi county twelve miles from Charleston, was laid out in 1883 and for a number of years was almost entirely dependent upon saw mills and other wood working establishments. The country about the town has been opened up in recent years and it is now supported very largely by the farming community. It has Methodist, Christian and Catholic churches, cotton gin, several general stores and other business establishments and one newspaper, the *East Prairie Eagle*, a well edited and newsy county paper. The town is situated on the Cairo branch of the St. Louis Southwestern Railway. The New Bank of East Prairie has a capital stock of $15,000 and was organized in 1905.

BERTRAND

Bertrand is a village on the Cairo branch of the Iron Mountain six miles from Charleston. It was laid out in 1859 by H. J. Diehl. It has stores, a church and school. The Bank of Bertrand was chartered in 1906 and its capital is $15,000.

Other villages in Mississippi county are Whiting, a saw-mill town, Sands and Wolf Island. Bird's Point, the famous old town settled in early days by a member of the Bird family for whom it was named has practically ceased to exist having been washed away by the river on whose bank it was situated.

GIDEON

One of the fastest growing towns in New Madrid county is Gideon which is situated on the St. Louis & Gulf Railroad about three miles east of the Dunklin county line. Fifteen years ago its site was in the midst of the unbroken forests of the Little River lowland. In 1900 a mill was located at this place by the firm of Gideon & Anderson. A town sprung up about the mill and it became a prosperous community. It was incorporated as a village in 1906. Among the early settlers were W. P. Anderson, M. S. Anderson, Frank E. Gideon and M. V. Mumma. The first merchants in the place were Gideon & Anderson, the owners of the mill. There are now general stores and other business establishments. There are also two sawmills, a stave factory, handle factory and planing mill. The town has electric light supplied by the mill company. There are two churches—Methodist and Baptist, a four-room school building, and seven acres of land has been set aside for a park. The country about Gideon is exceedingly fertile, and as it is drained and cleared will be supported by a fine farming community. Its population is 702.

Parma

In 1900 the first settlers moved to the site of the present town of Parma, New Madrid county. This town is eight miles northwest of Malden on the line of the St. Louis Southwestern Railway between Cairo and Malden. It is not a great way from an earlier village which was known as Lotta. The site of the new town of Parma was determined by the crossing of a line of the Frisco Railroad at this point. The presence of the two railroads and construction of mills for the working up of the great timber supplies, brought a considerable number of people to the town. It was situated in rather a low place and before drainage ditches were cut, was subject to constant overflow. This has been remedied, however, by the cutting of the ditches so that its site now is a very good one. The timber is being rapidly cut out and farming land opened up in the vicinity. Among the early settlers were: William Webb, Sol Hon and H. L. Boaz. Boaz and Wrather Brothers were among the early merchants. In 1905 owing to the wealth of the town and its importance it was incorporated and F. P. Wrather was the first mayor. The town now has six general stores and a number of other business interests, among them a handle factory and two large veneering factories. The financial interests of the town are cared for by the Bank of Parma, established in 1905, with a capital of $10,000. The more important buildings are the I. O. O. F. hall, recently constructed and the new brick school building erected in 1910, containing eight rooms and thoroughly equipped. The town has electric lights. Good sidewalks have been built in the central part of the town and some work done towards the paving of the streets. The population is now 905.

Lilbourn

One of the fastest growing towns in Southeast Missouri is Lilbourn in New Madrid county, situated at the junction of the St. Louis Southwestern and the St. Louis & San Francisco railroads. The first town in the vicinity was called Papaw Junction and was situated about a mile west of the present site of the town where the New Madrid branch joined the main line of the St. Louis Southwestern. The town was incorporated in 1904, its first mayor being R. T. Waring. Waring was one of the first settlers and also one of the early merchants of the town, others being D. H. Wilkison and R. F. Baynes. The town has eight general stores and besides these several factories, broom, stave, handle, brick and tile plant and two saw-mills. There is one bank in the town known as the Bank of Lilbourn which was chartered in 1910 and has a capital of $10,000. The town is lighted with electric lights and is growing very rapidly. It is situated in the midst of good farming country and has unusual railroad facilities. The population as given by the census of 1910 is 274 but now the citizens claim a population of 1,200. The town has recently made a number of public improvements including over five miles of granitoid sidewalks.

Como, on Como lake, is a village in New Madrid county on the St. Louis Southwestern. It has timber interests and is in the midst of what is destined to be a fine farming country. Canalou is on the Gulf branch of the Frisco. It was settled as a sawmill town when the Houck road was constructed in 1902. It has extensive timber interests, a saw mill, store, and several minor business interests. Hyman, Mathews, and Risco are other villages in New Madrid county.

Morehouse

Morehouse, in the extreme northwest corner of New Madrid county, had its origin in the location here of large saw mills when the Cairo branch of the Iron Mountain made possible the handling of the vast quantities of timber found about the town and surrounding country. For many years the place was merely a saw-mill town. It is on the bank of Little River which overflows most of the place. The surrounding country was almost wholly timbered, and much of it not capable of being cultivated without being drained. With the building of the Gulf Railroad, the clearing away of the timber, the drainage and subsequent cultivation of the lands, and the protection of the town from overflow by the building of levees along the course of Little River, the place began to develop. It is now a thriving and prosperous town of 1,700 people, with good streets, sidewalks, well built business blocks, churches, a good brick school building, a superior hotel, and one of the largest saw-mill plants in the state. In this mill, which is owned by the Himmelberger-Harrison Lumber Company are cut vast quantities of cypress and gum lumber. The town bids fair to grow and to become even more prosperous as more of the land is subjected to cultivation as it is of unsurpassed fertility.

Hayti

At the junction of the main line of the Frisco with the Caruthersville and Kennett branch, six miles from Caruthersville, is the town of Hayti, Pemiscot county. It began to be a town at the time of the building of the railroad from Kennett to Caruthersville and has had a rapid growth since. It now has a population of 1,057. Its business interests consist of a number of general stores, two banks and several manufacturing establishments devoted to wood working principally. It has a good system of public schools, several churches and a city hall which is above the average for towns of this size. There is one paper, the *Hayti Herald*, which is edited by William York.

Pascola

Pascola, an unincorporated village in Pemiscot county, is situated on the Frisco Railroad between Kennett and Hayti. It began to be a town on the building of the railroad from Kennett to Caruthersville in 1894 but previous to that time there had been settlers living in the immediate vicinity of the town since 1879. The earliest of these were Tim Ingram and Mrs. Sarah Brown. The town was incorporated in 1899, the first mayor being A. Russell. The merchants in the early period were John Swails and Edward Harrison. There are now three general stores and one stave factory. The town is largely dependent upon the agricultural community around.

HOLLAND

In 1871 J. C. Winters and J. W. Holland settled on the site of the present town of Holland in Pemiscot county. Winters is still a resident of the town but Holland, for whom it was named, is dead. It was twenty years before the place was anything more than simply a little group of farms; not until the opening of the Frisco Railroad between St. Louis and Memphis was there any considerable activity in building up of the town. This was in 1901 and the first incorporation was made in May, 1903; Samuel E. Redmond was the first mayor. Besides Winters and Holland, Joe and J. L. Lester, J. E. Butler and James Mills were among the first who moved into the town. The first merchants were W. A. Sanford, Holland Supply Company, A. L. Watson and G. S. Mirick. There are now five general stores and the usual number of blacksmith shops, restaurants and other small establishments. In addition to these there are two cotton gins and a saw mill in the town. One of the local institutions of which the town is proud is the telephone exchange owned by the Citizens Co-operative Telephone Company of Holland. The population is about 400, having increased very rapidly in the last two or three years. This is due to the development of the surrounding country, which is of unusual fertility.

STEELE

Steele is an unincorporated village in the southern part of Pemiscot county. It was named for L. L. Steele. Some of the persons who lived there during its first years were William Wilford, Jesse VanHoy, G. E. Moore and Henry Flowers. The first merchants were F. T. Jackson Store Company and George W. Freese. The business interests of the town are now represented by seven general stores, three cotton gins, a saw-mill and a grist mill. The Bank of Steele was chartered in 1904, and has a capital of $10,000. The town is in the midst of fine farming country and gives every evidence of continued prosperity. It now has a population of 600 and is situated on the Frisco Railroad.

Cottonwood Point on the river, in Pemiscot county, was for a long time an important shipping point for the adjacent country. Much traffic came to the place from Pemiscot and even Dunklin counties on the construction of a road across the Little River swamp. The town prospered on account of this business, a number of large stores and other business establishments sprung up, churches were built and a school maintained. Tyler, to the south, experienced a similar growth in a smaller degree. Both of these towns lost their importance in a large measure by the building up of Caruthersville to the north of them and the construction of the Frisco Railroad through the county west of them.

Deering and Wardell are important saw-mill towns, and other villages in Pemiscot county are Game on the Frisco, Stancil, Stewart and Covington and Kennedy.

CLARYVILLE

The town of Claryville in Perry county was settled in 1869 and incorporated as a town in 1871, the first mayor being V. P. Tucker. The first merchant in the town was E. J. Rhodes. There are now three general stores, but no factories of any kind and the town is dependent upon the farming community about it. It has a population of 140.

Lithium

Lithium, same county, was surveyed as a town in 1882. At that time the settlers were Dr. Henry Clay Tish, Richard P. Dobbs and James G. Christian, all of whom came to Missouri from Illinois. The town was incorporated in 1883 and the first mayor was Richard C. Lisenby. The first store was opened by Brown and Hartley in the spring of 1883. A public bath house was built by Thomas King in the same year. The location of the town was determined by certain mineral springs. They were very popular and the town grew very rapidly for about a year. There are two of these springs of water both of them being highly prized on account of medicinal qualities. One of them belongs to the town and the other is owned by Mrs. Richard P. Dobbs. The town is situated on the Cape Girardeau, Perryville & Ste. Genevieve Railroad and is two miles from the Frisco. These are two churches in the town, a Baptist church organized in 1885, and a Catholic church organized in 1896. The town has two general stores, a flour mill, a grist mill, a blacksmith shop, brick yard and a feed stable. Its population is 98.

Wittenberg

Wittenberg, in Perry county, was laid off as a town and incorporated in 1867. It is situated at the mouth of Brazeau creek and as its name indicates is a settlement of German Lutherans. It is a shipping point on the river and is a station on the Frisco from St. Louis to Memphis.

Longtown, an inland village of Perry county, was laid out in 1871. It has a church, school and three stores. Seventy-six is a flourishing village on the Frisco with a population of 367. It was for a long time only a shipping point on the river and was called Seventy-six Landing. With the construction of the railroad it assumed new importance. It has a flouring mill, stores and churches.

Schumer Springs, a village in Perry county two miles from the line of the Cape Girardeau & Chester Railroad, is a health resort famous for the medicinal character of its waters.

Other villages in the county are Menfro on the Frisco with a population of 365, Uniontown, Yount, Frohna and Farrar.

Bunker

Bunker is a new town on the line between Dent and Reynolds counties. The first settlements in the neighborhood of the town were made about 1840, but there was not even a village before 1907. The town was incorporated in 1909 and Dr. J. B. Gordon was the first mayor. It is now a thriving town with eight general stores and one large saw mill. The town is lighted with electric lights and has a population of 106. It is the terminus of the Missouri Southern Railroad which runs from Leeper in Wayne county.

Ellington

Ellington, while not the county seat of Reynolds county, is the most important town except for the transaction of legal business. It is near the center of the county and is on the Missouri Southern Railroad. It is a thriving business community with mills, stores, churches and a good school. There are two banks in the town. The Bank of Ellington was incorporated in 1905 with a capital of $25,000 and the Farmers State Bank in 1909. It has a capital of $25,000 also. These amounts show the extent of the interest of the community. The town is largely supported by timber and farming interests.

NAYLOR

Naylor is a village in Thomas township in Ripley county. It is on the main line of the Iron Mountain Railroad and is the western terminus of the Doniphan branch. Its population is 406. There are two churches, a school and about ten business establishments of various kinds. The Bank of Naylor was chartered in 1903 and has a capital stock of $10,000.

Other villages in Ripley county are Fairdealing, Ponder, Gatewood, Pine and Poyner.

FLAT RIVER

The largest city in St. Francois county is Flat River. Settlement was made here early in the history of the county and lead mines opened just before the war. The lead interests were not greatly developed until after the building of the Mississippi River and Bonne Terre Railroad. The mines were developed rapidly then and they are so extensive and so rich as to cause the growth of a large community supported in large part by them. There are farming interests also, but they are of much less importance than the mines. The town now has another railroad—the Illinois Southern—which passes through extending between Bismarck and Ste. Genevieve. Flat River is the northern terminus of the St. Francois county interurban line. Its transportation facilities are thus unusually good and the prosperity of the town greatly enhanced by them. There are about 100 business establishments including stores, mills, mines, wagon shops and minor establishments. The Bank of Flat River was chartered in 1907 and has a capital of $15,000. The Miners & Merchants Bank was chartered in 1899 and its capital is also $15,000. The school system is one of the best in this part of the state. The town is a typical mining community, differing from all others of Southeast Missouri outside the Lead Belt.

DESLOGE

DesLoge is an unincorporated village of St. Francois county. It has a large and constantly growing population due to its large mining interests, but has never assumed a municipal organization. The Bank of DesLoge was chartered in 1902 and has a capital of $10,000. The Citizens Bank dates from 1907 and its capital is also $10,000. The town has recently erected a fine new school building, one of the best and most modern in Southeast Missouri. It maintains a good system of schools and is a progressive and thriving community.

LEADWOOD

Leadwood is another unincorporated village of the Lead Belt in St. Francois county. Its population is large though no municipal government has been organized. The village of Iron Mountain is in Iron township in St. Francois county. It is situated at the foot of Iron Mountain and is fourteen miles southwest of Farmington. The town is owned in large part by the mining company which owns Iron Mountain. There are stores, churches, a school and a population of 180. At one time it was a large community having more than 1,000 people, but with the cessation for many years of active work on the iron mines the population dwindled away.

ELVINS

Another of the great mining communities is Elvins. It forms practically a part of Flat River, being situated but a little further south and west. It is organized as a separate municipality, however, and has a population of

2,071. It depends upon its mines and the railroad traffic, being situated on two lines of railroad—the Mississippi River & Bonne Terre, and the Illinois Southern. It is reached also by the St. Francois county interurban line. The Bank of Elvins was organized in 1900 with a capital stock of $15,000.

BONNE TERRE

Bonne Terre is in the northwestern part of St. Francois county about thirteen miles from Farmington. Until after the close of the Civil war it was simply a collection of miners' huts or tents, there having been mining carried on for a number of years. It received its name from the French words meaning "good land," applied to the district because of the fact that lead ore was scattered through the clay of the region and could be obtained by simply washing. This particular clay with the lead ore disseminated through it was called "bonne terre." The little village came to have this name and it was retained by the first postoffice that they established and still applies to the town. It was in the year 1864 that the mine of Bonne Terre which had been operated in a very successful manner, passed into the hands of a number of men who organized the St. Joseph Lead Company and began very soon to carry on mining operations on a much more extensive scale than formerly. They employed large numbers of men and the town consequently grew rapidly. It was under the direction of this company that the first extensive shafts were sunk in the earth for the obtaining of lead in Southeast Missouri.

The growth of the town and the prospect

IN THE BONNE TERRE LEAD MINING DISTRICT

that it had become an important place induced the St. Joseph Lead Company to provide for its wants. They had the town surveyed, laying out a number of large lots and wide streets. The policy of the company was to keep all the business in the town practically in their own hands and they were not willing to sell property but followed the plan of leasing it for long periods of years; owing to this restriction and to the further fact that property would not be leased for the carrying on of any business which the company wished to conduct, the large part of the population grew up on the land outside of the town itself. In February, 1883, and in March, 1885, the town was seriously damaged by fire and the Lead Company's works were largely destroyed on each of these occasions.

The principal industry of the town is, and has been from the very first, lead mining. The number of persons engaged in this business has made the town a good market for all the produce of the surrounding country. The largest lead smelter in the United States is in Bonne Terre and there are a large number of other business establishments in the town, their number being about a hundred, including banks, flouring and planing mills, brick yards, machine shops, hotels and stores. The town has organizations of the principal secret orders and is well supplied with churches, there being Catholic, Congregational, Methodist Episcopal and Methodist Episcopal South. The Catholics maintain a school and the public schools are among the best in this part of the state.

Not only is the city unique among Southeast Missouri cities because of its unincorporated condition and lack of municipal government, more than any other town in the section it is developing a distinctive character of architecture. There are a number of buildings which are quite different from those now found in any other of the towns. One of these is the building occupied by the St. Joseph Lead Company as a store. It is English in its style, the first story being of brick and the second of frame and plaster. Another building of marked individuality is the Congregational church, a new and handsome building of the English style. This church is set in the midst of a beautiful lawn and forms an altogether charming addition to the town. The central school building is also very different from that of most school buildings. Another unique and charming building is the Memorial library. This is a small building, but handsomely constructed and well suited to its purpose. The Mississippi River & Bonne Terre Railroad maintains extensive shops and roundhouses here. The population is more than 5,000, though no exact estimate can be made as the place is not incorporated.

BISMARCK

Bismarck, a town at the intersection of the Belmont branch with the main line of the St. Louis, Iron Mountain & Southern Railway, in St. Francois county, was laid out in 1868 by C. T. Manter, P. R. VanFrank, J. H. Worley and E. H. Cordell. The town was supported by the farming interests about it and possessed some advantages in transportation. Its population is now 848. The principal industries are the stores, hotels and flour mills. In 1877 the town was incorporated by the county court, the first trustees being William H. Gulliver, Benjamin Schoch, C. C. Grider, George H. Kelly and A. H. Tegmeyer. The Bank of Bismarck was organized in 1902 and has a capital of $25,000.

DELASSUS

Delassus is situated two miles west of Farmington on the Belmont branch. It was laid out by A. DeLassus in October, 1869. For many years it was the principal shipping point for both Farmington and Doe Run. It is now connected with Farmington and other towns in the lead belt by interurban railway. It was the residence for many years of A. DeLassus who was a descendant of Lieutenant Governor DeLassus.

Seven miles south of DeLassus on the Belmont branch is a little town known as Knob Lick. Its importance is due to the fact that it is a shipping point for the granite quarries in this part of St. Francois county. Just west of the village of Knob Lick is one of the granite peaks of the St. Francois mountains and here for many years have been quarried large quantities of granite. Some of this granite is worked into paving blocks and some of it into building and monumental blocks of various kinds.

Libertyville is the present name of one of the oldest settlements in St. Francois county. This was Cook's Settlement in the southern part of the county. It is removed from the railroad and has a few general stores and blacksmith shops, flouring mill, church and schoolhouse.

Doe Run

In 1880 Doe Run, an unincorporated village in St. Francois county, had not been founded. Its site was the pasture land and orchards. About 1885 lead was discovered in that vicinity, and after prospecting it was found that the region was rich in lead ore. The Doe Run Lead Company was organized and commenced a mine there. They operated a number of shafts and built large reduction works for handling the ore. The mine attracted large numbers of settlers and the town grew rapidly. It is the southern terminus of the Mississippi River & Bonne Terre Railroad Company and is at a distance of three miles from the Belmont Branch of the Iron Mountain.

Oran

Oran is in Sylvania township, Scott county, on the Belmont Branch of the Iron Mountain and on the St. Louis & Gulf Branch of the Frisco. The first settlement here was called Sylvania. It was laid out as a town in 1868 and was first called St. Cloud. At a later time it was named Oran. It is on the level sandy ridge just east of the Scott county hills. There are large deposits of yellow ochre and at one time a paint factory was operated here. It has five general stores, other minor business establishments, large flouring mill, and the Bank of Oran with a capital of $25,000. The public school building is a brick structure of eight rooms and is well equipped. The present population of the town is 1,023.

Fornfelt

The two towns of Fornfelt and Illmo, Scott county, owe their existence to the building of the Thebes bridge and the consequent construction of the St. Louis, Southwestern Railway to this bridge. The first persons who made their home in what is now Fornfelt, were G. S. Cannon and A. Baudendistel. The town dates its settlement from September, 1904, and was incorporated as a town in the following May, the first mayor being Charles Hamm. At the present time there are four general stores together with some other business interests of minor character. There is one box factory which employs about a hundred and fifty men and turns out a large amount of box material. The Bank of Edna is one of the principal institutions of the town. It was organized in 1905 and has a capital of $15,000. Among the more important buildings are the two brick schoolhouses and the building occupied by the bank. The town is lighted by electricity and other improvements in the way of sidewalks and streets have been made. The possession of the railroad yards of the St. Louis Southwestern and St. Louis, Iron Mountain & Southern is shared by Fornfelt and Illmo, as the yards are between the two towns. They consist of round houses and machine shops and employ several hundred men forming one of the reasons of the prosperity of the towns. Fornfelt has experienced a rapid growth, sixty residences having been erected during 1911.

ILLMO

Just as is true of Fornfelt, Illmo owes its existence to the building of the Thebes bridge. It was settled in 1904 and incorporated in 1905, the first mayor being Phillip Ruebel. Among the first settlers were J. P. Lightner, Casper Roth and Charles Will. The merchants during the early period were B. Thomas, D. T. Titwell and Beggs Brothers. At the present time there are eight general stores and one factory. The Bank of Illmo is in a flourishing condition and takes care of the financial interests of the town. There is an electric light plant which supplies the residences, business houses, and also lights the streets. The more important buildings are the Southern Hotel, Lightner's Opera House and Crews building. The town of Illmo is the division headquarters for the St. Louis Southwestern and St. Louis, Iron Mountain Railroads.

CROWDER

The first settlers in Crowder, Scott county, were James Marshall, James H. Marshall, J. H. Denbow, W. H. Page, Lee and W. C. Wellman, E. Virgin, W. J. Page, S. W. Wisdom, T. A. Cooksey, S. P. Marshall, T. A. McCutchen, William Utley, Dr. C. C. Harris and Major McKinley. The first settlement in the town was made in 1897 and the town was incorporated in 1902, the first mayor being Sterling P. Marshall. The first stores in the town were conducted by James Marshall & Brother, Huddleson Store Company, and J. A. Rifner. There are now three general stores in the town. Besides these the principal business interests consist of a saw mill, hoop mill and stave factory. The town is situated in the midst of a farming community and draws its support from the farms about it. There is still more land to be opened up and no doubt the town will experience a growth with the cultivation of this land. The population is now 288.

KELSO

Kelso was settled in 1882 and incorporated as a town in 1904, the first mayor being A. L. Drury. Among the early settlers were John Blattle and Charles Roberts. The first merchants in the town were George G. Wright and A. Baudendistel. There is now one general store and the principal manufacturing establishment is a flour mill. The Farmers & Merchants Bank was established in 1903 and has a capital stock of $10,000. The town is in Scott county and is situated on the main line of the St. Louis Southwestern Railroad, and is also the southern terminus of the Cape Girardeau & Thebes Bridge Railroad.

BLODGETT

The settlement of Blodgett in Scott was made in 1869. It is situated on the Belmont branch of the St. Louis, Iron Mountain & Southern Railway. The men who laid out the town and were among its first residents were: W. B. Congleton, B. F. Marshall and Charles L. Stubbs. Marshall and Stubbs and W. R. Sherer were the early merchants. The town was incorporated in 1900 and Z. T. Wright was made the first mayor. There are now two general stores besides some drug stores and other business establishments. Both the general stores are of unusual size considering the population of the town, carrying stocks of goods which would be a credit to a city. The Blodgett Bank, which was organized in 1901, with a capital of $15,000, looks after the financial interests of the town. The present population is 422. Blodgett is situated in the midst of fine farming country and enjoys the distinction of shipping more watermelons than any other station in the world. During the season of 1911 there were shipped 600 cars of this fruit.

Morley

Morley is a town on the Belmont branch of the Iron Mountain in Scott, and was for a number of years the shipping point for the county seat, Benton. It was laid out as a town in 1869 and incorporated in 1872, the first mayor being James Bardwell. The first merchants were B. D. Gaither, W. A. Cade, Hughes and Watkins and J. T. Anderson & Brother. There are now three general stores and two cotton gins. The first mill was built by F. C. Martin & Brother. The town is situated in the midst of fine farming country and ships a great deal of surplus produce every year, including many cars of melons. The soil in the immediate vicinity of the town seems to be especially suited for the production of canteloupes. The Scott County Bank was organized in 1891 and has a capital of $15,000. The population is 494.

Chaffee

The town of Chaffee, in Scott county, was laid off in August, 1905. The land on which the town is situated was purchased by officials of the Frisco Railroad and laid off into town lots. Shortly after its establishment the town was made the division point of the Frisco road and the repair shops removed to this point from Cape Girardeau. The first mayor of the town was R. J. Wright and its first merchants were Wright Mercantile Company and H. A. Osman. Besides the smaller establishments, such as restaurants, drug stores, etc., there are four general stores in the town, all of them carrying complete stocks of goods. There are also two factories, one a general lumber manufacturing company, the other is engaged in the manufacture of hoops. Chaffee State Bank was organized in 1906 with a capital of $10,000. The town is lighted with electric lights. Among the important buildings are the Astoria Hotel, bank buildings and the offices of the railroad company. The town now has a population of 2,082.

Vanduser

Vanduser in Scott county is on the St. Louis & Gulf branch of the Frisco and is the terminus of the Bloomfield branch. It has a population of 338. The Bank of Vanduser was organized in 1907 and its capital stock is $10,000. The town is supported by the farming country around it which is very fertile and productive.

Dexter

Dexter is situated not far from the center of Stoddard county. It is on the east side of Crowley's ridge, the site of the town being about seventy-five or one hundred feet higher than the level plains to the east and south. It was laid out as a town in 1873. The advantages of the place for a town are very great and immediately after the site was surveyed a sale of lots took place and stores began to be opened. Among the early merchants were: R. P. Liles & Co., William Edwards, J. N. Miller, Sisel & Plaut, and Riggins & Co. At a later time the leading merchants were Miller, Ladd & Co., Dowdy & Co., Edw. Webber, T. N. Doherty, R. A. Sisler & Co., J. J. Dowdy, T. S. Ulen, A. E. Bohlcke, E. E. Carter and J. R. Clark. Copper & Jorndt were millers. Miller, Ladd & Co. also operated a grist mill and cotton gin, and were dealers in cotton.

The great advantage which Dexter possessed at the early period and the cause of its rapid growth was the railroad. It was located on the Cairo branch of the Iron Mountain between Bird's Point and Poplar Bluff. It thus had connection with the river and with the main line of the Iron Mountain to St. Louis. The transportation problem, the greatest which had to be solved for towns and communities in this part of the state when they were situated away from the river, was not troublesome in the early history of Dexter. Consequently it grew rapidly. It was in a position to seize a large part of the trade from Stoddard and Dunklin counties which had formerly gone to Cape Girardeau and New Madrid. To the south of Dexter was the great sand ridge over which travel was easy. It was separated from Dunklin county by Taylor and Gum sloughs, it is true, but these were easily crossed so that no real obstacle was interposed except distance. This was much less than the citizens of that country had previously travelled to market so that there soon poured into Dexter a constantly increasing stream of cotton and other produce especially from Dunklin county. Much of the country around the town was suitable for wheat growing and a mill was built which brought wheat from places many miles distant. Much of this wheat had formerly been carried to Cape Girardeau or Bloomfield.

Not only was much produce brought to the town. Those who came to sell their products bought large quantities of goods. The greater part of the country to the south was supplied with practically all imported goods from Dexter. This trade brought wealth to the town. Its merchants were prosperous and added to their stocks.

The first blow to the prosperity of the town came with the building of the Little River Valley & Arkansas Railroad from New Madrid to Malden. The latter town was nearer to the cotton regions and soon absorbed much of the trade which had formerly come to Dexter.

Two things, however, contributed to the growth of the town perhaps more than was lost. One of these was the building of St. Louis Southwestern Railway north from Malden, first to Delta, later to Gray's Point and eventually to Thebes. This provided railroad competition and direct connection by through trains to St. Louis. The other fact important in the development of the town was the drainage movement which resulted in the opening of vast quantities of the richest and most productive lands. These lands were naturally tributary to Dexter and the increased trade which they brought added to the town's wealth. Large wood-working plants were erected and are still in operation.

For years there was bitter rivalry between Dexter and Bloomfield. The latter town was without railroad facilities for years after Dexter had acquired them, but it was the county seat, was older and seemed more firmly established. The people of Dexter made efforts to move the county seat to their town. Failing in this they secured the passage of a law requiring two sessions of the circuit court to be held in Dexter and two in Bloomfield each year. To provide a place for the meetings of the court they erected a fine brick building. The arrangement was not found satisfactory and the law was repealed. The building which was thus left vacant was sold to the Christian church for use as a college building. After some efforts to establish a college the church sold it to the public school and it is now in use as a high school building.

The schools of Dexter have always been

among the best. The first organization for a public school was made in 1874 and from that time much interest and attention has been given to the schools. At the present time there are two good brick buildings, a well organized system of grade schools, and a good four years high school.

Besides the two railroads Dexter has some good public roads. From Dexter to Bloomfield a distance of seven miles there is a fine rock road, and there are other good roads also. At present there are about seventy business establishments of various kinds. They include large general stores, drug stores, furniture and hardware stores, saw mills, heading and stave factories, handle factories, other minor establishments and two banks. The Bank of Dexter was organized in 1892 and has a capital stock of $50,000. The Citizens Bank, organized in 1903, has a capital of $30,000. There are the usual church organizations with good buildings. The town has good streets, sidewalks, water-works, electric lights, and all the conveniences of modern cities of its size. Its present population is 2,322.

Advance

Advance in the extreme northern part of Stoddard county is on the Hoxie branch of the Frisco. It has a population of 621 and is a thriving and prosperous town. The farming country around it is very productive and its people are enterprising. The Bank of Advance was chartered in 1902. Its capital is $20,000. The Advance Exchange Bank with a capital of $15,000, was chartered in 1909. Advance has good public schools, about twenty business establishments, the usual church organizations.

Bell City

Bell City in Stoddard county, is a town on the St. Louis Southwestern, laid out soon after the building of that line. Its present population is 316. It has one bank with a capital of $10,000. There are churches, a public school, hotel, four stores, and other smaller business establishments.

Brownwood, situated at the crossing of the Zalma and Bloomfield branch and the Hoxie branch, is a saw mill town.

Ardeola, Idalia, Dudley, Headquarters and Avert are other Stoddard county villages.

Bernie

The town of Bernie in Stoddard county, is situated on the main line of the St. Louis Southwestern Railroad between Dexter and Malden. The first settlement was made there in the year 1878. It was incorporated as a village in 1890 and as a city in 1908, the first mayor being L. J. Turner. Among the early settlers were A. H. Slayton, W. L. Smith, Morgan Wood, T. J. Bailey, T. L. Whitehead, W. S. Russell, J. A. Walker, W. L. Schutt, M. C. Dooin and J. M. Barnett. The early merchants were W. L. Smith, W. L. Schutt, M. C. Dooin, McFadden, Louis Klein and T. L. Whitehead. There are now eighteen general stores in the town and also a cotton gin and grist mill. The financial interests of the town are cared for by the Bank of Bernie which was chartered in 1901, and has a capital stock of $20,000. The town has just completed the erection of a $10,000 public school building and is conducting a good school including a high school. Besides the general interests which we have mentioned there are other minor business establishments including a drug store and undertaking establishment. There are Baptist, Christian, Methodist and General Baptist churches. The population of the town is 742.

PUXICO

The first settlement at Puxico in Stoddard county was made September 29, 1883, and the town was incorporated June 2, 1884. The first mayor was E. L. Hawks. Among the early settlers were J. A. Hickman, E. L. Hawks, W. C. Clark, George Eaton, Henry Jeffords, Prior Daniels, John W. Reed, William Gray and H. B. Purcell. The business interests of the town were, for the first period, in the hands of J. A. Hickman, John Reed, H. B. Purcell and T. J. Moss. There are now four general stores, handle factory, flour mill, electric light plant, canning factory, saw mill, and planing mill. Among the important buildings are the opera house, three churches, brick school building and a lodge hall. The town is situated on the Hoxie branch of the Frisco Railroad and has a population of 814. The Bank of Puxico was organized in 1898 and has a capital stock of $25,000. One newspaper, the *Puxico Index*, is published in the town.

IRONDALE

Irondale, in Washington county, was laid out in 1857 by Hon. John G. Scott, who erected a large iron furnace there. It is on the Iron Mountain Railway, ten miles southeast of Potosi, the county seat.

There are three churches, Catholic, Cumberland Presbyterian, and Methodist, a public school, hotel, five stores, and a mill. The Bank of Irondale was organized in 1901 with a capital stock of $10,000. The population is now 338.

MINERAL POINT

Mineral Point is a village in Washington county, four miles east of Potosi and is the terminus of the Potosi branch of the Iron Mountain Railway. It was laid out in 1857 by the Hon. John Evans. It has a school, a Methodist Episcopal church, a hotel, four stores, and its population is 290.

RICHWOODS

Richwoods is a village in Washington county near the Jefferson county line. It has recently taken on new life and is becoming more important. A bank called the Bank of Richwoods, was organized in 1910 with a capital stock of $10,000. There are ten business establishments, a church, and a mill. The population is about 300. Other villages and towns are Baryties, Tiff, Hopewell, Shirley, Summit, and Undine.

CHAONIA

Chaonia, in Wayne county on the Hoxie branch of the Frisco, is a town which sprung up around a saw-mill about 1899. After the timber was cleared away the farming interests began to support the town and it is now growing. The population is 363. There are stores, a church, mills, and the Bank of Chaonia with a capital stock of $10,000. It was chartered in 1907.

LEEPER

Leeper in Wayne county, is the junction point of the Missouri Southern with the Iron Mountain. It was named in honor of Col. W. T. Leeper, a northern soldier in the Civil war. At one time it was the seat of extensive saw mills, but these have disappeared. It is now supported by farming and railroad interests. There are four stores, a hotel, churches, and other establishments. The population is 360.

MILL SPRING

Mill Spring, a few miles south of Leeper on the Iron Mountain, was once an important lumber manufacturing town. The mills have closed down and the town is supported only by the farming country. It is near a large and beautiful spring from which it takes its name. The spring was once used to furnish power for the mill. The population is now given as 360.

WILLIAMSVILLE

Williamsville, an important town in Wayne county, is situated at the junction of the Iron Mountain main line with the Williamsville, Greenville and St. Louis Railroad, and also on the Hoxie branch of the Frisco. Its transportation facilities are such as to make it a good town in time, as the country develops in a farming way. For years it was supported by mills which used up the large forest of pine timber. Later the iron industry became important and large reduction works were built for handling the iron ore. These have not yet proved permanent and the town depends largely upon its railroad and farming interest. There are five stores, a mill, two hotels, churches and the Williamsville State Bank with a capital of $10,000, which was chartered in 1905.

SECTION VII

Educational Institutions

CHAPTER XXXI

EARLY SCHOOLS

WORK OF THE SUBSCRIPTION SCHOOLS — ACADEMIES AT STE. GENEVIEVE, JACKSON, POTOSI, NEW MADRID, PERRYVILLE, POINT PLEASANT, CAPE GIRARDEAU, BLOOMFIELD, POPLAR BLUFF AND CHARLESTON.

Up to 1804 when Louisiana became a part of the territory of the United States there had been but few attempts made to provide schools. We have seen that occasional schools were conducted in Ste. Genevieve and in the Ramsay settlement in Cape Girardeau district and perhaps in a few other places. These schools, however, were very inefficient. They were conducted for only a very short period of time, usually only two or three months, and were taught by whatever persons seemed able to spare the time. The course of study included only the merest rudiments of education and each school was conducted entirely separate and distinct from all the others. There seems to have been no effort made to preserve a record of the work done by students and when school was begun in any year no attention was given to what had been accomplished before.

With the transfer to the United States and consequent inflow of settlers from the states east of the river more attention came to be paid to the matter of education. It was natural that this should be the case. These settlers had lived where schools were held in high esteem and where efforts were being made to provide systems of education. They accordingly made every effort to establish schools as far as that was possible.

The history of the development of education from this time is concerned with two movements: The first of these was a continuation of the method formerly in use, that is, to provide schools independent of the state. Alongside of this there was a movement to form a system of public education which seems to have come into the state from Virginia and perhaps owes its existence more to Thomas Jefferson than to any other one man. The movement for state education found expression in the act of purchase itself and all through the history of the state we find that people are giving their attention to the matter of building up the public schools. In spite of many attempts, however, and much work accomplished, it is hardly possible to speak of an organized system of public schools before the period of the Civil war. In fact, it was not until 1874 that really adequate provision came to be made for public education. Before that time the public schools existed side by side with private schools and were in most places of far less importance in the educational history of the country than the latter.

Work of the Subscription Schools

It is intended here to give an account of the attempts to provide schools independent of the state and later to discuss the growth of the public schools system itself. As has been said, a few schools had been conducted in scattering settlements before the transfer to the United States. These schools were taught by teachers who were paid by subscription, or else by some priest or nun of the church.

Private schools in Southeast Missouri of an elementary character were usually either subscription schools or else the elementary department of an academy. There were two kinds of academies, those chartered by the state and those which existed without a charter.

What we have termed subscription schools were probably the most common form of the early elementary schools. They were taught usually by men who claimed certain attainments in learning and for a longer or shorter period devoted themselves to instruction. These teachers were professional teachers in that they supported themselves in part by teaching but most of them turned their attention during the greater part of the year to other pursuits. These schools were usually conducted in the winter time when it was impossible to do much of anything else while in other seasons of the year both teacher and pupils were otherwise engaged. There were two principal methods of organizing and conducting such schools. Either a teacher provided room in some dwelling house and secured, by personal canvass, a sufficient number of subscribers to make it worth while to conduct the school (the patrons having no organization of their own), or else, and more commonly, those families in the community which desired to send children to school banded themselves together, appointed one of their number as trustee and provided a place for conducting the school. This trustee was empowered by the voluntary association which he represented, to employ a teacher and to exercise a degree of supervision over his actions. This was the most common plan and it is perhaps not too much to say that in many parts of Southeast Missouri the schools thus organized and conducted were the most important factors in educational work during all the period preceding the war. Even after the war this plan was still used in many places. The writer well remembers that his first school days were spent in such a school. The house had been built by voluntary association of neighbors who appointed one of their number as a trustee. He hired the teacher and when necessary discharged him. The house itself was well built and for the time, excellently seated and furnished. This was at a period long after the war.

The state exercised no control over these schools and of course contributed nothing to their support. No license to teach was required of those who conducted them, and accordingly the only requirements to be met by the would-be teacher were such as were established in the community itself. These requirements varied in the different communities, and from time to time. Quite naturally, however, they were not usually high. In many cases, especially in the early days, those who taught were almost wholly incompetent. They possessed but the merest smattering of knowledge and in some cases the moral standards set for them were very low. In another chapter we have quoted from Peck as to the character of some who conducted schools. Such conditions were inevitable, however. It was entirely beyond the limited means of the community to pay sufficient salary to attract men of education and ability as teachers, even had there existed the ability to set up standards by which to judge the work of the school.

In the more populous and wealthy communities were to be found schools of a much better character conducted by men of learning and enthusiasm. Many of the educated ministers of the country like Peck and Flint taught schools such as we have described. Their work was of high grade and through their efforts there gradually grew up standards by which the work of the schools was measured. Jackson early became famous for its good schools and had among its early teachers were Henry Sanford, Edward Criddle, Mrs. John Scripps, Mrs. Wathen, Mrs. Rhoda Ranney and Dr. Barr.

The most famous and perhaps the best of the early schools was that known as the Asylum, conducted near Ste. Genevieve. It was opened in 1815 by Joseph Hertich. Hertich was a native of Switzerland and brought with him to this country the ideas of Pestalozzi. He seems to have been a born teacher and his school soon became famous on account of the superior grade of teaching which he did. A large number of his pupils afterward became famous. Among them were General A. C. Dodge of the United States army, his brother, Henry Dodge, afterward a member of the United States senate, and Lewis F. Linn, the famous senator from Missouri. It is doubtful if any other school in Southeast Missouri since that time has had so large a number of boys who afterward reached eminence in one station or another.

These subscription schools improved as the years passed and the country grew in wealth and population, making possible better salaries. The establishment of academies, seminaries and colleges, in Southeast Missouri, together with the more liberal salaries, made it possible for men who wished to teach to prepare themselves for the work. There was, however, still great room for improvement. In many of the communities of this part of the state, as well as in other sections, we find schools conducted by men of very little education. Schools were conducted for but a short time and had only a very limited course of study. There is appended here a copy of an agreement drawn up between a teacher and the patrons regarding the conduct of school. It is inserted as showing some of the manner in which these schools were arranged for, and also as casting light on the conditions of education in some parts of the state.

A true copy a Shool article Commenced on the 14th of July 1847 in Greenville Township Wayne County Mo. by Thomas Taylor for six months.—

1st. I Thomas Taylor promise to teach they Children of this Neighborhood to the number of Twenty five if that many can be made up, or will commence with twenty to teach six months at the rate of Two dollars and fifty cents per scholar per quarter or three months. I will teach spelling, reading, writing, the rudiments of arithmetic, then the single rule of three, double rule of three Practice, Tare and tret, simple Interest and compound Interest, also teach the vernacular Language, teach five days in each week and if any time is lost by Thomas Taylor by sickness or otherwise to be made up before the Experation of Teaching.

2nd. We the undersigned employers to this article promise to pay to Thomas Taylor the above sum per scholar on or before the experation of teaching. I will receive Cash, Pork, Beefhides, Deerskins, Mink skins, Raccoon skins or any fur if good, also woolen Jeans Cloth, shirting cloth or Young Cattle one year not over, a young Beef Steer or Cow. The defirent articles as above to be delivered me at Mr. Eli Cowans an on or before the experation. the Schoolhouse to be Comfortably fixed with a good roof writing Tables or Benches. also seats Benches to sit on. Fuel furnished when needed.

Employers Names	No. of scholars	Remarks
Samuel Sutherlin	2	
E. W. Cowan	2	
Conrad Shearheart	2	
Cornelius Mabrey	2	
Isam Sutherlin	1	
James Kirkpatrick	5	
Andrew H. Forister	1	
Wm. Lee	1	
Ferbley Lee	1	
William Hawes	2	
John Days (three months)	1	
Samuel Baker	1	

SCHOOL REGULATIONS

1st They scholars to come to school at half past 7 o Clock in the morning or as soon after as circumstances will permit.

2nd They will come with clean hands and face hair Combed.

3rd When assembled at the school house there will be no Discoursing of laughing, but every scholar to attend to their lessons and study

4th When at play they will play without hurting one another. Climbing trees throwing stones or going into water will be prohibited

5th It is hoped that every scholar will be Guided by these Rules.

Signed T Taylor, tutor.

In judging these subscription schools it must be kept in mind that they were wholly voluntary schools. They were defective and failed in large part to accomplish the work which ought to have been done. Their terms were short, their equipment inadequate, and there existed no standards for those who taught in them; and yet they were the outgrowth of a local feeling favorable to education. This part of the state was working out its educational problems for itself, every community independent of every other community and of the state. People devoted time and money to the solution of the problem of education. Other schools organized on a different plan, better equipped with standards imposed from above would have been much superior in many ways. It is doubtful, however, if such schools had been conducted whether they would have met the needs of the communities in which they existed as well as did the crude and inefficient schools developed by the people themselves. Out of these schools there has grown a system of education which is justly the pride of Missouri. That system is a growth, it was not manufactured and imposed upon the people, but is the expression of their own feeling and the working out of their own ideas along the line of education.

Side by side with these subscription schools there were developed in certain communities, church or parochial schools. Wherever there were strong organizations of Catholics or Lutherans there were always to be found these schools. They were attached to the church in some way, usually a separate building was provided for them, and they were conducted by a priest of the church or by one of the nuns. These schools are still to be found in this part of the state. In all the Catholic communities are separate parochial schools conducted under the direct supervision of the church itself. The largest of these schools, as well as the oldest, is that at Ste. Genevieve, which has an enrollment of more than three hundred pupils every year.

ACADEMIES

The early settlers in Missouri were not content with the establishment of subscription schools for elementary education, they also began the development of schools of secondary character as well. The south, from which Missouri received a large number of immigrants at the period when Missouri was being populated, held to what has been denominated the academy idea; that is to say that education was not necessarily provided by the state for the masses of the people but that provision should be made by private munificence for the erection and maintenance of academies where were educated the children of the well-to-do. This idea was of course a development of the English notion concerning education. The academies that sprung up over the South and in the North also were feeble copies of the great English public schools which were of course not public schools at all, but schools in which the children of the rich and of the noble were educated. This had developed in the South side by side with the idea of public education. We find the public schools spoken of somewhat contemptuously at times as the free schools. When serious attention began to be given to education in Missouri the earliest attempts were to found academies. These academies were secondary schools according to the plans on which they were organized, but they all had attached to them a department for elementary instruction. It is estimated that within the whole state there were chartered at least 110 academies before the year 1875.

The first academy chartered in southeast Missouri was that at Ste. Genevieve. In 1808 the governor and other territorial officers granted to certain citizens of Ste. Genevieve a charter for the establishment of an academy. Certain restrictions were placed upon the trustees. They were to make no religious test in the employment of teachers, they were not to have theology taught, and they were to provide free instruction to children of the very poor and of Indians. A stone building for the use of the school was begun at this time but not completed until later. No school was conducted under the charter until Bishop DuBourg opened a school in 1818.

In 1854 the old building which had been begun and only partly completed for the academy was finished by General Firmin A. Rozier, the school was conducted under his direction and was in a flourishing condition until it was suspended on account of the war; it was not reopened after the war. This building was remodeled and occupied by General Rozier as a residence. In 1837 the Loretto Sisters established a school for girls called the school of Our Lady of Mount Carmel, this school was conducted in the building known as the Detchemendy house. In 1858 the Sisters of St. Joseph opened a school known as the St. Francois de Sales Academy; it was conducted in a frame building until 1872 when a large four-story brick structure was erected.

In 1817 the territorial assembly chartered an academy at Potosi and another at Jackson. The trustees of the school at Potosi were authorized to conduct a public lottery for its support.

From this time until 1875 academies flourished. Some account of the more important and famous ones is given here.

The first school house in Jackson was a small log building erected upon the site of the present school lot, soon after the establishment of the town. The commissioners conveyed this lot in accordance with the special act of the territorial assembly of January 30, 1817, to Joseph McFerron, Zenas Priest, Thomas Neale, Joseph Seawell and Thomas Stewart as trustees. In 1820 a charter of incorporation was granted to the Jackson Academy with David Armour, Joseph Frizzell, Thomas Neale, V. B. DeLashmutt and William Surrell as trustees; nothing was done, however, concerning this school further than the simple act of incorporation. There were a number of private schools conducted; the first grammar school was taught by Henry

Sanford, other teachers were Mrs. John Scrips, Mrs. Edward Criddle, Mr. Wathen and Miss Rhoda Ranney. The Jackson Academy was incorporated again in 1839, the trustees being P. R. Garret, Edward Criddle, Nathan Vanhorn, John Martin, Johnson Ranney, Charles W. Welling and N. W. Watkins. The academy opened with J. G. Gardiner as principal and Miss Elmira Gregory assistant; Mr. Gardiner was a very skillful teacher and the school became one of the leading schools in this part of the state; he was succeeded, after five or six years, by Rev. D. E. Y. Rice. The academy was operated until the war; at that time it was transferred to the Methodist church but owing to some bitter feeling the act of transfer was not confirmed and after the close of the war the buildings and grounds were transferred to the trustees of the public school.

The Potosi Academy was rechartered December 24, 1824. Like the other institutions of its kind it was empowered to take and hold property and to establish and conduct a school. No religious restrictions were made in employment of teachers and all students who offered themselves were to be received. The first body of trustees of this academy had among its members men who were very influential in the early history of Missouri. These trustees were William H. Ashley, Lionel Browne, John Rice Jones, Moses Austin, David Wheeler, Moses Bates, Benjamin Elliott, James Austin, William Perry, John McIllvaine, Andrew Scott, John Hawkins and Abraham Brunke.

An academy was chartered at New Madrid January 11, 1841. It did not differ in the scope of its powers, its purposes or the limitations thrown about it, from the other academies in the state; its trustees were Robert G. Watson, Henry Toney, Richard Jones Waters, Alphonso Delorederi, Richard Barkley, Robert D. Dawson and Frederick C. Butler.

February 25, 1845, the general assembly incorporated an academy to be conducted at Perryville, with the following trustees: James Rice, Reuben Shelby, Ferdinand Rozier, James A. Rutledge, Edward M. Holden, Hiram Block, Dr. Wheeler, Albert G. Abernathy, William McCombs and John Layton.

Three days after the incorporation of the academy at Perryville a similar institution was incorporated to be conducted at Point Pleasant, in New Madrid county; its trustees were Urban C. Spencer, John Woodward, H. D. Maulsby, Thomas S. Bancroft, Godfrey LeSieur and John Martin.

In 1830 the people of Cape Girardeau elected George Henderson, Abner Vansant, Ezra J. Dutch, Alfred P. Ellis and Levi L. Lightner as trustees to purchase a lot and build a school house. They bought the lot at the corner of Fountain and Merriweather streets, now occupied by the Lorimier school, and on this lot erected a small brick building. In February, 1843, a school known as Cape Girardeau academy was incorporated, with Hiram L. Sloan, P. H. Davis, W. S. Watson, E. B. Cassilly, I. R. Wathen, Thomas J. Rodney and B. M. Horrell as trustees. In 1849 the school known as the Washington Female seminary was incorporated; its trustees were George Trask, Edward Dobbins, Noah Handy, John B. Martin, John D. Cook, Wilson Brown and Samuel A. Hill. Both these institutions were maintained until the Civil war. Among the principal teachers in them were Lyman B. Andrews, L. H. Andrews, and J. J. Gardiner. They both occupied the old building known as the Ellis Hotel.

The first schools in Bloomfield were taught in the Methodist church. In 1853 the Bloomfield Educational Society was organized with S. G. Kitchen, Orson Bartlett, Henry Miller, D. B. Miller and Michael A. Wilson as trustees. They proceeded to erect a two-story frame building and conducted a seminary until the war. After the close of the war the only schools in the town, for a time, were some private schools taught at the seminary building.

The first school in Poplar Bluff was established in 1869 by the Butler County Educational Society, a corporate body, with Green L. Poplin, J. W. Baldwin, James Tolds, J. M. Henderson, J. M. Spence, B. F. Turner, J. S. Ferguson and G. T. Bartlett as trustees. The school which was conducted was known as the Black river Seminary; the first principal was H. McKinnon, and was conducted in a two-story frame building erected for school purposes. This seminary was succeeded by the public schools.

In 1870 the Charleston Classical Academy was opened in Charleston. It was the enterprise of a number of leading citizens of the town that led to the formation of a company and the foundation of the academy. A large brick building was erected for the school, which was under the supervision of Justin Williams. The academy, however, did not prosper. The feeling among the people was in favor of public schools by this time, so the academy was closed, and the building was rented to the public school.

CHAPTER XXXII

PUBLIC SCHOOLS

FOUNDATION OF PUBLIC SYSTEM—THE STATE COMMISSION—SALE OF LANDS—LAWS OF 1853—PROVISIONS OF 1874—GROWTH OF THE SYSTEM — SOUTHEAST MISSOURI TEACHERS' ASSOCIATION—FIRST SCHOOLS IN VARIOUS COUNTIES.

Jefferson's idea that the state, in order to preserve itself, must provide for the education of all of its children was brought to Missouri by immigrants from Virginia. It found expression in the act which provided for the transfer of Louisiana to the United States. In that act it was said that the government of the United States would care for the education of the people. When the dissatisfied settlers in the district of Louisiana assembled at St. Louis soon after the transfer and drew up a memorial of grievances to Congress, one of the things included in that memorial was a request that Congress should provide means of support for the public schools. The establishment of the academy at Ste. Genevieve in 1808 by the governor and territorial judges, while not a provision for public education, expressed in part the desire of the people for schools which should be, to a certain extent at least, under public supervision.

FOUNDATION OF PUBLIC SYSTEM

In 1812 the Congress of the United States created Missouri a special territory of the second class and in the act it was said "that schools and the means of education shall be encouraged and provided for from the public lands of the United States within the territory as Congress may direct." Missouri remained a territory for eight years after this time but there was very little accomplished in the way of provision for the support of schools; some things, however, were done looking in the direction of public education. In 1817 the territorial legislature incorporated the city of St. Louis as a special school district with seven trustees to manage affairs, and to this special school district Congress donated some valuable tracts of land which lay within and near the town and was known as United States common lands. This donation should have been of very great value in supporting the schools, but the lands were badly managed so that the income derived from them was very small.

When the Missouri Compromise was framed in 1820 and the state was authorized to frame a constitution it was declared in the act of Congress that schools should be forever encouraged in the new state and the legislature of the state was directed to take steps to preserve from waste or damage such lands as have been or should hereafter be granted for the use of schools. A further provision of this act was "one or more schools shall be established in each congressional township as soon as necessary and the children of the poor shall be taught free."

When Missouri was finally admitted into the Union in 1821, the act of admission set aside every sixteenth section of land within the state, together with seventy-two sections of saline land for school purposes. The lands thus granted amounted to 1,254,200 acres and it was directed that the land was to be sold and the proceeds invested for the use of the schools. This was a princely donation and coupled with the direction to establish township schools seems to have been enough to put a system of education in actual operation within the state. Several things prevented this, however, one of them was the inherent difficulty in creating a system of schools at a single stroke together with the fact that the lands, although vast in extent, were at that time not very valuable. The lands thus granted, however, have since become exceedingly valuable, but at that time it was practically impossible to sell them at even a nominal price.

These things prevented any rapid progress among the schools for a number of years. In 1825 the state legislature made the first contribution to the school law of the state. The act was designed to carry out the provision in the congressional act of the admission and provided that each congressional township should form a school district to be under the control of the county court in school matters. A further provision set aside all rents from school lands and all fines, penalties and forfeitures as a school fund.

In this same period extending from 1820 to 1833 the legislature established about fifty schools similar in character to the one established in the city of St. Louis. The support of these schools, however, was a very great problem and a difficult matter owing to the circumstances which we have mentioned. In almost every case they had to depend upon private donations and tuition fees.

THE STATE COMMISSION

In the year 1833 a great forward step was taken in the matter of public education within the state. On the 26th day of January of that year the legislature passed an act authorizing the governor to appoint a commission of three persons whose duty it was to study public education and to draw up a plan for public schools. This was during the administration of Governor Daniel Dunklin of Washington county, and he appointed as such commission Joseph Hertich, John J. Lowery and Abel R. Corbin. Hertich was the famous teacher of the private school called the Asylum, near Ste. Genevieve, and was perhaps as well informed on matters pertaining to elementary education than any other man in the state. This commission made a report in 1834 to the governor and through his efforts it was adopted by the general assembly in 1835. This report, as adopted by the assembly, provided for a system of schools. Among its provisions were the creation of a board of commissioners for literary purposes; it was to consist of the governor, secretary of state, auditor, treasurer, and attorney general. This was really the first state board of education, though it was not known by that name. It was further provided that schools should continue at least six months in each year and that school expenses should be paid from the school funds of each county, these funds to be the sums derived from the rent of the school lands and from fines and forfeitures, and the people of the county were authorized to vote, by two-thirds majority, a tax of three and one-third cents on each one hundred dollars for school purposes. The schools were to be under the official direction of a board of three trustees in each district, who were empowered to employ teachers, appoint visitors, and make other necessary arrangements for the school. The report also arranged a curriculum for the schools and directed that reading, writing and arithmetic, geography, English grammar and other branches should be taught as the funds might justify. Theology was excepted and excluded in positive terms from the list of subjects which might be taught in these schools.

Sale of Lands

In 1837 the general assembly provided that the funds derived from the sale of the saline lands and the fund known as the United States revenue fund, should be invested in stock of the Missouri State Bank. The income from this stock was set aside for school purposes, but it was directed by the legislature that it should not be distributed among the schools until the amount invested amounted to $500,000. This amount was reached in 1842 and the first distribution of the fund among the schools was made in that years. Sixty cents for each pupil was distributed among the thirteen counties of the state at that time.

In spite of these things which had been accomplished in the matter of education the people of the state were still concerned over the question and the legislature still gave attention and time to public schools. In 1839 it was enacted that a common school fund should be constituted and permission to sell the sixteenth section of the state lands was again given. Out of this provision of the law have grown the permanent school funds of the state. It was further provided that there should be chosen a state superintendent of schools who was to be elected by the senate and house of representatives for a term of two years. One of the duties of this state superintendent was the distribution of the state school moneys among the several counties of the state which maintained public schools.

Laws of 1853

These were the important provisions which laid the foundation for a public school system in the state, but they have been added to and the whole of the school law revised in 1853. At that time the schools were under the supervision of the state superintendent elected by the people and there was provided in each county a county commissioner of common schools. It was the duty of the latter officer to license teachers and to visit the schools in his county. The unit for the schools was still the congressional township, which, however, could be divided into school districts by vote of the people, and each district was authorized to select three trustees who were empowered to employ the teachers and supervise the financial affairs of the district.

It was provided, too, at this time, that twenty-five per cent of the general revenue of the state and the dividends from the funds invested in the Bank of the State of Missouri were to be apportioned to the several counties on a ratio based on the enumeration of children of school age. It was also provided that orphans and children of indigent parents might attend school free.

An effort was made at this time by the state superintendent to provide a uniform course of study for the schools; the effort, however, was unsuccessful. At this time there were in the entire state about 2,500 school districts and 300,000 children of school age, of whom only 125,000 were enrolled in the schools. It has been pointed out by competent students of the educational history of the state that the great defect in all of this legislation was the failure to provide for a direct tax on property for school purposes. Such a tax could be levied provided it received a two-thirds vote in the entire county. This provision made it practically impossible to levy such a tax.

PROVISIONS OF 1874

Soon after the constitution was adopted for Missouri in 1865, it was found necessary to reconstruct the school system which had fallen to pieces during the Civil war. An elaborate system was worked out and embodied in the constitution adopted in that year. This system, while commendable in many ways, had what was practically a fatal defect in that it did not put the responsibility for the conduct of the schools and their support directly upon the people in the several districts. It was not until the year 1874 that the present system of Missouri schools was finally worked out. The legislature recognized the importance of thrusting the responsibility of the schools upon the people themselves. The school district was made the unit and to the people in the district was committed the power to vote taxes and to carry on the schools. With some modifications this system survives to the present day. It has its defects and the time has possibly come when a larger unit than the present school district is both desirable and necessary.

GROWTH OF THE SYSTEM

Since 1875, when the system was outlined, there has been a very great change in the educational situation in Southeast Missouri. All territory has been organized into school districts and in practically every district a school house has been built and a school is maintained for at least six months in every year. The people no longer depend upon subscription schools, the wealth of the entire community is taxed to support a school open to all the children of the district. The teachers are no longer selected in a haphazard way, but are required to secure a license to teach from the state before being permitted to give instruction in the public schools. The first great work of this period was the organization and development of a system of elementary schools all over this section of the state; the past fifteen years have seen the development of secondary education in a manner commensurate with the growth of elementary schools before that time. Up till about 1895, very little attention was paid in Southeast Missouri to public high schools; they were practically unknown here. Since that time high schools have been developed in all the larger towns, well equipped and providing a good secondary education for those who attend them. Even the smaller towns are doing some high school work so that there is to be found scarcely a single community with a population of as many as 300 that does not carry on from one to three years of high school work. These high schools are exerting as great influence as almost any other single thing for the improvement of the graded schools. At the present time there are fourteen schools in Southeast Missouri which have been classified as first class, and there are thirty-six other schools doing high school work.

In 1908 the general assembly passed two laws which are exerting a great influence upon the school system. One of these provided that in every county there should be elected a county superintendent of schools, to whom was to be given general supervision of the schools. No other step in the history of the schools has exerted a greater influence for their uplift than the provision for supervision. Along with this law providing for county superintendents, was passed a law known as the compulsory attendance law, requiring children between the ages of eight and fourteen to attend school, unless excused by reason of ill health or other necessities. This law, while defective in some ways, has undoubtedly exerted an influence favorable to more uniform attendance in the schools.

As we have intimated, there is a feeling that we have outgrown the old form of organization which makes the small district the unit of school work and certain provisions of amended school laws make it possible for districts to combine either for the support of an elementary and high school or simply for the purpose of supporting a central high school, the elementary schools in the district being retained as formerly. So far, this possibility of consolidating districts has not been made use of in Southeast Missouri; it seems, however, that before long a number of districts will make use of this authority and unite for the support of better schools.

One other thing in connection with the public school system that is worthy of note is the custom of graduating from the schools those students who complete eight years of common school work. It is believed that this graduation aids school attendance, and so far as it has been tried it bears out the promise which it made. In those counties where the graduating of eighth grade pupils is encouraged and the exercises made interesting it becomes less and less difficult to keep the older students in the school. This movement seems to have been originated in Southeast Missouri and this part of the state is keeping up with the rest of the state in this particular matter. In 1910 there were graduated from the rural schools more than 1,000 pupils.

It is a far cry from the old subscription schools of early territorial Missouri with their lack of equipment, short terms, inadequate courses of study and usually incompetent teachers giving the poorest and most meagre instruction to a handful of students, to the great educational system of Southeast Missouri as it is today. In 1910, twenty counties in this part of the state kept in operation 1,305 schools, in which more than 90,000 pupils received instruction. These schools were conducted for the most part in fairly good houses with reasonable amount of equipment and by teachers whose experience is something of a warrant for their ability to instruct. Once the possibilities of education were confined to the favored few whose wealth and social position enabled them to procure such education as the times afforded, but now the door of the schools has been opened to practically every child in this part of the state and he may procure, at the state's expense, not only a primary education but a good secondary education. Generous provision has been made for giving academic and professional training. Many problems in education are yet unsolved and perhaps unsolvable, yet it is clearly evident that the progress in these matters in the one hundred years of school history has been little short of marvelous. What further developments may be made it is not possible to predict. There seems an evident determination, however, on the part of the people to provide such a system of education as makes it possible for every child to be instructed not only in common schools but also in secondary schools.

Southeast Missouri Teachers' Association

Two agencies should be mentioned here which have contributed much to the rapid growth of schools and educational sentiment. These are the State Normal School at Cape Girardeau, and the Southeast Missouri Teachers' Association. The history of the former is given in another place and only a few words may be said regarding the latter. It was hoped that a complete account of its early history might be given. Owing to the unfortunate loss of its early records this is impossible. The association was organized in 1874 and owes its existence to the initiative of Rev. N. B. Henry, at that time a teacher in this part of the state. From the first it has held annual meetings and by its insistence on standards, its inspirational meetings, its forum for the exchange of ideas, has promoted the best interests of education in this part of the state. Its thirty-seventh annual meeting was held in Farmington in November, 1911. More than 400 teachers were in attendance; and in enthusiasm, value of its program, and general uplift to those in attendance it equaled if it did not surpass any previous meeting. This session was presided over by Supt. W. H. Hargrove of Bloomfield.

It is readily seen from a study of the actual schools that the various acts of the general assembly favoring education at public expense failed to establish actual schools. The great drawback through all these years was the lack of funds. Private schools and academies supplied about all the facilities for education given to the youth of this part of the state. In some sections these were wanting so that no chance for schooling was afforded.

First Schools in Various Counties

Butler county seems to have had only a few scattered subscription schools until the establishment of the Black River Seminary, and the public schools system was not really put into operation till 1875.

In Carter county there were a few private schools before 1874. In that year it was reported to the state superintendent of public schools that there were in the county 531 children of school age, 99 of whom were in school; at the same time there were said to be 25 teachers who were working at an average salary, for male teachers, of $16 a month and for female teachers for $10 a month. The report further disclosed the fact that there were three school houses in the entire county having a total valuation of $265, or an average of $53 each.

The public school system of Cape Girardeau, which has now come to be recognized as the equal of any in the state, owes its existence in its present form to the action of the city taken on the 24th of January, 1867. At that time there was a law in Missouri by which any city or town might organize for school purposes with certain special privileges. In order to avail themselves of the opportunity offered by this law a number of the leading citizens of Cape Girardeau issued a call for an election to determine whether the city should organize its schools in accordance with the terms of this act. The proposition was carried unanimously and a board of education was chosen. It consisted of George H. Cramer, H. G. Wilson, M. Dittlinger, G. G. Kimmell, N. C. Harrison and J. M. Cluley. The board employed F. M. Grove, who was then county school commissioner, as the principal of the school, and Mrs. E. Wooden and H. Cluley as assistants. The first term was opened April 1, 1867, in the basement of the Presbyterian church. In the following September another room was rented on Good Hope street and four assistant teachers were employed; in the next year the number was increased to eight. The superintendent at that time was William C. Provines, who held the position until 1870, when he was succeeded by D. L. Morrison. The Lorimier school building was completed in September, 1872. It was erected by D. F. Tiedeman at a cost of $15,000. This building was occupied by the public school and for a time by the normal school after the organization of the latter. The superintendents, in addition to those mentioned, have been J. B. Scott, Mrs. Hope, J. Q. A. Kimmell, W. T. Carrington, James H. Van Amburg, A. V. Hamilton, T. E. Joyce, E. E. McCullough, H. S. McCleary, C. T. Goodale, F. L. MacChesney, A. W. Lawson, John Laidlaw and G. H. Reavis. At the present time there are four schools besides the colored school. There has recently been organized a high school.

Private schools and the Arcadia high schools supplied the educational needs of Iron county prior to 1866. In that year an effort was begun to establish public schools.

The first school in Jefferson county was established in 1806 by Benjamin Thompson on Sandy Creek. School lands were sold in the county by the year 1821, but not in sufficient quantities to provide any real school funds. The townships were not organized into school districts until 1841, and the public schools were not really effective before the war.

The early schools of Madison county were all of the subscription variety except some parochial schools, one for girls and one for boys, carried on by the Catholic church. It is said that the system of public schools was not really organized so as to be effective until 1880.

The earliest school in Mississippi county was taught on Mathews Prairie. It was called Indian Grove school. The first teacher was Hartford Hayes. Other teachers connected with this school were John C. Thomas and James L. Moore. The public school system was organized in 1871.

St. Francois county had one of the first schools in this section. It was taught by Mrs. Sarah Murphy, in the Murphy settlement, about 1800. It was of course a private school conducted by this noble woman because she saw the great need of some schooling for the children of the community. The first public school in the county was organized at Farmington in 1870. At this time a two-story building was erected for the school.

Public schools in Jackson were established in 1867. The board of trustees was composed of Charles Welling, president; Jacob Kneibert, Jacob Tobler, James W. Cannon. Charles M. E. Slack and C. H. Friedrichs. The board employed James Alderson as the principal. The following year A. W. Milster was chosen principal, with Margaret A. Goode and Rev. Frederick Kies assistants. The academy building was used for the school until 1882 when the present brick building was erected. Among the early principals and superintendents were Rev. James Reid, A. S. Coker, A. R. Byrd, James A. Brooks and T. M. Wilson.

The public schools in Ste. Genevieve were not organized until 1856, though ten years previously a board of directors of common schools, consisting of Elroy S. LeCompte, Felix Valle, Francois C. Rozier, Eugene

Guibord and Ichabod Sergeant, had been appointed. When the school was first opened in 1856, it occupied what was known as the old Fort building. The first house was erected in 1860 and was afterward occupied by the colored schools. The present school house in Ste. Genevieve was erected in 1874, at a cost of $6,000. In the early days there was only one teacher, but the schools were graded in part soon after the war.

The public school system of Bloomfield was organized in 1871. The first board of directors was composed of H. H. Bedford, Samuel Montgomery, George S. Pollard, William Litton, John E. Liles and John L. Buck. The first teacher employed in the public school was B. B. Allen. The school was taught in the seminary building until 1886, when a frame house was erected, which has since then been superseded by a substantial brick structure. The present system of schools is recognized as being a very good one.

The next public school organized in Stoddard was that at Dexter. This was in 1874. Out of this early school has grown the fine system of the present day.

One of the first public schools in this part of the state was organized in Liberty township, Washington county, in 1854. The public schools system was reorganized about 1870. The other counties in the district had similar experiences with their schools. It is not now possible to give the date of the organization of the first public school in all of them, but in no case does it precede those we have given and in all of them the date of the real foundation of the system is about 1870.

CHAPTER XXXIII

INSTITUTIONS OF HIGHER LEARNING

ST. MARY'S SEMINARY—ST. VINCENT'S COLLEGE—WILL MAYFIELD COLLEGE—ELMWOOD SEMINARY—FARMINGTON COLLEGE—MARVIN COLLEGIATE INSTITUTE—CARLETON COLLEGE—ARCADIA COLLEGE—THE STATE NORMAL SCHOOL AT CAPE GIRARDEAU.

Efforts were made from time to time to provide educational institutions in the southeast equipped to do college work. These attempts were at best but partly successful in most instances. It was inevitable that such should be the case. The backward condition of the elementary and secondary schools made it difficult to secure sufficient students to support a college and there was experienced great difficulty in securing funds for these schools from other sources. Some of the schools succeeded. In spite of discouragement and obstacles those connected with them persevered and wrought work of the utmost value to this section.

ST. MARY'S SEMINARY

The earliest institution for higher learning actually put on foot here, is St. Mary's Seminary at Perryville, in Perry county. This was an enterprise of the Catholic church and had behind it the wealth and compact organization of that church. Out of this effort grew the St. Vincent's College at Cape Girardeau, which for many years, was the great college of this part of the state, and St. Mary's Seminary to this day is a great and flourishing theological school. We have already given something of the early history and struggle of this seminary under Bishop Dubourg, its founder.

As we have noted, the seminary was open for the reception of students in 1818. At that time there was only a single log cabin, and Father Rosati has preserved for us, in his diary, a picture of the activities that went on within this single room. In one corner of it there was a kitchen, another part a laundry, in still another corner a sleeping apartment, while another part was given over to the students for their use in study and recitation. However, the seminary was not long confined to a single building. The necessity for such a school and the evident earnestness and ability of the men in charge of its work, resulted in the gathering of funds and the erection of other buildings. The second one of these was a large two-story log structure in which the seminary found much more convenient and comfortable quarters. From time to time the equipment in buildings was added to as need was found in the growth of the institution itself. Here were educated not only those men who were being trained for the priesthood but others who desired to pursue a college education under the direction of the church. The first students, as we have seen, were brought from Italy, coming with Bishop Dubourg, but other students were attracted to the institution and it soon found that all that could be accommodated were ready for the mission.

The first students of the college from Missouri were the sons of Joseph Pratte and Frederick Rozier, of Ste. Genevieve. Others came at various times from Kaskaskia, Cahokia, St. Louis, and Louisiana. Within a very short time the attendance had reached eighty students and in 1833 it was one hundred and thirty. The course of study covered a period of six years and included Latin, Greek, history, mathematics, chemistry, natural philosophy, astronomy, geology, English, French, German, Italian and Spanish. Christian doctrine and music were also taught and the last year of the course was devoted to the study of mental philosophy, embracing logic, metaphysics, cosmology, psychology, natural theology and ethics. This was the course required of college students, and in addition to it the theological students, who were candidates for the priesthood, were required to pursue a three years' course in theology, scripture, canon-law, ecclesiastical history and other subjects fitted for the training of priests.

These courses of study were maintained at St. Mary's from its opening in 1818 until 1844. At that date St. Vincent's college was founded at Cape Girardeau and the classical or collegiate departments of St. Mary's were transferred there.

St. Mary's was supported in a very large party by the fee for board and tuition. This varied from two to three hundred dollars for each student during the year of ten months. The equipment for the college in laboratories and libraries was in part donated and in part purchased by money given for the purpose. The library soon amounted to about 20,000 volumes and the laboratory equipment was good considering the time.

The professors and students were accustomed to do missionary work in the surrounding country, and it was a member of the faculty, Father John Timon, as we have seen, who began work in Cape Girardeau.

Since the transfer of the collegiate department of St. Vincent's, St. Mary's has been conducted as a seminary for the education of priests. It has a large and well-equipped plant, in striking contrast to its first humble buildings, and is a well-conducted and powerful institution.

St. Vincent's College

St. Vincent's had its beginning in a day school which was opened October 22, 1838, by Father Odin. He and another priest and a lay-brother conducted the school for two years. Sessions were held in buildings used for the church. In 1840, Father Odin was succeeded by Rev. Michael Domenech. At that time the day school was in a flourishing condition and Father Domenech determined to turn it into a college. The site for the college had already been purchased, being included in the tract of forty acres bought from Robert Daugherty. The stone for the building was quarried in 1842 and other preparations made for its erection, which was begun in the spring of 1843.

On the 27th day of February, 1843, the general assembly incorporated St. Vincent's College under the title of the president and faculty of St. Vincent's College. The incorporators, all of whom were priests of the Congregation of the Mission, were Revs. John Timon, John Brandt, H. Figari, Joseph Paquin, J. F. McGerry and John Odin. The college was granted the authority to confer degrees and literary honors such as were customarily granted by schools and colleges.

The corner-stone of the building was laid by Rev. John Timon, who had originated the work in Cape Girardeau, and who was afterward bishop of Buffalo, N. Y. The site of the building is a beautiful one, standing back five hundred feet from the river bank on a gently rising slope of one hundred feet above low water mark. The building itself is of stone and brick, one hundred feet long and forty feet wide and three stories high. To this building there were added, in 1853, the south wing, of the same size as the original building.

In May, 1844, the collegiate department of St. Mary's was transferred to St. Vincent's. The first faculty of the college were: Rev. H. Figari, president; Rev. M. Barbier, vice-president; Rev. J. F. McGerry, prefect of discipline; Rev. H. Cercos, procurator, and Rev. J. Richini. To this faculty there were soon added Messrs. Amat, Penco, O'Reilly, Knowd, Tierman, Burlando, McGinnes, Chandy, Verrina, Burke and Pasqual. President Figari resigned in October, 1844, and was succeeded by Rev. Thaddeus Amat. In November, 1845, President Amat was made president of St. Mary's Seminary, and Rev. A. Penco became president of St. Vincent's. He was very popular as president, and held the position for six years. He was succeeded by Rev. R. Hennessy, this was in 1851, and

St. Vincent's College

President Hennessy died in 1853. The next president was Rev. H. Masnan, who served one year, and was followed by Rev. S. V. Ryan. Rev. Thomas J. Smith became the next president, on the resignation of Father Ryan in 1858. During the years 1858 and 1859, the archbishop of St. Louis, Rev. P. R. Kenrick, and the bishops of the province of St. Louis requested the Vincentian Fathers to open a seminary for the exclusive use of students for the priesthood. The proposition was made to the trustees of St. Vincent's

College and accepted by them, and accordingly, in 1859, the college opened as a strictly ecclesiastical seminary. This brought about a change in the presidency, and Father Smith was succeeded by Father James McGill. Not much change was made in the curriculum of studies, except the addition of senior courses of philosophy and theology. The course was practically the same as that maintained at St. Mary's; it covered a space of six years and was concerned with practically the same studies. Great stress was laid upon the teaching of languages, both ancient and modern, and the commencement programs contained exercises, both original and selected, in Greek, Latin, Italian, Spanish, French, German and English.

Some of the men who were connected with St. Vincent's in these early years won for themselves high standing, both as scholars and teachers. One of these was the Rev. James Knowd. For more than twenty years he was professor of higher mathematics at St. Vincent's. He was not only skilled in mathematics, but also in instruction. The mathematical course extended during the entire six years of the college work. Professor Knowd was a correspondent for the Smithsonian Institution at Washington, and before the establishment of a weather bureau was accustomed to keep and transmit to the Smithsonian, weather observations.

Another man who won distinction was Rev. John F. McGerry, professor of natural science. He was especially interested in botany and gathered together in the gardens and greenhouses of the college a most remarkable collection of flowers and rare plants. These gardens were one of the show places of the town and were visited by a great many persons.

The students of the college came from many places in the west. The first students were those transferred from St. Mary's Seminary. They were about seventy-five in number and the average attendance was between one hundred and one hundred and fifty; the greater part of these students coming from Louisiana and from the towns of St. Louis and Ste. Genevieve.

Not a great many students were graduated for the examinations required of the applicant for graduation were very rigid. The first graduate was Angelo Navarro, of San Antonio. He received his degree July 29th, 1847. At the commencement of 1849, Charles Rozier, of Ste. Genevieve, and J. A. Leveque, of Baton Rouge, La., were graduated.

The founding and maintenance of the college in its early years was a matter of very great difficulty. The great flood of 1844, shortly after the transfer of the students to the college, proved a severe trial. A part of the support of the institution was expected to come from the college farm, which lay south of town, and which at the time of the flood was covered with a crop of wheat and corn and vegetables. The high waters, however, covered the farm to a depth of eight to ten feet and entirely destroyed the crops. The fences, too, were swept away, and most of the livestock was drowned. The college itself was too high above the river to be directly injured, but one effect of the flood after it had receded was an epidemic of sickness which broke out among the students. More than a hundred persons were sick at the same time, and there were two deaths, both members of the faculty, Revs. H. Raschini and H. Cercos.

Two memorable calamities befell the college in these years. In the winter of 1843-1844, a steamboat, called the Sea Bird, was caught in the floating ice and tied up by her officers below the ledge of rocks in front of the college. She was loaded with 1,500 kegs of powder. On the night of February 4th, the boat was discovered to be on fire, and at about midnight the captain of the boat aroused the people in the college and warned them of the danger which confronted them. They dressed as hurriedly as possible and ran out of the buildings and away from the river toward the west. The last man had hardly left the building when a terriffic explosion was heard. No one was hurt, but all were pretty badly shaken by the force of the explosion. The building itself was considerably damaged; every pane of glass was broken, the doors were torn from their hinges and broken into splinters, and every foot of plastering from ceiling and walls was torn down; the roof was lifted several inches, but settled back into place with but little injury. The windows and doors were closed with sheets and blankets until new ones could be secured from St. Louis. The plastering was not replaced until the following summer.

The second calamity which befell the college occurred on the 27th of November, 1850. On that date a tornado of terrific force struck the building. All the outhouses, tailor shop, shoemaker shop, clothes room, baker shop and barns were literally torn to pieces and blown away with the storm. The roof of the college itself was cleared away and not a particle of it was ever found. The walls of the southwest corner of the main building and both gables were blown down. No one was killed except an old colored man who lived in the house in the garden, though several persons were slightly injured. The students were sent away and the college closed for four months, during which time the necessary repairs were made.

On the 15th of June, 1861, at a meeting of the faculty, it was decided that it was for the best interests of the college to suspend its operations owing to the war. A resolution was passed that the examinations should take place immediately and that the students should quit the college as soon as possible. This action of the faculty was taken because of the great state of excitement then existing in Southeast Missouri. There were companies of soldiers drilling on the streets of Cape Girardeau and there were rumors that the town would be the scene of a battle between the forces of the north and the south. There was strong feeling even among the citizens of the town and it seemed that any attempt to carry on the work of the college would expose its students to danger.

The examinations were held and the usual commencement exercises were dispensed with. Following the examinations the students returned at once to their homes, most of them entering the armies of the north or south. About twenty students, however, remained at the college, and most of the faculty. On the 25th of July it was determined by the faculty to send the students who still remained, in charge of the procurator, Rev. F. Guidry, to the college farm. This action was taken because of the rumor that the city was to be attacked by the Confederate troops. The students remained at the farm until August 10th. On this date they were recalled, for it had been decided that it was for the best interests of the college to open session in September as usual. There had been talk of the college buildings being taken by the United States government as a military hospital. The college authorities very naturally opposed this and it seemed their opposition would be most effective if the college were in operation.

The session began September 1st, 1861.

most of the students in theology and philosophy returned, but not very many of the college students. At this time Rev. James McGill was president and other members of the faculty were: Rev. Joseph Alizeri, Rev. James Knowd, Rev. J. F. McGerry, Rev. Felix Guidry, Rev. William Ryan, Rev. A. J. Ryan, Rev. T. D. O'Keefe, Rev. P. M. Regan, Rev. J. T. Landry and Rev. T. M. O'Donoughue.

One member of the faculty, however, did not long remain. This was Rev. Abram J. Ryan. He resigned his place in college and became a chaplain in the Confederate army. Here he devoted himself to his work as chaplain and to writing poems which have made his name famous. Father Ryan was one of the most noted men ever connected with the faculty of St. Vincent's.

The college continued its operations throughout the war; the attendance was not large but the faculty managed to keep the institution open and the buildings occupied. After the war the faculty were called upon to take the test oath under the Drake constitution and upon their unanimous refusal they were arrested and taken to Jackson. Their trial was postponed from time to time, however, to await the decision of another case. The other case was finally determined by the supreme court of the United States, which held that the provisions in the Drake constitution requiring the taking of the test oath were unconstitutional. This put an end to the case against the members of the faculty.

The college continued its work after the war but found itself handicapped by a considerable debt that had accumulated and also by the necessity of drawing students from different sections of the country than formerly. Before the war more than fifty per cent came from Louisiana; after the war, however, very few Louisiana students were in attendance. In 1866 Rev. Joseph Alizeri was president and Rev. M. Dyer was vice-president.

Owing to the destruction of one of the buildings of St. Mary's seminary at Perryville, the college students at St. Mary's were transferred to St. Vincent's. This indicated a change in the character of St. Vincent's college, which, since 1859, had been purely ecclesiastical. Although the theological department was still continued, classical courses were begun and also commercial courses began to receive attention. From this time until 1893 these three courses of study, theological, classical and commercial, were carried on side by side in St. Vincent's; each course was independent of the other.

The college course continued to be six years in duration and led to the degree of Bachelor of Arts; two years further study entitled a student to the degree of Master of Arts. The curriculum was much the same as that established at the founding of the college in 1844. The same is true of the theological course, which included those subjects which have come to be recognized as standards of those preparing for the priesthood.

In 1868 Anthony Verrina became president of the college. He was followed in 1875 by Rev. J. W. Hickey. President Hickey resigned in 1884. Among his successors have been: Rev. P. McHale, 1884-1886; Rev. P. V. Byrne, 1886-1889; Rev. F. V. Nugent, 1889-1893; Rev. J. J. Murray, 1893-1894; Rev. G. H. Dockery, 1894-1896; Rev. J. Linn, 1896-1898; Rev. E. M. Hopkins, 1898-1900; Rev. J. A. Layton, 1900-1901.

Rev. J. F. McGerry, who has been referred to as one of the most distinguished able members of the faculty, died in 1873. He had been a member of the college faculty for thirty years; in fact his services began at the founding of the institution. At the time of his death he was eighty years old and had been a teacher for more than fifty years. He was held in the highest esteem by the trustees of the college, by the members of the faculty and by the students.

In 1871 plans were made for a new building to be erected west of the study hall. The structure was to be 100 feet by 40 feet and three stories high. The first story was to be a gymnasium; second, an exhibition hall, and third as a chapel.

Since 1902 the college has not had an active existence. There have been several members of the faculty always in attendance at the college and usually some students have taken the courses, especially those in theological training, but no effort has been made to extend the equipment or to gather a large number of students. This has been due in part to the fact that the Congregation of the Mission, under whose control the college exists, have concentrated their efforts to the upbuilding of institutions in other places. It is the intention at the present time to dispose of the whole college plant and to purchase property elsewhere. The decision to sell the historic buildings and holdings of the college was arrived at because of the fact that the situation is no longer suitable for school purposes. In one way it is a most beautiful site, lying as it does, on the bank of the river and affording a most delightful view, but in another way the situation is no longer desirable for school purposes; it is on the railroad, and lies at the edge of the factory district of the town; the buildings, while ample, are old and no longer meet the requirements of school work. It is to be hoped, however, that arrangements may be perfected by which this college, one of the oldest west of the Mississippi river, may be retained in Cape Girardeau and may once more secure that position of influence and importance which it once held. The institution at present is in charge of the Rev. Father Thomas Levan.

WILL MAYFIELD COLLEGE

This institution, now situated at Marble Hill in Bollinger county, was organized February 10, 1878, by Dr. W. H. Mayfield and Dr. H. J. Smith. At that time it was known as the Mayfield-Smith Academy, and was located at Smithville in Bollinger county. No effort was made at first to erect a building for the school and it was carried on in rented rooms; there were no endowments and the expenses were met by tuition fees principally and in part by gifts. There were 22 students at the first session. In 1879 work was begun for a building, but the work was discontinued and in 1880 the school was removed to Marble Hill. At that time Rev. A. M. Johnson became connected with the school and began the work of raising funds for the construction of a building. The Baptists to whom he appealed had come to feel the need of an educational institution such as he planned and they contributed liberally to the institution. A good building of brick was erected upon commanding situation on the top of a hill in Marble Hill and the work of the school in its new location began. Since that time it has prospered. A dormitory building has been erected, the grounds which are naturally beautiful have been improved, and the courses of instruction strengthened. The present head of the school, Mr. J. H. Hendricks, is succeeding in carrying on the institution with really remarkable success. Much of the credit of the school's prosperity belongs to Rev. W. A. Davault, who has been connected with it for many years and has been untiring in his devotion to it. The school is supported largely by tuition fees and voluntary gifts.

ELMWOOD SEMINARY

Elmwood Seminary, under the control of the Presbyterian church in Farmington, was established through the work of Rev. James A. Creighton, at one time supply of the Farmington Presbyterian church. While engaged in the duties of this position he became impressed with the importance of an institution in Southeast Missouri under the control of the church for the education of women. He accordingly prepared plans for the institution and submitted them to the Presbyteries of Potosi and St. Louis in April, 1886. The plans were approved by the two Presbyteries and Mr. Creighton began the work of securing property and buildings for the location of the school. He was successful in securing the property in Farmington known as the Cayce place, and the school was opened in September, 1886, in the old residence on this place. It was conducted in this building for several years, but it became evident that if the school was to succeed to a very great extent a new building must be erected suited to school purposes. The work was undertaken in September, 1889, and the building completed in June, 1890.

This building is 45x80 feet in size and four stories in height, including the basement. Together with the heating, lighting and furnishing it cost about $20,000, all of which was contributed, with the exception of $500, by the people of Farmington.

The new seminary which was called Elmwood, was placed in charge of Rev. A. W. Wilson, who was not only a minister, but also an experienced teacher, and was fortunate at the time in having two daughters to assist him in the work of instruction. Circumstances, however, compelled him to resign the position after some years of successful work and he was succeeded by Miss Sallie H. Holliday, under whose direction the school had a very prosperous period of growth. Presidents of the institution since that time have been Miss Helen Montgomery, Miss Maude Montgomery, and Miss Lula May Winn, who is now at the head of the school. The attendance averages about 120 and the school is known for the close attention given to its students and the thoroughness of its work. It fills a distinct place in the educational system of the southeast.

FARMINGTON COLLEGE

For a time an institution known as Farmington College was conducted in Farmington by E. F. Jennings. It was established in September, 1886, and was under the control of the Franklin Association of Baptist churches. The school was conducted in a two-story brick building which stood on the lot now occupied by the new high school building. This building had been erected in 1883 by J. S. Gashwiler who erected it and conducted a school until 1886. This Farmington College had a precarious existence for several years. It usually had an enrollment of 75 or 100 students but was never in a prosperous condition. The building was destroyed by fire about 1894, was later rebuilt and again was destroyed by fire, and the school finally closed about the year 1900.

MARVIN COLLEGIATE INSTITUTE

Marvin Collegiate Institute, an educational institution under the control of the Methodist Episcopal church, South, was organized in 1867 at Caledonia in Washington county. For many years the institute, which was then called Bellevue Collegiate Institute, was operated at Caledonia and had a successful existence. As public high schools, however, came to be common through this part of the state it was felt that the buildings and equipment at Caledonia were not sufficient to enable this school to compete with the high schools. There was an agitation for a change of location. It was felt that since Caledonia was not located on a railroad the school would always be handicapped on that account. Fredericktown offered a building to cost $25,000 and ten acres of land on condition that the school be established at that place. This offer was accepted in 1894 and in September, 1895, the school was transferred to the new building at Fredericktown. Since that time the school has been successfully carried on. It is not organized as a college and confers no degrees, though it does do a certain amount of college work. The president of the school now is Rev. C. M. Gray. The building is a substantial brick structure, well suited to the purposes for which it was erected, and in addition to this main structure there is a dormitory for girls.

Carleton College

This institution was founded by Miss E. A. Carleton in April, 1854, under the name of Carleton Institute. From 1854 until 1878 it was conducted in the country eight miles north of Farmington. In 1859 the institution was incorporated by the general assembly under the title of Carleton Institute and was given authority to conduct a school and to grant degrees. The institution was successful from the beginning, Miss Carleton herself being a successful teacher and organizer. In 1878 the school was removed to Farmington and installed in its new building December 2nd. This building stands on an attractive site comprising about 16 acres lying just east of the town. The building itself is a four-story brick of about 30 rooms. It was sufficient to house the school until 1884, when an addition 57 feet long and four stories high was made to the main building, which is called the Henry Annex in honor of Henry Carleton, and contains a chapel, library, museum, laboratory and other rooms.

Arcadia College

In 1849 a school was established at Arcadia and called the Arcadia high school. It soon acquired a reputation for good work and was well patronized. It was later chartered by the legislature as Arcadia college. In 1870 a large four-story brick building was erected and the school grew rapidly. It came under the control of the Methodist Episcopal church for a number of years, but was not self-supporting. An effort was made at one time to sell the buildings and plant to the state for the establishment of third normal school afterward located at Cape Girardeau. This attempt failed and the college was finally transferred to the Ursuline Sisters who have conducted it since 1878 as the Ursuline academy. It is pleasantly situated, has a good library of about 1,200 volumes, and is a prosperous institution.

State Normal School

The institution which more than any other has influenced education in Southeast Missouri is the Missouri State Normal school, third district, at Cape Girardeau. It was the third of the Normal schools established in the state Kirksville was established in 1869, Warrensburg in 1871, and the act of the legislature which created the third Normal school was approved March 22, 1873. It may thus be seen that the three Normal schools are the result of the same forces and the same agitation for improvement of teaching.

This agitation was the result, in large part, of the work of Joseph Baldwin, the founder and first president of the Kirksville Normal school. While we may not withhold from President Baldwin the just credit which belongs to him for his work in establishing Normal schools in the state, it is very evident that the demand for improved teaching would have eventually led to the organization of schools for the training of teachers. The necessity for such training is too great for a public school system to become very effective without the organization of schools devoted especially to this work.

After the organization of the Normal schools at Warrensburg and Kirksville it was plainly evident that a third school was needed to supply that great section of the state lying south of the Missouri river and east of Jefferson City. Accordingly the legislature provided for the establishment of such

STATE NORMAL SCHOOL

a school to be located within the bounds of Southeast Missouri. Under the provisions of this act the first step to be taken in the organization of the school was the creation of a board of regents, which was to consist of the state superintendent of schools, the secretary of state and the attorney general, who were to hold a place on the board *ex-officio*, and four members to be appointed by the governor of the state. Shortly after the approval of the act a board of regents was appointed. It was composed of John Monteith, state superintendent of public schools; E. F. Weigel, secretary of state; H. C. Ewing, attorney general, ex-officio members, and George W. Farrar, of Iron county; Jacob H. Burrough, of Cape Girardeau; T. J. O. Morrison, of New Madrid county, and Charles C. Rozier, of Ste. Genevieve county. The board was organized by the selection of John Monteith as chairman and E. F. Weigel as secretary.

These officers of the board were elected at its first meeting in Jefferson City September 30th, 1873. This meeting of the board had been called for the purpose of organization and for the reception of bids for the location of the new school. On the following day, October 1st, the board opened and received bids from those communities in the state which desired the location of the normal. Byrd township in Cape Girardeau county, the city of Cape Girardeau and Iron county were the only bidders. Byrd township offered $50,000 in bonds, $14,450 in cash and about 240 acres of land. The bonds, however, were conditioned on the passage of an enabling act by the legislature. The city of Cape Girardeau's bid included $50,000 in bonds, $6,885 in notes and cash, and lands worth about $10,000. Iron county offered the plant of Arcadia College upon which a valuation of $75,000 was placed, and nearly 7,000 acres of land.

After these bids were opened the board heard statements from various interested persons concerning the bids and then by a vote declared that the offer from Byrd township of Cape Girardeau county should be considered no bid, since under the provision of the law creating this school the board could not consider bonds which the township had no authority to issue.

This narrowed the question to a decision between Cape Girardeau and Iron county. At subsequent meetings of the board held in the city of Cape Girardeau and at Arcadia in Iron county, hearings were held on the question of these two bids. Many citizens of Cape Girardeau, prominent among them being Louis Houck and A. D. Leech, appeared before the board urging the selection of Cape Girardeau and offering to purchase the bonds at various prices. At the meeting held in Arcadia some persons appeared and urged the location of the school there, but a protest was received from other citizens of the county urging that the school should not be brought to Arcadia. The matter was decided at a meeting held October 28th, 1873, when, by a vote of four to three, Cape Girardeau was selected as the site of the school.

Having determined that the school should be located at Cape Girardeau, the board took up the question of the particular site in the town. Two offers were made, one by Mr. Fagan of the hill known as Fort A, the other by Mr. Lansmann, of the hill known as Fort B. The board surveyed both these sites and listened to various persons urging one place or the other, and finally selected Fort B as the most suitable place for the school.

At its meeting in St. Louis on October 28th, 1873, the board determined to appoint an executive committee with full power to take such steps to establish the school and to employ teachers as might be found necessary. The state board of education and Mr. Jacob Burrough of Cape Girardeau, were appointed as such committee. It was later determined to accept an offer made by the public school of Cape Girardeau to turn over to the Normal school a part of the public school building and to begin a session there. The board employed Mr. L. H. Cheney as principal and fixed his salary at the sum of $2,000 per annum. Mrs. Cheney was made an assistant, while Mr. Burrough and Professor Cheney were empowered to select such other assistants as were found necessary. The tuition or incidental fee was fixed at $3.00 for each of three terms during the year.

The board advertised for plans for the erection of a school building and at a meeting in St. Louis on January 14th, it opened these plans and selected the one submitted by C. B. Clarke, of St. Louis. At subsequent meetings the board received from Architect Clarke the plans and specifications for the building and advertised for bids for its construction. The sum of $39,000 was fixed as the maximum amount which would be spent on the building. The bids were opened at Jefferson City on March 25th, 1874, but all of them were rejected, for all were above the sum of $39,000. The board then determined to make such changes in the plans for the building as would bring the cost within the fixed sum, exclusive of the heating, seating and architect's fees. After this was done arrangements were made for the erection of the building and Jacob Burrough, Principal Cheney, and Otto Buehrmann were appointed as a building committee to supervise the erection of the building. Work on the building was finished in the spring of 1875 and was occupied by the school that year.

This building, which at the time of its erection was the finest single building of its kind in the state, was of the modified Gothic style of architecture. It was 163 feet long and 72 feet wide and three stories in height. It contained ten recitation rooms with other necessary rooms and an auditorium on the first floor, capable of seating about five hundred. It was rather ornate in appearance, having a number of towers and spires upon it and was only fairly well adapted to the purpose for which it was intended. This building was the home of the school until it was destroyed by fire in 1902.

Before the completion of the building, arrangements had been made for opening the school in the fall of 1873 in a portion of the public school building. Mr. L. H. Cheney, an experienced and able teacher, had been employed a principal of the Normal and instructor in professional training. Associated with him was his wife, Mrs. Frances A. Cheney, a woman of great ability and force of character and an experienced and successful teacher. Under Principal Cheney's guidance the first year of school was successful. There were enrolled 57 students, 28 of them being women and 29 men.

The equipment of the school was very limited, in fact for the first year it was practically nothing at all. It was the intention, however, of Mr. Cheney and the board to equip the school as rapidly as possible with the necessary things for successful teaching.

The faculty for the next year was composed of Principal Cheney, R. P. Rider, who taught language and mathematics; Mrs. Cheney, instructor in history and geography; G. T. Lemmon, instructor in natural history and drawing; and L. C. Schleich, instructor in German. The session this year was held in the public school building until near its close when the school was transferred to the newly completed Normal building. This year the attendance reached 164, showing a considerable and gratifying growth and bearing testimony to the fact that such a school was needed and filled a vacant place in the educational system.

Near the close of this school year of 1874-75, the school was transferred to the new building. There was great rejoicing on the part of all connected with the school at the change. The board of regents had provided for some equipment for instruction in science and had begun the work of accumulating a library. It must not be supposed, however, that the surroundings were, even in the new building, such as are to be seen today. Fort B, the site of the building, was a bare hill, cut off in nearly every direction by deep gullies so that there was little of the beauty of situation that it to be seen today. The gullies were so deep and the ground so rough that it was found necessary to build a bridge as an approach to the building. The mud was deep in many places and there was an absence of shade and grass that was very trying for some years. In spite of these handicaps and unfavorable conditions the school prospered under the guidance of Principal Cheney.

Great sacrifices were made at times by those connected with the institution in order to advance it and to carry on its work. Not infrequently the members of the faculty in the early days were called upon to travel over the district attending meetings of the teachers and soliciting students. Travel in Southeast Missouri in those days was not altogether pleasurable. There were very few railroads and the bulk of the travel was by wagon and over roads that were far from good.

The school, at its organization, did not possess a practice or model school, though it was the intention of the regents that such a school should be organized as soon as found possible. It was not within their power to provide such a school until the beginning of the session in 1876. At that time arrangements were perfected for the organization of a school in which students might teach under competent supervisors. This feature of the Normal school was stressed in its advertisements as offering an opportunity for students to do actual work in teaching and thus to become prepared for its duties. It was not found practicable, however, to continue a practice school longer than the close of the session of 1878-79. From that time on for a number of years the school had no opportunity for giving actual training in teaching to its students. An attempt was made from time to time to supply this deficiency by calling on the members of the senior class to take charge of certain of the elementary classes under the eye of a member of the faculty. It is useless to say this plan was not found to be of any great value though it was continued for a number of years.

At the close of the year 1873-74, the first year of the school, a public exercise was held in Turner's hall, June 25, 1874. That program is reproduced here, as it will probably be of interest to the alumni and others interested in the institution.

Music.
Chorus—Vacation Song.
Oration—No Man Should Live for Himself Alone, Alex. H. Miller.
Essay—The Power of Trifles, Belle Green.
Music.
Duet—In the Starlight, Ida Burrough and Mary Ross.
Essay—Cape Girardeau in 1900, Mollie Holmes.
Oration—Paddle Your Own Canoe, Charles K. Hayden.
Music.
Instrumental Duet, Emma and Ida Burrough.
Essay—Ancient America, Julia Moon.
Essay—Celebrated Rivers, Elizabeth Hines.
Essay—School Days, Geo. Kenrick.
Music.
Chorus—Gladsome Song.

Essay—Mary, Queen of Scots, Ida Burrough.

Oration—Education and the Educator, Ashley S. Coker.

Music.

Duet—Beautiful Venice, Ellen Wray and Mollie Holmes.

Address, by Prof. Oren Root, Jr., of Glasgow.

Music.

Chorus—What Shall the Harvest Be?

A catalogue issued in 1874, which was the first, sets out the courses of study which were to be pursued. The division into elementary course and advanced course, which still obtains in the school, was begun at this time. The elementary course was divided into five classes known as sub-junior class, junior class, middle class, sub-senior class, and senior class. The studies pursued by the sub-junior class were arithmetic, geography, botany, reading, composition, penmanship, chemistry, drawing and vocal music. In the junior class most of these subjects were continued with the addition of United States history, natural philosophy, and grammar. In the middle class, algebra, physiology, zoology and the constitution of the United States were taken up. These subjects were continued during the sub-senior year and in addition physical geography, analysis of words, school law of Missouri, and geometry were studied. The senior class of the elementary course studied geometry, natural philosophy, school economy, methods in teaching, composition and drawing, or bookkeeping, and vocal music.

The advanced course was also organized in four classes known as class D, class C, class B, and class A. In class D the students were occupied with algebra, Latin or German, general history, natural philosophy, composition, drawing, and music. In class C these studies were continued except that geometry was substituted for algebra, one term of English literature for general history, and chemistry for natural philosophy. In class B, the mathematical subject studied was trigonometry, in science it was geology, while work in Latin or German and English literature together with minor subjects was continued. In class A, students studied analytical geometry, logic, and astronomy and continued their work in Latin or German and in minor subjects.

Arrangements were made also for a sub-Normal class and the courses were so arranged that students were admitted to the advanced course after completing the studies of the sub-senior class of the elementary course.

A study of this curriculum shows that very little attention was given to the study of pedagogy and there was little opportunity provided for election. It was held by those in authority in the Normal school of that day, that students should be required to take certain specified subjects. It was before the day of election in school studies.

In the spring of 1875 the first students completed the elementary course. They were: Ida Burrough, Ada Jaquith, Martha R. Moon, John T. Harris, Jefferson W. Limbaugh, William Ragland, and William A. Ranney.

The first graduate from the advanced course was Miss Emma E. Cowdon. She was granted a diploma in 1877. In 1878 the advanced class had three members: Eugene T. McNeely, Theodore H. Polack, and Miss Ellen Wilson.

The school grew steadily under the administration of Principal Cheney and he continued in charge until his untimely death in

1877. He was killed by an explosion and was buried in the old Lorimier cemetery in Cape Girardeau.

For the year 1877-78 the board chose as principal Mr. C. H. Dutcher, an experienced teacher and former member of the faculty of the Warrensburg State Normal school. Mrs. Cheney remained in the faculty as instructor of geography and history. Associated with these were DeWitt Roberts, instructor of mathematics; Lillie E. Skaats, instructor in rhetoric, German and drawing, and Martha R. Moon, instructor in arithmetic and penmanship. It was announced that members of the senior class would act as assistants. Principal Dutcher was an active and energetic man and associated with himself several men who had great influence in moulding the character of the school. The attendance continued to increase and the courses of study were enlarged so that the school experienced a healthy growth. Among the men who were later associated with Mr. Dutcher and who had great influence, were Nelson B. Henry, teacher of English language and literature, and A. E. Douglas, a teacher of Latin and assistant in the English department.

In 1881 Principal Dutcher resigned his position to accept a position in the Warrensburg State Normal and was succeeded by Richard C. Norton. The title of the head of the school was changed at this time from principal to president, a title which is still in use.

Mr. Norton came to the Cape Girardeau Normal from Warrensburg and had had experience as a teacher in many different positions. He remained with the school until the fall of 1893, serving as its president for twelve years. It is not too much to say that President Norton exerted a remarkable influence in shaping the character of the school and putting it on a firm basis in the thought and affection of the people of Southeast Missouri. During his administration the attendance increased from 225 in 1881-82, to 392 in 1891-92. This attendance of 392 was the high water mark in what we call the old Normal school, meaning by the term that part of the school's history before the destruction of the old building by fire.

President Norton gathered around him a group of men and women who were well suited to the work of the school and who exerted a great influence upon its growth. The head of the department of science was W. D. Vandiver who was afterward president of the school. John S. McGee was professor of mathematics. He was also president at a later time. The English department was in charge of James Underwood Barnard, one of the ablest and strongest of the group. Mr. Barnard was afterward a member of the faculty of the University of Mississippi, later head of one of the great public schools of Kansas City, where he died in 1909. Besides these there were others whose names and work became familiar to many hundreds of students. L. G. McConachie was for a time in the history department. He later became a member of the faculty of Wisconsin University and a writer on the science of government. Mrs. S. F. Fuhri was a member of the English department, as was Miss Nellie Gordon. It was during President Norton's administration that Miss Winifred Johnson began that connection with the school which was to continue for so many years and to do much to make the school popular. The department of music was in charge of Otto Eckhardt, long a member of the faculty and known to all the students for his untiring interest in their various activities.

It must be remembered in considering the

work of the school in these early years that while it was established as a state institution and supported by state appropriation, it lacked one of the advantages which the State Normal schools now possess. There was no provision in the act establishing Normal schools within Missouri making the elementary certificate or the Normal diploma a teacher's certificate. The students who completed either of the two courses were required to pass an examination just as was done in the case of other persons before being granted license to teach. Arrangements were made with Dr. R. D. Shannon during his term as state superintendent for the conducting of examinations of students who completed courses of instruction. It was not, however, until 1887 that provision was made in the law by which the Normal certificate and Normal diploma became licenses to teach, one for a term of two years and the other for life. It is plainly evident that such a provision was a distinct inducement to students to attend a Normal school, provided they expected to become teachers. Coupled with this provision was another which made as one of the conditions of entering, the taking of an obligation to become a teacher in the public schools of Missouri.

President Norton severed his connection with the school by resignation in the spring of 1893. His successor was Willard D. Vandiver who had been for several years the professor of physics and chemistry. Under Mr. Vandiver's administration the school progressed, but he remained for only four years, being succeeded at the end of his term by Professor J. S. McGhee. Professor McGhee had been connected with the school since 1880, being the head of the department of mathematics. He, too, held the position for two years. In 1899 the board elected as president Mr. W. S. Dearmont, at the time of his election superintendent of schools at Kirkwood. President Dearmont is a graduate of the University of Missouri and had had a most successful experience as a teacher and as superintendent. He entered upon the work of his position with great enthusiasm and soon came to have an understanding of the situation that enabled him to lay plans which have resulted in the growth of the institution.

On the night of April 2nd, 1902, the building was destroyed by fire. The origin of the fire is not known, but the loss was total, there being practically nothing saved from it. There were fears expressed that the destruction of the old building would result in very great injury to the school and there were suggestions also that the school should be removed from Cape Girardeau. Prior to the destruction of the building, the board of regents had determined to erect another building to be used as a science and training school building. The general assembly had appropriated $20,000 for this purpose at its meeting in 1901 and the board of regents had let the contract for its erection on September 9th, 1901.

After the destruction of the old building of the school there was no cessation of the work, provision being made for the holding of the school in the court house and in the churches of the town until Science Hall was completed. On its completion the school occupied it as the sole building. The old building had been insured and the funds paid by the insurance company were used by the board to erect a new stone building, which is now known as the Training School building. This was completed September 1st, 1903, and with Science Hall, offered comfortable and commodious quarters for the school.

Perhaps the greatest service which President Dearmont has rendered to the school was made possible by his clear insight into the opportunities presented by the destruction of the old building. Under his leadership a determined effort was made to secure from the general assembly an appropriation large enough to build a Normal school plant which would be capable of housing the school for many years. After strenuous efforts had been made the general assembly for 1903 appropriated the sum of $200,000 for the erection of the new main building. There was added to this in 1905 the sum of $186,000 to complete and furnish the new building and to erect a power house and manual training building. The new building, known as Academic Hall, was completed and occupied by the school in February, 1906. The building was dedicated with appropriate exercises on May 24th of that year.

This dedication was one of the most impressive events in the history of the school. Addresses were delivered by former Governor Dockery, by Hon. Louis Houck, president of the board of regents, by President Dearmont of the school, and by President E. B. Craighead, of Tulane University. Invitations had been sent out to former members of the faculty, many of whom attended. One of the pleasant features of the occasion was the presence of C. H. Dutcher, the second principal of the school. To him, President Dearmont resigned for the day his office, and delivered to him, on the rostrum of the school, the gavel of the presiding officer.

Since the completion of the main building there has been erected a power plant and manual training building, both of which have been fully equipped. The manual training is one of the best and most carefully arranged in the country. It is fully equipped for teaching all branches of the manual arts.

No account of the Normal school plant would be complete without mentioning the two dormitories. These are not yet the property of the state. They were built by the Normal Dormitory Company, a private corporation which rents them to the state. It is highly probable that they will become the property of the state before the close of the year 1912.

All the buildings of which we have spoken, six in number, are built of Cape Girardeau limestone. They are the most substantial character, all of them well planned and comfortably furnished. Academic Hall, the main building, is perhaps the best single school building in the state. It is 260 feet long with a depth of 186 feet. It contains, in addition to the class rooms, gymnasiums, art room, music rooms, library, offices, society halls and ladies' parlor.

The equipment for teaching science is ample. Laboratories for physics, chemistry, botany, physical geography and physiology are to be found in Science Hall. Besides the school has a completely furnishment department of domestic science and domestic art.

An examination of the present courses of study offered by the school reveals perhaps as great a growth and development as is evidenced by the growth of the school's material equipment. We have set out previously the course of study as offered in the first catalogue issued by the school in 1874.

In 1890 the school was still organized in six departments, as had been the case for several years previous to that time. These departments were: 1st, the professional department; 2nd, department of language; 3rd, department of mathematics; 4th, department of geography and history; 5th, department of natural science, and 6th, department of penmanship and drawing.

The professional department was organized to include work in the following subjects: School economy, methods of teaching, natural science, mental and moral philosophy, history and philosophy of education, logic, graded schools, institute work, etc., and practical teaching.

The language and literature department included work in English, comprising rhetoric and English and American literature, and two years in Latin. In addition to these, elocution was taught in each year of the course.

The mathematical department gave instruction in arithmetic, algebra, geometry, trigonometry, surveying, and astronomy. The work in surveying included some practical work with the compass and the course in astronomy was accompanied by experimental observations through a telescope.

The department of natural science and natural history did work in physical geography, physics, chemistry, geology, mineralogy, botany, zoology, physiology, and history of science. The equipment for teaching these sciences at that time was limited, though judged by the standards of the time, it was not wholly inadequate.

The department of geography and history gave instruction in descriptive geography, United States history, general history, and civil government. There was also a brief course in English history.

In the art department penmanship was taught, also drawing, bookkeeping, and vocal music.

A comparison of these with the courses offered at the present time indicates the expansion in this direction. The Normal school of today is a teacher's college and is organized into three great departments; one, the elementary professional department, the completion of which gives to the student the elementary certificate good for a period of two years; the advanced professional department, which leads to the Normal diploma, and the college department, organized after the usual form of colleges and leading to one of three degrees, Bachelor of Arts, Bachelor of Science, or Bachelor of Education.

In addition to this the school is divided into departments according to subjects. The department of education, which offers courses in pedagogy, in the teaching of common branches, in psychology, principles of teaching, school management, history of education, kindergarten teaching, primary teaching, supervision of country schools, play ground and school hygiene, and theory and practice of physical training.

The department of philosophy offers courses in sociology, especially psychology, logic, history of philosophy, ethics, theory of school organization, control and philosophy of the elementary school curriculum.

The department of languages offers courses in Latin, Greek, German, French, Spanish, and English.

The department of history offers courses in history of Europe and America.

The department of mathematics gives instruction in mathematics including analytical geometry and calculus.

The department of physics and chemistry is equipped for teaching these sciences after the most approved method, having good laboratories for both.

The department of biology and of geography are well prepared for instruction in these subjects.

One of the large departments in the school is that of agriculture and industrial training. It is organized to give instruction in agriculture, manual training, in domestic science and domestic art.

There is also a department of physical

training, one of art, and one of music. All these departments have thoroughly organized courses and are fully equipped to carry on the work in their various subjects.

The present condition of the Normal school as attested by its buildings and grounds, which are now valued at more than $600,000, by its faculty of forty-four teachers, by its attendance of students, which for the school year 1911-1912 was 1,001, is most encouraging to the friends of public education in Southeast Missouri.

During the thirty-nine years of the school's history it has graduated more than 600 students and has enrolled more than 14,000. Its students are found in the greater number of teaching positions throughout this part of the state and are exerting constantly a wider and deeper influence upon the course of education here.

Within a short time after the organization of the school, literary societies were formed by the students. The first of these, which seemed to have been organized in 1875, were the Union Literary, the Humboldt and the Arion. They were under faculty supervision, but were conducted almost entirely by the students themselves. Membership was open to both boys and girls and the programs were of a general literary character. For a good many years the societies were advertised in the catalogue as one of the means of general culture.

In 1876 the three old societies were disorganized and two new ones were formed; these were the Adelphi and the Zenonian. They were patterned after the former societies and continued to be the only ones of the school until 1879 when a third society called the Philomathean was organized. In 1888 a fourth society called the Van Guard came into existence. These societies held their meetings usually in the afternoon and there was no special place provided for their meetings; they usually occupied some one or other of the various class rooms of the school and they seem to have exerted no great influence on student life.

In 1892 it was determined by the students to organize societies on a slightly different pattern. The initiative in the movement was taken by the members of the class of 1893. It was felt by many of the students that societies would prosper more greatly if only men or only women were admitted to membership. Accordingly, there was organized as the first of the new societies, the Webster. One reason for the change was that it might be made possible for evening meetings to be held; it was felt that the society would have a more distinct character and a greater influence if it became possible to hold meetings in the evening. After the organization of the Webster Society its meetings for a time were held on Saturday evenings in a room rented in the Masonic Temple, which had just been completed. In the same year the first of the girls' societies, the Sorosis, was organized. The following year the Bentons came into existence and a little later the Clio was formed.

Even after the organization of the new societies it was found necessary, during the greater part of the time, to hold their meetings in the class rooms of the Normal school. In 1894 there were built for the use of the societies, four halls. They were in the form of additions to the chapel, were well furnished, and well suited to the purpose for which they were intended. They were occupied until the destruction of the building in 1902. On the completion of Academic Hall, rooms were set aside for the use of these societies, which they still continue to occupy.

It was not until after the organization of

the present societies that inter-society contests were held. They have now become a feature of society work.

In addition to these societies there exists an organization of the students somewhat broader in character, known as the Oratorical Association. Its membership is made up of representatives of the four societies and has control of the various contests between the societies and also with other schools. Under its auspices are held declamatory, oratorical and debating contests in the school, and inter-school debates and the oratorical contests with other Normal schools. Since the participation of the school in these contests it has won an enviable place.

Besides the literary societies already mentioned, there are several other student organizations connected with the school which add much to the value of school life. One of these is the Young Women's Christian Association, which was organized for the first time in 1890, and since that time has been one of the features of student life. It holds weekly meetings of a devotional character and also advances the social interests of its members and other students in the school. At the present time a student secretary is employed, who gives to the work of the association a considerable part of her time.

The Young Men's Christian Association was organized in the school in 1900; since that time it has had a steady growth and now has a membership of more than a hundred. As is the case with the Y. W. C. A., the association holds weekly devotional meetings and also looks after the social life of students as far as possible. The association at present conducts a number of Bible study classes in the school and also in the various Sunday schools of the town and has a committee on self help whose officers are directed to aid students who are making their way in the school.

Another one of the student organizations is the band. This was organized in 1906, under the direction of H. L. Albert, who was the first director. It has a membership of thirty and is one of the features of student life that adds very much to the pleasure and interest of the school.

One of the activities of students which deserves notice is the publication of a paper. A number of papers have been published at different times, but none of them have been placed upon a firm financial basis until the beginning of the publication of the *Capaha Arrow* during the school year of 1910-11. It is now in its second year and receives sufficient patronage in the way of subscriptions and advertising to warrant the continuance of its publication. The *Arrow* gives opportunity for the expression of the student views and for experience in journalism that is quite valuable.

A German society known as the Schiller Verein has existed among the students for several years. It gives an occasional program, all its exercises being contributed in German.

Besides the organizations mentioned there exist a number of others having in view the promotion of different objects; all of them adding something to the life of the school and furnishing a part for training in organization and management that is much needed and appreciated.

LIBRARY

Early in the history of the school the board determined that it was essential to its work to equip a library. The first record which appears of its action along this line is authority granted to the executive committee to buy a set of the American Encyclopedia. A little later we find the sum of $300 was set aside to be used in the purchase of books and laboratory apparatus. The collection of books continued to grow until in 1876 there were 1,200 volumes belonging to the school. The catalogue of 1892 sets out that the school has two libraries, one a general collection of 1,100 volumes of literature and the other a reference library containing 700 volumes. Under the old organization of the school the library was far from being as useful as it might have been made. The reference library was usually open for the use of students, but the general collection was usually closed. It was kept in a locked room and was really a circulating library which was opened for issuing books only once a week. By the time of the fire in 1902, there had been gathered about 3,000 volumes. With very few exceptions these volumes were all destroyed; the only ones being preserved were those which happened to be out of the building on the night of the fire. The school proceeded to buy about 1,000 volumes of a general character and these formed the library until the school moved into the new Academic building in 1906. The general assembly made some liberal appropriations for the purchase of books and the library has grown to now about 9,000 volumes and 7,000 unbound pamphlets.

Not only has the library grown in the actual number of books but has become thoroughly organized and catalogued so that it is accessible to the students at all times.

Enrollment

The enrollment of the school, as we have seen, has grown steadily from fifty-seven in its first year to 1,001 in the year 1911-12. This large enrollment and the large number of students who have been sent out as graduates from the various courses indicates the place which the school occupies in the educational system of Southeast Missouri. The greater number of its more than six hundred full graduates have taught in the public schools of Southeast Missouri for longer or shorter periods. There is scarcely a school in this section of the state that has not employed at some time a former student of the Normal, and many of the best teaching positions are now filled, and have been for years, by students of this school. Its educational ideals and standards have been communicated to most of the communities in this district. It is not too much to say that its work more than any other influence has contributed to the improvement of the educational situation in this part of the state.

The present faculty: Washington Strother Dearmont, A. M., Litt. D., president and professor of education.

Winifred Johnson, A. B., professor of history.

Benjamin Franklin Johnson, A. M., professor of mathematics.

Henry Stephen Moore, A. B., professor of American history and economics.

Benjamin Glime Shackelford, A. M., professor of physics and chemistry.

Edwin Andrew Hayden, B. S., Ph. D., professor of philosophy and education.

Robert Sidney Douglass, A. B., LL. B., professor of European history.

Homer Lawson Roberts, professor of biology.

Joseph Anthony Vaeth, A. B., professor of modern languages.

Arthur Winn Vaughan, B. S., professor of public speaking.

Edgar Augustus Cockefair, M. S., professor of agriculture.

Henry Frank Schulte, A. B., professor of physical training.

Ewell Martin Carter, B. S., in Ed., field and extension worker.

Frederic Hugo Doeden, A. B., A. M., professor of education and superintendent of training school.

James Arthur Dunn, A. B., A. M., professor of Latin and Greek.

Maud Montgomery, A. M., professor of modern languages.

Myrtle Knepper, A. M., assistant professor of mathematics.

Jeptha Riggs, A. M., assistant professor of English.

Eleanor Tyler, A. B., instructor in Latin.

Arthur Clay Magill, B. Pd., assistant professor in chemistry.

Elizabeth Parker Hunt, Ph. B., instructor in public speaking.

Arthur Louis McCarthy, A. B., assistant professor of mathematics.

Charles Lamb, director of manual training.

James Monroe Sitze, B. Pd., instructor in stenography, typewriting, bookkeeping, penmanship.

Nora Naeter, director of piano and violin.

Mary Louise Booth, assistant in manual training.

Emily Pitman Wilburn, B. L., instructor in drawing.

Mabel Flint, instructor in public school music.

Lora Alza Harvey, instructor in voice.

Mary Geraldine Allen, B. S., instructor in physical training.

Mary Turner Chapin, instructor in domestic science.

Ida May Shilling, B. S., instructor in domestic art.

Joe Mathews, B. Pd., assistant in piano.

Martha Catherine Shea, A. B., critic teacher and instructor in method in upper grades.

Estaline Wilson, critic teacher and instructor in method in upper grades.

Emma Jane Howarth, A. B., critic teacher and instructor in method in intermediate grades.

Rachel Elizabeth Gregg, B. S., critic teacher and instructor in method in primary grades.

Elma Williams Ealy, B. Pd., critic teacher and instructor in method in kindergarten.

Bertha Edith Rector, B. Pd., training school assistant in primary grades.

Sara Jane Weber, B. Ph., training school assistant in upper grades.

Olga Anna Huters, B. Pd., regents' scholar and assistant in modern languages.

Sadie Trezevant Kent, B. Pd., librarian.

Christine Isabella Wheeler, secretary and stenographer.

Edward Felix Vaeth, bookkeeper and registrar.

Mary Mildred Steel, preceptress.

Board of Regents

The board of regents has been fortunate to have had the service of a number of men able and devoted to its interests: T. J. O. Morrison, Jacob Burrough and Charles C. Rozier, members of the first board of regents, rendered valued service in the beginning of the school's work; of these, perhaps the man whose influence was felt most in the life of the school was T. J. O. Morrison. Besides these there have been a number of others whose services deserve recognition; two of these stand out with especial prominence in considering the history of the school. In 1881 Leon J. Albert of Cape Girardeau, became connected with the school as a member of the board of regents and has continued his connection with it since that time. During these years he was faithful in attendance at the meetings of the board, was a member during a great part of the time of the executive committee, and gave to the school the best service which his great financial ability and experience made possible.

Perhaps the man most closely associated in the minds of most people with the work of the Normal school is Hon. Louis Houck, who became a member of the board of regents in 1886 and is still a member and has been for 24 years the president of the board. In fact, Mr. Houck's interest in and connection with the school began long before he became a member of the board. It was due in part to his active and intelligent interest that Cape Girardeau was selected as the site for the school and during all the years of the school's existence he has had an interest in its welfare. Since his connection with the board of regents, and especially since he became its president, he has devoted to the work of the school much of his time and thought. Few weeks have passed in recent years in which Mr. Houck has not devoted some hours to the consideration of the needs and wants of the school. It was his presence on the ground, and his wide experience in affairs that made possible the erection of the present school plant at a cost, very generally considered, extremely low. Mr. Houck has given personal attention to the work of the school and it is not too much to say that to him perhaps more than to any other one person the school owes its success. No doubt the generous dealings of the legislature with the school has come in part, at least, because of Mr. Houck's connection with it. His wide acquaintance with men of affairs has inspired confidence in the wisdom and ability with which the school would be conducted.

The present board is composed of Hon. Louis Houck, president, C. D. Matthews, Jr. vice president, Leon J. Albert, secretary, Him C. Schult, Moses Whybark, Edward A. Rozier and William P. Evans, *ex- officio*, R. B. Oliver of Cape Girardeau is the board's treasurer and the executive committee is composed of Louis Houck, Moses Whybark and Leon J. Albert.

FORMER PRESIDENTS

Principal C. H. Dutcher was born February 17, 1841, in Pike county, Illinois, his parents being natives of New York. He was reared on the farm and after completing the course of study in the country schools he spent a year at Christian university at Canton and then became a student at Kentucky university, where he was graduated in June, 1864, with the degree Bachelor of Arts. During part of his college life he served as a volunteer nurse in the hospital organized in the buildings of the university. After his graduation he taught school at Danville, Kentucky, and then at other points in that state. In 1872-73 he was principal of the city schools of Kirksville, Missouri, and in the latter year was elected a member of the faculty of the Kirksville State Normal school, teaching Latin and science; he held this position until 1877, when he became principal of the State Normal school at Cape Girardeau. As we have seen, his administration, which was conservative and businesslike, enabled the school to become thoroughly established. He held the principalship for three years and then engaged for a time in banking. In 1881 he became a teacher in the State Normal school at Warrensburg, holding the position until 1892, when he resigned. Mr. Dutcher is a member of the Christian church and a man of highest character and ideals. He was not only a successful administrator and executive, but also an able and successful teacher. Under him the school prospered and won a place in the educational system of the state.

President Richard Chapman Norton, LL. D., was born in Ohio in 1840. He was educated in the public schools and Hiram college, where one of his teachers was James A. Garfield, afterwards president of the United States. After Mr. Norton was graduated in the year 1861, he immediately enlisted in the army and served throughout the war. In 1866 he came to Missouri and was for a time connected with a railroad as a surveyor and engineer. He then accepted a position as superintendent of public schools in Trenton, Missouri, a position which he held for two years. He then became a member of the faculty and vice president of the State Normal school at Warrensburg, remaining there until he came to Cape Girardeau in 1880. After his resignation from the presidency of this school he was for a time connected with the Kirksville Normal, then he retired to his home near Trenton, and spent the last years of his life quietly there. In all he was connected with the Normal schools of the state for nearly a quarter of a century and few men impressed themselves more upon the young men and women with whom they came in contact.

Mr. Norton exercised a remarkable influence over students, especially young men. His influence had for its secret an uprightness of character and unfailing earnestness of purpose which were the foundations of a noble and successful life. Every student knew that in him could be found a wise and faithful counselor and friend. He was called "Uncle Dick" by the students and this was an expression of the real affection in which he was held.

On the resignation of President Norton in 1893 the board selected as his successor Willard D. Vandiver, a native of Virginia. Mr. Vandiver had been engaged in school work for many years. He was graduated from Central College in 1877 and was immediately elected professor of mathematics in Bellevue Collegiate Institute at Caledonia. After three years' connection with the institution he became its president. His administration was very successful and he attracted the attention of school authorities on account of his success in this institution. In 1889 he was made professor of science in the Normal school. Here again he was successful in his work and on the presidency of the school becoming vacant, he was elected to that position. Mr. Vandiver remained at the head of the institution for only four years. His administration was marked by great progress in the school. He terminated his connection with it to accept a position as a member of Congress for the 14th congressional district as a Democrat. Since that time he has been active in political life, serving three terms in Congress and then being appointed insurance commissioner of the state of Missouri. He is now connected with an insurance company of St. Louis.

John S. McGee, who was president from 1897 to 1899, was a native Missourian. He was born in 1849 and spent most of his early life in Wayne county. He was educated in an academy at Greenville and in the State Normal school at Kirksville. After his graduation from the latter he was elected to the principalship of the public schools at Pierce City, a position he filled for two years. In 1879 he became professor of mathematics in the State Normal school at Cape Girardeau. Here he made a place for himself in the life of the school and became known as one of the strong men of the faculty. On the resignation of President Vandiver in 1897, Mr. McGee was chosen as the head of the school. He gave to the duties of this office the same careful thought and untiring effort which had distinguished his work as a teacher. He retired from the position in 1899 and devoted himself to other pursuits. He became interested in real estate in Cape Girardeau and acquired a competence. His death, which occurred in 1903, brought sadness to many men and women who had found in him not only a wise and capable teacher, but also a sympathetic and helpful friend.

PLACE OF THE NORMAL SCHOOL

Two ideas are held regarding the position of the Normal school in the system of public education. One of these, and perhaps the older idea, is that it should be a school devoted solely to the preparation of teachers, especially for the elementary schools. Those who hold to this idea would limit the Normal schools in equipment and buildings and would also limit their courses of study to include about as much of academic work as is given in a high school, and in addition to this certain pedagogical training.

The other idea is that a Normal school should have for its first duty the preparation of teachers, but not only teachers for the elementary schools, but also teachers for all grades of school maintained in the system; and that in addition to its work in the preparation of teachers, the plant and equipment of the Normal school should be used, as far as is consistent with its principal purpose and mission, to bring within the reach of all the people of the district a general college education. Those who hold to this idea as the purpose and aim of the Normal school maintain the position that the buildings and equipment and faculty of these schools should be of the best, that so far as is consistent with the maintenance of a school system the Normal schools should be colleges in which instruction is given not only in pedagogical subjects, but in all the subjects requisite to a liberal education. This view is justified by the consideration that teachers need a broader and more thorough education than is to be had in the high schools and that the preparation of efficient teachers demands and requires Normal schools to widen their courses of study and to bring to their students the inspiration and help that comes from contact with higher education. It is felt too that not only does this consideration justify the maintenance of a college curriculum, but it is also justified by the further fact that to fail to make of the Normal schools a college is in reality to miss an opportunity and in thus far to waste the funds invested in the Normal school. There seems no reason why regular college work may not be carried on by the Normal school faculty not only without interference with pedagogical work of the institution but even with an actual strengthening of that special work.

It is this second view of the wider function of the purpose of the Normal schools that is maintained by the Normal school at Cape Girardeau. It is taking a foremost position among the Normal schools of the entire country on this question, and its courses now include not only purely pedagogical material, but also thoroughly organized college work.

SECTION VIII

Present Conditions

CHAPTER XXXIV

SOCIAL LIFE AND INDUSTRIES

Isolation of Many Communities—Deprivations Suffered — Houses — Food — Dress — Household Implements—Schools and Churches—Amusements — Unity of Feeling—Treatment of Disease—Versatility of the Pioneer — Development of Character — Farming—Mining—Manufacturing.

There are many persons now living, whose recollection goes back into the period which we are now considering. They have a just appreciation of the situation and circumstances under which the inhabitants of this part of the state lived up to this time. To those of the younger generation, however, it is a very difficult matter to reconstruct conditions of life that prevailed in many parts of Southeast Missouri. It is especially true of those towns and villages which were situated at a distance from the river. They presented, in many respects, a scene of primitive life that is almost beyond the comprehension of those who did not actually live that life. When we consider that such towns as Greenville in Wayne county, Poplar Bluff in Butler county, Kennett in Dunklin county, and Fredericktown in Madison county, were situated at great distances from the river; that there were no railroads reaching them, and that the roads which formed the sole means of travel for their inhabitants were, in many cases and at many times, almost impassable, we see something of the hard conditions of life in many of these places. It is true that in all of them stores were opened with considerable stocks of goods, and that communication was kept up more or less regularly with the towns on the river, but in spite of this fact, these and similarly situated places were in a state of what seems today very great isolation.

There are great numbers of people who can remember when their homes were at a distance of twenty-five to one hundred miles from the nearest town, and when the annual, or semi-annual visit to the town was the occasion of the only real shopping expedition that the women of the family made during the entire year. All the manufactured articles, with the exception of the simplest, including cloth, tools, household implements, and furniture, such supplies of food as were not grown on the place itself, were brought from these distant towns in wagon or on horse-back over indifferent roads.

This situation led to some customs which seem peculiar to those of the present day. The prices of many things were inordinately high, as compared with the prices now. This was true of such a small thing as the match, and it was no unusual thing for the household to be entirely without matches, and to depend upon the flint and steel, or upon a supply of fire borrowed from some neighbor to rekindle that which had gone out from carelessness. On many shelves, or mantles, there stood in these days a vessel containing rolls of paper called lamp-lighters, which were held in the fire that blazed on the hearth, and then used to light the candle or the lamp. Other articles of the most frequent use, and seemingly entirely indispensable, were rarely seen inside the houses of many people in this period.

The houses of the settlers were, in the early part of the period we are considering, built very largely of logs. The same house plan followed in Virginia and the Carolinas and brought westward by the American settlers was still in use. By 1850, however, there were in operation saw-mills, enabling the more enterprising of the inhabitants to construct frame houses and, accordingly, we find that from this time on, frame houses became more and more common. These houses built during this period, while simple in plan, and free from much ornamentation, were usually built of the quality of lumber which it is now no longer possible to secure. Timber was the cheapest commodity on the market, and where a saw-mill was available at all, it was possible to secure at a very low cost, lumber sawed from the finest and straightest of trees.

These houses, whether frame or logs, were still heated by the fire-place. There were a few stoves, for during this period the open iron stove known as the "Franklin" made its appearance in Southeast Missouri, and found favor in some places, but the great dependance was upon the open fire-place. The chimneys were built in some counties of stone, but in most cases they were still of what was known as the "stick and dirt" type. Brick was coming to be used for the same purposes in places, and there were occasional brick houses being erected, though they were as yet by no means common.

The food of the people was simple, but abundant. In more remote settlements game was still to be found in very great abundance, and supplied, in considerable measure, food for the family. Wild turkey and venison, and some of the countless varieties of wild fowl, bacon, and less frequently beef, were the staple meats. Bread made from flour was used more and more extensively, but during all of this period the bread that was most commonly used by the American settlers was corn bread. There was as yet no general use of many varieties of vegetables or fruits. Orchards were planted in places, and kitchen gardens were cultivated by some, but these were the exception and not the rule. Dependence was placed on the plainer and more substantial items of diet which we have mentioned. These remarks, of course, do not apply to the French settlements, for they retained that taste and skill in cookery and the preparation of food which has always distinguished the French.

The dress of the American settlers during a great part of this period was still of the home-spun cloth, such as we have described in speaking of the dress of an earlier time. Toward the close of the period, as we have indicated, there came more and more into use clothing made from cloth imported into the country. Even at this time, however, the cloths themselves were cut and made up in the home. Not many of the people wore clothes made by tailors or in great manufacturing establishments. This was especially true of the clothing of the men. Of course in the larger towns, where something of a society prevailed, men of substance were accustomed to have their clothes made in the cities by tailors, but this was by no means the usual thing in Southeast Missouri before the war. If the cloth itself were not woven in the home, it was bought and then turned into the various articles of dress. While there were many disadvantages in this situation, it had some advantages. One was the possibility of securing cloth that possessed unusual wearing qualities.

The household implements were primitive in character. Cooking, during the greater part of this period, was almost universally done on the open fire. The kitchen of the house contained, instead of a range, a fireplace, and on this the women of the house cooked the food that was used. The frying-pan, the kettle, and the baking oven were the utensils used. Those who never tried the experience cannot appreciate the trials of the housewife who prepared dinner for a large family in this way. It was before the day of the sewing machine, or at least the use of the machine was not common in this part of the state. Almost all sewing was done by hand. This took a great part of the time of the busy housewife, for she not only mended the clothes of the household, but also made them in the first instance.

It has been set out in other chapters that during this period there was a constant growth in schools and in church organizations. While there was no such careful organization of public schools as now exists, and no such opportunities offered for education as the children of the present day enjoy, still there were few communities, even in the most remote counties, where schools were not conducted for at least a part of the year, and there were not many places where the pioneer preacher did not penetrate, bringing with him the gospel.

The amusements were not different from those of the present period. The dance and the social party, attendance upon meeting, picnics, barbecues, were the principal gatherings attended by both sexes. The men found amusement in shooting at a mark with the rifle, in hunting and fishing, in such humble sports as marbles and pitching horseshoes. There were also certain athletic contests, and it was no uncommon thing for the men of the neighborhood to engage in wrestling and in the jumping match. This was before the day of baseball, but the men had a game, out of which baseball probably developed, which was called "town ball."

One thing which marked the social life of the early settlers in outlying districts, and which has practically disappeared, was the unity of feeling. This was manifested in many ways. Most often it took the form of co-operative work. If a house was to be raised, or the logs on a piece of ground were to be "rolled," the work was not left to be done by the man interested, and those whom he might employ, but the neighbors on every hand gathered in to assist him. The raising of a new house was the term applied to putting up the logs on the ordinary log structure, and setting up the rafters for the roof. This was accomplished by a collection of men who spent the day in hard work and also in pleasant companionship. The men who came for this, or other work, were often accompanied by their wives, who, while their husbands were busily engaged in the field or on the new house, assisted the hostess in the preparation of the bountiful dinner which was one of the main features of the day. This method of work extended also to such work as wheat threshing. This feeling of the unity of the neighborhood found expression, however, not only in this work together, but also in a certain care for the interests of each individual. The man who fell sick might be at a distance from a physician, and at a very much greater distance from a trained nurse, but he was certain to have the attention and help of those who lived about him. It was not an infrequent thing for a man who fell sick and whose crops thereby suffered to find that the kindly disposed of his neighbors had gathered together and worked his crop out for him.

This feeling, which was found in almost every neighborhood, went far toward ameliorating the hard conditions in which men and women passed their lives. Unfortunately, this spirit has been lost in most communities in this part of the state. There exists but little trace of the friendly, neighborly spirit which found expression in the ways which we have mentioned. Today, the man who has extra work to do no longer looks to his neighbors and friends, but counts himself fortunate if he is able to hire persons to work for him.

We have seen in discussing the various settlements that there were physicians living in many of them. In spite of this fact, however, one of the great hardships endured by many people of this section of the state, was the absence of medical treatment and of the proper supply of medicines. It was not at all unusual for families to live at great distances from the nearest physicians. This state of things, of course, caused much suffering which might have been avoided, had it been possible to have secured a physician's service. It resulted, however, in the study of simple diseases and the making of simple remedies in practically every home. Some member of the family had to take upon himself the responsibility for the simple treatment of diseases, and the housewife usually prepared a supply of home remedies. There were certain herbs and barks that were held in high esteem for the treatment of common complaints.

In considering the situation of the people in this time, we must not forget that it was not a day of division of labor, at least not in the rural communities. There were carpenters and blacksmiths and other mechanics in the larger towns, but just as was the case with the physicians, people who lived in the more remote counties were compelled to dispense with the services of these. This resulted in the all-around knowledge and in the ability to do a great many things which distinguished men who lived along the frontier. Since it was often impossible to secure a carpenter or a blacksmith, and since carpenter work and blacksmithing had to be done, it fell out that men who needed the work learned to do it for themselves. There are now living in Southeast Missouri many men of the older generation who could turn their hands to various kinds of work. They could build a house or a fence or construct furniture. They could sharpen a plow or weld a broken rod, and do many other similar things, which we are accustomed to think of as being solely within the province of the professional workman. This all-around skill which was developed from the very necessity of the case, was one of the compensations for the lack of schools and formal education. The boy in the remote community might be unable to attend school more than a few weeks in the year, and the school which he attended was not equipped for doing a high grade of work, but he found in his home the stimulus for learning many useful things and the opportunity and even necessity for practicing them. To use the carpenter's tools, or those of the blacksmith, to be able to mend harness or shoes, or to turn his hand to do a number of other things, was supposed to be a part of the boy's education and preparation for life. And it must not be forgotten in estimating character and intellectual development of the man of this period, that such a training as this not only fits the hand and the eye for the performance of their tasks, but also has its effect in developing intellect and the formation of character. We have sometimes misjudged the men of other generations, and of lesser opportunities, because we have considered that the mind may be developed only by contact with books and schools. It is not true, of course, that all manner of labor has a great effect in the development of the mind, but it is true that the practice of the different trades and professions which we have mentioned, under the circumstances of pioneer life, does have a very great effect in mental growth and development. Out of the seemingly unfavorable conditions, the elementary condition of the schools in Southeast Missouri during this period, there came many men who have real breadth of intellect and force of character, and may not be unworthily compared to many who have had much greater advantages and much better opportunities.

This life developed men of very great initiative and wonderful power. It was during this period that the west attracted such great numbers of people by the discovery of gold in California. Thousands of Missourians, some of them from the southeast, made their way to the west and took part in all the stirring scenes of that time. These men, owing to their early training and the character which it had developed, made their mark in every part of the new country. The Missourian became a well known character and was regarded as one of the highest types of men in the west. It is a curious and interesting exercise to look through the records of western life and to see how many Missourians have filled important places and played great parts in the building up of the west. All along the coast, from Canada to Mexico, are to be found Missourians and their descendants. The characters which were developed in them by the pioneer life in the state fitted them excellently for the work of the country.

One of the most interesting accounts having to do with this period was written by Judge Robert Goah Watson of New Madrid county. Judge Watson, who came to New Madrid very early in its history as a trader with the Indians, became one of its most prominent and influential citizens. He accumulated considerable property through his trading enterprises and was a man who always stood up for the best interests of his community. He wrote late in his life an account setting out the experiences which he had in the new section of the country. It is an interesting bit of biography and it casts considerable light on the surroundings and life in New Madrid county.

One of the things of which he speaks with special emphasis is the existence in the early days of undesirable people. Not only were such gangs of robbers as the Mason and Murrell band, if not tolerated, at least allowed to continue their operations for a good many years, but there were in addition to these open and notorious outlaws, a large number of men who, for one reason or another, had left their homes and who had vicious and evil habits that they brought to the new country. They considered themselves to be outside of the domain of law and order and to have a license to conduct themselves as they chose. It was exceedingly difficult to reduce them to orderly living. They formed a considerable part of the population and by their boldness they imposed themselves upon the quieter and better class. There were many crimes committed by them, more especially the crime of counterfeiting and forgery. Judge Watson says that it became a matter of the greatest difficulty to determine whether a bill or check or a piece of money was really valuable or whether it was only a counterfeit or a forgery.

This condition of affairs lasted until the better citizens of the county determined for the safety of the county, for the sake of their good names and self protection, to rid themselves of these undesirable persons. Accordingly, they banded themselves together into an organization, not unlike the later vigilance committees of California. They served notice on those who were giving trouble that they would be summarily dealt with, that they need no longer expect to be tolerated or allowed to continue their nefarious practices. At first it seemed that resistance would be made and that blood would flow as a result of this action. The better citizens, however, stood firm for their rights and finally those whose presence was not desired slunk away and the country was left much better off than it had been.

INDUSTRIES

During these years the principal industries in the country continued to be farming and mining. A great deal of farming land was opened, and the products of the soil increased in number and value. Agriculture was studied more carefully, and the great fertility of much of the soil enabled the growing of large crops. The great majority of the population were directly dependent upon the produce of the soil. This was true even in the mineral section, for while many persons worked at times in the mines, there was no great number, even in that district, who were not also directly interested in the cultivation of the soil. The better lands of Southeast Missouri, which are to be found in the alluvial soil of the Mississippi bottoms, began to be opened up during this period. The building of the levee in Pemiscot county was an evidence of the growing appreciation of value of this soil. In Butler, Stoddard. Dunklin and Mississippi counties, there were large tracts of land being put into cultivation during this period. It is impossible to give any accurate statistics as to the value of the produce of the soil, for the reason that no such statistics were gathered during part of this time. It was not until the census of 1860 that the government began to make inquiry into the occupations of men and to take account of the things which they grew or manufactured. It was long before the organization of the bureau of labor or of the labor department of the state government, and no particular attention was paid to the gathering or preservation of statistics having to do with these matters. The growth of the population, however, enables us to decide that production was increasing rapidly because the country was self-supporting. It grew practically everything necessary for the life of the people.

The crops were not greatly different from those that are now grown, though hardly so varied in character. Corn and wheat were the staples, and connected with these was the cattle growing industry. The range had not disappeared as yet, and it was still possible to raise stock profitably at very little cost. It was during this period that cotton made its appearance in the counties in the extreme southeast.

One handicap under which farmers labored was the lack of transportation facilities. Except for those situated on the river, it was a matter of the very greatest difficulty to transport their surplus products to market, and we may not be surprised that the growth of the country away from the river, in spite of all its natural advantages, was slow until the era of railroad construction began. A study of the statistics of population set out in the table accompanying another chapter, shows very conclusively the influence of river transportation in the development of the country. If these figures are compared with similar figures published in another chapter the influence of railroads in the development of the interior is very plainly seen.

Farming, however, was not the only, though it was the most important, industry followed by the people of the section. There were considerable numbers of men engaged in buying and selling. More and more the people came to depend upon the imported goods, especially clothing and dry goods. During the earlier part of this period, the home was the factory where there was manufactured all that was needed for the comfort of its members. This, however, was changed by the close of the period which we are considering. The development of steamboat transportation and the consequent ease and cheapness with which goods might be transported, enabled those who lived in the counties bordering the river, to secure manufactured goods at a fraction of their former cost, and they came more and more to be dependent upon articles so secured. This habit, or fashion, of using things imported from other parts of the country spread slowly but surely, to those settlements and towns lying away from the river. To supply the wants of these people there was a considerable number of persons engaged in merchandising. In contrast to the settlements made prior to this period we find that one of the first houses in every town was occupied by one enterprising trader with a considerable stock of goods.

The wheat raised on these farms was cut by hand. It was before the day of farming machinery. The first implement used in wheat cutting was the sickle. This was a curved blade with handle, which was held in the right hand while the left hand grasped the heads of the wheat. These were then cut off at the top of the stalk and carried from the field. Sometimes the scythe was used, and later the cradle was invented. The cradle consisted of a long, heavy scythe blade, to which was attached a number of wooden fingers, each as long as the blade, and projecting above it. When the wheat was cut, the cradle caught the stalks, and these were then removed by the person using the implement. The handfuls of grain thus gathered were placed together to form a bundle or sheaf. The instrument appears awkward and of little use, judging by the standards of today, but it was used for many years and harvested great crops of wheat.

The scythe was also used to cut whatever hay was grown on the farm. This, too, was work requiring time, and seems today to have been inadequate for the purpose for which it was used.

Other farming machinery and implements were of like character. The wooden plow was still in use in some places. The first improvement over the wooden plow in general use was the steel point, then the whole of the point and mold board were made of steel. Of course, the wooden implement, or even the one with steel point was vastly inferior to the modern plow, and work accomplished by it not to compare in quality with that done today. The modern cultivator and disc harrow were as unknown as the self-binder.

The wheat which was thus harvested by hand, was threshed, usually, by the flail, or by being trampled upon by cattle. After it was dry it was placed on the floor of the barn, or on a specially prepared piece of ground, and then beaten upon with sticks, in order to shatter the grains from the head. When this was done the straw was raked away, and then the wheat was winnowed. This was accomplished by taking it up in shovels and throwing it into the air, so that the chaff was blown away by the wind.

This wheat was ground into flour at the little mills which made their appearance at a number of places in this section. Practically all of them at first were water mills, and were to be found only in those counties in the Ozarks. The people who lived in the alluvial section were compelled to take their wheat for great distances to these mills.

Corn was ground both by water mills, such as are used for the grinding of wheat, and also at mills operated by other power, usually horse power. These horse-power mills sometimes consisted of a great, flat wheel set at an angle on which horses and sometimes cattle were tied. Their walking set the wheel in motion, and this was geared to the machinery of the mill. Corn was not infrequently ground also in hand mills owned by many families.

The mining interests were large during this period though they did not develop as rapidly as they did later. The lack of capital to provide proper machinery as well as inadequate transportation facilities prevented the development of the region to the extent possible in a later period. Some of the richest lead regions were not yet discovered. The great Flat river district was not yet developed in full, and the very rich deposits at Doe Run had not yet been touched. The first furnace at Bonne Terre, afterward the site of the greatest mine in the entire southeast, was not erected until about 1856, and the production was very limited until near the close of the war, when the St. Joseph Lead Co. was organized and began to push the work of development. The older mines were still worked, but they did not produce anything like the immense quantities of lead later taken from them.

Manufacturing began to have importance toward the close of this period. Perhaps the most important manufactured product during these years was flour. Water mills were erected at various places in the counties of the upland and wheat was brought to them from all over the district to be ground. Toward the close of the period the first steam mill in the section was erected at Cape Girardeau. During this period, also, the demand for lumber caused the building of saw mills. Previously when lumber was desired, it was sawed from the log by hand. The first saw mills were water mills or else were driven by horse power.

Another manufactured article was brick. At Cape Girardeau, Jackson, Perryville, Fredericktown, and the towns in the hills houses began to be built of brick. Clay existed in many places suitable for brick-making and this industry began to develop.

There were distilleries in places, and much whiskey was made. Tan yards were common also. Lime began to be manufactured. The manufacture of pig lead and of shot had long been carried on in the mineral region and grew in quantity during this period.

To a certain extent every farm house was a factory where many articles of domestic use were made. Cloth was woven, thread spun, clothing made, furniture and many household implements and tools were constructed. All these processes of manufacture whether carried on in the home or the factory added to the independence and fostered the development of the country.

CHAPTER XXXV

RELIGIOUS HISTORY—Continued

CATHOLICS — METHODISTS: QUARTERLY MEETINGS, CIRCUITS AND DISTRICTS—BAPTISTS: ASSOCIATIONS—EVANGELICAL LUTHERANS—PROTESTANT EPISCOPAL CHURCHES—CONGREGATIONALISTS—GERMAN EVANGELICAL AND GERMAN METHODIST CHURCHES—NEW SCHOOL PRESBYTERIANS—CUMBERLAND PRESBYTERIAN CHURCHES — CHRISTIANS (DISCIPLES OF CHRIST)—SOUTHEAST MISSOURI PRESBYTERIAN CHURCHES—PRESBYTERIANISM IN 1854-64—1864-1874—DIVISION IN PRESBYTERY—DECADE FROM 1884 TO 1894—HISTORY SINCE 1894.

In a former chapter we have discussed the beginning of religious work within the bounds of Southeast Missouri by those religious denominations which entered this part of the state prior to its admission to the Union. We now have to continue the story of the development of the work in these churches, and the beginning of the work of other denominations which entered the state in the period we have under consideration.

Our attention is given first of all to the development of the work of the Catholic church, the oldest of the religious organizations within the state. It will be recalled that Bishop Dubourg, who was appointed to the diocese of New Orleans, which included Upper Louisiana, in 1815, brought with him on his return from Rome, a number of zealous, earnest priests and students, who came to take up and carry on the work of the church in this state. The most famous of these who accompanied the bishop were Father De Andreis and Father Rosati, both of whom, as was the bishop himself, were members of the Congregation of the Mission. Father De Andreis became vicar general of the diocese with headquarters in St. Louis, and assisted in the organization of St. Mary's Seminary at Perryville. Later, the work of carrying on this seminary was entrusted to Father Rosati. Among the men associated with these whom we have mentioned, in their work of evangelization, were: Father J. M. Odin and Father John Timon. Father Odin became the first bishop of Galveston and later archbishop of New Orleans. Father Timon, who was ordained in 1825, was assigned to the work in Perry and Cape Girardeau counties. He often preached in the courthouse at Jackson, and it was through his efforts that a mission was established in the town of Cape Girardeau. When this mission had been established, and it became necessary to purchase property on which to erect buildings to carry on the work, a tract of land just south of the town was purchased from a man named Daugherty; it was bought in the name of the Vincentian Fathers. It is the tract of on which St. Vincent's church and St. Vincent's College in Cape Girardeau now stand. At first the services were held in Daugherty's house, later a store-house was purchased and modified so as to be suitable for the celebration of religious services. The mission became a regularly organized parish in 1836, at which time Father Odin was installed as the priest in charge. It was but a short time until plans were made for the erection of a suitable church building. This was completed and dedicated July 19, 1852. It stands facing the river and is a commodius brick structure, in the Gothic style of architecture, and is still in use. It has been remodeled and thoroughly overhauled at various times, so as to keep it in condition for the use of the congregation.

The settlement of St. Michaels, in Madison county near the present site of Fredericktown, was a distinctly Catholic settlement. It was made in 1802, and about the year 1820 a church building was erected on the site of the new village. It was simply a missionary station and no regular parish priest was attached to it. After the removal of the town from St. Michaels to the present site of Fredericktown, the church which was built of stone was taken down and moved to a new town; this was in 1827. After the removal, a regular parish was organized and Father Francois Cellini was appointed to take charge of the work. He was one of the men who had come with Bishop Dubourg from Italy in 1817. He was a man of unusual attainments and ability. Before coming to America he had served as a surgeon in the Italian army and had been knighted on account of his services in that capacity. When he became parish priest in Fredericktown he continued the practice of his former profession among his parishioners, and he possessed such skill as a surgeon that he was often called upon to practice in different parts of the country. He also engaged in the manufacture and sale of certain proprietary medicines known as Cellini's Balm and Cellini's Bitters. Father Cellini was succeeded in 1842 by P. D. Savelli, who remained until 1845. At this time, Father Tucker, a native of Perry county, was appointed parish priest. He organized a movement for the erection of a brick church and a new residence for the priest. These were completed in 1858. He remained in charge of the parish until his death in 1880.

In 1838, there was erected at Perryville, a church known as St. Mary's church. This was in connection with St. Mary's College, and the priests in charge of the church have ordinarily been members of the faculty of the college. This church building is of stone and is a very beautiful and commodious structure.

The first church in Washington county was built at Old Mines about 1825. It was built by the Catholics and was a log building. This was torn down in 1830, and a brick structure erected. The church in Potosi was organized in 1828, and the present church building was erected in 1862.

In 1845 a Catholic church was organized in Benton, and a house erected to be used as a church. The lot on which the church was placed was given by a gentleman named Meyers. In 1850 this church was burned.

In 1848 a log church was built at New Hamburg which was superseded in 1857 by a handsome stone structure. This church was destroyed by fire during the war, but was replaced by a more costly and beautiful one.

In 1856 a Catholic church was organized at Leopold, in Bollinger county. The priest who conducted the organization was John Van Lluytelaar; the members of the church were J. G. Sonderen, J. Scharenbourg, John and Jacob Holweg, Armond Jansen, Herman Elfraut, W. Wardraeker, J. W. Tuling, T. Meyer, A. Rickhoff, Clement Beel and John

Derbraak. The first church building was of logs, but it was soon replaced by a large frame building.

The second Catholic church in Cape Girardeau was the German church. It had been the desire of the German families in the town to have a separate organization and in 1858 J. Meyer and J. Goetz were appointed as a committee to consult with Archbishop Kenrick as to the advisability of establishing a separate congregation for German speaking Catholics. All that was accomplished at the time was the purchase of a lot by ten men who were interested in the establishment of the new church. Nothing more was done toward the organization until after the close of the war. The delay probably would not have taken place, had it not been for the difficulties that arose at that time, occasioned by the war itself.

In 1867 Father Rainerius Dickneite began an agitation for building of the church. The priest of St. Vincent's at that time was Father L. C. Meyer. He gave to the subject of building all the weight of his influence, and a new building committee was appointed, composed of J. Lansman, Charles Fuerth, J. Schwepker, H. Sander and J. Goetz. This committee purchased a lot on Frederick street for $650, and the work of erecting the building was begun March 25, 1868. The building cost $14,000. A schoolhouse for the parochial school was built in 1882, and the priest's residence in 1885. The school has been conducted by Sisters of the Order of St. Francis. The pastors of this parish have been Rev. J. Herde, Rev. Gells, Rev. W. Hinssen, Rev. J. Schmidt, Rev. S. Kleiser, Rev. W. Sonnonschein, Rev. Francis Willmer, and Rev. E. Pruente. Father Pruente has been in charge of the parish since December 30, 1881, and his labors have been unusually successful. The church now has a large membership.

The church of St. Augustine was organized at Kelso in 1878. The members of the organization had formerly belonged to the church at New Hamburg. Immediately after the organization, a frame building was erected and used for a number of years, then superseded by the present brick structure.

The St. John's church at Leopold has more than 600 communicants, and has maintained a school since 1872.

In 1870 a church was built at Farmington and a congregation of about twenty families organized by Henry Milsepen, who was the German vicar-general. For a time there was no resident priest, the first one being Rev. John Daley. He had charge of the church at French Village also. For a period of about ten years Farmington and Iron Mountain parishes were united under the care of the same priest. About 1885 the church at Farmington had grown so as to require the services of a priest for all the time. The church has a good brick building and a school building also.

The first Catholic church at Bonne Terre was built by Father Daley, the land having been given by members of the Whilebon family. The church was not conveniently located, however, being at a distance from the town. In 1881 the Desloge Lead Company gave a lot, upon which a brick building was erected, at a cost of $3,000. Rev. E. J. Dempsey was the first resident priest, and the principal work of establishing the church was performed by Father M. C. Walsh. Through his exertions a fine school building was erected in 1885, and a priest's residence a few years later. Father Walsh was a native of Ireland, but came with his parents to America in infancy. His parents determined to fit him for the priesthood, and he was educated in St. Patrick's school, in St. Louis, and was later sent to St. Mary's Seminary, at Perryville. He was graduated from St. Vincent's College at Cape Girardeau in July, 1862, and was ordained to the priesthood. He spent the first years of his ministry in north Missouri, but from about 1881 he was active in a number of counties in Southeast Missouri. The great growth of Catholicism during this period is due in part to the earnest efforts of Father Walsh.

The German Catholic church of Perryville, known as St. Boniface, was established in 1870, and the present brick building was erected shortly after that time.

The church of Our Lady of Perpetual Help, at Pilot Knob, was established about the beginning of the war. There had been a settlement at Pilot Knob since the transfer to the United States, and beginning in 1846, Father Tucker, the parish priest at Fredericktown, had held occasional services in the homes of members at Pilot Knob. In 1861 Mrs. Catherine Immer began the work of raising funds for a church building. The first contributor to this fund was Archbishop Kenrick, of St. Louis. The church was completed early in the year 1864, and in that same year was injured by an explosion during the battle of Pilot Knob. Some of the early priests were Father Hennessey, afterwards Bishop of Wichita, Kansas, and L. C. Weinert. Father Weinert remained with the church for many years and was esteemed one of the ablest and most devoted pastors the church had. In 1881 a parochial school was established in connection with the church, and at this time a great-granddaughter of Joseph Pratte is a teacher in this school. It was to Joseph Pratte that the land on which the town now stands was originally granted by the Spanish government, which grant was afterwards confirmed by the United States in 1834. In 1882 the church purchased land and established a cemetery. It celebrated the fiftieth anniversary of the establishment of the church June 5, 1912. A number of former priests took part in this celebration.

Besides the churches already mentioned, there are the following Catholic churches in Southeast Missouri: St. Joseph's, at Uniontown; St. Joseph's Chapel, at Arcadia; St. Philomena's, at Bloomsdale, in Ste. Genevieve county; the Church of the Nativity, in Bois Brule Bottom; the Church of Our Lady, in Claryville; the Church of St. Lawrence, in Ste. Genevieve county; Ste. Anne's, at French Village, in St. Francois county; St. Joseph's, at Zell, in Ste. Genevieve county; St. Mary's, in Ste. Genevieve county; Sacred Heart, at Poplar Bluff; the Immaculate Conception, Jackson; St. Mary's at Charleston; St. Francois de Sales, in Mississippi county; the Immaculate Conception, at New Madrid. Besides these there are organizations at Doniphan, Malden, Caruthersville, Glennonville, Bismarck, Bloomfield, De Soto, Dexter, East Prairie, Festus, Caruthersville, Greenville, Irondale, Iron Mountain, Maxville, the oldest church in Jefferson county, organized in 1850; Kimmswick, Old Mines, the oldest church in Washington county, Potosi, and Richwoods.

Not only was the Catholic church the first in the territory of Southeast Missouri, it has always been one of the most powerful. Its compact organization, its wealth, and the zeal and devotion of its priesthood have given it a place among the people of this part of the state. This is especially true in the French settlements like Ste. Genevieve, New Madrid, and Cape Girardeau. Some of the German settlements as well are strongly Catholic.

Other German communities were settled by Lutherans and their influence has continued paramount in these places.

The Catholic church has given great attention to the matter of education. In this field it was the pioneer. St. Mary's Seminary at Perryville, is the oldest institution of learning in the entire state, and St. Vincent's College at Cape Girardeau the oldest college. Besides these the church has supported parochial schools in all communities where the number of Catholics warrants it. A large and growing membership, virtual control of the religious situation in certain parts of the section, valuable property, and numbers of schools attest the position won for this church during the years of its history.

Up to 1821 the Methodists had established one district called Cape Girardeau District, and the following circuits: Bellevue, Saline, St. Francois, Spring River, White River, Cape Girardeau and New Madrid. At that date Thomas Wright was the presiding elder of the district. The church grew slowly during the years. Some of the congregations were prosperous and sent out new organizations, but some of them were almost at a stand for a number of years. No great advance was made until about the year 1835. By that year some new circuits had been added, among them: Farmington, Greenville and West Prairie. At that time Uriel Haw was Presiding Elder. A mission was established at Bloomfield in 1837, which in another year became a circuit of the church. In 1839 Jacob Lanius was the Presiding Elder. Cape Girardeau circuit was supplied by Nelson Henry and Edward Allen, New Madrid by Uriel Haw and James G. T. Dunleavy, Bloomfield by N. B. Evans, Greenville by Lysander Wiley, Farmington by Melville Will, and Ste. Genevieve by Samuel S. Colburn.

About the year 1835 there began a movement for the building of church houses. At that time there were, perhaps, fewer than one-half dozen church buildings belonging to the Methodists in all of Southeast Missouri. One of the early buildings was Yorke Chapel; this was in Perry county, about five miles from Perryville and was erected in 1825. It was afterward replaced by a stone building which is still standing. In 1835 a chapel, which was known as Mt. Zion, was built in the Virginia settlement four miles from Fredericktown. About the year 1830 a church was organized in Matthew's Prairie, in Mississippi county and a small log house was erected on the land of Elizabeth Smith. The names of the members of this church have been preserved. Some of them were: Absolum McElmurry and wife, Elizabeth Smith, Elijah Bruce, Samuel Duncan and family, William Bush, Joseph Moore and wife, James Moore and wife, Charles Moore and wife, Richard and Mary Crenshaw, Uriel Haw and wife, and Isaac Vernon and wife. It will be seen that some of these were members of families still prominent in Mississippi county. Uriel Haw afterward became one of the prominent ministers of the church and served at various times as Presiding Elder of the Cape Girardeau District. His grandson, Marvin T. Haw, is a minister of the Methodist church and has been stationed at various places in Southeast Missouri.

In 1838 this house was burned and two or three years later a church building was erected at Charleston. This was occupied until 1856, when it was torn down and a brick building put in its place. This, too, was burned in 1870 and was immediately rebuilt.

Some of the other early churches in Mississippi county were Kay's Chapel, Haw's Chapel and Rush Ridge Chapel.

A church building was erected at Jackson about 1841. The trustees of this church were: Greer W. Davis, David H. Davis, Caleb Green, Welton O'Bannon, John D. Cook, Hiram Gilliland and William T. Randol. The lot for the church was given by Greer W. Davis.

The first Methodist church house in Cape Girardeau was erected about 1842. It was blown down by a storm in 1851 and the next building was a small frame house on the corner opposite where the Episcopal church now stands. This house was destroyed by a snow storm in 1856, the weight of the snow crushing the structure.

The first church building in Bloomfield erected by the Methodists was a small house put on a lot donated by the county, this was in 1842. Edmund Wood, Thomas Neale, Samuel Sifford, Thompson Couch and John Eaker were trustees of the church.

In 1838 a church was built at Fredericktown, and occupied the site of the present church building. Some of the early members were: T. F. Tong, F. T. Overfield, Thomas Cooper, Wm. M. Newberry and Andrew Russell with their families.

Our information concerning the condition of the church at this period is derived in large part from a copious diary which was kept by Jacob Lanius, the Presiding Elder of the Cape Girardeau District in 1839 and '40. A perusal of this old diary indicates more plainly than anything else the difficulty under which the ministers of that early day labored. Some extracts from it are given ("History of Southeast Missouri," Page 536).

"Thursday, November 14—Started from my New Madrid quarterly meeting, and after a ride of thirty miles through steady rain reached Brother Caleb Crain's near Jackson. Here is a society of about twenty members in a tolerable state of prosperity only. The next day passed through Jackson, a little old village, and took breakfast at the house of Greer Davis, a member of the bar, and a respectable member of our church. Traveled thirty miles today and lodged at the house of old Mother Houts, near Benton, the county seat of Scott county. Here the church once prospered but is now in moral ruins.

"16th and 17th—Held the first quarterly meeting for New Madrid circuit at Pleasant Plains meeting-house in Sandy Prairie. Brothers Haw and Dunleavy, the pastors of the circuit, and Henry and Owens attended as ministers in holy things. Two professed faith in Christ. This circuit has nearly 400 members, but religion is at very low ebb. This is a land of swamps and earthquakes, so that you have no access to the circuit save by crossing a swamp. I crossed on a levee three miles long. The land is very fertile, but the country sickly.

"23d and 24th—Held the first quarterly meeting for Cape Girardeau Circuit at McKendree Chapel, three miles from Jackson. Some good omens.

"30th—Held quarterly meeting for Farmington Circuit, which embraces my residence, in the town of Farmington. Here Methodism once flourished, but now lies in ruins. A class of only about twenty, no meeting-house, and under the necessity of occupying the Presbyterian church. Some deep feeling on Sabbath, but all the seed fell on 'stony ground.'

"December 14th—Held quarterly meeting for Ripley Mission at Brother Sharp's on Current River. Congregation small, only four families in two miles. Country as sparsely settled, prospect dark.

"21st—Held quarterly meeting for Greenville Circuit at old Father Dee's cabin, seven miles south of Greenville. On Sabbath we occupied Bowman's Chapel, near the dwelling, but the cold weather and smoke operated very much against us. However, when I called for mourners at night about one dozen came forward.

"28th—Held quarterly meeting for Bloomfield mission in the town of Bloomfield. Here we occupied the courthouse, an unfinished edifice that does honor to the county. The meeting was pretty good, the love feast most excellent. The church numbers about twenty members and is doing pretty well. This mission is also surrounded by swamps. In going to it I crossed a dismal swamp about three miles wide.

"January 4, 1840—Held quarterly meeting for Ste. Genevieve Circuit in the New Tennessee settlement in Ste. Genevieve county, at the house of John McFarland's family, an itinerant now a local of our church, one of the best of human kind. This meeting was a blessing to many in the church, but the wicked seemed little affected. I never preached much harder in my life, but all to no purpose, seemingly. This meeting closed my first round in the district. The district numbers about 1,200 members, the great mass of whom are measurably destitute of the power of godliness, though the most of them have the form, or a part of it at least, and are strictly moral. There is a want of vital religion. The preachers have pruned the church since conference, and I hope God will follow this wholesome course with His blessing.

"11th and 12th—Held a two days' meeting at Fredericktown at which time the district stewards were expected to meet. . . .

Second quarterly meeting for Cape Girardeau Circuit appointed for February 1, in the town of Cape Girardeau, but, the creeks being up, and the whole face of the country being covered with a sheet of ice, I was compelled to turn back, after having started, and so failed to reach the meeting, but I have since learned that the Lord was with them, and some good was done. A little revival of religion began in Farmington during the holidays, and as a result of it eight persons joined the church and three the Baptist church. Left home on Wednesday morning, and after traveling through mud and water almost impassable succeeded in reaching the seat of New Madrid quarterly conference. The meeting was held in Lewis' Prairie, two and one-half miles from the old town of that name; Brothers Haw and Dunleavy attended and assisted in the work. Thirteen were at the altar of prayer on Sabbath night, and eight united with the church. This was the best meeting of the year, and we left the best prospect that has appeared in the district.

"February 15th—This was the time for the Bloomfield quarterly meeting, but I failed to attend owing to ill health. I learn that the meeting was very good. Four were admitted on trial, and the church was refreshed by the Spirit.

"March 14th and 15th—Held the second quarterly meeting for Greenville Circuit at Brother Robert McCullough's in Wayne county. Here I found a society of about twenty members and a little congregation. The class is in a pretty good condition at present, seem all alive and full of some kind of fire. I trust it is the right kind. Several came forward as mourners, and one old lady joined the class. Brothers M. Wiley and Christian Eaker afforded ministerial aid on the occasion.

"March 21st and 22d—Held quarterly meeting for Ste. Genevieve Circuit at Yorke Chapel in the Abernathy settlement in Perry county, five miles from Perryville, the county seat. Here we have a society of seventy-three whites and more than thirty blacks, but alas, how cold and formal! Very few appeared to enjoy the life and power of religion. Only two additions to the church. The brethren here dwell in ceiled houses, while the house of God lies in ruins, the foundation only having been laid. I hope before the close of the year the church will be completed.

"March 28th—Held the second quarterly meeting for Farmington Circuit at Fredericktown, Brothers H. Baird and L. Wiley assisting as ministers; congregation respectable and attendance good in spite of unfavorable weather; six mourners one night, and three accessions to our ranks. This completes my second round. It was more interesting than the first. Have missed three quarterly meetings on account of the difficulty of traveling.

"April 4th and 5th—Assisted Brother Wiley of Farmington Circuit with a two days' meeting at John White's among the Dutch (my countrymen) on Castor. This meeting was the best this year, about twenty mourners on Sabbath night, some of whom were converted and quite a number received into the church.

"11th—Commenced the quarterly meeting for New Madrid Circuit in Benton, the county seat of Scott; the congregation small and careless, and the professors cold. This was once a numerous society, but removals and deaths have reduced almost to a unit. Satan seems to have his seat here and intemperance reigns.

"18th and 19th—Held a two days' meeting in the town of Cape Girardeau, assisted by Brothers Henry, Dunleavy and Owens. Here we are much opposed by Catholics, and Protestants are struggling for existence; have no meeting house but are trying to build one.

"25th and 26th—Held a two days' meeting in the town of Jackson. Here we are compelled to worship in the courthouse, but are erecting a convenient church. Large congregation on Sabbath. This is another hard place. But few Christians and many speculators in religious principles.

"May 30th and 31st—Held the third quarterly meeting for Cape Girardeau Circuit in Eaker's settlement on Crooked Creek amongst my countrymen, the Dutch. Here we have a large society, but many members are in a lukewarm state. This region was once the kingdom of Bacchus. One passes an old still-house, and sometimes a new one every two miles.

"June 20th and 21st—Held the third quarterly meeting for Ste. Genevieve Circuit in New Tennessee. One was received on trial. Arrangements are being made to build a stone chapel. It is much needed, for we worship in a dwelling-house or under a grove at present.

"July 3d and 5th—Held the last quarterly meeting for the New Madrid Circuit, in Mathews Prairie, Scott county. It was a camp-meeting. Owing to the premature coming of the sickly season only four families camped out of a class of sixty whites and forty blacks. On Sabbath the congregation was the largest I have addressed for two years, say 1,000 persons. A few professed faith.

"11th and 13th—Held quarterly meeting for the Farmington Circuit at a new chapel called Mt. Zion, in the New Virginia settlement, four miles from Fredericktown.

"September 30th—Have closed the last round of the district—the camp-meeting round. Much good was done at some of these meetings, especially at that at Yorke Chapel, in Perry County. More than twenty united with the church there, and quite a number were savingly converted."

Work of the church moved on with what must have seemed to those engaged in it very great slowness, but there was a constant and steady growth in every part of this section of the state. New societies were organized, new circuits were established, and supplied with preachers and here and there over the district new houses of worship were built. At first these houses were small, sometimes of logs, oftener there were frame buildings, but we are able to see a constant improvement in the character of the buildings themselves. More and more the people were impressed with the idea that the church house ought to be in keeping with the character of the community and was inevitably a reflection of the conditions existing.

One thing that halted to an extent the work of the Methodist church in Missouri was the controversy over slavery. This fierce and bitter struggle concerning the ownership of slaves was not confined to the political arena, it extended to the homes of the people and even into the church organizations. Perhaps no other church suffered more severely on account of this contention than did the Methodists. When the General Conference met in New York in 1844 it passed a resolution known as the Finley Resolution which suspended Bishop Andrew of Georgia from the exercise of his office on the ground that he was an owner of slaves. He was not to be reinstated as a bishop of the church until he had disposed of these slaves. This resolution was adopted on the first day of June, and, on the 5th, the southern members of the General Conference presented a declaration in which it was said that they believed the continual agitation of slavery and abolition in the conferences of the church and especially the suspension of Bishop Andrew from his office would result in a state of things which would render the continuance of the jurisdiction of the General Conference over the conferences of the South inconsistent with the success of the ministry in the slave-holding states.

This declaration, which was signed by all the members of the Southern Conference and by one member from the Illinois Conference, was referred to a committee with instructions to provide a plan for adjusting difficulties which had arisen over the subject of slavery, or, if that were found to be impossible, a plan for a friendly division of the church. After some deliberation this committee reported that it was impossible to settle the difficulties of the situation and recommended that the church should be divided. A conference of delegates from the organizations of the church in those states where slavery existed was held in Louisville, Ky., May 1st, 1845. It was presided over by Bishops Soule and Andrew and the final result of its work was a declaration that the Southern Conference should become a separate church under the name of the Methodist Episcopal Church, South.

The next meeting of the Missouri Conference following the action at Louisville was held in Columbia, Missouri, September 24, 1845. Bishop Soule presided and he delivered an address asking the Missouri Conference to unite with the Southern Church. After a discussion and delay it was finally voted that the Missouri Conference should become a part of the Methodist Episcopal Church, South. At this conference John K. Lacey was appointed Presiding Elder for the Cape Girardeau District. The appointment for the circuits were: Cape Girardeau, A. Peace; Crooked Creek, J. O. Wood; New Madrid,

J. H. Headlee; Charleston, L. P. Rowland; Bloomfield, E. E. Deddge; Greenville, H. N. Watts; Fredericktown, N. B. Peterson; Ste. Genevieve, P. B. Markle; Ripley, J. Eaker; Black River, R. M. Stevenson.

The enumeration of the circuits contained in the Cape Girardeau District at this time indicates the growth experienced by the church. In 1847 a new conference was organized called the "St. Louis Conference," and a new district, Greenville District, was formed from the western part of the Cape Girardeau District.

From this time until the breaking out of the Civil war, in 1861, the church experienced a steady growth. It is hardly possible to give an entire list of the preachers who supplied the various circuits at that time. The Presiding Elders for Cape Girardeau District from 1852 to 1861 were: J. M. Kelly, J. H. Headlee, J. C. Berryman, Wesley Browning, H. S. Watts, J. McCarry, M. R. Anthony. The Presiding Elders of the Greenville District from 1852 to 1857 were: N. B. Peterson, J. R. Burk, J. L. Burchard. In 1857 there was a reorganization of the districts and the western district was called "Potosi." Its Presiding Elders were H. N. Watts and J. C. Thompson.

The work of the church was very greatly interrupted by the Civil war. There were no regular appointments made in 1861, and there were no meetings of the St. Louis Conference during the war. Services continued to be held at Charleston, Bertrand, Big Lake and Rush Ridge. Many of the churches were destroyed and the organizations disbanded under the stress of the war.

In 1865 Southeast Missouri was organized into the Iron Mountain District, and W. S. Woodward was appointed as the Presiding Elder. The appointments on the circuits for that year were as follows: Richwoods, G. C. Knowles; Fredericktown, J. S. Frazier; Perryville, J. M. Proctor; Jackson, not filled; Charleston, H. N. Watts; New Madrid, L. W. Powell; Greenville, S. A. Blakey; Grand Prairie, James Copeland; Bloomfield, J. C. Thompson.

In 1866 the old districts of Cape Girardeau and Greenville were restored, but in 1868 the name of the latter was changed to Potosi. In 1871 the districts were named Iron Mountain and Charleston, and in 1873 a new district called Poplar Bluff was established.

In 1887 Charleston District contained the following stations: Charleston, established in 1872; membership, 253; value of church, $6,000; C. M. Hensley, pastor. Cape Girardeau, membership, 132; value of church, $1,200; W. Mooney, pastor. Farmington, membership, 185; value of church, $3,200; W. F. Wilson, pastor. New Madrid, membership, 153; value of churches, $2,800; E. F. Seuter, pastor. Fredericktown, membership, 216; value of churches, $3,400; J. W. Robinson, pastor. Sikeston and Bertrand were for several years prior to 1887 under one charge. They had a membership of 348, and churches to the value of $3,300. Sikeston was a station under the care of V. J. Millis. The circuits within the Charleston District were as follows: Commerce, including Commerce, Macedonia, Head's schoolhouse, Campbell's schoolhouse and Lusk's chapel, S. A. Mason, pastor; Morley, including Morley, Oran, Blodgett, Sandy Prairie and Cross Plains, S. H. Renfro, pastor; Point Pleasant, including Point Pleasant, New Hope, Union, Ruddell's Point, Mound and Beech Grove, supplied by A. G. Horton; Bertrand, including Bertrand organized in 1844; East Prairie, organized in 1865; Thrower's Chapel, organized in 1880, and Diehlstadt, organized in 1886, W. H.

Blalock, pastor; Belmont, including Haws chapel, Rush's Ridge, Concord and Locust Grove schoolhouse, supplied by R. G. Parks; Caruthersville, S. Richmond, pastor; Lutesville, including Lutesville, Glen Allen, Union, Ebenezer, Bethel, Point Pleasant, Eaker's chapel, Gravel Hill, Hickory Grove, Killian schoolhouse, Sedgewickville and Trinity, S. C. Biffle, pastor; Jackson, including Jackson, Arlington, Rock Hill and McKendree, H. A. Smith, pastor; Oak Ridge, including Oak Ridge, Shiloh, New Salem, Salem, Millersville, Goshen, Shawneetown, Oak Hill, Neely's Landing and McLain's, J. K. Mathews, pastor; also three or four churches in Cape Girardeau county, supplied by local preachers; Yorke chapel, T. Lord, pastor; Farmington, J. A. Russell, pastor; Marquand, T. W. Glass, pastor, and New Prospect, supplied by M. M. Blaese. The total membership of Charleston district in 1887 was 6,004. In 1880 it was 2,954.

In the Poplar Bluff district there was but one station, Poplar Bluff, which for some time was united with the church at Dexter under the care of one pastor. It had been a station since 1884. W. E. Boggs was pastor. Among the circuits in the Poplar Bluff district were: Grand Prairie, including Brannum, Liberty, Harkey's chapel and Cotton Plant, R. A. McClintock, pastor; Williamsville, including Shiloh, organized about 1830; Walton's chapel, a branch of Shiloh, organized in 1887; Freeland (in Carter county), Chapel Hill, organized about 1873; Prospect, organized in 1885; Dee's chapel, organized in the "thirties;" Williamsville, organized about 1884, and Cool Springs, organized in 1888, Geo. H. Adams, pastor; Piedmont, including Piedmont, organized about 1876; Des Arc, organized in 1882, and Mill Springs, Webster Full, pastor; Clarkton, including Malden, organized in 1881; Clarkton, Knight's schoolhouse, Salem, Zion and Gravel Hill, J. A. Jenkins, pastor; Arcadia, including the churches in Iron county, H. C. Fleenor, pastor; Bloomfield, R. Walton, pastor, and Piketon, L. W. Pickens, pastor. The total membership in 1887 was 5,260.

Since 1887 the growth of the church has been steady and rapid. It has kept pace with the growth of population. It is not possible to give in detail the changes in pastoral relations during these years. The information is readily available in the published reports of the church. A summary of the present condition of the church, together with the names of the various organizations, the pastors and membership of each is given in the form of tables. From these it appears that in the territory of Southeast Missouri in 1911 there were forty-six stations and forty circuits, with a total membership of 21,307. These figures testify to a wonderful growth since McKendree chapel was established and even since the war.

Under the present organization of the church most of the churches in Southeast Missouri are members of three districts of the St. Louis conference. These districts are Poplar Bluff, Farmington and Charleston. A few of the churches are in West Plains district of the same conference and some others in West Plains district.

The tables given below show the location of church organization together with the minister in charge and the membership of the church.

The Presiding Elder of Charleston District is Rev. Robert L. Russell and the organizations, pastors and membership in his territory are as follows:

S. M. Clack, Anniston Ct., 431.
J. C. Denton, Benton, 117.
H. W. King, Bertrand, 349.
J. C. Thogmorton, Blodgett, 161.
A. S. J. Baldridge, Caruthersville, 439.
Del. Longgrear, Caruthersville Ct., 88.
P. G. Thogmorton & J. F. Holland, J. P., Charleston, 604.
Lenord Gray, Charleston Ct., 315.
I. L. Holt, Cape Girardeau, 517.
A. C. Stovmont, Chaffee, 264.
O. S. Tallent, Commerce & Macedonia, 215.
T. G. Fallin, Cottonwood & Cooter, 418.
R. D. Kennedy, Cairo, 153.
S. A. Bennett, Deering.
E. F. McDaniel, East Prairie, 262.
H. H. S. DuBois, Edna & Illmo, 99.
I. Q. McCorkle, Hayti, 111.
Clarence Burton, Jackson, 480.
A. W. Darter, Lilbourn Ct., 124.
S. M. Roberts, Morley & Richwoods, 403.
W. H. Jordan, New Madrid, 135.
C. E. Harris, New Madrid Ct.
Elmer T. Clark, Oran, 165.
T. E. Smith, Parma, 103.
J. T. Evitts, Portageville Ct., 125.
O. J. Furguson, South Cape Girardeau, 41.
A. U. Burris, Steel Ct., 221
J. M. Bradley, Sikeston, 170.
J. C. Montgomery, Vanduser Ct., 181.
J. L. Wolvarton, Mathews, 267.
Total, 7,258.

Farmington district is presided over by Rev. Henry P. Crowe and there are twenty-five stations in this territory of the church as follows:

Wm. Court, Farmington, 371.
C. N. Clark, Fredericktown, 530.
J. R. Bullington, Potosi, 134.
N. B. Henry, Bonne Terre, 353.
J. P. Stubblefield, Flat River, 319.
Elmer Peal, Lavins, 305.
Arthur Trotter, Des Loge, 137.
A. S. Coker, Arcadia, 112.
L. D. Nichol, Esther, 199.
Wm. Stewart, Bismark & Hickory Grove, 277.
R. Walton, Caledonia & Irondale, 170.
J. N. Sitton, Leadwood & Frank Clay, 137.
H. C. Hoy, Lutesville & Glen Allen, 260.
D. M. Margrave, Oak Ridge Ct., 306.
O. A. Bowers, Marquand Circuit, 313.
A. N. Walker, Whitewater Circuit, 226.
H. A. Showmaker, Libertyville Circuit, 193.
E. G. Brent, Mineral Point Circuit, 129.
B. L. Wright, York Chapel Circuit, 113.
F. A. Hearn, Neely's Landing Circuit, 232.
R. S. Warren, Sedgewickville Ct., 259.
S. C. Bockman, Fredericktown Ct., 193.
B. W. Bynum, Belleview Ct., 205.
M. M. Blaese, Marble Hill Ct., 284.
J. A. Wood, Farmington Ct., 360.
Total, 6,117.

There are twenty-six stations in the Poplar Bluff district and the present presiding elder is Rev. J. R. H. Vaughan.

J. T. Ricketts, Advance Ct., 101.
F. M. Mayfield, Bernie Ct., 181.
R. M. Ownby, Bell City Ct., 367.
Linus Eaker, Bloomfield Ct., 194.
Thomas Lord, Campbell, 172.
J. B. Wilburn, Clarkton Ct., 261.
J. D. Doherty, Cardwell Ct., 141.
W. J. Heys, Dexter, 245.
R. E. Foard, Doniphan, 233.
L. L. Johnston, Doniphan Ct., 235.
C. L. Fry, Essex & Sadler's Chapel, 131.
S. C. Biffle, Greenville Ct., 309.
J. W. Ham, Harkey's Chapel & Senath, 350.
J. S. Newson, Holcomb Ct., 405.
F. Eaker, Hornersville Ct., 320.
W. J. Velvick, Kennett, 303.
W. L. King, Lowndes & Coldwater, 366.
E. T. Reid, Morehouse, 179.
J. T. Self, Malden, 394.
J. L. Batton, Naylor Ct., 381.

W. A. Tetley, Poplar Bluff, 307.
C. L. Kirkendall, Poplar Bluff Ct., 198.
A. R. Sanders, Pine Ct., 272.
E. Jones, Sherry Ct., 162.
T. W. Glass, Williamsville Ct., 302.
J. C. Reid, C. Francis, Zalma Ct., 220.
Total, 6,822.

De Soto district has for its Presiding Elder Rev. J. W. Worsnop. Of the organization in this district the following are within the territory covered in this history.
E. J. Rinkel, De Soto, 208.
J. P. McDonald, De Soto Circuit, 228.
Geo. J. Evans, Festus, 317.
D. R. Davis, Hematite Circuit, 101.
J. R. Kincaid, Plattin Circuit, 256.

West Plains district has for its Presiding Elder William A. Humphrey. The following organizations are considered here.
H. L. Taylor, Ellington Circuit, 344.
Geo. Jaycox, Lesterville Circuit, 90.

The church has entered upon an era of great expansion in this part of the state. This is evidenced not only by the large increase in numbers, the greater influence possessed by the church in all social and moral questions, but also by the remarkable improvement in church buildings. In the last ten years the church has erected a number of buildings of great cost, well-planned and constructed and adapted to the work of the church as it is now carried on. Cape Girardeau, Jackson, Charleston and Sikeston, have recently erected churches each costing more than $40,000, and each of permanent and enduring materials. The church at Cape Girardeau is built of native stone. It is of Gothic architecture, handsomely finished and furnished, has a large auditorium, Sunday school rooms, a kitchen and dining rooms, offices and all the equipment necessary to the work of a modern church.

The church at Jackson is of brick and equally as well adapted for its purpose. The Charleston church is of stone, and is one of the best in this section.

Perhaps the best building owned by the church in this part of the state is that at Sikeston finished and occupied in 1912. It is built of brick of the modified Romanesque style, has a handsome auditorium with domed roof, is finished in handsome woods, and beautifully lighted and seated. The auditorium contains one of the largest pipe-organs in the state. There are many rooms for Sunday school purpose so arranged as to be thrown into the main portion of the church as occasion demands.

Other churches of the St. Louis Conference, outside of St. Louis are almost equal to these. That at Dexter is of recent erection and is a handsome and dignified structure.

In another chapter an account has been given of the educational work of the church in supporting Marvin Collegiate Institute at Fredericktown. In all that pertains to the welfare of society at large the church in Southeast Missouri takes an active and efficient part.

To the heroic pioneer preachers of the Methodist church is due a large debt of gratitude for the work which they accomplished in this part of the state. At a time when frontier conditions prevailed over the entire section these men faced the perils and hardship of the wilderness in discharge of the duty which rested upon them. Through the period of growth that preceded the Civil war, while the wilderness was being subdued, towns built, farms cleared, and the state entering on its marvellous career of prosperity and civilization, one of the strong forces that wrought for progress and advancement was the influence of these men. They preached and taught in every community, planted, not alone the seeds of Christianity, but also higher ideals of social service, of education and organization. During the trying period of the war and the years of bitterness and strife that succeeded it, when industry was paralyzed, organizations ended, when lawlessness prevailed, they still labored, and upheld the principles which had been planted by the fathers. They fostered education, and at early day when schools were few, money scarce and the difficulties great they established Bellevue Collegiate Institute, and in spite of every difficulty and discouragement, kept it alive and growing, and so shaped its course and work that it has developed into the Marvin Collegiate Institute of our own day, a splendid and vigorous school destined to become a powerful influence in the life of the church. To every other great movement they have lent aid and influence, so that their work is indelibly woven into the life of the state, and its power seen on every page of its history.

In spite of all other activities their chief interest has been the work of the great church which they have built up here. The numbers, the power, the wealth of that institution testifies to the success which they achieved.

It is not possible to preserve the names of all these men nor to accord to them the credit they deserve for their great achievements. To Jesse Walker, perhaps, belongs the honor of first place among the preachers of the church, at least in point of time. He it was who first planted the seed of Methodism in this great territory and the story of his work, the long and dangerous miles he travelled, his devotion, the success of his labors will always be a stirring chapter in the history of the church. H. S. Watts, famous as Rough and Ready, with his blunt honesty, his unfailing courage, his ready wit, his unflinching devotion to his work, who wrought as circuit rider and presiding elder, will always be remembered with pride by his church. U. L. Haw, whose long life of labor as minister and presiding elder did much for the church, contributed not alone his own life of active service but a family to continue his work. His son, Dr. James L. Haw, was one of the most prominent laymen of the church interested and devoted to its work. His son, Marvin T. Haw, the secretary of the St. Louis Conference continues the traditions of the family and his years of successful ministry recall the best days of his grandfather.

The Henrys, father and son, gifted men, able to lead, eloquent of speech, scholarly, have had a powerful influence upon the development of the church and its work.

J. C. Berryman, a prince of preachers, and a master organizer, will always be honored. T. M. Finney, Henry Hanesworth, were among a multitude of honored names.

Methodist Episcopal Church

Although the Missouri Conference at its meeting in 1845, voted by a large majority to unite with the Southern Church, some members of the Conference were opposed to this change and determined to abide in their relation to the older organization. Two of the men who made this decision were: Rev. Anthony Bewley and Rev. Nelson Henry. Some of the men who did not wish to unite with the Southern Church left the state and took up work in other places. Some, however, remained and these held a convention on Spring River, December 25, 1845. They tried to arrange plans for carrying on the work in Missouri and Arkansas. The only ministers left at that time were: George Sly, David Thompson, Joseph Doughty, Mark Robertson, Anthony Bewley and Nelson Henry. They were unable to accomplish very much, but in 1848 the Missouri Conference of the Methodist Episcopal church was reorganized. It was divided into three districts, one of which included the most of Southeast Missouri and a large part of Arkansas. Nelson Henry was Presiding Elder of this district and under his direction a mission was organized at Bloomfield.

The first quarterly meeting in the district was held at the house of W. W. Norman, October 14, 1848. Nelson Henry was the Presiding Elder and John W. McKnight was the pastor of the church. Another quarterly meeting was held later at the house of Jonas Eaker in 1849. J. J. Buren was presiding elder and W. W. Norman was pastor of the church. This arrangement was kept up during the next few years. The circuit with Norman as its pastor, included practically all of Southeast Missouri. In 1852 D. M. Smith was Presiding Elder and E. N. Lowe was the pastor.

It is probable that the first church erected by the Methodist Episcopal church after the division was the one at Bloomfield. It was built under the supervision of a committee consisting of W. W. Norman, H. C. Rich and J. C. Bottom; this was in 1853. The church carried on services not only at Bloomfield, but at Grand Prairie, Big Lake, Gravel Hill, Spring Creek, Dick's Creek, Poplar Creek and Mt. Zion. Some of the ministers who served the church during this period were: John McKnight, Richard Thornton, J. S. Gooch, Thomas Golding, Asa D. West, Hiram Lipe and Francis Beggs.

It was unfortunate for the cause of religion that this division occurred in the Methodist church. The activity of the old church in Southeast Missouri was productive of bitter feeling, and serious obstacles were placed in the way of those having the work in charge. On more than one occasion ministers were denounced and even attacked by the persons opposed to the abolition sentiment expressed by the ministers. Southeast Missouri, at this time, was very largely pro-slavery in sentiment,—in fact this was true of the greater part of the state, and the well known fact that the Methodist Episcopal church was opposed to the institution of slavery, operated to bring strong opposition to the work of its ministers. This is shown very conclusively in the failure of the legislature to issue a charter to the school which the church purposed to establish in Jackson. In 1854 a society in Jackson, which was in charge of a school there, offered buildings and grounds to the Missouri conference, provided the conference would guarantee the establishment of a good school. This offer was accepted by the church and the school was begun. In order that the school might be on a permanent basis, application was made to the legislature for a charter of incorporation, but the bill was defeated by a vote of sixty to thirty-six on the express ground that the church was opposed to slavery.

All the circuits in Southeast Missouri were attached to the St. Louis District, and Rev. Samuel Huffman was the Presiding Elder of this district from 1858 until the beginning of the war. There were regular circuits at that time at De Soto, where F. S. Beggs was the pastor in charge, at Jackson, where J. Linan was pastor, at Fredericktown, where J. E. Baker was pastor, and Bloomfield, which was under the charge of F. S. Beggs. The society at McKendree chapel, in Cape Girardeau county, which was the oldest Methodist church in the state, remained faithful to the old organization and within this county there have been a considerable number of its adherents.

In 1864 the Farmington circuit, embracing the counties of St. Francois, Ste. Genevieve, and parts of Iron, Madison, Washington and Jefferson, was reorganized, with Rev. N. J. Giddings as the Presiding Elder. This circuit was divided in 1866. One year later the church purchased a building at Farmington, formerly occupied by the Christians, and used it as a place of worship. In 1887 there were churches at Perryville, Cedar Fork, Cross Roads, St. Mary's and Independence.

At the present time there are in Southeast Missouri the following church organizations, all of which are contained in the Farmington district which is a part of the St. Louis Conference, besides the names of the organizations there are given the pastors of the different places at the present time: Belgrade, C. W. Jennings; Bloomfield, O. R. Sides; Bloomfield circuit, D. W. Fields; Bonne Terre, A. Tremayne; Chapin, V. L. Miller; Cornwall, M. W. Krieger; Courtois, J. H. Hicks; De Soto, Arthur A. Halter; De Soto circuit, Albert Maynard; Doe Run, Jesse J. Pruitt; Farmington, J. W. Borah; Flat River, D. E. Barrett; Fruitland, A. H. Barnes; Irondale & Graniteville, Robert Treganza; Ironton, W. T. Street; Lutesville, D. R. Cole; Mountain View, C. V. Bryan; Patten, ———; Perryville, M. O. Morris; Poplar Bluff, F. E. Duboys; Poplar Bluff circuit, G. W. Davis; Puxico, J. A. Kirkman.

BAPTISTS

In 1821 the Bethel Association of the Baptist church had fourteen churches and a membership of 417. Some of these churches were in Arkansas and they were later dismissed to form a new association in that territory.

In 1825 Pendleton church was organized in a settlement six miles west of Farmington. The settlement was made up of immigrants from Pendleton district, South Carolina, and the church became a member of Bethel Association in 1826. At that time James Holbert was pastor, remaining as such until 1838 when he was succeeded by Elder William Polk.

Bethel Association held its meeting in 1827 at Providence church in Fredericktown, September 22 to 24th. The sermon was preached by Elder D. Orr; Wingate Jackson was the moderator and Simeon Frost, clerk. There were present messengers from nine churches: Providence, Bellevue, St. Francois, Hepzibah, New Hope, Pendleton, Crooked Creek, Little Flock and Liberty. The minutes of this association show that there had been 17 baptisms during the year and that there was a total membership of 227.

The meeting of the association in 1837 was with the Pendleton church in St. Francois county and in 1838 at Hepzibah church in Ste. Genevieve county. In 1840 the meeting was held with Bethel church, in 1841 the association met with New Hope church in St. Francois county. At that time a church known as the Colony church in a settlement five miles east of Farmington was received as a member of the association. In 1859 the association met in New Hope church in St. Francois county. The sermon was preached by Elder William Polk who was also moderator. There were three new churches received—Mount Zion, Locust Grove and White Oak Grove. At this time there were 19 churches in the association with a total membership of 834.

Bethel Association did a great work in organizing new associations. In 1824 nine churches were dismissed to form the Cape Girardeau Association. In 1829 it dismissed four to form an association in Arkansas. Two were dismissed in 1831 for the Franklin Association and nine in 1859 to form the Central Missouri Association. Finally many of the churches in the association joined others, some churches were led off to other doctrines and the association ceased to exist as an organized body of Baptists.

The Cape Girardeau Association of Baptists was organized at Hebron, Cape Girardeau county, June 12th to 14th, 1824. The following churches took part in the forming of the association: Bethel with 41 members, Dry Creek with 28 members, Tywappity with 11, Clear Creek in Illinois 66, Apple Creek 15, Ebenezer 17, Big Prairie 19, Hebron 26, Shiloh in Illinois 28, Jackson 8, making a total membership in the association of 248.

From 1824 to 1832 the meetings were held regularly, a good spirit was manifest and much work accomplished. The association was a missionary association and was constantly raising funds and providing ways for missionary work. From 1832 to 1860 the association changed in character. In 1832 there were twenty churches located in Cape Girardeau, Scott, Mississippi and Perry counties. At the meeting in 1840, eight of the twenty churches comprising the association withdrew and formed what was called the New Cape Girardeau Association. It was composed of churches at Cape Girardeau, Mount Zion, Harmony, Mount Moriah, Pleasant Grove, Cypress, Pleasant Hill and Little River. The division in the association had arisen over the question of missions; twelve churches had adopted anti-mission principles, while the eight which formed the new association, held to the former ideas of the importance of missionary work. This New Cape Girardeau Association, as it was called, had a prosperous history from 1840 to 1860. As in the case of all other denominations in this part of the state, the war brought to the Baptists very great difficulties and discouragements. Many of the ministers were driven away from home or else were compelled to give up preaching for a time. From 1864 to 1867 there was only one minister in the territory of the Cape Girardeau Association engaged in preaching. This was the Rev. John H. Clark, who had been licensed to preach by the Cape Girardeau church in 1842 and continued his active labors as a minister until his death in 1869.

The Cape Girardeau Association met in 1864 at Hubble Creek church. Only nine churches were represented. They reported 58 members having been baptized during the previous year, but 48 of these were from one church, Pleasant Grove. The meeting of 1865 was held under very great difficulties. The test oath was enforced and none of the ministers were willing to take it. Accordingly they had to preach in violation of the constitution of the state. There were nineteen churches at this time on the list of the association, but only six of the number sent messengers to the meeting. New ministers were added to the association from 1867 to 1870. Among them were G. F. Brayton, J. G. Shearer, James Reed, J. S. Jordon, Jonas Hoffman, B. L. Bowman and J. T. Ford.

In 1876 there were twenty churches in the

association, but they dismissed some of these to form a new association in Scott county. In 1878 the association was composed of twenty churches in the counties of Cape Girardeau, Scott, Mississippi, Perry and New Madrid. The total membership was 557. The ministers at that time were T. A. Bowman, John T. Ford, C. B. Ford, J. F. Godwin, Z. A. Hoppas, J. M. Warren and W. H. Welker.

In 1881 the meeting was held at Cape Girardeau. Elder J. Hickman was moderator and T. A. Bowman, clerk. There were at that time fourteen churches with a membership of 426.

By successive divisions the Cape Girardeau Association has come to include only the territory of Cape Girardeau and Perry counties. The meeting in 1911 was held at Crosstown in Perry county.

In 1911 the Cape Girardeau Association reported sixteen churches having a membership of 1,560. They were: Allenville, 24; Burfordville, 37; Cheney Fork, 48; Cape Girardeau, 329; Leroy, 53; Gravel Hill, 62; Round Pond, 49; Iona, 77; Jackson, 296; Lithium, 82; New Bethel, 116; Niswonger, 28; Oak Ridge. 158; Pleasant Grove, 123; Bethlehem, 74; Whitewater, 42.

Of the churches of this association Jackson is the oldest. It was organized April 30, 1824, largely from members of Bethel church and it finally absorbed the best and most progressive element of that church. Cape Girardeau church was organized in 1834 by Elder Thomas P. Green with nine members. The pastors of the church before the war were T. P. Green, J. H. Clark, Samuel Baker, S. H. Ford, W. F. Wilson, James S. Green, A. Sherwood and J. C. Maple.

This church at Cape Girardeau, which is the most important owing to its situation of the church in the association, has had a most interesting history. Owing to the unfortunate circumstances most of the old records of the church were destroyed, but Mrs. J. C. Maple, who was for many years a member of the church in the early period, wrote a sketch of the early history which is reproduced here through the kindness of Dr. J. C. Maple. It contains much of interest and importance concerning these early years.

"This sketch of the early history of the church," says Mrs. Maple, "must be largely reminiscent; made up from the recollections of a child, and of what was told her, and of occurrences that I remember. The church records having been lost, I may be able to review some things that will prove of interest to the present membership.

"Rev. R. S. Duncan, in his history of Missouri Baptists gives the date of the organization August 13, 1834, with nine members. The church was instituted in the little brick schoolhouse that stood almost directly west of the present residence of L. J. Albert, Sr. The track of the Cape Girardeau and Chester railroad runs near the location of the building.

There is now no means of knowing the names of the original nine, but I feel confident that John Juden, Sr., John Juden, Jr., Abbie Block Juden, his wife, and Captain William Surrell and his wife, Ann Surrell (nee Juden), were among the number. Rev. Thomas P. Green was instrumental in bringing about the organization and was its first pastor. John Juden, Jr., was the first clerk and senior deacon and continued to fill both offices until his removal to New Orleans, La., a few years later.

"The church must have taken steps very promptly to secure a house of worship, and the brick building on Lorimier street was erected. It was the first and for a long time the only Protestant house of worship in the city.

"An occurence, connected with the first services held in this house, served for a long time to fix dates of events, by the habitual saying 'these things occurred before or after the floor of the church gave way.' The late Mrs. Louisa Rodney, who had a remarkable memory for dates, told me it was in 1839. Mrs. Mary La Pierre connecting the time with some items of family history corroborates that date. If they are correct, I was only two and a half years old, yet some of the events were indelibly fixed in my mind.

"The Cape Giarardeau Association was to hold its annual session with the church, and the workmen were very much hurried to get the house in condition to be used. Situated on a hill that sloped to the south, it was very easy, and inexpensive to arrange for a basement room half way under the building. The floor above was to be supported by substantial pillars but there was not time to finish the basement and temporary supports were arranged. A stump, that had not been removed served as a base for one of these improvised pillars. My impression of the day is that it was very bright and beautiful and the house was crowded to its utmost capacity. The people were also dressed in their very best attire. The pews were not in, but temporary seats had been made of planks.

"I remember very distinctly sitting by my mother, and looking at Rev. Mr. Edwards who was preaching the introductory sermon, when suddenly the floor seemed to sway under me, and when I looked up I saw the red-top-boots of my brother—the late C. G. Juden—go out of the window south of the pulpit. Then my father said to my mother, 'Sit here until I come back,' and took me in his arms and placed me upon the lap of Uncle Thomas Juden who was sitting on the pulpit steps. From this safe haven I looked with bewilderment upon a panic, such as is seldom witnessed.

"The first law of nature seemed to have asserted itself, for every one was trying to escape from the building regardless of everything and everybody else. Clothing was torn, slippers lost, bonnets crushed, jewelry torn away and broken, while many bruises and hurts were inflicted by the merciless crowd. It is strange, but true, that no one was seriously injured.

"After almost every one had left the building, my father, after getting my mother out unhurt, came for me. Uncle Thomas told him that I had been a good girl and did not cry. This praise was very pleasant to me, but I think it was not goodness, but the sight of that screaming, struggling mass of humanity so bewildered me that I forgot I could cry.

"Investigation showed that the prop placed on the stump had acted as a wedge, and so split it that the floor had sagged only a little way, but enough to produce the fright of the entire audience. The damage to the floor was easily repaired, and the length of time the build has stood, and the many, many times it has been filled by attentive worshipers prove how substantially it was built.

"The membership of the church must have increased rapidly between the time of its organization and the opening of the house of worship. Besides those I have already mentioned I recall the names of Mr. and Mrs. William Johnson, his mother, Mrs. Johnson. Cynthia Johnson, wife of Thomas Johnson. Mr. and Mrs. Thomas Baldwin, Mr. and Mrs. Campster, whose stone residence still stands near the Campster schoolhouse, Mr. and Mrs.

Thomas Joyce, Mr. and Mrs. Thomas Anderson—(Mr. A. was a half-brother of the late Dr. W. B. Wilson), Mr. and Mrs. Baker Gorden, Mrs. Clark, a sister of Mrs. Gorden. This Mrs. Clark's son, John Henry Clark, Mr. Clark's sister, Mrs. Samuel Gorden, Mrs. Smarr, another sister of J. H. Clark, Mrs. Alfred Ellis, Mr. and Mrs. Sutton, Mr. and Mrs. Case, Mr. and Mrs. Thomas Juden, Mr. and Mrs. G. W. Juden (the father and mother of Mrs. J. C. Maple, who wrote this sketch), Mrs. Wathen who was one of the early teachers in this community, and her daughter, Mrs. Wheeler, Mrs. Captain Watson, Mr. Porter, who came from Hickman, Kentucky, and after a few years residence here returned to Hickman, Joseph Gorden and wife, William McKnight and wife, parents of Mrs. Emma Kimmel, and others whose names I do not now recall.

"There were some things in connection with the building of the house of worship, which I remember to have heard discussed that make me quite certain that Mr. Anderson and Mrs. Ellis came into the church at an early date, if they were not constituent members.

"Captain Ellis, though not a member of the church, was a staunch Baptist in principle and a man of large means. He made a liberal contribution to the building fund and offered in addition a lot on the east side of Lorimier street north of Broadway for the use of the church if they would build thereon. Mr. Anderson was a man of limited means, but offered the lot on which the house was built, stating that this was all he was able to give. The church accepted this offer, hoping that Captain Ellis would increase his contribution, at least, to the value of the lot. Perhaps he was a little sensitive over the matter; at any rate, he did not increase his contribution. The choice proved to be an unfortunate one, for after some years it cost the church large sums of money to prevent the house from being undermined by the constant washing away of the earth forming a deep ditch. That ravine offers a lesson of the importance of taking things in time. A little ditch was formed by the rains in the garden of Mr. Ollar which joined the church lot on the west and ran towards the east. The people were used to hills and hollows, and were unconcerned about the small ravine thus formed.

"The church had preaching every Sunday. Each family had its own pew, and it was the custom for parents and children to sit together. The pews were also supplied with Bibles and hymn books. Another custom, which we would do well to follow today, was when the pastor read the scripture lesson, the congregation was reading it too; thereby impressing it upon their minds, through two channels, the eye and the ear.

"A Sunday school was established at an early day. I have no recollection of the time when I first went to Sunday school, but I remember my father going with me every Sunday. He took his children to the Lord's house, and after school closed, he usually took us for a little walk, but returned and we were all seated in the family pew before the preaching service began. In those days it was not optional, with the children, whether they attended church services or not, at least I never learned it. I do not remember the name of the superintendent.

"As has been said Thomas P. Green was the first pastor. I think it must have been shortly after his death that Dr. Russell Holmon of Alabama visited the church and preached for a few weeks, to the delight and edification of the membership. He received a hearty call to the pastorate, but did not accept. The facts in regard to Dr. Holmon I obtained from letters of my father written to my mother, in August, 1843, while she was absent from home at a health resort.

"I think the church must have been without a pastor for some time, for my father died in August, 1844, and Rev. Edward Hempstead was sent for to preach the funeral sermon.

"John Henry Clark was ordained in December, 1844, and following his ordination supplied the pulpit for a few months. I remember his ordination. He preached a sermon previous to the laying on of hands from the text, 'Mary Hath Chosen that Good Part which shall not be taken away from her'—Luke 10-42.

"Rev. Samuel Baker a native of England, then a young man, became pastor. He in after years attained high eminence as a man of great learning. Was pastor of churches in New York City, in Chicago and other cities. His last years were spent at Russellville, Kentucky.

"S. H. Ford became pastor in 1845. He entered the editorial field at Louisville, Kentucky, a few years later; was editor and proprietor of the 'Christian Repository,' a monthly magazine, for more than fifty years. His wife, Sallie Rochester Ford, attained equal eminence with her distinguished husband as an author.

"Rev. W. F. Nelson was for a time professor in a theological seminary, while Dr. Adiel Sherwood was an author and college president of several institutions of learning. Thus we see, in that day the church had the best talent in its pulpit.

"On October 4, 1857, J. C. Maple was ordained at the call of this church. He had been stated supply from the first of July preceding this date.''

Dr. Maple served as pastor in 1860. During his term there were about 100 members of the church and Thomas Juden and Thomas Baldwin were deacons and the latter was church clerk. Dr. Maple gave up the care of the church in 1860 and removed to Jackson. Here he engaged in teaching school until the outbreak of the war. The school was closed at that time and he then preached part of the time at Jackson and part of the time at Cape Girardeau until 1864. On his removal to Kentucky in that year, he severed his connection with the church for a time.

Between 1864 and 1874 there were a number of pastors, among them Rev. Mr. Bray and J. S. Jordan. In the latter year Dr. Maple returned to the church and served as pastor for three years.

Among the pastors since that date have been Rev. J. Hickman, Rev. Mr. Daniels, C. J. Tate, Rev. Mr. Duvall, J. O. Willett, and A. M. Ross. The present pastor is F. Y. Campbell.

The church worshipped in the old house on Fountain street until 1894, when a new house was constructed at the corner of Broadway and Spanish. This was during the pastorate of Mr. Daniels. Later an addition was made to the house under the pastoral direction of C. F. J. Tate. This house is still in use though the congregation has purchased a new lot and plans the erection of a more suitable building.

Among the other organizations in the association were Union church organized in 1832, Pleasant Hill in Scott county, organized in 1828; Pleasant Grove in Perry county in 1839, Mount Moriah in Scott county in 1830, Apple Creek in 1820, Ebenezer in the big bend of the Mississippi, Cape Girardeau county in 1821, Cypress in Scott county in 1821, Hubble Creek in 1861, Harmony in Mississippi county in 1830, reorganized in 1855, Little River, later called Sylvania, in 1845 in Scott county, and Goshen near Oak Ridge in 1841.

Franklin Association was organized at the house of J. C. Duckworth in the year 1832. At that time there were ten churches represented, ten ministers and a total membership of 374. The territory embraced in the association consisted of the counties of Franklin, Washington, and parts of Jefferson, St. Francois, Gasconade, and Crawford.

The second annual meeting was held at Potosi in Washington county in 1833. There were at that time 13 churches and a membership of 544.

In 1835 the association met at the Providence church in St. Francois county, there were then 20 churches, 15 ministers and a membership of 797. By 1839 there were 26 churches, and among the prominent ministers were John Hutchings, Uriah and Josiah Johnson, Isaac Benning, Z. Jennings, Simeon Frost, J. C. and P. P. Brickey, J. H. Banbo, and James Glenn.

In 1844 the session was held at Union church in Ste. Genevieve county. After cutting off a large number of churches, thirteen remained with a total membership of 1,482.

Among the prominent churches of this body were Black River situated on the middle fork of Black river, organized in 1833 by Elder H. Lassiter. Among its preachers have been R. S. V. Caldwell, H. M. Smith, J. N. Russell and J. R. Pratt.

Another of the old churches was Liberty, called Bellevue, organized June 9, 1816, by Elder Felix Redding, who was its first pastor. This church was anti-missionary but was organized as a missionary church in 1829 being called Liberty. Old Mines was organized in 1834 in Washington county by James Williams with a membership of 16. Union church in Ste. Genevieve county was organized May 7, 1832, by Elder James Williams, T. B. Green and James Cundill.

The most prominent minister of the period of this association was James Williams, who was a native of Kentucky and came to St. Louis and later to New Madrid, where he suffered the loss of property in the earthquake of 1811. After the earthquake he removed to Cape Girardeau county and began the work of preaching about 1816. He then moved to Madison county and in 1832 to Washington county. Through his work a number of churches were organized in these various counties and he was a very active and able man. He died in Jefferson county in 1861.

Franklin Association in 1910 had 25 churches with a membership of 2,911. The churches were: Bismark, 126 members; Bonne Terre, 176; Belleview, 33; Big Creek, 34; Cove, 42; Cantwell, 56; Chestnut R'ge, 91; Doe Run, 141; Desloge, 164; Elvins, 224; Flat River, 459; Farmington, 184; Genevieve, 40; Hopewell, 105; Ironton, 168; Irondale, 41; Knob Lick, 20; Leadwood, 289; Liberty, 55; Little Vine, 73; Providence, 47; Herculaneum, 90; St. Francis, 87; Union, 153; Mt. Zion —

Black River Association was organized with churches dismissed from Cape Girardeau Association, in 1835 at Greenville, in Wayne county. The churches entering into the organization were Black River, Cherokee Bay, Columbia, Big Creek, Bear Creek, and Greenville. There was an aggregate membership of 188. The ministers were Henry McElmurry, William Macom, and S. Winningham,

Elder McElmurry was moderator and S. J. McKnight, clerk. Within a few years Elder William Little, B. Clark, and N. G. Ferguson were added to the list of ministers.

This association was an aggressive and active one and grew rapidly. Its territory included the counties of Wayne, Stoddard, Dunklin, and Madison with parts of other counties. In 1850 the association dismissed twelve churches principally in Wayne county to form a new association and in 1857 five churches were dismissed to form Cane Creek Association in Butler county. This left 18 churches in Black River Association and its territory was reduced to Stoddard and Dunklin counties.

At the meeting of 1860, which was held at Bloomfield in Stoddard county, there were messengers present from the following churches: Providence, Bloomfield, Gravel Hill, Bethany, Mount Pleasant, Grand Prairie, Kennett, Bethlehem, Pleasant Valley, Palestine, Shiloh, Oak Grove, Mount Union, White Oak Grove, New Hope, Duck Creek, Pleasant Grove, Ebenezer, Point Pleasant, Friendship, Union, Concord and Casterville. There were 125 baptisms reported for the previous year and a total membership of 962.

The ministers belonging to the association were R. P. Paramore, Samuel Walker, Edward Allen, F. W. Miller, W. B. Howell, A. E. Watson, W. W. Whayne, William Macom, James H. Floyd, Lewis L. Stevens, John Miller, and Jonathan Snider.

In 1881 a meeting was held at Bloomfield at which time R. P. Owen was moderator and C. B. Crumb was clerk. At that time the ministers of the association were David Lewis, B. F. Bibb, W. H. Dial, T. B. Turnbaugh, R. H. Douglass, T. Hoben, M. B. Baird, L. D. Cagle, J. J. Wester, J. H. D. Carlin, and M. J. Whitaker.

The following synopsis of the first forty-four meetings is taken from the minutes of 1880: 1st. Anniversary held at Greenville Sept. 3rd, 4th and 5th, 1836. First sermon by Bro. McElmurry. Wm. Street, moderator, and Wm. W. Settle, clerk. 8 churches and 228 members.

2nd. Anniversary held with Columbia church Randolph county, Ark., Sept. 30th, 1837. First sermon by Bro. McElmurry. Wm. Street, moderator, Wm. W. Settle, clerk. 9 churches, 252 members.

3rd. Anniversary held at Providence church, Stoddard county, Mo., Oct. 27th, 28th and 29th, 1838. Wm. Street, moderator, and Wm. W. Settle, clerk. Churches 10, members 287.

4th. Anniversary held at Mt. Pleasant church, Wayne county, Mo., Sept. 7th, 8th and 9th, 1839. First sermon by Bro. McElmurry. H. McElmurry, moderator, Elisha Landers, clerk. Churches 11, members 312.

5th. Anniversary held with Black River church, Wayne county, Mo., Sept. 12th, 13th, and 14th, 1840. First sermon by Bro. McElmurry, E. Rhewbottom, moderator, and E. Landers, clerk. Churches 12, members 320.

6th. Anniversary held with Black River church, Wayne county, Mo., Sept. 11th, 12th and 13th, 1841. First sermon by Bro. W. W. Settle, W. W. Settle, moderator, Elisha Landers, clerk. Churches 13, members 357.

7th. Anniversary held with Black River church, Sept. 10th, 1842. First sermon by Wm. Macom. Elisha Spiva, moderator and Elisha Landers, clerk. Churches 12, and 322 members.

8th. Anniversary held with Black River church Sept. 9th, 10th and 11th, 1843. First sermon by Bro. B. Clark, M. A. Short, moderator, Elisha Landers, clerk. Churches 11, members 625.

9th. Anniversary held with Black River church, Sept. 7th, 8th and 9th, 1844. First sermon by Bro. Wm. B. Kere, Wm. B. Graham, moderator, Pinckney Graham, clerk. Churches 15, members 694.

10th. Anniversary held with Black River church, Sept. 12th, 13th and 14th, 1845. First sermon by Bro. N. G. Ferguson. A. A. Shorter, moderator, Pinckney Graham, clerk. Churches 21, members 345.

11th. Anniversary held with Black River church, Sept. 11th, 12th and 13th, 1846. First sermon by N. G. Ferguson. David Pruit, moderator, Solomon Kitrell, clerk. Churches 23, members 798.

12th. Anniversary held with Mars Hill church, Wayne county, Mo., Oct. 2nd, 3rd and 4th, 1847. First sermon by Bro. N. G. Ferguson, Carter J. Graham, moderator, E. Landers, clerk. Churches 21, members 957.

13th. Anniversary held with Mars Hill church, Sept. 29th and 30th, 1848. First sermon by E. Landers. Carter T. Graham, moderator, and Elisha Landers, clerk. Churches 20, members 1,162.

14th. Anniversary held with Mars Hill church Oct. 6th, 7th and 8th, 1849. First sermon by R. P. Paramore. R. P. Paramore, moderator, and Pinckney Graham, clerk. Churches 22, members 1,227.

15th. Anniversary held with Cedar Creek church Wayne county, Mo., Aug. 31st and Sept. 1st, and 2nd, 1850. First sermon by Wm. W. Settle. R. P. Paramore, moderator, Pinckney Graham, clerk. Churches 24, members 1,079. At this session twelve churches were dismissed to form St. Francis Association, which they did October, 1850.

16th. Anniversary held with Stoddard (now Bloomfield) church Sept. 5th, 6th, 7th and 8th, 1851. First sermon by Martin Epps. R. P. Paramore, moderator, R. P. Owen, clerk. Churches 11, members 634.

17th. Anniversary held with Cane Creek church September 3rd, 4th, 5th and 6th, 1852. First sermon by Sanders Walker, Sanders Walker, moderator, R. P. Owen, clerk. Churches 12, members 595.

18th. Anniversary held with Union church Randolph county, Arkansas, Sept. 2nd, 3rd, 4th and 5th, 1853, on the plantation of Deacon Duckworth who died a few weeks before the meeting, but left ample arrangements for the attendants. First sermon by R. P. Paramore. R. P. Paramore, moderator, R. P. Owen, clerk. Churches 12, members 592.

19th. Anniversary held with Antioch church, Butler county, Mo., Sept. 1st, 2nd, 3rd and 4th, 1854. First sermon by Martin Epps, R. P. Paramore, moderator, R. P. Owen, clerk. Churches 16, members 793.

20th. Anniversary held with Bloomfield church Aug. 31st and Sept. 1st, 2nd, and 3rd, 1855. First sermon by Martin Epps, Martin Epps, moderator, R. P. Owen, clerk. Churches 15, members 922.

21st. Anniversary held with Kennett church Dunklin county, Mo., Sept. 5th, 6th, 7th and 8th, 1856. First sermon by Mathew J. Reed, S. Walker, moderator, Given Owen, clerk. Churches 16, members 938.

22nd. Anniversary held with Bloomfield church Sept. 4th, 5th, 6th and 7th, 1857. First sermon by R. P. Paramore, R. P. Paramore, moderator, R. P. Owen, clerk. Churches 18, members 1,095.

Cane Creek, Black River, Antioch, Mars Hill and New Hope churches were dismissed to form Cane Creek Association.

23rd. Anniversary held with New Liberty church, New Madrid county, Mo., Sept. 3rd, 4th, 5th and 6th, 1858. First preacher, S. Walker, S. Walker, moderator, R. P. Owen, clerk. Churches 16, members 797.

24th. Anniversary held with Oak Grove

churches, Sept, 2nd, 1859. Introductory sermon by R. P. Paramore, S. Walker, moderator, R. P. Owen, clerk. Churches 20, members 825.

25th. Anniversary held with Bloomfield church August 31st, 1860. Introductory sermon by S. Walker, S. Walker, moderator, R. P. Owen, clerk. Churches 23, members 963.

26th. Anniversary was held with Palestine church but on account of the war only two or three churches were represented. No minutes of session obtained.

27th. For 1862, and 28th for 1863, and 29th for 1864, and 30th for 1865 prevented by war.

31st. Anniversary held with Palestine church Sept. 14th, 1866. Introductory sermon by L. L. Stevens, L. L. Stevens, moderator, J. B. Rese, clerk; only 4 churches represented.

32nd. Anniversary held with Oak Grove church Sept. 13th, 14th, 15th and 16th, 1867. Introductory sermon by James E. Floyd, L. L. Stevens moderator, Given Owen, clerk. Churches 18, members 946.

33rd. Anniversary held with Liberty church Sept. 18th, 19th and 20th, 1868. Introductory sermon by L. L. Stevens, L. L. Stevens, moderator, M. V. Baird, clerk. Churches 27, members 1,313.

34th. Anniversary held with Bethany church Sept. 24th, 25th and 26th, 1869. Introductory sermon by L. L. Stevens, L. L. Stevens, moderator, C. B. Crumb, clerk. Churches 27, members 1,360.

35th. Anniversary held with Oak Grove church Sept. 16th, 17th and 18th, 1870. Introductory sermon by L. L. Stevens, L. L. Stevens, moderator, C. B. Crumb, clerk Churches 30, members 1,726.

36th. Anniversary held with Shady Grove church Sept. 15th, 16th and 17th, 1871. Introductory sermon by L. L. Stevens, L. L. Stevens, moderator, M. V. Baird, clerk. Churches 30, members 1,628.

37th. Anniversary held with Land Mark church. Minutes lost.

38th. Anniversary held with Oak Grove church Sept. 12th, 14th, and 15th, 1873. Introductory sermon by Tilford Hogan, David Lewis, moderator, M. V. Baird, clerk. Churches 25, members 1,434.

39th. Anniversary held with Palestine church Oct. 2nd, 3rd and 4th, 1874. Introductory sermon by M. V. Baird, David Lewis, moderator, C. B. Crumb, clerk. Churches 26, members 1,354.

40th. Anniversary held with Little Vine church Sept. 24th, 25th and 26th, 1875. Introductory sermon by David Lewis, David Lewis, moderator, C. B. Crumb, clerk. Churches 27, members 1,252.

41st. Anniversary held with Bloomfield church Sept. 22nd, 23rd and 24th, 1876. Introductory sermon by J. H. D. Carlin, R. P. Owen, moderator, C. B. Crumb, clerk. Churches 24, members 1,294.

42nd. Anniversary held with Oak Grove church July 20th, 21st and 22nd, 1877. Introductory sermon by J. H. D. Carlin, M. V. Baird, moderator, C. B. Crumb, clerk. Churches 24, members 1,257.

43rd. Anniversary held with Shady Grove church July 27th, 28th and 29th, 1878. Introductory sermon by David Lewis, David Lewis, moderator, C. B. Crumb, clerk. Churches 18, members 959.

44th. Anniversary held with Antioch church July 26th, 27th and 28th, 1879. Introductory sermon by J. H. D. Carlin; David Lewis, moderator, C. B. Crumb, clerk. Churches 18, members 649.

45th. Anniversary held with Four Mile church July 23rd, 24th and 25th, 1880. Introductory sermon by M. J. Whitaker, M. V. Baird, moderator, C. B. Crumb, clerk. Churches 22, members 923.

The meeting in 1885 was held at Oak Grove church in Dunklin county. Eld. R. H. Douglass was moderator and C. B. Crumb, clerk. There were 25 churches represented and the total membership was 1,018. The introductory sermon was preached by Rev. S. M. Brown.

The fifty-first annual meeting was held at Philadelphia church in Stoddard county in 1886. Eld. R. H. Douglass was moderator, and R. P. Owen, clerk. The introductory sermon was preached by the moderator. Eighteen churches reported 978 members.

About 1890 the association was divided, the churches in Stoddard county organizing the Stoddard county association and those in Dunklin county retaining the original organization and name.

Among the older churches of this association are Bloomfield, organized in 1846; Oak Grove, in 1858; Liberty, 1866; Shady Grove, 1866; Four Mile, 1866; Kennett and Cotton Plant.

This association is now confined to Dunklin county. In 1910 there were 24 churches in organization with a total membership of 2,449. The churches were: Bible Grove, 76; Caruth, 75; Cardwell, 202; Campbell, 144; Clarkton, 208; Friendship,—; Gideon, 17; Holly Grove, 66; Holly, 36; Holcomb, 90; Hornersville, 276; Kennett, 289; Little Vine,—; Lulu, 98; Malden, 119; New Prospect, 74; Oak Grove—; Octa, 97; Palestine, 115; Parma, 80; Senath, 148; Shady Grove, 82; Stanfield, 73; Varner River, 91.

The man, who more than any other perhaps, contributed to the prosperity of the Baptist church in this association was Elder J. H. Floyd, who was a native of Clark county, Missouri, born in 1832. Together with his father's family he came to Dunklin county about 1850 and began the work of preaching in 1858 continuing in the ministry there, with the exception of one year, until his death in 1874. He was a man of very great energy and not only preached continually, having charge usually of three or four churches, but also supported himself by farming. Doubtless to his labors is due more than to that of any other man the growth which the church experienced in those years.

Another of the early ministry was John W. Brown, who died in August, 1868, after having spent a number of years in the work of the church.

Still another one was L. L. Stephens, who served for a number of times as moderator of the association and also as missionary. He died in 1874.

Among the ministers who contributed very greatly to the success of the churches in this association were M. V. Baird, M. J. Whittaker, R. H. Douglass, and J. N. Richardson. Eld. Richardson came to the association from Arkansas though a Tennessean by birth. He was a careful student, an original thinker, and a powerful and pleasing speaker.

One of the influential citizens of Dunklin county is and has been for a number of years Rev. Martin V. Baird, who was born in Wilson county, Tennessee, June 7, 1837. He came with his father's family to Missouri in 1860; he had received a good education before coming to Missouri and after living for a time in Dunklin county he was licensed as a minister of the Baptist church and began his active work in 1870; from that time until the present he has been one of the foremost ministers of that denomination in that county. At one time or another he has been pastor of practically every Baptist church in the county, and his influence for good has been strong in every community. In addition to his work as a minister, which has given him a wide acquaintance, he has been a successful farmer and owns a large and well improved farm. In 1860 he was married to Ollie B. Hopper; to them were born two sons, Walter B. and Thomas J. Both these young men were educated at the Normal School at Cape Girardeau; both became influential teachers in their county and both met early an untimely death.

Rev. Mr. Whittaker was a self-made man, an earnest, devoted minister, possessing a most commendable influence in his community. He was a native of Kentucky, born in 1832. He was for a time a teacher before coming to Missouri. In 1854 he removed to Dunklin county and in 1874 was ordained as minister of the Baptist church. He served as pastor of a number of churches in his home county. He was also a farmer and nurseryman. He served in the Confederate army for a time and was present at one of the skirmishes at Bloomfield.

Rev. R. H. Douglass was a member of one of the pioneer families of Dunklin county. He was a native of Kentucky, born in 1839. He came with his parents to Dunklin county in 1850. He received the school training common to pioneer countries such as Dunklin county then was. At the breaking out of the war he enlisted and served until its close. He was a member of the famous cavalry regiment, the Second Missouri, and participated in all its great battles and marches.

After the war he returned to the farm and won for himself a competence. He was always an active and devoted member of the church and was finally ordained as a minister. On taking up this work he felt the handicap of the lack of sufficient education and set himself to the work of self-cultivation. Gifted with a good mind, great physical and mental endurance, and a determined will, he acquired a good education through his own endeavors.

He was an eloquent and forceful speaker being gifted with a high degree of magnetism and a power of clear exposition. He labored as pastor and evangelist with great success, but it was as an exponent and teacher of the great doctrines of his church that he excelled. Here few men surpassed him in the power and clearness with which he presented his convictions of truth. Due as much to his uncompromising stand and able exposition as to any other cause is the prosperous condition of the Baptist church in the Black River Association.

Personally he was a man of the highest ideals and the firmest convictions of right. No man who knew him doubted his absolute and unqualified sincerity.

He was twice married. The first time to Rebecca J. Wagster. One child of this union survives, T. J. Douglass, of Kennett. The second marriage was to Mrs. Mary E. (Lamb) Richardson, who survives him. Mr. Douglass died in 1904 at his home in Caruth.

The Concord Association is the second association of the name to be organized in the state; the first, was in Cooper county. The one in Southeast Missouri was composed of churches in Iron and Reynolds counties and was organized in December, 1867, at Big Creek church. The other churches taking part in the organization were Bethlehem, Mount Zion, and Pilgrims Rest; these churches had a membership of 298. The moderator of the association was Isaac Lane and the clerk was E. C. Smith.

In 1858 this association met at Pilgrims Rest church in Iron county and received the following new churches: New Prospect, Pleasant Exchange, Mount Gilead and Sugar Tree Grove. The ministers at this meeting were Isaac Lane, R. Seal and D. Warren; Isaac Lane was moderator again and Thomas Dickson was chosen clerk. The next year's meeting met at Big Creek church in Iron county, one other organization was added, this being Highland church. The third annual meeting was with Bethlehem church in Reynolds county in 1870. At this time there were only 6 churches in the association, but the next year, 1871, Denning Chapel, Pleasant Valley, Locust Grove, White Oak Grove, Black Oak Grove and Friendship churches were received. The meeting was held at Pleasant Exchange in Reynolds county; Samuel S. Beard was moderator. In 1874 the association consisted of 16 churches with a membership of 584 and 6 ordained ministers.

The territory of this association is now in Franklin and Reynolds counties. The association had 21 churches in 1910 with a membership of 1,468. The churches were: Centreville, 95; Dickens Valley, 90; Lesterville, 136; Pine Dale —; Bethany, 34; Bethlehem, 85; New Hope, 20; Dry Valley, 47; Oak Grove, 71; Redford, 122; Ellington, 149; Lone Cedar, 50; Logan Creek, 54; Roland Hill, 83; Corridon, 12; Van Buren, 68; Cedar Grove, 196; Sinking Creek, 28; Hopewell, 41; West Fork, 47 and Black River —.

Bethel Association was continually sending off groups of churches for the establishment of other associations. In 1860 a group of churches in Iron county consisting of Mount Pleasant, Big Creek, Pilgrims Rest, White Oak Grove, Sugar Tree Grove, Mount Gilead, Mount Zion and Locust Grove organized an association called the Central Missouri Association. The ministers concerned in this organization were William Polk, Harry Young and James Ritter. All of these churches had been members of Bethel Association and were dismissed from that organization in 1859. This association met in 1860 at Mount Zion in Washington county; at that time Isaac Lane was moderator and David Adams was clerk. There were 13 churches in the association at this time, 8 of which were represented at the meeting reporting a total membership of 367. The ministers were N. Adams, Isaac Lane, G. W. Bay and P. McCracken.

The next year Central Missouri Association met at Pleasant Grove in Iron county; there were 13 churches represented reporting a total membership of 528. Seven of these churches were then dismissed to form a new association called Concord.

In 1874 the Central Missouri Association had 9 churches with a total membership of 283, and there were 5 ordained ministers. The churches constituting the association were no longer confined to Iron and Washington counties, but were scattered over Dent, Reynolds and Madison counties as well. This association is now disbanded and the churches are in other organizations.

Jefferson County Association was organized at Bethlehem church, October 8, 1853; there were representatives present from Bethlehem, Swashing, Mount Zion, Calvary, Sandy and Little Maramec, all of them being in Jefferson county. The ministers of the association were James Williams, Washington Stevens, William McKay, J. C. Hudspeth, Sullivan Frazier and John H. Hensley; James Williams was the moderator of this first meeting. The meeting of 1856 was held with Swashing church; three new churches were added to the association. The meeting of 1869 was held at Mount Zion church, the moderator being W. Stevens, who also preached the opening sermon. There were at this time 17 churches connected with the association, only 13, however, sent any report which showed a total membership of 791. The meeting for 1870 was at Sandy church where three more churches were admitted. In 1871 Mount Zion and Valle Mines churches were admitted to the association; at the meeting with Swashing church at this time the total membership was 1,390 and there were 22 churches on the roll of the association. In 1881 the meeting was with Little Maramec church and the reports showed that there were 20 churches.

The oldest church in Jefferson county is Bethlehem church which was organized in 1829, about 8 miles northwest of Hillsboro. Two ministers, Lewis and James Williams, were the oldest preachers and assisted in the organization of this church; in 1840 there were 60 members. The first house of worship was built in 1843; it was a log house and was 20 x 24 feet.

Another of the old churches was Lebanon which was organized with 7 members in 1833 by James Cundiff and Walter W. Tucker. While a member of the Jefferson County Association the church was situated in Ste. Genevieve county; the first minister was J. C. Renfro, who continued as pastor for many years. The first building erected by this church was a log building which dated from about 1835.

Swashing church was organized in July, 1843, with 6 members; W. Stevens was the first pastor. This church is about 10 miles southeast of Hillsboro and 2 miles from DeSoto.

Pilgrims Rest church was organized in November, 1854, with 7 members, by John Hudspeth. It was on Dry Creek in Jefferson county.

Hopewell in Washington county was organized by Elder W. Stevens, September 24, 1855, with 7 members, the first pastor being William McKay.

Cedar Hill church was organized by W. Stevens, April, 1856, with 7 members; it is in Jefferson county northwest of Hillsboro.

In 1910 Jefferson County Association reported the following churches having a combined membership of 1,169: Bethlehem, 64; Blackwell, 31; Cedar Hill, 14; Cantwell, 62; Festus, 139; Grubville, 30; Highland, 81; House Spgs. —; Hillsboro, 27; Lebanon, 64; Moontown —; Mt Hermon, 76; New Harmony, 19; Oakland, 30; Oak Grove —; Pleasant Ridge, 78; Plattin —; Pilgrims Rest, 159; Providence, 40; Swashen, 106; Temperance Rest, 143.

In 1850 representatives of 12 churches, formerly members of the Black River Association, met at Castor church in Madison county and organized the St. Francois Association. The churches were situated in Wayne and Madison counties and perhaps one or two in Bollinger county. The first meeting of the association after its organization was held at Little Vine church in Madison county in 1851. At this meeting Zion church in Wayne county and Salem church in Bollinger county were admitted to membership. The ministers of the association were C. T. Graham, W. W. Settle, J. Duncan, J. P. Wallis, A. Hughes, R. S. Eaton and S. M. Randoff. Other ministers who later worked in this association were L. D. Bennett, A. G. Tidwell, A. R. L. Meador, A. Land, L. Langley, S. Farr, W. H. Mattox, M. W. Taylor and E. J. Bunyard.

The association grew steadily up to the breaking out of the war when there were 29 churches, in 1863 there were only 10 churches reported at the meeting in Big Creek church in Madison county, with only 326 members in the association. In 1874 there were 37 churches in the association with 1,400 members. In 1876, 10 churches were dismissed to form the Wayne County Association. At the meeting in 1878 there were representatives present from 24 churches chiefly in Madison and Bollinger counties with a membership of 1,200. At this time the ministers of the association were J. C. Hornsby, William London, H. F. Tong, L. W. Revelle, A. Tidwell, F. M. Holbrook, M. Robins, V. T. Settle, B. L. Bowman, J. F. Rudy, and J. C. Hembree.

The oldest church in the association was Big Creek church organized in May, 1835, about 18 miles south of Fredericktown. The first church house was built in 1854; the first pastor of the church was Henry McElmurry; he was succeeded by C. T. Graham, who served as pastor for 22 years.

Castor church was organized in 1845 by Elders Graham, Settle and Eaton. Little Vine church was organized in 1846 with 21 members. Marble Hill church was organized in 1848.

The first church of Fredericktown seems to have been organized in 1870 by Elder W. W. Settle and Silas Livermore; there were 31 members at the time of the reorganization in 1872.

Among the prominent ministers of this association were the following: Carter T. Graham, who was a native of North Carolina and who came to Madison county in 1822, was a well educated man and while he preached for a great many years, supported himself principally by farming. He died in September, 1861; Anderson Hughes was a native of Tennessee but settled in Wayne county while very young; he preached for a number of years and died in 1863.

One of the most influential of the men of this association was W. W. Settle, who came to Missouri from Tennessee in 1833. He first lived in Bollinger county and later in Madison county; he became a preacher in 1839 and up to the time of his death in 1870, was a very active, energetic worker as a minister.

One of the early preachers of this association was Pinkney Graham, who was a native of Kentucky and came to Southeast Missouri in 1826 and was for many years an influential minister.

Twenty-four churches reported to the association in 1910. They had a combined membership of 2,009. They were: Big Creek, 82; Brush Creek, 87; Castor, 22; Ebenezer, 71; Fredericktown, 444; Friendship, 107; Granite View, 19; Glen Allen, 102; Little Whitewater, 136; Marble Hill, 156; Marquand, 113; Miller's Chapel, 41; Moore's Chapel, 46; Mt. Carmel, 43; Mt. Pisgah, 116; Mt. Pleasant, 47; New Salem, 73; Shetley's Creek, 93; Trace Creek, 93; Twelve Mile, 116; Union Light, 19.

The association known as Cane Creek Association was formed in 1857 by 5 churches formerly members of Black River Association; for a considerable time the association had churches in Butler, Carter and Ripley counties in Missouri as well as some churches in Arkansas. In 1867 there were 14 churches reported, in 1874 there were 24 churches with a total membership of 632, in 1875 there were 22 churches.

There were 29 churches in the association in 1910 with a combined membership of 2,115. They were: Amity, 46; Antioch, 73; Black Creek, 71; Bethel, 75; Belleview, 31; Bethlehem, 33; Bay Springs, 94; Concord-Elsinore, 26; Cane Creek, 30; Doniphan, 353; Friendship, 44; Grandin, 125; Harmony, 25; Lone Star, 41; Lone Hill, 90; Mt. Carmel, 53; Melville, 7; New Prospect, 49; Naylor, 91; New

Hope, 106; Providence, 23; Poplar Bluff, (1st) 211; Poplar Bluff (2nd), 266; Paradise Ridge, 20; Rocky Point, 57; Sylvan, 53; Spring Hill, 62; Center Hill —; Fairdealing —.

The Maramec Association was organized November 11, 1870, by 6 churches in Washington county; these churches were Oak Hill, White Oak Grove, Crossroads, Little Spring, Mount Vernon and Fourche a Renault. The moderator of this association was J. R. Hamlin and M. T. Walker was clerk. There were 143 members. The ministers of the association were M. O. Gibson, J. R. Hamlin and H. M. Smith. The second meeting was held at Oak Hill in 1871; there were 11 churches and 302 members. In 1879 there were 10 churches and 319 members. The early ministers, besides those mentioned, were H. M. Smith and Gideon Seymore.

The oldest church of this association was Fourche a Renault which was organized in January, 1829, under the name of Mount Zion; its first pastor was James Williams and there were 6 members at the time of the organization. Like most other of the early churches, its first meeting house was a log structure built in 1844.

White Oak Grove church in Washington county was organized April 9, 1842.

Maramec Association was composed of 14 churches in 1910, whose membership was 821, divided as follows: W. Oak Grove, 83; Steelville, 136; Shoal Creek, 131; Liberty —; Courtois, 56; Mt. Olive, 50; Cross Roads, 76; Bourbon, 45; Huzzah, 61; Mis. Ridge, 17; St. Joseph, 36; Fourche a Renault, 29; Emmaus, 62; Bethel, 86.

Charleston Association was organized in 1876 with 4 churches; Morley, New Hope, Richwoods and Sylvania. These churches were all in Scott county and they had a membership of 146. In 1879 there were 9 churches with a total membership of 239. The ministers at this time were I. E. Anderson, Lewis Dickinson, W. K. Rainbolt, W. B. Richardson and J. G. Shearer; the latter was moderator.

In 1880 the session had held at Blodgett in Scott county; there were then 10 churches with 313 members; the churches were in Scott, Mississippi and New Madrid counties.

There were 20 churches in the association in 1910 with a combined membership of 1,693. They were: Bethel, 26; Bethany, 130; Blodgett, 41; Charleston, 282; Chaffee, —; Diehlstadt, 63; East Prairie, 108; Fornfelt, 21; Harmony, 76; Hickory Grove, 63; Hopewell, 41; Morley, 165; New Bethel, 128; Oran, 237; Pleasant Hill, 41; Rock View, 57; Savannah, 81; Sikeston, 32; Unity, 53; Vanduser —.

In 1910 there were 14 churches in Washington County Association with a total membership of 716. They were: Mt. Zion, 47; Breton Creek, 25; Lost Creek, 52; Pleasant Grove, 74; Missionary Ridge, 34; Fourche a Renault, 39; Shoal Creek, 36; Bunker Hill, 128; Hickory Grove, 39; Liberty, 51; Emmaus, 16; W. Oak Grove, 59; Potosi, 30; Hazel Creek, 17; Macedonia, 30.

The Stoddard County Association had 21 churches in 1910 whose total membership was 971: Advance, 79; Bloomfield, 101; Dexter, 158; Duck Creek, 133; Idalia, 43; Liberty, 57; Little Vine, 50; New Hope, 34; Philadelphia, 140; Providence, 306; Puxico, 58; Little Flock, 12.

In New Madrid Association there were 19 churches in 1910, having a membership of 1,403. They were: Caruthersville, 258; Cotton Wood Point, —; Como, —; Dry Bayou, —; Evergreen, 45; Holly Grove, 50; Holland, 65;

Hayti, 100; Macedonia, —; Micola, 70; Oak Grove, 80; Portageville, 90; Steele —; Shiloh, —; Tyler, —; Little River, 39; New Zion, 50; Pierce's Chapel, 36; Crockett Chapel, 40.

In 1875 it was determined to divide St. Francois Association, and 10 churches in Wayne county were dismissed to form a new association, in October of that year known as Wayne County Association. The ten churches had a membership of 1,444, and the ministers were Isaac Lane, A. R. L. Meador, J. W. Wilson, J. B. Mattox, M. A. Taylor and David Cheats. Five more churches were added in 1875 and in 1878 the total membership was 678.

There were 30 churches in the association in 1910 with a membership of 1,754. They were: Bear Creek, 47; Bethel, 24; Beulah, 64; Big Brushy, 33; Big Lake, 103; Black River, 105; Cedar Creek, 107; Chaonia, 49; Cullen's Sw. —; Des Arc, 8; Greenville, 155; Hodge's Fer., —; Lebanon, 180; Little Lake, 75; Liberty Hill, 22; Leeper, 34; Mt. Olive, 51; Mt. Pleasant, 70; Mt. Zion, 77; New Life, 37; New Prospect, 78; Philippi, 34; Piedmont, 193; Trace Creek, 72; Virginia, 21; Oak Grove, —; Patterson, 57; Williamsville, 91; Rocky Grove, 23; Low Valley, 14.

The Methodists and Baptists have been peculiarly fortunate in being able to do pioneer work in this section. More than the ministers of other denominations they have been able to get out into the country and organize and develop churches away from the towns and centers of population. No other denominations have quite equalled them in this respect. Accordingly we find the country districts of Southeast Missouri dotted over with Methodist and Baptist churches.

The Baptists were first in the field. Tywappity church was the first non-Catholic religious organization in this part of the state, and Bethel the second. Both were Baptist organizations. From the organization of these early churches until now, the denomination has prospered. There are now in Southeast Missouri, 281 churches with an aggregate membership of about 25,000. The ministers of the church have been in the forefront of every good and worthy movement, education has been fostered by them, they have created and supported Will Mayfield College at Marble Hill besides lending support to other educational institutions. The denominations seem entering on an era of increased prosperity as is attested by the erection of better buildings, the liberal support accorded the church, and the widening of its plan of work.

The church in this section has enjoyed the service of a long line of earnest and able men. To their ability and industry is due much of the place the denomination now occupies in the religious affairs of Southeast Missouri.

LUTHERANS

When the German colony was formed in Perry county in 1838, there was organized the first society of the Evangelical Lutheran church in this part of the state. A number of small communities made up this colony, and at first a number of pastors ministered to the wants of the communities. Wittenberg and Frohna had for their ministers Rev. Ernst Gerhard, Wilhelm Keyl; Altenberg's minister was Gotthold Heinrich Loeber. The minister of Seelitz community was Rev. Moritz Burger, while Rev. Carl Frederick Wilhelm Walther ministered to Dresden and Johannesburg. At a later period, however, it was found impossible to support so many pastors and the communities were combined. In 1839 there was established another community called Putzdorf. This was about eight miles from

Altenberg, and the pastor here was Carl Frederick Gruber.

Most of the settlers of this colony were poor, and were subjected to very great hardships in a new country, hardships which they were not fitted to undergo. It is, however, a striking commendatary upon their earnestness and piety, that in spite of the difficulties which surrounded them, from the very first, they began and carried on the work of preaching, building church houses, and even the formation of a Christian school. It was under the leadership of Rev. Carl Frederick Wilhelm Walther that the foundations for a college were laid at Altenberg. This college had only a one-story log building at first, but the school was opened and conducted within it and continued until the year 1849. Up to this time it was the sole property of the colonists of Perry county and was conducted by them and supported by their gifts. In this year it was transferred to the synod of the church and removed to St. Louis; it is now known as Concordia Seminary. In 1839 the college erected a parsonage and in 1841 a school house, in addition to the college. This school employed one teacher, H. F. Winter for more than twenty-five years. In 1844 the colony erected a stone church building which is still standing.

Two incidents which occurred in the history of this colony disturbed the work of the church. One of these was the great attack of cholera in 1849. The pastor of the church, Rev. Mr. Loeber, remained and cared for those who were sick and those who died, until he, too, fell a victim on August 19, 1844. The other disturbing incident was a discussion over doctrinal matters which took place in 1856. The pastor of the church G. A. Schieferdecker, was dismissed from his post and on his refusal to vacate the parsonage, was sued by the church and compelled, by law, to give to give up the place.

The Evangelical Lutheran church in Cape Girardeau dates its origin to the year 1854. In that year the church was constituted with eight members, among them being: Caspar and Louis Roth, Ernst Mantz, Charles Doesselman and Anthony Schrader. They adopted the constitution of the church on June 1, 1854, and in 1855 began the erection of the first building. It was of brick and very small.

The man who was instrumental in founding this church, and who was its first pastor was the Rev. A. Lehman, who was succeeded in 1856 by Ernst Harms. He was pastor of the church until August, 1859, and for the next nine years, the Rev. Mr. Riedel was in charge.

During this period other churches of this denomination were organized at various places in Southeast Missouri, most of them, however, in or near Cape Girardeau. One of these was Trinity church at Dissen, in Apple Creek township. Its organization was made in the year 1848 with these members: Fred Leeving, Louis Kaiser, Edward Engelman, Gottlieb Krause, Henry Grossheider, John Beck, Caspar Klaus and Henry Wehnmiller. The pastor of the church was F. J. Blitz. The congregation erected a log building for church purposes and used it until during the Civil war. The successors of Rev. Blitz as pastor were: F. Reidel, G. Gruber. F. W. and John H. Harmening.

There was also a church organized about 1860 at Kurreville. In Randol township, Cape Girardeau county, a church was organized at Hanover in 1852. They immediately erected a frame building which was used by the church for many years. The first pastor of this church was Daniel Bertling. In 1857 a church was organized at New Wells, by A. Schieferdecker. The principal members of the church at that time were: Joseph Meyer, G. Starzinger and M. Koessel. Zion Lutheran church was organized in 1857 at Gravelton. The first pastor of the church was Rev. John R. Moser, who served until 1870. There were about twenty-five members of the church at the time of its organization, and it became one of the largest and most prosperous churches of its denomination in this part of the state. In 1850 a church was organized in Kelso township, Scott county, and named Eisleben church. The men instrumental in this organization were: David Roth and Daniel Raubel.

In 1887 Rev. J. F. Köstering became the pastor at Altenburg, and was succeeded by Rev. A. G. Grimm. There was also organized a congregation at Frohna and at Uniontown and Perryville. The latter was organized in 1867 by Rev. Mr. Besel. This church erected a school building and also a church. The first regular pastor was Rev. C. H. Demetrio, who was called in 1869. He was succeeded by Rev. Wm. Matthes. This church has a good brick building and a brick schoolhouse.

The Lutheran church of Ste. Genevieve was incorporated by the circuit court on May 11, 1867. The petitioners were Christian Lucke, Henry Wilder, Phillip Medast, Charles Weiss, F. C. Fertner, August Wilder, Wiliam Mavoss and F. A. Klein. In 1875 a brick building was erected and a school since that time.

The church at Farmington, known as St. Paul's, was organized in 1874 by Rev. C. F. Obermeyer. The first house of worship was a small frame structure, erected the same year.

About 1859 the church was organized at Iron Mountain, and at a somewhat later date the congregation at Pilot Knob.

Trinity church at Egypt Mills was dedicated in 1881 by H. Guemmer.

A church was organized at Tilsit in 1866 and called Emmanuel. Rev. G. A. Muller was the first pastor. There were about 15 members.

Zion Evangelical Lutheran church was organized at Gravelton in 1857 by Rev. John R. Moser, with a membership of 25. Two of the prominent members of the church at this time were Judge Law Cloninger and Maj. M. N. Abernathy. The second pastor of the church was Rev. P. C. Henkel. He was succeeded by L. M. Wagner. A fine church edifice was erected in 1878, and a parsonage, near the church, in 1885. Under the leadership of Pastor Wagner a school, known as Concordia, was established and is still conducted.

At the present time there are church organizations at Festus, Ste. Genevieve, Poplar Bluff, Bismarck, Pilot Knob, Pocahontas, Jackson, Cape Girardeau, Gordonville, Farmington, Altenburg, Perryville and Kimmswick. Most of these organizations are in a flourishing condition and this denomination is making progress in Southeast Missouri.

EPISCOPAL

In 1887 there were only three Protestant Episcopal churches in Southeast Missouri—at Cape Girardeau, Ironton and De Soto. The first Episcopal minister who came to the southeast was Rev. Thos. Horrell, who came from Maryland to Cape Girardeau county in 1818. There was no church organization at that time, but he held services at different houses and baptized a number of people. He resided in Cape Girardeau county for only a short time and then went to St. Louis. In 1876, George Moore, a native of New York, located at Cape Girardeau, and through his influence a house of worship was built at the corner of Fountain and Themis streets. It was a brick structure and cost about $3,000. He became the first rector of the church and was succeeded by Rev. T. F. C. James, who was installed in 1882. The present rector is the Rev. C. F. Maltus.

The church at De Soto was organized in 1865. St. Paul's church was organized at Ironton as a mission in 1869, when Judge John W. Emerson was warden, and there were only two communicants, Mrs. Markham and her daughter. In 1887 the membership of the church had grown to 39, and a neat frame building was erected, costing about $600.

In 1890 Grace Episcopal church was organized in Crystal City. The Pittsburgh Plate Glass Company donated about three acres of ground to the church and upon this site was erected a handsome brick structure. It is open for use by all denominations. It is maintained principally by the Plate Glass Company, and is one of the most beautiful spots in Southeast Missouri.

At the present time there are organizations at De Soto, Cape Girardeau, Crystal City and Ironton.

CONGREGATIONAL

The first Congregational church in Southeast Missouri was organized at Arcadia about 1840. After an existence of a few years, however, the members adopted the Presbyterian confession of faith and became connected with the Potosi Presbytery of that church. The next organization was that at De Soto. Later churches were formed at Bonne Terre and Grandin. These are the only organization within this territory. The church at Bonne Terre has recently erected a beautiful and commodious building. It stands in the center of a large plot of ground, very attractively laid out in trees and flowers. The building itself is of brick and follows the English style of architecture. It presents a pleasing contrast to the usual forms of church buildings.

GERMAN EVANGELICAL

The history of the German Evangelical church in Southeast Missouri began in 1836. At that date a number of families from Switzerland made their homes near Rodney's Mill, in Cape Girardeau county. Two members of this Swiss colony, Benedict Mullett and Benedict Schneider, bought a mill, while the others were engaged, principally in farming. They were devout people and kept up religious services in the absence of any regularly organized church or of a pastor. For a number of years they were accustomed to meet at private residences to hold these informal services. The first pastor was called, and the church organized about 1847. The pastor was the Rev. J. Koebler. In 1851 they built and dedicated a small log house for church purposes. This was the only organization of the Evangelical church in this part of the state before the war.

The church at Jackson was organized in May, 1867, with 28 members and the following trustees: Charles Hohrenberg, Jacob Frederick, Adam Hoffman and Hermann Geyerd. F. Kies was the first pastor. The church fell into difficulties owing to a debt on the building and certain internal dissensions, and no regular pastor was employed for about fifteen years. In 1886 a reorganization was made and since that time the church has continued its work.

At present there are organizations at Cape Girardeau, De Soto, Allenville, Altheim, Dexter, Dutchtown, Jackson and Tilsit.

GERMAN METHODISTS

The first organization of German Methodists in Southeast Missouri was probably the church at Gordonville, which was organized in 1848. In the same year Apple Creek chapel was made a mission and was attached to the congregation which was formed about six miles southwest of Jackson. The original officers of the church at Gordonville were: Phillip Ruhl, presiding elder; Christian Bartels, Frederick Schleuter, August Gunther, Conrad Boettler and Henry Doris, stewards; and John Antonsen, Dietrich Brase and Henry Doris, trustees. The officers of the church in the early times were Charles Hollman, Frank Horstman, Jacob Mueller, Thomas Hoyer, Christopher Hoech and Henry Schultze. The first building for this congregation was a simple frame house erected in 1849. It served the purposes of the church until it was replaced by a brick building in 1875. The original members of Apple Creek church were: William Schultze and wife, Heinrich Tuschoff and wife and Heinrich Westmeir and wife. William Schultze was the local minister, and Tuschoff was the steward and superintendent of Sunday school. The pastors of this church were: Charles Hollman, 1849; Frank Hortsman, 1851; Jacob Mueller, 1853; Theodore Heyer, 1854; C. Hoech, 1856; Henry Schulze, 1860. The first house of worship erected by the congregation was a small frame building which is still standing. It was dedicated by Rev. Jacob Mueller. This church was continued as a mission until 1863, when a parsonage was erected and the mission became a circuit.

Later a church was organized at Whitewater. The church at Cape Girardeau is perhaps the largest of these organizations in Southeast Missouri. It has a good brick building and is a flourishing and influential body. It was organized as a mission in 1867 and connected with Apple Creek until it was made a station in 1884.

The German Methodist church at De Soto was organized in 1851 by Rev. John G. Kost.

PRESBYTERIANS

The Presbytery of Missouri was formed by the Synod of Tennessee and held its first meeting at St. Louis on December 18, 1817. It then included all the territory in the United States west of the meridian passing through the mouth of the Cumberland river, the only ministers in the Presbytery being Solomon Giddings, Timothy Flint, Thomas Donnell and J. W. Mathews. In 1831 the Synod of Illinois was formed and the Presbytery of Missouri was divided into three Presbyteries, St. Louis, Missouri and St. Charles. The next year the Synod of Missouri was formed and held its first meeting at St. Louis on the second Thursday in October, 1832; there were forty churches in the organization and eighteen ministers. In 1837 the general assembly of the Presbyterian church passed what was known as the Excision Act, severing all ecclesiastic relations with several synods and causing the organization, in 1838, of what was popularly known as the New School General Assembly. This act led to a division of synods and Presbyterian churches throughout the United States. In 1839 the Presbytery in Missouri divided also; on the division of the St. Louis Presbytery each faction should retain the original name. At its meeting in 1843 the Synod of Missouri (Old School) passed a resolution allowing the organization of the Presbytery of Potosi.

SOUTHEAST MISSOURI PRESBYTERIAN CHURCHES

At a meeting of the Synod of Missouri in St. Louis, October 23, 1843, it was ordered that the churches in Southeast Missouri should be organized into a Presbytery called the Presbytery of Potosi. The meeting for the purpose of effecting this organization was held in the Presbyterian church in Farmington April 2, 1844. The assembly was called to order in the old brick church building which afterward became the property of the Disciples or Christians. The opening sermon was preached by Rev. John T. Cowan and after the sermon the organization was perfected. There were three ministers present, John F. Cowan, D. E. Y. Rice, and James M. Covington. There was only one other minister within the bounds of the Presbytery, John McLean. The elders present were John McNeely, of the 1st Apple Creek church, Peter Statler of Whitewater church, Seth Hall of the 2nd Apple Creek church, Robert Sloan of Bellevue and Potosi, John D. Peers of Farmington, William Patterson of Clark's Creek, and Peter Whittenberg of Steelville. The churches not represented were Brazeau, Pleasant Hill, Jackson and Castor, making a total within the bounds of the Presbytery of five ministers and twelve churches. It will be noticed that the Presbytery was somewhat larger than the territory of Southeast Missouri, as we have defined it, for it included thirty-three counties in this part of the state. During the first ten years following the organization of the Presbytery the ministers received were as follows: In 1845, Amos H. Rogers, who had charge of the Farmington church; Assel Munson, who was received in June, 1845, and for 23 years was in charge of the 1st Apple Creek church, afterward becoming a member of the St. Louis Presbytery, but returning to Potosi Presbytery in April, 1870, where he supplied the Potosi and Irondale churches until his death in 1876; J. T. Paxton, who was received into the Presbytery in April, 1853, and supplied the church of Farmington; A. A. Mathis, on the same date, and was supply at Bellevue and afterward pastor at Brazeau; John McLean, one of the ministers of the Presbytery was a member for five years, but during that time was not in charge of any church.

During these ten years two new churches were organized, one at Cape Girardeau and one at Benton in 1852. During the same period Jackson, Castor and the 2nd Apple Creek churches were dissolved, so that at the close of the first decade there were five ministers and eleven churches.

PRESBYTERIANISM IN 1854-64

During the second decade, extending from 1854 to 1864, there were a number of changes in the ministry of the church. The Rev. D. E. Y. Rice died in 1854; he had been a member of the Presbytery for more than ten years and served as a stated clerk, was pastor at Pleasant Hill and Cape Girardeau and, as we have seen, was president of the Washington Female Academy. In 1854, Rev. John F. Cowan was dismissed from the Presbytery after a service of more than 20 years. In 1855 J. H. Moore was ordained as a minister and supplied Brazeau for a number of years. At the same time J. G. Wells was ordained and was made principal of Pleasant Hill Academy. W. F. P. Noble was also made a minister, but seems to have had no charge;

Julius Spencer was ordained in 1863 and remained in the Presbytery until 1869, supplying Bellevue and Potosi churches, and later establishing an academy at Irondale. From other Presbyteries, there were received Thomas C. Smith for the Farmington church, L. P. Rowland for Clark's Creek church, and also as a missionary, Francis Patton for Cape Girardeau church; H. F. L. Laird for Potosi church, G. C. Cannon for Bellevue and Potosi churches; John Donaldson for the 1st church at Ironton; David E. Curtis for Farmington and New Madrid, and D. A. Wilson for Potosi and Ironton.

During this period there were a number of changes in church organizations. The Arcadia Congregational church having adopted the Presbyterian Confession of Faith, was received in April, 1856, and the name was changed to the First Presbyterian church of Ironton. In 1857 the churches at New Madrid and Bloomfield, which had been organized by Rev. L. P. Rowland, were enrolled.

One of the strong and influential advantages of the work of the church during this period was its educational interests. The academy at Pleasant Hill under the direction of Rev. M. M. Fisher and later of Rev. J. G. Wells, seems to have exerted a considerable influence on the course of church matters and to have developed a number of ministers for the church. At the close of this decade within the Presbytery there were seven ministers and sixteen churches, which shows a growth, though but a slow growth during the period.

1864-74

The third decade, from 1864 to 1874, also saw a number of changes in the churches. Four men were ordained as evangelists, C. W. Alexander in October, 1867, who served as supply of the First Apple Creek church and Brazeau church for 13 years; W. B. Y. Wilkie, who was ordained in April, 1876, and for three years was supply to New Madrid and Sikeston churches; O. W. Gause was ordained July 9, 1871, and was at first the supply at Jackson and Pleasant Hill churches and later the pastor of Cape Girardeau church, and William McCarty was ordained the same day, July 9, 1871, and served first as an evangelist and preached also at Jackson, New Madrid, and Sikeston, and also supplied for the churches at Lakeville and Clarkton. Later he supplied at the First Apple Creek church and Brazeau and still later of Potosi. Irondale and South Bellevue.

Besides ministers ordained there were received from other Presbyteries George W. Harlan, who was received in October, 1865, and served as supply at Farmington, Clark's Creek and Syenite; Thomas C. Barret, who was received in October, 1866, and was supply of Bellevue and South Bellevue churches and later of Cape Girardeau; John Branch was received in January, 1868, but had no regular assignment; W. W. Faris, received in 1870, served one year as pastor of the Cape Girardeau church.

During this period the following changes in church organization were made: In May, 1864, the church at Jackson was reorganized by Rev. A. Munson with 18 members; the church at Irondale was organized in August, 1868, by a committee consisting of Rev. George W. Harlan and Rev. T. C. Barrett and Elder John Adams; there were 10 members in this church in 1867, Robert Sloam and John A. McCormick being elders; the South Bellevue church was organized in December, 1869; the Sikeston in July, 1870; the Charleston in 1871; the Clarkton church in 1872, and the Lakeville church in 1873. During the same period the Benton and Bloomfield churches were dissolved because they were in a disorganized state; the Whitewater church was dropped from the roll because it was withdrawn from connection with the church organizations and had become affiliated with the Northern Presbyterian church.

Just as is true in the history of every other church organization in the state, the Civil war period was an exceedingly trying one. Not only were buildings burned and many members of the congregation killed and their property destroyed so that the organizations were themselves almost destroyed, the bitter feelings engendered by the war and the contest from slavery made themselves felt in the conference, synod and associations of various church bodies.

The troubles in the Presbyterian church became acute at the meeting of the general assembly in 1861 and were intensified by the adoption of a resolution known as the Ipso Facto Order, in 1866. This Ipso Facto Order summoned the signers of a certain declaration and testimony which had been presented to the general assembly as a protest against certain of its members to appear before the assembly of 1867 and answer for their conduct in signing this declaration. It was also part of this order that such persons were forbidden to sit in any court higher than the session and enjoined all Presbyterians to look out for this order and not to enroll any such persons as members of their respective courts under penalty of immediate dissolution.

When the Potosi Presbytery met in 1868, Rev. John Branch introduced a resolution that only such delegates as avow their adherence to the general assembly be permitted to take seats as members of the Potosi Presbytery. This resolution was promptly rejected, whereupon Rev. John Branch and Rev. Julius Spencer gave notice that they withdrew from the jurisdiction of the Presbytery.

Prior to this meeting of the Potosi Presbytery the Synod of Missouri had divided, owing to an attempt to carry out this Ipso Facto order, the division having been made in October, 1866. The minority of the Potosi Presbytery, after the withdrawal of Branch and Spencer, sent a memorial to the synod in which they expressed their adherence to the assembly of the church and they secured from the synod an order for the meeting of the Potosi Presbytery in Ironton April, 1869. This order of the synod was in violation of the arrangements made by the Presbytery itself at a stated meeting appointed by the Presbytery. in Farmington September, 1868, and was to be held in the First Apple Creek church in April, 1869.

DIVISION IN PRESBYTERY

This, then, affected a division of the Presbytery; the majority of the members retained the records and met in the First Apple Creek church on the 22nd of April; the meeting was composed of three members and representatives of thirteen churches; the minority met in the First church at Ironton on the same date and there were present five ministers and representatives of four churches.

There were thus two bodies, each claiming to be the Potosi Presbytery. One of them, which we have called the majority, was independent for three years, not being represented in any of the synods of the church. In 1872, however, when it seemed that the division could not be cured, the majority connected itself with the Independent Old School Synod of Missouri. This synod, as its name indicates, was at the time occupying a neutral position, not being attached either to the

Presbyterian church of the North or of the South, and it was the hope of this association who were guilding the destinies of the synod, that a connection between the two divisions of the church might be effected. Abandoning this hope, however, at a meeting of the Potosi Presbytery in Jackson in April, 1874, it was determined to send commissioners to the general assembly of the Presbyterian church in the United States, commonly known as the Southern Presbyterian church. The commissioners chosen at the meeting were Rev. T. C. Barret and Elder E. Virgil Conway. The meeting of the assembly was held at Columbus, Mississippi, and the commissioners from Potosi Presbytery were received and the connection established between the bodies.

At the beginning of the fourth decade of the history of the Potosi Presbytery in April, 1874, there were on its roll six members and seventeen churches. The ministers were: A. Munson, George W. Harlan, T. C. Barret, C. W. Alexander, William McCarty and Andrew W. Gause. The churches were: Bellevue, Potosi, Farmington, Brazeau, First Apple Creek, Clark's Creek, Pleasant Hill, First Ironton, Cape Girardeau, New Madrid, First Jackson, Irondale, South Bellevue, Charleston, Sikeston, Lakeville and Clarkton. Two of these churches, however, those of Ironton and Pleasant Hill, though they were on the roll, were no longer regarded as a part of the Presbytery since they had attached themselves to the Northern Assembly and were dropped from the roll in October, 1874.

During this period of the church the ministers received and ordained were these: J. V. Worsham, ordained November 12, 1874. He preached at Clarkton and New Madrid and was supply at Apple Creek and Brazeau and was later the general evangelist of the Presbytery. A. W. Milster, who became connected with the Presbytery in June, 1876, and served as supply at Bellevue and South Bellevue churches, was later pastor at Bellevue; John M. Rhea, also received in June, 1876, was for a time supply at New Madrid church; Robert Morrison, preached at Potosi and Irondale, was received in April, 1877; Uncas McCluer, who was received in September, 1877, preached at New Madrid, Clark's Creek, Clarkton and other points; John B. Rubey received April, 1878, and supplied a number of churches; William M. Stratton, received in 1881, and served as supply at Potosi and Irondale; Joseph A. Graves, received in April, 1881, and preached as supply at Cape Girardeau, New Madrid and Clarkton; Weisel Beale ordained in September, 1881, was pastor at Apple Creek and supply at Brazeau, New Madrid, Clarkton, Kennett, Jackson and Oak Ridge; James H. Creighton, received in September, 1882, preached at Farmington for six years; J. W. Roseborough, received in September, 1882, and supplied at Cape Girardeau and Pleasant Hill; John Brown, received in April, 1883, but had no regular work; Horace B. Barks, received in April, 1884, and preached as supply at Bellevue and South Bellevue.

Only one church was organized during this period, that of Watervalley in August, 1879. In April, 1878, the churches at Lakeville and Sikeston were disbanded and Charleston church was disbanded in March, 1882, leaving on the roll seven ministers and thirteen churches.

Decade from 1884 to 1894

During the decade which extended from 1884 to 1894, the changes in the ministers of the church were as follows: James V. Worsham was received in September, 1884, and supplied at Brazeau and Apple Creek for three years and was also evangelist for a time; Henry C. Brown, received in September, 1885, was supply at Bellevue and South Bellevue churches for one year; Samuel W. Mitchell, received in September, 1885, and served as supply at Jackson, Apple Creek, Potosi, Irondale; Eber G. Mathews was supply at Cape Girardeau for one year; A. W. Wlison, received October, 1886, was president of Elmwood seminary six years and was supply of Doe Run church for two years; J. L. Leonard, received May, 1887, and supplied Bellevue and South Bellevue churches; Josiah F. Curtis, received April, 1888, was supply at New Madrid church four years; Samuel T. Ruffner, received in August, 1888, supplied at Farmington church, and W. T. Howison, received April, 1889, was pastor of Potosi and Irondale and supply of Bismarck and South Bellevue; William Flynn, D. D., received April, 1889, and was for a time supply of Cape Girardeau church; John W. Primrose, D. D., received in January, 1891, and served as evangelist for nearly three years; W. W. Killough, received in April, 1891, and served as supply at Apple Creek, Pleasant Hill and Brazeau church for a number of years; S. Addison McElroy, received in September, 1891, was pastor of the church at Cape Girardeau until 1898; Weisel Beale, received in April, 1891, and for five years supplied Apple Creek and Jackson churches; John E. L. Winecoff received September, 1891, and was supply for churches at Clarkton and Kennett; M. D. W. Granger, received October 13, 1892, was for several years supply at Bellevue and South Bellevue churches; J. D. Fleming, ordained in November, 1893, and made pastor of New Madrid church.

HISTORY SINCE 1894

In 1904 the reports made to the Presbytery show that there were then twelve ministers and twenty-four churches in its territory. In 1912 the ministers within the Presbytery were George W. Harlan, stated clerk of the Presbytery, Josiah F. Curtis, M. H. Kerr, pastor of Potosi, F. L. Delaney, stated supply at Malden and at Clarkton, F. E. Flow, pastor at Kennett, J. D. Harley, pastor at Charleston, William C. Beattie, stated supply at Brazeau and First Apple Creek, J. R. C. Brown, J. F. Curtis, C. E. Hicock, pastors at Farmington, W. W. Killough, pastor at Pleasant Hill and Perryville and stated supply at Oak Ridge, J. F. Lawson, pastor at Cape Girardeau, Lynn F. Ross, pastor at Jackson, Newton Smith, pastor at Caledonia, Bellevue and Ironton and stated supply at Bellgrade. Thomas H. Watkins, pastor at Caruthersville, and James V. Worsham, stated supply at Ste. Genevieve.

The first Presbyterian church which was organized in Missouri was at Bellevue, in what is now Iron county. The church was constituted by Rev. Salmon Giddings on August 3rd, 1816. It was called at that time, Concord church. There were thirty members in the organization and the elders were William Sloan, Robert M. Stephenson and Joseph McCormick. It is not only the oldest church in the state, but was for a number of years a most prosperous one. In 1844 it had a total of 175 members; fifty years later, in 1894, it had ninety members.

Brazeau church was organized in what is now Perry county, September 12, 1819, by Rev. David Tenney with 20 members. It was reorganized in July, 1890, with 62 members, and in 1894 it had 100 members.

The First church of Apple Creek was organized by Rev. Salmon Giddings, May 20th, 1821, with 41 members. The ruling elders were Mitchel Fleming, John Gilliland and Oliver Harris. Its membership had grown to 92 in April, 1844; in 1894 it had 85 members.

Farmington church was organized May 18, 1832, by Rev. Joseph Sadd and Rev. Thomas Donnell with seven members; Alexander Boyd was the elder of the church. In April, 1844, this church had 89 members and its elders were John D. Peers, Milton P. Cayce and Newton F. Cayce. In 1844 this church had 160 members.

Rev. Mr. Sadd continued as minister of the church until April, 1835, when he removed to Scott county. His successors were Thomas Donnell, Luther Vandoren, James M. Covington, who filled the pulpit of the church until 1844; among the other men who have been pastors were Rev. Amos H. Rogers, Rev. James T. Paxton, Rev. David E. Curtis, Rev. George W. Harlan, Rev. James A. Creighton and Rev. Mr. Ruffner. The first house of worship built by the Farmington church was dedicated in 1836 and was rebuilt and rededicated in 1868; this house was sold to the Christian congregation and a new house built, which is still occupied.

The Presbyterian church at Cape Girardeau is dated by some of the church authorities, in 1851, but it seems that there was an organization formed at a much earlier date. In 1835 the Rev. J. F. Cowan, who was the pastor at Apple Creek church, visited Cape Girardeau and gathered together eight members whom he constituted into a church. It was made a part of the Presbytery of St. Louis. It is not possible to give the names of the members, except that it is known that Charles Welling, afterward a member of the church at Jackson, was one of the early members and a Captain Dutch and family were also members. It is doubtful whether the organization ever succeeded in accomplishing anything, for there was preaching only at intervals by pastors of other churches and at a meeting of the Presbytery at Brazeau in Perry county in May, 1839, the Cape Girardeau church was struck from the list, its officers and members having moved away. In August, 1842, Rev. Robert G. Barret, then pastor at Apple Creek, visited Cape Girardeau and preached to a good congregation. He says that at that time the population of the town was about 400; that there were only two church houses in existence, one of them owned by the Baptists and the other by the Catholics. The Methodists had an organization in the town, but no church building. Rev. Mr. Barret reported that he found only one Presbyterian in the town, a woman.

The Potosi Presbytery met at Whitewater in April of 1850 and appointed a committee composed of D. E. Y. Rice, A. Munson and Elder A. Caldwell to organize the Cape Girardeau church. This organization was perfected and the church was received into the Presbytery August 31, 1850. The first pastor of the charge was Rev. D. E. Y. Rice, who served from 1850 to 1854. During his term as pastor of the church he was also president of the Washington Female academy, which he established and conducted in Cape Girardeau. The church went through the usual vicissitudes, being reorganized in 1855, at which time there were 18 members, the elder of the church being A. Flynn. For a time it was without a pastor, but from 1857 to 1859 it was served by the Rev. F. Patton. After his resignation two or three different ministers spent a few months in the service of the church, but on the breaking out of the war the organized work practically ceased for a time. Some of the sermons during that period were preached by the Rev. A. Munson, of Apple Creek church. In 1868, the church was visited by Evangelist W. H. Parks, who served them as a supply for several months. In 1869 Rev. Mr. Drake became the pastor, but remained for only six months; during his pastorate, however, the church had a constant growth. In 1870 W. W. Faris was chosen as pastor; from 1873 to 1875 the pastor was O. W. Gause; from 1875 to 1880 T. C. Barret, one of the most active and energetic men ever connected with the church, was pastor; from 1881 to 1885 the pastor was J. W. Roseberge; from 1886 to 1888, Rev. E. G. Mathene; from 1899 to 1891, Lellwyn Humphreys; 1901-02, J. L. Allsworth. The church was without a pastor for some time and then called Rev. Robert S. Brown, who remained, however, for only a short pastorate; from 1905 to 1910, Rev. Adolphus Kistler was pastor; he was succeeded by Rev. E. F. Abbott, who resigned in 1911.

The fifth church organized in the bounds of Southeast Missouri was Potosi church, which was formed July 21, 1832, by Rev. Thomas Donnell. There were six members in the organization, and Henry Pease was the elder. In 1844 it had 49 members and in 1894, 85 members.

Pleasant Hill church was formed by a group of members from the First Apple Creek church and was organized in April, 1841. It was first called South Apple Creek church, but the name was changed in September of the same year. In 1845 it afforded 75 members and in 1894 there were 90 members.

Clark's Creek church was organized in 1842 by Rev. James M. Covington. In 1844 it had 15 members, in 1894, 52 members.

The eighth church in Southeast Missouri was organized at Jackson, February 7, 1843, by Rev. Robert G. Barret with seven members; Dr. Franklin Cannon and James J. Gardiner were the elders of the church. In April, 1844, there were 11 members. During the war this church was disorganized, but was reconstituted May 15, 1864, by Rev. A. Munson. There were at this time eight members, and Charles Welling was the elder. In 1894 there were 95 members.

Pleasant Hill church was formed by a colony from the First Apple Creek church and organized in April, 1841; it was at that time called the South Apple Creek church, the name being afterward changed. The elders of the church were Ebenezer Flynn, E. W. Harris, E. L. Adams and Elam Harris. For a number of years after the Civil war this church was connected with the St. Louis Presbytery from which it was received into Potosi Presbytery in April, 1893. In April 1894, it had ninety members and four elders. During the period from 1850 to 1860 a very flourishing school was taught at Pleasant Hill. It was established by the Rev. Mr. Bidler, with Robert Caldwell as assistant. After one year, Professor Andrews assumed the management of the institution. He was succeeded by J. G. Wells, who remained until the beginning of the war. It was through his work that the school grew, as he was a very able and successful teacher.

The pastors of South Apple Creek, or Pleasant Hill church, as it is known, were J. L. Frary, 1841 to 1843; D. E. Y. Rice, 1843 to 1851; A. Munson, 1851 to 1865; James Stafford, 1865 to 1872; O. W. Gauss, 1872-73; John Branch, 1873-74; C. W. Alexander, 1874 to 1878; J. B. Rubey, 1878-79; P. B. Keach, 1879 to 1883; J. W. Roseborough, 1883.

The New Madrid Presbyterian church was

organized September 20, 1856, by Rev. L. P. Rowland. The members of the organization at that time were Thomas L. Fontaine, Catherine Davis, David Welschance, Elizabeth Welschance, Elizabeth Hatcher, Harriet Hatcher and Susan Duncan. At first the services were held in the Baptist church, but in 1875 a frame church building was erected. Among the pastors of the church were W. B. T. Wilkie, William McCarty, Uncas McCluer, J. A. Graves, J. H. Rhea, Weisel Beale and J. L. Curtis.

The Presbyterian church at Clarkton was organized December 1, 1872, though there had been preaching there for many years before that time. The church was formed by Rev. W. B. T. Wilkie and Rev. William McCarty and Elder W. A. Ponder; the members were Z. B. Penney, V. H. Harrison, elders; John H. Stokes, Charles E. Stokes, Clement McDaniel, Mrs. B. D. Austin and Mrs. Lucretia Stokes; the pastors of the church have been J. V. Worsham, Uncas McCluer, J. A. Graves, J. C. Buchanan and Weisel Beale. A church house was constructed in 1875 and dedicated April 3, 1882.

The church at Kennett was organized in June, 1887, by Rev. J. W. Roseborough and Rev. W. Beale. There were 41 members of the original organization, the elders of the church being Thomas E. Baldwin, and D. Y. Pankey. In 1894 the church had 60 members.

The Presbyterian church at Oak Ridge was organized October 31, 1884, by Rev. W. Beale and Rev. J. W. Roseborough. The members of the church were Oliver S. Harris and wife, Martha A. McNeely, Julia Hatcher, J. M. Bollinger, Elizabeth Bollinger, James C. and Mary A. Henderson; J. C. Henderson was also the elder of the church. In 1894 this church had 29 members.

Watervalley church in Wayne county was organized in May, 1879, by Rev. George W. Harlan and Rev. John B. Rubey and Elder Samuel Black. There were 13 members originally; John F. Miller was the elder.

Syenite church was organized in June, 1885, by Rev. George W. Harlan and Rev. James A. Creighton and Elder George W. Williams with 36 members and four elders.

Doe Run church was organized April 26, 1891, by Rev. A. W. Wilson and Rev. S. T. Ruffner and Elder James McCormick, with 11 members; Dr. F. L. Keith and S. G. Templeton were elders. In 1894 the church had 15 members.

The church at Bismarck was organized April 29, 1891, by Rev. J. W. Primrose with 13 members; Charles T. Martin and W. Scott Dent were the elders. In 1894 this church had 15 members.

Irondale church was organized in August, 1869, by Rev. George W. Harlan and Rev. T. C. Barrett. There were 11 members in the organization and Robert Sloan and John A. McCormick were the elders.

Sikeston church was organized in February, 1894, by Rev. Frank Mitchell, with 11 members, and B. L. Barnes and Thomas R. Brown as elders.

The church at Point Pleasant was organized March 18, 1894, by Rev. J. D. Fleming, with 11 members; the elders of the organization were James S. Law and Henry Bishop.

Northern Presbyterians

When the synod of Missouri divided in 1840 a call was issued for a gathering of those members of the synod who afterwards came to be known as New School Presbyterians, this meeting was held in Hannibal, October 7, 1841, and arranged for a meeting of the synod in St. Louis on April 8, 1842.

At this meeting there were present thirteen ministers and three elders who represented the New School element in the presbytery of St. Louis and that of St. Charles. After a short time matters were so arranged that there were four presbyteries in Missouri, by 1845 they were in a flourishing condition. This branch of the church, however, was hampered very greatly in Missouri by the opposition of the General Assembly to slavery. After the resolution passed by the General Assembly in May, 1857, at its session in Cleveland all the churches of the New School throughout the South, except those in Missouri, were separated from the General Assembly of the church. The Synod of Missouri decided first to stand independent but in 1859 it renewed its allegiance to the General Assembly and was later joined to the Synod of Kansas.

In 1870 the Synod of Missouri, New School, and that part of the Synod of Missouri, Old School, which remained in connection with the Northern General Assembly united, they then created a Presbytery of Potosi which they declared to be the legal successor of the original presbytery of that name, thus denying to the adherents of the Southern Church the right to use the name of Potosi Presbytery. The territory of this body was defined to include twenty-two counties of Southeast Missouri, and its first meeting was held September 20, 1870, at Whitewater church in Bollinger county; in 1872 the presbytery had six ministers and thirteen churches and 494 members.

The oldest church of this presbytery is Whitewater in Bollinger county, which was organized June 24, 1832, under a tree on the banks of Whitewater river. Its organization was the result of the visit of Rev. Joseph M. Sadd who had been sent to Missouri in 1830 by the American Missionary Society. While traveling over the country he visited the German colony in Bollinger county, most of the residents in this vicinity were members of the German Reformed church and their pastor for many years had been the Rev. Samuel Whybark who, however, had died shortly before the visit of Rev. Mr. Sadd and the congregation was left without a pastor. As there are no great doctrinal differences between the German Reform church and the Presbyterian church many of the members of the Reform went into the new organization; the names of the members of Whitewater church were Mathias Bollinger, Peter Statler, David Conrad, Moses Bollinger, Mary Statler, Sally Yount, Polly Bollinger, Rebecca Conrad, Sally Statler, Elizabeth Bollinger, Peter Ground, Peggy Ground, Sophia Whybark, Sophia Yount, Sally Conrad and Peggy Bollinger. Mathias Bollinger and Peter Statler were ordained as elders of the church. At first the congregation met in the house of Moses Bollinger and later they fitted up an old still house for services; after a time a log building was erected and dedicated as a church. The pastor, Mr. Sadd, remained until 1835 and he was succeeded by Thomas Donnell, James M. Covington, Robert G. Barret, Amos H. Rodgers, John J. Cowan, A. Munson, J. H. Moore, L. P. Rowland, D. E. Curtis and A. A. Mathias. These pastors bring the record of the church up to 1861. There seems to have been no regular services held between 1861 and 1867. In the latter year Rev. John Branch became pastor and served until 1872. Since that time other pastors have been Rev. Rowland, McCoy, E. P. Keach. From this congregation went off other churches—one at Bristol, one at Marble Hill and a third at Smithville.

The church at Marble Hill was organized

in 1868. The original members were Levi E. Whybark and wife, Samuel W. Whybark and wife, J. J. Conrad and wife, Mrs. Murdock, Kaziah E. Sutherlin and Urriah D. Titus. A meeting house was erected by them in 1868.

In 1880 a church was organized at Fredericktown, and on March 21, 1880, one at Poplar Bluff by J. W. Allen of St. Louis. The Poplar Bluff congregation erected a house of worship in 1884 at a cost of $2,000.

The churches of this branch of the Presbyterian church are affiliated with the Northern Presbyterian General Assembly. Their work has prospered but has hardly kept pace with the work of the Southern Church.

Recently an effort has been made to unite the Cumberland church—a venerable organization with the General Assembly of the Northern Church. The great bulk of the Cumberland churches were merged with the church of the North. Some refused to enter the larger organization and out of this attempted merger came much bitter feeling and a number of suits to determine the ownership of church property. Some of the Cumberland churches in Southeast Missouri followed the majority of churches of that connection into the Northern church but others have maintained their separate existence.

An account is here given of some of the Cumberland churches in this part of the state.

Cumberland Presbyterians

There are a number of Cumberland Presbyterian churches in Southeast Missouri. The oldest one of these was organized at Clarkton in Dunklin county, in 1855 by Rev. G. W. Jordan. The members were: Jacob Trout and wife, William Pickard and family, Thomas P. Hord and wife, John Agnew and family and John Timberman and wife. In 1856 the congregation erected a meeting house of hewn logs and in 1866 they built a substantial frame structure which was dedicated in 1887 by Rev. B. G. Mitchell. Among the pastors of this church have been G. W. Jordan, J. N. Roberts, E. J. Stockton, James McKnight, Rev. Mr. Cobb and W. W. Spence. This church was for a time known as West Prairie church.

A church was organized at Dexter, March 21, 1870, under the name of Mount Union church, the elders of the organization were Abner Warren, John Sitton and D. W. Mays. The name of the church was changed to Dexter church in 1875 and it was reorganized in 1879 with M. P. Riggin and L. O. Glascock as elders

A church was organized at Malden in Dunklin county, July 10, 1884, by Rev. W. W. Spence, who became the pastor of the church. There were about 20 members in the original organization.

In 1887 a church was organized at Kennett.

On November 12, 1858, four ministers, James Kincaid, S. Brown, J. W. Jordan and W. B. Province and several elders met at West Prairie church in Clarkton and organized West Prairie Presbytery. The new presbytery was under the jurisdiction of McAdoo Synod, which included 9 congregations and 360 members. Its territory extended into Arkansas until in 1877, when 4 of the churches were dismissed to the White River Presbytery and the southrn boundary of the West Prairie Presbytery was made to coincide with the southern boundary of the state. In 1888 there were within the presbytery a total of 21 churches with 641 members. The churches with their membership at that time were as follows: Bloomfield, 17; Canaan in Dunklin county, 59; DeLassus, 6; Dexter, 54; New Providence, 21; Doniphan, 97; Irondale, 26; Malden, 45; Mount Carmel, 18; Patterson, 41; Pleasant Grove, 13; New Hope, 33; Piedmont, 16; Pilgrims Rest, 24; Union, 44; West Prairie, 67; Blackwell, 12; Kennett, 9; Kennett Branch, 8; Good Hope, 10 and Mount Horeb, 21.

The ministers belonging to the Presbytery in the same year were: C. M. Eaton, W. H. Cook, W. W. Spence, E. H. White, J. M. Birdwell, Henry Hillman and P. Langford.

The Cumberland Presbyterian church at Clarkton in Dunklin county was organized about 1850 and they begun the erection of their church house in 1853 and finished it in 1855. It was built of hewn logs and was two stories in height, the second story being used for a Masonic hall. The house was built before there was a saw mill in the county and all the lumber for the doors, the floors and the finishing of the house was sawed by hand, the seats in the church were long benches. In 1883 the congregation erected a new frame building at a cost of about $1,600. One of the early pastors of the church was Rev. T. S. Love, who preached for them during the Civil war. He was succeeded by J. H. McKnight, during his pastorate the church grew rapidly and in 1868 had a membership of 175.

It was this congregation which had a peculiar experience during the war. On a Sunday while they were engaged in worship the house was surrounded by a band of guerillas whose leader announced to them that they did not wish to disturb the congregation but that they did want to exchange clothes with the men. Resistance was out of the question so the men left the building and exchanged clothing with the guerillas. One young man, who was more thoughtful than the rest, saved his boots by putting them in the stove in which there was no fire, before he left the room. The rest of the men had their choice of going home barefoot or wearing the worn-out shoes discarded by the guerillas.

Another of the early organizations of this church was Canaan organized at Gibson in 1862. Its first pastor was E. J. Stockton. Among its elders and prominent men have been M. J. Benson, W. R. and S. T. Weathers and John C. Agnew. In 1895 this church had 110 members and was an active flourishing body. There is also a Cumberland Presbyterian church at Kennett and one at Malden.

Christians

The first church of Disciples, or Christians, which, as we have seen, was organized in 1822 by William McMurtry near the village of Libertyville, grew slowly during the years and in 1844 erected its first building. This was a frame building which was replaced in 1860 by a brick structure. The pastors of this church were: William McMurtry, John C. Farmer, Sterling Price, A. G. Lucas, B. F. Wilson, T. E. Sheppard and J. G. Dillard.

About 1825 a church was organized in Madison county, three miles east of Fredericktown, called Antioch. Among the early members of this church were: George and Jacob Nifong, Ephraim Potter, Joseph Bennett, James Marshall and their families.

About 1844 a church was organized in the New Tennessee settlement in Ste. Genevieve county. Among its members were: Richard Griffith, J. M. Powell, Valentine Underwood and Peter Bloom.

In 1854 a church was organized at Farmington through the efforts of Elder S. S.

Church. This congregation erected a large brick building, but it finally passed out of their hands, and became the property of the Methodist Episcopal church.

Rev. Thomas Douthitt reorganized the congregation in 1875 and it purchased the house of worship formerly used by the Methodist Episcopal church, South. The church prospered and now has a handsome and commodious brick building.

The Poplar Bluff church was organized in 1877 through the efforts of Elder E. Childress. There were about twenty members in the organization but it gradually lost numbers and finally became extinct. Rev. G. A. Hoffman reorganized it in 1887, at which time there were twenty-two members. It has grown very greatly and is now a large and powerful organization.

The Dexter church was founded by Elder Thomas Sheppard in 1879. The membership was small at first and no house was erected until 1883. The congregation is active and growing now.

In 1886 a church was organized at Malden. A good frame building was erected which was afterward destroyed by fire caused by lightning. It was replaced with the present comfortable building. About the same year the church at Kennett was organized. It has a frame building and is actively engaged in church work.

The great growth and expansion of the church has been the work of the last thirty years. Up to that time the denomination was of comparatively small numbers in this part of the state, but it has grown to be one of the large and influential church organizations. It has been found impossible to secure detailed information concerning the foundation of the various congregations or their present membership.

There are many other churches in Southeast Missouri besides those we have mentioned. There are congregations at Charleston, East Prairie, Festus, Fredericktown, Caruthersville, Greenville, Hematite, Marble Hill, Morley, Naylor, Marquand, Mine La Motte, Higdon's chapel, Bismarck, Knob Lick, Bonne Terre, Mill Springs and DeSoto. The DeSoto church was founded in 1868.

CHAPTER XXXVI

RAILROADS

BEGINNING OF RAILROAD AGITATION—COMPANIES FORMED—THE FIRST RAILROAD—ST. LOUIS, IRON MOUNTAIN & SOUTHERN—CAIRO & FULTON—PRESENT CONDITION OF THE IRON MOUNTAIN—THE CAPE GIRARDEAU, PILOT KNOB & BELMONT—THE HOUCK LINES—THE 'FRISCO SYSTEM—THE ST. LOUIS SOUTHWESTERN—THE ILLINOIS & MISSOURI BRIDGE COMPANY—MISSISSIPPI RIVER & BONNE TERRE RAILROAD COMPANY—THE WILLIAMSVILLE, GREENVILLE & ST. LOUIS RAILROAD COMPANY—ST. LOUIS, KENNETT & SOUTHEASTERN—THE ST. LOUIS & MISSOURI SOUTHERN—THE PARAGOULD SOUTHEASTERN — THE ILLINOIS SOUTHERN—THE MISSOURI SOUTHERN—THE PARAGOULD & MEMPHIS—THE BUTLER COUNTY RAILROAD—THE ST. FRANCOIS COUNTY INTERURBAN.

During this period of Missouri history the organization of railroad companies was begun. Up to this time there had been no particular interest in railroad building, but the decade extending from 1850 to 1860 was filled with railroad projects of almost every conceivable kind. Railroads were projected from place to place throughout the state. Many companies were organized, most of which were without any tangible capital and were, therefore, unable to construct railroads. Southeast Missouri was no exception to the situation in the state as a whole. There were a great number of railroads projected, and but few of them ever built.

One of these was a company called Mine La Motte & Mississippi Railroad, with a capital of $300,000.00, for the purpose of building a road from Mine La Motte to some point on the Mississippi river not lower than Pratte's Landing. Another railroad was projected from St. Louis to Caledonia, in Washington county, by way of Potosi. This company had a capital of $2,000,000. Another one was to run from Caledonia to Cape Girardeau by way of Iron Mountain, Mine La Motte and Jackson. It was called the Southern Railroad and was capitalized at $1,000,000.00. The Southeastern Railroad, with a capital of $200,000.00 was projected from New Madrid to Commerce, in Scott county, and the Washington & Ste. Genevieve Railroad was planned to be built between Washington and Ste. Genevieve. All of these mentioned were organized in 1836 and 1837, but none of the companies possessed either money or credit enough to construct the railroads proposed.

The first railroad company which actually built a railroad in Southeast Missouri was the St. Louis & Iron Mountain Railway Company. The first work done looking to the building of this road in this part of the state was the survey from St. Louis to Iron Mountain made in 1852 by J. H. Morley. The object of the promoters of this scheme was to make available the great quantities of iron ore then supposed to be contained in Iron Mountain. Iron had been mined in considerable quantities in the vicinity of Iron Mountain for a number of years. In fact the first record we have of the working of iron mines in Iron county is prior to 1820, but during all of these years the work of digging out the ore and developing these mines was very greatly handicapped by the lack of proper transportation facilities. It was necessary to transport the ore overland from the mines to the river. The ore was carried on horseback or in carts and wagons and the transportation cost was very great. It was to provide better means for shipping the product of these mines that this first railroad in Southeast Missouri was projected. This first survey, in 1852, resulted in very little being done. In January, 1853, there was chosen for the St. Louis & Iron Mountain Company a board of directors. This board immediately ordered the making of a new survey for the road. After many delays the road was finally built as far as Pilot Knob, in Iron county.

The state of Missouri had provided that any railroad company in the state might receive state aid. This aid was given in the form of lands, or in the form of the credit of the state itself. The credit of the state was loaned to these railroad enterprises through the device of guaranteeing the bonds of the railroad. A bill which became law, provided that the state should grant two dollars in bonds for every dollar expended by any railroad company, not to exceed $400,-000.00. The Iron Mountain Railway Company received both grants of lands and guarantee of the large amount of its bonds. This, however, did not meet the expectation of its promoters and they soon fell into financial difficulties. The road became unable to pay the interest on its bonds, and on September 22d, 1866, the railroad was sold at public auction, and was purchased for the state itself. It was operated by three commissioners appointed by the governor until January 12th, 1867, when it was again sold, and was purchased this time by McKay, Simmons & Vogel. They later transferred it to the man who more than any other was instrumental in providing for the people of this section of the state their first railroad, Thomas Allen. Under his management the road was extended and was put upon a paying basis. The first extension south was that which came to be known as the Belmont branch. This particular line of railroad was built from both ends toward the middle and it was completed August 14th, 1869, the last rail being laid in the middle of the tunnel in Bollinger county.

On February 9th, 1853, the President of the United States approved an act of Congress which granted to the states of Missouri and Arkansas the right of way and lands to aid in the construction of the railroad from a point on the Mississippi river opposite the mouth of the Ohio by way of Little Rock to the Texas boundary near Fulton, Arkansas. Not only was the right of way granted through all government lands, but every alternate section of land designated by even numbers contained in a strip six miles in width on each side of the track was also conveyed. The act carried with it a proviso that it should expire by limitation within ten years.

The people of Southeast Missouri were,

very naturally, anxious to take advantage of this liberal offer of assistance, and accordingly a meeting was called of the citizens of Charleston and such others as might be interested, to begin work looking to the construction of the road. This meeting was held June 9th, 1853, in the court house at Charleston, and was presided over by Judge Noah Handy, as chairman. John C. Thomas was secretary. It was determined first of all to discover the cost of constructing the railroad across the swamp along the line of the projected road from Cairo to Fulton. George Whitcomb, Harrison Hough, H. M. Molder, H. M. Ward, A. M. Bedford, John Byrd and Felix Badger were appointed as a committee to investigate this cost of construction. It was then determined to call together a large number of citizens from the southeast and also from Kentucky and Tennessee, to further consider the possibility of building the road. This meeting was held at Benton, Missouri, November 14th and 15th, 1853. Not much was done at the meeting, further than to adopt resolutions advocating the building of the Cairo & Fulton road by way of Bloomfield, and asking that the St. Louis & Iron Mountain Railway Company extend their road to a crossing with the Cairo & Fulton.

On September 12th, of the same year, the Cairo & Fulton Railroad Company had been organized in Stoddard county, with John M. Johnson as president. The capital stock of the new corporation was fixed at $1,500,000.00, divided into 60,000 shares of the par value of $25.00 each. The incorporators of this railroad did not have the means to build it, and it had been provided before the act of incorporation to secure from some of the interested counties subscriptions to the capital stock of the railroad. These subscriptions were to be paid in land at a value of $1.00 per acre. Subscriptions were received from the counties, as follows:

Stoddard County	$150,000
Butler County	100,000
Dunklin County	100,000
Scott County	50,000
Ripley County	19,500
Total	$419,500

In accordance with the terms of the agreement made, the county courts of the counties mentioned conveyed to the Cairo & Fulton Railroad Company, lands at the value of $1.00 an acre to the amounts mentioned. This transfer of large bodies of land at a minimum price, resulted in very great loss to the counties, and in long continued litigation.

A meeting was held in Charleston in 1853 to determine whether it was possible to proceed to survey the line of the new railroad. The meeting asked the county court of Mississippi county to provide funds not to exceed $500.00, for the purpose of a survey. This the county did, but the survey was not made. The Cairo & Fulton Railroad Company had, in the meantime, been incorporated by the state of Arkansas, and the chief engineer, J. S. Williams, had made a survey of the road through Arkansas and extended his survey through Missouri and reported to the legislature of Missouri in February, 1855. Immediately following this report, the legislature proceeded to incorporate the Cairo & Fulton Railroad Company in Missouri, and to pass an act to issue bonds of the state to the new company, equal to the amount that it had expended, but not to exceed $250,-

000.00. This bill was vetoed by the governor, but was later passed over his veto and became a law.

In 1856 the company elected Orson Bartlett as president, and a new survey of the line was made, beginning, this time, at Bird's Point. In 1857 new officers were chosen and the contracts were let for the grading of the road from Bird's Point to Charleston. The first actual work was done on October 1st, 1857. H. J. Deal, who was the contractor, threw the first shovel of dirt on that date. The work of construction proceeded slowly, and it was not until April 1st, 1859, that the first train reached Charleston. The engine on this train had been named Sol. G. Kitchen, in honor of Sol. G. Kitchen, of Stoddard county, who was one of the men most interested and active in securing the road. On the 4th of July, 1859, there was held a great celebration in honor of the formal opening of the road.

By the beginning of the war, in 1861, there were about twenty miles constructed, and at that time it fell into the hands of the government and was used for military purposes, which resulted in the loss of the greater part of the rolling stock. This prevented the road from earning even enough to pay the interest on the state bonds, which fell into arrears. The holders of the bonds caused a sale of the road in 1866, which was bought by commissioners for the state, who later sold the road to McKay, Simmons & Vogel, the same persons who bought the St. Louis & Iron Mountain. They paid the state the sum of $350,000.00, and then transferred the road to Thomas Allen, the president of the Iron Mountain System. It was later extended to Poplar Bluff, and was known as the Cairo, Arkansas & Texas road. It is still popularly called the "Cat Road," the word being formed from the initial letters of Cairo, Arkansas and Texas. It remained a separate organization until 1874, when it was consolidated with the St. Louis, Iron Mountain & Southern, and was afterward designated as the Cairo branch.

For many years the Iron Mountain System was the only great system in Southeast Missouri. In fact, for years it was the only system. After the war, when the road came into the possession of Mr. Thomas Allen it entered upon a period of prosperity and expansion. When the war closed the road extended only as far south as Pilot Knob in Iron county. Shortly after Mr. Allen's purchase of the road in January 1867, it was transferred to a corporation known as the St. Louis & Iron Mountain Railroad Company. This company was formed by Mr. Allen and his associates and was incorporated July 26, 1867. Mr. Allen was made its president, a position he held for many years.

This company proceeded to construct a line from Pilot Knob to Belmont, a distance of 120 miles. This line opened up the counties of St. Francois, Madison, Bollinger, Scott and Mississippi. The principal towns along it were Farmington, two and one-half miles distant, Fredericktown, Oran, Morley and Charleston.

Between 1870 and 1874, the company constructed a branch called the Arkansas branch from Bismark to the Arkansas line at Moak, a distance of 184 miles. This road passed through Iron, Wayne and Butler counties, the principal towns springing up along it, being Ironton, Piedmont, Williamsville and Poplar Bluff.

In 1872, Thomas Allen conveyed to the St. Louis & Iron Mountain Railroad Company the property of the Cairo, Arkansas &

Texas Railroad Company, which consisted of a line from Cairo to Sikeston. The company then proceeded to rebuild this line and extend it to Poplar Bluff, a distance of 70 miles.

Acting under the charter granted to the Cairo & Fulton Railroad Company and acquired by the Iron Mountain, the latter company constructed a line from Moak through Arkansas to the Texas line at Fulton, Ark. These two companies were consolidated under the name of the St. Louis, Iron Mountain & Southern Railroad Company in June, 1874. This line from St. Louis to Fulton, Arkansas, a distance of 681 miles, became the main line of the company and the line from Bismarck to Belmont became known as the Belmont branch.

In 1883 a company was organized, known as the Jackson Branch Railroad Company, to build a line from Allenville, on the Belmont branch, to the Mississippi river, at Grand Tower, by way of Jackson, the county seat of Cape Girardeau county. This line was constructed by the Iron Mountain as far as Jackson and was later consolidated with the Iron Mountain System. Later a branch was constructed from Mineral Point to Potosi, in Washington county, to provide transportation for the mineral products of that region.

The Iron Mountain company later constructed a line from Poplar Bluff to Doniphan, in Ripley county, by way of Naylor, in the same county. This road is now operated as a part of the Cairo branch, through trains being run from Bird's Point to Doniphan.

Close relations have always existed between the Iron Mountain System and the St. Louis Southwestern, or Cotton Belt, as they are both owned in large part by members of the Gould family. The Iron Mountain System, about 1900, constructed a line called the Valley line, from East St. Louis to Gale, Illinois, opposite Gray's Point, the northern terminus of the Cotton Belt. On the construction of the Thebes bridge these roads formed a continuous line from Texas and Arkansas points to St. Louis. It also provided connection with the main line and branches of the Iron Mountain. The Cotton Belt connects with the Belmont branch at Delta, with the Cairo branch at Dexter, and with the main line of the Iron Mountain at Paragould, Arkansas. A traffic agreement was entered into between these roads by which Cotton Belt trains entered St. Louis over the tracks of the Valley line, and Iron Mountain trains used the tracks of the Cotton Belt from Dexter to Thebes. This last arrangement was made because the Cotton Belt and Valley lines afford what is practically a water-level route to St. Louis, while the Iron Mountain above Poplar Bluff passes through a hilly country. Much of the freight from Arkansas and Texas is diverted at Poplar Bluff over the Cairo branch to Dexter, then by way of the Cotton Belt and Valley lines to St. Louis. The immense importance of the Thebes bridge is made apparent by this arrangement.

Plans are under way at this time providing for the double tracking of much of the main lines of the St. Louis, Iron Mountain & Southern and the St. Louis Southwestern. The Iron Mountain continues to be, as it has been since its construction, one of the most important factors in the development of southeast Missouri. Its main line provides unrivaled transportation facilities for the western tier of counties and its various branches serve much of the remainder of the territory.

In 1859 the Cape Girardeau, Pilot Knob & Belmont Railroad Company was organized to construct a road from Pilot Knob to Belmont, by way of Cape Girardeau. William C. Ranney was made president of the company, arrangements were perfected and a large private subscription obtained for the stock of the company. The county of Cape Girardeau voted to take two hundred thousand dollars worth of the company's stock. It seemed that the railroad would be built and it probably would have been but for the breaking out of the Civil war. Nothing was done during that period, but after the close of the war the matter was taken up again. A company was organized, known as the Cape Girardeau & State Line Railroad Company, with intention to build a road from Cape Girardeau to some point on the Arkansas line. The company was organized April 27th, 1869, with the following directors: G. C. Thilenius, John Albert, T. J. Rodney, Robert Sturdivant, John Ivers, A. B. Dorman, M. Dittlinger, L. F. Klostermann, William Woeleke, F. Hanny, M. M. Kimmell, A. D. Leech, H. Bader, C. Hirsch, William Regenhardt, William Hamilton, J. Vasterling and Casper Uhl. G. C. Thilenius was made president, John Ivers, vice-president, and S. G. Kitchen, manager.

The company started off with very flattering prospects, there was a large private subscription to the bonds and the city of Cape Girardeau voted to take a hundred and fifty thousand dollars worth and the township of Cape Girardeau the same amount. The bonds were sold and with the money the work of construction was begun. Through bad management, however, the funds were exhausted before a single mile of the road was finished. It was then determined to build the road by contract. Accordingly an agreement was entered into with Governor Fletcher and his associates to build the road, and for their services they were to receive a deed to the roadbed, provided they completed twenty-five miles by December 1, 1871.

Governor Fletcher then proceeded to organize a company known as the Illinois. Missouri & Texas Railway Company and issued bonds to the amount of $1,500,000 secured by mortgage on the property of both companies. The bonds found no sale however, and it became impossible to secure funds. The project of building the road was abandoned for ten years. A considerable amount of work had been done in building bridges and in laying ties and throwing up a roadbed; all these suffered very materially during the years when nothing was done, the wood work decayed and the roadbed was washed away by the rain and grew up in brush.

In 1880 a man became interested in the railroad whose name is associated with most of the successful railroads built in Southeast Missouri, Louis Houck. He entered into a contract with the Cape Girardeau & State Line Company, which still controlled the old roadbed, by the terms of which he was to complete the road from Cape Girardeau to Delta by January 1, 1881, and was then to receive a title to all the property of the old company. He was successful in carrying out his agreement and the Cape Girardeau & State Line Company transferred to him the title to the road. By August, 1881, he had extended the road to Lakeville, in Stoddard county, and in 1882 it reached Brownwood. In this year the name of the company was changed to the Cape Girardeau & Southwestern Railway Company. In 1883 it was built to Idlewild; in 1884 it reached Wappapello, in Wayne county, a distance of fifty-one miles from Cape Girardeau. In 1886 the road acquired by lease the Brownwood & Northwestern Railroad, which extended from Brownwood to Zalma, a distance of nine miles. This Brownwood & Northwestern had been built by William Brown. In 1887 the road was extended from Wappapello to Chaonia, a distance of seven miles.

In 1891 Mr. Houck became interested in a railroad that had been built from Campbell, on the Cotton Belt, to the county seat of Dunklin county. This road had been constructed by E. S. McCarthy and associates. Mr. Houck acquired a controlling interest in this road, reconstructed it, and continued its operation. In 1893-1894 he built a railroad from Kennett to Caruthersville, in Pemiscot county, a distance of 25 miles, giving the people of the southern part of Dunklin county a more direct outlet to the Mississippi river than they had had before. In 1896-1897 he constructed a railroad from Kennett, by way of Senath, to Leechville, in Arkansas, opening up a country before distant from railroads and a country among the most fertile and valuable in Southeast Missouri.

In 1898 he built a railroad from Brownwood to Bloomfield, in Stoddard county. Up to this time Bloomfield had been a purely inland town having no railroad connections at all. This brought connection with the Cape Girardeau & Southwestern which, with its connections, formed a trunk line through southern Missouri. In the same year the road from Bloomfield to Zeta, in Stoddard county, on the Cotton Belt, was rebuilt.

In 1894 Mr. Houck began the construction of one of the most important of his railroads. It was known as Houck's Missouri & Arkansas Railroad, and was to extend from Cape Girardeau to a connection with the St. Louis, Kennett & Southern at Gibson, in Dunklin county, a distance of 100 miles. This enterprise required until 1900 for its completion. This link made the railroads owned by Mr. Houck into a system, since all of them were now connected.

This system of railroads covered part of Southeast Missouri south of Cape Girardeau. In 1905 a railroad was constructed from West Chester, on the Mississippi river, to Perryville, the county seat of Perry county. In 1898 a road connecting St. Mary's and Ste. Genevieve was built. These were the beginnings of a system north of Cape Girardeau, but for a time were left unconnected. In 1902 all of Mr. Houck's railroads south of Cape Girardeau were consolidated under the name of the St. Louis & Gulf. They embraced the lines running to Hunter and from Cape Girardeau to Kennett. Caruthersville, and a stretch of railroad eight miles in length from Pascola to Deering, which had been built in 1901.

Shortly after the consolidation of these various railroads the ownership of them was transferred from Mr. Houck and his associates to the St. Louis & San Francisco Railroad Company, but Mr. Houck's activity in railroad building did not cease with this transfer. He had parted with the control and ownership of most of his railroad property, but still owned the road from West Chester to Perryville and that from St. Mary's to Ste. Genevieve. It was his intention to make these the beginnings of a new system to cover the country north of Cape Girardeau which was without railroad facilities. It is rather remarkable that the counties of Ste. Genevieve, Perry and St. Francois, among the old counties of the state, were among the last to secure adequate railroad facilities. Carrying out his purpose, in 1904 he formed a company known as the Cape Girardeau & Chester Railroad Company and built a railroad from Cape Girardeau, by way of Jackson, to Perryville, connecting with the road from West Chester at the latter point. This system of railroads extending from Cape Girardeau to West Chester was about 65 miles in length. In 1906 the Saline Valley Railroad was incorporated and work begun on the line from Saline Junction, where the Cape Girardeau & Chester crossed Saline creek, to Farmington, in St. Francois county. This is a distance of 35 miles and the railroad was completed into Farmington in 1912.

The Cape Girardeau & Thebes Bridge Terminal Railway Company was incorporated in 1907 and constructed a line from Cape Girardeau to Kelso, on the main line of the St. Louis Southwestern, a short distance from the Thebes bridge; this line is seven miles in length. At the present time all the lines owned by Mr. Houck are being consolidated under one management into a road extending from the Thebes bridge to Farmington, in St. Francois county, a distance of about 110 miles. In addition to this line there is a branch from Saline Junction to West Chester. It is evident that the system of railroads here indicated is destined to form an important link in a north and south line probably from St. Louis to Thebes, or even further south.

It is difficult for us to give a just idea of the importance of the work of Louis Houck in Southeast Missouri. At a time when many localities in the section had absolutely no railroad facilities, at a time when people did not appreciate the importance of railroads in the destiny of the country, when capital was scarce and difficult to obtain for railroad purposes, Mr. Houck, who was then a lawyer with no great amount of capital, but with a vision which extended into the future and saw the development of Southeast Missouri and the part which railroads were destined to play in their development, began the construction of railroads. Through his efforts railroads have been built in Cape Girardeau, Scott, Stoddard, Bollinger, Dunklin, Pemiscot, Perry, Ste. Genevieve and St. Francois counties. In many of these counties the Houck railroad was the first constructed. The advantages which were accrued to the section from these railroads are immeasureable. A study of the tables of population and surplus products establishes conclusively the importance of these lines. The benefits the country derived from their building was not confined to the railroads themselves, the very evident fact that they were building up the country and that they were carrying great quantities of freight and large numbers of passengers was inducement for other railroad owners to extend their systems into southeast Missouri. When these enterprises were begun the section was touched by but two railroads, the Belmont branch of the Iron Mountain and the Cairo & Fulton; all the other railroads have been built subsequently to the beginnings made by Louis Houck.

One of the two great trunk lines of Southeast Missouri is the St. Louis & San Francisco system. It acquired by purchase the system known as the St. Louis & Gulf, which had been built by Louis Houck. The lines of this system extended south from Cape Girardeau through the counties of Scott, New Madrid, Dunklin and Pemiscot, to Caruthersville, on the Mississippi. The principal towns on the main line of the road were Commerce, Benton, Morley, Morehouse, Parma, Clarkton, Holcomb, Kennett, Hayti and Carutheraville. In addition to the main line there were several branches. One of these ran from Clarkton to Malden. Another extended from Gibson north to Campbell and Caligoa. A third branch extended south from Kennett to Leechville, Arkansas, passing through Senath and near Cardwell. A fourth extended eight miles from Pascola to Deering.

When the 'Frisco took over the ownership and operation of these roads it proceeded to improve the main lines with heavier steel, taking up the branch running north from Campbell to Caligoa and rebuilding it to Bloomfield to connect with the line from Brownwood.

The 'Frisco acquired at the same time the Houck lines running southwest from Cape Girardeau to Hunter, in Carter county, where connection was had with the Current River Railroad. A branch from this line extended from Zalma, in Bollinger county, to Bloomfield, in Stoddard county, crossing the main line at Brownwood. There was also a line from Bloomfield to the St. Louis Southwestern at Zeta, in Stoddard county.

The 'Frisco improved these lines also. The Zeta branch was extended to Vanduser, in Scott county, and a new line was built from Mingo, near Puxico, through Poplar Bluff, Naylor and Pocahontas, Arkansas, to a connection with the 'Frisco's Memphis and Kansas City line at Hoxie. This line is at present being greatly improved and will become one of the most important branches of the system.

The great work of the new system was the construction of an entirely new line. This was called the St. Louis, Memphis & Southeastern and extends from St. Louis to Memphis. This line passes to the west of the Iron Mountain south of St. Louis until it reaches the river at Crystal City. From this point it follows the river to Cape Girardeau. It diverges at the latter place from the river and follows the Sikeston ridge after crossing "Nigger Wool" swamp. This road reaches some of the important towns in the eastern tier of counties. It was the first railroad in Ste. Genevieve and greatly stimulated activity and growth in that town. It gave the first direct rail connection that Cape Girardeau had with St. Louis and Memphis and the great prosperity of the town dates from this time. South of Cape Girardeau, Sikeston. Portageville, Lilbourn, Hayti and Caruthersville are served by this line, and through its numerous branches, it is of great importance to many other towns.

The 'Frisco system also secured the entrance of the Chicago & Eastern Illinois, an allied railroad, into Southeast Missouri. This road crosses the Mississippi at Thebes and runs trains into Cape Girardeau from Chicago.

The 'Frisco has always adopted a liberal policy toward Southeast Missouri and has aided all the forward movements in its territory. It has provided good service in the main and its presence in this territory has meant much for the people. It now reaches by main line or branches nearly every one of the twenty counties in Southeast Missouri and provides transportation facilities for much of the region.

One of the enterprises of Southeast Missouri about which there has been considerable controversy was the proposed plan of building a plank road from Point Pleasant, in New Madrid county, to Clarkton, in Dunklin county. Just before the war a company was organized for this purpose, known as the Blanton Plank Road Company, and it secured from New Madrid county a large grant of land. The company did considerable work and opened up the road, but it was destroyed during the war and nothing was done toward rebuilding it by that company. In 1875 Oscar Kochtitzky, the registrar of the land office, George B. Clark, state auditor, and A. M. Shead, who was the agent of the Glasgow Ship Building Company, obtained the charter and franchise of the Blanton Road Company. It was their intention to rebuild this plank road and to secure a confirmation of the land grant from New Madrid county to themselves. After securing the charter, however, they determined to build a narrow-gauge railroad and applied to New Madrid county for a transfer of the land for this purpose. The county court of New Madrid county assented and the company proceeded to build the railroad. It was begun in October, 1876, and in February, 1878, it was completed between New Madrid and Malden. After being operated for a short time as a narrow-gauge railroad, it was rebuilt as a standard gauge and extended to Cairo. Shortly after this was done it came under the control of a group of capitalists headed by S. W. Fordyce, of St. Louis, and was reorganized as the St. Louis, Arkansas & Texas Railroad and extended to Texarkana, on the line between Arkansas and Texas. Through trains were run between Cairo and Texarkana in 1882. It soon became a part of the Gould system and in 1888 a branch was built from Malden to Delta. This branch was afterwards extended to Gray's Point, on the river, and later to the Thebes bridge. It is now operated as the main line of the system and the company is known as the St. Louis Southwestern Railroad Company.

One of the great movements in this part of the state in railroad matters was the building of a bridge across the Mississippi river at Thebes. In 1900 a corporation called the Southern Illinois & Missouri Bridge Company was organized for the purpose of constructing such a bridge. It was composed of men representing the Illinois Central Railroad, the St. Louis Southwestern, the St. Louis, Iron Mountain & Southern, the St. Louis & San Francisco, and the Chicago & Eastern Illinois. Charles G. Warner was president of the company, Myron J. Carpenter vice-president, and Charles N. Hillard secretary.

It was determined to build a bridge at Thebes. The location was determined by a number of considerations. The St. Louis Southwestern had failed to secure an entrance to Cape Girardeau and had located its northern terminus at Gray's Point, near Thebes. The Missouri Pacific and Iron Mountain, also part of the Gould system, had built the Valley line from St. Louis south along the Illinois side of the river to connect with the St. Louis Southwestern. The other roads indicated, had interests in the same territory. These facts had something to do with the selection of the site. The determining factor, however, was the character of the river banks. At Thebes the river is narrow and the bluffs are at the water's edge on both sides. This afforded an opportunity to build a bridge without the necessity for long approaches. The character of the soil was such as to provide a firm foundation, as native rock is found at comparatively shallow depths both in the river itself and on either side. These two features make the site chosen an ideal one. In fact it is one of the best if not the best point for a bridge to be found on the entire river. This site was chosen and the company proceeded to erect here a double track cantilever bridge of massive proportions.

There are five spans. The center or cantilever span is 671 feet long, each of the other spans is 521 feet. The approaches are built of concrete, one of these concrete arches having a span of 100 feet. The entire length of the bridge including approaches is 3,910 feet. It is 65 feet above high water mark and 108

violence of the river floods, or attacks of ice. It forms a link in one of the most important highways of travel from southwest to north and east. The volume of traffic carried across it is already enormous and is constantly increasing.

The Mississippi River & Bonne Terre Railway possesses an unusual interest owing to the way in which the road was constructed. It was built to provide transportation facil-

MISSISSIPPI RIVER BRIDGE, THEBES

feet above low water mark. From the lowest point of the pier foundations, which reach to bed-rock, to the topmost chord is 231 feet.

The bridge was designed and constructed by the engineering firm of Noble & Modjeski. It was dedicated with appropriate ceremonies on May 25, 1900, in presence of a large number of railroad officials and other persons. The strength of the bridge was tested by running upon it a string of locomotives. It has been in constant use since that time and has never been affected by heavy traffic, the

ities for the products and supplies of the St. Joseph Lead Company at Bonne Terre. Up till 1880 this company, which operated one of the largest lead mines in the world, depended upon wagons for hauling between their mines and the St. Louis & Iron Mountain Railway. In that year the St. Joseph Lead Company and the DesLoge Lead Company built a narrow-guage railway thirteen and a half miles long between the mines and Summit, a point on the St. Louis & Iron Mountain. The cost of construction was divided between the two lead companies, the St. Joseph Lead Company paying two-thirds and the DesLoge one-third. The business of the lead companies increased very greatly so that the narrow-guage railway no longer provided sufficient facilities for transportation. It was determined to construct another road, and in 1888 a charter was granted to the Mississippi River & Bonne Terre Railway Company. It was to extend from Riverside, on the Mississippi river twenty-five miles below St. Louis, to Bonne Terre and later to DesLoge. The line was completed in March, 1890, and the Summit railway was abandoned. The road was changed to standard guage in 1894. Later an extension was built from Bonne Terre to Doe Run, crossing the Belmont branch of the Iron Mountain at Doe Run Junction. The road is at present forty-seven miles in length, and while it is an independent line, having no connection with other roads, its road-bed and equipment are equal to most trunk lines, and it carries an enormous business considering the length of the road.

In 1894, the Holliday-Klotz Land and Lumber Company, a corporation owning vast bodies of timber and operating extensive mills in Wayne county, undertook the construction of a railroad from the Iron Mountain at Williamsville to Greenville, the county seat of Wayne county and the site of their mills. The road was a costly one as the country is very hilly. It was built, however, and served the purpose for which it was constructed. Upon the practical exhaustion of the pine timber about Greenville, the mills were closed down there and the road extended further into the county to open new bodies of timber. The present terminus is Cascade, thirty-five miles from Williamsville. The road serves a large part of Wayne county.

The St. Louis, Kennett & Southeastern was built in 1906 from Campbell, on the St. Louis Southwestern Railroad in Dunklin county, to the county seat, Kennett. Later Piggott, Arkansas, was made the northern terminus. The road was built by a group of Dunklin county capitalists. Among them were R. H. Jones, Virgil McKay, J. B. Blakemore, W. D. Lasswell and D. B. Panker. It was built to develop large bodies of timber lands owned by these and other men. The land when stripped of its timber is very valuable farming land and the road aids in opening it up for settlement. Railroad bridges have been constructed across Varner and St. Francois rivers and the road is being put into condition to handle the large traffic originating in its territory.

In 1911 a road was completed from Marston, in New Madrid county, to New Madrid, the county seat. It was built principally by capitalists of the latter place under the leadership of E. S. McCarthy, a well-known railroad promoter and builder. Among the men interested were L. A. Lewis, Mr. Garanflo, A. B. and Lee Hunter and Murray Phillips. It provides a connection for New Madrid with the 'Frisco main line. Formerly the town had depended entirely upon the St. Louis Southwestern system which has a branch from Lilbourn. The new road is called the St. Louis & Missouri Southern. It is eight miles in length and is one of the best built roads in this part of the state. It operates what is probably the only parlor car in the state for which no extra charge is made. The unusual character of the road leads to the belief that it is meant to form a link in a new north and south system, probably extending from the bridge at Thebes, into Arkansas. Plans are already on foot for immediately increasing its mileage to eighty, and the probabilities are that actual work on the construction will soon be begun.

The Paragould Southeastern is a line of railroad extending from Paragould, Arkansas, to the southeast, crossing the St. Francois river near Cardwell, in Dunklin county. It is built across the south end of Dunklin county, reaching Little river at Hornersville. A few miles east of Hornersville it turns to the south and enters Arkansas and has its eastern terminus at Blytheville, near the Mississippi. This road opens up immense tracts of farming and timber land in Dunklin county and has been a prime factor in the building up of Cardwell and Hornersville. It was built and originally owned by local capitalists under leadership of E. S. McCarthy. It is now owned by the Gould system and is operated by the St. Louis Southwestern.

About 1905 the Illinois Southern, an Illinois road with headquarters at Chicago, entered this territory. It was built from Salem to a point opposite Ste. Genevieve. It was constructed through Ste. Genevieve and St. Francois counties to Bismarck, in the latter county, on the main line of the Iron Mountain. The road passes through the richest mineral section of the state. One of its important stations is Flat River, in the very center of the lead belt. The road is well built and operated after the best methods. It unites the great system of the Iron Mountain and 'Frisco; serves a rich county and offers an outlet to Chicago. It is destined to be an important link in an east and west line, and will be of great benefit to the section which it serves.

The Missouri Southern, which extends from Leeper, in Wayne county, on the main line of the Iron Mountain, nearly through Reynolds county to Bunker, was built by a saw-mill company having large timber interests in the territory traversed by the road. A large steel bridge across Black river was built at Leeper and the road was well constructed. Its present terminus is Bunker, in Reynolds county. Plans have been formed for its extension to the 'Frisco at Salem, in Dent county, but it is probable that it will become a branch of the Iron Mountain.

The Paragould & Memphis Railroad, extending from Paragould, Arkansas, through the south part of Dunklin county to Manila. Arkansas, is 118 miles long. It was developed from a tram road built to facilitate the handling of timber by the Decatur Egg Case Company, a large corporation with headquarters at Cardwell. Out of this tram road has grown the Paragould & Memphis. The president of the road is John W. Vail, of Cardwell, Mo., and most of the other officers are residents of the same town. Although its line is principally in Arkansas, it is distinctly a Missouri enterprise. Its successful development has been due in part to the energy and ability of the men who built it and in part to the fact that it opened up immense tracts of valuable timber and farming land previously without railroad facilities.

The Butler County Railroad Company operates a short line in Butler county, Missouri, and Arkansas. It extends from Linstead and Lowell Junction, on the Iron Mountain, to Arkansas points and is operated as a timber road in large part. The present president of the road is R. M. Parker.

About 1905 a company composed of business men and capitalists of St. Francois county was organized for the purpose of constructing an electric line through the lead belt. That section has an enormous population and it was thought by the promoters that an interurban line would be of great benefit to the country and also a paying investment. The line was built from Flat River, on the Illinois Southern and the Mississippi river and Bonne Terre railroads, south and west to Farmington, the county seat, and then to DeLassus, on the St. Louis, Iron Mountain & Southern. The road was well-built and first-class equipment provided for it. The expectations of its builders were fully met as it at once received a heavy traffic.

It not only carries passengers, but operates freight and express service as well. It has become of immense inportance in its section and will be an important link in the interurban line which will doubtless be built in the near future from St. Louis south through Southeast Missouri.

At the present time this is the only interurban line in the section. The Cape Girardeau & Jackson Interurban Company was organized in 1905, but up to this time it has not extended its lines outside the city of Cape Girardeau. Its plans are to unite the latter place with Jackson and also with the towns near the Thebes bridge. The development of the country in wealth and population, and the demand for better transportation will doubtless lead to the building of other electric lines within a few years, some of which are already under consideration.

CHAPTER XXXVII

GENERAL STATUS

Location — Area — Topography — Timber — Industries — Transportation — Towns — Population — Schools — Wealth — Bollinger — Butler — Cape Girardeau — Carter — Dunklin — Iron — Jefferson — Madison — Mississippi — New Madrid — Pemiscot — Perry — Reynolds — Ripley — St. Francois — Ste. Genevieve — Scott — Stoddard — Washington — Wayne.

The sketches embraced in this chapter are designed to present a general pen-picture of the counties of Southeast Missouri embraced in this work. The counties are given in alphabetical order.

Bollinger county joins Cape Girardeau on the west. It contains 394,240 acres, about one-third of which is under cultivation; the other two-thirds being unimproved and covered with timber. The principal timbers are oak, hickory and walnut on the hills, and gum and cypress in the valleys of the rivers and streams. The county is almost wholly agricultural in character, the chief products being those of the farm. In addition to these products a large amount of lumber is shipped out every year. In 1910 there were shipped more than nine million feet of lumber. The north part of the county is rolling, partly broken and there is a considerable area of uncultivated land that is capable of cultivation. The southern part of the county extends unto the edge of the lowlands.

The population of Bollinger county is principally American born, there being only a few negroes, and not a great many settlements have any large number of foreign immigrants. The population in 1910 was 14,576, and the assessable wealth of the county is $2,797,570. There are 89 school districts, employing 94 teachers and the number of children enumerated in 1910 was 4,781.

The principal towns are Marble Hill, which is the county seat, and Lutesville; besides these there are Glen Allen, Bessville, Sturdivant, Zalma and some other smaller places.

The principal streams in the county are Crooked Creek, South Fork, and Little Whitewater, and the county is traversed by the Belmont branch of the St. Louis, Iron Mountain & Southern and the St. Louis & San Francisco railroads.

There are no factories in the county except some saw mills, stave factories, flouring mills and other similar institutions. The total value of manufactured products including railroad ties was $389,072 in 1910. There is some water power which will probably be used at some time. There are no mineral products, except kaolin, which is taken out in quantities near Glen Allen and some good lime stone found in a number of different places.

Butler county joins Arkansas on the south and it is divided into two parts by the Mississippi escarpment. Northwest of this part the country is rolling, while in the southeast are found the swamps of Black and St. Francois rivers. The county contains 716 square miles of territory, about one-half of which is alluvial soil. A great deal of the land in the county is well timbered, much of it being very valuable on this account.

The principal streams in the county are Black river and St. Francois river which run entirely through it and which have many small tributaries, many of them being creeks of pure and clear water. The principal exports of the county are farm products and lumber. In 1910 there were exported three million feet of lumber. There are some manufacturing establishments, principally those in Poplar Bluff. These are principally wood working establishments engaged in the manufacture of staves, lumber and heading. There is also a foundry and a factory for making adding machines. Besides these there are several flouring mills and other manufacturing establishments of minor importance. The total value of manufactured products in 1910 was more than $2,000,000.

The railroads of the county are the St. Louis, Iron Mountain & Southern main line; the Cairo, Arkansas & Texas branch of the Iron Mountain, and the Doniphan branch; besides these, there is the St. Louis, Memphis & Southeastern, a branch of the Frisco which runs through the county.

IN THE THICK TIMBER

The population of Butler county is 20,627 and the taxable wealth is $4,148,435. There are 78 school districts employing 118 teachers, and the school system of Poplar Bluff is one of unusually high rank.

The principal town in the county is Poplar Bluff, which has a population of about 6,000. The other towns are principally saw mill towns and small stations on some line of railway.

Cape Girardeau county is situated about

100 miles south of St. Louis on the Mississippi river. It is divided into two parts, the greater portion of the county being in the Ozark plateau, but part of the southern half is in the alluvial bottoms of the Mississippi river. At one time a large part of the county was heavily timbered. Most of this timber has been removed, however, and the land is in cultivation. There are some small tracts of oak and gum, but the timber is no longer of any very great value. The area of the county is 540 square miles, more than two-thirds of which is under cultivation. The soil of the county is productive even on the hills. In the bottoms of the Mississippi and other streams the land is very rich. The principal products are those of the farm. Some lumber is shipped out, amounting to four million feet in 1910. There is no coal mined in the county, but large quantities of lime stone is quarried and there are a few kaolin pits, and in some places crystal sand is taken out for glass manufacturing purposes.

There are a number of manufacturing establishments, wood working plants, mills, shoe factory, and a large cement plant; besides these there are some important quarries where large quantities of lime stone are removed.

The county, exclusive of the city of Cape Girardeau, produced manufactured products in 1910, amounting to $4,150,667. The largest single item was flour. In the same year the city of Cape Girardeau had products amounting to $2,773,432, the largest single item being shoes.

The population of the county is 27,621 and the assessable valuation $174,382. There are 80 school districts in the county employing 140 teachers, and the school system is a well organized one. The county has the Third District State Normal school, St. Vincent's college and academy at Cape Girardeau. There are good high schools at Jackson and Cape Girardeau.

The county seat is Jackson, which is a thriving prosperous town, and the largest town is Cape Girardeau, with a population of about 9,000. Besides, there are the following towns: Allenville, Appleton, Burfordvills, Dutchtown, Egypt Mills, Fruitland, Gordonville, Millersville, Neeleys Landing, Oak Ridge, Pocahontas and Whitewater. The county is well supplied with transportation facilities. Besides the Mississippi river there are the following railroads: St. Louis, Iron Mountain & Southern, St. Louis & San Francisco, St. Louis Southwestern and the Cape Girardeau & Chester.

Carter county is one county north of the Arkansas line and is five west of the Mississippi river. It has an area of 323,000 acres, much of which is still timbered. There are three different classes of land in the county, hill land, table land and creek bottoms. Seventy-five per cent of the land in the hills is rocky and at least one-fourth of the area of the county is still unimproved. The principal productions are farm products and timber, there having been thirteen million feet of lumber shipped out in 1910, besides large quantities of railroad ties and posts. The largest sawmill in the state is at Grandin. It has a capacity of 285,000 feet a day and employs more than 1,200 men. The total of manufactured products in 1910 was $316,070.

The soil is adapted to fruit growing and the probabilities are that within the not distant future there will be large orchards in the county. Much iron ore is found in two different sections of the county and there are traces of lead and copper, but not in sufficient quantities to warrant their being mined.

The population is 5,504 and the assessable wealth is $1,523,380. The population is largely American, there being but few negroes or foreign immigrants. There are 32 school districts in the county employing 37 teachers.

Perhaps the scenery in Carter county is equal to or superior to that in any other of the counties of Southeast Missouri. The county is divided by Current river, one of the most beautiful streams in the state. There is much unused water power on this stream that will doubtless be developed soon. There are two railroads in the county, the St. Louis, Memphis & Southeastern and the Current River branch of the 'Frisco.

The largest town in the county is Grandin, which is principally a saw mill town and owned by the mill company; Van Buren, the county seat, is situated on Current river and is surrounded by hills.

Dunklin county has an area of 500 square miles, not more than one-half of the area being under cultivation. At one time the county was almost entirely covered with a dense growth of timber, consisting of oak, maple, sycamore, poplar, cypress, gum, ash, walnut and pecan. Large quantities of timber still exist, though much of it has been cut. With the exception of a strip about two miles wide and ten miles long, extending across the northwest corner, being a part of Crowley's ridge, the land is level. The soil is alluvial and part of it comprising the great ridge running south from Dexter, is sandy loam immensely productive. The soil of Little river bottoms and St. Francois river bottoms is a heavier soil, also productive. Much of this land was made usable only by drainage; many miles of ditches have been dug and much land reclaimed in this way.

The principal productions are those of the farm. It is the great cotton growng county of the state and in fact is the greatest cotton producing county in the United States. Besides cotton, large quantities of corn, wheat and melons are grown. The factories are wood working plants, cotton oil mills, and brick yards, flour mills, ice plants and other similar plants. In 1910 the manufactured products of the county amounted to nearly $2,000,000. The most important item was cotton, valued at $510,897, followed by lumber, cooperage and oils in almost equal amounts.

The county has the St. Louis & Southwestern Railroad, the 'Frisco, and St. Louis, Kennet & Southeastern. The largest town in the county is the county seat, Kennett, and other principal towns are Malden, Campbell, Clarkton, Holcomb, Cardwell, Hornersville and Senath.

The population of the county is 30,228, and the total taxable wealth is $5,876,187. The principal part of the population is American born, seventy-five per cent of whom own their own homes. There are many churches in the county and a good system of public schools. There are 74 school districts employing 134 teachers, and each of the larger towns maintains a high school.

There are 550 square miles in Iron county, much of it being in the Ozark mountains. The best land is found in the valleys where the soil is alluvial, but there is also some good farming land on the hills. In the southwest part of the county the land is very broken and rocky; at the present time only a small percentage is under cultivation. The principal productions of the county are its farm products and the products of the quarries. There are lead mines in the county, though not of very great importance, but there are a number of granite quarries and large deposits of granite which are not yet being mined. The manufactures of the county amounted to the sum of $176,929 in 1910. The principal items in this amount were stone, cooperage, and flour. The Arcadia valley is one of the most beautiful spots in Missouri and Ironton and Arcadia, two towns of this valley, are famous as summer resorts. Mines are worked at Pilot Knob, Shepard Mountain, Cedar Mountain and a few other places; besides these, marble and kaolin are also mined.

The county is traversed from north to south by the main line of the St. Louis, Iron Mountain and Southern Railroad. The principal towns are Graniteville, a famous quarry town; Ironton, the county seat, Arcadia, Pilot Knob, and DesArc. The population of the county is 8,563 and its total amount of taxable property is $2,359,457. There are 47 school districts employing 55 teachers.

There are 640 square miles in Jefferson county and practically all the surface gives evidence of mineral deposits. The land is generally high and rolling, much of it broken by streams. There are considerable areas of fertile bottom lands and the best part of the county is in the northwest section. About one-third of the area of the county is under cultivation and the principal productions are farm products and those which come from various mines. In 1910 there were one thousand car loads of stone, granite, lead, zinc and sand shipped out of the county. There are also large manufacturing plants, one of the largest lead smelting plants in the world is in Herculaneum, while at Kimswick is an important lime plant, and Crystal City is famous for the manufacture of plate glass. Besides these other products of the mines such as zinc, lead and clay are mined and worked up in the community. The nearness to St. Louis makes the raising of garden products and orchard products profitable, as well as the dairy industry.

There are a number of famous springs in the county, some of them mineral springs said to have medicinal values, among them Sulphur Springs and Mineral Springs. There are other resorts along the Mississippi river.

Transportation facilities are afforded by the Mississippi river, the St. Louis, Iron Mountain & Southern and the St. Louis & San Francisco railroads. The population is 27,878 and the total taxable wealth $6,056,147. There are 87 school districts, employing 133 teachers.

The principal town is DeSoto, largely a railroad town, with a population of about 5,000; the county seat is Hillsboro, one of the oldest towns in the county. Besides these the principal towns are Crystal City, Festus, Herculaneum, Kimswick, Riverside, Victoria and Selma.

The manufactures of the county are very extensive. In 1910 they reached the total of $8,111,433. By far the largest item in this great amount was the products of the smelters which in themselves amounted to more than $5,000,000. Glass was another big item, being more than $1,500,000. Other large items were the products of the car shops, shoes and flour. This enormous total makes Jefferson the most important manufacturing county in the southeast.

The chief industrial interest of Madison county is mining. There are large deposits of lead, cobalt, copper, granite, marble and iron in the county. One of the oldest mines in Southeast Missouri, Mine La Motte, is in

Typical Stone Quarries

Madison county. It has been operated for about 140 years continuously. There are 492 square miles in the county and of that about one-sixth is under cultivation, farming being the interest second in importance.

The population of the county is 11,273 and the taxable wealth $2,608,295. There are 55 school districts, employing 77 teachers.

The land is rolling and much of it is timbered, white oak and pine still being found in many places. The river bottoms are fertile, the land on the hills is much less so, but it is well adapted to fruit growing, which will probably become one of the leading industries of the county. Big and Little St. Francois rivers and Castor river water the county, and besides these there are a number of fine springs. Those at White Spring are considered to have a medicinal value.

The principal manufacturing establishments are saw mills, flouring mills, stave factories, distilleries, ice plant and quarries. The principal town is the county seat, Fredericktown; besides this Marquand and Mine La Motte are also important. The total manufactured products in 1910 amounted to $53,274. The principal items were the products of the smelters, lumber and flour.

Mississippi county is about one hundred and sixty miles south of St. Louis, on the Mississippi river. It contains 275,000 acres of land, nearly one-half of which is in cultivation. It is practically all level land lying within the alluvial plains of the Mississippi river. There is much sand in the soil in most of the county, but not enough to prevent it from being very productive. A part of the land near Charleston was originally prairie and is the most fertile land in the county. Other parts were originally heavily timbered with black and red oak, cypress, gum, cottonwood, sycamore and hickory. There were many other varieties of timber but these were the most important commercially. Some of this timber still remains. More than 6,000,000 feet of lumber was exported in 1910.

Part of the land is subject to overflow from the river. Levees have been built to protect from floods, which will be adequate except for most unusual floods. The sand which everywhere forms a sub-soil aids very greatly in drainage.

The county is well improved. Good barns and residences are found in all the older settled portions of the county.

The chief industry is farming. The land is well adapted to the growing of corn and wheat, large quantities of both being produced. These two crops furnish exports worth more than a million dollars each year. Alfalfa is also grown and is becoming more important as a crop. Second in importance to farming is the timber interest. The principal manufacturing plants are flour mills and woodworking establishments. Lumber, staves, heading, handles and spokes are manufactured in the latter plants. The manufactured products reached a total of $1,158,801 in the year 1910. The largest single item of this total was flour, which had a value of $871,075. Cooperage was next in importance.

The county has three railroads. The Belmont branch of the Iron Mountain, the Cairo, Arkansas & Texas branch of the same system, and the main line of the 'Frisco. The river which forms the eastern boundary affords transportation facilities also.

The principal town is Charleston, the county seat, which has a population of 3,144. Bertrand, East Prairie, Whiting and Anniston are other important places.

The population of the county is 14,557 and its taxable wealth is $3,939,516. There are 45 school districts, employing 75 teachers. The high school at Charleston is a well-organized and well-attended institution.

The usual church organizations are found in the county and the population is known for its industry, thrift and sobriety.

There are 620 square miles in New Madrid county, about one-fourth of the area being under cultivation at the present time. A part of it is in the sandy loam of the Sikeston ridge and a large part in the heavy soil of the Little river bottoms. The principal industry is farming. The county was once covered with a heavy growth of timber, much of which has been removed. There are still large bodies of valuable timber which is rapidly being cut. The principal products in the north part of the county are corn and wheat, in the south part, cotton. Alfalfa is beginning to be grown in large quantities and will probably become one of the leading products of the county. The value of manufactured articles in 1910 was $1,682,959. The important products were lumber, cotton and cooperage. A large part of the land was at first not susceptible to cultivation because overflowed by the Mississippi river. The government levee and local drainage ditches have reclaimed large parts of the land.

The river affords transportation and the St. Louis & San Francisco, St. Louis, Iron Mountain & Southern and the St. Louis & Southwestern railways, all of which have branch lines as well as the main line.

The present population is 19,488 and the total taxable wealth is $4,485,765. The principal towns are New Madrid, the county seat, with a population of about 1,900; Lilbourn, Morehouse, Portageville, Point Pleasant, Marston, Gideon and Parma. There are 50 school districts in the county, employing 85 teachers, and a number of the towns have well organized high schools.

CORN MEASURED BY HORSES

In the extreme southeast corner of the state, bordering the Mississippi river and extending to the Arkansas line, is Pemiscot county, with an area of 480 square miles, about one-sixth of which is being cultivated. The land is all level and is alluvial soil. There are immense quantities of timber remaining in Pemiscot county though it is rapidly being removed. In 1910 fully thirty million feet of lumber was shipped out of the county. The land is extremely fertile and is adapted to the growth of corn, wheat and other grains, the production of cotton, and especially to the growth of alfalfa, which in all probability will become the leading crop of the county. The principal factories are those devoted to the handling of timber, cotton and cotton seed oil. The total value of manufactured articles in 1910 was $1,840,612. The most important of these products were cotton, lumber, cooperage and oils.

The county has only the St. Louis & San Francisco Railway system, including a number of branches. The population is 19,559 and the total taxable wealth is $3,369,219. There are 48 school districts in the county, employing 70 teachers.

Caruthersville, the county seat, is a town of about 3,500 and is a flourishing and prosperous community. Besides Caruthersville, Hayti, Cottonwood Point, Pascola and Steele are the most important communities.

Perry county is on the Mississippi river, about 60 miles south of St. Louis. It contains 436 square miles of surface, most of which at one time was covered with a heavy growth of cottonwood, oak, walnut, willow and gum timber. At the present time more than half the area of the county is under cultivation. Most of the land is rolling, some of it broken. There are considerable areas of level land in the river bottoms and on top of the hills. The eastern part of the county is Mississippi bottom bordered by bluffs; the roughest part of the county is in the southeastern and ex-

SIMPLY A BIG OIL TANK

Missouri Orchards in Bearing

treme west. On the west side of the county is a small lake called Silver lake. There are several creeks, but no navigable streams, except the Mississippi. There are good springs in the county. Lithium Springs in the north and Schumer Springs in the south are said to possess medicinal properties.

The principal interest of the county is farming. There are some lead deposits and some fine stone. Lithographic stone is found ten miles west of Perryville. At one time iron ore was mined in the county, but this is no longer done. The forests yield considerable products in the shape of lumber and railroad ties. The principal crops grown are wheat and hay and considerable attention is also paid to the growing of fruit. The soil seems adapted to fruit growing and it is probable that the orchard interests of the county will increase. Considerable attention is also given to stock raising and to poultry farming. There are a number of factories of one sort and another, some of which are saw mills, flouring mills, distilleries and creameries, brick yards, ice plants and other minor factories. The largest item in the manufactured products of the county in 1910 was flour, which had a value of nearly $200,000. The total value of all manufactured articles was $320,736.

The Mississippi river forms one great highway of commerce, and the county has the main line of the 'Frisco from St. Louis to Memphis and also is traversed by the Cape Girardeau & Chester Railway. There are many good roads in the county. The total length of gravel roads is about 100 miles.

The present population is 14,989 and the total taxable wealth is $3,383,273. There are 61 school districts in the county, employing 73 teachers.

The largest town in the county is the county seat, Perryville, with a population of about 1,500. Other towns are Altenberg, which was founded about 1847 by German Lutherans and was the original site of Concordia seminary; Wittenberg, Longtown, Lithium, Crosstown, Brazeau, Frohna, Yount and Uniontown.

Reynolds county is situated in southern Missouri, being three counties north of Arkansas and five west of the Mississippi river. Its area is 830 square miles, or more than a half million acres. It was originally covered by forests of pine and oak; there were other species of timber also, but these were the principal ones. Not more than one-tenth of the entire area is in cultivation. The surface as a whole is mountainous, the soil that can be successfully cultivated is found in the river bottoms, where it is very rich. In the hilly part, the soil is poor and much of it has rock. In some few cases there are entire quarter sections of almost solid rock.

The principal industry in the county is lumbering. Large amounts of lumber and railroad ties are shipped out of the county every year. Farming interests follow, but these are less extensive owing to the small area in cultivation. The only factories in the county are wood-working establishments, flour and grist mills. Stock raising is carried on to a considerable extent, as stock may be grown in the woods with very little expense in many cases. No effort has been made to develop the mineral resources, which are large. There are fine beds of red granite, sandstone and some deposits of iron ore, and at some time the mineral resources of the county will become of very great importance. Lumber, ties and cooperage made up the greater part of the value of manufactured products which in 1910 reached a total of more than half a million dollars.

Black river runs through the county on the eastern side and has a number of small tributaries, the largest being West Fork of Black river. There are a number of springs and an opportunity is afforded for the use of water power which will doubtless receive attention in the future. Another industry which will probably be developed is fruit growing, as much of the soil in the county is capable of being put into orchards.

The population of the county is 9,592 and its taxable wealth is $2,369,791. There are 63 school districts, employing 63 teachers; 3,099 children of school age are enumerated in the county.

At the present time there is only one railroad in the county, the Missouri Southern, which runs from Leeper, in Wayne county, on the Iron Mountain, to Corridon, near the central part of the county. Most of the other sections of the county are served by the Iron Mountain Railroad in Wayne and Iron counties.

There is no incorporated town in the county. The county seat is Centerville and the largest town, perhaps, is Ellington, on the railroad. Some of the other smaller places are Bunker, Lesterville and West Fork; of these towns Bunker is a railroad town and is situated in the midst of a large pine forest where large mills cut a great deal of timber during the year.

The county is attractive on account of its scenery and also the opportunity for forming summer resorts, and for hunting and fishing. The streams are full of fish and there is still game to be found in some portions of the county.

Ripley county is on the Arkansas line, 60 miles west of the Mississippi river. It contains 640 square miles of land, about one-third of which is in cultivation. Large parts of the county are still covered with timber, the principal timbers being yellow pine, white oak, black oak and red gum. The southeast part of the county is in the low lands of Black river. The Mississippi escarpment, a line of bluffs, runs diagonally through the county. The northwest part of the county is hilly and even mountainous. Owing to this situation the eastern part of the county is more densely settled and at the present time the land is more valuable. Farming and timber working are the principal industries of the county. The shipments of lumber and other timber products are large, perhaps the largest saw-mill in the state is located at Grandin, in Carter county, but near the Ripley county line. There are large mills also at Doniphan that saw and dress large quantities of lumber. Besides these there are some portable mills which are moved from place to place over the county.

The manufactured products of the county had a value of $376,677 in 1910. The only large item in this total was lumber and cooperage, with a value of $289,830.

The eastern and southern part of the county is almost wholly agricultural in its interest. The principal farm products are cotton and corn. Some livestock is raised and the county is within the fruit belt. In time orchard products will become one of the important features of the county. There are considerable deposits of iron ore scattered over the western half of the county though there are no large attempts made at handling ores. Owing to the improved methods of handling ore and its increased value it is probable that the mining interests of the county will develop rapidly in the near future. It has been said of the Ripley county farmer that he is also a manufacturer and a miner. He tills the soil, pastures livestock on a ranch, with an axe he makes railroad ties, and with a pick axe he collects iron ore. This statement, however, applies to the farmer living outside of the alluvial section of the county, where the soil is rich and productive as any to be found in the state.

The population of the county is 13,099, the taxable wealth is $2,879,028. There are 74 school districts, employing 87 teachers. There are two lines of railroad in the county, the St. Louis, Iron Mountain & Southern, a branch line from Poplar Bluff to Doniphan, and the Hoxie branch of the St. Louis & San Francisco, which crosses the southeast corner of the county.

The county seat is Doniphan, with a population of more than 2,000, and a most delightful town, situated near Current river. Other important towns are Naylor, at the crossing of the 'Frisco and the Iron Mountain, having some manufactories; Varner, Fair Dealing, Ponder and Currentview. The school system is well organized in Ripley county, especially so in Doniphan, which supports a good public school, including a well organized high school.

The principal streams are Little Black river, which runs through the northeastern part of the county, Logan creek and Current river, which runs through the county from north to south dividing it into almost equal parts. There are some smaller streams tributaries of these and a number of fine springs and the possibility of developing water power on a number of them. Current river is perhaps the most beautiful stream in the state.

St. Francois county is fifty miles south of St. Louis and one county west of the Mississippi river. It contains an area of 410 square miles, about one-third of which is devoted to agriculture. There are two classes of land in the county, a high rolling section occupying a large area in the southwest corner and broken regions adjacent to the principal streams and then an area which is gently rolling found in the eastern and southern part of the county. These lands on this plateau are free from stone and quite fertile indeed. The only poor land in the county is found in the extreme southwest corner. That along the border of the streams is rich and fertile as any in the state.

St. Francois county, like most of the other counties in the state, had at one time a very heavy growth of timber, the most valuable being white oak. Much of this timber has been removed however, especially along the line of railroads. Besides white oak there were considerable quantities of black oak. red oak, sugar maple, walnut, cherry and hickory, besides these there were gum, pine and elm. There is still some pine timber as well as some other varities in the county.

The principal interest of the county is mining. It is the center of the lead district of Missouri. Besides lead, in the forms of disseminated ore, zinc, iron, nickel, copper and granite, limestone and sandstone exist in workable quantities. Of these minerals the most important is lead. St. Francois county has produced more than 70 per cent of the lead of Missouri for a great many years. During the year 1910 there were produced 211,845 tons of lead, large quantities of barytes, iron ore, sand, granite and other mineral products.

The farming interests of the county are

also large. The chief products grown are wheat, corn and hay. Livestock is raised, making large shipments every year of cattle, hogs and sheep. Considerable attention is given to orchards and gardens. The principal factories are flouring mills which manufacture large quantities of high grade flour, saw mills, planing mills, ore reduction works, granite quarries and brick factories. The total of manufactured products in 1910 was $7,305,825. Of this amount the products of the smelters furnished $6,556,423. The other large items were flour and the products of the car shops. St. Francois is surpassed in the value of manufactured products by only one county in the southeast—Jefferson. It is first in population, wealth and total value of all products.

The railroads in the county are the St. Louis, Iron Mountain & Southern main line, the Belmont branch which runs through the county, the Missouri Southern, from Ste. Genevieve to Bismarck, and the Mississippi River & Bonne Terre, from Doe Run to Riverside, in Jefferson county. Besides these the St. Francois County Interurban line runs from De Lassus through Farmington to Flat River.

The population of the county is 35,738 and its total taxable wealth is $9,969,403. There are 63 school districts, employing 168 teachers, and an enumeration of more than 10,000 children of school age.

The principal incorporated towns in the county are Farmington, the county seat, near the central part of the county and having a population of about 2,673, and Flat River, in the mining district, with a population of 5,012. Besides these incorporated towns there are a number of towns in the lead belt with large populations which are not incorporated. The largest of these is Bonne Terre, with more than 5,000 people. Others are Doe Run, Des Loge, Elvins, Esther and Leadwood, which are mining centers. Bismarck, on the Iron Mountain Railroad, has a population of 848; and De Lassus, Iron Mountain, Knob Lick, Libertyville and Syenite. Syenite is the site of a great granite quarry, the largest in the state, and is situated just west of Knob Lick. Farmington has large manufacturing interests and is the seat of Carleton College, Elmwood Seminary and State Hospital No. 4, for the insane.

Ste. Genevieve county is fifty miles south of St. Louis, on the Mississippi river. There are 450 square miles of land surface, about one-third of which is cultivated. A large part of the surface is rolling, and much of which is covered with timber, but along the Mississippi river and other water courses there are extensive tracts of bottom land. This is alluvial soil and is very fertile and productive. The upland, where it is farmed, is well adapted to wheat growing. In the alluvial soil corn and fruit are grown. About 60 per cent of the county has timber products, the chief timbers being black oak, though there are quantities of white oak, walnut, hickory and pecan.

The chief interest of the county is farming. The principal products are wheat and corn, though a large area is given up to the growing of hay. Livestock interests are extensive, and considerable attention is given to poultry raising, and dairying and horticulture are important items. The mineral interests of the county are also extensive, there being deposits of copper, lead, zinc, iron, glass sand, kaolin, marble and building stone. All of these exist in quantities large enough to make mining a commercial possibility. The building stone is especially valuable.

Some fine marble is found near the central part of the county and the large deposits of glass sand are of importance. At one time a plate-glass factory was projected for Ste. Genevieve to use this sand. It was not erected, however. Most of the sand that is taken out is sent to Crystal City. The principal products are marble, brick and lime. There are several small nurseries and a number of vineyards where wine is produced, and other smaller manufacturing interests are also represented. The manufactured products of the county in 1910 were worth $1,199,039; the principal item being flour. Lime was also a large item.

The county is bordered on the east by the Mississippi river, which has as tributaries within the county the river Aux Vases, Establishment, Bois, and Saline creeks. There are a number of fine springs in the county also. The Mississippi river affords transportation facilities and the county is traversed by the main line of the St. Louis & San Francisco, by the Cape Girardeau & Chester, and by the Illinois Southern.

The population of the county is 10,607 and the total taxable wealth is $2,940,924. There are 54 school districts, employing 59 teachers. The population of the county is about one-half German and German descent and the other half is made up of both French and Americans. Ste. Genevieve, the county seat, is the largest town in the county and the oldest in the state. St. Mary's has a population of about 800 and there are some other smaller towns, among them being Brickeys, New Offenberg and Zell.

Scott county is situated on the Mississippi river, and is about 140 miles south of St. Louis. It contains an area of 277,760 acres, nearly one-half of which is in cultivation. It was at one time heavily timbered, the principal varieties being gum, white oak, black oak, maple, cypress, cottonwood and poplar. There are still 100,000 acres of timber, most of which, however, has been cut over and the most valuable timber removed. The county is level with the exception of the range of hills known as the Scott county or Commerce hills. These are in the northeast corner and are part of the Ozark plateau. The soil is fertile, especially so on the ridge known as the Sikeston ridge, and the principal crops are wheat and corn, though melons are also grown extensively. Perhaps Scott county produces more watermelons and cantaloupes than any other county in the state. The chief shipping point for melons is Blodgett, which in 1911 shipped more than six hundred cars of melons.

There are some minerals found in the county, among them iron, limestone, sandstone and several varieties of clays, including pottery, brick and clay suitable for making paint. Yellow ochre also occurs on the west side of the hills near Oran. Iron does not occur in commercial quantities, though there are traces of it in a number of places. The total value of manufactured articles in 1910 was $2,115,796. Flour, feed and meal made up $1,126,556 of this amount. The products of car shops and lumber were the other large items.

The county is well supplied with transportation facilities. Heavy freight is moved on the Mississippi river, which forms the eastern border of the county, and it contains several railroads. The Belmont branch of the St Louis, Iron Mountain & Southern, and also the Cairo branch, the main line of the 'Frisco between St. Louis and Memphis runs through the county, as does the St. Louis & Gulf branch of the 'Frisco. The extreme southern part of the county is crossed by the St. Louis Southwestern system.

The principal town is Sikeston, on the 'Frisco and the Iron Mountain. It is one of the fastest growing towns in this part of the state, and now has a population of about 3,500. It is a center of unusually fine farming country, and one of the principal industries of the town is the manufacture of flour. There are two large flouring mills, and a high grade of flour is produced. Besides its flouring mills there are some woodworking plants which are using up the timber in the vicinity. Benton, one of the oldest towns in the county, is the county seat, situated about one-half mile from the St. Louis & Gulf. Commerce, on the Mississippi river, has a population of about 700, and is a freight shipping point, and has a flour mill and cooper plant. Oran, which is a railroad junction, is also an important shipping point, especially for melons and wheat. Morley is the third town in size, having a population of 600; it is also a railroad junction, and is the center of the cantaloupe country of the county. Besides these, there are some smaller towns, Diehlstadt, New Hamburg, Vanduser, Gray's Point and Kelso.

The population of the county is 22,372 and its total taxable wealth is $5,773,958. There is a good system of public schools, there being 54 school districts, employing 103 teachers. A large part of the population of the county is American, though there are some settlements of Germans made before the war.

Stoddard county is one of the largest counties in the state, having 840 square miles, or more than half a million acres. The middle part of the county, north to south, is hilly, being a part of Crowley's ridge, which swings in a broad curve from near Bell City through Arkansas to Helena. On the east edge of this ridge in Stoddard county the average height is about 100 feet, and the Cotton Belt railroad follows this ridge on the east side for a long distance. On the west the ridge slopes gradually to the level of the Black river and St. Francois bottoms. The ridge land is about one-half of the area of the county. Its soil is yellow-red clay, mixed with sand, and it is underlaid with a gravelly clay. About fifteen per cent of this ridge land is still timbered, the greater part of it being in cultivation. East of the ridge is the lowland of Little river bottom, of which the very much greater part is not yet improved. Stoddard county is developing its swamp land very rapidly by a system of drainage. The soil thus reclaimed is alluvial soil of a high degree of fertility. West of Crowley's ridge is the swamp of Black river and St. Francois, which resembles in general characteristics that of Little river.

The principal productions of the county are farm products, corn and wheat being the most important, and timber. At one time the timber interests were very extensive, and large quantities of staves and heading, as well as lumber, were manufactured at Bloomfield, Dexter and other points. Of late years, however, the timber is well cut out, except in the swamps. Even here, the best timber has been cut. About one-half of the area of the county is still timbered. Besides the staple crops mentioned, cotton is grown in the south part of the county, and is ginned at two or three points. Flour is manufactured, especially at Dexter and Bloomfield. A good grade of pottery clay is found near Bloomfield and there is an establishment for making pottery there. The manufactured products of the county reached a total of $1,676,351 in 1910. The large items were flour, lumber, cooperage and cotton.

The county has the following railroads: the St. Louis, Iron Mountain & Southern, Cairo branch; the St. Louis Southwestern and the 'Frisco. Most of the county is well supplied with railroad facilities.

The principal towns are Dexter and Bloomfield. The latter is the county seat, and is supported largely by farming interests since the removal of the wood-working plants. Dexter is now the largest town, made so largely because of its superior shipping facilities and in part by the fact that large bodies of timber are still available near Dexter. The population of the county is 27,807, and its total taxable wealth is $6,452,077. There are 107 school districts, employing 151 teachers, and the school system of the county is one of the best in Southeast Missouri.

Washington county, one of the oldest in the state, is fifty miles south of the Missouri river and about forty west of the Mississippi. It is in the heart of the mineral district, and its principal industry is mining. The county contains 780 square miles, or nearly half a million acres, and of this immense area only about 100,000 acres, or one-fifth, is farmed. The remainder of the county, amounting to about 400,000 acres, is still timbered, the principal varieties being oak, yellow pine, hickory, maple and walnut. White oak is the most abundant timber and the most valuable. It amounts to about 35 per cent of the remaining timber, and black oak, found chiefly in the western and southwestern parts of the county, amounts to about 25 per cent.

There are three general classes of lands in the county. In the northeast part there is a table land where is to be found the most valuable of farming lands. The surface is gently rolling and well drained. The soil is gravelly clay, sometimes covered with rocks. The sub-soil is usually a red clay. This is fairly productive land and is well adapted to fruit growing. In the southeast part of the county there are also some high, rolling lands suitable for farming, while in the western part the land is broken, the only farm land in this county being found in the valleys of the streams.

There is scarcely a mineral known to Southeast Missouri that is not found in considerable quantities in Washington county. Of these minerals the most valuable and important is lead. Lead mines have been operated in the county from about 1780, when the mine known as Mine a Breton was discovered near the present site of Potosi. This is the center of the lead mining district. Another is about Old Mines, and another is found at Palmer, in the western part of the county. In the early times, mines were worked on the Mineral fork of Big river.

The production of lead is no longer as large as it once was, but in 1910 nearly 1,000 tons of lead ore were shipped from the county. Besides lead, barytes, zinc, iron, copper, clay, limestone and sandstone are found in paying quantities, and all of them are being mined and exported. In 1910, 25,000 tons of barytes were shipped from the county. In 1910 there were manufactured in the county products to an amount of $308,096. The large items were cooperage, flour, mineral products and lumber.

The only railroad in the county is the St. Louis, Iron Mountain & Southern, which touches the western edge, and a branch of this system extending from Mineral Point to Potosi. The county has a fine system of roads which extend in every direction from Potosi.

There are more than sixty miles of good rock roads within the limits of the county.

There are a number of streams, the most important being Big river, but Indian creek, Fourche a Renault and Mine a Breton creeks are also important streams. There is an opportunity for the development of water power on some of these.

Potosi, the county seat, is the principal town in the county. Its population is 840. It has a flour mill, stave factory and mining interests. Irondale is a mining town in the east part of the county, and Caledonia, the old seat of Marvin institute, has flour mills and mineral interests. Other towns are Belgrade, Richwoods, Shirley and Blackwell. The population of the county is 13,378, and its total taxable wealth is $3,250,410. There are 71 school districts, employing 84 teachers. The nearness to St. Louis makes possible the growing of vegetables in a profitable way, and also makes residence in the county much more pleasant than it would otherwise be.

At one time Wayne county embraced about one-fourth of the area of the state. It has been reduced by the formation of other counties until its area is now about 500,000 acres. Of this only a small part, less than one-fifth, has been put into cultivation. The remainder is largely timbered land. At one time the whole county was covered with an immense forest, principally pine, oak, cottonwood, gum and maple. The greater part of the valuable timber has been removed, though there is still some pine and oak to be found. The land is hilly, being mountainous in the northwest part where the county joins Iron county. There are some river valleys, approximating about 15,000 acres, that are exceedingly productive. The other soil in the county consists of upland and is of two kinds, limestone, which is free from surface rock (this centers around Patterson), and then there is a gravelly clay, where considerable rock occurs, found in most other parts of the county. All the land in the county which may be farmed at all is fairly productive.

The principal interests in the county are farming and lumbering, though mining employs a considerable number of men also. The principal crops are corn and wheat. At one time the county produced more pine lumber than any other county in the state. There were then immense mills at Greenville and Williamsville, employing thousands of men. With the practical exhaustion of pine timber, however, these large mills have ceased to exist, and the timber is worked up by smaller mills which can be moved from place to place. The value of the county's manufactured products in 1910 was $396,770. The largest item was lumber. Other important products were flour and cooperage.

The largest town is Piedmont, which is a division point on the main line of the Iron Mountain. It is in the western part of the county. The county seat, Greenville, is on the St. Francois river and is connected with the Iron Mountain system by the Williamsville, Greenville & St. Louis Railroad, an independent line, built in order to carry the immense quantities of lumber manufactured at Greenville to the railroad at Williamsville. Williamsville is the third town in the county. It has timber and farming interests, and there are also some iron mines in the vicinity.

The population of the county is 15,181, and its total taxable wealth $2,979,166. There are 73 school districts, employing 95 teachers.

The transportation facilities are good in the western and southern parts of the county. The main line of the Iron Mountain runs near the western line, and the south part of the county is crossed by the 'Frisco and the Missouri Southern extends from Leeper into Reynolds county. There are a number of streams, the principal one being the St. Francois river, which runs through the county from north to south, dividing it into practically equal parts. Black river is in the western part of the county, and is paralleled through a considerable part of its length by the Iron Mountain railroad.

The population of the county is very largely American born. In 1905 there were only 126 foreign born persons and only 115 negroes. The value of manufactured products in 1910 was $396,770. Of this amount, lumber and flour represented about three-fourths.

CHAPTER XXXVIII

THE NEWSPAPERS

Cape Girardeau — The First Paper — Bollinger — Butler — Carter — Dunklin — Iron — Jefferson — Madison — Mississippi—New Madrid — Pemiscot — Perry — Reynolds — Ripley — St. Francois — Ste. Genevieve — Scott — Stoddard — Washington — Wayne — The Great Work of Newspapers.

This chapter is intended to give an account of the newspapers of this district. It is hardly possible that it is entirely full and accurate, because of the difficulty in ascertaining all the facts concerning some of the early papers. It does include within it, however, a mention of the principal papers that have been published from time to time in this part of the state, and it is believed that it has a record of all the papers now being published. Newspaper enterprise began in Southeast Missouri at a very early date. The settlers soon felt the need of some medium for the exchange of news, and a forum for the discussion of public questions. It was, perhaps, this latter need that led to the founding of the earliest papers, for it was not until the great discussion which arose from the admission of the state into the Union, and the formation of its constitution, that a paper was published here.

So far as can now be ascertained, the first paper in Southeast Missouri, and the second one published outside of the city of St. Louis, was the *Missouri Herald*, the publication of which was begun in 1819, at Jackson, by T. E. Strange. Strange soon transferred the paper to James Russell who, in 1825, sold it to William Johnson. Johnson changed the name of the paper to the *Independent Patriot*, and later to *The Mercury*. In 1831 it passed from Johnson to R. W. Renfroe and Greer W. Davis, who published it for a short time under the title of the *Jackson Eagle*. In 1835 its name was changed to the *Southern Advocate and State Journal*. It was moved to Cape Girardeau and published there at first by Dr. Patrick Henry Davis, and later by Robert Burns. In 1845 it was returned to Jackson and was now called the *Jackson Review*, being published by Wagner and McFerron. In 1849 its name was again changed to the *Southern Advocate*, the publisher being H. S. McFarland. McFarland published it only until 1850 when it went into the hands of J. W. Limbaugh, who renamed it the *Southern Democrat*. It was Democratic in politics, and its motto was "The constitution in its purity, the bulwark of American liberty." Limbaugh continued its publication until his death in 1852. At that time the name was changed to the *Jeffersonian*, and the publication continued by Robert

Brown. In 1853 it was succeeded by the *Jackson Courier*, of which Joel Wilkinson was editor and proprietor. Wilkinson continued its publication until the breaking out of the Civil war, when the newspaper was suspended.

On August 4th, 1871, ther appeared the first issue of the *Missouri Cash Book* at Jackson. It was founded by W. S. Malone, and he continued as editor and proprietor until June, 1875. For a time it was conducted by the Cash Book Publishing and Printing Company. They sold it to D. D. Hampton, who died within a year of his purchase. It was then published by A. S. Coker, and later by Coker & Honey, until January, 1882, when Coker sold his interest to F. A. McGuire. In June, 1883, McGuire became the sole proprietor, and has continued the publication up to this time.

The *Cash Book* is unique among the older papers of this section in that it has never changed either in name or political faith. It was established as a Democratic weekly and has continued as such up to the present. It is one of the oldest papers in this part of the state issued under its original management, and is an influential and ably conducted journal. Mr. McGuire's long association in the newspaper world has given him a fund of information about newspapers and newspaper men that is exceedingly valuable.

The *Deutscher Volks Freund* was established in 1886, the first number appearing on March 11th. Its editor was Frederick Kies, and it was published in the German language. The publication has continued down to the present time. Mr. Kies still conducts it with distinguished ability, and the paper has a large circulation among the German population of Cape Girardeau and surrounding counties. For several years Mr. Kies has published in connection with it an English paper called the *Jackson Items*.

The *Comet* was issued at Jackson for a short time, about 1895, by W. S. Wilkinson. It was a Populist paper and soon disappeared.

The first newspaper printed in Cape Girardeau was *The Patriot*, established in 1836 by Edwin H. White. White was a Whig and published his paper in the interest of that party; however, he experienced the usual difficulty attendant upon newspaper publication in Southeast Missouri and suspended his paper after a short time. In 1843 John W. Morrison established another Whig paper called *The South Missouri*. The *Western Eagle* and *Marble City News* were published in 1866, and *Democracy*, by William Gruelle. James Lindsay for a few years edited a paper called *The Censor* about 1846, and a paper called *The Argus* was established in 1869 and published for a short time. The first German paper was the *Westliche Post*, established in 1871. The *Courier* began to be published in 1878 and the *Mississippi Valley Globe* in 1872. The *Cape Talk* was published for a while in 1856 and a religious paper called *The Baptist Headlight* in 1896.

In 1876 a paper called *The Democrat* was established as a weekly and later made a daily about 1888, and published for many years by Benjamin H. Adams. Publication of *The Democrat* was discontinued in 1907. The *Southeast Gazette*, a weekly, was established in 1898 by Joseph Flynn and continued by him for several years. In 1893, *The New Era* began but was published only for a short time. It was published by Minton & Shelton. In the same year D. L. Hoffman published a paper which he called the *Re-*

view. It was independent in politics. In 1895, Larey & Hoffman issued a few numbers of a paper called the *Spice-Box*. It was a Democratic weekly. In 1899, C. D. Tresenwriter established the *Progress*. He continued its publication until 1908. The *Progress* was Democratic in political affiliations. In that year, too, D. L. Hoffman issued some numbers of the *Optimist*.

In 1901, the Cape Girardeau News Publishing Company began to publish a daily and weekly called the *News*. Its publication was soon discontinued.

In 1900, *The Republican* was established. One year later it came into the hands of Naeter Bros. They began to issue it as both a daily and weekly and soon established it as the leading newspaper in Cape Girardeau. At the present time it is issued from a well-equipped plant and is one of the leading papers of the state.

In 1911, the *Herald*, which had been published at Jackson since its establishment in 1899, by B. F. Lusk, was removed to Cape Girardeau and it is now edited by Fred Goyert.

In 1907 Dix Walker established the *Oakridge Indicator* and continued it for a number of years. In the same year *The Whitewater Times* began to be published at Whitewater. It had a brief existence.

It seems that the first paper in Bollinger county was the *Standard*, which was established about 1868 by a Mr. Osborne. He continued its publication for only a short time and then sold it to Col. Lindsay Murdoch, the Civil war veteran. Col. Murdoch continued in charge of the paper until 1874, when he sold it and it was removed to Fredericktown. It was, of course, a Republican paper. The first Democratic paper was the *Herald*. Thomas Johnson was the owner and editor of the *Herald* and he strongly opposed Murdoch and the *Standard*. In 1883 this paper was also sold and was taken to Ironton.

In 1881, George W. Harrington established a paper which he called the *Reflector*. After a short time he sold it to James G. Finney, who published it for many years as the *Press*. At the present time the *Press* is owned by Hill & Chandler and edited by Dean B. Hill. It is a Democratic paper and has an established place.

The *Palladium* was a paper established in 1878 by P. T. Pigg. After two years he sold it to the *Herald*. After J. G. Finney disposed of the *Press* he published the *Times* for several years, beginning in 1896. All the papers mentioned were conducted in Marble Hill, the county seat.

The only other paper in Bollinger county is the *Lutesville Banner*. It was established in 1891. It was edited by a number of persons, among them Thomas R. Green. The present editor is F. A. Wiggs. The *Banner* is Republican in politics.

The first paper in Butler county was the *Black River News*, established at Poplar Bluff in 1869, under the management of G. L. Poplin and G. T. Bartlett. Bartlett's connection with the paper was soon terminated and it was then called *Poplin's Black River News* until 1874. W. T. Kitchen and George H. Kelly purchased the paper at that time and changed the name to the *Headlight*. It became the *Poplar Bluff Citizen* in 1877 under the management of George H. Crumb, and still continues under that name. Two new papers were established in Poplar Bluff in 1875, one the *Black River Country* and the other the *New Era*. They lasted for only a few months. In 1879 the *Southeast Missourian* was begun, but was later sold to the owners of the *Citizen*. Judge John G. Wear, a lawyer, began the publication of the *Renovator* in 1882, but he, too, sold to the *Citizen* about two years later. In 1887 the office was purchased by W. L. Oury, and in April, 1888, George H. Crumb issued the first number of the *Republic*. The publication of this paper was continued for only a short time.

After Mr. Crumb's retirement from the *Citizen* it was conducted by a number of editors. George H. Kelly held the place for a time. He was succeeded by Thomas M. Johnson, and he by George H. Thomas. In 1882 the paper came into possesion of Hedges & Batterton, with Batterton as editor. During their ownership Richard L. Metcalfe, later a famous newspaper man of Lincoln, Nebraska, was a writer for the paper. Joe C. Berner became the owner in 1895 and established the daily edition in 1897. Later it absorbed a paper called the *Democrat* and the consolidated paper is known as the *Citizen-Democrat*. The present publishers are Ferguson & Adams and the paper has both a daily and weekly edition and is a prosperous and flourishing enterprise.

There were many other newspaper ventures during the years that the *Citizen* was being developed. One of these was a real estate trade journal called the *Southern Land Owner*, which was conducted for a time by E. R. Lentz. It was devoted to the interests of the real estate business in surrounding communities. Another was the *Advocate*, published in 1893 by W. L. Oury.

The *Republican* was founded in 1890 by J. T. Davidson. It was devoted to the interests of the Republican party in opposition to the *Citizen*, which was Democratic in politics. For a number of years it was conducted by L. F. Tromley. At present the *Republican* is published by D. L. Burnside and has both weekly and daily editions. It is one of the progressive and influential papers in this part of Missouri.

There is only one paper published in Carter county. This is the *Current Local*, which was founded in 1884. It is a Democratic weekly and is owned and edited by Oliver W. Chilton.

In 1907, when Grandin was perhaps the greatest saw-mill town in the state if not in the world, Elbert C. White established a Republican paper there which he called the *Grandin Herald*. It received considerable support for a time but was not permanently successful and finally had to be discontinued.

The first newspaper published in Dunklin county was the *Dunklin County Herald*, established in 1872 at Kennett. In the same year the *Missouri Democracy* was removed from Cape Girardeau to Clarkton and these two were afterward consolidated and published at Kennett.

In 1872 a paper called the *Advertiser* was established at Clarkton by Albert & Baldwin. It later became the property of Charles E. Stokes who changed its name to the *Enterprise* and improved it in many ways. In 1876 this paper was moved to Kennett, but like the previous ventures it was discontinued after a short time.

The next paper published in the county was called the *Dunklin County Advocate* and was established in October, 1877, at Clarkton, by W. R. McDaniel. It later came under control of John W. Baldwin and was moved to Kennett. In 1879 it was purchased by Charles E. Stokes and removed to Malden.

Here its name was changed to *Malden Clipper*. It was then taken to Kennett in 1886, and its publication discontinued in 1887.

The publication of the *Kennett Clipper* was begun in March, 1888, by R. H. Jones, who had had previous newspaper experience in Dexter and in Malden. After some years, Ligon Jones, a brother of R. H., became interested in the paper and they continued it until April, 1903, when it was sold to the Dunklin County Publishing Company, a corporation. This publishing company continued to issue the paper, at first under the editorship of O. S. Harrison for about five months. E. P. Caruthers was then made editor and the name of the paper was changed to the *Dunklin Democrat*. Since that time it has continued under the management of Mr. Caruthers and has been published a total of 980 weeks without having missed a single number. The *Democrat* is an able and influential paper and is conducted along business lines. It is published in a well-equipped plant belonging to the publishing company.

In 1902 the *Dunklin County Mail* was established at Kennett, by Rev. J. H. Peay. He continued its publication for a time and the office was closed. The property came into the hands of a company which issued it for a time as the *Dunklin County Herald*. Later it disappeared.

When the *Malden Clipper* was moved to Kennett in 1886 John P. Allen and R. G. Sandidge began the publication of the *Dunklin County News*. Others were interested in its management from time to time. T. L. Roussin, who had experience with a number of southeast papers, was interested in it for a time. One of the men trained under him was Casper M. Edwards, who secured control of the *News*, organized a company called the Edwards Publishing Company and carried on its publication for a number of years. Edwards was a brilliant and forcible writer. He finally disposed of the paper to the Malden Printing Company and Daniel J. Keller became its editor and manager. Under his management the *News* became a prosperous and influential paper. He continued its publication until 1910, when he was succeeded as editor and manager by Lyman F. Jackson, who continues its publication.

During all its existence until the present management the *News* has been Democratic, but it is now conducted as an independent paper.

About 1895 E. G. Henderson, of Arkansas, brought a paper to Malden called the *Evening Shade*. He continued its publication as a Democratic weekly for a short time and then moved it away. Other attempts have been made to conduct papers in the town but all of them met with very limited success until the *Merit* began to be issued in 1904.

The first issue was gotten out July 1, 1904, by R. L. White and J. C. Shores. White was editor and manager of the paper and in September, 1910, became also the sole owner by the purchase of the interest of Shores. The *Merit* is independent in politics, has established a place for itself, and is in a prosperous condition.

The *Campbell Citizen* was established in 1901 by C. D. Bray and Jas. Sanders. It was published during the first few years by a number of persons, being transferred from hand to hand. In December, 1901, it came under the control and ownership of B. W. Overall and son, and they have continued its publication ever since that time. The *Citizen* is a Democratic paper and devoted very largely to the building up of Campbell and the immediate vicinity. A few years before the founding of the *Citizen* D. L. Mabie had issued a few numbers of a paper he called *The Independent*. It was not successful and was soon discontinued.

Senath, in Dunklin county, has had a varied experience with newspapers. About 1902 Jas. A. Bradley established a paper which he called the *Star*. It was soon discontinued. Later a paper called the *Farmers' Union Advocate* was issued for a while. Other papers followed. Some of them suffered financial shipwreck. At present the *Leader* is being issued by John Mann.

The first paper published in Arcadia was *The Arcadia Prospect*, with A. Coulter as proprietor and W. L. Favor as editor. This was in 1859. After a short time it was removed to Ironton and in 1861 the publication was discontinued. One year before this time *The Furnace* had been established in Ironton by James Lindsay. *The Furnace* was a Free Soil paper, but it, too, was discontinued in 1861. About the breaking out of the war a religious paper known as *The Baptist Journal* was established by Rev. William Polk, but he, too, was forced to discontinue during the war. In 1865 *The Ironton Forge* was started by Eli D. Ake, using the material which had formerly belonged to *The Furnace*. This was the entrance upon newspaper life of probably the oldest editor in this part of the state. In 1866 *The Forge* was sold to G. A. and J. L. Moser, who called the publication *The Southeast Missouri Enterprise*, but discontinued its publication in 1873. In 1866 *The Review*, a Democratic paper, was founded by R. E. Craig. The name of the paper was changed to the *Iron County Register* in July, 1867, with Thomas Essex and W. H. Winfield as editors. This paper was purchased in 1869 by Eli D. Ake and C. K. Miller. In 1871 Mr. Ake became the sole proprietor and since that time has owned and edited the *Iron County Register*, perhaps the longest continuous control of any paper in Southeast Missouri. Mr. Ake is regarded as the dean of newspaper men in this section, not only because of his long service, but also because of his real ability as an editor. *The Register* is one of the most influential papers of this section. In 1870 Robert L. Lindsay established a campaign paper called *The Liberal* at Ironton, and *The Commonwealth*, an independent religious paper, was conducted by Crawford and Duncan for a few months in 1874. *The Herald*, a Democratic paper established in 1884, by John Smith, which suspended publication in a short time, was another Ironton enterprise.

In 1897 the *Republican* was established by G. H. Broadwell. It was later edited by C. A. Byers and was discontinued about 1902. Byers transferred the office to Arcadia and established the *Arcadia Valley Enterprise*. *The Enterprise* is a Republican paper and is at present under the control of Fuller Swift.

A non-political paper called *Columbian Reciprocity* was published for a short time in Ironton about 1893. It had no particular patronage and was soon discontinued.

The first newspaper in Jefferson county was established at DeSoto in 1859 by E. E. Furber. He continued its publication until forced to suspend by the breaking out of the war. No attempt was made to conduct another paper in DeSoto until 1869, when C. D. Clarke established a paper which he called *The Republican*. It was Republican in politics, but its publication was suspended within a short time.

In 1890 a company was organized at

DeSoto to publish a paper called the *DeSoto Facts*. Just as in other cases it was discontinued after a time.

In 1893 the Mitchim Publishing Company began to issue a paper which they called the *Press*. The editor was J. F. Mitchim, who was for a long time connected with newspaper enterprise in Southeast Missouri, editing at various times a number of papers. The *Press* is still published and is edited by C. C. Mitchim, who became editor in 1906. It is a Democratic paper with a wide circulation and considerable influence.

The only other paper now published at DeSoto is the *Jefferson County Republican*, a Republican paper edited and published by W. E. Crow.

The oldest and one of the most influential papers in Jefferson county is the *Jefferson County Democrat* at Hillsboro. It was established immediately after the war in 1865, and has been continuously published since that time. A family of newspaper men have been identified with this paper. The member of this family now in control is R. W. McMullin. Mr. McMullin has a wide acquaintance with Missouri history and has a valuable collection of historical material of various kinds.

The *Jefferson County Record*, also published at Hillsboro is the Republican rival of the *Democrat*. Its editor is John H. Reppy. Mr. Reppy is a practicing lawyer, but is a man of literary turn of mind, has a wide acquaintance with the history of the state and publishes a good paper. The *Record* is the successor of the *New Era*, which was established at Hillsboro in 1903 by the New Era Publishing Co.

Festus, in Jefferson county, has two papers at the present. The *Festus News* is a Democratic paper published by H. L. Marbury; the *Tri-City Independent* is Republican in politics and is published by W. P. Brent.

For a number of years J. J. Wilson published a paper at Hillsboro, which he called the *Jefferson County Crystal Mirror*. It was a Republican paper and for a time received considerable support, but finally ceased to be issued.

The first paper in Madison county was called the *Espial*. It was established in 1847 by James Lindsay, and was the first Free Soil paper in the state. Its publication ceased after a very short time. In 1885 the *Fredericktown Journal* was established by W. H. Booth, but was discontinued in September, 1861, and no other paper was published in the town until after the close of the war. S. Henry Smith established the *Conservative* in 1866, and sold the office to Charles E. Barroll two years later, who changed the name to the *Bee*. In a short time this paper was purchased by E. P. Caruthers, and in 1875 he combined it with the *Plaindealer*, which was established by William Gosner in 1874. From 1876 to 1882 the paper was published by W. J. Collier. At a later date it passed into the control of O. K. Clardy. The next paper established in Fredericktown was the *Standard*, the publication of which was begun in 1887 by E. D. Anthony. Among other papers which were published for a short time were the *Jeffersonian*, edited by H. M. Williams, the *Farmer & Miner*, by C. W. Dunifer, and the *Clarion*, by Perry D. Martin.

A paper called the *Advertiser* was published at Mine LaMotte for a short time in 1877.

The *Fredericktown Democrat* was established in 1893 by Geo. B. Pressgrove. It was later published by Pressgrove & Gale. About

1897 R. L. Daniel secured control of the paper and it was shortly afterward combined with the *News*. This paper was established in 1889. It was a Republican paper and its editor was E. L. Purcell, who has been connected with it since that time. The *Democrat-News* is one of the influential papers of its section.

The *Tribune* was established in 1900 by Ed. Costello. He was succeeded as editor by T. A. Bowman. The next man who controlled the paper was E. P. Francis, who still continues its publication. The *Democrat-News* is Democratic in politics, while the *Tribune* is Republican.

The first paper published in Marquand was *The Echo*, which was established by A. V. Cashion, now the editor of the *Perry County Republican*. Cashion was the editor and the plant was owned by Thomas Estes. *The Echo* appeared for only two years, from 1890 to 1892. After its discontinuance, Marquand was without a paper until in October, 1910, when Dean Gibson established the *Marquand Leader*. This paper is independent in politics and is devoted to local interest, principally.

The first newspaper in Charleston, Mississippi county, was *The Courier*. It was established by George Whitcomb in the latter part of the year 1857. It was ably conducted and a very creditable paper. It was established as an independent paper and was one of the few Southeast Missouri papers that continued to be published during the war. Even *The Courier*, however, was subject to frequent interruptions. From 1858 to 1872, the management was in the hands of W. F. Martin, who was also during part of the time, its editor. The plant was sold in 1872, on the death of Mr. Martin, to Frank M. Dyer, who published *The Courier* until 1877, when he sold it to C. M. Dunifer. In 1875 *The Charleston Gazette* was established by George M. Moore, and the two papers were consolidated under the name of the *Charleston Gazette* in 1877. In a short time Dunifer withdrew from the firm and established a new paper called *The Sentinel*, which two years later was removed to Arkansas. Moore sold the *Charleston Gazette* to a joint stock company and they sold it to W. H. Campbell. Campbell operated the paper something like a year and then sold it to Andrew Hill, and in April, 1886, the office, material and press were removed to Malden.

In 1865 George Martin, a son of W. F. Martin, who had published *The Courier* for many years, began the publication of a little sheet which he called *The Enterprise*. Martin was then only 15 years old and his sole help in working the paper was another boy about his own age named M. V. Golder. Martin continued the publication of *The Enterprise* until 1892, when he sold it to his brother, John F. Martin. In 1902 the paper was transferred to Colonel P. B. Moore and from that time until 1907 was under the management of S. G. Tetweiler. Tetweiler combined it with the *Democrat*, which he published since 1887. In the year 1907 R. E. Douglas became the editor and proprietor of the paper and has continued its publication ever since that time. It is Democratic in politics and it is probable that *The Enterprise* has had the longest continuous existence under the same name of any paper in this part of the state. At one time the paper was published as a daily. This was during the time of the management of John F. Martin.

The other paper published in Charleston is the *Republican*, whose editor is G. N. Stille.

As its name indicates it is a Republican paper, and together with *The Enterprise*, gives Charleston a good news service.

But one other paper is published in Mississippi county. This is the *East Prairie Eagle*, published at East Prairie. It was established in 1905 by Guy E. Cooksey as *The Leader*, and is now published by David Bright. *The Eagle* is Democratic in politics.

There have been other papers published from time to time in Charleston. One of these was a Democratic sheet called *The Call*. It was published in 1893 by H. D. Lutz. Another was *The Star*, whose editor for a time was F. A. Wiggs.

In 1846 John T. Scott, a lawyer from Tennessee, came to New Madrid and established the first newspaper there. It was called *The Gazette*. In 1850 Mr. Scott sold the paper to Mr. Barber, and he transferred it a year later to Hopkins & Nash. The publication was continued by them until 1854, when they were succeeded by John C. Underwood, who changed the name to *The Times*. The breaking out of the war caused the suspension of this paper, as it did of nearly all others published in the southeast, and the publication was never continued. About 1867, Albert O. Allen began the publication of *The Record*, which he has owned since that time, with the exception of a few months, when it was under the control of Frank Jones. Mr. Allen gave up the editorial control of the paper, though not its ownership, in 1886, when he became swamp land commissioner of the state and later state auditor. During these years E. A. Wright was in editorial charge. In 1906 Mr. Allen returned to New Madrid, and since that time has conducted the paper himself. *The Record* is not only one of the oldest, but also one of the most influential papers in the southeast. Mr. Allen's wide acquaintance, his familiarity with state affairs, his long residence in the southeast, enable him to conduct a paper creditable in every way.

In 1872 a firm known as Masterson & Mulkey established a newspaper called *The Chronicle*. They continued its publication for about eighteen months.

In 1895 W. W. Waters, a member of one of the old pioneer families of New Madrid, began the publication of a paper which he called the *Southeast Missourian*. The venture was successful from the first and Mr. Waters soon acquired a standing among newspaper men. He continued its publication until about 1904, when he became connected with the administration of the State Hospital for the Insane at Farmington and was succeeded in control of *The Missourian* by E. A. Wright, who had long been associated with *The Record*. Mr. Wright continues the publication of this paper and is firmly entrenched in the newspaper world. Both *The Record* and the *Southeast Missourian* are Democratic in politics.

The first paper established in Morehouse was the *Morehouse Sun*, which James L. Bailey began to publish in 1905. It was later transferred to Claude B. Hay and the name changed to *The Hustler*. This was about 1907. It is now an independent paper and is edited by C. Harvey Burgess. *The Parma Victor* was established about 1905 and is now published by A. L. Stearnes. The *Portageville Critic* was established in 1905 by Charles N. Walker. It is a Socialist paper with a large circulation. There had been one other attempt at running a paper in Portageville. J. Blake Taylor began to publish a paper, which he called *The Push*, in 1903, but it was discontinued after a short time.

The first paper in Pemiscot county was the *Gayoso Democrat*, established in 1871 by B. H. & T. S. Adams. For a time it was published at Cape Girardeau. In 1872 it became the property of W. S. Carleton and Maj. Geo. W. Carleton was made editor. It was published then at Gayoso. Its name was changed in 1875 to the *Southeast Missouri Statesman*. For a number of years it passed from hand to hand, coming back into the possession of Major Carleton, who continued it for many years. In 1879 it was again called *The Democrat*. In 1892 it was finally transferred to Caruthersville. Here it was published by a number of persons. In 1893 W. D. Schult became the editor. He was soon succeeded by G. B. Gale. About 1897 Del Loggrear became connected with the paper and directed it for some years. The paper finally, in 1900, came into possession of W. R. Lacey, under whose management it entered upon an era of prosperity. It is now published twice a week, has its own brick building, and well appointed office. It has always been a Democratic paper.

When W. D. Schult gave up his control of *The Democrat* he established *The Press*. Later, Corridon Garrett became its editor, remaining in the position until about 1904. *The Press* was finally discontinued. Previous to his connection with *The Press* Garrett had conducted a paper called the *Southern Scimetar*.

The Republican is published in Caruthersville in Pemiscot county by Frank Abernathy. Mr. Abernathy is also the owner of the paper and has been since the first publication, August 12, 1910. It is the only Republican paper in Pemiscot county. Other Republican papers have been established from time to time, but have been unsuccessful. The present paper, however, has won its place and seems to be firmly established.

The *Pemiscot Argus* was established at Caruthersville by the Argus Printing Company, a corporation. Its editor is Harvey E. Averill, and the paper is independent in politics and favors temperance. It is the successor of a paper established in 1898 at Hayti by C. S. York. From the time of its establishment until 1907 it was published at Hayti, being at various times forced to suspend publication. In the latter year it was removed to Caruthersville in charge of Amos Huffman. It suspended publication again in November, 1907, and in February, 1908, it came into the possesion of the present proprietors and has been published continuously since that time. *The Argus* is a well edited and an influential journal.

The first paper published in Hayti was started in 1897. It was called the *Hayti Signal*, but its publication was discontinued after a time. In 1898 another effort was made to establish a paper and this was called the *Pemiscot Argus*, which was afterward removed to Caruthersville, where it is still published. In October, 1908, Mr. York began the publication of a paper at Hayti under the name of *Hayti Herald*. It has continued since that time, being owned and edited by Mr. York and is Democratic in politics.

The *Southern Pemiscot News* was established in Steele in the south part of Pemiscot county in 1910 by G. Clarence Smith, who still continues its publication. *The News* is independent in politics and is devoted to the furtherance of the interests of Steele and surrounding country.

The first paper published at Perryville was called *The Union*. This was formerly the *Fredericktown Conservative*, but was moved to Perryville in 1862 by W. H. Booth, who continued the publication for twenty years.

John B. Robinson established the next paper in 1875, and called it *The Forum*. A year or two later he transferred it to a stock company and in March, 1880, it was succeeded by the *Perry County Sun*, under the management of John B. Holmes. The owners of this paper subsequently purchased *The Union* and the combined papers were under the direction of John B. Davis. In 1886 the *Perryville Chronicle* was established by E. H. Elliff.

The Sun passed from one control to another for several years. At one time it was published by S. Henry and Harry A. Smith, the former a veteran of the newspaper field in this section as editor. At the present time it is published by Zoellner & Zoellner. It is Democratic in politics and is well established in the esteem of a wide circle of readers.

The *Perry County Republican* was started at Perryville in 1889. It was a Republican paper published in opposition to *The Sun*. For a time it was edited by F. W. Hempler. At the present time *The Republican* is under control of A. V. & C. E. Cashion and is an influential sheet.

Besides these two papers, which are still published, there have been other newspaper ventures in Perry county. *The Democrat* was established in 1898 and published for a time by the Democrat Publishing Company. An older paper was called *The Chronicle* and was published for a time by E. H. Elliff, beginning in 1886.

The first paper in Ripley county was *The Doniphan Prospect*, established about 1874. It was followed at a later date by *The News*. These two were combined in 1883 as the *Prospect-News*. The editor of the combined papers for a time was R. E. Douglass. At the present time the *Prospect-News* is published by J. P. Campbell. Associated with him is J. P. Morrison. The paper is a weekly and is Democratic in politics.

In 1895 *The Headlight* was established. It was conducted for a time by J. W. Presson. In 1898 D. C. Cunningham began to publish a Democratic paper which he called *The Hustler*. The name was later changed to *The Democrat*, and it is still published by Mr. Cunningham. Both the *Prospect-News* and *The Democrat* are well conducted papers.

It was December 8, 1905, that F. A. Vire began the publication of the *Doniphan Republican* and has continued as its owner and publisher since that time and the paper owns a well equipped office and is installed in its own building.

In 1910 Dr. M. M. Lane established the *Naylor Nail* at Naylor, Ripley county, and has continued its publication up to the present time. *The Nail* is Democratic in politics.

Several other attempts had been made to establish a paper at Naylor. Mobley & Company published *The Advocate* for a time in 1893. This was a Democratic paper. About 1905, J. E. Slattery began to publish a Republican sheet called *The Republican*. Both were later discontinued.

A Populist paper was published at Barfield, Ripley county, for a time, beginning in 1895. Mobley & Lilley were the proprietors. On the collapse of the Populist movement in Missouri the paper was discontinued.

The first paper established in Reynolds county was the *Reynolds County Outlook*. It began to be published in 1877 at Centreville and its publication has been continued to the present time. For a number of years it was conducted by A. P. Shriver. It is now owned and edited by T. D. Shriver. *The Outlook* is Democratic in politics. The second paper in the county is *The Headlight*. Its editor and owner is W. S. Tussey. *The Headlight* is also a Democratic paper.

The *Ellington Press* was established in 1906 at Ellington, Reynolds county. After some changes of ownership, *The Press* came into the charge of R. Daniels, who has continued to be both editor and proprietor. Mr. Daniels was for a number of years a teacher and also a member of the state legislature. He is a Democrat and *The Press* sustains the policies of that party.

In 1892 Dr. W. C. Bowles was publishing a paper in Centreville which was called *The Reformer*. It was discontinued in 1894, but revived again in 1898. He published it for a number of years, but it was finally discontinued.

The first paper published at Farmington, St. Francois county, was the *Southern Missouri Argus*, which was established in April, 1860, by Nichol, Crowell and Shuck. Nichol was a native of Kentucky, Crowell was from Massachusetts, and Shuck a Missourian. Their purpose in establishing *The Argus* was to support that wing of the Democratic party that favored the nomination of Stephen A. Douglas. In 1861 they sold the paper to Joseph Brady, who called it *The Missouri Argus*, and published it until 1866, when he transferred it to his two sons, J. J. Brady, Jr., and S. B. Brady. After a few years they changed the name to the *Farmington Herald* and in 1872 they removed the paper to DeSoto. In 1871 Washington Hughes began the publication of *The New Era* at Libertyville in St. Francois county. He soon removed it to Farmington and continued its publication until 1876. He then sold it to George W. Herrington, who in a few years removed to Marble Hill. The *Farmington Times* was established in 1874 by C. E. Ware and I. H. Rodehaver. They published *The Times* until 1875, when R. H. Sylvester became editor of the paper in place of Mr. Ware. T. D. Fisher was made its editor in January, 1879, and in 1881 he purchased the entire interest in the paper and has been its owner and editor since that time. In March, 1886, I. H. Rodehaver began to publish a paper known as the *St. Francois County Democrat*. It was Democratic in politics, but in November of that year it was sold to John Hartshorn, who published it in the interest of the Republican party.

About 1903 *The Times* was combined with *The Herald* under the name *Times-Herald*, and was published with this title for several years, but finally the old name was resumed. *The Times* is one of the oldest and ablest papers in this part of the state. Mr. Fisher is an editor of unusual gifts as well as an able business man. *The Herald*, which was consolidated with *The Times* was established in 1892 by J. J. & S. H. Lews. It remained in their hands for some time, being edited for a while by C. R. Pratt.

The Republican paper of Farmington for many years was *The News*. This was issued for the first time in 1883 by T. P. Pigg. Mr. Pigg continued his connection with the paper for many years, but finally disposed of it to the present proprietors, the Farmington News Publishing Company.

The editors of *The News* are Harry and Clint Denman. *The News* pursues a somewhat different policy from most of the county papers, as it is a purely local paper and publishes no news outside of St. Francois and adjoining counties.

About 1903 R. M. Yost began to publish in Farmington a weekly Democratic paper called *The Progress*. He did not long continue it, however. The *Farmington Eagle* was later published for a time by E. C. Barroll.

The *St. Francois County Republican* is the title of a Republican paper now being issued at Farmington by the veteran editor, T. P. Pigg. He established it in 1911.

The *Bonne Terre Star* was established by H. M. Butler about 1896. Within a short time he transferred it to I. L. Page, who has continued its publication to the present time. *The Star* is Democratic in politics.

The *Lead Belt News* is published at Flat River by Melbourne Smith. It is a Democratic paper and was established in 1901 by Ward & Gibson. Later it was published by W. H. Lewis, who became associated with C. R. Pratt under the name of Pratt & Lewis.

The *Labor Herald* is published at Elvins by the Lead Fields Publishing Company. The publication of *The Herald* was begun in 1905 by the Elvins Printing Company. Later the paper was owned by Cameron & Raines. The *Labor Herald* is Republican in politics.

The *Lead Belt Banner* is published at Leadwood by the same company which issues the *Labor Herald*. It is Republican in politics.

The *Bismarck Gazette* is a continuance of the *Washington County Gazette* which was established in Irondale about 1904. In 1906 it was transferred to Bismarck and its name changed. In 1908 the paper was sold to George H. Bisplinghoff who continues its publication at the present time. *The Gazette* is Democratic in politics.

In 1907 the *DesLoge Sun* was established by Frank Abernathy at DesLoge in St. Francois county. It was sold to Claude E. Abshier in 1908 and is still published by him. *The Sun* is independent in politics and is devoted principally to the building up of the town and surrounding country.

The *Bonne Terre Register* was established in 1888 by J. M. Kirkpatrick, who continued the publication until 1890, when he sold the plant to E. H. Elliff. In 1890 B. A. Roy bought *The Register* and combined it with *The Democrat*. He continued its publication until 1911, when the paper was sold to its present owner and editor, J. H. Wolpers. *The Register* is Republican in politics and is a live, active and progressive paper.

Besides the papers mentioned there have been a few others established in St. Francois county which did not long survive. A paper called *The Sunnyside* was issued at Bonne Terre for a time in 1905 and 1906.

In 1821 there was begun the publication of a newspaper in Ste. Genevieve. It was called the *Correspondent and Record,* and its editor was James Foley. The *State Gazette* was established in Ste. Genevieve in 1833 by William B. Baker. Later, there was published for a short time, the *Missouri Democrat* in the same town. None of these papers was published more than a very short time. In 1849, Concannon and Lindsay began the publication of a paper called *The Pioneer*. They transferred it later to James H. Dixon. From 1850 to 1851 Charles C. Rozier published a paper called *The Creole*, which was then transferred to St. Louis. In 1854 *The Independent* was established by Amable Rozier, and the *Missouri Gazette* in 1859, by E. K. Eaton. O. D. Harris began the publication of the *Pleasant Dealer* in 1860, and the Provost-Marshal caused its discontinuance in 1861. Halleck and his brother published *The Representative* in 1865 for a short time. In 1868 the *News Advertiser* was established by G. L. Setts. *Fairplay* was published for the first time in June, 1872, by S. Henry Smith. In 1882 he transferred the paper to

Valle Harrold, and he published it from 1880 to 1884. Henry Shaw then carried on the paper until 1886, when it was transferred to Joseph Flynn. Flynn soon disposed of his interest in the paper and it passed into the hands of Henry J. Janis, a member of the old pioneer French family of that name. It is now ably conducted by Jules J. Janis. *Fairplay* is a Democratic paper and is well established in the esteem of the people of Ste. Genevieve and wields an influence there.

In 1882 Joseph A. Ernst began the publication of the *Ste. Genevieve Herald*. It was published in both English and German and has continued to the present under the control of Mr. Ernst. It is a popular and influential journal, and is independent in political affiliations.

St. Marys has had a number of papers published at various times. Among these were *The Times* and *The Progress*, published for a time between 1902 and 1906. At the present *The Review* is the only paper published there. It is independent in politics and is edited by C. R. Bartels. It was established in 1906.

The first newspaper in Benton, Scott county, was the *Benton Record*, established by George M. Moore in July, 1879. The editor was Louis Diehl. He was succeeded by Jefferson Shelton, and he by S. Henry Smith. Smith purchased *The Express*, a paper which had been established by T. S. Adams, and combined the two under the name of the *Express Record*. He sold the papers in August, 1886, to J. F. Mitchim.

The Dispatch was the first newspaper published in Commerce, and it was established in 1867 by Wm. Ballentine and H. P. Lynch. The paper was continued, going through a number of changes of ownership, until the county seat was moved to Benton. In March, 1885, a paper called the *Scott County Agricultural Wheel* was begun with Rev. S. A. Mason as editor. Publication was continued for only a short time.

The first newspaper in Sikeston was called *The Star*, and was established by J. F. Mitchim in January, 1884. He was succeeded as editor by W. S. Mitchim.

In 1893 Heckam & McClintock began the publication of a religious paper at Sikeston. It was called the *Methodist Advocate*, but was discontinued after a short time.

In 1894 *The Democrat* began to be issued at Sikeston. It was a Democratic sheet and was published by E. R. Larey. *The Budget* was established by Guy Cooksey in 1898.

At present there are two Sikeston papers. *The Herald* is Democratic and is published by John B. Huffman.

The Standard was established in 1911 by Naeter Brothers of Cape Girardeau. It is independent in politics and is devoted largely to local news and to the building up of the interests in Scott county.

The *Chaffee Signal* was established at Oran, Missouri, April 15, 1910, as the *Oran Leader*. It was moved to Chaffee on August 26 of the same year and its name changed to *Chaffee Signal*. The editor and proprietor is C. E. Mattocks and the paper is Democratic in politics.

One of the veteran editors of Southeast Missouri is Phil A. Hafner, editor of the *Scott County Kicker* at Benton, Missouri. This is a Socialist paper published by the Workers Printing Company. Mr. Hafner was at one time in his life a conductor on the street railway in St. Louis, and while engaged in this business became impressed with the idea that he would like to own and edit a newspaper. The idea grew upon him and he went so far as to select a name for his proposed newspaper. He decided that if he ever should publish a newspaper it should be called *The Newsboy*, the name being suggested by the newsboys who are always bright and always much in evidence on the street cars. In 1888 Mr. Hafner was able to carry out his plan and established at Benton, Missouri, *The Scott County Newsboy*. He continued the publication until in 1901 when its name was changed to the *Scott County Kicker*, under which name it has since been published.

The *Scott County Banner* is published at Morley in Scott county, the editors being R. L. Buck and R. L. Reed. The paper was established at Oran under the name of the *Scott County Citizen* in 1905, and in 1908 it was removed to Morley and was continued under that name until 1911, when it came into the possession of Buck and Reed and its name was changed to *The Banner*. It is published as a Democratic paper.

The *Illmo Headlight* is published at the new and growing town of Illmo. It is a Democratic sheet and is issued by Tim Hosmer, a veteran editor of this section.

The *Scott County Democrat* is published at Benton by T. F. Rucker. It is Democratic in politics and gives the news of the county seat of Scott county in general.

Stoddard county's first paper was called *The Herald*, and was established in 1858 at Bloomfield by A. M. Bedford, of Charleston. The editor in charge of the paper was J. O. Hull. The purpose in establishing this paper was to further the construction of the Cairo & Fulton railroad. The publication was continued until the breaking out of the war, when the office was destroyed and publication stopped. *The Argus* was established in Bloomfield in 1866 by James Hamilton, who carried on the paper until 1873. The next paper was under the management of George H. Crumb and O. C. Jones. This paper was called *The Messenger* and was published from 1874 to 1877. At that date it was consolidated with the *Dexter Enterprise*. The *Vindicator* was established in 1878 by T. L. Roussin. He sold it to Buck and Miller, who employed H. N. Phillips as editor. Later, the paper was purchased by Charles E. Stokes, and it was again transferred in 1882. The purchaser at this time was Ligon Jones. Jones published the paper for a time and it then changed hands several times. At one time Connelley & Moseley were in control, then J. O. Turnbaugh, and later it passed to the charge of M. S. Phelan. At the present time *The Vindicator* is edited by Stephen Chapman. It is a Democratic paper and has a well established circulation.

The first Republican paper in Bloomfield was *The Cosmos*, established in 1896 by Bear & Ollar. Ollar's interest was later purchased by Walter S. Bear, who continued publication for some time and then was succeeded by N. A. Moseley, an accomplished lawyer and one-time congressman of Bloomfield.

About 1905 Tim Hosmer, who has been connected with southeast newspaper enterprises for many years published a paper at Bloomfield called *The Enterprise*.

The *Stoddard County Republican* is a new paper, having been established October 1, 1910. O. B. Parrott is the editor and the paper is owned by a stock company known as the Republican Printing Company. It is published at Bloomfield and is Republican in its politics.

Charles E. Stokes, whose name is associated with a number of newspapers in this section, began the publication of *The Enterprise* at Dexter in February, 1875. Two years later he purchased the *Bloomfield Mes-*

senger and consolidated the two papers under the name of the *Enterprise-Messenger*. He continued the publication under this name until 1887, when he transferred it to R. H. Jones, and then founded a paper he called the *New Southeast*. After a short time he removed it to St. Louis. Jones changed the name to *The Dexter Messenger* and the paper was afterwards bought by Hill and Watkins in 1894. The present owner and editor, Webb Watkins, bought out the interest of Mr. Hill in 1899. *The Messenger* is Democratic in politics and is not only one of the old papers of this section, but also one of its influential papers as well.

The *Dexter Statesman* is published at Dexter, its editor and proprietor being Edmund P. Crowe. The paper is classed as an independent Democratic paper. *The Statesman* was formerly the Sikeston, Missouri, *Enterprise*, which was established in Sikeston in 1883. *The Enterprise* was published and controlled by a number of people, the last of whom was M. G. Gresham, by whom it was sold to E. P. Crowe in 1910. Crowe removed the entire plant to Dexter and has continued the publication of the paper since that time.

The *Puxico Index* was established by E. J. Hickman in 1895. Later it was published for a time by G. N. Wynenger. It is at present under control of Marion Harty. The *Index* has always been Democratic in its political affiliations.

The *Essex Leader* is published at Essex in Stoddard county and is owned and edited by D. O. C. Brydon. The publication of the paper was begun May 15, 1908, by Mr. Brydon, who has owned it continuously since that time. It is a live paper and very much devoted to the agricultural and business interests of Essex and the surrounding country.

Advance has no paper at present, though for a time one was published there. This was the *Advance Guard*, which was established in 1903 by G. M. Brydon. He continued it for some years.

The *Bernie Star*, an independent paper, was established in 1905 by J. B. Daniels. Later John Russell published it. Others interested in it were DeWitt Henderson and O. B. Parrott. The present editor is Claud Wilkins, and *The Star* is independent in its politics.

The first newspaper published in Washington county was *The Miners' Prospect*, established at Potosi September, 1846, by Phillip G. Ferguson and F. A. Dalla. It was an independent paper and passed out of existence in 1849. The next paper established in the county was *The Washington County Miner*, which was published by N. P. Buck, beginning in 1856 and was discontinued in 1861. After the war, George B. Clark established *The Washington County Journal*, in 1867, and transferred it to Eli D. Ake in 1872. He soon removed it to Ironton. The *Potosi Independent* was established in 1873 by Frank Harris, who published it until his death in 1886. It was sold to Henry C. Bell in 1888. The *Potosi Free Press* was started by Jesse W. Homan in 1886, but was soon discontinued. In 1888 *The Potosi Eagle* began a publication as an independent paper and had a struggle for existence for a few years and finally passed out of existence. Another paper was *The Republican*, established in 1887, and published for a short time. The *Washington County Journal* was established in August, 1894, by F. M. Deggendorf. *The Independent* and *The Journal* have had an unusual history. Since Henry C. Bell purchased *The Independent* in 1886 he has continued its publication without change, and Mr. Deggendorf has been in charge of *The Journal* since he became connected with it in 1894. These long terms of service bespeak unusual success in the conduct of papers, as measured by the standards of Southeast Missouri. *The Independent* is Democratic while its rival, *The Journal*, is Republican in politics.

There have been some other ventures in the newspaper field in Washington county, which have not proved so successful. About 1901, Will D. Wright began to issue two papers at Belgrade. One of these was an independent paper called *The Messenger*, and the other was religious and was named the *Farmington District Messenger*. They were soon discontinued. Soon afterward Dean Gibson began the issuance of the *Washington County Gazette* at Irondale. The office was later removed.

The first newspaper published in Piedmont, Wayne county, was called *The Banner*. It was founded in 1872 by Banks and Crawford. They soon sold out, however, to S. B. Sprowl, who removed the paper to Patterson and published it under the name of *Patterson Times* until 1876; he then came back to Piedmont with the paper and after a few months discontinued its publication. In March, 1878, *The Vindicator* was established by B. E. H. Warren. About the close of that year *The Vindicator* was sold to T. L. Roussin and moved to Bloomfield, where it was published under the title of the *Bloomfield Vindicator*. In 1885 G. Y. Gale established *The Piedmont Rambler* and somewhat later the paper became known as *The Piedmont Leader* and was published by W. B. Harris. The office with all of its material was destroyed by fire in 1888. In 1892 *The Piedmont Weekly Banner* was established by Dr. J. N. Holmes,

who continued its publication for a time and then sold out to Charles Mitchim. After Mitchim's ownership the paper was published for a time by Rev. Mr. Wilson, W. H. Lewis and others. In 1905 Lewis sold *The Banner* to the present owner and editor, Bristol French. Mr. French proceeded to put the office in good condition, equipping it with modern machinery and presses. *The Banner* is a Democratic paper.

Some other ventures at Piedmont have been *Crucible*, a religious paper published by the Christian Publishing Company. This was in 1893 and the enterprise came to an end within a few months. John Marsh at about the same time published *The Herald*, which was a Republican paper. It, too, soon disappeared.

A number of papers have been published in Greenville, Wayne county. The first of these was *The Reporter*, established about 1869, by C. P. Rotrock and afterward published by Frank C. Neely & Company. A. W. Banks began the publication of the *Greenville Democrat* in March, 1872. This paper, however, was afterwards removed to Piedmont in 1876. The *Weekly Journal* was established by J. N. Morrison, who continued its publication about two years and was succeeded by John T. Rhodes. Rhodes sold the paper in 1881 to A. T. Lacey and he in turn transferred it to John G. Settle in 1886. It then passed into the control of J. N. Holmes, who at the same time conducted with great success the *Piedmont Banner*. It was afterward transferred to a number of persons. Clarence Carleton published it for a time, as did C. C. Mitchim.

It is now owned by G. W. Stiver and William B. Kennedy. Mr. Kennedy is the editor of the paper, which is Democratic in politics.

The *Greenville Sun* was established in 1894 by S. A. Bates. It was issued as the organ of the Republicans in Wayne county, the rival paper, *The Journal*, being Democratic. Later the paper was published by J. S. Marsh. At the present time its editor is Chas. Barrow. It is still Republican in politics.

The *Williamsville Iron News* was established in 1905. The principal purpose in publishing the paper was to push the iron ore industry in the county, which had its center at Williamsville. It is independent in politics. Before *The News*, W. D. Wright had published an independent paper called the *Buzz-Saw*, which was soon discontinued.

The record of newspapers in this section, incomplete as it must be, is a long one. It includes the names of many papers, some of them at present prosperous and active, many others long since discontinued and almost, if not quite, forgotten. Such a list indicates the strong attraction which newspaper work has for many men, and the feeling of the necessity of the establishment of papers in this part of the state.

To the men who have labored at the great task of giving this section adequate newspaper facilities is due a great debt. The task of circulating newspapers here was a herculean one. The wrecks which strew the path of journalistic progress is sufficient attestation of that fact. It was a task which must be performed. Few appreciate the tremendous importance of the local paper in the development of the life of a community. Too often it is referred to with a sneer and compared to its great disadvantage with the metropolitan daily. Its limitations are apparent. Much less apparent, but far greater is its usefulness to the community. It is safe to say that the newspapers of Southeast Missouri have been one of the strong forces for upbuilding this section. No great movement for public improvement has been pushed to success or doubtless could have been pushed to success without the aid and support of the local papers. They have formed the medium of exchange for ideas, a forum for discussion, a means of comparison of one part of the territory with another. Drainage, railroads, education, religion, all of these and scores of other enterprises have received help from the papers.

Too often this contribution to the good of the public has been gift for which no adequate return has been received. The papers which have ceased to exist here did not go out of existence because their editors desired to give up their work. In most cases the failure was due to a lack of financial support. Small subscription lists and little advertising have caused the downfall of most of the papers that are no longer published.

As one goes over the roll of the papers he is struck by the number of times that a few names occur. Certain members of the profession have had experience in many places and on many papers. These were the men for whom the life of the editor had an attraction too strong to be resisted. Not meeting with the desired success in one place they have sought it in another. The conclusion is forced upon us in many cases that some really quit the profession because of lack of returns from it and then found its lure too strong. Sometimes they have at last found the opportunity for which they sought and achieved that prosperity which their talents and industry richly deserved. Others were less fortunate and finally drifted away from the work they loved, into other fields.

It is not possible to review the work of all the worthy men whose names live on the pages of the papers of this section. From T

E. Strange, that first member of the profession in this part of the state until this present time, there have always been men whose lives and work have adorned the profession of letters. Whitcomb and Martin, of Charleston, McGuire and Kies, of Jackson, Ake of Ironton, Fisher of Farmington, Bell and Deggendorf, of Potosi, Allen of New Madrid, Caruthers of Kennett, Roussin and Holmes, of Piedmont, Flynn of Cape Girardeau, Watkins and Stokes, of Dexter, Mitchim of DeSoto, McMullin of Hillsboro, Ernst and Janis, of Ste. Genevieve, among the older men have been distinguished for ability, long service and great usefulness. Other men have contributed to the total of journalistic usefulness in great measure also. The younger men of this day are pressing the work and advancing the profession to greater influence. Some of the most powerful and successful papers are now in the hands of men who have not been long connected with the profession in this part of the state.

It remains to be said that it is a matter of deep regret that there is not to be found complete files of all these papers. They contain much of the history of the times. Out of them must be dug much of that intimate acquaintance with the course of events and lives of men which makes the story of a country's progress real and vital.

CHAPTER XXXIX

SOME BIOGRAPHIES

Louis Houck—Lownes H. Davis—Robert H. Whitelaw — William B. Wilson — Judge John W. Emerson—Samuel S. Hildebrand—Samuel Byrns—B. B. Cahoon—James D. Fox—J. J. Russell—H. J. Deal—Absalom McElmurry — William Dawson — Joseph Hunter—John A. Mott—Robert A. Hatcher—Eliza A. Carleton—William Carter —Placide DeLassus—James R. McCormack—Milton P. Cayce—Gustavus St. Gem—Charles S. Hertich— M. L. Clardy— Marshall Arnold — James P. Walker — N. B. Henry—F. P. Graves—Firmin Desloge.

A separate volume of this history is given to the biographies of men and women who have had to do with making history in this part of the state. It is concerned largely with those who are still in active life. A few men whose work has ended, and a few who for special reasons have been prominently connected with the development of Southeast Missouri by reason of official or business relations, are mentioned in the following pages. The list includes only those connected with the history of the period since the war. Others who were active before that time have been discussed in other sections of this work.

Perhaps Southeast Missouri owes more to Louis Houck, of Cape Girardeau, than to any other one of its citizens for it was due to his energy and ability that this section of the state was supplied with railroad facilities. The impulse toward development given by the network of railroads constructed by him has had a remarkable influence in building up the country and in causing the construction of other lines and systems of railroads. Mr. Houck is a native of Illinois and is now seventy-one years of age. His early life was spent in Illinois and part of it in his father's printing office. He received two years' training at the University of Wisconsin and then published a paper for a time, but later began the study of law in 1862 in the office of William H. Underwood. Until 1868 he practiced law at Belleville and in that year removed to St. Louis and became assistant United States attorney under General John W. Noble. He became a resident of Cape Girardeau in 1869, engaging in the general practice of law until 1881. Mr. Houck became known as one of the most active and resourceful attorneys in Southeast Missouri. He was a diligent student and a man of unlimited energy. In addition to his work as a practitioner he published a number of legal texts and was also the editor of the 15th volume of Missouri Reports.

Although his profession had absorbed his energy to a considerable extent and although he found himself amply fitted for its work, Mr. Houck turned to other fields of labor. He had become interested in the resources of this section of the state and determined to begin the building of railroads. From 1881 up to the present time he has been engaged in this work. In the chapter on railroads an account is given of his activities. Southeast Missouri owes to him, however, more than simply a debt for railroad building. It is due as much to his ability as a writer as to any other one cause that the resources and opportunities of Southeast Missouri have been made known to the state at large. Numbers of articles have been contributed by him to papers and magazines in which he has set out with force and skill the situation actually existing in this part of the state. During all the years of his active life here he has given most intelligent attention to collecting material relating to the history of the state. His private library is one of the best and largest in Missouri and in spite of the numerous occupations which have engaged him, he has devoted himself to the preparation of an adequate account of the early days in Missouri. His history of Missouri from the earliest time to the formation of the state government is a monumental work which represents years of study, the accumulation of a great deal of material, and the expenditure of large sums of money. It is not a mere composition from second-hand authorities but has resulted from patient inquiry into sources of early history. A companion work, The Spanish Regime, is an account of the Spanish rule, containing translations of all the old documents relating to the government of Missouri during the Spanish period, many of these having never before been translated.

It is doubtful, however, if the great work which Mr. Houck has wrought both as a railroad builder and as a student of history outweighs his service to the state as a regent of the State Normal School at Cape Girardeau. For more than a quarter of a century he has been president of the Board of Regents and during that time has been active and untiring in his work for that great institution. To him perhaps, more than to any other one man is due the credit for its buildings and continued growth. He has given it the best service of his life and his wide experience, his untiring energy and the respect and confidence in which he is held by a large circle of acquaintances throughout the state have enabled him to secure a consideration for the claims of the school not possible otherwise to be obtained.

Lownes H. Davis was born at Jackson December 14, 1836. He received a good education, being graduated at Yale College in 1860, and at the Louisville Law School in 1863. After his graduation he began the practice of law at Jackson, and in 1868 was elected prosecuting attorney, serving for four years. Later he was a member of the State Legislature and in 1878 was elected to the 46th Congress and was twice reelected. He is a Democrat and recognized by his associates as a man of ability and uprightness of character.

Robert H. Whitelaw is a native of Virginia, coming to Cape Girardeau with his parents in 1862. He was educated in the public schools and in the law school of the University of Michigan. He began the practice of law at Cape Girardeau and in a short time became interested in politics. He was prosecuting attorney of Cape Girardeau from 1874 to 1878, and from 1881 to 1885 was a representative in the general assembly. In 1890 he was elected to congress serving one term and then returning to Cape Girardeau to take up the practice of law. Since 1899 he has been city attorney of Cape Girardeau.

William B. Wilson was born near Appleton, January 12, 1831, his family having been residents of Cape Girardeau county since 1808. Dr. Wilson was educated in private schools and in the medical school of the University of New York, from which he graduated in 1852. After his graduation he began the practice of medicine in Cape Girardeau and continued it until his death in October, 1900. He was a very prominent citizen of Cape Girardeau and was well known especially for his connection with the Masonic order, in which he held high rank. He was regarded as a very upright and able man and while never engaging in politics, held a number of positions, having been a member of the council, school director, and member of the board of regents of the State Normal School.

Judge John W. Emerson, a native of New England, came to Missouri as a millwright; he made his home in Arcadia and after a time began the study of law with Judge Pipkin; after his admission to the bar he became a very successful lawyer. He was a soldier during the war and at its close was appointed a judge of the 15th judicial circuit, serving for only a short time, however. Judge Emerson was not only a good lawyer but possessed considerable literary ability, having written several poems and a number of essays and addresses. His former home in Arcadia is one of the most beautiful places in Missouri and it was under a tree at this place that Grant received his commission as a brigadier general.

The troublesome period of the Civil war and the times immediately following it produced a number of men whose names became widely known on account of their exploits as leaders of bands, sometimes of soldiers and sometimes of guerrillas. No man in Southeast Missouri achieved a wider reputation of this sort than Samuel S. Hildebrand, who was a member of a pioneer family of Missouri, the Hildebrands being some of the earliest settlers of Jefferson county. At the time of the breaking out of the war a brother of Samuel Hildebrand. named Frank, was hanged by a vigilance committee in Ste. Genevieve county. This and other wrongs stirred the sense of injustice in Hildebrand and he set out to achieve a desperate revenge. The men who were instrumental in hanging his brother Frank. were shot and killed one after another. He took part in the war on the southern side and became very famous on account of his operations; he held a major's commission in the Missouri State Guard, issued by General Jeff Thompson. At the close of the war he continued his depredations and finally left Missouri and made his way to Arkansas and then to Texas. His later history is in doubt; some say he became a resident of Illinois where he was killed, other accounts have it that he is still living. Hildebrand was tall, rawboned with high cheek bones, a pallid complexion and blue eyes that were cold and expressionless. He was a man who probably had no fear, possessed great determination and was a most excellent marksman. He became thoroughly acquainted with the country in which he operated and possessed some of the Indian ability to know the country and to make his way about it from one place to another. There is a cave on Big river near the north line of St. Francois county, known as Hildebrand's cave; its entrance is about 40 feet above the head of the stream and it can be approached by. only one man at a time. It is said that

Hildebrand made this cave his headquarters at various times, especially on one occasion when he was recovering from a gun shot wound.

Samuel Byrns, a native of Jefferson county, was born March 4, 1848. He was reared on the farm, received a good English education, studied law, was admitted to the bar and began the practice of his profession at Hillsboro. He soon became known as a good lawyer, established a practice, and took an active part in politics. In 1876 he was a presidential elector and cast a vote for Tilden and Hendricks. In 1877 he was a member of the house of representatives of the legislature. In 1878 he became a member of the senate and served four years. He was a member of the Democratic state committee from 1886 to 1888, and in the latter year was again a presidential elector, voting for Cleveland. He became a member of congress in 1890 and served with distinction. At the close of his first term he returned to the practice of law. He was always interested in public affairs and a leading figure in everything looking to the upbuilding of the community.

Benjamin Benson Cahoon was born in 1846, in Delaware. After receiving a common school education and being admitted to the practice of law in the District of Columbia, he came to Fredericktown in 1868. Shortly after his arrival he was married to Miss Bell LeCompte of Ste. Genevieve, who was a member of one of the old French families of Missouri. Mr. Cahoon built up a large law practice and was soon recognized as one of the leading attorneys in Madison county. He was elected prosecuting attorney in 1870, but after the close of his term he declined to become a candidate for any other office. He has always been interested in party movements, being a Republican but is a man of liberal views. It was due in part to his work that the liberal movement in Missouri to enfranchise former Confederate soldiers was successful. One of his interests is in connection with the development of water transportation and the improvement of the Mississippi river.

James D. Fox was born in Madison county January 23, 1847. He was educated in the common schools at Fredericktown and at St. Louis University, was admitted to the bar in 1866, and began the practice of law at Fredericktown. He came to be known as a good lawyer and established a large practice. He was elected judge of the 27th judicial circuit in 1880, and held the position until 1904, when he was elected a member of the supreme court, a position which he still holds. Mr. Fox is a Democrat.

Joseph J. Russell, of Charleston, Missouri, was born August 23, 1854, and is a native of Mississippi county. His grandfather, James A. Russell, came to Mississippi county from Maryland in 1836. Joseph J. Russell was reared on a farm and attended a country school; at the age of nineteen he began to teach and continued his education at the Charleston Academy. In 1876, after having studied law in the office of Moore and Hatcher, he was admitted to the bar and was afterward graduated from the law department of the University of Missouri. He was successful in the practice of law from the beginning and acquired a large and valuable practice. Mr. Russell was school commissioner of Mississippi county for two years and prosecuting attorney from 1880 to 1884. In 1884 he was a presidential elector on the Democratic ticket and in 1886 he was a representative from Mississippi county in the general assembly of the state and served as speaker of the house. In 1900 he was elected to congress as a representative of the 14th congressional district and was again elected to the same position in 1910. He has won for himself a place in congress by his ability and close attention to the duties of his position. He is held in high esteem by those who know him well and is regarded as one of the ablest men in this part of the state.

One of the pioneer families of Southeast Missouri is the Deal family. The oldest one of this family to live in this part of the state was Colonel H. J. Deal, who was born in Pennsylvania in 1829. He learned the tanner's trade and worked at this until he was nineteen years of age when he went west. At first he was employed for a time in Farmington, Iowa, then for two years he lived in St. Louis. In 1856, after his marriage, he came to Charleston in Mississippi county. At first he engaged in the business of building levees and digging ditches, but in 1857 he took a contract for building the Cairo & Fulton Railroad. At the breaking out of the war he had finished building twenty-seven miles of this road, but nothing further was done in contract work during the war. The representative in congress from this district at that time was Robert A. Hatcher, who resigned his position, however, and attached himself to the fortunes of the South. Mr. Deal was elected to succeed him; he served for one year and then became a member of the state senate. In 1868 he was elected representative from Mississippi county in the legislature, and was later re-elected for another term.

During the war Colonel Deal was appointed by the governor to enlist men in a number of counties in Southeast Missouri; he was given the rank of colonel of enrolled militia and served in the capacity of a recruiting officer during the war. On the close of the war Colonel Deal once more took up his former work of contracting. In 1866 he began the work of building fifty miles of the St. Louis & Iron Mountain Railroad; this work he completed within a year. In 1867 he finished up the work of the Cairo & Fulton Railroad to Poplar Bluff. In 1881 he took a contract for building one hundred and ten miles of the St. Louis, Arkansas & Texas Railroad, which he completed in 1882; after that time he turned his attention to farming and stock raising. He secured large tracts of land in Mississippi county which became very valuable and up to the end of his life he was interested in farming in all of its branches. Colonel Deal was a public spirited citizen and always interested in whatever work was to be done for the improvement of his community and his county; his interest was manifested on more than one occasion by building public roads at his own expense.

In 1806 Absalom McElmurry, a native of Kentucky, moved from that state to Southeast Missouri. In a short time he removed to Little Rock, Arkansas, but returned to Mississippi county, Missouri, in 1813. He was the first judge of the county, being appointed in 1843. His eldest son, Thomas S. McElmurry, was born near Charleston, in 1815; he was reared on the farm and attended the public schools in the vicinity. After becoming a man, he interested himself in politics and held a number of offices in the county. at one time he was interested in the mercantile business, but during the latter part of his life he devoted himself to farming. Judge McElmurry lived to a great age and was one of the best known citizens of the county. He had an unusual experience in that he lived in a territory under the Federal government, under the Confederate government and in three different counties and yet all the time on the same farm.

The Dawson family has been for many years one of the most prominent in New Madrid county. Dr. Robert D. Dawson, a native of Maryland, who came to New Madrid county in 1800, was the founder of the family in Missouri. He was one of the most prominent citizens in this part of the state. William Dawson is his grandson; he was educated in the Christian Brothers College of St. Louis. After some experience as a teacher he was admitted to the practice of law and engaged in the practice in New Madrid. He was elected sheriff in 1870, and re-elected in 1872, he then served three terms in the legislature, and in 1884 was elected to congress as a representative of the Fourteenth Congressional district. Mr. Dawson is a Democrat and holds the esteem of those who are acquainted with him.

One of the most prominent citizens of New Madrid county was Joseph Hunter. He was a native of Scott county, a son of Hon. Abraham Hunter, he was born in 1823, coming to New Madrid in 1843. His second wife was Elizabeth Russell of Cape Girardeau county, a member of one of the pioneer families of that county. Mr. Hunter was engaged in farming until the breaking out of the Civil war, when he joined the Second Missouri Cavalry and served until its close. He then returned to New Madrid county, where he resided until his death. His descendants are prominent in the county until this time.

John A. Mott was a native of Kentucky and came to New Madrid in 1852. He was born in 1826 and grew to manhood in Hickman, Kentucky, spending his youth in school and in his father's store. In 1850 he went to California and spent two years in the mining region returning to New Madrid in 1852. For several years he was engaged in the mercantile business and as an employee of the American Express Company and also as a farmer. In 1858 he was appointed clerk and recorder of the circuit court, a position which he held for more than thirty-five years. He died in 1908.

In 1848 Robert A. Hatcher came to New Madrid and took a position as clerk on the steamer Selma; within a short period, however, the boat was sold for debt and Mr. Hatcher began the study of law with William S. Moseley, who had been the captain of the Selma. He was a man who made friends rapidly and had a turn for political life as is shown by the fact that two years after coming to New Madrid he was elected representative in the legislature. After serving one term he resigned and engaged in the mercantil business with D. V. LeSieur; he found this employment uncongenial, however, and sold out his business and began the practice of his profession. He was very successful and established a good practice. During the war Mr. Hatcher's sympathies were with the South and he became a member of the Confederate congress. At the close of the war he returned to the practice of law at New Madrid until his election to congress in 1872, a place he held for four years. In 1877 he removed to Charleston where he lived until the time of his death.

One of the women who during this period of our history exercised a good influence on affairs, was Eliza A. Carleton. She was born in Montgomery county, Virginia, in 1826. She received a common school education in Virginia and was afterwards sent to school in South Bend, Indiana. She came to Missouri with her grandfather and in the spring of 1843 began her work as a teacher. This was in district No. 31, at Hickory Cabin schoolhouse in Perry township, St. Francis county. Miss Carleton received $3.00 in trade or $2.00 in cash for each pupil taught. With the proceeds of her teaching she attended Arcadia College and was graduated with the degree Master of Arts. Miss Carleton was a teacher at heart, and after her graduation continued the work. She was impressed with the necessity of some further opportunities for education than were offered then to the youth of Southeast Missouri. Being a woman of initiative and development, Miss Carleton determined to build such a school herself. Accordingly, in April, 1854, she opened a school eight miles north of Farmington, under the name of Carleton Institute, it being so called in honor of her father. About thirty pupils attended this school which was incorporated by an act of the legislature, March 4, 1859. To the work of this institution she gave her entire time and attention. In 1878 this school was moved to Farmington where was erected a large and commodious brick building in the midst of attractive surroundings. Up till her death Miss Carleton remained in close connection with the school and lived to see it become a prosperous and influential institution. She was a consistent and devoted member of the Methodist Episcopal church and through her work undoubtedly influenced for good the lives of many young people in this part of the state.

The Carter family came to Missouri from South Carolina. The head of the family was Zimri Carter, who made a settlement on Current river, in what is now Carter county, about 1813. Zimri Carter was one of the most influential and prominent men in Southeast Missouri. He was judge of the county court and the county was named for him. One of the children of the family was Hon. William Carter, born in 1830. He was educated in the common schools and also at Arcadia College. He then attended a Louisville law school and was graduated in law in 1855, beginning his practice at Potosi and then removing to Farmington in 1862. In 1864 he was elected circuit judge of the 20th circuit, which included the counties of Washington, Iron, St. Francis, Madison, Perry and Ste. Genevieve. He held this office until in 1874; he was then elected a member of the general assembly of the state where he was made chairman of the judiciary committee. Since that time he has devoted himself to the practice of law, but has held other positions of honor at the same time. For a number of years he was one of the curators of the University of Missouri.

Placide DeLassus was born in New Orleans June 28, 1839, and was the grandson of Charles de Hault DeLassus, who was lieutenant governor of Upper Louisiana at the time of the transfer to the United States. Governor DeLassus received many grants of land from the Spanish government; one of these was a tract in St. Francois county, Missouri, on which the village of DeLassus was located. The family was a very prominent one in Missouri, some of them living in St. Francois county and others in Perry county. Placide DeLassus was educated in New Orleans and in France. He served throughout the war in the Confederate army. He lived for a time after the war in St. Louis where he married Miss Mary Clark, the daughter of

Henry L. Clark. In 1868 he moved to De-Lassus in St. Francois county, where he continued to live until his death. He owned during all his life the greater part of the grants made by the Spanish government to his grandfather.

One of the prominent persons of Southeast Missouri during this period was General James R. McCormack, of Farmington, Missouri. He was born August 1, 1824, in Washington county. He was educated in the common schools and in Transylvania Institute in Kentucky. He was graduated from the Memphis Medical College and practiced medicine for a time in Wayne county and in Perry county. On the breaking out of the war he was appointed surgeon of the Sixth Infantry of Missouri. These men were enlisted for a term of six months and at the expiration of their term, Dr. McCormack was made brigadier general for Southeast Missouri. The brigade consisted of seven regiments and General McCormack remained in command until the close of the war. He was regarded as a good officer and was held in esteem by his superiors. At the close of the war he practiced his profession for a time at Arcadia and later became a citizen of Farmington, Missouri. General McCormack had some experience in politics, having been a member of the constitutional convention in 1861 and later serving in the state senate and in 1867 being elected to fill a vacancy in the United States congress. He was interested in public affairs in his community and was regarded as one of its most prominent and influential citizens.

Milton P. Cayce was a Virginian, having been born in that state in 1804. He was reared on a farm and then served as a salesman in a store. He came to Farmington in 1832 and began the conduct of a general store. He continued as a merchant for more than fifty years and during that time accumulated considerable property. Besides his mercantile business he was also a contractor and the owner of a flouring mill. He had other interests, among them a tan yard and several farms. The first ice house in St. Francois county was built by Mr. Cayce, and he is said to have owned the first piano. Mr. Cayce was a Democrat and served for more than twenty years as county treasurer. He was also a sheriff at one time in the county and was a member of the constitutional convention in 1861. Few men in the history of Farmington occupy a higher place in the esteem and respect of the citizens than did Mr. Cayce.

One of the interesting men of this period was Captain Gustavus St. Gem. He was a member of the old St. Gem family, one of the earliest families to emigrate from France to America. They seem to have located in Ste. Genevieve about 1780, and that during all the rest of the history of the town were among its prominent citizens. Gustavus St. Gem was educated at St. Vincent's College at Cape Girardeau. On returning from college he engaged in business in Ste. Genevieve for a time and then removed to Washington county, where he became interested in mining. During the war he was an officer in the Federal army and served with credit during the entire time. He was captain of Company K of the Forty-seventh Missouri Infantry. In 1878, President Hayes appointed him collector of customs in St. Louis. Captain St. Gem lived to be very old and died having the universal respect of his friends and neighbors in Ste. Genevieve.

Dr. Charles S. Hertich was the son of Joseph Hertich, a native of Switzerland. He was born in Ste. Genevieve in 1821. His father was the master of the famous school in Ste. Genevieve known as The Asylum. It has been pointed out in another place that this school was the first in Missouri to put into practice the principles of education set out by Pestalozzi. Dr. Hertich was educated in this school himself and afterwards became a teacher in it, assisting his father. He then studied medicine at Burlington, Iowa, and later at the St. Louis Medical College. He was for a time a United States surgeon to the Indians at Long Prairie, Minnesota. During the war he served as post surgeon of Ste. Genevieve. From the close of the war until 1878, he continued the practice of medicine in Ste. Genevieve, at that time he was afflicted by a stroke of paralysis which kept him partially helpless until his death. His wife was a daughter of Ferdinand Rozier.

Martin L. Clardy was born in Ste. Genevieve county April 26, 1844, and was educated in the common schools, in St. Louis University and in the University of Virginia. After his graduation he began the study of law and devoted himself to its practice, making his home for a number of years in DeLassus in St. Francois county. He acquired considerable political experience and in 1882 was chosen a member of congress as a Democrat and was twice reelected; after the conclusion of his third term in 1888, he removed to St. Louis, where he became one of the principal attorneys for the Missouri Pacific Railroad Company. Mr. Clardy is recognized as one of the leading lawyers and politicians of the state.

Marshall Arnold, one of the best known lawyers in Southeast Missouri was born in St. Francois county on October 21, 1845. He lived the usual life of a farmer boy, received an education in the common schools and in Arcadia College. In 1870 he was a teacher in Arcadia College. He served for a time as deputy clerk of the county, circuit, and probate courts of St. Francois county and during this time began the study of law. He later removed to Scott county where he opened a law office and soon established a reputation as an able lawyer. He was elected prosecuting attorney and later served two terms in the legislature of the state. In 1884 he was presidential elector on the Hancock ticket and in 1890 was elected to congress from the 14th congressional district as a Democrat. He was reelected in 1892 by a very large majority. but was defeated in 1894 by N. A. Moseley, a Republican. Since that time Mr. Arnold has devoted most of his energy to the practice of his profession. He is recognized as one of the ablest criminal lawyers in this section of the state and is a forceful and eloquent speaker.

James P. Walker was born in Lauderdale county, Tennessee, March 4, 1851. He came to Missouri early in his life and made his home in Stoddard county. Mr. Walker soon won the confidence of the people and came to be known as a man of marked ability. In 1886 he was nominated by the Democrats for congress from the 14th district and was elected by a large majority. In congress he made a splendid record for himself and seemed to be entering upon a career of great usefulness and influence. Before the close of the term, however, he died, putting an end to a very promising life.

Nelson B. Henry, a minister of the Methodist Episcopal Church South, was born July 23, 1848, near Burfordville, Missouri. He is a grandson of John D. Cook, one of the pioneers of Missouri and for a number of years a circuit judge of this state. The father of Nelson B. Henry was also a Methodist preacher and for many years one of the most prominent in Southeast Missouri. Mr. Henry, who is now pastor of the Methodist church at Bonne Terre, was reared on the farm, received a good education, being graduated from the State Normal School at Kirksville in 1876. After his graduation he became principal of the high school at Oak Ridge, serving two years. In 1878 he became a member of the faculty of the State Normal School at Cape Girardeau, teaching English and literature and holding the position until 1886, when he was elected to the chair of pedagogy in the University of North Carolina. From this position he resigned to become president of the Pueblo Collegiate Institute at Pueblo, Colorado, in 1888. Here he remained until 1892 when he was elected president of the Bellevue Collegiate Institute at Caledonia. He filled this position two years and then resigned to become the presiding elder of the Farmington district. He held this position one year and then became president of the Marvin Collegiate Institute at Fredericktown. Mr. Henry assisted in the organization of this school and did much to develop it. He resigned, however, after a few years and entered upon the work of the ministry, which he still continues. While he was teacher of the high school at Oak Ridge in 1876 he began an agitation which resulted in the organization of the Southeast Missouri Teachers Association of which he became the first president.

Another man who has been closely associated with the development of the lead industry in Southeast Missouri is F. P. Graves, who was born in Rochester, New York, in 1849. After receiving a good education he came to Missouri and found employment in the St. Joseph lead mines at Bonne Terre; this was about the year 1869. Before coming to Missouri he had had some experience in lead mines in Massachusetts. When he first became connected with the St. Joseph Lead Company he worked in the mill and the shops, but after two years was made cashier of the company and held this position for seventeen years. In 1887 he became connected with the Doe Run Lead Company, assisting in its organization and becoming its secretary and assistant superintendent. Under his direction the company prospered greatly and the Doe Run mines became one of the chief lead producing centers in this part of the state. Mr. Graves has found time from his connection with the lead industry to take an intelligent and active interest in public affairs. He served as postmaster at Doe Run from 1887 to 1891 and has been a consistent party worker though never a candidate for public office. Mr. Graves gathered one of the finest collections of minerals in the state, and it has been a feature of a number of great expositions in this country.

Firmin DesLoge, whose name is connected with the development of the mining district of Southeast Missouri, was born at Potosi in Washington county. His father was a native of Nantes, France, who came to Potosi while a young man and engaged in a mercantile and lead-mining business. Firmin DesLoge was educated at Potosi and at St. Louis University, and began his business career as a clerk for the firm of John B. Valle & Company of St. Louis. In 1867 he gave up his position and turned his attention to mining operations at Potosi. He was one of the first men to become interested in the mining prospects of St. Francois county. He purchased land adjacent to the plant of the St. Joseph Lead Company and built a smelting plant for the corporation known as the DesLoge Lead Company. Mr. DesLoge managed this company until it was sold in 1887 to the St. Joseph Lead Company. During his connection with this corporation he helped to build the first railroad, the Bonne Terre & Mississippi Valley Railroad, which penetrated the lead regions to St. Francois county. Later Mr. DesLoge bought property which had belonged to the Bogy Lead Mine Company and the St. Francois Mining Company and organized a new corporation known as the DesLoge Consolidated Lead Company. The Bonne Terre Railroad was extended to these mines which were operated on a large scale. Not only was he interested in the development of the mining industry in which he acquired considerable wealth, but Mr. DesLoge was interested in public affairs; he served as treasurer of Washington county and on various occasions was a director of public schools. The town of DesLoge, now one of the prosperous mining communities of St. Francois county, was named in his honor.

JUDGE THOMAS EDWARD BALDWIN. There is one mystery in this brief life and that mystery is death. What we call history is a long procession of human beings, reaching back into the ages, who arrive on this earth, act, hate, love, accumulate, strive and then go back. Each one of us has one spark of life and then death, the mystery of the unknown. The thought of death should stimulate a man to better work and harder work, that he may shine in some way while his little spark is still a light. Whether Thomas Edward Baldwin ever reflected just along these lines or not, the fact is that he made the most of his life while he was here and when the spark went out, reflections from it still remain.

He was born in Cape Girardeau, Missouri, October 23, 1849, and died May 27, 1904, at Kennett, Missouri. His father, Thomas Baldwin, was born in Scott county, Missouri, November 16, 1810. He married Elizabeth Lobdell, and both died in 1859, when the Judge was but ten years of age. John Baldwin, father of Thomas, was born in Berkeley county, Virginia, October 26, 1771; and married Rachel Wellbourne, January 28, 1796, in Washington county, Georgia. The family came from Georgia to Missouri in 1803, locating at what, in the early days was known as Baldwin's Landing, in Scott county, Missouri. John Baldwin was a descendant of one of three brothers who, in 1643, came from England and settled at New Haven, Connecticut. One of these brothers later removed to Virginia and is the progenitor of this branch of the family.

Judge Baldwin was as a boy thrown upon his own resources and got what education was possible in the schools of Cape Girardeau, where he remained until twenty-one years of age. He then came on the old road to Clarkton, Dunklin county, Missouri, where he clerked in a store owned by Mr. Whitelaw. Previous to that time, however, he had clerked for Leech and Company at Cape Girardeau. Young as he was, he was appointed Circuit and County Clerk to fill a vacancy soon after coming to Clarkton, which necessitated his living in Kennett. Subsequently in 1878, he was elected and in 1880 re-elected to the same office and by that time had decided to remain in Kennett. In 1882 he was elected probate judge, serving four years, during the last two of which he was also county treasurer.

Judge Baldwin became a partner of W. F. Shelton in a general store at Kennett in 1886, under the firm name of W. F. Shelton & Company.

For four years he remained in the store as book-keeper and credit man, at the end of which time he sold out his share to his partner, buying a drug store on the site of the present Baldwin Drug Store. The store had formerly been owned by the late Dr. A. B. Mobley. After conducting the drug store for two or three years he erected a brick block, in which he installed his drug store. His building and the one erected by W. F. Shelton about the same time, 1892, were the first brick buildings in Kennett. He continued to manage the drug store until 1896, when he sold out to O. S. Harrison, who had been his druggist. He next became interested in real estate and was for years agent of the Great Chouteau lands, but in addition to this he bought and sold on his own account. At one time he owned several thousand acres of swamp land, four thousand acres in one tract. At the time of his death he owned two thousand acres and a three hundred and twenty acre farm near Kennett that he had cleared. He laid out Rose Park Addition to Kennett, selling the lots himself. He was an organizer of the Bank of Kennett, being its president until a few months before he died, his interest still remaining in the bank. He was always ready to do anything he could for the betterment of the town and also served the county as its representative in the state legislature. He was a Democrat, always active in county and local campaigns.

In 1872 he married Mary J. Pankey, daughter of Dr. G. Pankey. Her father was born at Richmond, Virginia, where he received his education, being brought up on the farm. He became a tobacco grower and dealer in the south, owning a great number of slaves to cultivate and pick the tobacco. He always treated them in the most considerate manner and they were devoted to him. He married Miss Sally Jones, a charming Southern woman, a native of Richmond like himself. All business was beginning to be very much demoralized in the south and Mr. Pankey was losing money on his plantation. He therefore sold off everything he possessed, except his slaves. These he brought with him to Missouri, settling at Clarkton, where he bought a small farm and started a store. In 1861, when the war broke out, he raised a regiment for the Confederate army, he being its Colonel. He served throughout the war, at the end of which time he set his slaves free, but they never lost the feelings of affection and devotion towards him, but would have cheerfully laid down their lives for him at any time. One of them, Charles Birthwright, with his wife Bettie, live in Clarkton and are leaders among the colored people of that town. Colonel Pankey lived in Cardwell, Missouri, later, where he died in January, 1910, at the age of seventy-four, his wife having died many years before. The Colonel served the county as county collector. He was a man who had served the country both in the army and in civil affairs. He was very well known all over the state and was universally respected. D. B. Pankey, the son of the Colonel and brother to Mrs. Baldwin, is well known in Kennett, having served it in many capacities. He was clerk of the county and one time mayor. He was one of the organizers of the bank and is its cashier still. He has seen it grow in wealth and reputation. He is president of the electric light company, having helped to organize it. He is president of the Kennett Store Company and of the St. Louis, Keokuk & Southeastern Railroad Company and is treasurer of the Dunklin Publishing Company. Mrs. Baldwin's sphere of usefulness has been her home, but she has been every whit as effective as her father and her brother, though in a more retired way. She has brought up a family of six children, all of whom are a credit to her. Sallie May Baldwin, the eldest child, is now the wife of L. P. Tatum, a merchant in Kennett. Edward Y. is cashier of the Campbell Lumber Company and a director in the Kennett Bank. Ernest Albert is proprietor of the Baldwin Drug Store, formerly owned by his father. Paul is a physician, having received his degree of Doctor of Medicine at the Washington University, medical department, in 1904. He is now practicing medicine in Kennett and making a success, as the son of such a father and such a mother must needs do. Lillian Ballard is just graduated from the Synodical College at Fulton, Missouri, in the class of 1911. Josephine, the youngest, is at present attending the public school of Kennett.

Mr. Baldwin is a Mason and also a member of the Independent Order of Odd Fellows. He was a member of the Presbyterian church, having been an elder from the time of its organization, twenty-five years ago, when the Reverend Beale was its first minister. During all these years, with all his business activities, it was the church which received his interest above all else. His greatest pleasure was in working for the church and it is needless to say that practically the whole responsibility of the church rested on his shoulders. When a man is both capable and willing, he is sure to have more thrust upon him than he really ought to carry. He was superintendent of the Sunday-school, knowing personally every teacher and scholar. Each one felt that in Mr. Baldwin he was sure to find a sympathetic confidant, one who had the faculty of entering into the feelings of others, no matter how much opposed they were to his own feelings and beliefs. He was a friend to any one who needed his help, giving money, time and of himself. It is now seven years since he passed on into the unknown, but the work he organized is still going on, the children he guided in the Sunday-school are fast growing up, but they have not forgotten him. He has gone, but his influence will never die. That is the thought that must have been of comfort to his family during these years, as they live the kinds of lives that he would have had them live, trying to be the kind of men and women that he would have had them be.

OTTO KOCHTITZKY, as he commonly writes his name, or Otto von Kochtitzky, as he is entitled to write it, is perhaps the best authority on swamp land values and drainage in Southeastern Missouri. He was born in South Bend, Indiana, May 4, 1855, and comes of a family well-known both in this country and abroad. His father, Oscar von Kochtitzky, was for some years state auditor, and was connected with many public enterprises.

The son Otto was educated in the public schools and the Jefferson City high school. Upon taking up active work for himself he became interested in surveying and qualified himself for the work of a civil engineer. He was for a time surveyor of New Madrid county, and thus became acquainted with the great opportunities offered by the swamp lands of the section. He was interested in building the Little River Valley and Arkansas Railroad from New Madrid to Malden, the beginning of the present St. Louis Southwestern System. He was one of the first men in the section to see the possibilities of drainage in the swamps of Little River and made a thorough study of the topography of the country and of the history and development of drainage in similar sections, especially in Indiana and Illinois. In spite of great discouragements arising from the inherent difficulties of the situation, the indifference of the people of the district, Mr. Kochtitzky persevered in his efforts to establish a system of drainage which should reclaim the overflowed lands of Little River. He carried on a campaign of education, became associated with the Luce family, which made the first attempts at constructing drainage canals on a large scale, and was finally successful in having much of the swamp land territory organized into districts and the work of drainage actually begun. Under his direction many miles of canals were constructed and much land reclaimed. His efforts in this respect resulted in the organization of the Little River Valley Drainage Company, which has for its object the construction of a diversion channel which shall turn the waters of Whitewater, Crooked Creek and other streams which enter the lowlands from the Ozark plateau into the Mississippi river just south of the city of Cape Girardeau, thus preventing this water from spreading over the lowlands; and the digging of a large drainage canal to carry off the water which falls on the swamps of Little river. This is a most ambitious scheme, which calls for the expenditure of several million dollars and which will probably result in reclaiming large bodies of land. Mr. Kochtitzky was for a time the chief engineer of this company and did most of the preliminary work of organization.

His chief attention at the present time is given to the development of large tracts of valuable lands which he has acquired and to the work of contracting in the digging of drainage ditches.

Mr. Kochtitzky has never been greatly interested in politics, though he was a delegate to the Democratic convention in 1896 that nominated Palmer and Buckner, being the only representative from the Thirteenth Congressional district of Missouri.

For a number of years he has made his home at Cape Girardeau, having formerly lived at a number of places in this section. He, with his family, is a member of the Presbyterian church.

Mr. Kochtitzky has done much for Southeastern Missouri. He is intimately acquainted with the country, is a clear and convincing writer, and has rendered very valuable service in making this section of the country known in other places and its opportunities appreciated. Few citizens of Missouri have contributed as much to the upbuilding of his great section of the state. One of the matters about which he has strong convictions is the New Madrid earthquake of 1811-'12. He does not believe that in any way affected the level of the country, changed its watercourses, or left other permanent effects. He dissents from the views expressed in another part of this work, holding that they are based on imperfect data.

C. E. BURTON. It is one of the rarest occurrences in this commercial age that a man of marked business ability takes a place in the ranks of our educators. The teaching profession engages citizens of the loftiest intellectual and moral qualifications, but those who follow it seldom find opportunity to exercise their talents in the business world. Wayne county is singularly fortunate in having at the head of her school system a man who is at once a born teacher and conspicuously successful in commercial pursuits, Mr. C. E. Burton, of Piedmont.

C. T. Burton, the county superintendent's father, was born in Tennessee August 15, 1852. At the age of twenty he left his native state and went to Kentucky, where he conducted a store and engaged in farming. His marriage to Miss Ellen Walker, a native of the Blue Grass state, took place in 1874. Mrs. C. T. Burton was born in Carlisle county in the year 1854. Seven years after their marriage Mr. and Mrs. Burton moved to Missouri, locating first on a farm near Piedmont and later moving into the town. Here Mr. Burton established a mercantile business, which he conducted until 1908, when he retired. He and his wife are now living in Piedmont and it is their good fortune to have the four children who are now living of the six born to them all residing in Piedmont and its environs. These are: Maud, Mrs. Charles McFarland; Artie, Mrs. C. F. Shelton, and Daisy, still at home, besides C. E. Burton, of this sketch.

Kentucky was the birthplace of Mr. C. E. Burton and the year of his nativity was 1877. Until he was four, he lived on the Kentucky farm. After his parents came to Missouri, he attended the Piedmont high school, from which he graduated at the age of sixteen. The next year he began teaching. At nineteen, Mr. Burton graduated from Wayne Academy and has continued his work of teaching and studying ever since. He has taught in the grades and in the high school, and is familiar with every part of the work of the entire curriculum from the primary grade to the university.

Three years ago, Governor Folk appointed Mr. Burton to fill out four months of J. K. Clubb's unexpired term as county commissioner. In the spring of 1909 he was elected a county commissioner and in August, 1909, Mr. Burton qualified as county superintendent. In 1911 he was again elected to the superintendency without opposition. Mr. Burton has unusual qualities both as a man and as an instructor. He is a born teacher and an eminently progressive one. His efforts to elevate the standard of the Wayne county schools are unremitting. Under his regime some of the rural schools have added the first year of high school work to their course of study, and the high school graduates are admitted to several colleges without examination. Mr. Burton's educational training beyond the common schools has been acquired by his own efforts.

On Christmas day of 1896 Mr. Burton was married to Miss Lula Bell Shelton, of Iron county, Missouri. Four children have blessed this union, all of whom are still in their parents' home; Celeste Cynthia, Inez Emory, Donald Clarence and Marjorie Florence. Both Mr. and Mrs. Burton are members of the Methodist church, South. In politics Mr. Burton is a Democrat and in a social way, a member of the Modern Woodmen's lodge of Piedmont.

In a business way Mr. Burton has been a successful dealer in real estate. He is also a property holder of some prominence in the county. His holdings include a residence in Piedmont and two hundred and ten acres of land near the town, on which he has a summer cottage. In addition to this he has a residence in Greenville.

LUTHER P. TATUM, a successful merchant of Kennett, was born in Howard county, Missouri, January 3, 1863. He is the son of A. C. and Susan Franklin Tatum, who were natives of Virginia and Kentucky, respectively. L. P. Tatum, after acquiring an education in the schools of his native county, came to Kennett while a young man and immediately engaged in business. He had even then the natural ability which makes men successful merchants and was successful from the first. The Kennett of that day was very different from the city of today. It was a struggling town of four or five hundred people and only a few men among them. Mr. Tatum, however, saw the great possibilities of the town.

In 1883 he formed a partnership with an older brother, James F. Tatum, under the firm name of Tatum Brothers. This soon became one of the leading mercantile firms of Dunklin county. It acquired the most desirable corner in the town, erected a commodious brick building, and was in a position to profit by the great growth of the town and its increased prosperity which followed the building of its first railroad. The business is still conducted by Mr. Tatum under the firm name, although the senior partner is dead. Out of this business Mr. Tatum has acquired a comfortable fortune and is a man of influence in his community.

In September, 1893, he was married to Miss Sallie M. Baldwin, daughter of Judge Thomas Baldwin, one of the most prominent and influential men of the county. They live in one of the most beautiful and costly homes in the county, and have the respect and esteem of all their acquaintances.

LEE SHELTON. One of the most successful and enterprising merchants of Southeastern Missouri is Lee Shelton, of Kennett, a member of the firm of Shelton & Company. He was born at Kennett, January 11, 1875, and is the son of Joseph Jackson Shelton, who was born in 1836. He was educated in the public schools, in Bellevue Collegiate Institute at Caledonia, in college at Farmington and St. Louis and received a good business training at a business college in Quincy, Illinois.

Mr. Shelton's father died many years ago and he was reared by his uncle, W. F. Shelton, the shrewdest and most successful business man of Dunklin county. Under his training Lee Shelton acquired a knowledge of actual practical business which has enabled him to carry on the large establishment of his firm in a most successful manner. This firm probably sells as many goods as any other in the southeast and probably buys more cotton than any other. In addition to his interest in this mercantile business he is heavily interested in many other enterprises, many of the larger undertakings in Dunklin county being financed by his firm. He has recently erected a large office building on a prominent corner in Kennett, which is as well equipped as those found in the large cities.

Mr. Shelton finds time from his large enterprises to give attention to public matters. He has served as a member of the board of aldermen of Kennett, and has been for many years one of the most valued members of the board of education.

Mr. Shelton is married and has a beautiful home in Kennett.

WASHINGTON S. DEARMONT. There is much of consistency in the paraphrase of a familiar quotation which is made to express the sentiment that "education makes the man, the want of it the fellow," for the entire basic differentiation between the various social grades is made through the training of mental powers. The progress of civilization has been accomplished by men of strong mentality and well disciplined faculties, and there is no vocation which is of so great importance and that imposes so great responsibility as that of the teacher, whether his work be in the more rudimentary grades or in the broad field of exalted scholarship. Numbered among the able and valued factors in educational work in the state of Missouri is Professor Washington Strother Dearmont, who is the honored president of the Missouri State Normal School at Cape Girardeau and whose career in the domain of pedagogic endeavor has been one of signal success. He has proved a most able administrative officer in his present position, in which also he has found ample scope for the most effective work along scholastic lines. None of the normal schools of the state has a higher reputation than that at Cape Girardeau and at no period in its history has its standard been higher than under the regime of its present chief executive, who has at all times held the confidence and high regard of the student body and who has been able to infuse the utmost enthusiasm into all departments of the work of the institution, by gaining the zealous co-operation of the various members of the corps of instructors and earnest and appreciative application on the part of the students who have availed themselves of the advantages of this admirable school.

Dr. Dearmont finds a due mede of pride and satisfaction in reverting to the historic Old Dominion as the place of his nativity and he is a scion of a family that was founded in that commonwealth in the colonial epoch. He was born in Clarke county, Virginia, on the 22d of September, 1859, and is a son of Peter and Mary (Bell) Dearmont, both of whom were born and reared in Virginia, the former being of staunch English lineage and the ancestral line of the latter being traced back to staunch Irish stock.

Peter Dearmont was a successful agriculturist in his native state until the ravages of the Civil war wrought disaster to him, as to so many other citizens of Virginia, which was the stage of action on the part of the contending forces for many weary months, as history well records. In 1871 he sought a new field of effort and removed with his family to Holt county, Missouri. There he purchased a farm in the vicinity of Mound City and with the passing of the years he was enabled, through industry and good management, to again gain independence and substantial prosperity, though he did not acquire wealth. He is now venerable in years and is living virtually retired on a farm near Mound City, Holt county, Missouri. His sterling integrity of character has given him the confidence and high regard of his fellow men and his life has been one of usefulness and honor in all its relations. He is a staunch advocate of the principles of the Democratic party and his religious faith is that of the Presbyterian church, of which his wife likewise was a zealous member. The latter was summoned to the life eternal in 1900, at the age of sixty-three years, and her memory is revered by all who came within the sphere of her gentle influence. Of the children five sons and one daughter attained to years of maturity, and of the number Dr. Dearmont, of this review, is the eldest.

Dr. Dearmont clearly recalls the scenes and incidents of his boyhood days on the old homestead plantation in Virginia, and he is indebted to the common schools of his native commonwealth for his rudimentary educational discipline. He was a lad of twelve years at the time of the family removal from Virginia to Holt county, Missouri where he was reared to adult age under the sturdy and invigorating discipline of the home farm, in the work of which he gave effective assistance, the while he availed himself of the advantages of the public schools of the locality and period. His ambition to secure a liberal education was early quickened and was one of definite action. The financial resources of his parents were limited and thus he depended upon his own exertions in gaining the funds which enabled him to complete his higher academic education. When nineteen years of age Dr. Dearmont gained, in a district school, his first practical experience in the pedagogic profession, and by his continued and effective labors as a teacher in the public schools he provided for the expenses of his collegiate courses. In 1880 he was matriculated in the University of Missouri, at Columbia, in which he was graduated as a member of the class of 1885 and from which he received the degree of Bachelor of Arts. He continued to teach in the public schools after his graduation and finally completed an effective post-graduate course in his alma mater, the state university, which conferred upon him in 1889 the degree of Master of Arts. For eight years he taught in the schools of Mound City, in his home county, and during the last five years of this period he held the position of principal. From 1893 until 1899 he was superintendent of the public schools of Kirkwood, St. Louis county, and no better evidence of his success in his chosen profession could be given than that afforded in his selection, in 1899, for his present important office, that of president of the Missouri State Normal School at Cape Girardeau, where his labors have been admirably directed and where he has gained unquestioned distinction and prestige as one of the leading factors in connection with educational activities in the state which has been his home from his boyhood days and in which he has secure vantage ground in popular confidence and esteem. He has made of his profession not a means to an end but a distinctive vocation which he has deemed worthy of his unequivocal devotion, with the result that his success has been marked and his rewards unstinted in the sense of good accomplished. In recognition of these services, the degree of Doctor of Literature was conferred on him by Westminster College.

Subordinating all other interests to the demands of his chosen vocation, Dr. Dearmont naturally has had no desire to enter the turbulent stream of practical politics, though he takes a broad-minded interest in public affairs and gives his allegiance to the cause of the Democratic party. He is a valued member of the Missouri State Teachers' Association and many other educational organizations and both he and his wife are zealous and devoted members of the Presbyterian church. He is affiliated with the Knights of Pythias. Dr. and Mrs. Dearmont are valued factors in connection with the best social activities of their home city and their influence in this connection is refined and benignant, as is it also in the various other relations of life. Their circle of friends is coincident with that of their acquaintances and their home is a center of gracious hospitality.

On the 31st of May, 1890, was solemnized the marriage of Professor Dearmont to Miss Julia Lee McKee, of Mound City, Holt county. Mrs. Dearmont was born at Maryville, Missouri, and is a daughter of Horace N. and Sarah (Scott) McKee. He now maintains his home with a daughter at Bigelow, Missouri, and is living retired. The mother died in 1899. Dr. and Mrs. Dearmont have three children,—Russell Lee, Julian Scott and Nelson Strother.

ARTHUR C. BOWMAN. Prominently identified with a line of business enterprise that ever has important bearing on the civic and material progress and prosperity of any community, Mr. Bowman is one of the leading representatives of the real-estate business in the fine section of country to which this history is devoted. He is manager of the Southeast Realty Company, of Cape Girardeau, and he has shown marked discrimination and initiative and administrative ability in directing the affairs of this company, whose operations have reached a broad scope, involving the handling of farm, city and village properties throughout the various sections of southeastern Missouri. Mr. Bowman is a man of ambition and resourceful energy, as has been amply demonstrated in his independent career. He depended upon his own resources in the securing of higher academic education and became a successful and popular factor in the work of the pedagogic profession, to which he devoted his attention for several years. He is a scion of one of the sterling pioneer families of southeastern Missouri and he has well upheld the prestige of the honored name which he bears. Thus there are many points that render most consonant his recognition in this publication—especially on the score of his being at the present time one of the representative business men of the younger generation in Cape Girardeau, where his circle of friends is coincident with that of his acquaintances.

Arthur Caswell Bowman was born on a

farm in Lawrence township, Bollinger county, Missouri, on the 24th of October, 1880, and is the third in order of birth of the ten children born to Miles W. and Catherine (Snider) Bowman, both of whom were likewise born and reared in Bollinger county, where the respective families were founded in the early pioneer days. Groves Washington Bowman, the paternal grandfather of him whose name initiates this review, was a native of North Carolina and he became one of the early settlers in Bollinger county, in southeastern Missouri, where he engaged in agricultural pursuits and where he passed the residue of his life. He contributed his quota to the development and upbuilding of this favored section of the state and was a man who ever commanded unqualified popular esteem. The lineage of the Bowman family is traced back to staunch Holland Dutch origin and representatives of the name were numbered among the early settlers of North Carolina, where they took up their abode in the colonial epoch of our national history.

Miles W. Bowman was reared to maturity in Bollinger county and was afforded the advantages of the common schools of the locality and period. He was there identified successfully with agricultural pursuits for many years and for thirty years he also conducted a general merchandise store in the little hamlet of Glen Allen, Bollinger county, where he was a citizen of prominence and influence and where he continued to reside until about 1894, when he removed to the city of Cape Girardeau, where he has since maintained his home and where he is now living virtually retired from active business. He is a staunch Democrat in his political proclivities and his religious faith is that of the Methodist church, of which his noble wife likewise was a zealous member. Mrs. Bowman was born and reared in Bollinger county, where her father, the late Josiah Snider, established his home in the pioneer days. Mrs. Bowman was summoned to the life eternal in 1895, secure in the affectionate regard of all who had come within the sphere of her gentle influence, and of her four sons and six daughters two sons and one daughter died in childhood. Concerning the surviving children the following brief record is entered: Clara is the wife of Will E. Walker, of Timpas, Colorado; Lee L. is a representative member of the bar of Cape Girardeau; Arthur C. is the immediate subject of this review; William O. is assistant cashier of the First National Bank of Cape Girardeau; Mollie C. is the wife of Theodore E. Head, who is engaged in the real-estate business in the city of Dallas, Texas; May is a popular teacher in the public schools of Timpas, Colorado; and Vesta, who remains with her father, is attending the Normal school of Cape Girardeau.

Arthur C. Bowman passed his boyhood days in his native county, where he gained his initial experience in connection with the sturdy discipline of the farm and where he was afforded the advantages of the public schools of the little village of Glen Allen. Later he continued his studies in the public schools of Cape Girardeau, and for the purpose of securing funds to pursue higher academic studies he worked on farms and at other occupations during vacation seasons. Thus his ambition was one of definite purpose and action, and after completing the elementary course in the Missouri State Normal School at Cape Girardeau, he engaged in teaching in the country schools, to which line of work he devoted his attention for two years, and in connection with which he received a compensation of forty dollars a month. From this diminutive salary he saved sufficient amount to permit the completion of his regular academic course in the state normal school which he had previously attended and in which he was graduated as a member of the class of 1902. For one year thereafter he held the position of first assistant principal of the public schools of Sikeston, Scott county, after which he served two years as principal of the high school at Norwood, Wright county. During the following school year he continued his effective pedagogic work, in charge of the grammar department of the Douglas County Normal School. In the meanwhile he had passed about one year in travel through various sections of the west.

In 1907, believing that other fields of endeavor would afford better opportunities than continued service in the pedagogic profession, Mr. Bowman turned his attention to the real-estate business, in which he became associated with his brother Lee L., at Cape Girardeau, under the title of the Bowman Brothers Realty Company. He continued as active manager of the business until September, 1910, when he sold his interest in the same to his father, and assumed his present office, that of manager of the Southeast Realty Company. He has made a close study of real-estate values and is an authority in this line, so that he has been most successful in his operations in the handling of realty of all kinds. The company with which he is now identified has built up a large and important business, the ramifications of which extend throughout the various counties of southeastern Missouri, and he is showing marked circumspection and discrimnation in the adminstration of its affairs, the while his sterling character and correct methods have gained to him the implicit confidence of those with whom he has had dealings. He is progressive, alert and aggressive as a business man, and as a citizen is loyal and public-spirited. A man of broad mental ken, and of genial personality, he has gained a wide circle of friends in this section of the state, and has a secure place in the esteem of all who know him.

In politics Mr. Bowman accords a staunch allegiance to the cause of the Democratic party and he takes a broad-minded interest in public affairs, especially those of local order. He is affiliated with Cape Girardeau Lodge, No. 639, Benevolent & Protective Order of Elks, and for two years has been secretary of the Commercial Club of Cape Girardeau. In religion he is a Methodist. Mr. Bowman still remains in the ranks of eligible bachelors and is a popular factor in both business and social circles in his home city.

WILLIAM LEE BARRETT. In the many important lines in which southeastern Missouri has made great strides in the past decade, none is more noteworthy than that of education, and one of the chief factors in the attainment of this supreme benefit is Professor William Lee Barrett, superintendent of the schools of Poplar Bluff, Missouri. He is by no means one content with "letting well enough alone," but is a constant student of the best educational methods and has succeeded in keeping abreast of the most modern and enlightened thought and impressing this upon the schools in his charge.

Mr. Barrett was born near Nevada, Story county, Iowa, December 27, 1870, the son of John Thomas and Margaret (Seabold) Barrett. He was one of a family of two children, his only brother, Jesse Cross Barrett, living at Poplar Bluff, Missouri. He spent his youth in his native county, receiving his preliminary education in the district schools and subsequently matriculating at Drake University, from which institution he was graduated in 1895 with the degree of Bachelor of Scientific Didactics.

Mr. Barrett taught in the district schools of Ringgold county, Iowa, for three years, and in 1893 assumed the principalship of the Primrose, Iowa, public schools, in which position he continued until elected superintendent of the Birmingham, Iowa, schools in 1896.

In 1899 he was chosen principal of the Fort Madison (Iowa) high school, building up one of the most remarkable secondary schools in the state, and continued in that capacity until elected to his present position in 1905, having successfully served in the ensuing six years as superintendent of the Poplar Bluff schools. He is well and favorably known not only in this part of the state, but in those sections of Iowa in which he has lived and labored as a particularly enlightened instructor and one who ever makes it his object to keep the highest ideals constantly before the mind of the student. He is one of whom it may be said that he was born as well as made to the high calling to which he has chosen to devote his life.

Mr. Barrett has taught in summer normals and institutes for years, and attends regularly the district, state and many of the national educational associations. He is at the present time a member of the state educational council and also of the executive committee of the State Teachers' Association.

Mr. Barrett is a member of the Christian church, and is one of the most valued and useful of its members, serving at the present time as Bible school superintendent and member of the church board. He is a loyal Mason and exemplifies in his life those ideals of moral and social justice and brotherly love for which the order stands. He is a member of several of the Masonic orders and has served in several official capacities. He belongs to the R. R. Y. M. C. A. and is at the present time a member of the local board of directors.

Mr. Barrett established a happy household by his marriage, on August 11, 1902, to Bertha E. Lightfoot, of Fort Madison, Iowa, their two young sons, John Willis and Paul Burdette, having been born September 4, 1909, and May 30, 1911, respectively. Professor and Mrs. Barrett are highly esteemed members of society and play a useful part in the many-sided life of the community to whose interests they are signally loyal.

WILLIAM L. TUCKER. Talented and cultured, William L. Tucker, of Bloomfield, probate judge for Stoddard county, has won prestige as an attorney-at-law and has been an important factor in promoting the highest interests of town and county, his influence having been especially marked in educational affairs. He was born January 31, 1871, in Shelby county, Indiana, and was educated, principally, in Ohio, completing his early studies at the National Normal University at Lebanon and taking a special course under Professor Albert Holbrook, a noted educator.

Mr. Tucker subsequently taught school three years in Indiana, from there coming, in April, 1895, to Stoddard county, Missouri, where he continued his pedagogical labors for five years, teaching first at Advance, then at Idalia, and later being for two years principal of the Bloomfield Public School. He was really the founder of the Bloomfield High School as it now stands, having systematized the course of study, introduced new methods, and having secured as its first superintendent one of his classmates in the Ohio Normal University, Professor I. H. Hughes, an able and progressive teacher, who did much to elevate the standard of the school, placing it on a high plane of achievement.

While teaching Mr. Tucker began reading law, and after his admission to the Missouri bar, in 1900, was associated with the well known Judge Thomas Connelley. He made a specialty of laws relating to real estate and land titles, becoming an authority on lands and on drainage, and for ten years carried on a fine civil practice. Being elected judge of probate, Mr. Tucker assumed the duties of his office on January 1, 1911, and is performing them with characteristic ability and fidelity.

Politically Mr. Tucker is prominent in the Democratic ranks, and in addition to being active in campaign work has served as a delegate to judicial, congressional and state conventions. He has rendered efficient service both on the local school board and in the city council. Fraternally he is a member of the Independent Order of Odd Fellows; of the Modern Woodmen of America; and of the Knights of Pythias, in which he is especially active in lodge work.

Mr. Tucker married, in Bloomfield, in 1897, Minnie Cone, a successful school teacher and a half-sister of Ralph Wammack. Mr. and Mrs. Tucker have five children living, namely: Vivian, Kent, Ralph, William L. and Evangeline. Mrs. Tucker is a woman of culture and refinement, and a consistent member of the Baptist church.

HON. JAMES L. FORT. Bringing to the practice of his profession a well trained mind and habits of industry, which have won for him genuine success, Judge James L. Fort, of Dexter, for twelve years judge of the Twenty-second judicial circuit, took his seat upon the bench exceptionally well equipped for its duties, not only by scholarship and ability, but by natural gifts and temperament, and his wise decisions in various cases of importance have had a permanent bearing upon the development of Southeastern Missouri. A native of Illinois, Judge Fort was born February 18, 1854, in Johnson county, where he received his rudimentary education.

Judge Fort comes of a family whose traditions date back to the early history of Virginia and Maryland. According to the tales handed down from father to son the family was founded in this country by three brothers who came over from Ireland and settled in these two states. The paternal great-grandfather of Judge Fort was a native of Virginia, who had crossed the mountains and settled in Kentucky as a planter at a very early day. He settled in Christian county, and there his son Garrie was born. Garrie Fort became a planter and spent the whole of his life in Kentucky, though he never became very prosperous. He married Miss Condor, and died during middle age, while his wife survived him many years, dying at the age of seventy-five. The father of Judge Fort was Mears P. Fort and was born in Christian county, Kentucky. There he was reared and there he married, removing to Johnson county, Illinois, in 1853. He became a farmer, and pursued that occupation up to the time of his death, which occurred in 1882, when he was fifty-eight years of age. His wife was Anna Hester, who was a native of Virginia. Her father was James Hester, and her mother's maiden name was Keaton. Both of them were natives of Virginia, and they removed to Kentucky in 1837. There, in Trigg county, they settled, and the husband became a planter. Mrs. Fort and her husband were the parents of twelve children, five of whom are living today. She lived to be seventy-four years old, dying in 1898.

Migrating to Stoddard county, Missouri, in February, 1880, James L. Fort taught school during the long winter seasons, and worked on the farm during seed time and harvest, for four years. In 1884 he began reading law, and in 1886, soon after his admission to the

Missouri bar, was elected prosecuting attorney of Stoddard county. In this capacity he won a fine reputation for professional knowledge and skill, and when, in 1898, he was nominated for judge of the Twenty-second judicial circuit he was elected over his Republican opponent by a plurality of votes amounting to nearly five thousand, nine hundred. This circuit consisted at that time of Carter, Ripley, Butler, Stoddard and Dunklin counties. In 1901 the legislature placed Carter county in another circuit, and in 1904 a new circuit, which included Ripley and Butler counties, alone, was made, and the two remaining counties constituting the Twenty-second judicial circuit since that time. On the 1st of January, 1899, Judge Fort assumed the duties of his new office, and during the ensuing twelve years served his constituents ably and faithfully, the truth of facts and the principles of law involved in the cases brought to his notice seldom eluding his keen perceptions, while justice was ever the constant motive of his wise decisions. The twelve years that Judge Fort was on the bench formed one of the most important periods in the history of Stoddard county and of Southeastern Missouri. During that time the great drainage system that is such an important factor in increasing the property value of this region was successfully inaugurated, and many legal questions arising from its development were adjudicated before him, his rulings thereon being invariably wise and just. Many important criminal cases were likewise tried before Judge Fort, he having been called upon at different times to pass sentence upon men convicted of capital crimes.

In the well remembered case of the Illinois and Missouri Bridge Company versus Smith, the new question of the right of the bridge company to construct beyond the point where the bridge proper touched solid ground at grade above high water mark, came before the Judge, who decided that no such right existed. The supreme court reversed the decision by a divided court, but in a trial for damages for land taken for such a purpose a jury, under Judge Fort's instructions, awarded $10,000 for damages sustained, and the award was also allowed by both the State Supreme Court and the United States Supreme Court.

In 1908 Judge Fort, at the earnest solicitations of his friends, became a candidate for the Democratic nomination for governor of Missouri, his platform being one of the best and cleanest ever constructed, its three principal planks having been as follows: "Aggressive honesty in public affairs; strict enforcement of all laws; and suppression of the liquor traffic by constitutional prohibition." He made a vigorous campaign, which resulted in the Democratic platform coming out very strong for local option.

On January 1, 1911, Judge Fort retired from his position as Judge, and has since been prosperously engaged in the practice of his chosen profession at Dexter, where he has an extensive and lucrative clientele. Progressive and public spirited, he lends his influence towards the establishment of beneficial projects, being in favor of the good roads movement, and in advancement in every line of improvements, believing firmly in a wonderful future for Stoddard county; the "Garden Spot" of Missouri.

Judge Fort was married on the 2nd of August, 1874, to Miss Lizzie Whitesides, a native of Johnson county, Illinois. She is a daughter of John S. and Peinnina (Harrel) Whitesides, and she was reared and educated in her native county. Her mother was a native of Johnson county, and her father was born in the state of Kentucky and came to Illinois during pioneer days, becoming a wealthy farmer. Judge and Mrs. Fort have had seven children: Anna is the wife of Byron Champion, of Dexter; Will J. lives in Dexter; Candace married Judge Green, of Bloomfield, Missouri; Gertrude lives at home; Myrtle died at the age of three; Winifred married J. E. Mulvey, of St. Louis; and Reverdy, the youngest, is still at home. Both the Judge and his wife are members of the Methodist Episcopal church, South.

WILLIAM C. STADY, postmaster at Essex and mayor of the city, is a man who by his untiring efforts and indomitable energy has done much toward the improvement and advancement of the city, and has always availed himself of the advantages of his position as a public man to influence the people to act for the best interests of the community. A native of Missouri, he was born January 20, 1871, in Bollinger county, and was there reared on a farm. His father, Christian Stady, was born in Germany, while his mother, whose maiden name was Mary Miller, was born in America, of German parentage.

Leaving home on attaining his majority, William C. Stady worked out by the month for a time, and was afterwards engaged in general farming on his own account until 1903. Locating then in Essex, he was clerk in the store of William J. Hux, continuing in mercantile pursuits for several years. Being appointed postmaster at Essex on March 20, 1909, Mr. Stady assumed charge of the office about two weeks later, on April 7, succeeding the former postmaster, James R. Grant, who had been forced to resign the position on account of ill health. He has since devoted himself carefully to the duties devolving upon him in this capacity, having charge, in addition to the local service, of one star route going out from the Essex office.

Mr. Stady has ever evinced a warm interest in the promotion of the leading interests of town and county, and has served three years in the village Council, and is now a member of the Board of Education, and with his fellow-associates has done good work, the public schools of Essex being exceptionally fine for a town of its size. In April, 1911, Mr. Stady was elected mayor, and is not only pushing the improvements already inaugurated, including the laying of cement walks, but has paid off the indebtedness of the town and has money credited to the village in the local bank.

Mr. Stady has been twice married. He married first, in Bollinger county, Mary A. Henderson, who died in early womanhood, leaving one child, Mettie M. Mr. Stady married for his second wife, in Stoddard county, Electa E. Page, and to them three children have been born, namely: Merrill, Lillian and Kathleen. Fraternally Mr. Stady is a member of the Independent Order of Odd Fellows; and of Essex Lodge, No. 705, A. F. & A. M., in which he has passed all the chairs excepting that of worthy master. Mrs. Stady is a woman of devout Christian principles, and a member of the Methodist Episcopal church.

WILLIAM HENRY MILLER, one of the most successful lawyers in southeastern Missouri is also president of the Southeast Missouri Trust Company at Cape Girardeau, Missouri. The men of his acquaintance are so accustomed to thinking of him as being away up at the top notch that they almost forget that he was not born that way. We fall into or climb up to close fitting positions in the activities of life, according to our varying sizes and values. All cannot be generals; most of us find our places in the ranks of soldiers. In either capacity there is full incentive for our best endeavors as well as fitting recompense for the highest grade of service. Civilizations in their early stages maintained a premium on brawn and perseverance. As they grow older physical supremacy gives way to intellectual. America is rapidly emerging from the rule of muscular force and untutored intelligence to the sway of trained minds. In this age men who labor are valued by the amount of cash they can produce. The amount of wealth is largely governed by the intelligence brought to bear upon it. Mr. Miller has produced and is producing cash. He has acquired and is acquiring prominence amongst the men who know. This condition has not been brought about by accident, but is due to Mr. Miller's natural abilities and his unbounded capacity for work.

William Henry Miller was born in Cape Girardeau county, Missouri, September 28, 1856. His grandfather, Henry Miller, was a native of North Carolina and he came to Cape Girardeau county in 1808, locating on a farm twenty miles west of Cape Girardeau. He was one of the pioneers of the county and saw it grow from a collection of scattered hamlets into the cities and towns of which it is now composed. The Miller family originally came from Germany and were early settlers in North Carolina. Andrew Miller, son of Henry and father of William Henry, was born December 20, 1825, on the farm in Cape Girardeau county, on which his father first located on his arrival in Cape Girardeau county. The farm is situated near Millerstown, which was named in his honor. He is now eighty-six years old and has spent his entire life on the farm, first where he was born and later on his wife's farm, where he now lives. He married and later managed the farm on which his wife was born and where he now lives. She died in 1856, the year that her son William Henry was born. Of her three sons and one daughter who all grew to maturity, only two are living now, William Henry and his brother E. S. who is a farmer.

William Henry Miller's boyhood days were spent on the farm on which his mother was born, adjoining the farm on which his father was born and where his grandfather lived. He attended the public schools of his district until he was eighteen years of age, when he spent two years at the Southeastern Normal School. He then determined to become a lawyer and to that end he entered the state university and graduated from the law department in 1879, immediately commencing the practice of law. He located at Jackson, Missouri, and became the first president of the Cape Girardeau County Savings Bank at Jackson, Missouri. For fourteen years he was attorney for the Cotton Belt Railroad and was also attorney for the Southern Illinois and Missouri Bridge Company at the time of its organization. He still holds this office. He served four years as member of the state board of law examiners of Missouri. He is a director of the street railway company.

October 5, 1881, was a notable one with him, as on that day was solemnized his marriage with Elizabeth Bollinger Welling a native of Jackson, Missouri. One son was born to this union, Julien Gale, who followed law as his profession and is now practicing in Cape Girardeau.

William Henry Miller is a member of the Masonic order, is a Knight Templar and also a Shriner. He is a member of the Benevolent and Protective Order of Elks in which organization he is past excellent ruler. Mr. Miller is still president of the bank in Jackson, having held that office since 1893. There is now a capital of fifty thousand dollars in the bank with sixty-five thousand dollars surplus. He is also president of the Southeast Missouri Trust Company, which has a paid up capital of five hundred thousand dollars, and one of the directors of the Sturdivant Bank, being chairman of the discount committee. He is a loyal member of the Democratic party, but has never desired public office. As a life long resident of southeastern Missouri it is natural that he should be intensely interested in any enterprise that affects the welfare of his native state. He has made a decided success of his life, both financially and from a higher standpoint, for he has been of use to his fellow men. He is a citizen of whom the county is proud and one whom it delights to honor.

ALEXANDER THOMAS DOUGLASS, who was at the head of the family in Dunklin county, was a native of Virginia. He was born in Bedford county in that state April 5, 1811, being the son of Robert Henry and Permelia (Noel) Douglass. The family was originally from Scotland and it seems that the second "s" in the name was added in this country to distinguish different branches of the family.

The children of Robert Henry and Permelia Douglass besides Alexander Thomas, were Louvina, who became the wife of a man named Penny in Callaway county, Kentucky; Catherine, who married Matthew Senter of Tennessee and removed to Southeast Missouri; and Alfred Hill Douglass, who afterward lived in Cheatham county, Tennessee.

Alexander T. Douglass was married at Moscow, Kentucky, to Elizabeth Mott in 1838. The entire family moved from Virginia to Montgomery county, Tennessee, in 1830. At various times they lived near Fulton, near Union City, Tennessee and in Callaway county, Kentucky. The family was related to the Callaways in whose honor Callaway county was named. While living in Kentucky they were associated with the family of Daniel Boone and at one time Sue Callaway, a cousin of Alexander T. Douglass, and Daniel Boone's daughter May, were captured by the Indians and after a thrilling pursuit were rescued.

In 1850 the family consisting of father, mother and children moved to Dunklin county, where they engaged in farming, the land which was settled by them was near the site of the present town of Caruth. Mr. Douglass made his home at this place until the time of his death in 1876.

Dunklin county was at this time a frontier county. The first settlers were still living and the population was exceedingly small; conditions of life were hard in many respects, but Mr. Douglass was a bold, vigorous, hardy, and enterprising man and soon accumulated a competence. He was held in the highest respect and confidence by his neighbors, and while never a politician or candidate for office, was appointed to positions of trust, at one time being made a special commissioner for the sale of county lands and at another time being vested with authority to adjust certain difficult matters in the early history of the county. In person he was a tall well proportioned man of commanding presence and bearing and possessed a wonderful strength and power of endurance; he died in 1876, as previously stated, from an attack of erysipelas.

His wife, Elizabeth Mott, was born in Kentucky, June 12, 1821. Her family was one of the pioneer families of that state and many of its members are still living there. One of her sisters, Mrs. W. H. Helm, lives at Kennett. Mrs. Douglass died at Senath, February 1, 1899. To Mr. and Mrs. Douglass there were born the following children: Rev.

R. H. Douglass, who died at Caruth in 1904; William, who died as a young man; J. M. and A. W. of Senath; Mrs. Hettie Satterfield of Helena, Arkansas; Mrs. Jennie Lawson of Cape Girardeau; Mrs. C. P. McDaniel and Mrs. Lucy Baird of Senath.

JUDGE JAMES M. DOUGLASS, of Senath, Missouri, was born in Fulton county, Kentucky, October 27, 1847. He is the son of Alexander T. and Elizabeth (Mott) Douglass He came with his parents to Dunklin county in the year 1850. The family settled on Grand Prairie, not far from the site of the present town of Caruth. Dunklin county was only sparsely settled at that time and the life was largely that of a frontier country. Schools were few then and opportunities for education were very limited. Pioneer life is wonderfully stimulating to both body and mind, however, and it is always true that some education may be had under the most adverse circumstances. The boy who desires to learn finds some way opened to him. It was true in this case. He had always a desire for an education and a just appreciation of its importance. This led him to take advantage of such schools as were afforded and to pursue his studies at home. Thus, in spite of the limitations of early life, he was able to acquire a business education, being a life-long student, and is a well informed man.

His principal occupation has been that of a farmer and stock raiser, although he has always been interested in other things as well. In 1879 he was elected county assessor, and made a very careful study of property values. The assessment he made was accordingly one of the fairest and best ever made in the county. A few years later he was elected a member of the county court, serving two terms of two years each. Here his well known good judgment and his knowledge of conditions in the county made his services especially valuable to the people. Since the expiration of his term of office he has never been a candidate for other official positions, but he has always maintained an intelligent interest in politics.

He was one of the organizers of the Cotton Exchange Bank of Kennett and served as its president for five years. At the expiration of that time he assisted in the organization of the Citizens Bank of Senath, serving as its president until he was forced to spend some years away from the county on account of his health. He is now president of the Bank of Senath. His business operations have enabled him to accumulate a competency, and he owns several hundred acres of fertile farm land.

Judge Douglass moved to Senath in 1881, before it was dignified by the name of "town." At that time the present site of the town of Senath was a dense forest, and many are the changes which he has seen worked in that place. He has been one of the foremost men of the town of Senath since its organization many years ago, and has contributed his full quota toward the growth and upbuilding of the town, much of the credit for the present standing of Senath as a thriving and prosperous community of right belonging to Judge Douglass.

On Christmas day, 1881, he was married to Miss Belle Phelan, a daughter of William G. and Belle (Randol) Phelan. The father of Mrs. Douglass was a native of Ireland, having been educated there for the Catholic priesthood, but became a lawyer instead of taking holy orders, and for many years practiced law in southeast Missouri. The mother was a member of the Randol family of Scott county, one of the oldest and best known families in the state.

Judge Douglass and his wife are the parents of five children: J. Mott, who is a member of the drug firm of Bradley & Douglass at Senath; Thomas G., who is superintendent of schools at Senath; Miss Frances, a teacher in the Senath schools; Allen M., who is a consulting chemist, now located in Midland, Michigan; and Margaret, a student in the State Normal School at Cape Girardeau.

The Judge is an active member of the Baptist church, and fraternally is a Mason.

GILBERT OWEN NATIONS was born in Perry county, Missouri, on August 18, 1866. His father, James W. Nations, fought under the stars and stripes in the Civil war as a private in Company F, Fiftieth Missouri Volunteer Infantry, and after the close of the war he engaged in the milling business, taught school and did considerable surveying and civil engineering, having held the office of county surveyor of Ste. Genevieve county, Missouri, for eight years. In 1861 James W. Nations was married to Miss Caroline L. Hart, of Perry county, Missouri. Of this union seven children were born, five of whom, including the subject of this sketch, are living.

Gilbert grew up amid the rugged hills of

Ste. Genevieve county, where his parents made their home in his early childhood. Besides the indifferent educational advantages then offered in the rural schools of that neighborhood, he did much systematic home study; and at the age of ten years he had gained considerable notoriety among the neighbors on account of his attainments in arithmetic, geography and other common-school branches of study. In his eighteenth year he entered the State Normal School at Cape Girardeau, Missouri, and completed the sophomore year in ten months. After teaching in the public schools of home county a few terms he became a student in the National Normal University at Lebanon, Ohio, then under the presidency of Alfred Holbrook, and completed the course in the College of Science. Returning to Missouri, he resumed the work of teaching in the public schools, holding the superintendency of schools for several years successively at Crystal City and at Farmington.

On December 6, 1886, he was married to Miss Sarah E. McFarland, of Coffman, Missouri. Their oldest child, Heber, is a graduate of the Cape Girardeau State Normal School and is married and engaged in the real estate business at Flat River, Missouri. Heber is twenty-two years younger than his father. Six younger children, Zora, aged twenty; Gustavus, aged eighteen; Myrtle, aged fifteen; Paul, aged twelve; Florence, aged ten, and Carl, aged seven, complete the family circle of Judge Nations and his estimable wife in their delightful home in Farmington. The entire family except Carl, are members of the Christian church, in which the Judge has been an elder for nearly twenty years.

In 1894 the subject of this sketch was examined by the State Superintendent of Public Schools, assisted by the faculty of the Warrensburg State Normal School, and was given a first grade state teacher's certificate, valid for life. He also passed successfully the examination given by the City Superintendent of Schools of St. Louis to those applying for principalships in that city, besides completing a year of regular post-graduate work at Hiram College for which he was awarded an appropriate degree.

While teaching at Farmington he studied law and was admitted to the bar in the spring of 1902. In the same year the Republican party nominated him for the office of probate judge, and he was elected by nearly a hundred majority, though the county went Democratic by nearly three hundred majority. No other Republican nominee had then carried the county in thirty years. At the close of his term he was renominated and re-elected in the face of a substantial Democratic majority.

In his habits and tastes, Judge Nations is a commoner. He stands uncompromisingly for clean politics and the rights of the people. He is opposed to the control of our politics and institutions by predatory wealth. While favoring the principles of the Republican party, he believes it to be the duty of voters to favor the election of the men who are honest and capable and who will render the best service to the public. As a lawyer he is rapidly gaining an enviable reputation and is building up a clean and lucrative practice. Those who know him believe intensely in his personal and professional honesty. An eloquent and forceful public speaker, he has become one of the most influential men in southeast Missouri.

WILL MAYFIELD COLLEGE at Marble Hill, Missouri, is one of the favorably-known, carefully conducted and enlightened institutions of learning of the state. It is the outcome of what was formerly known as the Mayfield-Smith Academy and was founded in 1878 by W. H. Mayfield and Dr. Smith, at Sedgewickville, Missouri. In 1880 the school was moved to Marble Hill and chartered. Professor T. W. Tate was the first principal in charge of the school at Sedgewickville and twenty-two pupils were enrolled in 1878 and 1879. Elder A. M. Johnson was the first principal at Marble Hill in 1880 and 1881.

The school was successively under the administration of Drs. Graham, Graves, Dobbins, Mingo and F. J. Hendershot, until 1903, when it was re-chartered as the Will Mayfield College. It has now at its head that excellent educator, Professor A. F. Hendricks, of whom further mention is made in the Hendricks biography on other pages of this work.

The school has been fostered and supported by the Missionary Baptist of South-Eastern Missouri Associations. In 1877 plans were projected by Messrs. Shurtleff, Mercer, Jewell and Mayfield for the founding of the school. On February 10, 1878, a fund of one thousand one hundred dollars was provided by Elder H. F. Tong, district missionary, and another fund or addition to the former, reaching the amount of one thousand four hundred dollars, was provided at Big Creek by the St. Francois Association, in September, 1878, and a committee consisting of W. H. Mayfield, J. Q. A. Whitener, and E. E. Graham was selected to effect an organization and select a site.

The first board of trustees consisted of the following gentlemen: J. Frank Sitze, W. H. Mayfield, E. P. Settle, Alexander Jennings, H. M. Williams and William Sparkman. Those zealous in fostering the college were: W. H. Mayfield, F. M. Wells, J. Frank Sitze, A. J. Mayfield, H. F. Tong, E. L. Graham, Francis Graham, Henry Cheek, Enoch Robertson, F. C. Shell, J. Q. A. Whitener, J. W. Revelle, J. C. Heinbrey and E. R. Graham. F. M. Wells is president of the present board of trustees, and Jesse A. McGlothlin, secretary.

The college is supported entirely by tuition and the Baptists of South-Eastern Missouri. The Baptists of sixteen counties are interested and students are drawn from the surrounding counties. Under a re-charting clause recently enacted, it is impossible for the college to remain in debt, and it is thus placed upon a remarkably firm financial foundation. A large and attractive boarding-hall (Rosemont Hall) in charge of Mrs. Hendricks will house thirty-six girl students comfortably.

Professor W. A. Devault is vice-president of the college and a faculty of seven teachers is employed. Two degrees are conferred, namely: Bachelor of Science and Bachelor of Arts. Twenty-three graduates were reported for the year 1911 and one hundred and seventy students were continuously enrolled in 1910-1911. Strong departments of music and elocution are maintained in the institution, thus sending forth an appeal to students so inclined. A high moral training is an important feature, the methods of the college proceeding on the thought that morality in the best sense can be taught only through the inculcation of high ideals constantly kept before the minds of the student.

The college buildings, which are commodious structures, are situated on a commanding wooded height, and are situated in a healthful locality, excellent drinking water of the mineral sort similar to that obtained from the Marble Hill mineral well furnishing a strong recommendation to parents to whom the health of their sons and daughters is dear.

PROFESSOR A. F. HENDRICKS. There is no profession open to man so fraught with equal responsibility and opportunity to serve the race as that of the educator, for in equipping the young for their work in life he has somehow to combine all professions, and in the greater number of individuals that pass through his hands at the most pliant periods of their careers, he holds the responsibility for the mental, moral, and physical vigor of each recurring "next generation." One of the educators of southeastern Missouri whose calibre justifies his high calling is Professor A. F. Hendricks, the president of Mayfield College. He is a man in whom high ideals and exceptional vision are happily united with a broad experience and keen sense of practical values, a combination of qualities needed but rarely found in the field of education.

Professor A. F. Hendricks was born February 1, 1870, in James county, Tennessee, the son of Nathan and Mary J. Hendricks. His father was a skilled mechanic, and both the parents, knowing the inestimable value of a thorough education, were vastly interested that their son should enjoy its benefits. After having finished his preparatory work in the public schools of Birchwood, Tennessee, the son attended the seminary at Shumach, Georgia, and then went to Dayton University in Tennessee. Following that Professor Hendricks went to the Valparaiso University, at Valparaiso, Indiana, graduating there in the class of 1904. He returned the next year and took post-graduate work in the same college. In the year 1906 his desire to be thoroughly prepared for his life work led him to take graduate work in the University of Chicago. In his career as an educator Professor Hendricks has been in many places. In 1905-1907 he was principal of the Lutesville schools. His first teaching was done in 1893, in Hamilton county, Tennessee, and he had charge of the Morgantown schools for three years, following by two years at the head of the Dayton city schools. In 1907 he was elected to the presidency of Will Mayfield College, and his incumbency of this office has been such as to bring honor both on himself and on the institution whose policies he directs. Since his advent, an addition to the college buildings has been made at a cost of six thousand dollars, and the annual report shows an attendance of one hundred and seventy students, in all departments, the academic course of four years and the college departments, both the scientific and the classical courses.

Will Mayfield College is under the control of the Saint Francis Association of the three counties. It is supported in its running expenses by the tuitional fees. Under its new charter, recently obtained in the place of the original charter, it is not allowed to incur any indebtedness, so that the college is now on a solid financial basis. All the buildings and rooms have been repaired, and all are furnished complete. The college confers two degrees, B. S. and A. B. In 1911 there were twenty-three academic graduates and two graduates from the college receiving the degree of B. S., and there were seven teachers on the instructing corps. Besides its regular curriculum, Will Mayfield College has a department of music and of elocution. Its dormitory, of which Mrs. Hendricks has charge, can accommodate thirty-six girl students. The personnel of the student body is made up largely of residents of Bollinger and adjoining counties. President Hendricks holds both the degrees of B. S. and A. M. He is also one of the members of the Southeastern Missouri Educational Association. Much might be said of Professor Hendricks' work as president. It is certain that the college is establishing a reputation of which Marble Hill may well be proud. His efforts are building up the institution, and the annual attendance has steadily increased since his advent.

On September 22, 1897, was solemnized the marriage of Professor Hendricks to Miss Dora Pence, of Ellijay, Gilmer county, Georgia. She is a daughter of L. B. and Lydia Pence, and was reared and educated in the Cracker state. Their marriage was celebrated in Dayton, Tennessee. Professor and Mrs. Hendricks have no children. Mrs. Hendricks has entire charge of Rosemont Hall, the students' dormitory.

Fraternally Professor Hendricks is affiliated with the Ancient Free and Accepted Masons, the Independent Order of Odd Fellows, the Knights of Pythias and the Modern Woodmen of America. Both he and his wife are devout members of the Baptist church.

HON. STERLING H. MCCARTY. Prominent among the representative lawyers and public men of southeastern Missouri stands Sterling H. McCarty, member of the law firm of Duncan & McCarty, of Caruthersville, Missouri, one of the strong combinations of legal talent in this section. He has also had an opportunity to "give a taste of his quality" as a legislator, having been elected to represent Pemiscot county in the forty-sixth general assembly of the state of Missouri. He belongs not to the class of modern politicians whose sole aim seems to be self-advancement, but gives his time and energies for the good of his fellow men and for securing wise legislation that will benefit the entire state. In politics he is of stanch Democratic convictions and has ever proved ready to do anything, to go anywhere to support the cause of the party to which he pins his faith.

Mr. McCarty is a native of Kentucky, his birth having occurred in Henderson county, January 8, 1876, the son of John and Belle (Hicks) McCarty. His identification with Missouri dates from 1889, when the family removed to this state. He was educated primarily in the common schools and subsequently entered the normal school at Cape Girardeau. Later he was appointed a cadet at the United States Naval Academy at Annapolis, Maryland, where he had the advantage of its splendid discipline. In the meantime having come to the conclusion to adopt the law as his profession, he entered the law department of Washington University at St. Louis, Missouri, and graduated with the degree of LL. B. When it came to engaging in the active practice of the profession for which he is so eminently well fitted, he decided upon Caruthersville and here his career has been of the most satisfactory character.

The Hon. Mr. McCarty has had military experience, as well as naval, having enlisted and served as a volunteer during the Spanish-American war, as a member of Company C, First Regiment Pennsylvania Volunteers. He taught his first school when eighteen years of age, in Stoddard county, Missouri, and in 1901 was elected county school commissioner of Pemiscot county, being at the time superintendent of the Hayti (Missouri) schools. He has been honored in his professional life and served as judge of the probate court of Pemiscot county from October, 1904, to

January 1, 1911. His election to the state legislature from Pemiscot county occurred in November, 1910. He took an active part in the session, being chairman of the committee on constitutional amendments and permanent seat of government; served as house chairman of the committee to investigate the fish and game department; as a member of the committee on elections; and the committee on wills and probate law.

Mr. McCarty is a popular and prominent lodge man, being a thirty-second degree Mason and a member of the Eastern Star, and a member of the Modern Woodmen of America, of the Elks and the Redmen. He has not yet become a recruit to the Benedicts and maintains his residence in Caruthersville.

WILLIAM ARTHUR COOPER. One of the rising young attorneys of Washington county is William Arthur Cooper, whose brilliant gifts and definite achievements thus early in life presage a career of more than usual usefulness and honor. He has for several years held the office of prosecuting attorney and is one of the leaders of local Republicanism, being one of the most loyal and unswerving of the adherents of the "Grand Old Party." Mr. Cooper was born May 26, 1882, on a farm in the western part of Washington county.

His father, William Cooper, was an Ohioan and was the son of Eugeneous W. Cooper, who was a fisherman and collier by trade, a Republican in politics and a member of the Baptist church. At about the time William reached his majority he left the parental roof-tree and came to Missouri, where he purchased a farm and took his place among the state's agriculturists. He was married April 16, 1881, to Miss Mary Elizabeth Crump, of Washington county, daughter of Fendall F. Crump and Margeline (nee Sanders) Crump, and their two sons are William Arthur and Claude Fendall. He has continued engaged in farming throughout his life and also acted as postmaster at Brazil for a number of years, meeting the duties of the office with all faithfulness. He is Republican in politics and in his religious views he is of the Baptist persuasion. Although he is interested in public affairs and gives heart and hand to all measures likely to result in general welfare, he is by no means an office seeker. He and his wife reside on the old homestead farm in the vicinity of Brazil.

William A. Cooper, prosecuting attorney of Washington county received his early education in the common schools and subsequently attended the Steelville Normal School. He taught school for about four years. Meanwhile, however, he came to the decision to make the law his life work and studied for the profession under the tutorship of Judge E. M. Dearing, of Potosi, and Hon. A. L. Reeves, of Steelville. He was admitted to the bar in 1904 and shortly thereafter hung up his professional shingle at Potosi and there entered upon his practice, in a short time winning the confidence and clientage of his fellow townsmen. He was recognized as of the proper material for office and served one term as justice of the peace; he was also alderman and city clerk of Potosi and his services in those capacities made appropriate his appointment by Governor Hadley (October 1, 1909) to the office of prosecuting attorney to fill the unexpired term of S. G. Nipper, resigned. In the following year he was elected to the same office on the Republican ticket. In this office he has won remarkable distinction as an able lawyer and an efficient officer.

On October 23, 1904, Mr. Cooper was united in marriage to Miss Irene Blount, of Palmer, the lady of his choice. They have one daughter, Helen Mary. Mr. Cooper is not a member of any church, although a strong supporter of the cause of Christianity. His wife and child are members of the Methodist Episcopal church, South.

PROFESSOR FREDERICK ARTHUR CULMER. One of the valued members of the faculty of Marvin College is Professor Frederick Arthur Culmer, Ph. B., LL. B., A. M., who holds the chair of English and History in that institution of learning. He is looked upon as one of the most talented and enlightened of the educators of this section of the state and he is also a clergyman of the Methodist Episcopal church, South. He first assumed his professorship in Marvin College in 1907, continued through that year; was again appointed in 1910, and has been but recently appointed for continued service.

Professor Culmer was born in the county of Kent, England, December 2, 1883, the son of George Culmer, gentleman, now retired for many years, and his wife, whose maiden name was Nellie Brenchley. The family is one of the oldest and most dignified in England, its history having been traced back to 862 A. D. A part of the family, which is of Danish origin, removed to Holland in some political crisis and in that country the spelling of the name has been changed to Kulmer.

Professor Culmer received a high school education in his native country and at the age of twenty came to America, via Canada. In course of time he found his way to Knob Lick, Saint Francois county, Missouri, and there worked for a short time in a stone quarry. Although so young a man, he had already been active in church work as an exhorter and he now and then, after coming to the state, engaged in this. He was at first content with very humble positions and for some time drove a delivery wagon for the J. T. Evans department store at Elvins, Missouri. He continued thus employed until the meeting of the district conference of the Methodist Episcopal church, at Oak Ridge, Missouri, when he was licensed to preach. He then filled the pulpit at Arcadia until the annual conference of the church at DeSoto, Missouri. Subsequent to that he accepted a home with Rev. T. W. Shannon, of Fredericktown, his duties in the household being to care for the conservatory and grounds. Meantime he attended Marvin College for two years, and his ability and character were so apparent that in the third year he was offered the position of assistant instructor of mathematics, while at the same time pursuing his studies. In 1907 he was graduated with the Ph. B. degree, and in the ensuing year was elected to the chair of mathematics. In the year subsequent he took a special course in theology at Vanderbilt University, Nashville, Tennessee, and the next year matriculated at Morrisville College, where he pursued studies and at the same time taught English. In 1909-10 he accepted a call as pastor of the Park Avenue Methodist Episcopal church, South, of Rich Hill, Missouri. His pastorate there was of the most successful and satisfactory character, and during it the present beautiful church was erected at a cost of twenty thousand dollars. Desiring to resume his career as a college instructor, Professor Culmer was proffered and accepted the chair of English and History at Marvin College, and he is at the present time the incumbent of the same. He is a thorough as well as an ambitious student and from boyhood has lingered willingly at the "Pierian spring." Like so many other students he has found correspondence courses profitable and finished his incompleted studies by means of correspondence with Oskaloosa College, Oskaloosa, Iowa, his A. B. and A. M. degrees being obtained in this way. He received his LL. B. degree by correspondence work with the Illinois College of Law, and his Ph. B. degree from Marvin Collegiate Institute, now Marvin College. He is now pursuing his studies leading to the degree of Doctor of Philosophy.

Professor Culmer established an independent household by his union with Miss Allen-Philips, of Higginsville, Missouri, daughter of the late Rev. Lamartine Philips, for thirty-three years pastor of the Methodist Episcopal church, South, in the Southwestern Missouri Conference. The subject and his wife share their delightful home with a baby daughter, Fredonia Linnell, born December 7, 1910.

Rev. Lamartine Philips was a native of Roachport, Howard county, Missouri, and received his education in the Randolph-Macon College of Virginia. He prepared for both the law and the ministry, and he remained in the work of the latter until his death, on January 11, 1908, at the age of fifty-four years. This reverend gentleman, whose work was cut short when almost in the prime of life, is interred in Mt. Washington cemetery, Kansas City, Missouri. The Philips family is one of the oldest in Missouri. Mrs. Culmer's mother, whose maiden name was Verlinda Norfleet, was a native of Kentucky.

Mrs. Culmer was reared in southwestern Missouri and is a cultured and admirable young woman. She received her musical education at Sedalia College of Music, where she spent four years and at Independence, Missouri, where she pursued her studies for three years. She devoted seven years to advanced piano study and is an artiste.

EDWARD D. ANTHONY, whose name occupies a conspicuous place on the roll of Missouri's eminent lawyers, during some three decades' connection with the bar of the state has won and maintained a reputation for ability that has given him just preeminence among his professional brethren. In the law, as in every other walk of life, success is largely the outcome of resolute purpose and unfaltering industry,—qualities that are possessed in a large degree by Mr. Anthony. The official headquarters of Mr. Edward D. Anthony are in the Telephone Exchange Building, at Fredericktown, Missouri. He is attorney for the Security Bank of this city and at one time was attorney for a number of mining companies in this section of the state, in addition to which he is also interested in the Citizens' Telephone Company at Fredericktown.

A native son of Missouri, Mr. Anthony was born in Madison county, this state, the date of his birth being the 8th of July, 1856, and he is a scion of a fine old pioneer family in this state. His parents, Joseph F. and Martha J. (Stevenson) Anthony, were likewise born in Madison county, Missouri, the former in 1818 and the latter in 1835. The father was a son of William J. Anthony, a native of Tennessee, whence he removed to Missouri in the year 1816, locating on a farm three miles east of Fredericktown. The mother is a daughter of Hugh B. Stevenson, who came to Missouri from North Carolina in the year 1820. Mr. Stevenson was a farmer and stockman by occupation and his fine old estate is still in the possession of his descendants. Mrs. Martha J. Anthony survives her honored husband and she is now residing, at the age of seventy-six years, at Fredericktown. Joseph F. Anthony was summoned to the life eternal in 1883, at the age of sixty-six years. He gained distinctive prestige as a farmer and stockman. In 1849 he made the overland trip to California and subsequently was a lieutenant in the Mexican war, in which he participated in a number of important engagements. During his life time he made three trips to California, where he owned considerable mining property and some valuable real estate in San Francisco. He suffered a very heavy loss in the San Francisco fire of the early 50s. The various members of the Anthony family in Missouri are all devout members of the Christian church, and it is interesting to note at this juncture that pioneers of the name in Madison county, Missouri, established a church of that denomination as early as 1824. A beautiful new Christian church is now being built at Fredericktown. Mr. and Mrs. Joseph F. Anthony became the parents of five children, Eliza, the wife of Charles Remmert, of St. Louis, Missouri; Julia, Mrs. Theo. Underrine, of Madison county, Missouri; Sterling P., a merchant at Webb City, Missouri; James F. maintains his home in Madison county, Missouri; and Edward D., the immediate subject of this review.

Edward D. Anthony was reared to maturity in Madison county, where he has always resided, and his rudimentary educational training consisted of such advantages as were afforded in the public schools of Fredericktown. Subsequently he attended the state normal school for two years and eventually he began to read law under the able preceptorship of B. B. Cahoon, of Fredericktown. He was admitted to practice at the Missouri bar in March, 1881, and since that time has won renown as a versatile trial lawyer and well fortified counselor at Fredericktown, where he has been engaged in the active practice of his profession for fully a score of years. Mr. Anthony is a stockholder in the Security Bank, for which substantial monetary concern he is attorney, and he is general manager and principal owner of the Citizens' Telephone Company, at Fredericktown. He is a business man and lawyer of unusual ability and as such his services are in great demand in this section of the state. In a fraternal way he is affiliated with the time-honored Masonic order, the Independent Order of Odd Fellows, the Modern Woodmen of America and the Modern Brotherhood of America. In religious matters he is a devout member of the Christian church, to whose philanthropical work he is a most liberal contributor. In politics he is a Democrat, warmly advocating party principles, although he is not an active politician. He has devoted himself assiduously to his profession and has not sought political office. As a man he is thoroughly conscientious, of undoubted integrity, affable and courteous in manner and has a host of loyal and devoted friends.

Mr. Anthony was happily married in 1880, to Miss Laura Nifong, a native of Fredericktown, Missouri, and a daughter of J. T. and Amanda (Caruthers) Nifong, the former a general merchant and farmer. An uncle of Mrs. Anthony's, Mr. Samuel Caruthers, was congressman from this district. Mr. and Mrs. Anthony have two daughters, namely: Edith, wife of S. S. Clarke, a mining engineer of Saint Francois county, Missouri; and Anna, wife of H. H. Martin, engaged in mining operations in Saint Francois county. Mr. Martin has mined in British Columbia and many other districts. They have one son, Edgar Anthony Martin, born September 14, 1911.

CHARLES POPE POSTON, M. D. Other men's services to the people and state can be measured by definite deeds, by dangers averted, by legislation secured, by institutions built, by commerce promoted. The work of a doctor is entirely estranged from these lines of enterprise and yet without his capable, health-giving assistance all other accomplishments would count for naught. Man's greatest prize on earth is physical health and vigor. Nothing deteriorates mental activity as quickly as prolonged sickness—hence the broad field for human helpfulness afforded in the medical profession. The successful doctor requires something more than mere technical training—he must be a man of broad human sympathy and genial kindliness, capable of inspiring hope and faith in the heart of his patient. Such a man is Dr. Charles Pope Poston, who for the last quarter of a century has enjoyed distinction and success as a skillful physician and surgeon of Bonne Terre and vicinity. The years have told the story of a useful career due to the possession of innate talent and acquired ability along the line of one of the most important professions to which a man may devote his energies,—the alleviation of pain and suffering and the restoration to health. The Poston family is one noted for its gifted physicians, the father of the subject, Dr. Henry W. Poston, of Irondale, having been a well-known pioneer doctor, and one of his sons, Dr. Harry Poston, well maintaining the honored prestige of the name. As a citizen he is interested in the success of good government and aids in the promotion of business and social harmony by a straightforward course as a citizen.

Dr. Poston is a native of the state, his birth having occurred at Irondale, Washington county, on the 28th of September, 1854. He is a son of Dr. Henry W. and Casandria (Ashburn) Poston, natives of Missouri and Kentucky, respectively. Dr. Henry W. Poston practiced at Irondale for about thirty-five years and was a credit to his profession. He died when sixty-four years of age, and he was also a farmer, active Democrat and Presbyterian. Dr. Henry Poston was a native of St. Francois county, Missouri, and his father, Henry, was a native of North Carolina and came to Missouri, St. Francois county, in 1806. He was a civil engineer and farmer, and owned quite a large tract of land, operating same with slaves. When it came to choosing a life work young Charles Pope Poston decided, with little difficulty, to follow in the paternal footsteps. He had received his preliminary education at Irondale and Westminster College at Fulton, Missouri, and took his medical course at Washington University in St. Louis. Since his graduation he has practiced at Bonne Terre, and there and in the surrounding country he enjoys the highest general confidence. It is of such men as he that Alexander Pope penned his famous couplet, "A wise physician, skill'd our wounds to heal, is more than armies to the public weal." Dr. Poston specializes in gynecology and internal medicine and has been chief surgeon for the St. Joseph Lead Company, and for the Mississippi River & Bonne Terre Railway Company for thirty-five years, when he resigned, and his son Harry P. was appointed to that position.

Dr. Poston married on the 26th day of September 1883, the young woman to become his wife and congenial life companion being Miss Mahala Cunningham, of Farmington. Their union has been blessed by the birth of nine children, seven of whom are living at the present time. They are as follows: Harry P., M. D., of whom mention is found on other pages of this work), Marie Louise, Charles H., Florence N., Virgil, Frank D. and Stanly. The older children are all college graduates.

Dr. Poston subscribes to the articles of faith of the Democratic party, with which he has been affiliated since his earliest voting days. He is a prominent member of the Masonic fraternity and emulates in his own living those fine ideals of moral and social justice and brotherly love for which the order stands.

ANDREW T. SCHULTZE. In these days of intensified farming agricultural reports tell us that a comfortable living may be made from ten acres of good land, planted to advantage. Whether our average farmer would agree to this we know not, but all will agree that a comfortable living, with some for luxuries, can be obtained from several hundred acres of rich southeastern Missouri land, than which there is no better in the Union. The subject of this sketch, Andrew T. Schultze, is not only owner of a large farm three miles east of Washington, in Franklin county, Missouri, but he is closely allied with several other successful business enterprises.

The father of Andrew T. Schultze was Andrew Schultze, Sr., who was a native of Germany, his birth having occurred at Leunburg in 1810. It was the wish of his parents that he enter the ministry, and accordingly he supplemented the education obtained at the common schools in his native land by a course in the theological department of the University of Berlin, from which he was graduated. Being especially fond of the languages, he devoted all his spare time to mastering Greek, Latin, French and several other European tongues, all preparatory to his engaging in the ministry of the Evangelical church. However, "the best laid plans of mice and men gang aft agley," and Andrew Schultze decided to visit the United States and, if this new country pleased him, to settle here. Accordingly he immigrated to the United States, and in 1849 settled in Missouri, near the present homestead of his son, the aforementioned Andrew T. Schultze. He immediately adapted himself to the new world methods and manners, and made himself agreeable to all his neighbors, who esteemed and respected him for his splendid educational equipment, and at the same time loved him for his manly character and striking personality.

At the breaking out of hostilities in the Civil war period Mr. Schultze supported the flag of the Union, but, being too old to enlist in active service, he could do no more than enthuse those about him in the cause. He was thus strongly Republican in politics, but veered off with the liberal element of that party during the Greeley campaign, later, however, coming back into the fold of his parent party. His extreme popularity and the confidence reposed in him by the citizens of Franklin county is best evidenced by the fact that in November, 1872, Mr. Schultze was nominated for county judge by the Democratic party, and elected, chiefly upon the local issue of opposition to the payment of the road bonds which had been wrongfully saddled upon the county. He died the next month, however, December, 1872, before assuming his official position, and this sudden demise delayed for several years the final adjustment of the matter.

Though Mr. Schultze never entered religious work as had been originally planned, yet his interest in everything good continued unabated, and he did much in a quiet way for the betterment of conditions in his immediate community, and was one to whom much credit is due in the building of the present Evangelical church in Washington. Mr. Schultze was married in Germany to Johanna Kaiser, born in 1830, and to them were born the following children: Bertha, the widow of William Daetweiler, of Franklin county; Andrew T., whose biography follows; Charles, of Arizona; Fredrick, who died at fourteen years of age; Adolph, who died at the age of forty; Rudolph, now a resident of Union, Missouri; Otto, living on the old homestead in this county; Ernst, of Union; Louise, who died when fourteen years of age; and Anna, wife of George Hausmann, of Washington. Mrs. Andrew Schultze, Sr., is still living in Franklin county, Missouri.

The man who has before him a living example of honesty, integrity, manliness and innate culture is bound to live up to that standard. With such a father Andrew T. Schultze could not be less a man. His birth occurred March 19, 1854, in Franklin county, so that he has lived all his life in southeastern Missouri. Though the educational facilities in Missouri at that time were not what the father had had in Germany, yet he determined that his son should be educated as well as possible. Young Andrew therefore attended private schools and public schools at Washington, the high school at Hermann, and later took a commercial course in one of the business colleges of St. Louis. Having a love for nature and nature's handiwork, our subject had early decided that he would follow in his father's footsteps a little farther, and would adopt farming as his life work, and with the exception of two years passed in Colorado, 1883-84, in the cattle business, Mr. Schultze has carried out his original plans.

As before stated, the attractive farm which was originally the old Bell homestead, three miles east of Washington, is now owned and operated by Andrew T. Schultze, but Mr. Schultze does not confine his interests entirely to agricultural pursuits. He is president of the Farmers' Mutual Insurance Company of Franklin county; is a stockholder in the National Cob Pipe Works of Union; and is president of that thriving institution, the Franklin County Bank, established in November, 1909, and associated in this business with F. W. Hawley, as vice-president and C. M. Ellis, as cashier. The bank has a capital stock of thirty thousand dollars, and a large clientele among the farmers adjacent to Washington. During the past years Mr. Schultze has served the government as carrier for route No. 1, rural mail service, which he organized.

In politics Mr. Schultze was reared under the banner of the Republican party, but after much reading and study he could not find it consistent with his belief to uphold high tariff, so cast his influence and his ballot with the Democratic party, which he still supports. He is genial and affable and enjoys many social hours with his fellow members in the ranks of the Modern Woodmen and the Turnverein. The family are members of the Evangelical church.

Mr. Schultze was married in Franklin county, December 28, 1888, to Miss Alvina Bergner, a daughter of George Bergner, a native of Saxony, a man of much mechanical genius, being by vocation a lock and a gunsmith, and a holder of many patents for invention. To Mr. and Mrs. Schultze have been born the following children, Alvina, Nellie H. and Cora V., also Johanna, who died when about ten years of age.

HARRY L. MACHEN. Whether the elements of success in life are innate attributes of the individual or whether they are quickened by a process of circumstantial development, it is impossible clearly to determine. Yet the study of a successful life is none the less profitable by reason of the existence of this uncertainty and in the majority of cases it is found that exceptional ability, amounting to genius, perhaps, was the real secret of the pre-eminence which many envied. So it appears to the student of human nature who seeks to trace the history of the rise of Harry L. Machen, a typical American of the best class. He is yet a young man but has achieved a success that many an older resident of Cape Girardeau might envy. He is the popular and efficient incumbent of the office of cashier of the Sturdivant Bank of this city.

A native of Sikeston, Scott county, Missouri, Mr. Harry L. Machen was born on the 5th of February, 1880, and he is a scion of a fine old Bluegrass family. His father, Henry L. Machen, was born in Lyon county, Kentucky, in the year 1843. When a lad of eighteen years of age, Harry L. Machen enlisted as a soldier in the Confederate army, becoming a member of a western Kentucky company, in Cobb's Artillery, and serving with all of valor and faithfulness as a soldier for a period of two years. He participated in a number of important engagements marking the progress of the war and was active in the battle of Shiloh, being one of the few survivors of that sanguinary campaign. He was taken prisoner by the Federal army and for a time was held in duress in the Delaware prison. After the close of the war he resided in his native state of Kentucky until the year 1877, at which time he removed to Missouri, settling in Scott county, where he was one of the largest and most influential farmers of the southeastern section of the state. He was also largely interested in the lumbering business. In 1891 he retired from active participation in business affairs and removed to Dexter, Missouri, where his demise occurred on the 1st of July, 1893, at the comparatively early age of fifty years. The paternal grandfather of him to whom this sketch is dedicated was Colonel B. Machen, who served on the staff of General Longstreet in the Confederate army. Colonel Machen was a prominent resident and a public-spirited citizen of Lyon county, Kentucky, and after the war he was honored with election to membership in the United States senate, in which capacity he served with all of honor and distinction. Henry L. Machen married Emma Wyatt, the ceremony having been performed in Lyon county, Kentucky, in 1876. To this union were born four children, of whom the subject of this sketch is the eldest. The others are: Margaret, who is now Mrs. James G. Reynolds; Edward Kirby Machen, who died November 7, 1902; and Mary Florence, who resides at home with her mother and brother.

After the death of the father, the Machen family removed to Cape Girardeau, where Harry L., who was then a lad of thirteen years of age, completed his rudimentary educational discipline. For a period of three years he was a student in the State Normal School, at Cape Girardeau, Missouri, and at the age of eighteen years he entered the Sturdivant Bank, where he has remained to the present time. In 1902 he was made assistant cashier of that substantial and highly reliable financial institution and on the 1st of March, 1909, he was promoted to the position of cashier. The Sturdivant Bank is the oldest monetary concern of its kind in southeastern Missouri, having been established in 1866, by Colonel Robert Sturdivant, one of the early pioneers in this section of the state. The bank has always enjoyed a good business and has successfully passed through three panics. It has a very conservative policy and through shrewd management has won a well merited reputation as one of the finest financial institutions in this part of the country. Prior to Colonel Sturdivant's acquisition of this bank it was a branch of the State Bank of Missouri. Up to 1882 it was a private corporation but in that year it was incorporated as a state bank, with a capital stock of thirty thousand dollars. Later the capital was increased to fifty thousand dollars and in 1902 to one hundred thousand dollars. The surplus and undivided profits amount to forty-five thousand dollars. The stockholders of the Sturdivant Bank are some of the wealthiest and most reliable citizens of southeastern Missouri and the splendid reputation enjoyed by the bank is largely the outcome of the sterling attributes of the officials and board of directors. Mr. Machen is strictly a self-made man and in addition to the duties devolving upon him as cashier of the above bank he is a director and one of the large stockholders in the Elks Realty Company. He is also a stockholder in the Cape Girardeau Park Association, and has a fine farm in New Madrid county.

In a fraternal way Mr. Machen is affiliated with the local lodge of the Benevolent and Protective Order of Elks and his religious faith is in harmony with the tenets of the Presbyterian church. In politics he accords an unswerving allegiance to the cause of the Democratic party and while he has never manifested aught of ambition or desire for the honors or emoluments of public office of any description he was persuaded at one time to accept the temporary position of city treasurer, after the impeachment of the regular incumbent of that office. He is not married and resides with his mother and sister in their beautiful home at 315 Bellview street. In all the relations of life Mr. Machen has so conducted himself as to command the unalloyed confidence and esteem of his fellow citizens and at Cape Girardeau he is universally admired and respected for his straightforward and honorable business career.

HENRY T. WEST, one of Kennett's prominent business men, is also identified with the political life of the town. It is not often that there are united in one man the qualities which make a successful farmer, an enterprising business man and a jurist, but Judge West is the unusual exception. During the thirty years and more that he has been a resident of Dunklin county, the Democratic party has found in him one of its most stalwart supporters, and a brief review of his life will serve to recall to the minds of his friends and acquaintances his business and public career of faithfulness, ability and honor.

Henry T. West was born November 30, 1852, in Williamson county, Illinois, where his father was a leading merchant and county official. After attending the public schools of his home locality and obtaining valuable experience as a farmer, on December 15, 1878, the stalwart young man of twenty-six left his native state and came to Missouri, where he likewise devoted himself to agricultural pursuits. He located on a farm five miles north of Kennett, but at the time of his coming the land was in its primitive condition, covered with a thick growth of timber. During the twelve years following his arrival Mr. West cleared a great portion of the land, brought it under cultivation, built good fences and made many other improvements. In 1890 he established a general merchandise business at Kennett, under the firm name of West & Bailey. For six years, under able management, the enterprise prospered, but in 1896 the store was destroyed by fire and the partnership was dissolved. In the course of the following years he twice entered into business in Kennett, and in April, 1902, he opened the store which he owns to-day. He carries a complete line of groceries of all kinds, but he aims to carry only one quality, and that the best. Mr. West's third and last venture in the mercantile field has already been of longer duration than either of his previous undertakings, and it has met with success from the very outset.

Mr. West has been married twice; his first wife was Miss Pauline Jane Ralls, to whom he was united on September 26, 1873, just before he had attained his majority. During the seven years of married life which followed three children were born to the couple, and in 1880 Mrs. West died in Dunklin county. The names of the three children are as follows: W. H., the eldest, the present assessor of Dunklin county; Daisy, who died at the age of eighteen; Lul, who did not survive infancy. In 1881 Mr. West celebrated his second marriage, to Miss Rosalie T. Greer, a native of Scott county, Missouri, where she passed her maiden life. Mrs. Rosalie West became the mother of nine children, five of whom died in infancy; one, Rosa, survived until she was fifteen years of age, and the three living children are as follows: Martha M., who was educated in the schools of Kennett, and is now a teacher in that place, after having taught two years at Senath, Missouri; Grace and Ruth, who are still pupils in the public schools.

Mr. West is affiliated with the Independent Order of Odd Fellows, in which society he is a past noble grand and its present treasurer. He holds membership with the Christian church of Kennett; for a period of forty years has been connected with the Disciples and during that time he has ever been an active worker for the local church which he attended; indeed, Mr. West is so constituted that he is bound to take an active part in connection with any enterprise in which he believes. This is as true in regard to politics as it is with religious matters. He finds in the Democratic platform the elements of good government, and, such being his views, he has been constant in upholding the Democratic party, which in its turn has shown its appreciation of his support and of his abilities and character by bestowing honors on him. It is well to state, however, that none of the offices which he has filled have been sinecures, but on the contrary have required the intelligent care which they have received at his hands.

In 1902 Mr. West was elected chairman of the board of trustees of Kennett; after serving on the board for the ensuing five years he declined re-election and was released from office the following two years. His services, however, were too valuable for him to be allowed to continue inactive in that regard, and in 1908 he was re-elected to the board of trustees, in which capacity he has served continuously ever since. Many of the improvements which have appeared in Kennett during the last few years are the direct result of his influence and efforts. For six years he served as police judge of Kennett, performing the duties pertaining to that office in the most scrupulous manner; but in such a quiet, effective way did he go to work that he was able to accomplish splendid results without making enemies. At the close of his six years' term, he was held in the highest esteem by both Republican and Democratic parties alike. He served two terms as justice of the peace, the first four years from January, 1897, to January, 1901, and he was again elected in the fall of 1906, serving from January, 1907, to January, 1911. In 1910 Mr. West was the regular Democratic nominee for the office of probate judge, and was elected by a large majority. He took office on the first of January, 1911, since which time his efforts have been directed towards the fulfilment of the duties of his office, of the importance of which he has the highest realization.

Judge West does not claim to be anything of a public speaker, as he believes that for him at least actions are more effective than words. He is generally to be found on convention committees, where he can be depended on to work for the Democratic cause and for the public good in general. Perhaps the reason that Mr. West has been able to win the confidence of the people to so large an extent is because, in his eyes, no duties are trivial. Anything which he undertakes he performs as if that duty were of the utmost importance. A man with such a high sense of responsibility is sure to accomplish great things in the world, as has been the case with Judge West.

HIRAM P. GEASLIN, justice of the peace at Hornersville, is an able citizen of Dunklin county whose career of usefulness is highly appreciated by his fellow citizens. The energy and ambition which accomplish things unaided by outside influences and in spite of difficulties have been his throughout his life, and relying on these qualities he has attained an honored position in his community.

Born on a farm in Lawrence county, Arkansas, October 19, 1873, he lost his father when he was two years old, and he lived at home with his mother until he was twenty-two. His mother died in 1899, her last years having been spent near her son and his wife. Up to the time he was seventeen years old he attended the public schools, including two years in the Sulphur Rock high school, and then began a career as teacher. He taught a summer term and during the winter continued his education, and taught about four months each year for seven years. When he was twenty-two he was elected assessor of his county, being in this office four years or two terms. He lived at Lynn while holding this office, which required about three months of each year, and part of the remaining time he spent in teaching.

On the expiration of his last term as assessor he moved to Dunklin county in 1902 and established a mercantile business in Branum. There was one other store in the village, and he had a good share of the patronage of that community. Mr. Geaslin has been a resident of Hornersville since 1906. Soon afterward he was elected justice of the peace and has held this office to the present time. In 1910 he was one of the five candidates on the Democratic ticket for nomination to the office of probate judge, and came in second. He is a potential candidate for 1914. In 1911 he established the only collecting agency in the southern part of Dunklin county. During his official and private business career he has acquired a practical training in the law, and for several years he has represented that profession in Hornersville. He is a tactful man of affairs, resourceful and energetic, and has the confidence of the entire community. Fraternally he is a member of the Independent Order of Odd Fellows and the tribe of Ben Hur.

In 1895, at the age of twenty-two, he married Miss Joann L. Penn, who died October 13, 1904, leaving three children: Bon, born in 1897; Paul, born in 1899, and Dessie, born in 1903. On March 2, 1905, Mr. Geaslin married Miss Grace A. Rodgers, of Hornersville, and they have three children: Sanford, born in 1906; Pleas, born in 1908; and Oliver, born in 1910.

ARTHUR V. CASHION. Perry county, Missouri, figures as one of the most attractive, progressive and prosperous divisions of the state, justly claiming a high order of citizenship and a spirit of enterprise which is certain to conserve consecutive development and marked advancement in the material upbuilding of this section. The county has been and is signally favored in the class of men who have contributed to its development along commercial and editorial lines and in the latter connection the subject of this review demands recognition as he has been actively engaged in the newspaper business during the greater part of his active career thus far. He owns and publishes the *Perry County Republican* in connection with his cousin Charles E. Cashion and this paper is recognized as one of the most enterprising and progressive publications in southeastern Missouri.

A native of Perryville, Missouri, Arthur V. Cashion was born on the 29th of February, 1868. He is a son of Archibald H. Cashion, whose birth occurred on a farm eligibly located some five miles south of Perryville. The parents of Archibald H. Cashion were William and Sally Cashion, both of whom died when their five boys were very young. These boys grew up on the old homestead farm in Perry county and when the dark cloud of Civil war obscured the national horizon all of them enlisted for service, their sympathies being with the North. Archibald H. Cashion was a member of the Fifth Missouri Cavalry and he participated in a number of important engagements marking the progress of the war. He served under General John McNeal and from the office of corporal was later promoted to the rank of lieutenant. After the close of the war and when peace had again been established throughout the country he returned to Perry county, where he again devoted his time and energies to farming operations. In the election of 1866 he was elected sheriff and collector of Perry county and after serving in those capacities for a period of four years he returned to his farm where he resided for a number of years. Just prior to the outbreak of the war between the states he had married Miss Margaret Brewer and they set up housekeeping on a farm adjoining the old Cashion estate. Mr. and Mrs. Archibald H. Cashion became the parents of eight children and the devoted wife and mother was called to eternal rest in the year 1906. In 1896 Mr. Cashion was honored by his fellow citizens with election to membership in the state legislature, as a representative of Perry county, serving two terms, and while a member of that august body he served on a number of important committees. After his retirement from the legislature he was appointed postmaster of Perryville, an office he filled with great credit to himself for a period of nine years. He is now living retired at

Perryville and while he has attained to the venerable age of seventy-two years he still retains in much of their pristine vigor the splendid physical and mental qualities of his prime. He is a grand old man and one well worthy of the high degree of popular confidence and esteem accorded him by all with whom he has come in contact.

Arthur V. Cashion is indebted to the public schools of Perryville for his early educational training and at the age of sixteen years he entered upon an apprenticeship to learn the printer's trade, working for a period of three years in the office of the *Perry County Sun,* under John B. Davis. In 1887 he removed to Marquand, in Madison county, Missouri, where he clerked in a store for a short period and where he later managed and edited the *Marquand Echo.* The *Echo* was a Republican paper and Mr. Cashion had charge of it during the Harrison campaign. In 1890 he returned to Perryville where he entered the office of the *Perry County Republican,* which was then owned and conducted by Charles E. Cashion, a cousin of the subject of this review. Later Mr. Cashion bought the plant of the *Perry County Republican* from his cousin and from 1891 until 1898 he conducted this paper individually. In 1898 Charles E. Cashion again became interested in the publication of the paper and in that year he was admitted to partnership in the conduct of the *Perry County Republican.*

On the 28th of December, 1889, was recorded the marriage of Mr. Cashion to Miss Ida Finger, the ceremony having been performed at Marquand, Missouri. Mr. and Mrs. Cashion have three sons, Elbert T., Medford and Benson, the two latter of whom remain at home. Elbert is assistant cashier in the Bank of Eudora, Arkansas. The Cashion family are devout and consistent members of the Presbyterian church in their religious faith and they contribute liberally of their time and means to all philanthropical movements projected in the community.

Mr. Cashion is a stanch Republican in his political views and it may be noted here that the Cashion cousins, through the medium of their paper, exerted a very strong influence in the building of the beautiful Perry county courthouse, which is located at Perryville and which is a great attraction in the way of beautifying the town. For nine years, from 1899 to 1908, Mr. Cashion was a member of the Perryville school board. In a fraternal way he is a valued and appreciative member of the local lodge of the Modern Brotherhood of America and he is a man whose many excellent attributes make him a valuable adjunct to the citizenship of Perryville.

BENJAMIN HOODENPYLE MARBURY. It is said that the poet is born, not made, but the successful lawyer has to be both born and made—made by close application, earnest effort, by perseverance and resolute purpose. The abilities with which nature has endowed him must be strengthened and developed by use, and only by merit can the lawyer gain a permanent position. And further than this, it is the tendency of the age to devote one's energies to a special line, continually working upward and concentrating his efforts toward accomplishing a desired end,—so in the career of Benjamin H. Marbury, who has risen above the average in his specialty and is one of the most prominent and successful of criminal lawyers. He also represents a number of important corporations and does a general practice.

Benjamin H. Marbury was born in Warren county, Tennessee, October 30, 1865, the same being the district of the nativity of his father, also Benjamin Marbury, whose eyes first opened to the light of day September 20, 1840. The elder gentleman, who was a physician by profession, was also educated for the law. His earlier training was secured in the Cumberland University at Lebanon, Tennessee, and to obtain his preparation in medicine and surgery he matriculated in the medical college which afterwards became the medical department of Vanderbilt University. being graduated from that institution in 1868, with the degree of M. D. He subsequently became surgeon for the Sewanee Coal Mine of Tracy City, Tennessee, and there remained until 1873, in which year he went to Mississippi county, Missouri, and within its boundaries he practiced medicine until his death, which lamentable event occurred November 20, 1875. He was a communicant of the Methodist Episcopal church, South, and in politics was a supporter of the men and measures of the Democratic party. He was married in Scott county, Missouri, to Rachel Anne Lusk, daughter of William M. Lusk, a farmer of that locality, and their love story was not without the pleasant element of romance. Benjamin Marbury, the elder, was a Confederate soldier under General Braxton Bragg.

In the year of the great struggle between the states he was captured at Franklin and was put a prisoner on board a boat which was landed at Scott's Landing. He escaped by jumping off the boat with four messmates, and while a fugitive he met Mr. Lusk, his father-in-law to be, and, both being Masons, a firm friendship was cemented. The elder gentleman took him to his home and there he met the daughter of the house, the two young people falling immediately in love. They were married in May, 1862. Three sons were born to bless this union, they being: Horatio L., editor of the *Festus News* at Festus, Missouri; Benjamin H.; and Dr. Alexander B., a dentist at Charleston. Dr. Marbury was a prominent and talented physician and well merited that term which has come to mean all of good, "a Southern gentleman."

Benjamin H. Marbury received his early education in the public schools of Mississippi county and later matriculated at Bellevue College, located at Caledonia, Missouri, and was graduated from the same in 1887, with the degree of B. S. Like so many of our successful men he taught school for several years and became president of St. Charles College, at St. Charles, Missouri. He completed his literary and legal education in Washington University at St. Louis, Missouri, and was admitted to the bar at Petosi, Missouri, in 1895. In 1897 he came to Farmington and here success has awaited him. He was elected prosecuting attorney in November, 1903, and served until 1905. Generally recognized as a proper man for public office, he was made a candidate for judge of the St. Louis Court of Appeals in September, 1910, but was beaten by Charles Bates. At the present time he is attorney for the St. Louis Smelting & Refining Company and also for the Farmers Bank, the Flat River Ice & Cold Storage Company, and the Peoples' Bank of Delose. As a member of the firm of Marbury & Hensley he conducts a very successful general practice, Mr. W. L. Hensley, his partner, being United States congressman from the Thirteenth Missouri district. Mr. Marbury has won considerable fame in this locality as a gifted criminal lawyer. During the one term in which he was prosecuting attorney he convicted over forty men, one for the death penalty. The aggregate sentence of the remaining thirty-nine amounted to over one thousand years. He proved a stanch and strenuous judge,—the friend of good government.

Mr. Marbury laid the foundation of a happy home and ideally congenial life companionship when on September 3, 1895, he was united in marriage to Annie Eversole, of Caledonia, Missouri, daughter of William G. and Rebecca A. Eversole. Mr. and Mrs. Marbury share their hospitable and attractive home with three children—Virginia, Leonard Rutledge and Anna. Mrs. Marbury is a direct descendant of Chief Justice John Rutledge, of South Carolina. The subject is in direct descent from Felix Grundy, the celebrated Southern statesman, United States senator from Tennessee in 1829-1838 and attorney general from 1838 to 1840. Mr. Marbury is a gifted orator and possibly inherits his silver tongue from his distinguished forebear. Fraternally he is a member of the Knights of Pythias, Cristal Lodge, No. 50, of Farmington; politically is a Democrat; and he and his family are members of the Methodist Episcopal church, South.

GEORGE KRONE, formerly of the firm of Hooper & Krone, now serving his second term as mayor of Senath, has public official, his achievements in developing and advancing the material interests of the community bringing to the people a realization that the affairs of the city are their affairs, and at all times entitled to their consideration. A native of Kentucky, he was born August 13, 1878, in Calloway county, where he resided until eighteen years of age.

In 1896 Mr. Krone came to Senath, Missouri, arriving here four months later than his mother, and where he also had a brother living, J. W. Hall, who is still a resident of this city, and one of its earliest pioneer citizens, he having come here before there were any railways in this section of the country. Forced by circumstances to earn his own living, he worked by the month as a farm hand for two years, and the next two years found employment in a shop. Ambitious then to embark in business on his own account, Mr. Krone bought a team on credit, and began draying, an industry in which he was prosperously engaged for eight years, doing almost the entire draying for the town. During the last two years in which he was thus engaged he also dealt in feed, ice and coal, building up a trade which demanded so much of his time that he gave up the draying in its favor, since September, 1910, being junior member of the firm of Hooper & Krone. Mr.

Krone is a keen, far-sighted man of business, and through his own efforts has accumulated a good property. He has two hundred and thirty-eight acres of valuable farming land, the greater part of which is under cultivation, and is operated by tenants. He has also erected several business houses and residences in Senath. In April, 1909, Mr. Krone was elected mayor of Senath, and served the city so ably and faithfully that in April, 1911, he was re-elected to the same high position.

Mr. Krone married, July 28, 1901, Fanny Barr, who was born in Texas, but was brought up near Senath, Missouri, where her father was engaged in farming until his death. The union of Mr. and Mrs. Krone has been blessed by the birth of one child, Jewel. Religiously Mrs. Krone is a member of the Christian church. Mr. Krone is an active member of the Democratic party, and fraternally he belongs to the Benevolent and Protective Order of Elks; to the Modern Woodmen of America; and to the Woodmen of the World.

EDWARD B. RECK. Fourteen years postmaster of Lutesville with an average absence from the office of less than a day a year is the enviable record of Edward B. Reck, born in Cape Girardeau, September 1, 1869. Both his father, Frederick Reck, and his mother, Adelina, were natives of Missouri and of Cape Girardeau county. The former was born near Appleton and the latter near Shawneetown. Mr. Reck's grandfather, George Reck, was born in Germany, likewise his grandmother, Catherine Reck. George Reck was a shoemaker in the "fatherland" and followed that trade in Cape Girardeau county, where he had an extensive business, and was also engaged in farming. After serving ten months in the militia, Frederick Reck enlisted in the Union Army, May 2, 1863. He belonged to Company C, second Missouri Light Artillery. He served in the war until December, 1865, and then spent six months fighting the Indians. The campaign was one of incessant activity. Engagements were numerous and often desperate. Mr. Reck was in the fight at Jefferson City and the one at Glasgow, besides a number of lesser engagements and numberless skirmishes. After being mustered out of service in 1866, Mr. Reck married Miss Adeline Whiteledge and resumed his occupation of farming, in which his good management and hard work made him more than ordinarily successful. Edward B. is one of the three children of Mr. and Mrs. Frederick Reck, the others being: John A. Reck, a physician of Oklahoma City, Oklahoma, and Cora, wife of Mason F. Kinder, of Marble Hill, Missouri.

Like most of the successful men of his generation, Edward B. Reck spent his boyhood on his father's farm. He attended the public schools and had the additional advantage of a course in the Pocahontas high school. He remained with his father until he was twenty-four years old and then went to farming for himself on his father's home place of seventy acres. In August, 1893, he moved to Lutesville and for three years worked there as a laborer. In 1897 Mr. Reck was appointed postmaster, which office he still holds. The Lutesville postoffice is no sinecure, as all the mail for the southern part of the county must pass through the Lutesville office. Formerly Mr. Reck handled the mail for the following offices, Marble Hill, Leopold, Dongola, Zalma, Huxis, Hahn and Lutesville. The distribution is now made through Marble Hill, Zalma and Hahn. Mr. Reck sorts out the mail for the four or five offices for which Zalma is the distributing point. The Lutesville office has been burglarized twice during Mr. Reck's term of service.

Mr. Reck was first married to Rosa Schatte, of Cape Girardeau county, on Christmas day of 1892. Rosa was the daughter of John and Mary Schatte, old residents of the county but natives of Germany. The death of Mrs. Reck occurred March 14, 1897. In 1898 Mr. Reck's union with Mrs. Julia A. Yount took place. She is the daughter of Henry Schenimann, of Cape Girardeau county, where he was a successful merchant, also a farmer and stock raiser. Henry Schenimann came to America from Germany in 1844 with his father, D. Schenimann. The boy was but nine years old at the time. The family settled in Cape Girardeau county, where Mrs. Reck's father grew up. Mr. Henry Schenimann served three years in the enrolled militia in the Civil war. He afterwards engaged in mercantile business at Neely's Landing. His daughter Julia became the wife of W. C. Yount, a merchant of Patton, Missouri, on March 27, 1895. One child, Miss Willie C., was born of this union, which was tragically ended before their first anniversary, for Mr. Yount was shot March 14, 1896.

The eldest of Mr. and Mrs. Reck's four

children, Alpha O., was born February 11, 1899. Their son Fred E. was eleven on the sixteenth of December, 1911. Inez Glorine was born April 27, 1903, and Hope Otelea on the seventeenth of the same month, six years afterward.

Though Mr. Reck is so constantly on duty at the postoffice, he has other interests in which he is active. He is a stockholder in the Bollinger County Bank and has been second vice-president of it for eight years. He owns a fine residence property in Lutesville and is prominent in the lodges of that town, being a member of the Ancient Free and Accepted Masons, the Royal Arch Masons and the Modern Woodmen. In politics he is a staunch adherent of the Republican party. His religious preference is for the Presbyterian church, of which he and his wife are both members.

WILBUR M. WELKER, the superintendent of the Bollinger county schools, was born in this county June 9, 1883. His father, J. A. Welker, is a farmer now residing at Bloomfield. Randolph Welker, the grandfather of Wilbur M., was also born in the county, where his father, Wilbur's great-grandfather, came from in North Carolina.

The second of a family of nine children, Mr. Wilbur M. Welker was kept busy on his grandfather's farm when not attending school. Until he was twenty years old his life was spent in this fashion. In 1903 he began to teach school and has followed this profession ever since. Two years in the district schools, two in the schools of Marble Hill and three years in Bessville have filled up his seven years' experience.

As Mr. Welker is ambitious, he has spent the time not occupied in the school-room in studying. Part of two different years he attended Will Mayfield College. By taking courses in the spring and the summer terms at the State Normal at Cape Girardeau, he obtained the degree of Bachelor of Pedagogy from that institution. In April, 1911, Mr. Welker was elected county superintendent for four years. He is in charge of eighty-nine schools in Bollinger county.

On December 23, 1906, occurred the marriage of Mr. Welker and Miss Clara Walker, daughter of Richard A. Walker, of this county. They have two children, Vera Vern, born 1907, and Paul Lee Alexander, two years younger. The family reside upon a place of forty-three acres, which they own. Mr. Welker is a member of the Missouri Teachers' Association and keeps abreast of all educational movements. Fraternally he is connected with the Independent Order of Odd Fellows and with the Modern Woodmen of America.

B. P. BURNHAM, now serving in his second term as county superintendent of the schools of Iron county, has gained much distinction as an educator in this section of Missouri, and during his long connection with the schools of this locality has succeeded in greatly raising the standard of education and promoting the efficiency of the system as a preparation for the responsible duties of life. Indeed, the constant aim and the general character of Mr. Burnham's life work are summed up in the famous dictum of Sidney Smith,—that "The real object of education is to give children resources that will endure as long as life endures; habits that time will ameliorate, not destroy; occupation that will render sickness tolerable, solitude pleasant, age venerable, life more dignified and useful, and death less terrible."

A native of Reynolds county, Missouri, B. P. Burnham was born on the 9th of April, 1875, he being a son of Martin L. and Mary (Sloan) Burnham, the former of whom is now living at Ellington, Missouri, and the latter of whom was summoned to the life eternal in 1876. Martin L. Burnham was born on Current river, in Missouri, his father, Samuel Burnham, having come to that section of the state in the ante-bellum days. Samuel Burnham was a native of Indiana, while his wife, nee Miss George, was born in Missouri, and he was a gallant soldier in the Confederate army during the Civil war. He died at his home in Reynolds county, Missouri, about 1870, his old farm near Ellington being still in the possession of his descendants. He was an extensive farmer and stock-raiser during the greater portion of his active career. Martin L. Burnham was likewise engaged in farming operations for a number of years but he is now identified with the hotel business at Ellington, where he is a man of mark in all the relations of life. He is a devout member of the Missionary Baptist church. His wife, whose maiden name was Mary Sloan, was born near Belleview, in Iron county, this state, a daughter of Alexander and Mary Elizabeth (Wyatt)

Sloan, who came from Tennessee to Missouri about 1830. Mrs. Burnham died before she had reached her thirtieth year and the subject of this review was her only child.

Mr. Burnham was reared to the invigorating discipline of the old homestead farm and his preliminary educational training consisted of such advantages as were afforded in the public schools of Reynolds county. Subsequently he attended the Marvin Collegiate Institute, at Fredericktown, Missouri, and for a time he was also a student in the state normal school at Cape Girardeau. On the 9th of April, 1902, he was graduated in the Gem City Business College, at Quincy, Illinois. For six years he was engaged in teaching in Reynolds county and from 1902 to 1909 he was a popular and successful teacher in Iron county. He was elected county school commissioner in April, 1909, serving in that capacity until he qualified as superintendent of the schools of Iron county, assuming charge of the responsibilities connected with that office on the 16th of August, 1909. In April, 1911, he was elected as his own successor for the office of county superintendent for a term of four years, and he is acquitting himself with all of honor and distinction in discharging the duties of that important position. As a teacher Mr. Burnham had charge of the schools at Belleview, Annapolis, Granite, Pilot Knob and other places in the state.

On the 9th of August, 1905, was solemnized the marriage of Mr. Burnham to Miss Letha M. Moyer, whose birth occurred in Iron county and who is a daughter of A. G. Moyer, of Belleview. This union has been blessed with one child, Edwin B., whose natal day is the 14th of September, 1906.

In politics Mr. Burnham is a Democrat. His interest in political questions is deep and sincere and he gives a hearty support to all projects advanced for the good of the general welfare. In a fraternal way he is affiliated with Camp No. 421 of the Independent Order of Odd Fellows, at Annapolis, and with the Belleview lodge of the Modern Woodmen of America. In their religious faith Mr. and Mrs. Burnham are devout members of the Methodist Episcopal church, South, to whose good works they are most liberal contributors of their time and means. They are popular and prominent in connection with the best social activities at Ironton, where their beautiful home is the scene of many attractive gatherings.

LEON J. ALBERT. A representative of a family whose name has been prominently and worthily identified with the history of southeastern Missouri for more than half a century, Leon J. Albert has long held distinctive prestige as one of the active and influential business men of the city of Cape Girardeau, which place has represented his home since his boyhood days and in which he holds secure vantage ground in popular confidence and esteem. He is essentially one of the representative citizens of Cape Girardeau county, his influence has permeated the civic and business activities of this favored section of the state, and his activities have been directed along normal and legitimate lines. In point of consecutive identification with the more important business interests in Cape Girardeau he is now one of the older business men in this city, where his capitalistic interests are of broad scope and importance. He has stood exponent of the highest civic ideals and the utmost loyalty and few residents of Cape Girardeau have wielded larger or more beneficent influence in the promotion of the best interests of the community. He served seven years as mayor of his home city and has held other positions of public trust,—preferments that bear patent evidence of the high regard in which he is held in the community that has so long been his home and the center of his productive activities. Here he is president of the Sturdivant Bank, the oldest and most substantial financial institution of this section of the state, and he has been actively concerned with the same for forty years, being the oldest banker in Missouri south of St. Louis. He is also a member of the directorate of the Southeast Missouri Trust Company and has other large interests in Cape Girardeau.

Leon J. Albert was born at Portland, Jefferson county, Kentucky, on the 6th of November, 1840, and the village in which he was thus ushered into the world is now an integral part of the city of Louisville. He is a son of Nicholas and Anna (Hoin) Albert, both of whom were natives of France and the marriage of whom was solemnized in the city of Louisville, Kentucky. Nicholas Albert was born in Alsace-Lorraine, France, a district that became a German province as a result of the Franco-Prussian war, and there he was reared to years of maturity. He received excellent educational advantages and, reared on the border between France and Germany, he had virtually equal facility in the use of both the French and German languages,—a knowledge that proved of great value to him during his subsequent business career in America. His mother died in her native land and after he himself had established his residence in the United States his venerable father, John Albert, joined him and passed the residue of his life in Louisville, Kentucky.

Nicholas Albert gained his initial business experience in his native land, where he continued to maintain his home until 1830, when, as a young man, he embarked on a sailing vessel and set forth to seek his fortunes in the United States. After a long and weary voyage he landed in the city of New Orleans, whence he proceeded to Kentucky and located in the city of Louisville. There he was given a municipal office, largely due to his familiarity with the French and German languages, and in the '40s he removed with his family to Jackson, Cape Girardeau county, Missouri, where he engaged in the general merchandise business, in company with his brother. In 1852 he removed to Cape Girardeau, the judicial center and metropolis of the county, and here he soon gained precedence as one of the leading merchants of the county. He was a man of marked ability and sterling character, commanded the high regard of all who knew him and was an influential factor in local affairs of a public order. He was well known throughout the county and was the confidential advisor of its French and German citizens, the while he was deeply appreciative of the institutions and advantages of the land of his adoption, to which his loyalty was ever of the most unequivocal type. He was called to various offices of local trust and at the time of his death was incumbent of the position of United States gauger for his district. He was summoned to the life eternal in August, 1874, at the age of sixty-eight years, and his name merits enduring place on the roster of the sterling citizens who have aided in the development and upbuilding of this favored section of the state of Missouri. In politics he gave his support to the cause of the Democratic party and both he and his wife were devout communicants of the Catholic church, in whose faith they were reared. Mrs. Albert died in 1872, at the age of fifty-six years, leaving four sons and one daughter, all of whom attained to years of maturity, and three of whom are now living.

Leon J. Albert, the second in order of birth of the five children, gained his rudimentary education in Louisville, Kentucky, and he was about twelve years of age at the time of the family removal to Missouri. He continued to attend school at Cape Girardeau, this state, and was about twelve years old when the family home was established in the little city, where he has maintained his residence during the long intervening years, within which he has risen to a position as one of the representative citizens of the section of the state to which this history is devoted. Here he continued his higher academic studies in St. Vincent's College. After leaving this institution he was for a time employed as clerk in his father's mercantile establishment and later he was for two years a clerk on boats of the St. Louis & Memphis Packet Company, operating a line of steamboats between the two cities mentioned. After severing his connection with this company Mr. Albert became associated with his uncles, John and Sebastian Albert, in the wholesale grocery business at Cape Girardeau, and with this line of enterprise he was thus identified from 1864 until 1871, in which year he assumed the position of cashier in the bank of Robert Sturdivant, which was then a private institution. In 1882 the bank was incorporated under the laws of the state, under the title of the Sturdivant Bank, and Mr. Albert continued to serve as its cashier until January, 1902, when he was elected president of the institution, of which office he has since continued incumbent. He has wielded much influence in the upbuilding of this solid and popular banking concern, which bases its operations on a capital stock of one hundred thousand dollars and which now has a surplus fund of twenty-five thousand dollars. From dates designated it will be seen that Mr. Albert has been consecutively identified with the executive affairs of this bank for a period of forty years, and additional significance is given to this statement by reason of the fact that the Sturdivant Bank is the oldest in the state south of St. Louis. Its management has ever been along careful and conservative lines and it has successfully weathered the various financial panics of localized or national order, without the slightest questioning of its ability to liquidate all its obligations at any period in its history. The bank has done much to conserve the best interests of the community in which it is located and those identified with its management have at all times been citizens of the highest standing.

In addition to being one of the principal stockholders in the bank of which he is president, Mr. Albert is also one of the leading principals in the Southeast Missouri Trust Company, of Cape Girardeau, which was organized and incorporated in 1906 and which has a paid up capital stock of five hundred thousand dollars. He was one of the organizers of this corporation and has been a valued member of its directorate from the beginning. He is also a stockholder and director in the Cape Girardeau Water Works Company and the local electric-light company. Every enterprise and measure projected for the general good of the community has received the earnest co-operation of Mr. Albert and no citizen of Cape Girardeau has shown more distinctive loyalty and public spirit. Though he has had naught of ambition for public office, he yielded to the importunities of his fellow citizens and consented to become a candidate for the office of mayor of his home city. He was first elected to this position in 1877 and he served as mayor for seven years,—a fact that offers the best voucher for the efficiency and acceptability of his administration of municipal affairs,—an administration marked by due conservatism and wise progressive policies. Mr. Albert has shown a specially lively interest in educational affairs and he has served consecutively as a member of the board of regents of the Missouri State Normal School at Cape Girardeau since 1885. He was appointed to this office by Governor Francis and has thrice been reappointed. During more than a quarter of a century of such identification with this fine state institution he has been indefatigable in the promoting of its interests and the maintaining of its facilities at the highest standard. Besides serving as mayor of his home city Mr. Albert has held other municipal offices and also county offices, his election to each of which was made entirely without solicitation or effort on his part and his acceptance of which was prompted solely by a sense of civic duty. In politics he accords unwavering allegiance to the Democratic party and both he and his wife are communicants of the Protestant Episcopal church. He is one of the appreciative and valued members of Cape Girardeau Lodge, No. 639, Benevolent and Protective Order of Elks.

In the year 1864 was solemnized the marriage of Mr. Albert to Miss Clara Given Haydock, of Livingston county, Kentucky, and she was summoned to eternal rest on the 25th of December, 1900. Of the nine children of this union six are now living, and concerning them the following brief data are given: Hattie is the widow of S. R. Nelson, of Chillicothe, Missouri, and she has three children. Leon, Jr., who is engaged in banking at St. Louis, Missouri, married Miss Mary Juden, and they have three children; Alma is the wife of William W. Wood, of Baltimore, Maryland, and they have three children; Harry, who is a resident of St. Louis, Missouri, where he is engaged in the real estate business, married Miss Charlotte Peironnett, and they have two children; Clara is the wife of Henry Coerver, of Olathe, Colorado, and they have one child; and Leland is engaged in commission business at Cape Girardeau. Helen, who is deceased, became the wife of Melbourne Smith, of Farmington, Missouri, and is survived by one child, so that Mr. Albert has a total of thirteen grandchildren, in whom he takes the deepest interest, as may well be inferred. On the 4th of April, 1907, Mr. Albert contracted a second marriage, by wedding Miss Lee Cairns, who was born and reared in Missouri and who proves a gracious chatelaine of his beautiful home in Cape Girardeau.

JOSEPH F. CHILTON, the present prosecuting attorney of Madison county, Missouri, has gained a position of distinctive priority as one of the representative members of the bar of the state and he served for one term as representative from his district in the Missouri state legislature. He has gained success and prestige through his own endeavors and thus the more honor is due him for his earnest labors in his exacting profession and for the precedence he has gained in his chosen vocation.

A native of Fredericktown, Missouri, Joseph F. Chilton was born on the 8th of February, 1872, a son of Septimus W. and Julia (Newberry) Chilton, the former of whom is now living in retirement at Fredericktown and the latter of whom was summoned to the life eternal in 1888. The father was born near the Missouri-Arkansas state line and he passed his boyhood and youth in Madison county. He was early bereft of his parents, both having died on the same day, when he was a child of but six months of age. Practically rearing himself, his early educational training consisted of such advantages as were afforded in the public schools of Madison county. At the age of sixteen years he enlisted as a soldier in the Confederate army, serving with all of honor and distinction in the cause of the South for a period of four years. After the close of the war he returned to Madison county, locating at Fredericktown, where he engaged in commercial gardening. He has always been a stanch Democrat in his political proclivities and in his religious faith is a devout member of the Methodist Episcopal church. In 1867 he married Miss Julia Newberry, and to them were born two children,—George, who remains at home with his father; and Joseph F., whose name forms the caption for this review.

After completing the curriculum of the public schools at Fredericktown, Joseph F. Chilton was a student in the Missouri State Normal School, for a time, then turning his attention to the study of law. For two years he attended the Chicago College of Law, at Chicago, Illinois, being graduated therein as a member of the class of 1897 and duly receiving his degree of Bachelor of Laws. He was licensed to practice law in Missouri in 1898 and in that year initiated the active work of his profession at Fredericktown where he soon succeeded in building up a large and representative clientage and where he has gained recognition as one of the leading lawyers in Madison county. In 1906 he was honored by his fellow citizens with election to membership in the lower house of the state legislature, serving in that capacity for one term, during which time he was assigned to a number of important committees. In the fall of 1910 he was elected prosecuting attorney of Madison county and in that connection he is giving most creditable service. He is a man of unusual ability and splendid equipment along the line of his chosen vocation and has already achieved phenomenal success in the legal profession.

In 1900 Mr. Chilton wedded Miss Maude May, who was likewise born and reared at Fredericktown and who is a daughter of Frank and Amanda (Newcum) May. The Newcum family were early pioneers in Madison county. Mr. and Mrs. Chilton have four children, whose names and respective ages, in 1911, are here entered,—Wilma, ten years; May, eight years; Julia, six years; and S. W., three years.

In politics Mr. Chilton is a stanch Democrat and in a social way he is affiliated with the Masonic order, being a valued member of the Order of the Eastern Star, and he is also connected with the local lodges of the Independent Order of Odd Fellows and the Knights of Pythias. The religious faith of the Chilton family is in harmony with the tenets of the Methodist Episcopal church, in whose faith they are rearing their children.

CHARLES B. PARSONS. As steadfast as the granite hills of his native state was the character of the late Charles Bunyan Parsons, and, measured by its accomplishment, its beneficence, its altruism and its uprightness, his life counted for good in every relation. Bringing to bear the powers of a strong and versatile personality, his optimism was of the true constructive order and through his well directed endeavors as a member of the world's noble army of productive workers he gained large and worthy success. His course was ever guided and governed by the highest principles of integrity and honor and he merited and received the confidence and esteem of his fellow men. His splendid abilities were prolific in their influence upon the industrial and civic development and upbuilding of Southeastern Missouri, and here the great success which he gained had its basis in his close and influential association with the development of the great mineral resources of this section of the state. His early labors in this connection implied self-denial, strong initiative and executive ability admirably applied, and a confidence and courage to which no obstacle was held insuperable. But above his great achievements in connection with material things, the great mind and heart of the man made him exemplify the higher ideals of human existence, and he never failed in his stewardship or in his helpful interest in his fellow men. It can well be realized that such a man merits consideration in a work of the province assigned to the one at hand, and it is gratifying to be able to perpetuate in this volume a record of his life and labors and to offer a tribute to his memory. In the preparation of this memoir recourse is taken largely to a memorial published, for private circulation, soon after his death, and it is not deemed necessary to utilize formal designation of quotation in drawing from such source.

Charles Bunyan Parsons was born at Benson, Rutland county, Vermont, on the 26th of February, 1836, and died at his home in Riverside, Jefferson county, Missouri, on the 28th of January, 1910, secure in the lasting esteem of all who knew him. He was a scion of a family, of staunch English origin, that was founded in New England, that cradle of so much of our national history, in the early colonial days, and he came from a long line of educated and talented folk. His grandfather, Reuben Parsons, was a man of fine intellectual attainments and wielded benignant influence in the community in which he lived. His maternal grandfather, Judge Chauncey Smith, was a citizen of distinctive prominence and influence in Vermont, where he acquired great wealth, as gauged by the standard of the locality and period. He served in a magisterial or judicial capacity for a number of years and for several years represented his county in the state legislature of Vermont. Concerning him, with incidental reference to the grandson, Charles B. Parsons, the following pertinent statement has been made: "He was a large contributor to the needs of all worthy persons and causes, a trait of character strongly developed by his grandson, Charles B. Parsons."

Henry Augustus Parsons, father of him whose name initiates this memoir, was likewise a native of Benson, Vermont, where he was born on the 19th of August, 1790, and where he was reared and educated. He was prominent in the social and religious life of the town, and, being a fine musician, was for forty years a member of the local church choir. He was closely identified with the various interests of his home town, and as a member of the state militia he was with the troop that went from Benson to meet General LaFayette, in 1824, on the occasion of the visit of the distinguished nobleman to the land whose gaining of independence he had so signally aided in the war of the Revolution. By vocation Henry A. Parsons was a saddler and harness manufacturer, and he continued to follow this line of enterprise in his native town until impaired health compelled him to seek a change of climate. He first removed to Brighton, New York; thence to Rochester, that state, where he remained until 1854, when he removed with his family to Michigan, where he passed the residue of his life, his death having occurred at Hillsdale, that state, on the 22d of January, 1862. His cherished and devoted wife, whose maiden name was Elizabeth Smith, was born at Benson, Vermont, on the 12th of April, 1791, and died at the home of her son Charles B. subject of this review, in Bonne Terre, Missouri, on the 30th of November, 1884, at the venerable age of ninety-three years. Concerning her the following appreciative words have been written: "She was a woman of great force of character and loveliness of disposition. She came to Bonne Terre, Missouri, after the death of her husband and her declining years were spent in the pleasant home of her son. She passed to the life eternal well beloved by all who had known her." Henry A. and Elizabeth (Smith) Parsons became the parents of six sons and five daughters, all of whom are now deceased except the youngest daughter, Emily, who married General C. C. Doolittle, brother of Mr. Parsons' wife. Of the eleven children Charles B. was the youngest. Two of the sons, Lafayette and Chauncey, were graduated in the collegiate institution at Castleton, Vermont, and in the medical college at Pittsfield, Massachusetts. Both practiced their profession in Michigan, and another brother, Reuben, was just entering upon the practice of the same profession when he sacrificed his life during the great cholera epidemic of 1849. Dr. Lafayette Parsons served as a member of the Michigan legislature, and late in life he removed to Adair county, Iowa, where he died at the age of eighty-three years.

When it was deemed expedient for the family to remove to Michigan, Henry Parsons was sent on ahead to begin the work of clearing the homestead which had been secured in the midst of the forest in St. Joseph county, Michigan. A few weeks later Charles B. Parsons, who was at the time seventeen years of age, and who had been afforded the advantages of the Rochester schools, set forth for the new home to join his brother Henry and help in the clearing. He started with a team and a load of household goods for this overland trip.

Concerning this memorable journey the following description has been given: "With only his dog for company, he made the dreary trip of more than five hundred miles, crossing the Niagara river into Canada and recrossing the boundary into the United States at Detroit. In due time he arrived at the clearing made by his brother. Three weeks later his brother Henry was killed by a falling tree, and this proved a tremendous disaster to the surviving brother,—a beardless boy, alone in the big woods with only a few neighbors for help. Alone, the boy continued the work, cleared the land and built the home. When everything was ready, with that minute attention to details which was one of his characteristics, he sent for his parents to join him, and with them he remained on the farm until he was twenty-one years of age.''

Upon thus attaining to his legal majority Mr. Parsons determined to work his way through college. This ambition he found virtually impossible to realize, and he became a teacher in the public school in the little village of Burr Oak, Michigan. Thereafter he devoted three years to the study of dentistry and after mastering the same he engaged in practice at Hillsdale, Michigan. Soon, however, he subordinated all other interests to tender his aid in defense of the Union, whose integrity was menaced by armed rebellion. Upon the first call for volunteers for service in the Civil war Mr. Parsons enlisted in Company E, Fourth Michigan Volunteer Infantry, and before the regiment left the state he was made second lieutenant of his company. His command proceeded directly to the city of Washington and participated in the first battle of Bull Run. Mr. Parsons was promoted first lieutenant on the 1st of September, 1861, and on the 1st of the following July was made captain of his company. In the command of General McClelland he took part in all the battles incidental to the campaign of that gallant leader and he distinguished himself by conspicuous and meritorious service until impaired health compelled him to retire, on the 27th of March, 1863, in which month he duly received his honorable discharge. It should be noted that he ever retained a deep interest in his old comrades in arms, and that he indicated the same by his membership in the Grand Army of the Republic and the Military Order of The Loyal Legion.

In 1864 Mr. Parsons accepted a position with a mining company at Northampton, Massachusetts, where he retained this incumbency for three years, at the expiration of which the mines ceased operation. At Northampton he formed the acquaintance of J. Wyman Jones who, with associates, had recently purchased the LaGrave mines in Missouri, and Mr. Parsons was engaged to visit the mines and make a personal investigation of the same, with subsequent report to the owners. He accomplished the work assigned to him and upon his return to the east made his report to the directors of the company. He was soon afterward tendered the position of superintendent of these mines, but he considered it inexpedient to accept the place, owing to the remoteness of the mines from advantages of civilization to which his wife and family were accustomed. Concerning his final decision and action the following record has been made and is worthy of perpetuation: "Mrs. Parsons, who was ever her husband's trusted confidante and adviser, displaying that spirit of devotion and self-sacrifice which in all the years of their married life made her a tower of strength to her husband, urged him to accept the position, declaring, like Ruth of old, 'Whither thou goest I will go,' and the decision was made. Mr. Parsons came west and assumed charge May 1, 1867, leaving his family at DeSoto, then a small town, until June 26th, when he brought them to Bonne Terre and installed them in half of the only frame house in the place. Thus it was that this kind, gentle and capable man came to Bonne Terre and came to be associated with and bound up in the life history of nearly every one of our people.'' Continuing, this local estimate gives further words of deep appreciation and honor: "Standing at the brow of one of our hills and looking over our beautiful, modern little city of six thousand people; viewing the clouds of smoke rising from the largest lead mine in the world; noting our handsome schools, beautiful churches and peaceful homes nestling amid bowers of shade,—is it to be wondered that the people of this place, through the long months of Mr. Parsons' illness, gave their daily thoughts to the suffering man whose genius had made Bonne Terre a possibility, and is it strange that as life's sands ran low, the desire of Mr. Parsons should be that his remains be laid at rest among those who for nearly forty-five years had been near and dear to him, and that when the final summons came it was felt as a personal loss to everyone in Bonne Terre?''

It is not within the province of this publication to enter into details concerning the upbuilding of the great industrial enterprises with which Mr. Parsons' name was so long and conspicuously identified, but it should be noted that no other one man has done so much to develop the great lead resources of this section of the state and that his labors were of herculean order in this connection. In these early days adverse conditions, circumstances and influences compassed him in his endeavors, but with characteristic courage, tenacity of purpose and fertility of expedient he pressed forward along the course he had defined, with the result that the years gave him tribute and splendid reward. He was the dominating power in the upbuilding of one of the greatest industries of the kind in the world, and it is due to him largely that the St. Joseph Lead Company gained precedence as the largest lead-mining concern of all in existence. Such accomplishment denotes the great executive and constructive ability of the man and through his labors in this connection he did much for mankind, the while gaining for himself and family a comfortable fortune of nearly two million dollars,—representing the just reward of long years of earnest and indefatigable toil and endeavor. Further reference to the mining industry is not demanded in this connection, as the subject is amply considered in the generic history on other pages. None but a strong man could show such results in the mastering of circumstances, and these results tell their own story. However, there is consistency in making the following brief extract from the published memorial to which reference has been made in a preceding paragraph: "To the task of making available the immense lead deposits Mr. Parsons devoted himself and his every energy. The first shaft to the lower deposits was started the latter part of March, 1870, and with the first load of rock hoisted from its underground bed there arose the stupendous problem of crushing, separating and smelting. No blazed trails were there to follow, and in the still watches of the long nights Mr. Parsons wrestled with the problems, sometimes discouraged and disheartened but ever persistent and ever exhibiting to the world a smiling face, so that only his loved ones knew of his trials and discouragements, and no one knew that the helpful, courteous superintendent, who was always ready with a kind word, a helpful suggestion, a hearty handshake, or an order on the store to supply some poor fellow with a pair of shoes, was for months unable to look into the future for a single day with hope of reward, and was only kept to his hard task, was only enabled to face each new day with confidence, by the cheerful counsel and support of that splendidly equipped wife and mother who had been more than willing to leave home, friends and social enjoyments to come with him into the wilderness of the west. These years, and the many years which followed them, were years filled with ceaseless vigil, burning life's candle at both ends; always planning, always looking forward, and, withal, always willing to lend a helping hand to the weak or to give from his store to those in need.'' This indeed represents a triumphant life, and all who knew Mr. Parsons not only revere his memory but also realize that none ever was more worthy of success.

The very nature of Mr. Parsons was one of breadth and liberality, and he gave of himself to the furthering of every measure and enterprise tending to advance the material and social welfare of his home community, and also the entire district in which his interests centered. Thus he was concerned with railroad development, with the exploitation of all public utilities and with the upbuilding of various industrial and commercial enterprises of magnitude and importance. He was one of the large stockholders and active executives not only in the St. Joseph Lead Company but also in the Mississippi River & Bonne Terre Railroad Company, the Doe Run Lead Company, the Bonne Terre Farming & Title Company, and the Farmers' & Miners' Trust Company, of Bonne Terre.

In politics Mr. Parsons gave a staunch allegiance to the Republican party, and he was zealous in the furtherance of its cause, the while it was a distinct pleasure to him that he lived to see St. Francois county cast a majority of Republican votes. He was a delegate to the national convention that first nominated William McKinley for the presidency and was active in the local councils of his party.

In the advancement of educational facilities he took an abiding interest and he served for many years as a valued member of the Bonne Terre school board. He never sought political preferment and it was largely a matter of extraneous expediency that caused him to hold the office of postmaster of Bonne Terre from April, 1876, to October, 1885. He had deep reverence for the spiritual verities and was instant and liberal in the support of all religious activities in which, though himself a member of the Congregational church, he recognized neither sect nor creed, as he realized the value of the work of all denominations. The present fine edifice of the Congregational church in Bonne Terre is his gift to the people of his home city. From the previously mentioned memorial are taken the following appreciative words: "Perhaps the characteristics which endeared him so generally to the people of this community were his never-failing courtesy and that kind consideration which never varied, whether the occasion was a presidential reception or that of helping some poor foreigner from the gutter, or compelling some poor workman to accept a loan which his keen perception told him was needed."

The death of Mr. Parsons caused an entire community to mourn, and all classes and conditions of men and women in Bonne Terre showed their deep sense of personal loss and bereavement. They mourned not the successful man, not the man of wealth and influence, but felt that they were bereft of a true friend, the man of deep human sympathy and tolerance, the man whose was the faith that makes faithful in all things. His funeral was conducted by Rt. Rev. Daniel Tuttle, the venerable bishop of the Missouri diocese of the Protestant Episcopal church, and this honored prelate was assisted by the pastor of the Congregational church in Bonne Terre, Rev. H. L. Hartwell. Interment was made with Masonic honors, as Mr. Parsons was long identified with this time-honored fraternity.

It may be noted that the sons of Mr. Parsons have succeeded to and assumed active supervision of his varied industrial and other capitalistic interests, in the control of which they are showing themselves worthy of the honored name which they bear. They are also men of sterling character and high civic ideals.

There can be no wish to lift the gracious veil that gave seclusion to a home whose every relation was ideal, but it is consistent to enter a brief record concerning the domestic relations of Mr. Parsons,—relations that were marked by the greatest of solicitude and beauty. While serving as a soldier in the Civil war Mr. Parsons was granted a furlough, and within this period, on the 5th of February, 1862, was solemnized his marriage to Miss Jane E. Doolittle, the accomplished daughter of M. J. and Elizabeth (Camp) Doolittle, and a sister of General Charles C. Doolittle, who gained distinction in the Civil war, in which he entered service as a member of the same company as did the subject of this memoir. Mrs. Parsons survives her honored husband and still resides in the beautiful home at Riverside, near Bonne Terre. She was reared and educated in New York city and Brooklyn and brought into the wilds of Missouri, when she came here with her husband, the fine elements of culture that had been gained in her associations in the east. For three years previous to her marriage Mrs. Parsons was the leading soprano in the choir of Rev. Theodore L. Cuyler's church at Brooklyn. Mr. and Mrs. Parsons became the parents of eight children, of whom five are living: Roscoe R. S. and Gerard S., who have succeeded their father in the various positions of the latter's large interests; Jessie H., who is the wife of Ben Blewett, superintendent of the public schools of St. Louis, Missouri; Mabel T., who is the wife of Dr. George Knapp, of Vincennes, Indiana; and Miss Bertha S., who remains with her widowed mother. Roscoe R. S. Parsons is now general manager of the St. Joseph Lead Company; vice-president of the Doe Run Lead Company; vice-president of the Mississippi River & Bonne Terre Railroad Company; and president of the Farmers' & Miners' Trust Company of Bonne Terre. Gerard S. Parsons is assistant general manager of the St. Joseph Lead Company and treasurer of the railroad company above mentioned.

PROFESSOR WILLIAM LESLIE JOHNS. It is not to be gainsaid that there is no office carrying with it so much responsibility as that of the instructor who moulds and fashions the plastic mind of youth; who instills into the formative brain those principles which, when matured, will be the chief heritage of the active man who in due time will sway the multitudes, lead armies, govern nations or frame the laws by which civilized nations are governed. To say that all learned men are capable of filling this high and important office is by no means the truth. One is inclined frequently to believe that the true educator is born and not made; he must have a vast knowledge of human nature; he must know not only what is in books, but what is in man also; he must understand his pupil and deal with his kind according to his individuality.

William Leslie Johns, superintendent of the Flat River schools, was born July 3, 1872, at Grubville, Jefferson county, Missouri. The family is one which has been identified with the state for many years, the birth of the subject's father, William Alfred Johns, having occurred in Robertsville, Franklin county, Missouri, in the year 1839. The early life of the elder gentleman was spent on his father's farm and he received his education in the common schools. He adopted agriculture as his own vocation and was thus engaged throughout the course of his useful and active life. At the time of the Civil war he was a member of the state militia and at the termination of the great conflict he again took up farming. The subject's mother was Mary Ann Sullens, of Fenton, Jefferson county, Missouri, daughter of Isaac Sullens, a farmer and Methodist circuit rider. To this union, which occurred in 1861, nine children were born, William Leslie being the sixth in order of birth. The father passed on to his reward in 1877, but his devoted wife and helpmeet has survived him for more than a generation and is still living, her residence being maintained at Grubville, Jefferson county, Missouri. The father was in his political conviction an adherent of the policies and principles of the "Grand Old Party" and his religious faith was that of the Methodist Episcopal church. His lodge relations extend to the time-honored Masonic order.

The early life of William L. Johns was passed on his father's farm in Jefferson county and in youth he had the usual opportunity of the farmer's son to become familiar with the many strenuous duties of farm life. He attended the public schools and having come to the conclusion to become an instructor, he entered the Cape Girardeau Normal School and was graduated from that institution in 1907, with the degree of B. P. D. His first work in the pedagogical profession was as a teacher in the country schools, and this was of seven years' duration. For three and one-half years he was principal of the DeSoto grammar schools and, recommended by his excellent work at that point, he was called to Flat River, where in the capacity of superintendant of schools he has given the utmost satisfaction. The Flat River schools are fully accredited and a diploma received from the high school admits without further ado to the state university.

Professor Johns laid the foundation of a happy and cultured household when, in 1897, he was united to Emma Cole, of Blackwell, Jefferson county, daughter of Joshua and Anne Cole, the former a well-known farmer of Jefferson county. Mr. and Mrs. Johns share their pleasant home with two young sons,—Delos Cole and Burdette Theron. In his political adherence Professor Johns is aligned with what its loyal admirers are pleased to call the "Grand Old Party;" he is a Baptist in his religious affiliation, and his lodge relationship is extended to the Independent Order of Odd Fellows.

ROY STONE MARLOW. Among the leading young citizens of DeSoto must assuredly be mentioned Professor Roy Stone Marlow, superintendent of the Moorhart Commercial College of this place. He has been a prominent factor in educational work of this section of southeastern Missouri since his graduation from college, having been a teacher in the public schools of Montgomery county for five years previous to preparing himself for the duties of his present responsible position as the head of one of the noted Moorhart chain of colleges. His success in preparing young men and women for positions of a commercial character has been remarkable, and in addition to his professional ability he is esteemed as a good citizen and popular member of society.

Professor Marlow was born in Martinsburg, Missouri, June 7, 1882. He is the son of W. H. Marlow, who was born December 9, 1851, at LaGrange, Missouri. The latter's mother died when he was but a few months old and he was reared to the age of twelve years by two aunts. At about that time his father met his death in the Civil war. He had married again and had a family of small children, but young Marlow, although only a boy himself, returned to his father's home to manage the farm, and there he remained until he attained his majority. He then removed to a farm in Callaway county and there, when about twenty-seven, established a home of his own by marriage, Miss Laura Peery becoming his wife. Three children were born to them, namely: Thomas, Roy S. and Ora Elizabeth. Some years later the father went into the hotel business at Martinsburg, Missouri, and he remained there until four years prior to his demise. The last five years of his life were spent in retirement at Montgomery City, Missouri, and he died, universally regretted, in 1908. He was a loyal and consistent Democrat, having given allegiance to the party since his earliest voting days; he held membership in the Christian church; and was affiliated with the Mutual Protection League. The mother was born in Callaway county, September 4, 1857, and is making her home with her son in De-Soto.

Roy Stone Marlow spent his early life on the farm in Callaway county and through actual contact and experience became familiar with agricultural life in all its phases. He received his preliminary education in the public schools of Martinsburg, graduating therefrom, and also in a special class from the high school of Montgomery City in 1900. Following this he took special work in the University of Missouri and taught in the high school for a period of five years, giving the greatest satisfaction to all concerned. He then took special work in Central Wesleyan College at Warrington, Missouri, and finished the same in 1907, in which year he received a degree from that institution. It was in the year named that Professor Marlow became associated with Mr. George Washington Moorhart in his business college work, and ever since that time he has been a part of the teaching force of those excellent institutions, teaching a year at Cape Girardeau; two years at Farmington and two years at De-Soto where he resides at the present time. The student enrollment averages forty.

Professor Marlow was married in 1907, Miss Ellen Marie Robertus, of Warrenton, Missouri, becoming his wife, and both young people are held in high regard in the community. They have two young sons,—John William and Addicks Ransom. The subject is a member of the Christian church; enjoys fellowship with the Independent Order of Odd Fellows; and follows in the parental footsteps in the matter of politics, being a stanch Democrat.

The Moorhart Business College of DeSoto is situated on a hill overlooking the city and is surrounded by beautiful grounds.

JAMES A. HENSON. The name of James A. Henson, judge of the probate court, has been identified in an honorable and useful fashion with the various interests of Washington county since 1898. He is an almost life-long resident of Missouri and lived in Gasconade county for many years previous to coming to Potosi. He is a veteran of the Civil war and one of the pillars of local Republicanism, standing high in party councils. Mr. Henson was born in the state of Indiana, September 20, 1838, and is the son of Larkin Henson, who was a native of South Carolina, born about 1794. The elder gentleman was a carpenter and builder and was married at about the age of twenty-one years to Susan Hollandsworth. To their union were born five children, of whom Judge Henson was the second in order of birth, and an enumeration of the number is as follows: Eliza, deceased; James; Robert; Jeanetta, now Mrs. William Davis; and Albert. The father, who was a man of advanced years at the outbreak of the Civil war, was so thoroughly in sympathy with Southern traditions and institutions that he enlisted in the Confederate army, and his death occurred during the great conflict. He was a stanch Democrat in politics and a member of the Baptist church.

When Judge Henson was but a few months old the family removed to Missouri and located in Gasconade county, where he grew to manhood. He received his early education in the subscription schools and his first experiences as a wage-earner were as a worker on various farms. At the outbreak of the Civil war he joined the Union army under General Grant and saw a good deal of hard service, participating in the battles of Wilson Creek and Vicksburg and many lesser engagements. He was a member of Company F, First Missouri Light Artillery, and he was a brave and valiant soldier, who with the passage of the years has lost no whit of interest in the comrades of other days, being prominent in all the "old Boy" doings. When the war was over he returned to Gasconade county and engaged in farming, and he continued thus engaged until 1898, when he removed to this county. After coming to Potsoi he conducted a dairy for Dr. Noll and then made a successful run for office, receiving the election for justice of the peace and serving in that capacity with faithfulness and efficiency from 1899 to 1903. He was then elected judge of the probate court, which office he still holds, having been twice elected. In many ways he has demonstrated the public spirit which makes him so good and patriotic a citizen, and he never fails to yield hearty support and co-operation to any measure that has appealed to him as likely to be conducive to the public good.

In January, 1862, Mr. Henson was united in marriage to Mary S. Davis, daughter of

Garrett Davis, their marriage being solemnized at Gasconade county, Missouri. The wife died in 1866, leaving two young children, Milford and Marshall. He was again married in 1872 to Dora Roberts, of Missouri, daughter of Asa Roberts, and this union resulted in four children,—James E., Lillian, Fred and Laura. Judge Henson is well and favorably known in the community, where he is agreeably recommended by his daily living; and his family are useful and popular members of society. He is a Baptist in religious conviction, and is a member of Becket Post, No. 38, at Hopewell, Missouri.

HENRY A. HERKSTROETER, the efficient postmaster of Washington, is a native son of the place and was born and reared among the younger generation of the business men of this city, his birth occurring March 29, 1874. His father is Casper H. A. Herkstroeter, a clothing merchant and tailor of Washington. The elder gentleman is a native of Germany. Like so many of his countrymen he concluded to cast his fortunes with the New World and arrived on our shores previous to the war between the states. Shortly afterward he located in the city of St. Louis, where he served an apprenticeship as a tailor, and while residing there he married Miss Minnie Gast, a daughter of Ernst and Christina Gast, of Washington, Missouri. This resulted in his establishing a home here and he opened a tailor shop. His business grew and expanded with the development of the country and he now owns and manages a large ready-made clothing house, while at the same time carrying on a tailoring establishment. He is still the proprietor of this business and has reached the age of seventy-eight years. The subject is one of a family of six children, as follows: Christina, wife of L. H. Kamp, of St. Louis; Henry A., the subject of this review; Emma, who married E. A. Kamp and resides in Webster Grove, Missouri; Louisa, of Washington; Ed. C., of St. Louis; and Miss Minnie, who is at home.

After the termination of his school days, Mr. Herkstroeter learned the trade of cutter in his father's shop and with the exception of two years spent in St. Louis, where he was also engaged in the tailoring business, he continued as an assistant to his father until his retirement to assume the duties of postmaster of Washington. In his political conviction Mr. Herkstroeter is a stanch and stalwart Republican and stands high in party councils. He served as councilman for the Fourth ward for two years and was a member of the county Republican central committee and acted as its treasurer for the space of six years, being ever ready to do anything, to go anywhere for the good of the cause with which he is aligned. He was appointed postmaster on July 15, 1908, by President Roosevelt (in vacation) and was re-commissioned by President Taft, December 14, 1908, for a term of four years, and he has given satisfactory service as a servant of Uncle Sam.

Mr. Herkstroeter laid the foundation of a happy home life when, on October 28, 19.. he was united in marriage to Miss May Werner, daughter of Charles H. Werner. Their family history corresponds in several points, for Mrs. Herkstroeter's father is also a tailor and by birth a German. The two children of the Herkstroeter household are daughters—Leona and Helen. The subject takes pleasure in his relations with the Independent Order of Odd Fellows.

HERBERT PRYOR. In considering what Herbert Pryor, superintendent of public schools, has done for Kennett it is only necessary to recall the progress that the schools have made under his regime.

Herbert Pryor was born in Pike county, Missouri, August 11, 1879. His boyhood was for the most part spent in Paynesville, where he was educated in the public schools. He then attended the local academy and later the Missouri State University. He had begun to teach when he was only eighteen years of age and worked his way through college. He taught in Pike county, being assistant principal of the academy and principal of the public schools of Paynesville for three years. He came to Kennett as superintendent in the fall of 1906 and has just closed the fifth year of his work here. The public school has an enrollment of seven hundred pupils, with a corps of sixteen teachers. The course is of high grade and is accredited in the university. The class of 1911 was the sixth to graduate. All the teachers have had normal training and they are almost all home teachers; it is the aim of Superintendent Pryor to train the graduates that they may be prepared to fill vacancies in the staff of teachers as they occur. During the last five years the salaries of the teachers have nearly doubled and six additional teachers have been installed. During the past five years the high school has increased from seventeen pupils to eighty-six. The seating capacity of the old building is not sufficient to accommodate the additional pupils and a new high school building is contemplated.

In June, 1908, Mr. Pryor married Miss Agnes Harrison, of Kennett, daughter of Dr. V. H. Harrison, now deceased. She is a teacher in the high school. Mr. and Mrs. Pryor have one daughter, Sue Elizabeth.

Mr. Pryor is in the Methodist Episcopal church, while his wife belongs to the Presbyterians, thus both the churches are gainers. Mr. Pryor belongs to the order of Masons. He is desirous to be right up with the most approved modern methods of teaching and takes every opportunity to compare notes with other educators. He attends the summer terms of the University and is working for his A. M. degree. To the casual observer, the fact that the high school has increased its number of scholars might mean that the population is larger; if the percentage of increase were proportionately large in the graded schools that might be the natural inference. The fact is, however, that during the past six years the high school has increased its scholars much more than the graded schools. The fact of the matter is that the course has been made more practical, so that whereas many pupils left school while they were half way up in the grades, now a large proportion take the high school course. In this way Kennett is turning out boys and girls to become more efficient citizens than ever before, for the true use of education is to increase efficiency. Mr. Pryor is doing a great work.

WILLIAM R. EDGAR. The senior partner of the law firm of Edgar & Edgar may be said to "come naturally" by his prominence in the enterprises for the development of Ironton, for he is an American of the old stock, the son and grandson of pioneers who settled and developed new country. The family came originally from Scotland and settled in Rahway, New Jersey, in 1720. They gave more than one soldier to the American cause, during the Revolution. Something over a century later—in 1830—William R. Edgar, father of the present William R., Sr., married and went to Tipton, Cedar county, Iowa. His wife was Rebecca Tichenor, a Presbyterian of English descent and a native of Lebanon, Ohio. They were successful in the new country, where they engaged in farming. It was in Tipton that William R. Edgar was born in 1851 and there that his mother died.

In 1866 the family moved to Iron county, where the father continued his work of farming until his death in 1879. The son William R. is the only surviving member of that family. Mr. Edgar was educated at Arcadia College. He graduated from that institution in 1871, during the presidency of General L. M. Lewis, a noted divine and a lawyer of unusual eloquence. Four years later he graduated from the law department of Washington University. He then taught for three years in Arcadia College and was one year principal of the Ironton public schools. Since 1879 he has devoted his entire attention to the practice of law. He was a partner of the late J. W. Emerson, formerly one of Ironton's prominent lawyers. Later he was with George W. Benton for one year. The present law firm was organized April 10, 1911. In addition to their extensive library, Edgar and Edgar have a complete set of abstracts of Iron county.

Mr. Edgar has served several terms as prosecuting attorney and during president Cleveland's first administration was four and a half years receiver of the U. S. land office, then located at Ironton but now removed to Springfield. He has always been a power in the Democratic party of the county and has been a delegate to several national conventions and at the last election was presidential elector.

He married Miss S. P. Whitworth, daughter of the late I. G. Whitworth, mentioned elsewhere in this work. She was born in Iron county and educated at Arcadia College. Mr. and Mrs. Edgar have five children: Maude married Lieutenant Jurich, of the U. S. Army Cavalry, and since his death in San Francisco in 1908 she has resided in Ironton. William R., Jr. of the firm of Edgar & Edgar, was educated in Ironton and in the Benton law school of St. Louis. He was chief clerk in the law department of the Missouri-Pacific Railroad, under General Attorney M. L. Clardy. He resigned this position to form the present partnership. There are two other sons, James D., aged twenty-one, a graduate of the Western Military Academy, and Robert Lee, aged eleven. The other daughter, Miss Mary C., is also at home.

Mr. Edgar is president of the Iron County Bank of Ironton, organized in 1897. For the first year of its existence Mr. I. G. Whitworth was president, but since that time Mr. Edgar has held the office continuously. He is no less prominent socially than professionally. He is master of the Star of the West Lodge, No. 133, A. F. & A. M. The son is also a member of the A. F. & A. M.

JOHN A. PELTS. The Pelts family is one of the best known of the old Dunklin county families and a citizen who bears the name with credit as one loyal to the best interests of the community is John A. Pelts, a man of quiet though forceful character, a native son of the county and an agriculturist, whose farm of eighty acres he redeemed from the virgin forest and brought to a high state of improvement. Mr. Pelts, who is a son of that prominent farmer-citizen, the late Joseph Pelts, of whom more extended mention is made on other pages of this record, was born March 20, 1857, at the family homestead situated not far distant from his present comfortable home in the vicinity of Vincent, Dunklin county, Missouri. Here he was reared and in the district school received his education. In choosing a vocation he followed in the paternal footsteps and since young manhood has engaged in farming. He has expended much time and labor upon his farm, which is new land and which he cleared and has brought to a fine state of improvement.

Mr. Pelts was married September 16, 1884, the young woman to become his wife being Miss Lou Cook, who was born at Nashville, Tennessee, July 23, 1864, the daughter of Jesse S. and Nancy J. (Sparks) Cook. The father was a Union soldier and one of the martyrs of the "Great Conflict," his death upon the battlefield occurring in the month of September, 1864. He was a young man at the time. The widow removed with her two children, Lou, now Mrs. Pelts, and Thomas M., residing in Stoddard county, from Tennessee to Alabama in 1866, and there she resided until 1874, when she came to Clarkton, Dunklin county, Missouri. In this state she lived for a good many years, being well-known and highly respected in the community in which she made her home. The demise of this good woman occurred in January, 1900, at the home of her daughter, her years numbering sixty-two at the time of her summons to the Great Beyond. She was a member of the Missionary Baptist church.

To Mr. and Mrs. Pelts have been born six children, an enumeration of the number being as follows: The oldest children, Alma and Osa, were twins; Osa died in infancy, and Alma is now the wife of David Brandon of Waco, Texas. Rachel is the wife of Joseph Nesler, of Vincent, Missouri. Miss Eulah and Lee Shelton are at home and Ray died at the age of one year.

Mr. Pelts was previously married to Miss Mary Taylor, who died some twenty-eight years since, leaving one son, William T. now a farmer residing near Vincent, Missouri. This young man took as his wife Miss Alice Stephens and they share their pleasant home with three sons, namely: Oakley, Alton and Herbert.

In the question of politics John A. Pelts has always been a firm supporter of Democratic policies and principles and like every intelligent voter he endeavors to become familiar with all matters effecting the public welfare. Fraternally he is a member of the Woodmen of the World, of Caruth, Missouri. Mrs. Pelts is a member of the Circle at Caruth and also of the Missionary Baptist church.

JOSEPH PELTS. For many years, more than half a century in fact, one of the best-known, best-liked and most influential men of this section was the late Joseph Pelts, whose identification with Dunklin county dated from that day in 1854 when, wearing "the rose of youth upon him," he took up his residence within the county. By vocation an agriculturist, he was a man of many interests and it is characteristic of his energy and enthusiasm that at the age of seventy years he organized a stock company at Kennett for gold-mining and was on his way to the gold-fields at or near Alton, Missouri, when his death occurred and the company lost its leading spirit.

He was a veteran of the Civil war, and although by birth a Hoosier, the years of his residence in this state prior to the "Great Conflict" so enlisted his sympathies with the institutions of the South that he gave his services to the Army of the Confederacy. He and the late Robert H. Douglass were comrades in the same company, and neither of them ever lost interest in reviewing the stirring, but lamentable experiences of the dark days of the '60s. The death of this gentleman occurred at Doniphan in the winter of 1906-07, but his memory will long remain green, recalling the poet's words:

"To live in hearts we leave behind,
Is not to die."

Joseph Pelts was born in Indiana in the '30s and passed his boyhood and early youth in that state, there receiving his public school education. In 1854, when about seventeen years of age, with his parents and the other members of the family he removed to Dunklin county, Missouri, making the journey overland by team and locating at first near Clarkton. His parents were William and Mary Pelts. The father was a horseman who handled thoroughbreds and racers and who was a well-known figure in Clarkton and its neighborhood.

Joseph Pelts adopted agriculture as his life work and in due time married, his chosen lady being Martha Baker, a native of this county and a daughter of James B. and Drusilla Baker, Dunklin county pioneers and farmers. This admirable woman died at the old home at about the age of fifty-five years, but two of her sisters are living, namely: Mrs. Delilah Hicks and Mrs. Esther Gorgas, both of Dunklin county. Both Joseph Pelts and his wife were members of the Missionary Baptist church, and the former was a stalwart Democrat, who gave unswerving allegiance to the party and participated in its political bouts with interest. They became the parents of a family of nine children, eight of whom were sons and one a daughter, and of which number four brothers are living at the present time, namely: John A., Robert A., Joseph E. and Charles Lee. The deceased children are: James W. (eldest in order of birth), Nathaniel D., George R., Lewis and Frances E.

When Joseph Pelts arrived in Missouri many of the difficult conditions which were the portion of the pioneer still prevailed. There were no near markets and he hauled his produce to Cape Girardeau, requiring eight days with ox teams to make the round trip. Elk, deer and the like were abundant and he made fine use of his opportunities, being a great hunter. He was a man of distinct personality and public-spirit and well worthy of representation in this volume devoted to the makers of Southeastern Missouri.

CHARLES LEE PELTS, a well-known farmer in Dunklin county, began in a small way but has been very successful. He was born in Dunklin county, Missouri, on the place upon which he now lives, on January 3, 1874, and he is a son of Joseph Pelts, of whom more extended mention is made on other pages of this work. He went to school at Shady Grove and lived on the farm with his father, his mother having died when Charles was very young. When he was sixteen his father married again and Charles then began to work around on the different farms. Up to the time when he was twenty-one he had earned very little and spent what he did make. At the end of eight years he owned forty acres of land, having bought from his father the farm where he was born and spent his childhood days. At the time he took the farm it was very much run down, but he at once set to work to improve it. He built fences, put up a good house and now owns one hundred and fifty acres of land, on which he raises cotton, corn and peas and cattle.

When he was twenty-one years of age Mr. Pelts married Sadie Bedwell, who died on giving birth to her child. The child lived only a short time. Eight years later he married Minnie Bailey, by whom he had two children,—Lula and Ethel. On St. Valentine's Day, 1908, he married Eva Shailand, by whom he had one child, Lee Rogers.

Mr. Pelts is a Democrat, and is always happy to see his party come out ahead. He may surely feel that he has done well, as he has made all that he has through his own efforts, except an interest in a forty acre farm. He is indeed to be congratulated on the success of his efforts and the community for the possession of so good a citizen.

HORACE D. EVANS. Through his own character and accomplishment Horace D. Evans, cashier of the Lead Belt Bank, at Bonne Terre, St. Francois county, has well upheld the prestige of a name that has been identified with the annals of Missouri history for more than a century. His father attained to marked distinction in public affairs and was called upon to represent this state in the state senate, besides which he served in other offices of distinctive public trust. He was long one of the representative men of Missouri and was a scion of one of the honored pioneer families of this commonwealth.

Horace Dell Evans was born at Steelville, the judicial center of Crawford county, Missouri, on the 11th of June, 1859, and is the fourth in order of birth of a family of six children, of whom two are now living. William Evans, grandfather of him whose name initiates this review, was born in Jefferson county, Tennessee, on the 27th of December, 1793, of sterling Welsh lineage, and the family was founded in America in the Colonial era of our national history. William Evans was about seven years of age at the time of his removal to Missouri with his aunt, and records show that on the 12th of June, 1800, the family located in St. Francois county, on the site of the present thriving little city of Farmington, the capital of the county. Here William Evans was reared to maturity under the scenes and influences of the pioneer epoch, and he gained his full quota of experience in connection with life on the frontier. He married Miss Mahala George, and of their eight children Ellis G., father of the subject of this sketch, was the third in order of nativity. William Evans was a man of strong character and sterling integrity, so that he proved a potent factor in connection with the development of St. Francois county along both industrial and social lines. Here he continued to reside until his death, which occurred on the 31st of July, 1851, and his devoted wife was summoned to eternal rest on the 21st of September, 1872, their names meriting enduring place on the roll of the honored pioneers of southeastern Missouri.

Ellis G. Evans was born on the family homestead at Big River Mills, St. Francois county, on the 10th of July, 1824, and his early education was secured in the common schools of the locality and period. His father was one of the early teachers in the schools of this county and was a prominent figure in educational affairs in this section of the state. Thus Ellis G. Evans had the privilege of receiving instruction from his honored father, who likewise was a man of superior intellectuality. His natural heritage of alert mentality was amplified by his own application to reading and study and he became a man of exceptionally broad intellectual ken, mature judgment and well fortified opinions. As a youth he served an apprenticeship to the carpenter's trade in the city of St. Louis, and through his work at his trade he laid the foundation for the substantial success which he eventually gained in connection with the productive activities of life. It is worthy of record that he cast his first vote, in 1845, in support of delegates to the convention which formulated a new constitution for the state. He finally engaged in the general merchandise business at Steelville, Crawford county, and he became prominently concerned with the industrial and civic upbuilding of that section. He was one of those interested in the building of the old Merrimac iron works near Steelville and his co-operation was given in the promotion of many other enterprises of important order.

Major Ellis G. Evans, both by reason of impregnable integrity and fine mental gifts was well fitted for leadership in thought and action, and his interest in public affairs soon brought him into prominence in political affairs in his native state. When the dark cloud of civil war cast its pall over the national horizon his loyalty to the Union was of the most perfervid order, and he became in the climacteric period leading up to the great struggle between the north and south, one of the organizers of the Republican party in Missouri. He served as vice-president of the party's first state convention in Missouri, that of 1856, and he ever afterward continued a stalwart advocate of the principles and policies for which the "grand old party" stood sponsor. He was a member of the Missouri constitutional convention of 1865, when the institution of human slavery was forever prohibited in the state by the provisions of the new constitution. He gave effective service in behalf of the Union during the progress of the Civil war, as he served as major on the military staff of Governor Fletcher and was provost marshal and paymaster at Rolla, this state, during the major part of the conflict through which the integrity of the nation was perpetuated. In 1866 he was elected to represent the twenty-second senatorial district of Missouri in the United States senate, in which he served until 1870, and in which he wielded most distinctive influence during the period of reconstruction in the south. In 1871 Major Evans was appointed register of the United States land office at Booneville, and shortly after his retirement from this office he endured a stroke of paralysis that rendered it impossible for him to walk thereafter, though he retained his mental vigor unimpaired until the close of his long and useful life. Subsequently to enduring this affliction Senator Evans served twelve years as a member of the Republican state central committee and continued to exert potent influence in political affairs in the state, the while no man held to a higher degree the confidence and esteem of his associates, not only in political circles but also in all other relations of life. He was for some time editor of the *State Times*, published as the semi-official organ of the Missouri legislature. He was a man who stood "four square to every wind that blows," and his name is held in lasting honor in the state which represented his home throughout his life and to which his loyalty was ever of the most incisive order. He passed the closing years of his life at Cuba, Crawford county, where he died in 1889, secure in the high regard of all who knew him. His cherished and devoted wife was summoned to the life eternal in 1886, and of their six children one son and one daughter are now living. His marriage to Miss Emily H. Treece, a native of Ohio, was solemnized at Brush Creek, Crawford county, Missouri, on the 20th of July, 1850, and his wife was a daughter of one of the honored pioneers of that section of the state. Both were consistent and zealous members of the Methodist church.

Horace D. Evans, whose name initiates this article, gained his early educational discipline in the public schools of Rolla and Booneville, and in the former place he entered upon an apprenticeship to the printer's trade, in the office of the Rolla *Herald*. He familiarized himself with the esoteric mysteries of the "art preservative of all arts" and incidentally gained a training that proved a most valuable supplement to his prior education. In 1879 he went to the city of St. Louis, where he was a clerical employe in the office of the city assessor and collector until 1883, when he received an appointment to the railway mail service, with which he thereafter continued to be identified for a period of thirteen years, as an efficient and valued employe. In 1896 he resigned his position and assumed the position of bookkeeper in the Farmers & Miners Bank of Bonne Terre, where he has since maintained his home and where he has risen to prominence as one of the representative business men and influential citizens of St. Francois county. In 1899 he became associated in the organization of the Lead Belt Bank, of which he has since served as cashier and in which he is a stockholder. His effective administration has had marked influence in the upbuilding of the substantial business of this popular institution, which bases its operations on a capital stock of fifteen thousand dollars and which is one of the solid banking houses of this section of the state.

Mr. Evans has also identified himself with other enterprises that have conserved industrial and commercial stability and progress and as a citizen he is most liberal and public-spirited,—ever ready to lend his influence and co-operation in the furtherance of measures tending to enhance material and civic prosperity. He is treasurer of the Bonne Terre Building & Loan Association, is a member of the directorate of the Bonne Terre Lumber Company, and is a director of the Bank of Herculaneum, at Herculaneum, Jefferson county. He is president of the Commercial Club of Bonne Terre, an organization of high civic ideals and one that has been most influential in promoting the best interests of the thriving little city.

In politics Mr. Evans has never swerved from the faith in which he was reared and he is aligned as a stalwart in the local camp of the Republican party, in whose cause he has given yeoman service. He was elected chairman of the Republican county committee of St. Francois county in 1904 and was re-elected in 1906 and 1908. He seems to have inherited much of his father's discrimination in the maneuvering of political forces and gave most effective service along this line during his incumbency of the position noted, as has he also as a member, from the state at large, of the Missouri state central committee of his party, with which he has been thus actively identified since 1904. He served five years as a member of the board of education of Bonne Terre, and here he is affiliated with the Masonic fraternity and the Knights of Pythias. Both he and his wife hold membership in the Congregational church in their home town, and are liberal in the support of the various departments of its work.

On the 28th of December, 1887, Mr. Evans was united in wedlock to Miss Annie Towl, a daughter of William Towl, a prominent merchant and lumber manufacturer at Annapolis, Iron county, this state. Mr. and Mrs. Evans have two children, Emily T. and Claire, both at home.

JOSEPH A. MINTRUP. No member of the business community has a greater responsibility than the banker, and any community or city is much to be congratulated which has at the head of its finances men of thorough training, true worth and moral dependability. No banker of southeastern Missouri is more closely typical of what is required in the financial manager and leader to inspire and retain business and commercial confidence than Joseph A. Mintrup, cashier of the Citizens' Bank of Union, Missouri. From every possible viewpoint Mr. Mintrup is a man of the finest citizenship, public spirited, altruistic, ever ready to give his support to all measures likely to result in general benefit. He is one of the standard bearers of the local Democratic party and as a public official has a record of the most meritorious character. He was for a number of years postmaster of Washington and for twelve successive years held the office of county clerk of Franklin county with credit to himself and honor to his constituents. The length of time he held this important position is sufficient in itself to show how well he performed its duties, and doubtless much further public usefulness lies before him, for he is a man in the prime of life. By his private life as well as his public services he has endeared himself to the people of Franklin county, for he grew up in the county from the age of five years and his whole career is an open book.

Mr. Mintrup was born in St. Louis county, Missouri, April 28, 1862. He is of German stock, his father, Francis Mintrup, having been a native of the German state of Hanover, now a part of the province of Prussia, where his birth occurred in 1822. Like the majority of his countrymen he was of the stuff of which the best citizenship is made, and his stalwart, fine Teutonic characteristics have come to his son as a heritage. He and a brother, Joseph, came to the decision to make a hazard of new fortunes in the land across the Atlantic in their youth and saying farewell for all time to their parents and brothers and sisters they sailed, two brave and adventurous spirits, for America, some years previous to the outbreak of the Civil war. In course of time they found their way to Missouri and located in Washington, where they became useful citizens, married and reared families and both now sleep beneath the sod of that section. Francis Mintrup, ideal patriot and lover of liberty, was in sympathy with the Union and when the long-lowering war cloud broke in all its fury in the early '60s of the nineteenth century, he enlisted in a Missouri regiment of the Federal army, only served a very short time when discharged on account of disability. In 1867 he established himself in business at Washington with his brother, and together they operated a planing-mill until the demise of Francis Mintrup in 1869. The young woman whom he chose as his wife and the bearer of his name was Miss Mary Narup, an admirable lady who has survived her husband for these many years, making her residence at the family home. The children are as follows: Miss Annie, of Washington, Missouri; Joseph A., of this notice; Kate, wife of Edward Jasper, of Washington; and Henry and August, of Chicago, Illinois.

In the Washington public schools and in the well-known Catholic institution at St. Mary's, Kansas, Joseph A. Mintrup received his education. When a youth he learned the printer's trade on the Franklin County Observer at Washington, and proving faithful and efficient in little things, he in course of time acquired a partnership in the paper and eventually became the editor. He evinced no inconsiderable gifts as an exponent of the Fourth Estate, but sold the plant and entered mercantile life, joining the J. L. Hake Shoe Company at Washington and becoming secretary of the same. He remained thus associated until the beginning of President Cleveland's second administration, when he received the appointment of assistant postmaster of Washington, and a year later was appointed chief of the office. He filled the position until June, 1898, when he was replaced by a Republican and not long afterward engaged in the real estate and insurance business.

At the fall election in 1898 Mr. Mintrup was chosen county clerk on the Democratic ticket, overcoming a Republican majority of several hundred and winning the office with one hundred and seventy-five votes to spare. His first service of four years so justified the confidence of the people that he was reelected for another term, which was succeeded in turn by another. He retired from office in January, 1911, with twelve years of successful political life to his credit. Resuming private life, he entered the domain of finance, becoming cashier of the Citizens Bank of Union, March 1, 1911, and in addition to this office he is secretary of the official board.

Mr. Mintrup married in Washington, Missouri, December 29, 1891, his wife being Miss Amelia Wehrmann, whose father, Louis Wehrmann, was for many years postmaster of Washington and a leading citizen of that place. He was a German by nativity, a Republican in politics, and he was engaged in the real estate business. The children of Mr. and Mrs. Mintrup are five in number and as follows: Mamie, Louis, Lillie, Frances and Doherty. The family is a popular one and the home is the center of a gracious and attractive hospitality. Mr. Mintrup is a communicant of the Catholic church and a member of the Knights of Columbus and the Benevolent and Protective Order of Elks.

J. THOMPSON BLANTON. In that particular portion of Iron county in which his home is situated and where he is best known, J. Thompson Blanton, farmer, stockman and veteran of the Civil war, stands as one of the important and highly esteemed members of his community. Here he has resided for many years, since 1858, to be exact, and although not a native of the county, he has resided in the state all his life with the exception of a period spent in farming in the state of Nevada and during his war service. The attractive Blanton homestead is situated some seven miles southeast of Ironton and is one of the highly improved estates of Iron county.

Mr. Blanton was born in Madison county, Missouri, on the Saint Francois river, October 24, 1843, and is the son of Benjamin F. and Ailsey (Berryman) Blanton. The mother was a niece of the Rev. J. C. Berryman, a detailed sketch of whose life appears elsewhere in this work. She died in 1869, aged about seventy years. Her father, whose farm included what is now Arcadia, was Josiah Berryman, a prominent man of his day. He came to Missouri at the same time as his clergyman brother, who was the founder of Arcadia College. Benjamin F. Blanton was born in Lincoln county and removed to Madison county as a young man, locating on the Saint Francois river, near Wayne county, that being the scene of his marriage. He subsequently removed to Arcadia Valley and died in Dunklin county, at the age of about seventy years. He whose name inaugurates this record is the second in order of birth in a family of ten children, of whom four are now living. The other surviving members of the family are: Mrs. Michael Deguira, of Fredericktown; William H., of the vicinity of that place; and Moman, who is a Fredericktown resident.

Mr. Blanton passed the roseate days of boyhood and youth in Madison county, and there received his schooling. When about seventeen years of age he came to Iron county, which has ever since been the scene of his residence, with the exception of the time spent in the far west, above alluded to. He engages in general farming and also in the stock business, and in both departments has met with success, his methods being up-to-date and well-directed. When the Nation went down into the dread Valley of Decision in the '60s, Mr. Blanton enlisted in the Confederate army, as a member of Company C, Ninth Missouri Infantry, his enlistment taking place in Arkansas. The young man of nineteen was firmly convinced of the logic of the severing of the states from the national government if its rulings were against their conviction and he proved a loyal and valiant soldier. He participated in several engagements, but was fortunate enough not to receive a wound. When peace was restored to the stricken country, he went to Nevada and there for four years engaged in farming, in a rich valley, four hundred miles south of Salt Lake. The charms of Missouri remained strong with him, however, throughout his period of absence and he returned to Iron county, and bought the property upon which he has ever since resided. This consists of three hundred and twenty acres and is valuable and well situated.

In October, 1871, Mr. Blanton was united in marriage to Miss Caroline F. Kinkead, who was born in Saint Francois county, in October, 1852, and is a daughter of Andrew B. and Rebecca C. (Elgin) Kinkead, who came to the state in their youth and were married in Saint Francois county, which continued to be their home for the rest of their lives. The father died before the Civil War, but the mother survived until February, 1906, when she passed away at the age of ninety years. He was a tanner and farmer by occupation. He was born in Kentucky and the mother in Virginia, and they were both consistent members of the Christian church. Mrs. Blanton is one of a family of seven children, but of this number only one brother, Nicholas A., a farmer in St. Francois county, survives in addition to herself.

The union of Mr. and Mrs. Blanton has been blessed by the birth of the following children: Beatrice is the wife of M. P. Gregory, of Madison county and the mother of two children, Helen and Corena; Pauline died at the age of two years; Benjamin B., deputy sheriff of Iron county, is a citizen of Ironton; Gerard, a farmer of Madison county, married Miss Belle Freeland and their two daughters are Winifred and Charlene; Courtright R. is at home; Sophie is the wife of James L. Freeland, a farmer of Iron county, and their two sons are Nicholas and Josiah; M. Deguire is at home, as are also the twin brothers, Langdon E. and James E., and the youngest member of the family, Ailsey Litia.

In evidence of the zeal and energy of Mr. Blanton is the fact that his farm had but twenty acres cleared when he bought it and at the present day some two hundred acres are under cultivation. It is one of Iron county's finest farms, is adorned with a fine, commodious dwelling, and its buildings and fences are of the most substantial character. In the matter of politics Mr. Blanton has always been a Democrat, having given his suffrage to the party since his earliest voting days. He is a member of the Masonic order of Blanton and exemplified its high ideals in his own living. Mrs. Blanton retains her membership in the Christian church of Libertyville, Saint Francois county, and the various members of this popular family enjoy high standing in the community in which their interests are centered.

JIMER E. RICE. Among the citizens of southeast Missouri who began their careers dependent entirely on their own ability and energy and have since attained positions of influence and independence, one of the best known examples in Dunklin county is Mr. Jimer E. Rice, the banker.

He is a native son of Dunklin county, where he was born March 1, 1870. He attended the county schools, and then entered the State Normal, where he studied part of four years. He had assistance in only the first year and then taught to earn the money for the rest of his education. After graduating he taught four years, and made himself known as a reliable, intelligent young man worthy of larger responsibilities. He was then made deputy county collector, and after four years in that office was elected by the people of the county to the office of county treasurer, and served two terms.

He was a resident of Kennett practically all his life until he located in Hornersville. Buying an interest in the Bank of Hornersville in 1908, he moved to this town and entered upon his duties as cashier and member of the board of directors. This bank was organized by Mr. Langdon in 1901 and conducted as a private institution five years, being incorporated in 1906. It is one of the three banks south of Kennett, and its business is growing rapidly. The capital has been increased from five to ten thousand dollars, and in the last five years it has accumulated a surplus of five thousand dollars. Besides his active connection with the bank, Mr. Rice is a dealer in real estate on his own account, and his investments have been very profitable. He is the owner of farm land three miles south of Hornersville and some near Kennett, and has considerable town property. All this has been the rewards of his own efforts and business management, and few citizens of the county can point to a better record of success than he. In politics he is Democratic, and was the choice of that party when he served as a county official. He and his family are members of the Methodist church, South.

Mr. Rice married, June 23, 1895, Miss Lillian J. Brower. Their children are: Nola, born in June, 1896; and David B., born November 19, 1907. Fraternally Mr. Rice is a member of the Masonic lodge at Hornersville.

EDWARD W. FLENTGE. How difficult it is for a young man to choose the line of work he intends to follow throughout his life. What a little thing will often cause him to decide and something just as small may cause him to change his mind. A single stone may turn the rivulet of water to the right or to the left. It is sometimes said that Providence shapes our careers. Undoubtedly something outside of ourselves has something to do with the general direction of a man's life, but the getting on is a purely private affair. Each individual is fated to work out his own career. If he is qualified by nature he cannot be kept down; if deficient he cannot by hook or crook be boosted up. Opposition, adversity and hard luck are powerless to keep a big man in a small place and no set of outside conditions can keep a small man in a big place. The best we can do is the least we can offer. Such has been and is the maxim of Edward W. Flentge, the postmaster of Cape Girardeau. He has attained a prominence in the county and his high position has been reached by reason of his natural capabilities, united with the efforts he has untiringly put forth.

He was born in St. Louis, Missouri, March 2, 1863. His grandfather, William Flentge, was born in Germany, there received his education and was married. He was a cabinet maker by trade, but was not making very much money. He decided to come to America, bringing his wife and son with him. He came direct to Cape Girardeau, but not meeting with success right away he moved to Jackson, where he lived the rest of his life. His son, Henry, spent the first eight years of his life in his fatherland, when he came to America with his parents. He attended school in Cape Girardeau and learned the carpentering trade. When he was only seventeen he was injured by a fall and was sent back to Germany. As soon as he was well again he felt that he should like to study medicine. He attended a medical school, graduating from Marx College. After he returned to America he located at Cape Girardeau where he practiced medicine in Wayne and Cape Girardeau counties. During the Civil war he moved to St. Louis, where he established a large practice. In the fall of 1875 he moved to Texas, locating in McLennan county. He remained there for about two years and again moved to Rancho, Texas, thence to Oregon and California, where he died in 1903, being over seventy years old. While he was in Germany studying medicine he had met Teresa Heisen, a young German girl. They were married, she returning to America with him. She lived to be only forty-eight years old, leaving behind her three sons and her husband. At present only two of the sons are living, of whom Edward is the second. Mr. Flentge was a successful physician, but he was of a roving turn of mind, not staying in one place long enough to build up a very large practice.

Edward's boyhood days were spent in Wayne and Cape Girardeau counties, where he attended the public school. When he was twelve years old he went with his parents to Texas and attended school there for about two years. When he was seventeen years old he came back to Missouri alone, attending the state normal school and locating at Cape Girardeau. At the close of his school life he became a clerk in the store of H. P. Pierronett in Cape Girardeau, remaining with him in different capacities until December, 1888. At that time he engaged in business for himself, forming a partnership with Mr. Wood, the style of the firm being Flentge & Wood. They did a general merchandise business doing a flourishing trade until 1907. On the first of June in that year Mr. Flentge sold out his share of the business and became connected with the Cape Girardeau Brass Book Company, being secretary of the same. Since then he has filled many positions of honor, being at this time president of the Rock Tobacco Company of Cape Girardeau and secretary and treasurer of the Painter Realty Company. On the nineteenth of December, 1903, he was appointed postmaster, having held the position ever since. He is a member of the Commercial Club at Cape Girardeau and was its vice president for several years.

In 1884 he married Miss Sadie E. Taylor a native of Cape Girardeau to which union one son and two daughters were born. The daughters died in infancy. John E., the son, married Mabel Hash and is now a resident of Cape Girardeau.

Mr. Flentge is a member of the Masonic order. He is a Republican in political belief and has always been a most active worker for and with his party. He was a member of the city council for two terms and was two terms county collector. In 1906 he was a candidate for railroad and warehouse commissioner, but the Democratic candidate was elected. Mr. Flentge has been practically a life long resident of southeastern Missouri and has always been active in the business and political life of the state. Unlike his father, he found the greatest satisfaction in remaining in one place, feeling that by so doing he could not only gain a better living for himself and his family, but he could form more lasting friendships, he could make his presence felt in the community and thereby be given opportunities to be of use in the county and state. Such has been Mr. Flentge's desire, to serve his fellow citizens and to fulfil to the best of his ability the duties which he undertook.

T. R. R. ELY. The Honorable T. R. R. Ely, one of the most prominent lawyers in the county, has had wide and varied experience in his profession. A man with strong opinions on all public questions, he has always had the courage to express them. While in the legislature he had the most exalted views of his office and the obligations it involved. He was not there to pander to public sentiment or so to trim his sails that he might arouse a popular feeling among the people of his district, but to represent the people as he felt they should be represented. He felt that if it were otherwise and he were to be restricted in his views and their expression and obliged to wait to find out whether they pleased the people or not, he would infinitely rather go back to private life and become a private citizen, with the right to express his views untrammeled and unquestioned by anybody on earth, with the right to try to formulate public sentiment along the lines of his ideas. A man with such decided views could not fail to be an important factor with his party and in the community in general.

T. R. R. Ely was born in Atchison county, Missouri, January 19, 1860, where his boyhood days were spent until he reached the age of sixteen. He attended the Stuartsville, De Kalb county, school and the academy conducted by the Reverend Perry of the Presbyterian church. He then went to Westminster College at Fulton, where he stayed two years, taking a general course, followed by a law course at the State University, graduating in the class of 1881. As soon as he was graduated he came to Kennett, upon the recommendation of Joseph Russell, a fellow student, who is now a prominent member of congress. The bar was at that time mainly composed of outside men from other counties, but it was a rich practice. The following year, in 1882, Mr. Ely was elected prosecuting attorney and during his term of office he did such good work that two years later, at the next election, he was reelected. The country around Dunklin was very wild at that time, much wickedness going on in the county. During his term Mr. Ely sent forty-four men to the penitentiary, really the enforcement of law in that part of the country began with his regime; from that time on there was a complete change, the better class of people standing by him and giving him the advantage of their support. They had only needed a leader, long having felt that a change was needed, but not having sufficient initiative to go ahead and make any change by themselves. In 1886 Mr. Ely was elected to represent Dunklin county in the legislature. During his term of office he pushed the bill setting apart one-third of all revenues for the school support, one of the most important acts of legislature. At the expiration of his term he resumed his practice in Kennett, having all the work he could possibly attend to. In 1904 he was elected to the senate in the twenty-second senatorial district, including Dunklin, Butler, Ripley, Wayne, Curtis, Bollinger and Cape Girardeau counties. It is needless to say that he worked hard, for he was so constituted that he could not undertake a thing and not go into it with all his might. It was through his energetic pushing that the appropriation of ten thousand dollars was made to make a topographical survey of the five swamp counties. The amount was expended by commission of the governor; this was the first step towards drainage in that district, resulting in some twenty-five drainage districts being formed in Dunklin county alone. This simply aroused public interest, as at that time there was not a canal in existence. They have all been made since that first start. He was a member of the board of regents of the State Normal School at Cape Girardeau, at the time when the new school was being built. He always took the deepest interest in all matters pertaining to education and only resigned his position on the board to fill the position of senator, where a wider scope was offered his capabilities. Since he left the senate he has devoted most of his time to his practice, being a member of the firm of Ely, Kelso & Miller at Cape Girardeau, in addition to his own practice in Kennett. His aid is called for in most leading cases and the side that is fortunate enough to secure his services is pretty sure to come out ahead. He has been wonderfully successful in his practice.

One would imagine that the Honorable T. R. R. Ely would have no time for anything but his law work, but such is not the case. He has been most active in politics all of his life, the Democrats having a strong advocate in him. He was a delegate to the Denver Convention to nominate Bryan, the state committee obtaining his services as a stump speaker. He has an unusual gift of oratory; his language is excellent, but that is not the reason that his speeches are so convincing; he never advocates anything that he does not believe in, and thus he puts his whole force into what he says. It is very hard for anyone to listen to him and not agree with him at least while he is talking. He has great executive ability and is vice president of the Bank of Kennett. He stands high in the Masonic order, being a member of the Blue Lodge and of the Chapter at Kennett, of the Council at Malden and of the Commandery at Malden. He is a past worshipful master in the Blue Lodge. He also belongs to the Independent Order of Odd Fellows and to the Modern Woodmen of America. He owns farm lands to the extent of twenty-two hundred acres, having cultivated a great proportion of this land himself, it being wild when he bought it. He rents most of the land to tenants, but oversees some of it himself. He is a member of the Presbyterian church and in that as in everything else he has to do with he is an active worker. He has laid out two additions to Kennett, on which he has laid out lots and built residences. He only has fine homes on the addition, owning a beautiful place himself. All of these enterprises are in the nature of work, but Mr. Ely is just as enthusiastic about his recreations. He is of the opinion that his efficiency is increased by relaxation, which he takes principally in the form of hunting. He belongs to the club of West Kennett on the St. Francis river. Any man might be proud of the law practice that the Honorable T. R. R. Ely has built up and feel that that constituted a man's life work. His connection with education in the county would satisfy the ambition of the majority of people, while his political connections, both in the legislature and in the senate, would cause a less enterprising man to feel that he need do nothing else for the rest of his life. If he had not been such a successful lawyer, he would have made a reputation as a farmer. If he had done nothing but handle his addition in Kennett he might still feel that he had done something for his county, but when all these different activities are combined in one man, the result is an all around man of whom his town, county and state are proud, whom his acquaintances are proud to know and to whom all are proud to take off their hats. There is no more useful member of the community than the Honorable T. R. R. Ely.

ORTON COLMAN LYNCH, superintendent of the public schools of Farmington, deserves credit as a strong element in the educational progress of the county. One of the most progressive, able and enlightened of educators, he presents the potent combination of fine ideals and an executive capacity which contrives to make realities out of them. Since the beginning of his career in the judicial center of Saint Francois county—1907—a great improvement has been made in the local school system; a fine new high school building erected; and the higher department of the schools raised from an unrecognized condition to a fully accredited high school with full recognition.

Professor Lynch was born in Harrison county, West Virginia, on the 20th day of April, 1874, his father, Hiram Lynch, having been a native of the same locality. The father, who was at different times in his career a teacher and educator, was reared on a large cattle farm which belonged to his father. He attended the public schools of his locality and period and also for two years was a student at a college in Lebanon, Ohio. He engaged as a school teacher for a short time and then adopted farming as his occupation, continuing permanently as an exponent of the great basic industry. He was married in 1868 to Eleanor Williams, of Sycamore, West Virginia, daughter of John Williams, who answered to the double calling of farmer and Methodist circuit rider. To this union were born six children, three of whom are living at the present time. The first Mrs. Lynch died in the early '80s, when the subject was a small boy, and in 1883 the father was married to Miss Flora Maxwell, of Weston, West Virginia. Four children were the fruit of the second union. In 1885 the father removed with his family from West Virginia to Missouri and located in Fraklin county, where he again engaged in farming and where he is today located, secure in the enjoyment of the respect and confidence of the community. He is one of the stalwart supporters of the "Grand Old Party," as its admirers are pleased to call it; he is a popular member of the Independent Order of Odd Fellows and the American Order of United Workmen; and he is a zealous and valued member of the Methodist Episcopal church.

Orton C. Lynch entered the Academy of West Virginia, at Weston, where he received his elementary education, and after prosecuting his studies at that place until about ten years of age he then attended the public schools in Franklin county, Missouri, until entering Carlton Institute, of Farmington, Missouri. After a period of study there he became a student at the Missouri State Normal at Warrensburg, and is continuing his work by courses in the University of Chicago, correspondence study department, Chicago, Illinois. In 1899 he received his degree (that of B. S. D.) at the Normal School and in addition to his other training he attended for one year the Missouri State University at Columbia. A part of his education had been interspersed with his actual pedagogical work and he had taught in various schools, gaining the many advantages which only experience can give. After quite finishing his preparation he was for eight years connected with the public schools of Tipton, Missouri, four years as principal of the high school and four years as superintendent of the entire school system. He came to Farmington in 1907 to accept the position of superintendent here and this he retains at the present time, his work here having been of the most satisfactory character. In addition to his general supervision he is instructor in mathematics and science. The new high school building which he was materially instrumental in securing was finished in 1911 and is a model of convenience and modernity.

Professor Lynch was married on the 5th day of June, 1901, at Warrensburg, Missouri, to Miss Mary G. Scott, of that place. Mrs. Lynch is a daughter of Rev. William G. Scott, a well-known Presbyterian minister. To their happy union has been born three sons, whose names are Orton, William and Wallace.

In politics Professor Lynch is a liberal Prohibitionist, voting more for the man than party; he is a member of the Methodist Episcopal church; and he is sufficiently social in nature greatly to enjoy his relations with the Independent Order of Odd Fellows and the Modern Woodmen of America.

ALBERT L. JOHNSON. In a history devoted to the representative men and women of Southeastern Missouri who have contributed to its upbuilding and prosperity and whose lives reward closest inspection no one is more appropriately included than that fine

which, with the exception of ten acres, being covered with a heavy growth of timber. To clear the timber-covered land, of course, entailed a vast amount of labor. On the farm was a horse-power saw mill, which he operated a few months and then installed an engine, running both a saw-mill and grist mill and so efficiently that he had a great amount of patronage in the neighborhood. He was bringing his affairs to a very satisfactory footing when the Civil war, so long threatening, became a terrible reality, and life all over the country was changed and altered from the even tenor of its course. Soon after the first guns were fired at Sumter, Mr. Johnson enlisted in the army of the Confederacy, believing the cause it defended to be just and all the institutions of the South being very dear to him. His military career was eventful. In March, 1863, he was captured by Union forces and after being held a prisoner at St. Louis for three months was exchanged and joined his regiment in Virginia, on the Chesapeake Bay, thereafter serving with his command in East Tennessee until after the termination of the great conflict.

Returning to his farm on July 1, 1865, Mr. Johnson found that his barn had been burned, his stock taken off by the Federals and that he was in debt fifteen hundred dollars for his mill and land. Nothing daunted, however, he soon resumed his agricultural and industrial labors, clearing and improving his farm, which was an excellent one, and, as his means allowed, buying more land, at one time having title to seven hundred and twenty acres, the greater part of which was valuable and advantageously situated. At the time of his death he owned six hundred and sixty acres of land and the little burg of Octa, three miles northeast of Senath, its entire site being his, with the exception of two lots. He also owned considerable property in Senath, his holdings there consisting in a lot and store building on Front street (the building being twenty by eighty feet in dimension) and five good lots on other streets. He had other interests of importance, owing five shares in the Citizens Bank of Senath, of which he has been president since its organization and being a stockholder in the Caneer Store Company. Mr. Johnson's commodious dwelling-house on his farm was an attractive and substantial one, and a previous two thousand dollar residence had been destroyed by fire. Toward the close of his life he gave over the more strenuous duties of managing his farms into other hands, and at the time of his death rented all of his farms, with the exception of his forty acre homestead. His homestead was virtually the centre of a little settlement, for he had thirteen tenant houses on his place for the use of his renters, all of these houses being within a mile and a half of his own home. From the beginning of his career he always maintained a saw mill and grist mill on his farm, which he himself operated. He was a man of remarkable executive ability, able to manage successfully large forces and essentially progressive in the adoption of new ideas. It will not be gainsaid that he was one of the most successful and widely known citizens of Dunklin county, and one whose influence will be greatly missed in the many-sided life of the community.

Politically Mr. Johnson had always been identified with the Democratic party, to whose causes he gave hand and heart and he was at one time prominent in public life, serving as county judge for six years shortly after the war and subsequently being justice of the peace for twenty years. Fraternally he was affiliated with the time-honored Masonic order, which he joined in 1867, his membership being with Helm Chapter, R. A. M., of Kennett. At one time he was a member of the Independent Order of Odd Fellows. In his own life he followed the fine principles of Masonry and at his death the order conducted the last ceremonial rites and consigned the body to the grave. Religiously he was affiliated with the Methodist Episcopal church, South.

Mr. Johnson married, in 1875, Louisa Bailey, who died five years later, leaving three children, namely: Corrinner V., is the wife of Joseph Tackeberry, of Dunklin county, and they have five children: James A., Katie, Ernest P., Minnie B. and Dudley; Minnie B., wife of Henry Jones, until her father's demise lived with him, presiding over his household wisely and well. They have had eight children: Stella, Della, Clarence and five who died young; and Jennie who died at five years of age. Like himself, Mr. Johnson's children are respected and prominent and very loyal to the institutions of Dunklin county.

HONORABLE ROBERT GIBONEY RANNEY. Although the man without ancestors, who succeeds in making his own way in the world has doubtless a great deal to contend with, he is without the obligations which are imposed on the descendant of a family which has always amounted to something. The feeling of *noblesse oblige* determines many actions. If a man is conscientious this feeling is his safeguard, although he may chafe under the obligations at times. The Honorable Robert Giboney Ranney has not only lived so as to satisfy his family and his fellow men, but has also lived up to the standard set forth by his father and his grandfather; he has made his life count for something; he has not only made a competency for himself and his family, but he has done honor to the name; he has been of assistance to individuals; he has aided in the advancement of his state and his country.

He was born at Jackson, Cape Girardeau county, Misouri, December 15, 1849. His grandfather was Stephen Ranney, a native of Connecticut, who served in the Revolutionary war and also in the war of 1812. He held the office of Attorney General under Governor Hendricks. He spent the last years of his life in Cape Girardeau county and was buried at Jackson, Missouri. He had a large, powerful frame and was physically a very strong man. He was married four times, his last wife, grandmother of our subject, being Elizabeth Hathorn of Salem, Massachusetts.

William C. Ranney, father of Robert and son of Stephen, was a native of Whitehall, New York. He came to Cape Girardeau county, Missouri, about 1826, where he soon made his presence felt, being a lawyer by profession. He was the first common pleas judge in the county, having been appointed by the legislature,—a most unusual occurrence. He was a member of the legislature and was state senator. During the whole of his residence in Cape Girardeau he was active in public affairs, feeling the deepest interest in the growth and advancement of the state in which he was one of the early settlers. He lived to be eighty-three years old and was hale and hearty up to the time of his death. He, like his father, was possessed of a very strong physique and weighed two hundred and seventy-five pounds. He married Elizabeth Giboney, a native of Missouri. Her father, Robert Giboney, came to Missouri with his father, Alexander Giboney, about 1796 from their home near Harper's Ferry, in Virginia. They came by wagon to Cape Girardeau county, bringing with them the few necessities of life. They were pioneers to Cape Girardeau county, where they obtained grants of land and located there. These tracts of land are still in the ownership of the descendants. Mrs. William C. Ranney lived to the age of eighty-one, having borne four sons to her husband, three of whom are living now. The eldest son was Stephen, named after his grandfather; Robert Giboney was the second; William Alexander, named after his father, the third, and Herbert Hathorn, the youngest.

When Robert was a baby his parents moved to a farm five miles southwest of Cape Girardeau; there Robert was brought up and s soon as he was old enough he attended the district school. He learned how to do all sorts of farm work, thereby laying a foundation for conscientious fulfilment of duty that has been of good service to him through life. He was sent away to attend the Kentucky Military Institute when he was seventeen years old. He remained there four years and when he returned home he taught one year. He had by this time made up his mind that he wished to study law as had his father and uncle, Johnson Ranney before him. He was desirous of starting in their footsteps but would make others for himself, branching out in other directions from those taken by his ancestors. After reading law with Louis Houck he attended the law school at the Missouri University, graduating in the class of 1873. Louis Houck had formed such a high opinion of his ex-scholar's abilities that he took him into partnership. The two did business together until 1880, when Robert's state of health compelled him to retire from the practice of law. He moved on to a farm and continued to actively superintend its management until 1894. He found the outdoor life was just what was needed to build up his health, but was in no hurry to return to his professional life, rather preferring the quiet, simple life of a farmer. In 1894, however, the interests of his family decided him to move to Cape Girardeau and again practice law. His knowledge and capabilities were such that he was eminently successful. In 1908 he was elected judge of the Common Pleas Court, which position he now fills. He had previously been a Justice of the Peace, while he was engaged in farming.

In 1876 he married Lizzie Giboney, by

whom he had five children, two of whom lived to maturity, viz., Louise, wife of Clyde Harrison of Cape Girardeau, and Robert Clifton, also living in Cape Girardeau. Mrs. Ranney died in 1892. In 1894 Mr. Ranney married Emma Wathen, by whom he also had five children, all of whom are living, as follows: Wathena, Roberta, Ralph G., Mary and Maud.

The Judge is one of the oldest born citizens of southeastern Missouri, where he has spent the whole of his life, with the exception of his school days, when he went both south and east. He has always been a firm upholder of Democratic principles, believing that in them are the principles of good government. He believes in party spirit, not because he is prepared to endorse everything that is done by his party, but he does heartily endorse its great principles. He thinks and reasons for himself and is most tolerant of the opinions of others, to whom he grants the same right of free thinking and acting. Although he is decided in his own views he does not necessarily think all others are wrong. He is a man with a keen sense of justice and right, a man who has helped to make of Cape Girardeau the power that it now is in the state.

HORACE D. BENEDICT. Americans are beginning to realize the moral as well as the historical significance of genealogical foundations. A nation which relies upon the record of its homes for its national character cannot afford to ignore the value of genealogical investigation as one of the truest sources of patriotism. The love of home inspires the love of country. There is a wholesome influence in genealogical research which cannot be overestimated. Moreover, there is a deep human interest to it. The Hon. Horace Dryden Benedict, present mayor and prominent business man at Fredericktown, Missouri, is a scion of an old, old English family, his genealogy in England being traced back to the eleventh century. The original progenitor of the name in America settled at Rotterdam, Connecticut, having immigrated to that place at a very early day. Subsequently members of the family removed to Canada and on their return to the United States settled in St. Lawrence county, New York, where they were engaged largely in surveying. The great-grandfather of him whose name forms the caption for this review was killed in the war of 1812 by Indians and a number of his forebears were gallant soldiers in the war for independence.

The career of Horace D. Benedict has been varied and interesting in the extreme, as will be noted in ensuing paragraphs. He was born in Jefferson county, New York, on the 11th of January, 1843, and is a son of Amasa and Waty (Reynolds) Benedict, both natives of New York. When the young Horace was two years old his parents removed from the east to northern Ohio, where he was reared to adult age. During his life time he had resided in twenty-six different states and for a time he also maintained his home in Canada. As a young man he learned the trade of telegraph operator and for a number of years he was in the employ of the Missouri Pacific Railroad Company, also doing construction on that and other roads.

At the time of the inception of the Civil war Mr. Benedict was fired with boyish enthusiasm for the cause of the Union and enlisted at the first call for volunteers, becoming a member of the Fourteenth Ohio Regiment. Three months later he enlisted for three years in the Third Ohio, and while a member of that regiment was captured at the battle of Iuka and sent to prison at Vicksburg, where he was held in duress for nearly three months. He saw much hard service but was never seriously injured. He participated in the Atlanta campaign and received his discharge and was mustered out of service in November, 1864. After the completion of his military service Mr. Benedict returned to Ohio, whence he removed to St. Louis, Missouri, in the following year. In the latter city he entered the Military telegraph service and later engaged in railroad construction work, as previously noted. On the 1st of July, 1888, he located at Fredericktown, where he engaged in contracting and building work, having a large number of men in his employ and also handling all kinds of building supplies. In the early '90s he became interested in the old Madison County Bank at Fredericktown, serving as vice-president and manager of that institution for a number of years. This concern was later disposed of to the trust company. For several years past Mr. Benedict has lived retired, contenting himself with a general supervision of his extensive holdings. He is the owner of nine beautiful residences in St. Louis, the rental from which is a snug fortune in itself. He is also the owner of two fine residences at Fredericktown.

In October, 1866, Mr. Benedict was united in marriage to Miss Mary Hallett, who was born and reared in Ohio. Concerning their children the following record is here offered,—Truman L. is owner of the telephone exchange at Clarendon, Texas, and he is married to Maud McAlpin, of Gurdon, Arkansas, and has four children, viz., Myrle R., Grace T., Mary H. and William R. He was formerly connected with railroad construction work. Russell Pope is connected with a telegraph company at St. Louis. He married first Miss Katie Hill, of Fredericktown, Missouri, who died January 25, 1908, leaving one daughter, Mary H., aged eleven years in June, 1911. His present wife was Miss Anna Weatherwax. Horace, Jr., married Carolyn Brock, of Frankfort, Kentucky, and travels for the Thomas Law Book Company, of St. Louis. Norma is the wife of Louis F. Alt, who is in the license collector's office of St. Louis. They have one child, Benedict Alt, aged two years.

Mr. and Mrs. Benedict were married in Lucas county, Ohio, and for thirteen years followed farming near Toledo, Ohio. Then, in 1880, they removed to Marshall, Texas, where Mr. Benedict was engaged in construction work, under his half-brother, C. W. Hammond, who was superintendent of the whole Gould system, telegraph and construction work. He was a prominent man in those circles and was an old resident of St. Louis. He died in 1899, at his home at St. Louis. Mr. and Mrs. Benedict had little to start with except energy and ambition, and their united efforts have been crowned with success.

In politics Mr. Benedict is a stanch advocate of the cause of the Republican party in national issues but in local affairs he maintains an independent attitude, voting for men and measures meeting with the approval of his judgment. In 1910 he was elected mayor of Fredericktown, being incumbent of that office at the present time. He is proving a most efficient administrator of the municipal affairs of the city and has instituted many improvements during his regime. In the time-honored Masonic order he has passed through the circles of both the York and the Scottish Rite branches, being a member of the Commandery and Consistory at St. Louis. He retains a deep and abiding interest in his old comrades in arms and signifies the same by membership in Hiram Gavitt Post, Grand Army of the Republic. He and his family are consistent members of the Methodist Episcopal church, South. The life history of Mr. Benedict is certainly worthy of commendation and emulation, for along honorable and straightforward lines he has won the success which crowns his efforts and which makes him one of the substantial residents of Fredericktown.

MOSES H. TOPPING, M. D. One of the eminent citizens of Flat River, Saint Francois county, Missouri, is Dr. Moses H. Topping, a physician widely known for his high attainments in his profession, and who in addition to his general practice is extensively engaged in surgery among the miners. Dr. Topping is also president of the Bank of Flat River, and it is largely due to his discrimination and well directed administrative dealing that this institution has become one of the substantial and popular smaller banking houses of the state of Missouri.

Dr. Topping is a Virginian by birth, the place of his nativity having been Elizabeth City county, of the Old Dominion, and its date November 6, 1874. His father, James S. Topping, was also born in Virginia, and like most of the young men of his day and generation he was a soldier in the Civil war, having entered the army of the Confederacy at the early age of sixteen years. He saw some of the most active service of the war and participated in some of the closing events, having been with General Lee at the fall of Richmond. After the war he adopted the Republican policies and was throughout his life a useful and public-spirited citizen. He engaged in the wholesale wood, coal and stock food business and followed this actively until his demise, March 16, 1895, in Elizabeth City county, Virginia. He was married at about the age of twenty-nine years to Alice Jane Hawkins, daughter of Captain James Hawkins, of Elizabeth City county, Virginia. The Hawkins family is of English descent. Dr. Topping was the youngest of three children born to these worthy people, the others being James B., of Harriston, Virginia; and Alice Virginia, now Mrs. M. T. Webber. The father was a consistent member of the Baptist church and a popular and prominent lodge man, his fraternal affiliations extending to the Knights of Pythias, the Masons and the Redmen.

The preliminary education of Dr. Moses H. Topping was received in the public and high schools at Hampton, Virginia. His higher training was of a varied and extensive character, including attendance at the Suffolk Military Academy; a year at William and Mary College at Williamsburg, Virginia; and two years at the Physicians and Surgeons College at Richmond. It was while he was a student at the latter institution that its name was changed to the University College of Medicine. He finished his preparation for his profession at the Louisville Medical College, there graduating and receiving his degree. He went to Oklahoma to begin active practice, but remained there but a short time, in 1897 removing to Missouri and settling in Desloge, Saint Francois county. After a residence in that town he came on to Flat River, where he has ever since remained, and where his ability has received enthusiastic recognition. Dr. Topping is president of the Bank of Flat River, as mentioned previously, and he has held this high position ever since its organization, in which he was instrumental. He is likewise president of that flourishing concern—the Lead Belt Amusement Company. Dr. Topping is a stanch adherent of the Republican party, of which he is a disciple by inheritance and personal conviction, and he is a valued member of the Baptist church, assisting to the best of his ability in its good works. No movement calculated to result in bettered conditions for the whole of society fails to secure his support, and he is in truth at the head of many such. He has social proclivities, finding pleasure in association with his brethren, and his lodge affiliations extend to the Benevolent and Protective Order of Elks and the Knights of Pythias.

On May 4, 1898, Dr. Topping established a happy household by his union with Amanda C. Blue, daughter of John W. Blue, a prominent Saint Francois county agriculturist and one of the pioneer settlers of southeastern Missouri. Her grandfather, John W. Blue, was mayor of Farmington previous to the Civil war. The union of Dr. and Mrs. Topping has been blessed by the birth of three children, Vannesse, Virginia and Norman H., and their home is the center of gracious hospitality.

GEORGE T. DUNMIRE, the postmaster at Kennett, has had a most interesting career. The educators of the present day are urging military training as a means of making better citizens. What Mr. Dunmire might have been without his military service it is hard to say, but at least the lessons he learned while in the army have been of more value to him than any experience gained before or since.

He was born in Mercer county, Pennsylvania, April 21, 1837. He received his education in his native town and when the Civil war broke out he joined the One Hundred and Forty-second Pennsylvania Regiment, serving from August 8th until the close of the war. He was in the battle of the Potomac and at Appomattox, serving as Commissary Sergeant for a time. After the war was ended he went back to Pennsylvania, where he stayed until 1866, when he located at what is now known as Cumberland City, Kentucky, the Coal Company having established the postoffice there. In 1870 he left there to go to Springfield and a year later returned to Pennsylvania. After three years there he went to Indiana, remaining about a year, and thence to Birmingham, Kentucky, where he remained until 1878, when he came to Malden, Missouri, where his brother-in-law, C. P. Phillips, had been in the mercantile business from its start. After remaining with Mr. Phillips for a year and a half, Mr. Dunmire went to Paragould, Arkansas, but his stay there was short lived, only lasting one year. He came to Kennett in 1884 and has been here ever since. For two years he was in the general store business, then he became a building contractor, continuing thus until 1901, when he was with his son in the drug store. In 1907 he was appointed postmaster under President Roosevelt. He has fitted up a nice postoffice and has one rural free delivery. During the four years of service he has devoted himself to the duties of postmaster and has fulfilled them to the satisfaction of the people in general.

In 1868 Mr. Dunmire was married in Kentucky to Vienna M. Phillips. Three children were born to the union, two of whom reached maturity, but only one is living now, John H., the druggist at Kennett. In addition to his drug business Mr. John Dunmire is the assisting postmaster and has received the appointment as postmaster. Hattie E. married Leonard Loeffeler of Hayti, Missouri, and died when a young woman.

Mr. Dunmire has been connected with the Masons for forty-four years, having joined the order in Kentucky in 1867. He is still a worker in the lodge. He is affiliated with Kennett Lodge, No. 68, A. F. & A. M., Helm Chapter, No. 117, of Kennett, and Campbell Council, No. 30, of Campbell, Missouri. He is a member of the Methodist Episcopal church in Kennett. Mr. Dunmire is what is known as a Black Republican in St. Louis, but he has hosts of friends with the Democratic party, notwithstanding the active work he has always done for the Republicans. During the years that Mr. Dunmire has been in Kennett he has seen many changes in the county, most of them for the better. He is one of the most loyal citizens of Kennett, standing ready at all times to do his best for its betterment. He began his life in the service of Uncle Sam in the army and hopes to end it in the same service in the postal department.

BURWELL FOX. One of the native Ohioans transplanted to the great state of Missouri is Burwell Fox, a prominent educator now serving as county superintendent of schools, and a gifted writer and editor. He is a man not only of ability, but also of high ideals of citizenship, and although a Democrat in politics, at the election for his present office he received a large majority in a strongly Republican county,—assuredly an eloquent tribute. He was educated for the law and practiced his profession in Lebanon, Ohio, in which city he also served as mayor and police judge.

Professor Fox was born near Lebanon, Warren county, Ohio, December 8, 1849, and his father, John C. Fox, was born in the vicinity of Lebanon. The grandparents were of Scotch-English stock. John C. Fox lived in the Buckeye state in the days when the wilderness had but recently yielded to the strength and daring of the first brave pioneers and he himself grew to manhood on a farm in his native county and there acquired those habits of industry and thrift which distinguished his later life. He answered to the two-fold calling of carpenter and farmer, and subsequently he removed to Indiana, his farm being practically the forest. In 1857 he died from the effects of a horsekick. He married Anne Wayne Brownley, a native of the Old Dominion. Three children were born to them. The eldest died in infancy; Sarah F. is now Mrs. John T. Barr; and Burwell is the subject of his brief biographical record. The mother died one month after the death of her husband, and the two children were left alone in the world at a very early age. In religious conviction the elder Mr. Fox was a Baptist and he was a stanch Whig.

Burwell Fox was but seven years of age when he became fatherless and motherless. The home in Indiana was of course broken up and he went to live with an aunt and uncle, Burwell and Catherine Bassett, who resided in his native Lebanon. He received an education in the public schools of Lebanon and through the kindness of Mr. and Mrs. Bassett found it possible to prepare for the legal profession, to which he was inclined. His studies in this line were pursued at Lebanon, Ohio, and in 1870 he was admitted to the bar at that place and shortly afterward he commenced to practice, and took his place among the representative members of his profession. In 1872 he gave Lebanon an excellent administration as mayor and he held the office of police judge until 1876, in which year he departed for Missouri.

Professor Fox located at once in Washington county and since coming here his field of most active usefulness has been the pedagogical. From 1893 to 1897 he was United States commissioner at Ironton, Missouri, and he subsequently resumed teaching. In 1909 he was elected to his present important office as county superintendent of schools and in 1911 was reelected to the same office. The triumph of his personality over politics has been previously told. He is a splendid enlightened officer and well maintains the dignity and responsibility of the superintendency. He has the work exceedingly well systemized and can instantly look up the record of any teacher or school. His career as an instructor has also included three years as principal of the Potosi schools.

Professor Fox was first married November 13, 1878, Miss Kitty I. Harguss, a member of a Kentucky family, becoming his wife. She died in 1889, at Arcadia, Missouri, and the one child born to the union is also deceased. On June 29, 1892, he was united to Miss Maria A. Russell, of Ironton, daughter of Theodore P. and Emily (Guild) Russell, and they share their delightful, cultured home with a son, who bears his father's name. A younger son, Pitkin, died at the age of three. They are members of the Presbyterian church and act in harmony with all salutary measures.

Professor Fox's literary talent has been before alluded to. He has been successful as a magazine writer, being particularly gifted in the field of fiction and he at one time assisted in the editing of the *Iron County Register* and the *Potosi Independent*.

JOHN J. MAUTHE. Among the prominent and representative citizens of Pacific, John J. Mauthe holds deservedly high place in popular confidence and esteem, his fellow townsmen having paid him the highest compliment within their power of considering him a worthy son of that splendid and honorable citizen, the late William Mauthe. He holds the office of cashier of the Citizens' Bank of Pacific, having held this position since 1909, and has proved himself an efficient, alert and well-trained banker, whose discrimination and well directed administrative dealing have been of no inconsiderable value in building up its fortunes. He comes of German stock and in him are to be discovered those excellent characteristics which make the Teutonic one of our most admirable sources of citizenship. In addition to his banking interests he is identified with the mercantile life of the place.

Mr. Mauthe is a native son of Pacific, his birth having occurred here January 14, 1873, the son of William Mauthe, an antebellum settler who spent his active life as a merchant and who died in the harness, January 18, 1901. The father was born in Germany, in 1826, and came to America to seek a home among a people more free and independent than the people of the Fatherland. He located in Pacific and built up a good mercantile business, and was identified, besides, in the most praiseworthy manner with the civic affairs of the place. He served as postmaster during the Civil war and was at times connected with the town board. He was a Republican and was a loyal supporter of the cause of the Union in the troublous days of the great conflict between the states. William Mauthe married Susan Kiburz, who was also a native of Germany, and this worthy lady is still a resident of Pacific. The issue of their union was as follows: Miss Annie Mauthe, of Pacific, a member of the mercantile house of Mauthe & Company; William, who is engaged in the bottling business at DeSoto, Missouri, and who is president of the German-American Bank there; August F., who was cashier of the Citizens Bank of Union, Missouri and who died at that place in January, 1910; Louis F., who died at Pacific in January, 1905, and who was engaged in the bottling business, married Miss Lena Burger and at his death left a family of six children, whose names were Raymond, Lorine, Dewey, Harold, Gertrude and Louise, Mrs. Gus C. Rau, of Pacific; Louisa, who married Charles Hufschmidt, of this place, and is deceased; and John J., the immediate subject of this record.

John J. Mauthe gained his schooling in the public schools of Pacific and when about seventeen years of age he entered his father's store as one of the fixtures of that institution. He mastered the details of the retail mercantile business and when his father passed away he became the active head of the concern. The firm of Mauthe & Company includes himself and his sister Miss Annie, who is a most able and judicious business woman. Although Mr. Mauthe is not associated as intimately with the business as in youth, he retains a connection with it and to him is largely due the fact of its permanence and the same confidence as under the old regime which it enjoys in the community.

When the Citizens' Bank was brought into existence in 1909 Mr. Mauthe, who was one of the promoters, was invited to take the place of cashier. The bank was chartered in that year; buildings were erected, and it opened business on August 30 of the same year, with a capital of fifteen thousand dollars. Its other officers are James Booth, president, and L. R. Dougherty, vice president, and it has already gained prestige as a sound and substantial monetary institution.

Mr. Mauthe is also one of the directors of the electric light company of Pacific and is a member of the board of directors of the Pacific Home Telephone Company. Like his father, he is identified with the Republican party, but unlike that well-remembered gentleman he has never been connected with office. The fraternal order of Knights of Pythias knows Mr. Mauthe as one of its members, but business connections preclude his giving his time to the work of this or other fraternal societies.

On December 28, 1904, Mr. Mauthe was

happily married to Miss Margaret Carroll, daughter of P. W. Carroll, of Cape Girardeau, Missouri, a concrete contractor and decorator. They have no children. Mr. and Mrs. Mauthe enjoy a prominent place in the best social life of the place and are very loyal to the interests of Pacific.

DANIEL E. CONRAD is the son of David R. and Mary (Bollinger) Conrad, who are also the parents of Peter Conrad, whose life is briefly outlined in this work. Daniel was the thirteenth child of the family of which Peter was the eldest. As has been stated, the grandfather came to Missouri from North Carolina in 1820. Daniel was born in 1859, on February 27.

David Conrad owned several hundred acres of land and as he was not only a man of wealth but also of culture, he took pains with the education of his children. Daniel went to the county schools and afterwards to the State University at Columbia. When twenty-two years of age he married and began to farm for himself. He first managed his father's farm for a few years and then operated a portion of the farm for himself. In 1890 he bought one hundred and seventy-five acres of land and now has five hundred and fifty-five acres of land on Whitewater creek, of which two hundred and fifty acres are under cultivation. Besides this Mr. Conrad is farming his sister's farm of two hundred acres. Sixty acres of this is in cultivation. Agriculture is a pursuit which Mr. Conrad follows according to scientific methods, as he is a progressive farmer. He has a modern residence on his place, put up in 1901. Stock engages part of his attention and he owns eighteen horses and mules, forty-three head of cattle, one hundred and twenty hogs and twenty-seven sheep.

Mrs. Conrad's maiden name was Ella Statler, the daughter of Robert Statler. She and Mr. Conrad have had the following children: Ora, born June 14, 1883; Howard Dale, July 23, 1885; David R., August 9, 1887; Ella Ethel Irene, February 11, 1889; Mary Kathleen, December 31, 1890; Hazel, November 30, 1892; Chalmers F., December 3, 1894; Gyle D., May 14, 1896; and Corliss Dewey, March 1, 1898. Mr. and Mrs. Conrad are members of the Presbyterian church.

ALFRED HOWARD AKERS. Few men are better and more favorably known in Saint Francois county than Alfred Howard Akers, who has been identified with this section since the year 1884 and who holds the position of county principal and superintendent of schools. He held the office of county school commissioner for fourteen years and no one is more thoroughly in touch with educational matters or better able to cope with the various problems arising.

Mr. Akers was born in the Valley of Virginia, near the city of Roanoke, October 12, 1855. His father, Henry Akers, was born in the vicinity of Lynchburg and was reared on a farm, receiving the limited education to be acquired in the country schools. He was married at the age of twenty-two years to Katie Garnet, daughter of Allen Garnet, a farmer located in that vicinity, and they became the parents of three children, namely: A. H., the immediate subject of this review, Walter; and Bessie. In politics the father was an old-line Whig and he subsequently became a Democrat. He was Baptist in religious conviction and a member of the time-honored Masonic fraternity. He passed away at the age of sixty years.

Until the age of fifteen years Mr. Akers was reared upon the farm and received his earlier education in a private school, located not far from his home. When arrived at his fifteenth birthday he was sent to the Agricultural and Mechanical College at Blacksburg, Virginia, and after a four years' preparatory course there he matriculated in the University of Virginia, where he remained two years. With a view to entering the field of educational endeavor, Mr. Akers took a brief normal course at Farmville, Virginia, and ever since then he has been engaged in teaching school. In 1884 he came to the state of Missouri and for the past eighteen years he has been principal and superintendent of schools in this county. In 1909 he was elected county superintendent and at the next election succeeded himself, being the present incumbent of the office. He enjoys a splendid reputation for ability, judgment and progressiveness in educational circles and has done much in this important field.

On the 1st day of September, 1886, Mr. Akers was united in marriage to Alice Wescott, of Saint Francois county, daughter of J. W. and Mary J. Wescott. Mr. and Mrs. Akers are the parents of the following seven children: J. Clyde, Jessie V., Wilbur D., Waldemar F., Alfred Howard, Christine and

Julian. The head of the house is Democratic in politics; his fraternal relations extend to the Masons, the Redmen, the American Order of United Workmen and the Knights of Pythias; and his church is the Baptist.

In evidence of Mr. Akers' successful elevation of the standard of the county schools is the fact that there are three fully accredited ones among them and ten are doing high school work.

MANN RINGO. Mr. Ringo's entire attention is given to the banking business, specifically to the Iron County Bank, of which he has been a director since its organization in 1896 and cashier since 1897. Other officers of the organization are William R. Edgar, president, whose biography appears elsewhere in this volume, Eli D. Ake, vice-president, and Arthur Huff, assistant cashier. These gentlemen and William H. and I. G. Whitworth constitute the board of directors. The bank was organized by the present stockholders with a capital of ten thousand dollars and has now a surplus of fifteen thousand dollars and has been incorporated as a state bank.

Mr. Ringo was born September 25, 1864, in Mississippi county, southeastern Missouri. His parents, J. M. and Fredonia (McGregor) Ringo, had come to Missouri nine years before from western Kentucky. The father was a native of Kentucky, but the mother was born in Tennessee. After settling in Missouri, J. M. Ringo became a merchant farmer and was prominent in the political affairs of the county. He served as district judge of the county court and also as county treasurer of Mississippi county. He died in 1893, at the age of sixty-five years, after the death of his wife. Both were members of the Baptist church.

Mr. Mann Ringo has two brothers and three sisters. Mr. D. M. Ringo is a merchant farmer and a stock and grain dealer. He resides in his father's adopted home, Mississippi county. Mr. S. P. Ringo is a merchant in Ironton. The sisters are Mrs. W. A. Fletcher, of Arcadia, Miss Nannie Ringo, primary teacher in the same place, and Mrs. Louis Miller, also of Arcadia.

Mr. Ringo has spent his active life in the Arcadia valley. He was educated at the Normal in Cape Girardeau, graduating in the class of 1886. The two years following he taught school. In 1888 he was elected to the legislature and served two terms. During Cleveland's second administration he was appointed receiver of public moneys for the U. S. land office. Since 1897 he has been cashier of the bank and an executive officer.

He married Miss Annie Newman, a native of Ironton. She is the daughter of the late Thomas Newman, whose widow and family still reside in Ironton. Mr. Newman was a house and sign painter, a native of England, but a resident of Ironton from 1864 until his death, in 1907. Mr. and Mrs. Ringo have two daughters, Miss Lucille, aged sixteen, and Miss Fredonia J., aged eighteen. Both are attending their father's old school, the Normal at Cape Girardeau.

Mr. Ringo's retirement from the field of active politics has in no way weakened his adherence to the Democratic party, whose policies have always embodied his political convictions. Though banking is his exclusive business, he finds opportunity to maintain his affiliation with the Masonic order.

SAMUEL B. KIEFNER. Civilization will hail riches, prowess, honors, popularity, but it will bow humbly to sincerity in its fellows. The exponent of known sincerity, singleness of honest purpose, has its exemplification in all bodies of men; he is found in every association and to him defer its highest offices. Such an exemplar whose daily life and whose life work have been dominated as their most conspicuous characteristic by sincerity is Samuel B. Kiefner, who is a business man of prominence and influence at Perryville, Missouri, and who is the present able and popular incumbent of the office of postmaster of this city.

Samuel B. Kiefner was born on a farm near Kaiser's Ridge, in Allegany county, Maryland, on the 20th of October, 1863, and he is a son of John and Catherine (Lakel) Kiefner, both of whom are now living in retirement at Perryville, where the former was long engaged in the furniture and undertaking business. John Kiefner was born in Germany in the year 1834 and he accompanied his grandfather to America when he was a lad of sixteen years of age. Settlement was made at Baltimore, Maryland, where John entered upon an apprenticeship at the cabinet maker's trade and where, on the 25th of December, 1854, was recorded his marriage to Miss Catherine Lakel. This union was prolific of eleven children, five of whom are living, in 1911, the subject of this article being next youngest of those who survive. Elsewhere in this volume appears a sketch of the life and career of Charles E. Kiefner, younger brother of Samuel B. Kiefner.

Samuel B. Kiefner, of this notice, was a child of but two years of age at the time of his parents' removal to Perryville, to whose public schools he is indebted for his preliminary educational training. At the age of eighteen years he undertook to learn the ins and outs of the carpenter's trade and two years later, in 1883, he accompanied his parents to Kansas, where the family home was maintained for the ensuing four years. During three years of that time Mr. Kiefner was foreman of a street-car barn at Wichita, Kansas, and in 1889 he removed to Des Moines, Iowa, where he resided for one year, at the expiration of which he went to Keokuk, Iowa, where he was employed as clerk for the street-car company from 1890 to September, 1891. On the date last mentioned he returned to Perryville and here was engaged in the work of his trade until the fall of 1903. He then organized the Union Store Company, which was incorporated under the laws of the state with a capital stock of twenty-five thousand dollars and which is officered as follows,—Samuel B. Kiefner, president; H. M. Geile, vice president; and Charles J. Litsch, secretary and treasurer. For a time he had charge of the furniture and undertaking department of this concern but on the 22nd of May, 1906, when he was appointed postmaster of Perryville, he was obliged to relinquish that work. In his political convictions Mr. Kiefner is a stanch supporter of the principles and policies promulgated by the Republican party and while he has never shown any great ambition for political preferment he was a member of the Perryville board of aldermen from 1896 to 1898. In 1906, as previously noted, he was appointed postmaster of Perryville, by President Roosevelt, and he was re-appointed to that office by President Taft in 1909. In fraternal circles he is affiliated with the United Brotherhood of America, the Ancient Order of United Workmen and the Modern Woodmen of America. For a period of three years he was a member of the Perryville school board and his religious support is given to the Presbyterian church, in whose faith he was reared.

In the year 1889, at Wichita, Kansas, was celebrated the marriage of Mr. Kiefner to Miss Clara B. Armstrong, who was reared and educated at Wichita. Mr. and Mrs. Kiefner became the parents of six children, all of whom are living except Clarence, who was summoned to the life eternal in 1901. The names of the other children are as follows,— Maud, Leroy, Carl, Burton, and Nellie. Maud is assistant postmistress at Perryville and Leroy is a popular and successful teacher in the public schools of this place. Mrs. Kiefner is a woman of charming personality and she and her husband are everywhere accorded the highest regard of their fellow citizens on account of their exemplary lives and sterling qualities.

DR. ROBERT P. DALTON, one of the most promising young doctors at Cape Girardeau, is a life long resident of southeastern Missouri. His family on both sides were amongst the oldest settlers in Missouri. The time has passed when youth is any handicap to a man,—even a physician—nor is age any detriment. The world demands that a man shall deliver the goods, having no fault to find with him as long as he does that. It is only when he fails that attention is called to his years. Dr. Dalton has shown the people in Cape Girardeau that he has ability of an unusual order, combined with integrity of a still rarer kind. He, like a number of other young men, was not decided what road he would travel to success, but when he did decide he quickly got on to it and is making up for lost time by his rapid progress along it.

He was born at Frederickstown, Missouri, on the last day of the year 1876. His grandfather, John P. Dalton, was born in Ripley county, Missouri, his father having been one of the pioneers of southeastern Missouri. John P. Dalton was a farmer and also a blacksmith, a common enough combination years ago. His son, also named John, was a native of Frederickstown, Missouri, where he received his education. He studied medicine and became a practicing physician, as also a preacher of the Gospel. A physician has many opportunities to speak a word in season regarding the spiritual life as well as the corporeal, but Dr. Dalton was not satisfied with that, he felt the necessity of proclaiming in a public way the teachings of the Bible. He married Fannie Best, a young woman born in Perry county, Missouri. She was the daughter of Jonathan Best, one of the first settlers of southeastern Missouri, whither he came from North Carolina. He was a farmer both in his native county and in Missouri. Dr. and Mrs. John Dalton had eleven children, of whom two daughters died in infancy, the remaining nine living to grow to maturity, seven sons and two daughters. The two youngest of the family died at about the age of twenty-one.

Dr. Robert P. Dalton was the second child of his parents. His childhood was passed on the farm at Frederickstown, where he was born. As soon as he was old enough to attend school, he had to walk a distance of five miles each way, to the little log school house, known as the Killday or McKenzie school. He received his preliminary education at this school, after which he went to the Underwood school, which was four miles in another direction from his home. Both school houses were built of logs, the desks were formed of a log split in two, having peg legs. The instruction however, was not as primitive as the buildings, as Robert learned a good deal at these two schools. He next attended the Greenville high school, in Wayne county, going from there to Hales College at Gravelton, Missouri, where he took a general course, graduating in 1896. He had not yet decided to become a physician, but he believed in the advantages of a first class education, no matter what course he pursued. After leaving college he was engaged in the drug and grocery business at Patton, Missouri, in which he continued for about four years. In 1900 he had made up his mind that he was not cut out for a mercantile career, but felt a very decided leaning towards the medical profession. He sold out his business, entered a medical college at St. Louis, Missouri, graduating therefrom in 1904, having taken the full four years medical course. The same year he came to Cape Girardeau, immediately starting to practice. He has been here ever since, with a steadily increasing practice. He is a member of the Cape Girardeau County Medical Society and of the State Medical Association.

On September 7, 1892, the Doctor married Miss Sue E. Swindell, the daughter of Sam J. Swindell. There have been no children born to Dr. and Mrs. Dalton.

The doctor is a member of various fraternal orders, as follows: the Modern Woodmen of America, the Knights and Ladies of Security, the Modern Americans. Politics do not greatly interest Dr. Dalton, his time being fully occupied by his practice, his societies, his family and his needed recreation. He has already shown himself to be a power for good in the community.

JOSEPH SCOTT WOLFF, D. D. S.—One of the best known members of the dental profession in Southeast Missouri, as well as mayor of Festus and a public citizen of broad and strong character, Dr. Joseph S. Wolff comes of an old, substantial Pennsylvania family which has included not a few distinguished members in the east and southwest. His father, Rev. A. T. Wolff, was born in Westmoreland county, that state, and was recognized until his death, in 1905, at the age of forty-nine, as one of the eminent Presbyterian clergymen in the country. The elder man spent his early boyhood and youth on the old Pennsylvania farm and as a hardworking pupil in the neighborhood schools, afterward realizing his ambition for a higher education by completing a course at Union Seminary, Alliance, Ohio. At his graduation therefrom he became pastor of a small church at Sandy Lake, Pennsylvania, and not long afterward accepted a call from the First Presbyterian church of Alton, Illinois. He acceptably filled the pulpit of that strong organization for seven years, and then served as pastor of the Calvary Presbyterian church of Detroit, and the North Presbyterian church of St. Louis. In the discharge of the duties attaching to these responsible charges, Dr. Wolff had become so widely admired and loved both as a faithful pastor and an eloquent pulpit orator that he received an urgent call to assume pastoral charge of the largest Presbyterian church in Edinburgh, Scotland, the old-world stronghold of the denomination. Although deeply appreciative of the honor, his home ties and stanch Americanism, as well as his firm conviction that he could do more good in the United States where his influence had been so long exerted —these considerations forced him to decline the proffered Edinburgh pastorate. For some time, however, he lectured abroad under the Slayton Lyceum Bureau, and became widely known in Great Britain. He also became very prominent as a Mason and at one time was grand state orator for Illinois.

In 1875 Rev. A. T. Wolff was united in marriage with Miss Margaret S. Young, of Oakland Cross Roads, Pennsylvania, and of the six children born to him, the Doctor was the eldest. His mother is still living, also two brothers and one sister, residents of St. Louis.

Dr. Wolff is also a native of Westmoreland county, Pennsylvania, where he was born June 14, 1878. He first received a common school education, but pursued his professional courses at Washington University, St. Louis, from which he graduated, in 1905, with the degree of D. D. S. For the succeeding two years he engaged in practice in that city, and then moved to Festus, his present residence and his lucrative and progressive field of professional labor.

That Dr. Wolff's honors do not end there, has already been intimated. To particularize—he was first elected mayor of Festus in 1909, and re-elected in 1911, and his administrations have been so conducted as to earn him the respect of all parties, albeit his personal support has always been given to the Democracy. He is one of the leading fraternalists of this section of the state. The Red Men, Odd Fellows, Modern Woodmen and Select Knights have all afforded him evidences of their esteem, and at the present time he is presiding officer (Great Sachem) of the Improved Order of Red Men, State of Missouri. And his advancement has never been of the drifting nature, but rather of the propelling and pushing kind, often against strong contrary currents. Owing to a serious decline in his father's health, he was compelled to work his way through college. Both figuratively and literally, he had to fight hard to get his education, for, soon after the completion of his freshman year at Washington University, he enlisted for service in the Philippines, and served as regimental commissary sergeant for two years and seven months. This delayed his graduation until 1905, but showed his stamina and added to his deserved popularity as a man.

In the year of his graduation Dr. Wolff was married to Miss Antoinette Nengle, of Festus, Missouri, and their three children are Scott Emmerson, Marguerite Antoinette and Marie Wolff.

OLIVER B. GWYN is at the head of the Conran Cooperage Company, one of the industrial enterprises which play an important part in the prosperity of the county, his relation to this thriving concern being that of president and general manager. Although a Kentuckian by birth, he has resided in this state for a number of years and here has enjoyed excellent fortunes. Mr. Gwyn, who is a son of E. B. and Margaret J. (Lynch) Gwyn, natives of Kentucky, was born in Hickman county of the Blue Grass state January 27, 1874. His father was a painter by occupation and the subject resided beneath the home roof until the age of fifteen years. He is one of a family of five children. At the age mentioned Mr. Gwyn went to Clay county, Arkansas, and located in Rector, where the young fellow, who had started out quite alone in the world, secured a position in a saw-mill, and remained thus engaged for four years. The kind of work he secured when a boy had no inconsiderable influence upon his subsequent career, for he has been for a number of years in the milling business. After that he found farm work to do and while thus employed he was married in 1898 to Miss Ada Deniston, daughter of James and Mary E. (Welch) Deniston, their marriage occurring in the vicinity of Rector. Mrs. Gwyn was born there November 1, 1873. For a time after his marriage Mr. Gwyn continued to farm, but he finally concluded that he could not make enough money as a farmer and so took up another line of enterprise—milling, with which he was already familiar. He came to Missouri in 1899, locating in Dunklin county, in the town of Paulding, and there took a contract to stack lumber for three years. He then engaged with the Paulding Stave Company and continued in this line until 1906. During this time he carried on business in both Paulding and Geneva, at the latter place with the Buffalo Stave Company. In 1906 he went into business in Boynton, Arkansas, just across the line from his former Missouri residence, again operating a mill for one year. During the same year he moved to Kennett. He sold the Boynton mill in 1908. In January, 1909, he put in a new plant at Gideon, New Madrid county, but in the following October he sold the same, and in the following January put in a new mill at Conran, which he still operates. This has a capacity of forty-five thousand slack barrel staves a day and is an up-to-date and paying concern. Mr. Gwyn also built a mill in Marston, Missouri,—the Marston Cooperage Company, which he operated for nine months and then resigned from its management to more fully devote his energies to the constantly growing business of the Conran concern. This is an incorporated business, and Mr. Gwyn is president and general manager. In addition to this large interest he has considerable town property and also six hundred and sixty acres of land near Conran, which is being cleared and farmed. He is very loyal to Missouri, in which state all of his success has been achieved.

Mr. and Mrs. Gwyn have an interesting family of seven children. Bessie attends Hardin College, and Frank, Judge, Myrtle, Tom, Burley and Dan are all at home. Mrs. Gwyn and five of the children, Bessie, Frank, Judge, Myrtle and Tom, are all members of Missionary Baptist church. Mr. Gwyn is one of the most enthusiastic of local lodge men and holds membership in no less than six orders. He is a Mason, being affiliated with the time-honored order at Cardwell and having attained to the thirty-second degree, and he also belongs to the Independent Order of Odd Fellows, the Knights of Pythias, the Woodmen of the World, the Modern Woodmen of America and Ben Hur. He is the friend of good government and of a public spirited type of citizenship.

JOHN MARSHALL FINNEY, M. D. At a very early age a boy begins to make plans for his future career; he is positive as to the direction this career will take, but very frequently before he has finished his schooling he branches out into something entirely different; sometimes the change is brought about by a series of circumstances over which he has no control. Sometimes he himself undergoes such radical changes that he no longer feels any inclination towards those things he formerly loved. In the case of John Marshall Finney, when he was in the grammar school he had already decided on his profession and he never changed his mind. Since that time everything he studied or read was selected with a view to his chosen profession.

He was born at Vienna in Johnson county, Illinois, February 18, 1852, and was the son of G. P. and Rachael (Latham) Finney, both of whom were born in Illinois. The Finney family originally came from Virginia and were early settlers in Illinois. Mr. and Mrs. Finney had three children, one daughter and two sons, of whom John Marshall is the youngest. His brother, W. N. Finney, is a resident of California. Mr. Finney died when he was forty-three years of age and his wife at about the same age.

After his mother's death, when he was eleven years old, John Marshall Finney went to live with an uncle, Dr. J. F. Latham, a farmer of Saline county, Illinois. After he had finished the grammar school course, he attended the Ewing College, preparatory to the study of medicine. When he was only sixteen years of age he went to Eldorado, Illinois and there read with a doctor and practised under his instructions. He next attended a medical college in St. Louis, where he also practiced. In 1873 he came to Missouri, after practicing in Illinois for a short time, and located at Marble Hill. After three years of successful practice, he located at Laflin in Bollinger county, but very near to Cape Girardeau county. His practice was in both counties. For thirty years he kept up this hard life, traveling long distances to visit his patients. In 1906 he came to Cape Girardeau, with the intention of giving up his visiting and intending to have only an office practice. He established a drug store in the town, carrying a very full line of drugs of all descriptions and medicines. His patients will not, however, be contented to let him devote his time to his drug store, but they come to him from long distances, although he only visits in Cape Girardeau. For the past twenty years he has been a member of the Southeastern Missouri Medical Society, being one of the oldest practitioners in this part of southeastern Missouri.

In 1877 he married Mary G. Manning, daughter of George and Louisa Manning of Leopold, Missouri. Dr. and Mrs. Finney had a family of eleven children, nine of whom are living now (1911), as follows: John Marshall, Jr., a physician near Leopold, Missouri; Norman J. in the United States Army, located at the Philippine Islands; Louisa Ann, wife of J. H. Price of Orange, Texas; Francis M., attending normal school at Cape Girardeau; Rachael, Julia, George G., William Paul and Mary Gertrude are all at home with their parents. Norman was the only child who was not born in southeastern Missouri. He was born in St. Louis, while the doctor was living there attending medical college in 1884, taking a special course of study.

The doctor is a member of the Masonic Order and is a master Mason. He is a Democrat in political sympathies; he is greatly interested in politics, but holds no office, nor has he any desire for political honors for himself. He finds his time fully taken up with the duties of his own profession and the management of his drug store. He has been in practice in southeastern Missouri for thirty-seven years, much of the time in Cape Girardeau. He is naturally known all over the state by his professional brethren and his office, at 709 Broadway, is visited by physicians from all over the two counties. We sometimes feel that a man has mistaken his calling in life, that he would have made more of a success in some other position. That is not the case with Dr. Finney; one feels that he is a perfect success as a physician and he would not have done his best work in any other profession.

FRANCIS MARION WELLS. There is no finer satisfaction in life than to look back, when success has come, and see that achievement has been wrought, not on the foundation of the fortunes of one's forebears, but upon the firmer basis of innate progressiveness, perseverance and courage undaunted in the face of all obstacles. Such is the satisfaction that F. M. Wells, the well-known banker of Marble Hill, must take, when still in the prime of life, when he glances back over his noteworthy career of sixty years.

Mr. Wells was born in those days of clouded premonition, when the Missouri Compromise and its attendant circumstances had already split the country into the North and the South, January 6, 1850, in Bradley county, in eastern Tennessee. He was the son of Eli and Mary (Brandon) Wells, the former a native of the Big Bend state and the latter a descendant of Colonial stock, born near Rome, Georgia. The parents lived upon their farm, and there followed the great basic industry of agriculture. In 1858 the father brought his generous family of eleven children to Stoddard county, Missouri. Of the seventeen children born, six had deceased in Tennessee. Eli Wells had made an early venture in the mercantile business, but reverses in that field had necessitated a second choice, and he selected farming, being engaged first on the farm of his brother James, well-known as a successful agriculturist.

On the 2d of April, 1863, occurred the death of Eli Wells, and a large family was left to carve out its own fortunes without the guidance or assistance of a father. Francis Marion was then thirteen, and during the remainder of the war period, he being the oldest boy at home, upon his sturdy boy's shoulders rested the responsibility of the support of the large family. Two of the older boys were off at the war following the Union flag, while Francis Marion and a younger brother, by renting a farm, were cheerfully performing the tasks of farm labor and keeping the family together until peace should be declared and the older boys return. Of such stuff are men made, those early chapters but foretell the spirit of his later life.

After farming in Stoddard county and in Scott county, Mr. Wells came to Bollinger, where after farming for a year he entered the general merchandise store of Bollinger and Slinkard, located at Bollinger's Mill (now Zalma) in the capacity of clerk, and he made no change in his position for five years.

On March 24, 1874, Mr. Wells was united in marriage to Miss Rachel C. Bollinger, daughter of Joel and Ann Elizabeth Bollinger, stanch pioneers of the region. Mr. and Mrs. Wells became the parents of two children, Francis R., born in January, 1875, died in early infancy, and Charles A., born June 1, 1877, is now a prominent physician, with a flourishing practice, at Pascola, Pemiscot county, Missouri, in which place he has resided for twelve years. In 1877 Mr. Wells, through an appointment by the county court, became collector to fill the unexpired term of Mr. Hopkins. He served two years, and then was elected to the same office for three consecutive terms, a speaking comment of the efficient and honorable service rendered by Mr. Wells.

In 1885 Mr. Wells opened mercantile establishments at Lutesville and Marble Hill. On March 10, 1886, Mrs. Wells was called to the Great Beyond, leaving her husband with her little son Charles, then a child of nine.

For three years, from 1887 until 1889, Mr. Wells was interested in the handling of live stock, and managed a large trading business in the same, carrying on extensive operations throughout southeastern Missouri. In 1889 the governor of Missouri selected him to fill the unexpired term of county clerk and in 1890 the citizenship of the county mindful of the record of Mr. Wells as county collector, again elected him to public office and for six years he was county clerk of Bollinger county, and no man has ever held the office with more general satisfaction to the community. In 1906 he was elected presiding Judge of the County Court, serving four years, making altogether eighteen years of public service in county office.

When the Bollinger County Bank was organized Mr. Wells, ever on the alert where the welfare of the county is concerned, was actively concerned in the establishment of a reliable local monetary institution, and subsequently became its president. In 1897, upon the resignation of Cashier B. F. Stevens, he accepted the cashiership, thus giving in all fifteen years of service. Besides his interest in the Bollinger County Bank he is also a stockholder in the Bank of Marble Hill, and with some six others he maintains a controlling interest in the Advance Telephone company, an enterprise that started with a capital stock of $20,000, and has since, through wise executive policies, been built up to $44,000. Besides his handsome residence and town lots in Marble Hill, Mr. Wells' real estate holdings include town lots in Oklahoma, a one hundred and twenty acre farm and an interest in a farming property amounting to three hundred and sixty acres. Besides this he holds the enviable record of having been identified with Mayfield College for twenty years, having been president of the Board of Trustees for that length of time.

On September 29, 1887, Mr. Wells laid the foundation for his present happy household by his marriage on that date to Miss Lucy E. Swift, daughter of Thomas and Hannah A. (Wilkinson) Swift, of Cape Girardeau county. Six children have been born to this union, four of whom survive, as follows:— William F., born September 20, 1888, is now a cashier of the Bank of Patton, which he organized with a capital of ten thousand dollars; Marie, born January 24, 1896; Emma Jane, born April 19, 1899; and Harry Hubert, born March 17, 1902. Mr. and Mrs. Wells and their family are members of the Baptist church, and Mr. Wells is a deacon in the Marble Hill church. Fraternally Mr. Wells is affiliated with that historic order, the Ancient Free and Accepted Masons.

It is interesting to note, not only for the fact itself but for the lesson it may possibly teach the younger generation, bred among less trying scenes than those of war and frontier pioneering, that Mr. Wells never actually attended school except for the trifling period of six months, but like many another indomitable soul of the sixties and seventies, when circumstances demanded that the daylight hours be given to toil, he undertook to educate himself at night, and it is no mere figure to say that he studied by "midnight oil." Mr. Wells indeed deserves the loyal affection and high respect with which he is regarded throughout the county and beyond its limits.

EDGAR PREWITT CARUTHERS. There are but ten persons on the Midway Islands, a recent acquisition of the United States, yet they are not lonesome, for these Islands are used as a cable station, and the news of the world passes daily through their hands. The man who brings this news to our doors in readable form has performed a public benefaction, which should be highly appreciated. Such a man is Edgar Prewitt Caruthers, who was born in southeastern Missouri, in St. Francois county, October 27, 1854, a son of Solomon D. and Mary Jane (Harris) Caruthers. The father, Solomon D., was a native of Madison county, Missouri, coming here with his father, David L. Caruthers, from Tennessee in 1820. The mother was a native of Kentucky, her father being Squire Samuel Perrin Harris, of Irish descent, who came to Missouri at an early day. The branch of the Caruthers family to which this subject belongs were of Scotch-Irish stock, and were settlers in North Carolina before the Revolution.

The immediate subject of this review, Edgar P. Caruthers, obtained his education in the common schools of his native state. In early life he decided to adopt the printer's trade as his life work, and, in accordance with this idea, went into a printer's office at Fredericktown, where he mastered the intricacies of this business and became the owner of the *Bee* there when but a mere boy. Later he was employed for six years in the treasury department of Missouri, and then became a reporter on a St. Louis newspaper. He then removed to Medicine Lodge, Kansas, where he published a paper for eight years, and takes credit as the "discoverer" of Jerry Simpson. He then returned to Missouri and located at Carthage, where he was engaged in the printing business for two years, when he removed to Kennett, in the same state, taking charge of the Dunklin *Democrat* in 1893, since which time he has been its editor and publisher, and he is quite proud of the fact that it has not missed an issue during all that time.

Mr. Caruthers was first married in 1874, the lady of his choice being Mary L. Fleming, of Fredericktown, Missouri, and of this union there are four children living,—Mrs. Will A. Jones, of Kennett; Albert B. Caruthers, for the past five years in the Canal zone in the government employ; Robert L. Caruthers, an attorney of Haskell, Oklahoma; and Mrs. Wallace E. Barron, of Calico Rock, Arkansas. Mr. Caruther's first wife died in 1890. Four years later he was united in the holy bonds of wedlock to Miss Minnie Chandler, who lived but four years, her demise occurring in 1898. There were two children by this marriage, both of whom are deceased. He was again married, Mrs. Electra Townsend becoming his wife. No children were born of this union, and Mrs. Caruthers has passed on to her eternal life. In politics Mr. Caruthers is an earnest and unswerving Democrat, and in fraternal relations is an esteemed member of the Royal Arch Masons.

WILLIAM L. COLE is the prosecuting attorney of Franklin county, an able and successful advocate in criminal practice and a powerful factor in political affairs not merely in Franklin county, but throughout the entire state of Missouri. Although not yet come to middle life, Mr. Cole's achievements in his profession and in the domain of political affairs mark him as belonging to the chosen band of leaders who are shaping the policies and directing the forces which are lifting the commonwealth to a still higher plane of enlightenment and prosperity.

A native of Franklin county, Mr. Cole's natal day is the 30th of March, and the year of his birth was the centennial, 1876. Gerald, his birthplace, was the final home of his parents. His father was also indigenous to this county, his native place being four miles east of Washington.

W. N. J. Cole, the father of the present attorney, was born in 1831, spent his life as a farmer, was fairly educated for that time and was always actively interested in public education. Upon public questions he agreed with the Democrats until the time of the Civil war, when the issue of Secession drove him into the Republican party. Mr. Cole's mother was formerly Mrs. Susan Cooper, widow of a Mr. Cooper who came to Franklin county immediately after the Rebellion. Prior to her marriage to Mr. Cooper she was Miss Susan Smith, whose father was a Kentuckian. She was the mother of three children by her first marriage and her issue by Mr. Cole were: George L., superintendent of schools at Marshfield, Missouri; Charles A., superintendent of schools at Union, Missouri; Jacob E., a farmer of Franklin county; William L., of this review, and Emma J., who died in the county as the wife of William Williams. Mrs. Cole passed away in 1882 and her husband followed her in 1904.

The Franklin county branch of the Cole family was founded by Jacob Cole in 1813. He was born near Charlestown, West Virginia, in 1795. In 1798 he accompanied his father to Missouri. He lived in St. Charles county until the age of eighteen. As a pioneer he became one of the best known citizens in this part of Missouri. His business was distilling liquor and farming. His marriage took place in Franklin county, where he lived until 1882. W. N. J. Cole was the youngest of his eleven children.

William L. Cole, the subject of this sketch, received his elementary education in the country near his birthplace, and then attended the Owensville Normal. He taught in the district schools of Franklin and of Gasconade counties until he was chosen principal of the schools in Pacific, Missouri. While filling this position, he devoted all his spare time to the study of law, completing his preparation by taking the summer course in law at the State University in Columbia. In 1900 he was admitted to the bar in Hermann before Judge Hertzel, but continued to teach until 1904, when he began to practice his profession in Pacific. Mr. Cole was a member of the bar in that town until he was elected prosecuting attorney of his county in November, 1906. He succeeded Hon. O. E. Meyersick in this office and established his residence in the county seat. Twice reelected he has maintained the reputation of Franklin county for the conviction of violators of the law, some of the notorious criminals of the age having been overtaken by justice in the Franklin county court.

Gifted by nature in the art of public speaking, Mr. Cole easily found place for his talents in the practice of law. The state Republican committee eagerly availed itself of so capable and convincing an expounder of the doctrines of the party and invited him to take part in the compaign of 1904. Since that time he has participated in every campaign; he has served the county, the state and the congressional committees, and he has been a recognized power in the organization of his party and in its success at the polls.

Mr. Cole has attained some prominence in Woodcraft, having filled the chair of consul in Union, attended stated conventions of the order and been delegate to the Head Camp at Buffalo, New York. In the Masonic order he has sat in the Grand Lodge as delegate both in St. Louis and in Kansas City. He and his wife hold membership in the Eastern Star.

On November 28, 1906, Mr. Cole was married to Miss Agatha Bucher at Pacific, Missouri. Her father was Jacob Bucher, a Swiss by birth, while her mother was Miss Agatha Zetch, born in Germany. Mr. and Mrs. Cole have no children.

The outline of Mr. Cole's career would present to one unacquainted with him the idea of a successful and popular lawyer, adroit in the handling of men and affairs. Mr. Cole is all of this and much more. No account of his achievements would picture the force and directness of his character nor the geniality of his manner, which is yet utterly devoid of the remotest trace of fawning or flattery. All in all, Mr. Cole's frequent selection for office may be said to be simply the natural tribute to his personal popularity and capabilities.

GEORGE W. REDDEN. It has been the pleasant fortune of George W. Redden, leading photographer of Farmington, to have obtained the highest prestige in his particular field of endeavor. He is in truth one of the state's leading photographers and is an artist in the truest sense of the word, his productions having that quality which distinguishes the work of the really artistic temperament from the commonplaceness of him who merely understands the mechanism of the camera and fails to reproduce the individuality of his sitters. More than this, he is a man of fine inventive ability, and his method of photographic printing, known as the "Redden Way" is known over the entire country. He has also invented a number of other devices in this field.

George W. Redden was born July 26, 1868, on a farm near the town of St. Aubert, now Mokane, Callaway county, Missouri. He is the son of Wiley S. and Mary Jane (Level) Redden. The father was a native of middle Tennessee, and his father, Willian Redden, was born in North Carolina, and went to Tennessee as a young man. The grandfather was a farmer and slave-holder and he was called to the life eternal when about fifty years of age. He was a descendant of an old and well known North Carolina family. The father was reared and educated in Tennessee and resided there at the time of the breaking out of the Civil war. There were four brothers in the family and all of them were brave young fellows whose first thought was of enlisting. But there was so much to say on both sides of the great question which pressed for settlement that they were a little undecided upon which side to enlist. The four gathered in the yard of the old home and, seated on a log, talked the matter over, long and earnestly. At last they sadly separated, one brother going to enlist in the Union army and the other three joining the army of the Confederacy. The first fought throughout the entire war, being wounded at the battle of Gettysburg. This brother who joined the cause of the Union was the subject's father, Wiley S. Redden, and among his adventures was a period of incarceration in Andersonville prison. He escaped at one time from the prison, but was recaptured.

After the termination of the war, Wiley S. Redden, settled at St. Aubert, Callaway county, Missouri, and in 1867 he was united in marriage to Miss Mary Jane Level. Six children came to bless their union and of this number three died in infancy. The three surviving are George W., of this review; Samuel G., of St. Charles, Missouri; and Charles A., of Memphis, Tennessee. Mr. Redden remained upon the farm until his death, in 1878, at the age of forty-seven years, this resulting from blood poison, with which he became afflicted from the wounds received while a soldier. His widow now resides at Fredericktown.

The boyhood days of George W. Redden were passed upon the home farm and there he learned the helpful lessons of industry and thrift. He attended the district schools and the schools of Fulton and subsequently became a student in Westminster College. He entered the photograph business at the age of twenty years, for several years being a journeyman workman, employed by some of the leading photographers of the United States, his ability becoming at once apparent. He was established at Fredericktown for eleven years and during that time acted as official photographer of the mines, quarries, clays, timbers, and timber products, securing pictures of the foregoing for the Missouri Commission of the St. Louis World's Fair, and serving with credit to himself and the state. As previously mentioned Mr. Redden is the inventor of the Redden photographic printing machine and several other devices for shortening the long process and securing easier and better work. He is now having them manufactured and sold on royalty.

On September 4, 1892, Mr. Redden was united in marriage to Miss Ora Gross, of Sedalia, Missouri, daughter of A. P. M. and Ella Nevada (Gay) Gross, both natives of Dade county. The father is deceased, but Mrs. Gross now makes her home in Los Angeles, California. Mrs. Redden received her education in the Sedalia public schools. They have a quartet of interesting children, namely: Allan C., Elizabeth, Anthony and Charles Greer. The subject is a Republican and a Royal Arch Mason and he and his wife are affiliated with the Christian church.

LIN GRISHAM. As president of the Consolidated Store & Manufacturing Company, the main headquarters of which important concern are at Fredericktown, Missouri, Lin Grisham is actively identified with mercantile and manufacturing interests in southeastern Missouri. He is deeply interested in community affairs and his efforts have also been a potent element in the business progress of this section of the state. He has with ready recognition of opportunity directed his labors into various fields, wherein he has achieved success, and at the same time has promoted a business enterprise that has proved of more than local value, largely promoting the commercial activity of the state. A brief history of this gigantic concern will appear in a succeeding paragraph.

Lin Grisham was born in Wayne county, Missouri, on the 10th of April, 1869, and he is a son of James and Margaret (Andrews) Grisham, who came to Missouri from Tennessee in the year 1854. The father was born in the state of Tennessee in the year 1837, and as a young man he was interested in farming, continuing to devote his attention to that line of enterprise until 1882. Since that time he has been engaged in the mercantile and milling business in Wayne county, Missouri, but at the present time he resides at Fredericktown. He was county judge of Wayne county for a period of eight years and also served with the utmost efficiency as associate judge for a period of two years. The mother of the subject of this review was descended from old Virginia stock and her father at one time was a sailor on the Atlantic ocean. He established the family home in Wayne county, Missouri, in an early day and there passed the residue of his life. Mrs. James Grisham was summoned to eternal rest in 1911, at the venerable age of seventy-six years. Mr. and Mrs. Grisham became the parents of seven children, concerning whom the following brief data are here inserted,—Frank is a farmer and miller at Caledonia, Missouri; T. M. resides at Fredericktown, Missouri; J. S. was formerly state representative from Colorado and he is now sheriff of Las Animas county, that state; W. F. is an extensive rancher and stock dealer in Colorado, owning barns at Trinidad and Pueblo; John is engaged in business at Fredericktown; Ida is the widow of Dr. Montgomery, of Wayne county, and she resides with her father; and Lin is the immediate subject of this review.

To the public schools of Wayne county, Missouri, Lin Grisham is indebted for his preliminary educational training. As a youth he became associated with his father in the latter's extensive mercantile enterprises, and during the intervening years to the present time he has devoted considerable attention to general merchandising and lumbering. The Consolidated Store & Manufacturing Company, of which he is president, was organized in 1910, and it represents a merging of four different mercantile corporations. The Company has stores in Cape Girardeau, Madison, Wayne and Bollinger counties. It has a capital stock of eighty-three thousand dollars and its official corps is as follows:—Lin Grisham, president; R. H. Davis, vice-president; C. A. Grisham, secretary and treasurer; and the board of directors includes T. M. Grisham, R. H. Davis, John Grisham and Lin Grisham, of Fredericktown, and T. H. Wiseman, of St. Louis. Since its organization the Company has opened five new stores and now conducts sixteen individual concerns in the four counties mentioned above. The offices of the company are located in a fine concrete structure at Fredericktown, the same being situated on West Main street. As president of this great corporation Mr. Grisham has displayed unusual shrewdness and excellent executive ability and under his able management it has been decidedly prosperous. In addition to his mercantile interests Mr. Grisham is a member of the board of directors of the Bank of Fredericktown and he is also a member of the board of curators of Marvin College.

In Wayne county, Missouri, in 1892, was celebrated the marriage of Mr. Grisham to Miss Josie Dixon, a native of that county and a daughter of Benton Dixon. Mr. and Mrs. Grisham have two sons,—Leonard, whose birth occurred in 1893; and Lloyd, born in 1897 and at present a student in Marvin College.

In politics Mr. Grisham is aligned as a stalwart supporter of the principles and policies for which the Republican party stands sponsor. He is not a politician, practically speaking, but he has given splendid service as a member of the Central Republican committee. In the Masonic order he is a member of Marcus Lodge, No. 110, Free and Accepted Masons; and Solomon Chapter, Royal Arch Masons. In their religious faith the Grisham family are devout members of the Methodist Episcopal church, South, to whose good works, they are liberal contributors of their time and means.

CHRISTIAN E. STIVER. The present able and popular incumbent of the position of city engineer of Cape Girardeau is Christian E. Stiver, who was elected to that important office in April, 1911. He is a prominent business man of the younger generation who has achieved success as the result of his own well directed endeavors and he is a citizen who is ever on the alert and enthusiastically in sympathy with all movements projected for the progress and improvement of this section of the state, where he has maintained his home since March, 1909.

A native of the fine old Keystone state of the Union, Christian E. Stiver was born in the city of Philadelphia, Pennsylvania, on the 19th of January, 1884. He is a son of Charles L. and Sarah (Hagey) Stiver, both of whom were likewise born in Philadelphia and both of whom are now living, their home being at Nazareth, Pennsylvania. Of the two children born to Mr. and Mrs. Stiver the subject of this article is the eldest and his brother, Ellwood H. Stiver, is attending college. In his youth Christian E. Stiver was afforded excellent educational advantages. After completing the curriculum of the public schools of his home community in Philadelphia he was matriculated as a student in Nazareth Hall, a military academy at Nazareth, Pennsylvania. In 1901 he was a student in the Lehigh University, at Bethlehem, Pennsylvania. He entered Lafayette College, at Easton, Pennsylvania, in 1904, in the engineering department of which excellent institution he was graduated as a member of the class of 1907. In March, 1909, he came to Cape Girardeau, where he accepted a postion with the Cape Girardeau Portland Cement Company as engineer. In June, 1909, however, he left that concern and took up railroad survey work. In September of the same year he entered the employ of the Kettle River Company, a paving concern in this city, and in July, 1910, he again turned his attention to railroad surveying. In April, 1911, he was honored by his fellow citizens with election to the office of city engineer and he is now serving in that capacity with the utmost efficiency.

In his political convictions Mr. Stiver is aligned as a stalwart in the ranks of the Republican party and his religious faith is in harmony with the teachings of the Methodist Episcopal church. In a fraternal way he is affiliated with the local lodge of the Benevolent & Protective Order of Elks and he is also connected with the Sigma Nu college fraternity. He is a young man of splendid mentality and fine moral fiber and in all the relations of life he has so conducted himself as to command the unalloyed confidence and esteem of all with whom he has come in contact. He is genial in his associations, affable in his address, generous in his judgment of his fellow men, and courteous to all. As a citizen and enthusiast of his town, it is but just to say that communities will prosper and grow in proportion as they put a premium on men of his mould.

WILLIAM S. C. WALKER. Distinguished for his umblemished record as a man and a jurist is William Samuel Crittenden Walker, circuit judge of the Twenty-second Judicial Circuit. Judge Walker is the son of Thomas C. and Susan F. (Crittenden) Walker, both representatives of old Virginia families and natives respectively of Lancaster and Essex counties of the Old Dominion. He was elected to the bench in 1910 and assumed the duties of his high office in January of the ensuing year. His reputation as one of the prominent lawyers of Dunklin county has been reinforced with the passing years, during which he has appeared in connection with many of the important cases brought before the state and federal courts, and his standing has been stamped with approval by his elevation to the bench.

Judge Walker was born at Tappahannock, Virginia, August 22, 1859. After finishing his public school course in his native town he entered William and Mary College, from which he was graduated with the degree of Bachelor of Arts in 1877. He next took up the study of law at the University of Virginia and received the degree of Bachelor of Laws in 1880. He practiced law in the Old Dominion, the scene of his first professional labors being in his native county, and in 1889 he came to Dunklin county, where he has ever since remained and where his life and achievements have amply recommended him. For four or five years he was in practice with H. N. Phillips, now of Poplar Bluff, and subsequently he entered into partnership in the practice of the law with D. R. Cox, of Malden, this association continuing throughout the decade included between the years 1897 and 1907. From 1901 to 1905 he was prosecuting attorney of the county, being twice elected to the office without opposition. His tenure of office in that capacity was thus of four years' duration. In 1910 he was elected circuit judge, as previously mentioned, and he has already had opportunity to prove that the choice of the people was by no means at fault. In his political convictions Judge Walker is a Democrat, and he has ever been very loyal in his support of the principles and policies for which the party stands.

Judge Walker stands high in Masonry, belonging to the Blue Lodge and Chapter, and lives up to the fine ideals which the ancient and august order teaches. He holds membership in the Knights of Pythias and the Independent Order of Odd Fellows. He is a member of the Missionary Baptist church in Kennett.

Judge Walker was first married in 1891, to Marion B. Phillips, the daughter of Colonel H. N. Phillips. She died after five years of married life, leaving one daughter, Rose M. In 1900 he married Miss Belle McCarroll. She became the mother of one son, Henry, and died in 1904.

Judge Walker is a quiet, unassuming student of the law. He is slow to form opinions, but when he has become sure of his ground he acts accordingly and nothing can make him swerve from the right as he sees it.

OBA HALEY, M. D. For the past thirty-five years Dr. Oba Haley has been engaged in the practice of medicine and for at least a quarter of a century he has maintained his professional headquarters at Fredericktown, Missouri, where he controls a large and representative patronage and where he is honored and esteemed by all with whom he has come in contact. The years have told the story of a successful career due to the possession of innate talent and acquired ability along the line of one of the most important professions to which man may devote his energies,—the alleviation of pain and suffering and the restoration of health, which is man's most cherished and priceless possession. This is an age of progress in all lines of achievement and Dr. Haley has kept abreast of the advancement that has revolutionized methods of medical and surgical practice, rendering the efforts of physicians of much more avail in warding off the inroads of disease than they were even at the time when he entered upon his professional career.

Dr. Haley was born at Steeleville, in Crawford county, Missouri, on the 25th of November, 1847, and he is a son of Henry and Emma (Key) Haley, the former of whom was born in Tennessee and the latter of whom claimed Steeleville, Missouri, as the place of her birth. The father was reared to maturity in the vicinity of McMinnville, Tennessee, and as a young man came to Crawford county, this state, where was solemnized his marriage to Miss Emma Key and where he passed the greater part of his active career as a farmer and stockman. William Haley, grandfather of the Doctor, was likewise a farmer by occupation and he came to Crawford county, Missouri, in the latter '40s. His father was a soldier in the English army and he served as such in the war of the Revolution. During that conflict he was captured and imprisoned in the United States and at the close of the war he decided to make his home in this new country. Henry Haley was a valued and appreciative member of the time-honored Masonic order. He was called to eternal rest in 1879, at the age of sixty years. The mother of the Doctor was a daughter of Oba Key, a pioneer Missourian and a native of Kentucky. Mrs. Henry Haley passed to the great beyond in 1879, at the age of fifty years. Dr. Haley was the first born in a family of eight children—six boys and two girls, of whom all the sons are living. William M. Haley is a prominent real-estate man in St. Louis, Missouri, where he has resided for the past thirty years; John and Wilson Haley are engaged in the general merchandise business at Steeleville, Missouri; Basil conducts a meat market at West Plains, Missouri; Jerry maintains his home in Texas; and Oba is the immediate subject of this review. Concerning the two sisters,—Mary died at the age of eighteen years, in 1880; and Delia, who became the wife of Reuben Summers, resided for a number of years in East St. Louis, where her death occurred in 1893; she is survived by her husband and two daughters.

Dr. Haley, of this notice, was reared to adult age at Steeleville, his preliminary educational training having been completed with a course in the Steeleville Academy. For three years thereafter, from 1864 to 1867, he was employed as a clerk in the general store of the Merrimac Iron Works. From 1864 to 1867 he attended school in Phelps county, Missouri, and in 1869 he began to read medicine under a noted physician at Steeleville, Missouri. In 1872 he was matriculated as a student in the old St. Louis Medical College, in which excellent institution he was graduated as a member of the class of 1873, duly receiving his degree of Doctor of Medicine. Subsequently he attended the medical department of the University of Missouri, in which he was graduated in 1879. He initiated the active practice of his profession at Bellevue, Missouri, where he remained for the ensuing ten years, coming thence to Fredericktown, in 1886. During the period of his residence at Fredericktown he has achieved unusual success as a skilled physician and surgeon and he holds prestige as one of the finest doctors in Southeastern Missouri.

Dr. Haley has been twice married, his first union having been to Miss Martha A. Brooks, who died in June, 1904. To this marriage were born three children,—Claude B., who is engaged in the newspaper business at Cincinnati, Ohio; Henry L., who is a civil engineer at Los Angeles, California; and Lucy, who is the wife of Dr. Keller, of Willisville, Illinois. In 1908 Dr. Haley wedded Mrs. Birdie Law, nee Nifong, who had one child by her first marriage, namely,—Jamie, who died at the age of six yars.

In connection with the work of his profession Dr. Haley is affiliated with the Madison County Medical Society; the Southeastern Missouri Medical Society, the Missouri State Medical Society and the American Medical Association. He has served as president of the Southeastern Missouri Medical Society. He was local surgeon for the Iron Mountain Railroad from 1886 to 1896, and was also Secretary for ten years of the United States Pension Board. In a fraternal way he is connected with the Independent Order of Odd Fellows and in politics he accords a stalwart allegiance to the principles and policies promulgated by the Democratic party. Dr. Haley commands the hearty admiration and esteem of his fellow practitioners by reason of his strict adherence to the unwritten code of professional ethics and as a citizen he is essentially loyal and public spirited, doing all in his power to advance the general progress and improvement.

LOUIS KRUEGER. The present able and popular incumbent of the office of clerk of the common pleas court at Cape Girardeau, Missouri, is Louis Krueger, who has resided in this city during all of his life and who is here honored and esteemed by all with whom he has come in contact by reason of his fair and straightforward business dealings. Mr. Krueger was born at Cape Girardeau, on the 11th of September, 1874, and he is a son of William and Elizabeth (Schrader) Krueger, both born in Brunswick, Germany. Both parents came to the United States in early youth, settling at Cape Girardeau, where they became acquainted and eventually married. As a young man Mr. William Krueger turned his attention to the meat-market business, stock buying and farming, and he was identified with those lines of enterprise during the major part of his active career. He died November 4, 1880, his wife, now Mrs. Hitt, living in Cape Girardeau. Mr. and Mrs. Krueger became the parents of six children, of whom the three daughters are deceased.

The sons all reside in this city,—Louis is the immediate subject of this review; Martin O. is most successfully engaged in the hardware business and is mentioned on other pages of this work; and William H. is janitor of the Federal building.

Louis Krueger was reared to adult age at Cape Girardeau, where he attended the Loirmier Public School until he had reached the age of seventeen years. He then entered the State Normal School, and later Bryant & Stratton's Business College at St. Louis. After completing his education he taught school for two years, and then entered the office of Cape Girardeau Water Works and Electric Light Company where he remained for two years. He gave his attention to the hardware business for a short time. For a number of years he was secretary of the Cape Girardeau and Jackson Gravel Road Company, but a few years ago resigned that position. He has an interest in a farm, and as above stated, is the clerk of the common pleas court at Cape Girardeau at the present time.

In his political convictions Mr. Krueger is aligned as a stalwart supporter of the principles and policies for which the Republican party stands sponsor. On the 1st of January, 1911, he was honored by his fellow citizens with election to the office of clerk of the court of common pleas, in discharging the duties of which important position he is acquitting himself with all of honor and distinction. Mr. Krueger is a man of sterling worth and unquestioned integrity; he looks upon a public office as a public trust and as a result of his varied experiences and broad information is eminently well fitted for public honors. In fraternal circles Mr. Krueger is affiliated with the local lodges of the Benevolent and Protective Order of Elks, the Royal Arcanum and the Sons of Veterans, he being eligible for membership in the last organization by reason of his father's service as a gallant and faithful soldier in the Union army of the Civil war. Mr. and Mrs. Krueger are noted for their geniality and in their comfortable, attractive home hospice is given to all comers. They are held in high regard by their fellow citizens and possess scores of friends.

At Jackson, Missouri, in the month of March, 1903, was solemnized the marriage of Mr. Krueger to Miss Helen Jaeger, who was born and reared in this place and who is a daughter of Joseph and Elizabeth Jaeger, the former a native of Germany and the latter a native of Cape Girardeau. Mr. and Mrs. Krueger are the parents of two daughters: Helen, whose birth occurred in 1905, and Louise, born in 1908.

ALFRED A. VITT, of Union, represents one of the pioneer families of Franklin county. His father, John T. Vitt, was a native of Prussia, born at Siegen in 1809. A man of university training, Mr. Vitt was induced to come to America by the "Giesener Auswanderings Gesellschaft," a society for the promotion of immigration to the United States. The opportunity to become a citizen of the republic and to enjoy its privileges appealed to John T. Vitt and in 1834 he came to Franklin county. Four years later he returned to Prussia for his bride, Cornelia Schmidt, and the couple formed the nucleus of a family that has been modestly identified with Franklin county's history for more than seventy years.

John T. Vitt had entered a tract of government land in 1834, but later became a merchant in the town of Union and remained in the mercantile business until 1856. In 1859 he built a steam grist and merchant mill at Union and he continued to operate the mill with the assistance of three of his sons until 1868, when he retired. Always an active business man, he was an equally conscientious public official. A resident of Union when it was incorporated, he was made one of its first trustees. In the early days he filled the office of justice of peace and was several times chosen county judge. He was among the original Fremont Republicans and had few colleagues here during that memorable campaign. Three of his sons served in the Union army: Adolphus H., who died in Union, leaving a family of six children; Herman W., whose home is still in Union; and Alfred A. The other children of John and Cornelia Vitt are Edwin, who passed away in 1878, and Mrs. Bertha E. Clark, of Union. Cornelia Vitt died in 1884 and John T. Vitt in 1889.

Alfred A. Vitt was born near Union, Missouri, February 28, 1844, the historic "high water" year. His education was concluded before the outbreak of the Civil war and he gave evidence of his patriotism by enlisting in Company A of the rifle battalion attached to the First Regiment, Missouri Infantry

Volunteers, commanded by Colonel Frank P. Blair, in April, 1861. Company A was commanded by Captain L. E. Konieuzeski. The enlistment was for ninety days, and upon its expiration Mr. Vitt returned home. He served in and around the St. Louis arsenal and marine hospital—Meramec Station on the Missouri Pacific Railroad and Rolla, at that time the terminus of the Southwestern Branch, now the Frisco Railway. He witnessed the capture of General Frost's Confederate Camp Jackson at St. Louis by General Lyon, on May 10, 1861, which event saved St. Louis to the Union. From August, 1861, until some time in 1864 Mr. Vitt remained out of the zone of hostilities, working in his father's mill. In that year he enlisted in the Forty-seventh Missouri Infantry, commanded by Colonel Thomas C. Fletcher, afterward governor of the state. Until May, 1865, Mr. Vitt was in active service in the war. His company helped to build the fort at Pilot Knob, Missouri, and after General Sterling Price's raid they were sent up the Missouri river on a boat with a detachment of artillery, to prevent the crossing of bands or independent companies from the north side of the river to join Price's army. His regiment was subsequently ordered into Tennessee, when General Thomas at Nashville called for aid. Before the Forty-seventh reached that point, Thomas had cut Hood's army to pieces, so that the services of the regiment were diverted to other points in Tennessee, where it did active military duty until the spring of 1865, when it was ordered home to be mustered out at Benton Barracks, St. Louis.

Resuming business as a civilian, Mr. Vitt assisted his father in the mill until the fall of 1866, when he engaged in the stove and tinware business in Union. He learned the tinners' trade and followed that business until May, 1868. At that time his father decided to retire and Alfred A. and his brother Herman W. purchased the mill. In 1880 he became sole proprietor and has since conducted the business. Other matters have claimed his attention in the ensuing forty odd years, among which was the organization of the Citizens' Bank of Union. Mr. Vitt was the first president of this bank; later he acted as its cashier from January 4, 1910, to March 1. 1911, and is still a member of the board.

In politics Mr. Vitt has, like his distinguished father, always acted with the Republicans, of which party he has been an honored and prominent figure, being twice chosen chairman of the Republican County Committee. He has been mayor of Union and has represented his county in the general assemblies of 1907 and 1909. During his first term he was a member of the committee on private corporations and that of claims, local bills and miscellaneous business. In the second session he was a member of the committee on roads and highways, wills and probate law and private corporations, and chairman of the committee on labor. The legislation towards good roads claimed Mr. Vitt's special interest and the measures passed during his service in the legislature are now bearing fruit. Another of Mr. Vitt's achievements was the bill empowering counties to levy a special tax for the erection of a court house or other public buildings without resorting to bonded debt, inasmuch as he was the author of the bill, now a law in Missouri.

On March 5, 1866, Mr. Vitt was married to Miss Mary Jane White, a daughter of John White, who came to Missouri from Pennsylvania. Mrs. Vitt's mother was Elizabeth Ferguson. Mrs. Vitt died February 10, 1886. Of the children born to the subject and his wife, Fred married Miss Caroline Pisane and resides in Union; Jessamine is Mrs. J. W. Ream, of Portland, Oregon; Mary M. married Edward Muench, of Union, where Gertrude E. (Vitt) Shelton also makes her home. One son, Tracy G., is dead; the others are Eugene B., a locomotive engineer of St. Louis, Missouri; and John T., a civil engineer, now at Evansville, Indiana, in the employ of the C. & E. I. Railroad Company.

Mr. Vitt is a Knight of Pythias and a Mason, and has served as a delegate to the Grand Lodge of both orders. Well informed and unusually interested in the general welfare of the community, which he has served in such varied capacities, Mr. Vitt is a worthy representative of an admirable race. He is hale and hearty and very active for one of his years.

F. G. CLIPPARD. The postmaster and merchant farmer of Leopold is a Missourian and the son of Missourians. He was born in Bollinger county, in 1854, his parents being G. W. and Sorintha Clippard. Like most of the district's prominent citizens, Mr. Clippard spent his early life working on his father's farm. At the age of eighteen he left the farm to work for his uncle in the mercantile business and remained here for ten years, always an efficient and careful worker.

In 1872 Mr. Clippard and his sisters inherited jointly an estate of one hundred and thirty-five acres. The brother bought out his sisters and operated the farm for twenty years. In 1892 he sold this farm and bought two hundred and seventy-five acres near Laflin, Missouri. Mr. Clippard is also the owner of one hundred acres near Leopold. In the town itself he holds three and a half lots besides a large general merchandise store. He has conducted this mercantile business since 1892 with notable success.

Mr. Clippard was married in 1876, to Miss Katie Manning, daughter of Herman and Fronie Manning, natives of Germany. Six children were born of this marriage, three of whom are still living: E. W., aged twenty-six; Early, aged nineteen; and Mary Clippard, aged twenty-three. The mother of these children died in 1901. In 1903 Mr. Clippard married Miss Josephine Geroniskie, a native of Germany. Two daughters have been born to them, namely: Ella, born in 1904, and Alma, born in 1907.

Mr. Clippard is a communicant of the Roman Catholic church. Politically he is a loyal and consistent Democrat. His efficiency in office is indicated by the fact that he has been postmaster since 1902.

THOMAS W. SCHULTZ, court stenographer for the Twenty-second judicial circuit, is a young man who has attained prominence not only in Kennett, but throughout Dunklin county. If we should look for the cause of his success we might recall the fact that in his veins flows the blood of Germany, France and America, and Mr. Schultz has inherited from each country qualities which largely account for his advancement. Combined with the industry of the Germans we find in his personality the vivacity of the French and the enterprise of the Americans.

Mr. Schultz was born at Hornersville, Dunklin county, December 16, 1881. This also is the native county of Francis M. Schultz, his father, who was born June 11, 1838, and his grandfather was one of the pioneers of this section, whither he came about 1830. Previous to this date he had resided in Stoddard county for a period of nine years, having migrated from Tennessee to Missouri in 1821. Tennessee was the commonwealth to which Grandfather Schultz owes his birth and his early education, but although his family had been amongst the early settlers of that state, his ancestors originated in Germany. After coming to Dunklin county Mr. Schultz was uniformly successful and was accounted one of its most substantial and honorable citizens. The homestead there became endeared to him, being the one in which he was married and where his children were born and reared to childhood years. Before they had grown to be young men and women, however, the father died, leaving the children to be brought up by their mother, who lived to see them all doing well, and she died on the farm where her married life had so profitably and happily passed.

The son, Francis, after the death of his father, spent much of his early life with the Indians along Little river, taking keen delight in the companionship of those untutored but intelligent people. When a young man, Francis M. Schultz was married to Angeline Dunaway, who was born in New Madrid county, near Portage, and descended from an old French family of pioneers who had settled along the Missouri river in that section of the state. At the outbreak of the Civil war Mr. Schultz enlisted in the Confederate army and served until hostilities ceased. After he was mustered out he went to Hornersville, Dunklin county, where he settled on a farm and has since followed agricultural pursuits continually. There he and his wife still live, content to feel that they are performing their modest part for the good of the community. Mr. Schultz has always been a good Democrat, at all times staunch in the support of his party, but personally having no desire for political office.

Thomas W. Schultz, as noted, was brought up on his father's farm. As soon as he was of proper age he was sent to the public schools at Hornersville, and after finishing their prescribed course entered a business college at Quincy, Illinois, August 31, 1910, where he received a thorough training, especially in stenography. In 1899, when eighteen years of age, he commenced work in the post-office and general stores and was thus employed for the ensuing eight years. At the expiration of that time, in 1907, he located at the town of Senath, where he earned a fine reputation as an insurance agent. In this capacity his French blood came to his practical assistance, for his fluent speech and persuasive manners made it difficult for anyone to long turn a deaf ear to the propositions he laid before them. Although Mr. Schultz was defeated for circuit court clerk in the Democratic nominating caucus, Judge Walker appointed him to the office of court stenographer of the twenty-second district, in which capacity he is serving now. In every way he is one of the bright young men of this section, whose steady advance is taken as a matter of course.

On the 8th day of December, 1908, the year after Mr. Schultz entered the insurance field, his marriage to Miss May McCluer was solemnized at her native town of Senath.

DONALD H. CAMERON. Taking cognizance of the name of the able and popular editor of the *Mining Herald,* of Elvins, St. Francois county, there can be no measure of conjecture as to his ancestral lineage, for both his personal and family names bear unmistakable evidence of the sturdy Scotch derivation, and the family history gives record concerning the valiant deeds of the fine old Cameron clan of the Scottish highlands, within which oppression has been hurled back to keep the boon of liberty. Mr. Cameron, as editor and publisher of the *Mining Herald,* has made that paper an effective exponent of local interests, especially of the mining industry in the section of the state in which it is published, and it ranks as one of the vigorous and excellent weekly papers of southeastern Missouri.

Donald Hilliard Cameron was born at Woodville, Victoria county, province of Ontario, Canada, in 1878, and is a son of Duncan and Lovisa (Irish) Cameron, whose marriage was there solemnized in the year 1862. The father was born in the staunch Scottish settlement in Glengarry county, province of Ontario, in the year 1841, and was reared to the sturdy discipline of the great basic industry of agriculture. He became a marine engineer, however, and for many years was identified with navigation interests on the Great Lakes. He continued to reside in Canada until his death, on the 17th of December, 1897, and his widow still maintains her home at Port Arthur, province of Ontario. Duncan Cameron well exemplified the canny traits of the race from which he was sprung, and his independence, sterling integrity and mature judgment made him a strong and noble character. He commanded the respect of all with whom he came in contact and lived a life of signal honor and usefulness. He was a staunch Tory in his political allegiance and was a member of the Presbyterian church, of which his widow also has long been a devoted adherent. Of the nine children Donald H., of this review, was the seventh in order of birth.

The childhood and youth of Donald H. Cameron were passed in his native province, —principally at Woodville and Orillia—and his early educational discipline, secured in the public schools, was effectively supplemented by a course of study in the collegiate institute in the village of Orillia. It has been consistently said that the training of a newspaper office is tantamount to a liberal education, and the consistency of this statement has been exemplified in the career of Mr. Cameron, who instituted his association with the "art preservative of all arts" when he was a lad of fifteen years. He entered, at the age noted, the office of the *Orillia News Letter,* in which he served a practical apprenticeship to the printer's trade and with which he continued to be identified for five years, after which he was employed at his trade and as a reporter on various papers in his native province,—principally in the city of Toronto.

In the year 1902 Mr. Cameron came to Missouri and located in St. Louis, but in the following year he established his residence in Elvins, St. Francois county, where he assumed the position of editor of the *Labor Herald.* In March, 1910, was effected a reorganization of the controlling company and the name of the paper was changed to the *Mining Herald,* under which title it has since been effectively conducted, with Mr. Cameron as editor and manager. The *Herald* is staunchly aligned in support of the principles and policies for which the Republican party stands sponsor, and with this party Mr. Cameron has been actively identified since he became a naturalized citizen of the United States, in 1908. He is a vigorous and resourceful writer and the editorial and news columns of the *Herald* amply indicate his ability in this line. As a citizen he is liberal and progressive, and his personal popularity shows conclusively that he has measured up to the demands of the metewand of objective approbation. In April, 1911, there came distinctive evidence of the confidence and esteem reposed in him in his home community, as he was then elected mayor of Elvins, in which position he is giving a most careful and progressive administration of municipal affairs. Both he and his wife hold membership in the Presbyterian church and he is affiliated with the Independent Order of Odd Fellows and the Knights of Pythias.

In July, 1906, was solemnized the marriage of Mr. Cameron to Miss Kate Langdon, daughter of Mrs. Mary Langdon, of Elvins, and she is a popular factor in connection with the social activities of her home community. Mr. and Mrs. Cameron have no children.

AARON PALMER. One of the most active and prosperous agriculturists of Dunklin county, Aaron Palmer owns and occupies a valuable farm in the town of Senath, where he has won an enviable reputation as an honest man and a good citizen, and as one who has contributed his full quota towards the advancement and development of one of the richest agricultural regions of Southeastern Missouri. A son of William and Pamelia (Miller) Palmer, he was born in Carroll county, Tennessee, February 4, 1845, on the home farm.

William Palmer was born and reared in South Carolina, but as a young man settled in Carroll county, Tennessee, where he lived until 1849, when he came to Missouri, locating in Stoddard county, near Bloomfield. He was of English ancestry on both sides of the house, as was his first wife, the mother of the subject of this sketch. She died on the farm near Bloomfield, in 1854, leaving three children, namely: Aaron Palmer, the subject of this sketch; and a son and a daughter that are now living in California. William Palmer was subsequently twice married, and had one other child, Mrs. Martha Hays, of Dunklin county.

Brought up in Stoddard county, Aaron Palmer lived at home for a few years after his father's second marriage. At the age of thirteen years, however, he began working out for wages, finding employment on different farms in Missouri and Tennessee. In 1862, during the most exciting period of the Civil war, he came to Dunklin county with two yoke of steers, which he drove sixty miles in three days, his father, who had large herds of stock and was a southern sympathizer, coming here for protection, as things were pretty warm for him in Stoddard county. Mr. Palmer himself subsequently fought for a few months in the Confederate army, being a member of Marmaduke's Cavalry, which was stationed principally in Arkansas.

At the close of the conflict Mr. Palmer came to Dunklin county in search of remunerative employment, having no capital save willing hands, a courageous heart and a strong determination to win success in the battle of life. About four years later he had succeeded so well in his efforts that he felt warranted in taking unto himself a wife. She had some land and a few head of cattle, and they settled near his present home. A year or two later Mr. Palmer purchased eighty acres of the land now included in his farm, and in its management met with such eminent success that he has since made frequent purchases of other land, and is now owner of eight hundred acres of land in Dunklin county, nearly all of which is in one body, he being now one of the largest owners of improved land in the entire county. When Mr. Palmer located in Senath there were no roads in the vicinity, nothing but paths, and only one building had then been erected in the town. The country roundabout was heavily timbered, his first dwelling place having been erected in the woods, and having been made of logs, with a stick and mud chimney. At the end of seven years Mr. Palmer traded his original property, selling to a man at Cotton Plant, and subsequently made another deal with Will F. Shelton, Sr., of Kennett. He is now occupying a large, seven-room cottage, and on his farm has fifteen tenant houses, which are occupied by his renters, who devote their time and attention to the raising of the crops common to this region. Mr. Palmer himself doing now but little of the actual labor of the farm.

Mr. Palmer has been twice married. He married first, in September, 1869, Parlee Cook, who died in 1895, leaving six children, namely: Nancy; Thomas J.; Martha; Charles, living at home; George, also at home; and Tennie. Mr. Palmer married for his second wife, Mrs. Rachel T. Culp, nee Hardin, a widow with three children, namely: Henry, Janetta and Alfred. In his political relations Mr. Palmer is a Democrat, and religiously he is an active and trustworthy member of the Primitive Baptist church.

WILLIAM F. BERGMANN. The name Bergmann suggests commercialism to the people of Cape Girardeau. Not only is William F. Bergmann a go-ahead business man, but his father before him was a merchant. William imbibed business principles in his babyhood; he observed them in his boyhood and he has practiced them in his maturity. The people of Cape Girardeau feel that they have a proprietary interest in him, he having spent the best part of his life in their midst. They have watched his development and that of his business. They have seen him grow from being simply the son of his father to a man who has made his own career, not being willing to live on the reputation of his father, however good that might be.

William F. Bergmann was born at Cape Girardeau, Missouri, August 6, 1876. His father, of whom mention is made on other pages of this work, is William C. Bergmann.

William Bergmann is the eldest son of his parents and to him Cape Girardeau means home,—the place where he was born, went to school, attended the state normal school and where his parents still live and he has made his own home. He began his business life as a traveling salesman in the millinery business, being employed by a St. Louis house. In 1902 he went into business for himself and has continued in the same place and along the same line ever since. He carries a large and complete stock of groceries, dry goods and furnishings, employing fifteen clerks to carry on his growing trade.

In June, 1902, he married Fannie Harker, a native of Winfield, Kansas. One daughter, Madeline, was born to this union.

Mr. Bergmann is a member of the Commercial Club of Cape Girardeau and is a very active member. He belongs to the Benevolent and Protective Order of Elks, standing high with the members of that organization. He is one of the most prominent men of the city, not only in the business world, but also in his social life. Those same characteristics which have made him so successful in a commercial way have also won him friends.

J. FRANK MEADOR. There is no lawyer in Wayne county who has a higher standing than Mr. Meador, its prosecuting attorney, and throughout his interesting career his actions have been beyond criticism—no one has been able to cast any aspersions on his character either in his private or public capacity. Since his first entry into the field of law he has set himself to run the course with singleness of purpose. His goal has not been a crown of glory for himself, but the performance each day of such duties as he saw. This course he has kept without deviating to the right or to the left. To men of such calibre honors will come without being sought—as indeed they have to Mr. Meador—but in his mind the satisfaction which results from the knowledge of time well spent means much more than the positions of honor which have been awarded him.

Mr. Meador was born in Wayne county, near Patterson, on the 1st day of December, 1880. James F. Meador, the father of J. Frank, is a native of Macon county, Tennessee, where his birth occurred in 1842. Grandfather Joseph Meador was a native of Virginia, where he married Miss Luiza Rhodes, and the young couple migrated to Tennessee, where they reared their family. In 1859 they moved to Wayne county, Missouri, settled on some wild land which they improved and brought into a high state of cultivation. Their son, James F. Meador, was about seventeen years of age when he accompanied his parents from Tennessee to Wayne county, Missouri; he had acquired all the education he ever received in the district school in Tennessee, and on his arrival in Wayne county he commenced farming on the place which he now operates. He has devoted most of his time to agricultural pursuits, to the support of the Baptist church, of which he and his wife are both members, and to the rearing and educating of his children. Mrs. James F. Meador's maiden name was Anna Kinder, and she was born in Wayne county, Missouri, in 1849; her parents hailed from Pennsylvania and were of German descent. Of the ten children who were born to Mr and Mrs. James Meador eight are living, as follows: Adolph, a physician located in Iron county, Missouri; J. Frank Meador, the subject of this biography; Mannie, wife of William Atuip, of Wayne county, Missouri; Ninnie, married to C. C. Ward, of Wayne county, Missouri; Callie, whose husband is George Bell, of Hiram, Missouri; Luna, wife of William Chilton, Bismarck, Missouri; Pearl, residing in Wayne county, Missouri, with her husband, James Biggerstoff; and Walter, at home with his father, who is living on his farm on the St. Francois river, situated one mile distant from the land which Grandfather Meador took up on his arrival in Wayne county.

J. Frank Meador was reared on his father's farm and when he was old enough he attended the district school in his neighborhood, remaining there until he was sixteen years old. He then entered the state normal school at Cape Girardeau and after a two years' course in this well-known institution he entered the state university at Columbia, Missouri, from whose law department he was graduated in 1901. He had not attained his majority at the time of his graduation, and was therefore not eligible to practice, so for a few months he taught and then took up his residence at Mountain Grove, Wright county, Missouri, where for eighteen months he practiced law. In 1903 he removed to Van Buren, Carter county, Missouri, remained there in legal practice until 1905, when he removed to Greenville, Missouri. In the fall of 1906, when he was less than twenty-six years old, he was elected to the office of prosecuting attorney of Wayne county; in 1908 his record had been so entirely satisfactory that he was reelected, and again in 1910 he was the Democratic nominee and was elected for the third time. He is now serving his third term, and is but thirty-one years of age.

Mr. Meador was married to Miss Willa Hixson on the 3rd day of August, 1902. She is a daughter of Jerry and Elizabeth (Coleman) Hixson, both of whom are still living. Mr. and Mrs. Meador are the parents of two daughters,—Violet and Fern. The husband and wife are members of the Baptist church, where they have many friends. Mr. Meador's career so far may be characterized as brilliant, and inasmuch as he is a young man, he may expect a future of still greater prominence.

FRANKLIN A. WIGGS, a citizen of distinctive prominence and influence at Lutesville, Missouri, is owner and editor of the well known publication, the *Lutesville Banner*, a Republican paper, whose unusual success and wide renown are the direct result of Mr. Wiggs' well applied efforts.

A native of the state of Illinois, Mr. Wiggs was born in Union county, on the 2nd of August, 1857, and he is a son of William and Mary E. Wiggs, both of whom are deceased, the father having passed away in 1903 and the mother in 1899. William H. Wiggs was a native of Virginia and his wife was born in North Carolina, both having come to southern Illinois in early life. The father was a farmer by occupation and he and his wife were the parents of eight children, of whom the subject of this review was the first born. Franklin A. Wiggs passed his boyhood and youth on the old homestead farm in Union county, Illinois, and his preliminary educational training consisted of such advantages as were afforded in the district schools of that county. At the age of seventeen years he was matriculated as a student in Ewing College, at Ewing, Illinois, spending the ensuing seven years in preparatory and collegiate work in that excellent institution. Owing to illness, however, he was unable to complete his course and was obliged to go to Colorado to recuperate. Returning to Illinois in 1882, he located at Ewing, where he was engaged in the general merchandise business until 1890. While in college he had worked for a time in the printing office of a Baptist paper, and thus, being somewhat familiar with that particular line of enterprise, he opened a job-printing office at Chester, Illinois, in 1890, continuing to conduct the same for five or six months.

In the latter part of 1890 Mr. Wiggs removed to Mountain View, Missouri, where he was unfortunate in investments, losing a great deal of money in the panic of 1893. For a time thereafter he was engaged in the job and blank printing business at Mountain View and subsequently he edited the *Mountain View Times*, achieving a fair amount of success along these lines of enterprise. In 1900 he removed his printing plant to Charleston, Missouri, where he established the *Charleston Star*. Disposing of the latter publication in 1904, he bought out the plant of the *Lutesville Banner*, a Republican newspaper which boasted a Washington hand press and a subscription list. Mr. Wiggs is now the owner of a fully equipped plant, modern in all its appointments and fitted out with power and type-setting machines. The *Lutesville Banner* has grown from a second rate paper to be one of the most influential newspapers in southeastern Missouri and its prestige is due entirely to Mr. Wiggs' excellent management. In addition to his printing plant, he is the owner of some fine property at Lutesville, the same including a beautiful residence.

On the 12th of October, 1887, at Sailor Springs, in Clay county, Missouri, was solemnized the marriage of Mr. Wiggs to Miss Dean Sailor, a daughter of Thomas N. and Rebecca J. Sailor, residents of Sailor Springs, Illinois. This union has been blessed with one child, William S., whose birth occurred on the 25th of November, 1892. In religious matters the Wiggs family give a loyal support to the Presbyterian church, of which they are devout members, and in a fraternal way Mr. Wiggs is a valued and appreciative member of the local lodge of the Modern Woodmen of America. In politics he accords a stalwart allegiance to the principles and policies for which the Republican party stands sponsor and he is ever on the alert to do all in his power to advance the best interests of Lutesville, where he is a man of mark in all the relations of life.

O. H. STOREY. A wide-awake, brainy man, possessing good business qualifications, O. H. Storey occupies a position of note among the enterprising and progressive citizens of Senath, and as treasurer and general manager of the J. M. Baird Mercantile Company is associated with one of the city's leading industries. He was born June 22, 1888, in White county, Illinois, where he acquired an education and training that well fitted him for a business career.

In 1907, ere attaining his majority, Mr. Storey secured a position as cashier with the Caneer Store Company, in Senath, Missouri, and was afterwards cashier for awhile in the Bank of Senath. Leaving that position, he served in the same capacity at the Citizens' Bank in Senath, until the incorporation, in 1910, of the J. M. Baird Mercantile Company, of which he is treasurer and general manager. This company, of which a brief account is given elsewhere in this work, in connection with the sketch of the late J. M. Baird, was incorporated in 1910, with a capital of $30,000, and a surplus of $60,000, and with the following named officers: Mrs. J. M. Baird, president; Mrs. O. H. Storey, vice-president; Miss Hettie Baird, secretary; and O. H. Storey, treasurer and general manager. The company carries a stock valued at $30,000, with annual sales amounting to upwards of $75,000, dealing not only in hardware, agricultural implements and vehicles of all descriptions, but in cotton, owning and operating a finely-equipped cotton gin, and doing a business in cotton that amounts to about $65,000 a year.

Mr. Storey married June 30, 1909, in Senath, Huldah C. Baird, eldest daughter of the late James M. and Lucy (Douglass) Baird, and they have one child, Hattie Lucille Storey.

NAPOLEON B. WATTS. Success along any line of endeavor would never be properly appreciated if it came with a single effort and unaccompanied by some hardships, for it is the knocks and bruises in life that make success taste so sweet. The career of Napoleon B. Watts, who has long maintained his home at Fredericktown, Missouri, but accentuates the fact that success is bound to come to those who join brains with ambition and are willing to work. Mr. Watts received but meager educational advantages in his youth and his early start in life was of the humblest order. Through persistency and a fixed determination to forge ahead, however, he has succeeded in building up a fine success for himself in the business world of southeastern Missouri. At the present time, in 1911, he is president of the Security Bank at Fredericktown and in politics has figured prominently, having been county clerk for a period of eight years.

Napoleon B. Watts was born in Madison county, Missouri, on the 13th of February, 1848, and he is a son of Reuben and Nancy C. (Sites) Watts, both of whom were likewise born in Madison county. The paternal grandparents of the subject of this review were natives of Culpeper county, Virginia, whence they migrated to Missouri about the year 1818. Captain James Watts, the grandfather, was an officer in the war of 1812 and he was summoned to the life eternal in 1846, at the age of forty-eight years. He was the owner of a tract of fine land in the southeastern part of Madison county and at the time of his demise his son Green Watts inherited the estate. Reuben Watts was a Methodist Episcopal minister and a farmer, he having entered and improved a farm adjoining the old homestead, this farm now being owned by Mr. N. B. Watts. He died in Madison county in 1876, at the age of fifty-seven years. Nancy C. (Sites) Watts was a daughter of John Sites, who came to Missouri in 1818. He was a prosperous farmer in this section of the state but died in the ante-bellum days. He was a native of North Carolina and was descended from stanch old German stock. Mrs. Watts passed to the great beyond in March, 1911, at the venerable age of eighty-seven years. In the agnatic line Mr. Watts, of this notice, traces his ancestry to old English stock. Of the nine children born to Mr. and Mrs. Reuben Watts but three are living at present, namely, Mrs. Mary J. Whitener, of Madison county, Missouri; Mrs. Missouri C. Bess, likewise of Madison county; and Napoleon B., the immediate subject of this review.

Mr. Watts passed his boyhood and youth on the old homestead farm, his education consisting of such crude advantages as were afforded in the schools of the locality and period. At the age of twenty-two years he launched out into the business world on his own account, engaging in the general merchandise business. Subsequently he turned his attention to farming and in 1882 was honored by his fellow men with election to the office of county clerk, serving with the utmost efficiency in that capacity for a period of eight years. In 1882 he established his home at Fredericktown, where he has since resided. In 1890 he became interested in the banking business and was instrumental in the organization of the Madison County Bank, one of the most substantial monetary concerns in southeastern Missouri. Mr. Watts acted as cashier until 1901. The security of the bank had been previously incorporated with a capital stock of ten thousand dollars and the original officers were: Val Schlesinger, president; J. F. Anthony, cashier. In April, 1904, the capital was increased to twenty thousand dollars and the institution reorganized as a state bank. In January, 1901, Mr. Watts became cashier, continuing in that office until January, 1910. The present officers are: N. B. Watts, president; E. H. Day, vice president; J. W. Blanton, cashier; and J. F. Glaves, assistant cashier. Under the shrewd management of its eminently capable officers, the bank has prospered in every connection, as shown by a recent statement, in which the surplus and profits amount to $4,513.38; the deposits, $170,165.53; the cash on hand, $58,090.96; and the loans and discounts, $136,587.95. In January, 1910, Mr. Watts was elected president of the bank and ably fills that position at the present time. In addition to his banking interests he has extensive farming interests in Madison county, Missouri, being the owner of the fine old farm on which he was born and reared.

In the year 1870 was celebrated the marriage of Mr. Watts to Miss Luraney I. Whitener, a daughter of the late J. Q. A. Whitener, a prominent farmer and merchant in Madison county for a number of years prior to his death. Mr. and Mrs. Watts have two children, concerning whom the following brief data are here inserted. Duty S. is cashier of the Marquand Bank and he is also interested in farming in the vicinity of that place. He married Josie Hahn and they have five children, Ethel I., Bessie, Russell, Bryan and Charles. Minnie is the wife of Judge F. J. Parkin, former incumbent of the office of presiding county judge of Madison county.

In politics Mr. Watts is an uncompromising supporter of the cause of the Democratic party and as previously noted he served as county clerk for eight years. He was a member of the Fredericktown school board for a period of years, from 1884 to 1910, resigning in the latter year. As a result of his enthusiastic interest in educational affairs the schools of this city have been materially benefitted, many of the improvements along that line being due to his initiative. Socially he is a valued member of the local Knights of Pythias lodge and in religious matters he is a devout member of the Congregational Methodist church, in the different departments of whose work he is an active factor. The beautiful Watts home is located on College avenue, in the southwestern part of the town.

MARTIN C. KRUEGER. In view of the nomadic spirit which is gradually growing to animate all classes of American citizens to move restlessly about from place to place, it is most gratifying to come in close touch with one who has passed practically his entire life thus far in the place of his nativity, where his exemplary life has won him the unalloyed confidence and esteem of those who have been familiar with his career from earliest youth. Martin C. Krueger was born at Cape Girardeau, Missouri, on the 17th of January, 1877. His father was born at Bremen, Germany, and his mother, Elizabeth

(Schraeder) Krueger, was a native of upper Prussia. Mr. and Mrs. Krueger immigrated to America as young people and their marriage was solemnized at Cape Girardeau, where were born to them six children—three boys and three girls. The daughters are all deceased, as are also the parents, and the three sons are now living at Cape Girardeau. Martin C. Krueger is the immediate subject of this review; Louis Krueger is the present able incumbent of the office of clerk of the common pleas court and on other pages of this work appears a sketch dedicated to his career; and the third son is the present janitor at the Federal Building. The father was engaged in the butcher business during a goodly portion of his active career and at the time of the inception of the Civil war he served with valor and distinction as a member of the Missouri Home Guards.

The rudimentary educational training of Martin C. Krueger was obtained in the Lorimer School at Cape Girardeau and subsequently he was a student in the Normal School for a period of two years. After leaving school he was variously engaged for a time, eventually entering into a partnership alliance with Mr. Heinze, his father-in-law, to engage in the hardware business. A splendidly equipped establishment is now conducted at Cape Girardeau, under the firm name of Heinze & Krueger, and the same commands an extensive and most profitable trade. In addition to his business affairs Mr. Krueger is an enthusiastic collector of Indian relics, his collection being one of the rarest and most complete in this section of the country. Most of his specimens were picked up in the close vicinity of this city and a number of them are extremely valuable on account of their antiquity. In his political convictions Mr. Krueger is aligned as a stalwart in the ranks of the Republican party, and while he has never manifested aught of ambition for the honors or emoluments of public office of any description he was at one time incumbent of the position of city assessor, having been in tenure of that office from 1900 to 1902. In fraternal channels he is affiliated with the local lodge of the Benevolent and Protective Order of Elks and he is also a valued and appreciative member of the Sons of Veterans, by reason of his father's service in the Civil war.

On the 26th of September, 1899, was solemnized the marriage of Mr. Krueger to Miss Alma Heinze, who was reared and educated at Cape Girardeau. Mrs. Krueger was a woman of rare charm and attraction and at the time of her death, in 1901, just two years after her marriage, her loss was deeply mourned by a wide circle of admiring and affectionate friends. In his religious faith Mr. Krueger is a consistent member of the Lutheran church, in whose faith he was reared, and he is a liberal contributor to all kinds of philanthropical work. He is a man of broad sympathy and generous impulses and as a business man and citizen is accorded the highest regard of all with whom he has come in contact.

JOSEPH M. BRASHER. Judge Brasher is a Tennesseean by birth, and his journey through this changing scene was begun on March 22, 1851. His parents resided on a farm and their son grew up in that environment, early taking a responsible part in the conduct of the home place. His parents, John L. and Martha Davis Brasher, were in moderate circumstances, and although they suffered somewhat from the war, they were able to give their son a fair education for that time. As he was more than ordinarily apt, and was fond of reading, he made the best possible use of such advantages as he enjoyed.

At the age of twenty-one Mr. Brasher came to Pemiscot county and bought a farm near Cottonwood Point. Being a farmer of enterprise, he soon had acquired an estate of three hundred and twenty acres. The Judge still owns this large farm, although he and his family now reside in Caruthersville.

Mr. Brasher had always been a consistent and ardent Democrat, and before he had been long in the county he was recognized as one of the strong men of the party. His interest in public affairs was always of the sort which is concerned primarily with the advancement of the general welfare and this the people were quick to recognize. The capacities in which he has served the county are many. For years he was a member of the school board, and during that time he did not merely attend the meetings and consider that he had fulfilled his duty, but he studied the needs of the schools and set himself to supply them wherever possible. In 1878 he was elected justice of the peace and served for four years. At the close of this period he was chosen to fill the office of judge of probate, and for another four years he filled that office. He was then selected to represent his district in the legislature, and at the capital he worked zealously to carry out the views of his constituents. In 1898 Mr. Brasher was elected district judge of the county court, and in 1906 he was elected presiding judge. After four years in this office he was again selected as candidate for the position of probate judge and in November, 1910, was elected for four years.

To those who are acquainted with Judge Brasher, this frequent selection for judicial positions is most natural, for he has all the qualities which are desirable for that calling. He is an excellent judge of evidence and also of human nature. He is fearless in the rendering of his decisions, and is scrupulously just and impartial in all cases. Personally he is a man of genial manners and possesses a large share of that courtesy which we characterize as being of the old school. In the Judge's case, this manner is the expression of a truly kind and sympathetic nature, one which attracts and keeps friends wherever he meets them.

In Caruthersville, the present home of the Brasher family, the Judge is prominent in fraternal circles. He holds membership in the Masonic order, in the Woodmen and in the Red Men. The family attend the Methodist Episcopal church, South, of which Mrs. Brasher is a member, the Judge being a member of the Baptist church. Previous to her marriage to Mr. Brasher, Mrs. Brasher was Mrs. Mary S. Pate, of Cottonwood Point, whose father was Judge Jesse Huffman, of that city. Her union with Mr. Brasher occurred in 1875 and they have a family of three daughters and one son.

EDWARD A. STIERBERGER, M. D., of Union, Franklin county, Missouri, represents the medical profession here and is supreme in this field as a practitioner. Rare, indeed, is the instance where a single physician holds in the palm of his hand the confidence and goodwill of an entire community, and when such a situation is encountered the solution must lie in the individual himself. It is not so far to seek. Acute in his perceptions, widely read in his profession and skillful in applying his acquirements to practical use, his value as a physician and surgeon is of the highest character.

Dr. Stierberger is indigenous to the environment of Union. Here his birth occurred on April 16, 1875, and the people to whom he now ministers so successfully have known him in every phase of life from babyhood up. His childhood training was secured amidst the scenes in which he now lives and labors. His one-time playmates are now his patrons and the seniors of his childhood are now his social and business companions. These unbroken early attachments coupled with his recognized proficiency in his profession, explain, perhaps, why Dr. Stierberger stands alone and without a colleague in Union.

The family to which Dr. Stierberger belongs was established in Franklin county by his father, Charles R. Stierberger, who came here from St. Louis about the year 1859. He was of German birth, his nativity having occurred in Prussia in 1824. He possessed those fine national characteristics which make the German nation one of America's most desirable sources of immigration and his business associations served to make him widely known. When he died in 1876 he was a man scarcely past his prime. He was twice married. His first wife was Miss Elizabeth Giebler, of Union, and to them were born the following children: The late Charles R. Stierberger, of Union; John, who passed away unmarried; Mrs. Emile Szymanski, of Union; Mrs. Amanda Brown, wife of Postmaster Clark C. Brown, of Union; Mrs. Clara Allersmeyer, deceased; and Miss Mattie Stierberger, for many years one of the teachers in the Union public schools. After the demise of his first wife Mr. Stierberger married Miss Lizzie Lindner, who survives him, making her residence at Union, Missouri. Her parents were Albert and Marie (Kline) Lindner, and she was born at Union, Missouri.

Dr. Stierberger, immediate subject of this biographical record, is the only child of the second marriage. He received his preliminary education in the common schools and is one of the many strong practical men who have secured some of their most valuable early impressions in a printing office. When a young lad he secured a position in the office of the *Tribune* and spent the following five years in that field of activity, adding much of value to his fund of general information and leaving its portals better fortified and with greater capabilities than when he entered it.

The mind of the young fellow had been busy with the great question of a future vocation and it was finally solved in favor of medicine. His first studies were pursued under the direction of Dr. Bridgeford in Union and he subsequently became a student in the old Marion Sims Medical College in St. Louis, which later on was to be incorporated in the St. Louis University. He received his degree in 1897 and his first location for professional work was in Sioux City, Iowa, where for two years he had charge of a hospital. Following this he spent six months in Cherokee, Iowa, and a like period in St. Louis before coming to his home town and entering the practice here. In 1898 he took a post-graduate course in the institution from which he had received his degree, it being his laudable ambition to keep abreast of the strides in discovery made constantly in his particular field. Since 1898 he has been occupied with his professional duties and with unconsciously cornering the medical business of the county seat. It will scarcely be doubted that there is not to be found a busier young physician in all Missouri.

Dr. Stierberger holds membership in the Franklin County Medical Society, in the Missouri State Medical Society, and in the American Medical Association. He is local surgeon for the Rock Island Railway Company at Union and belongs to the Association of Railway Surgeons. Nor is his activity limited by his profession, for he has substantial business connections, these confined chiefly to financial investments. He is a stockholder of both the Bank of Union and the Citizens' Bank and is vice-president and a director of the former.

In politics Dr. Stierberger acts with the dominant party of Franklin county. He asserts himself as a good citizen should when questions of public policy come up for adjustment at the polls or elsewhere, but has never manifested ambition for public office himself. His social proclivities are such that he finds great pleasure in his lodge relations, which extend to the Knights of Pythias, the Benevolent and Protective Order of Elks and the Modern Woodmen. He is unmarried.

CHARLES F. BIDEWELL. In 1854 Henry Bidewell came to Bollinger county from England. He acquired a farm of two hundred and forty acres in that county and only interrupted his pursuit of agriculture to fight in the Union army. He married Lucrecia Killion, a native of Missouri, and they had eleven children. Charles F. is the second of the eleven children, seven sons and four daughters, of whom but four are living, the two sisters being married and are now Mrs. W. H. Hobbs, of Stoddard county, Missouri, and Mrs. Arthur George, also of Stoddard county. Their home farms join similarly to those of the brothers, Charles and George Bidewell.

Mr. Charles Bidewell was born December 9, 1871, in Bollinger county, and lived on his father's farm until he was twenty-three years of age. A year later his father died, and Charles disposed of his share of the estate to his brother George, whose life appears elsewhere in this volume.

He then bought fifty-one acres of land near Dongola, to which he soon added two hundred and fifty-one and a half acres. At present he farms three hundred and two and a half acres. On this large estate he carries on general farming and stock raising.

Mr. Bidewell was married in 1895 to Miss Ursula Simpkins, whose parents, Rufus and Flora Simpkins, are natives of Indiana. Four boys and one girl were born to Ursula and Charles Bidewell, who are still living. The daughter, Nora, was born in 1901. The names and dates of birth of the sons are as follows: Walter A., 1896; Ora G., 1905; Leamon, 1908; Elvin, 1910.

A popular and public-spirited citizen, Mr. Bidewell is a member of the Masonic order and of the Modern Woodmen. He is a communicant of the General Baptist church. While in no sense a politician, Mr. Bidewell holds the political faith of his father and is a Republican.

J. W. SEXTON. Does Dunklin county go a hunting, it asks J. W. Sexton to be its master. Does it require a competent, honorable man to look after its funds it elects J. W. Sexton. Is it asked for one of its most up-to-date farmers. J. W. Sexton is the man it names. Are the Democrats looking for some one to fill the office of clerk of the county court, J. W. Sexton is the obvious selection. Thus in all kinds of activities in the county Mr. Sexton is a leader.

He was born in Kennett, January 28, 1859. His father, Lafayette Sexton, was born in Lexington, Kentucky, and was brought up in Kentucky and Missouri, coming to Missouri with his mother in 1840 and settling then in Bollinger county. His father had died in Kentucky about —. In 1858 Lafayette and his mother came to Kennett. She died at Hot Springs, Arkansas, whither she had moved. Lafayette lived one mile from Kennett, on land that he received from the Government. He spent almost all the rest of his life on the farm, which he used for the purposes of stock raising. He enlisted in the Confederate army when the Civil war broke out and after seeing considerable service came home on furlough. During this time he was stricken with the cholera and died October 30, 1863. Soon after he came to Kennett, he had married Nancy G. Evans, nee McCullough, a widow, born in Frankfort, Kentucky. Her parents, Benjamin W. and Mary (Glasscock) McCullough, came to Missouri in 1832. They settled one mile south of Kennett and obtained Government grants of land. He became a land owner in the county that was then known as Stoddard's county and died on his farm at the age of fifty. His widow survived him many years, living until she was eighty years old. Only one of their children is living still, William McCullough, living in Breckenridge county, Kentucky. Nancy McCullough had married John H. Evans when she was a young girl and had borne him four children, Franklin, Ellen, Callie and Kate, all of whom are dead. Mr. Evans was a native of Kentucky, of Welsh descent, but the marriage took place in Missouri. After she married Lafayette Sexton she became the mother of two children, J. W. and R. E., the latter a merchant at Malden, Missouri. Mrs. Sexton had practically to raise the six children alone, as her first husband had died when his four children were small and Mr. Sexton, too, died young. She died in 1900, having lived a life of usefulness for her children. Both Mr. and Mrs. Sexton were members of the Methodist Episcopal church.

When J. W. Sexton was only four years old his father died, so that he never remembers having had a father's care. His mother, however, did all in her power to take the place of both parents and in his turn J. W. Sexton cared for her until the time of her death. When he was twenty-one he took charge of the farm and continued a farmer for many years. In 1898 he was elected county treasurer, which office he filled for the term of two years. At the expiration of his term he went back to farming, devoting most of his farm to stock raising. On November 2, 1910, he was elected to the office of clerk of the circuit court, assuming the active duties of the office January 1, 1911. He was nominated by the Democratic party, for which he had always been an active worker, in conventions and elsewhere. He devotes himself to his office, fulfilling the duties involved in an exemplary manner.

In 1885, when he was thirty-six years old, Mr. Sexton married Mrs. Anna Floyd, a young widow in Dunklin county. She was the daughter of W. T. Meredith. Two children have been born to the union, Kate and Ruth.

Mr. Sexton is a member of the Mutual Protective League and of the Modern Woodmen of America, standing high with the members of both those organizations. As a relief from his strenuous duties he spends his vacations either hunting or fishing, being an expert in both of these sports. Mr. Sexton is a thoroughly capable man and besides this is conscientious, a combination which cannot fail to result in success. He is very popular both socially and in his business relations, as he has the ability to command love as well as respect.

JESSE M. ELVINS. With the history of St. Francois county the name of Elvins has been long and prominently identified, and the subject of this memoir well upheld the prestige of the same through his sterling character and large and worthy accomplishment. The thriving little city of Elvins, this county, was named in his honor and he was long numbered among the influential citizens of this favored section of the state, where he did much to further civic and industrial progress.

Jesse Mahagan Elvins was born in St. Francois county, on the 12th of May, 1841, and he died at his home in Doe Run, this county, on the 25th of April, 1910, secure in the high regard of all who knew him. He was a son of Moses and Sarah (Flannigan) Elvins and a grandson of William Elvins, who was a native of England, a clockmaker by trade and the founder of the family in America. In the year 1840 Moses Elvins established his home in Farmington, St. Francois county, Missouri, and here he continued to reside until his death. He became one of the prosperous farmers of the county and also had other interests of important order. He was a man of the most inflexible integrity and ever commanded the confidence and esteem of his fellow men. His wife survived him by a number of years. Jesse M. Elvins was reared and educated in his native county and as a youth he served an apprenticeship to the carpenter's trade, to which he continued to devote his attention, as a contractor and builder, for many years, within which he contributed materially to the upbuilding of various towns and villages in the county, as did he also through his various real-estate operations, which reached wide scope. He had much to do with the development of the lead industry in this district and was the virtual founder of the present fine little city which perpetuates his name. He supervised the construction of the lead mills at Bonne Terre and Doe Run and was known as a business man of ability, enterprise and scrupulous integrity. His progressive policies and thorough business methods enabled him to achieve large and worthy success in connection with his various undertakings, and no citizen in the county commanded more secure vantage ground in popular confidence and esteem. He was signally true and loyal in all the relations of life and his name merits an enduring place of honor on the roster of those who have contributed in conspicuous measure to the development and prosperity of his native county, within whose gracious borders his entire life was passed. He was aligned as a staunch supporter of the cause of the Republican party and was admirably fortified in his opinions as to matters of public import.

In the year 1861 was solemnized the marriage of Mr. Elvins to Miss Zelma Politte, a representative of one of the old and distinguished French families of Missouri. Mrs. Elvins, a woman of most gracious and gentle personality, was summoned to eternal rest on the 5th of January, 1885, secure in the affectionate regard of all who had come within the sphere of her influence. Of the seven children of this union three died in infancy and Rice, the fourth in order of birth, died in 1899. The surviving children are Linn, William and Politte, and concerning the last mentioned specific record is given on succeeding pages of this work. The loved wife and mother was a devout communicant of the Catholic church and her life was marked by kindly words and generous deeds. On the 11th of December, 1888, Jesse M. Elvins contracted a second marriage, by his union with Miss Elizabeth Mehring, who survives him, as does also the younger of their two children, Charles Parsons Elvins. The elder son, Jesse Pierce, died at the age of five years.

Measured by its rectitude, its strength and its definite accomplishment, the life of Jesse M. Elvins counted for much, and his name will be held in lasting honor in the county which ever represented his home and the center of his varied interests.

HON. POLITTE ELVINS is engaged in the practice of law and the banking business in the city of Elvins, St. Francois county. A staunch and active Republican, he represented the thirteenth congressional district in the sixty-first congress of the United States, in which he made an admirable record and in which he had the distinction of being the youngest member.

Mr. Elvins was born at French Village, St. Francois county, Missouri, on the 16th of March, 1878, and is the youngest of the three surviving children of Jesse M. and Zelma (Politte) Elvins. On preceding pages of this publication is entered a memoir to his honored father, and the family data incorporated in said article are such as to render it unnecessary to repeat the same in the present sketch. Mr. Elvins is indebted to the public schools of his native county for his early educational discipline, which was supplemented by a course in Carlton College and the University of Missouri, at Columbia, from which he received the degree of Bachelor of Laws in 1899, being forthwith admitted to the bar.

On the 25th of November, 1901, he was married to Miss Florence Kells, of Arcadia, Missouri. Mr. and Mrs. Elvins are popular factors in the social activities of the community and their pleasant home is known for its generous hospitality.

JOHN H. HIMMELBERGER. Among the men of fine initiative and constructive powers who are contributing materially to the industrial and civic stability and progress of southeastern Missouri, a place of no slight prominence must be accorded to this well known and public-spirited citizen of Cape Girardeau, where he is president of the Himmelberger & Harrison Lumber Company and where he has other capitalistic interests of important order. Sterling character, alert and progressive ideas and marked civic loyalty and liberality make Mr. Himmelberger a valuable factor in the various activities of the community, and he is distinctively one of the representative business men of the fine little city in which he maintains his home.

A scion of staunch German stock long and worthily identified with the history of Pennsylvania, Mr. Himmelberger finds a due sense of pride in reverting to the fine old Keystone state of the Union as the place of his nativity. He was born at Myerstown, Lebanon county, Pennsylvania, on the 30th of October, 1861, and is a son of Isaac and Catherine (Haak) Himmelberger, both of whom were born and reared in that sturdy old commonwealth, where the respective families were founded in an early day. In 1867 Isaac Himmelberger removed with his family to Logansport, Indiana, where he owned and operated a sawmill and was otherwise prominently identified with the lumber business for more than a decade. In 1879 he came to Missouri and established his business at Buffington, Stoddard county, continuing, however, to reside at Logansport, Indiana, in which place he continued in the same line of enterprise and built up a prosperous business. He passed the closing years of his long and useful life at Logansport, and was sixty years of age when he was summoned to eternal rest, in July, 1900, secure in the high regard of all who had known him. His widow now maintains her home in Logansport, and he is survived also by one son and three daughters. The father was a stalwart Republican in his political proclivities, was a man of sincerity and strong individually, and his religious faith was that of the Universalist church. His widow has long been a devoted member of the Reformed Lutheran church.

John H. Himmelberger was a lad of six years at the time of the family removal to Logansport, Indiana, in which thriving little city he gained his early educational discipline by duly availing himself of the advantages of the excellent public schools, in which he completed the curriculum of the high school. In the meanwhile he began to assist his father in the operation of the sawmill and other details of the lumber business, and he thus continued after the removal to Buffington, Missouri, at which time he was eighteen years of age. Through this means he gained a thorough knowledge of all details of this important line of industrial enterprise and was well equipped for successful operations in an independent way. In 1885 his father admitted him to partnership, and this alliance continued about a decade, within which he won his spurs as a practical and successful business man of excellent constructive ability. In 1895 he became one of the interested principals in the organization of the Himmelberger-Luce Land & Lumber Company, at Morehouse, New Madrid county, this state, and he was chosen its secretary at the time of incorporation. This company continued operations in the lumber business and the handling of timber lands until 1904, when it was succeeded by the Himmelberger & Harrison Lumber Company, of which he has since been president. This company is incorporated with a capital stock of six hundred thousand dollars and its operations are of broad scope and importance, including the ownership of valuable timber lands and the manufacturing of lumber through the agency of a well equipped and thoroughly modern plant located at Morehouse, Missouri. The enterprising spirit of Mr. Himmelberger and associates was significantly manifested in 1907, when they instituted the erection of the Himmelberger & Harrison building, on Broadway, in Cape Girardeau. This is a fine, modern structure of brick and stone, is five stories in height and is conceded to be the finest office and bank building in the city. Here are maintained the offices of the Southeast Missouri Trust Company, which is one of the substantial and popular financial institutions of this section of the state and of which Mr. Himmelberger is a director. It is one of the strongest institutions of the kind in this part of the state and bases its operations upon a paid-up capital stock of five hundred thousand dollars. He has been a valued factor in the directing of the policies of this institution, of which he is vice-president and which has done much to further the financial prestige of Cape Girardeau. Mr. Himmelberger is also a member of the directorate of the Sturdivant Bank at Cape Girardeau and of the Bank of Morehouse at Morehouse, Missouri, where he still retains other interests, and he has also identified himself with various other enterprises in his home city of Cape Girardeau and he stands exemplar of the most progressive civic policies, as he is ever ready to lend his aid and influence in the furtherance of measures and enterprises projected for the general good of the community. He is the president of the Board of Supervisors of the Little River Drainage District. This drainage district has for its object the draining and reclamation of five hundred thousand acres of wet and over-flowed lands in Cape Girardeau, Scott, Stoddard, New Madrid, Pemiscot and Dunklin counties. He enjoys unqualified popularity in both business and social circles in his home city, and here he is affiliated with the Benevolent and Protective Order of Elks and the Independent Order of Odd Fellows. Both he and his wife are members of the Presbyterian church.

January 1, 1889, marked the solemnization of the marriage of Mr. Himmelberger to Miss Mary A. Kesling, who was born and reared in Cass county, Indiana, of which Logansport is the judicial center. She is a daughter of Oliver and Kate (Pannebaker) Kesling, who still reside in that county, where the father has long been a representative farmer and honored citizen. Mr. and Mrs. Himmelberger have four children, Harry I., Charles, John and Katharine.

GEORGE K. WILLIAMS. One of the most widely known and most important names to be encountered in connection with the lead district of this part of the state is the name of George K. Williams, of Farmington, Missouri, who is acting superintendent for the Potosi Mines Company, of Boston and New York, with mines located at Leadwood. He also served under two gubernatorial administrations as state mine inspector, his thorough knowledge of mining making him a man admirably incumbent of the office which in a state of such vast mineral resources of Missouri is an important one.

Previous to his present association, Mr. Williams was for fifteen years with the Doe Run Lead Company, and it was his portion fairly to grow up in an atmosphere of mines and mining, for his father was a man of importance in the field. That gentleman, George M. Williams, was born in St. Francois county, March 4, 1830. He early became a miner and driller and possesses the distinction of being the first man to do drilling at Bonne Terre with a churn drill, the same striking disseminated lead ore.

St. Francois county was the scene of the birth of George K. Williams, and the date of his advent on this mundane sphere was September 9, 1864. He received his education in the schools at Bonne Terre, and, finishing the school at the age of seventeen years, he entered upon his career in some comparatively unimportant capacity in the mines. In a short time he accepted a position with the Doe Run Lead Company, at Doe Run, Missouri, and was sent to the Flat River district with the first prospecting diamond drill to Flat River, and struck the first deep disseminated lead ore that was struck in the Flat River district. This being at the depth of four hundred feet.

The greater part of Mr. Williams' connection with the Doe Run Lead Company was in the Diamond drill department. He was appointed state mine inspector by Governor A. M. Dockery, governor of the State of Missouri, in 1901, and was re-appointed in 1905 to that office by Governor Joseph W. Folk, holding the position until February 15, 1909, and in the eight years in which he had mining affairs in the state in his hands and under his supervision he proved himself without possibility of doubt to be the right man for the place, knowing the mining situation as it is given to few to know it and possess it,—splendid judgment in addition.

In December, 1910, he and his associates took up the Jacob Day land which was located in the Leadwood district, consisting of three hundred and fifty-seven acres, and sold it to Boston and New York capitalists. The property was tested with a diamond drill and a shaft is being sunk near the center of the property, and is called the Alma Shaft, being named after his daughter. Mr. Williams, who is superintendent of the Boston and New York Company, is, of course, directing the work.

Mr. Williams married in 1897 Miss Barbara Adams, of Irondale, Missouri. She is the daughter of Richard Adams, superintendent of the Old Irondale Company. Mr. and Mrs. Williams have two sons and one daughter—Naive, Alma and Richard,—thus sharing their delightful home with a trio of young people.

Mr. Williams is Democratic in politics, giving heart and hand to men and measures. He and his family attend the Methodist Episcopal church, South, and he exemplifies in his daily living the fine principles promulgated by the Masonic Lodge, in which he is entitled to wear the white-plumed helmet of the Knight Templar.

DR. JOHN F. WAGNER, a progressive young medical practitioner of Greenville, Wayne county, is a son of the widely known educator, Professor L. M. Wagner. The father was born in Washington county, Tennessee, on the 1st of April, 1851, and received a theological education at Mosheim College, one of the first institutions of higher learning established in that state east of the Alleghany mountains. Soon after his graduation he commenced preaching in Missouri under the auspices of the Lutheran synod. At the same time, in order to eke out a livelihood, he taught school, most of this work in that state being in connection with various parochial institutions connected with his church.

Professor Wagner first came to Missouri in 1877, locating in the northern part of what is now Cascade, Wayne county, where he founded Concordia College, in which so many of the professional men of that section of the state have received the early literary training which fitted them to assume the higher courses of their education. While conducting that select institution Professor Wagner also preached to many scattering charges and those without regular pastors. He was thus busily and worthily employed until 1909, when he retired from professional work altogether and entered the employ of the Williamsville, Greenville & St. Louis Railroad at Cascade, his present occupation. The Professor also cultivates and operates a farm, and has been serving on the local Board of Education since 1900. He had previously been a member of the County Board of School Commissioners for three terms, and there has never been a time since he became a resident of Wayne county that he has failed to show his unbounded interest in her educational progress, or that her people have failed to show their faith in his ability and high-minded motives. His wife (formerly Miss Emma Whitener) is also living and highly respected as an intelligent and lovable woman. Of their nine children, the following seven are living: Virda, now the wife of Zark Souderman; John F., of this biography; Effie, who became Mrs. William E. Pabor, of Fredericktown, Missouri; Harry, a citizen of Cape Girardeau; and Otto, Gus and Irving, still living at home.

John F. Wagner was born at Gravelton, Wayne county, on the 20th of December, 1882; was reared on the family homestead; educated in his preparatory courses at his father's school (Concordia College), and in 1902 was matriculated at the American Medical College, St. Louis, from which he graduated in 1906. He established himself in practice at Cascade in 1906, but finally located at Greenville, where he has founded a substantial and a high-grade professional business. He continues the family tendencies in his adhesion to the Lutheran church, as well as in his general support of Democratic principles and policies. His professional relations are with the Missouri Eclectic Medical Society and the National Electric Medical Association, and his fraternal connections are with the Modern Woodmen of America.

Dr. Wagner was married, March 7, 1911, to Miss Stella Rhodes, born in Greenville, a daughter of John F. and Sarah (McGhee) Rhodes, who have spent their lives here. Mr. Rhodes has filled nearly all county offices, including that of Representative, and owns a fine farm near Greenville, Missouri.

JESSE A. McGLOTHLIN, the present circuit clerk and county recorder of Bollinger county, Missouri, is a man whose position as one in whom all who know him impose implicit trust, and whose name has come to be synonymous with progressive enterprise, makes it impossible to omit his name from any record of the history of Southeastern Missouri. He was born in Reynolds county on his father's farm, March 10, 1869. His father, Joseph McGlothlin, was a native Hoosier, while his mother, prior to her marriage Miss Louisa Allison, was born in the state of Tennessee. In 1879 the family moved to Wayne county, this state, and there Jesse A. McGlothlin lived until his twentieth year. His early education he obtained in the district schools of the locality, meantime being a willing assistant in the various duties of the home farm.

At eighteen Jesse McGlothlin inaugurated his independent career as a school-master, his first school being in Carter county. In Wayne, Bollinger and Madison counties he was known as a leading member of the pedagogic profession. He augmented his early education during his teaching career by attendance at Concordia College at Gravetta, and also at Hales College in Wayne county for two years.

In 1899 McGlothlin became interested in the mercantile business, and he entered a dry-goods store at Glen Allen, in which establishment he remained until 1906. After seven years he left Berry's employ and was elected in that year, on the Republican ticket, to the offices of circuit clerk and county recorder for a term of four years. So efficient and honorable was the record of his first term's service that he was re-elected to the same office, and he is now serving his second term.

Mr. McGlothlin's active interest in educational matters has never wavered, and he is now wielding his influence for what is best in that field as a member and secretary of the board of directors of Mayfield College. The old Snyder farm of seventy-one acres adjoining the municipality of Marble Hill is now in Mr. McGlothlin's possession, and is prospering under his management.

On October 7, 1894, was solemnized the marriage of Mr. McGlothlin, the lady of his choice being Miss Dora L. Rhodes. She was born and reared in Bollinger county, the daughter of Robert and Georgia (Floyd) Rhodes, prominent residents of that county. Four children have been born to the union of Mr. and Mrs. McGlothlin, namely: Maud, born in 1895; Helen, born in 1897; Lee A., born in 1901; and Jesse Robert, born in 1910. In their religious affiliation, the McGlothlin family are identified with Baptist church. Fraternally Mr. McGlothlin is a member of that historic order, the Ancient Free and Accepted Masons, and belongs to both the Independent Order of Odd Fellows and the Modern Woodmen of America.

CAPTAIN W. I. MCDANIEL. A venerable and respected resident of Senath, Captain W. I. McDaniel, now living with his son, C. P. McDaniel, of whom a brief personal account is given elsewhere in this work, fought bravely in defense of the Confederacy during the Civil war, and now bears upon his body a scar which resulted from a wound received on the field of battle. A native of Tennessee, he was born November 14, 1827, in Sumner county, but as an infant was taken by his parents to Natchez, Mississippi, where he lived until six years of age.

Returning to Obion county, West Tennessee, in 1834, he continued his residence there for nearly forty years, serving in the meantime for awhile as captain of a company of State Militia, having been commissioned by Isham G. Harris, war-Governor of Tennessee. On September 9, 1861, he enlisted as a private in the Thirty-third Tennessee Regiment, of which he was elected first sergeant. After the battle of Perryville Captain McDaniel was promoted to the rank of second lieutenant, and subsequently, at Shelbyville, Tennessee, was chosen as the bravest man of his company, owing to an order issued by the Confederate Congress that each and every company in that division should elect or appoint the bravest man in the company. At Missionary Ridge, while serving as second lieutenant, he had charge of his company, as he had had much of the time during his enlistment, even at the battle of Chickamauga leading his company. He was subsequently confined in the hospital four months, and on rejoining his regiment assumed the same position, and held it until the close of the war, having command of Company D. The Captain saw many hard-fought engagements, at Shiloh twenty-one of the sixty-six men of which he had command being either killed or wounded. At the engagement at Franklin, Tennessee, Captain McDaniel received a severe wound from a bayonet, and still carries the scar that ensued. He was often detailed on special duty with squads of men of whom he had charge, serving under different commanders, including General Clark, who was afterwards governor of Mississippi; Brigadier General A. P. Stewart; and under General Strahl, who lost his life at the battle of Franklin. The brigade to which the Captain belonged assisted in protecting the rear of Hill's army on its retreat from the battle of Nashville, keeping up a constant fight with the enemy. He subsequently surrendered at Raleigh, North Carolina, with Johnston's men, and there took the oath of allegiance.

After his surrender Captain McDaniel returned to his old home in western Tennessee, which he had visited but twice during the entire war. His good wife, however, had visited him after the battle of Stone River, having ridden on horseback one hundred and fifty miles to do so, carrying a young child with her, crossing several rapid streams and fording some, and after meeting the enemy in the road riding straight through the Federal lines.

Coming to Dunklin county, Missouri, in 1870, Captain McDaniel resided at Clarkton for six years. Moving then to Texas, he was for several years employed as a builder and a painter in Frio county. At a recent reunion in Little Rock, Arkansas, the Captain was there met by his son, C. P. McDaniel, who brought him to Senath, and he is now spending the closing years of his long and useful life with this son.

C. P. McDANIEL. The wide-awake, busy little town of Senath owes its strong vitality and its great popularity to the enterprise and active spirit of its broad-minded and keen-sighted business men, who are putting forth practical efforts to aid its growth in every line of industry. Prominent among the number thus employed is C. P. McDaniel, the leading furniture dealer and undertaker of this part of Dunklin county. He was born April 30, 1851, in Fulton county, Kentucky, but was taken to Obion county, Tennessee, when but a year old, and resided there until 1869, when he made his way to Dunklin county, Missouri, which seemed to offer special inducements to a young man of vim and energy, being in the center of a rich and highly productive country.

Locating in Clarkton, Mr. McDaniel there followed his trade of a blacksmith for nearly thirty years. Coming from there to Senath in 1897, he was here not only the "Village Blacksmith" for six years, but was also successfully engaged in the undertaking business. Giving up his smithy in 1903, Mr. McDaniel has since built up a substantial trade as a dealer in furniture, having gained an extensive and lucrative patronage in Senath and vicinity, his systematic and upright methods attracting customers from all parts of the county. This business he is carrying on successfully in connection with undertaking, in both lines being well patronized.

Mr. McDaniel has been twice married. He married first, at Union City, Tennessee, Ozella B. Starrett, of Dunklin county, Missouri, a daughter of Robert C. Starrett, an early settler of Clarkton. She died at Clarkton, Missouri, in 1894, after twenty years of happy married life, having four children. namely: Florence E., wife of F. E. Williams, of Malden, Missouri; Edna May, wife of Alexander T. Douglass, of Senath; Clara Ann, of Senath; and Arthur S., who is engaged in business with his father. Mr. McDaniel married in 1900, in Senath, Huldah C. Douglass, an aunt of Robert Sidney Douglass, editor of this work, and a sister of Rev. Robert Douglass, pastor of the Baptist church at Senath.

Mr. McDaniel is not identified with any political organization, but takes an active interest in the advancement of local affairs. Fraternally he is a member of the Independent Order of Odd Fellows. He is a member of the Baptist church, to which Mrs. McDaniel also belongs, and in which she is and has ever been an active worker, even as a young girl having taken a great interest in the Sunday school work. She attends the Baptist Association meetings, in which she is frequently an earnest speaker. A stanch advocate of temperance, Mrs. McDaniel at one time addressed the court on the matter of local option, presenting a remonstrance so effectively that she carried her point without the assistance of an attorney.

Mr. McDaniel is a son of Captain W. I. McDaniel, a venerable and highly esteemed resident of Senath, of whom a brief biographical sketch precedes this.

ROBERT A. ANTHONY. Among the distinctively prominent lawyers and jurists of the state of Missouri, none is more splendidly equipped for the work of his profession than Judge Robert A. Anthony, whose home and business headquarters are at Fredericktown, Missouri. Throughout his career as a distinguished attorney and well fortified counselor he has, by reason of unimpeachable conduct and close observance of the unwritten code of professional ethics, gained the admiration and respect of his fellow practitioners, in addition to which he commands a high place in the confidence and esteem of his fellow citizens. He has served as judge of the Twenty-seventh judicial circuit of Missouri and for four years was prosecuting attorney for Madison county.

A native of the Lone Star state, Judge Anthony was born in Kaufman county, Texas, the date of his birth being the 10th of March,

1859. He is a son of Patrick Henry and Elizabeth (Matthews) Anthony, both of whom were born and reared in Madison county, Missouri. The father was born in 1826 and he died at Fredericktown in 1878. He was a farmer and millwright by occupation and at the time of his demise was the owner of considerable valuable farming property. He resided in Texas from 1854 until 1865, and in that state was an extensive plantation and slave owner. He lost heavily during the Civil war and shortly after the close of that sanguinary struggle returned to Missouri, where he operated saw and grist mills for a number of years. His father was Samuel Anthony, who came to Missouri from Tennessee in 1816. Samuel Anthony was a farmer and he reared to maturity a large family of children, a number of whose descendants reside in Texas and Missouri. Patrick H. Anthony was one of the forty-niners who made the perilous overland journey to California, where he was fairly successful in his mining ventures. Elizabeth (Matthews) Anthony, mother of the Judge, was born in Madison county, Missouri, as already noted, and she was descended from stanch French stock, her mother having been a Miss Tesreau. She died in 1890, at the age of fifty-four years. Her father was Samuel C. Matthews, a farmer in Madison county during the greater part of his active career: He died in 1861. Mr. and Mrs. Anthony were devout communicants of the Catholic church, in the work of which denomination they were most active factors and in whose faith they reared their children.

Judge Anthony was a child of seven years of age at the time of his parents' return to Madison county, Missouri, to the public schools of which place he is indebted for his early educational training. As a young man he read law under the able preceptorship of Judge Fox, at Fredericktown, and he was admitted to the bar in 1884. He initiated the active practice of his profession in this place and for a number of years was associated in the practice of law with Emmet Williams, now of the Bankers Trust Company, of St. Louis. He was also associated in law work with H. Clay Marsh, who is now a farmer in Madison county. At the present time Judge Anthony is a member of the well known law firm of Anthony & Davis, the same being assistant attorneys for the Missouri Pacific Railroad Company, representing that concern in seven counties in southeastern Missouri.

In March, 1905, Judge Anthony was appointed, by the Supreme Court of Missouri, as commissioner to take testimony and try the case of the state of Missouri versus the Standard Oil Company of Indiana, the Waters-Pierce Oil Company of Missouri and the Republic Oil Company of New York, the charge being a combination, conspiracy or trust to monopolize and control the oil business in the state of Missouri. After some two years' investigation of the case in the states of Missouri, Oklahoma, Iowa, Ohio, New York and Illinois, Judge Anthony held the companies above named to be guilty and so reported the case to the Supreme Court of the state, which affirmed and adopted that decision. The report and opinion covered over three hundred pages in book form and showed judicious foresight and remarkable knowledge of the science of jurisprudence on the part of Judge Anthony. It is conceded to be one of the most important cases ever taken up in Missouri. The prosecution was instituted by the then attorney general of Missouri the present Governor Hadley. Judge Anthony was appointed, in 1902, by Governor Dockery, as circuit judge of the Twenty-seventh Judicial Circuit of Missouri, to fill out the unexpired term of Judge James D. Fox. He served as circuit judge for a period of two years and from 1886 to 1890 he was prosecuting attorney for Madison county. He has always been aligned as a stalwart in the ranks of the Democratic party, in the local councils of which he has been an active and zealous worker. He is affiliated with a number of professional and fraternal organizations of representative character and in all the relations of life has so conducted himself as to be popular with all classes of people. He is possessed of a cheery, kindly disposition and is intensely religious.

In 1888 was solemnized the marriage of Judge Anthony to Miss Jennie Wiley, who was born in Peoria, Illinois, whence she accompanied her parents to Madison county, Missouri, at the age of fifteen years. For some time prior to her marriage she was a popular and successful teacher in the public schools of Madison county. She is a woman of gracious personality and is deeply beloved by all with whom she has come in contact. Judge and Mrs. Anthony have no children. They are communicants of the St.

Michaels Catholic church, at Fredericktown, this mission having been established at a very early day. It did not become a regular pastorate until 1830, however. At the present time the church has a membership of one hundred and fifty Catholic families and in addition to a fine church it also has two good school buildings, a pastor's residence and a home for the Sisters, who conduct the school. The present pastor is Rev. Father McCartney.

LOUIS STEIN, actively identified with milling interests in Southeastern Missouri, makes his home at Cape Girardeau, where he is general manager of the Cape City Mills. He is deeply interested in community affairs and his efforts have also been a potent element in the business progress of this section of the state. He has with ready recognition of opportunity directed his labors into various fields wherein he has achieved success, and at the same time has promoted a business enterprise that has proved of more than local value. In 1911 he was given proof of the high regard of his fellow citizens in that he was then elected city treasurer of Cape Girardeau, an office he is filling with the utmost credit to himself and his constituents.

Louis Stein is a native of Cape Girardeau, where his birth occurred on the 12th of August, 1864, and he is a son of Christian and Margaret (Mertz) Stein, both of whom were born and reared in Germany, where was celebrated their marriage and whence they immigrated to the United States in the year 1859. Settlement was first made at New Orleans, where the family home was maintained for one year, at the expiration of which removal was made to a more northern section on account of Yellow fever epidemic. Coming to Missouri, the father settled at Commerce, where he entered the employ of James Whitelaw, a prominent miller in that place. Three years later, in 1863, the family located at Cape Girardeau, where Mr. Stein began to work for G. C. Thelineus, in the flour-mill business. His cherished and devoted wife passed away in 1892, but Mr. Stein is still living, 1911. They were the parents of seven children, six boys and one girl, of whom Louis was the fifth in order of birth.

In the German school at Cape Girardeau Louis Stein received his early educational training and this discipline was later supplemented by a course of study in the normal school. When eighteen years of age he entered the employ of the F. Fiedemann Company, at Jackson, Missouri, as miller. Four years later he was proffered and accepted a position as expert miller for the Barnard & Leas Manufacturing Company, at Moline, Illinois. In 1887 he assumed charge of all the mills of the Cape County Milling Company and three years later he came to Cape Girardeau, where he has since resided and where, in 1897, he organized the Cape City Mills, of which he is now in charge. He is a business man of splendid ability and his success in his chosen line of work has been on a parity with his own well directed endeavors. In his political affiliations he is a stanch advocate of the cause of the Democratic party, in the local councils of which he is a most active factor. In 1905 he was elected a member of the city council and he served in that capacity for a period of two years during Mayor Whitelaw's administration. In 1911 he made the race for and was elected city treasurer, meeting with practically no opposition. He is showing himself a capable administrator of the fiscal affairs of the city and in this connection is giving the utmost satisfaction to his constituents. Mr. Stein is a charter member of the Commercial Club of Cape Girardeau and he is also a valued and appreciative member of the organization known as the Sons of Veterans, being eligible for representation therein by reason of his father's service in the Civil war. In a fraternal way he is connected with the Modern Woodmen of America, the Ancient Order of United Workmen and the Knights and Ladies of Security. His religious faith is in harmony with the tenets of the Presbyterian church, in which he is president of the board of deacons.

In the year 1886 was solemnized the marriage of Mr. Stein to Miss Marguerite Barrett, who was reared and educated at Cairo, Illinois. To this union have been born three children, whose names are here entered in respective order of birth,—Harvey, Carroll and Marguerite,—all of whom remain at the parental home. The Stein family are well known and popular in the best social circles of Cape Girardeau and here they are accorded the unalloyed confidence and esteem of their fellow citizens.

BARBEAU ANDREW ROY is one of the strong, practical men who have had a helpful experience in that popular and immensely valuable educational institution known as journalism. Beginning life as a teacher, in 1890 he came to Bonne Terre and entered the newspaper field, eventually becoming editor of the *Bonne Terre Register,* and probably no one factor has been as potent as his influence through the eloquent columns of his paper in changing the county from Democratic to Republican. After eighteen years he abandoned the Fourth Estate and became in January, 1910, postmaster of the city, the office now being one of the four largest in Southeastern Missouri.

Mr. Roy's father, Ferdinand A. Roy, was born in Prairie du Rocher, Randolph county, Illinois, June 5, 1817. He came to Missouri in 1844, when a young man, and was employed by a Mr. Deloge, of Potosi, Missouri, in his mercantile business. In the early '50s he removed to Sainte Genevieve county, where he went into a business association with Francis A. Rozier, in the line of merchandise, and later embarked independently in the same business, carrying it on for some time, including the Civil war period. He was a man held in respect and confidence, and after retiring from business his usefulness was by no means at an end and he held several offices, being county judge and for fifteen years justice of the peace. The last years of his life were passed with his daughter, Mrs. Joseph Flynn, of Cape Girardeau, Missouri, the date of his death being February 18, 1898. He was married at about the age of thirty-two years to Rosine Goin and ten children were born to them, only two being alive at the present time, namely: Ferdinand Roy, Jr., of Prairie du Rocher, and the subject. The church of this well-remembered gentleman was the Catholic and in politics, unlike his son, he was a stanch Democrat.

Barbeau Andrew Roy was born November 25, 1866, in Sainte Genevieve, Missouri, and within its pleasant boundaries he passed his early life. He received his education in the common and high schools and after finishing such advantages as they had to offer he taught school for a time in Sainte Genevieve county and then went on to South Dakota, where he engaged in the mercantile business. In 1890 he came to Bonne Terre and here entered into the newspaper business with his brother-in-law, Joseph Flynn, the two gentlemen editing and publishing the *Bonne Terre Democrat.* In the fall Mr. Roy bought out the interests of Mr. Flynn and continued in publication of the paper alone until 1893, when he bought the *Bonne Terre Register* and consolidated the two papers under the name of the *Register,* the policy of the sheet being Republican. He continued in command until May, 1908, when he sold the *Register* to Mr. George Stanfill. He proved himself a talented and influential editor and the *Register* flourished under his regime. After quitting the newspaper field, Mr. Roy entered for a time the accounting department of the Mississippi River & Bonne Terre Railroad, where he remained until he was appointed postmaster in January, 1910, and which office he holds at the present time. The postoffice has made rapid and definite strides, for it was but a short time ago third class. In July, 1910, six months after Mr. Roy became its head, the office was entered as second class and it is now one of the four largest offices in Southeastern Missouri. Mr. Roy, as all are ready to agree, has ever discharged its duties with promptness and fidelity.

Mr. Roy was married on the 20th day of January, 1897, to Onna G. Thomure, of Bonne Terre, and their happy and congenial union has been blessed by the birth of two children, namely: Edgar L. and Lucian T. Mr. and Mrs. Roy are communicants of the Catholic church and the head of the house is affiliated with the Knights of Columbus, of which he holds the important office of state secretary. He is also a member of the Commercial Club and stands as a thoroughly helpful and public spirited member of society.

HENRY C. VOSSBRINK is the efficient recorder of Franklin county, in Boone township of which his birth occurred November 25, 1872. His father, John H. Vossbrink, was born in Hanover, Germany, and came to the United States as a youth in 1845, locating in St. Louis, where he completed his trade as a tailor and then engaged as clerk in a furniture store, spending eleven years of his early manhood in St. Louis. He was born in 1830 and was under thirty years of age when he came out to Franklin county. Here he abandoned his trade and adopted as his own the great basic industry, engaged in the wholesale cultivation of wheat and succeeded in building up a splendid estate. He is now a resident of the community of Gerald.

John H. Vossbrink has given a graphic illustration of what industry and perserverance can accomplish upon the farm. The aim of his life has been the achievement of financial independence, and while this has been in process of accomplishment, he has infused habits of industry and thrift into the younger generation of his household. He has kept away from politics, except in the capacity of the voter, and as such is aligned in harmony with the Republican party. He married Wilhelmina Keller, who survives, and the issue of their union are as follows: Louis H.; Edward C.; Julia C., wife of Julius Wulfert; Emma E., who married Dr. A. T. Kessler; John W.; William H.; Henry C.; George H.; Julius A.; and Minnie A., now Mrs. W. H. Linstromberg.

Henry C. Vossbrink was educated in the public school and is an excellent German student, having acquired the parental tongue with unusual aptitude. At the age of eighteen years he began his career as a business man by forming a partnership with one of his brothers at Shotwell, near the family home. They established a thriving mercantile business and continued the same for four years. A change in conditions caused him to seek employment in St. Louis and he spent eighteen months there as a street car conductor. Subsequently he spent a period engaged in the retail liquor business at St. Louis and after spending a few months as a clerk in Sullivan he associated himself with a brother in Tolona, Missouri, and there spent a year. Following this he spent nine months at Shotwell engaged in clerking and then went to Washington, Missouri, where he tended bar for two years. He passed the next twelve years as bartender for Kramolowski in Union and terminated it when he assumed the office of recorder in 1911.

Mr. Vossbrink was reared to loyalty to the principles of what its admirers call "The Grand Old Party," and his residence at several points in Franklin county gave him an unusually large acquaintance and an enthusiastic one, so that when he became a candidate for office, support came to him from many sources. He made the race before the primary against five competitors and distanced them all for the nomination, winning the election from his Democratic opponent by better than the party vote. He is making a record as a popular official.

Mr. Vossbrink is one of the directors of the Bank of Union; is interested in the Helling Manufacturing Company and was its secretary and treasurer for more than three years. He is also a stockholder in the National Cob Pipe Works of Union and is an important figure in the Masonic Blue Lodge and the Modern Woodmen.

On January 27, 1900, Mr. Vossbrink married in Union Miss Ida E. Gehlert, daughter of an old settler of Franklin county, Louis H. Gehlert, who was of German blood and birth. Mr. and Mrs. Vossbrink share their delightful home with a daughter and son, namely: Meta W. and J. Henry.

FELIX G. LAMBERT. In the forefront of the enterprising group of citizens whose efforts have established and maintained the progress and prosperity of Bollinger county stands Felix G. Lambert. He practically built Dongola, and though that is perhaps his most notable achievement it is by no means his only one. He was born November 13, 1847, in Cape Girardeau county, Missouri, and both of his parents were natives of Missouri. His father, Ira B. Lambert, died when Felix G. was but two years old, in the year 1849. After this sad event the mother, Polly Lambert, moved to Cape Girardeau county, where she had inherited about two hundred acres of land. Here she later married Brazilas Estes. Her death occurred in 1865, when Mr. Lambert was but eighteen years old. Up to this time he had followed the usual course of the sons of that generation, assisting in the farm work and attending the district school.

The year after his mother's death Mr. Lambert started out to work for himself. Though young, he was a keen business man and one who had the genius for management, which is largely the ability to work hard and look after details. He bought a grist mill in Cape Girardeau county, which he ran for twelve years and developed into a most profitable business. After selling this mill Mr. Lambert bought one hundred and sixty acres of land in Bollinger county. He continued to add to his farm acreage until he is now farming two hundred and twenty acres. Both stock raising and general farming engage his attention.

In 1882 he came to his farm near Dongola which at that time was a settlement of one house. Since that date the history of the town has been mostly of his making. His first contribution to the industrial resources of the village was a saw mill. With this start, the town sprang up and has continued to grow steadily. Mr. Lambert's enterprises did not end with the saw-mill. He built a planing mill and a grist mill, both of which attracted desirable citizens to the town and increased its value as a place of residence and as a business centre.

Though pre-eminently a business man, Mr. Lambert is a citizen who takes the liveliest interest in all public questions, and one who is ready to fulfill all duties whether of public or private import. Of this he has given evidence by his twelve years' service in the offices of the county. He was eight years justice of the peace and four years public administrator. In politics he is a Democrat, and is regarded as a most influential member of his party, because of those qualities which make for his eminence in all things in which he engages.

Mr. Lambert has been married three times. His first wife was Levina Mayfield, daughter of Elisha Mayfield, a native of Missouri. She died in 1879, leaving a son, Shelby, three years old. Mr. Lambert was later united to Amanda Plummer, daughter of George Plummer, born in Ohio. Her son, Grover Cleveland Lambert, was born in 1886. He is now married to a daughter of Missouri, whose maiden name was May Zimmerman. Amanda Plummer Lambert died in 1888. Mr. Lambert's third wife was Mrs. Sarah V. Brown, nee Smith, a Kentuckian by birth. She passed to her reward in 1909.

JOHN H. BRADLEY was born near Senath, Dunklin county, Missouri. His parents were Reuben and Anna Aletha (Myracle) Bradley. Reuben was born near Vincit, in Dunklin county, January 7, 1847, and when he was very small both of his parents died. When he was seventeen years old he enlisted in the Confederate army, in which he served until the close of the Civil war. After he was mustered out he returned to Dunklin county, where he bought a farm at Senath and he was a farmer all of his life. His wife died in 1890 and he has recently come to live with his son at Kennett. Mr. Bradley never laid claim to being a politician, but he worked for all matters of public advancement. He has a family of three sons, all of whom have made successes of their lives. The eldest is James A., the clerk of Dunklin county. John Henderson is the second, while the third, Milton Miliard, has a drug store at Smith.

John received his general education in the public schools and in the Cape Girardeau Normal, after which he took a law course at the State University, from which he was graduated in the class of 1902. In 1908 he was elected prosecuting attorney, serving in 1908 and 1909, living in Kennett. In 1910 he was re-elected, without opposition.

On the 6th of October, 1903, Mr. Bradley married Miss Hettie Horner, of Caruth, Dunklin county. Four children have been born to this union, two of whom died in infancy. The two living are Lethe and Eugene.

Mr. Bradley has done excellent work during his service as prosecuting attorney and as he is but a young man, just at the beginning of his career, he will doubtless rise still higher in his profession, thereby finding opportunity to be of greater service to the state.

HARRY A. MILLER. The junior member of the well known and popular mercantile firm of Miller Brothers, of Elvins, St. Francois county, is one of the representative young business men of this county, which has been his home since his boyhood days and in which his circle of friends is coincident with that of his acquaintances. He was born in the city of Nashville, Tennessee, on the 22d of May, 1886, and is a son of Rulien and Ida (Bloom) Miller, concerning whom more specific mention is made in the sketch dedicated to their elder son, Isadore W., on other pages of this work, said son being senior member of the firm of Miller Brothers and being a resident of Desloge, St. Francois county.

Harry Abraham Miller was a lad of thirteen years at the time when his parents removed to Missouri and established their home at Elvins. He had previously attended the public schools and after coming to Missouri he was enabled to continue his studies in the city schools of St. Louis. His initial business experience was gained in his father's well ordered mercantile establishment at Elvins and upon attaining to his legal majority he was admitted to partnership in the enterprise, which was thereafter conducted for two years under the firm name of Miller & Son. The father then sold his interest to his elder son, Isadore W., and the two brothers have since continued the business with ever increasing success. Harry A. Miller has the direct management of the establishment, which is admirably equipped and in which is carried a large and comprehensive line of general merchandise. Fair and honorable dealings have gained to the concern an appreciative patronage and he whose name initiates this sketch has a secure place in the confidence and esteem of the community. He is also interested with his brother in the conducting of a prosperous mercantile business at Leadwood, in the same county. He is vigorous and alert as a business man, liberal and progressive as a citizen, is a Republican in his political proclivities, and is affiliated with the Ancient Order of United Workmen.

On the 27th of June, 1909, was solemnized the marriage of Mr. Miller to Miss Minnie Magidson, of St. Louis, who presides most graciously over their pleasant home, which is further brightened by the presence of their little daughter, Mildred.

DR. EDWARD GRIFFIN. Among the prominent and valued citizens of Flat River and Saint Francois county stands Edward Griffin, who is particularly well entitled to a place in this volume devoted to representative men and women of southeastern Missouri as a talented member of his profession—the dental—and as president of that flourishing monetary institution, the Miners & Merchants Bank. By no means one to be content with the theory of "letting well enough alone," he is a constant student of his profession and has well succeeded in keeping in touch with the steady march of progress which is the result of dental investigation. The bank of which he is the head holds a position of prominence among the monetary institutions which emphasize and exert marked influence in conserving the financial stability and commercial prestige of the city.

Dr. Edward Griffin is still to be numbered among the younger generation, his birth having occurred in Sainte Genevieve county, March 20, 1879. The father, George Griffin, was born in Knoxville, Tennessee, in 1841, and was a soldier of the Civil war, serving for the whole four years in the army of General Thomas and participating in many notable engagements, among them being the battles of Lookout Mountain, Missionary Ridge and Shiloh, and was with Sherman on his famous march to the sea. After the war he came to the state of Missouri and located in the western part of Union township, in Sainte Genevieve county, where he has ever since been engaged in farming, although his fine ability has by no means been solely devoted to the great basic industry. He was judge of the Sainte Genevieve county court for two years and has the distinction of having been the first Republican judge ever elected in that county. A man of fine citizenship, he is widely known and everywhere honored. He was married in 1866 to Sarah J. Haines, of Knoxville, Tennessee, and to their union eight sons and daughters were born, Dr. Griffin being the seventh in order of birth.

The early education of Edward Griffin was obtained in the public schools of Sainte Genevieve county and he attended for one term the old Baptist College at Farmington. He went thence to the Dental College at St. Louis and there prepared for the work he had elected to follow. In the year 1901 he was graduated from the Washington University at St. Louis, Missouri, taking the degree of D. M. D., and soon thereafter he located at Flat River and there hung out his professional shingle, and in the intervening decade has built up a large and enthusiastic practice as one of the leading dentists of the section. In 1906 he became director of the Miners & Merchants Bank and two years later he received the compliment of being elected to the presidency of that financial institution. Dr. Griffin previously was secretary and treasurer of the Flat River Ice & Cold Storage Company, but upon becoming identified with the bank he has severed that association to devote his attention to his other concerns. Although by no means an office seeker, Dr. Griffin is active in local politics, giving hand and heart to the man and measures of the Republican party, to which he has given his suffrage since his earliest voting days. At the time of the recent Prohibition campaign he acted as president of the Amendment County Committee of Flat River.

On the 7th day of April, 1903, Dr. Griffin formed a happy life companionship by his union with Marietta Sebastian, of Flat River, daughter of R. Sebastian, a blacksmith and wagon maker of this place. Their home is one of the popular gathering places of the community and they are particularly valuable factors in society. They are members of the Christian church, the subject being a deacon of the same. Dr. Griffin is a member of the ancient and august Masonic order and is also affiliated with the Modern Woodmen of America.

ISAAC N. DAFFRON. A widely known and highly esteemed citizen and public official is Isaac N. Daffron, county collector of Wayne county, Missouri, and a blacksmith by trade. With the expiration of his present and third term in the responsible position mentioned he will have served twelve years in that capacity, and he is well recommended by his services which have been a credit to himself and a benefit to the community. He is a native son of Wayne county, his birth having occurred in Benton township October 23, 1860. Mr. Daffron is the son of Smith and Elizabeth (Gilbert) Daffron, the former of whom was born in the vicinity of Ringgold, Georgia, in 1819, and died at the age of fifty-three years. The mother was born in Tennessee July 19, 1829, and is still living, a venerable and worthy woman whom makes her home with the subject. After the death of Smith Daffron she was married a second time, to William Stokley, who is now deceased. The subject is one of three children, two of whom survive. His brother, Thomas E., resides in Piedmont, Missouri. The father of him whose name inaugurates this review came from Georgia to Missouri in the year 1857 and located upon the farm which a few years later was the birthplace of his children. He secured three hundred and twenty acres of wild land, which he cleared and brought to a state of cultivation. He was a blacksmith and carpenter by trade and he followed these callings throughout his life, also engaging in milling, having purchased a water power grist mill partially finished, whose construction he completed. He was a man successful in all his business undertakings and his citizenship was admirably public-spirited. In his political convictions he was in harmony with the teachings of the Democratic party and he and his wife belonged to the Missionary Baptist church. Smith Daffron and a Mr. Ivy practically built the first church and the first school-house in this part of Wayne county.

Isaac N. Daffron was reared on his father's farm and gained his preliminary education behind a desk in the district school room. Having finished its curriculum, he matriculated at the state normal school at Cape Girardeau and there spent a profitable year and a half. He then started in to learn the trade of his father, that of blacksmithing, a smattering of which he had already gained under the tutelage of his brother. He was of Piedmont when a blacksmith of that place was deserted by his assistant and Mr. Daffron was asked to help out—which the young fellow consented to do. What was supposed to be a temporary arrangement lasted for a number of years. The first week he received twenty-five cents a day and the second one dollar a day, a hasty advancement which speaks well for his ability. Mr. Daffron worked in all eleven and one-half years in the blacksmith business, the last five years of this period for himself. He has always had a good business, for his work is good and reliable, but he has not always managed advantageously for himself and he does not have the competence which he deserves. In 1896 he was elected county assessor and removed to Greenville, where he served in the office for a term of four years. That was his first experience in public life and he was well recommended by his services. His efficiency was not forgotten and in 1902 he was elected county collector and succeeded himself at the elections in 1906 and 1910. He is not without some experience in the pedagogical field, having taught school for a time in his young manhood. He has been a Democrat since his earliest voting days and he is very loyal to the interests of the party. His fraternal affiliations extend to the Knights of Pythias and the Modern Woodmen of America.

Mr. Daffron was married October 23, 1887, to Georgia E. Miller, who was born in Cape Girardeau county, Missouri, August 18, 1866. Mr. and Mrs. Daffron's union has been further cemented by the birth of three daughters, namely: Nellie, wife of Scott Judy, of Garnett, Kansas; Clara and Ann, at home.

JAMES F. TATUM. We all of us look towards the future as having something greater in store for us than that we have already experienced, or at least if such is not the case we are to be pitied. Every man hopes for a future better than the present or the past. In the case of James F. Tatum, he has already realized the future, some two years ago; of that we know nothing, but we do know what his past has been.

He was born January 5, 1850, in Howard county, Missouri. He was a son of the late A. C. Tatum, who moved from Virginia to Howard county, Missouri, soon after his marriage. There James received his education and after he left school he started into business, first working for a relative at St. Charles, traveling through the state as a tobacco salesman. His travels brought him to Dunklin county, where he saw the possibilities for a young man and he entered the mercantile business in Dunklin county, being one year at Malden and then in Kennett until three years ago, when he retired and turned the business over to his two sons, Frank and

Ira, who removed the stock to Clarkton. There they are successfully following in the footsteps of their father.

Mr. Tatum was married in 1877, to Miss Lillie Bragg, daughter of the late Captain W. G. Bragg and a sister of Mrs. Sturgis and Mrs. Towson and of that wonderful family of nine splendid "Bragg girls," as they were known. W. G. Bragg of this city is a brother of Mrs. Tatum. Luther P. Tatum, the merchant and capitalist at Kennett, is a half brother of James F. Tatum, and Mrs. Nannie Newby is his cousin. Of the six children born to Mr. and Mrs. Tatum five survive him, as does their mother. John the fourth son, died about eleven years ago. Frank and Ira are in business at Clarkton, while Richard M. is in business here. Susie, the only daughter, is just blossoming into womanhood and is a student of William Woods College, Fulton. Bernie is at Central College at Fayette, Howard county, Missouri.

Mr. Tatum died December 13, 1909, not having quite attained his three score years. He had been in failing health for two years, though he was up and able to attend to business. He was a member of the Masonic order, being a member of the Kennett lodge, No. 68, Ancient Free and Accepted Masons. The funeral service was conducted by the Masons, Dr. Paul Baldwin being the presiding master. Mr. Tatum had for years been a member of the Christian church and religious services at the home were conducted by Elder Rolley Ney, pastor of the Christian church, assisted by the ministers of the Presbyterian, the Baptist and the Methodist Episcopal churches. The fact that these ministers of different denominations came to pay him their last tribute is significant of the liberal attitude Mr. Tatum bore towards all religious bodies. He believed in any organization which had for its aim the betterment of mankind and inasmuch as there are all kinds of men, it takes all kinds of religious creeds to reach them. At the time of his death Mr. Tatum was a member of the Kennett school board, having always taken the deepest interest in all educational matters. He was vice president of the Bank of Kennett and was interested in much Kennett property, for he was well off in this world's goods. He was thoughtful for others, as is evidenced by his having a fifteen thousand dollar life insurance policy. He was a man of deliberation and good judgment, was reliable and honorable and inasmuch as his past has been full of thoughts for others, full of kindly deeds, we can feel that the future which he is already experiencing must be in keeping with his past, therefore we rejoice. Since he left us, time has to a certain extent mercifully softened the keenest first feelings of loss which his widow and children felt, yet they feel, as does the whole of Kennett and Dunklin county, that it is impossible to exactly fill his place, be his successor in the business and church spheres ever so good. He was a man who had the loftiest ideals and he came as near to attaining them as it is possible for any one to do.

SAM J. McMINN. A man firmly established in the business and social life of the county and intimately connected with the history of its development in Sam J. McMinn, now the assistant cashier in the Consolidated Bank, formerly the People's and the Bollinger County Banks. He was born in Buchanan, Missouri, in the southwestern part of Bollinger county, the date of his nativity being August 11, 1869. He is the son of W. A. and Elizabeth C. (Burk) McMinn. His father was a native of the county, and well known for his wise administration of the office of county judge. His grandfather, Samuel McMinn, was a native of North Carolina, who left the old North state in 1819 to try his fortunes in the then far western territory of Missouri. After the death of W. A. McMinn his wife, the mother of the subject of this brief personal review, continued to make her home on the old home farm, where she still lives. During his early life Sam J. McMinn attended the public schools of the county, and also did his share of the work on the parental farm. Following that took a course at the Kentucky University in Lexington, Kentucky, and was graduated from that institution.

In 1893 he began the business career that has made his name a guarantee of stability in any undertaking, and entered the merchandise and milling business at Zalma with his brother, Andrew J. McMinn. The two brothers operated the mill for their father, and managed the store as their own venture until 1897. In that year their father passed to the "Great Beyond," and left his affairs entirely in the hands of his sons.

From 1897 until 1899 Mr. McMinn took charge of the farm, an occupation which he gave up at his election on the Democratic ticket to the office of circuit clerk, an office in which he gave honorable and highly efficient service, which is evidenced by the fact that he was returned to office upon the expiration of his first term, thus making his tenure of that office eight years. In 1907 he entered the People's Bank in the capacity of assistant cashier, soon becoming cashier, a position of trust and responsibility which he held until the consolidation of the bank with the Bollinger county institution, June 7, 1911, upon which he assumed the position of assistant cashier of the Consolidated Bank. Besides stock in the bank, Mr. McMinn is a director and one of the principal stockholders of the Peoples Telephone Company, an Independent Company now operating in Bollinger, Wayne, Madison, Cape Girardeau, Iron and Stoddard counties; is also a stockholder and director of the Lutesville Milling Company; has a half interest in a tract of farming and woodland of one thousand nine hundred and seventy acres, and himself owns one thousand eight hundred and fifty acres and some fine residence property in Marble Hill.

In 1903 was solemnized the marriage of Mr. McMinn to Miss Maude Conrad, the charming and accomplished daughter of Judge Conrad, of Bollinger county. She was summoned to eternal rest in April, 1909, leaving one son, Samuel Joseph, Jr., born in 1904.

Mr. McMinn's cordial personality finds natural outlet in his fraternal relations, and he is a prominent member of the esteemed Masonic order, being affiliated with the A. F. & A. M. at Fredericktown, the Commandery at Cape Girardeau, and having taken the thirty-second degree, Scottish Rite, at Saint Louis. Mr. McMinn is also a member of the Benevolent and Protective Order of Elks, the Independent Order of Odd Fellows and the Knights of the Maccabees, in all of which he maintains an active interest.

T. C. McHANEY. A prosperous druggist of Senath, and one of its substantial and prominent business men, T. C. McHaney is an important factor in promoting its advancement, and is held in high repute as a man and a citizen. He was born April 22, 1876, in Henderson county, Tennessee, where he was bred and educated.

Beginning life for himself at the age of seventeen years, Mr. McHaney entered a drug store as a clerk, and proved himself so well adapted for the business that he made himself familiar with its every detail, in due course of time becoming a skilled pharmacist. In 1901 he located at Senath, Missouri, where he has since built up a large and lucrative trade, his patronage having steadily increased from year to year. He has made wise investments in real estate, and now owns a farm of eighty acres lying about two miles from Senath, and this he rents to tenants, who devote almost the entire tract to the growing of cotton.

Mr. McHaney married, April 20, 1903, Grace Sando, who was born in Indiana, but was brought up in Dunklin county, Missouri, her early home having been near Cotton Plant. The following children have been born of their union, namely: Robert, Neal, James, Elizabeth and Nellie. Politically Mr. McHaney is an earnest suporter of the principles of the Democratic party, and in local campaigns is quite active. Fraternally he belongs to the Woodmen of the World. Mrs. McHaney is a most estimable woman, and a valued member of the Christian Church.

FELIX J. PARKIN. A citizen of prominence and influence at Fredericktown, Missouri, is Judge Felix J. Parkin, who gave efficient service for a period of four years as county judge of Madison county, retiring from that office in 1910. At the present time he is engaged in the abstract business, having launched out into that line of enterprise in 1900. Judge Parkin was born in Madison county, Missouri, on the 18th of September, 1859, his parents being Joseph T. and Mary (Lanpher) Parkin. The father, who is still living, resides at Fredericktown and the mother passed to the life eternal in 1876, at the age of thirty-seven years. Joseph T. Parkin was likewise born in Madison county, this state, and he is descended from stanch English stock, his father, Joseph Parkin, having immigrated to America from England prior to the year 1818. On his arrival in the United States Joseph Parkin proceeded directly to Missouri, locating in Madison county, where he entered a tract of government land, the same consisting of six hundred and forty acres. At one time he operated a grist mill in Madison county and he was the first miner in southeastern Missouri to use powder. He and his brother, Thomas Parkin, with others, came together from England. The Parkin brothers conducted a mill one mile west of Fredericktown, in 1838, and subsequently they were engaged in mining and milling enterprises for a number of years, using negroes for the work. Both these pioneer brothers are buried in the family cemetery on the old farm near Fredericktown.

Joseph T. Parkin was reared to the invigorating discipline of his father's farm and his rudimentary educational training consisted of such advantages as were afforded in the schools of the locality and period. He was identified with agricultural pursuits during the greater portion of his active career but he is now living in virtual retirement at Fredericktown, enjoying to the full the fruits of his former years of earnest toil and endeavor. In 1858 was solemnized his marriage to Miss Mary Lanpher, who traced her ancestry to stanch French extraction, her mother having been a member of the celebrated Nifong family. Mr. and Mrs. Joseph T. Parkin became the parents of two children,—Lizzie, who married Robert Murray and who died in 1884; and Felix J., the immediate subject of this review.

Judge Parkin passed his boyhood and youth at Fredericktown, where he attended the public schools. At the age of eighteen years he went to Colorado, where he maintained his home for fourteen years and where he was most successfully engaged in mining operations. For a period of four years he was circuit court clerk and recorder in Ouray county, Colorado. Eventually disposing of his interests in that state, he returned to Missouri, in 1891, engaging in farming operations in Madison county for the ensuing nine years. In 1900 he turned his attention to the abstract business and it is worthy of note here that he has the only complete set of abstract records in Madison county, the same including all the old records. In politics Judge Parkin is an unswerving advocate of the principles and policies for which the Democratic party stands sponsor and while he is not an office seeker he is deeply and sincerely interested in community affairs. In 1907 he was elected judge of Madison county and he was the able and popular incumbent of that important office for a period of four years, retiring therefrom at the close of 1910.

In 1890 was recorded the marriage of Judge Parkin to Miss Minnie Watts, a daughter of Napoleon B. Watts, a sketch of whose career appears on other pages of this work, so that further data concerning the family history is not deemed essential at this juncture. Mr. and Mrs. Parkin are the parents of three children, whose names and respective ages, in 1911, are here entered,—Maurice, seventeen years; Lelia, fourteen years; and Reva, seven years. In their religious faith the Parkin family are devout members of the Baptist church and they are popular factors in connection with the best social activities of Fredericktown, where their spacious and attractive home is recognized as a center of gracious refinement and hospitality. In a fraternal way the Judge is an appreciative member of the local lodge of the Independent Order of Odd Fellows. He is a man of broad human sympathy and generous impulses and in the various walks of life is honored and esteemed as a man of high ideals noble principles.

WILLIAM C. BERGMANN. The United States ranks as the foremost nation of the modern civilized world. It has served as the melting pot of the best characteristics of all other nations and the outcome is a fine sterling American citizenship consisting of strong and able bodied men, loyal and public-spirited in civic life, broad-minded and honorable in business, and alert and enthusiastically in sympathy with every measure tending to further the material welfare of the entire country. The great Empire of Germany has contributed its fair quota to the upbuilding of this great nation and among its representatives in this country are to be found successful men in every walk of life, from the professions to the prosperous farmer and business man. William C. Bergmann, whose name forms the caption for this article, was born in Germany but he has resided in the United States since he was a child of eight years of age. He has maintained his home at Cape Girardeau for fully a half century and here he has long been engaged in the general merchandise business. He is a fine old veteran of the Civil war and as a citizen and well known business man he commands the unqualified confidence and esteem of all with whom he has had dealings.

William C. Bergmann was born at Brünswick, Germany, on the 16th of February, 1841, and he is a son of Dr. Staats Henry Bergmann, who held distinctive prestige as a skilled physician and surgeon at Cape Girardeau during the period of his residence in this city. Dr. Bergmann was married to Miss L. C. Lehne in his native land and to them were born five children, three of whom were born in Germany and of whom the subject of this sketch was the second in order of birth. In 1849 the Bergmann family immigrated to the United States and settlement was made immediately in Cape Girardeau county, Missouri, where for the ensuing few years the father was engaged in agricultural operations. Dr. Bergmann removed to this city in 1851 and here he was engaged in the practice of his profession until the time of his demise, in 1862. The mother was summoned to the life eternal at an advanced age.

To the public and private schools of Cape Girardeau William C. Bergmann is indebted for his preliminary educational training. When eighteen years of age he left school and engaged in the portrait business, continuing to be identified with that line of enterprise for a period of three years. At the time of the inception of the Civil war he tendered his services as a soldier in the Home Guards, serving in that capacity for a period of three months. In 1863 he enlisted in the Eighth Provisional Regiment of the Missouri Militia, in which he was first sergeant for six months. As a Union soldier he saw some hard fighting and after the close of the war, when he had received his honorable discharge, he returned to Cape Girardeau, where he engaged in the general merchandise business. In this connection he had been exceedingly prosperous and his present large, well-equipped establishment is recognized as one of the finest of its kind in the entire city. A large and representative trade is controlled and the business is now largely in the hands of Mr. Bergmann's sons, W. F. and A. W. Bergmann.

In the year 1868 Mr. Bergmann was united in marriage to Miss Mary C. Eggimann, whose birth occurred in this county and who is a daughter of B. Eggimann, and to them have been born nine children.

While not a politician, strictly speaking, Mr. Bergmann gives a stanch allegiance to the principles and policies for which the Republican party stands sponsor. He is always ready to do all in his power to advance the best interests of the community in which he resides and while he has never manifested aught of ambition for the honors or emoluments of public office of any description he was honored by his fellowcitizens, in 1900, with election to the office of city treasurer. He was the popular and highly efficient incumbent of that position for a period of nine years and during all that time discharged the duties connected therewith with all of honor and distinction. He is deeply and sincerely interested in educational affairs and for eleven years was a member of the board of education. In their religious belief the Bergmanns are devout and valued members of the Lutheran church and they are popular and prominent factors in connection with the best social activities of the community. Thrifty and industrious, Mr. Bergmann is eminently well deserving of the admirable success it has been his to achieve and it is with pleasure that a history of his life and career is here inserted.

DAVID W. BREID is one of the representative attorneys of this part of Missouri and is a member of the Franklin Realty Company of Union. He is a native of the state and was born near Fulton, Callaway county, February 1, 1873. Nicholas Breid, his father, was a farmer, and was born in Trier, Prussia, in 1830. Like many another of his countrymen he hearkened to the call of Opportunity from the shores of the New World and arrived in this country shortly before the Civil war. He located in Juniata county, Pennsylvania, and entered the volunteer army of the United States, spending two of the dread years of the great conflict between the states in Sherman's army, battling with the forces of the Confederacy. Soon after the war he brought his family to Missouri and engaged in farming in the vicinity of Fulton, where he was gathered to his fathers in 1892. He married Susan Cleck, a daughter of David Cleck, of Juniata county, Pennsylvania, and the surviving children of their family of twelve are as follows: Isaac R.; Charles; Mary, wife of John R. Level; Dr. Jacob, who is in the government service at Washington, D. C.; William; David W., immediate subject of this record; Samuel; Martha, now Mrs. Pease; and Helena, wife of Gooch Bartley. All save David W. and Dr. Jacob are residents of Callaway county, Missouri.

Mr. Breid spent nearly the first thirty years of his life upon the farm of his birth. He acquired his education in Avalon College, Trenton, Missouri, after completing the curriculum of the country school, and then spent several winters as a teacher in the rural schools near his home. In 1902 he left the farm and took a position with the meat inspection department of the government at St. Louis, spending six years in the service. While there he prepared himself for the law by night study and school attendance and was admitted to the bar by the supreme court of Missouri in 1907. In 1909 he removed to Union and identified himself with the Franklin county bar. He soon afterward entered the real estate business and is associated with Mr. A. W. Hoffman in exploiting the lands of this county. The Franklin Realty Company works in harmony with the migration department of the Rock Island Railway and a thrifty and vigorous new citizenship is being introduced into the county on this account.

In the matter of political conviction Mr. Breid is a Republican and stands high in party councils. He is active in public life and in times past has served as justice of the peace in Union. At the present time he is assistant prosecuting attorney of the county under William L. Cole, and he is police judge of Union and city attorney of St. Clair. He is interested in the success of good government and aids in the promotion of social and professional harmony by a straightforward course as a citizen.

Mr. Breid laid the foundation of a happy union when on January 4, 1904, he was married to Miss Maytie Rose Freiberger, daughter of Godfrey Freiberger, their wedding being at Fulton, the bride's home. They have no issue.

In his fraternal association Mr. Breid is past venerable consul of the Modern Woodmen and is affiliated with the Independent Order of Odd Fellows.

GEORGE BIDEWELL presents that happy combination of farmer and scholar which, though not unusual, is seldom found in the measure that makes a successful teacher out of a fine farmer.

The subject of the present sketch was born May 18, 1885, a son of Henry and Lucrecia Bidewell. As stated elsewhere in this work, Henry Bidewell was a native of England, who came to this county in 1854. Upon the inception of the Civil war, his convictions brought him to the Union army. He joined Company K, Third Missouri Mounted Cavalry, in 1861 and remained in the war until its close, seeing much active service.

George grew up on his father's farm and attended the district school. He still lives on the extensive homestead which his father acquired, having bought out the shares of the other heirs. Like his brother he follows both general farming and stock raising on the two hundred and forty acre farm.

At the age of nineteen Mr. Bidewell entered Will Mayfield college at Marble Hill. Here he took a year's course and obtained a teacher's certificate. He has taught for four years and is still engaged in that profession.

In March, 1906, his marriage to Miss Jane Crites was solemnized. Mrs. George Bidewell is the daughter of J. M. and Adeline Crites and the sister of Charles Crites, another of the substantial farmers of Bollinger county, whose life is also briefly outlined in this work. Two of the three children born to Mr. and Mrs. George Bidewell are still living: Cletis, born in 1906, and Ivan, born in 1910. Mr. Bidewell's fraternal affiliations include the Ben Hur lodge and the Modern Woodmen. In politics he is aligned with the Republican party.

DAVID W. OWEN, proprietor of a fine farm and home in Dunklin county, was in debt when he began his career some twenty years ago. Depending on his own industry and good management, he has left his success to the destinies presiding over this great Southeast Missouri country, and it has rewarded him with a generous share of its general prosperity and fruitfulness.

He was born in Greene county, Arkansas, October 3, 1869. His parents were farmers, and along with most other residents of that section were poor. School facilities were meager, and he got about three months each year. When he was nineteen, in 1888, he married Miss Mary Rowe in Greene county. His liabilities showed a debt of thirty-six dollars, and his resources included nothing material, only the spiritual qualities of courage and industry possessed by his wife and himself. After their marriage they moved west to Lawrence county, Arkansas, where he made a crop on poor land, and in 1890 he came to Dunklin county, and for three years share-cropped north of his present place. He then bought a team on credit and began farming on a rented place. For six years he was on fifty-five acres near Hornersville, and during this time managed to get ahead a little. His next move was to the Uncle Nap Wilkins' farm a mile north of his present homestead, and he farmed at first fifty-five acres, then ninety-two acres, and the last year one hundred and fifteen acres. In 1900 he had bought forty acres now comprised in his present estate. It was all in the woods when he bought, and while he continued farming as a renter up to 1905 he improved his other place, and when he moved to it in 1905 he was owner of eighty acres, which he at once began to clear up. He built his present comfortable cottage home of five rooms and also a good barn, sixty by sixty feet, has fenced his fields, and has all his original place in cultivation. In 1910 he purchased eighty acres more, half of which is in cultivation. He leases sixty acres of his place to a tenant. Corn is his principal crop, and he is known through the country-side as an industrious and prospering farmer and citizen, who has earned all he has. To supplement his income at different periods he has baled hay and hauled logs.

Mr. Owen affiliates with the Independent Order of Odd Fellows, the Modern Woodmen of America and the Mutual Protective League of Hornersville. In politics he is a Democrat, and is a member of the Methodist church, South. He and his wife are the parents of the following family: Suda, born December 30, 1890, now the wife of Thomas Hitt; Viola, born in 1891, died at the age of fifteen; Charles, born in 1893; Mary, born in 1897; Mattie, born in 1899; and Thomas, born in 1901.

Mr. Owen's parents were Rev. John Sylvester and South Carolina Owen, the former a minister of the Methodist Episcopal church, South, during all of his active life. He was born in Tennessee and died at Caruthersville, Missouri, in 1899, aged fifty-five years. He was a Mason and active in lodge affairs. His wife had died at the age of forty-two years, in 1887, in Arkansas. David W. Owen was the second of ten children, of whom six are living: Daniel, of Mississippi county, Arkansas; Lucinda (Lomax), of Dunklin county, Missouri; Willie, also of Dunklin county; Catherine (Busby), of Noble, Clay county, Arkansas; Walter, of Dunklin county, Missouri; and Caretha (Pitts), also of Dunklin county, Missouri. Mrs. David W. Owen was born in Greene county, Arkansas, in 1872, a daughter of John and Sarah Rowe, both now deceased, but early residents and farmers of Greene county, Arkansas.

JOHN T. MCKAY, practicing attorney at Kennett, is a man who has distinguished himself in the field of law, even as his father was noted as an educator. The father's achievements lie all in the past, but to the son, in addition to the deeds which may already have been accredited to him, belongs the precious present, the time when he can prepare for the future, the time when he can continue to work out that success which does not come unasked, but must be wrought out by ambition, plus preparation and work.

A brief survey of the early history of John T. McKay and his immediate ancestors will give us a fuller realization of his present status. Forty-two yars ago, January 11, 1869, John T. McKay was ushered into the world, the scene of his arrival being New Madrid county, Missouri. The grandparents of the subject of this sketch, Walter McKay and Mary (Holcomb) McKay, were natives of Georgia, where they spent the early years of their lives, were educated and married. In 1833, a few years after their marriage, Mr. and Mrs. Walter McKay left their home and came to Missouri, where they settled on a farm in New Madrid county. There they reared their children to maturity, educating them in the subscription schools of their vicinity. Mr. McKay gained the confidence of the people in the community, as is evinced by his election to the office of sheriff of the county, a position which he filled in an eminently satisfactory manner.

His son, John McKay, was born in the Georgian home of his parents, but had only hazy recollections of his southern birthplace, as he was only three years old when he came to Missouri with his parents. The early years of his life were spent in New Madrid county, where he attended the subscription schools, being self educated. He virtually spent his life as a teacher, for which he was admirably qualified both by nature and training. John McKay was possessed of the faculty of realizing the difficulties of the student and could explain all his perplexities in the most clear, concise manner. In addition to this, he was a disciplinarian of the highest type, as he was not only able to maintain order, but at the same time secure the good will and respect of his pupils. For a period of thirty years Mr. McKay taught in New Madrid, Stoddard and Dunklin counties, losing none of his force and interest during those several years of faithful work. He taught up to the age of sixty-seven, only two years before his death, his last professional work being in the preparatory schools of Dunklin county. He died in 1898, ending a life of self-sacrifice, as does every teacher who spends his years in unremitting efforts to develop the capabilities of others, for which abnegation, as a rule, the educator receives none of the credit. John McKay was twice married, his first wife being Miss Mary Adams, like himself a native of Georgia, who had come to Missouri with her parents when she was a young girl. She died in 1865, leaving two children to be the companions of their father, Virgil and Fernando. The latter died in 1884 and Virgil is a prominent attorney of Kennett, of whom mention is found elsewhere in this work. His second marriage was to Mary F. Adams, a native of Missouri, who died in 1879, leaving four children: Annie L., wife of J. H. Ham; John T.; Benjamin A.; and Ola O., wife of W. J. Allison.

John T. McKay, one of the four children mentioned, spent the first four years of his life in New Madrid county, where he was born, his father then moving to Stoddard county, Missouri. When he was eleven years old his mother died and the same year his father brought his family to Dunklin county. There John T. McKay attended the public schools and afterward entered the normal school at Cape Girardeau. Without any deliberate planning on his part, it seemed natural that he should follow in his father's footsteps and enter the educational field, and when he was only eighteen he commenced to teach. Before long, however, he discovered that he had not the inclination to follow teaching, but was possessed of very decided tastes and capabilities in other directions. All his tastes seemed to point towards law as the calling in which he could best find scope for his talents. As he did not possess the funds to take a regular college course, he began to read law during the time he could spare from his teaching, working far on into the night in his eager desire to become proficient. His progress was not as speedy as it would have been if he could have devoted his whole time to study, but after ten years of teaching and of close application to his legal studies he was admitted to the bar before Judge Wear, in September, 1897. The success which was the immediate result of his admission to the bar and the commencement of practice was ample justification of Mr. McKay's choice of a profession.

On April 4, 1910, he formed a partnership with John H. Bradley. Mr. McKay has gained distinctive recognition and high reputation by reason of his broad and exact knowledge of jurisprudence and his ability in applying this information effectively, both as a trial lawyer and as a counselor.

On the 28th day of June, 1894, Mr. McKay was united in matrimony to Miss Lucy Laden, the daughter of R. A. Laden, an influential resident of Kennett. To the union of Mr. and Mrs. McKay one child was born, Weltha. Mrs. McKay died January 8, 1901, and on January 28, 1902, Mr. McKay was married to Miss Ethel McHaney, whose birth had occurred in Tennessee, but her education had been obtained in Kennett, where she lived until she was married and has since continued in the town where she has passed most of the years of her short life.

If we were called upon to decide which profession is the more worthy, that of a lawyer or a teacher, we should be utterly at a loss, but comparisons are unnecessary; both are noble professions and both call forth the highest quality of ability and endeavor. Mr. McKay, as an influential lawyer, holds the power to do an immense amount of good for the state of Missouri, and being a loyal Missourian, he is availing himself of every opportunity. He is especially devoted to Dunklin county, where he has spent practically his entire life and where he has a great future before him.

CARR HARTSHORN. It is indeed a pleasure to the publishers of this work to offer in its pages an appreciation of the young men of southeastern Missouri, to whom this portion of the state must look for its future prosperity and prestige. Among the able young men of Saint Francois county is eminent Carr Hartshorn, cashier of the Bank of Elvins and former postmaster of the place. Mr. Hartshorn is a man of varied abilities and he preceded his present manner of usefulness as a teacher, clerk in a grocery establishment, assistant postmaster and then incumbent of the office.

Carr Hartshorn, whose name inaugurates this review, was born August 13, 1877, and is a son of John Hartshorn, who was born in St. Louis county, Missouri, December 20, 1830. The senior Mr. Hartshorn came to Saint Francois county in 1872, a few years previous to the birth of the subject. In March, 1875, he was united in marriage to Susan Adeline Evans, and to their union were born three children, namely: Carr, David, of Kansas City, Missouri, and Susie, deceased. The mother was a daughter of David and

Catherine Evans, pioneer farmer-folk of Saint Francois county. The father of the subject came to Saint Francois county as a school teacher and afterward engaged in newspaper work, becoming the editor of the *Saint Francois County Democrat*. John Hartshorn, although a prominent man, was not an office holder, for he was a Republican in his views, and in his day a Republican had little chance in local politics. He belonged to the Independent Order of Odd Fellows and he and his wife were consistent members of the Presbyterian church. This gentleman died in April, 1895, and his cherished and devoted wife was summoned to the life eternal in August, 1906.

Carr Hartshorn passed his early life in Farmington and after receiving his preliminary education in the public schools of that city he attended a trio of collegiate institutions, namely: Elmwood, Carlton and Baptist Colleges, his name being enrolled at these for short terms. His education acquired, he taught school for a couple of years and then accepted a position in a grocery concern at Farmington. His identification with Elvins dates from July, 1899, and in the years intervening he has accomplished much. For a time he worked in a local grocery—that of J. C. Westover—and at the same time engaged in the duties of assistant postmaster, to which office he was appointed. He was subsequently appointed to a similar position at Desloge, but eventually returned to Elvins and found employment in the Evans & Howell Store Company. After remaining there for a time he was appointed postmaster by President Roosevelt, in the month of January, 1908, and has held that office to the present time. In 1911 he became cashier of the Bank of Elvins, and in addition to the important duties of this post, he also carried on a large fire insurance business. He owns considerable real estate and is helpfully interested in all that pertains to the prosperity of Elvins and Saint Francois county.

On the 7th day of August, 1902, Mr. Hartshorn was happily married to Mary Belle Dunklin, of Flat River. Their union has been blessed by the birth of three children, whose names are Harold, John Carr and Helen.

The family are Calvinistic in their religious conviction and attend the Presbyterian church, to whose good causes they willingly contribute their assistance. The fraternal relations of the subject extend to the Ancient Free and Accepted Masons, the Independent Order of Odd Fellows, the Knights of Pythias and the Modern Woodmen of America. In politics he gives warmest allegiance to the Republican party and is a very active member of the county Republican committee, to which he has belonged for fully ten years.

Dr. Gustav B. Schulz, the prominent physician and surgeon of Cape Girardeau, is universally respected. He is considered a most skilled surgeon by the members of the profession, indeed he specializes in that branch. This has not been the result primarily of deliberate intent; he has not sought the specialization, but rather it has been thrust upon him by reason of his marked abilities in that line. The man, in the medical profession, who specializes before he has had much experience in general practice, is apt to make a mistake. It is only after he has established his general practice that his ability along certain lines is apt to show itself. So it was with Dr. Schulz.

He was born in Wittenberg, Perry county, Missouri, September 13, 1870, and was the son of a physician, Dr. F. B. Schulz, who was a native of Germany, where he received his education, both general and medical. He came to America when he was a young man and after a short stay in New York, he went to Texas, where he practiced medicine. There he met and married Augusta Zedler, a young German girl who had come to America with her parents locating in Texas. There Augusta received her education. In 1876 Mr. and Mrs. Schulz came to Missouri and located in Cape Girardeau. He soon gained repute as an able physician and he remained at Cape Girardeau in active practice until the time of his death in 1908, having survived his wife by ten years.

Gustav came to Cape Girardeau with his parents, his four half brothers and sisters and his six full brothers and sisters when he was six years old. He entered the public schools, then St. Vincent's college and the state normal school. At that time he had no intention of following in the footsteps of his father, but rather had let his choice of a profession wait until circumstances should decide. After leaving the state normal school he entered a drug store, but it was only a very short time before he decided that he did not care to be a business man, but that on the other hand he felt strong desire to study medicine. He stayed at the store for two years, studying hard all the spare time he could get. He then entered the St. Louis University and graduated from its medical department in 1892. After spending one year in the city hospital he located at Altenburg, Perry county, Missouri, where he remained for ten years and a half, engaged in general practice. In December, 1903, he came to Cape Girardeau, where he has been ever since. Although he is a general practitioner, his abilities in the surgical line have caused him to be considered somewhat of a specialist. He is a member of the Cape Girardeau County Medical Society, of the Missouri State Medical Society and of the American Medical Association. He is a member of the state board of health and of the city board of health. He is a Republican of a very decided character. He is greatly interested in all matters pertaining to public welfare and especially in educational ways. He realizes the advantages to be gained from an education, the culture that it gives, the satisfaction that is gained by its possession, apart from the dollars and cents that it helps one to gain. He is president of the board of education, always active in promoting the welfare of both pupil and teacher. He is a man who is only at the beginning of his career, but he has already made his presence felt in the county.

BENJAMIN H. HUGHES. "Some men are born to greatness; some achieve greatness, and some have greatness thrust upon them." The "greatness" which Mr. Hughes enjoys has been achieved my him. Born and reared on a farm, it was entirely owing to his own capabilities that the responsible position which he so ably fills was bestowed on him, and was even thrust on him a second time.

Mr. Hughes was born October 24, 1875, in St. Francis township, Wayne county, Missouri. He belongs to the Hughes family who are so well known as pioneers in Wayne county. Mr. Hughes' grandfather, William Hughes, was a native of Virginia, where he was educated and learned the blacksmith trade. He was there married and thence came to Missouri, locating near Lodi, Wayne county, on some wild land which he proceeded to bring under cultivation. There his first wife died and he married a second, Miss Delphia Brown, and to this union A. C. Hughes (father of Ben. H.) was born, February 2, 1849, in Cedar Creek township. Grandfather Hughes trained his son in the knowledge of farming and also blacksmithing, and with these two industries Mr. A. C. Hughes has occupied himself. When a young man he purchased a farm four miles west of Greenville, Missouri, and settled on the wild, uncultivated prairie, which he gradually cleared and improved until it became a productive farm. His wife was Martha Rodgers, born in Carter county, Missouri, who died when she was thirty-three years of age, in 1886. Mr. and Mrs. A. C. Hughes became the parents of seven children, five of whom are living, and all are residents of Wayne county. Their names are as follows,—W. W., living near the old homestead which his grandfather owned in St. Francis township; Benjamin; Joseph D.; G. W.; and Lulu, the wife of William H. Lane. Father Hughes is living a retired life on the farm which his son superintends, and where the father spent so many years of his life and where he still retains the interests of his youth. He has always been a stanch Democrat, but has never desired any public office for himself. He has for years held membership in the Missionary Baptist church—the church in which he and his young wife worked together during the short years of their wedded life.

Ben. Hughes obtained his education in the district school of the township and after leaving school he assisted his father with the work of the farm, remaining at home until 1906. In the fall of 1906 he was elected to the office of treasurer of Wayne county, and that his services in the capacity of treasurer were eminently satisfactory is evinced by the fact that in 1908 he was reelected to the same office to serve a four-year term. In January, 1910, he became cashier of The Iron Exchange Bank for a year.

Mr. Hughes was married to Miss Sarah Eads on the 11th day of April, 1901. Mrs. Hughes is a daughter of J. N. Eads, formerly a prosperous farmer in Wayne county, where he died in the year 1907. Mr. and Mrs. Hughes are the parents of five sturdy sons,— Ralph, Robert, Raymond, Roy and Russell; they lost one son, Richard, by death. Both husband and wife are members of the Baptist church, where they have many friends. Mr. Hughes has always been aligned as a Democrat, and in a fraternal way he is affiliated with the Masonic Order, the Independent

Order of Odd Felows, the Rebekahs and the Modern Woodmen of America. His is a personality that wins friends and admirers in all his relations of life—political, fraternal, religious and social.

G. B. SNIDER, cashier of the Bank of Marble Hill and one of the leading citizens of the town, is as popular as he is influential. Throughout his career his maxim has been to do the duty which lies nearest, not worrying about what the next might be, and it is because of this simplicity of action that Mr. Snider has made such an unmitigated success of his life up to the present time, He has by no means reached the limit of his capabilities, and it is safe to predict that inasmuch as he has heretofore filled all positions in a highly satisfactory manner, that he will continue to have greater responsibilities thrust upon him.

Mr. Snider's birth occurred January 27, 1880, near Laflin, Bollinger county, on the old homestead which has been in the family for one hundred years or more. Early in the nineteenth century George Snider (one of G. B. Snider's ancestors) came from his home in North Carolina and took up a tract of land in Bollinger county, which he received by government grant; he cultivated the land and built the house which has remained in the family ever since. His son was Andrew Snider, who married and farmed in Bollinger county and there reared his family; one of his children was George P., the father of G. B. Snider. Mr. George P. Snider passed his whole life on the old homestead, engaged in agricultural pursuits. As a young man he married Miss Martha E. Clippard, and to this union one son, G. B., was born. The father died when their son was a mere child and in course of time the mother married again. She is now living in Kennett, the wife of Dr. W. B. Finney of that town.

G. B. Snider received his preliminary educational training in the public schools and was graduated from the State Normal at Cape Girardeau in 1900. When he was twelve years old he accompanied his mother to Kennett and remained there until 1902, when he returned to Marble Hill in Bollinger county. The last two years of his residence in this county he was the editor of the *Bollinger County Times*. In 1902 he sold his interest in the paper, moved to Laflin and entered the mercantile business. In 1906 he commenced his connection with the Bank of Marble Hill, serving successively as bookkeeper, assistant cashier and later as cashier, which responsible position he still occupies. Mr. Snider was one of the original stockholders, as the bank was organized in 1906, with C. A. Sanders, M. D., as its president. During the five years of its existence the stockholders have each year received dividends and the capital is now fifteen thousand dollars. Today (1911) the deposits amount to fifty-one thousand dollars and the bank is doing a thriving business under the management of its efficient cashier. Mr. Snider has other interests besides his bank connection; he is a stockholder of the Advance Telephone Company and is the owner of two hundred and seventy-five acres of land in Bollinger county and another tract of one hundred and twenty acres in Dunklin county.

On the 17th day of December, 1903, Mr. Snider was united in marriage to Miss Anna Drum, a daughter of Senator Robert Drum, of Marble Hill. Mr. Snider is affiliated with the Masonic fraternal order and with the Benevolent and Protective Order of Elks, his direct membership in the former being in the Blue Lodge at Marble Hill, Ancient Free and Accepted Mason, and he holds membership with the Elks at Cape Girardeau. His is the personality that gains friends, who respect him for his sterling characteristics and esteem him for his genial, affable manners.

W. T. CANEER, JR. Possessing in an eminent degree the energy, keen foresight and sound judgment that ever command success in the business world, W. T. Caneer, Jr., general manager of the Caneer Store Company, holds a place of note among the leading merchants of Senath, and is numbered among the representative citizens of Dunklin county. A native of Tennessee, he was born July 29, 1866, in Gibson county, near Milan, where the days of his youth were spent.

Soon after attaining his majority Mr. Caneer spent a year in Missouri, and was so well pleased with its future possibilities that when looking about for a permanent location he came to Dunklin county, in 1894 locating in Senath, which has since been his home. The following four years he was employed as a clerk in the store of Caneer & Karnes, and then, with his brothers, bought the entire business, which was conducted for several years under the firm name of Caneer Brothers, he being manager of affairs.

In 1904 the Caneer Store Company was incorporated, with a capital of fifty-two thousand dollars, and is now doing an immense business, its trade extending not only throughout the southern portion of Dunklin county, but over a large portion of Arkansas. This business was founded by J. I. Caneer, who at the inception of the town of Senath established the first mercantile house in the place, it being a small building, sixteen by twenty-four feet. He began on a modest scale, and afterward enlarged his stock and his operations. In 1891 Mr. J. I. Caneer became sole proprietor of the business, which increased so rapidly that more commodious quarters were needed, and he erected a large frame building, which soon proved none too large for his extensive trade. In 1898 he with his two brothers, W. T. Caneer and A. A. Caneer, engaged in business together under the firm name of Caneer Brothers, W. T. Caneer becoming manager of the store and A. A. Caneer, bookkeeper, collector, etc. Mr. J. I. Caneer, who had been instrumental up to that time in the upbuilding of the business, simply holding a third interest in it. Mr. J. I. Caneer was a man of wonderful resources, and in addition to having managed a business amounting to about fifty thousand dollars a year had also made much money in the buying and selling of lands, and is now living retired in Los Angeles, California, although his financial interests are mainly in Missouri, as he retains an interest the Caneer Store Company and owns upward of a thousand acres of land in Dunklin county.

The Caneer Store Company is owned mostly by Senath people, and has the following named gentlemen as officers: A. W. Douglass, president; E. Baker, vice-president; A. T. Douglass, secretary; A. A. Caneer, treasurer; and W. T. Caneer, Jr., general manager. The store building which the firm occupies has a hundred feet frontage, and is one hundred and fifteen feet deep, a part of it being two stories in height, and in addition has outside warerooms. The Company carries on a general supply business, handling tools and implements of all kinds, its stock being valued at thirty-two thousand dollars, while its sales in this line amounts to upwards of one hundred thousand dollars annually. The firm likewise handles hay, feed and cotton, buying and ginning about fifteen hundred bales of the latter production each year, its sales from cotton exceeding one hundred and twenty-five thousand dollars a year.

Mr. W. T. Caneer is also interested in Missouri lands, Caneer Brothers owning large tracts that are under cultivation and are highly productive. He is also a stockholder and the vice-president of the Citizens' Bank of Senath. He is a stanch Republican in politics, and fraternally is a member of the Independent Order of Odd Fellows and of the Woodmen of the World.

Mr. Caneer married, in 1903, Kate Lawson, a daughter of the late Moses Lawson, of Kennett, who was for many years a prominent attorney and county official of Dunklin county. Mrs. Caneer passed to the higher life November 19, 1909, leaving no children.

PETER R. CONRAD traces his ancestry in a direct line back to the Revolution. He is the son of David, son of Peter, son of Rudolph, son of Peter, who probably came to America from Prussia about 1750. Rudolph and his brother Jacob went from the neighborhood of Harrisburg, Pennsylvania, to Lincolnton, North Carolina, during the Revolutionary days. Both brothers were soldiers in the Revolutionary war and probably witnessed the battle of Cowpens, accounts of which have been handed down to the children of the third and fourth generation; how the men rode two by two to battle under the gallant General Greene.

Rudolph Conrad was three times married. His first marriage was with a Miss Schuford. The issue of this union was one child, Daniel. By his union with Miss Shell, Rudolph had five children, Peter, Jacob Lewis, Mary (Kline), Susan (Baumgarten) and Charlotte (Plott). His third marriage was to Miss Stockinger, and their children were John Lewis, Ephraim, Rebecca, Elizabeth. Peter, the paternal grandsire of Peter R. of this sketch, married Sarah Abernathy, of North Carolina, and came to Missouri in 1820. David Conrad, the father of Peter R., was the oldest of his seven children. The others were Elizabeth, Jacob, William, Clarissa, George and Martha. The Conrads are a remarkably long-lived race and all these children except David and Martha lived to be over eighty. The latter died at the age of seventy-five and the former in 1890, at seventy-nine. George is supposed to be still living near Grinnell, Iowa, at the age of ninety-one. The father of this family was a cabinet maker by trade. He had been apprenticed to a worker in this craft when a boy, being bound out for a number of years, as was the custom of the time. When he came to Marble Hill he settled near an uncle, Casper Shell, who gave him five acres of land, planted in corn. Peter was very poor at the time of his arrival in the county, but before he died he accumulated a fair competence and a comfortable home. He died in August, 1842, at the age of sixty-two.

David R., son of Peter and father of Peter R., was born January 5, 1811. He married in 1833 Miss Mary Bollinger and lived and died on the farm now occupied by Daniel E. Conrad. This was a part of the old Spanish grant purchased by David R. from Frederick Slinkard. David Conrad had thirteen children, including Peter R., of this review; Jacob, who died on December 7, 1905, at the age of seventy; Moses, who passed away at sixteen years of age; Elizabeth, still living; John; Sarah and Priscilla, both deceased; Clarissa, wife of William Heitman; George E., born in 1852; Benton, who died at the age of nineteen; and Frances Jane, wife of Trustin Gideon.

Peter R. Conrad was educated in the county schools and at home. He had the advantage of the instruction of his parents, both of whom were well educated and cultured. Peter spent nearly two years at Pleasant Hill Academy, north of Jackson. He lived with his father until he was twenty-six years old, this being in the year 1860. At that date he began to farm for himself, but interrupted this peaceful pursuit a year later to enter the Union army.

The First Missouri Engineers was Peter Conrad's regiment and he gave three years of service to the country which his great-grandfather had helped to make an independent nation. He served as a sapper and a miner and in the signal corps, in the railroad repair work, in railroad building and in road making. In the course of performing this important work Mr. Conrad saw much hard service and was present at the bombardment of Fort Henry.

After the war agriculture again claimed Mr. Conrad's attention. He now owns two hundred and forty acres of land, one hundred of which is fine cleared land on Whitewater creek. He owns considerable live stock, including a small herd of sheep. A large fruit orchard is one of the most valuable sections of his farm.

Mr. Conrad does not permit his work to absorb all his attention. He is a man of broad culture and wide reading. Geology is one of his favorite studies and he has studied the geological formation of the region with which he is thoroughly familiar. He is famed as a collector of minerals and Indian implements, as well as other curios. His collection of stone implements used by the Indians is one of the finest private collections in the state.

Mr. Conrad has been twice married. His first wife was Anna Nugent, daughter of John H. Nugent, of West Virginia. Their marriage took place in May, 1860, and the union lasted until Mrs. Conrad's death, twenty-one years afterward. They had nine children, seven of whom are living. The names and dates of birth of the children are as follows: Rudolph, June 3, 1861; William, September 15, 1865, and died at the age of nine; John I., May 20, 1867; George, May 28, 1870; Mary, July 10, 1872; Albert, February 28, 1875; Arthur O., February 25, 1877; Augusta, February 22, 1878; and David, born June 2, 1869, who died in infancy.

In 1886 Mr. Conrad was married to Emma Griffith, the adopted daughter of Dr. C. N. Griffith. Mrs. Conrad is a native of Denmark. Her mother died on the ocean coming to America and her father in St. Louis in 1852. The infant daughter Emma was adopted by Dr. and Mrs. Griffith, of Iron county. Mr. and Mrs. Conrad have two children living, Frances Eleanor and Julius C. Two others, a son and a daughter, died in infancy.

Mr. Conrad is a member of the fast diminishing Grand Army of the Republic. He is of the political party of Lincoln, Grant and McKinley. In religious doctrines, he subscribes to those of the Presbyterian church, of which he is an honored and valued member.

MICHAEL DE GUIRE. Great men are great in their methods. As contrasted to ordinary men, they draw their plans on a larger scale —think in bigger units—trudge to further horizons—climb longer hills—contest in greater arenas, and accept no compromise from opportunity. It is the size of the game as well as the size of the man that spells success. Michael De Guire is a scion of one of the oldest pioneer families in Missouri, his father having come to what is now Madison county as early as 1790. He has ever been imbued with the ancestral spirit of enterprise and through his well directed endeavors has achieved a marvelous success as a business man and miller. He has lived retired from participation in active affairs since 1903, and while he has now attained to the age of seventy-four years he is still hale and hearty and manifests a keen interest in community affairs.

Michael De Guire was born in Madison county, Missouri, on the 5th of November, 1837, and he is a son of Paul and Sarah (Nifong) De Guire, the former a native of Ste. Genevieve, this state, and the latter a native of North Carolina. Paul De Guire was a son of Paul De Guire, who came to America from France prior to 1800 and settled on a farm in the vicinity of Fredericktown. Paul De Guire, with three other French families, hewed the road through the wilderness to Madison county, theirs having been the first wheeled vehicle to come over the trail. Paul De Guire, whose birth occurred in 1792, died in 1875, at the venerable age of eighty-three years. He was engaged in lead-mining, smelting and shipping during the greater part of his active career, his product having been manufactured and sold after being shipped to the Mississippi river, where it commanded a price of two and a half cents per pound. He had a number of slaves and hired other negro help to carry on his business. He was also an extensive farmer. He married, in 1821, Sarah Ann Nifong, whose birth occurred in North Carolina, in 1805, and who was descended from German ancestors. She came to Missouri as a child and died in 1887, at the age of eighty-two years. She and her husband were both devout comunicants of the Catholic church. Of their nine children the subject of this review was the fifth in order of birth and but three are living at the present time, namely,—Mrs. Elizabeth Allen, of Kansas City, Missouri; Mrs. Sarah Putnam, of California; and Michael, of this notice. At this juncture it is interesting to note that Paul De Guire owned the first hand-mill for grinding corn in this section of the state. The subject of this sketch still has the top stone in his possession, this being a very historical relic, as it represents part of the first mill of any description in Madison county.

Michael De Guire was reared to the pioneer life of his native place and his rudimentary educational training consisted of such advantages as were afforded in the schools of the locality and period. In 1854, at the age of seventeen years, he accompanied two of his brothers, A. A. and Henry, on the overland trip to California. A. A., G. W. and Henry De Guire went to California in 1849, being members of a company of twenty-five, of whom A. A. De Guire was the last survivor, his death having occurred on the 4th of June, 1911, in his eighty-third year. A. A. De Guire crossed the plains again in 1862, driving cattle, and he made two more trips in '63 and '64. In the latter years of his life he made three trips by railroad, making in all seven round trips to California. Michael De Guire remained in California from 1854 to 1858, devoting his time to mining enterprises and achieving marked success. With the exception of nineteen years he has spent his entire life in Madison county, having maintained his home in Fredericktown since 1876. For thirteen years he was engaged in the milling business in St. Francois county and subsequently he was identified with that line of enterprise in Madison county, devoting forty years to that particular project. He started out with a fifty barrel mill and for thirty years conducted a two hundred barrel mill, this mill being now operated by others, at Fredericktown. In 1877 he built a brick mill in this place and owned the same until 1903, when he retired. He recently sold a fine farm directly north of the town and he resides in his beautiful home on West Main street, where he has lived for the past twenty years.

On the 19th of December, 1861, Mr. De Guire was united in marriage to Miss Elizabeth Blanton, a native of Iron county, Missouri, and a daughter of Benjamin Blanton, who was born in Kentucky and who became a farmer in this state in an early day.

Mr. and Mrs. De Guire became the parents of two daughters, concerning whom the following data are here inserted,—Fannie married H. D. Christoff, who is a druggist at Fredericktown, and they have four children. Charles, John, Norman and Consuelo; and Flora, who is the wife of W. R. Nifong, of Oklahoma City, where he is a civil engineer, employed in setting up refrigerating and ice plants. They have two children, Jennie and Robert.

In politics Mr. De Guire is a Republican,

with Prohibition tendencies. He has never been ambitious for public office of any description but has served with efficiency as a member of the board of school directors. In their religious faith he and his family are devout members of the Methodist Episcopal church. Mr. De Guire is strictly a self-made man, having himself built the ladder by which he rose to affluence. All his business dealings have been characterized by fair and honorable methods and as a citizen he commands the unalloyed confidence and esteem of his fellow men.

SAMUEL BOUTIN. If those who claim that fortune has favored certain individuals above others will but investigate the cause of success and failure, it will be found that the former is largely due to the improvement of opportunity, the latter to the neglect of it. Fortunate environments encompass nearly every man at some stage of his career, but the strong man and the successful man is he who realizes that the proper moment has come, that the present and not the future holds his opportunity. The man who makes use of the Now and not the To Be is the one who passes on the highway of life others who started out ahead of him, and reaches the goal of prosperity in advance of them. It is this quality in Samuel Boutin that has made him a leader in the business world and won him an enviable name in connection with contracting and building affairs at Cape Girardeau, where he is recognized as a citizen whose loyalty and public spirit have ever been of the most insistent order.

Samuel Boutin was born in Windham county, Vermont, on the 19th of July, 1852, and he is a son of Joachim Boutin, who was born at Point Levis, Canada, the date of his nativity having been 1804. The grandfather of him to whom this sketch is dedicated immigrated to America from his native land of France in the latter part of the eighteenth century. After being reared and educated in Canada Joachim Boutin came to the United States, locating in the state of Vermont, where he turned his attention to agricultural operations. In 1826 was recorded his marriage to Miss Martha Warner and to them were born ten children, of whom Samuel was the seventh in order of birth and five of whom are living at the present time, in 1911. The father was summoned to the life eternal in the year 1879 and the mother passed away in 1883.

In the public schools of his native state of Vermont, Samuel Boutin received his elementary educational training. In 1872, at the age of twenty years, he decided to seek his fortunes in the west and in that year established his home at Hampton, Iowa, where he became interested in the contracting and building business, being associated in that line of enterprise with his brother, C. W. Boutin, until 1887. In the latter year he removed to Centerville, Iowa, where he was superintendent of bridge-building for the Keokuk & Western Railroad Company for the ensuing fourteen years. In 1901 he went to Gary, Oklahoma, where he was general roadmaster for the Choctaw & Northern Railroad for about one year, at the expiration of which he came to Cape Girardeau to accept a position as superintendent of bridges and construction work on the St. Louis & Gulf Road. In 1903 his territory was extended over the third district of the Frisco system and he remained with that road until March, 1905, at which time he went to Muskogee, in the Indian Territory, where he was roadmaster over the Midland Valley. In September, 1905, he returned to this city, where he was employed as general foreman by the Frisco system to build the Chaffee yards. In 1907 he was in Georgia with the Fall City Construction Company and soon thereafter was forced to give up railroading on account of the impaired condition of his health. In 1908 he came back to Cape Girardeau and here opened offices as contractor and builder. He has been eminently successful in this line of enterprise and by reason of his extensive experience has won renown for the excellent quality of his work.

At Hampton, Iowa, in the year 1874, Mr. Boutin was united in marriage to Miss Julia Crawford, who was born in Canada, a daughter of William Crawford. Mr. and Mrs. Boutin are the parents of four children, concerning whom the following record is here offered,—Maud is the wife of C. R. Porter, a prominent lawyer and politician at Centerville, Iowa; Lottie is now Mrs. A. S. Duckworth, her husband being engaged in the lumber business at Cape Girardeau; Ralph G. is a dentist by profession and is engaged in that work at Harper, Kansas; and Charles W. is auditor for the Bell Telephone Company in this city. In their religious faith the Boutin family are devout members of the Presbyterian church and they are popular factors in connection with the best social activities of Cape Girardeau.

In his political affiliations Mr. Boutin is aligned as a stalwart in the ranks of the Republican party but aside from membership in the city council he has not been active in politics. In the time-honored Masonic order he is a valued and appreciative member of St. Marks Lodge, Free & Accepted Masons; Royal Arch Masons; and St. John's Commandery, No. 21, Knights Templar. He is also connected with Za-Ga-Zig Temple, Ancient Arabic Order of the Nobles of the Mystic Shrine. Mr. Boutin is a man of fine mentality and broad human sympathy. He thoroughly enjoys home life and takes great pleasure in the society of his family and friends. He is always courteous, kindly and affable and those who know him personally accord him the highest esteem. His life has been exemplary in all respects and he has ever supported those interests which are calculated to uplift and benefit humanity, while his own high moral worth is deserving of the highest commendation.

CHARLES AUSTIN COLE. It is not to be gainsaid that there is no office carrying with it so much of responsibility as that of the instructor who moulds and fashions the plastic mind of youth; who instills into the formative brain those principles which, when matured, will be the chief heritage of the active man who in due time will sway the multitudes, lead armies, govern nations or frame the laws by which civilized nations are governed. To say that all learned men are capable of filling this high and important office is by no means the truth. One inclines to the belief that the true instructor is born and not made; he must have a vast knowledge of human nature; he must know not only what is in books, but what is in man, also, that is, he must understand his pupil and deal with his mind according to his individuality.

Professor Charles Austin Cole is one of the able and efficient educators of Franklin county and is superintendent of the Union public schools. He was born in this county and is descended from one of the earliest of the pioneers among the territorial settlers along the Missouri river. The honor of bringing the family patronymic into the state belongs to Jacob Cole, the grandfather of the subject, who came hither in 1797 from Lexington, Kentucky. Jacob Cole devoted his activities to pastoral and agricultural pursuits and was one of the highly known and highly honored men of his section.

Jasper Cole, a son of Jacob, was born in Missouri in 1831. Following in the footsteps of his father, he adopted as his own the great basic industry and beyond his assumption of the duties of the office of justice of the peace he had little connection with public affairs. During the Civil war his sympathies were with the Union and its preservation and he did his part as a member of the Missouri State Militia. He was Republican in politics. The death of this prominent man occurred at Shotwell in 1904, when his years numbered seventy-three. He married Mrs. Susan Cooper, widow of John Cooper and a daughter of Joseph Smith, a Kentuckian. Four sons and a daughter were born to the union, making a large household, for Mrs. Cole had the following children by her previous marriage with Mr. Cooper: John Thomas; Elizabeth, first Mrs. Seaton and afterward Mrs. Cowan; and James. The subject is the eldest in order of birth of the Cole family.

The country schools served to provide Charles A. Cole with his elementary education. He left his desk in the rural school to preside over a school of the same kind as its teacher and thus began what proved to be a life work in the domain of public education. While teaching he strengthened himself by home study and as a student in private schools, and advanced in the pedagogical profession to supervisor of graded schools. Normal training in the state institution at Cape Girardeau aided him materially in grasping the essentials of success as a teacher and manager in graded work, which he began as principal of the schools in Union in 1893. After a year he was elected principal of the schools of Washington and remained in such capacity for four years. He returned to Union at the end of that period and has since carried on his work here.

As an educator in the broadest sense Mr. Cole has acquitted himself creditably. For four years he was county school commissioner and during his regime the old practice of holding county institute prevailed and he was in command of the work of training the county teachers, as provided then by law. Since the abolishment of the old plan he has conducted a summer school in Union for teachers, and such as feel the need of a practical review of the common branches and of advice on method and management for a number of weeks each vacation season are afforded this great advantage. An experience of more than twenty years in the schoolroom has made Professor Cole a master in training both the pupil and the teacher. His high scholarship has been awarded recognition by a state life certificate issued by State Superintendent William T. Carrington.

In politics Mr. Cole is a Republican and his inclination to participate actively in the bouts of his party in the county have been occasionally gratified. He won the Republican nomination for county clerk from a competitor who had been incumbent of the office for sixteen years and who had held other offices as long, totaling thirty years continuous office holding, but was defeated in the election by the disloyalty of his beaten opponent to the party ticket. He has served as secretary of the county central committee and has mingled frequently and fraternally among the public men of both his county and state.

Mr. Cole was married in Franklin county, December 24, 1891, his chosen lady being Miss Cora Fitzgerald, a daughter of W. H. and Talitha Fitzgerald, who were among Franklin county's old settlers. The first Mrs. Cole died March 3, 1905, the mother of three children: Raymond W., Edith M. and Herbert Allan. For his second wife Mr. Cole married Miss Minnie Faughnder, daughter of George W. and Sarah Faughnder, who came to Missouri from the Old Dominion. Their union was celebrated August 29, 1906, and their home is one of the attractive and hospitable abodes of the town. There are no children.

Fraternally Mr. Cole holds membership in the State Teachers' Association of Missouri and he is past chancellor of the Knights of Pythias. He is one of the elders of the Union Presbyterian church.

CHARLES M. CRITES. Born July 6, 1887, Mr. Charles Crites has most of his history yet before him. His parents, J. M. and Adeline Crites, were both born in Bollinger county, this state. J. M. Crites bought a quarter section of land near Dongola in 1901, being an experienced farmer during his entire active life.

His death in 1910, aged fifty-six years, has left the two sons, Charles and Henry to manage the farm. Stock and general farming engage the attention of the two young men. Mr. Crites is a Republican in politics, and while not active in political circles is none the less counted one of the influential citizens of Dongola, both personally and politically.

J. W. TIMBERMAN, the county sheriff, is a man who stands high in the esteem of the people of Kennett. For a man to make a success of his life under any circumstances is a subject for congratulation, but when he has all the difficulties to encounter that Mr. Timberman has surmounted he may justly be proud of himself. As a matter of fact, however, Mr. Timberman is a very modest man in regard to his own attainments and capabilities.

He was born near Clarkton in Dunklin county, January 25, 1872. His father was Mathew Timberman, a native of Virginia, who came to Missouri, where he bought a farm. He died in 1875. He married Margaret A. Rayburn, whose family had come from Mississippi. She has always remained with her son, J. W. Three daughters were also born to Mr. and Mrs. Timberman.

J. W. Timberman had the misfortune to lose his father when he was only six years old. His mother was left with the task of bringing up the little family of three girls and a boy. J. W. very early felt the responsibility of the family resting on his shoulders, as he tried in every way to spare his mother as much as possible. He was not able to get very much schooling himself, but he has educated his three sisters. He has done all kinds of work to keep things going. For ten years he operated a saw mill near Kennett. He worked on the farm which his father had bought near Clarkton, farming in the summer and clerking in a store in the winter. He moved to Kennett for the sake of his sisters, so that they could have more advantages in the way of education. In 1908 he was elected to the office of sheriff of the county, his term commencing January, 1909, and lasting four years. He is a representative Democrat and active in primary work. He is a member of several fraternal orders, the Independent Order of Odd Fellows, the Modern Woodmen of America, Ben Hur and the Masons. Mr. Timberman has never married, perhaps he has not yet found time or has not seen the right lady. His mother and he have always been most devoted to each other. He has found time in the midst of his busy life to devote a short period to the sports of hunting and fishing, being an adept at both.

THEODORE LEWIS BUNTE, JR. A well known citizen and enterprising business man of Saint Francois county is Theodore Lewis Bunte, Jr., cashier of the St. Louis Smelting & Refining Company, one of the important industrial concerns represented in this section. He was born September 27, 1874, at St. Louis, Missouri. He is of Teutonic extraction, his father, Theodore L. Bunte, Sr., having been born in Hanover, Germany, March 30, 1845, and the subject shares in those fine characteristics which have made the German one of our most valuable sources of immigration. The father came to America at the age of twenty-seven years and located in St. Louis, where he engaged in mercantile business. The year 1889 marks an era in his career, for in that year he abandoned the mercantile field and went into the smelting business with the St. Louis Smelting & Refining Company, engaging in general smelting. In 1873, the year after his immigration to this country, the father married Miss Bertha May, also from Germany, and to their union have been born three children, namely: T. L. Bunte, Jr.; Alma B., wife of W. H. Nance, and Lewis H. The father remained associated with the St. Louis Smelting Company until 1904, in which year he went back to his old occupation, the mercantile business, and he is thus engaged in St. Louis at the present time. He is in harmony with the policies and principles of government for which the Democratic party stands sponsor, and he is a member of the Lutheran church.

Theodore L. Bunte, Jr., spent his early life amid the scenes of his birth—the city of St. Louis. He received his education in the excellent public schools and was graduated from the high school. Very soon thereafter he entered business life and almost from the first he exhibited that fine executive capacity and acumen that has insured his success. He has been with the same company throughout the entire course of his career, first becoming associated with them in 1892, the year he finished school, and remaining with them in St. Louis until 1900. In that year Mr. Bunte came to Saint Francois county, representing the same company with which he now holds the office of cashier, headquarters being located at the lead mines. It is not to be gainsaid that much of the prosperity of the concern in this locality is due to the part he has played in its management.

Mr. Bunte was married in 1898, Miss Louise A. Jacobi, of Kirkwood, Missouri, becoming his wife and the mistress of his household. Their union has been further cemented by the birth of two children,—Marie and Lewis. Mr. and Mrs. Bunte are valued members of the Presbyterian church and are active in the best social life of the community. In politics Mr. Bunte is an adherent of the Democratic party and his fraternal interests extend to the Ancient Free and Accepted Masons, the Independent Order of Odd Fellows and the Order of Columbian Knights, in which three organizations he is a prominent and popular member.

ABNER BARROW. To owe one's success neither to chance nor to the happy circumstance of the fortunate struggles of one's forebears, but to be able to look back over one's life and see success coming as the result rather of innate talent, grit and manly persistence is a great thing. Few men are afforded this satisfaction, but Abner Barrow, now the honored and successful postmaster of Greenville, can recall the day when he came to Wappapello with the discouraging capital of thirty-five cents, from which small beginning he has wrought an ample competence for himself and his family, as well as gained the sincere respect and hearty liking of the community where he makes his home.

Abner Barrow was born in Jackson county, Illinois, June 29, 1858, a son of Marion and Elizabeth (Thomason) Barrow, both of whom were also natives of Jackson county. Besides the subject of this brief personal review they were the parents of the following children: Abner, John, James (deceased), George, Ed., Charles, Ellsworth, Frank, and Annie, the third child, is the wife of Ben F. Hill, of Hiram, Missouri. With this large family of brothers and one sister he was reared among the homely but pleasant surroundings of the Illinois farmstead, and enjoyed the educational advantages of the neighboring schools. After his marriage in 1882, to Miss Lewella Jones, the young couple started life on a small farm, but in the year 1886 he and his wife and his parents felt the call to a newer country, and, migrating to the state of Missouri, first settled in Wappapello, this state. From that time the elder Mr. Barrow worked as a tiller of the soil, dying in Greenville in February, 1893, at the advanced age of sixty-seven years. He had taught school in Illinois for many years. His wife survives him, and at present makes her home in Greenville. She is still young in appearance, although the date of her birth was in June, 1839.

Upon his settlement in Wayne county Abner Barrow engaged in the tie business, and was associated in his initial venture in that occupation with the Frisco & Hauck Railroad. Following that, he came to Greenville and took a tie contract for Mr. Halliday, whose section boss he subsequently became during Mr. Halliday's active interest in the building of the W. G. & St. L. Railroad. During the winter of 1892 Mr. Barrow managed the laying of the ties and steel through Greenville.

In this connection it is a pleasure to recall that Greenville owes much the same sort of gratitude to Mr. Barrow that Ohio owes to the famous "Johnny Appleseed," whose early efforts are responsible for most of the oldest apple orchards in that state, for it was Mr. Barrow who set out most of the maple trees that are at the present time one of Greenville's most attractive features. Before returning to work for Mr. Halliday in 1896 Mr. Barrow turned his attention to the occupation that had been his father's during his boyhood days in Illinois, and for a brief time returned to farming.

In the year 1897 he entered upon his first taste of public service, and accepted the position of postmaster, which position he held until 1904, when he resigned to further serve the public in the position of sheriff, to which office he was twice elected, for two terms of two years each. On April 8, 1909, he was again appointed to the postmastership of Greenville, and he returned to his former post.

By his first marriage Mr. Barrow became the father of six children, four of whom now survive, as follows: Lyman, of Bonne Terre; Malta, of East St. Louis; Waldo and Blanche. Three of the sons, Lyman, Malta and Waldo, with their uncle, Ellsworth Barrow, form the Barrow Quartette, well known in musical circles throughout southeastern Missouri. Lyman Barrow is a trombonist of ability and great renown, having toured the country as a trombone soloist two seasons with Wheeler's Marine Band, appearing in almost every state of the Union. He has been in the ranks of professional musicians for the past fourteen years. Malta Barrow has had long experience with various bands and orchestras throughout the country and has appeared as saxophone and trombone soloist on various occasions. Waldo Barrow has been a professional musician since twelve years of age, and is one of the youngest musicians appearing in concert to-day. His work is proclaimed by press and public of the highest type. Ellsworth Barrow, the uncle, was for a number of years a teacher of wind instruments.

In June, 1897, Mr. Barrow, of this review, contracted his second marriage, and Mrs. Alice (Baird) Barrow became the mother of one son, Ray, now at home. She died in September, 1909, aged thirty-six years. On March 27, 1911, Mr. Barrow was united in marriage with Mrs. Rachel Goodwin. Both Mr. and Mrs. Barrow are valued and devoted members of the Missionary Baptist church.

That Abner Barrow is indeed "one of the most popular and best-liked men in Greenville," as has often been said of him, is attested by the number of his appreciative and enthusiastic fraternal affiliations. He is a member of the time-honored Masonic order, a member of the Independent Order of Odd Fellows, a member of the Modern Woodmen of America and of the Court of Honor. In his political affiliations he avows a stanch allegiance to the "Grand Old Party," whose interests he has ever been ready to serve and to represent.

DR. JOHN D. PORTERFIELD, now retired from active practice, although he is not an old man, is one of Cape Girardeau's most respected citizens. A professional man, and above all a physician, may be looked upon as making more or less a sacrifice of himself to aid humanity and the cause of science. He receives less monetary returns for his work than a business man and yet as a general thing he has expended much more time and money in preparation for his career than has the business man. The physician who looks upon his profession as merely a means of livelihood is an utter failure. Monetary considerations had very little to do with Dr. Porterfield's choice of a calling. From the very beginning of his training he has felt that he wanted to learn all that it was possible for him to learn in regard to diseases and their cures. A most profound reader and thinker, he hailed every new discovery with the deepest interest.

He was born in Venango county, Pennsylvania, July 15, 1843. His father, Dr. Robert L. Porterfield, was also a physician, a native of Pennsylvania. He practiced in Pennsylvania and Illinois, locating in Danville about 1848. His father, William Porterfield, was of Scotch-Irish descent and served during the Revolutionary war. Dr. Robert Porterfield married Ann Donaldson, a native of Pennsylvania, of Scotch-Irish descent.

Dr. John D. Porterfield has little recollection of his Pennsylvania home amongst the mountains, as his parents moved away when he was very small. He was educated at Marietta, Ohio, and also attended the Jefferson Medical College at Philadelphia and the Missouri Medical College in St. Louis, Missouri. In 1864 he came to Cape Girardeau, but only stayed a very short time, not long enough to become established in his profession. He went to Commerce, Missouri, where he stayed for twenty-three years, practicing all the time. In 1888 he came to Cape Girardeau, where he has lived ever since. He has been in practice in southeastern Missouri longer than any physician in the state. About 1906 he retired from practice, leaving the carrying on of that work to his sons.

In 1866 he was married to Sarah Hall, who died in 1872. The following year he married Fannie B. Cullum, who came from Mobile, Alabama. To this union were born one daughter and three sons. The sons have all followed their father's profession, thus making three generations that have given themselves to the medical profession. Elmo, the eldest son, is practicing in St. Louis. John D., Jr., has taken his father's practice in Cape Girardeau. Lowry is a physician and surgeon in Chicago. All three sons are graduates of the Chicago University and Rush Medical College. Their sister Bulah C., is the wife of Harry H. Coffman, son of Dr. John Coffman, a practicing physician of southeastern Missouri.

In addition to his professional duties, the Doctor has taken an active part in public affairs. He was mayor of Cape Girardeau for one term. He is at present president of the Cape Girardeau Water Works and Electric Light Company. He was one of the organizers and is a director in the Southeast Missouri Trust Company and has other interests in farm lands. He is a prominent Mason; having joined that order in 1866, he has taken the thirty-second degree in Scottish rite masonry, one of the first men in southeastern Missouri to have that degree. He is also a member of the Elks, with a high standing in that organization. He was at one time Exalted Ruler and he took an active part in the erection of the new building, having raised the money to build same. The Doctor has lived in southeastern Missouri for forty-seven years, twenty-three years of that time in Scott county and the other twenty-four in Cape Girardeau county. Although he does not treat patients any more, he is by no means an idle man, but on the other hand is most active in all public affairs. Not only did he devote so many years of his own life to the science of medicine, but he has left three sons to carry on the work. There is no man in the county who has a wider reputation and no man who stands higher in the respect and affections of those with whom he comes in contact.

CARROLL P. BENNETT. Greenville owes a double debt to Carroll P. Bennett, for not only is he conspicuous as the scion of a family long known in Wayne county as sturdy supporters of all that was advanced for the best interests of the community, but, by his own enthusiasm and untiring energy he has led others after him, and has always shown, both in industry and public affairs, that quality of leadership which inspires others to go and do likewise.

Born near Coldwater on St. Francois river, Wayne county, December 14, 1871, he was the son of John L. and Mary (Mathes) Bennett. His father was born on Bear creek, Wayne county, March 7, 1845, and died at Piedmont February 11, 1906. His mother was also born on Bear creek, the date of her nativity being September 14, 1845, and she is still living, at Greenville, Missouri.

Not only were his father and mother born on Bear creek, but also his paternal grandfather, Larkin Bennett, 1810 being the year of his birth, and he survived to the ripe old age of eighty-seven years, his demise not occurring until 1897. His wife, who prior to her marriage was Miss Mary Hughs, came to Wayne county with her father who migrated to that district at an early date and there entered a farm. The father of Larkin Bennett and the great-grandfather of the citizen to whom this record is dedicated was a native of North Carolina, who migrated from that state, moving first to Kentucky, and subsequently to Wayne county, where he located on section 30.

The maternal grandfather of Carroll Bennett, Milburn Mathes, was a native of eastern

Tennessee, who came early to Wayne county and died before his prime. His marriage with Jane Ivy is tinged with a bit of pioneer romance that helped to make bright those days of not too easy life in the sparsely populated districts of the middle southwest. She had started with her father and brother to found a home in the state of Kentucky, when she met, loved and consented to become the bride of Milburn Mathes.

Carroll P. Bennett was one of two children. His sister, who became Mrs. Jennie Barnett, died in 1906. He spent his early life in the invigorating and strength-giving environment of the home farm, and so satisfactorily did he complete his work in the common schools of the district that he in turn became teacher instead of the taught, and occupied the pedagogue's desk until 1898. In that year he came to Greenville and compiled a set of abstract books. He then entered the real estate and insurance business. Considering the fact that to all who know him "his word is as good as a U. S. bond," and that he has insight and farsightedness combined with an unusual portion of that quality of electric energy that marks the successful American business man, it is no wonder that every enterprise he undertakes prospers. Besides his substantial business interests already mentioned, he is the owner of two or three farms in Wayne county, and is vice-president of the Wayne County Bank.

On December 22, 1895, Mr. Bennett established the charming home that is now his by his marriage to Miss Effie Smith, born in Wayne county, near Piedmont. She is a daughter of William R. Smith, a prominent farmer of Wayne county and at one time sheriff and probate judge of the county. To them have been born three children, Hal, Mary and Hiram. Politically Mr. Bennett is recorded among the able and valued members of what its devoted adherents love to term "the Grand Old Party."

ALBERT A. FARNSWORTH is one of the well-known and representative farmers in Bollinger county. Since he first engaged in agricultural pursuits the status of a farmer has undergone a radical change and the man himself is viewed in a very different light from that in which we used to regard him years ago. A farm and a mortgage used at one time to be synonymous terms, and a man burdened with debt is not apt to be beautiful either in looks or disposition. Now all of this has been changed and "back to the farm" means a return to efficiency, health and life; we reach the farm by going forward, not by going backward. The business of the farmer who produces food must be regarded as a fine art, not to be left to the whipped-out and the discouraged, as in former times. Much of this changed condition has come about within the recollection of Mr. Farnsworth, and it is due to the work and example of such as he that ideas in regard to farmers have become so modified.

Mr. Farnsworth was born August 18, 1865, in Johnson county, Missouri, the son of Christopher L. and Nancy Caroline (George) Farnsworth, natives of Greene county, Tennessee. In the fall of 1854 Mr. and Mrs. Christopher Farnsworth came to Henry county, Missouri, with the idea of becoming permanently located there, but in the spring of 1855, they determined to move to Johnson county, where they raised their first crop that season. After harvest they bought a tract of land in Cass county, where they resided until General Ewing's command was issued to vacate the border counties, in 1863. They then returned to Johnson county and lived there until death summoned the father, March 7, 1909, while his widow still maintains her residence in the county. Mr. and Mrs. Christopher Farnsworth were the parents of ten children, nine of whom are living.

Albert A. Farnsworth, the seventh of the family in order of birth, was reared on his father's farm in Johnson county and attended the district school in his neighborhood. After completing his schooling he assisted with the work of the farm and remained at home until 1890, at which time he was twenty-four years of age. He then rented from his father a farm in Johnson county of one hundred and seventy acres in area, where he lived until March, 1910, the year following his father's demise. He removed to Bollinger county, and with the savings he had accumulated and his share of his father's estate he bought four hundred acres of land near Scopus, Bollinger county. This tract was only in his possession a very short time before he re-sold it to the original owner and bought instead two hundred and twenty acres of fine land between Marble Hill and Lutesville. Seventy acres of this tract is bottom land and the remainder hill land, admirably adapted for the uses to which Mr. Farnsworth puts it. He raises horses, mules, cattle, sheep and hogs; also corn, grass, Kaffir corn and cow peas, thus utilizing all of his farm. He is regarded as one of the most enterprising, progressive farmers in his section of the country.

In 1890 Mr. Farnsworth married Miss Florence Redford, born March 6, 1872, the daughter of W. W. and Mary E. (Rutledge) Redford, of Henry county, Missouri, and they now have a family of three children,— Nellie P., born in 1891, married to J. W. Gibson, of Johnson county; Cyrus Paul, born in 1894; William Ernest, born in 1898. Mr. and Mrs. Farnsworth lost two children by death, one, Archeles Earl, the twin brother of William Ernest, dying at four and one-half months and Albert Clyde, died at seven weeks.

Mr. Farnsworth is a member of the Independent Order of Odd Fellows and both he and Mrs. Farnsworth are members of the Missionary Baptist church. He is a devout Christian worker and consistently religious in his every day life.

E. BAKER. It is the lot of some men to be born great, while others have to achieve greatness, and Mr. E. Baker of Senath, was clearly destined to be the architect of his own fortune. He began life for himself on a low rung of the ladder of attainments, but by sturdy industry, untiring energy and a diligent use of his faculties and opportunities has met with well deserved success in his agricultural operations, his large farm being one of the best cultivated and most productive of any in the vicinity. Born in Pontotoc county, Mississippi, December 9, 1853, he there lived on his father's farm for ten years, having no educational advantages whatever.

When ten years old he accompanied his parents to Tennessee, and from that time until attaining his majority he assisted his father on the home farm. In 1874 his parents came to Missouri, but after a year's residence in this state they moved to Texas. Mr. Baker remained in Dunklin county when his parents settled in Texas, and although he had no capital, with the exception of thirteen dollars in cash and a Texas pony, he bought sixty acres of the land included in his present estate, paying four dollars an acre for it, buying it on credit. He continued work, however, as a farm laborer the following year, but at the end of that time married, and, with his bride, assumed possession of his land. Laboring resolutely, he cleared and improved a good farm, and from time to time judiciously invested in other land, having now a fine farm of four hundred and forty acres, the greater part of which is in a high state of culture, having been cleared and made productive through his own efforts. In 1904 Mr. Baker added to the improvements already inaugurated a substantial house, which, with the three barns on the place, make a good set of farm buildings. Mr. Baker's farm is carried on by tenants, being rented to different people, there being five good tenants on his land, which is devoted principally to the raising of corn and cotton.

Mr. Baker married, in Dunklin county, Missouri, in 1876, Fannie Romines, a native of this part of Missouri, and into their home four children have been born, namely: Zella, wife of Clarence Hutchins, of Dunklin county; Willie, wife of Edward Wallace, one of Mr. Baker's tenants; Maddie; and Charles, at home. Politically Mr. Baker is a sound supporter of the principles of the Democratic party, and for nine years has served as school director. Religiously he is a member of the Methodist Church, and an active worker in Harkey's Chapel, having been trustee fifteen and steward fourteen years, and still holds the office of trustee.

FRANK SCHULTE is a noble illustration of what Independence, self-faith and persistency can accomplish in America. He is a self-made man in the most significant sense of the word, for no one helped him in a financial way and he is self-educated. As a young man he was strong, vigorous and self-reliant. He trusted in his own ability and did things single-handed and alone. Today he stands supreme as a successful business man and a loyal and public-spirited citizen. Most of his attention has been devoted to mining and prospecting enterprises and at the present time he is vice-president of the Bank of Fredericktown, an institution that has benefitted greatly by his shrewd counsel.

A native of the great Empire of Germany, Mr. Schulte was born near the city of Berlin, on the 10th of May, 1842. He is a son of Anton and Elizabeth Schulte, who immigrated to the United States in 1845, bringing with them their family for four sons and two daughters, of which Frank was the youngest. Anton Schulte, after his arrival in America, proceeded directly to Madison county, Missouri, where he engaged in mining operations, entering the employ of the Flemings, owners of the Mine LaMotte. For a number of years he worked for that company on the ten per cent royalty basis but later he turned his attention to farming. In 1861 his health became impaired and he lived retired from that year until his death, in 1867. His cherished and devoted wife passed away in 1866. They were devout communicants of the Catholic church and to the rigid principles of that denomination reared their children. Only two of their children are living at the present time, namely,—Frank, of this notice; and Anton, a farmer near Fredericktown. Joseph Schulte died in 1899, his active career having been devoted to mining and farming; he was also associated with his brothers Frank and John in the general merchandise business at Fredericktown for a number of years and in 1850 he made the overland trip to California, where he mined for a time. John Schulte was a merchant and miner in Madison county during his life time and he died in February, 1883. Elizabeth Schulte, who married John A. Weber, a merchant at Farmington, Missouri, died in 1880; and Gertrude was the wife of Jacob Lohrey, a merchant at Middlebrook, this state. She died in 1897.

Frank Schulte was reared to adult age in Madison county, where he attended the public schools up to the age of sixteen years. For a year and a half thereafter he worked at the carpenter's trade and later he spent several years as a blacksmith. In 1864 he enlisted as a soldier in Company F, Fiftieth Missouri Regiment, serving for twelve months under Captain Robert Lindsay in the Union army. He was mustered out of service in the spring of 1865 and immediately returned to Madison county, where he has since resided. For a time he was identified with mining ventures and later he engaged in the general mercantile business, continuing therein until 1880. In the latter year he again became interested in mining and prospecting, along which lines he has achieved marvelous success. He developed the Buckeye and the Madison (now the Phoenix) mines, both of which are located in Madison county, and he has prospected extensively in this county for lead. In all his ventures he has met with unqualified success and the same is due, not merely to good fortune, but to energy and perseverance. Since 1906 he has been vice-president of the Bank of Fredericktown, in which substantial monetary institution he has invested a great deal of money.

In Madison county, in 1895, Mr. Schulte was united in marriage to Miss Amanda Miller, who was born in Iron county, this state, and who is a daughter of Henry and Margaret Miller, both natives of Germany. Mrs. Schulte's father died in 1885 and her mother resided in the Schulte home until her death, July 1, 1911, at eighty-one years of age. Mr. and Mrs. Schulte have no children. Mrs. Schulte is a consistent member of the Lutheran church. In a fraternal way Mr. Schulte is affiliated with the Independent Order of Odd Fellows. In politics he is a stalwart supporter of the cause of the Republican party but has never manifested aught of desire for political preferment of any description, preferring to devote his undivided attention to his extensive business affairs. He is held in high esteem by his fellow men, who honor him for his exemplary life and his sterling integrity and worth.

Dr. George W. Walker, physician and surgeon at Cape Girardeau, has practiced his profession in this city for nearly six years and has gained high favor among a large and representative patronage. He is a practitioner of equipment equal to that of the best, and he has been a devoted student of his profession for the past decade. His broad knowledge of his science and sympathetic manner have given him rank among the most skillful and popular physicians and surgeons in this city.

A native of the state of Illinois, Dr. Walker was born near Jonesboro, that state, on the 26th of January, 1876, and he is a son of William W. and Sarah I. (Williford) Walker, both of whom were likewise born in Illinois, the former on the 3d of April, 1849, and the latter on the 1st of February, 1850. The father was a farmer during the major portion of his active career but in December, 1901, he came to Cape Girardeau, where he is now living virtually retired, enjoying to the full the fruits of his former years of earnest toil and endeavor. Mr. and Mrs. William W. Walker were the parents of eleven children, of whom the Doctor was the third in order of birth and the ninth of whom are living, in 1911.

The rudimentary educational discipline of Dr. Walker was obtained in the country schools of Union county, Illinois, and subsequently he pursued a course of study in the Indiana State Normal School, at Danville. For five years thereafter he was engaged in teaching school in his native county and at the expiration of that period he entered the

Hospital College, at Louisville, Kentucky, where he pursued a two-year medical course. He was then matriculated as a student in the Washington University, at St. Louis, Missouri, and in that excellent institution he was graduated as a member of the class of 1903, duly receiving his degree of Doctor of Medicine. Immediately after graduation he initiated the active practice of his profession at Jonesboro, Illinois, where he succeeded in building up a large and representative patronage and where he continued to maintain his home and professional headquarters for the ensuing two years. On the 1st of August, 1905, however, he decided to seek greater fame and fortune in the west and that date marks his advent in Cape Girardeau, where he has resided during the intervening years to the present time and where he is recognized as a physician and surgeon of unusual skill.

At Jonesboro, Illinois, in the year 1897, was solemnized the marriage of Dr. Walker to Miss Effie M. Fulenwider, who was born at Jonesboro, Illinois, in 1877, and who is a daughter of William M. Fulenwider, long a representative citizen of Jonesboro. Dr. and Mrs. Walker have three children,—Marie, Helen and Louise, all of whom are attending school in this city. In their religious faith the Walker family are consistent members of the English Lutheran church, to whose charities and benevolences they are most liberal contributors.

In politics Dr. Walker is aligned as a stalwart supporter of the principles and policies for which the Democratic party stands sponsor and while he is not actively interested in local politics he manifests a deep and sincere interest in all matters projected for the good of the general welfare. In the grand old Masonic order he is affiliated with St. Mark's Lodge, No. 93, Free & Accepted Masons, of which he is past master. Dr. Walker is a man of broad human sympathy and kindly, genial manner and it may be said concerning him that the circle of his friends is coincident with that of his acquaintances.

J. M. PORTERFIELD, like many other young men, did not know exactly what he wanted to make his life work when he started out on his career. He commenced as a physician, next gave his attention to carpentering, and subsequently turned to the farm as the place where he would like to spend the rest of his days. There is an old saying that "a rolling stone gathers no moss," but if Mr. Porterfield will pardon our likening him to a stone, we would say that he has not only gathered moss, but he has found time to dispense some to others who were less fortunate than he.

Mr. Porterfield hails from a farm in Hardin county, Tennessee, where he was born July 31, 1849. He is the son of W. C. and Ursula Porterfield, who were natives of Eastern Tennessee, where he followed the occupation of farming all of this life. In earlier life he had followed carpentering. J. M. Porterfield is the seventh child in order of birth of the thirteen children who were born to his parents. He received his preliminary educational training at the district school in the neighborhood of his father's farm, and at that time the school was a subscription one. After he had completed the course which was required he entered the college at Savannah, Tennessee, and more as the result of accident than deliberate choice, he prepared himself to be a physician, in the medical department of the Savannah College. This college only offered a two years' course at that time, so that after he had learned all the medical knowledge which the college afforded, he entered the office of Drs. L. E. Covey and J. D. Wagner, and under the preceptorship of these able physicians Mr. Porterfield read medicine for a year. He then went to Vanderbilt University, at Nashville, for a six months' term, and this completed his course. He was then a certified practitioner, and he established himself in Cerrogordo, Tennessee, where he built up a very fine practice during the eleven years that he stayed there. He found the life a hard one, however, as his patients were scattered over an area of eight or ten miles, which necessitated his making very long trips to visit them. After eleven years of this life Mr. Porterfield decided that he was not following the line of work for which he was best fitted, either in taste or abilities—although he had been remarkably successful, but he decided to give up his practice. He removed from Tennessee to Arkansas, where he took up his residence in Paragould and began to do carpentering. From a boy he had always shown great aptitude for all kinds of wood work, and his success was immediate and steady. While he was living in Cerrogordo, Tennessee, he had accumulated some property, and when he moved from the state he sold this, but he did not buy any more in Arkansas, rather devoted his whole attention to his carpentering business. He only stayed in

Paragould a short time, and then moved to Piggott, Arkansas, but his stay there was of short duration also, and he pressed on to Missouri and located at Senath, when there were only a few scattered houses there; he helped to build the town, and at the expiration of three years he felt that his desires were turned in the direction of the farm. He bought the place which he occupies to-day,— a mile and half southeast of Caruth, where he farms eighty acres of land, forty acres of which belong to his wife and the other forty acres he bought. When he first moved on to the farm it was very much run down, but he has greatly improved it, having built fences and put up a new barn. He grows cotton and corn, and also raises stock on his land, and is very successful.

Mr. Porterfield has been twice married. On October 13, 1876, he was united in marriage to Miss Sallie C. Welch, of Savannah, where the Doctor was in college. After just twenty years of married life she died in Arkansas, leaving five children,—Eldridge, who is now a contractor and architect in Piggott, Arkansas, and is married to Miss Lulu Wheeler; Mary, the second child, who is the wife of John Stevens, of Malden, Missouri; Ella, who is married to Tom Clifton of Dunklin county; and Vivian, who lives with her sister Marsella, the wife of William Pitts, near Caruth. On the 18th of January, 1900, Mr. Porterfield married Mrs. Nancy A. Pruett, a widow with five children. One child, Archie, has been born to the union of Mr. and Mrs. Porterfield, and he is just ten years old, a student in the public school.

Mr. Porterfield is a member of the Methodist Episcopal Church, where he is an active worker. He is a Democrat, and although he has no desires for political honors for himself, he has at different times been most active in working for some of his friends. All that Mr. Porterfield owns is the result of his own efforts. As a rule it is not a good thing for a man to make change of occupation, but it is much better to change than it is to continue in work which is distasteful, and in the case of Mr. Porterfield his varied experiences have helped to broaden his character and to make him the efficient member of the community that he is at present.

FREDERICK W. STUMPE. For a decade past the Bank of Washington, Missouri, has had its official head Frederick W. Stumpe, who is a native of Missouri, though his father came from Germany. This is an especially happy combination—American aggressiveness and push combined with German thrift and conservatism, and it has served to inspire with confidence those who desired to invest their savings in the Bank of Washington. Indeed, Mr. Stumpe has been extremely successful in handling money to good advantage,—not only his own, but that of his patrons, and he can justly take a pardonable pride therein.

As above stated, Mr. Stumpe was born in Missouri, upon a farm three miles south of the city of Washington, the date of his birth being November 6, 1852, a son of Henry W. and Mary (Marquard) Stumpe. Henry W. Stumpe and his wife were both natives of Osnabruck, Germany, where they were married, but hearing of the glories of America they decided to try their fortunes in that country, so, in 1833 they immigrated to the United States and settled in Franklin county, Missouri. Here Mr. Stumpe devoted his time and talents to farming, which formed his life occupation. He died in 1868, at the age of sixty years, his wife surviving him until May, 1886, when she, too, passed to the Great Beyond. The issue of this union was Mary, wife of W. H. Gallenkamp and mother of Judge Gallenkamp, the surveyor of the port of St. Louis; Henry, who was one of the first volunteers from Missouri in the Civil war, and who later passed his life as a merchant in Washington; Julia became the wife of Judge Robert Hoffman, of Washington; Louisa married Arnold Godt, and died in Washington; Charlotte passed away in 1868 as the wife of John Wentyne, of St. Louis; and Frederick W., the immediate subject of this review.

Frederick W. Stumpe left the farm during his early youth, as agricultural pursuits did not tempt him as a life vocation, and entered private school in Washington, where he acquired his educational training. He first tasted the fruits of his own labor employed as a painter, but instead of following this occupation he accepted a clerkship, which position he retained until 1875, when he was appointed assistant cashier of the Washington Savings Bank, the first and only bank in that city. He immediately discovered that the handling and investing of money was his forte, and decided to make the banking business his life vocation. In July, 1877, this institution failed and Mr. Stumpe was appointed its assignee, and so successfully did he manage its tangled affairs that the depositors were practically paid in full.

That same year the Bank of Washington was organized, its promoters being F. W. Stumpe, Leopold Wattenberg, F. A. Hendrich, John B. Busch and H. D. Hibbler, the two latter gentlemen having but one share each. The capital of the institution was ten thousand dollars, and Leopold Wattenberg was chosen president, while Mr. Stumpe was appointed assistant cashier. In 1890 Mr. Stumpe was promoted to cashier, and in 1901 he was elected president to succeed Mr. Wattenberg. The success of its managements can best be grasped from its present condition, the capital stock having been increased to fifty thousand dollars, while its surplus is double its present capital. Mr. Stumpe has other business interests, being one of the directors of the Washington Building and Loan Association, a concern which has made a phenomenal record as a fiduciary institution, and he is also a director of the Washington Water Company.

In politics Frederick W. Stumpe gives his preference to the Republican party, his fellow-citizens having shown their trust in him by electing him to the offices of city clerk and city treasurer, respectively. He is a member of that old established fraternity, Ancient Free and Accepted Masons, and is a past master of Washington Lodge, No. 25.

On October 9, 1878, a marriage ceremony was performed uniting Frederick W. Stumpe and Amelia Wilhelmi in the holy bonds of wedlock. Mrs. Stumpe was the daughter of Julius Wilhelmi, a native of Mannheim, Germany, who came to this country in early life. He was a Union refugee from Arkansas during the period of the Civil war, and was later sheriff and collector of Franklin county, Missouri. Mr. and Mrs. Frederick W. Stumpe were the parents of the following children: Earna, the wife of Jasper N. Tankersly, of Chicago, manager of the interests of the McMillan Company, of New York; Miss Adele, of Washington; Robert W., who is in business in St. Louis; and Miss Elsie, of Washington. Mrs. Stumpe was called to her eternal home July 25, 1899. She was a devoted wife and mother and beloved by all who knew her. The two daughters, Misses Adele and Elsie, preside graciously over the home of our subject, which is a gathering place for the social activities of Washington.

D. J. CONRAD. It was "the embattled farmers" who "fired the shot heard round the world" at Concord Bridge and ever since America has drawn her best soldiers from her farms. Patriotism flourishes in the country. The life of D. J. Conrad is an instance of the response that the call to arms evokes from the man who owns and works his fields. His father, J. J. Conrad, was a veteran of the Civil war, whose military career in no way interfered with his being a successful agriculturist, and the son, born in 1872, emulates his parent in zeal for the two pursuits.

Reared on his father's large farm, D. J. Conrad attended the schools of the county. At the outbreak of the Cuban war he enlisted, joined the Sixteenth U. S. Infantry and served eight months in Cuba. He was mustered out of the Cuban army January 17, 1899. Eight months later he again enlisted in the Philippine war. His regiment was the Thirty-eighth U. S. Volunteer Infantry, in whose ranks he served seventeen months in the Philippine Islands. He returned to Bollinger county after his discharge and took up his work of farming again.

Upon his father's death in 1903 he became possessed of one hundred and fifty acres of land, mostly in timber, though he has added eighty acres of timber. The father owned at one time some four thousand acres, which is still owned in the family. Like most of his neighbors, Mr. Conrad raises stock besides doing general farming. He spent one year in the west, leaving Missouri in March, 1903. From 1905 to 1907 he was sheriff of Bollinger county, an office whose duties he discharged with characteristic thoroughness. At the time of the disturbance in Mexico, in 1911, Mr. Conrad was sent to Texas and served in the camp of instructions. He was called out by the Adjutant General of Missouri.

The marriage of Mr. Conrad and Miss Ida Kinder took place December 30, 1908. Ida Kinder was the daughter of A. A. and Mary Kinder, both natives of Missouri. Mary Burns Conrad, the only child of Mr. and Mrs. D. J. Conrad, was born November 9, 1909.

Mr. Conrad belongs to the Masonic order, being a member of the lodge at Marble Hill, Missouri. He is also actively connected with the Army and Navy Union at St. Louis, Missouri. Mr. Conrad's church preference is the Presbyterian, where he regularly attends. Politically he is known as a thorough-going Republican.

REV. ELISHA CALVIN BUTLER. One of the most necessary characteristics for a man to be possessed of in order to make a success of his own life and of those things which he undertakes is to be intensely in earnest. This is one of the most noticeable traits about the Rev. E. C. Butler, pastor of the Kennett Missionary Baptist Church. If one follows his career one cannot fail to see that he has accomplished almost miraculous results by reason of his own personality. Others have the same message to tell, but they are not able to obtain the listeners, simply because they have not the power to speak with the conviction that strikes home. Mr. Butler accomplishes those things which he sees possible day by day, thus opening up avenues to new efforts and new results. A brief survey of his history may prove of interest.

He was born in Carroll county, in western Tennessee, January 8, 1869, and was brought up on the Tennessee farm. After the completion of his preliminary education he attended Ewing College, Ewing, Illinois; not having at that time felt himself drawn towards the ministry, he began to teach at the age of twenty-two, teaching in the country schools in Tennessee for three years. He had also taken a two years' course at the Holiday Independent Normal School in Benton county, Tennessee. After teaching for a short time in Tennessee he decided that for him the way to do the most good in the world was to become a minister. He was especially interested in the mission side of the ministry and he attended the Missionary Baptist College at Ewing, where he took a theological course. He had, however, preached before this and had also been ordained; he felt, however, that the college work would make him more fully equipped for his career. As soon as he left college he entered upon his pastoral work, locating first at Steeleville, Illinois, in Randolph county, and Tamaroa, Illinois, taking charge of the pastoral duties at both these last named places at the same time. His next charge was at Cobden, Illinois, coming in 1906 to Dexter, Missouri, where he remained three years as local pastor. During this time the church was remodeled and the attendance was doubled. He organized the Baptist Young Peoples Union, which still continues to be a live enthusiastic society. He owns a Gospel tent, in which he holds meetings. During the series held in Dexter there were twenty-four conversions. He held a series of four meetings in the county, outside Dexter, one resulting in thirty-eight conversions one in forty-seven and still another in thirty-one. The result of these meetings, in addition, or perhaps because of the impression produced in the hearts of the people, resulted in the building of a thousand dollar church at Idalia, Missouri. It was erected within sixty days after the close of the meetings and was fully paid for at the time of its dedication. This was certainly striking while the iron was hot. It is the experience of so many of the evangelistic preachers of the country that the people who are converted during special meetings do not continue in the road in which they started. The Rev. Elisha Butler has probably found a cure for that; he, as in the case cited above, immediately gets the new converts started to do something, not giving them a chance to backslide; then when once in the work, the chances are very much in favor of the large majority remaining steadfast, as there is constantly something to do to keep their interest alive. He held meetings at the Tatum school house, near Dexter, Missouri, where there were forty-seven conversions; a church resulted, which is called Butler's Chapel. He witnessed two hundred conversions in five meetings in Stoddard county, Missouri. All of this work was accomplished within three years, and in October, 1909, he came to Kennett, as the result of a most urgent invitation from the Baptist church. Since he came to Kennett he has spent most of his time in connection with the local church. Since his arrival the Kennett church has added twenty by baptism and thirty-two by letter, as the result of constant, day by day effort on the part of Mr. Butler. The church is now being enlarged, to accommodate the growing enterprises. Six Sunday-school rooms are being added, for the modern teaching that has been inaugurated. The present membership of the church is about two hundred and eighty-nine. The young people in particular are becoming interested and are doing effective work. Although Mr. Butler is absolutely devoted to the local church and finds full scope for his energies, he still continues the tent work, for which he is so admirably suited.

On April 20, 1897, Mr. Butler was married to Miss Josie Parham, a native of Montgomery county, Illinois. She is in perfect sympathy with her husband in all of his efforts and is herself active in the church. Besides being president of the Woman's Missionary Union, she is active in the general work of the church. Mr. and Mrs. Butler have one daughter, Verdie Charleve, who is now twelve years old and attending the Kennett public school. Their other child, Loran Parham, died when he was two years old, while Rev. Butler was pastor at Dexter, Missouri.

Mr. Butler is a member of the Independent Order of Odd Fellows. It is probable that his association with this order has been of great assistance to him in his church work, as he can the more readily adjust himself to different classes of men. He has a fine library, composed chiefly of books pertaining to his work, but not exclusively, as Mr. Butler believes in having about him all the broadening influences that are possible. If a minister would be effective, he must be able to be "all things to all men," not in the way of toadying to them in the least, but he must have the faculty of entering into their feelings and be able to view things from their standpoints. Mr. Butler naturally has this faculty and he has cultivated it so that it has developed to an unusual extent. He is doing a great work and as he is still a young man, is probably only at the beginning of his career. From Mr. Butler's standpoint the most successful life is the one that has accomplished the most good and from that attitude his friends would say that he is most successful. He is not a rich man, which is the gauge of a business man's success—the ability to make money—but he has riches of a more lasting nature, treasures which can never be stolen nor lost. The people in Kennett love both Mr. Butler and his wife and appreciate every effort they are making. His work as pastor at Kennett, Missouri, closed in October, 1911.

EMIL CHARLES SCHRAMM. A young man of splendid business intelligence and enterprise is Emil Charles Schramm, manager of the Schramm Wholesale Grocery Company, of Flat River, an important and flourishing concern with capital stock estimated at forty thousand dollars. He is also connected with one of Saint Francois largest monetary institutions, the Miners & Merchants Bank, being a stockholder and director in the same. Mr. Schramm is a native of Sainte Genevieve county, Missouri, his birth having occurred within the boundaries of that neighboring county May 11, 1881. His father, Henry Schramm, was born in Germany, March 22, 1843. He secured his education in the rightly famed schools of that country and like so many German youths of his generation, served an apprenticeship as a baker. At the age of nineteen years he came to America and located in Sainte Genevieve county, Missouri, but did not pursue the trade he had learned, instead securing land and devoting his energies to the great basic industry. He early established a household by marriage, the young woman to become his bride being Miss Phillipine Herter, of Sainte Genevieve county, daughter of Henry Herter. To their union were born twelve children, of whom ten survive at the present time, Emil C., the immediate subject of this review, being the ninth in order of birth. Mr. and Mrs. Schramm, the elder, reside in St. Francois county at the present time, making their home upon the farm which is dear to them by many happy associations and enjoying the respect of the community in which they have so long been valuable factors. The elder Mr. Schramm is Republican in politics and Lutheran in religious conviction.

Emil C. Schramm enjoyed the experience, usually considered an advantage rather than otherwise, of spending his early years upon the farm and assisting in the duties there to be encountered which bring the boy and girl, in the words of the Hoosier poet, "near to Nature's heart." He received his education in the public schools of East St. Louis and later entered the business department of Carleton College, whose course he finished at the age of twenty-two. Soon afterward he entered the Schramm Wholesale Grocery House, managed by A. O. Schramm, a brother, first engaging in the duties of the position of stockman and subsequently as salesman. In 1908 the subject became manager of the Schramm Grocery Company at Flat River and in the subsequent time has met with no small amount of success in this capacity. As mentioned in a preceding paragraph, he is also connected with the Miners & Merchants Bank.

Mr. Schramm became a recruit to the Benedicts when, on the 26th day of September, 1906, he was united in marriage at Farmington to Miss Mamie Braun, of Farmington, daughter of Charles and Elizabeth (Mell) Braun. Mr. and Mrs. Schramm are the parents of one son, Leonard. The subject gives hand and heart to the policies and principles for which the "Grand Old Party" stands and is Lutheran in religious faith. He and his wife maintain a pleasant home and hold high place in popular confidence and esteem.

The Schramm Wholesale Grocery Company was established in the year 1903, and is capitalized for forty thousand dollars. This company makes the entire lead belt its territory and does a business of the highest class, being indeed one of those excellent concerns which contribute in very material fashion to the prosperity and prestige of the section.

WILLIAM N. HOWARD, M. D. In all the county of Cape Girardeau there is no man who is more respected and loved by old and young, by rich and poor alike, than is Dr. William N. Howard. For years his life has been spent in seeking to benefit others. His one ambition has been and still is to serve his fellow men. His maxim is to look up, not down, to look forward not back, but lend a hand. His knowledge of human nature has taught him to look upon the errors of others in sorrow not in anger. He is a man whom to see is to admire.

He was born in Cape Girardeau county, Missouri, November 26, 1862. He is the son of James M. Howard, a native of North Carolina and one of the early settlers in Missouri, whither he came with his parents when he was a small boy. The family located on a farm near Appleton, on which one of the sons still lives. James M. Howard married Sarah Day who was also born in North Carolina and was the daughter of Nighten Day of that county. When Sarah was very small her parents moved to Cape Girardeau county, where they farmed, settling near Oak Ridge. Mr. and Mrs. Day have four sons and two daughters, who all live in the neighborhood of their old home. Mrs. James M. Howard died in 1909, having borne five sons and two daughters. The little girls both died in infancy. Four of the sons are living now, of whom Dr. William is the third. The grandfather of William N. Howard and father of James M. Howard was named John. He was of Scotch English descent and was born in North Carolina. He came to southeastern Missouri and located on a farm near Appleton. Two of his sons were also farmers.

William N. Howard's boyhood days were spent on his father's farm, where he learned something of the farm life and attended the district school. After he had been educated as highly as his father thought was necessary, he started out to make a career for himself. He had not at that time decided to become a physician, but first did some surveying for the railroad, in 1884. Three years later he began to study medicine, entering the St. Louis Medical College, from which he graduated in 1890. Immediately following his graduation, he came to Cape Girardeau, where he has been in practice ever since. He is a member of the Cape Girardeau Medical Society, the Southeastern Missouri Medical Society, the Missouri State Medical Society and the American Medical Association.

In 1896 his marriage to Adda Wilson, daughter of Gilbert Wilson of Cape Girardeau county, was solemnized. To this union was born one daughter, named Sarah after the Doctor's mother.

Dr. Howard is a Democrat and although he is greatly interested in public affairs, he has evinced no desire for honors for himself. He is a member of the Knights of Pythias and of the Masonic Order, holding membership in the Blue Lodge Ancient Order Free and Accepted Masons. He is a life long resident of Cape Girardeau county and has been in practice in this city for over twenty years, having a general practice and also doing surgical work for the railroad. There is only one physician in Cape Girardeau who has been in practice a little longer than Dr. Howard, but there is no one who is more loved. He is very much interested in educational work and is a member of the board of education, on which he does very admirable work. He realizes that it is on the schools that the future of his native county depends. He has the interests of the children greatly at heart.

THOMAS J. SWEAZEA. It is a pleasure to the biographer to include in these sketches of important citizens of southeastern Missouri one who is not only prominent for his prestige as the grandson of a pioneer and as a respected member of the legal profession, but one who is also as firmly intrenched in the affection and high regard of the many who know him personally as Mr. Thomas J. Sweazea, of Piedmont.

The paternal grandfather of Thomas Sweazea, William Sweazea, was born in the state of Tennessee, and migrated to this state in 1808, locating near the Black river, where he entered and bought a large and fertile tract of land, which he tilled and made his home until 1850, the year of his death. George Mann, the maternal grandfather of Mr. Sweazea, a native of South Carolina, also early felt the impulse to try life on what was then the frontier, and came from his native state to the Black river district. William Sweazea, the father of the subject of this brief record, was born and reared in Wayne county, where until 1865 he undertook farming on a small tract of land on the Black river, but in that year he removed to Reynolds county. There he purchased another tract of land and spent the remainder of his life in its improvement, so that in 1901, when he died at the venerable old age of seventy-three years, he having been born in 1832, it was an important agricultural and stock raising estate. His wife, before her marriage, was Amanda Mann, a native of Reynolds county. Her birth occurred in 1832, and she passed to her eternal reward in 1880. Her husband was ever a loyal member of the Democratic party, and both were devout members of the Baptist church. Besides Thomas J., their children were as follows: William A., now of Wayne county; Sophronia, wife of Robert Benson and makes her home in Alabama; and Margaret, wife of M. L. Sanders, of Leeper, this state.

Thomas J. Sweazea was born on his father's farm on October 14, 1870. He remained on the home farm until he was within one year of his majority, and took advantage of the educational opportunities afforded by the district schools of those early days. When he was twenty he entered Carleton College, at Farmington, Missouri, where he remained until 1893. He then made practical use of his education and taught a school with such success that in 1895 he was elected county commissioner for a term of two years. His first experience as candidate for the office of county clerk of Reynolds county not resulting in the possession of the honor, he ran again in 1903 and this time easily won the office. In 1907 his political service to his county was continued as a member of the Forty-fourth General Assembly, as representative from the Reynolds county district, and he is still remembered for his able participation in the making of wise legislation for his native state.

Following his term of office, he removed to Salem, where he prepared himself for his profession by reading law, with such success that in 1909 he was admitted to the bar. He again changed his residence, coming to Piedmont, where he opened his office and made the beginnings of his present fine patronage. He has continued his public service as a member and secretary of the school board of Piedmont, where he has rendered needed service as an advocate of better and more efficient schools.

Besides his profitable law clientage, Mr. Sweazea owns a farm not far from Piedmont. On June 6, 1895, he insured for himself a gracious companionship and happy home by his marriage with Miss Ella Malloy, who was born May 30, 1871, near Piedmont, a daughter of John and Mary (Warren) Malloy, of Wayne county. Four children have since come to their pleasant home, namely: Doyle J., Pearl, Ava and Opal T.

Mr. Sweazea adheres firmly to the principles and policies of the party of Jefferson and Jackson. Both he and his wife support the tenets of the Baptist church.

THOMAS MARTIN JACKSON, member of the bar of Southeast Missouri and a successful attorney of Desloge, has had a varied and useful career both in the law and in the ministry. Born in Monroe county, Kentucky, January 14, 1860, and spending his early years on a farm, he received an education in the country schools, in the Glasgow Normal School and Business College at Glasgow, Kentucky, and the Southern Normal School and Business College at Bowling Green, Kentucky, and after his graduation from the latter entered educational work. For thirteen years he was a successful teacher in Kentucky, Missouri and Arkansas. During six years of this period he carried on his studies for the bar in a law office, and was admitted to practice April 28, 1892, at Russellville, Arkansas, and later enrolled in the supreme court of Missouri.

For six years he was engaged in active practice. He then devoted his service to the ministry of the Methodist church, South, and for sixteen years was a traveling minister for that denomination. Finally, on account of his wife's health, he returned to the practice of law in 1908, and has since enjoyed a liberal business at Desloge. During his ministry he occupied some of the leading pulpits of the state and was also a presiding elder in that church. In politics he is a Republican.

Mr. Jackson's father was George W. Jackson, who was born in Washington county, Tennessee, March 29, 1836. His early life was spent on a farm in his native state until the war, when he joined the Union army, Company B, Fifth Kentucky Cavalry, and was a member of Sherman's army during its march to the sea. After the war he settled on a farm in Kentucky. Before entering the service he married Miss Rebecca A. Ford, a daughter of Thomas and Mary Elizabeth Ford, of that state. Eleven children were born of their marriage, Thomas M. being the second in order of birth. George W. Jackson moved to Missouri in 1880, locating near Farmington, where his active years were spent in farming, and he lived retired in that town until his death, in 1910. His wife preceded him to the other world about twenty years. In politics he was a strong Republican, was affiliated with the G. A. R. post, and was a member of the Baptist church.

Mr. Thomas M. Jackson married, February 27, 1890, Miss Jennie Fowler, a daughter of George P. and Lavina Fowler, farmers of St. Genevieve county, Missouri. Mr. and Mrs. Jackson have four children: Clemmie, Harry F., Grace M. and Catherine.

W. A. DAVAULT. The great Apostle Paul, when describing the ideal preacher of the gospel, says, he must be "apt to teach," a characterization which cannot fail to impress all who know Rev. W. A. Davault, vice-president of Will Mayfield College, as being an especially fitting description of the Professor. It is not given to many men to wield so wide an influence; to be in such close touch with the younger generation, the students of the college, and at the same time to be pastor of three Baptist churches, and perhaps few men could fulfill such responsibilities. Certainly Professor Davault is rightly regarded as a power for righteousness, culture and all that makes for the higher life.

By descent Professor Davault belongs to the Huguenots who settled in North Carolina when persecution drove them from France and who have given America so many theologians, scholars and statesmen. The founder of the American branch of the family was a Baptist missionary. In 1804 James Davault, grandfather of W. A., came to Bollinger county, where he was one of the earliest settlers. Christian J. Davault, son of the pioneer and father of the subject of this sketch, was a farmer and also a soldier in the Civil war, in the Union army. He was once captured and later paroled. He was in active service at the close of the war, having enlisted three times, always in a Missouri regiment. He died in 1899, in the county where he was born and where he spent the most of his life. His wife was born in Perry county, the daughter of William Adison Walker. Her family, too, were pioneers of this county, coming from Virginia early in the nineteenth century. The Walkers are of English origin.

W. A. Davault's native town is Perryville, Missouri, where he was born January 25, 1865. His boyhood days were spent on the farm assisting his father and attending the district school. He began teaching at the age of nineteen, an occupation for which he had prepared himself by study in both public and private schools and one for which he kept himself at the best by constant study. In 1894 he graduated from the academic course of Will Mayfield College; in 1901 Mr. Davault took his B. S. degree from the same institution, and received his A. M. degree in 1911.

Mr. Davault has not confined his interest in education to merely acquiring knowledge or even to imparting instruction. He has given many years of faithful and intelligent service to the administrative branch of the department of public education. His service as school-commissioner of Bollinger county began in 1895. He served in this capacity until 1899. During the same period he was chosen as conductor of the district teachers' institute, doing most efficient work the whole four years in both offices. In 1903 the Professor was again elected school commissioner and served six years, making five terms in all which he has given to this work.

During all this time he was active in the ministry, having missed but twenty appointments in twenty-two years since he was ordained for the Baptist ministry in 1889. He is now moderator of the St. Francis Baptist Association of southeast Missouri. He gives half of his time to preaching at Marble Hill. The other half he divides between the Baptist churches at Glen Allen and Marquand.

The Rev. Davault has been teaching in Will Mayfield College since 1893, with the exception of some years spent in teaching in the public schools. His service to that institution has been recognized by his appointment to the vice-presidency of the college, which office he has held since 1900. His work as an instructor is in the departments of History and Psychology.

The marriage of Mr. Davault to Miss Margaret E. Williford occurred in 1887. Mrs. Davault is the daughter of George S. Williford, a native of Tennessee. Six children have been born to the Professor and his wife, one son and five daughters. The son, Dr. Webster W. Davault, has chosen the profession of medicine and will graduate from the Barnes Medical School of St. Louis in 1912. Before entering upon this special training. Dr. Davault took his A. B. degree at Will Mayfield College. He was born in 1889, four years before Miss Miriam Eula Davault. Miss Davault graduated from the college where her father and brother received their degrees both in music and in the academic department. She is at present engaged in teaching at Sikeston, Missouri. Three younger daughters, Helen Emma, Willa Anastasia and Lula Ionia, are aged sixteen, thirteen and nine, respectively, and the fifth, Mildred Anna, made her advent into the home September 10, 1911.

Professor Davault is a valued member of the Modern Woodmen of America. His many professional and social duties have not caused him to grow indifferent to his immediate surroundings. He owns a fine residence and six lots in Marble Hill.

R. E. JENNINGS. Noteworthy among the prosperous agriculturists of Dunklin county is R. E. Jennings, of Senath, who through his own persistent energy and industry has acquired a good farming property, which he is managing with most satisfactory pecuniary results. A native of Texas, he was born in Dallas June 27, 1865, but a short time before the death of his father.

Taken then by his widowed mother to Virginia, he lived for awhile in the Old Dominion, and later accompanied his mother to Tennessee, from there, at the age of fourteen years, coming to Dunklin county, Missouri, where the death of his mother occurred in 1898. Although he had received but a meager education, R. E. Jennings was forced to begin working for wages as soon as old enough to be of use to any one, and the first seven months after coming to Missouri was employed on a farm in the vicinity of Kennett. He subsequently worked as a farm hand in various places, principally in Dunklin county, and by dint of perseverance and thrift accumulated sufficient money to warrant him in purchasing a farm. Assuming possession of his present farm of forty acres in 1904, Mr. Jennings has made improvements of an excellent character, increasing its value to one hundred and fifty dollars an acre, it being one of the best and most highly productive estates in the neighborhood.

Mr. Jennings has been twice married. He married first, in 1886, Beulah C. Wright, who died a few months later, on November 30, 1886, leaving no children. He married for his second wife, January 8, 1888, Cassa B. Harkey, who was born August 13, 1872, and is a sister of W. R. Harkey, of whom a brief biographical sketch may be found on another page of this work. Mr. and Mrs. Jennings are the parents of three children, namely: Annie, born March 31, 1893; Walter, born October 18, 1894; and Raymond, born February 28, 1905. Politically Mr. Jennings is a stanch adherent of the Democratic party, and fraternally he is a member of the Woodmen of the World.

GEORGE W. LANPHER, SR., has for many years been a leading and influential citizen of Fredericktown and his former activity in business affairs, his co-operation in public interests and his zealous support of all objects that he believes will contribute to the material, social or moral improvement of the community keeps him in the foremost rank of those to whom the city owes its development. His life has been characterized by upright, honorable principles and it also exemplifies the truth of the Emersonian philosophy that "the way to win a friend is to be one." His genial kindly manner wins him the high regard and good will of all with whom he comes in contact and while he has lived in retirement for the past ten years he is still hale and hearty.

A native of Madison county, Missouri, George W. Lanpher was born at Mine LaMotte on the 12th of February, 1837, and he is a son of George and Elizabeth (Nifong) Lanpher, the former a native of Ohio and the latter a native of Missouri. The father came to this state as a young man, was a carpenter by trade, and after his marriage settled at Mine LaMotte, where he was interested in mining projects until his death, in 1845, at the early age of thirty years. For a short time he also conducted a tavern at Fredericktown, where he likewise served as postmaster. Mrs. Lanpher was a daughter of George Nifong, who settled in Bollinger county, Missouri, having removed thither from North Carolina. Mr. Nifong was a farmer by occupation and during the closing years of his life resided on a fine estate near Fredericktown, where he died in 1870. Mrs. Lanpher died in 1885, at the age of seventy-seven years; in early life she was a member of the Christian church but later affiliated with the Methodist denomination. Mr. and Mrs. Lanpher became the parents of seven children, of whom four grew to maturity and three of whom are living at the present time, namely,—Felix, of Cape Girardeau; Mrs. Amanda Moore, of Ironton, Missouri; and George W., of this notice.

George W. Lanpher, Sr., the immediate subject of this review, was reared to maturity at Fredericktown, where he attended the common and subscription schools. As a mere youth, in 1854, he accompanied a band of fellows on the overland trip to California, where he remained until the latter part of 1857 and where he was interested in mining ventures. After his return to Madison county, Missouri, he farmed for eight or ten years, his fine homestead, a mile and a half west of Fredericktown, being now operated by a son. In 1872 he was elected to the office of assessor of Madison county and later he was chosen as county sheriff and collector, serving in the latter offices for four years. In 1879, in company with Michael DeGuire, he built the mill at Fredericktown, continuing to operate the same for a period of twenty-one years, at the expiration of which he disposed of his interest therein to William Gudger. Since 1901 he has lived in virtual retirement.

On the 14th of October, 1858, was recorded the marriage of Mr. Lanpher to Miss Eliza Virginia Parkin, whose birth occurred in Madison county, August 28, 1838, and who is a daughter of Joseph and Emily (Johnson) Parkin. Joseph Parkin was born in England, whence he removed to Virginia in an early day, settling at Wytheville. He was twice married, Mrs. Lanpher having been a child of his second union. On his trip to America, Joseph was accompanied by two brothers, one of whom died at sea, en route, and the other, Thomas, who died in Missouri shortly after the Civil war. Mr. Parkin was a farmer and miner by occupation and he died in the vicinity of Fredericktown in 1845, at the age of sixty years. Emily (Johnson) Parkin was a sister of Thomas and William Johnson, former residents of Cape Girardeau. She was born at Louisa Courthouse, Virginia, removing thence to Mt. Sterling, Kentucky, and coming from the latter place to Missouri as a girl. Mrs. Lanpher has one brother and a sister living and one brother deceased, namely: Joseph resides at Fredericktown; Emily is the wife of Dr. Reuben Fugate, of Farmington, Missouri; and Aylette B. was a soldier in the Confederate army and lost his life during the Civil war, at Farmington, this state.

Mr. and Mrs. Lanpher became the parents of seven children, of whom five are living at the present time, in 1911. Emma is the wife of M. E. Blanton, of Fredericktown; they had four children—James, William, Charles (who died at four years of age), and Almeda. William, who had been attending the State University at Columbia, Missouri, died at the age of twenty-three years, at Fredericktown, Missouri. Edgar is a farmer near Fredericktown; he married Patty Wiley and they have three daughters—Belle, Eliza V. and Dorothy. Lillian married Samuel Buford and she died on the 17th of August, 1909, being survived by four children—Frank, Charles, George L. and Nellie Jane. Annie is the wife of William H. Blanton and they reside on a farm one mile north of Fredericktown; they have three children—Lillian, Walter and Clyde. Charles A. is engaged in the general merchandise business at Fredericktown; he married Belle Hoffman and they have two children—Eliza Elizabeth and Charles, Jr. George W., Jr., operates his father's farm near Fredericktown; he married Annie Nevada Graham and they have one child, Alma.

In politics George W. Lanpher, Sr., is a stalwart in the ranks of the Democratic party, in the local councils of which he has been a most active factor, serving with efficiency in a number of important offices of public trust and responsibilty, as previously noted. For the past fifty years he has been a valued and appreciative member of the time-honored Masonic order, being the oldest living member of the lodge at Fredericktown. He and his wife are both connected with the Order of the Eastern Star and in their religious faith are consistent members of the Christian church.

ROBERT F. WICHTERICH, M. D. During the years which mark the period of Dr. Wichterich's professional career he has met with gratifying success and during the period of his residence at Cape Girardeau he has won the good will and patronage of many of the best citizens here. He is a thorough student and endeavors to keep abreast of the times in everything relating to the discoveries in medical science. Progressive in his ideas and favoring modern methods as a whole, he does not dispense with the time-tried systems whose value has stood the test of years. There is in his record much that is worthy of the highest commendation, for limited privileges and financial resources made it necessary that he personally meet the expenses of a college course. In doing this he displayed the elemental strength of his character, which has been the foundation of his success. He now stands very high in the medical profession of the state and is in the fullest sense of the term a self-made man. Dr. Wichterich is also engaged in the drug business at Cape Girardeau, where he has resided during most of his life thus far.

A native of this city, Dr. Robert Felix Wichterich was born on the 23d of March, 1868, and he is a son of Nicholas Wichterich, whose birth occurred at Bünn, Germany, on the 12th of March, 1827. Reared and educated in Germany, Nicholas Wichterich attended the gymnasium and University of Bünn, making a special study of astronomy. He was a school mate of Carl Schurz and participated in the Rebellion of 1848, coming to America immediately after the close of that struggle. Shortly after his advent in the United States he located at Cape Girardeau, Missouri, where in 1860 he engaged in the milling business, continuing in that line for thirteen years. He was active in politics, being city treasurer for thirty-two years, thus demonstrating the respect and esteem accorded him by his fellow townsmen. He died January 9, 1900. He was lieutenant of the Home Guards at the time of the Civil war and his political allegiance was given to the Democratic party. He married Miss Eliza Molitor and to them were born three children, of whom the Doctor is the youngest. The others are Kathryn, who is now Mrs. Antone Kammer, and John H. Mrs. Wichterich is still a resident of Cape Girardeau, being eighty-three years of age.

Dr. Robert F. Wichterich received his rudimentary educational training in the public and parochial schools of Cape Girardeau and as a young man he attended St. Vincent's College. Subsequently he was matriculated as a student in the Memphis Hospital Medical College and still later he attended the St. Louis College of Physicians & Surgeons, and the Barnes Medical College, in which latter institution he was graduated as a member of the class of 1899, duly receiving his degree of Doctor of Medicine. Dr. Wichterich was registered as a pharmacist in April, 1889, before the state board of pharmacy and thereafter he was engaged in the drug business at Cape Girardeau for a time in company with Dr. J. H. Rider. For three years, from 1885 to 1887, he was engaged in the drug business at Marshall, Texas, where he was connected with the Texas & Pacific Railroad Hospital. After being graduated in Barnes Medical College Dr. Wichterich settled permanently at Cape Girardeau, where he initiated the active practice of his profession and where he soon succeeded in building up a large and lucrative patronage. In 1907 he again engaged in the drug business in conjunction with his professional work and he is now the owner of a very fine drug store. In his practice Dr. Wichterich makes a specialty of internal medicine, never advising surgery except in most urgent cases. He is an ardent follower of the unwritten code of professional ethics and by reason of his splendid ability and straightforward methods has won the unqualified regard and admiration of his fellow practitioners.

In June, 1902, was recorded the marriage of Dr. Wichterich to Miss Elma Taylor, who was born ar ' reared at Cape Girardeau and who is a daugnter of J. W. Taylor, long a prominent and influential citizen of ths place. Dr. and Mrs. Wichterich have no children. In his religious faith the Doctor is a devout communicant of the Catholic church and a liberal contributor to many philanthropical organizations.

In politics Dr. Wichterich is aligned as a stanch supporter of the cause of the Democratic party and while he is not desirous of political preferment of any description he manifests a deep and sincere interest in all matters affecting the general welfare. After his father's death, in 1900, he filled out the latter's unexpired term as city treasurer. For the past eight years he has been a member of the board of health of Cape Girardeau and in that connection he has been a means of improving the sanitary conditions of the city. He was president of the Cape Girardeau Medical Society for one year and he is also connected with the Missouri State Medical Society. In a fraternal way he is affiliated with the local lodges of the Benevolent & Protective Order of Elks and the Knights of Columbus. Dr. Wichterich is a man of high ideals and generous impulses. He is considerate of others' opinions and sensibilites and is ever ready to lend a helping hand to those less fortunately situated than himself.

HENRY ALLEN MAY. Too much honor and esteem cannot be given to a physician who counts his time and pleasure as naught in comparison with the aid he can give to suffering humanity, who foregoes his night's rest, perhaps, and buffets a driving snowstorm to render assistance to one of our loved ones. Dr. Henry Allen May, of this review, has passed his entire life in Franklin county, Missouri, and has, doubtless, during the last decade and more, done just such service for many who will read this history.

Robert H. May, grandfather of our subject, was the founder of this Franklin county family and the progenitor of all the older members of this family. He was born August 7, 1792, in Charlotte county, Virginia, and removed from that state to Missouri, locating at Gray Summit, where he lived until March 13, 1870, when he was called to the Great Beyond. This old pioneer married Mary R. Portwood, of Virginia, and to them were born seven sons and two daughters, as follows: Stephen T., William H., Robert H., Jr., John R., James A., Joseph F. and Edward B. F., the two daughters, Mary A. E. F. and Martha, dying unmarried.

James A. May, one of the large family of Robert H. May, was born in 1827, on a farm near Gray Summit, Franklin county, Missouri, and he followed his father's vocation, that of farming, while he lived. His allegiance to the Southern cause precluded his enlisting in any other than the Confederate army when hostilities broke out, and he had many thrilling adventures during his war record. He was a prisoner of war in the hands of the Federals, and was wounded at the battle of Gettysburg. James A. May married Sarah Frances Hundley, a daughter of W. A. Hundley, a pioneer of Franklin county from the Old Dominion state, the locality from whence also came the Mays. The children born to this union were James Arthur, a lawyer of Pacific, Missouri; Annie Lee, the wife of W. H. Miles, of Gray Summit; and Henry Allen, the subject of this sketch. The mother of these children died July 23, 1880, when she was but little more than thirty-one years of age; the father had died nine years previously, in December, 1871.

Dr. Henry Allen May was thus left without parents at a very tender age, his birth having occurred at Gray Summit, Franklin county, Missouri, on the 14th of April, 1872. At the death of his mother, this eight-year-old boy was taken care of by his relatives, and he spent the first two years in the home of his uncle, Edward B. F. May. Upon the death of this gentleman he went to live with another uncle, Thomas B. North, where he remained for some years, acquiring his educational training in the common schools of that locality. After finishing the prescribed work of the public school he spent two years in the State University of Missouri, and, having decided that he would become a physician, he took up the study of medicine at Beaumont Hospital Medical College, a school which later was merged with the St. Louis University, and graduated from that institution, receiving his certificate of Doctor of Medicine in 1894. The next year young Dr. May located at Washington, where he has since successfully practiced his profession, attaining a considerable clientele and an ever-growing circle of admirers, who have every confidence in the skill and professional acumen of Henry A. May. The Doctor holds membership in the Franklin County Medical Society, the Missouri State Medical Society and the American Medical Association. Fraternally he is affiliated with the Ancient Free and Accepted Masons and the Modern Woodmen of America, while in politics he, like his ancestors, is a supporter of the principles and policies of the Democratic party. Dr. May is also one of the proprietors of that interesting sheet, the *Franklin County Observer*.

On February 5, 1895, our subject married Miss Clara Ming, who was born Setember 8, 1868, a daughter of the late Judge James M. Ming, an honored citizen of Frankiln county. Judge Ming was born in Virginia, in 1824, where he married Jemimah Osborn, a native also of that state, and from there they removed to Missouri early in life. He rendered invaluable and undying service to the citizens of Franklin county when he, as county judge, declined to make the levy of taxes for the payment of the bonds of the fraudulent Budd and Decker road, and, because of such refusal, he was imprisoned by the court and thus suffered for his loyalty to his county and his allegiance to the principles of right. The children of Judge James M. and Jemimah (Osborn) Ming were as follows: Eugene, who has sat upon the bench of the county court of Franklin county and wore the ermine which his father graced and rendered hallowed by his righteous decisions, and he is now engaged in farming; William, who married Miss Celeste Jeffries; Emmet, deceased, who married Miss Emma Wallis; Fannie, deceased, who was united in marriage with Dr. J. R. Wallace, and passed away at Washington, Missouri, in June, 1904; and Clara, who married Dr. May, our subject. Judge Ming was not only respected and beloved as a public official, but was a man of fine character, being, as he always asserted, a "self-made man" in the truest sense of the word. He made a success of whatever he undertook, believing in that old and trite but true axiom: "What's worth doing at all is worth doing well." He was a staunch Democrat in his political proclivities, having served Franklin county for three terms in the legislature. He passed away March 22, 1908, his wife having preceded him to that "Far Country," her demise occurring October 2, 1903.

Returning to the immediate subject of this sketch, Dr. Henry Allen May, we would chronicle the fact that Dr. and Mrs. May have one daughter, Susie Frances, and these three form a home circle which is in every way ideal, and their friends, be they rich or poor, are ever accorded a genial welcome to their home.

JACOB M. DECK. That true American, Thomas Jefferson, is credited with saying: "Let the farmer evermore be honored in his calling; for though he labor in the earth he is one of the chosen people of God." Jacob M. Deck, of Bollinger county, Missouri, comes of a family of farmers, men of honor and good citizens and he stands as a representative of the third generation of his family in this county, the first of the name having been one of the brave and dauntless pioneers who turned out of the trodden highways and cut new paths, laying them straight and clean. Mr. Deck was born one mile northwest of the town of Glen Allen, Bollinger county, Missouri, on the 18th day of April, 1858. He is the son of Frederick and Margaret E. (Clubb) Deck, natives of Missouri, and his paternal grandfather, Isaac Deck, was a native of North Carolina. Isaac Deck was the founder of the family in the state, his arrival in Bollinger county occurring in 1805. He secured six hundred acres of land, which he entered and homesteaded, and he changed the wilderness into a fertile farm, upon which he lived and reared his children. His son Frederick, father of the immediate subject of this biographical record, died March 20, 1865, and left three hundred and forty acres to be divided among his four heirs. Mr. Deck became the possessor of the entire estate, buying the shares of the other three heirs. However, he later sold forty acres and now owns all but that amount of the old Isaac Deck homestead.

Upon this fine old farm the subject was born and reared and here has passed all his life. He attended the district school and like most farmers' sons early became familiar with the many mysteries of seedtime and harvest. When it came to choosing a vocation he concluded to follow in the paternal footsteps and he has achieved success, being well-to-do and prominent.

Mr. Deck married in 1880, the lady of his choice being Eliza J. Sites, born in Madison, a daughter of Emanuel and Susan (Yount) Sites, natives of Missouri. Their union has been blessed by the birth of a number of children, seven of whom are living, namely: Ira Walter, born in 1881, married to Rue Reason; Dora, born in 1883, married to E. A. Lincoln; Isaac Jacob, born in 1886; Mary Ann, born in 1887, is the wife of Jesse H. Winters and now lives at Hotchkiss, Colorado; Archie M., born in 1891; Nellie, born in 1896; and Beulah, born in 1898. The cheerful and hospitable Deck household is one of the most popular of the community. Mr. Deck is a tried and true Democrat and in his religious conviction is in harmony with the teachings of the Missionary Baptist church. He is a member of the Woodmen lodge.

Mr. Deck is the only one living of a family of ten children, and he has but one aunt living, Mrs. Catherine Sullivan, who was also one of a large family, one of the younger children. She is now past eighty-five years of age.

CHARLES E. KIEFNER. An enumeration of the men of the present generation who have won success and public recognition for themselves and at the same time have honored the state to which they belong, would be incomplete were there failure to make prominent reference to the one whose name initiates this paragraph. He holds distinctive precedence as a contractor and builder at Perryville, Missouri, as a man of broad and varied attainments and as a valued and patriotic citizen. He is distinctively a man of affairs and one who has wielded a wide influence. A strong mentality, invincible courage and a most determined individuality have so entered into his makeup as to render him a natural leader of men and a director of opinion. He has ever manifested a deep and sincere interest in community affairs and for three sessions represented his district in the state legislature of Missouri.

A native son of Perryville, Missouri, Charles E. Kiefner was born on the 25th of November, 1869, and he is a scion of an old and honored German family, his father, John Kiefner, having been born in Bavaria on the 6th of April, 1834. John Kiefner was reared to the age of sixteen years in his old fatherland and he received an excellent primary education in the public schools of Germany. In 1850 he immigrated to the United States in company with his grandfather and they located in the city of Baltimore, Maryland, where the young John learned the cabinet maker's trade. In 1865, just after the close of the Civil war, John Kiefner decided to establish his home in the west and in that year he came to Perryville, where he opened up a furniture and undertaking business, continuing to be engaged in that line of enterprise for a period of forty years. On the 25th of December, 1854, at Baltimore, was solemnized his marriage to Miss Catherine Lakel, who traces her origin back to sterling German stock. Mr. and Mrs. Kiefner became the parents of eleven children, five of whom are living at the present time, in 1911. On other pages of this work is dedicated a sketch to Samuel B. Kiefner, an older brother of the subject of this review. Mr. and Mrs. Kiefner are now living at Perryville, where they are retired from the active affairs of life and where they are enjoying to the full the fruits of their former years of earnest toil and endeavor. They are a fine old couple and are everywhere beloved for their admirable qualities and genial kindliness.

Charles E. Kiefner was educated in the public schools of Perryville and at the age of fourteen years he accompanied his parents to Kansas, where they resided for the ensuing four years. During this period Mr. Kiefner learned the carpenter's trade and upon his return to Perryville, at the age of twenty-one years, he opened offices as a contractor and builder. In 1894, when the railroad was extended into Perryville he entered into a partnership alliance with Mr. Tlapek in the lumber business, in which line of enterprise he has continued to be interested during the long intervening years to the present time. As a captain of industry he is a man of shrewd executive ability—one who sees and grasps an opportunity in time to make the most of it. But all his attention has not been devoted to business enterprises. He is a stanch Republican in his political proclivities and his first public office was that of alderman of Perryville. So well did he discharge his duties in this connection that later he was elected mayor of the city, serving in that capacity for a period of four years, from 1899 to 1903. In 1902 Mr. Kiefner was further honored by his fellow citizens in that he was then elected to represent Perry county in the Forty-third general assembly of Missouri. He was elected as his own successor in that office for the two succeeding sessions and he finally retired from the legislature in 1908. He was assigned to membership on important committees of the house and was a faithful and earnest worker in the deliberations of both the floor and committee room. At the present time, in 1911, he is president of the Republican county committee. In every possible connection Mr. Kiefner has contributed his fair quota to the progress and upbuilding of Perryville and Perry county at large and as a citizen no one commands a higher degree of popular confidence and esteem than does he.

On the 10th of July, 1895, Mr. Kiefner was united in marriage to Miss Jettie Luckey, who was born and reared at Brazeau, in Perry county and who is a daughter of Robert Luckey, a representative farmer at Brazeau, now deceased. Mr. and Mrs. Kiefner are the fond parents of five children, whose names are here entered in respective order of birth,—Charles H., Edwin L., Frank W., John and Kathryn. In their religious faith the Kiefner family are devout members of the Presbyterian church, to whose charities and benevolences he is a most liberal contributor.

In a fraternal way Mr. Kiefner is affiliated with the time-honored Masonic order and with the Modern Woodmen of America, in addition to which he is also a valued and appreciative member of the local lodge of the Ancient Order of United Workmen. His is a noble character, one that subordinates personal ambition to public good and seeks rather the benefit of others than the aggrandizement of self. Genial in his associations, he is considerate of others' feelings and sensibilities and is always ready to lend a helping hand to those in distress.

Kos Little is known in Kennett as the "Spoke Man." By that they do not mean that he is always talking, on the contrary, he does not talk unless he has something to say and then he knows how to say it. One cannot fail to have the most profound admiration for those men who do their work and hold their peace—giving us faith in their abilities. They mind their own business. Such a one is Kos Little, the manufacturer of spokes.

He was born in Weakley county, Tennessee, October 27, 1869. He is a son of T. I. and Sarah (Roberts) Little, both residents of Tennessee, being natives of Kentucky and Tennessee, respectively. T. I. Little has always been and is still actively interested in spoke manufacturing and banking. Both are members of the Cumberland Presbyterian church. There were eight children born to them, viz.: J. D. (deceased), T. M., J. W., Kos, Mrs. Maud (Jeter), Maggie (deceased), Dr. R. M. and Mrs. Mary Gray (Banks). Kos Little was educated in his native county and after his schooling was ended he spent two years in the United States Revenue Service; then moved to Paducah, Kentucky, and engaged with his brother, J. W. Little, in manufacturing spokes. His father and three older brothers are all engaged in the spoke manufacturing business. He learned all about the business, learning how to select the timber, how to cut it and move it to the factory. He used hickory almost exclusively for his spokes. He was in the business with his brother in Paducah for eight years, coming to Kennett in 1901 to establish a plant here. He sells about thirty thousand dollars worth of spokes each year, manufacturing buggy, carriage and automobile spokes, all made of hickory. He employs thirty men and his expenses for operating are about twenty-five thousand dollars a year. In addition to this business he is president of the Merchant Oil Company of Kennett, selling oil for tanks, etc. He is vice president of the Kennett Building and Loan Association, which is doing a great deal for Kennett. He owns some town property, on which he puts up the buildings. He is interested in educational work and has served on the city board.

Mr. Little married Mary Jones in Greenfield, Tennessee, November 7, 1894, and one daughter, Louise, has been born to the union. When Mr. Little takes a vacation, he generally spends it at Dawson Spring, Kentucky.

George Henry Bisplinghoff. Three years ago (in 1908) when George Henry Bisplinghoff, editor and publisher of *The Bismarck Gazette*, first secured control of that newspaper, he had the distinction of being the youngest newspaper proprietor in the state of Missouri. Now, although but twenty-four years of age, he has manifested that he is of the stuff of which the ideal member of the Fourth Estate is made. The *Gazette* is interesting, reliable, sound and advanced in its views and is experiencing a steady growth. Mr. Bisplinghoff is loyal to Bismarck with the loyalty of a native son, for it was within its borders that his birth occurred on February 10, 1887. His father, Henry Bisplinghoff, was born in Wayne county, Missouri, in 1858, and is of German descent. The grandfather, August Bisplinghoff, was, in truth, one of the early settlers of the state. He was born in Elberfeldt, Germany, in 1829, and came to the "land of promise"—America—in early life, locating in Missouri and engaging first in surveying and then devoting his energies to farming. He was never elected to the position of government surveyor, but was appointed to the same by Governor Brown. This interesting and honored gentleman, who is now eighty-two years of age, divides his residence between Bismarck and Fredericktown, and although advanced in years still retains his physical and mental faculties in much of their pristine vigor. The father of the subject came to Missouri just previous to the Civil war and settled in Patterson, in whose vicinity the grandfather conducted a farm. In 1885, some two years before the birth of the subject, he removed to Bismarck, where he still resides. He married Cornelia Jordan, daughter of William Jordan, of Potosi, and to their union eight children were born, six of whom are living, George Henry being the second in order of birth of the living children. The father since becoming identified with Bismarck has been engaged in the drug and general merchandise business. He is one of the stalwart Democrats of the county and is affiliated with the Court of Honor, while the family is connected with the Methodist Episcopal church, South.

The early life of George Henry Bisplinghoff was passed in Bismarck and to the schools of the city is he indebted for his education in its preliminary stages. He subsequently matriculated in Marvin College at Fredericktown, and was graduated from the Will Mayfield College at Marble Hall in 1905, taking the degree of Bachelor of Science. After graduating he returned to Bismarck and in April, 1908, he bought the office of *The Bismarck Gazette.* Although young in years, he has given evidence in the management of its affairs of a sound judgment and an editorial ability of decidedly promising order. The paper, independent in policy, has a local subscription list of five hundred, and its advent into the many homes of the little city and its environs is each week eagerly awaited.

Mr. Bisplinghoff still resides at the parental home, having not yet become a recruit to the Benedicts. He is Democratic in his political faith, as his father and grandfather have been before him, and his lodge membership is with the Masons, the Odd Fellows, the Court of Honor and the Rebekahs.

HARRY E. ALEXANDER, although a young man, has already shown the citizens of Cape Girardeau the mettle there is in him. He is a man who is calculated to be a power for good in the community. Most people are consumed with anxiety as to what others will think of their actions and will govern their conduct according to other people's ideas of what it should be. On the other hand, some men are utterly regardless of what other people may think and in order to show their disregard for public opinion they go ahead and do exactly the opposite to the approved, generally accepted methods of procedure. Mr. Alexander is one of the small class of men who have hit the happy medium. He takes pains to find out in his own mind the course he intends to follow and he pursues that course, regardless of all other considerations. It is through such men that reforms come and without them there would be no progress.

He was born in Cape Girardeau county, February 3, 1880. His grandfather, William E. Alexander, was a native of Mecklinburg county, North Carolina, and was of Scotch-Irish descent, his ancestors having come to America from Scotland. In 1830, when William E. was a lad of eleven years of age, his father and mother brought him to southeastern Missouri; they located in Cape Girardeau county, where they were one of the pioneer families of the county. William was educated in the county and achieved success. For many years he was public administrator in the state. His son, Oliver Alexander, was born in Cape Girardeau county, where he was educated, engaged in farming and was married to Lillian L. Woods, also a native of Cape Girardeau county. She was the daughter of Rufus Woods who came from North Carolina about the same time that William E. Alexander came. The Woods family packed all their worldly belongings on wagons and made the journey from North Carolina to Missouri by that slow, laborious method. The family originally came from Scotland and like the Alexander family were of Scotch-Irish descent.

Harry is the eldest of three children, having a brother and sister. His boyhood days were spent on his father's farm, where he learned to work, his father believing in the value of early training in habits of industry and responsibility. He did not, however, intend to be a farmer, but to be a lawyer like his grandfather. He was sent to the district school, where his natural abilities and diligence combined soon won him recognition. He attended high school and then the State normal school at Cape Girardeau, after which he went to the state university at Columbia, but did not complete the course there. Instead he went to Austin, where the state university of Texas was located and graduated from the law department there in 1902. The following year he came to Cape Girardeau, where he began to practice law. He was alone for six years, but in 1909 he formed a partnership with Senator Lane, a lawyer who had already become prominent as a lawyer and a statesman. The firm has met with unprecedented success.

In 1905 Mr. Alexander married Miss Myrtle Jackson, the daughter of Dr. Robert J. Jackson, of Bloomfield, Missouri. Two children have been born to this union, Genevieve Lucille and William E., named after his great grandfather.

In 1907 Mr. Alexander was elected state attorney, which position he held until 1911. He is a firm supporter of the Democratic party, believing that that platform embodies the principles of good government. He is a member of the Benevolent and Protective Order of Elks, of the Eagles. of the Knights of Pythias and the Modern Woodmen of America. Being a life long member of Cape Girardeau county, it is natural that Mr. Alexander should be vitally interested in the welfare of that county and of southeastern Missouri generally. He is by no means inclined to rest on his oars, but is ready to assume any responsibility and undertake any work that will promote the well being of the community and of the state. Personally he has the attributes which assure a man of success in anything he undertakes.

E. L. CLEVENGER. One of the public-spirited citizens of Piedmont is the agent and yard master of the Iron Mountain Railway, E. L. Clevenger. He is the eldest of three sons of Henry and Susan (Horwood) Clevenger, of Fulton county, Pennsylvania. The other two brothers live in Washington, D. C., and in San Francisco, respectively. The parents died in Pennsylvania, the father at the age of sixty-four and the mother in Pennsylvania, when thirty-nine years old.

E. L. Clevenger was born in Fulton county, Pennsylvania, February 6, 1870. When he was six years old his parents took him from the farm to town and sent him to school until he was fourteen years old. At that age he started work in a tan yard and four years later he came west. For a time Mr. Clevenger worked on farms in Iowa, but in December of 1891 he came to Missouri as an operator of the Iron Mountain Railway at Annapolis and has continued in the railroad work in this state ever since. From Annapolis he was transferred to Blackwell, Missouri; in 1894, was sent to Williamsville as agent, and in 1902 he was promoted to his present position at Piedmont.

In this town Mr. Clevenger has worked untiringly for the improvement of the schools. He was first elected to the school board in 1908. He was reelected in 1911 and chosen president in recognition of his hard work for the cause of education. Both Mr. and Mrs. Clevenger are active members of the Christian church. Mrs. Clevenger was formerly Miss Margaret Suddeth, of Prairie City, Iowa. She became Mrs. Clevenger September 4, 1892. Mr. and Mrs. Clevenger have four children, Ruby, Helen, Marjorie and Edrice, all at home.

Politics has no part in Mr. Clevenger's business, but he is a staunch Republican in matters of political policy.

JOHN C. DALE. Distinctly a man of affairs, with a wide and successful experience in business and service in public office, Mr. Dale is best known in the county as a lumber merchant. His parents, James L. and Sarah J. Dale, were natives of Tennessee, who came to Missouri in 1847 and located in Wayne county, near Piedmont. Here John C. Dale was born May 16, 1857, the first of a family of four children of whom three are still living. Both parents are deceased.

Until eighteen years of age Mr. Dale lived on his father's farm. At that time he went to Greenville and spent the next four years as deputy clerk, deputy sheriff and collector under James F. Hatton. At the conclusion of this period he kept books for Mr. Fred Evans, of Piedmont, and later was employed in the same capacity by Mr. H. N. Holliday, of Williamsville. Mr. Holliday was then planning the Holliday Railroad, later built to Greenville.

After spending four years in mercantile business in Piedmont, Mr. Dale went to Texas in 1885. He remained there ten years, the entire time working in the clerical department of the Southern Pacific Railway. In 1895 he returned to Missouri where he has remained ever since. Saw mills, a stave factory, real estate, the insurance business and lastly the tie and lumber business have claimed his attention during these last sixteen years. Mr. Dale operated saw mills for three years and in 1900 he became superintendent for the Pioneer Cooperage Plant at Lutesville, which was established over forty years ago. He kept this position for six years, until he resigned it to engage in a successful real estate and insurance business. Mr. Dale spent the period from 1905 to 1909 at the last mentioned business, and then went into the lumber and railroad tie business. In a normal season his son Harry is his official tie and lumber inspector and buyer. Mr. Dale himself is the owner of three hundred and fifty acres of timber and farm land in Bollinger county, besides one and three-fourths acres and a fine residence in Lutesville.

The marriage of Mr. Dale to Miss Anna Dennis, of Wayne county, occurred August 1, 1879. Miss Dennis was the daughter of William Dennis, former sheriff of Wayne county, a personal friend of Sam Hildebrand and a Confederate soldier. Mr. and Mrs. Dale have seven children living: Maudie, wife of S. E. Chandler, was born in 1883. Hattie, a bookkeeper in Shreveport, Louisiana, was born in 1885. The third daughter, Martha V., is the wife of J. H. Byrd, of Kansas City, Missouri, and was born in 1888. Ollie, born 1890, is with the Consolidated Store and Manufacturing Company. James Harry, mentioned earlier in this sketch, was born in 1893. Lillie and Charles were born in 1897 and 1900 respectively.

A good mixer and a man of deserved personal popularity, Mr. Dale is active in several fraternal organizations. He is a member of the A. F. and A. M., of Marble Hill, and of the chapter and commandery at Cape Girardeau, in which he has taken fourteen degrees. He is also affiliated with the I. O. O. F., the K. O. T. M. and with the A. O. U. W. Mr. and Mrs. Dale are members of the Presbyterian church.

In politics Mr. Dale is a Republican, and, as earlier stated, he is not without experience in public office. It was while he was serving as deputy sheriff of Wayne county that the capture of the New Madrid desperadoes was planned and executed. The leaders in this dangerous undertaking were James Hatton and John Davis. Mr. Dale, who was absent on official business, was fifteen minutes late in arriving at Greenville, and Messrs. Hatton and Davis had already followed the desperadoes out of town and caught up with them at the rendezvous, Jim Lee's residence, where they were eating a late breakfast. Hatton and Davis had held up both robbers in the dining room, but unfortunately they relaxed vigilance and both were shot. Hatton recovered, but Davis died as the result of an operation performed in the hope of saving him from the effects of the robbers' bullets. Altogether, Mr. Dale's career has been one of unusual interest.

WILLIAM W. HUBBARD. An industrious and enterprising farmer of Dunklin county, William W. Hubbard is prosperously engaged in his free and independent occupation on one of the pleasantest homesteads in Senath, where he has lived for nearly a decade. Coming on both sides of the house from Irish ancestry, he was born September 27, 1858, in Brownsville, Haywood county, Tennessee, where his parents settled on leaving Virginia, their native state. His father, who died while yet in the prime of life, in 1861, was a stage driver until after the building of railroads throughout Tennessee, when he embarked in the grocery business, which he carried on successfully until his death. His widow married a second time, but did not live very long thereafter, passing away in 1872.

After his mother's death William W. Hubbard, who had acquired his early education in the subscription schools of Tennessee, went to live with his grandmother and two aunts, who had been left almost destitute through the ravages of the Civil war, and his grandmother subsequently lived with him until her death, in 1896, at the venerable age of eighty-nine years. Selecting farming as his life occupation, Mr. Hubbard settled in White county Arkansas, about 1879, remaining there until 1903, being employed in agricultural pursuits all of the time with the exception of four years when he was engaged in railroad work, being foreman of a section gang a part of the time. For four years after locating in Dunklin county, in 1903, Mr. Hubbard rented land, but has since resided on his present farm, and in its management has been quite successful, having a large part of it cleared and under cultivation, much of which is now rented to tenants. He intends to clear and improve the whole of his land and fence it, a work in which he has already made rapid progress, his farm bidding fair to become one of the most desirable pieces of property in the neighborhood.

Politically Mr. Hubbard is affiliated with the Republican party, and fraternally he is a member of the Woodmen of the World, in which he has held various offices, and of the Woodmen's Circle, an auxiliary of the former organization.

Mr. Hubbard married, in January, 1889, in White county, Arkansas, Elizabeth Allen, who was born in Tennessee, January 24, 1867, a daughter of J. M. and Emma (Sparkman) Allen. Her father is now living in Senath, but her mother died in 1878, when Mrs. Hubbard was a girl of eleven years. Mr. and Mrs. Hubbard have four children, namely: Russell B., born July 23, 1890; Walter C., born January 27, 1892; John B., born November 11, 1896; and Pauline, born December 25, 1908.

JAMES R. ROMINES. Missouri boasts, and with reason, of its wonderful agricultural resources, and that it has become such a successful farming country is attributable to the fact that men of acknowledged abilities have identified themselves with the cultivation of the soil. James R. Romines, a farmer by nature, by inheritance and from choice, stands prominent in the state which he has helped to make famous.

Mr. Romines was born August 2, 1870, on a farm near Vincit, and is the son of Thomas and Lulu (Rogers) Romines. The father, familiarly called "Tom," was a native of Tennessee, where he spent the first few years of his boyhood, then came to Missouri with his parents, where he later entered the agricultural field. He secured a tract of land on Horse Island, with the idea of cultivating it, but he was not very successful; thinking that he would accomplish better results in some other location, he moved to Vincit, but a short trial convinced him that if anything he would find the Vincit farm less desirable than the one he had formerly worked on, so back he went to Horse Island. He stayed this time for a period of seven years, his previous experience enabling him to achieve a fair success, but he was by no means satisfied. At the expiration of seven years of uphill work, he disposed of the Horse Island place and again pulled up his stakes, moving this time to a farm two and a half miles northeast of Caruth. He was a hard worker, but somehow or other he was not able to do more than make both ends meet—land was new and there were few conveniences in that section of the country. He died in 1880, leaving fifty acres of land to his twin brother Will, and this tract represented the result of his years of work; Will died some years ago, and the property remains in the family, owned by his children. The early history of Mrs. Tom Romines was identical with that of her husband, in that she was born in Tennessee and had come to Missouri with her folks some years before her marriage, which took place at Caruth. To their union two children were born, Ellen, who married Wesley Winters, of Vincit, and James R., the subject of this sketch. Mrs. Thomas Romines maintains her home with her daughter at Vincit.

When James R. Romines was very small the family moved from Vincit to Horse Island, as above noted, remaining there until James had passed his sixth birthday and was about ready to commence his school life. At that time he accompanied his parents to Caruth; his father was poor and the roads in the neighborhood of his new home were very bad, so the result was that the lad received very little education in the way of schooling, but he did receive a thorough training in all kinds of farm work, so that in 1890, when at the age of twenty he started out to carve his own career, he was equipped with a working knowledge of the various classes of agricultural pursuits, which stood him in good stead. Leaving home with a capital of ten dollars, he passed the ensuing three years as a farm hand, working for the farmers in the neighborhood of Caruth. He did not draw on his capital, but on the other hand he constantly added to it all that he could possibly save, and at the expiration of three years he bought a tract of land on Horse Island and commenced farming operations on the place. After two years' steady cultivation of the soil he had made many improvements in the farm, and he was able to dispose of it at a profit. For the following four or five years he rented a place, and in the meantime he watched for an opportunity to become permanently located. He bought forty acres of land near Kennett, his present home, but he now owns a tract of sixty acres, and inasmuch as the land has doubled in value since he bought it, he is worth three times as much as when he first came to Kennett. He has done much to bring his farm to a high state of cultivation,—has put up new fences, built new outbuildings and generally improved the place. In addition to managing his own land, he rents about eighty acres yearly, making about one hundred and fifty acres of land which he farms, raising cotton and corn for the most part, but he also devotes part of his land to stock raising.

On the 8th of January, 1890, Mr. Romines married Josephine Akers, who was born in Alabama, in 1872, where her father was engaged in farming. She is a daughter of Leb and Jane (Stone) Akers, both natives of Alabama and both are deceased, as are Mrs. Romines' three brothers and three sisters. The Akers family moved to Vincit, Missouri, in 1874, when the little Josephine was a mere child, and as a matter of course she made the acquaintance of James Romines, her neighbor. To the union of the young people two children were born, Hersel, whose birthday was on St. Patrick's Day, 1896, and Nolar, born May 23, 1900.

Mr. Romines is a Democrat in political sympathies. He is a member of the Woodmen of the World, being affiliated with the Caruth lodge, in which he has held office at different times. He was for years active in the different enterprises of the Shady Grove Mission Baptist church, standing high in the regard of its members, as with the farmers in the community where he has spent all of his life. Mrs. Romines is a member of this church.

THOMAS B. SHARP, who is ably filling the office of marshal of Fredericktown, Missouri, has been the popular and efficient incumbent of a number of important offices of public trust and responsibility since his arrival in this place, in 1892. He was sheriff of Madison county for four years and for two years was county collector. He is loyal and public-spirited in his civic attitude and is ever on the qui vive to do all in his power to advance the best interests of this section of the state.

Mr. Sharp was born in Iron county, Missouri, some five miles south of Ironton, the date of his nativity being the 28th of July, 1855. His father, John Q. A. Sharp, was a son of Robert L. Sharp and he died in 1888, at the age of sixty-two years. John Sharp was a small boy when his father worked at the mine LaMotte. As a youth he became interested in a colliery, engaging in the manufacture of charcoal until the Pilot Knob mine was started, when he secured employment in it as a miner. He also owned a farm sixteen miles southwest of Fredericktown, on the St. Francis river, where he resided during the closing years of his life, his death having occurred in 1888. He married Miss Jane Sutton and they became the parents of six children, of whom the subject of this review was the third in order of birth and four of whom, two sons and two daughters, are living at the present time, in 1911.

To the public schools of Iron and Madison county Thomas B. Sharp is indebted for his preliminary educational training. He was a child of ten years of age at the time of his parents' removal from Iron county to the vicinity of Fredericktown, where he has since passed the greater portion of his life. For three years he was engaged in ranching and stock-raising in Texas and he holds a reputation for being the first man in Madison county to feed a carload of stock here. He is the owner of considerable farming property in Madison county and he also owns land in Oklahoma, his holdings in this county amounting to eight hundred acres, the same containing timber and valuable mineral deposits. A portion of this land is under cultivation. In 1892 Mr. Sharp was honored by his fellow citizens with election to the office of sheriff of Madison county and that year marks his advent in Fredericktown. His work as sheriff covered a period of four years and during that time he was instrumental in greatly raising the standard of law and order in the county. In 1896 he was elected county collector and in 1908 was chosen for the office of city marshal. He was re-elected to the latter office in 1910 and is serving in that capacity at the present time. In politics he is an uncompromising supporter of the principles and policies promulgated by the Democratic party, in the local councils of which he is an active worker.

On January 27, 1877, Mr. Sharp wedded Miss Alma S. King, whose birth occurred in Madison county and who is a daughter of Alexander King, a farmer near the St. Francis river. Mr. and Mrs. Sharp are the parents of four children, concerning whom the following brief data are here recorded: Millie Emeline is the wife of William T. White, a farmer in Madison county, and they have one child, Thomas; Robert L. remains at the parental home; Flavia Eveline is a stenographer in the Third National Bank building at St. Louis; and George Gilbert is in the United States Marine service, his headquarters being at Norfolk, Virginia.

In fraternal circles Mr. Sharp is a valued and appreciative member of the time-honored Masonic order and he is also affiliated with the Independent Order of Odd Fellows, the Knights of Pythias, the Modern Brotherhood of America and the Modern Woodmen of America. In religious matters he is a consistent member of the Methodist Episcopal church. The life of Mr. Sharp is a noble illustration of what independence, self-faith and self-reliance can accomplish in America. He is absolutely self-made and for that reason his admirable success in the business world of this section of the state is the more gratifying to contemplate.

GEORGE W. TARLTON, M. D. One of the prominent and well known physicians and surgeons of Cape Girardeau, Missouri, is Dr. George W. Tarlton, who in connection with his medical work, conducts a large and flourishing drug business at Cape Girardeau.

Dr. George W. Tarlton was born in the state of Kentucky, just across the river from New Madrid, the date of his nativity being the 13th of October, 1849. He is a son of Alexander C. Tarlton, who was born in 1828, at the old Tarlton home in Wayne county, about four miles northeast of Wappapello, on which beautiful estate he was reared and where he was engaged in agricultural operations during the greater part of his active business career. In 1864, on the 18th of

December, he was murdered by a band of guerrilas, who entered the home on Sunday evening, saying: "You d—— black Republican, ain't you ashamed of yourself?" The mother of the Doctor was Arzula Phillips in her girlhood days and she was born and reared in the vicinity of New Madrid. Alexander C. Tarlton was twice married and by his first marriage he became the father of four children, of whom the Doctor is the only survivor at the present time, his two sisters and one brother having died in infancy. The second marriage was prolific of six children, of whom three are now living.

Dr. Tarlton attended school in his native place until he had reached the age of fifteen years when he left home and came to Cape Girardeau, which city has continued to represent his place of residence during the long intervening years to the present time, with the exception of a period of two years, from 1881 to 1883, during which time he lived in Wayne county. For three years he was a student in the state normal school, at Cape Girardeau. In 1871, at the age of twenty-one years, he engaged in the drug business, continuing to follow that line of enterprise until 1879, in which year he was matriculated as a student in the St. Louis Medical College, in which excellent institution he was graduated as a member of the class of 1881, duly receiving his degree of Doctor of Medicine. Immediately after graduation he entered upon the active practice of his profession at Pocahontas, later removing to Oak Ridge. In 1890 he returned to Cape Girardeau, where he now controls a large and lucrative patronage and where he is also engaged in the drug business. In connection with his life work he is a valued and appreciative member of the Southeastern Medical Society and of the Cape Girardeau Medical Society. In the time-honored Masonic order he is affiliated with the Scottish Rite branch and he is also a valued member of the local lodge of the Woodmen of the World. His religious faith is in harmony with the tenets of the Baptist church and in politics he accords an unswerving allegiance to the principles promulgated by the Democratic party.

Dr. Tarlton has been twice married, his first union having been to Miss Addie Penny, the ceremony having been performed on the 18th of March, 1880. Mrs. Tarlton was called to eternal rest four and a half months after her marriage and on the 29th of November, 1882, was solemnized the marriage of the Doctor to Miss Maggie Morton, who was born and reared at Pocahontas, Missouri. To this union have been born four children, concerning whom the following brief data are here incorporated,—David W. P. Tarlton is a dentist by profession and he is engaged in that work at Marshall, Arkansas; Lou B. is a teacher at Cape Girardeau; Ann, who is the wife of George Cochran, resides at Hoxie, Arkansas; and Mary Katrina, fourteen years of age, is a student in the local high school.

GUY F. KAHMANN. It is to be doubted whether a man in a position of great trust realizes the confidence and esteem thus exhibited by his friends and fellow citizens. Guy F. Kahmann of this review holds just such a position, but he is deeply conscious of the trust reposed in him as cashier of the First National Bank of Washington, and labors valiantly and well to uphold that confidence.

Our subject came from good old German stock, thrifty, alert and honest, his father, Christopher H. Kahmann, having been born in Hanover, Germany, in 1828. He came to the United States when but a small boy of eleven years, but there is no record of where his youth was passed or what were his educational advantages, but his later business success marked him as a man of unusual and extraordinary acumen, being endowed with a capacity for affairs of broad scope. Mr. Kahmann was a leading citizen of Washington for many years, being the proprietor of the pork-packing business in that city, instituted in 1856 and continued until his death in 1883 and then until 1887 under his successor, Guy F. Kahmann. when it yielded to the pressure of the great packing interests of St. Louis and Kansas City and became extinct. Christopher H. Kahmann married Anna Mense, a daughter of Gerhard Uhlenbrock Mense, who was engaged in the saw and grist-mill business in Franklin county for many years, coming to that county in 1833. The children born to this union were as follows: George H., who died in Kansas City in February, 1911, a prominent contractor of that city; William. who was a lawyer and a publisher, and passed away in Washington in October, 1893; Guy F., the immediate subject of this review; Annie, the wife of Charles Wynne, of New York city; Cassilda, who married John B. Busch, of Washington; and Joseph F., of

Kansas City, special agent for the London and Lancashire Insurance Company.

Guy F. Kahmann, our subject, was born in Franklin county, Missouri, September 6, 1858, the son of Christopher H. and Anna (Mense) Kahmann. He received a sure foundation for whatever business he chose to adopt in having received good educational advantages, than which there is no greater heritage. He entered Pio Nono College in 1873 in Milwaukee, Wisconsin, and completed the commercial training in that college to prepare him for practical life. As above stated, he became a member of the firm of C. H. Kahmann & Son, of which his father was the founder in 1856, and continued in this business until 1887, carrying on the business himself some four years after his father's demise. After the abandonment of this pork-packing industry he associated himself with the firm of H. Tibbe & Son Manufacturing Company, the predecessors of the Missouri Meerschaum Company of Washington, and was its secretary and treasurer for nearly a quarter of a century, his ability and value in this concern being evidenced by the length of time of his association with it.

The First National Bank of Washington was organized by E. C. Stuart, of Cape Girardeau, in 1900, and in 1910 our subject was chosen cashier, succeeding Mr. E. C. Stuart, who is now connected with the Third National Bank of St. Louis, at which time he severed his connection with the Missouri Meerschaum Company. The other officials of the bank are: A. Kahmann, president, and E. C. Stuart and E. H. Otto, vice-presidents. Its capital stock and surplus is at the present time, 1911, $38,000.00, and deposits, $250,000.00, and its board of directors comprise some of the most successful business men of Washington and community. This bank is a sound and safe moneyed institution of this part of Missouri.

Mr. Guy F. Kahmann was united in the holy bonds of wedlock with Miss Regina Wellenkamp, a native daughter of Franklin county, this marriage being solemnized in Washington on the 11th of September, 1883, and Mrs. Kahmann being the daughter of Henry and Katharine (Menkhaus) Wellenkamp, the former an early merchant of Washington. To this union have been born six children, as follows: Walter H., assistant cashier of the First National Bank of Washington; Regina; Leander, who is with the Roberts, Johnson & Rand Shoe Company of St. Louis; Raymond J.; Othmar M.; and Rosa L., deceased.

While Mr. Kahmann has never desired to avail himself of the honors or emoluments of office, he has ever kept in touch with party politics, and is firmly allied on the side of the Democratic party. He devotes much time to his family and his friends, and consequently has not found leisure to join any fraternal organizations. The Kahmann family are members of the Catholic church. The home of Mr. and Mrs. Kahmann is one of the most pleasant and hospitable in Washington, and the latch-string is always out not only to their friends but to any one in distress or trouble.

SAMUEL THOMAS MCGEE is one of the prominent farmer-citizens of Bollinger county and he is also a veteran of the Civil war, his military record in the great conflict being a thrilling one whose recountal has brought to many a youthful cheek the glow of interest and enthusiasm. He is a native son of Missouri, his birth having occurred in Washington county on the 2nd day of February, 1842, and his parents were Samuel and Elvira (Thompson) McGee, both natives of the state. The scene of the father's birth was Washington county and that of the mother's Cape Girardeau. He is of Irish descent, both his paternal grandparents having claimed Erin as their birthplace. Their names were Felix and Elizabeth McGee. The great-grandfather, Patrick McGee, was also a native of Ireland, as was his wife, Rosa. His great-grandfather Dennis was born, lived and died in Ireland. The birth dates of the father and mother of Mr. McGee were 1813 and 1815.

Mr. McGee was reared upon a farm and has spent almost his entire life amid rural surroundings. A young man less than twenty years of age at the outbreak of the Civil war, he was none the less one of the first to enlist, in 1861 joining Company B, Sixth Missouri Infantry under the command of William Tecumseh Sherman, and Captain John W. Fletcher, as a member of the First Brigade, Second Division of the Fifteenth Army Corps, Army of the Tennessee. A brief resume of his service includes many of the great and decisive events of the struggle between the states. He was in the engagement at Chickasaw Bayou, Mississippi, when Sherman was repulsed; the battle of Arkansas

Post; at Champion Hill and Jackson, Missouri; he was present at the siege of Vicksburg and participated in the battle of Missionary Ridge, near Chattanooga, Tennessee. He was in the forced march from Chattanooga to Knoxville, in eastern Tennessee, when General Burnside was surrounded by General Longstreet. He then started with Sherman on the march to the sea in the spring of 1864, and after that was in one continual fight until June 24, 1864, at which time he received his discharge.

Upon the termination of his career as a soldier Mr. McGee returned to Jefferson county, Missouri, and in 1870 bought eighty acres of land in the vicinity of Glen Allen, Missouri. Since then he has added twenty-four acres, his property now consisting of one hundred and four acres. It is an excellent farm, fruitful and well improved and it is very dear to Mr. McGee, who has made his home upon it for forty-one years.

On October 1, 1863, Mr. McGee was happily married to Mary A. Brinley, daughter of Michael and Catherine (Baldwin) Brinley, natives of Missouri. Mrs. McGee passed to the life eternal June 29, 1880, after becoming the mother of the following children: Elvira, born in 1865, wife of R. A. Porter; Sarah Elizabeth, born in 1866, the wife of Edward Stanton; Patrick F., born in 1868, died 1890; Jessie, born in 1870, wife of Phineas Haynes; Minerva, born in 1872, wife of James Stewart; William Jackson, born in 1874, died in 1904; and Andrew M., born in 1879, and married to Ida Cole. He was married a second time, to Rachel Browner, daughter of William and Lydia Browner, natives of Tennessee and Kentucky, respectively, their union being solemnized May 7, 1881. The two sons of this union are Jasper Samuel, born in 1883, and married to Grace Sample; and Thomas Sherman, born in 1894.

Mr. McGee and his worthy wife are affiliated with the Methodist Episcopal church and the former is an influential Republican who has from time to time held public office acceptably. He was deputy sheriff of Bollinger county for two years; justice of the peace for twelve years; and public administrator four years. He is interested in all things likely to benefit the community, and the county finds in him one of the valuable citizens.

JAMES A. ROGERS, of Kennett, is a man of the highest sense of honor, which has never been besmirched. He is exceptionally fair minded in all of his conclusions, having the unusual ability to see both sides of a question. His history has been an interesting one.

He was born in Giles county, Tennessee, in 1848, on the 6th of November, the son of John and Susannah Rogers, both natives of South Carolina. They lived in Tennessee until 1860, when they came to Dunklin county, Missouri. They bought land at Caruth and also cotton gins, operating the same for about four years. They then bought the Redman farm at Vincit, six miles south of Kennett, where they both died and were buried on the farm. He was sixty-four when he died and she was seventy-five at her death. They had a family of five children, three of whom are living now. Louisa married Tom Romines and is now his widow. She has one son, James. The other daughter is Emma, who married Mr. Snipes of Kennett.

The third child living is James A., who spent the first twelve years of his life in Tennessee, coming to Dunklin county when he was twelve years old. For four years they lived on Horse Island, farming. He then moved six miles south of Kennett. From the time he first moved to Missouri he did not have a great deal of schooling, but helped his father on the farm and with the cotton gins. He lived at home until he was twenty-six years old, for the last five years of that time taking full charge of the farm, part of which his father had deeded to him and he still owns it. He lived on the farm until 1910, when he moved into Kennett. He had one hundred acres of land to start out with, to which he added as he was able until he had three hundred and one and a half acres, the large proportion of which he cleared himself. He sold part of this large farm, now owning two hundred and sixty acres on which he has built a new house and buildings. The farmers around say that Mr. Roger's farm is the best one in that section of the country. He grows grain and cotton on his land. For a few years he operated a cotton gin, but gave that up long ago. Vincit post office and general store were on his farm, he being postmaster from 1895 to 1902. He is a Democrat, but aside from casting his vote at election times he does not take any active part in politics.

In 1879 he married Lavisa Barger, daughter of Philip and Jane Barger. They came from Indiana to Missouri in the fifties, their daughter Lavisa having been born since their removal to Missouri. Mr. Barger was killed by the guerillas during the Civil war, as they were believed to be in sympathy with the South. Mr. and Mrs. Rogers have had three children. The eldest is Audrey, who was educated in the state normal school at Cape Girardeau and has been a teacher for the past seven years, now teaching in the Kennett school with great success. Thomas, the elder boy, also attended the state normal and died October 30, 1909, when he was twenty years old. The youngest child is Ray, who is at present a high school student.

Mr. Rogers is not a member of any church, but his family attend the Baptist church. He is interested in education, perhaps all the more because his own schooling was of necessity rather meagre and what he knows he has had to gather from reading and observation as he went along. He has made a point of giving his children the best education that he could, realizing the advantages that it would be to them, no matter what line they might follow in after years. Mr. Rogers is very devoted to the county where he has lived practically all of his life, and the county is fully appreciative of Mr. Rogers and all that he has done in a quiet way for its improvement; he is widely known and as universally respected.

MOSES BURETTE BARBER, M. D., of Flat River, is one of the foremost professional and business men of southeastern Missouri. During his career as a physician and surgeon his practice has grown to the extent of his ability to care for it, and in addition many important business interests require his attention.

Dr. Barber was born at Frohne, Perry county, Missouri, August 30, 1869, and spent his early life on a farm in that county and in Wayne county. His early education was secured in the public schools and at the Carlton Institute and Farmington Baptist College, and thus equipped he entered educational work and for seven years taught school, during the last two years being principal of the Mine La Motte public schools. For two succeeding years he was engaged in the drug business at Bonne Terre. Having in the meantime taken up the study of medicine, he took his degree of Doctor of Medicine at the Barnes Medical College on April 12, 1899. His entrance in this profession was at Flat River, where he has resided for the past twelve years.

Dr. Barber was the organizer of the Flat River Ice & Cold Storage Company and is its president. This company, which is capitalized at fifty thousand dollars, has two plants, one at Bonne Terre and one at Flat River. He also was one of the organizers and is a stockholder in the Central Steam Laundry at Flat River. For two years he was president of the Miners and Merchants Bank, of which he is still a director. His real estate holdings include property in Flat River and extensive interests in New Mexico.

Dr. Barber belongs to one of the old families of southeastern Missouri. His father, Richard H. Barber, who is still a resident of Madison county, was born at Brazeau, Perry county, January 4, 1845, and has enjoyed a career of prosperity, being the owner of large amounts of real estate. He is a member of the Presbyterian church and the Independent Order of Odd Fellows, and in politics is a Democrat. He married, October 23, 1868, Surena Cline, of Frohne, Missouri, daughter of Moses and Caroline Cline, farmers and early settlers of Perry county. Her mother, Mrs. Cline, was one of the first members of the Baptist church in this state, and lived to the age of eighty-six. Mrs. Barber died July 22, 1909, having been the mother of seven children, of whom Dr. Barber is the oldest.

In politics Dr. Barber is Democratic, is a member of the Methodist Episcopal church, South, and affiliates with the Modern Woodmen of America and the Modern Americans. He is also a member of the American Medical Association, the Missouri State Medical Association, the Southeastern Missouri Medical Society and the St. Francois County Medical Association. He was married, August 29, 1895, to Miss Mollie E. Turley. She taught in the public schools of St. Francois county for ten years before her marriage. Her parents are Wesley and Emeline Turley, her father being one of the pioneer farmers in the lead belt. Three children have been born to Dr. and Mrs. Barber. The two living are Anson B. and Virginia E.

LUTHER HENRY WILLIAMS. Among the most prominent and able financiers of Saint Francois county is Luther Henry Williams, cashier of the Farmers' Bank, a monetary institution in whose organization he participated; a director of the Mines' Supply Company at Flat River; and interested in the National Bank of Commerce of the city of St. Louis and the Bankers Trust Company of St. Louis. The Farmers' Bank is one of the monetary institutions which emphasize and exert marked influence in conserving the financial stability and commercial prestige of the county and its judicial center and Mr. Williams has shown marked discrimination in the management of its affairs.

Mr. Williams is a native of Saint Francois county, his birth having occurred within its pleasant boundaries on November 21, 1869. His father, George McGahan Williams, was born in this county, March 4, 1831. The senior Mr. Williams, owing to educational conditions of his time, received but a limited training, this, such as it was, being secured in the common schools of the locality and period. He passed his early days on the farm and in truth has devoted his life-long activities to the great basic industry. He established a household of his own in 1855, when he was united in marriage to Amelia Thomasson, of St. Francois county, a daughter of Gabriel and Sally Thomasson, the former of whom was a prominent agriculturist. To this union nine children were born, six of whom are living at the present time. The devoted wife and mother was summoned to the life eternal in 1885, but the father survives, a venerable gentleman, well-known in the locality. He remained upon his farm until he sold it to the Theodora Lead Company, about the year 1894, which marks the time of his retirement from active farm life, and he now makes his home in Farmington. In political questions he gives heart and hand to the men and measures of the Democratic party, which he has supported since his earliest voting days, and his religious conviction is that of the Southern Methodist Episcopal church.

Luther Henry Williams had what is generally considered the good fortune to pass his early life upon the farm, and in the common country schools he received his preliminary education. When it came to choosing a life work he found that he had no ambition to follow in the paternal footsteps, and at the age of twenty-one years he left the farm and went to work in the mines, running a diamond drill. He was engaged in this wise for four years, at the end of which time he concluded to prepare himself for a business career and to this end he went to St. Louis and entered the Bryant & Stratton Commercial College, and having finished this he entered the mercantile business at Flat River in association with his brothers, George K. and John T. In 1898 the Messrs. Williams sold out and after a short period of leisure the subject entered upon his first banking experience, as an employe of the Miners' & Merchants' Bank at Flat River, he taking the office of assistant cashier for the first year and in the two years following holding that of cashier. In 1904 he assisted in the organization of the Farmers' Bank at Farmington, and was made cashier of the institution, which place he now holds. As mentioned in a preceding paragraph he is a director of the Miners' Supply Company at Flat River and also interested in the National Bank of Commerce in St. Louis and The Bankers Trust Company of St. Louis.

On the 20th day of April, 1898, Mr. Williams was happily married to Nelly Pearl Moody, of Irondale, daughter of William Moody, an engineer and mechanic. The union of Mr. and Mrs. Williams has been blessed by the birth of six children, namely: Gwendolyn, Luther Wallace (deceased); George Harry, Franklin, Mary Lucile and Corinne.

Mr. Williams is an interested and popular member of the great Masonic order and exemplifies in his own life its noble principles, while his church home and that of his worthy wife is of the Southern Methodist denomination. Politically he is a stalwart supporter of the Democratic party, having been aligned with the same since his earliest voting days.

ROBERT H. WHITELAW, one of the successful lawyers of Cape Girardeau, is as popular as he is influential. Throughout his career his maxim has been to do the duty which lies nearest, not worrying about what the next step might be. It is because of this simplicity of creed that Mr. Whitelaw has made such an unmitigated success of his life up to the present time. He has by no means reached the limit of his capabilities, although he has accomplished enough to satisfy a less enterprising man. However, it is safe to predict that inasmuch as he has heretofore filled all offices to the satisfaction of both his own and opposing parties, he will continue to have responsibilities thrust upon him.

He was born in Essex county, Virginia, January 30, 1854, and is the son of Thomas Whitelaw, a planter in Virginia, in which state he was born. He was possessed of a large plantation on which were many slaves, but he was a believer in the rights of the colored man and was a most considerate master.

In 1859, foreseeing the struggle that was imminent between the north and the south, he set free his slaves and sold his plantation, coming to Cape Girardeau in 1859. He bought a farm there but died in 1863, while the war was still in progress. He married Emily Reynolds, a young Virginia girl, who bore him three children, the last one costing her her life. She died in 1856, leaving her husband, her two little boys and baby girl to mourn her loss.

When Robert was only five years old, his father took him and his little brother to Cape Girardeau, leaving the daughter in Virginia. Robert has very little recollection of the little mother who left them when he was two years old, of the plantation where he was petted and scolded by turns by his colored mammy and of the journey from Virginia to Cape Girardeau. He has, however, very distinct recollections of the first school which he attended, of the death of his father when he was only nine years old and of the sense of desolation which overwhelmed him at being left without father or mother at that early age. He attended the public schools of Cape Girardeau and later the academy of St. Louis, Professor Wyman being the principal at that time. He then went to Ann Arbor, where he took a law course at the University of Michigan. He graduated in 1874 when he was just twenty years old and located in Cape Girardeau. He soon established a practice, and, young as he was, in 1876 he was elected prosecuting attorney of Cape Girardeau county. This office he held until 1879. He was elected to the legislature, representing Cape Girardeau county, serving for two terms. He was a member of Congress in 1890 and 1891 and has been prosecuting attorney for many years.

In 1877 he married Katie Block, the daughter of Zalma Block of Cape Girardeau. Mr. and Mrs. Whitelaw have three children living, as follows: Helen, the wife of Lieutenant R. G. Rutherford, now stationed at Madison Barracks, New York. Matilda, the second child, is the wife of Captain Allen R. Williams and is also stationed at Madison Barracks, New York. Thomas G., the youngest child and only son, is in business in St. Louis.

Like his father, Mr. Whitelaw has always been a Democrat and most active in the interests of his party. Although not born in Cape Girardeau, he has very little remembrance of his native place and his affections are all with southeastern Missouri, which has been to him a foster parent, taking the place of father and mother. He is a man who has done incalculable good in the county and his efforts have been appreciated by the citizens of Cape Girardeau.

BRISTOL FRENCH. To the editor is confided singular responsibility. He is the moulder of public opinion, and it is his privilege to be heard on questions of public welfare by more people than any public speaker could possibly hope to reach. The *Piedmont Banner* is indeed fortunate to have as its publisher and editor Mr. Bristol French, who, though yet a young man, brings to his task a varied experience in the newspaper field as well as a courageous sense of his responsibility to the public whom he informs through the pages of the *Piedmont Weekly Banner*.

He was born in Houston county, Tennessee, February 2, 1877. His father was John French, a member of an old Tennessee family, and his mother was a daughter of Colonel John Morris, who was a military officer in both the Mexican and Civil wars. Until the opening of the Spanish-American war he was engaged in the newspaper business, connected with the *Erin News* in his home town of Erin, Tennessee. At the call for volunteers, he at once enlisted with the First Tennessee Volunteers, and went with that company to the Philippine Islands, where he spent nineteen months in the service, during which time he served as sergeant major in the second battalion and sergeant in his own company. His army career, however, in no way interfered with his life work, as he was an active correspondent for the Nashville papers during his stay in our insular possessions. Upon his return, he was associated first with the *Memphis News Scimitar*, and later with the *Memphis Commercial Appeal*. In 1904 Mr. French took his present position, and purchased the *Piedmont Weekly Banner*, which sheet was established by Dr. J. N. Holmes in June, 1892.

He was married in 1905 to Miss Nettie Williams, of Piedmont, Missouri, and to this union have been born two children. Politically Mr. French favors the policies advocated by the Democratic party, and both personally and officially, is counted a valuable member of his party.

C. A. WALKER has risen from clerk to the position of leading hardware merchant in the county by the qualities of business sagacity and initiative, combined with a genius for hard work. He was born in Illinois, in 1869, on the 16th of July. His parents, C. T. and Louise Walker, are still living on a farm in that state.

Mr. Walker spent the first twenty-one years of his life in Illinois. He helped his father on the farm and secured his education in the meantime in the district schools and in the normal at Carbondale, Illinois. In September, 1890, he came to Lutesville and secured employment as clerk for George E. Clark & Son. Mr. Walker learned the business thoroughly in the following six years and rose steadily in it, so that in 1897 he was able to purchase a hardware business in Marble Hill. In 1910 he sold out his interests in Marble Hill and went to Colorado, intending to make his home in that state, but decided to return to Missouri. In January, 1911, Mr. Walker purchased the interests of Clark & Son and is engaged in managing that extensive business. The house carries a line of hardware, agricultural implements, furniture, lumber, shingles, cement and lime, and transacts the bulk of the trade in these lines in Lutesville and in Bollinger county. In addition, Mr. Walker is a stockholder in the Bollinger County Bank and in the Bank of Marble Hill. His residence is one of the attractive homes of Lutesville.

Mr. Walker's wife was Miss Nellie Clark, daughter of George Clark, the former employer of Mr. Walker. Mr. George Clark was a pioneer merchant of Lutesville, coming to that town in 1872 from Marble Hill, where he had located five years previously. Mr. and Mrs. Walker have two children: George Earl, born in 1893, and Charles Dean, in 1897.

Mr. Walker has attained high honor in the Masonic order. He was made a Blue Lodge Mason at Marble Hill, Missouri, and joined the Chapter at Fredericktown. He went into the Commandery at Cape Girardeau, and into the Consistory at St. Louis, taking thirty-two degrees in all. In addition he is a member of the Modern Woodmen and of the Odd Fellows in Lutesville. He takes an active interest in his lodges and in the Presbyterian church, of which Mrs. Walker is a member and a valued adherent.

J. OLIVER EUBANKS. A thrifty and well-to-do agriculturist of Hollywood, J. Oliver Eubanks is the proprietor of a fine farm, which in regard to its appointments compares favorably with any in the locality, the neatness and orderly appearance of the property showing conclusively that the owner has a thorough understanding of his business and exercises excellent judgment in its management. A Missourian by birth, he was born on a farm in Douglas county, January 8, 1877, and lived there until three years of age. In 1880 his father and his half-sister were killed by lightning, and his mother subsequently married a second husband and removed to Stoddard county, Missouri, where her death occurred in 1892, on the farm which she had there purchased.

Until sixteen years of age J. Oliver Eubanks worked on his mother's farm in Stoddard county, near Puxico, in the meantime obtaining a practical education in the district school. He subsequently worked for wages on neighboring farms for a number of years. Coming then to Dunklin county, he invested his money, all of which, with the exception of forty-two dollars that he received from his mother's estate after attaining his majority, he had earned by the sweat of his brow, in farming land in Hollywood. Mr. Eubanks first purchased forty acres on time, and later bought forty acres of adjoining land, and of this he has cleared about sixty-three acres himself, and placed it under culture, and when he first came to the place he also cleared land for other people, becoming quite expert in the pioneer task. For a number of years after assuming possession of his property Mr. Eubanks lived in a rude shack, but he has since erected a substantial, eight-room house and good farm buildings, and is now devoting his energies to the growing of corn and cotton, crops which he finds most profitable. Mr. Eubanks also owns an eighty-acre farm lying one and three-fourths miles northeast of Cardwell, on which he has made valuable improvements, that land being rented out. He is also now contemplating the purchase of one hundred and twenty acres of land adjoining his farm near Cardwell, an investment which will eventually prove of value.

Mr. Eubanks married first, in 1892, on his present farm, Nellie Horner, the daughter of an early settler of Hollywood. She passed to the higher life a few years later, leaving four children, namely: Nettie, Melvin, Elmer and Herman, all of whom, with the exception of the eldest child, are at home. Mr. Eubanks married in 1900 Ora Sanders, and they are the parents of three children, namely: Ruth, Rose and Floyd. Politically Mr. Eubanks is a Democrat, and fraternally he belongs to Senath Camp, No. 256, W. O. W.

WILLIAM M. GUDGER. At this juncture in a volume devoted to the careers of representative citizens of southeastern Missouri, it is a pleasure to insert a brief history of the life and work of William M. Gudger, who has ever been on the alert to forward all measures and enterprises projected for the general welfare and who is the present efficient incumbent of the office of president of the Madison County Milling Company, an enterprise which reflects credit on Fredericktown.

William M. Gudger is strictly a self-made man, the admirable success which he has achieved in the business world of Madison county being the direct result of his own well applied endeavors. He was born in the vicinity of Nashville, Tennessee, the date of his nativity being the 29th of May, 1869. He is a son of John and Nancy (McCreary) Gudger, both of whom were natives of North Carolina, whence they removed to Tennessee a short time after their marriage. In the early '70s they decided to move still further west, and accordingly came to Missouri, settling at Fredericktown. They were the owners of a fine plantation in Tennessee in the antebellum days but the ravages of the war practically ruined them. The father was identified with farming operations during the greater part of his active career and he was summoned to the life eternal in 1908, when past seventy years of age. The mother died in 1884, in her forty-fifth year. John Gudger was a devout Methodist in his religious faith and his wife was a member of the Baptist church. Mr. and Mrs. Gudger were the parents of five children, two of whom are deceased. Those living are:- Henry, who is engaged in the railroad business in Texas; Lulu, who is the wife of Henry Robinson, of St. Francois county, Missouri; and William M., the immediate subject of this review.

Mr. Gudger grew to young manhood at Fredericktown, where his preliminary educational training consisted of such advantages as were afforded in the public schools. After leaving school he launched out into the business world on his own account, early becoming interested in milling enterprises. He had no capital to start with but by hard work and careful management he finally forged ahead and today he is recognized as one of the most prominent and influential citizens in this place. He is president of the Madison County Milling Company, which important concern was incorporated under the laws of the state of Missouri in 1903. In November of that year the present mill was erected and since that time a splendid business has been controlled. The Company is incorporated with a capital stock of twelve thousand dollars and the officers are as follows: W. M. Gudger, president; George O. Smith, secretary; and Henry Ward, director. The capacity of the mill is one hundred and fifty barrels of flour per day and two of the leading brands of flour in this section of the state are turned out, namely, "Pride of Madison" and "Lily of the Valley." A force of five men are constantly employed and ninety per cent of the wheat ground comes from local customers. Mr. Gudger was formerly associated in the milling business with Messrs. DeGuire and Lanpher, being a member of the DeGuire Milling Company at Fredericktown for some eighteen years. His long association with milling enterprises has made him expert in that particular business and under his careful and wise management the Madison County Milling Company has prospered wonderfully.

In the year 1894 was celebrated the marriage of Mr. Gudger to Miss Elizabeth Hunter, a native of St. Francois county, Missouri, and a daughter of English parents, who came to America about the year 1873. Mrs. Gudger's father was long engaged in teaching in this part of the state and he is now residing at Fredericktown. Mr. and Mrs. Gudger have no children living.

In politics Mr. Gudger is a loyal supporter of the principles of the Democratic party and for six or seven years he was a member of the city council of Fredericktown. He is now serving on the school board. In Scottish Rite Masonry he has attained to the thirty-second degree and he is also a member of Moolah Temple, Ancient Arabic Order of the Nobles of the Mystic Shrine. He is likewise connected with the Independent Order of Odd Fellows and Mrs. Gudger is a member of the Daughters of Rebekah. In their religious faith they are devout communicants of the Protestant Episcopal church, to whose good work they are liberal contributors.

MOSES ROSENTHAL, M. D., in his professional service has been prompted by a laudable ambition for advancement as well as by deep sympathy and humanitarian principles that urge him to put forth his best efforts in the alleviation of pain and suffering. He has gained recognition from the profession as one of its able representatives and the trust reposed in him by the public is indicated by the liberal patronage awarded him. Since 1903 Dr. Rosenthal has been a valued citizen of Cape Girardeau and here he is universally admired and respected for his high order of ability and for his loyal and public-spirited interest in all matters affecting the general welfare.

At Scranton, Pennsylvania, occurred the birth of Dr. Moses Rosenthal, the date of his nativity being the 15th of May, 1858. He is a son of Julius Rosenthal, who was born and reared at Stolp, Germany, whence he immigrated to the United States about the year 1855. Julius Rosenthal was born in the year 1825 and he was summoned to the life eternal in 1892. For a time after his arrival in this country he resided in the city of St. Louis, Missouri, where he was engaged in the general merchandise business. At the time of the inception of the Civil war he gave evidence of his intrinsic loyalty to the cause of the south by enlisting as a soldier in the Confederate army. In 1865, just after the close of the war, he went to Jackson, Tennessee, where he was engaged for a number of years in the mercantile business and where he continued to reside until his demise. In 1857 was solemnized his marriage to Miss Henrietta Ackerman and this union was prolific of four children, of whom the Doctor was the first born and of whom he is now the only survivor. By a former marriage Julius Rosenthal had one child, Benjamin, a resident of Kentucky.

Dr. Rosenthal was a child of seven years of age at the time of the establishment of the family home at Jackson, Tennessee, where his preliminary educational training consisted of such advantages as were afforded in an old Catholic school. Subsequently he was matriculated as a student in the Southern Baptist Union University, at Jackson, Tennessee, in which excellent school of learning he was graduated as a member of the class of 1875. For two years after completing his collegiate course he was engaged in business with his father but in 1877, deciding upon the medical profession as his future life work, he began to study for the same under the able preceptorship of Dr. Joseph Thompson, at Paducah, Kentucky, the latter having been a surgeon in the Confederate army under General Sidney Johnson. From Paducah Dr. Rosenthal removed to St. Louis, Missouri, where he attended the Missouri Medical College, in which well equipped institution he was graduated in 1880, duly receiving his degree of Doctor of Medicine. Prior to his graduation and during his residence in Kentucky he had been admitted to the medical fraternity of the old Bluegrass state and for a short time he was associated with Dr. Thompson in a general practice. Immediately after graduation he opened offices in the city of St. Louis, where he resided until 1882 and where he was successful in building up a large and lucrative patronage. On account of ill health, however, he was forced to give up his practice in the Missouri metropolis and he then went to Pemiscot county, this state, remaining there for a period of two years, at the expiration of which, in 1885, he removed to Kennett, in Dunklin county. He maintained his home in the latter place until 1903 and in that year came to Cape Girardeau, where he controls an extensive practice and where he is a man of prominence and influence in all the relations of life. Since coming to this city Dr. Rosenthal has pursued post-graduate courses in St. Louis, Chicago and New York. He is interested in and is a valued member of a number of representative medical organizations of representative character, including the Southeastern Missouri Medical Society, in which he has been honored with a number of important official positions. He is surgeon for the C. G. & C. Railroad Company and is everywhere held in high esteem for his splendid ability in the field of one of the most helpful professions to which man may devote his energies.

In January, 1882, at St. Louis, was celebrated the marriage of Dr. Rosenthal to Miss Affie Nickerson, who was born at Pawtucket, Rhode Island, on the 16th of May, 1860. Dr. and Mrs. Rosenthal have no children. In religious faith Mrs. Rosenthal is a consistent member of the Presbyterian church. They are popular and prominent factors in connection with the best social activities of Cape Girardeau.

In his political proclivities Dr. Rosenthal is an uncompromising advocate of the principles and policies set forth by the Democratic party and while he has never mixed much in local politics he served at one time with all of efficiency as coroner of Dunklin county. In fraternal circles he is affiliated with the

Benevolent & Protective Order of Elks and with the Modern Woodmen of America. Dr. Rosenthal's professional career excites the admiration and has won the respect of his contemporaries, and in a calling in which one has to gain reputation by merit he has advanced steadily until he is acknowledged as the superior of most of the members of the medical fraternity in this part of the state, having long since left the ranks of the many to stand among the successful few.

HARRY A. GUESS. An essentially prominent and influential business man at Flat River, Saint Francois county, Missouri, Harry A. Guess is manager of the Federal Lead Company, an important mining concern of this county. Though a native Canadian, Mr. Guess has resided in the United States and Mexico since 1901, and during the intervening years to the present time he has been engaged along mining and metallurgical lines.

Harry A. Guess was born, November 21, 1875, at Kingston, in the province of Ontario, Canada. He is a son of Charles Wellington and Sarah (Shorey) Guess, both natives of Canada, where the former was born in the year 1846, and the latter in 1848. The Guess family traces its ancestry back to stanch English and Irish stock. Charles W. Guess was identified with agricultural pursuits during the major portion of his active career but retired from business in recent years and is now living at Napanee, Canada. Mr. and Mrs. Guess became the parents of three children, whose names are here entered in respective order of birth,—George A., Harry A., and Ross W. George A. Guess is metallurgical superintendent of the Cerro de Pasco Mining Company, at La Fundicion, Peru, South America; Harry A. is the immediate subject of this review; and Ross W. is cashier of the Bank of Montreal, at Glace Bay, Canada. In politics the father is a liberal and in his religious adherency he is a devout member of the Methodist Episcopal church, in whose faith he reared his children.

To the public schools of his native place Harry A. Guess is indebted for his early educational training, which was followed by a course in the Sydenham Collegiate Institute, at Sydenham. Subsequently he was matriculated as a student in Queens University, at Kingston, in which excellent institution he was graduated as a member of the class of 1895, duly receiving the degree of Master of Arts and also the University medal in chemistry. He was also graduated in the School of Mines at Kingston and thereafter he passed two years in British Columbia, in the southern part of which province he was engaged in survey and assay work. For a time he had an office in British Columbia but in 1897 he returned to eastern Canada, where he became manager of the Ottawa Gold Milling & Mining Company, at Kewatin, province of Ontario, remaining there until 1901. In the latter year he came to the United States and assumed charge of the concentrating plant of Silver Lake Mines at Silverton, Colorado—a Guggenheim property—continuing there for the ensuing three years. During the year 1904 to 1905 he had charge of special experimental work for the Cananea Consolidated Copper Company, at Cananea, Mexico. Subsequently he was manager of the Silver Lake Mines, at Silver Lake, Colorado, and in 1907 he became general milling superintendent for the Guggenheim interests in the United States and Mexico, retaining the latter position to the present time. Since 1908 he has also been manager of the Federal Lead Company and of the Central Experimental plant at Flat River. In connection with the latter concern he is interested in devising the best processes of treatment for all difficult ores and products from the various properties of the Guggenheim interests in the United States and Mexico. He is a member of the Colorado Scientific Society; Society of Chemical Industry; American Chemical Society; and the American Institute of Mining Engineers.

Mr. Guess was married on the 19th of June, 1901, to Miss Eva Young, of Winnipeg, Canada. Mr. and Mrs. Guess have one son, Shorey Guess, born on the 16th of April, 1907. They are popular and prominent in connection with the best social activities of Flat River, where their spacious and comfortable home is the center of many attractive gatherings and where they are held in high regard by all. In their religious faith they are members of the Presbyterian church, to whose philanthropical work they are liberal contributors.

UPTON L. WEIRICK. One of the important industrial enterprises that contribute materially to the commercial prestige of the city of Washington, Missouri, is the Missouri Meerschaum Company, of which that prominent and valued citizen, Upton L. Weirick, is president. He is one of the aggressive and thoroughly up-to-date business men who are aiding in the up-building of the city, and while his own affairs are of engrossing nature he still finds time to concern himself with the matters effecting the general community in an admirably public-spirited fashion. Although a native of the Buckeye state, Mr. Weirick has been a resident of the city for a quarter of a century, his identification with it dating from the year 1886. In this period he has built up an extensive business and his specialties, "Tibbes Missouri Meerschaum Patent Corn Cob Pipes" and the "Only Genuine Detmold Corn Cob Pipes," are known and enthusiastically recommended in whatever country and clime are found devotees of Lady Nicotine. This concern is a definite factor in the industrial and commercial prestige of Washington and the subject's representation in a work of this nature is indeed fitting.

Upton L. Weirick was born at Dalton, Ohio, October 7, 1847, but passed the roseate days of childhood and youth in Tiffin, Seneca county, that state. He is a son of Jesse Weirick, a Tiffin carriage manufacturer, who died in that place in 1871, after a life of industry and usefulness. The maiden name of the mother was Eliza Flenner, and he was one of a family of six children. Young Upton received his education in the public schools and previous to entering commercial pursuits he worked at painting and blacksmithing. He had had some training as a clerk before he embarked in merchandising at Tiffin, and in that place he conducted a store for four years. Retiring from this, he represented the Buckeye Tobacco Company of Toledo, Ohio, as a traveling salesman for eight years and then settled down in Kansas City. Becoming interested in mining and the development of mining territory, he took an interest in the Niles-Augusta mine at Leadville and helped develop the property to a commercial proposition, and in 1879 he disposed of his stock. His next move of importance was embarking in the cattle business in western Nebraska. He located not far distant from Fort Robinson and for a number of years continued there successfully, in 1885 selling out his stock at the topnotch of cattle prices and seeking other channels for his capital.

It was upon returning to Kansas City that Mr. Weirick became interested in the manufacture of cob pipes, and he was so favorably impressed with the possibilities in this field that he invested extensively in the business of H. Tibbe & Sons at Washington. With his entry into the business the name was changed to the H. Tibbe & Sons Manufacturing Company and eventually to the Missouri Meerschaum Company. Since 1886 he has made his home here and has large real estate interests here and in Kansas City, Missouri.

Mr. Weirick laid the foundation of a happy household and congenial life companionship when, on November 25, 1885, he was married at Kenton, Ohio, to Mrs. Flora B. Mille, daughter of Judge T. H. Bagby, a widely known citizen of that place. Their charming home is situated upon the grassy bluff overlooking the Missouri river, where they share the blessings of prosperity with their friends and neighbors, not forgetting the derelicts and those to whom fortune has been less kind. They are friends and supporters of the Episcopal church and are held in high regard in the community.

In politics the Weiricks have for many years espoused the faith of Thomas Jefferson, but the present representative of the family confines his political action to the advocacy of protection policies at national elections.

H. B. McCLENDON. Faithfulness to duty and strict adherence to a fixed purpose in life will do more to advance a man's interests than wealth or advantageous circumstances. The successful men of the day are they who have planned their own advancement and have accomplished it in spite of many obstacles and with a certainty that could have been attained only through their own efforts. One of the well and favorably known farmer-citizens of Bollinger county is H. B. McClendon, who is engaged in general farming and stock raising and who has been identified with this section since 1887. He is a native of Randolph county, Alabama, his birth having occurred there on the 16th day of August, 1853, his parents being Wiley and Sarah McClendon, natives of Georgia and South Carolina, respectively. Mr. McClendon was reared upon his father's homestead farm, his time, like that of the majority of his rural associates, being divided between assisting in the work of the farm and pursuing his study of the common branches behind a desk in the district school. He began farming independently in young manhood and for some years was engaged in that calling in his native state. His coming to Missouri, as previously mentioned, dates from the year 1887, when he ser-ered old associations and removed to Bollinger county, of whose advantages he had heard good report. Here he bought two hundred and forty acres of land, five miles west of Glen Allen, and this has ever since been his home and the scene of his activities. Although this gives the greater part of his attention to general farming, he also raises stock and at the present time owns sixteen head of cattle, fifteen hogs and thirty sheep. He believes in the future of Bollinger county and takes a helpful interest in all affairs of public import.

Mr. McClendon laid the foundations of a happy marriage by his union on the 7th day of September, 1902, to Anna Pridy, one of Bollinger county's daughters. Her parents are J. T. and Betty Pridy. They share their home with one daughter, Enla, born in 1903.

Mr. McClendon is a stanch and stalwart supporter of the policies and principles of the Democratic party and for two years served as marshal of Alexandria City, Alabama, representing the law and its restrictions with entire efficiency. He is one of a family of nine children, the other members being Cynthia, Joseph, Mary, Wyley, Samantha, Eliza, Clamanda and William.

DR. N. F. KELLY. "The evil that men do lives after them, the good is oft interred with their bones." Considering that one never hears so many good things about a man as at the time of his funeral, at first glance it seems as if the immortal bard were incorrect in his statement, but if we take it in the broader sense, that evil has more lasting effects than good, it is true to some extent. Dr. Norris F. Kelly, father of Will V., did many acts of kindness, performed many acts of goodness, made many worthy efforts towards the betterment of his fellow citizens, which now, three years after his death, live in the hearts of his friends. The results have not all been buried with him, but have been inculcated in his son and many others with whom the Doctor had intimate relations.

Norris F. Kelly was born in North Carolina, April 20, 1850, and came to Dunklin county when a boy, about 1868, when he located at Clarkton, his brother John having preceded him and become a man of note in the county. N. F. Kelly studied medicine under the late Dr. V. H. Harrison and was later graduated at the Missouri Medical College, St. Louis. Immediately after his graduation he engaged in the practice of medicine, locating in Kennett in 1871. Since then he has lived here constantly except a few years that he spent at Senath. He built up an extensive practice, partly on account of his skill and partly because of his personality.

Early in the seventies the Doctor married Miss Ruth Bragg, daughter of Captain Bragg and sister of W. G. Bragg and of Mrs. J. F. Tatum, Mrs. Bettie Sturgis, Mrs. Mattie Towson and the large family of daughters of Captain Bragg. Three children were born of the union, only one of whom lived to maturity, Will V. Kelly. Mrs. Kelly died in the late eighties. Several years afterwards he was married to Miss Bow White, of Jerseyville, Illinois, but she lived only a few years.

Dr. Kelly was a leading citizen in Kennett for many years and at one time owned much valuable property, but he could never become what is known as a wealthy man. He considered that money was made to spend and he lived with a great degree of comfort, besides expending much in helping those less fortunate than he. He was not ostentatious in his giving, but as a rule only the recipients of his kindness knew anything about them. The Doctor was a lover of political excitement and was never happier than in a contest for his friends. His power was felt many times in the county and district. He was several times treasurer of the county and was coroner for several terms. He was chairman of the Democratic county committee for a considerable time. He was a warm-hearted man and no one who came to him in trouble would be turned away without his trying in some slight manner to ease the burdens. Besides his son, he left two sisters in North Carolina to mourn his loss when he died on August 4, 1908, in his native place. He was a man whose memory will long be cherished, even as it has been during these three years.

William V. Kelly was born in Kennett July 8, 1875. He attended the public schools and then entered the insurance business, establishing an agency in Kennett in April, 1908, dealing with general and fire insurance. He is a well read man, thoroughly well up in insurance and a student of human nature. It is this last ability which causes him to be so successful. He knows when to talk to a man and when to let him alone and he knows the kind of talk that will suit a particular man. He is still a young man, with much of his career still before him and judging from his past record, this career will be a noteworthy one, full of achievements and worthy acts.

FRANK LEO LONG, M. D., is a prominent young physician of Doe Run, and has acquired high rank in the profession and an excellent practice in this vicinity. His family have been identified with southeastern Missouri more than half a century, and its members have been honored citizens and able workers in various lines of activity.

He was born in Jefferson county, November 18, 1882. His father, W. T. Long, who was born in the same county in July, 1855, is one of the best known railroad men in this part of the state. He spent his early life on a farm, being educated in the common schools and when about thirty-five began railroading. With the exception of four years when he was sheriff of Jefferson county, he has been conductor on the Iron Mountain railroad for the last twenty-five years. He is a member of the Brotherhood of Railway Trainmen and the Order of Railway Conductors, and in politics is a Democrat. His mother was a cousin of the late Senator Hearst of California. He was married about 1878 to Miss Emma Goodin, of Jefferson county, and of their eight children six are living, the Doctor being the third in the family.

The early life of Dr. Long was spent in Jefferson county, and he graduated from the DeSoto high school in 1900. The following year he entered the medical department of the Washington University at St. Louis and took his degree in medicine in 1904. His first two years of practice was in DeSoto, after which for three years he was a member of the medical staff at the Farmington asylum until a change in politics occurred. Since then he has been a resident of Doe Run, where in addition to a large general practice he does the surgical work for the M. R. & B. T. railroad and the Doe Run Lead Company. He is a member of the County, State and American Medical Societies. In politics he is a Democrat, is a member of the Presbyterian church, and affiliates with the Ancient Order of United Workmen, the Court of Honor and the Masonic order.

On March 31, 1909, Dr. Long married Miss Genevieve Browne, of DeSoto, Missouri. They have one child, Frank L., Jr.

www.ingramcontent.com/pod-product-compliance
Lightning Source LLC
Chambersburg PA
CBHW080536230426
43663CB00015B/2614